Date Due

OCT 0 9 2007			

WITHDRAWN

BRODART   Cat. No. 23 233   Printed in U.S.A.

The Flora of Canada
Part 3 — Dicotyledoneae (Saururaceae to Violaceae)

National Museum of Natural Sciences
Publications in Botany, No. 7(3)

Published by the
National Museums of Canada

Staff editor
Bonnie Livingstone

Musée national des Sciences naturelles
Publications de Botanique, n° 7(3)

Publié par
Les musées nationaux du Canada

The Flora of Canada

Part 3 — Dicotyledoneae (Saururaceae to Violaceae)

H.J. Scoggan

Class II *DICOTYLEDONEAE* (*see* p. 94)

SAURURACEAE (Lizard's-tail Family)

SAURURUS L. [1856] Lizard's-tail

Stem jointed, naked below, to over 1 m tall, commonly forking, from extensively creeping aromatic rhizomes. Leaves cordate-ovate, entire, alternate, rather succulent, to about 1.5 dm long, the long petioles sheathing at base. Flowers small, white, perfect, 3 or 4 mm long, in slender peduncled tip-nodding spikes to 3 dm long. Perianth none. Stamens usually 6 or 7, hypogynous, with long slender filaments. Fruit subglobose, indehiscent, strongly rugose, 2 or 3 mm thick; (Ont. and sw Que.).

S. cernuus L. Water-dragon, Swamp-lily
/T/EE/ (Hel) Swamps and shallow water from Minn. to s Ont. (N to the Ottawa dist.; Gillett 1958; *see* s Ont. map by Soper 1956: fig. 4, p. 75), sw Que. (Montreal dist.; CAN; MT), Conn., and R. I., s to Tex. and Fla.

SALICACEAE   (Willow Family)

Dioecious trees or shrubs with simple, alternate, commonly narrow, stipulate leaves, the individual plants unisexual. Flowers small, lacking a perianth, solitary in the axils of small scale-like bracts in staminate or pistillate aments (catkins). Staminate flowers consisting of 1 to many stamens. Pistillate flowers consisting of a single pistil. Style 1, or the often lobed stigma sessile. Fruit a 1-locular many-seeded ovoid capsule, the seeds tipped with long silky down.

1   Buds with several overlapping scales; floral bracts mostly lacerate; disk below each
     flower cup-shaped; aments soon arching or pendulous; leaves commonly ovate or
     deltoid . . . . *Populus*
1   Buds with a single scale; floral bracts entire or subentire; disk below each flower
     consisting of 1 or 2 glands; aments ascending or divergent, rarely drooping; leaves
     commonly linear to lanceolate . . . . *Salix*

POPULUS L.   [1872]   Poplar, Aspen, Cottonwood.   Peuplier

(*See* treatment of hybrids at end)

1   Leaves about as broad as or broader than long, deltoid or cuneate-deltoid to
     rhombic, rotund-ovate, or cordate-reniform, the petiole commonly at least as long as
     the blade.
     2   Leaves white- or grey-tomentose beneath, palmately angulate-lobed with 3–5
          coarse blunt lobes and few teeth, their nearly terete petioles tomentose; young
          branchlets canescent; capsules to 5 mm long, tomentose, on pedicels 1 or 2 mm
          long; bark greyish white, smooth (or cracked at the base of the trunk); (introd.) . . . .
          . . . . *P. alba*
     2   Leaves glabrous (or essentially glabrate at maturity), their petioles more or less
          strongly flattened in cross-section.
          3   Capsules lanceolate to lance-ovate in outline, to 6 mm long, on pedicels 1 or
               2 mm long, their subtending scales deeply 3–5-cleft; pistillate catkins to about
               1 dm long; stamens less than 15; leaves broadly ovate to rhombic or
               suborbicular (or those of vegetative shoots even reniform), their margins
               finely toothed or undulate, the petioles strongly flattened; buds shiny but
               scarcely resinous; bark smooth or smoothish, whitish to greenish-grey;
               (transcontinental) . . . . *P. tremuloides*
          3   Capsules relatively broader, to about 1 cm long, on pedicels mostly at least 3
               mm long, their subtending scales fringed with 9 to many narrow or thread-like
               segments; stamens commonly more numerous; bark rough except near the
               top of the trunk.
               4   Scales of catkins with 9–11 slender segments; stigmas appressed-reflexed
                    against the ovary; capsules 2-locular; leaves rhombic, finely dentate,
                    lacking basal glands at the broadly cuneate base; (introd.) . . . . *P. nigra*
               4   Scales of catkins fringed with very many thread-like segments; stigmas
                    with spreading lobes; capsules 3–4-locular; pistillate catkins to about 1.5
                    dm long; leaves deltoid, bearing 2 or 3 glands at the subtruncate to
                    truncate base, their margins more or less translucent and cartilaginous,
                    the teeth ending in a callous incurved tip, the petioles laterally flattened;
                    overwintering terminal buds heavily glutinous; (s Alta. to Que.) . . . . *P. deltoides*
1   Leaves mostly longer than broad, glabrous or nearly so at maturity, the petiole
     commonly shorter than the blade.
     5   Leaves averaging 3 or 4 times longer than broad, cuneate-based, finely callous-
          crenate, only slightly paler beneath than above, their petioles commonly less
          than 1/3 as long as the blade, somewhat dorsiventrally compressed; scales of
          catkins laciniate-fringed; capsules 2-locular; stamens less than 20; buds
          resinous; bark rough; (s Alta. and sw ?Sask.) . . . . *P. angustifolia*

5 Leaves mostly not more than twice as long as broad, broadly cuneate to
subtruncate or rounded at base, their petioles commonly more than 1/3 as long
as the blade.

  6 Leaves very coarsely toothed with at most about 15 remote unequal deltoid
teeth on each margin, their coriaceous blades narrowly to broadly ovate, their
petioles laterally compressed; scales of catkins deeply 5–7-cleft; stamens less
than 15; buds canescent-pubescent; bark smooth, whitish to greenish-grey;
(SE Man. to N.S.) . . . . *P. grandidentata*

  6 Leaves entire to rather finely toothed; scales of catkins fringed with numerous
thread-like segments; stamens usually many; buds resinous; bark rough (or
smooth near the top of the trunk).

    7 Leaves only slightly paler beneath, broadly cuneate or rounded at base,
their petioles dorsiventrally compressed; capsules glabrous; (S Alta.) . . . .
. . . . [*P. acuminata*]

    7 Leaves paler beneath, very resinous and balsamic-fragrant (often rust-
tinged beneath in dried specimens), broadly cuneate or rounded to
truncate or even cordate at base, their petioles terete or nearly so;
(transcontinental) . . . . *P. balsamifera*

[P. acuminata Rydb.]
[This species of W N. America (Oreg. to SW Alta. and S.Dak., S to Calif. and Mexico) is now
generally considered to be a hybrid-complex between *P. angustifolia* (*see* treatment of hybrids at end) and other species. *See* Hitchcock et al. 1964:34. MAPS: Canada Department of
Northern Affairs and Natural Resources 1956:104; Preston 1961:128; Hough 1947:99.]

P. alba L.   White or Silver-leaved Poplar
Eurasian; commonly planted and spreading by sprouts from the roots; known from B.C.
(Henry 1915; Vancouver Is.), S Alta., S Man. (Waskada, W of Turtle Mt.), Ont. (N to the Ottawa
dist.), Que. (N to Ste-Anne-de-la-Pocatière, Kamouraska Co.; QSA), Nfld., N.B., P.E.I., and N.S.

P. angustifolia James   Narrow-leaf Cottonwood
/T/W/ (Ms) Streambanks, plains, and foothills from Oreg. to Mont., S Alta. (Lethbridge
and Pincher Creek to the Cypress Hills), and SW ?Sask. (Cypress Hills; CAN), S to E Calif., N
Mexico, N.Mex., and Nebr. MAPS: Hosie 1969:130; Preston 1961:128, and 1947:102; Canada
Department of Northern Affairs and Natural Resources 1956:102; Hough 1947:101.
    The above maps all indicate a rather extensive area in S Sask. (Hough's map also including
extreme SW Man.). Breitung (1957a), however, doubts the occurrence in Sask., believing that
records from that province are probably based upon an 1895 collection in CAN (John Macoun, 16256; "along Frenchman's Creek, Cypress Hills), accompanied on the same sheet by
a specimen of *P. balsamifera* taken by Macoun in 1896 in S Alta., and that the possibility exists
of an accidental interchange of data. However, its presence on the Alta. side of the Cypress
Hills argues for a probable occurrence on the Sask. side.

P. balsamifera L.   Balsam-Poplar, Hackmatack, Taccamahac.   Liard
/ST/X/ (Ms) Moist woods, ravines, shores (often pioneering on gravel bars), and prairie
parklands (in association with *P. tremuloides* and *Quercus macrocarpa*), the aggregate species from N Alaska–Yukon (*see* Hultén 1943: map 400, p. 563; *P. tac.*) to the Mackenzie R.
Delta, Great Bear L., Great Slave L., L. Athabasca (Alta. and Sask.), northernmost Man.–Ont.,
Que. (N to S Ungava Bay and the Côte-Nord), Labrador (N to Ramah, 58°54′N), Nfld., N.B.,
P.E.I., and N.S., S to Oreg., Nev., Colo., Nebr., and Pa. *See* T.C. Brayshaw, Can. Field-Nat.
79(2):91–95. 1965, and L.A. Viereck and J.M. Foote, Can. Field-Nat. 84(2):169–73. 1970. MAPS
and synonymy: *see* below.
1 Staminate flowers with 12–20 stamens; pistillate flowers producing 2-valved,
glabrous, lanceolate capsules . . . . ssp. *balsamifera*
  2 Leaves broadly cuneate to rounded or subcordate at base, they and their
petioles glabrous; [*P. michauxii* Dode; *P. tacamahacca* Mill.; incl. *P. candicans*

Ait.; transcontinental; MAPS: Hultén 1968*b*:331; Hosie 1969:124; *Atlas of Canada* 1957: sheet 41; Canada Department of Northern Affairs and Natural Resources 1956:94; Fowells 1965:497; Preston 1961:126; Little 1971: map 148-N; Raup 1947: pl. 21; Hough 1947:105; Halliday and Brown 1943: fig. 9, p. 368; N.C. Fassett, Ann. Mo. Bot. Gard. 28: map 29, p. 365. 1941; Munns 1938: map 72, p. 76] . . . .
. . . . var. *balsamifera*
2 Leaves subcordate to cordate at base, slightly pubescent along the veins beneath, their petioles also slightly pubescent; [var. *fernaldiana* Rouleau; *P. michauxii* of auth., not Dode; ?Alta. and Sask. to Nfld. and N.S.] . . . .
. . . . var. *subcordata* Hylander
1 Staminate flowers with 40–60 stamens; pistillate flowers producing 3-valved, pubescent, subglobose to globose capsules; [*P. trichocarpa* T. & G.; *P. balsamifera* var. *californica* Wats.; incl. the phase with larger, more acuminate leaves, var. *hastata* (Dode) Brayshaw (*P. hastata* Dode, as to type; *P. tri.* var. *hast.* (Dode) Henry); S Alaska–SW ?Yukon–B.C.–SW Alta.; MAPS (mostly as *P. trichocarpa*): Hultén 1968*b*:332; *Atlas of Canada* 1957: sheet 41; Canada Department of Northern Affairs and Natural Resources 1956:96; Fowells 1965:508; Preston 1961:126, and 1947:98; Munns 1938: map 73, p. 77; Little 1971: map 153-N; Hosie 1969:128] . . . .
. . . . ssp. *trichocarpa* (T. & G.) Brayshaw

P. deltoides Marsh.   Cottonwood, Necklace-Poplar
/T/(X)/   (Ms)   Streambanks at low elevations from S Alta. (N to Calgary; CAN) to S Sask. (N to Saskatoon; Breitung 1957*a*, *P. sarg.*), S Man. (N to Vermilion River, N of Riding Mt.; CAN), S Ont. (N to the Ottawa dist.; *see* S Ont. map by Fox and Soper 1953: fig. 13, p. 8), SW Que. (N to Champlain Co.; John Macoun 1886), and W New Eng., S to Colo., Tex., and Fla. MAPS: Hosie 1969:126; Canada Department of Northern Affairs and Natural Resources 1956:98; *Atlas of Canada* 1957: sheet 41 (aggregate species); Fowells 1965:515; Preston 1961:124; Munns 1938: map 74, p. 78, and map 75 (*P. del. virginiana*), p. 79; Little 1971: maps 149-W and 149-E.
  The western plant (Alta. to Man.) is commonly referred to var. *occidentalis* Rydb. (*P. occ.* (Rydb.) Britt.; *P. monilifera* var. *occ.* (Rydb.) Henry; *P. sargentii* Dode; *P. ?canadensis* Michx. f., not Moench; *P. ?laevigata* Ait., not Willd.; an often lower and slightly broader-leaved tree, the twigs commonly yellowish rather than greyish, the bud-scales minutely ciliate rather than glabrous). MAPS: Canada Department of Northern Affairs and Natural Resources 1956:100 (*P. sarg.*); Fowells 1965:519; Preston 1947:110.

P. grandidentata Michx.   Large-toothed Aspen
/T/EE/   (Ms)   Dry woods, slopes, and recent burns from SE Man. (Shoal L., SE of Winnipeg near the Ont. boundary; WIN; reported from Sandilands Forest Reserve, SE of Winnipeg, by Lowe 1943) to Ont. (N to Batchawana Bay at the E end of L. Superior and New Liskeard, ca. 47°30′N), Que. (N to Tracadigash Mt., Carleton Co., Gaspé Pen.; CAN; RIM), N.B., P.E.I., and N.S., S to Minn., Mo., Tenn., and N.C. MAPS: Canada Department of Northern Affairs and Natural Resources 1956:92; Fowells 1965:502; Meusel, Jaeger, and Weinert 1965:112; Preston 1961:122; Hough 1947:111; Halliday and Brown 1943: fig. 9, p. 368; Munns 1938: map 70, p. 74; Little 1971: map 152-N; Hosie 1969:122.

P. nigra L.   Black Poplar (of Europe)
European; this species, particularly the Lombardy poplar (var. *italica* Du Roi; *P. dilatata* Ait.; (Fr.: peuplier d'Italie or peuplier de Lombardie); branches strictly erect rather than spreading) is widely planted as an ornamental or windbreak in N. America and locally spreading by roots. It appears to be definitely recorded as spreading from original plantings in Canada only in Essex Co., S Ont., where reported from Pelee Point by Dodge (1914; "Occasionally planted . . . and spreading by root") and from Pelee Is. by Core (1948; "widely escaped"), and in P.E.I. ("At Eldon, and to some extent at Springfield West and Wellington, root suckers form spreading colonies"; D.S. Erskine 1960). Other reports or collections, as from B.C., Que., Nfld., N.B., and N.S., and more northerly localities in Ont., do not specify the plant as an escape.

P. tremuloides Michx.   Trembling or Quaking Aspen.   Tremble
/ST/X/   (Ms)   Dry or moist woods, prairie parklands, burns, and clearings from N Alaska and N -cent. Yukon (*see* Hultén 1943: map 401, p. 563) to the Mackenzie R. Delta, Great Bear L., SW Dist. Keewatin, northernmost Man.–Ont., Que. (N to ca. 57°N), Labrador (N to Cartwright, 53°42′N; GH), Nfld., N.B., P.E.I., and N.S., S to Baja Calif., N.Mex., N Mexico, Mo., Tenn., and Va. [*P. tremula sensu* Cochran 1829, not L.; incl. the following minor phases, based chiefly upon leaf-shape, this often not constant even on different parts of the same tree: f. *betuloides* Rousseau; f. *nana* Cock.; f. *reniformis* Tid.; var. *aurea* (Tid.) Daniels *(P. aurea* Tid.); vars. *intermedia, magnifica,* and *rhomboidea* Vict.; var. *vancouveriana* (Trel.) Sarg. (*P. van.* Trel.)]. MAPS: Hultén 1968*b*:332; Fowells 1965:524; Meusel, Jaeger, and Weinert 1965:112; Preston 1961:122; Dansereau 1957: map 1B, p. 33; Canada Department of Northern Affairs and Natural Resources 1956:90; Raup 1947: pl. 20; Hough 1947:109; Halliday and Brown 1943: fig. 9, p. 368; Munns 1938: map 69, p. 73; Little 1971: map 154-N; Hosie 1969:120.

Populus Hybrids

The following hybrids between species of *Populus* have been reported from or collected in Canada:

P. alba × *P. grandidentata:* (× *P. rouleauiana* Boivin, the type from Longueuil, Chambly Co., Que.); also reported from Ont. by Boivin (1966*b*).
P. alba × *P. tremula* (of Europe): *P. canescens* (Ait.) Sm. (*P. alba* var. *can.* Ait.) may be of this origin.
P. alba × *P. tremuloides:* (× *P. heimburgeri* Boivin, the type from Masson, Hull Co., SW Que.).
P. angustifolia × *P. balsamifera:* (× *P. brayshawii* Boivin, the type from Lethbridge, Alta.).
P. angustifolia × *P. deltoides* var. *occidentalis, P. fremontii,* or *P. sargentii:* (*P. acuminata* is probably of this origin); SW Alta. (the following maps indicate an area in extreme SW Sask. but Breitung (1957*a*) excludes it from the flora of that province; the report from Spruce Woods Forest Reserve SE of Brandon, Man., by Shimek 1927, is probably based upon *P. balsamifera*): MAPS (*P. acum.*): Canada Department of Northern Affairs and Natural Resources 1956:104; Preston 1947:104, and 1961:128; Hough 1947:99. × *P. acuminata* nm. *andrewsii* (Sarg.) Boivin (*P. andrewsii* Sarg.) is reported from SW Alta. by Boivin 1966*b*. It seems possible that the two nothomorphs are a reflection of hybridization of *P. angustifolia* with the three purported alternate parents.
P. angustifolia × *P. tremuloides:* (× *P. sennii* Boivin, the type from Lethbridge, Alta.).
P. balsamifera × *P. deltoides:* various degrees of genetic infiltration between these two parents apparently produce two hybrids: × *P. jackii* Sarg. (*P. manitobensis* Dode), reported from Alta. to SW Que. by Boivin 1966*b;* and × *P. gileadensis* Rouleau (*P. ?ontariensis* Desf.; *P. candicans* of auth., not Ait.); Ont. to Nfld. and N.S.
P. balsamifera × *P. tremuloides:* S Ont. (Soper 1949).
P. balsamifera var. *subcordata* × *P. tremuloides:* (× *P. dutillyi* Lepage, the type from the Kenogami R., Ont., at 50°28′N).
P. balsamifera × *P. trichocarpa:* reported from Alaska and NW Yukon by L.A. Viereck and J.M. Foote (Can. Field-Nat. 84(2):169–73. 1970; general range of the purported parents in the area shown in their map, fig. 1, p. 171, stations of these and their intermediates in the area indicated in their map, fig. 2, p. 172; compare the present treatment under *P. balsamifera*).
P. deltoides × *P. nigra* var. *italica:* (× *P. eugenii* Simon-Louis, the Carolina Poplar; collections (undoubtedly from planted trees) in MT from Que. (Montreal; Longueuil; Rimouski) have been placed here. A purported hybrid between *P. balsamifera* and × *P. eugenii* (× *P. rollandii* Rouleau) is known from the type locality, St. Helen's Is., Montreal, where undoubtedly planted.
P. deltoides var. *occidentalis* × *P. tremuloides:* (× *P. bernardii* Boivin, the type from Estevan, Sask.).

SALIX L.   [1873]   Willow.   Osier, Saule

(Ref.: Raup 1943, 1959; Schneider 1918–21; *see* treatment of hybrids at end)
1   Leaves mostly regularly crenate-serrate or dentate nearly or quite all around the
     margins (but smaller leaves of many species often essentially entire); catkins usually
     appearing as the leaves unfold (coetaneous) or sometimes only after they are well
     grown (serotinous), but occasionally appearing before the leaves unfold
     (precocious).
    2   Capsules typically pubescent (rarely glabrate in age); stamens 2; catkins
       terminating short leafy-bracted lateral peduncles (or sessile on the twigs in
       S. arbusculoides) . . . . *GROUP 1*
    2   Capsules glabrous at least at maturity and usually nearly or quite from the first;
       catkins usually terminating short leafy-bracted lateral peduncles.
       3   Bracts of catkins whitish, yellowish, or pale brown, deciduous before ripening
          of the capsule . . . . *GROUP 2* (p. 553)
       3   Bracts of catkins pale brown to reddish-brown, dark brown, or blackish (at
          least toward summit), persistent until withering of the capsule . . . .
           . . . . *GROUP 3* (p. 554)
1   Leaves typically entire or with small scattered gland-teeth, or serrate only toward
     base (but the largest leaves or those of vegetative shoots of many species often
     conspicuously toothed).
    4   Capsules glabrous nearly or quite from the first; anther-filaments mostly glabrous
       (hairy only in *S. setchelliana*); catkins mostly terminating short leafy lateral
       peduncles (sessile on the twigs in *S. calcicola* and *S. richardsonii*) . . . .
        . . . . *GROUP 4* (p. 556)
    4   Capsules typically pubescent (occasionally glabrate in maturity).
       5   Catkins falsely terminal on naked peduncles opposite the terminal leaf of
          short shoots of the season, serotinous (expanding after the leaves are well
          grown); capsules sessile or nearly so, their subtending bracts typically
          densely pilose or villous; anther-filaments pilose at base; staminate and
          pistillate flowers both with 2 basal glands; stigma subsessile; leaves usually
          entire or nearly so, broadly elliptic or oval to subrotund. . . . . *GROUP 5* (p. 558)
       5   Catkins lateral on the previous year's wood (some of those of the western
          S. barrattiana also terminating shoots of the previous year), sessile or more
          commonly on leafy-bracted peduncles.
          6   Leaves usually glabrous or nearly so by the time of full expansion.
             7   Catkins mostly expanding before the leaf-buds unfold (precocious),
                sessile or on leafy-bracted peduncles; staminate flowers with (?always)
                a single basal gland . . . . *GROUP 6* (p. 558)
             7   Catkins mostly expanding as the leaves unroll (coetaneous) or after
                they are well grown (serotinous), on leafy-bracted peduncles
                (or sometimes sessile in *S. bebbiana*) . . . . *GROUP 7* (p. 559)
          6   Leaves persistently more or less densely pubescent at least beneath.
             8   Catkins mostly expanding before the leaf-buds unfold (precocious),
                mostly sessile on the branches (occasionally on a short peduncle with
                a few small bract-like leaves) . . . . *GROUP 8* (p. 560)
             8   Catkins mostly expanding as the leaves unroll (coetaneous) or after
                they are well grown (serotinous), sessile or on leafy-bracted peduncles . . . . .
                 . . . . *GROUP 9* (p. 561)

GROUP 1

1   Leaves subsessile or on petioles rarely over 5 mm long, entire to remotely sharp-
     denticulate, linear to broadly lanceolate; bracts of catkins pale, commonly yellowish,
     soon deciduous, the catkins terminating short leafy-bracted peduncles; anther-
     filaments densely long-villous toward base.

2 Stigma-lobes to about 1 mm long, they and the style together about 1.5 mm long; (s B.C. and sw Alta) . . . . *S. fluviatilis*
2 Stigma-lobes relatively short and stout, essentially sessile; (transcontinental) . . . .
. . . . *S. exigua*
1 Leaves more definitely petioled.
  3 Low prostrate shrub, the trailing branches and the bases of the petioles usually bearing long white hairs; leaves thin, green above, pale and glabrous beneath, elliptic or obovate, to nearly 6 cm long; fruiting catkins to 8 cm long, terminating leafy-bracted peduncles, their bracts blackish; capsules at least 4 mm long, subsessile or very short-pedicelled; style about 1 mm long; (Alaska–Yukon–Dist. Mackenzie) . . . . *S. chamissonis*
  3 Taller, ascending to erect shrubs or small trees.
    4 Leaves soon glabrate, green on both sides (sometimes slightly paler on the strongly reticulate-veined lower surface), mostly elliptic-lanceolate, glandular-serrate, to 8 cm long; twigs purplish brown; fruiting catkins to about 6 cm long, terminating leafy-bracted peduncles, their bracts yellowish; capsules to about 8 mm long, on pedicels to 2 mm long; style to 1.3 mm long; anther-filaments hairy toward base; (B.C. to Que.) . . . . *S. maccalliana*
    4 Leaves glaucous or silky-pubescent beneath, not conspicuously reticulate-veined; style less than 1 mm long or nearly obsolete.
      5 Pedicels at least 2.5 mm long; fruiting catkins to 4 cm long, terminating leafy-bracted peduncles, their bracts yellowish or brown; capsules silvery-silky; anther-filaments hairy at base; leaves linear or lanceolate; twigs green or olive-brown; (B.C. to N.S.) . . . . *S. petiolaris*
      5 Pedicels at most about 2 mm long; fruiting catkins to 5 cm long, their bracts dark brown to blackish; anther-filaments glabrous; leaves appressed-silky-pubescent beneath, finely serrulate; twigs brown or reddish brown.
        6 Leaves narrowly lanceolate, to 1 dm long, dark green above, lustrous beneath with minute silky hairs; catkins precocious, terminating leafy-bracted peduncles; capsules at most 5 mm long, on pedicels to 2 mm long; (Ont. to N.B. and N.S.) . . . . *S. sericea*
        6 Leaves elliptic or elliptic-lanceolate, mostly less than 6 cm long, paler green above, delicately silky beneath; catkins mostly coetaneous, sessile or on very short peduncles; capsules to 7 mm long, on pedicels at most 1.2 mm long; (B.C. to Man.; reported from L. Mistassini, Que.) . . . . . .
. . . . *S. arbusculoides*

GROUP 2 (see p. 552)

1 Leaves subsessile or on petioles rarely over 5 mm long, entire to remotely sharp denticulate, linear to broadly lanceolate; bracts of catkins pale, commonly yellowish, soon deciduous, the catkins terminating short leafy-bracted peduncles; anther-filaments densely long-villous toward base.
  2 Stigma-lobes to about 1 mm long, they and the stipe together about 1.5 mm long; (s B.C. and sw Alta.) . . . . *S. fluviatilis*
  2 Stigma-lobes relatively short and stout, essentially sessile; (transcontinental) . . . .
. . . . *S. exigua*
1 Leaves distinctly petioled.
  3 Flowers and capsules tufted in apparent whorls along the axis of the catkin; staminate flowers with 3–7 stamens and 2 basal glands; capsules to 5 mm long, long-pedicelled; bracts of catkins yellowish; leaves to 1.5 dm long, long-acuminate.
    4 Leaves deep green on both sides, linear-lanceolate to lanceolate, often somewhat curved, those of the sprouts subtended by broad glandular-serrate stipules; branchlets brittle at base; pistillate flowers with 1 basal gland; style nearly obsolete . . . . *S. nigra*

    4   Leaves pale green above, more or less glaucous beneath, lanceolate to ovate-lanceolate; stipules minute or none; branchlets tenacious, flexible; pistillate flowers with 2 basal glands; style to 0.5 mm long; (B.C. to Que.) . . . *S. amygdaloides*

3 Flowers and capsules spirally arranged.

    5 Petioles glandless or merely glandular-viscid near the leaf-blade when young; leaves linear to lanceolate; staminate flowers with 2 basal glands, the anther-filaments pilose at base; style short or nearly obsolete; (introd.).

        6 Capsules less than 2 mm long, sessile; pistillate flowers with 2 basal glands; stamens 3 or more; leaves pale beneath, silky when young, finely serrate; young petioles viscid near the blade . . . . [*S. babylonica*]

        6 Capsules at least 3 mm long, short-pedicelled; stamens 2.

            7 Young petioles viscid near the leaf-blade, this to 4 cm broad, rather coarsely undulate-serrate, green on both sides; twigs brittle at base; pistillate flowers with 2 basal glands . . . . *S. fragilis*

            7 Young petioles not viscid; leaf-blades at most 3 cm broad, finely serrulate; twigs not brittle at base; pistillate flowers with 1 basal gland; (var. *vitellina*) . . . . *S. alba*

    5 Petioles usually with a pair (or more) of conspicuous glands on the upper side near the junction with the reticulate-veined, finely and regularly glandular-serrate, narrowly to broadly lanceolate blade; staminate and pistillate flowers with 2 basal glands, the former with typically about 5 stamens; style at most 0.5 mm long; pedicels 1 or 2 mm long.

        8 Leaves distinctly glaucous beneath, acuminate.

            9 Pistillate catkins to about 1 dm long, appearing with the leaves; capsules to 7 mm long; leaves to about 1.5 cm long, acuminate, commonly about 4 times as long as broad; tall shrub or small tree to 7 or 8 m tall, with reddish shining twigs; (B.C. to Sask.) . . . . *S. lasiandra*

            9 Pistillate catkins at most about 3.5 cm long, appearing with the leaves or later; capsules to 1 cm long; leaves to about 1 dm long and 3.5 cm broad, short-acuminate, commonly not more than 3 times as long as broad; shrub to about 4 m tall, with yellowish-brown shining glabrous twigs; (transcontinental) . . . . *S. serissima*

        8 Leaves green on both sides, only slightly paler beneath; fruiting catkins to over 6 cm long, appearing with the leaves.

        10 Mature leaves short-acuminate; pedicels about twice as long as the upper gland; capsules 5 or 6 mm long, conic-subulate; (introd.) . . . .
. . . . *S. pentandra*

        10 Mature leaves caudate-acuminate (with slender-tapering tips); capsules conic-ovoid, on pedicels 1 or 2 mm long.

           11 Pistillate catkins to about 1 dm long; capsules to 7 mm long, on pedicels to 2 mm long; leaves mostly lanceolate, to about 1.5 dm long and commonly about 4 times as long as broad, gradually narrowed to tip; shrub or small tree to about 5 m tall; (B.C. to sw Sask.) . . . . *S. lasiandra*

           11 Pistillate catkins at most about 5 cm long; capsules less than 7 mm long, on pedicels about 1 mm long; large shrub commonly less than 3 m tall; (transcontinental) . . . . *S. lucida*

GROUP 3 (*see* p. 552)

1 Leaves distinctly pubescent at least beneath (or only tardily glabrate); twigs rather persistently pubescent; stamens 2, their filaments glabrous; style to 1.5 mm long.

    2 Pedicels shorter than the bracts; fruiting catkins at most about 6 cm long; capsules to 8 mm long; twigs and leaves densely grey-villous; (SE Man. to S Labrador, Nfld., and N.S.) . . . . *S. cordata*

    2 Pedicels nearly equalling or surpassing the bracts; fruiting catkins to 1 dm long;

capsules to 1 cm long; twigs and leaves densely white-pubescent; (Ont. to Nfld.
and N.B.) . . . . *S. laurentiana*

1 Leaves glabrous or soon glabrate; twigs glabrous (or pubescent only when young).
 3 Catkins borne on naked peduncles opposite the terminal leaf, the fruiting ones to
  about 1 cm long; capsules about 4 mm long, short-pedicelled; style nearly
  obsolete; leaves elliptic, crenate, to about 2 cm long, reticulate beneath, on
  petioles to 4 mm long; low prostrate shrub, essentially glabrous throughout;
  (Nfld.) . . . . [*S. leiolepis*]
 3 Catkins lateral on the previous year's wood, usually on leafy-bracted peduncles.
  4 Stem and main branches filiform, subterranean and rooting at the nodes, the
   ascending branches commonly less than 1 dm high, bearing usually about 3
   or 4 shining, slender-petioled, oval to orbicular, shallowly crenate-serrate
   leaves to 3 cm long, these green on both surfaces; capsules commonly less
   than 8, short-pedicelled, to 6 mm long; style about 0.5 mm long; (Dist.
   Mackenzie to Labrador, Nfld., and E Que.) . . . . *S. herbacea*
  4 Stem and main branches stouter, above the ground.
   5 Dwarf, prostrate, northern and montane shrub with trailing branches
    forming dense mats; leaves firm, shining above, glaucous beneath, elliptic
    to ovate, remotely glandular-serrate, at most about 2.5 cm long; staminate
    flowers with 2 basal glands and 1 stamen; pistillate flowers with 1 basal
    gland; style about 0.5 mm long; slender fruiting catkins to about 3 cm
    long; capsules 3 or 4 mm long, short-pedicelled; (s Baffin Is., Que.,
    Labrador, Nfld., and N.S.) . . . . *S. uva-ursi*
   5 Taller, erect or ascending shrubs or trees (*S. myrtillifolia* sometimes
    straggling); leaves mostly longer; stamens 2, their filaments glabrous;
    staminate and pistillate flowers each with 1 basal gland.
    6 Bracts of catkins whitish; fruiting catkins to over 7 cm long; capsules to
     8 mm long, on pedicels about 3 mm long; style to 1 mm long; leaves
     typically broadly oval or ovate, rounded or subcordate at base, pale
     and strongly reticulate beneath, with persistent balsamic fragrance;
     (transcontinental) . . . . *S. pyrifolia*
    6 Bracts of catkins brown to blackish at least at tips; leaves not balsamic.
     7 Leaves lance-oblong to oblong-obovate, conspicuously reticulate
      on both sides, dark green and lustrous above, serrulate or
      crenulate-serrulate; style to 1 mm long; capsules to 6.5 mm long, on
      pedicels to 1.5 mm long; (transcontinental) . . . . *S. myrtillifolia*
     7 Leaves not conspicuously reticulate, often glaucous beneath,
      mostly somewhat more coarsely toothed.
      8 Leaves yellowish green above, broadly lanceolate, acuminate, to
       about 7 cm long; twigs yellowish, becoming grey; capsules 4 or 5
       mm long; style at most about 0.5 mm long; (Dist. Mackenzie and
       Alta. to Ont.) . . . . *S. lutea*
      8 Leaves deeper green above, to over 1 dm long; twigs mostly
       brownish or reddish.
       9 Capsules to 1 cm long; style to 1.5 mm long; catkins on leafy
        peduncles commonly about 1 cm long; leaves lanceolate to
        somewhat obovate-oval; (Ont. to Nfld. and N.B.) . . . *S. laurentiana*
       9 Capsules at most 8 mm long; style usually less than 1 mm
        long; fruiting catkins subsessile or on short bracted
        peduncles; leaves lanceolate to oblong-lanceolate or
        oblanceolate.
        10 Pedicels 3 or 4 mm long; capsules to 7 mm long; pistillate
         catkins to about 6 cm long, on leafy peduncles; leaves
         lanceolate or oblanceolate, to about 1 dm long,
         commonly about 3 times as long as broad; shrubs usually
         2 or 3 m tall; (the Yukon–B.C. to NW Sask.) . . . *S. mackenzieana*

10 Pedicels at most about 1.5 mm long; pistillate catkins sessile or on very short leafy peduncles; leaves commonly less than 3 times as long as broad.

    11 Capsules to 8 mm long; leaves ovate to obovate, to about 6 cm long, mostly not more than twice as long as broad, usually distinctly cordate (sometimes merely rounded) at base; (Alaska–B.C. to James Bay) . . . . *S. monticola*

    11 Capsules at most about 6 mm long; leaves to over 1 dm long, mostly at least 3 times as long as broad; (var. *rigida;* Man. to Nfld. and N.S.) . . . . *S. cordata*

GROUP 4 (see p. 552)

GROUP 4 (see p. 552)

1 Stems prostrate and trailing, the branches sometimes rooting and stoloniferous; leaves to 2 or 3 cm long, glabrous or finally nearly so; catkins appearing with (coetaneous) or after (serotinous) the leaves, on short leafy lateral peduncles.

  2 Style 1 or 2 mm long; fruiting catkins to 3 cm long, their scales red-brown; leaves broadly ovate to rotund, green above, glaucous beneath, entire; branches often with slender subterranean stolons; (Alaska–Yukon–B.C.; *see* treatment of the *S. ovalifolia* complex) . . . . [*S. stolonifera*]

  2 Styles mostly not over 0.5 mm long.

    3 Leaves green on both sides, entire; scales of catkins dark brown to black; pedicels very short.

      4 Leaves elliptic to ovate, to 2 cm long, rather prominently veined and strongly marcescent, their skeletonized remains clothing the stems for several years and forming a large part of the mat; fruiting catkins to 3 cm long; (Alaska–Yukon–Dist. Mackenzie) . . . . *S. phlebophylla*

      4 Leaves ovate to roundish, usually less than 1 cm long, delicate, the dried ones persisting for about a year; fruiting catkins commonly not over 1 cm long and with only 5 or 6 capsules; (Alaska–Yukon–w Dist. Mackenzie) . . . . *S. rotundifolia*

    3 Leaves glaucous beneath, green above, not strongly marcescent; scales of catkins red-brown to dark brown.

      5 Fruiting catkins to 3 cm long, their scales red-brown; pedicels very short; leaves obovate to rotund, entire, glaucous beneath; (Alaska–Yukon–N B.C.) . . . . *S. ovalifolia*

      5 Fruiting catkins to 2 cm long, their scales dark toward tip; pedicels to 3 mm long; leaves obovate, entire or serrate toward base; (Alaska to Dist. Keewatin and N Man.) . . . . *S. arbutifolia*

1 Stems mostly ascending to erect (if prostrate and spreading, the branches neither stoloniferous nor rooting, but the stems may be stoloniferous).

  6 Capsules on pedicels to 3 or 4 mm long, the style nearly obsolete or at most 0.3 mm long (*S. lasiolepis* may sometimes be sought here); catkins appearing with the leaves, to about 2 cm long, on short leafy lateral peduncles; leaves shining green above, commonly glaucous beneath; twigs glabrous; shrubs usually less than 1 m tall.

    7 Bracts of catkins yellowish, glabrous or nearly so; capsules glabrous from the first, on pedicels to 4 mm long; leaves broadly oblanceolate to obovate-oblong, to 4.5 cm long and 2 cm broad; (transcontinental) . . . . *S. pedicellaris*

    7 Bracts of catkins dark toward tip, hairy; capsules sometimes pubescent when young, on pedicels at most 3 mm long; leaves elliptic to obovate, to about 3 cm long; (Alaska to Dist. Keewatin and N Man.) . . . . *S. arbutifolia*

  6 Capsules subsessile or on pedicels at most about 1.5 mm long (or 2 mm in *S. lasiolepis*); bracts of catkins distinctly long-hairy or ciliate.

    8 Leaves linear to linear-lanceolate, revolute-margined, white-tomentose

beneath; twigs glabrous or glabrate; fruiting catkins commonly 1 or 2 cm long, on short leafy peduncles; (spread from cult. in Que. and N.S.) . . . . . . *S. elaeagnos*

8 Leaves oblanceolate or elliptic to broadly obovate, glabrous or sparingly pubescent beneath when young; twigs more or less pubescent at least when young; fruiting catkins mostly longer; (native species).

  9 Style commonly 2 or 3 mm long; catkins precocious (appearing before the leaves), sessile on the twigs, their blackish scales about 2 mm long; capsules sessile or very short-pedicelled, to 9 mm long; leaves glabrous or soon so, green above, glaucous beneath; twigs stout, the young ones densely hairy; terminal winter-buds to 1 cm thick; (arctic, subarctic, and alpine regions).

    10 Stipules oblong-ovate to suborbicular, entire or with numerous very fine glandular teeth; leaves broadly ovate to rotund, short-pointed, rounded or subcordate at base, mostly entire, the midrib broad and conspicuous, the petiole relatively short and broad; stigmas entire; (sw Dist. Mackenzie; mts. of ?Alta.; Man. to Nfld.) . . . . *S. calcicola*

    10 Stipules lanceolate, with conspicuous gland-tipped teeth; leaves narrowly ovate to obovate-oblong, acutish at apex and base, usually glandular-serrate, the midrib and longer petioles narrower; stigmas distinctly 2-cleft; (transcontinental in arctic, subarctic, and alpine regions) . . . . *S. richardsonii*

  9 Style less than 2 mm long; catkins usually on leafy-bracted peduncles (or often subsessile in *S. hookeriana, S. lasiolepis,* and *S. piperi*); capsules on pedicels to 0.5 mm long or more; twigs and terminal buds more slender; (B.C. and Alta.; *S. farriae* also in N Man.).

    11 Leaves essentially glabrous when fully expanded, glaucous beneath (or often green beneath in *S. setchelliana*); capsules to 6 or 7 mm long.

      12 Bracts of catkins pale yellow, to 4 mm long, ciliate on the margins, sometimes notched at apex; pistillate catkins to 2 cm long, coetaneous; capsules short-pedicelled; styles about 0.3 mm long; anther-filaments hairy; leaves somewhat fleshy or leathery, gradually tapering to a subpetiolar base, acute to rounded or retuse at summit, entire or irregularly glandular-serrate, shining above, to about 6 cm long and 2 cm broad; shrub prostrate but the pruinose branches sometimes ascending to 6 dm; (Alaska–Yukon) . . . .
. . . . *S. setchelliana*

      12 Bracts of catkins dark brown or blackish, to 1 or 2 mm long, long-hairy as well as ciliate; capsules on pedicels to 1.5 cm long; style relatively long; anther-filaments glabrous; leaves more distinctly petioled; twigs at first pubescent but soon glabrate, not pruinose; plants mostly taller.

        13 Fruiting catkins at most 3.5 cm long, coetaneous or serotinous, on leafy peduncles; style to 0.7 mm long; staminate catkins slender; leaves entire or nearly so, commonly not over 5 cm long and 2 cm broad, acute at apex, tapering or somewhat rounded to the short petiole; plant commonly less than 1 m tall; (Alaska–B.C. to Man.) . . . . *S. farriae*

        13 Fruiting catkins to over 1 dm long, sessile or short-peduncled (the bracteal leaves often less than 1 cm long), precocious or coetaneous; style to about 1.5 mm long; staminate catkins commonly about 1.5 cm thick or more; leaves entire or slightly crenate-serrate, to over 1 dm long and 5 cm broad, acute to broadly rounded at summit, relatively long-petioled; plants commonly over 2 m tall; (s ?B.C.) . . . . [*S. piperi*]

    11 Leaves more or less pubescent at least on one side when fully expanded (but often finally glabrate), entire or finely crenate; plants

commonly over 1 m tall; (mts. of B.C.; all except *S. lasiolepis* also in the mts. of Alta.).

14 Leaves more densely and persistently hairy above than beneath, to about 8 cm long and 3.5 cm broad; fruiting catkins to 6 cm long, coetaneous or serotinous, their bracts dark brown or blackish; capsules to 6 mm long, the style to 1.5 mm long; branchlets blackish; shrub to 2(4) m tall . . . . *S. barclayi*

14 Leaves more densely and persistently hairy beneath than above (but finally often glabrate).

15 Catkins coetaneous or serotinous, the fruiting ones to about 6 cm long, their bracts rather light brown; capsules to 6 mm long, their styles rarely over 1 mm long; leaves to about 8 cm long and 3.5 cm broad, loosely long-woolly-villous especially beneath, commonly paler beneath but not at all glaucous; plants rarely over 3 m tall . . . . *S. commutata*

15 Catkins more or less precocious, their bracts dark brown or blackish; leaves to over 1 dm long, more or less densely pubescent or finally glabrate, the lower surface then strongly glaucous; plants to about 6 m tall.

16 Fruiting catkins to 6 cm long; capsules to 5 mm long, the style less than 1 mm long; pedicels commonly about 2 mm long; leaves typically oblanceolate, mostly not over 2.5 cm broad, rather densely short-hairy when young, at maturity usually glabrous above and strigose-puberulent beneath; (?B.C.) . . . . [*S. lasiolepis*]

16 Fruiting catkins to 12 cm long; capsules to 8 mm long, the style to about 1.5 mm long; pedicels shorter; leaves commonly broadly elliptic to broadly obovate, to over 5 cm broad, more or less densely villous-tomentose or finally glabrate . . . . *S. hookeriana*

GROUP 5 (see p. 552)

1 Petioles to about 3 cm long, usually several times surpassing the subtended bud and 2/5 to nearly as long as the leaf-blade; leaf-blades conspicuously reticulate beneath, entire or nearly so, sparingly silky beneath or glabrous, to about 4 cm long; fruiting catkins to 3 cm long; capsules densely white-pubescent, to 4 or 5 mm long; branches prostrate or barely ascending, mat-forming and often rooting; (transcontinental) . . . .
. . . . *S. reticulata*

1 Petioles less than 1 cm long, shorter than or only slightly longer than the subtended bud.

2 Leaves typically densely clothed beneath with long, white, silky, appressed hairs (or glabrate in age), the closely crenate blades to 8 (but commonly not over 4) cm long, dark green and deeply impressed-veined above; fruiting catkins to 5 cm long; capsules to 7 mm long; branches erect-ascending, stout, to about 1 m tall; (transcontinental) . . . . *S. vestita*

2 Leaves glabrous or becoming glabrate, to about 2.5 cm long, conspicuously reticulate-veined beneath; fruiting catkins less than 2 cm long; capsules less than 5 mm long; branches prostrate or somewhat ascending, often rooting.

3 Bracts and ovaries glabrous; leaves crenate; (Nfld.) . . . . [*S. leiolepis*]

3 Bracts and ovaries pubescent; leaves entire; (Que., SE Labrador, and N Nfld.) . . . . .
. . . . [*S. jejuna*]

GROUP 6 (see p. 552)

1 Leaves (or some of them) subopposite, linear-oblanceolate, finely rugose-reticulate on both surfaces, more or less glaucous and purple-tinged, entire or minutely

dentate, to about 1 dm long; branches slender and flexible, often reddish or purplish, usually glabrous; catkins often paired, sessile or nearly so, slenderly cylindric, their bracts dark-tipped; anther-filaments and often the red anthers coalescing; capsules ovoid, to 3 mm long, sessile; style very short; (introd.) . . . .
. . . .*S. purpurea*

1 Leaves evidently alternate; filaments and anthers distinct.
  2 Pedicels at most 1 mm long; catkins sessile or on leafy-bracted peduncles, their bracts to 2 mm long, blackish toward tip; filaments glabrous; style to about 1.5 mm long; leaves oblanceolate to elliptic, entire or finely serrate; (transcontinental) . . .
  . . . .*S. phylicifolia*
  2 Pedicels to over 1.5 mm long.
    3 Catkins sessile or on very short leafy peduncles, the fruiting ones to 5 cm long, their bracts blackish; capsules to 9 mm long; style commonly about 0.5 mm long; pedicels at most about 1.5 mm long; anther-filaments glabrous; leaves oblanceolate to obovate, rounded or obtuse at apex, commonly in a fan-like arrangement at the ends of the twigs, sometimes more or less silvery- or rusty-pubescent beneath; (Alaska–B.C. to Man.) . . . .*S. scouleriana*
    3 Catkins sessile on the twigs, the fruiting ones to over 1 dm long, their bracts dark red or brown to blackish; capsules to 12 mm long; style about 0.8 mm long; pedicels usually over 1.5 mm long; anther-filaments pilose at base; leaves lanceolate to elliptic or obovate, acute, more or less regularly alternate toward the ends of the twigs; (transcontinental) . . . .*S. discolor*

GROUP 7 (see p. 552)

1 Bracts of catkins yellowish or yellowish brown, not darkened at tip; anther-filaments hairy at base (except sometimes in *S. glauca*); stems spreading to erect; (transcontinental).
  2 Style very short (less than 0.5 mm long); pedicels 2–4(5) mm long; staminate and pistillate flowers each with 1 basal gland; pistillate catkins to 5(6) cm long; leaves to 8 cm long and 3 cm broad . . . .*S. bebbiana*
  2 Style at least 0.5 mm long (to 0.8(1.5) mm); pedicels at most 2 mm long; staminate flowers with 2 basal glands (the pistillate with 1).
    3 Leaves suberect and overlapping, rarely over 1.5 cm broad, commonly 2 or 3 cm long, the thick petioles shorter than the larger of the axillary buds, at most 2 mm long; catkins commonly less than 2.5 cm long; capsules 5 or 6 mm long; stigma subsessile; bracts merely pilose . . . .*S. brachycarpa*
    3 Leaves scarcely overlapping, to over 3 cm broad, on slender petioles over 2 mm long; catkins to about 7 cm long; capsules to 1 cm long; style usually less than 1 mm long; bracts usually more copiously villous . . . .*S. glauca*
1 Bracts of the catkins brown to blackish or black-tipped.
  4 Stems creeping, the slender prostrate branches rooting and mat-forming; leaves marcescent for 1 or more years, mostly not over 2 cm long; fruiting catkins to about 3 cm long; capsules to 5 mm long, nearly sessile; (mts. of B.C.).
    5 Leaves obovate to subrotund or even slightly reniform, typically rounded or retuse at apex; (Alaska–Yukon–Dist. Mackenzie–N B.C.) . . . .*S. polaris*
    5 Leaves mostly rather narrowly elliptic and acute; (SW B.C.) . . . .*S. cascadensis*
  4 Stems mostly ascending to erect (if prostrate in *S. arctica*, the branches rarely rooting).
    6 Pistillate catkins erect on the prostrate branches, to 1 dm long; pedicels about twice as long as the short, broadly truncate glands; anther-filaments hairy toward base; leaves to about 4 cm long, usually dark green and shining above, the numerous lateral veins sometimes nearly perpendicular to the midrib; dried branchlets brittle; (transcontinental) . . . .*S. arctophila*
    6 Pistillate catkins merely ascending; branchlets flexible.
      7 Capsules sessile or very short-pedicelled, to 1 cm long, the style to over 2 mm long; anther-filaments glabrous; leaves mostly elliptic to obovate, to

about 5 cm long and 2 cm broad; stems prostrate, seldom rising more than 1(2) dm above the ground; (transcontinental in arctic, subarctic, and alpine regions) . . . . *S. arctica*
  7   Capsules relatively long-pedicelled, the style usually shorter; stems ascending to erect; (plants more southern).
    8   Anther-filaments glabrous; fruiting catkins to about 1 dm long; capsules to 1 cm long; pedicels to 1.5 mm long; style to 1.5 mm long; leaves to over 1 dm long and about 6 cm broad; twigs glabrous to densely ashy-tomentose; (Ont. to Nfld. and N.B.) . . . . *S. laurentiana*
    8   Anther-filaments hairy toward base; fruiting catkins rarely over 5 cm long; capsules to 6 mm long; pedicels to 2.5 mm long; leaves to about 8 cm long and 1.5 cm broad; twigs glabrous and often very glaucous; (western species).
      9   Leaves at first silky, usually sooner or later glabrate or sometimes more or less persistently hairy especially beneath; staminate catkins commonly about 1 cm long; pistillate catkins rarely over 2.5 cm long; style at most about 0.5 mm long; (s B.C.) . . . . *S. geyeriana*
      9   Leaves slightly appressed-hairy when unfolding, soon glabrate; staminate catkins to about 3.5 cm long; pistillate catkins to about 5 cm long; style to 0.9 mm long . . . . [*S. lemmonii*]

GROUP 8 (see p. 552)

1   Twigs, leaves, and capsules white-woolly with a dense dull tomentum; capsules to 7 mm long, the style to about 1.5 mm long; pedicels to about 1 mm long; fruiting catkins to 5 cm long, subsessile, their bracts pale brown; leaves mostly oblanceolate or narrowly oblong, to over 1 dm long; (transcontinental) . . . . *S. candida*
1   Twigs and leaves not white-woolly (if tomentose, the tomentum silvery or silky).
  2   Capsules sessile or on pedicels to about 1 mm long, the style elongate.
    3   Leaves to over 2.5 dm long, lance-linear, long-attenuate, silvery-satiny beneath; capsules sessile or nearly so, minutely puberulent, to over 6 mm long; bracts of catkins black-tipped; (introd.) . . . . *S. viminalis*
    3   Leaves usually less than 12 cm long; capsules 4 or 5 mm long, on short pedicels to about 1 mm long; bracts of catkins brown to blackish.
      4   Leaves silvery-tomentose beneath with short straight appressed hairs, usually oblanceolate, acute or obtuse at apex and base, to about 7 cm long and 2.5 cm broad; capsules silvery-silky; fruiting catkins sessile on the twigs; (s Yukon–B.C.–Alta.) . . . . *S. subcoerulea*
      4   Leaves silky-tomentose beneath with longer, scarcely straight, slightly appressed hairs, linear-lanceolate to lanceolate or oblanceolate, acuminate at apex, acute or obtuse at base, to about 12 cm long and 1.5 cm broad; capsules densely whitish-pubescent; fruiting catkins subsessile or subtended by a few small leaves; (Sask. to Labrador, Nfld., and N.S.) . . . . *S. pellita*
  2   Capsules on elongate pedicels; catkins sessile; style very short; leaves narrowly to broadly oblanceolate to obovate, to about 1 dm long.
    5   Stipules of sprouts or suckering branches semilanceolate to semiovate or wanting; capsules to 9 mm long, on glabrous pedicels; fruiting catkins to 8 cm long; young anthers reddish or purplish; leaves typically oblanceolate to broadly obovate, sparsely to densely ashy-pubescent beneath with short soft hairs (or sometimes glabrate); (Alta. to s Labrador, Nfld., and N.S.) . . . . . *S. humilis*
    5   Stipules of sprouts semicordate; leaves more or less dentate; capsules 6 or 7 mm long, on pubescent pedicels; leaves to about 1 dm long; (introd.).
      6   Leaves elliptic to broadly ovate, broadest near the middle, mostly rounded or subcordate at base, the upper surface soon glabrate and shining; staminate catkins expanding from the base upward; anthers yellow, their filaments smooth or slightly hairy at base . . . . [*S. caprea*]

6 Leaves elliptic-lanceolate to obovate, obtuse at apex, mostly broadest above the middle, permanently pubescent on both surfaces; staminate catkins expanding from the apex downward; anthers reddish, their filaments more hairy at base . . . . [*S. cinerea*]

GROUP 9 (*see* p. 552)

1 Bracts of catkins dark brown to blackish or black-tipped; pedicels usually not over 1 mm long; fruiting catkins to over 5 cm long; anther-filaments glabrous.
  2 Stamen 1 (by fusion of 2); style less than 1 mm long; fruiting catkins sessile or sometimes on short leafy peduncles, their bracts 1 or 2 mm long; leaves typically broadly oblanceolate to obovate, to over 1 dm long, densely woolly or silky beneath with a silvery, shiny or satiny pubescence, greener above (or finally glabrate); (s Alaska–B.C.–?Alta.) . . . . *S. sitchensis*
  2 Stamens 2.
    3 Catkins sessile or with 1 or 2 small leaves on a short peduncle, their bracts about 1 mm long; style to 0.8 mm long; leaves elliptic-lanceolate to elliptic, delicately silky beneath with short appressed hairs; (Alaska–B.C. to Man.; reported from L. Mistassini, Que.) . . . . *S. arbusculoides*
    3 Catkins sessile on the twigs, their bracts to 3 mm long or longer; styles commonly 1 or 2 mm long.
      4 Leaves thickly felted beneath or on both sides with a white tomentum, the midvein beneath (where visible) yellowish; stipules rather distantly glandular on the margins; capsules densely white-hairy, to 8 mm long, on pedicels 1 or 2 mm long; (Alaska–B.C. to Man.) . . . . *S. alaxensis*
      4 Leaves whitish or light greyish-hairy on both sides, somewhat silky in appearance, the midvein not yellowish; stipules densely glandular on the margins; capsules white-silky, about 6 mm long, sessile or on very short pedicels; (Alaska–Yukon–Dist. Mackenzie–B.C.–Alta.) . . . . *S. barrattiana*
1 Bracts of catkins rather uniformly yellowish to yellow-brown.
  5 Pedicels 2–4(5) mm long; capsules to 9(12) mm long; style very short or obsolete; staminate and pistillate flowers each with 1 basal gland; anther-filaments hairy toward base; leaves broadly oblanceolate to ovate or obovate, to 8 cm long and 3 cm broad; catkins sessile on the twigs or on peduncles rarely over 1 cm long bearing leaves seldom over 1(2) cm long; (transcontinental) . . . .
. . . . *S. bebbiana*
  5 Pedicels at most about 2 mm long, the capsules often subsessile; staminate flowers with 2 basal glands (or presumably so); pistillate flowers with 1 basal gland (or presumably so); catkins on leafy-bracted peduncles.
    6 Leaves narrowly elliptic to elliptic-oblanceolate, mostly acutish at both ends, dark green and impressed-nerved above, thinly to densely long-silky beneath, to about 6 cm long; fruiting catkins to 2.5 cm long; capsules densely short-silky, 3 or 4 mm long, gradually tapering to the slender style, distinctly pedicelled; anther-filaments glabrous; (Labrador and Que.) . . . . *S. argyrocarpa*
    6 Leaves and capsules not as above; capsules sessile or subsessile; anther-filaments hairy toward base; (transcontinental).
      7 Leaves suberect and overlapping, rarely over 1.5 cm broad, commonly 2 or 3 cm long, the thick petioles shorter than the larger of the axillary buds, at most 2 mm long; catkins commonly less than 2.5 cm long; capsules 5 or 6 mm long; stigma subsessile; bracts of catkins merely pilose . . . . *S. brachycarpa*
      7 Leaves scarcely overlapping, to over 3 cm broad, on slender petioles over 2 mm long; catkins to about 7 cm long; capsules to 1 cm long; style usually less than 1 mm long; bracts usually more copiously villous . . . *S. glauca*

S. alaxensis (Anderss.) Cov.
/aST/WW/eA/ (Mc) Moist tundra and gravels (common on river sandbars and lake shores), the aggregate species from the Aleutian Is. and coasts of Alaska–Yukon–Dist. Macken-

zie to N Banks Is. and Melville Pen., S to cent. B.C. (S to Hazelton, 55°15'N; CAN; isolated in the mts. of SW Alta.), Great Slave L., and NE Man. (known only from Churchill); E Asia. MAPS and synonymy: *see* below.

1 Leaves thickly covered on both surfaces with a whitish tomentum, pale green to greyish above, to 6 cm long and 3.5 cm broad; stipules to 7 mm long; capsules about 6 mm long; [*S. silicicola* Raup, the type from L. Athabasca, Sask.; also reported from S Dist. Mackenzie by Boivin 1966*b*; MAP: Raup 1959: map 20, p. 13] . . . .
. . . . var. *silicicola* (Raup) Boivin
1 Leaves glabrous or glabrate and bright green above, white with a dense matted felt-like pubescence beneath, to 1 dm long and 4 cm broad; stipules to about 2 cm long; capsules to 8 mm long.
  2 Twigs permanently white-woolly; leaves mostly oblanceolate and acutish; [incl. var. *obovalifolia* Ball; *S. speciosa* H. & A., not Host nor Nutt., and its var. *alaxensis* And.; *S. ?lapponum sensu* Hooker 1838, not L.; Aleutian Is. and Alaska (type from Kotzebue Sound) to Southampton Is., S to cent. B.C., W Alta., S Dist. Mackenzie, and Churchill, Man. (the inclusion of W Labrador in the range by Hultén 1943, is undoubtedly erroneous); MAPS (aggregate species): Hultén 1968*b*:356; Raup 1959: map 20, p. 13, 1947: pl. 21, and 1930: map 15 (incomplete), p. 202; Porsild 1957: map 120, p. 175] . . . . var. *alaxensis*
  2 Twigs soon glabrate, usually pruinose (covered with a bluish waxy bloom); leaves mostly obovate and obtuse; [*S. longistylis* Rydb., the type from the mouth of the Klondike R., the Yukon; f. *long.* (Rydb.) Boivin; *S. ?drummondiana* Barratt in part (*see* Raup 1959:92); perhaps general throughout the range; MAP: Hultén 1968*b*:356] . . . . var. *longistylis* (Rydb.) Schn.

S. alba L. White Willow
Eurasian; much planted as a windbreak and shade tree in N. America and thoroughly natzd.; known from S Man. (Brandon; Winnipeg; Beausejour, about 25 mi NE of Winnipeg), Ont. (N to Sioux Lookout, about 175 mi NW of Thunder Bay; CAN), Que. (N to Rimouski, Rimouski Co., and the Gaspé Pen. at Matapédia; MT; RIM), Nfld., N.B., P.E.I., and N.S. The following taxa are known in our area:
1 Branchlets and leaves persistently silky-hairy, the branchlets olivaceous to brown; capsules nearly sessile . . . . var. *alba*
1 Branchlets and leaves promptly glabrate.
  2 Branchlets brown; [reported from S Ont. by Soper 1949, and from P.E.I. by D.S. Erskine 1960] . . . . var. *calva* Mey.
  2 Branchlets yellow; [*S. vitellina* Strokes; the common N. American phase, possibly a hybrid between *S. alba* and *S. fragilis;* reports from Labrador (Schrank 1818; Meyer 1830; Schlechtendal 1836) undoubtedly refer to some other species] . . . . var. *vitellina* (L.) Stokes

S. amygdaloides Anderss. Peach-leaved Willow
/T/X/ (Mc (Ms)) Moist ground and shores from S B.C. (Osoyoos L.; Kootenay L.) to S Alta. (Milk River; Lethbridge; Medicine Hat), Sask. (N to Hudson Bay Junction, 52°52'N; Breitung 1957a), Man. (N to Lynn Lake, ca. 57°N), Ont. (N to Renfrew and Carleton counties), Que. (N to Ville-Marie, 47°20'N), and Vt., S to Oreg., N.Mex., Tex., Kans., and Pa. [*S. nigra amygdaloides* And.]. MAPS: Preston 1961:132; Hough 1947:75; Munns 1938: map 77, p. 81; Little 1971: map 189-N.

S. arbusculoides Anderss.
/ST/WW/ ((N) Mc) Woods, thickets, and rocky barrens from N Alaska–Yukon (*see* Hultén 1943: map 438, p. 567) to the Mackenzie R. Delta, Great Bear L., and E-cent. Dist. Keewatin, S to S-cent. B.C.–Alta., cent. Sask. (S to Waskesiu Lake, 53°55'N), and cent. Man. (S to the Nelson R. about 150 mi S of Churchill; CAN). [*S. acutifolia* Hook.; *S. humillina* And.]. MAPS: Raup 1959: map 28, p. 13, and 1947: pl. 22.

In the original description (Kongl. Svenska Vetensk. Akad. Handl. 6:147. 1867), N.J. Andersson included Labrador in the range but later (DC. Prodr. 16(2):248. 1868; *S. humillina*) questioned this locality. It is reported from L. Mistassini, Que., by Dutilly and Lepage (1947) and collections in CAN, MT, and RIM appear to belong here. However, this range extension is not accepted by Raup (1959). Var. *glabra* And. (*S. saskatchewana* Seem.; *S. tyrrellii* Raup; leaves glabrous rather than moderately short-appressed-pilose beneath) occurs throughout the range.

S. arbutifolia Pallas

/aSs/WW/eA/ (N) Wet or swampy ground from the coasts of Alaska–Yukon–Dist. Mackenzie to cent. Dist. Keewatin (N to the Back R. at 65°35′N; CAN), S to the E Aleutian Is., S Alaska, Great Bear L., and northernmost Man. (S to Nejanilini L. at 59°22′N; CAN; *S. fuscescens* var. *reducta* reported from Moosonee, S James Bay, Ont., by Dutilly, Lepage, and Duman 1954, but this locality not accepted by Raup 1959); E Asia. [*S. fuscescens* And. and its var. *reducta* Ball]. MAPS: Raup 1959: map 23, p. 13; Meusel, Jaeger, and Weinert 1965:115 (very incomplete for N. America).

According to Skvortsov (*see* Hultén 1968a), the names *S. arbutifolia* and *S. fuscescens* are not strictly synonymous and at least the Alaskan plant should bear the latter name (incl. *S. rhamnifolia* H. & A., not Pallas).

S. arctica Pallas   Arctic Willow

/AST/X/GEA/ (Ch) Moist or dry tundra and rocky or gravelly exposed places from the coasts of Alaska–Yukon–Dist. Mackenzie throughout the Canadian Arctic Archipelago to northernmost Ellesmere Is. and northernmost Ungava–Labrador, S to N Alta. (L. Athabasca), SE Dist. Keewatin, cent. Que. (S to ca. 55°N; isolated on Mt. Albert and Mt. Blanc, Gaspé Pen., E Que.), and Nfld., and in the mts. of the West through B.C. and SW Alta. to Calif. and N.Mex.; W Greenland N of ca. 76°N, E Greenland N of ca. 70°N; Eurasia. MAPS: combine the maps by Hultén 1968b:340 (ssp. *arctica* and ssp. *crassijulis*) and p. 341 (ssp. *torulosa*); Porsild 1957: map 125, p. 176; Raup 1959: map 7, p. 11, and 1947: pl. 21.

This is a very plastic species and much further work is required before the many segregates that have been split off from it can be satisfactorily coordinated and their ranges defined with precision. In constructing a key to western varieties, Raup (1959) comments that "It should be emphasized that these forms are poorly defined, and that the following key will do little more than indicate trends." Perhaps the most useful treatment would be along the lines adopted for the *S. glauca* complex by Argus (1965), the many segregates of which he groups together geographically into Eastern, Western, Beringia, and Rocky Mountain phases. Keeping in mind the fact that "It is hardly possible to quote synonyms, as every group mentioned under one name necessarily includes several sometimes rather different types" (Hultén 1943), the following taxa are here included in the species-complex: *S. arctica* vars. *brownei, groenlandica* (in part), and *petraea* And.; *S. anglorum* and its vars. *antiplasta, araioclada,* and *kophophylla* Schn.; *S. obcordata, S. pallasii,* and *S. subcordata* And.; *S. crassijulis, S. diplodictya,* and *S. torulosa* Trautv.; *S. cuneatifolia* Flod.; *S. cuneata* Turcz.; *S. hudsonensis* Schn.; *S. petrophila* Rydb.; and *S. sphenophylla* Skvortzow.

S. arctophila Cockerell

/aST/X/G/ (Ch) Mossy tundra, streambanks, lake shores, and alpine barrens from the coasts of Alaska–Yukon–Dist. Mackenzie–Dist. Keewatin to S Ellesmere Is. and northernmost Ungava–Labrador, S to Great Bear L., Great Slave L., NE Sask. (Hasbala–Patterson lakes dist. at ca. 59°30′N; G.W. Argus, Can. Field-Nat. 80(3):134. 1966), N Man. (S to Churchill), Ont. (S to W James Bay), Que. (S to E James Bay, the Côte-Nord, Anticosti Is., and Shickshock Mts. of the Gaspé Pen.), Nfld., and Mt. Katahdin, Maine; W Greenland (type locality) N to ca. 78°30′N. [*S. chloroclados* Flod.; *S. arctica* var. *groenlandica* And. (*S. gr.* (And.) Lundstr.) in part]. MAPS: Hultén 1968b:342; Raup 1959: map 7, p. 11; Porsild 1957: map 123, p. 176.

Forma *lejocarpa* (And.) Fern. (ovaries and capsules glabrous rather than pubescent) occurs sporadically throughout the range. [*S. arctica* var. *groenlandica* subvar. *lej.* And., the type from Greenland].

S. argyrocarpa Anderss.

/ST/E/ (N) Swampy ground, shores, and alpine or subalpine meadows of Que. (Richmond

Gulf, ᴇ Hudson Bay, to ɴᴇ Ungava Bay, s to ᴇ James Bay, Knob Lake at 54°48'N, the Côte-Nord, and Shickshock Mts. of the Gaspé Pen.) and Labrador (ɴ to Bowdoin Harbour, 60°24'N) to the White Mts. of N.H. [*S. ambigua* Tuckerm.; *S. labradorica* Schw.; *S. ?depressa, S. ?fusca,* and *S. ?repens* of Canadian reports, not L.]. ᴍᴀᴘ: Raup 1943: pl. 4 (ɴ area).

The reports from Fort Franklin, on the Mackenzie R., and from the Nipigon R., Ont., by John Macoun (1886) undoubtedly refer to other species. The citation from Ste-Luce, Rimouski Co., ᴇ Que., by Ernest Lepage (Nat. can. (Que.) 69(12):273. 1942; as also, perhaps, that from Trois-Pistoles, Temiscouata Co.) is based upon *S. candida* f. *denudata* (relevant collection in MT).

[S. babylonica L.]   Weeping Willow
[Eurasian; planted as an ornament or windbreak in N. America, where thoroughly established and locally spreading to streambanks and shores, as in s Ont. (Dodge 1914; with the note, however, "Planted in abundance and thriving along roads near Lake St. Clair. Not noticed as spreading.") and sᴡ Que. (ɴ to the Montreal dist.). Collections from P.E.I. (Southport; NSPM; ACAD; not listed by D.S. Erskine 1960) and N.S. (Grand Pré Park, Kings Co.; ACAD; not listed by Roland 1947) are probably from planted individuals, such being reported from N.B. by Fowler (1879; 1885; "cultivated for ornament"). According to Boivin (1967*a*), most of our material (except possibly some reported from s Ont.) is based upon *S. alba.*]

S. barclayi Anderss.
/ST/W/   (N (Mc))   Streambanks, wet meadows, and lake shores from the Aleutian Is. and ɴ Alaska–Yukon–ᴡ Dist. Mackenzie through B.C. and the mts. of sᴡ Alta. to Wash., ?Oreg., ɴ Idaho, and ɴᴡ ?Mont.; the type is from Kodiak Is., Alaska; (concerning a report from ᴇ Asia, *see* Hultén 1943). [Incl. f. *angustifolia,* f. *grandifolia,* and f. *rotundifolia* And.; *S. conjuncta* Bebb; the report from ᴇ Que. by M.L. Fernald (Rhodora 9(105):160. 1907; Tabletop Mt., Gaspé Pen.) is based upon *S. laurentiana* f. *glaucophylla,* relevant collections in CAN and GH]. ᴍᴀᴘs: Hultén 1968*b*:353; Raup 1959: map 14, p. 12, and 1947: pl. 21.

S. barrattiana Hook.
/ST/W/   (Mc (Ms))   Moist open slopes, boggy meadows, streambanks, and lake shores (ranges of Canadian taxa outlined below), s to Glacier National Park, Mont. ᴍᴀᴘs and synonymy: *see below.*
1   Leaves rather thinly long-hairy on both sides when young but becoming glabrate, finely serrulate to subentire; style to 3 mm long; [*S. tweedyi* (Bebb) Ball; s B.C.: Falkland, about 35 mi sᴇ of Kamloops; Hitchcock et al. 1964] . . . . var. *tweedyi* Bebb
1   Leaves persistently villous-tomentose on both sides (more densely so and grey beneath), entire or nearly so; style to 2 mm long.
  2   Stipules persistent as marcescent remains subtending the leaves; [type from Brintnell L., Mackenzie Mts., sᴡ Dist. Mackenzie; reported also from Alaska and the Yukon] . . . . var. *marcescens* Raup
  2   Stipules promptly deciduous; [incl. vars. *angustifolia* and *latifolia* Anderss.; *S. albertana* Rowlee; ɴ Alaska–Yukon–ᴡ Dist. Mackenzie–B.C.–ᴡ Alta.; ᴍᴀᴘs (aggregate species): Hultén 1968*b*:355; Raup 1959: map 17, p. 12, and 1947: pl. 21] . . . . var. *barrattiana*

S. bebbiana Sarg.   Long-beaked Willow.   Chaton or Petit Minou
/ST/X/eA/   (Mc)   Moist to wet thickets and streambanks, the aggregate species from ɴ-cent. Alaska–Yukon–Dist. Mackenzie to Great Bear L., Great Slave L., L. Athabasca (Alta. and Sask.), Man. (ɴ to Churchill), northernmost Ont., Que. (ɴ to sᴇ James Bay, John L. at 54°49'N, the Côte-Nord, Anticosti Is., and Gaspé Pen.), Labrador (ɴ to the Hamilton R. basin), Nfld., N.B., P.E.I., and N.S., s to Ariz., N.Mex., Nebr., Pa., and Md.; Siberia. ᴍᴀᴘs and synonymy: *see below.*
1   Capsules to 12 mm long, on pedicels to about 8 mm long; fruiting catkins to 8 cm long and 3 cm thick; leaves scarcely rugose, soon glabrate; [*S. rostrata* var. *lux.* Fern., the type from Bic, Rimouski Co., ᴇ Que.; also known from Charlevoix and Gaspé counties, ᴇ Que.] . . . . var. *luxurians* Fern.

1 Capsules to about 9 mm long, on pedicels to about 5 mm long.

  2 Fruiting catkins to 8 cm long; pedicels less than 4 mm long; young leaves gland-toothed, heavily tomentose; branchlets densely and permanently pubescent [*S. rostrata* var. *pro.* Fern., the type from near Bay of Islands, w Nfld.] . . . .
. . . . var. *projecta* (Fern.) Schn.

  2 Fruiting catkins to 5 cm long; pedicels to 5 mm long.

    3 Leaves densely and permanently pilose-tomentose beneath, to 4 (on sterile sprouts 6) cm broad; branchlets densely pubescent into the 2nd year; [*S. rostrata* var. *cap.* Fern., the type from Tourelle, Gaspé Pen., e Que.; Que. (Megantic and Rimouski counties; Côte-Nord; Gaspé Pen.; Anticosti Is.), Nfld., and N.S. (Digby, Pictou, Inverness, and Cape Breton counties)] . . . .
. . . . var. *capreifolia* Fern.

    3 Leaves at first grey-pubescent, soon glabrate or nearly so, those of fertile branches to 3 cm broad; branchlets often glabrate by the 2nd year; (transcontinental).

      4 Mature leaves plane and scarcely reticulate beneath; [incl. var. *depilis* Raup; *S. rostrata* var. *per.* (Rydb.) Fern. (*S. per.* Rydb.)] . . . .
. . . . var. *perrostrata* (Rydb.) Schn.

      4 Mature leaves reticulate-rugose beneath; [*S. rostrata* Rich., not Thuill.; *S. livida* var. *occidentalis* Gray; *S. fusca sensu* Hooker 1838, not L.; MAPS: Hultén 1968*b*:358 (*S. depressa* ssp. *rostrata*); Raup 1959: map 21, p. 13, and 1947: pl. 21 (aggregate species)] . . . . var. *bebbiana*

S. brachycarpa Nutt.

/aST/X/ (N) In a wide variety of habitats (including saline, calcareous, and serpentine) from lowland to alpine elevations (ranges of Canadian taxa outlined below), s in the mts. of the West to Oreg., Idaho, Utah, and Colo. MAPS and synonymy: *see* below.

1 Pistillate catkins subglobose or, if subcylindrical, then densely flowered; numerous catkins borne below vegetative shoots; style to 0.8 mm long; leaves densely pubescent on both surfaces, their arrangement fan-like because of the short shoot-internodes; branches mostly thick and stout; [*S. desertorum* var. *stricta* And.; *S. stricta* (And.) Rydb.; *S. ?chlorolepis* Fern.; incl. vars. *psammophila* Raup, *sansonii* Ball, and *glabellicarpa* Schn. (this glabrous extreme very closely resembling *S. chlorolepis* Fern., supposedly endemic to Mt. Albert, Gaspé Co., e Que., and the hybrid-swarm between it and *S. brachycarpa* (× *S. gaspeensis* Schn.; *S. chlorolepis* var. *antimima* Schn.; *S. br.* var. *ant.* (Schn.) Raup) reported from Mt. Albert by Argus 1965:131); cent. Dist. Mackenzie (Norman Wells) and B.C. to northernmost Ungava and e James Bay; e Que. (Gaspé Co. and Anticosti Is.); MAPS: Hultén 1968*b*:348; Argus 1965: map 5, p. 106, and map 6, p. 107; Raup 1959: map 10, p. 12] . . . .
. . . . ssp. *brachycarpa*

1 Pistillate catkins narrowly cylindrical, loosely flowered; few catkins borne below vegetative shoots; style to 0.5 mm long; leaves appressed-pubescent beneath, thinly pubescent or becoming glabrate above, acute-attenuate; branches thin and flexible . . . . ssp. *niphoclada* (Rydb.) Argus

  2 Shrubs usually erect; leaves to 3(4.5) cm long; pistillate catkins to 3(5) cm long, their narrowly oblong bracts yellowish; branchlets densely yellowish-tomentose; [*S. niphoclada* Rydb. (type from the lower Mackenzie R., Dist. Mackenzie) and its var. *muriei* (Hult.) Raup; *S. glauca* ssp. *niph.* (Rydb.) Wiggins; *S. muriei* Hult.; *S. lingulata* And.; *S. brachycarpa* var. *mexiae* Ball; Alaska–Yukon–Dist. Mackenzie (e to Great Bear L.) and northernmost B.C. (s to ca. 59°30′N); MAPS: on the above maps by Argus and Raup for ssp. *brach.;* W.J. Cody, Nat. can. (Que.) 98: fig. 18 (*S. niph.*), p. 152. 1971; Porsild 1957: map 121 (*S. niph.*), p. 176; Hultén 1968*b*:349] . . . . var. *niphoclada*

  2 Shrubs prostrate; leaves less than 3 cm long; pistillate catkins to 2.5 cm long, their broad bracts reddish, drying blackish; branchlets thinly pubescent, reddish brown; [*S. fullertonensis* Schn.; *S. niph.* var. *full.* (Schn.) Raup; coast of w Dist.

Mackenzie to Banks Is., Victoria Is., and E Dist. Keewatin (S to ca. 61°N; type from Fullerton, N Hudson Bay); MAPS: on the above maps by Argus for ssp. *brachycarpa*] . . . . var. *fullertonensis* (Schn.) Argus

S. calcicola Fern. & Wieg.
/aST/(X)/   (N)   Calcareous rock and barrens: SW Dist. Mackenzie (J.W. Thieret, Can. Field-Nat. 76(4):207. 1962); mts. of SW ?Alta.; SE Dist. Keewatin and N Man. to cent. Baffin Is. and northernmost Ungava–Labrador, S to N Ont. (S to the mouth of the Severn R., Hudson Bay, at ca. 56°N), James Bay (type from South Twin Is.), Que. (coasts of Hudson Bay to S James Bay and of Hudson Strait to S Ungava Bay; isolated on calcareous cliffs of Tabletop Mt., Gaspé Pen.), and N and NW Nfld. [*S. lanata* ssp. *calc.* (F. & W.) Hult.; incl. vars. *glandulosior* Boivin and *nicholsiana* Polunin; *S. richardsonii* of E Canadian reports, not Hook.; *S. rich.* var. *macouniana* Bebb]. MAPS: Raup 1959: map 18, p. 12; Porsild 1957: map 116, p. 175; Fernald 1925: map 56, p. 323, and 1929: map 16, p. 1492.

The closely related *S. wiegandii* Fern., endemic to W Nfld., is perhaps best considered a phase of *S. calcicola,* from which it may be distinguished as follows:
1   Ovaries, capsules, and pedicels glabrous; leaves oblong to suborbicular, glabrous or
    soon glabrate . . . . *S. calcicola*
1   Ovaries, capsules, and pedicels minutely tomentose; leaves narrowly to broadly
    oblong, flocculent-tomentulose; [NW Nfld., the type from Ingornachoix Bay; MAP:
    Raup 1943: pl. 3] . . . . *S. wiegandii* Fern.

S. candida Fluegge   Hoary Willow
/ST/X/   (N)   Bogs and swampy places (usually calcareous or alkaline) from S-cent. Alaska and S Yukon to Great Bear L., Great Slave L., L. Athabasca (Alta. and Sask.), Man. (N to Churchill), northernmost Ont., Que. (N to the Leaf R. watershed at ca. 58°N, L. Mistassini, the Côte-Nord, Anticosti Is., and Gaspé Pen.), Labrador (N to the Hamilton R. basin), Nfld., N.B. (CAN), P.E.I. (Tignish, Prince Co.; CAN; not listed by D.S. Erskine 1960), and N.S. (Black River, Inverness Co.; E.C. Smith and J.S. Erskine, Rhodora 56(671):247. 1954; not listed by Roland 1947), S to S B.C. (Marble Range, NW of Clinton), Idaho, S.Dak., and N.J., and in the mts. of the West to Colo. [*S. incana* Michx., not Schrank]. MAPS: Hultén 1968b:357; Porsild 1966: map 46, p. 72; Raup 1959: map 19, p. 12.

Forma *denudata* (And.) Rouleau (the leaves becoming glabrate) occurs throughout the range. The obscure *S. cryptodonta* Fern. of Que. and Nfld. is perhaps best considered a phase of *S. candida,* from which it may be distinguished as follows:
1   Style very short or obsolete; pedicels to 2.5 mm long; leaves oblong-lanceolate,
    somewhat rugose, their revolute margins with obscure gland-tipped teeth; [Que.
    (L. Mistassini; Mingan Is. of the Côte-Nord; L. Matapédia, Gaspé Pen.) and Nfld.
    (type from East Branch, Humber R.); MAPS: Dutilly and Lepage 1945: fig. 10, p. 284;
    Raup 1943: pl. 3 (somewhat incomplete)] . . . . *S. cryptodonta* Fern.
1   Style slender and elongate; pedicels at most 1 mm long; leaves linear-lanceolate to
    oblong, plane, their revolute margins entire or undulate . . . . *S. candida*

[*S. capraea* L.]   Goat-Willow
[Eurasian; cult. in N. America and spreading to thickets; reported from Nfld. by Rouleau (1956), perhaps on the basis of its report from there by Bachelot de la Pylaie (1823), but some other species, perhaps *S. bebbiana* var. *capreifolia,* is probably involved.]

S. cascadensis Cockerell   Cascades Willow
/T/W/   (Ch)   Alpine meadows and talus slopes near or above timberline from SW B.C. (Mt. McLean, near Lillooet; Marble Range, NW of Clinton; Mt. Brent, near Penticton) and Mont. to ?Oreg., Utah, and Colo. [*S. tenera* And., not Brown].

S. chamissonis Anderss.
/Ss/W/eA/   (Ch)   Grassy tundra and damp slopes of Alaska (N to the Seward Pen.; *see*

Hultén 1943: map 408, p. 564), s Yukon (MacMillan Pass; CAN), and NW Dist. Mackenzie (Rich-ardson Mts.; Peel R. to LaPierre House; CAN); E Asia. MAPS: Hultén 1968b:354; Raup 1959: map 16, p. 12.

[S. cinerea L.]   Grey Willow
[Eurasian; spreading from cult. in N. America and reported from N.S. by Fernald *in* Gray (1950; not listed by Roland 1947). A sterile collection in CAN from N.S. (Bridgewater, Lunenburg Co., where taken along roadsides by John Macoun in 1910 and distributed as *S. capraea*) may form the basis of Fernald's report, which should be validated by further collec-tions.]

S. commutata Bebb
/sT/W/   (N (Mc))   Wet places at moderate to rather high elevations from s Alaska–Yukon (*see* Hultén 1943: map 429, p. 566) and SW Dist. Mackenzie (Brintnell L.; CAN) through B.C. and the mts. of SW Alta (Waterton Lakes; Breitung 1957b) to N Calif. and Wyo. MAPS: Hultén 1968b:353; Raup 1959: map 16, p. 12, and 1947: pl. 21.

Var. *denudata* Bebb (leaves becoming glabrate), the glabrescent extreme, occurs through-out the range. According to Hultén (1943), it is possibly a hybrid between *S. commutata* and *S. myrtillifolia.*

S. cordata Michx.   Heartleaf Willow
/ST/EE/   (N (Mc))   Gravelly or sandy shores, dunes, and low thickets (ranges of Canadian taxa outlined below), s to Kans., Ark., Miss., and N.C. MAPS and synonymy: *see* below.
1   Branchlets and petioles densely velvety-grey-villous; leaves densely silky- or grey-villous especially beneath, less than 3 times as long as broad; stipule-teeth at first gland-tipped; pedicels shorter than the bracts; [*S. adenophylla* Hook.; *S. syrticola* Fern.; NE ?Man. (Groentved 1937, on the basis of a sterile specimen); Que. (N to NE James Bay, L. St. John (type locality), the Côte-Nord, and Gaspé Pen.; reported from Anticosti Is. by Schmitt 1904), Labrador (N to Goose Bay, 53°18′N), Nfld., N.B., and N.S.; MAP: Raup 1959: map 16 (the Goose Bay, Labrador, station should be ‛indicated), p. 12] . . . . .var. *cordata*
1   Branchlets, petioles, and leaves typically glabrous or glabrate; leaves relatively narrow; stipules rarely gland-tipped; pedicels equalling to much longer than the bracts.
  2   Leaves gradually tapering or gradually rounded at base, to about 8 times as long as broad; [*S. rigida* var. *ang.* (Pursh) Fern.; Ont. (N to Ottawa; John Macoun 1886), Que. (Rimouski, Rim. Co.; MT; tentatively reported from L. Timiskaming, ca. 47°30′N, by Baldwin 1958), and N.S. (Sunny Brae, Pictou Co.; CAN, verified by Ball)] . . . . var. *angustata* (Pursh) Gray
  2   Leaves broadly rounded to subcordate at base, to 6 times as long as broad . . . .
      . . . . var. *rigida* (Muhl.) Carey
    3   Branchlets, petioles, and midribs of leaves soft-pubescent; [var. *?abrasa* Fern.; collections in RIM from cent. Ont. (Mattice, 49°37′N) and Que. (Missinaibi, Pagwa, and Kenogami rivers and the Gaspé Pen.); var. *abrasa* also reported from Nfld. and N.S. by Fernald *in* Gray 1950] . . . .
        . . . . f. *mollis* (Palm. & Stev.) Fern.
    3   Branchlets, petioles, and leaves glabrous or soon glabrate; [*S. rigida* Muhl.; *S. cordata* Muhl., not Michx.; *S. coactilis* Fern.; SE ?Man. (Löve and Bernard 1959; this report referred to *S. lutea* by Boivin 1967b), Ont. (N to Attawapiskat, W James Bay at ca. 53°N), Que. (N to Rupert House, SE James Bay, 51°29′N, the Côte-Nord, and Gaspé Pen.; reported from Anticosti Is. by John Macoun 1886), s Nfld., N.B., P.E.I., and N.S.; MAP: Raup 1959: map 12, p. 12] . . . . . . f. *rigida*

S. discolor Muhl.   Pussy-Willow.   Petit Minou or Chaton
/sT/X/   (Mc)   Swampy thickets and shores, the aggregate species from B.C. (N to Fort St. John, 56°10′N) to Alta. (N to McMurray, 56°44′N), Sask. (N to Prince Albert), Man. (N to the Hayes R. about 100 mi SW of York Factory), Ont. (N to W James Bay at 51°44′N), Que. (N to

Richmond Gulf, Hudson Bay, at ca. 56°30′N, L. Mistassini, and the Côte-Nord), Labrador (N to the Hamilton R. basin), Nfld., N.B., P.E.I., and N.S., s to Idaho, S.Dak., N Mo., and Md. MAPS and synonymy: see below.

1 Branchlets more or less pubescent; leaves broadly lanceolate to narrowly ovate or obovate, to about 5 cm broad, often rusty-pubescent on the veins beneath; [var. *eriocephala* of auth., not *S. eriocephala* Michx.; Ont. (N to sw James Bay at ca. 52°N), Que. (near Quebec City; L. St. John; Côte-Nord; Anticosti Is.), N.B. (St. Stephen, Charlotte Co.), and N.S. (Yarmouth, Yarmouth Co.)] . . . . var. *latifolia* And.
1 Branchlets and leaves glabrous or soon glabrate.
   2 Branchlets dull; leaves broadly elliptic, broadly oval, or broadly obovate, to about 6 cm broad; [Que. (N to Rimouski Co., the Côte-Nord, Anticosti Is., Gaspé Pen., and Magdalen Is.; CAN; GH), Nfld., and P.E.I. (Alberton, Prince Co.); reported from Man. and N.B. by Fernald *in* Gray 1950, and from cent. Ont. by Dutilly, Lepage, and Duman (1954; w James Bay at 51°27′N). It is considered to be nearly or quite identical with var. *latifolia* by Raup (1943)] . . . . var. *overi* Ball
   2 Branchlets lustrous; leaves mostly elliptic or elliptic-oblanceolate, acutish at apex, mostly less than 3 cm broad; [incl. f. *rigidior* And. and var. *prinoides* (Pursh) And. (*S. prinoides* Pursh); transcontinental; MAPS (aggregate species): Raup 1959: map 25, p. 13, and 1943: pl. 4 (NE area); Braun 1935: fig. 3, p. 355; Hough 1947:93]. The maps by Braun and Hough indicate a NW limit in extreme SE Sask. However, Raup's 1959 map extends the area to the Peace River dist. of E B.C., noting that the ranges of *S. discolor* and the scarcely separable western *S. scouleriana* overlap in the forested country between N Man. and that region . . . . . .
. . . . var. *discolor*

S. elaeagnos Scop.
Eurasian; spread from cult. in Que. (Fernald *in* Gray 1950; *S. incana*), N.S. (Barrington Passage, Shelburne Co., where taken by John Macoun in 1910, with the annotation "cultivated and run wild"; CAN), and New Eng. (Fernald *in* Gray 1950). [*S. incana* Schrank, not Michx. nor Schleich.].

S. exigua Nutt.   Sandbar-Willow
/ST/X/ (N (Mc)) Streambanks and alluvial soils (often pioneering on bars and beaches), the aggregate species from N Alaska and cent. Yukon (*see* Hultén 1943: map 404, p. 564; *S. int.*) to Great Bear L., Great Slave L., L. Athabasca (Alta. and Sask.), Man. (N to York Factory, Hudson Bay, ca. 57°N), northernmost Ont., Que. (N to s James Bay, L. St. John, and the Gaspé Pen.), and N.B. (not known from P.E.I. or N.S.; *S. interior* reported from Nfld. by Reeks 1873, but not listed by Rouleau 1956), s to Calif., N Mexico, Tex., La., Ill., and Del. MAPS and synonymy: see below.

1 Capsules to 5(6) mm long, typically sessile or nearly so; pistillate catkins mostly dense and short (commonly not over 5 cm long but occasionally to 1 dm).
   2 Leaves entire or with a few scattered small teeth, more or less persistently hairy; ovaries and capsules often hairy; bracts of catkins mostly narrow and pointed; [*S. argophylla* Nutt., the pubescent extreme; *S. longifolia* vars. *argyrophylla* And. and ?*sericans* Nees; *S. hindsiana* var. *tenuifolia* And.; s B.C., s ?Alta., and s ?Sask. (*see* C.R. Ball, Can. Field-Nat. 40(8):174. 1926)] . . . . ssp. *exigua*
   2 Leaves mostly rather strongly toothed, often relatively broad, soon glabrate; ovaries and capsules glabrous; bracts of catkins mostly broad and blunt; [*S. melanopsis* Nutt. and its var. *tenerrima* (Hend.) Ball; *S. bolanderiana* Rowlee; reported from Revelstoke, B.C., by Henry 1915, and from Banff, Alta., by Hitchcock et al. 1964] . . . . ssp. *melanopsis* (Nutt.) Cronq.
1 Capsules to 9 mm long, thinly silky or often glabrate, distinctly pedicelled; mature pistillate catkins loose and often elongate (to 8 cm long), their bracts tending to be pointed at apex; leaves relatively strongly veined . . . . ssp. *interior* (Rowlee) Cronq.
   3 Ovaries hairy at least when young (but the capsules often glabrate). . . . . . . var. *interior*
      4 Leaves glabrous or promptly glabrate, typically linear to narrowly lanceolate; [*S. interior* Rowlee; *S. longifolia* Muhl., not Lam.; *S. luteosericea* Rydb.;

S. exigua var. *lut.* (Rydb.) Schn.; *S. rubra* Rich., not Huds.; Alaska–B.C. to N.S. (reported from Nfld. by Reeks 1873, but not listed by Rouleau 1956); MAPS (all as *S. interior*): Hultén 1968b:362; Raup 1959: map 2, p. 11; C.R. Ball, Madroño 10: fig. 1 (incl. var. *ped.*), p. 82. 1949; Hough 1947:85 (incomplete northwards)] . . . . f. *interior*
   4   Leaves more or less permanently silvery-silky, often broader; [range of the species] . . . . f. *wheeleri* (Rowlee) Rouleau
 3   Ovaries essentially glabrous from the first; [*S. longifolia* var. *ped.* And., the type from the Saskatchewan R. of Alta.–Sask.–w Man.; *S. int.* var. *ped.* (And.) Ball; *S. linearifolia* Rydb. in part; Alaska–B.C. to Que.; MAP: Porsild 1966: map 48 (*S. int.* var. *ped.*), p. 72] . . . . var. *pedicellata* (And.) Cronq.

S. farriae Ball
/aST/WW/ (N (Mc)) Wet meadows, lake shores, and streambanks at low to moderately high elevations from N Alaska (*see* Hultén 1943: map 426, p. 566; the report from the Yukon by Hitchcock et al. 1964, requires confirmation) and the Mackenzie R. Delta (CAN) through the mts. of B.C. (type from Field) and Alta. (NW to the Caribou Mts. at 58°54′N; isolated in NE Man. at York Factory, Hudson Bay, ca. 57°N) to Oreg., Idaho, and Wyo. [*S. hastata* var. *farriae* (Ball) Hult.]. MAPS: Hultén 1968b:351 (*S. hastata*); Raup 1959: map 13, p. 12.
    This is an obscure species to which has been referred many plants apparently trending toward other species such as *S. barclayi* and *S. mackenzieana* and possibly of hybrid origin. C.R. Ball (Madroño 6(7):230. 1942) believes it to be most closely related to *S. pyrifolia,* this argued against by Raup (1959). Var. *microserrulata* Ball (leaves more distinctly toothed than those of the typical form; type from Banff, Alta.) may reflect introgression from *S. myrtillifolia.* The Alaskan plant is referred by Hultén (1943) to var. *walpolei* (Cov. & Ball) Ball (*S. wal.* Cov. & Ball; *S. hastata* L.), differing from the typical form, according to Raup (1959), "in having more pubescent branchlets, brown seasonal shoots, somewhat larger and broader leaves with more conspicuous serration, and longer catkins."

S. fluviatilis Nutt.   River Willow
/t/W/ (Mc) Streambanks and alluvial soils, the aggregate species from s B.C. (Schneider 1919, as *S. sess.;* reports from elsewhere in Canada–Alaska require confirmation, perhaps being referable to the *S. exigua* complex) to Oreg.
 1   Leaves lance-linear to lanceolate or elliptic, to about 1.5 dm long and 1.5 cm broad (commonly 15 or 20 times as long as broad), silvery-strigose or subsilky with appressed hairs when young, soon more or less glabrate; capsules rather sparingly short-villous or becoming glabrate . . . . var. *fluviatilis*
 1   Leaves lanceolate to lance-elliptic or oblong, to about 1 dm long and 3.5 cm broad (rarely over 7 times as long as broad), copiously and rather persistently villous or villous-puberulent with loose hairs; capsules densely long-villous; [*S. macrostachya* Nutt.; *S. sessilifolia* Nutt. and its vars. *villosa* And. and *hindsiana* (Benth.) And., not var. *sericans* f. *hindsiana sensu* Boivin 1966b; s B.C.] . . . . var. *sessilifolia* (Nutt.) Scoggan

S. fragilis L.   Crack-Willow
Eurasian; spread from cult. to roadsides, borders of woods, etc., in N. America, as in Alta. (N to Athabasca Landing, 54°43′N), Man. (N to The Pas and Flin Flon), Ont. (N to the Ottawa dist.), Que. (N to the Gaspé Pen.), Nfld., N.B., P.E.I., and N.S.

S. geyeriana Anderss.
/T/W/ (Mc) Wet meadows and streambanks at low to high elevations from s B.C. (Vancouver Is.; CAN; V; reported from Kootenay by Henry 1915) to Calif. and Colo.
 1   Twigs strongly glaucous; leaves tending to be persistently pubescent; [Kootenay, SE B.C.; Henry 1915] . . . . var. *geyeriana*
 1   Twigs only slightly or not at all glaucous; leaves generally more quickly glabrate; [*S. mel.* (Henry) Jones; *S. macrocarpa* Nutt.; SW B.C.: type from Shawnigan, Vancouver Is.; reported from New Westminster by Henry 1915] . . . . var. *meleina* Henry

S. glauca L.

/aST/X/GEA/ (N) Moist places and open rocky barrens and slopes (ranges of geographical phases in Alaska–Canada outlined below), s through the mts. of B.C.–Alta. to s Utah and N N.Mex., farther east s to s-cent. Sask., s Man., s James Bay (Ont. and Que.), E Que. (s to the Côte-Nord, Anticosti Is., and Gaspé Pen.), and Nfld.; w Greenland N to ca. 76°N, E Greenland near the Arctic Circle; Iceland; Eurasia. MAPS: Raup 1959: map 10, p. 12, and 1947: pl. 21 (aggregate species); combine the maps by Hultén 1968*b*:346 (ssp. *acutifolia*), p. 347 (ssp. *callicarpaea* and ssp. *desertorum*), and p. 348 (ssp. *glabrescens*); Hultén 1958: map 167 (ssp. *call.*), p. 187; Porsild 1957: map 122 (*S. cordifolia* vars. *call.* and *intonsa*), p. 176; Raup 1943: pl. 2 (*S. cord.* and vars.). Additional MAPS (of geographical "phases") and synonymy: see below.

G.W. Argus (Contrib. Gray Herb. Harv. Univ. 196:1–142. 1965) has greatly enlightened our understanding of this difficult species-complex by grouping its numerous intergrading elements into four "phases" characteristic of four fairly distinct geographical areas (*see* his MAP 2, p. 63). The following key is taken with little change from his paper.

1 Leaves to 1 dm long, narrowly to broadly oblanceolate (to 4 times as long as broad); stipules to over 1 cm long; pistillate catkins to 7 cm long, their bracts pale brown.
  2 Leaves silky-villous or sometimes glabrate beneath; stipules usually prominent; pistillate catkins stout, long-cylindrical; [*S. glauca* vars. *acutifolia* (Hook.) Schn. *(S. villosa* var. *acut.* Hook.), *aliceae* Ball, *glabrescens* (And.) Schn., *perstipula* Raup, and *stenolepis* (Flod.) Polunin, and ssp. *desertorum* var. *sericea* Hult.; *S. glauca* × (*monticola*) *pseudomonticola* (*S. padophylla* Rydb.); *S. ?stuartiana sensu* Hooker 1838, not Sm.; *S. seemannii* Rydb. in part; intergrading with the Beringia phase; Alaska–Yukon–Dist. Mackenzie (E to Great Slave L.); MAP: Argus 1965: map 2, p. 63] . . . . WESTERN PHASE
  2 Leaves pubescent on both surfaces, becoming glabrate above, never silky-villous beneath; stipules variable in prominence; pistillate catkins shorter and sometimes slender; [ssp. *glauca; S. glauca* ssp. *desertorum* (Rich.) And. (*S. des.* Rich.); *S. seemannii* Rydb. in part; coastal Alaska–Yukon–w Dist. Mackenzie (Mackenzie R. Delta); MAP: Argus 1965: map 2, p. 63] . . . . BERINGIA PHASE
1 Leaves generally less than 5 cm long, elliptical to obovate (to 3 times as long as broad); stipules to 4 mm long; pistillate catkins to 4 cm long.
  3 Shrubs to 1.5(3.5) m tall, their branchlets at first pubescent but becoming glabrate and often pruinose; leaves oblanceolate to narrowly elliptical, occasionally with some rust-coloured hairs; bracts pale brown to blackish; [*S. glauca* vars. *poliophylla* (Schn.) Raup (var. *acutifolia* f. *poliophylla* Schn.), *pseudolapponum* (Seem.) Kelso (*S. pseud.* Seem. and its var. *subincurva* Kelso), and *villosa* (Hook.) And. (*S. villosa* Hook.); *S. glaucops* And.; *S. desertorum* var. *elata* And.; *S. athabascensis* and *S. fallax* Raup, in part; mts. of B.C.–Alta. to SE Dist. Keewatin and s Man.; MAP: Argus 1965: map 2, p. 63] . . . .
. . . . ROCKY MOUNTAIN PHASE
  3 Shrubs to 1(2) m tall, prostrate, their branchlets finely pubescent or white-tomentose (pruinose in N Que. and Baffin Is.); leaves elliptical to oval or obovate, lacking rust-coloured hairs; bracts pale brown; [*S. glauca* vars. *macounii* (Rydb.) Boivin (*S. macounii* Rydb.) and *stenolepis* (Flod.) Polunin (*S. sten.* Flod.) in part; *S. anamesa* Schn.; *S. atra, S. labradorica,* and *S. vacciniformis* Rydb.; *S. rydbergii* Heller; *S. cordifolia* and its f. *atra* (Rydb.) Schn. and f. *hypoprionata* Schn., and its vars. *callicarpaea* (Trautv.) Fern. (*S callicarpaea* Trautv.), *macounii* (Rydb.) Schn., and *eucycla, intonsa,* and *tonsa* Fern.; s Dist. Keewatin, N Man., and N Ont. to SE Baffin Is., N Que., Labrador, E Que. (Anticosti Is. and Gaspé Pen.), Nfld., and St. Paul Is., N.S.; MAP: Argus 1965: map 2, p. 63] . . . .
. . . . EASTERN PHASE

S. herbacea L.

/aST/EE/GEA/ (Ch) Damp tundra and mossy alpine regions on acidic rocks from Great Bear L. and the coasts of Dist. Mackenzie–Dist. Keewatin to Devon Is., Baffin Is. and northernmost Ungava–Labrador, s to N Man. (s to Churchill; not known from Ont.), Que. (s to SE Hudson Bay, Mollie T. Lake at ca. 55°N, and the Shickshock Mts. of the Gaspé Pen.), and

Nfld., and in the mts. to N.Y., N.H., and Maine; w and e Greenland n to ca. 79°N; Iceland; Spitsbergen; Europe; nw Siberia. [*S. polaris* of Labrador reports, not Wahl.]. MAPS: Hultén 1958: map 24, p. 43; Raup 1959: map 6, p. 11; Porsild 1957: map 114, p. 175; *Atlas of Canada* 1957: map 5, sheet 38; Meusel, Jaeger, and Weinert 1965:114; Böcher 1954: fig. 28 (top; bottom right), p. 111.

Forma *latifolia* Rousseau & Rouleau (the large-leaved extreme with leaves to 2.5 cm long and broad) is known from the type locality at Payne L., n Que., 59°27'N, 74°40'W.

S. hookeriana Barratt
/t/W/eA/ (Mc) Coastal sands and dunes (seldom more than 5 mi from salt water) from sw B.C. (Vancouver Is. and adjacent islands and mainland w of the Coast Range) to n Calif.; e Asia. MAP: Fernald 1925: map 23, p. 257.

According to Breitung (1957a), reports from Sask. probably refer to *S. scouleriana*. Polunin (1940) notes that his tentative referral to this taxon of collections from Akpatok Is., Ungava Bay, n Que., is based upon *S. calcicola*. Var. *tomentosa* Henry (ovaries and capsules pubescent rather than glabrous) is known from sw B.C. (the presumed type locality). Concerning the obscure Alaskan *S. amplifolia* Cov. (type from Yakutat Bay, the only known locality), Hultén (1943) writes, "It is closely related to *S. Hookeriana* Barr., from which it differs in having longer styles, large-leaved peduncles and the underside of the outgrown leaves tomentose on the midrib. It is remarkable that this plant, so far known only from Yakutat Bay, lies between the two separated areas of *S. Hookeriana* in W. America and E. Asia. In E. America *S. laurentiana* Fern. comes close to this type, and it seems probable that all three species are remnants of a pre- or interglacial species, split up by the ice."

S. humilis Marsh. Prairie Willow
/T/EE/ (N (Mc)) Open woodlands, thickets, and plains, the aggregate species from Sask. (n to Candle Lake, 53°50'N; Breitung 1957a; the report from Alta. by Boivin 1966b, requires confirmation, perhaps being based upon the citation from South Kootenay Pass by John Macoun 1886, the relevant collection in CAN proving referable to *S. scouleriana*) to Man. (n to Flin Flon), Ont. (n to w James Bay at ca. 52°N), Que. (n to e James Bay at ca. 53°45'N, L. Mistassini, the Côte-Nord, Anticosti Is., and Gaspé Pen.), se Labrador (n to the Hamilton R. basin), Nfld., N.B., P.E.I., and N.S., s to Wisc., Mich., N.Y., and n New Eng. MAP and synonymy: *see* below.
1 Leaves narrowly oblanceolate, acutish at apex; shrub to about 1 m tall; [incl. var.
     rigidiuscula And.; *S. tristis* Ait.; collections from s Man. and e Que. evidently belong
     here; reports from N.S. by Lindsay 1878, and John Macoun 1886, and from s Ont. by
     Soper 1949, require confirmation] . . . . var. *microphylla* (And.) Fern.
1 Leaves oblanceolate to obovate, rounded at apex; shrub to about 3 m tall; [incl. var.
     keweenawensis Farw.; range of the species; MAP (aggregate species; not including
     Alta. in the range): Raup 1943: pl. 4] . . . . var. *humilis*

[*S. jejuna* Fern.]
[Calcareous barrens and cliffs of se Labrador (Chateau Bay, ca. 52°30'N), ?Que. (Boivin 1966b), and n Nfld. (type from Pistolet Bay). MAP: Raup 1943: pl. 1.

This species may finally be merged with the *S. arctica* complex or assigned to a hybrid between that species and some other one.]

S. lasiandra Benth. Red Willow, Western Shining Willow
/ST/WW/ (Mc) Along streams at low to moderate elevations, the aggregate species from N-cent. Alaska and cent. Yukon (*see* Hultén 1943: map 403, p. 563; var. *lancifolia*) to Great Slave L., Alta. (n to L. Athabasca), and Sask. (n to Lac La Ronge, 55°10'N; Breitung 1957a), s to Calif. and N.Mex. MAPS and synonymy: *see* below.
1 Leaves essentially entire; [Big Bend, NE of Revelstoke, B.C.] . . . . var. *abramsii* Ball
1 Leaves finely and regularly toothed.
    2 Leaves glaucous beneath.
        3 Young branchlets glabrous or soon glabrate; [var. *lyallii* Sarg.; *S. lyallii* (Sarg.)
            Heller; *S. fendleriana* And.; *S. speciosa* Nutt. in part; *S. lucida macrophylla*

And.; Alaska–B.C. to Sask.; MAPS (aggregate species): Hultén 1968*b*:363; Raup 1959: map 1, p. 11, and 1930: map 22, p. 202; C.R. Ball, Madroño 10: fig. 1 (together with var. *lancifolia*), p. 82, 1949] . . . . .var. *lasiandra*

    3 Young branchlets usually densely pubescent; [*S. lancifolia* And., the type from Vancouver Is.; range of var. *lasiandra* and largely replacing it northwards] . . . . .var. *lancifolia* (And.) Bebb

  2 Leaves green on both surfaces (sometimes paler beneath but scarcely glaucous).

    4 Young branchlets glabrous or soon glabrate; [var. *parvifolia* Ball; *S. caudata* Nutt.; B.C. to SW Sask.] . . . . .var. *caudata* (Nutt.) Sudw.

    4 Young branchlets pubescent; [SW Dist. Mackenzie, the type from near Fort Simpson] . . . . .var. *recomponens* Raup

[S. lasiolepis Benth.]
[The report of this species of the W U.S.A. (Wash. and Idaho to Baja Calif., Mexico, and Tex.) from cent. B.C. by Hitchcock et al. (1964; Hazelton, ca. 55°15′N) requires confirmation, perhaps being based upon some closely related species such as *S. hookeriana*.]

S. laurentiana Fern.
/ST/EE/ (Mc) Thickets, gravelly slopes, beaches, and dunes (ranges of Canadian taxa outlined below), S to Ill., Ohio, N.Y., and Maine. MAPS and synonymy: *see* below.

1 Ovaries and capsules (at least at base) minutely tomentose; [?Ont. (reported from N Ont. by Fernald *in* Gray 1950, but Dutilly, Lepage, and Duman (1954; 1958) refer their James Bay reports (Dutilly and Lepage 1947) to the following taxon under the name *S. glaucophylloides*); E Que. (L. Mistassini; Côte-Nord; type from the Gaspé Pen.); MAP: Fernald 1925: map 23 (in ellipse), p. 57] . . . . .f. *laurentiana*

1 Ovaries and capsules glabrous; [*S. glaucophylloides* Fern. and its f. *lasioclada* Fern. and vars. *glaucophylla* (Bebb.) Schn. (*S. glaucophylla* Bebb) and *albovestita* (Ball) Fern. (*S. glaucophylla* var. *alb.* Ball); cent. Ont. (W James Bay N to ca. 53°N), Que. (N to Great Whale R., SE Hudson Bay, ca. 55°15′N, L. St. John, the Côte-Nord, Anticosti Is., and Gaspé Pen.), Nfld., and N N.B.; the report from SE Dist. Keewatin by Boivin 1966*b*, may refer to the very closely related *S. monticola,* which is otherwise known in that region only as far N as Churchill, Man. (*see* Raup 1959:71, and his map 15, p. 12, under the name *S. padophylla*); MAPS (*S. glaucophylloides*): Raup 1959: map 15, p. 12, and 1947: pl. 3 (incomplete)] . . . . .f. *glaucophylla* (Bebb) Boivin

[S. leiolepis Fern.]
[Known only from the type locality, mossy mounds on the calcareous tableland of Table Mt., W Nfld.; perhaps merely a glabrate phase of *S. vestita*; (*see* Schneider 1919:46–47).]

[S. lemmonii Bebb]
[The range of this species is given as Oreg. to Calif. and Idaho by Hitchcock et al. (1964; incl. *S. austiniae* Bebb). The inclusion of the Yukon, B.C., and Alta. in the range of *S. austiniae* given by Rydberg (1922) is probably based upon other species.]

S. lucida Muhl. Shining Willow
/ST/EE/ (Mc) Shores and swampy places, the aggregate species from Sask. (N to Nipawin, 53°22′N; Breitung 1957*a*) to Man. (N to York Factory, Hudson Bay, 57°N), Ont. (N to Sandy L. at ca. 53°N, 93°W), Que. (N to E James Bay at 53°50′N, L. Mistassini, and the Côte-Nord), SE Labrador (N to the Hamilton R. basin), Nfld., N.B., P.E.I., and N.S., S to S.Dak., Ill., Ohio, and Md. MAPS: *see* below.

    The extension of the range westwards to Alaska–Dist. Mackenzie–B.C. by Boivin (1966*b*) is probably through the inclusion of the closely related *S. lasiandra* Benth.

1 Branchlets and leaves glabrous or soon glabrate.

  2 Leaves lanceolate to lance-ovate, long-attenuate, to over 1.5 dm long and 5 cm broad; [range of the species; MAP: Raup 1959: map 1, p. 11] . . . . .var. *lucida*

  2 Leaves narrowly lanceolate, to 8 cm long and 2 cm broad; [Man. to S Labrador, Nfld., and N.S.; MAP (NE area): Raup 1943: pl. 1] . . . . .var. *angustifolia* And.

1 Branchlets and lower leaf-surfaces permanently pubescent with sordid or rusty
   hairs; [Ont. to Nfld. and N.B.] . . . . .var. *intonsa* Fern.

S. lutea Nutt. Yellow Willow
/ST/WW/ (Mc) Moist places and streambanks from w Dist. Mackenzie (N to Norman Wells,
ca. 65°15′N; W.J. Cody, Can. Field-Nat. 74(2):84. 1960) to Great Slave L., Alta. (N to
L. Athabasca), Sask. (N to Prince Albert), Man. (N to York Factory, Hudson Bay, 57°N), and
Ont. (Timmins, 48°28′N; SW James Bay), S to Calif., N.Mex., Nebr., and Iowa. [*S. missouriensis*
Bebb; *S. eriocephala* and *S. rigida* of Sask. reports, not Michx. nor Muhl., respectively]. MAPS:
Raup 1959: map 12, p. 12, and 1930: map 28, p. 203.

S. maccalliana Rowlee
/ST/(X)/ (N (Mc)) Damp meadows, streambanks, and lake shores from southernmost
Yukon (CAN) and Great Slave L. to B.C.–Alta. (type from Devil's Head L., near Banff), Sask. (N
to about 25 mi NE of Prince Albert), Man. (N to York Factory, Hudson Bay, 57°N), Ont. (N
shore of L. Superior; Longlac; Timmins; w James Bay N to ca. 53°N), and S-cent. Que. (E
James Bay N to ca. 53°N; L. Mistassini), S to a poorly defined limit in the w U.S.A. MAPS: Raup
1959: map 11, p. 12; Dutilly, Lepage, and Duman 1954: fig. 10 (NE area), p. 70.

S. mackenzieana (Hook.) Barratt
/sT/WW/ (Mc) Moist places, streambanks, and sandbars from s Yukon (Whitehorse and
Pelly R. Valley; CAN) and w Dist. Mackenzie (N to Fort Simpson, 62°51′N) through E B.C.,
Alta., and NW Sask. (L. Athabasca, the type locality of *S. turnori*) to Oreg. and Wyo. [*S. cordata (rigida)* var. *mack.* Hook., the type locality "Great Slave Lake and the Mackenzie River";
S. ?monochroma Ball; *S. ?prolixa* And.; *S. turnori* Raup]. MAPS: Hultén 1968b:351; Raup 1959:
map 12, p. 12.

S. monticola Bebb
/ST/(X)/ (Mc) Moist woods and streambanks from N-cent. Alaska to cent. Yukon–w Dist.
Mackenzie, Alta. (N to Athabasca Landing, 54°43′N), Sask. (N to 27 mi NE of Prince Albert),
Man. (N to Churchill), Ont. (Nipigon, Longlac, Hearst, Cochrane, New Liskeard, and w James
Bay N to Attawapiskat, 52°56′N; CAN), and w-cent. Que. (E James Bay at ca. 51°30′N and SE
Hudson Bay at ca. 56°N; CAN), S to Oreg., Ariz., N.Mex., and S.Dak. [*S. pseudomonticola*
Ball; *S. padifolia* Rydb.; *S. padophylla sensu* Raup and other Canadian auth., not Rydb. (*see*
synonymy under the "Western Phase" of *S. glauca*); *S. barclayi sensu* Fraser and Russell
1944, not And.]. MAPS (as *S. padophylla*): Hultén 1968b:354; Raup 1959: map 15, p. 12.

S. myrtillifolia Anderss.
/ST/X/ (N (Mc)) Damp woods, mossy thickets, and muskegs from cent. Alaska–Yukon to
Great Bear L., Great Slave L., L. Athabasca (Alta. and Sask.), northernmost Man.–Ont., Que.
(N to SE Hudson Bay at ca. 56°N and the Côte-Nord), Labrador (N to the Hamilton R. basin),
Nfld., and N.B. (near Hillsborough, Albert Co.; not known from P.E.I. or N.S.), S to S B.C.–
Alta., S-cent. Sask.–Man., and the N shore of L. Superior, Ont., and in the mts. of the West to
Calif., S Utah, Wyo., and ?Colo. [*S. novae-angliae* var. *myrt.* And.]. MAPS: Hultén 1968b:352;
Raup 1959: map 14, p. 12, and 1947: pl. 21.
   The western plant includes taller forms with larger leaves (to 4 m tall with leaves to 7 cm
long, rather than mostly less than 1 m tall and with relatively short leaves). It may be distin-
guished as var. *pseudomyrsinites* (And.) Ball (*S. pseud., S. curtiflora,* and *S. pseudocordata*
And.). Some of the material from Que. and Nfld. has been separated as var. *brachypoda* Fern.
(incl. *S. obtusata* Fern.), characterized by very short pedicels (those of the typical form to
1.5 mm long) and leaves with a distinctly glaucous lower surface. The habitally similar
S. nigricans Sm. (*S. myrsinifolia* Salisb.) of Eurasia is reported from Ont. by Gillett (1958;
Ottawa dist.) but a planted tree may be involved.

S. nigra Marsh. Black Willow
/T/EE/ (Ms) Moist woods, streambanks, and shores from Ont. (reported N to the Kaminis-

tikwia R. NW of Thunder Bay by John Macoun 1886; reports from Man. by Jackson et al. 1922, and Lowe 1943, require confirmation) to Que. (N to the Quebec City dist.) and S N.B. (not known from P.E.I. or N.S.), S to N Mexico, Tex., and NW Fla. [*S. ambigua* Pursh, not Ehrh.; *S. ligustrina* Michx. f.]. MAPS: Fowells 1965:650; Preston 1961:132; Hough 1947:79; Munns 1938: map 76, p. 80; Little 1971: map 190-N.

S. ovalifolia Trautv.
/aST/W/eA/   (Ch)   Chiefly coastal on tundra and rocky slopes from the Aleutian Is. and coasts of Alaska–Yukon–NW Dist. Mackenzie to cent. B.C. (S to Hazelton, ca. 55°15′N); NE Asia.

Included in the above statement of range and keyed out below are four species (?microspecies) perhaps best treated as elements of an *S. ovalifolia* complex. It may be noted that *S. glacialis* is listed by Hultén (1943) but is not mentioned in his 1968*a* and 1968*b* publications, so that his final concept of that species remains in doubt.

1   Ovaries and pedicels more or less densely pubescent; styles less than 0.5 mm long; [*S. glacialis* And., the type from between Point Barrow, Alaska, and the Mackenzie R. Delta; *S. ovalifolia* var. *camdensis* Schn.; MAPS: Raup 1959: map 9, p. 11; Hultén 1943: map 419, p. 565] . . . . [*S. glacialis* And.]
1   Ovaries and pedicels glabrous from the first.
  2   Styles 1.5–2 mm long; leaves obovate; [type from Glacier, SE Alaska; MAPS: Hultén 1968*b*:345, and 1943: map 418, p. 565] . . . . [*S. stolonifera* Cov.]
  2   Styles rarely over 0.5 mm long.
    3   Leaves orbicular, broadly rounded to subcordate at base; [*S. ovalifolia* var. *cyc*. (Rydb.) Ball; type from Alaska; MAP: Hultén 1968*b*:344] . . .[*S. cyclophylla* Rydb.]
    3   Leaves obovate-lanceolate to elliptic, cuneate at base.
      4   Leaves obovate-lanceolate, acute, yellowish green; [type from Kotzebue, Alaska; MAPS: Hultén 1968*b*:346, and 1943: map 420, p. 565; W.J. Cody, Nat. can. (Que.) 98(2): fig. 24, p. 155. 1971] . . . . [*S. arctolitoralis* Hult.]
      4   Leaves elliptic, mostly blunt, dark green; [*S. diplodictya* Rydb.; *S. flagellaris* Hult.; type from Alaska; MAPS: Hultén 1968*b*:343, and 1943: map 416, p. 565; Raup 1959: map 8, p. 11] . . . . *S. ovalifolia*

S. pedicellaris Pursh   Bog Willow
/ST/X/   (N)   Acid bogs and sphagnous shores, the aggregate species from SE Yukon and B.C. to Great Bear L., Great Slave L., L. Athabasca (Alta. and Sask.), Man. (N to Churchill), northernmost Ont., Que. (N to S Ungava Bay and the Gaspé Pen.), Labrador (N to the Hamilton R. basin), Nfld., N.B., and N.S. (not known from P.E.I.), S to Oreg., N Idaho, N Iowa, Ill., Pa., and N.J.

The following key (with MAPS and synonymy) includes two "microspecies" endemic to Quebec that are considered by C.R. Ball (Rhodora 52(613):8–18. 1950) to be of probable hybrid origin between *S. pedicellaris* var. *hypoglauca* and some other unknown species.

1   Creeping shrub, rooting at the lower nodes; capsules pubescent or glabrate, on pedicels 1 or 2 mm long; styles to 0.7 mm long; bracts short-hairy, dark brown; [*S. fuscescens* var. *heb*. Fern.; ?Alaska (Seward Pen.; *see* Hultén 1943:520, and his MAP 415, p. 565); E Que. (type from Mt. Albert, Gaspé Co.); also reported from the Larch R., N Que., by Dutilly and Lepage 1951*b*; MAPS: Raup 1959: map 23, p. 13; Hultén 1968*b*:345] . . . .[*S. hebecarpa* Fern.]
1   Erect shrubs; bracts light brown or yellowish; styles obsolete or at most 0.5 mm long.
  2   Pedicels scarcely 1 mm long; bracts more or less pilose; [type from Betchewun, Saguenay Co., Que., the only known locality, this indicated on the MAP by Raup 1943: pl. 4] . . . . [*S. simulans* Fern.]
  2   Pedicels 2–4 mm long; bracts glabrous . . . . *S. pedicellaris*
    3   Leaves linear-oblong to oblanceolate, acute at both ends, to about 1 cm broad, glaucous beneath; capsules distant, subulate, to 1 cm long; [N Alta. (Wood Buffalo National Park); Man. (Riverton, about 75 mi N of Winnipeg);

Ont. (Raith, near Thunder Bay; Kapuskasing; Sandy L. and Big Trout L., 53°–53°45′N)] . . . . var. *tenuescens* Fern.
3 Leaves broadly oblanceolate to obovate-oblong, obtuse or subacute, to 2.5 cm broad; capsules rather crowded, ovoid at base, to 8 mm long; [*S. myrtilloides* of most Canadian reports, not L.; transcontinental].
  4 Leaves glaucous-whitened beneath; [the common form northwards; MAPS: Hultén 1968*b*:350; Raup 1943: pl. 4 (NE Canada; a dot should be added for Chimo, S Ungava Bay] . . . . var. *hypoglauca* Fern.
  4 Leaves green on both surfaces; [*S. myrtilloides* ssp. *ped.* (Pursh) And.; MAP (aggregate species): Raup 1959: map 23, p. 13] . . . . var. *pedicellaris*

S. pellita Anderss.
/ST/EE/ (Mc) Streambanks and rich thickets from Sask. (N to Candle Lake, 53°50′N; Breitung 1957*a*) to Man. (N to York Factory, Hudson Bay, 57°N; the type is an early Bourgeau collection from "Lake Winipeg"), Ont. (N to Fort Severn, Hudson Bay, ca. 56°N), Que. (N to the George R., Ungava Bay, at ca. 58°N, and the Côte-Nord), Labrador (N to the Hamilton R. basin), Nfld., N.B., and N.S. (not known from P.E.I.), S to N Mich. and N New Eng. [*S. chlorophylla* var. *pell.* And.]. MAP: Raup 1959: map 27 (the area should be extended to Ungava Bay in Que.), p. 13.

According to Hitchcock et al. (1964), *S. pellita* is the eastern phase, apparently largely apomictic, of the western *S. drummondiana,* with which they merge it. *See,* also, Raup 1959:90–92. Forma *psila* Schn. (type from Que.–Nfld.; leaves becoming glabrate beneath) occurs throughout the range.

S. pentandra L.   Bay-leaved Willow
Eurasian; spread from cult. in N. America, as in S Ont.; also reported from Alta., Sask., Man., N Ont., Que., Nfld., P.E.I., and N.S., but apparently chiefly or wholly on the basis of planted trees.

S. petiolaris Sm.
/ST/X/ (N (Mc)) Meadows and wet ground, the aggregate species from B.C. (N to Dawson Creek, 55°46′N) and northernmost Alta. to Great Slave L. (J.W. Thieret, Can. Field-Nat. 75(3):115. 1961), Sask. (N to the Churchill R. at ca. 55°30′N), Man. (N to MacBride L. at ca. 57°N, 100°W), Ont. (N to the Albany R. SW of James Bay at 52°11′N), Que. (N to L. Waswanipi at 49°39′N), N.B., P.E.I., and N.S., S to Nebr., Pa., and N N.J. *See* M.L. Fernald (Rhodora 48(567):46–48. 1946), C.R. Ball (Bull. Torrey Bot. Club 75(2):178–87. 1948), and Raup (1959:84–85). MAP and synonymy: *see* below.
1 Capsules to 9 mm long; leaves to about 1 dm long, strongly serrate-dentate except at base, rarely silky; [*S. gracilis* var. *textoris* Fern.; range of the species] . . . . var. *petiolaris*
1 Capsules to 7 mm long; leaves mostly less than 7 cm long, entire or minutely dentate, more or less silky beneath; [vars. *angustifolia* And. and *rosmarinoides* (And.) Schn.; *S. gracilis* And.; *S. rosmarinifolia sensu* Hooker 1838, not L.; range of the species; MAP (aggregate species; *S. grac.*): Raup 1959: map 24, p. 13] . . . .
. . . . var. *gracilis* And.

S. phlebophylla Anderss.
/aSs/W/eA/ (Ch) Tundra habitats from the coasts of Alaska–Yukon and NW Dist. Mackenzie (Mackenzie R. Delta) to the E Aleutian Is. and S Alaska (type from Cape Mulgrave); Siberia. [Incl. f. *major,* f. *media,* and f. *minor* And.; *S. palaeoneura* Rydb.; *S. retusa sensu* Hooker 1838, not L.]. MAPS: Raup 1959: map 5, p. 11; Hultén 1968*b*:338, and 1943: map 410, p. 564.

S. phylicifolia L.
/aST/X/EA/ (Mc) Damp thickets and slopes, the aggregate species from the Aleutian Is. and coasts of Alaska–Yukon–Dist. Mackenzie–Dist. Keewatin to southernmost Baffin Is., northernmost Ungava–Labrador, and Nfld. (not known from the Maritime Provinces), S in the West through E B.C. and Alta. to the mts. of N Calif., Utah, and N.Mex., farther eastwards S to cent. Sask., Man. (S to Riding Mt.), W and E James Bay, E Que. (Côte-Nord, Anticosti Is., and Gaspé Pen.), and the mts. of N New Eng.; Iceland; Eurasia. MAPS and synonymy: *see* below.

1   Leaves mostly finely and more or less regularly serrate; catkins usually coetaneous, sessile or on prominently leafy peduncles; [sw ?Alaska and sw ?Yukon; *see* Raup 1959:87, and his MAP 26, p. 13] . . . . ssp. *phylicifolia*

1   Leaves entire or essentially so; catkins precocious, sessile or with a few small leaf-bracts at base . . . . ssp. *planifolia* (Pursh) Hiitonen

   2   Stipules persistent for several years as dried appendages on the old wood; [*S. fulcrata* var. *subglauca* And.; *S. pulchra* Cham. and its vars. *looffiae* and *palmeri* Ball and *yukonensis* Cham.; Aleutian Is. to Coronation Gulf and northernmost B.C. (s to 59°15′N); MAPS (*S. pulchra*): Hultén 1968b:359; Raup 1959: map 26, p. 13, and 1947: pl. 21] . . . . var. *subglauca* (And.) Scoggan

   2   Stipules deciduous after one growing season; [*S. planifolia* Pursh, the type being cult. specimens originating from Labrador; *S. phylicifolia* of most American auth., not L.; incl. the reduced montane *S. monoica* Bebb and *S. nelsonii* and *S. pennata* Ball; *S. ?chlorophylla* And.; the Yukon–B.C. to s Baffin Is., Labrador, Nfld., and mts. of N New Eng.; MAPS: Hultén 1968b:359; Raup 1959: map 26, p. 13, and 1947: pl. 22 (*S. plan.*); Porsild 1957: map 124 (*S. plan.*), p. 176] . . . . . var. *planifolia*

The E Que. endemic, *S. paraleuca* Fern., and the Nfld. endemics, *S. ancorifera, S. amoena,* and *S. pedunculata* Fern., are obscure species (?microspecies) that appear to have a close affinity with *S. phylicifolia* ssp. *planifolia* or may be of hybrid origin, perhaps with this species as one of the parents. Their purported distinguishing characters are outlined in the following key but they should probably not be accepted as distinct entities in the Canadian flora until better understood.

1   Twigs densely ashy-pilose or -velvety; young leaves pilose, the mature ones glabrescent, crenate- or undulate-dentate; fruiting catkins to 6 cm long, on peduncles to 1 cm long; style about 1 mm long; [*S. stenocarpa* Fern., not Gand.; type from Gaspé Co., E Que.; also known from Saguenay Co., Que.] . . . .
. . . . [*S. paraleuca* Fern.]

1   Twigs glabrous; leaves glabrous or promptly glabrate; fruiting catkins to 1 dm long, on peduncles to 3 cm long; [Nfld. endemics].

   2   Stigmas strongly reflexed, to 2 mm long, terminating a style about 1 mm long; pedicels scarcely 1 mm long; young leaves minutely pilose, glandular-dentate; [*S. ?latiuscula* of Nfld. reports, perhaps not Anderss.; *see* M.L. Fernald, Rhodora 28:126. 1929] . . . . [*S. ancorifera* Fern.]

   2   Stigmas ascending, about 0.5 mm long; young leaves glabrous, entire or undulate-crenate.

     3   Fruiting catkins to 1 dm long, their blackish bracts to 4.5 mm long; pedicels to 2 mm long; style over 1 mm long . . . . [*S. pedunculata* Fern.]

     3   Fruiting catkins to 7 cm long, their yellowish bracts 2 or 3 mm long; pedicels very short; style about 1 mm long . . . . [*S. amoena* Fern.]

[S. piperi Bebb]
[B.C. is included in the area of this species of the w U.S.A. (Wash. to Calif.) by Hitchcock et al. (1964), evidently on the basis of the report of *S. hookeriana* var. *laurifolia* Henry from that province by Henry (1915; the type presumably a collection from Vancouver). They note, however, that this is a form transitional between *S. hookeriana* and *S. piperi*. Until the discovery of typical *S. piperi* in Canada, it seems best to exclude it from our flora.]

S. polaris Wahl.
/aST/W/EA/   (Ch)   Mossy tundra habitats from the coasts of Alaska–Yukon–NW Dist. Mackenzie to Banks Is. and SE Victoria Is., s to the w Aleutian Is. and in the mts. to Mt. Selwyn, B.C., ca. 56°N; N Eurasia. MAPS: Hultén 1968b:337, and 1943: map 409, p. 564 (ssp. *pseud.*); Raup 1959: map 6 (ssp. *pseud.*), p. 11; Porsild 1957: map 119 (*S. pseud.*), p. 175.

The plant of w N. America and E Asia may be distinguished as ssp. *pseudopolaris* (Flod.) Hult. *(S. pseud.* Flod.; *S. polaris* var. *selwynensis* Raup), "characterized by light-coloured bracts with wavy hairs" (Hultén 1943).

S. purpurea L.   Purple Osier, Backet-Willow
Eurasian; originally introd. for basket-making and known from Ont. (N to the Ottawa dist.),
Que. (N to the Montreal dist.), Nfld. (Holyrood, Avalon Pen.; GH), N.B., P.E.I., and N.S. (some
collections presumably from trees spreading from their original plantings).

S. pyrifolia Anderss.   Balsam-Willow
/ST/X/   (Mc)   Moist thickets and borders of woods from B.C. (N to the Beatton R. at ca.
57°N; CAN) and Alta. to Great Slave L., Sask. (N to L. Athabasca), Man. (N to the Cochrane R.
at 58°13′N), Ont. (N to Sandy L. at ca. 53°N, 93°W), Que. (N to the Larch R. at ca. 57°35′N,
the Côte-Nord, and Gaspé Pen.), SE Labrador (N to the Hamilton R. basin), Nfld., N.B., P.E.I.,
amd N.S., S to Minn., Mich., N.Y., and New Eng. [Incl. var. *laeta* And.; *S. balsamifera* Barratt].
MAP: Raup 1959: map 17, p. 12.
    Var. *lanceolata* (Bebb) Fern. (leaves relatively narrow, tapering to base rather than rounded
or subcordate) "is found in some of the swamps of eastern Newfoundland to be so uniform
and to occur in such extensive areas that it seems well worth recognition." (M.L. Fernald,
Rhodora 16(186):116. 1914).

S. reticulata L.
/aST/X/EA/   (Ch)   Moist sandy, gravelly, or turfy places in calcareous areas, the aggregate
species from the Aleutian Is. and coasts of Alaska–Yukon–Dist. Mackenzie–Dist. Keewatin to
Banks Is., Devon Is., and northernmost Ungava–Labrador, S to S Alaska–Yukon, B.C. (S to
Queen Charlotte Is. and Hazelton, ca. 55°15′N), Great Slave L., N Sask. (Hasbala L. at ca.
59°30′N; G.W. Argus, Can. Field-Nat. 80(3):136. 1966), Man. (S to York Factory, Hudson Bay,
57°N), and W and E James Bay; isolated in the mts. of SW Alta. (Banff dist.) and in Nfld.; Spitsbergen; N Eurasia. MAPS and synonymy: *see* below.
1   Leaves typically broadly oval or obovate to suborbicular, broadly rounded at the
    summit, mostly less than twice as long as broad, strongly rugose beneath with a
    coarse reticulate venation.
    2   Ovaries and capsules densely white-pubescent; peduncles and bracts usually
        villous; branchlets and lower leaf-surfaces more or less persistently pubescent;
        [incl. f. *subrotunda* Ser. and the large-leaved extreme, var. *gigantifolia* Ball
        (f. ?*oblongifolia* Polunin); *S. orbicularis* And. in part; *S. nivalis* var. *saximontana*
        sensu Porsild 1943, not *S. saximontana* Rydb.; transcontinental; MAPS: Hultén
        1968*b*:336; Raup 1959: map 3, p. 11, 1947: pl. 21, and 1930: map 10, p. 202;
        Porsild 1957: map 118, p. 175; Meusel, Jaeger, and Weinert 1965:113] . . . var. *reticulata*
    2   Ovaries, capsules, peduncles, and bracts of the staminate catkins glabrous or
        only thinly pubescent; branchlets and leaves glabrous nearly or quite from the
        first; [ssp. ?*glabellicarpa* Argus; Queen Charlotte Is., B.C., the type locality of
        ssp. *glab.*; Labrador and N Nfld.] . . . . var. *semicalva* Fern.
1   Leaves narrower in outline, typically elliptic or obovate and more than twice as long
    as broad, acutish to broadly rounded at summit, less conspicuously rugose-
    reticulate; [*S. nivalis* Hook., the type a Drummond collection from the Rocky Mts.,
    probably of Alta.; incl. the larger-dimensioned extreme, *S. saximontana* Rydb.
    (*S. nivalis* var. *sax.* (Rydb.) Schn.) and *S. vestita* var. ?*nana* Hook.; mts. of B.C. (N to
    Hazelton, 55°15′N) and SW Alta.] . . . . var. *nivalis* (Hook.) And.

S. richardsonii Hook.
/aSs/X/eA/   (N)   Moist sandy or gravelly places and shores from the coasts of Alaska–
Yukon–Dist. Mackenzie (type from Fort Franklin on the Mackenzie R.) to Banks Is., Victoria
Is., and northernmost Baffin Is., S to S Alaska–Yukon–Dist. Mackenzie–Dist. Keewatin, Southampton Is., and S Baffin Is.; E Siberia. [*S. lanata* of Canadian reports, not L.; *S. lanata* ssp.
rich. (Hook.) Skvortz.; incl. vars. *angustifolia* and *latifolia* And. and the small-leaved extreme,
var. *mckeandii* Polunin]. MAPS: Hultén 1968*b*:355 (*S. lan.* ssp. *rich.*); Raup 1959: map 18, p. 12;
Porsild 1957: map 117, p. 175; Fernald 1925: map 56 (requiring considerable expansion),
p. 323.

S. rotundifolia Trautv.
/aSs/W/nA/   (Ch)   Tundra and alpine ledges and slopes from the N coast of Alaska (type locality) to the Aleutian Is., s Yukon, and s-cent. Dist. Mackenzie (Canol Road near the Yukon boundary at ca. 53°–54°N); Novaya Zemlya; N Asia. [Incl. f. *pilosiuscula* Schn. (× *S. pil.* (Schn.) Boivin)]. MAPS: Hultén 1968b:339; Raup 1959: map 5, p. 11.

Part of the material from the N. American area is referable to ssp. *dodgeana* (Rydb.) Argus (*S. dodgeana* Rydb.; lateral veins of the leaves prominent only beneath rather than on both surfaces, the intervening veinlets not visible). MAPS (*S. dodg.*): Hultén 1968b:338; Porsild 1966: map 47, p. 72; Raup 1959: map 5, p. 11.

S. scouleriana Barratt
/ST/WW/   (Ms)   Dry to moist woodlands, rocky slopes, and floodplains from cent. Alaska–Yukon–w Dist. Mackenzie to Great Slave L., L. Athabasca (Alta. and Sask.), and Man. (N to Lac Brochet at 58°38′N), s to Calif., N.Mex., and S.Dak. MAPS: Hultén 1968b:361; Raup 1959: map 25, p. 13, and 1947: pl. 21.

Var. *coetanea* Ball (catkins appearing as the leaves unfold rather than earlier) is known from the Yukon. Dist. Mackenzie, and B.C. (CAN). The hairy-leaved extreme, var. *poikila* Schn. (*S. flavescens* Nutt., not Host) is reported from Alaska and Vancouver Is. by Henry (1915) and from the Yukon by Hitchcock et al. (1964). A form with small-toothed (rather than essentially entire) leaves, var. *thompsonii* Ball, is known from sw B.C. (Vancouver Is. and adjacent islands; CAN).

S. sericea Marsh.   Silky Willow
/T/EE/   (Mc)   Moist thickets and streambanks from Ont. (Cornwall, Stormont Co. (TRT); shores of Georgian Bay, L. Huron (CAN); reported from Essex, Lambton, and Waterloo counties) to sw Que. (N to the Montreal dist.), N.B. (Queens and York counties; CAN; NBM; not known from P.E.I.), and N.S. (Yarmouth and Lunenburg counties; CAN; GH), s to Mo., Tenn., and S.C.

S. serissima (Bailey) Fern.   Autumn-Willow
/ST/X/   (Mc)   Wet or swampy ground (often calcareous) from w-cent. Dist. Mackenzie (N to Norman Wells, 65°17′N; W.J. Cody, Can. Field-Nat. 74(2):83. 1960) to L. Athabasca (Alta. and Sask.; not known from B.C.), Man. (N to York Factory, Hudson Bay, 57°N), Ont. (N to Big Trout L. and the w James Bay watershed, both at ca. 53°N), Que. (N to the E James Bay watershed at ca. 53°45′N and Anticosti Is.; not known from the Gaspé Pen.), SE Labrador (N to the Hamilton R. basin), and Nfld. (not known from the Maritime Provinces), s to Colo., N.Dak., Pa., and N.J. [*S. lucida* var. *ser.* Bailey; *S. ?erythrocoma* Barratt in part]. MAPS: Hultén 1968b:363; Raup 1959: map 1, p. 11.

S. setchelliana Ball
/Ss/W/   (Ch)   Sandy lakeshores and alluvia of Alaska (N to ca. 65°N; type from Muldrow Glacier) and sw Yukon (Kluane L. area; CAN). (*S. aliena* Flod.). MAPS: Hultén 1968b:337, and 1943: map 406, p. 507; Porsild 1966: map 49, p. 73; Raup 1959: map 4, p. 11.

S. sitchensis Sanson
/sT/W/eA/   (Mc)   Streambanks and moist woods from low to moderately high elevations (chiefly along the coast) from s Alaska (*see* Hultén 1943: map 440, p. 567; type from Sitka) and southernmost ?Yukon (a report from L. Lindemann requires confirmation) through B.C. (E to the Interior Plateau and the Selkirk Range; reported E to Alta. by Boivin 1966b) to E Wash., N Idaho, and ?Mont.; Siberia. [Incl. var. *angustifolia* Bebb (*S. pellita* var. *ang.* (Bebb) Boivin) and vars. *congesta* and *denudata* And.; *S. coulteri* And.]. MAPS: Hultén 1968b:361; Raup 1959: map 24, p. 13.

S. subcoerulea Piper   Blue Willow
/sT/W/   (Mc)   Moist ground and shores from SE Yukon (Raup 1959) through E B.C. and w Alta. (N to Athabasca Landing, near Lesser Slave L.) to s Calif. and N.Mex. [*S. drummondiana*

var. *sub.* (Piper) Ball and var. *?bella* (Piper) Ball (*S. bella* Piper)]. MAPS: Hultén 1968*b*:360; Raup 1959: map 27, p. 13.

For a discussion of this obscure species (perhaps best merged with *S. pellita*), reduced by Ball to varietal status under *S. drummondiana* (itself evidently a mixture of species referable in part to *S. alaxensis* var. *longistylis*), see Raup 1959).

S. uva-ursi Pursh   Bearberry Willow

/aST/E/G/   (Ch)   Exposed rocky and gravelly places (chiefly coastal) from S Baffin Is. (N to near the Arctic Circle) to Que. (S to E James Bay at 53°48'N, Knob Lake, 54°48'N, the Côte-Nord, and Shickshock Mts. of the Gaspé Pen.; reported from Anticosti Is. by Verrill 1865), Labrador, Nfld., and NE N.S. (St. Paul Is., off the N tip of Cape Breton Is.; GH; CAN), and in the mts. to N N.Y. and N New Eng.; W Greenland N to ca. 65°N, E Greenland N to ca. 61°N. [Var. *labradorica* And.; *S. cutleri* Tuckerm.]. MAPS: Porsild 1957: map 115, p. 175; *Atlas of Canada* 1957: map 16, sheet 38; Böcher 1954: fig. 6 (bottom), p. 31; Raup 1943: pl. 1.

Forma *phyllolepis* Fern. (bracts of the pistillate catkins changed to small leaves, the ovaries abortive) is known from the type locality, Table Mt., W Nfld.

S. vestita Pursh

/aST/(X)/   (N)   Calcareous rocky places: ?Alaska (*see* Hultén 1968*a*); mts. of SE B.C. and SW Alta. (N to Jasper; CAN) to Oreg. and W Mont.; NE Man. (Churchill S to York Factory, Hudson Bay, 57°N, and the Hayes R. about 100 mi SW of York Factory); N Ont. (coast of Hudson Bay between ca. 56° and 56°30'N); Belcher Is., SE Hudson Bay; Que. (Akpatok Is., Ungava Bay, S to SE Hudson Bay, L. Mistassini, Knob Lake, 54°48'N, the Côte-Nord, Anticosti Is., and Gaspé Pen.), Labrador (type locality; N to Nachvak, 59°06'N), and N and W Nfld. MAPS: Raup 1959: map 3, p. 11, and 1943: pl. 1 (NE area); Meusel, Jaeger, and Weinert 1965:113; Wynne-Edwards 1937: map 2, p. 24; Fernald 1925: map 15, p. 253, and 1918*a*: map 2, pl. 15.

The plant of B.C., Alta., and Man. is referred by Raup (1959) to var. *erecta* And. (leaves narrower and less strongly rugose than those of the typical form, the catkins to about 5 cm long rather than about 3 cm). Eastern plants with the leaves nearly glabrate at maturity may be distinguished as var. *psilophylla* Fern. & St. John. Forma *mensalis* Fern. (the dwarf extreme with leaves mostly not over 1.5 cm long and fruiting catkins only 5 or 6 mm long) is known from the type locality, Table Mt., W Nfld.

S. viminalis L.   Osier

Eurasian; spread from cult. in N. America, as in Ont. (collection in TRT from a beach at Whitby, Ontario Co.; reported from Belleville and near Toronto by John Macoun 1886), E Que. (Gaspé Pen.: collections in GH and CAN from the edge of a sandy beach at Rivière-Blanche, Matane Co.; collections in RIM from near Métis, Matane Co., and Ste-Adèle-de-Pabos, Gaspé South Co.), Nfld., N.B., P.E.I. (dry thickets and banks along Brackley Point road, Queens Co.; GH; CAN), and N.S. ("naturalized in roadside thickets" at Hasset, Digby Co.; also known from Kent, Cumberland, and Halifax counties and from Sable Is. and Cape Breton Is.).

Salix Hybrids

Following is a list of *Salix* hybrids that have been reported (in some cases only on herbarium sheets) from Alaska–Canada. In accordance with current practice, the names of the putative parents are given in alphabetical sequence. Many of the parent-species have been reported under names used in synonymy in the present work. Such synonyms are placed in brackets, followed by the parent name now generally accepted.

S. alaxensis × *S. glauca:* the ?Yukon (Hultén 1943).

S. alba × *S. fragilis:* *S. alba* var. *vitellina* may be of this origin; *see* under *S. alba.*

S. alba × *S. ludida:* (× *S. jesupii* Fern.); S Ont. (Cambridge, Waterloo Co.; OAC).

S. arctica × *S. brachycarpa:* South Twin Is., James Bay (Argus 1965; *see* his map 7, p. 129).

S. arctica × *S. herbacea:* Dist. ?Keewatin (Boivin 1966*b*).

S. arctica (var. *kophophylla*) × *S. brachycarpa:* Ungava–Labrador (CAN).

S. arctica (var. *koph.*) × *S. (cordifolia) glauca:* (× *S. waghornei* Rydb., the type from Red Bay, s Labrador); also known from Nfld.

S. arctica (var. *torulosa; S. ?crassijulis* Trautv.): hybrids between *S. crassijulis* and *S. barclayi, S. ovalifolia, S. phylicifolia* var. *subglauca (S. pulchra), S. richardsonii, S. rotundifolia,* and *S. stolonifera* are reported from Alaska by Hultén (1943).

S. arctophila × *S. (cordifolia* var. *callicarpaea) glauca:* E Que. (CAN).

S. arctophila × *S. uva-ursi:* N Ungava (Polunin 1940) and Labrador (Schneider 1921).

S. argyrocarpa × *S. (planifolia) phylicifolia* ssp. *planifolia:* (× *S. grayii* Schn.); a collection from Tabletop Mt., Gaspé Pen., E Que., has been placed here by Fernald.

S. barclayi × *S. commutata:* Skagway, Alaska (Hultén 1943).

S. barclayi × *S. discolor* var. *latifolia:* ?B.C. (Boivin 1966*b*).

S. barclayi × *S. glauca:* Alaska (Hultén 1943).

S. barclayi × *S. (pseudomonticola) monticola:* Alaska (Hultén 1943).

S. bebbiana × *S. candida:* ?Nfld. (Boivin 1966*b*).

S. bebbiana × *S. discolor:* (× *S. beschelii* Boivin, the type from near L. Opinicon, Ont.).

S. bebbiana × *S. humilis:* a collection in CAN from Halfway House, Cape Breton Is., N.S., has been tentatively placed here by Floderus.

S. bebbiana × *S. (glaucophylla) laurentiana:* E Que. (Bic, Rimouski Co.; CAN).

S. bebbiana × *S. lutea:* Alta. (Calgary; CAN).

S. brachycarpa × *S. candida:* (× *S. argusii* Boivin, the type from Churchill Man.); also known from Anticosti Is., E Que. (Argus 1965; *see* his map 7, p. 129). A hybrid between *S. brachycarpa* and *S. candida* f. *denudata* is also reported from Anticosti Is., E Que., by Marie-Victorin and Rolland-Germain (1969).

S. brachycarpa × *S. chlorolepis* (*see* note under *S. brachycarpa*): (× *S. gaspeensis* Schn., the type from Mt. Albert, Gaspé Pen., E Que.); *see* Argus 1965:131–134, and his map 7, p. 129.

S. brachycarpa × *S. glauca:* Dist. Mackenzie, Alta., Ont., and Que. (Argus 1965; *see* his map 7, p. 129).

S. brachycarpa ssp. *niphoclada* × *S. glauca:* Alaska–Yukon–Dist. Mackenzie–N B.C. (Argus 1965; *see* his map 7, p. 129).

S. candida × *S. pellita:* Sask. and Nfld. (CAN).

S. candida × *S. petiolaris* var. *rosmarinoides:* (× *S. clarkei* Bebb); cent. Sask. (Boivin 1966*b*).

S. capraea × *S. viminalis:* (× *S. smithiana* Willd.); near Charlottetown, P.E.I. (CAN); reported as naturalized on a clay bank at Baddeck, Inverness Co., N.S., by M.L. Fernald (Rhodora 23(275):257. 1921).

S. chamissonis × *S. ?arctica:* SE Yukon (Porsild 1951*a*).

S. chamissonis × *S. commutata:* SE Yukon (Porsild 1951*a*).

S. discolor × *S. humilis:* ?N.S. (Boivin 1966*b*); Nfld. (Robinson and von Schrenk 1896).

S. discolor × *S. pellita:* (× *S. pellicolor* Lepage, the type from St-Mathieu, Rimouski Co., E Que.).

S. flagellaris (S. ?arctolitoralis; see S. ovalifolia complex) × *S. ovalifolia:* Alaska (Hultén 1943).

S. geyeriana var. *meleina* × *S. sitchensis:* ?B.C. (Henry 1915).

S. glauca × *S. farriae:* Alaska (Hultén 1943).

S. glauca × *S. (pseudomonticola) monticola:* (× *S. padophylla* Rydb.); Dawson, the Yukon (Argus 1965; *see* his map 7, p. 129).

S. (cordifolia var. *callicarpaea) glauca* × *S. myrtillifolia* var. *brachypoda:* (× *S. ungavensis* Lepage, the type from W Nfld.); also known from Que.

S. glauca × *S. pedicellaris:* Dist. Mackenzie and Sask. (Argus 1965; *see* his map 7, p. 129).

S. glauca × *S. phylicifolia* (presumably ssp. *planifolia*): ?Labrador (Boivin 1966*b*).

S. herbacea × *S. uva-ursi:* (× *S. peasei* Fern.); E Dist. Keewatin (Polunin 1940).

S. hookeriana × *S. scouleriana* (var. *flavescens*): B.C. (Lulu Is.; Henry 1915).

S. humilis × *S. (planifolia) phylicifolia* ssp. *planifolia:* ?Côte-Nord, Que. (*see* St. John 1922, and Raup 1943).

S. lucida × *S. nigra:* (× *S. schneideri* Boivin, the type from Westfield, Ingleside, N.B.).

S. ovalifolia × *S. (glacialis) ovalifolia* var. *camdensis:* Alaska (Hultén 1943).

S. pedicellaris × *S. phylicifolia* (presumably ssp. *planifolia*): ?Sask. (Boivin 1966*b*).

S. pedicellaris var. *hypoglauca* × *S. pellita:* (× *S. jamesensis* Lepage, the type from Attawa-piskat, E James Bay, Que.; *S. pedicellaris* var. *?tenuescens* Fern.); collections in CAN from N Alta. (Wood Buffalo National Park), Man. (Riverton), and Ont. (Kapuskasing; Big Trout L. at ca. 53°45′N; Raith, near Thunder Bay; Sandy L., at ca. 53°N, 93°W).

S. pedicellaris var. *hypoglauca* × *S. ?sp.:* (× *S. ?hebecarpa* Fern.; *S. fuscescens* var. *heb.* Fern., the type from Mt. Albert, Gaspé Pen., E Que.); *see* C.R. Ball (Rhodora 52(613):8–18. 1950) and the key under *S. pedicellaris.*

S. petiolaris var. *rosmarinoides* × *S. sericea:* (× *S. subsericea* (And.) Schn.; *S. gracilis* var. *subsericea* And.); Sask. (Breitung 1957*a*); Ont. (Parry Sound, L. Huron; CAN; reported from the Ottawa dist. by Gillett 1958).

S. phlebophylla × *S. rotundifolia:* Alaska (Hultén 1943).

Four "microspecies" endemic to E Que. (*S. paraleuca*) and Nfld. (*S. amoena, S. ancorifera,* and *S. pedunculata* Fern.) have been keyed out following the treatment of *S. phylicifolia.* They all appear to be closely related to *S. phylicifolia* ssp. *planifolia* and, if actually distinct, have probably arisen through hybridization between that taxon, which occurs in the region, and some other species.

In addition to the above purported hybrids, one between *S. brachycarpa* and *S. lutea* var. *turnori* (Raup) Boivin (× *S. brachypurpurea* Boivin) is reported from the type locality, L. Athabasca, NW Sask., by Boivin (1967*b*). However, *S. turnori* Raup is an obscure species merged with *S. mackenzieana* in the present work. The hybrid between *S. brachycarpa* and *S. turnori* was already reported from L. Athabasca by Argus (1965; *see* his map 7, p. 129).

MYRICACEAE (Wax-Myrtle Family)

Shrubs with alternate simple resin-dotted fragrant leaves. Flowers small, unisexual, lacking a perianth, solitary in the axils of small bracts disposed in cylindric to globose aments (catkins). Stamens usually less than 10, sometimes more. Stigmas 2, subsessile. Fruit a drupe-like nutlet.

1 Leaves rather deeply pinnatifid, linear-lanceolate, dark green above, pale beneath, to about 12 cm long, subtended by semicordate stipules; nutlets in globular bur-like aments to 2.5 cm thick; (Ont. to P.E.I. and N.S.) . . . .*Comptonia*
1 Leaves entire or merely low-serrate toward summit, cuneate-oblanceolate to elliptic or obovate, lacking stipules; nutlets either in woody cone-like aments or solitary to few in waxy clusters . . . .*Myrica*

COMPTONIA l'Hér.   [1874]

C. peregrina (L.) Coult.   Sweet-fern
/T/EE/   (N)   Open sterile woodlands, sandy fields, and pastures from Ont. (N to Quetico Provincial Park, about 90 mi W of Thunder Bay, and Cochrane, ca. 49°N; *see* S Ont. map by Soper and Heimburger 1961:6; the report from SE Man. by Lowe 1943, requires confirmation) to Que. (N to L. St. John), N.B., P.E.I., and N.S., S to Minn., Ill., Tenn., and N Ga. [*Liquidambar* L.; *Myrica* Ktze.; *M. asplenifolia* of Canadian reports, not L.].

MYRICA L.   [1874]

1 Leaves evergreen, elliptic or elliptic-oblanceolate, mostly acute, from nearly entire to rather coarsely but remotely serrate the full length of the blade, finely black-dotted, pubescent beneath, to 8 (or even 10) cm long; pistillate aments borne in the leaf-axils, becoming 1 or 2 cm long; nutlets more or less waxy; shrub to 6 (or even 10) m tall; (Vancouver Is.). . . . .*M. californica*
1 Leaves deciduous.
  2 Aments borne at the summits of the previous year's branchlets, the pistillate ones becoming cone-like and up to 2 cm long in fruit; nutlets resin-dotted, 2-winged by fusion of the 2 thick ovate scales; leaves cuneate-oblanceolate, to about 6 cm long; (transcontinental) . . . .*M. gale*
  2 Aments borne on the old wood chiefly below the leafy tips, the pistillate ones consisting of dense clusters of bony globose wax-covered nutlets; leaves elliptic to oblanceolate or obovate, pale beneath and with scattered wax-atoms, often pubescent above and commonly pilose on the nerves beneath, to about 8 cm long; (Que. to Nfld. and N.S.) . . . .*M. pensylvanica*

M. californica C. & S.   Wax Myrtle
Native in the W U.S.A. from Wash. to S Calif. and planted along highways in W Oreg. Collections from SW B.C. (Vancouver Is.) are also probably from planted shrubs (collection in CAN from Clayoquot Sound; collections in CAN and V from "beside the road on a stump" near Ucluelet).

M. gale L.   Sweet Gale.   Bois-sent-bon or Piment royal
/ST/X/EA/   (N)   Shallow water and swamps, the aggregate species from N-cent. Alaska, the Yukon (N to Dawson; CAN), the Mackenzie R. Delta, and Great Bear L. to Great Slave L., S Dist. Keewatin, Que. (N to the Korok R., Ungava Bay, at 58°35'N), Labrador (N to ca. 56°N), Nfld., N.B., P.E.I., and N.S., S to Oreg., Minn., Tenn., and N.C.; N Europe; E Asia. MAPS and synonymy: *see* below.
1 Leaves mostly entire . . . . .var. *subarctica* Rousseau
  2 Leaves essentially glabrous; [type from the George R., Ungava, at ca. 55°N] . . . .
    . . . . .f. *subarctica*

2 Leaves distinctly pubescent beneath; [type from L. Mistassini, Que.] . . . .
. . . . f. *pubescens* Rousseau & Rouleau
1 Leaves with a few coarse teeth toward the apex.
    3 Leaves essentially glabrous; [range of the species] . . . . . . var. *subglabra* (Chev.) Fern.
    3 Leaves distinctly pubescent, at least beneath.
        4 Leaves copiously pubescent on both surfaces; [*M. tomentosa* (C. DC.) Asch.
          & Graebn.; N-cent. Alaska *(see* Hultén 1944: map 441, p. 779) and coastal
          B.C.; MAPS: Hultén 1968*b*:364, and 1958: map 199, p. 219] . . . .
          . . . . var. *tomentosa* C. DC.
        4 Leaves essentially glabrous above, more or less pubescent beneath; [*Gale
          palustris* (Lam.) Chev.; transcontinental; MAPS: Hultén 1958: map 199, p. 219;
          Porsild 1966: map 50 (aggregate species), p. 73; Meusel, Jaeger, and Weinert
          1965:117] . . . . var. *gale*

M. pensylvanica Loisel.   Bayberry, Candleberry
/T/EE/ (N (Mc)) Dry or wet sterile soil near the coast from E Que. (known only from Magdalen Is.; GH; CAN), St-Pierre and Miquelon, S Nfld., N.B., P.E.I., and N.S. to N.C.; an inland
station in S Ont. (Turkey Point, Norfolk Co.; ?introd.; *see* S Ont. map by Soper and Heimburger 1961:5). [*M. caroliniensis* and *M. cerifera* of Canadian reports, not Mill. nor L., respectively, relevant collections in several herbaria].

JUGLANDACEAE (Walnut Family)

Trees with large alternate odd-pinnate exstipulate leaves, the lanceolate to ovate or obovate leaflets gland-dotted beneath, commonly acuminate, shallowly serrate. Flowers small, unisexual, apetalous, the staminate ones in elongate aments (catkins), each consisting of a 2–6-lobed calyx adnate to a subtending narrow bract and bearing few to many stamens. Pistillate flowers solitary or in short terminal spikes, each subtended by a perianth-like cup-shaped involucre of united bracts and with a single inferior ovary with 2 plumose styles. Fruit a nut enclosed within a fibrous-fleshy or woody exocarp (husk).

1 Leaflets commonly 5 or 7 (sometimes 9), lanceolate to obovate, the terminal one usually the largest; staminate aments sessile, subsessile, or in peduncled clusters of 3 in the axils of bud-scales; nuts smooth, often angled; husk partly or completely dehiscent; pith of twigs not partitioned; (s Ont. and sw Que.) . . . . *Carya*
1 Leaflets commonly at least 11, lance- to ovate-oblong, the median ones usually the largest; staminate aments stout, solitary or 2 or 3 together, sessile in the axils of the previous year's leaves; nuts very rough; husk of fruit indehiscent; pith transversely partitioned . . . . *Juglans*

CARYA Nutt. [1882] Hickory. Hicorier or Caryer

1 Scales of overwintering buds paired, valvate, 4 or 6 in number; scars of bud-scales not confluent into a true ring; husk of fruit prominently keeled or winged at the sutures, the shell usually with powder-filled cavities.
   2 Clusters of staminate aments sessile or subsessile; scales of overwintering buds with tufts of bright-yellow hairs; fruit elongate, subterete, cylindric, the husk splitting to near base; nut 2-locular at base; leaflets up to 17 in number, the lower ones with recurving tips; (s ?Ont.) . . . . [*C. illinoensis*]
   2 Clusters of staminate aments peduncled; scales of overwintering buds sulphur-yellow-scurfy, lacking tufts of bright-yellow hairs; fruit flattened, about as broad as long, the husk splitting only to below middle; nut 4-locular in the lower half; leaflets commonly not more than 9, scarcely recurving; (s Ont. and sw Que.) . . . .
      . . . . *C. cordiformis*
1 Scales of overwintering buds pale brown or dark, imbricate, up to 12 in number; scars of bud-scales very narrow and confluent, forming a definite ring; husk usually wingless; nut-shell without cavities.
   3 Terminal bud rarely over 1 cm long, resinous, glabrous except for the ciliate margins; nut obscurely angled only toward summit; fruit mostly less than 3.5 cm long, the husk usually not over 4 mm thick.
      4 Young branchlets reddish brown, glabrous; leaflets 5 (rarely 7), glabrous or merely pilose on the nerves beneath, or the terminal one with conspicuous tufts of hairs beneath; bark close, becoming furrowed and ridged; husk tardily opening by 1 or 2 sutures or indehiscent, dark brown, shining; (s Ont.) . . . .
         . . . . *C. glabra*
      4 Young branchlets and expanded leaves yellowish-scurfy; leaflets usually 7; old bark often shaggy and separating into small plates or scales; husk promptly splitting to base, light brown, dull, warty; (s Ont.) . . . . *C. ovalis*
   3 Terminal bud commonly at least 1.5 cm long, bearing some appressed fragile hairs; nut 4–6-angled; fruit to over 3.5 cm long; husk splitting nearly to base.
      5 Leaflets 5 (sometimes 7), essentially glabrous at maturity, some or all of them with persistent dense tufts of hairs near the apex of the teeth; young branchlets minutely scurfy-pubescent, soon glabrate, reddish brown and lustrous; bark shaggily exfoliating in long plates; husk 3–12 mm thick; nut 4-angled, the whitish-brown shell 1 or 2 mm thick; (s Ont. and s Que.) . . . . *C. ovata*
      5 Leaflets 5, 7, or 9, the lower surface permanently pubescent; (s ?Ont.).
         6 Branchlets orange-brown or light tan, often puberulent; bark shaggily

Carya

exfoliating in long plates; leaflets 7 or 9, soft-pubescent beneath; nuts
strongly compressed, 4–6-angled, at least 3 cm long, with a yellowish- to
reddish-brown shell . . . . [*C. laciniosa*]
6   Branchlets usually tomentose; bark close and deeply furrowed, not
exfoliating; leaflets 5, 7, or 9, tomentose beneath with curly tufted hairs;
nuts only slightly compressed, 4-angled, at most 3 cm long, with a reddish-
brown shell . . . . [*C. tomentosa*]

C. cordiformis (Wang.) Koch   Bitternut, Pignut.   Noyer dur
/T/EE/   (Ms)   Wet to dry woods, streambanks, and swamps from SE Nebr. to Minn., Mich.,
Ont. (N to Carleton and Prescott counties; *see* S Ont. map by Fox and Soper 1954: fig. 26,
p. 100), SW Que. (N to Neuville, about 12 mi SW of Quebec City; *see* Que. map by Doyon and
Lavoie 1966: fig. 11, p. 817), and N.H., S to Tex. and Fla. [*Juglans* Wang.; *Hicoria* Britt.;
H. minima (Marsh.) Britt.; *C. amara* (Michx. f.) Nutt.]. MAPS: Fowells 1965:111; Gleason and
Cronquist 1964: fig. 14.7, p. 160; Preston 1961:144; Canada Department of Northern Affairs
and Natural Resources 1956:116; Hough 1947:53; Munns 1938: map 64, p. 68; Little 1971:
map 112-E; Hosie 1969:148.
A hybrid with *C. ovata* (× *C. laneyi* Sarg.) is reported from SW Que. by Raymond (1950*b*;
Montreal dist.). This is probably its nm. *chateaugayensis* (Sarg.) Boivin, reported from E Ont.
and SW Que. by Boivin (1966*b*).

C. glabra (Mill.) Sweet   Pignut
/t/EE/   (Ms)   Dry or moist woods and hillsides from S Ill. to S Ont. (N to Wentworth and Lincoln counties; see S Ont. map by Fox and Soper 1954: fig. 29, map 32, p. 105), Vt., and
E Mass., S to Miss., Ala., and Ga. [*Juglans* Mill.; *Hicoria* Sweet; *C. porcina* (Michx. f.) Nutt.].
MAPS: Hosie 1969:146; Fowells 1965:124; Canada Department of Northern Affairs and Natural
Resources 1956:120; Hough 1947:65; Little 1971: map 113-E; Munns 1938: map 68, p. 72. (According to 1969 revisions of material in CAN by Wayne Manning, most of the above material
may be referable to *C. laciniosa*).

[*C. illinoensis* (Wang.) Koch]   Pecan
[The report of this species of the E U.S.A. (N to Iowa and Ind.) from S Ont. by Landon (1960;
Norfolk Co.) requires confirmation. It may represent a planted tree. (*Juglans* Wang.; *J. (C.;
Hicoria) pecan* Marsh.). MAP: Fowells 1965:121; Little 1971: map 114-N.]

[*C. laciniosa* (Michx. f.) Loud.]   Kingnut, Big Shellbark
[Reports of this species of the E U.S.A. (Nebr. to N.Y., S to Kans., La., and Ala.) from S Ont.
require confirmation. Fox and Soper (1954; *see* their map 30, fig. 28, p. 104) cite it from Essex, Lambton, Kent, Huron, and Welland counties. These collections may have originated
from trees planted for furniture-wood. However, photographs accompanying collections in
TRT and GH indicate the possibility of the tree being native in the region, provided some
other species is not involved. (See *C. glabra*). The stations in S Ont. indicated in the map by
Hosie (1969:142) require confirmation.]

C. ovalis (Wang.) Sarg.   False Shagbark, Sweet Pignut
/t/EE/   (Ms)   Moist or dry woodlands, the aggregate species from Wisc. to S Ont. (Essex,
Lambton, Norfolk, Waterloo, Wentworth, Welland, and Lincoln counties; *see* S Ont. map by
Fox and Soper 1954: map 33, fig. 29, p. 105) and SW N.H., S to Ark. and Ga. MAP and synonymy: *see* below.
1   Petioles, rachises, and lower leaflet-surfaces permanently pubescent; [nm. *hir.*
(Ashe) Boivin; some of the above S Ont. reports probably belong here, the taxon
being reported from there by Boivin 1966*b*] . . . . var. *hirsuta* (Ashe) Sarg.
1   Petioles, rachises, and leaflets glabrous or soon glabrate.
2   Leaflets glandular-viscid beneath; husk of fruit with winged sutures, its inner
surface with a resinous odour; nut angled; [nm. *odorata* (Marsh.) Boivin;
Queenston Heights, Lincoln Co.; CAN] . . . . var. *odorata* (Marsh.) Sarg.

2 Leaflets not conspicuously glandular beneath; husk of fruit at most very narrowly keeled at the sutures; nut scarcely angled; [*Juglans* Wang.; *Hicoria* Ashe; *C. (H.) microcarpa* Nutt.; E U.S.A. only; MAP (aggregate species): Hough 1947:67] . . . .
. . . . [var. *ovalis*]

C. ovata (Mill.) Koch   Shagbark- or Shellbark-Hickory.   Noyer blanc
/T/EE/   (Mg)   Rich woods and bottomlands, the aggregate species from SE Nebr. to Minn., Ont. (N to Carleton and Russell counties; *see* S Ont. map by Fox and Soper 1954: fig. 27, p. 102), SW Que. (N to L. St. Peter in St-Maurice Co.; MT), and S Maine, S to E Tex. and Fla. MAPS and synonymy: *see* below.
1 Leaflets lanceolate to narrowly oblanceolate, not over 5 cm broad; fruit about 4 cm long; [S Ont.; Fernald *in* Gray 1950] . . . . var. *fraxinifolia* Sarg.
1 Leaflets broadly lanceolate, ovate, or obovate, the terminal one to 11 cm broad.
    2 Fruits relatively small, the nutlet strongly compressed laterally and at most 2 cm long; [S Ont. (Hamilton; TRT) and SW Que. (Vaudreuil, near Montreal; Marcel Raymond, Nat. can. (Que.) 74(5/6):168. 1947)] . . . . var. *nuttallii* Sarg.
    2 Fruits to 6 cm long; [*Juglans* Mill.; *Hicoria* Britt.; range of the species; MAPS (aggregate species): Canada Department of Northern Affairs and Natural Resources 1956:118; Little 1971: map 118-N; Gleason and Cronquist 1964: fig. 14.7, p. 160; Fowells 1965:128; Braun 1935: fig. 1, p. 352; Munns 1938: map 65, p. 69; Hough 1947:59; Preston 1961:140; Hosie 1969:140] . . . . var. *ovata*

[*C. tomentosa* (Poir.) Nutt.]   Mockernut
[Reports of this species of the E U.S.A. (N to Nebr. and Mass.) from S Ont., as by John Macoun (1886), Dodge (1914), Soper (1949), and Fox and Soper (1954; *see* their S Ont. map 31, fig. 28, p. 104; Essex, Kent, Lambton, and Welland counties) require confirmation, as does the inclusion of S Ont. in the range indicated by the following maps. Most or all such reports may refer to *C. ovata*. (*Juglans* Poir.; *J. (C.; Hicoria) alba* L.). MAPS: Hosie 1969:144; Fowells 1965:115; Canada Department of Northern Affairs and Natural Resources 1956:122; Hough 1947:63; Preston 1961:142; Munns 1938: map 67, p. 71; Little 1971: map 117-E.]

JUGLANS L.   [1881]   Walnut.   Noyer

1 Leaflets oblong-lanceolate, the terminal one usually present; leaf-scar with a downy pad at upper edge; petioles, young twigs, and oblong pointed fruit viscid-downy; pith dark brown; bark with smooth ridges; (Ont. to N.B.) . . . . *J. cinerea*
1 Leaflets oblong-ovate, the terminal one usually absent; leaf-scar without a downy pad; petioles, young twigs, and subglobose fruit puberulent or somewhat downy but scarcely viscid; pith light brown; bark with very rough ridges; (S Ont.; introd. in SW Que.) . . . . *J. nigra*

J. cinerea L.   Butternut, White Walnut.   Arbre à noix longues.
/T/EE/   (Ms)   Rich woods and river-terraces from N.Dak. to Ont. (N to Bruce, Renfrew, Carleton, and Russell counties; *see* S Ont. map by Fox and Soper 1953: fig. 14, p. 9), S Que. (N to Charlevoix and Montmagny counties; *see* the Que. northern-limits map by Marie-Victorin, 1935, and the Que. map by Doyon and Lavoie 1966: fig. 20, p. 819), and N.B. (planted in N.S.; not known from P.E.I.), S to Ark. and Ga. MAPS: Fowells 1965:208; Canada Department of Northern Affairs and Natural Resources 1956:110; Preston 1961:136; Hough 1947:51; Munns 1938: map 61, p. 65; Little 1971: map 133-E; Hosie 1969:134.

J. nigra L.   Black Walnut
/t/EE/   (Mg)   Rich woods from Minn. to S Ont. (N to Lambton, Waterloo, and S York counties; *see* S Ont. map by Fox and Soper 1953: fig. 15, p. 12, who consider trees north of these limits to have been planted), and W Mass., S to Tex. and Fla. MAPS: Hosie 1969:136; Fowells 1965:203; Canada Department of Northern Affairs and Natural Resources 1956:112; Gleason and Cronquist 1964: fig.14.7, p. 161; Preston 1961:136; Hough 1947:49; Munns 1938: map 62, p. 66; Little 1971: map 134-E.

BETULACEAE (Birch Family)

Trees or tall shrubs with simple alternate serrate straightish-veined leaves and deciduous stipules. Flowers small, unisexual, lacking a perianth or with a minute calyx, solitary or 2 or 3 together in the axils of scale-like bracts disposed in a many-flowered ament (catkin), or the pistillate flowers of *Corylus* at most 4 in a small head. Stamens 2 or more. Pistil 1. Styles 2. Ovary inferior. Fruit a 1-seeded nutlet or nut. (Corylaceae).

1   Scales of pistillate aments woody and enlarged in fruit; nutlets small and flat, winged
    or margined, lacking an involucre; staminate flowers with a 2–4-parted calyx.
    2   Bracts between nutlets and scales 3–5-lobed, woody, persisting after the fall of
        the 2 narrow-winged or coriaceous-margined nutlets; pistillate aments racemose;
        stamens 4 . . . .*Alnus*
    2   Bracts 3-lobed (rarely unlobed), thin, falling with or soon after the 2 or 3 narrowly
        to broadly winged nutlets; pistillate aments solitary in the leaf-axils; stamens 2 . . . . . .
        . . . .*Betula*
1   Scales of pistillate aments deciduous, the foliaceous involucre enclosing or
    subtending a single wingless nut; staminate flowers consisting of 3 or more stamens
    without a calyx.
    3   Involucre flat, 2–3-lobed, subtending the small nut; leaves oblong to narrowly
        oblong-ovate, sharply and often doubly low-serrate; small tree with blue-grey or
        ashy-grey smooth bark; (Ont. and sw Que.) . . . .*Carpinus*
    3   Involucre enclosing or enveloping the nut; leaves doubly serrate.
        4   Pistillate flowers at most 4 in a small head; involucre closely surrounding the
            nut and prolonged into a long slender beak or a broadly dilated flattened
            beak; shrubs or small trees . . . .*Corylus*
        4   Pistillate flowers several in aments; mature involucre inflated and bladdery,
            enclosing the small nut; tree with light-brown furrowed bark; (SE Man. to N.B.
            and N.S.) . . . .*Ostrya*

ALNUS Ehrh.   [1888]   Alder.   Aulne or Aune

1   Nutlets broadly membranous-winged.
    2   Catkins developing and flowering with the leaves on growth of the current
        season; body of nutlet usually less than half as long as broad, the wings broad;
        leaves typically finely and sharply serrate, glutinous, essentially glabrous or soft-
        pubescent beneath, their margins not at all revolute; bushy shrub commonly less
        than 4 m tall; (transcontinental) . . . .*A. crispa*
    2   Catkins developing and flowering before the leaves, produced on growth of the
        previous season; body of nutlet usually over half as long as broad, the wings
        relatively narrow; leaves sinuate and irregularly serrate-denticulate, deep green
        and glabrous or slightly hairy above, the lower surface rusty grey and usually
        more or less hairy, strongly gland-dotted, their margins always slightly revolute;
        tree to over 20 m tall, the bark thin, grey, smooth, the fresh wood tending to turn
        deep red; (SE Alaska–B.C.) . . . .*A. rubra*
1   Nutlets wingless; catkins developing and flowering before the leaves, produced on
    growth of the previous season; leaf-margins not revolute.
    3   Fruiting aments at most 5, very glutinous, to 3 cm long, long-peduncled, their
        scales with depressed terminal lobes; leaves very glutinous, flabellate-obovate to
        suborbicular, with at most 8 pairs of veins, their dentate or denticulate margins
        often somewhat lobed; (introd. in Ont., Nfld., and N.S.) . . . .*A. glutinosa*
    3   Fruiting aments 3–10, usually less than 2 cm long, sessile or short-peduncled,
        their scales with prolonged and ascending terminal lobes; leaves ovate or elliptic,
        with usually at least 9 pairs of veins.
        4   Leaves sinuate or lobed, broadly elliptic to ovate-oblong, rounded to
            subcordate at base, rounded to obtuse or slightly acute at tip; stamens

usually 4, the filaments rarely half as long as the anthers; shrubs mostly not
over 5 (but up to 10) m tall; (transcontinental) . . . . *A. rugosa*

4　Leaves only slightly if at all sinuate, elliptic to oblong-rhombic, acute to
rounded at each end; stamens at most 3, the filaments usually at least about
as long as the anthers; large shrub or small tree to about 20 m tall; (?B.C.) . . . .
. . . . [*A. rhombifolia*]

A. crispa (Ait.) Pursh　Green or Mountain-Alder.　Aulne vert
/aST/X/GEA/　(N (Mc))　Thickets, rocky shores, and moist slopes, the aggregate species
from N-cent. Alaska–Yukon (*see* Hultén 1944: map 447a, p. 779, and map 447c (ssp. *sin.*),
p. 780) and the Mackenzie R. Delta to Great Bear L., s-cent. Dist. Keewatin, Que. (N to Ungava Bay and the Côte-Nord), Labrador (N to Nachvak, 59°07′N), Nfld., N.B., P.E.I., and N.S.,
s to N Calif., Idaho, Mont., Minn., Mich., N.Y., and N.C.; w Greenland N to the Arctic Circle; NE
Europe; Asia. MAPS and synonymy: *see* below.
1　Leaves rounded or slightly cordate at base, more or less irregularly lobed in addition
to finely 1–2-serrate-dentate; [*A. sinuata* (Regel) Rydb.; *A. viridis* var. *sin.* Regel;
A. ?fruticosa Rupr. and its var. *sin* (Regel) Hult.; *A. sitchensis* (Regel) Sarg. (*A. vir.*
var. *sibirica* lusus *sit.* Regel); *A. alnobetula* of N. American auth. in part, not Koch;
incl. the laciniate extreme, ssp. *sin.* var. *laciniata* Hult.; cent. Alaska–s Yukon–B.C.–
w Alta.; MAPS (mostly as *A. sinuata):* Hultén 1968b:369; Hosie 1969:174; Canada
Department of Northern Affairs and Natural Resources 1956:152; Preston 1961:160,
and 1947:130; Meusel, Jaeger, and Weinert 1965:119; W.J. Cody, Nat. can. (Que.)
98(2): fig. 8, p. 148. 1971] . . . . ssp. *sinuata* (Regel) Hult.
1　Leaves generally more cuneate-based, finely 1–2-serrate-dentate but rarely
noticeably lobed . . . . ssp. *crispa*
2　Young branchlets, peduncles, and lower leaf-surfaces permanently and densely
soft-pubescent, the leaves to 12(20) cm long; [*A. mollis* Fern.; L. Superior, Ont.,
to s Labrador, Nfld. (type locality, as first region cited), and N.S.] . . . . . var. *mollis* Fern.
2　Young branchlets, peduncles, and leaves glabrous or only slightly pubescent, the
leaves commonly shorter.
3　Mature pistillate aments to about 2.5 cm long; [type from L. Athabasca, Sask.;
also reported from Alaska by Hultén 1944] . . . . var. *elongata* Raup
3　Mature pistillate aments at most 2 cm long . . . . var. *crispa*
4　Pistillate aments to about 1 cm long; leaves to about 5 cm long; [type from
Mt. Logan, Matane Co., E Que.; also known from the Adirondack Mts. of
N.Y.] . . . . f. *stragala* Fern.
4　Pistillate aments to 2 cm long; leaves to over 8 cm long; ascending shrub
to 3 m tall; [*Betula crispa* Ait., the type locality given as "Nat. of
Newfoundland and Hudson's Bay"; *A. viridis* of N. American auth., not
DC., and its var. *sibirica* Herder in part; *A. alnobetula* of N. American auth.
in part; incl. the narrow-leaved extreme, var. *harricanensis* Lepage;
transcontinental; MAPS: Hultén 1968b:368; Raup 1947: pl. 22; Meusel,
Jaeger, and Weinert 1965:119] . . . . f. *crispa*

A. glutinosa (L.) Gaertn.　Black Alder of Europe
Eurasian; spread from cult. and locally natzd. in N. America, as in s Ont. (Delhi, Norfolk Co.;
OAC; reported by Zenkert 1934, from near Port Colborne, Welland Co., where "spreading
from roots and established along creek . . . where planted about 50 years ago"), N.S. (Dennis
Pond, Yarmouth Co.; GH), and Nfld. (Birchy Cove, Bay of Islands, where taken by Waghorne
in 1876; GH). [*Betula glutinosa* L.; *A. vulgaris* Hill].
　An 1849 report from N.B. by J.E. Alexander *(L'Acadie; . . .,* vol. 2, p. 322. H. Colburn, Lon-
don) is probably based upon *A. rugosa* var. *americana,* as also the report from Labrador by
Schrank (1818).

[*A. rhombifolia* Nutt.]　White Alder
[This species of the w U.S.A. (Wash. and Idaho to Baja Calif.) is reported from s B.C. by John
Macoun (1886), Henry (1915), and Rydberg (1922), and that province is included in the range

depicted in the following maps. Boivin (1967a:639), however, notes Brayshaw's conclusion that all B.C. collections had been misidentified (material from Shawnigan, Vancouver Is., and Glacier, in Rogers Pass, proved to be *A. crispa* ssp. *sinuata*) except one from Agassiz, which probably originated from a cultivated tree. MAPS (the B.C. area should be deleted): Canada Department of Northern Affairs and Natural Resources 1956:148; Preston 1947:132; Munns 1938: map 86, p. 90.]

A. rubra Bong.   Red Alder
/sT/W/   (Ms)   Moist woods from the Alaska Panhandle (type from Sitka) through coastal B.C. to s-cent. Calif., inland to N Idaho. [*A. incana* var. *rubra* (Bong.) Regel, not *Betula-Alnus rubra* Marsh.; *A. oregona* Nutt.]. MAPS: Hultén 1968b:369 *(A. oreg.);* Fowells 1965:83; Preston 1961:158; *Atlas of Canada* 1957: sheet 41; Canada Department of Northern Affairs and Natural Resources 1956:146; Hosie 1969:170; Munns 1938: map 85, p. 89; Little 1971: map 104-N.

Var. *pinnatisecta* Starker (leaves deeply pinnatifid or even laciniate rather than merely sinuate or irregularly low-toothed) is known from sw B.C. (Inglewood, Vancouver Is.; Herb. V).

A. rugosa (Du Roi) Spreng.   Speckled Alder.   Verne or Aulne blanchâtre
/ST/X/EA/   (Mc (Ms))   Swampy ground, streambanks, foothills, and mountains up to moderately high elevations (ranges of Canadian taxa outlined below), s to Calif., N.Mex., Iowa, Va., and Pa.; Eurasia. MAPS and synonymy (together with a distinguishing key to the closely related *A. incana* of Eurasia): *see* below.

1   Leaves hoary with a permanent grey-velvety pubescence, mostly obtuse or subacute
    at the base; [*Betula alnus* var. *incana* L.; *B. incana* (L.) L. f.; Eurasia only, reports
    from Alaska–Canada referring to the following taxa] . . . .[*A. incana* (L.) Moench]
1   Leaves typically greener, essentially glabrous above, more or less pubescent or
    glabrate beneath; [N. America] . . . .*A. rugosa*
    2   Leaves simply serrate with very fine, almost regular teeth, glutinous when young,
        obovate-elliptic to obovate (mostly broadest at or above the middle), cuneate or
        slightly rounded at base, with weak cross-veins beneath; [*A. serrulata* Ait.;
        A. incana var. *serr.* (Ait.) Boivin; *A. rubra* (Marsh.) Tuckerm., not Bong.; N.S.
        (Yarmouth, Queens, and Halifax counties) and ?P.E.I. (McSwain and Bain 1891;
        probably extinct if once native there)] . . . . .var. *serrulata* (Ait.) Winkler
    2   Leaves mostly doubly serrate with teeth of irregular size (thus more or less
        lobed), scarcely glutinous, elliptic to ovate (mostly broadest at or below the
        middle), rounded or subcordate at base, prominently reticulate beneath.
        3   Bark not speckled; fruiting aments to 2 cm long; tall shrub or small tree to
            about 10 m tall; [*A. occidentalis* Dippel; *A. incana* ssp. *tenuifolia* (Nutt.)
            Breitung (*A. ten.* Nutt.); N-cent. Alaska–cent. Yukon–NW Dist. Mackenzie–
            B.C.–Alta. to Sask. (N to L. Athabasca) and extreme SW Man.; MAPS (mostly as
            A. tenuifolia, the last two incomplete northwards): Hultén 1968b:370; Raup
            1947: pl. 22; Preston 1961:160; Canada Department of Northern Affairs and
            Natural Resources 1956:150] . . . . .var. *occidentalis* (Dippel) Hitchc.
        3   Bark white-speckled with linear lenticels to 7 mm long; fruiting aments at
            most 1.5 cm long; shrubs (rarely somewhat tree-like) commonly not over 4 or
            5 m tall.
            4   Leaves glaucous or whitened beneath . . . . .var. *americana* (Regel) Fern.
                5   Lower leaf-surfaces densely velvety-pubescent; [range of f. *americana,*
                    the type from Grand Manan Is., Charlotte Co., N.B.] . . . . f. *hypomalaca* Fern.
                5   Lower leaf-surfaces essentially glabrous.
                    6   Leaves jagged-toothed or lacerate, ovate-lanceolate to narrowly
                        elliptic; [Nfld., the type from Norris Arm, near the mouth of the
                        Exploits R.] . . . . .f. *tomophylla* Fern.
                    6   Leaves low-toothed, relatively broad; [*A. americana* (Regel) Koch;
                        A. glauca Michx. f.; Sask. to N Man. (N to the Cochrane R. at
                        58°13'N), N Ont. (N to the Black Duck R., Hudson Bay, at ca.
                        56°45'N), Que. (N to Wawicho L. at 53°49'N and the Côte-Nord),
                        Labrador (N to the Sandwich R. at 53°40'N), Nfld., N.B., P.E.I., and

N.S.; MAP: Canada Department of Northern Affairs and Natural
Resources 1956:144; Hosie 1969:172 (*A. rug.*)] . . . . f. *americana*
4 Leaves green or tawny (not glaucous) beneath . . . . var. *rugosa*
7 Lower leaf-surfaces permanently soft-velvety-pubescent; [N.S.:
Yarmouth and Lunenburg counties] . . . . f. *emersoniana* Fern.
7 Lower leaf-surfaces essentially glabrous except along the veins;
[*A. incana* var. *virescens* Wats.; w N.S.; Fernald *in* Gray 1950] . . . . . f. *rugosa*

BETULA L.   [1887]   Birch.   Bouleau

(Ref.: J.R. Dugle 1966, and Can. Field-Nat. 83(3):250–52. 1969; *see* listing of hybrids at end)
1 Leaves of fruiting branches with 8 or more pairs of prominent veins; fruiting catkins
ovoid to thick-cylindric, 1 cm or more thick, subsessile, their bracts rather
persistent; wing of nutlet not broader than the seed-bearing body.
2 Bracts of fruiting catkins glabrous, about 6 mm long; bark of trunk reddish brown
to purplish black, not exfoliating, in age merely furrowed and ashy brown; (s Ont.
and s ?Que.) . . . . *B. lenta*
2 Bracts of fruiting catkins pubescent or the lobes at least ciliate, to 13 mm long;
bark yellowish brown or silvery grey, mostly loosely exfoliating; (Ont. to s Nfld.
and N.S.) . . . . *B. lutea*
1 Leaves of fruiting branches with 7 or fewer pairs of prominent veins; bracts of
mature fruiting catkins readily deciduous.
3 Samara-wings not broader than the seed-bearing body of the nutlet; fruiting
catkins rarely more than 3 cm long (to 4 cm in *B. fontinalis*), erect, sessile or
short-peduncled; leaves with rarely more than 5 pairs of veins; shrubs with
yellowish-brown to brown non-exfoliating bark.
4 Bracts of fruiting catkins unlobed, entire, oblong; nutlets wingless; leaves
flabelliform-obovate, to 1 cm long, glabrous, incised toward summit; stems
minutely ashy-tomentulose; (N Que., Labrador, Nfld., and N.S.) . . . . . . *B. michauxii*
4 Bracts of fruiting catkins 3-lobed; nutlets distinctly winged.
5 Branchlets typically glabrous (at most minutely puberulent) and
conspicuously dotted with wart-like resin-glands; leaves glabrous or
minutely glandular-puberulent; (transcontinental).
6 Samara-wing usually nearly or quite as broad as the seed-bearing
body of the nutlet; fruiting catkins to 4 cm long and 1 cm thick; leaves
rather sharply singly to doubly serrate, mostly ovate to suborbicular,
acute to rounded at apex, paler beneath, to 4.5 (or even 7) cm long;
branchlets with reddish resin-glands; shrub or small tree with shining
bark . . . . *B. occidentalis*
6 Samara-wing narrower than the body of the nutlet; fruiting catkins to
2.5 cm long and 7 mm thick; leaves broadly oval or obovate to
suborbicular, obtuse to rounded at apex, less sharply toothed, rather
leathery, green both sides, rarely over 3 cm long; branchlets densely
whitish-glandular-warty; shrub with dull bark . . . . *B. glandulosa*
5 Branchlets more or less densely puberulent or downy; samara-wings
mostly distinctly narrower than the body of the nutlet; bark dull.
7 Leaves orbicular to reniform (often broader than long), usually less
than 1.5 cm long; branchlets more or less glandular-warty; fruiting
catkins usually not over 1 cm long; (SE Baffin Is.) . . . . *B. nana*
7 Leaves relatively narrower in outline, ovate to obovate, usually mostly
longer; branchlets usually lacking resin-glands (but with wart-like
yellowish glands in *B. pumila* var. *glandulifera*); fruiting catkins to 3 cm
long; (transcontinental) . . . . *B. pumila*
3 Samara-wings usually broader than the seed-bearing body of the nutlet
(*B. borealis* may sometimes be sought here); fruiting catkins to 6 cm long, usually
longer-peduncled; leaves with up to 7 pairs of veins; trees or coarse shrubs.

8 Leaves caudate (tapering to a long tail-like tip), triangular (distinctly truncate at base), glabrous on both sides, doubly serrate; bracts of fruiting catkins divergent, puberulent on the back, their lateral lobes much longer than the terminal lobe; bushy tree to about 10 m tall, with close chalky-white bark; (Ont. to N.S.) . . . . *B. populifolia*

8 Leaves not prominently caudate-tipped.

9 Leaves glabrous or soon glabrate on both sides.

10 Branchlets bearing copious wart-like resin-glands; (var. *neoalaskana;* Alaska–B.C. to cent. Ont.) . . . . *B. papyrifera*

10 Branchlets glabrous or merely somewhat gummy; (introd.) . . . . . . *B. pendula*

9 Leaves more or less pubescent beneath at least on the veins or in their axils.

11 Leaves of the fertile branches typically acuminate, to about 1 dm long; branchlets nearly or quite devoid of resin-glands; fruiting catkins to over 6 cm long; bark exfoliating; (transcontinental) . . . . *B. papyrifera*

11 Leaves of the fertile branches merely acute, mostly less than 5 cm long.

12 Branchlets densely pubescent, usually glandless; bark exfoliating in layers; large tree with a single main trunk; (sw Greenland; introd. elsewhere) . . . . *B. pubescens*

12 Branchlets glabrous, bearing large resin-glands; bark not exfoliating; trunk commonly forking, the several narrow stems forming open clusters; (transcontinental) . . . . *B. occidentalis*

B. glandulosa Michx.   Dwarf or Scrub Birch
/aST/X/G/   (N (Ch))   Rocky slopes and alpine barrens (chiefly acidic) from the coasts of Alaska–Yukon–Dist. MacKenzie–Dist. Keewatin to Victoria Is., Baffin Is. (N to near the Arctic Circle), northernmost Ungava–Labrador (type from between Hudson Bay and L. Mistassini, Que.), N N.B. (Bald Mt.; GH), and NE N.S. (Ingonish Barrens, Victoria Co., Cape Breton Is.; ACAD; not known from P.E.I.), s (chiefly in the mts.) to N Calif., Colo., S.Dak., Minn., Mich., N.Y., and Maine; w Greenland N to ca. 65°N, E Greenland N to ca. 63°N. [*B. nana* vars *intermedia* Regel and *sibirica* Ledeb.; *B. ?ermanii sensu* John Macoun 1886, not Cham.; incl. f. *eucycla* Lepage]. MAPS: Hultén 1968b:365; Dugle 1966: fig. 4, p. 940; Meusel, Jaeger, and Weinert 1965:119; Porsild 1957: map 126, p. 176; Raup 1947: pl. 22.

B. lenta L.   Cherry-, Sweet-, or Black Birch.   Merisier rouge
/T/EE/   (Ms)   Rich woods from s Ont. (Lincoln and Welland counties; *see* s Ont. map by Fox and Soper 1954: fig. 30, map 34, p. 107; reported N to the Ottawa dist. by Gillett 1958) and s ?Que. (Fernald in Gray 1950; reports may refer to *B. lutea*) to Maine, s to Tenn. and Ga. [*B. carpinifolia* Ehrh.]. MAPS: Canada Department of Northern Affairs and Natural Resources 1956:132; Fowells 1965:99; Preston 1961:152; Hough 1947:125; Munns 1938: map 80, p. 84; Little 1971: map 106-E; Hosie 1969:158.

Specimens lacking fruiting catkins are difficult to distinguish from *B. lutea,* accounting for reports from Canada from outside the area outlined above. Such reports may be based in part upon *B. lutea* f. *fallax* Fassett, simulating *B. lenta* in its deep-brown close bark scarcely loosening into layers or plates

B. lutea Michx. f.   Yellow or Grey Birch.   Merisier
/T/EE/   (Ms)   Rich woods from Ont. (N to the NW and NE shores of L. Superior; CAN) to Que. (N to L. St. John and the Gaspé Pen.; reported from L. Mistassini by John Macoun 1886, and from Anticosti Is. by Verrill 1865), s ?Labrador (Fernald in Grey 1950), s Nfld., N.B., P.E.I., and N.S., s to NE Iowa, N Ind., Tenn., and N.C. [*B. alleghaniensis* Britt.; *B. excelsa sensu* Pursh 1814, not Ait.; *B. lenta* of Canadian reports in part, not L.; *B. ?nigra sensu* Cochran 1829, not L.]. MAPS: Hosie 1969:156 *(B. alleg.);* Canada Department of Northern Affairs and Natural Resources 1956:130; *Atlas of Canada* 1957: sheet 41 and map 13, sheet 38; Fowells 1965:104 *(B. alleg.);* Preston 1961:150 *(B. alleg.);* Hough 1947:127; Halliday and Brown 1943: fig. 11, p. 371; Munns 1938: map 81, p. 85; Little 1971: map 105-N.

Forma *fallax* Fassett (the deep-brown close bark simulating that of *B. lenta*) is reported from ?Ont. and Que. by Boivin (1967a; *B. alleg.* f. *fal.* (Fassett) Boivin). Var *macrolepis* Fern. (bracts of the pistillate catkins to 13 mm long rather than at most 8 mm) occurs throughout our area.

B. michauxii Spach   Newfoundland Dwarf Birch
/sT/E/ (N (Ch))   Bogs, heaths, and acidic peaty barrens of Que. (Knob Lake dist. at ca. 54°45′N, the type from between Hudson Bay and L. Mistassini; Côte-Nord; Anticosti Is.), Labrador (N to Cape Harrigan, 55°50′N), Nfld., St-Pierre and Miquelon, and N.S. (Brier Is., Digby Co.; Guysborough Co.). [*B. nana sensu* A. Michaux 1803, not L.; *B. nana* var. *?flabellifolia* Hook.; *B. terrae-novae* Fern.]. MAPS: Jacques Rousseau and Marcel Raymond, Rhodora 52(614): map 1, p. 30. 1950 (*see* discussion); Meusel, Jaeger, and Weinert 1965:119.

B. nana L.   Dwarf Birch
/aST/E/GEA/ (N (Ch))   Gravelly or rocky barrens and tundra: SE Baffin Is. near the Arctic Circle; W and E Greenland between ca. 62° and 75°N; N Europe; W Asia. MAPS: Hultén 1968b:365; Porsild 1957: map 127, p. 176; Jacques Rousseau and Marcel Raymond, Rhodora 52(614): map 1, p. 30. 1950; Meusel, Jaeger, and Weinert 1965:119.
[The closely related *B. exilis* Sukachev. of Alaska–Asia is referred to this species by Hultén (1944; *B. nana* ssp. *ex.* (Suk.) Hult.; MAP: Hultén 1968b:365), who notes that it seems to differ from the typical form only in its glandular, less pubescent branches. However, intermediate forms appear to indicate introgression with *B. glandulosa* and the problem requires further clarification.]

B. occidentalis Hook.   Black, Red, or Mountain Birch
/ST/X/ (Mc)   Woods, thickets, and shores from N-cent. Alaska–Yukon to the Mackenzie R. Delta, Great Bear L., Great Slave L., L. Athabasca (Alta. and Sask.), S Dist. Keewatin, Ont. (N to Big Trout L. at ca. 53°45′N and SW James Bay), Que. (N to S Ungava Bay, the Côte-Nord, and Gaspé Pen.), Labrador (N to Anatolak, 56°33′N), Nfld., and N.B. (Boivin 1966b; not known from P.E.I. or N.S.), S to N Calif., N.Mex., Nebr., and the mts. of N N.Y. and N New Eng. [*B. papyrifera (alba; microphylla)* var. *occ.* (Hook.) Sarg.; *B. fontinalis* Sarg.; *B. rhombifolia* Nutt. in part; *B. ?piperi* Britt.; incl. *B. papyrifera (alba; pubescens)* var. *minor* Tuckerm. *(B. minor* (Tuckerm.) Fern.)]. MAPS: Hultén 1968b:366, and 1958: map 47 *(B minor)*, p. 67; Dugle 1966: fig. 3 *(B. font.)*, p. 940; Canada Department of Northern Affairs and Natural Resources 1956:140; Preston 1961:154, and 1947:124 *(B. font.)*; Raup 1947: pl. 22; Hosie 1969:164.

B. papyrifera Marsh.   White Birch, Canoe- or Paper-Birch.   Bouleau blanc or Bouleau à canot
/ST/X/ (Ms)   Woods and rocky slopes, the aggregate species from N Alaska–Yukon to Great Bear L., S Dist. Keewatin, Ont. (N to Sachigo L. at ca. 54°N), Que. (N to Ungava Bay), Labrador (N to the Fraser R. at 56°38′N), Nfld., N.B., P.E.I., and N.S., S to Wash., Mont., Colo., Nebr., Minn., Pa., and N.Y. MAPS and synonymy: *see* below.
1 Leaves distinctly cordate-based; bracts of mature pistillate catkins to 1 cm long,
    their lobes mostly ascending . . . . var. *cordifolia* (Regel) Fern.
    2 Tall tree; [*B. cordifolia* Regel; according to Gleason 1958, probably a hybrid
       between *B. lutea* and *B. papyrifera;* Ont. to Que. (N to near Ungava Bay),
       Labrador, Nfld. (type locality of *B. cordifolia*), and N.S.; the report of *B. cordifolia*
       from Turtle Mt., Man., by Lowe 1943, requires confirmation] . . . . f. *cordifolia*
    2 Shrub to about 1 m tall; [type from Mt. Blanc, Matane Co., E Que.] . . . . . f. *nana* Boivin
1 Leaves tapering or merely rounded at base.
    3 Young twigs conspicuously resin-dotted; [var. *humilis sensu* Fern. & Raup, not *B. alba* ssp. *papyrifera* var. *humilis* Regel; *B. neoalaskana* Sarg.; *B. alaskana* Sarg., not Lesq.; *B. resinifera* Britt.; incl. *B. ?kenaica* Evans; the type of *B. alaskana* Sarg., basionym, is from Alaska; Alaska–B.C. to S Dist. Keewatin and cent. Ont.; MAPS: Hosie 1969:162 *(B. neo.);* Raup 1947: pl 22 (var. *humilis*); Dugle 1966: fig. 6 *(B. res.)*, p. 944; Hultén 1968b:367 (ssp. *humilis*)] . . . . . . var. *neoalaskana* (Sarg.) Raup
    3 Twigs mostly devoid of resin-glands.

4 Bracts of pistillate catkins to 1 cm long, with ascending lobes; samaras to
8 mm broad . . . . var. *macrostachya* Fern.
   5 Peduncles of pistallate catkins to 1.5 cm long; [E Que. to S Labrador, Nfld.,
   and N.S. (type from Hectanooga, Digby Co.)] . . . . f. *macrostachya*
   5 Peduncles of pistillate catkins to 3 cm long; [Gaspé Pen., Que., the type
   from Mt. Logan, Matane Co.] . . . . f. *longipes* Fern.
4 Bracts of pistillate catkins to 7 mm long, typically with divergent lobes;
samaras to 5 mm broad.
   6 Branchlets strongly drooping; leaves of fertile branches narrowly ovate to
   ovate-lanceolate, gradually tapering or only slightly rounded toward base;
   fruiting catkins often in clusters of 2, 3, or 4 on the spurs; [Que. to Nfld.
   and N.S.] . . . . var. *pensilis* Fern.
   6 Branchlets spreading or ascending; leaves of fertile branches broadly
   ovate, mostly rounded or truncate at base; fruiting catkins mostly solitary
   on the spurs . . . . var. *papyrifera*
      7 Pistillate catkins to 2 cm long, their bracts unlobed or with rudimentary
      lateral lobes; [var. *elobata* (Fern.) Sarg.; type from Mt. Albert, Gaspé
      Co., E Que.] . . . . f. *elobata* (Fern.) Boivin
      7 Pistillate catkins to over 6 cm long, their bracts 3-lobed; [incl. vars.
      commutata (Regel) Fern., *occidentalis sensu* Sarg. (*B. occidentalis*
      Hook. in part), and *recessa* Lepage; *B. alba* var. *pap.* (Marsh.) Spach;
      B. papyracea Ait.; *B. excelsa* of Canadian reports in part, not Ait.;
      transcontinental; MAPS (aggregate species): *Atlas of Canada* 1957:
      sheet 41; Canada Department of Northern Affairs and Natural
      Resources 1956:134; Hosie 1969:160; Fowells 1965:93; Little 1971:
      map 107-N; Preston 1961:148, and 1947:122; Hough 1947:121; the map
      by Dugle 1966: fig. 7, p. 949, indicates chiefly the western distribution;
      the map by Munns 1938: map 84, p. 88, indicates an occurrence only
      from E Man. eastwards] . . . . .f. *papyrifera*

B. pendula Roth   European Birch
Eurasian; occasionally spreading from cult. in N. America, as presumably in Man. (Spruce
Woods Forest Reserve and the banks of the Assiniboine and Souris rivers), Ont. (reported
from Toronto by Boivin 1966*b*, and from Wellington Co. by Stroud 1941), P.E.I. (roadside at
Charlottetown; PEI), and N.S. (Pictou, where "escaped from cult."; GH). Reports from else-
where in Canada may refer to cultivated trees.

B. populifolia Marsh.   Grey, Fire-, or Oldfield-Birch.   Bouleau rouge
/T/EE/ (Ms) Dry to wet sterile fields from Ont. (N to the Ottawa dist.) to Que. (N to the Quebec City dist.), N.B., P.E.I., and N.S., s to N Ind., N Ohio, and Va. MAPS (all indicating a range
too far northwards in Que.): Canada Department of Northern Affairs and Natural Resources
1956:138; Preston 1961:152; Hough 1947:119; Munns 1938: map 83, p. 87; Little 1971: map
108-N; Hosie 1969:166.

B. pubescens Ehrh.
/aST/–/GEA/ (Ms) Moist or wet habitats of SW Greenland, Iceland, and Eurasia; "Cult.
and spreading to roadsides, thickets, etc., Nfld. to N.E., w. to Mich." (Fernald *in* Gray 1950; *B.
alba*). [*B. alba* L. in part; incl. *B. tortuosa* Ledeb. (*B. pub.* (*odorata*) ssp. *tort.* (Ledeb.) Schn.)].
MAP: Hultén 1958: map 47 (*B. tortuosa*), p. 67.

B. pumila L.   Low or Swamp-Birch
/ST/X/ (N (Mc)) Bogs and wooded swamps (often calcareous; ranges of Canadian taxa
outlined below), s to Oreg., Wyo., N.Dak., Iowa, Ind., Ohio, and N.J. MAPS and synonymy: *see*
below.
1 Twigs and lower leaf-surfaces distinctly glandular-warty; leaves sparingly pubescent
   or glabrate, cuneate-obovate, conspicuously paler beneath, to 4 cm long, longer
   than broad; shrub to 3 m tall; [*B. glandulosa* var. *glandulifera* (Regel) Gl.; *B. nana*

var. *glandulifera* (Regel) Boivin (*B. glandulifera* (Regel) Butler); *B. glandulosa* var. *hallii* (Howell) Hitchc. (*B. hallii* Howell); cent. Yukon–w-cent. Dist. Mackenzie–B.C.–Alta. to Sask. (N to L. Athabasca), Man. (N to Churchill), Ont. (N to the mouth of the Black Duck R., Hudson Bay, at ca. 56°50′N), Que. (N to S Ungava Bay), and Labrador (N to the Hamilton R. basin at Goose Bay); (reported W to Alaska by Dugle 1966, but with no Alaska stations indicated on her map; not listed by Hultén 1944); MAPS: Dugle 1966: fig. 5 (*B. glandulifera;* Yukon–Ont. range), p. 944; the map for *B. pumila* by Meusel, Jaeger, and Weinert 1965, is applicable here] . . . . var. *glandulifera* Regel

1 Twigs and lower leaf-surfaces glandless.

2 Leaves of fertile branches broadly obovate to orbicular or reniform, scarcely paler beneath, commonly less than 2 cm long; prostrate or depressed shrub rarely over 6 dm tall; [*B. nana* var. *ren.* (Fern.) Boivin; *B. nana* var. *flabellifolia sensu* Fernald and Sornborger 1899, perhaps not Hooker; peaty tundra, exposed slopes, and alpine barrens in Que. (Knob L., 54°48′N, the Côte-Nord (type from Baie des Moutons), and Magdalen Is.), Labrador (N to Makkovik, 55°05′N), Nfld., and N.S. (St. Paul Is. and Inverness Co., Cape Breton Is.); reported from P.E.I. by D.S. Erskine 1960] . . . . var. *renifolia* Fern.

2 Leaves of fertile branches cuneate-obovate, pale green to whitish beneath, commonly over 3 cm long; upright shrub to about 3 m tall; [bogs and wooded swamps (often calcareous) in Ont. (N to near Ottawa), Que. (N to L. St. John, the Côte-Nord, Anticosti Is., the Gaspé Pen., and Magdalen Is.), S Labrador (Goose Bay), Nfld., N.B., P.E.I., and N.S.] . . . . var. *pumila*

Betula Hybrids

Following is a list of *Betula* hybrids that have been reported from Alaska–Canada. In accordance with current practice, the names of the putative parents are given in alphabetical sequence. Many of the parent species have been reported under names used in synonymy in the present work. Such synonyms are placed in brackets, followed by the parent name in current usage.

B. borealis × *B. pumila* var. *glandulifera:* (× *B. neoborealis* Lepage, the type from Moose Factory, S James Bay, Ont.); also known from Rupert House, S James Bay, Que.

× *B. caerulea-grandis* × *B. populifolia:* (× *B. caerulea* Blanch.); Halifax Co., N.S. Its nm. *cunninghamii* Boivin is reported from N.S. by Boivin (1966*b*). T.C. Brayshaw (Can. Field-Nat. 80(4):187–94. 1966) presents evidence to indicate that *B. caerulea* Blanch. and *B. caerulea-grandis* Blanch. are both members of a hybrid swarm originating from crosses between *B. papyrifera* and *B. populifolia*. Such hybrids may all be included under the name × *B. caerulea* Blanch. However, N.H. Brittain and N.F. Grant (Can. Field-Nat. 81(2):116–27. 1967) support the view that *B. caerulea-grandis* is a "good" species, hybridizing with *B. papyrifera* var. *cordifolia*.

B. fontinalis (occidentalis) × *B. glandulosa:* (× *B. eastwoodiae* Sarg., the type from Dawson, the Yukon; *B. glandulosa* × *B. resinifera sensu* Hultén 1944, in part); also reported by Dugle 1966, from Dist. Mackenzie, Alta., and Sask.

B. fontinalis (occidentalis) × *B. papyrifera:* (× *B. utahensis* Britt.; *B. subcordata* Rydb.; *B. papyrifera* var. *subcordata* (Rydb.) Sarg.; *B. glandulosa* × *B. resinifera sensu* Hultén 1944, in part); the Yukon–B.C.–Alta. (Dugle 1966).

B. glandulosa × *B. minor:* (× *B. dutillyi* Lepage, the type from Richmond Gulf, Hudson Bay, Que., at 56°10′N). *B. minor* (included above in *B. occidentalis*), itself, is considered by Gleason (1958) to be a hybrid between *B. glandulosa* and *B. papyrifera*.

B. glandulosa × *B. nana* ssp. *exilis:* Alaska (Hultén 1944).

B. glandulosa × *B. (glandulifera) pumila* var. *glandulifera:* (× *B. sargentii* Dugle, the type from Obed, Alta.; also reported by Dugle (1966) from Sask., Man., and Ont.

B. kenaica × *B. nana* ssp. *exilis:* Alaska (Hultén 1944).

B. kenaica × *B. (resinifera) papyrifera* var. *neoalaskana:* Alaska (Hultén 1944).

B. lutea × *B. pumila* var. *glandulifera:* (× *B. purpusii* Schn.); Bruce Pen., s Ont. (Fernald *in* Gray 1950).

B. nana × *B. pubescens:* (× *B. alpestris* Fries); Greenland.

B. papyrifera × *B. populifolia:* (× *B. caerulea-grandis* Blanch.; × *B. caerulea* nm. *grandis* (Blanch.) Boivin; *B. ?papyrifera* × *B. populifolia* (*see* × *B. caerulea-grandis* × *B. populifolia,* above); Que. (Montmorency Co. to the Gaspé Pen.), P.E.I. (Brackley Point, Queens Co.), and N.S. (Lunenburg and Halifax counties).

B. papyrifera × *B. (resinifera) papyrifera* var. *neoalaskana:* (× *B. winteri* Dugle, the type from Edmonton, Alta.); also reported by Dugle (1966) from Alaska–Yukon–Dist. Mackenzie and Sask.–Man.

B. papyrifera × *B. (glandulifera) pumila* var. *glandulifera:* (× *B. sandbergii* Britt.; *B. lutea* × *B. pumila* var. *glandulifera;* reported by Dugle (1966) from Alta. (L. Athabasca), Sask. (near Wallwort), and Man. (near Cypress River).

B. (resinifera) papyrifera var. *neoalaskana* × *B. (glandulifera) pumila* var. *glandulifera:* (× *B. uliginosa* Dugle, the type from Ponoka bog, 71 mi s of Edmonton, Alta.); also reported by Dugle (1966) from near Wizard Lake and Sangudo, s-cent. Alta.

B. populifolia × *B. pumila* var. *glandulifera:* (× *B. raymundii* Lepage, the type, as first collection cited, from LaColle, St-Jean Co., Que.); also reported from Farnham, Missisquoi Co., Que.

B. papyrifera × *B.* × *sargentii:* (× *B. arbuscula* Dugle, the type from Jasper National Park, Alta.).

CARPINUS L.   [1884]   Hornbeam, Ironwood.   Charme

C. caroliniana Walt.   Blue Beach.   Bois dur or Bois de fer
/T/EE   (Ms)   Rich woods and swamps from Ont. (N to Mattawa and Ottawa) to sw Que. (N to Bryson, s Pontiac Co., and the Montreal dist.) and New Eng., s to Ark., Tenn., and N.C. [Incl. var. *virginiana* (Marsh.) Fern.; *C. americana* Michx.]. MAPS: Canada Department of Northern Affairs and Natural Resources 1956:124; Preston 1961:164; Hough 1947:115; Munns 1938: map 78 (indicating the occurrence in N.B. and N.S. on the basis of early reports, the species now extinct there or reports perhaps referable to *Ostrya virginiana*), p. 82; Little 1971: map 109-N; Hosie 1969:152.

CORYLUS L.   [1886]   Hazel, Hazelnut, Filbert.   Noisetier or Coudrier

1   Fruiting involucre downy, relatively short, spreading and exposing the top of the bony-shelled nut; staminate aments distinctly peduncled; twigs, petioles, and involucres more or less glandular-bristly; (s Man. to sw Que.) . . . . *C. americana*
1   Fruiting involucre densely bristly, the bracts fused into a long tubular beak much exceeding the thin-shelled nut; staminate aments sessile or subsessile; twigs, petioles, and involucres essentially glandless; (transcontinental) . . . . *C. cornuta*

C. americana Walt.   American Hazel
/T/EE/   (Mc)   Forming thickets from s Man. (N to Fairford, about 110 mi N of Portage la Prairie) to Ont. (N to Huron, Northumberland, Dundas, and Stormont counties; *see* s Ont. map by Soper and Heimburger 1961:58), sw Que. (Boivin 1966*b*), and cent. Maine, s to Okla., Mo., and Ga.
   Reports from Sask. are excluded by Breitung (1957*a*). The glandless f. *missouriensis* (DC.) Fern. is reported from s Man. by Löve and Bernard (1959; Otterburne) and from s Ont. by Gaiser and Moore (1966; Lambton Co.).

C. cornuta Marsh.   Beaked Hazelnut
/T/X/   (Mc)   Rich thickets and borders of woods (ranges of Canadian taxa outlined below), s to cent. Calif., Kans., and Ga.

1   Tube of involucre usually less than twice the length of the nut; young twigs and
    petioles copiously hirsute; [s B.C.].
    2   Twigs and petioles only slightly glandular; [*C. rostrata* var. *cal.* DC.; *C. cal.* (DC.)
        Rose; s B.C.: Vancouver Is. and s mainland] . . . . var. *californica* (DC.) Sharp
    2   Twigs and petioles copiously stipitate-glandular; [type from Finlayson Arm,
        Vancouver Is., B.C.] . . . . var. *glandulosa* Boivin
1   Tube of involucre usually at least twice as long as the nut; twigs usually only slightly
    to moderately glandular-puberulent . . . . var. *cornuta*
    3   Involucre glabrous or only slightly bristly; [type from East Broughton, sw Que.] . . . . . .
        . . . . f. *inermis* Fern.
    3   Involucre densely bristly; [*C. rostrata* Ait.; incl. var. *megaphylla* Vict. & Rousseau;
        B.C. (N to Hudson Hope, ca. 56°N), Alta. (N to 58°43′N), Sask. (N to Prince
        Albert), Man. (N to Pipestone L., NE of L. Winnipeg), Ont. (N to the N shore of L.
        Superior and Pagwa, 50°01′N), Que. (N to N Labelle Co., L. St. John, Anticosti Is.,
        and the Gaspé Pen.), Nfld., N.B., P.E.I., and N.S.] . . . . f. *cornuta*

OSTRYA Scop.   [1885]   Ironwood, Hop-Hornbeam

O. virginiana (Mill.) Koch   American Hop-Hornbeam, Leverwood.   Bois dur, Bois de fer, or
Bois à levier
/T/EE/   (Ms)   Rich woods from SE Man. (N to Falcon L., E of Winnipeg) to Ont. (N to Ren-
frew and Carleton counties; reported N to Kenora by John Macoun 1886), Que. (N to Ste-
Anne-de-la-Pocatière, Kamouraska Co.; RIM), N.B., and N.S. (not known from P.E.I.), s to
Tex. and Fla. [*Carpinus virginiana* Mill., not Michx. f.; *C. ostrya* L.]. MAPS: Hosie 1969:150; Can-
ada Department of Northern Affairs and Natural Resources 1956:126; Preston 1961:162;
Hough 1947:117; Munns 1938: map 79, p. 83; Little 1971: map 146-N.

    All of the above maps except that by Hough erroneously indicate an occurrence in P.E.I.
Forma *glandulosa* (Spach) Macbr. (new branchlets stipitate-glandular rather than glabrous or
sparsely pilose and glabrate) is known from Que., N.B., and N.S.

FAGACEAE (Beech Family)

Trees with alternate simple straight-veined toothed or lobed leaves and deciduous stipules. Flowers small, unisexual, apetalous, with a small 2–8-parted calyx. Staminate flowers in aments (catkins) or small heads, each with 3 or more stamens. Pistillate flowers solitary or slightly clustered, each with a single pistil. Styles 3. Ovary inferior. Fruit a 1-seeded nut subtended by or enclosed within the accrescent involucre.

1   Fruit the familiar "acorn", the solitary, terete, globose to ovoid, pointed nut at most
    about half covered by the prickleless basal involucral cup; staminate aments
    distantly flowered, drooping; leaves with sharp or rounded coarse teeth or deep
    lobes . . . . *Quercus*
1   Fruit consisting of up to 3 or 4 flattened or 3-angled nuts enclosed in a prickly bur-
    like involucre dehiscent by as many valves as there are nuts.
    2   Nuts flattened on one or both sides, usually 2, 3, or 4 in each bur; staminate
        flowers in slender aments; leaves oblong-lanceolate, acutish to obtuse at base,
        coarsely and sharply serrate; rough-barked tree to about 30 m tall; (s Ont.) . . . .
        . . . . *Castanea*
    2   Nuts sharply triangular, commonly in pairs; staminate flowers in heads on
        drooping peduncles; leaves ovate to oblong-obovate, obtuse to subcordate at
        base, shallowly serrate; tree to about 30 m tall, with smooth ash-grey bark;
        (Ont. to N.S.) . . . . *Fagus*

CASTANEA Mill.   [1891]

C. dentata (Marsh.) Borkh.   Chestnut.   Châtaignier
/t/EE/   (Mg)   Dry gravelly or rocky, mostly acidic soils from Minn. to s Ont. (N to Lambton, Oxford, Wellington, and Halton counties; *see* s Ont. map by Fox and Soper 1953: fig. 16, p. 13), N.Y., Vt., N.H., and Maine, s to Miss., NW Fla., and Ga. [*Fagus-Castanea dentata* Marsh.; *C. vulgaris (sativa)* var. *americana* DC.]. MAPS: Hosie 1969:178; Canada Department of Northern Affairs and Natural Resources 1956:156; Meusel, Jaeger, and Weinert 1965:121; Preston 1961:168; Hough 1947:135; Munns 1938: map 89, p. 93.

In 1904, there appeared in New York City a chestnut-bark disease caused by the fungus *Diaporthe parasitica,* resulting in death of the tree through girdling of branches. By 1937, it was estimated that as many as 99 per cent of the trees in the United States had been killed. In a survey conducted in s Ont., W.S. Fox (Can. Field-Nat. 63(2):88–89. 1949) found not a single mature tree still alive and fruit-bearing. However, "Suckers are common everywhere, some bunched in clumps, some standing singly. Possibly some of these solitary specimens may be seedlings sprung from nuts planted by squirrels. These young trees range in height from one foot to ten feet, the dead and the living of all heights being about equal in number. It is clear then that the blight strikes as early as the plant's first two or three years. The vast majority are blasted before they reach six feet. Rare indeed is the one that exceeds twelve. So ubiquitous is the scourge that the odds against a chestnut escaping infection and attaining the size of a normal forest tree are overwhelming."

FAGUS L.   [1890]   Beech.   Hêtre

F. grandifolia Ehrh.
/T/EE/   (Mg)   Rich woods from Ont. (N to the N shore of L. Huron and Renfrew and Carleton counties) to Que. (N to Montcalm Co. at about 80 mi NW of Mont-Laurier and the Gaspé Pen.), N.B., P.E.I., and N.S., s to Tex. and Fla. [*F. ferruginea* Ait.; *F. sylvestris* Michx. f.]. MAPS: Little 1971: map 125-N; Canada Department of Northern Affairs and Natural Resources 1956:154; *Atlas of Canada* 1957: sheet 41; Meusel, Jaeger, and Weinert 1965:121; Gleason and Cronquist 1964: fig. 14.7, p. 160; Preston 1961:166; Fowells 1965:172; Hough 1947:133; Munns 1938: map 87, p. 91; Nichols 1935: fig. 5c, p. 408; Braun 1935: fig. 1, p. 352; Hosie 1969:176.

QUERCUS L. [1893] Oak. Chène

1 Leaves with sharp lobes, the principal veins excurrent as bristles; styles long and spreading; fruit maturing the second year, the inner surface of the shell tomentose; bark often dark, furrowed but rarely scaly; (Red and Black Oaks).
  2 Leaves loosely stellate-pubescent beneath and along the midvein above, shallowly to deeply lobed; scales pubescent, pale, relatively large, the uppermost loose, their free tips forming a loose marginal fringe; cup about 1/2 as long as the large (up to 2.5 cm long) ovoid acorn; winter-buds densely pubescent, strongly angled or grooved; (s Ont.) . . . .*Q. velutina*
  2 Leaves glabrous except sometimes for tufts of hairs in the axils of the veins beneath.
    3 Upper (innermost) scales of the pubescent cup (about 1/2 as long as the acorn) forming a loose marginal fringe; leaves variable, shallowly to deeply lobed; winter-buds densely pubescent, strongly 4-angled, to 1 cm long; (s Ont.) . . .
    . . . .*Q. velutina*
    3 Upper scales of cup (1/4 to 1/3 as long as the acorn) tightly appressed, not forming a definite fringe; winter-buds ovoid, rarely to 7 mm long, their scales glabrous or ciliate.
      4 Leaves relatively shallowly lobed, the longest lobes less than twice as long as the width of the broad median portion; (Ont. to N.S.) . . . .*Q. rubra*
      4 Leaves more deeply lobed, the longest lobes up to 6 times as long as the width of the median portion.
        5 Cup to about 1.5 cm broad, saucer-shaped, covering 1/4 to 1/3 of the nearly spherical acorn, this to 1.5 cm long; (s Ont.) . . . .*Q. palustris*
        5 Cup turbinate, covering 1/3 to 1/2 of the acorn, this to 2 cm long.
          6 Cup brown or chestnut-colour, finally glabrous and lustrous, to 2.2 cm broad; acorn ovoid to subglobose; (s ?Ont.) . . . . [*Q. coccinea*]
          6 Cup ashy grey, pubescent, at most 1.8 cm broad; acorn ellipsoid-cylindric; (s ?Man.; s?Ont.) . . . . [*Q. ellipsoidalis*]
1 Leaves with rounded or acute (but never bristle-tipped) lobes; stigmas subsessile; fruit maturing the first year, the inner surface of the shell glabrous; bark pale, often scaly; (White Oaks).
  7 Upper scales of cup awned, forming a marginal fringe; leaves with rounded teeth or lobes.
    8 Leaves deeply lobed, at least in the basal third or half, pubescent or glabrate; peduncles short or obsolete; cup sometimes covering more than 1/2 of the acorn; (Sask. to N.B.) . . . .*Q. macrocarpa*
    8 Leaves coarsely sinuate-crenate or often shallowly lobed, usually soft-downy and white-hoary beneath; fruiting peduncles to 6 cm long, much surpassing the leaf-petioles; cup 1/3 to 1/2 as long as the acorn; (s Ont. and s Que.) . . . .
    . . . .*Q. bicolor*
  7 Upper scales not awn-tipped; cup 1/3 to 1/2 as long as the acorn.
    9 Leaves coarsely sinuate-toothed but not lobed; acorns sessile or very short-peduncled; (s Ont.).
      10 Leaf-teeth rounded; leaves thinly pubescent beneath with appressed stellate hairs; acorn to 3.5 cm long . . . .*Q. prinus*
      10 Leaf-teeth ending in a minute projecting callus-tip; leaves normally densely pubescent or tomentose beneath; acorn at most 2 cm long . . . .
      . . . .*Q. prinoides*
    9 Leaves deeply lobed, the lobes rounded.
      11 Mature leaves essentially glabrous beneath, rather regularly lobed.
        12 Leaves cuneate to petioles mostly at least 1 cm long; fruiting peduncles very short or up to 4 cm long; (Ont., sw Que., and N.S.) . . .*Q. alba*
        12 Leaves cordate or truncate at base, subsessile or short-petioled; fruiting peduncles to 8 cm long; (introd.) . . . .*Q. robur*

11 Mature leaves usually pubescent beneath; acorns subsessile.
    13 Leaves greyish- or brownish-downy beneath, with stellate hairs
        intermixed, hard and harsh above, commonly with 2 or 3 lobes on each
        margin, the upper 3 lobes usually much the largest, truncate or slightly
        concave, constricted at base (the leaf thus suggesting a Swiss cross);
        branchlets tomentose; cup to half the height of the acorn; (s ?Ont.) . . . .
        . . . . [*Q. stellata*]
    13 Leaves usually rusty- to yellowish-pubescent beneath, with up to 7
        round-tipped lobes on each margin; branchlets at first usually densely
        rusty-pubescent, mostly glabrate; acorn-cup shallow; (sw B.C.) . . . .
        . . . . *Q. garryana*

Q. alba L.   White Oak
/T/EE/ (Mg) Dryish woods from Minn. to s Ont. (N to Chalk River, Renfrew Co., and the Ottawa dist.; *see* s Ont. map by Fox and Soper 1954: fig. 31, p. 109), sw Que. (N to Pontiac Co. and the Montreal dist.), and N.S. (Windsor, Hants Co.; J.S. Erskine, Acadian Nat. 1(4):147. 1944), s to Tex. and Fla. MAPS: Canada Department of Northern Affairs and Natural Resources 1956:160; Preston 1961:180; Hough 1947:165; Munns 1938: map 110, p. 114; Braun 1935: fig. 1, p. 352; Little 1971: map 157-E; Hosie 1969:182.
    The map by Preston erroneously indicates an extension into sw N.B. Forma *latiloba* (Sarg.) Palmer & Steyerm. (leaf-blades mostly cleft less than half-way to the midrib, the round-tipped broadly oblong lobes to over 3 cm broad) is reported from s Ont. by Soper (1949). A collection in OAC from Dundas, s Ont., has been referred to × *Q. deamii* Trel., a hybrid with *Q. prinoides* var. *acuminata*. A hybrid with *Q. macrocarpa* (× *Q. bebbiana* Schn.) is reported from sw Que. by Boivin (1966b).

Q. bicolor Willd.   Swamp-White Oak.   Chêne bleu
/T/EE/ (Ms) Swampy ground and streambanks from Nebr. to s Minn., s Ont. (N to Lambton, Peel, and York counties; *see* s Ont. map by Fox and Soper 1954: fig. 30, p. 107, and their note, p. 112, concerning more northern citations), sw Que. (N to the Montreal dist.), and s Maine, s to Okla., Ark., Ky., and Ga. [*Q. platanoides* (Lam.) Sudw.]. MAPS: Hosie 1969:188; Canada Department of Northern Affairs and Natural Resources 1956:164; Fowells 1965:625; Hough 1947:173 *(Q. plat.);* Munns 1938: map 116, p. 120; Little 1971: map 159-E.
    The above maps all indicate an extension northwards beyond that shown by Fox and Soper along the NE shore of L. Ontario and the N shore of the St. Lawrence R. in Ont. They believe that the tree may have once occurred in these more northern localities, where apparently now extinct. A hybrid with *Q. macrocarpa* (× *Q. schuettei* Trel.) is reported from sw Que. by Boivin (1966b).

[*Q. coccinea* Muenchh.]   Scarlet Oak
[Ont. is included in the range assigned to this species by Fernald *in* Gray (1950), perhaps on the basis of the report from s Ont. by John Macoun (1886; "In University Park, Toronto, are a few fine trees, but they become more numerous to the west and in the forest along the Niagara River and Lake Erie, it is an abundant tree."). The southernmost part of the Niagara Peninsula is also included in the following MAPS: Canada Department of Northern Affairs and Natural Resources 1956:176; Little 1971: map 161-E; Preston 1961:196; Hough 1947:147; E.J. Palmer, Am. Midland Nat. 27(3):733. 1942; Munns 1938: map 96, p. 100.
    Fox and Soper (1954), however, write that "After watching for Scarlet Oak in the field for many years and examining numerous herbarium specimens so labelled, the authors still have not found any clear-cut evidence that this species exists in Ontario today." If it once did, it is apparently now extinct.]

[*Q. ellipsoidalis* Hill]   Jack-Oak, Northern Pin-Oak
[Fernald *in* Gray (1950) includes s Man. in the range of this species, perhaps on the basis of its listing by Lowe (1943; "Rare. Along the Minnesota–Manitoba boundary."). MAPS by Preston (1961:198), Hough (1947:145), and Munns (1938: map 95, p. 99) indicate a possible occurrence in extreme s Ont. along the Detroit R. in Lambton Co., from where it is reported by

F. Mitchell (Ont. Nat. Sci. Bull. 7:61. 1912) but not listed by Dodge (1915) for that county. Fox and Soper (1954) do not mention the species in their treatment of the genus in s Ont.]

Q. garryana Dougl.   Garry or Oregon Oak
/t/W/   (Ms)   Dry prairies, foothills, and rocky bluffs from sw B.C. (s Vancouver Is. and adjacent islands and mainland E to Yale in the lower Fraser Valley) to Oreg. [*Q. jacobii* R. Br.; *Q. agrifolia sensu* Pursh 1814, not Née]. MAPS: Little 1971: map 166-W; Hosie 1969:184; Canada Department of Northern Affairs and Natural Resources 1956:170; *Atlas of Canada* 1957: sheet 41; Fowells 1965:596; Preston 1961:186; Munns 1938: map 112, p. 116.

Q. macrocarpa Michx.   Mossy-cup Oak
/T/EE/   (Mg)   Moist woods and bottomlands to dry prairie slopes and sand-hills from SE Sask. (N to the Qu'Appelle Valley; Breitung 1957a) to Man. (N to Cross Lake, N of L. Winnipeg; CAN), Ont. (N to the Kaministiquia R. W of Thunder Bay, the Kenora dist., and New Liskeard, 47°31'N), Que. (N to St-Marc, about 40 mi W of Quebec City; *see* Que. map by Doyon and Lavoie 1966: fig. 9, p. 817, and Que. N-limits map by Marie-Victorin 1935), and N.B. (St. John; St. Andrews; Grand Lake; Miscou Is.; not known from P.E.I. or N.S.), s to Wyo., Tex., Ala., and N.C. [Incl. var. *depressa* (Nutt.) Engelm. (*Q. mandanensis* Rydb.)]. MAPS: Hosie 1969:188; Canada Department of Northern Affairs and Natural Resources 1956:162; Fowells 1965:563; Preston 1961:180, and 1947:150; Hough 1947:169; Munns 1938: map 115, p. 119; Little 1971: maps 172-W and 172-E.

Q. palustris Muenchh.   Pin-Oak, Spanish Oak
/t/EE/   (Mg)   Swampy woods and bottomlands from Iowa to Ill., s Mich., s Ont. (N to Lambton and Lincoln counties; *see* s Ont. map by Fox and Soper 1954: fig. 34, p. 116), Pa., N.Y., and R.I., s to Okla., N La., Tenn., and N.C. MAPS: Hosie 1969:196; Canada Department of Northern Affairs and Natural Resources 1956:178; Fowells 1965:603; Preston 1961:198; Hough 1947:143 (the occurrence in s Ont. should be indicated); Munns 1938: map 93, p. 97; Braun 1935: fig. 1, p. 352; Little 1971: map 177-E.

Q. prinoides Willd.   Chinquapin-Oak, Dwarf Chestnut-Oak
/t/EE/   (Mg)   Dry rocky slopes and borders of woods, the aggregate species from Nebr. to Minn., s Ont., N.Y., and Maine, s to Tex. and N Fla. MAPS and synonymy: *see* below.
1   Leaves with at most 8 pairs of principal veins terminating in as many teeth on each margin; shrub or small tree to about 5 m tall; [s Ont.: Essex, Lambton, and Norfolk counties; *see* s Ont. maps by Fox and Soper 1954: fig. 33, p. 38, and Soper and Heimburger 1961:7] . . . . var. *prinoides*
1   Leaves with up to 13 pairs of principal veins terminating in as many teeth on each margin; tall tree; [*Q. prinus* var. *acuminata* Michx. (*Q. acuminata* (Michx.) Houba); *Q. muehlenbergii* Engelm.; s Ont. (N to N Lambton, SE Waterloo, Peterborough, Frontenac, and Leeds counties; *see* s Ont. map by Fox and Soper 1954: fig. 32, p. 113 *(Q. muehl.)*; MAPS (mostly as *Q. muehl.*): Hosie 1969:190; Canada Department of Northern Affairs and Natural Resources 1956:168; Preston 1961:190; Munns 1938: map 119, p. 123; Hough 1947:179; Little 1971: maps 173-W and 173-E] . . . . var. *acuminata* (Michx.) Gl.

Q. prinus L.   Chestnut-Oak, Rock-Chestnut-Oak
/t/EE/   (Ms)   Dry or moist upland or rocky woods (chiefly in acid soil) from cent. Ind. to s Ont. (N to Lambton and Lincoln counties; *see* s Ont. map by Fox and Soper 1954: fig. 33, map 39, p. 115) and sw Maine, s to N Miss., N Ala., and Ga. [*Q. montana* Willd.]. MAPS: Canada Department of Northern Affairs and Natural Resources 1956:166 *(Q. mont.)*; Fowells 1965:573; Preston 1961:188 (top); Hough 1947:177; Munns 1938: map 118 (*Q. mont.*; s Ont. occurrence not indicated), p. 122; Little 1971: map 179-E.

Q. robur L.   English Oak
European; much planted in the E U.S.A. and locally spreading to roadsides and borders of

woods, as in N.B. (Boivin 1966*b*), P.E.I. (D.S. Erskine 1960), and N.S. (Roland 1947). [*Q. alba sensu* Hurst 1952, not L.].

Q. rubra L.   Red Oak.   Chêne rouge
/T/EE/   (Mg)   Dry or upland woods (ranges of Canadian taxa outlined below), s to Okla. and Ga. MAPS and synonymy: *see* below.
1   Acorn-cup shallowly saucer-shaped (enclosing about 1/4 of the acorn), to 3 cm
     broad; bark of branches dark grey or brown; [*Q. rubra maxima* Marsh. (*Q. maxima*
     (Marsh.) Ashe; *Q. rubra (borealis)* var. *max.* (Marsh.) Ashe); reported from s Ont., s
     Que., P.E.I., and N.B. by Fernald *in* Gray 1950; a hybrid with *Q. velutina* (× *Q. porteri*
     Trel.) is reported from s Ont. by Soper 1949; MAPS: Fowells 1965:588; Hosie 1969:192;
     Hough 1947:139; Munns 1938: map 92 (var. *max.*), p. 96; Little 1971: map 180-N] . . .
     . . . . var. *rubra*
1   Acorn-cup deeply saucer-shaped to almost top-shaped (enclosing about 1/3 of the
     acorn), at most 2.5 cm broad; bark of branches paler grey; [*Q. borealis* Michx. f.;
     Q. ambigua Michx. f. (*Q. rubra* var. *amb.* (Michx. f.) Houba), not Humb. & Bonpl.;
     Q. ?banisteri (*Q. ilicifolia* Wang. of the E U.S.A.) *sensu* Hooker 1838, not Michx.; Ont.
     (N to the NW and NE shores of L. Superior and Haileybury, 47°27′N), Que. (N to
     L. Timiskaming at ca. 47°22′N and the Gaspé Pen.), N.B., P.E.I., and N.S.; MAPS
     (*Q. bor.):* Canada Department of Northern Affairs and Natural Resources 1956:172;
     Gleason and Cronquist 1964: fig. 14.7, p. 160; Munns 1938: map 91, p. 95] . . . .
     . . . . var. *borealis* (Michx. f.) Farw.

[Q. stellata Wang.]   Post-Oak
[This species of the E U.S.A. (N to Kans., Ohio, and Mass.) is reported from Canada by Hooker (1838; *Q. obtus.*) and from s Ont. by John Macoun (1886; Bay of Quinte, Hastings Co.; *Q. obtus.*). *Q. macrocarpa* is known from the Bay of Quinte and may be the basis of Macoun's citation. (*Q. obtusiloba* Michx., not Houba; *Q. minor* (Marsh.) Sarg.).]

Q. velutina Lam.   Black or Yellow-barked Oak, Quercitron
/t/EE/   (Mg)   Dry woods from Nebr. to s Minn., s Ont. (N to Huron, York, Peterborough, and Hastings counties; *see* s Ont. map by Fox and Soper 1954: fig. 35, p. 117), N.Y., and Maine, s to E Tex. and N Fla. [*Q. tinctoria* Bartr.]. MAPS: Hosie 1969:194; Canada Department of Northern Affairs and Natural Resources 1956:174; Fowells 1965:558; Gleason and Cronquist 1964: fig. 14.7, p. 161; Preston 1961:192; Hough 1947:149; Munns 1938: map 97, p. 101; Little 1971: map 183-E.
    Forma *pagodaeformis* Trel. (leaves with deep and very broad-based sinuses, their long, mostly acuminate lobes subentire or only slightly toothed, rather than the leaves usually less deeply lobed and more coarsely toothed) is reported from s Ont. by Landon (1960).

ULMACEAE (Elm Family)

Trees with simple alternate serrate leaves, these oblique at base. Flowers small, perfect or unisexual (or these intermixed), apetalous, with a commonly 3–7-lobed calyx, solitary, short-racemose, or in cymose clusters. Stamens as many as the calyx-lobes and opposite them. Stigmas 2, sessile or on short styles. Ovary superior. Fruit a thin-walled broad-winged circular samara *(Ulmus)* or a dark-red to nearly black drupe *(Celtis)*.

1   Fruit an ovoid, dark-red to purplish-black, thin-fleshed drupe with a large stone; flowers on shoots of the season, developing mostly with the leaves, at least partly staminate and fascicled, the fertile flowers commonly solitary, with or without stamens; leaves singly-serrate, with 2 prominent veins at the broad base in addition to the midrib; (s Man. to s Que.) . . . . *Celtis*
1   Fruit a thin flat broad-winged elliptic samara; flowers from buds of the preceding year, developing before the leaves, perfect, in fascicles or short racemes; leaves mostly doubly-serrate, copiously pinnate-veined, broadest near the middle . . . . *Ulmus*

CELTIS L.   [1898]   Hackberry, Nettle-tree.   Bois inconnu or Micocoulier

1   Leaves of fertile branches distinctly serrate to well below the middle (at least on the broader side), abruptly long-acuminate, yellowish green beneath, to about 13 (av. 8) cm long and 9 (av. 4.5) cm broad; mature drupes broadly ellipsoid or subglobose, commonly short-beaked, dark red to purple-black, to 13 mm long, on pedicels to over 2.5 cm long that usually markedly surpass the subtending petioles; stone to 9 mm long, conspicuously pitted; (s ?B.C.; Man. to Que.) . . . . *C. occidentalis*
1   Leaves of fertile branches entire or occasionally with a few low teeth above the middle, bluntish to merely short-acuminate, grey-green on both surfaces or darker green above, pubescent beneath, to about 8 cm long and 4 cm broad; mature drupes subglobose, beakless, to about 9 mm long, on pedicels at most 13 mm long that seldom (if ever) surpass the subtending petioles; stone to 7 mm long, shallowly and obscurely pitted; (s Ont.) . . . . *C. tenuifolia*

C. occidentalis L.   Hackberry.   Bois Inconnu
/T/EE/   (Ms)   Local in dry woods and in sandy or rocky places from s Man. (known only from near the s end of L. Manitoba; CAN; WIN) to Ont. (n to Smiths Falls and Ottawa; *see* Herbert Groh, Can. Field-Nat. 61(4):141. 1947) and sw Que. (n to Berthier, about 45 mi NE of Montreal; *see* Que. maps by Rouleau 1945: fig. 3, p. 26, and Raymond 1950b: fig. 36, p. 101), s to Okla., Ark., Tenn., and n Fla. [Incl. vars. *crassifolia* (Lam.) Gray (*C. crass.* Lam.) and *pumila* (Pursh) Gray; *C. ?reticulata* Torr.]. MAPS: Canada Department of Northern Affairs and Natural Resources 1956:188; Fowells 1965:140; Preston 1961:222, and 1947:160; Hough 1947:193; Munns 1938: map 121, p. 125; Little 1971: maps 121-W and 121-E; Hosie 1969:206.

The report of the closely related *C. douglasii* Planch. from B.C. by Rydberg (1922) requires confirmation. Hitchcock et al. (1964) assign it a range from Wash. and Idaho to s Calif. and Ariz. Some of our material may be referable to var. *canina* (Raf.) Sarg. (*C. canina* Raf.; leaves relatively thin and smooth; drupes distinctly longer than broad, becoming dark brown to blackish, rather than nearly spherical, greyish brown to orange-red; pedicels to 3.5 cm long rather than commonly less than 1.5 cm). According to Gleason (1958), however, the two forms are sometimes found on the same tree.

C. tenuifolia Nutt.
/t/EE/   (Mc)   Dry cliffs and slopes from Kans. to Mo., Ind., s Ont. (Lambton and Huron counties; *see* s Ont. map by Fox and Soper 1953: map 16, fig. 17, p. 14), and Pa., s to Okla., La., and n Fla. [Incl. var. *soperi* Boivin; *C. pumila* of auth., not Pursh].

ULMUS L.   [1896]   Elm.   Orme

1   Calyx divided to below the middle; flowers appearing in autumn in axillary clusters; fruit glabrous; leaves to 5 cm long; (introd.) . . . .[*U. parvifolia*]
1   Calyx short-lobed; flowers appearing in spring before the leaves.
2   Flowers slender-pedicelled, soon drooping; fruits longer than broad, densely ciliate; bud-scales merely dark-margined; (native).
3   Fruit notched at least half-way to the seed, glabrous except for the ciliate margins; flowers subumbellate or corymbose; buds glabrous; leaves often scabrous above, very oblique at base, their petioles commonly over 5 mm long; branches not corky-winged; (Sask. to N.S.) . . . . *U. americana*
3   Fruit shallowly notched, pubescent on the faces; flowers in elongating loose racemes; buds pubescent; leaves glabrous and very smooth above, usually less oblique at base and on shorter petioles; branches often corky-winged; (Ont. and s Que.) . . . . *U. thomasii*
2   Flowers subsessile or short-pedicelled, not drooping; fruits nearly or quite as broad as long, eciliate.
4   Fruit pubescent over the seed; stigmas pink; leaves very harsh above, ciliate, fragrant in drying, soft-downy beneath at least when young; twigs and pedicels scabrously pubescent; bud-scales downy with rusty hairs; (Ont., Que., and ?N.B.) . . . . *U. rubra*
4   Fruit glabrous throughout; stigmas white; (introd.).
5   Twigs often corky-winged, persistently pubescent; leaves smooth or scabrous above, pubescent with axillary tufts of hairs beneath; bud-scales minutely pale-pubescent; pedicels about 1 mm long; seed centred about two-thirds from the base of the fruit . . . . [*U. procera*]
5   Twigs not corky; leaves scabrous above, otherwise glabrous; bud-scales sparingly pubescent or glabrate; pedicels 2 or 3 mm long; seed central . . . . [*U. glabra*]

U. americana L.   American or White Elm.   Orme blanc
/T/EE/   (Mg)   Rich soil, especially along streams and in bottomlands, from Sask. (N to Cumberland House, ca. 54°N; Breitung 1957a) to Man. (N to Steeprock, about 100 mi N of Portage la Prairie), Ont. (N to the Kenogami R. at 51°06′N), Que. (N to Duparquet, ca. 47°30′N, L. St. John, and the Gaspé Pen.), N.B., P.E.I., and N.S., s to Tex., La., and N Fla.; reported by Henry 1915, as planted for shade in B.C. MAPS: Hosie 1969:200; Canada Department of Northern Affairs and Natural Resources 1956:182; *Atlas of Canada* 1957: sheet 41; Meusel, Jaeger, and Weinert 1965:124; Fowells 1965:725; Gleason and Cronquist 1964: fig. 14.7, p. 161; Preston 1961:216, and 1947:156; Hough 1947:183; Munns 1938: map 120, p. 124; Braun 1935: fig. 1, p. 352; Little 1971: maps 196-W and 196-E.

Reports from Nfld. (as by Gleason 1958, and the indication of sw Nfld. on most of the above-noted maps) require confirmation, the planted *U. glabra* being the only elm listed by Rouleau (1956). The typical form has glabrous or sparsely pilose branchlets, the leaves glabrous or scabrous above, glabrous or soft-pubescent and glabrate beneath. The following phases may be recognized:
1   Leaves harshly scabrous above.
2   Young branchlets pubescent; [Ont., E Que., and N.B.] . . . . .f. *alba* (Ait.) Fern.
2   Young branchlets glabrous; [Ont. and N.S.] . . . . f. *intercedens* Fern.
1   Leaves smooth or smoothish above.
3   Young branchlets pubescent; [Ont., E Que., and N.S.] . . . . .f. *pendula* (Ait.) Fern.
3   Young branchlets glabrous; [Ont., P.E.I., and N.S.] . . . . .f. *laevior* Fern.

[*U. glabra* Huds.]   Wych Elm
[Eurasian; tending to spread from cult. in the U.S.A. and reported from s Ont. by Soper (1949), from N.S. by Roland (1947), and from Nfld. by Rouleau (1956), but with no indication from these authors as to its spreading from original plantings. The report by Henry (1915) of

U. campestris L. and its corky-barked var. *suberosa* Loud. forming thickets at Cadboro Bay, near Victoria, B.C., may be referable here or to *U. procera.* (*U. campestris* L. in part; *U. montana* With.).]

[U. parvifolia Jacq.]   Chinese Elm
[Asiatic; reported from Lambton Co., s Ont., by Gaiser and Moore (1966) but with no indication as to its spreading from original plantings.]

[U. procera Salisb.]   English Elm
[European (possibly endemic to England); reports of *U. campestris* from s Ont. by F.H. Montgomery (Can. Field-Nat. 62(2):95. 1948; taken up by Soper 1949) may refer here or to *U. glabra,* but there is no indication of either species spreading from original plantings in Canada. A collection in Herb. V from Vancouver Is., B.C., originated from a planted tree. (*U. campestris* L. in part).]

U. rubra Muhl.   Slippery or Red Elm.   Orme rouge or Orme gras
/T/EE/   (Ms)   Rich soil (often calcareous) from N.Dak. to Ont. (N to the Batchawana R. E of L. Superior at ca. 47°N), Que. (reported N to near Quebec City by John Macoun 1886; *see* Que. map by Doyon and Lavoie 1966: fig. 10, p. 817), and ?N.B. (a sterile specimen in CAN from near St. Andrews has been placed here by Malte; not known from P.E.I. or N.S.), s to Tex. and w Fla. [*U. fulva* Michx.; *U. pubescens* Walt.]. MAPS: Hosie 1969:204; Canada Department of Northern Affairs and Natural Resources 1956:184; Fowells 1965:736; Preston 1961:218; Hough 1947:189 *(U. pub.);* Little 1971: maps 198-W and 198-E.

U. thomasii Sarg.   Rock- or Cork-Elm
/T/EE/   (Ms)   Rich upland woods (often calcareous) from S.Dak. to Minn., Ont. (N to the Ottawa dist.), sw Que. (N to Pontiac and Gatineau counties and the Montreal dist.; *see* s Que. maps by Rouleau 1945: fig. 2, p. 72, and Raymond 1950*b*: fig. 29, p. 80), and w New Eng., s to E Kans., Mo., and Tenn. [*U. racemosa* Thomas, not Borkh.]. MAPS: Hosie 1969:202; Canada Department of Northern Affairs and Natural Resources 1956:186; Fowells 1965:732; Preston 1961:218; Hough 1947:185; Little 1971: map 200-E.

U. pumila L.   Dwarf Elm
Asiatic; reported as an escape from cultivation in s Que. by Lionel Cinq-Mars et al. (Nat. can. (Que.) 98(2):196. 1971; Candiac, Laprairie Co., where taken along the river shore far from habitation). The species is not keyed out above but has the distinguishing character of nearly symmetrical leaves.

MORACEAE (Mulberry Family)

Large shrubs or medium-sized trees with milky juice and simple alternate leaves, the stipules early deciduous. Flowers small, apetalous, unisexual, in aments (catkins), racemes, or heads, the calyx 4-cleft. Stamens 4. Pistil 1. Style 1 (deeply parted in *Morus*). Fruit consisting of achenes buried in the fleshy or juicy calyx to form a syncarp (multiple fruit). (s Ont.).

1 Leaves ovate-lanceolate, acuminate, entire, shining, pinnately veined, to about 12 cm long; staminate flowers in loose short racemes; pistillate flowers in dense globose heads; multiple fruit somewhat orange-like but dry and hard, yellowish green, to 1.5 dm thick; stems with stout thorns 1 or 2 cm long; (introd.) . . . .*Maclura*
1 Leaves coarsely toothed and often lobed, palmately veined; staminate flowers in long loose aments; pistillate flowers in short-cylindric aments; multiple fruit juicy, resembling a blackberry . . . .*Morus*

MACLURA Nutt.   [1918]

M. pomifera (Raf.) Schneid.   Osage Orange.   Bois d'Arc
Native in the E U.S.A. from Tex. to Ark. and natzd. northwards; planted as a hedge in s Ont., where occasionally spreading in the counties neighbouring L. Erie (Essex, Lambton, and Norfolk counties; TRT; OAC). [*Toxylon* Raf.; *M. aurantiaca* Nutt.].

MORUS L.   [1913]   Mulberry.   Mûrier

1 Leaves glabrous or merely hairy-tufted in the axils beneath, often irregularly 3– several-lobed; fruit white to dark purple or black; (introd. in s Ont.) . . . .*M. alba*
1 Leaves downy beneath, glabrous or scabrous above, occasionally 2–5-lobed; fruit red or dark purple; (s Ont.) . . . .*M. rubra*

M. alba L.   White Mulberry
Asiatic; natzd. and spreading from cult. in N. America, as in s Ont.
1 Fruit white, pink, or pale purple; [s Ont.: Essex, Kent, Lambton, Lincoln, Welland, Wellington, and Bruce counties] . . . . .f. *alba*
1 Fruit dark purple to black; [*M. tat.* Pallas, not L.; s Ont.: Waterloo, Wentworth, York, and Wellington counties; TRT; OAC] . . . . .f. *tatarica* (Pallas) Ser.

M. rubra L.   Red Mulberry
/t/EE/   (Ms)   Rich woods from S.Dak. to Minn., s Ont. (Essex, Kent, Norfolk, Middlesex, Welland, Lincoln, Wentworth, Peel, and York counties; *see* s Ont. map by Fox and Soper 1953: map 17, fig. 17, p. 14), N.Y., and Vt., s to Tex. and Fla. MAPS: Hosie 1969:208; Canada Department of Northern Affairs and Natural Resources 1956:190; Preston 1961:226; Hough 1947:199; Munns 1938: map 123, p. 127; Little 1971: maps 139-W and 139-E.

CANNABINACEAE (Hemp Family)

Stems slender, erect or twining, to about 2 m long. Leaves opposite, deeply palmately lobed or palmately compound, serrate, stipulate. Flowers small, apetalous, unisexual, the loosely racemed or panicled staminate ones with 5 sepals and 5 stamens, the clustered pistillate ones with a cup-shaped entire calyx closely investing the 1-locular ovary. Style 2-cleft to base into filiform stigmas. Fruit a cluster of achenes (often glandular) subtended by accrescent bracts.

1   Stem erect, scabrous but not spinulose; leaves palmately divided into up to 7 (sometimes 9) serrate, linear to narrowly lanceolate, pubescent leaflets to about 1.5 dm long; pistillate flowers in small clusters on short leafy lateral branches from the upper leaf-axils; annual; (introd.) . . . .*Cannabis*
1   Stem twining, downwardly short-spinulose or almost prickly, the whole plant harshly scabrous; leaves deeply 3–7-lobed, serrate, palmately veined; pistillate flowers in compact cone-like axillary spikes, in fruit forming the familiar "hop" to about 6 cm long; perennial . . . .*Humulus*

CANNABIS L.   [1973]

C. sativa L.   Marijuana, Hemp.   Chanvre
Asiatic; introd. in N. America (chiefly in ballast and packing), as in Alta. (Spirit River, 55°47′N; Raup 1942), s Man. (street in Winnipeg, where probably planted; WIN), Ont. (N to the Ottawa dist.), Que. (N to the sw Gaspé Pen. at Matapédia; J. Rousseau 1931), and N.B. (Richibucto, Kent Co.; Taborville, Kings Co.).

HUMULUS L.   [1972]   Hop.   Houblon

1   Bracts of pistillate spikes with bristly-hispid margins, abruptly acuminate, scarcely glandular, much narrower than the fruits; principal leaves 5–7-lobed, the sinuses narrow and often closed; upper leaves usually 3–5-lobed; lower leaf-surface lacking waxy granules; petioles usually longer than the leaf-blades; stems harshly scabrous; (introd. in Ont. and Que.) . . . .*H. japonicus*
1   Bracts of pistillate spikes not bristly-hispid, mostly blunt, very glandular at base, covering the fruits; principal leaves 3-lobed, the sinuses broadly rounded; upper leaves commonly unlobed; lower leaf-surfaces bearing waxy granules; petioles usually shorter than the leaf-blades; stem less scabrous; (introd., transcontinental) . . . .*H. lupulus*

H. japonicus Sieb. & Zucc.   Japanese Hop
Asiatic; introd. and natzd. along roadsides, fence-rows, and in other waste places of N. America, as in s Ont. (N to Wellington and York counties; according to Montgomery 1957, often grown as an ornamental vine and sometimes locally common along riverbanks when discarded from gardens) and sw Que. (N to Wakefield, Gatineau Co., and the Montreal dist.).

H. lupulus L.   Common Hop
Eurasian (or possibly partly native in N. America); alluvial thickets, waste places, fence-rows, etc., of s B.C. (Vancouver Is.; Mission), Alta. (Moss 1959), Sask. (N to Runciman, ca. 53°N; Breitung 1957a), Man. (N to the Nw end of L. Winnipegosis), Ont. (N to the N shore of L. Superior), Que. (N to Anticosti Is. and the Gaspé Pen.), Nfld. (Rouleau 1956), N.B., P.E.I., and N.S. [Incl. the supposedly native *H. americanus* Nutt., the distinguishing characters evasive].

URTICACEAE (Nettle Family)

Herbs with simple, opposite or alternate, undulate to coarsely serrate, stipulate leaves, *Laportea* and *Urtica* beset with stinging hairs. Flowers small, commonly unisexual, apetalous, with 2–5 nearly or quite distinct sepals. Stamens as many as the sepals and opposite them. Pistil 1. Style or sessile stigma 1. Ovary superior. Fruit an achene commonly enclosed within the calyx.

1 Leaves alternate.
  2 Leaf-blades undulate, lanceolate, long-acuminate, cuneate at the short-petioled base; flowers in small axillary clusters; stigma sessile; achenes enclosed within the calyces; plant lacking stinging hairs; annual; (B.C. to Que.) . . . . *Parietaria*
  2 Leaf-blades coarsely serrate, broadly ovate, long-petioled; flowers in loose divaricately branched cymes from the upper leaf-axils; style 3 or 4 mm long; achenes nearly naked; plant beset with stinging hairs; perennial; (SE Sask. to St-Pierre and Miquelon and N.S.) . . . . *Laportea*
1 Leaves opposite.
  3 Plant beset with stinging hairs; calyx consisting of 4 nearly distinct sepals; stigma capitate; flowers clustered in racemes, spikes, or loose heads . . . . *Urtica*
  3 Plant lacking stinging hairs; leaves long-petioled, coarsely serrate.
    4 Flowers in long axillary spikes from the upper leaf-axils; achene completely enclosed within the tubular calyx; style long and filiform; leaves broadly lanceolate to ovate; stem to over 1 m tall; perennial; (Ont. and S Que.) . . . .
      . . . . *Boehmeria*
    4 Flowers in axillary cymes or cymose panicles; achene partly naked, surpassing the 3 nearly separate unequal sepals; stigma sessile and brush-like; leaves ovate, shining and translucent, broadly cuneate to rounded at base; stem decumbent at base, often bushy-branched, usually less than 4 dm tall; annual; (Ont. to P.E.I.) . . . . *Pilea*

BOEHMERIA Jacq. [1990] False Nettle

B. cylindrica (L.) Sw. Bog-Hemp
/T/EE/ (Grh) Moist or wet soil from Minn. to Ont. (N to the Ottawa dist.), SW Que. (N to Pontiac and Gatineau counties and the Montreal dist.), and Maine, S to Tex. and Fla. [*Urtica* L.; *U. ?capitata* L.].

LAPORTEA Gaud. [1980] Wood-Nettle

L. canadensis (L.) Wedd. Ortie du Canada
/T/EE/ (Grh) Moist woods and streambanks from SE Sask. (Gainsborough; Breitung 1957a) to S Man. (N to Selkirk, about 15 mi NE of Winnipeg), Ont. (N to L. Timiskaming), Que. (N to Rimouski and the S Gaspé Pen.; *see* Que. map by Doyon and Lavoie 1966: fig. 21, p. 820), St-Pierre and Miquelon, N.B., and N.S. (not known from P.E.I.), S to Okla., Ala., and Fla. [*Urtica* L.; *U. (Urticastrum) divaricata* L.].

PARIETARIA L. [2007] Pellitory

P. pensyivanica Muhl.
/T/X/ (T) Rocky or gravelly shaded places and waste ground from B.C. (N to Liard Hot Springs, 59°25'N) to Alta. (Boivin 1967b), Sask. (N to Kelfield, ca. 52°N), Man. (N to the NW end of L. Winnipegosis), Ont. (N to Cumberland and Hastings counties), SW Que. (N to the Montreal dist.; *see* Que. map by Robert Joyal, Nat. can. (Que.) 97(5): map B. fig. 2. p. 564. 1970; not known from the Atlantic Provinces), and New Eng., S to Mexico, Tex., and Fla.

PILEA Lindl.   [1984]   Richweed, Clearweed, Coolwort

P. pumila (L.) Gray   Petite Ortie
/T/EE/   (T)   Rich moist shaded places from Ont. (N to the Ottawa dist.) to Que. (N to the Montreal dist.), N.B., and P.E.I. (not known from N.S.), s to Tex., La., and Fla. [*Urtica* L.].
   Forma *fontana* (Lunell) Boivin (*P. font.* (Lunell) Rydb.; petioles shorter and fruits darker-coloured than those of the typical form) is reported from Ont., ?Que., and ?P.E.I. by Boivin (1966*b*).

URTICA L.   [1974]   Nettle.   Ortie

1   Tough-stemmed rhizomatous perennial to over 1 m tall; stipules to 1.5 cm long, erect; staminate and pistillate flowers usually in separate ample branched inflorescences many times longer than the petioles; perennial; (transcontinental) . . . .
   . . . . *U. dioica*
1   Soft-stemmed taprooted annual commonly not over 4 or 5 dm tall; leaves elliptic or oval, deeply incised-serrate, their stipules less than 5 mm long, spreading or reflexed; staminate and pistillate flowers intermixed in unbranched, more or less interrupted spikes or spike-like racemes mostly shorter than the leaf-petioles; annual; (introd.) . . . . *U. urens*

U. dioica L.   Stinging Nettle
/ST/X/E/   (Grh (Hpr))   Thickets, shores, and waste places (perhaps partly the introd. typical form of Europe), the aggregate species from cent. Alaska–Yukon (*see* Hultén 1944: map 450, p. 780) and B.C. to Great Bear L., Great Slave L., N Alta., Sask. (N to Windrum L. at ca. 56°N), Man. (N to Churchill), Ont. (N to Fort Severn, Hudson Bay, ca. 56°N), Que. (N to the Côte-Nord, Anticosti Is., and Gaspé Pen.), Labrador (N to Abel L. at 54°46'N, 66°48'W), N.B., P.E.I., and N.S., s throughout the U.S.A. to Mexico and S. America; introd. in sw Greenland; Iceland; N Scandinavia. MAPS and synonymy: *see* below.
1   Plants prevailingly unisexual; stem and petioles copiously beset with stinging bristles to 2 mm long; leaves very variable in shape and pubescence, the principal ones commonly broadly cordate-ovate, coarsely toothed; [Eurasia; MAP (aggregate species): Meusel, Jaeger, and Weinert 1965:124] . . . .[ssp. *dioica*]
1   Plants monoecious (but the flowers of any one clone mostly either staminate or pistillate) . . . . .ssp. *gracilis* (Ait.) Selander
   2   Leaves narrowly to broadly lanceolate (usually at least 3 times as long as broad), acute to rounded at base; petioles mostly less than 1/3 as long as the blades; inflorescence crowded above, some of its branches usually equalling or surpassing the subtending leaves.
      3   Plants densely pubescent or silky and usually more or less ashy in tone; [*U. holosericea* Nutt.; *U. gracilis* var. *hol.* (Nutt.) Jeps.; s B.C.] . . . .
         . . . . var. *holosericea* (Nutt.) Hitchc.
      3   Plants much less strongly pubescent, the stems sometimes merely bristly.
         4   Stems usually bristly only (at least near base), not otherwise hairy; leaves usually ashy-puberulent beneath; [*U. procera* Muhl.; Sask. to N.B. and N.S.] . . .
            . . . . var. *procera* (Muhl.) Wedd.
         4   Stems usually moderately hairy as well as bristly; leaves rather strongly hairy; [*U. dioica* var. *occidentalis* Wats.; s ?B.C.] . . . .[var. *angustifolia* Schlecht.]
   2   Leaves relatively broad (usually ovate-lanceolate to ovate and mostly less than 3 times as long as broad), the principal ones rounded to cordate at base; petioles mostly at least 1/3 as long as the blades; inflorescence not crowded, the panicle-branches mostly shorter than the subtending leaves.
      5   Stems copiously greyish-hairy and bristly with stinging hairs; leaves coarsely bristly and copiously puberulent beneath; [*U. californica* Greene; Wash. to Calif.] . . . .[var. *californica* (Greene) Hitchc.]
      5   Stems usually nearly or quite glabrous below (except for stinging bristles); leaves greenish, glabrous to sparsely pubescent.

6 Leaves usually very sparsely hairy or only weakly bristly, rarely over twice as long as broad and usually about twice as long as their petioles; stems subglabrous; [*U. lyallii* Wats.; s Alaska, B.C., and w Alta.; MAP *(U. lyallii)*: Hultén 1968*b*:371] . . . . var. *lyallii* (Wats.) Hitchc.

6 Leaves often moderately hairy, usually 2 or 3 times as long as broad and at least 3 times as long as their petioles; stems often hairy; [*U. gracilis* Ait.; *U. cardiophylla* and *viridis* Rydb.; transcontinental; the type locality of *U. gracilis* was given as "Nat. of Hudson's bay"; MAPS: Hultén 1968*b*:370, and 1958: map 202, p. 221; Porsild 1966: map 51 *(U. grac.)*, p. 73] . . . .
. . . . var. *gracilis*

U. urens L.   Burning Nettle, Dog-Nettle

Eurasian; waste places and around houses in B.C. (N to Chase, near Kamloops), Alta. (N to Beaverlodge, 55°13′N), Man. (Portage la Prairie; Winnipeg), Ont. (N to the Ottawa dist.), Que. (N to Anticosti Is. and the Gaspé Pen.), Nfld., N.B., P.E.I., and N.S.; s Greenland. MAP: Hultén 1968*b*:371.

SANTALACEAE (Sandalwood Family)

Rather low herbs from extensively creeping mostly subterranean stems, the erect simple flowering stems with simple alternate entire leaves. Flowers small, apetalous, perfect or the outer ones staminate. Calyx 5-cleft, its lobes whitish or greenish. Stamens 5, their anthers connected by a tuft of hairs with the calyx-lobes. Pistil 1. Style 1. Ovary inferior. Fruit dry or juicy, 1-seeded, indehiscent. (Transcontinental species).

1 Flowers several or numerous in terminal corymbs or panicles, all perfect; sepals ascending or erect, much longer than broad; fruit a dry nut-like drupe surmounted by the free summit of the calyx; leaves sessile . . . . *Comandra*
1 Flowers at most 3 or 4 in small cymes from the axils of the middle leaves, only the central one fruit-forming; sepals about as broad as long, spreading; fruit a red juicy false drupe; leaves short-petioled . . . . *Geocaulon*

COMANDRA Nutt.   [2112]   Bastard-Toadflax

C. umbellata (L.) Nutt.
/ST/X/ (Grh (Ch))   Dry hills and plains (often in sandy or gravelly places), the aggregate species from s-cent. Yukon and NW Dist. Mackenzie to Great Slave L., L. Athabasca, Man. (N to Flin Flon, ca. 55°N), Ont. (N to the N shore of L. Superior), Que. (N to the Côte-Nord, Anticosti Is., and Gaspé Pen.), SE Labrador (Red Bay, ca. 51°45′N; GH), Nfld., N.B., P.E.I., and N.S., s to Ariz., N.Mex., Tex., and Ga. MAP and synonymy: *see* below.
1 Calyx-lobes ovate-lanceolate to ovate, usually not over 2.5 mm long; leaves rather thin and usually only slightly if at all glaucous, their secondary veins mostly plainly visible in dried specimens; fruits to about 6 mm long; [*Thesium* L.; *C. richardsiana* Fern.; incl. var. *angustifolia* (DC.) Torr.; transcontinental] . . . . var. *umbellata*
1 Calyx-lobes rather narrowly lanceolate, usually 3 or 4 mm long; leaves thick and very glaucous, their secondary veins rarely visible; fruits to 1 cm long; [*C. pallida* DC.; s-cent. Yukon (*see* Hultén 1944: map 454 (*C. pallida*), p. 780) to NW Dist. Mackenzie, Great Slave L., and L. Athabasca, Sask., s in Canada to B.C., Alta., Sask., and Man. (N to Flin Flon; Lowe 1943); MAP: Hultén 1968b:372] . . . . var. *pallida* (DC.) Jones

GEOCAULON Fern.   [2112A *(Comandra)*]

G. lividum (Richards.) Fern.   Northern Comandra
/ST/X/ (Grh)   Damp coniferous forests and sphagnous bogs from N-cent. Alaska–Yukon (*see* Hultén 1944: map 453, p. 780) to Great Bear L., Great Slave L., L. Athabasca (Alta. and Sask.), northernmost Man.–Ont., Que. (N to s Ungava Bay and the Côte-Nord), Labrador (N to Nain, 56°33′N), Nfld., N.B., and N.S. (not known from P.E.I.), s to Wash., Minn., Ohio, and New Eng. [*Comandra* Rich.]. MAPS: Hultén 1968b:373; Raup 1947: pl. 22 (a dot should be added for Chimo, s Ungava Bay, Que.); J.G. Packer, Nat. can. (Que.) 98(2): fig. 1, p. 134. 1971.

LORANTHACEAE (Mistletoe Family)

ARCEUTHOBIUM Bieb.   [2091]   Dwarf Mistletoe

Plants parasitic on Pinaceae, but also with chlorophyll, often causing "witches' broom". Stems simple or branched, olive-green to reddish-brown or purplish, with minute opposite brown connate scale-like leaves. Flowers small, unisexual. Corolla none. Staminate flowers with a usually 3-parted calyx, the pistillate ones with a 2-toothed calyx. Ovary inferior. Fruit a 1-seeded drupe.

1   Stems rarely over 3 cm long and 1 mm thick (their segments at most 6 mm long); flowers blooming in the spring, both the staminate and pistillate ones usually in pairs at the stem-nodes and single when terminal.
    2   Stems brownish green or brown, rarely over 2 cm long, usually simple (if occasionally branched, the branches always simple); flowers all produced in one crop, the floral processes all at the same stage of development on a shoot; fruit maturing during the autumn of the same year; (E Sask. to Nfld. and N.S.; parasitic commonly on *Picea mariana,* less frequently on *P. glauca* and *P. rubens,* very rarely on *Larix laricina*) . . . .*A. pusillum*
    2   Stems usually olive- to bluish-green, to about 3 cm long, usually branched (but the branches themselves rarely branched, secondary branches, when developed, arising from superposed buds, their arrangement thus fan-like); flowers produced in several crops, the floral processes often in two stages of development on a shoot (buds and flowers or flowers and fruits); fruits maturing during the autumn of the second year; (S B.C.; apparently parasitic only on Douglas Fir (*Pseudotsuga menziesii*) . . . .*A. douglasii*
1   Stems commonly over 3 cm long and 1 mm thick (their segments commonly over 6 mm long), much branched, the branches themselves branched; flowers borne in several crops, the floral processes on a shoot often in two stages of development; fruits maturing during the autumn of the second year.
    3   Stems olive-green to orange-yellow or brownish, to over 1.5 dm long and often over 2 mm thick, the secondary branches arising from superposed buds in a fan-like arrangement; both the staminate and pistillate flowers usually in pairs at the stem-nodes and single when terminal; (S Alaska–B.C.; various forms parasitic on *Abies, Larix, Picea, Pinus,* and *Tsuga*) . . . .*A. campylopodon*
    3   Stems yellow-green, rarely over 7 cm long and 2 mm thick, the secondary branches arising from collateral buds (thus whorled rather than fan-like); both the staminate and pistillate flowers in pairs or whorls at the stem-nodes; (B.C. to W Ont.; apparently parasitic only on *Pinus*) . . . .*A. americanum*

A. americanum Nutt.   Pine Mistletoe
/T/WW/   (Ms (epiphytic))   Parasitic on branches of *Pinus* from B.C. (N to Dawson Creek, ca. 55°N) to Alta. (N to L. Athabasca), Sask. (N to Meadow Lake, 54°08′N), Man. (N to Grand Rapids, near the NW end of L. Winnipeg), and W Ont. (near Perrault Falls, in the Lac Seul region of the Kenora Forest Dist. NE of Kenora; Newsletter, Vol. 22, No. 51, p. 4–6, Ontario Department of Lands and Forests. 1969), S to Calif. and N.Mex. [*Razoumofskya* Ktze.; *A. oxycedri sensu* Hooker 1833, in part, not Bieb.].

A. campylopodum Engelm.
/sT/W/   (Ms (epiphytic))   Parasitic on branches of conifers from SE Alaska (Juneau; Sitka) through coastal B.C. to Mexico. [*Razoumofskya* Ktze.; *A. robustum sensu* John Macoun 1886, not Engelm.]. MAP: Hultén 1968b:372. The following forms have been maintained arbitrarily (note use of a quadruple lead 3):
1   Plant parasitic on *Pinus.*
    2   Shoots mostly orange or yellow (to brown) .f. *campylopodum*
    2   Shoots greenish; [*A. blumeri* Nels.] . . . . .f. *blumeri* (Nels.) Gill

1 Plant parasitic on genera other than *Pinus*.
3 Parasitic on *Picea* . . . . f. *microcarpum* (Engelm.) Gill
3 Parasitic on *Abies; [Arc. abietinum* Engelm.] . . . . f. *abietinum* (Engelm.) Gill
3 Parasitic on *Tsuga;* [*Razoumofskya tsug.* Rosend., the type from Vancouver Is.,
   B.C.; *A. douglasii* var. *tsug.* (Rosend.) Jones; *A. dougl. sensu* Henry 1915,
   not Engelm.] . . . . f. *tsugensis* (Rosend.) Gill
3 Parasitic on *Larix;* [*Razoumofskya laricis* Piper; *A. doug.* var. *lar.* (Piper) Jones . . . . . .
   . . . . f. *laricis* (Piper) Gill

A. douglasii Engelm.
/T/W/ (Ms (epiphytic)) Parasitic on branches of Douglas fir *(Pseudotsuga menziesii)* from
s B.C. (Sirdar and near Creston in the Kootenay Valley; Herb. V; reported from the Okanagan
Valley; reports from Alta. require confirmation) and Mont. to Calif. and N.Mex. [*Razoumofskya*
Ktze.].

A. pusillum Peck   Dwarf Mistletoe.   Petit Gui
/T/EE/ (Ms (epiphytic)) Parasitic on conifers (chiefly black spruce, sometimes white or
red spruce, rarely pine or tamarack) from E Sask. (Hudson Bay Junction, ca. 53°N) to Man. (N
to Grand Rapids, near the NW end of L. Winnipeg), Ont. (N to Hearst, 49°42'N), Que. (N to Tadoussac, Saguenay Co., and the Gaspé Pen.), Nfld., N.B., P.E.I., and N.S., s to Minn., Mich., N
Pa., N.J., and New Eng. [*Razoumofskya* Ktze.].

ARISTOLOCHIACEAE (Birthwort Family)

Herbs or woody twining vines with broad, entire or undulate, alternate or basal leaves. Flowers perfect, rather large and showy, regular or irregular, solitary or few on axillary peduncles. Petals none or 3, minute and awl-like. Calyx petaloid, the limb either very oblique and 1-lobed or nearly or quite regular and 3-lobed. Stamens 6 or 12. Pistil 1. Styles coherent in a column and expanded at summit into a 6-lobed stigma. Ovary at least partially inferior. Fruit a 6-locular capsule.

1 Twining vines or leafy-stemmed herbs; flowers either strongly oblique at summit or
  with a strongly bent tube; anthers 6, sessile, adnate to the stigma; (introd.) . . . .
  . . . . *Aristolochia*
1 Stemless herbs with long-creeping, branching, more or less pubescent rhizomes and
  a pair of cordate-rotund or -reniform long-petioled basal leaves; flowers red-brown,
  solitary in the leaf-axils, regular, to 3 or 4 cm long, the tube short, the lobes
  spreading to reflexed; pedicel stout, pubescent, to about 5 cm long; anthers 12,
  their filaments more or less distinct . . . . *Asarum*

ARISTOLOCHIA L.   [2174]   Birthwort.   Aristoloche

1 Perianth yellow, its tube straight, terminating in an ovate lobe on one side; flowers in
  axillary clusters; leaves at most about 1 dm long and broad; herb to about 1.5 m tall;
  (introd. in s Ont. and Que.) . . . . *A. clematitis*
1 Perianth brown-purple, strongly curved like a Dutch pipe, abruptly expanded into a
  flat 3-lobed limb; leaves to about 2 dm long and broad; high-twining shrubby vine;
  (introd. in s Ont.) . . . . [*A. durior*]

A. clematitis L.
Eurasian; introd. along roadsides and in waste places of N. America, as in s Ont. (Brantford; Guelph) and Que. (Montreal dist.; l'Ile d'Orléans, near Quebec City).

[A. durior Hill]   Dutchman's-pipe, Pipe-vine
[Native in the E U.S.A. and much cult. and locally natzd. eastwards to N.J. and New Eng.; reported from s Ont. by Stroud (1941; Wellington Co.), where probably merely a casual garden-escape. (*A. macrophylla* Lam.).]

ASARUM L.   [2170]   Wild Ginger.   Asarette

1 Calyx-lobes lance-attenuate or with tail-like tips to about 2 cm long; leaves
  deciduous, acute to rounded at apex; (SE Man. to N.B.) . . . . *A. canadense*
1 Calyx-lobes with tail-like tips to over 7 cm long; leaves more or less evergreen, acute
  to obtuse at apex; (B.C.) . . . . *A. caudatum*

A. canadense L.   Wild Ginger.   Gingembre sauvage
/T/EE/   (Grh (Hrr; Ch))   Rich woods and shaded calcareous ledges, the aggregate species from SE Man. (N to Lac du Bonnet, about 50 mi NE of Winnipeg; DAO) to Ont. (N to the Kaministiquia R. near Thunder Bay and New Liskeard, 47°31′N), Que. (N to the Gaspé Pen. near Matapédia and New Richmond; see Que. map by Doyon and Lavoie 1966: fig. 23, p. 820), and N.B. (not known from P.E.I. or N.S.), s to E Kans., Tenn., and N.C. MAP and synonymy: see below.
1 Calyx-lobes with caudate (tail-like) tips to 2 cm long, spreading.
  2 Calyx-lobes rather broadly ovate, to 2.5 cm long, distinctly narrowed to a slender
    tip to 1.5 cm long . . . . var. *canadense*
    3 Leaves broadly reniform, often abruptly short-acuminate, with a broad open
      sinus; [Ont. to N.B.; MAP (aggregate species): Meusel, Jaeger, and Weinert
      1965:126] . . . . f. *canadense*

    3   Leaves broadly ovate to subrotund, round-tipped, with a closed sinus; [reported from near L. Champlain in Missisquoi Co., s Que., by Marcel Raymond, Nat. can. (Que.) 70(11/12):270. 1943] . . . . f. *phelpsiae* Fern.

  2 Calyx-lobes narrowly to broadly lance-attenuate, to 3.5 cm long, tapering gradually from base to the slender tip; [*A. acum.* (Ashe) Bickn.; s Man. and sw Que.] . . . . var. *acuminatum* Ashe

1 Calyx-lobes scarcely caudate-tipped or merely mucronate.

    4   Calyx-lobes deltoid, at most 12 mm long, abruptly reflexed; [*A. refl.* Bickn.; reported from SE Man. by Fernald *in* Gray 1950, and from s ?Ont. by J.M. Macoun 1897:475] . . . . var. *reflexum* (Bickn.) Robins.

    4   Calyx-lobes attenuate, to 2 cm long, ascending or only tardily reflexed; [*A. ambiguum* (Bickn.) Daniels; s ?Ont.: J.M. Macoun 1897:475] . . . .[var. *ambiguum* (Bickn.) Farw.]

A. caudatum Lindl.   Western Wild Ginger

/T/W/   (Grh)   Rich woods from B.C. (N to Prince Rupert, ca. 54°N; E to Revelstoke and Nelson), Idaho, and Mont. to Calif. [*A. hookeri* Fielding]. MAP: Meusel, Jaeger, and Weinert 1965:126.

POLYGONACEAE (Buckwheat Family)

Herbs with stems swollen at the joints. Leaves simple, alternate, entire, usually subtended by sheathing, more or less scarious, cylindric stipules (ocreae; except in *Eriogonum*). Flowers small, chiefly perfect, apetalous. Sepals or calyx-lobes 3–6. Stamens commonly 4–9. Pistil 1. Styles or sessile stigmas 2 or 3. Ovary superior. Fruit a lenticular or 3-angled (trigonous) achene.

1 Flowers borne in tubular or campanulate involucres up to 6 mm long, the whole inflorescence subcapitate, umbellate, or cymose, subtended by an involucral whorl of scale-like to leaf-like bracts; perianth white, cream, ochroleucous, or yellow, commonly tinged with pink, rose, or purple, the 6 segments usually distinct nearly or quite to the swollen basal joint (in our species); stamens 9; styles 3; fruit a 3-angled achene; leaves entire, mostly petioled, usually more or less densely tomentose or woolly at least beneath (commonly greener or even glabrate above), sometimes marcescent, all in basal tufts (except for the leafy bracts subtending the inflorescences and peduncles of many species and the solitary whorl near the middle of the peduncles in *E. heracleoides*); stems (except in the annual *E. cernuum*) from a usually branching woody caudex, mat-forming or cushion-forming; (western species) . . . . *Eriogonum*

1 Flowers not borne in an involucre (but the minute flowers of *Koenigia* commonly subtended by a whorl of 2 or more separate leafy bracts); inflorescence mostly spicate, racemose, or paniculate (capitate in *Koenigia*); stigmas or styles 2 or 3; stamens 4–8; leaves subtended by sheathing stipules (ocreae).

  2 Stem scapose, the leaves all or chiefly basal, round-reniform, long-petioled; sepals 4, not enlarged in fruit, the outer pair spreading or reflexed; stigmas 2; achenes lenticular, flat, with a circular wing; flowers clustered in panicled racemes; (transcontinental in arctic, subarctic, and arctic-alpine regions) . . . . . *Oxyria*

  2 Stems alternate-leaved, the leaves narrower (basal leaves an opposite pair in *Koenigia* and occasionally forming a rosette in other genera).

    3 Flowers minute, in a terminal cluster usually subtended by an involucral whorl of 2 or more obovate leafy bracts; sepals 3; leaves ovate to oblong or obovate, often reddish purple, sessile or nearly so, less than 1 cm long; plant glabrous or somewhat pilose, often only a few cm tall; (transcontinental in arctic and subarctic wet habitats) . . . . *Koenigia*

    3 Flowers not subtended by involucral bracts; sepals usually 5 or 6, at least the inner ones often more or less enlarged in fruit.

      4 Achene broadly 3-winged, to 1 cm long, much surpassing the calyx; sepals 6; styles 3; basal leaves very large, subrotund, on stout edible petioles; stem hollow, to about 2 m tall; (introd.) . . . . *Rheum*

      4 Achene lenticular or 3-angled, included or somewhat exserted from the calyx.

        5 Sepals 6, the 3 outer ones spreading or reflexed, not enlarged in fruit, persistent at the base of the enlarged inner ones, at least one of these usually with a conspicuous callous tubercle ("grain") on the midnerve; stigmas 3; achenes 3-angled . . . . *Rumex*

        5 Sepals all ascending or erect and remaining subequal as they enlarge, often petal-like or with petaloid margins.

          6 Styles elongate and exserted, persisting as 2 indurated and reflexed connivent hooked achene-beaks; flowers greenish or reddish, in remote, finally deflexed clusters of 2 or 3 in slender spike-like terminal racemes to 4 dm long; calyx 4-parted, not enlarged in fruit; achenes lenticular; leaves lanceolate to ovate, acuminate at apex, acute to rounded at base, glabrous or roughly pubescent, to about 1.5 dm long, on petioles to 2 cm long; ocreae pubescent and long-ciliate; (s Ont. and sw Que.) . . . . *Tovara*

          6 Styles 2 or 3, deciduous, not hooked; calyx mostly 5-parted (sometimes 4- or 6-parted in *Polygonum*).

7 Pedicels jointed near base, recurving in fruit; flowers in loose terminal racemes, solitary in the axils of sheathing bractlets (ocreolae), the racemes solitary or panicled; styles 3; achenes 3-angled; leaves firm, linear-filiform, jointed near base and soon deciduous; stem slender and wiry, glaucous, to about 6 dm tall; (Ont. and Que.) . . . . *Polygonella*

7 Pedicels jointed at summit; flowers clustered in the axils of leaves or foliaceous bracts, in spike-like panicles or in corymbed or panicled racemes.

    8 Styles 3; achenes 3-angled, exserted or only loosely embraced by the soon withering calyx, this not enlarged in fruit; racemes in a terminal corymbiform cluster or additional ones solitary in the leaf-axils; leaves triangular-cordate or hastate; (introd.) . . . . *Fagopyrum*

    8 Styles 2 or 3; achenes lenticular or 3-angled, usually included in the closely embracing and enlarging calyx (if exserted, plants with narrow leaves) . . . . *Polygonum*

ERIOGONUM Michx. [2192] Umbrella-plant, Eriogonum

1 Inflorescence typically a usually open compound umbel or dichotomously branching open cyme, its primary peduncles themselves branching, the involucres solitary or capitate at the ends of the branches; perianth glabrous externally (rarely pubescent in *E. heracleoides*).

  2 Involucres glabrous, at most 2 mm long, 5-lobed (the lobes erect), solitary at the ends of slender, usually sharply reflexed peduncles; perianth at most 2 mm long; bracts subtending the inflorescence and individual peduncles scale-like, to about 2 mm long; leaves oval to orbicular, their blades to about 2 cm broad; scape to about 4 dm tall, glaucous or somewhat tomentose below, 3-forking below, 2-forking above, the inflorescence thus open-cymose; annual with slender taproot; (s Alta. and sw Sask.) . . . . *E. cernuum*

  2 Involucres usually copiously tomentose or woolly, to 5 or 6 mm long, solitary or clustered on erect or ascending peduncles; perianth commonly at least 3 mm long (usually not over 2 mm in *E. multiceps*); leaves linear to elliptic, oval, or ovate; perennials from usually branching woody caudices, the stems prostrate to ascending, cushion- or mat-forming; (B.C.).

    3 Peduncles mostly with a whorl of not greatly reduced leaves at about midlength in addition to the leaf-like bracts subtending the inflorescence; the several linear or lanceolate lobes of the involucres abruptly reflexed, 2 or 3 mm long; perianth narrowed to a slender stipitate base to 3 mm long above the joint at the top of the pedicel; leaves linear to narrowly lanceolate or oblanceolate, to 1(1.5) cm broad, up to 15 times as long as broad; stems forming clumps to about 6 dm broad and 4 dm tall; (B.C.) . . . . *E. heracleoides*

    3 Peduncles typically naked below the inflorescence, the foliage-leaves all basal or sub-basal; lobes of the involucres triangular-acute, erect, less than 2 mm long; perianth not stipitate above the joint; leaves mostly broader in outline.

      4 Inflorescence leafy-bracted at the lower forks (upper bracts gradually reduced), commonly 1 or 2 dm long, the branches strongly ascending, usually 3-forking at the lower nodes but 2-forking above, the strongly tomentose involucres all borne singly, usually 3-toothed (sometimes 4-toothed, very rarely 5-toothed); flowers usually creamy or pink; (s B.C.) . . . . *E. niveum*

      4 Inflorescence commonly lacking leafy bracts (bracts scale-like), usually less than 1 dm long, 2–3-forked and cymose (with the involucres borne singly) or umbellate (the involucres in part capitate at the ends of the branches); involucres occasionally glabrous, usually 5-toothed; flowers white or creamy to pink; (?B.C.) . . . . *[E. strictum]*

1 Inflorescence a usually simple congested or open umbel, the peduncles not branching, shorter (inflorescence subcapitate) or longer than the usually pilose, tomentose, or woolly, mostly 5-lobed involucres (umbel atypically compound in *E. umbellatum* and rarely in *E. flavum*); perennials.

    5 Inflorescence subcapitate to plainly umbellate, subtended by 2 linear bracts to 2 cm long; perianth and involucres both externally more or less glandular-puberulent and usually also crisp-pilose to woolly with often rust-coloured hairs, the broad lobes of the involucres erect, barely 1 mm long; leaves elliptic to oval, ovate, rhombic, or obovate, marcescent (plant cushion-like), the lower surfaces either woolly or glabrous and greenish yellow; crown simple to branched and woody; (mts. of ?B.C.) . . . .[*E. pyrolaefolium*]

    5 Inflorescence usually subtended by at least 3 bracts of various sizes; perianth usually not glandular (often slightly glandular-mealy at least below in *E. flavum*); leaves usually copiously tomentose or woolly beneath.

        6 Lobes of involucre usually reflexed, linear-lanceolate to oblong, 2 or 3 mm long, mostly about as long as the tube; perianth usually glabrous externally, cream or light to deep yellow, narrowed to a slender stipe 1 or 2 mm long above its joint with the pedicel; umbel subtended by a whorl of linear to oblanceolate leaf-like bracts; leaves spatulate to elliptic, oblong, or obovate, to 3(4) cm long; branches usually prostrate and forming loose mats to 6 dm broad; (B.C. and Alta.) . . . . *E. umbellatum*

        6 Lobes of the involucre erect (occasionally recurved in *E. ovalifolium*), broadly triangular, much shorter than the tube.

            7 Perianth glabrous, not stipitate (the segments free nearly or quite to the swollen joint, the outer ones often twice as broad as the inner ones); inflorescence subtended by at least 3 linear-lanceolate bracts (rarely 1 or more of the bracts leaf-like); leaf-blades from spatulate and less than 1 cm long to elliptic, oval, oblong, or rhombic and up to 2(3) cm long; branches prostrate and forming loose mats to 4 dm broad; (B.C. and Alta.) . . . .*E. ovalifolium*

            7 Perianth usually pilose, woolly, tomentose, or silky at least on the lower half; leaf-blades lance-linear or narrowly elliptic to oblanceolate or spatulate-oblanceolate.

                8 Involucres to 4 mm long, their lobes depressed, less than 0.5 mm long, much broader than long; perianth to 5 mm long, acute at base but scarcely stipitate; inflorescence subtended by a whorl of linear to leaf-like bracts; leaf-blades mostly less than 2 cm long, to 3 mm broad, often slightly revolute-margined; scapes rarely to 1 dm tall; stems prostrate, with the marcescent leaves forming thick mats or cushions; (mts. of s B.C. and sw Alta.) . . . . *E. androsaceum*

                8 Involucres to 6 mm long, their lobes at least 0.5 mm long and about as broad as long; leaf-blades to over 7 cm long; scapes mostly taller.

                    9 Perianth not stipitate at base, usually about 2 mm long, cream-colour and commonly pink- or rose-tinged or rarely yellow, usually strongly woolly on the lower half but sometimes almost glabrous; inflorescence subtended by a whorl of linear to semi-leafy bracts, usually a capitate cluster of several involucres but rarely the involucres short-peduncled; scapes commonly not over 1.5 dm tall; stems sprawling, marcescent-leafy, forming loose mats; (se B.C. to s Sask.) . . . .*E. pauciflorum*

                    9 Perianth narrowed at base to a stipe at least 0.5 mm long, pale to deep yellow (sometimes rose-tinged, very rarely red), pilose to silky externally and often slightly mealy-glandular (at least below); inflorescence subtended by a whorl of usually leaf-like bracts, its rays to about 3 cm long; scapes to 2(3) dm tall; branches of caudex

usually partially subterranean, densely covered with crowded marcescent leaf-bases and forming thick mats; (Alaska–B.C. to SW Man.) . . . . *E. flavum*

E. androsaceum Benth.
/T/W/   (Ch)   Open rocky foothills and subalpine slopes from the Rocky Mts. of SE B.C. and SW Alta. (N to Jasper) to N Mont. [*E. flavum* var. *and.* (Benth.) Jones; *E. caespitosum sensu* Hooker 1838, not Benth.].

E. cernuum Nutt.   Nodding Eriogonum
/T/WW/   (T)   Sandy hills and valleys from Oreg. and Idaho to S Alta. (Milk River; Medicine Hat; Empress; Writing-on-Stone) and SW Sask. (Abbey; Webb), S to SE Calif., Colo., N.Mex., and Nebr.

E. flavum Nutt.   Yellow Eriogonum
/T/WW/   (Ch)   Dry rocky prairies to alpine ridges and talus, the aggregate species from E-cent. Alaska and SE B.C. (N to Skookumchuck, near Kimberley at ca. 50°N; Eastham 1947) to S Alta. (N to Calgary; CAN), S Sask. (reported N to Carlton, about 35 mi SW of Prince Albert, by John Macoun 1886), and S Man. (N to St. Lazare, about 75 mi NW of Brandon; CAN), S to Oreg. and Colo. MAP and synonymy: *see below.*
1 Perianth-stipe slender, to 1.5 mm long; leaves relatively thin and usually distinctly greenish above; [*E. piperi* Greene; mts. of SE B.C. and SW Alta.] . . . .
. . . . var. *piperi* (Greene) Jones
1 Perianth-stipe usually thicker than the pedicel and less than 1 mm long; plant greyish-tomentose, the thick leaves greyish above, white beneath; [*E. crassifolium* Benth.; *E. polyphyllum* Small; range of the species; MAP: Hultén 1968*b*:374 (indicating the occurrence of var. *aquilinum* Reveal in E-cent. Alaska)] . . . . var. *flavum*

E. heracleoides Nutt.
/T/W/   (Ch)   Gravelly to loamy soil and rocky ridges from S B.C. (N to Lac la Hache, about 50 mi SE of Williams Lake; E to Lower Arrow L.) to Wyo. and W Mont., S to NE Calif., Nev., and Utah.

E. niveum Dougl.   Snow Eriogonum
/t/W/   (Ch)   Sandy plains and hillsides from S B.C. (N to Vernon) to cent. Oreg.–Idaho.

E. ovalifolium Nutt.   Silver-plant
/T/W/   (Ch)   Dry plains and ponderosa-pine woodlands to alpine ridges and talus slopes above timberline, the aggregate species from S B.C. (Manning Provincial Park, SE of Hope, to Flathead, near the Alta. boundary) and SW Alta. (Crowsnest Pass; South Kootenay Pass; Waterton Lakes) to N Calif. and N.Mex.
1 Scapes usually not over 6 cm tall; leaves (including the petiole) rarely over 1.5 cm long; involucres about 3 mm long; [*E. dep.* (Blank.) Rydb.; SW Alta. (Breitung 1957*b*; Waterton Lakes)] . . . . var. *depressum* Blank.
1 Scapes often over 1 dm tall; leaves (including the petiole) usually over 1.5 cm long; involucres commonly 4 or 5 mm long.
   2 Leaf-blades mostly oval to rhombic and less than twice as long as broad; [var. *purpureum* (Nutt.) Nels.; *Eucycla purpurea* Nutt.; S B.C. and SW Alta.] . . . .
   . . . . var. *ovalifolium*
   2 Leaf-blades oblanceolate or spatulate to oblong or obovate.
      3 Leaves at most 4 cm long, the blades generally at least twice as long as broad; flowers usually white or cream-colour to pinkish; [var. *ochroleucum* (Small) Peck (*E. ochro.* Small); mts. of S B.C.] . . . var. *macropodum* (Gandg.) Reveal
      3 Leaves to 6 cm long, the blades rarely twice as long as broad; flowers usually yellow; [var. *orthocaulon* (Small) Hitchc. (*E. orth.* Small); Alta.: Rydberg 1922] . . . . .
      . . . . var. *celsum* Nels.

E. pauciflorum Pursh
/T/WW/ (Ch) Open rocky ridges, blowouts, and badlands from SE B.C. (South Kootenay Pass on the B.C.–Alta. boundary; Henry 1915) to SW Alta. (Waterton Lakes; CAN) and S Sask. (Breitung 1957a), S to Mont., Wyo., Colo., and Nebr. [*E. gnaphalodes* Benth.; *E. multiceps* Nees].

[E. pyrolaefolium Hook.]
[This species of the W U.S.A. (Wash. and Mont. to Calif.) is reported as probably occurring in S B.C. by Hitchcock et al. (1964) but apparently no confirmatory collections have yet been made. The type of var. *coryphaeum* T. & G. (leaves lanate beneath rather than glabrous or merely greyish-pubescent) is from the "Summit of the Cascade Mts., about lat. 49°, on the east side", presumably in N Wash. but so close to the B.C. boundary as to warrant intensive search for it in that province.]

[E. strictum Benth.]
[The report of *E. proliferum* T. & G. (*E. strictum* ssp. *pro.* (T. & G.) Stokes; involucres usually tomentose rather than glabrous) from B.C. by Jepson (1951) requires confirmation. According to Hitchcock et al. (1964), the species attains its N limits in Wash., Idaho, and Mont.]

E. umbellatum Torr. Sulphur Eriogonum
/T/WW/ (Ch) Dry plains and foothills to alpine ridges and talus slopes, the aggregate species from B.C. (N to Kamloops) and SW Alta. (N to Banff; CAN) to S Calif. and Colo.
  The closely related *E. sphaerocephalum* Dougl. is tentatively reported from B.C. by Boivin (1967a). It and varieties of *E. umbellatum* reported from B.C. by Hitchcock et al. (1964) are keyed out below.
1 Leaves linear to linear-spatulate or oblanceolate; perianth strongly villous externally
  (rarely glabrous); [S-cent. ?B.C.; Boivin 1967a] . . . .[*E. sphaerocephalum* Dougl.]
1 Leaves broadly spatulate to obovate; perianth glabrous externally . . . .*E. umbellatum*
  2 Plant prostrate, the flowering stems rarely as much as 1 dm tall; flowers cream-
    colour to yellow, the umbels subcapitate . . . . .var. *hausknechtii* (Dammer) Jones
  2 Plant usually not prostrate, the flowering stems mostly at least 1 dm tall; umbel
    usually open.
    3 Flowers white or cream-colour; [*E. subalpinum* Greene] . . . .
      . . . . .var. *subalpinum* (Greene) Jones
    3 Flowers yellow . . . . .var. *umbellatum*

FAGOPYRUM Mill. [2202] Buckwheat. Sarrasin

1 Flowers white, 2 or 3 mm long, in clustered terminal racemes; achenes smooth and
  shining . . . .*F. sagittatum*
1 Flowers greenish, 1 or 2 mm long, in scattered elongate loose racemes; achenes
  dull, roughish, their sides grooved . . . .*F. tataricum*

F. sagittatum Gilib. Buckwheat. Sarrasin or Blé noir
Asiatic; spread from or persistent after cult. in N. America, as in Alaska (Fairbanks), Alta. (Edmonton), Sask., Man., Ont., Que., Nfld., N.B., P.E.I., and N.S. [*F. esculentum* Moench; *Polygonum (F.) fagopyrum* L.].

F. tataricum (L.) Gaertn. India-wheat. Sarrasin de Tartarie
Asiatic; spread from or persistent after cult. in N. America, as in Alta., Sask., Man., Ont., Que., Nfld., N.B., and N.S. [*Polygonum* L.].

KOENIGIA L. [2184]

K. islandica L.
/aST/X/GEA/ (T) Fresh, brackish, or saline sandy or silted shores and wet mossy places from the Aleutian Is. and N Alaska to cent. Yukon, N Dist. Mackenzie (Coronation Gulf), Devon

Is., and northernmost Ungava–Labrador, s to s Alaska–Yukon, NE ?B.C., Man. (Churchill; Schofield 1959; not known from Sask. or Ont.), Que. (s to E James Bay at 54°25′N), and Labrador (s to Gready Is., 53°48′N); isolated stations in SW ?Alta.; W and E Greenland N to ca. 77°N; Iceland; N Eurasia. MAPS: Porsild 1957: map 128, p. 176; Schofield 1959: map 8, p. 119; Hultén 1968b:373; W.J. Cody, Nat. can. (Que.) 98(2): fig. 3, p. 146. 1971.

OXYRIA Hill [2196]

O. digyna (L.) Hill   Mountain-Sorrel
/AST/X/GEA/ (Hr) Damp tundra, slopes, and alpine ravines from the Aleutian Is. and coasts of Alaska–Yukon–Dist. Mackenzie–Dist. Keewatin throughout the Canadian Arctic Archipelago to northernmost Ellesmere Is. and northernmost Ungava–Labrador, s to s Alaska–Yukon, Great Bear L., s-cent. Dist. Keewatin, Que. (s to SE Hudson Bay at ca. 56°N, Mollie T. Lake at 55°03′N, and the Shickshock Mts. of the Gaspé Pen.), s Labrador (s to ca. 52°N), Nfld., NE N.S. (Inverness Co., Cape Breton Is.; E.C. Smith and W.B. Schofield, Rhodora 54(645):222. 1952; not known from N.B. or P.E.I.), and the mts. of N.H., and in the mts. of the West to s Calif., Ariz., and N.Mex.; circumgreenlandic; Iceland; Eurasia. [*Rumex* L.; *Donia* R. Br.; *O. reniformis* Hook. f.]. MAPS: Porsild 1957: map 129, p. 177; Hultén 1968b:383; Meusel, Jaeger, and Weinert 1965:129; Raup 1947: pl. 22; Young 1971: fig. 10, p. 86.

POLYGONELLA Michx. [2203]

P. articulata (L.) Meisn.   Jointweed
/T/EE/ (T) Dry sands from Minn. to Ont. (N to the E shore of L. Superior and Renfrew and Carleton counties), Que. (N to Taschereau, 48°40′N, and the Quebec City dist.; the report from P.E.I. by McSwain and Bain 1891, requires confirmation; not known from N.B. or N.S.), and sw Maine, s to Iowa, Wisc., Ind., and N.C. [*Polygonum* L.; *Delopyrum* Small]. MAPS: J.H. Horton, Brittonia 15: fig. 15, p. 201. 1963; M.L. Fernald, Rhodora 42(502): map 23, p. 401. 1940.

POLYGONUM L. [2201] Knotweed, Smartweed.   Renouée

(Ref.: Löve and Löve 1956a; Styles 1962; Mertens and Raven 1965)
1   Flowers solitary or in small clusters in the leaf-axils (upper leaves often reduced and bract-like), the leaves and bracts jointed at base, sessile or very short-petioled; pedicels ascending; ocreae (sheathing stipules) finally 2-lobed or lacerate; styles (or stigmas) 3; achenes trigonous; mostly annuals (*P. paronychia* perennial).
  2   Inflorescence relatively compact, the flowers mostly crowded and often overlapping toward the end of the stem (this sometimes floriferous nearly to base) in the axils of the scarcely or only moderately reduced upper leaves (the upper leaves sometimes the longest), these much surpassing the flowers; (western species).
    3   Semi-shrubby, freely branched perennial, the prostrate to ascending branches readily rooting, densely clothed with the remains of the hyaline lacerate stipules; leaves narrowly oblong but usually strongly revolute and linear in outline; perianth white to pink, 4 or 5 mm long; achenes 4 or 5 mm long, black, smooth and shining; (sw B.C.) . . . . *P. paronychia*
    3   Herbaceous taprooted annuals, the stems and branches more or less strongly angled (or nearly terete in *P. confertiflorum* and *P. minimum*); perianth with a green midstripe and white or pinkish borders, commonly less than 2.5 mm long (mostly 3 or 4 mm long in *P. spergulariaeforme*).
      4   Leaves elliptic to obovate but pointed at each end, some usually half as broad as long; achenes very dark brown (almost black), shining; stems often not over 1 dm long (to about 2.5 dm); (B.C.–sw Alta.) . . . . . . *P. minimum*
      4   Leaves linear to narrowly oblong-lanceolate or -elliptic.
        5   Achenes black, smooth and shining.

      6   Perianth mostly 3 or 4 mm long; achenes more or less lanceolate, usually at least 3 mm long; styles usually united at base; stems to about 5 dm tall; (s B.C.) . . . .*P. spergulariaeforme*

      6   Perianth at most 2.5 mm long; achenes ovoid, usually about 2 mm long; styles distinct to base; stems to about 3.5 dm tall; (sw B.C.) . . . .*P. nuttallii*

   5 Achenes yellowish to very dark brown, often minutely striate lengthwise, mostly not shining.

      7   Bracts generally not white-margined, usually not more than 3 times as long as the flowers; functional stamens usually 8; (s B.C. and s Alta.). . . . .*P. watsonii*

      7   Bracts often white-margined, often more than 3 or 4 times as long as the flowers; functional stamens usually 3.

         8   Bracts mostly definitely white-margined, the upper ones often no longer than the flowers; stems to about 2 dm tall; (Sask.) . . . .*P. confertiflorum*

         8   Bracts only slightly or not at all white-margined, the upper ones usually surpassing the flowers; stems usually less than 7 cm tall; (mts. of s B.C. and s Alta.) . . . .*P. kelloggii*

2 Inflorescence a slender open raceme, the flowers not crowded toward the ends of the stems, these often floriferous nearly their whole length; upper leaves reduced to bracts that are often shorter than the ascending or reflexed flowers (*P. minimum, P. nuttallii,* and *P. spergulariaeforme* may sometimes be sought here).

   9 Flowers on ascending or spreading (but not reflexed) pedicels.

     10 Stems (and the strongly ascending branches) sharply angled, erect, to about 5 dm tall; leaves linear, firm, subulate-tipped, plicate with 2 longitudinal folds; flowers remote, mostly solitary, commonly subtended by small bracts in a spike-like inflorescence; achenes dark brown or dull black; (s Ont.) . . . .*P. tenue*

     10 Stems subterete, prostrate or erect, often striate or ridged; leaves flat or revolute, the bracteal ones mostly greatly surpassing the flowers . . . .*GROUP 1* (p. 623)

   9 Flowers on sharply reflexed pedicels; achenes black, smooth and shining; stems and branches sharply angled; annuals.

     11 Achenes mostly not over 2.5 mm long, usually less than twice as long as broad, commonly exserted from the perianth, this to about 2.5 mm long; leaves mostly 1 or 2 cm long; stems commonly less than 2 dm tall; (s B.C. and s Alta.).

       12 Principal leaves broadly elliptic to ovate, up to half as broad as long; pedicels to 2 mm long . . . .*P. austiniae*

       12 Principal leaves mostly linear-oblanceolate, less than 1/3 as broad as long, their margins often revolute; pedicels to 3 mm long . . . .*P. engelmannii*

     11 Achenes usually 3 or 4 mm long, at least twice as long as broad, rarely exserted; leaves linear to narrowly oblong, to 5(6) cm long; stems to 4(5) dm tall.

       13 Perianth mostly 4 or 5 mm long; pedicels 1 or 2 mm long; leaves nearly always at least 4 times as long as broad; (B.C.) . . . .*P. majus*

       13 Perianth rarely to 4 mm long; pedicels to 3(4) mm long; leaves sometimes less than 4 times as long as broad; (B.C. to Que.) . . .*P. douglasii*

1 Flowers in dense to loose spike-like racemes, these leafy-bracted only at or near base, solitary in the leaf-axils or at the top of the stem or 2 or more in a terminal panicle; leaves not jointed with the petiole, their ocreae mostly firm and rarely lacerate; styles 2 or 3; achenes lenticular or trigonous; annuals or perennials.

   14 Stem armed with reflexed prickles, weak and reclining on other plants; leaves broad; outer sepals neither keeled nor winged; annuals.

     15 Ocreae expanded into large leafy perfoliate blades; leaves broadly deltoid,

peltate on their petioles a few mm in from the truncate or subcordate base; (introd.) . . . . *P. perfoliatum*
15 Ocreae not expanded; leaves not peltate.
 16 Leaves sagittate (the basal lobes directed backward); flowers in subglobose heads; peduncles glabrous; style 3-parted; achenes sharply 3-angled; (E Man. to Nfld. and N.S.) . . . . *P. sagittatum*
 16 Leaves hastate (the basal lobes directed outward); flowers in short racemes; peduncles glandular-bristly; style 2-parted; achenes lenticular; (Ont. to N.S.) . . . . *P. arifolium*
14 Stems unarmed.
 17 Stems slender and commonly twining or trailing; principal leaves cordate or sagittate at base, less than twice as long as broad (often about as broad as long).
  18 Ocreae with a ring of reflexed bristles at base; leaves pilose beneath; flowers long-pedicelled, mostly in axillary and terminal panicles of slender open racemes (the axillary racemes sometimes solitary); sepals white, obscurely keeled; achenes shining; perennial; (Sask. to Nfld. and N.S.) . . . . *P. cilinode*
  18 Ocreae lacking bristles.
   19 Fruiting calyx to 5 mm long, scarcely winged; achenes to 4 mm long, dull; flowers in short axillary clusters or axillary and terminal interrupted spike-like racemes, on pedicels 1 or 2 mm long; basal lobes of leaves acutish; annual; (introd.) . . . . *P. convolvulus*
   19 Fruiting calyx to 1.5 cm long, broadly wing-angled; achenes to 6 mm long, shining; flowers in axillary clusters or in interrupted, usually leafy-bracted racemes to 2 dm long, their pedicels equalling or longer than the calyces; basal lobes of leaves roundish; perennial; (Sask. to Nfld. and N.S.) . . . . *P. scandens*
 17 Stems not twining.
  20 Stems very stout, erect, often somewhat woody at base, to over 2 m tall; flowers in small or large terminal and axillary panicles.
   21 Leaves lanceolate to ovate- or oblong-lanceolate, mostly 2 or 3 times as long as broad, the lower ones petioled, the upper ones short-petioled or subsessile; perennials.
    22 Fruiting calyces broadly winged; leaves tapering or rounded at base, to 1.5 dm long, the lower ones reduced to the sheaths; stems from a large branched crown surmounting a thick root; (Alaska–Yukon–Dist. Mackenzie; ?B.C.) . . . . *P. phytolaccaefolium*
    22 Fruiting calyces wingless; principal leaves truncate to cordate at base, to 2 dm long; stems reddish brown, rhizomatous; (garden-escape) . . . . *P. polystachyum*
   21 Leaves broadly ovate to subrotund, relatively long-petioled; (garden-escapes).
    23 Fruiting calyx not winged; achenes biconvex; flowers bright roseate; summit of at least some of the ocreae expanded into a horizontally divergent bristly-ciliate flange; leaves ovate to broadly oblong, sharply acuminate, the larger ones broadly rounded to cordate at base; soft-hairy annual with fibrous roots . . . . *P. orientale*
    23 Fruiting calyx wing-angled; achenes trigonous; flowers greenish or greenish white; ocreae tubular, not bristly at summit; essentially glabrous perennials with long stout rhizomes.
     24 Leaves round-ovate, truncate or slightly cuneate at base, abruptly cuspidate, commonly less than 1.5 dm long; stem to about 2.5 m tall . . . . *P. cuspidatum*
     24 Leaves cordate-ovate, to about 3 dm long, gradually tapering to tip; stem to about 3.5 m tall . . . . *P. sachalinense*

20 Stems relatively slender and low, herbaceous, erect or decumbent at base; leaves commonly many times longer than broad; inflorescence consisting of terminal and/or axillary spike-like racemes, these leafy-bracted only at the base.

  25 Leaves chiefly in a basal tuft, those of the stem few and much reduced; flowers borne in a solitary terminal spike-like raceme; styles 3; achenes trigonous; stem simple, from a short thick rhizome; perennials.

    26 Spike floriferous above, narrowly cylindric, the lower half often bearing only bulblets; stamens included; lower leaves typically lance-linear to narrowly oblong, acute or subacute, narrowed to base; (transcontinental) . . . . *P. viviparum*

    26 Spike floriferous throughout, thick-cylindric, lacking bulblets; stamens long-exserted.

      27 Basal leaves tapering or rounded to a long wingless petiole; achenes cuneate at base, pale brown; (s B.C. and s Alta.) . . . . *P. bistortoides*

      27 Basal leaves broadly rounded or cordate at base, the summit of the petiole broadly winged; achenes rounded at base, dark brown; (Alaska to Dist. Mackenzie; introd. in N.S.) . . . . *P. bistorta*

  25 Leaves cauline, not tufted at the base of the stem; racemes terminating the upper branches as well as the main stem; annuals or perennials.

    28 Ocreae (leaf-sheaths) normally fringed with bristles at summit . . . . *GROUP 2* (p. 624)

    28 Ocreae nearly or quite lacking apical bristles; styles usually 2 (sometimes 3); achenes usually lenticular (sometimes trigonous) . . . . *GROUP 3* (p. 625)

GROUP 1 (*see* p. 621)

1 Achenes shining or at least sublustrous.

  2 Fresh leaves conspicuously glaucous, linear-oblong, firm, crowded; sepals pink-margined, loosely ascending or slightly spreading, the outer one commonly flat, equalling or shorter than the inner 2; achenes to 4 mm long, exserted, becoming blackish; ocreae silvery, those of the lower nodes very conspicuous, to 1 cm long; (?N.B.; ?St-Pierre and Miquelon) . . . . [*P. glaucum*]

  2 Fresh leaves not conspicuously glaucous; ocreae rarely over 8 mm long; sepals erect, appressed to the achene.

    3 Achenes sublustrous, about 2 mm long, included or barely exserted; sepals with narrow white or roseate margins, closely appressed, the outer one hooded, nearly or quite concealing the inner 2 in fruit; pedicels included within the soon lacerate ocreae; leaves bluish green, linear-oblong, firm; (B.C. to N.S.) . . . . *P. prolificum*

    3 Achenes glossy, at least 2.5 (up to 6.5) mm long and commonly exserted; leaves linear to narrowly lanceolate or oblanceolate.

      4 Stems prostrate to loosely spreading or subascending, scarcely ridged when fresh, flexible; ocreae only tardily dissected; sepals with whitish or roseate margins, the outer one flat, equalling or shorter than the inner 2; (eastern saline shores) . . . . *P. oxyspermum*

      4 Stems erect, they and the strongly ascending branches conspicuously corrugate-ridged; ocreae soon deeply lacerate into veiny threads; sepals with yellow or roseate margins, the outer one hooded, nearly or quite concealing the inner 2 in fruit; (B.C. to N.S.) . . . . *P. ramosissimum*

1 Achenes dull.

  5 Perianth bottle-shaped, constricted just below the apex; sepals yellowish green, the outer one hooded and nearly or quite concealing the inner 2 in fruit; achenes about 3 mm long, included; leaves oblong, blunt, to 7 cm long and 2.5 cm broad; (transcontinental) . . . . *P. erectum*

5 Perianth not constricted below the apex; outer sepal commonly flat, not hooded, equalling or shorter than the inner 2.
    6 Achenes abruptly slender-beaked, granular, about 4 mm long, exserted; sepals with roseate margins; leaves fleshy, scarcely veiny, elliptic to narrowly elliptic-obovate, to 3 cm long and 1.5 cm broad; (sandy shores of the Pacific and Atlantic oceans and James Bay) . . . .*P. fowleri*
    6 Achenes neither abruptly beaked nor noticeably granular.
        7 Leaves of branches and stem subequal; fruiting perianth cleft to about the middle, the sepals with greenish-white or pink margins; achene to 2.5 mm long, 2 of its faces convex, the third face concave and shorter; (introd., transcontinental) . . . .*P. arenastrum*
        7 Leaves of branches much smaller than those of the stem; fruiting perianth divided nearly to base; achene with 3 equal concave sides.
            8 Stem-leaves subsessile or with petioles included within the ocreae; sepals with white, pink, or purple margins; achenes to 3.5 mm long; (introd.) . . . .*P. aviculare*
            8 Stem-leaves with petioles 4–8 mm long projecting from the ocreae; sepals with white or pink margins; achenes to 4.5 mm long; (sandy shores of Hudson Bay–James Bay and the Atlantic Ocean) . . . . . .*P. boreale*

GROUP 2 (see p. 623)

GROUP 2 (see p. 623)

1 Perennials with slender and tough forking rhizomes, often producing autumnal leafy basal offshoots; achenes lustrous.
    2 Summit of new ocreae expanded into a horizontally divergent herbaceous flange; spikes to 4 cm long and 2 cm thick, on glabrous peduncles; styles 2; achenes lenticular; leaves glabrous or nearly so; perennial by slender and tough forking rhizomes; (var. *stipulaceum* and its f. *hirtuosum;* transcontinental) . . . . .*P. amphibium*
    2 Summit of ocreae without a spreading flange; spikes slender, interrupted at base; styles 2 or 3; achenes lenticular or trigonous.
        3 Mature calyx glandular-punctate, white; ocreae strigose or glabrous; (B.C. to N.S.) . . . .*P. punctatum*
        3 Mature calyx not obviously punctate (the glands confined to the inner lobes of the sepals), roseate to purplish; ocreae strigose; (B.C.; Ont. to N.S.) . . . .
         . . . .*P. hydropiperoides*
1 Annuals with fibrous roots (some species occasionally perennial).
    4 Stem and peduncles glandular-bristly; leaves scabrous-hispid; calyx purplish or reddish; spikes slenderly cylindric, to 1 dm long, arching or recurving; styles 2; achenes lenticular, lustrous; (s Ont. and s Que.; introd. in N.B.) . . . .*P. careyi*
    4 Stem and peduncles not obviously glandular; leaves mostly smooth or nearly so; achenes lenticular or trigonous (or both types on the same plant).
        5 Mature calyx glandular-punctate; spikes slender, arching, usually much interrupted at base; styles 2 or 3; achenes lenticular or trigonous; upper leaf-axils commonly floriferous; (essentially transcontinental).
            6 Calyx greenish or purple-tipped; achenes dull; ocreolae (sheathing stipules subtending flowers) eciliate or short-ciliate, swollen and concealing cleistogamous flowers; plant intensely acrid or peppery . . . .
            . . . .*P. hydropiper*
            6 Calyx white; achenes lustrous; ocreolae ciliate, cylindric, without cleistogamous flowers . . . .*P. punctatum*
        5 Mature calyx not glandular-punctate; achenes lustrous.
            7 Spikes slender and more or less interrupted, often with remote fascicles extending down to the upper sheaths; leaves green above; (introd. in B.C., Ont., and Que.) . . . .*P. caespitosum*
            7 Spikes dense, thick-cylindric or ellipsoid, the longer ones definitely peduncled; ocreolae entire or short-ciliate.

8 Spikes less than 7 mm thick; mature calyx scarcely reticulate at base; achenes prevailingly 3-angled; leaves mostly green above; plant of sandy or gravelly pond-shores; (?N.S.) . . . . [*P. puritanorum*]

8 Spikes at least 7 mm thick; mature calyx prominently reticulate at base; achenes prevailingly lenticular; leaves often purplish-blotched above; plants of mostly weedy habitats; (introd.) . . . . *P. persicaria*

GROUP 3 (*see* p. 623)

1 Perennials with slender and tough forking rhizomes; upper leaves not markedly reduced; spikes terminal, solitary or paired (at most 3 or 4); styles 2; achenes lenticular; (essentially transcontinental).

2 Spikes thick-cylindric to ovoid, to 4 cm long and 2 cm thick; peduncles and ocreolae (sheaths subtending individual flowers) glabrous; terrestrial phases (var. *stipulaceum* and its. f. *hirtuosum*) with the summit of the new ocreae expanded into a horizontally divergent herbaceous flange . . . . *P. amphibium*

2 Spikes slenderly cylindric, to over 1.5 dm long and about 1.5 cm thick; peduncles and ocreolae pubescent; ocreae lacking a horizontally divergent flange . . . .
. . . . *P. coccineum*

1 Annuals with fibrous roots; upper leaves much reduced; spikes mostly numerous, terminal and axillary; styles usually 2; achenes usually trigonous.

3 Peduncles and axis of inflorescence with obvious stalked glands; spikes pink to purplish (rarely white); outer sepals obscurely nerved; (Ont. to N.S.) . . . .
. . . . *P. pensylvanicum*

3 Peduncles and axis of inflorescence glabrous or with sessile inconspicuous glands; outer 3 sepals in fruit strongly 3-nerved, each nerve terminating in an anchor-shaped fork (except in *P. pensylvanicum* var. *eglandulosum*).

4 Spikes green (rarely purplish), to 5 cm long, erect, the lateral ones mostly sessile or short-stalked; floral-axis copiously glandular; achenes about 3 mm long and about equalling the mature calyx, this not constricted at tip; (introd.) . . . .
. . . . *P. scabrum*

4 Spikes pink to purplish.

5 Plant glabrous throughout; calyx pale, about equalling the somewhat shining achene, this to 3.5 mm long; spike erect, to 1.5 cm thick; (var. *eglandulosum*; s Ont.) . . . . *P. pensylvanicum*

5 Plant often bearing sessile glands on the peduncles and lower leaf-surfaces; calyx pink to purplish, constricted above into a thick beak overtopping the achene, this not much over 2 mm long; spike often somewhat pendulous, not over 1 cm thick; (transcontinental) . . . .
. . . . *P. lapathifolium*

P. amphibium L.   Water-Smartweed

/ST/X/EA/ (Hel (Hpr)) Shallow water and shores, swamps, ditches, and wet meadows, the aggregate species from N-cent. Alaska, cent. Yukon, and the Mackenzie R. Delta to Great Bear L., Great Slave L., L. Athabasca (Alta. and Sask.), Man. (N to Churchill), Ont. (N to the Shamattawa R. at 54°47′N), Que. (N to the E James Bay watershed at 52°16′N, L. Mistassini, and the Côte-Nord), s ?Labrador (Fernald *in* Gray 1950), Nfld., N.B., P.E.I., and N.S., s to Utah, Colo., Nebr., Pa., and N.J.; Iceland; Eurasia. MAPS and synonymy: *see* below.

1 Summit of ocreae expanded into a horizontally divergent herbaceous flange bearing well-developed cilia or bristles; terrestrial or stranded forms with lanceolate, spreading to ascending, short-petioled leaves.

2 Leaves and new growth of stem essentially glabrous; [var. *hartwrightii* (Gray) Bissell; f. *hart.* (Gray) Blake; *P. (Persicaria) hart.* Gray; *P. natans* f. *hart.* (Gray) Stanford; *Persicaria nebrascensis* Greene; transcontinental; MAP (aggregate species; *P. amphibium*): Meusel, Jaeger, and Weinert 1965:130] . . . .
. . . . var. *stipulaceum* (Coleman) Fern.

2 Leaves villous; new growth of stem shaggily villous or hirsute; [var. *marginatum* f. *hirt.* Farw.; Alta. to N.S.] . . . . var. *stipulaceum* f. *hirtuosum* (Farw.) Fern.
1 Summit of ocreae lacking a flange, nearly or quite lacking marginal cilia.
  3 Terrestrial or stranded forms with lanceolate, spreading to ascending, short-petioled leaves.
    4 Leaves glabrous or sparingly appressed-pilose; ocreolae (sheaths subtending the pedicels) narrowly triangular; spikes to 2 cm thick; [Man. to Nfld. and N.S.] . . . . var. *stipulaceum* f. *simile* Fern.
    4 Leaves harshly scabrous on both surfaces with firm hairs less than 1 mm long; ocreolae broadly rounded-triangular; spikes to 1.5 cm thick; [introd. at Yarmouth, N.S.] . . . . var. *amphibium* f. *terrestre* (Leers) Blake
  3 Aquatic forms, the leaves mostly slender-petioled and floating, glabrous on both sides.
    5 Leaf-blades oblong-lanceolate, tapering gradually from near or below the middle to the apex, broadly rounded to subcordate at base; ocreolae deltoid or broadly rhombic; spikes to 1.5 cm thick; [f. *natans* (Moench) Stanford; Eurasia ?only] . . . . [var. *amphibium*]
    5 Leaf-blades elliptic to elliptic-oval, gradually tapering or rounded (rarely subcordate) at base; ocreolae elongate-triangular, acutish; spikes to 2 cm thick; [var. *natans* Michx. (basionym, the type from the L. St. John region of Que.), not Moench, nor f. *natans* (Moench) Stanford; var. *aquaticum* Torr., not Leyss.; ssp. *laevimarginatum* Hult.; *P. fluitans* Eat.; *P. natans* (Michx.) Eat.; *Persicaria ?canadensis* and *P. ?psycrophila* Greene; transcontinental; MAP (ssp. *laev.*): Hultén 1968*b*:387] . . . . var. *stipulaceum* f. *fluitans* (Eat.) Fern.

P. arenastrum Jord.
Eurasian; according to Mertens and Raven (1965), most reports of *P. aviculare* from N. America refer to *P. arenastrum,* which, on this basis, is introd. transcontinentally: N-cent. Alaska–Yukon (*see* Hultén 1944: map 474 *(P. bux.),* map 475 *(P. caur.),* map 478 *(P. heter.),* and map 480 *(P. negl.),* p. 782) to the Mackenzie R. Delta, Great Bear L., L. Athabasca, Man. (N to Churchill), northernmost Ont., Que. (N to Ungava Bay), Labrador (N to Nain, ca. 56°30′N), Nfld., N.B., P.E.I., and N.S. [Incl. reports of the following taxa, most of which can be considered identical with *P. arenastrum* or comprising part of the species-complex: *P. aequale, P. calcatum,* and *P. heterophyllum* Lindm.; *P. buxiforme* and *P. rubescens* Small; *P. caurianum* Robins.; *P. humifusum* and *P. ruvivagum* Jord.; *P. littorale* Link; *P. monspeliense* Pers.; *P. neglectum* Bess.; *P. provinciale* Koch].

P. arifolium L.   Halberd-leaved Tearthumb
/T/EE/ (Hp) Wet places (common in tidal marshes) from Minn. to Ont. (N to the Ottawa dist.), Que. (N to the Quebec City dist.; MT; reported from the Côte-Nord by St. John 1922), N.B. (Kent Co.; MTMG), P.E.I., and N.S., S to Ohio, Ind., and Fla.

The Canadian plant may be distinguished as var. *pubescens* (Keller) Fern. (var. *lentiforme* Fern. & Grisc.; *P. sagittatum* var. *pub.* Keller; achenes lenticular, to about 3.5 mm long and 2.5 mm thick, their faces not bossed, rather than achenes biconvex, to about 4 mm long and 3 mm broad, their faces bossed or bearing a stout projection in the middle).

P. austiniae Greene
/T/W/ (T) Dry to moist flats and riverbanks from SE ?B.C. (reported from South Kootenay Pass, on the B.C.–Alta. boundary, by J.M. Macoun 1895) and SW Alta. (Lake Louise, near Banff; CAN) to NE Calif., Idaho, and Wyo.

P. aviculare L.   Prostrate Knotweed
Eurasian; see *P. arenastrum,* to which Mertens and Raven (1965) refer most reports of *P. aviculare* from N. America except some collections from Alaska (Skagway), the Yukon (Moosehide Mt.), and Alta. (near Fort Saskatchewan); Greenland.

For varying treatments of the *P. aviculare* complex, *see* Mertens and Raven (1965), Löve and Löve (1956*a*), and Styles (1962).

P. bistorta L.   Bistort
/aST/W/EA/   (Hr)   Grassy tundra and ledges of Alaska–Yukon–w Dist. Mackenzie; Eurasia.
MAP and synonymy: *see* below.
1   Leaves broadly rounded or subcordate at base; plant to about 5 dm tall; [Eurasia;
    introd. in Colchester Co., N.S., where reported by M.L. Fernald (Rhodora
    24(285):173. 1922) as "somewhat naturalized (at least two obviously increasing
    clumps) in a field in Victoria Park, Truro."; MAPS (aggregate species): Hultén
    1968*b*:385; Meusel, Jaeger, and Weinert 1965:130] . . . . ssp. *bistorta*
1   Leaves cuneate at base; plant averaging lower; [*P. plumosum* Small, the type from
    St. Paul Is., Alaska; throughout Alaska–Yukon–w Dist. Mackenzie N to the Arctic
    coast; *see* Hultén 1944: map 473, p. 782] . . . . ssp. *plumosum* (Small) Hult.

P. bistortoides Pursh   Smokeweed, Bistort
/T/W/   (Hr)   Streambanks and moist or swampy meadows to alpine slopes from s B.C.
(near Chilliwack; Skagit R. valley; Manning Provincial Park, SE of Hope) and SW Alta. (Waterton Lakes; Cypress Hills) to s Calif. and N.Mex. [*Bistorta* Small].
    A collection in GH from near Millville, Nfld., has been placed here by Fernald but is consid-
ered by Eilif Dahl (Rhodora 64(758):120. 1962) as more probably referable to a species of *Rumex*.

P. boreale (Lange) Small
/aST/EE/GE/   (T)   Sandy, gravelly, or rocky coasts of ?Alaska (Fernald *in* Gray 1950), NE
Man. (Churchill; CAN; DAO), N Ont. (Cape Henrietta Maria, NW James Bay at ca. 55°N; CAN),
James Bay (South Twin Is., 53°08'N), Que. (Saguenay Co. and the Mingan Is. of the Côte-
Nord), Labrador (N to Nain, 56°33'N; GH), and Nfld.; w Greenland N to ca. 65°50'N; Iceland;
Scandinavia. [*P. aviculare* (*heterophyllum* ssp.) var. *bor.* Lange; *P. islandicum* Meisn.;
P. fowleri sensu St. John 1922, at least in part, not Robins., and *P. littorale sensu* Delabarre
1902, not Link, relevant collections of each in GH].

P. caespitosum Blume
Asiatic; locally natzd. along roadsides, shores, and in waste places of N. America, as in B.C.
and Ont. (Boivin 1966*b*) and in Que. (Rouleau 1947).
    Our plant is referable to var. *longisetum* (DeBruyn) Stewart (the ocreolae subtending the
pedicels with bristleform cilia equalling or longer than the sheathing body).

P. careyi Olney
/T/EE/   (T)   Thickets, swamps, clearings, and cult. ground from s Ont. (Georgian Bay region, L. Huron; CAN; reported from Waterloo Co. by Montgomery 1945) to SW Que. (swampy
field near Brome, Brome Co.; DAO), s to Minn., Wisc., Ind., and Del.
    This species is probably native in s Ont. and SW Que. It was also taken by the writer in 1956
from an extensive colony along a road embankment and dry ditch about 25 mi NW of Sussex,
Kings Co., N.B., where undoubtedly introd.

P. cilinode Michx.   Fringed Black Bindweed
/T/EE/   (Hp)   Dry thickets and rocky slopes from E-cent. Sask. (N to Flin Flon, ca. 55°N; the
report from w to Lesser Slave L., Alta., by John Macoun 1886, requires confirmation) to Man.
(N to Wekusko L., about 90 mi NE of The Pas), Ont. (N to Sandy L. at ca. 53°N, 93°W), Que. (N
to L. St. John and the Gaspé Pen.), Nfld., N.B., P.E.I., and N.S., s to Minn., Mich., Tenn., and
N.C. [*Bilderdykia* Greene].
    Forma *erectum* (Peck) Fern. (the stem erect, not greatly elongating and twining) is known
from Que., Nfld., N.B., and N.S.

P. coccineum Muhl.   Water-Smartweed
/sT/X/   (Hel (Hpr))   Quiet waters, shores, and wet ground, the aggregate species from SW
Dist. Mackenzie (J.W. Thieret, Can. Field-Nat. 75(3):115. 1961) and B.C.–Alta. to Sask. (N to
Runciman, ca. 53°N), Man. (N to Cross Lake, N of L. Winnipeg at ca. 54°30'N), Ont. (N to
Sandy L. at ca. 53°N, 93°W), Que. (N to Contrecoeur, about 40 mi NE of Montreal), P.E.I., and
N.S. (not known from N.B.), s to Calif., Mexico, Tex., Ark., and N.C.

1 Terrestrial forms with ascending stems; upper leaves merely rounded at base.
    2 Petioles attached near base of ocreae; leaves and upper part of stem glabrous or
       sparsely strigose; spikes rarely over 1 dm long; [f. *terrestre* (Willd.) Stanford;
       P. amphibium var. *emersum* Michx. (*P. emersum* (Michx.) Britt.); *P. amphibium*
       var. *muhlenbergii* Meisn.; *P. (Persicaria) muhl.* (Meisn.) Wats.; *Persicaria*
       coccinea (Muhl.) Greene; sw Dist. Mackenzie–B.C. to N.S.] . . . . var. *coccineum*
    2 Petioles mostly attached midway on the ocreae; leaves and upper part of stem
       densely ashy-pubescent; spikes to over 1.5 dm long; [*Persicaria pratincola*
       Greene; ?Alta., Sask., and Man.] . . . . var. *pratincola* (Greene) Stanford
1 Aquatic forms with glabrous floating leaves and branches.
    3 Leaves broadly lanceolate to ovate, acute, the upper ones cordate-based and up
       to 8 cm broad; [var. *aquaticum* Willd.; *P. muhlenbergii* f. *natans* Wieg.; Man. to
       P.E.I. and N.S.] . . . . var. *coccineum* f. *natans* (Wieg.) Stanford
    3 Leaves lance-acuminate, the upper ones tapering or merely rounded at base and
       usually not over 5 cm broad; [*P. (Persicaria) rigidulum* Sheld.; reported from near
       Moose Jaw, Sask., by Breitung 1957*a*, who, however, merges *P. coccineum* f.
       natans with it in synonymy; reported from Massacre, Ont., by E.E. Stanford,
       Rhodora 27(321):165. 1925] . . . . var. *rigidulum* (Sheld.) Stanford

P. confertiflorum Nutt.
/T/W/ (T) Dry to wet ground from Wash. and Mont. to sw Sask. (near Battle Creek, s of
the Cypress Hills, where taken by John Macoun in 1895; CAN, detd. Brenckle; reports from
B.C. and Alta. require confirmation), s to N Calif. and N ?Wyo.

P. convolvulus L. Black Bindweed. Renouée liseron or Chevrier
Eurasian; a common weed in cult. and waste ground from cent. Alaska (*see* Hultén 1944: map
476, p. 782), s Yukon, and s Dist. Mackenzie (W.J. Cody, Can. Field-Nat. 77(2):116. 1963)
through all the provinces to the U.S.A.; s Greenland. [*Bilderdykia* Dum.]. MAP: Hultén
1968*b*:384.

P. cuspidatum Sieb. & Zucc. Japanese Knotweed, Fleeceflower
Asiatic; a garden-escape in N. America, as in B.C. and Man. (Winnipeg), Ont. (N to the Ottawa
dist.), Que. (N to the Quebec City dist.), Nfld., N.B., P.E.I., and N.S. [*P. zuccarinii* Small].

P. douglasii Greene
/T/X/ (T) Dry to moist ground from B.C. (N to Smithers, ca. 54°30′N) to L. Athabasca
(Alta. and Sask.), Man. (N to Sasaginnigak L., about 125 mi N of Winnipeg), Ont. (N to Schrei-
ber, N shore of L. Superior), and Que. (N to the Laurentide region N of Montreal; Fernald *in*
Gray 1950), s to Calif., N.Mex., N.Y., and Vt.
    Some of the collections from the West (B.C. to sw Sask.) are referable to var. *latifolium*
(Engelm.) Greene (*P. tenue* var. *lat.* Engelm.; *P. montanum* (Small) Greene; leaves relatively
broad in outline and often over 4 mm broad, rather than linear or very narrowly oblong and
rarely as much as 4 mm broad).

P. engelmannii Greene
/T/W/ (T) Dry to moist soil from SE B.C. (reported from Southeast Kootenay by Henry
1915, and as abundant at Field by Ulke 1935) and sw Alta. (Waterton Lakes; Pincher Creek;
Livingston Gap) to Colo. and Idaho.

P. erectum L.
/ST/X/ (T) Dry open ground, roadsides, saline marshes, etc., from cent. Alaska–Yukon,
Dist. Mackenzie (Boivin 1966*b*), and B.C.–Alta. to Sask. (N to Prince Albert; CAN, *P. ach-
oreum,* detd. Brenckle), Man. (N to Gillam, about 165 mi s of Churchill), Ont. (N to the N shore
of L. Superior and sw James Bay), Que. (N to SE James Bay, L. St. John, and the Gaspé Pen.),
Nfld., N.B. (Woodstock, Carleton Co.; the report from P.E.I. by Herbert Groh, Sci. Agric.
7:391. 1927, is considered by D.S. Erskine 1960, to probably refer to some other species), and
N.S., s to Idaho, Colo., Kans., Mo., Tenn., and Ga. [Incl. *P. achoreum* Blake].

P. fowleri Robins.
/sT/D (coastal)/ (T (Hp)) Sandy or gravelly seashores and coastal salt marshes: s Alaska (*see* Hultén 1944: map 477, p. 782) through coastal B.C. to N Wash.; Ont. (w James Bay N to ca. 52°N) and Que. (E James Bay N to 53°50′N; s Ungava Bay; St. Lawrence R. estuary from Temiscouata Co. to the Côte-Nord, Anticosti Is., Gaspé Pen., and Magdalen Is.) to SE Labrador (N to Turner's Head, ca. 52°N; CAN), Nfld., N.B. (type locality; not known from P.E.I.), and N.S.; E ?Asia (*see* Hultén 1944). [*P. allocarpum* Blake; *P. aviculare* var. *buxifolium* Ledeb.; *P. littorale* var. *sitchense* Small; *P. maritimum sensu* Fowler 1885, not L., the relevant collection in GH]. MAPS: Hultén 1968*b*:391; Fernald 1925: map 25 (requiring considerable expansion), p. 257; J.G. Packer, Nat. can. (Que.) 98(4): fig. 2, p. 134. 1971.

[P. glaucum Nutt.]   Seabeach-Knotweed
["Sandy seabeaches, saline pond-shores and dune-hollows, local, Mass. to Ga." (Fernald *in* Gray 1950). The reports from St-Pierre and Miquelon by Rouleau (1956) and from w N.B. by Roland (1947) require confirmation.]

P. hydropiper L.   Common Smartweed.   Curage
/T/X/EA/ (T) Damp soils and ditches (both native and introd.) from SE Alaska (introd. at Juneau) and s B.C. (Hammond; New Westminster) to Man. (near Winnipeg and at Washow Bay, L. Winnipeg; reported N to Flin Flon, ca. 55°N, by Lowe 1943; not known from Alta.-Sask.), Ont. (N to the N shore of L. Superior), Que. (N to the Gaspé Pen.), Nfld., N.B., P.E.I., and N.S., s to Calif., Tex., and Ala.; Eurasia. [Incl. the long-pedicelled extreme, var. *projectum* Stanford]. MAP: Hultén 1968*b*:389.
   This is a weedy species and it is probable that much of our material derives from plants introd. from Eurasia. Indeed, the plant may be entirely introd. in N. America.

P. hydropiperoides Michx.   Water-pepper
/T/X/ (Hp) Wet ground, shores, and shallow water, the aggregate species from s B.C. (Vancouver Is.; Sumas; Agassiz; Chilliwack; Leanchoil, Kootenay dist.; not known from Alta.-Sask.–Man.) to Ont. (N to Quetico Provincial Park, about 100 mi w of Thunder Bay, and the Ottawa dist.), Que. (N to Mont-Laurier, about 80 mi N of Hull), N.B., and N.S. (not known from P.E.I.), s to Mexico, Tex., and Fla.; S. America. MAPS and synonymy: *see* below.
1 Spikes (or many of them) sessile and in clusters of up to 4 at the tips of erect
   peduncles; elongate bulblets often produced from sterile flowers; ocreae short-
   ciliate; [type from Springhaven, Yarmouth Co., N.S.; also known from Shelburne Co.] . . . .
   . . . . var. *digitatum* Fern.
1 Spikes borne singly at the tips of the inflorescence or along its branches; bulblets
   not produced.
   2 Ocreae eciliate or with cilia little over 1 mm long; [type from Sable Is., N.S.; also
      known from Shelburne Co.] . . . . var. *psilostachyum* St. John
   2 Ocreae with cilia at least 2 mm long . . . . var. *hydropiperoides*
      3 Leaves and stem distinctly strigose; [*P. hyd. macounii* Small; Ont. and Que.] . . . . .
         . . . . f. *strigosum* (Small) Stanford
      3 Leaves and stem essentially glabrous.
         4 Flowers white; [Ont. and Que.] . . . . f. *leucochranthum* Moore
         4 Flowers pink to purplish; [*P. mite* Pers., not Schrank; *P. persicarioides*
            HBK.; s Alaska (Circle Hot Springs, possibly introd.) to s B.C.; Ont. to N.B.
            and N.S.; MAPS (aggregate species): Hultén 1968*b*:388; Meusel, Jaeger,
            and Weinert 1965:131). A hybrid with *P. robustius* (*P. punctatum* var. *majus*
            of the present treatment) is reported from N.S. by M.L. Fernald (Rhodora
            24(285):175. 1922; Annapolis Co.] . . . . f. *hydropiperoides*

P. kelloggii Greene
/T/W/ (T) Meadows and wet places to dry subalpine slopes from s B.C. (Botanie Valley, Kamloops dist.; CAN, detd. Brenckle; reported from Lytton at 4,500 ft elevation by Eastham 1947; *P. unifolium* also reported by Eastham from Toad Mt., near Nelson, at 6,000 ft elevation)

and s Alta. (Redcliff; Cypress Hills) to N Calif., Ariz., and Colo. [*P. unifolium* Small]. MAP: L.C. Wheeler, Rhodora 40(476): map 4, p. 311. 1938.

P. lapathifolium L.   Willow-weed
/ST/X/EA/   (T)   Swampy thickets, shores, damp clearings, and cult. fields, the aggregate species from B.C.–Alta. (introd. in SE Alaska and SW Dist. Mackenzie) to Sask. (N to Hudson Bay Junction, 52°52′N), Man. (N to Churchill), northernmost Ont., Que. (N to E James Bay at 53°50′N, L. Mistassini, and the Gaspé Pen.), Nfld., N.B., P.E.I., and N.S., s to Calif., S.Dak., Minn., Pa., and N.J.; introd. in SW Greenland (as perhaps largely in the northern part of our area); Iceland; Eurasia. MAPS and synonymy: *see* below.
1   Leaves lanceolate, broadest near the base, attenuate to tip.
   2   Leaves green on both sides, to 2.5 dm long; spikes to 8 cm long, arching or drooping; [*P. incarnatum* Ell.; *P. nodosum* Pers.; *Persicaria oneillii* Brenckle; *Per. lap.* (L.) S.F. Gray; transcontinental, partly introd. northwards; MAPS (aggregate species): Hultén 1968*b*:389; Meusel, Jaeger, and Weinert 1965:131] . . . . var. *lapathifolium*
   2   Leaves white-pubescent beneath, at most about 1 dm long; spikes less than 4 cm long, erect; [var. *incanum* (Willd.) Koch; *P. tomentosum* var. *incanum* of auth., not *P. incanum* Schmidt; transcontinental] . . . . var. *salicifolium* Sibth.
1   Leaves broadest well above the base, not long-attenuate.
   3   Plant erect, to about 2 m tall; leaves oblong-ovate, to about 2 dm long; spikes to about 6 cm long; [Grindstone Is., Magdalen Is., E Que.] . . . . var. *ovatum* A. Br.
   3   Plant prostrate or depressed; leaves subrhombic, mostly not over 7 cm long; spikes to about 4 cm long; [Sable Is., N.S.] . . . . var. *prostratum* Wimm.

P. majus (Meisn.) Piper
/T/W/   (T)   Dry soils at low to moderately high elevations from s B.C. (Vancouver Is.; Osoyoos; Lytton; Spences Bridge; Cascade; Manning Provincial Park, SE of Hope) to N Calif., Idaho, and Mont. [*P. coarctatum* var. *majus* Meisn., not *P. punctatum* var. *majus* (Meisn.) Small; *P. tenue sensu* John Macoun 1886, as to B.C. reports, not Michx., relevant collections in CAN].

P. minimum Wats.
/T/W/   (T)   Dry soils at low to high elevations from B.C. (N to Bella Coola, ca. 52°20′N) and sw Alta. (South Kootenay Pass; Waterton Lakes) to N Calif. and Colo.

P. nuttallii Small
/t/W/   (T)   Dry plains and slopes from B.C. (N to Kimsquit, ca. 52°45′N; CAN, detd. Porsild) to NW Oreg. [*P. intermedium* Nutt., not Ehrh.].

P. orientale L.   Prince's-plume Lady's-thumb.   Monte-au-ciel
Asiatic; much cult. in N. America and spreading to roadsides and waste places, as in Ont. (N to the Ottawa dist.), Que. (N to the Montreal dist.), and ?N.B. (Westmorland Co.; NBM, possibly taken in a garden).

P. oxyspermum Mey. & Bunge
/T/E/EA/   (T)   Sandy and gravelly seashores and dune-hollows of E Que. (Anticosti Is. and Magdalen Is.; the report of *P. raii* from Turner's Head, SE Labrador, by J.M. Macoun 1895, is based upon *P. fowleri*, the relevant collection in CAN), Nfld., N.B., P.E.I., and N.S.; N Europe; NW Asia. [Incl. *P. acadiense* Fern. and *P. raii* Bab.; *P. maritimum sensu* Schmitt 1904, not L. (as also, probably, *sensu* Fowler 1879, and Saint-Cyr 1887); *P. robertii* of Canadian reports at least in part, not Loisel.]. MAPS: combine the maps by Hultén 1958: map 269 *(P. raii)* and map 270 *(P. oxy.)*, p. 289; combine the maps by Löve and Löve 1956*a*: fig. 15 *(P. raii)*, p. 507, and fig. 17 *(P. oxy.)*, p. 510.

P. paronychia C. & S.   Black Knotweed
/t/W/   (Ch)   Coastal beaches and dunes from SW B.C. (Vancouver Is. and adjacent islands; a report from Sitka, Alaska, requires confirmation) to N Calif.

Polygonum

P. pensylvanicum L.   Pinkweed
/T/EE/   (T)   Shores, thickets, clearings, and cult. ground, the aggregate species from Ont. (N to the Ottawa dist.; introd. in Alaska and perhaps at Agassiz, B.C.; reports from Man. are referred to *P. lapathifolium* by Boivin 1968) to Que. (N to Mont-Laurier, about 80 mi N of Hull, and the Mingan Is. of the Côte-Nord), N.B., and N.S. (reports from P.E.I. probably refer to some other species, perhaps *P. scabrum)*, s to Tex. and Fla. MAP and synonymy: *see* below.
1   Peduncles and axis of inflorescence glabrous (the whole plant glabrous); [reported by Core 1948, from Middle Is. of the Erie Archipelago, Essex Co., s Ont.] . . . .
. . . . var. *eglandulosum* Myers
1   Peduncles and axis of inflorescence covered with gland-tipped hairs.
    2   Leaves distinctly strigose on both surfaces; [Ont. to N.S.; introd. in Alaska and perhaps at Agassiz, B.C.; MAP: Hultén 1968*b*:387] . . . . var. *pensylvanicum*
    2   Leaves glabrous or at most sparsely strigose on the midrib beneath . . . .
    . . . . var. *laevigatum* Fern.
        3   Flowers whitish; glands of hairs yellowish; [N.B. and N.S.] . . . . . . f. *albineum* Farw.
        3   Flowers pink or roseate (presumably so in f. *pallescens*).
            4   Glands yellowish; [s Ont. and N.S.] . . . . f. *pallescens* Stanford
            4   Glands reddish; [N.B. and N.S.] . . . . f. *laevigatum*

P. perfoliatum L.
Asiatic; according to Fernald *in* Gray (1950), this species is becoming established in nurseries in Pa. It is known in Canada only from near Pitt Meadows in the New Westminster dist. of sw B.C., where forming roadside patches and taken by D. Faris in 1954 (Herb. V, detd. C. Frankton).

P. persicaria L.   Lady's-thumb, Heart's-ease
Eurasian; roadsides, damp clearings, and cult. fields of N. America, as in s Alaska and all the provinces (with the possible exception of Sask.); introd. in w Greenland N to ca. 70°N. [*Persicaria* Small; *P. pulchellum* Loisel.]. MAP: Hultén 1968*b*:388.
    Var. *ruderale* (Salisb.) Meisn. (*P. ruderale* Salisb.; stem prostrate or depressed rather than ascending or merely decumbent-based, the relatively short leaves rhombic-lanceolate rather than narrowly to broadly lanceolate, the spike usually less than 1.5 cm long rather than to over 4 cm) is known from Que., St-Pierre and Miquelon, Nfld., and N.S.

P. phytolaccaefolium Meisn.   Alpine Knotweed
/ST/W/eA/   (Ch)   Subalpine or alpine meadows, talus slopes, and ridges from N-cent. Alaska–Yukon (*see* Hultén 1944: map 471, p. 782; *P. alaskanum)* and the Mackenzie R. Delta to N Calif., Nev., Idaho, and Mont. (presumably through the mts. of B.C. but evidently not yet known from that province); E Siberia. [*Aconogonum* Small; *P. alpinum* vars. *alaskanum* Small (*P. alask.* (Small) Wight and its var. *glabrescens* Hult.) and *lapathifolium* C. & S.; *P. polymorphum sensu* John Macoun 1886, not Ledeb.]. MAPS (*P. alask.):* Hultén 1968*b*:386; Porsild 1966: map 52, p. 73.

P. polystachyum Wall.
Asiatic; a garden-escape in N. America, locally spreading to waste places and neglected yards; known in Canada from rubbish heaps and dumps near Yarmouth, N.S. (GH; CAN), and reported from B.C. by Calder and Taylor (1968; Graham Is., Queen Charlotte Is.).

P. prolificum (Small) Robins.
/sT/X/   (T)   Prairies, shores, brackish or saline marshes, and waste places from s B.C. (Eastham 1947; introd. at Whitehorse, the Yukon) to Alta. (N to Heart L. at 59°41′N; Raup 1936), Sask. (N to Saskatoon; Breitung 1957*a*), s Man. (Otterburne, about 30 mi s of Winnipeg), Ont. (N to Attawapiskat, w James Bay at ca. 53°N), Que. (N to l'Islet and Charlevoix counties), N.S. (not known from N.B. or P.E.I.), and Maine, s to Wash., Tex., Ark., and Va. [*P. ramosissimum* var. *pro.* Small; *P. autumnale* Brenckle]. MAP: Hultén 1968*b*:390.

P. punctatum Ell.   Water-Smartweed
/T/X/A/   (T (Hp))   Wet places and swampy ground, the aggregate species from s B.C. (N to Kamloops; not known from Alta.) to Sask. (N to Ile-à-la-Crosse, 55°27′N), Man. (N to Piney Is., L. Winnipeg), Ont. (N to the Ottawa dist.), Que. (N to Montmagny Co.), N.B., P.E.I., and N.S., s to s Calif., Mexico, Tex., and Fla.; Tropical America; s Asia. MAP and synonymy: see below.
1   Leaves fleshy, sparingly punctate, to 6 cm long, rounded to subacute at apex; plant
       to 2 dm tall; [fresh to brackish tidal shores of E Que. (type from near Lotbinière,
       Lotbinière Co.), N.B., and N.S.] . . . . var. *parvum* Vict. & Rousseau
1   Leaves not fleshy, strongly punctate, acuminate, to 1.5 dm long; plant to about 1 m
       tall.
       2   Annual with fibrous roots; [var. *leptostachyum* of auth., perhaps not (Meisn.)
              Small (*P. acre* var. *lept.* Meisn.); transcontinental; MAP: N.C. Fassett, Brittonia
              6(4): map 16, p. 378. 1949] . . . . var. *confertiflorum* (Meisn.) Fassett
       2   Perennial with tough rootstocks.
              3   Ocreae glabrous, fragile; ocreolae ciliate; spike loose and open except at
                     summit; achenes lenticular or trigonous; leaves to 3.5 cm broad; stem
                     slender; [*P. acre* HBK., not Lam.; the above-noted map by Fassett indicates
                     the absence of the typical form in Canada, reports being referable to the
                     other varieties] . . . .[var. *punctatum*]
              3   Ocreae strigose, firm; ocreolae eciliate; spike continuous except at base;
                     achenes trigonous; leaves to 4.5 cm broad; [*P. robustius* (Small) Fern.; N.S.;
                     see the above-noted MAP by Fassett] . . . . var. *majus* (Meisn.) Small

[P. puritanorum Fern.]
["Sandy or gravelly pond-shores, w N.S.; . . ." (Fernald *in* Gray 1950); collections from N.S. (Annapolis, Halifax, and Inverness counties; ACAD; CAN; GH) have been placed here but the species appears to be merely a reduced extreme of the Eurasian *P. persicaria*.]

P. ramosissimum Michx.   Bushy Knotweed
/T/X/   (T)   Sandy places, shores, and roadsides from SE Alaska and B.C.–Alta. to Sask. (N to Amisk L., near Flin Flon), Man. (N to The Pas), Ont. (N to w James Bay at ca. 52°N), Que. (N to E James Bay at ca. 52°N), N.B., P.E.I., and N.S., s to Calif., N.Mex., Tex., Mo., Pa., and Del. [*P. exsertum* Small; *P. interius* Brenckle and its var. *turneri* Brenckle].

P. sachalinense Schmidt   Sachaline, Giant Knotweed
Asiatic; persisting in or spreading from gardens to waste places, old fields, and roadsides as in sw B.C. (Vancouver Is. and Mayne Is.; Carter and Newcombe 1921), s Ont. (Montgomery 1957), Que. (l'Islet and Rivière-du-Loup counties), P.E.I. (Souris, Kings Co.; PEI), and N.S. (Queens and Cape Breton counties; ACAD; NSPM).

P. sagittatum L.   Arrow-leaved Tearthumb.   Gratte-cul
/T/EE/   (T)   Fresh to brackish marshes and wet meadows from s Man. (N to the E shore of L. Winnipeg at ca. 52°N) to Ont. (N to the N shore of L. Superior and Renfrew and Carleton counties), Que. (N to the Côte-Nord and Gaspé Pen.), Nfld., N.B., P.E.I., and N.S., s to Tex. and Fla. [*Tracaulon* Small].

P. scabrum Moench
Eurasian; introd. in cult. ground, waste places, shores, etc., in Alaska (Fairbanks; Talkeetna), s Dist. Mackenzie (Yellowknife; W.J. Cody, Can. Field-Nat. 70(3):111. 1956), s B.C. (Vancouver Is.; Queen Charlotte Is.), Alta. (Fort Saskatchewan; CAN), Sask. (N to Beauval, 55°09′N; Breitung 1957*a*), Man., Ont. (N to the N shore of L. Superior; collections from w James Bay N to ca. 53°N are tentatively placed here by Dutilly, Lepage, and Duman 1954), Que. (N to E James Bay at 53°50′N and the Gaspé Pen.), s Labrador (Goose Bay, 53°19′N), Nfld., N.B., P.E.I., and N.S. [*P. tomentosum* Schrank].

P. scandens L.   Climbing False Buckwheat
/T/EE/   (Hp)   Damp thickets, clearings, and shores from s Sask. (Cypress Hills and Swift

Current; CAN; reports from B.C. and Alta. require confirmation and may be based upon in-trod. plants) to s Man. (N to Matlock, about 30 mi N of Winnipeg; WIN), Ont. (N to Rainy L., near the Man. boundary w of Thunder Bay; CAN), Que. (N to L. St. Peter in Nicolet Co.), Nfld., N.B., P.E.I., and N.S., s to Tex. and Fla. [*Bilderdykia* Greene; *Tiniaria* Small; *P. dumetorum* var. *scandens* (L.) Gray; *P. ?cristatum sensu* Rouleau 1947, not Engelm. & Gray; *P. dumetorum* of Canadian reports at least in part, not L.].

P. spergulariaeforme Meisn.
/t/W/ (T) Dry to moist soils from s B.C. (N to Kamloops; CAN) to Calif. and Colo. [*P. coarctatum* Dougl., not Meisn.; *P. lineare* Hook.].

P. tenue Michx.
/t/EE/ (T) Dry open soil from s Minn. to s Ont. (Lambton and Norfolk counties; CAN and TRT, detd. Brenckle; a collection in CAN from Georgian Bay, L. Huron, has also been referred here tentatively by Brenckle) and s Maine, s to Tex., Ala., and Ga.

P. viviparum L.   Alpine Bistort
/AST/X/GEA/ (Gst) Moist tundra, meadows, and streambanks to alpine slopes, the aggre-gate species from the Aleutian Is. and coasts of Alaska–Yukon–Dist. Mackenzie–Dist. Keewa-tin throughout the Canadian Arctic Archipelago to northernmost Ellesmere Is. and north-ernmost Ungava–Labrador, s to N Alta. (L. Athabasca), N Sask. (Hansen L., 59°11′N), Man. (s to Swampy L., about 130 mi sw of York Factory), Ont. (s to the Severn R. at ca. 55°20′N), Que. (s to s James Bay, Rimouski Co., and the Gaspé Pen.), Labrador (s to Forteau, 51°28′N), and Nfld., and in the mts. of the West through B.C. and sw Alta. to Oreg., Utah, and N.Mex.; isolated in Minn. and N Mich., cent. Ont. (L. Nipigon and the N shore of L. Superior), and in the mts. of New Eng.; circumgreenlandic; Iceland; Eurasia. MAPS and synonymy: *see* below.
1 Plant robust, to over 6 dm tall, with relatively large bulblets and small calyces; [var. *?pseudo-bistorta* Rousseau; *P. (Persicaria) macounii* Small, the type from the Pribilof Is., Alaska; Alaska and E ?Que. (type of var. *pseudo-bistorta* from Anticosti Is.)] . . . .
. . . . var. *macounii* (Small) Hult.
1 Plant relatively slender, usually less than 4.5 dm tall . . . . var. *viviparum*
  2 Radical leaves oblong to oblong-ovate, blunt at apex, rounded or cordate at base; [range of the species] . . . . f. *alpinum* (Wahl.) Polunin
  2 Radical leaves lance-linear to -oblong, acute or subacute at apex, tapering to the base.
    3 Whole spike bulbiferous; [not yet reported from our area but to be searched for] . . . .[f. *bulbiferum* Beck]
    3 Spike bearing normal flowers.
      4 Spike entirely floriferous, bulblets wanting; [not yet reported from our area but to be searched for] . . . .[f. *florigerum* Beck]
      4 Spike bearing both flowers and bulblets; [*P. fugax* Small; *Bistorta viv.* (L.) Gray; *B. littoralis* and *B. ophioglossa* Greene; incl. monstr. *paniculata* Porsild, an apparently pathological phase with a branching spike, the type from Greenland; MAPS (aggregate species): Hultén 1968b:385; Porsild 1957: map 130, p. 177; *Atlas of Canada* 1957: map 2, sheet 38; Raup 1947: pl. 23; Meusel, Jaeger, and Weinert 1965:130] . . . . f. *viviparum*

P. watsonii Small
/T/W/ (T) Moist meadows and flats from s B.C. (near Rossland at 4,500 ft elevation; CAN), s Alta. (Hand Hills; CAN), and sw Sask. (Cypress Hills; CAN) to N Calif. and N.Mex. [*P. imbricatum* Nutt., not Raf.]. MAP: L.C. Wheeler, Rhodora 40(476): map 3, p. 311. 1938.

RHEUM L.   [2197]

R. rhaponticum L.   Rhubarb.   Rhubarbe
Asiatic; commonly persisting in old gardens in N. America and occasionally escaping, as in B.C. and Sask. (Boivin 1966b), Man. (Portage la Prairie; CAN), s Ont. (Lambton Co.; Gaiser

and Moore 1966), E Que. (collection in MT from sand-flats at St-Tharsicius, Gaspé Pen.; reported from Magdalen Is. by Leon Provancher, Nat. can. (Que.) 19(12):346. 1890), N.B. (Wolf Is.; R.B. Pike and A.R. Hodgdon, Rhodora 65(761):91. 1963), and N.S. (Quarry Road, Victoria Co., Cape Breton Is.; ACAD).

RUMEX L.   [2195]   Dock, Sorrel.   Doche

(Ref.: Rechinger 1937; Sarkar 1958)
1   At least the basal leaves with 2 large basal lobes, acid-tasting (*R. graminifolius* may sometimes be sought here); flowers dioecious, the plants unisexual; (introduced perennials; some forms perhaps native).
  2   Leaves sagittate, the basal lobes directed backward; sepals enlarged in fruit and much surpassing the achene, thin and veiny; stems tufted from a deep thick taproot . . . .*R. acetosa*
  2   Leaves hastate, the basal lobes directed outward; sepals scarcely enlarged in fruit; plant spreading by slender running rootstocks . . . .*R. acetosella*
1   Principal (basal) leaves mostly unlobed (sometimes slenderly hastate in *R. graminifolius*), tapering, rounded, or subcordate at base.
  3   Flowers dioecious (rarely polygamous), the plants thus unisexual; leaves acid-tasting; perennial caespitose plants from a taproot surmounted by a usually branched crown.
    4   Leaves linear, the blades of the basal ones to about 6 cm long and 5 mm broad, sometimes with hastate lobes; stems rarely over 2.5 dm tall; (Alaska) . . . .*R. graminifolius*
    4   Leaves lanceolate, the blades of the basal ones to over 1 dm long and 2.5 cm broad, never with hastate lobes; stems to over 5 dm tall; (mts. of B.C. and sw Alta.) . . . .*R. paucifolius*
  3   Flowers mostly perfect; leaves mostly relatively broader, never hastate, scarcely acid to the taste.
    5   Fruiting calyx to 3 cm broad, roseate, the valves lacking callous tubercles ("grains"), entire, strongly reticulate-veiny; pedicels shorter than the fruiting calyx, jointed near the middle; stipules upwardly dilated; leaves broadly lanceolate to oblong-elliptic or -oblanceolate; perennial from a deep-seated woody rootstock; (s Alta. to Man.) . . . .*R. venosus*
    5   Fruiting calyx smaller; stipular sheaths close; plants with a vertical taproot.
      6   Valves of fruiting calyx with prominent salient teeth or marginal bristles; pedicels distinctly jointed near or below the middle; stems usually lacking axillary branches.
        7   A plump callous grain usually present on the midrib of only 1 valve of the fruiting calyx (*R. pulcher* may be sought here); margins of valves with prominent teeth; pedicels much longer than the fruiting calyx, jointed somewhat below midlength; basal leaves narrowly to broadly ovate, subcordate or cordate at base, crenulate, to about 3 dm long and 1.5 dm broad, usually red-veined; stem firm; perennial; (introd.) . . . .*R. obtusifolius*
        7   A plump callous grain normally present on all 3 valves; leaves entire or merely undulate.
          8   Mature valves of fruiting calyx strongly reticulate, commonly 4 or 5 mm long, with relatively coarse marginal teeth shorter than the width of the valve; stems firm; perennials of fresh habitats; (introd.).
            9   Branches numerous, making a wide angle with the main stem (this to about 5 dm tall) and forming an entangled mass in fruit; pedicels about as long as the fruiting calyx, recurved, prominently jointed at or below the middle; leaves firm, pale green, the lower ones oblong-cordate or more or less fiddle-shaped, rarely over 1 dm long . . . .*R. pulcher*
            9   Branches usually making a narrow angle with the main stem (this to about 1.5 m tall) and not becoming entangled in fruit, the

dense inflorescence with ascending branches; pedicels much
longer than the fruiting calyx, jointed toward base; lower leaves
oblong, often truncate at base, obtusish at apex, undulate-
margined, commonly 1 or 2 dm long . . . . *R. stenophyllus*

    8 Mature valves not reticulate, commonly about 2 mm long, with
marginal bristles; pedicels jointed near base; basal leaves narrowly
to rather broadly lanceolate, truncate to cordate at base; stems soft
and hollow; native annuals or biennials of brackish or saline soil.

        10 Callous grain of valve ellipsoid, turgid, rounded at summit;
bristles about as long as the breadth of the valve; (saline
habitats from Que. to N.S.) . . . . *R. persicarioides*

        10 Callous grain linear-lanceolate, tapering to summit; bristles lon-
ger than the breadth of the valve; (transcontinental) . . . . *R. maritimus*

6   Valves of fruiting calyx entire or merely denticulate; perennials.

    11 Stem from a creeping rhizome, lacking a basal rosette of leaves; leaves
round-ovate to reniform-orbicular, the basal ones to about 3 dm broad;
all 3 valves of the fruiting calyx lacking a callous grain; mature pedicels
visibly jointed near base; (introd. in N.S.) . . . . *R. alpinus*

    11 Stem from a deep taproot and the previous year's basal rosette; leaves
relatively narrower.

        12 Stems ascending or decumbent at base, with axillary branches or
leaf-tufts; leaves linear- to oblong-lanceolate, tapering to the
petiole; pedicels distinctly jointed near the base.

            13 Well-developed callous grain present on only 1 calyx-valve;
lower leaves ovate- or oblong-lanceolate, commonly not more
than 4 times as long as broad; (s Ont.) . . . . *R. altissimus*

            13 Well-developed callous grains mostly 3, one on the midrib of
each valve.

                14 Fruiting pedicels clavate, strongly deflexed and straightish,
to 5 times as long as the valves; callous grains lanceolate;
(Ont. and Que.) . . . . *R. verticillatus*

                14 Fruiting pedicels filiform, curved, rarely more than twice the
length of the valves; callous grains broader in outline; (transcontinental) . . . . *R. salicifolius*

        12 Stems erect or ascending, mostly lacking axillary branches or leaf-
tufts; leaves often broader and often truncate or cordate at base.

            15 Well-developed callous grains 3, one on the midrib of each valve.

                16 Valves 2 or 3 mm long and about 1.5 mm broad, the callous
grain almost as broad; pedicels distinctly jointed somewhat
below midlength; fruiting racemes very slender, leafy,
interrupted, loosely spreading-ascending from below the
middle of the stem; principal leaves oblong-lanceolate to
oblong; (introd.) . . . . *R. conglomeratus*

                16 Valves at least 4 mm long and about equally broad, the
callous grains much narrower; fruiting racemes upright,
forming a compact panicle.

                    17 Leaves flat, oblong-lanceolate; valves suborbicular, to
8 mm long; callous grains narrowly lanceolate, acuminate,
their bases distinctly above the base of the valve; pedicels
obscurely jointed; (essentially transcontinental) . . . .
. . . . *R. orbiculatus*

                    17 Leaves with strongly wavy-curled margins, lanceolate;
valves broadly ovate, at most 6 mm long; callous grains
often unequal, the largest one ovoid, rounded at both
ends, its base even with the base of the valve or
projecting below it; pedicels distinctly jointed below
midlength; (introd.) . . . . *R. crispus*

15 Well-developed callous grain 1 or none.
    18 A small subglobose grain present near the base of the midrib of one of the valves; pedicels distinctly jointed near base; basal leaves lance-ovate, broadly rounded to truncate or subcordate at base; (introd.).
        19 Valves to over 6 mm long, the callous grain at most 1/3 as long as the valve; pedicels to about 1 cm long; inflorescence dense, the crowded upper whorls more or less confluent . . . .
. . . . *R. patientia*
        19 Valves about 3 mm long, the callous grain commonly more than 1/2 as long; pedicels usually less than 5 mm long; inflorescence lax, the whorls rather distant . . . . . [*R. sanguineus*]
    18 Callous grains wanting or rudimentary.
        20 Pedicels obscurely jointed below the middle; lower leaves truncate or subcordate at base.
            21 Stem at most about 4 dm tall; leaves linear-lanceolate to lanceolate, thickish, only the lowermost ones subcordate at base; panicle unbranched or with a few short branches; nerves of valves thickish and indistinct; whole plant often purple-tinged; (Alaska–Yukon–Dist. Mackenzie; NE Man.) . . . . .
. . . . *R. arcticus*
            21 Stem taller; leaves oblong-lanceolate to -ovate, mostly rounded to cordate at base and tapering uniformly to apex; panicle usually compound; (transcontinental) . . . .
. . . . *R. occidentalis*
    20 Pedicels distinctly jointed below the middle; (introd.).
        22 Mature valves rotund- or reniform-cordate, as broad as or broader than long; leaves tapering to base.
            23 Leaves narrowly lanceolate, their margins very strongly wavy-curled (appearing shallowly pinnatifid when pressed) . . . . *R. pseudonatronatus*
            23 Leaves oblong-lanceolate to oblong or narrowly ovate, flat or merely slightly undulate . . . . *R. longifolius*
        22 Mature valves broadly ovate, longer than broad; lower leaves truncate, subcordate, or cordate at base.
            24 Leaves with strongly wavy-curled margins, lanceolate; valves at most 6 mm long . . . . *R. crispus*
            24 Leaves flat-margined, the lower ones broadly cordate-oblong; valves commonly over 6 mm long . . . . . . *R. patientia*

R. acetosa L.   Garden- or Meadow-Sorrel, Sourdock.   Grande Oseille
Eurasian; introd. and natzd. in N. America, as in Alaska (N to the Seward Pen.; *see* Hultén 1944: map 456, p. 780; ssp. *alpestris*), NW Dist. Mackenzie (Richardson Mts.; CAN), B.C., Alta. (N to Banff), Sask. (Rosthern and Warman; Breitung 1957a), Man. (Winnipeg and Morden), Ont. (N to near Sault Ste. Marie and Ottawa), Que. (N to Charlevoix Co. and the Gaspé Pen.), Nfld., N.B., and N.S. (reports from Labrador require confirmation); S Greenland. MAPS and synonymy: *see* below.
    In addition to the taxa keyed out below, the closely related *R. rugosus* Campd. is reported from our area by Frankton and Mulligan (1970, the revised edition of Frankton 1955).
1 Ocreae entire (or ciliate only at the top in mature specimens); panicle-branches mostly simple; [var. *alpestris* (Scop.) Hartm.; *R. alpestris* (Scop.) Löve; Alaska–B.C.– W Alta.; S Greenland; MAPS: A. Löve, Bot. Not. (1944): fig. 2, p. 243. 1944; Hultén 1968b:377] . . . . ssp. *alpestris* (Scop.) Löve
1 Ocreae ciliate around the summit, even on young stems.
    2 Panicle-branches mostly simple; leaves dark green, up to 6 times longer than broad, sagittate (their basal lobes directed backward); [var. *pratensis* Wallr.;

transcontinental; MAPS: Hultén 1968b:377; Meusel, Jaeger, and Weinert 1965:127] . . . .
. . . . ssp. *acetosa*
2   Panicle-branches repeatedly forking, the panicle usually very dense.
    3   Leaves dark green, thick, at least 4 (to 14) times longer than broad, hastate
       (their basal lobes directed outwards); [*R. thyrsiflorus* Fingerh.; Ont. to N.B.
       and N.S.; MAP: Meusel, Jaeger, and Weinert 1965:127] . . . .
       . . . . ssp. *thyrsiflorus* (Fingerh.) Hayek
    3   Leaves light green, thin, at most about 4 times longer than broad, sagittate
       (their basal lobes directed backwards); [*R. ambiguus* Gren.; E Que.: Ste-Anne-
       de-la-Pocatière, Kamouraska Co.; RIM] . . . . ssp. *ambiguus* (Gren.) Löve

R. acetosella L.   Sheep-Sorrel, Common Sorrel.   Oseille or Surette
Eurasian; a pernicious weed in sterile fields of N. America, as in the Aleutian Is. and S Alaska
(*see* Hultén 1944: maps 457a and 457b, p. 780), the Yukon (Dawson; CAN), and all the provinces (in Alta., N to L. Athabasca; in Labrador N to the Hamilton R. basin); W and E Greenland
N to ca. 75°N. MAPS and synonymy: *see* below.
1   Leaves involute-margined, commonly at least 7 times as long as broad (excluding
   lobes); valves (perianth-segments) loosely investing the achene; stems more or less
   decumbent-based; [*R. tenuifolius* (Wallr.) Löve; E Que. and N.S.] . . . . var. *tenuifolius* Wallr.
1   Leaves flat-margined, commonly not over 4 times as long as broad (excluding the
   lobes).
    2   Valves closely investing the achene, unloosening from it with difficulty, the
       achene to about 1 mm long and about as broad; stems erect; [*R. angiocarpus*
       Murb.; transcontinental; MAP: Hultén 1968b:376] . . . . var. *angiocarpus* Murb.
    2   Valves loosely investing the achene, this easily detached, to 1.5 mm long; stems
       often more or less decumbent-based; [MAP (aggregate species): Meusel, Jaeger,
       and Weinert 1965:127] . . . . var. *acetosella*
       3   Most of the basal leaves unlobed; [E Que., Nfld., and N.S.] . . . .
          . . . . f. *integrifolius* (Wallr.) Beck
       3   Most of the basal leaves hastate, with a pair of divergent basal lobes; [incl. the
          coarse extreme, var. *pyrenaeus* (Pour.) Tim.-Lagrave; transcontinental; MAP:
          Hultén 1968b:375] . . . . f. *acetosella*

R. alpinus L.   Monk's Rhubarb, Butter Dock
Eurasian; natzd. in fields and meadows of N.S. (Rockville, Yarmouth Co., where noted by Fernald 1921, as "a very striking European species which has turned up casually in New England
but here is thoroughly naturalized."; CAN; GH; a collection in ACAD from Red River, Inverness Co., Cape Breton Is., has also been placed here).

R. altissimus Wood   Pale Dock
/t/(X)/   (Hs)   Alluvial or other rich soils from Colo. to Nebr., Minn., Mich., S Ont. (Simcoe
and York counties; CAN; TRT; collection in MICH from the region N of L. Huron; reported
from Walpole Is., Lambton Co., by Dodge 1915), N.Y., and N.H., S to Ariz., Tex., and Fla. MAP:
Sarkar 1958: fig. 19 (solid dots), p. 960.

R. arcticus Trautv.
/aSs/WW/EA/   (Hs)   Moist turfy tundra and shores of lakes and ponds from the coasts of
Alaska–Yukon (*see* Hultén 1944: map 458, p. 781) and Dist. Mackenzie (W to Bathurst Inlet,
Coronation Gulf) to S Alaska, s-cent. Yukon, Great Bear L., and SW Dist. Mackenzie; isolated
in NE Man. (Churchill; CAN); N Eurasia. [*R. occidentalis* var. *nanus* (Meisn.) Trel.; incl. var. *per-
latus* Hult.]. MAP: Hultén 1968b:379.

R. conglomeratus Murr.   Clustered Dock
Eurasian; roadsides, ditches, waste ground, and shores of N. America, as in SW B.C. (Van-
couver Is. and adjacent islands and mainland; CAN) and S ?Ont. (reported from Wellington
Co., by Stroud 1941, probably on the basis of a very immature specimen in OAC from
Guelph). MAP: Meusel, Jaeger, and Weinert 1965:129.

R. crispus L.   Yellow or Curly-leaf Dock
Eurasian; introd. in moist ground and waste places in Alaska–Yukon (*see* Hultén 1944: map 459, p. 781) and all the provinces (but not yet known from Labrador). [Incl. *R. elongatus* Guss.]. MAP: Hultén 1968*b*:378.
    A hybrid with *R. obtusifolius* (× *R. crispo-obtusifolius* Meisn.) is reported from Nfld. by Rechinger (1937) and a collection in CAN from Vernon, B.C., has been referred to it by Malte. It is also reported from Ont., Que., and N.S. by Frankton and Mulligan (1970, the revised edition of Frankton 1955).

R. graminifolius Lamb.
/aST/W/EA/   (Hs)   Gravelly or rocky tundra in the Aleutian Is. and Alaska (N to the Seward Pen.; *see* Hultén 1944: map 463, p. 781); NE ?Greenland; N Eurasia. MAP: Hultén 1968*b*:376.
    The report of this species as native in Nfld. by Fernald *in* Gray (1950) requires confirmation. (*See* note under *Luzula campestris*).

R. longifolius DC.
Eurasian; introd. in fields and waste places in the Aleutian Is. and SE Alaska (*see* Hultén 1944: map 460, p. 781; *R. dom.*), B.C. (Boivin 1966*b*), Sask. (N to Davidson, about 60 mi SE of Saskatoon), Man. (Otterburne, about 30 mi S of Winnipeg), Ont. (N to Michipicoten, E end of L. Superior; CAN), Que. (N to Anticosti Is. and the Gaspé Pen.), Nfld., N.B., P.E.I., and N.S.; S Greenland. [*R. domesticus* Hartm.]. MAP: Hultén 1968*b*:379.

R. maritimus L.   Golden Dock
/ST/X/EA/   (T (Hs))   Saline, brackish, or alkaline marshes and shores (and as a weed in waste ground), the aggregate species from SE Alaska and cent. Yukon to Great Slave L., L. Athabasca (Alta. and Sask.), Man. (N to Churchill), Ont. (N to Sachigo L. at ca. 54°N, 92°W, and Attawapiskat, W James Bay, ca. 53°N), Que. (N to NE James Bay at 54°37′N, Anticosti Is., and the Gaspé Pen.), P.E.I., and N.S. (not known from N.B. or Nfld.), S to Calif., N.Mex., Ark., Ill., and W N.Y.; S. America; Eurasia. MAPS and synonymy: *see* below.
1   Basal and lower stem-leaves flat, narrowly lanceolate, tapering gradually to a
    cuneate base; [introd. in the E U.S.A. and reported from Dawson, the Yukon, by
    Hultén 1944, where perhaps introd.; other reports of the typical form from our area
    apparently refer to the following taxon; MAP: Hultén 1968*b*:382] . . . . var. *maritimus*
1   Basal and lower stem-leaves narrowly to broadly lanceolate, with more or less
    crisped margins and truncate to cordate bases; [*R. fueginus* Phil.; *R. persicarioides*
    of W Canadian reports, not L.; transcontinental; MAP: Hultén 1968*b*:383]. The hybrid
    between *R. maritimus* and *R. stenophyllus* (× *R. alexidis* Boivin; type from Regina,
    Sask.) would presumably relate to var. *fueginus* . . . . var. *fueginus* (Phil.) Dusén

R. obtusifolius L.   Red-veined or Bitter Dock
Eurasian; introd. in usually moist ground in the Aleutian Is., S Alaska (Juneau), B.C. (Queen Charlotte Is.; Vancouver Is. and adjacent islands and mainland), Ont. (N to Ottawa), Que. (N to the Gaspé Pen.), Nfld., N.B., P.E.I., and N.S.; SW Greenland. [Incl. ssp. *agrestis* (Fries) Danser; *R. pratensis sensu* Fowler 1879 and 1885, not Mert. & Koch nor Dulac; *R. sanguineus sensu* McSwain and Bain 1891, not L.; *R. viridis sensu* Lindsay 1878, not Sm.]. MAP: Hultén 1968*b*:378.

R. occidentalis Wats.   Western Dock
/ST/X/   (Hs)   Wet ground and shores from the Aleutian Is. and S Alaska (*see* Hultén 1944: map 461a; *R. fenestratus*) to cent. Yukon, Great Bear L., Great Slave L., L. Athabasca (Alta. and Sask.), Man. (N to the Cochrane R. at 58°57′N), northernmost Ont., Que. (N to SE Hudson Bay, the Côte-Nord, and Gaspé Pen.), Labrador (N to the Hamilton R. basin), Nfld., and N.S. (Horseshoe L., Lunenburg Co.; ACAD; the report from N.B. by Fowler 1885, taken up by John Macoun 1886, requires confirmation; not known from P.E.I.), S to Calif., Tex., S.Dak., and Maine. [*Lapathum* Lunell; incl. vars. *labradoricus* (Rech. f.) Lepage and *perplexus* Lepage, and *R. confinis, R. fenestratus,* and *R. procerus* Greene]. MAPS: Hultén 1968*b*:380 *(R. fen.)*; Porsild 1966: map 53, p. 73.

R. orbiculatus Gray   Water-Dock
/T/X/   (Hs)   Wet ground and shores from s ?B.C. (Henry 1915; lower Fraser R.) to Alta. (Boivin 1966b), Sask. (N to Ile-à-la-Crosse, 55°27′N), Man. (N to Wekusko L., about 80 mi NE of The Pas), Ont. (N to the NW shore of L. Superior and s James Bay), Que. (N to the Côte-Nord and Anticosti Is.), Nfld., N.B., P.E.I. (Bunbury and Tracadie; CAN; GH), and N.S., s to Nebr., Ohio, and N.J. [Incl. the reduced extreme, var. *borealis* Rech. f.; *R. hydrolapathum* var. *americanum* Gray; *R. britannica* of most Canadian reports, not L.; *R. ?acutus* L.].

R. patientia L.   Patience-Dock.   Patience
Eurasian; introd. in waste places and thickets and along roadsides in the U.S.A. and known from Ont. (N to the Ottawa dist.). Reports from elsewhere in Canada require confirmation.
   R. confertus Willd., a closely related Asiatic species, is known from Canada only through a collection in CAN taken in 1953 by the writer from near Ethelbert, Man., distributed as *R. patientia,* revised by C. Frankton.

R. paucifolius Nutt.   Alpine Sheep-Sorrel
/T/WW/   (Hs)   Moist meadows and slopes at low elevations to above timberline from B.C. (N to Ootsa L. at ca. 54°N; Eastham 1947) and SW Alta. (N to near Jasper; CAN) to Calif. and Colo. [*R. geyeri* (Meisn.) Trel.].

R. persicarioides L.   Seashore Dock
/T/D (coastal)/   (T)   Saline or brackish marshes and shores, in the West from Wash. to Calif., in the East from E Que. (St. Lawrence R. estuary between the Quebec City dist. and Rimouski Co.; reported from Chambly Co. in the Montreal dist. by Rechinger 1937), N.B. (Miscou Is., Gloucester Co.; GH), P.E.I. (Queens Co.; GH), and N.S. (Broad R., Queens Co.; GH) to NE Mass.

R. pseudonatronatus Borbas
Eurasian; reported as introd. in Ont. by Gillett (1958; Ottawa dist.) and in the Yukon and from B.C. to Que. by Boivin (1968). [*R. fennicus* Murb.].
   A hybrid with *R.* (*salicifolius* ssp.) *triangulivalvis* (× *R. franktonis* Boivin, the type from Kindersley, Sask.) was first reported from that locality by G.A. Mulligan (Can. J. Bot. 37(1):89. 1959).

R. pulcher L.   Fiddle-Dock
Eurasian; introd. in waste places of the U.S.A. and reported from SW B.C. by Carter and Newcombe (1921; Mayne Is.). A collection from s Ont. (Toronto, where taken by Scott in 1904; CAN) has been referred by Boivin to the closely related *R. dentatus* L. of Eurasia. The two taxa may be distinguished as follows:
1   Lower leaves puberulent, cordate-based; pedicels jointed near the middle; [SW B.C.] . . . .
. . . .*R. pulcher*
1   Lower leaves glabrous, cuneate to truncate (rarely subcordate) at base; pedicels
    jointed below the middle; [Toronto, Ont.; also reported from Lethbridge, Alta., by
    Boivin 1968] . . . .*R. dentatus* L.

R. salicifolius Weinm.
/ST/X/EA/   (Hs)   Coastal sands, shores, alpine meadows, and rocky slopes, the aggregate species from cent. Alaska–Yukon (*see* Hultén 1944: map 467, p. 781; *R. sib.*) and NW Dist. Mackenzie to L. Athabasca (Alta. and Sask.), Man. (N to Churchill), Ont. (N to the Severn R. at ca. 56°N), Que. (N to the E Hudson Bay watershed at ca. 57°N and the Côte-Nord), SE Labrador (Hustich and Pettersson 1943; Abbe 1955), Nfld. (Rouleau 1956), N.B., P.E.I., and N.S., s to Calif., Mexico, Tex., Mo., Ohio, and New Eng. (?introd.); Eurasia. MAPS and synonymy: *see* below.
1   Perianth-valves thin, 1 or more usually covered by a large tubercle well over 2/3 as
    long and broad as the valve; [*R. pallidus* Bigel.; *R. subarcticus* Lepage;
    R. transitorius Rech. f.; s Alaska–Yukon–w Dist. Mackenzie–B.C.; NE ?Ont. and cent.

Que. (James Bay; Anticosti Is.); MAPS: Hultén 1968b:380 (*R. trans.*); combine the
maps by Sarkar 1958: fig. 22 (*R. pall.*), p. 964, and fig. 26 (*R. sub.*), p. 969] . . . .
. . . . ssp. *salicifolius*
1   Perianth-valves relatively thick, the tubercles (when present) commonly on all 3
    valves but usually not more than 1/2 as long as the valves and less than 1/2 as broad . . . .
    . . . . ssp. *triangulivalvis* Danser
    2   Tubercles wanting; [*R. hesperius* Greene; *R. utahensis* Rech. f.; *R. ?sibiricus* Hult.
        in part; ?Alaska–Yukon–Dist. Mackenzie; B.C. (Vancouver Is.; Carter and
        Newcombe 1921), Alta. (near Calgary), and Man. (Grand Rapids, near the NW end
        of L. Winnipeg); MAP: combine the maps by Sarkar 1958: fig. 24 (*R. utah.; also
        reported from S Yukon by Porsild 1951a), p. 967, and fig. 25 (*R. hesp.*), p. 968] . . . . . .
        . . . . var. *montigenitus* Jeps.
    2   Tubercles well developed.
        3   Valves about 4 mm long; [*R. (Lapathum) mex.* Meisn.; Utah and Colo. to
            Mexico, reports from our area referring to other entities; MAP: Sarkar 1958:
            fig. 19 (rings), p. 960] . . . . var. *mexicanus* (Meisn.) Hitchc.
        3   Valves mostly about 3 mm long (to 3.5 mm); [*R. sibiricus* Hult. in large part;
            range of the species; MAPS: combine the maps by Sarkar 1958: fig. 19 (dots;
            R. tri.), p. 960, and fig. 26 (dots; *R. sib.*), p. 969; the map for *R. mexicanus* by
            Hultén 1968b:381, is applicable here] . . . . var. *triangulivalvis*

[*R. sanguineus* L.]   Bloody or Red-veined Dock
[Eurasian; reports from Canada, as by Lindsay (1878; *R. viridis,* near Halifax, N.S.), John Macoun (1886; S Ont., N.S., and E Que.), and R. Campbell (Can. Rec. Sci. 6(6):342–51. 1895;
near St. John, N.B.) require confirmation, some of them proving referable to *R. obtusifolius*
(relevant collections in NBM and NSPM). (*R. viridis* Sm.).]

R. stenophyllus Ledeb.
Eurasian; reported from SW Alta. by Boivin (1966b), from S Sask. by Clarence Frankton (Can-
ada National Weed Committee, Western Section, Research Report, 1955, p. 121–25; a few mi
N of Swift Current and not uncommon elsewhere), from S Man. by D. Löve and J.-P. Bernard
(1959:389; Rhodora 60(710):54. 1958; near Otterburne, about 30 mi S of Winnipeg), and from
E Que. by Ernest Lepage (Nat. can. (Que.) 89(2):77. 1962; railway ballast at Rimouski).
[*R. obtusifolius sensu* Breitung 1957a, the relevant collection in DAO, rev. Frankton].

R. venosus Pursh   Winged or Veined Dock, Sour Greens
/T/WW/   (Grh)   Sand dunes and sandy riverbanks to dry gravelly soil and grasslands from
Wash. to S Alta. (Lethbridge; Dunmore; Grassy Lake; Medicine Hat), Sask. (reported N to Fort
Carlton, about 30 mi SW of Prince Albert, by John Macoun 1886), and S Man. (N to Fisher
Branch, about 75 mi N of Winnipeg), S to N Calif., N.Mex., Nebr., and Wisc. (?introd.). MAP: Sar-
kar 1958: fig. 16, p. 956.

R. verticillatus L.   Swamp- or Water-Dock
/T/EE/   (Hs)   Swampy ground and shallow water from Minn. to Ont. (N to the Ottawa dist.)
and Que. (N to the Gaspé Pen.), S to Tex. and Fla. MAP: Sarkar 1958: fig. 17, p. 958.

TOVARA Adans.   [2201]   Jumpseed

T. virginiana (L.) Raf.
/T/EE/   (Grh)   Rich woods and thickets from Minn. to Ont. (N to Waterloo Co.), Que. (N to
Beauport, near Quebec City; MT; reports from P.E.I. and N.S. require confirmation or the spe-
cies now extinct there; not known from N.B.), and N.H., S to E Tex. and Fla. [*Polygonum* L.].
MAP: Fernald 1929: map 4, p. 1488 (the Asiatic area should probably be deleted, Hui-Lin Li
(Rhodora 54(637):19–25. 1952) considering the plant of that area to be a distinct species,
T. filiformis (Thunb.) Nakai).

CHENOPODIACEAE (Goosefoot Family)

(Ref.: P.C. Standley, N. Am. Flora 21:1–93. 1916)
Herbs (or stems sometimes more or less woody) with simple, chiefly alternate (the lower often opposite), exstipulate leaves (*Salicornia* with minute opposite leaves). Flowers small or minute, greenish, perfect or unisexual, apetalous. Calyx usually 5-parted (in *Corispermum* and *Monolepis* reduced to a single sepal). Stamens commonly as many as the calyx-lobes and opposite them. Pistil 1. Styles or sessile stigmas commonly 2. Ovary superior. Fruit a 1-seeded utricle often enclosed by the calyx.

1 Stems leafless, fleshy and jointed, the leaves reduced to small appressed opposite scales; flowers sunk in hollows of the thickened upper joints of the stem, forming a narrow fleshy spike . . . . *Salicornia*
1 Stems leafy, scarcely fleshy, not jointed, the leaves all or chiefly alternate, not scale-like but sometimes linear; flowers not sunk in pits.
  2 Leaves filiform to linear, linear-lanceolate, or linear-oblong, entire, sessile.
    3 Stems armed with sharp rigid spines 1 or 2 cm long, yellowish white, becoming greyish; leaves linear-filiform or linear, to about 4 cm long; staminate flowers in cylindric terminal spikes to 3 cm long; pistillate flowers solitary in the leaf-axils; nearly glabrous branching shrub to about 3 m tall; (alkaline prairies from SE B.C. to S Sask.) . . . . *Sarcobatus*
    3 Stems unarmed.
      4 Calyx-lobes each terminating in a slender hooked dorsal spine; flowers solitary or in small clusters arranged in leafy-bracted short spikes in the upper leaf-axils; leaves linear-oblong or narrowly lanceolate, rather fleshy, 1 or 2 cm long; plant more or less finely tomentose or villous especially above, to over 1 m tall; annual; (introd. in S B.C.–Alta.) . . . . *Bassia*
      4 Calyx-lobes not terminating in a hooked spine.
        5 Plant permanently hoary with dense stellate pubescence and intermingling long hairs, the pubescence at first white, later reddish brown; flowers densely clustered in the upper leaf-axils, the 2-horned fruiting bractlets densely long-haired on the sides; leaves linear or linear-lanceolate, with revolute margins; stem woody at base; perennial; (S Yukon; S Alta. to SW Man.) . . . . *Eurotia*
        5 Plants not stellate-pubescent, or, if so, soon glabrate; leaves not revolute-margined; stem not woody but often rather hard; chiefly annuals (*Beta* usually biennial; 2 species of *Atriplex* perennial).
          6 Leaves spine-tipped, the principal ones filiform, to about 7 cm long; flowers usually solitary in the axils of the shorter and broader upper leaves; plant very bushy . . . . *Salsola*
          6 Leaves not spine-tipped, at most subulate-pointed.
            7 Leaves thick and somewhat fleshy, terete or plano-convex in cross-section; flowers sessile in groups of commonly 3 in the leaf-axils; calyx deeply 5-lobed, wingless, at maturity 1 or 3 of the lobes commonly more or less strongly keeled; seeds with a flattish-spiral embryo and scanty or no endosperm; stems procumbent, decumbent, or spreading-ascending, simple or branching from base . . . . *Suaeda*
            7 Leaves scarcely fleshy, flat at least toward base; seeds with embryo coiled into a ring around the usually copious endosperm; stems erect or ascending, usually bushy-branched; (plants commonly of dry sandy habitats).
              8 Flowers forming short dense leafy spikes in the leaf-axils; calyx subglobose, at maturity about 2.5 mm broad, star-shaped, each sepal incurved over the fruit and bearing a short dorsal wing; flowering branches and calyces villous, the long hairs reddish brown in age; leaves linear to linear-

lanceolate, more or less pubescent or glabrate, commonly
ciliate toward base; stem to about 1 m tall; (introd.) . . . . . . *Kochia*

   8 Flowers solitary in the axils of upper leaves or scarious-
margined bracts; fruiting-calyx not winged; plants rarely over
5 dm tall.

      9 Flowers in the axils of the upper leaves, each subtended
by a pair of conspicuous spine-like scarious whitish
bractlets; calyx deeply 5-lobed, the scarious sepals erect
or nearly so; leaves linear-spatulate, sharp-pointed,
broadened at the scarious-margined base, crowded,
about 1 cm long; stem at most about 2 dm tall; (introd.) . . . . . .
. . . . *Polycnemum*

      9 Flowers in the axils of lanceolate to ovate pointed
scarious-margined bractlets to about 1 cm long, forming
loose to dense terminal spikes; calyx a single delicate
sepal on the inner side; leaves linear to linear-lanceolate;
stem to about 6 dm tall . . . . *Corispermum*

2 Leaves relatively broader, often toothed or lobed, petioled or the upper ones
sessile.

  10 Leaves and stem stellate-pubescent; leaves lanceolate to elliptic-ovate, entire,
those of the flowering branches bract-like; flowers unisexual; calyx consisting
of 3 or 4 hyaline erect sepals; staminate fruit 2-winged at summit; spikes
slender, bractless, terminating the branches; mature bracts and calyx
becoming whitish and conspicuous; (introd. from B.C. to N.S.) . . . . *Axyris*

  10 Leaves and stem not stellate-pubescent, the leaves often toothed or lobed.

    11 Root becoming much enlarged and fleshy; calyx becoming hard and
woody in fruit, 2 or more of them cohering to form the dry "seed" of
commerce; flowers subtended by minute bractlets; (garden-escape) . . . . . [*Beta*]

    11 Root not markedly enlarged; calyx not becoming woody.

      12 Mature fruiting calyx red or purple, with a broad continuous
membranous horizontal wing; flowers very small and numerous, perfect
or pistillate, in a diffuse panicle; leaves oblong, irregularly sinuate-
dentate, the teeth tipped with a sharp point; branches angled and
striate; plant more or less cobwebby-pubescent or becoming glabrate;
(Sask. to Ont.) . . . . *Cycloloma*

      12 Mature fruiting calyx (when present) wingless or nearly so.

        13 Flowers mostly perfect or pistillate or a mixture of both, not
embraced between bractlets.

          14 Calyx a solitary green bract-like fleshy sepal; pericarp minutely
but strongly pitted; leaves scarcely mealy, hastate, passing
gradually into foliaceous bracts; stem branched from the base;
(Alaska–B.C. to Man.; introd. eastwards) . . . . *Monolepis*

          14 Calyx usually 5-parted, more or less enveloping the fruit; leaves
often sparsely to densely white-mealy beneath, entire or lobed;
branches ascending or prostrate . . . . *Chenopodium*

        13 Flowers unisexual, the pistillate (and their resulting fruits) embraced
between a pair of triangular to suborbicular appressed foliaceous
bractlets, these usually united at least at base.

          15 Bractlets of the pistillate flowers laterally compressed (each with
a distinct, minutely toothed dorsal keel), strongly 2-lipped at tip,
5 or 6 mm long; leaves rhombic-ovate to suborbicular, rounded
at apex, acutely sinuate-dentate, broadly cuneate to a long
petiole, at first sparingly mealy but soon glabrate, 2 or 3 cm long
and broad; stem prostrate or ascending, to about 4 dm long,
sparingly mealy; (s Alta. and s Sask.) . . . . *Suckleya*

          15 Bractlets of the pistillate flowers dorsiventrally compressed (thus
lacking a dorsal keel).

16 Stigmas 2 (rarely 3); fruit enclosed between 2 large flat
   bractlets; leaves often permanently mealy . . . . *Atriplex*
16 Stigmas 4 or 5; fruit (the "seed" of commerce) enclosed in a
   2–4-spined capsule-like body formed of the 2 bractlets; plant
   glabrous; (garden-escape) . . . . , ... [*Spinacia*]

ATRIPLEX L. [2229] Orach. Arroche

1 Plants perennial, shrubby or at least woody at base, much branched; leaves entire,
unlobed, linear or linear-spatulate to elliptic, oblong, or narrowly obovate, mostly
alternate (the lower ones often opposite), greyish-scurfy, to 5 cm long.
  2 Plants woody only at base, the younger stems herbaceous, rarely over 4 dm tall;
    fruiting bractlets not prominently winged lengthwise, indurate-spongy, from
    nearly smooth to prominently tuberculate, united to well above the middle, to
    7 mm long, their margins irregularly toothed; (Alta. to s Man.) . . . . *A. nuttallii*
  2 Plants woody almost throughout, usually over 4 dm tall; fruiting bractlets usually
    prominently winged lengthwise, undulate to sharply toothed, smooth; (?Alta.) . . . .
    . . . . [*A. canescens*]
1 Plants annual, herbaceous; leaves entire or toothed, mostly broader and commonly
hastate-based by a pair of outwardly projecting basal lobes.
  3 Plants soon green and glabrate (or the lower leaf-surfaces and the inflorescence
    permanently but sparingly mealy); leaves alternate above, opposite below (only
    the lowermost few opposite in *A. hortensis*); bractlets enclosing the pistillate
    flowers smooth.
    4 Leaves entire, not hastate-lobed, sessile, lanceolate to elliptic or ovate, acute
      or acuminate, cuneate to rounded at base, to about 3 cm long and 1 cm
      broad; bractlets of pistillate flowers about 2 mm long, united to tip, strongly
      mealy but otherwise smooth, the enclosed flower with a minute 3–4-parted
      perianth; stems spreading to erect, to about 3 dm long; (s Alta. and s Sask.) . . . . . .
      . . . . *A. dioica*
    4 Principal leaves usually more or less toothed (or at least hastate-lobed at
      base; if essentially entire, their bases commonly broad, subtruncate to
      hastate or cordate), at least the lower ones rather slender-petioled; bractlets
      of pistillate flowers to over 5 mm long, free to below the middle, the enclosed
      flower usually lacking a perianth.
      5 Pistillate bractlets to over 1.5 cm long and 1 cm broad; leaves lance-
        oblong to ovate-triangular, entire to undulate or sinuate-dentate, abruptly
        short-cuneate to cordate or slightly hastate at base, their blades to about
        2 dm long and 1 dm broad; stems to about 2.5 dm tall; (introd.) . . . . *A. hortensis*
      5 Pistillate bractlets smaller; leaves and stems smaller; (plants chiefly of
        saline and alkaline habitats).
        6 Spike-like inflorescence leafy-bracted to tip; fruiting bractlets to about
          8(12) mm long, united to about the middle, their sides obscurely
          pebbled; seeds to 4 mm broad; leaves triangular to ovate, very fleshy,
          entire or sinuate-toothed; (NW Dist. Mackenzie and the Hudson Bay–
          James Bay and Atlantic coasts) . . . . *A. glabriuscula*
        6 Spike-like branches of the inflorescence leafy-bracted only at base;
          fruiting bractlets mostly 1–5 mm long, united only at base, freely
          pebbled or tuberculate; seeds 1 or 2 mm broad; leaves less fleshy, at
          least the lower ones hastate and also often dentate; (transcontinental) . . . . .
          . . . . *A. patula*
  3 Plants copiously and permanently mealy or scurfy (especially on the lower leaf-
    surfaces and in the inflorescence), rarely over 1 m tall; leaves commonly not over
    5 or 6 cm long, mostly alternate (usually only the lowermost ones opposite),
    commonly oval or oblong to ovate, deltoid, or rhombic.
    7 Principal leaves prominently toothed, to about 3 cm long, they and the

branches usually all alternate (the lowest rarely subopposite); pistillate
bractlets to 1 cm long.

8   Stem prostrate or depressed, the lower branches horizontal; principal
    leaves rhombic-ovate, irregularly crenate-dentate; fruiting bractlets with
    many conspicuous free veins near the margins, toothed only near the
    whitish base, the limb subherbaceous; (introd. along sandy shores of E
    Que., N N.B., and P.E.I.) . . . . *A. laciniata*

8   Stem mostly erect, with ascending branches; principal leaves ovate to
    rhombic-ovate, deeply sinuate-toothed, greyish-mealy; fruiting bractlets
    finely reticulate, dentate to near apex; seeds at most about 2 mm broad;
    (introd.).

    9   Staminate flowers in the uppermost leaf-axils and in terminal spikes
        less than 1 cm long . . . . *A. rosea*
    9   Staminate flowers in leafless terminal spikes to 15 cm long . . . . . [*A. tatarica*]

7   Leaves often hastate-based, otherwise entire or only shallowly undulate-
    toothed.

    10 Pistillate bractlets to 1 cm long, hard and bony but with greenish, dentate
       to laciniate-tuberculate margins and usually conspicuously tuberculate
       faces; seed about 1 mm long; leaves to 5 (rarely 6) cm long, greyish-scurfy,
       the principal ones slender-petioled; (B.C. to Man.) . . . . *A. argentea*
    10 Pistillate bractlets less than 5 mm long.

       11 Pistillate bractlets only 2 or 3 mm long, united to tip, cuneate at base,
          rounded to truncate at summit, the summit bearing a few tiny teeth, the
          united lateral margins entire, the faces smooth or rarely obscurely
          tuberculate; leaves sessile or subsessile, to about 4 cm long; (B.C.) . . . .
          . . . . *A. truncata*
       11 Pistillate bractlets 3 or 4 mm long, broadly spatulate to oblong, ending
          in an entire greenish lobe, the faces short-tuberculate; principal leaves
          slender-petioled, to about 2 cm long, prominently 3-veined; (Alta.) . . . .
          . . . . *A. powellii*

A. argentea Nutt.   Saltbush, Silverscale
/T/WW/   (T)   Dry plains and alkaline flats from S B.C. (N to Kamloops; CAN) to S Alta. (Red
Deer R. and Medicine Hat; CAN), S Sask. (N to Mortlach, about 20 mi W of Moose Jaw), and S
Man. (N to Miniota, about 50 mi NW of Brandon), S to Calif. and Tex.; introd. eastwards, as in S
?Ont. (a collection in OAC from Lincoln Co. probably belongs here).

[*A. canescens* (Pursh) Nutt.]   Shadscale, Wingscale
[Saline flats of the W U.S.A. (N to Wash. and S.Dak.). The inclusion of Alta. in the range assigned to var. *aptera* (Nels.) Hitchc. (*A. aptera* Nels.; fruiting bracts at most about 8 mm long
rather than to about 2 cm, the plant low and spreading rather than usually well over 4 dm tall)
by Hitchcock et al. (1964) and Rydberg (1922; *A. aptera*) requires confirmation. (*Calligonum*
Pursh).]

A. dioica (Nutt.) Macbr.   Rillscale
/T/WW/   (T)   Dry plains and hills from Mont. to S Alta. (Hand Hills; Sunnynook) and S Sask.
(Elbow; Bracken; Val Marie; Wood Mountain), S to Wyo. and W Nebr. [*Kochia* Nutt.; *Endolepis*
Standl.; *E. suckleyi* Torr., not *Obione suckleyana* Torr., which is *Suckleya suckleyana* (Torr.)
Rydb.; *A. endolepis* Wats.].

A. glabriuscula Edmonston
/ST/(X)/GE/   (T)   Coastal sands and salt-marshes: NW Dist. Mackenzie (Porsild and Cody
1968); NE Man. (Churchill; CAN) and N Ont. (W James Bay N to ca. 54°30′N); Que. (E James
Bay N to 54°19′N; St. Lawrence R. estuary from Baie-St-Paul, Charlevoix Co., and Trois-Pistoles, Temiscouata Co., to the Côte-Nord, Anticosti Is., and Gaspé Pen.; a collection in MT
from the Boucherville Is., opposite Montreal, where probably introd. in ship-ballast, appears
referable here), S Labrador (Red Bay, ca. 51°45′N; GH), Nfld., N.B. (St. Andrews and Grand

Manan, Charlotte Co., and Miscou Is., Gloucester Co.; CAN; GH; not known from P.E.I.), and N.S. to s New Eng.; s ?Greenland (an immature specimen in CAN may belong here); Iceland; NW Europe. [*A. patula* ssp. *glab.* (Edmonston) Hall & Clements]. MAPS: Hultén 1958: map 266. p. 284; Meusel, Jaeger, and Weinert 1965:134.

Var *oblanceolata* Vict. & Rousseau (*A. patula* var. *ob.* (V. & R.) Boivin; leaves entire rather than acutely angled or toothed) occurs throughout the N. American area, which should probably be extended to include w Greenland N to 64°21'N, collections in CAN from that region having been placed here by Porsild.

A. hortensis L.   Garden Orach
Asiatic; a garden-escape to waste places and dumps in N. America, as in Alaska (Fairbanks), Dist. Mackenzie (Porsild and Cody 1968), B.C. (N to Kamloops; Eastham 1947), Alta. (N to Peace River, 56°14'N; Raup 1942), Sask. (Breitung 1957a), Man. (Brandon; Stonewall; Morris; Winnipeg), Ont. (N to Frontenac Co.; OAC), and Que. (N to Bonaventure Is., Gaspé Pen.; Groh and Frankton 1949a). [Incl. *A. nitens* Schk.]. MAPS: Hultén 1968b:399; Clarence Frankton and I.J. Bassett, Can. J. Bot. 46(10): fig. 5 (Canadian stations), p. 1313. 1968.

The crimson-leaved ornamental, var. *atrosanguinea* Hort., is reported by Breitung (1957a) as occasionally escaping in Sask.

A. laciniata L.
European; introd. (probably largely in ship ballast) along sandy shores of E Que. (Grindstone Is., Magdalen Is.; GH; CAN), NE N.B. (Miscou Is. and Youghal, Gloucester Co., and Fox Is., Miramichi Bay, Northumberland Co.; CAN), P.E.I. (Brackley Point, Queens Co.; CAN), and N.S. (DAO). [*A. sabulosa* Rouy; *A. arenaria* Woods, not Nutt.; *A. maritima* Hallier, not Crantz]. MAPS *(A. sab.):* Hultén 1958: map 267 (indicating additional stations in the Gaspé Pen., E Que.), p. 287; Fernald 1929: map 32, p. 1502.

Because of its apparently native habitat in E N. America, Fernald *in* Gray (1950) considers the plant to be native there. Hultén (1958) notes that, "Of this it must be said that a seashore plant must naturally occupy similar habitats in a country where it is introduced to those it occupies in the areas where it is indigenous." *See* note under *Luzula campestris.*

A. nuttallii Wats.   Moundscale
/T/WW/   (Ch)   Dry alkaline prairies and flats from Wash. to s Alta. (N to Lethbridge and Medicine Hat; CAN), s Sask. (N to Humboldt, 52°12'N), and s Man. (Brenda; Melita; Thornhill; North Star; Morden; Morris), s to N Calif., N.Mex., and Nebr.

A. patula L.   Spearscale
/ST/X/EA/   (T)   Saline, brackish, or rich soils and waste places, both coastal and inland, the aggregate species from Alaska (N to Kotzebue Sound; not known from the Yukon) and SW Dist. Mackenzie to northernmost Alta., Sask. (N to Tisdale, 52°51'N), Man. (N to Churchill), Ont. (N to NW James Bay at 55°07'N), Que. (N to E James Bay at ca. 54°N, the Côte-Nord, Anticosti Is., and Gaspé Pen.; not known from Labrador), Nfld., N.B., P.E.I., and N.S., s to Calif., Tex., and Fla.; Iceland; Eurasia. MAP and synonymy: *see* below.

1   Leaves linear, rarely over 4 mm broad, entire (rarely subhastate or slightly dentate); pistillate bractlets linear to narrowly lanceolate.

    2   Bractlets 3 or 4 mm long, usually denticulate-margined and tubercled on the back; [*A. littoralis* L.; cent. Ont. (Ekwan R. at 53°14'N); E James Bay; E Que., N.B., P.E.I., and N.S.; introd. in s B.C. (Vancouver Is.), s Man. (Otterburne, about 30 mi s of Winnipeg), and s Ont.] . . . . var. *littoralis* (L.) Gray

    2   Bractlets to over 1 cm long, entire, not tuberculate; [*Chenopodium zosteraefolium* Hook.; s Alaska–B.C.] . . . . var. *zosteraefolia* (Hook.) Hitchc.

1   Leaves more commonly lanceolate to oblong or ovate, often hastate or over 4 mm broad; pistillate bractlets lanceolate to deltoid.

    3   Leaf-blades mostly triangular-hastate; pistillate bractlets usually denticulate-margined and tubercled on the back; [*A. hastata* L.; *A. carnosa* Nels.; *A. lapathifolia* Rydb.; transcontinental, evidently both native and introd.] . . . . var. *hastata* (L.) Gray

3 Leaf-blades seldom hastate; pistillate bractlets smooth to denticulate-margined.
  4 Pistillate bractlets entire-margined, to over 12 mm long, usually smooth on the back; leaves lanceolate to oblong, unlobed; [*A. angustifolia* and *A. obtusa* Cham.; *A. ?drymarioides* Standley; *A. gmelinii* Meyer; Alaska–B.C. and NW Dist. Mackenzie; the similar, if not identical, var. *bracteata* Westlund (var. *subspicata* (Nutt.) Wats.; *A. subspicata* (Nutt.) Rydb.) is known from S Man. and Cape Breton Is., N.S.] . . . . var. *obtusa* (Cham.) Peck
  4 Pistillate bractlets denticulate, usually not over 6 mm long, often tuberculed on the back; leaves various, often denticulate-margined and slightly hastate-lobed at the base; [*A. ?alaskensis* Wats.; transcontinental, apparently both native and introd.; MAP (aggregate species): Hultén 1968b:398] . . . . var. *patula*

Two Asiatic species, *A. heterosperma* Bunge and *A. oblongifolia* Waldst. & Kit., are reported as introd. in Canada by Clarence Frankton and I.J. Bassett (Can. J. Bot. 46(10):1309–13. 1968). They are keyed out below to distinguish them from *A. patula* and *A. hortensis,* with which they might be confused.

1 Pistillate flowers of two kinds, some with horizontal seeds and a 3–5-lobed perianth, the rest with vertical seeds and 2 bractlets, the veins of the latter meeting above the base; [introd.] . . . .*A. hortensis*
1 Pistillate flowers all of one kind, all with vertical seeds and 2 bractlets, the veins of the latter meeting near or at the base.
  2 Bractlets broadly rhombic, entire or denticulate, smooth or tuberculate on the back . . . .*A. patula*
  2 Bractlets elliptical or rotund-cordate, usually entire, smooth; (introd.).
    3 Leaves broadly triangular-hastate; bractlets to 6 mm long, rotund or rotund-cordate; [*A. micrantha* Mey.; reported by Frankton and Bassett as introd. in B.C. (Osoyoos; Keremeos; Princeton; Kelowna; Vernon; Spences Bridge; Kamloops), Alta. (near Stirling), Man. (near Winnipegosis), and S Ont. (Kingston)] . . . .*A. heterosperma* Bunge
    3 Leaves mostly lanceolate to narrowly ovate-hastate; bractlets to 13 mm long; [reported by Frankton and Basset as introd. near Hedley, B.C.] . . . .
    . . . .*A. oblongifolia* Waldst. & Kit.

A. powellii Wats.
/T/W/ (T) Alkaline flats and badlands from Mont. to S Alta. (Pendant d'Oreille; Rosedale; Steveville, on the Red Deer R.) and S.Dak., S to Ariz. and N.Mex.

A. rosea L. Tumbling Orach
European; roadsides and waste places of N. America, as in S B.C. (several stations N to McLure, about 25 mi N of Kamloops) and S Ont. (Lincoln, Wentworth, and York counties); reported from near Halifax, N.S., by Lindsay (1878) and John Macoun (1886).

[A. tatarica L.] Tatarian Saltbush
[European; reported by Gleason (1958) as "occasional on ballast and in waste places at Atlantic seaports." Not yet known from Canada but to be looked for.]

A. truncata (Torr.) Gray
/t/W/ (T) Usually on strongly alkaline soils from S B.C. (Kamloops; near L. Windermere, Kootenay Valley; Donald, Columbia Valley) and Mont. to E Calif. and N.Mex. [*Obione* Torr.].

AXYRIS L. [2234]

A. amaranthoides L. Russian Pigweed. Ansérine de Russie
Eurasian; roadsides, waste places, and cult. fields of N. America, rapidly spreading, as in S Dist. Mackenzie (J.W. Thieret, Can. Field-Nat. 77(2):126. 1963) and B.C.–Alta., Sask. (N to Windrum L. at ca. 56°N), Man. (N to Churchill), Ont. (N to Longlac, N of L. Superior at 49°47'N), Que. (N to L. St. John, the Côte-Nord, and Gaspé Pen.), N.B., P.E.I., and N.S. (Windsor, Hants Co.; GH).

BASSIA All.   [2239]

B. hyssopifolia (Pall.) Ktze.
Eurasian; introd. in waste places of N. America, as in s B.C. (Penticton; Kootenay L.; Monte Creek; Kamloops), s Alta. (Moss 1959), and s ?Sask. (reported from alkaline soil along railway tracks at Swift Current by A.C. Budd, Blue Jay 10(4):24. 1952, but a duplicate of this collection in CAN is referable to *Kochia scoparia*).

[BETA L.]   [2221]

[B. vulgaris L.]   Beet
[A cultigen, presumably derived from the European *B. maritima* L. (*B. vulg.* var. *perennis* L.). Noted by Hitchcock et al. (1964) as sometimes persistent in waste places of N. America where, however, it does not become established. There are collections in Herb. V. from s B.C. (Chimney Creek, s of Williams Lake; roadside at Clinton).]

CHENOPODIUM L.   [2223]   Goosefoot, Pigweed.   Ansérine

(Ref.: Wahl 1952; Aellen and Just 1943; P.C. Standley, N. Am. Flora 21:9–32. 1916)
1   Plants typically glandular and strongly aromatic; seeds all or chiefly horizontal; (introd.).
   2   Leaves to 1.5 dm long or more, subentire to laciniate-pinnatifid, tapering at both ends, their lower surfaces dotted with yellow waxy atoms; panicles open; calyces only slightly if at all glandular; stem to 1.5 m tall, glabrous or merely with a waxy bloom; plant ill-scented . . . . *C. ambrosioides*
   2   Leaves mostly not over 5 cm long, subtruncate at base, sinuate-pinnatifid with obtuse or rounded lobes; calyces copiously stipitate-glandular; stem at most about 6 dm tall; plant sweet-scented . . . . *C. botrys*
1   Plants non-glandular, often farinose.
   3   Flowers in dense globose clusters to 1.5 cm thick, becoming fleshy and red in age, the clusters forming stout interrupted spikes; seed vertical; testa (seed-coat) minutely punctate-pitted; leaves mostly triangular or triangular-hastate and irregularly sinuate-dentate; plant glabrous; (transcontinental) . . . . *C. capitatum*
   3   Flowers in smaller clusters, not becoming markedly fleshy nor usually red.
      4   Seed usually vertical, the fruit then laterally flattened (but some of the seeds occasionally also horizontal in the same terminal and subterminal clusters, the fruit then flattened from the top).
         5   Leaves densely farinose beneath with short inflated hairs, to about 5 cm long, sinuate, slender-petioled; testa as in *C. rubrum;* (transcontinental, introd.) . . . . *C. glaucum*
         5   Leaves green, glabrous or only sparingly farinose beneath.
            6   Seeds about 1.5 mm broad, all vertical, the testa irregularly roughened; stigmas to about 1 mm long; leaves triangular-hastate, entire or shallowly sinuate, to 1.5 dm long; (introd.) . . . . *C. bonus-henricus*
            6   Seeds at most 1 mm broad, some of them horizontal, the testa non-radially reticulate and minutely pitted; stigmas barely evident; leaves rhombic-ovate or obovate, the principal ones hastate or coarsely toothed, the upper ones linear to lanceolate and subentire.
               7   Flower-clusters less than 4 mm thick; calyx not becoming reddish; seeds nearly always erect; terminal spike commonly branching; (essentially transcontinental in salt marshes or saline soils) . . . *C. rubrum*
               7   Flower-clusters often over 4 mm thick; calyx often becoming reddish; seeds occasionally horizontal in the same clusters as the normally erect seeds; terminal spike commonly simple . . . .
. . . . [*C. chenopodioides*]
      4   Seed usually horizontal, the fruit then flattened from the top (*C. glaucum* may

often be sought here; seeds sometimes vertical and horizontal in the same clusters of flowers, the fruit then laterally flattened).

8 Principal leaves linear to narrowly ovate, 3 or more times as long as broad, at most 2 cm broad across the basal lobes; seeds black and shining.

    9 Leaves linear or nearly so, commonly more or less fleshy, 1-nerved, to about 4 cm long and 5 mm broad, entire or the lowest subhastate; (B.C. to Man.; introd. elsewhere) . . . . *C. leptophyllum*

    9 Leaves lanceolate to ovate-lanceolate, 3-nerved; seeds about 1 mm broad.

        10 Pericarp firmly attached to the seed, the latter flattened on top and rather prominently exposed at maturity; leaves thickish; (B.C. to Sask.) . . . . *[C. hians]*

        10 Pericarp loosely attached to the seed, this rounded on the back and often covered by the sepals.

            11 Leaves thin, ovate-lanceolate, entire or, if lobed at base, the terminal lobe tapering and usually at least 1 cm broad; (s Ont. and sw Que.) . . . . *[C. foggii]*

            11 Leaves thickish, lanceolate to ovate-lanceolate or oblong, entire or, if with prominent basal lobes, then the terminal lobe lanceolate and less than 8 mm broad; (var. *oblongifolium;* s Alta. to s Man.) . . . . *C. leptophyllum*

8 Principal leaves ovate, deltoid, or deltoid-rhombic, rarely more than 3 times as long as broad, pinnately veined, entire or variously toothed.

    12 Sepals with definite apiculate tips; seeds black and shining, about 1 mm broad, exposed, the testa with close radially elongate pits with sinuous margins; leaves thin, oblong or oval, entire; plant green throughout or very sparsely farinose, flower-bearing nearly to base, the stem 4-angled; (introd.) . . . . *C. polyspermum*

    12 Sepals without definite apiculate tips; leaves variously toothed or entire.

        13 Principal leaves entire or merely with a pair of entire basal lobes.

            14 Branches weak, often prostrate; leaves thin, deltoid-rhombic, broadly rounded above the unlobed base, acutish or abruptly short-acuminate; sepals rounded on the back, united for at least 3/4 of their length; pericarp adherent to the minutely reticulate dull seed; plant ill-scented; (introd.) . . . . *C. vulvaria*

            14 Branches erect or, if spreading, not weak or prostrate; leaves rhombic to roundish-ovate, the larger ones hastate-lobed at base; sepals keeled on the back, united less than 1/2 their length; pericarp free from the smooth shining seed; plant not ill-scented; (B.C. to Man.) . . . . *C. fremontii*

        13 Principal leaves (at least the lower ones) shallowly to deeply toothed above the basal lobes.

            15 Glomerules (except in late stages) containing flowers and fruits in all stages of development; seeds shining, with low ridges radiating from the centre, over 1 mm broad, the pericarp usually readily separable; panicle loose, terminal, its branches essentially leafless; leaves thin; stem to about 1.5 m tall; (B.C. to N.S.) . . . . *C. hybridum*

            15 Glomerules containing flowers and fruits all at about the same stage of development; stem usually lower; (introd.).

                16 Leaves lustrous above, deltoid-rhombic, prominently sinuate-dentate with large acutish teeth; stigmas stout, at most about 0.1 mm long.

                    17 Seeds dull, finely punctate, over 1 mm broad, their margins acute . . . . *C. murale*

17 Seeds shining, minutely reticulate, about 1 mm broad,
their margins obtuse . . . . *C. urbicum*
16 Leaves dull or opaque above, rhombic-ovate, gradually
reduced upward to lanceolate entire bracts; stigmas long or
short but not stout.
18 Leaves oblong-ovate, prominently serrate, at least 3 times
as long as broad; seeds at most 1.2 mm broad . . . . *C. strictum*
18 Leaves typically rhombic or rhombic-ovate, less than 3
times as long as broad; seeds to 1.5 mm broad . . . . . . *C. album*

C. album L.   Lamb's-quarters, Pigweed.   Poulette grasse or Chou gras
Eurasian; a very common weed of waste and cult. ground in N. America and known from
Alaska–Yukon–Dist. Mackenzie and all the provinces (N to L. Athabasca, Churchill, Man., and
the Hamilton R. basin, Labrador); S Greenland. MAPS and synonymy (together with distinguishing keys to five closely related "microspecies" here included in the *C. album* complex): *see* below.
1   Leaves broadly linear to narrowly ovate, conspicuously toothed, their sides parallel
above the basal lobes at least to the next pair of teeth; sepals fused to or slightly
above the broadest part of the fruit; pericarp (seed-coat) adherent to the seed, finely
and regularly reticulate; seeds 1 mm broad; [introd. in S Ont.; Gaiser and Moore
1966] . . . . *C. serotinum* L.
1   Plants without the above combination of characters.
2   Leaf-blade about as broad as long, thickish, the basal lobes often 2-parted;
sepals united up to or above the broadest part of the fruit; seeds and pericarp
with essentially smooth surfaces; [introd. in Ont.] . . . . *C. opulifolium* Schrad.
2   Leaf-blade to over twice as long as broad; sepals not united up to the broadest
part of the fruit.
3   Seed and pericarp with essentially smooth surfaces; [introd., transcontinental; MAP: Hultén 1968b:395] . . . . *C. album*
4   Leaves relatively thin, chiefly less than twice as long as broad, their teeth
scarcely sharp.
5   Branches mostly ascending; flower-clusters chiefly contiguous; leaves
broadly ovate; [incl. *C. paganum* Rchb., the least farinose phase] . . . .
. . . . var. *album*
5   Branches spreading; flower-clusters more remote; leaves lanceolate to
narrowly ovate; [*C. lanceolatum* Muhl.] . . . .
. . . . var. *lanceolatum* (Muhl.) Coss. & Germ.
4   Leaves thicker, generally twice as long as broad and sharply toothed . . . .
. . . . var. *stevensii* Aellen
3   Seed and pericarp prominently honeycomb-reticulate.
6   Seeds at most 1.5 mm broad; sepals strongly keeled or even wing-keeled;
style-base often prominent; leaves thin to coriaceous; [*C. dacoticum*
Standl.; *C. zschackei* Murr.; *C. boscianum* Moq. in part; introd. from Sask.
to Ont.; MAP (ssp. *zsch.*): Hultén 1968b:395] . . . . *C. berlandieri* Moq.
6   Seeds to 2 mm broad; sepals less prominently keeled; style-base less
prominent or lacking; leaves relatively thin.
7   Seeds to 2 mm broad; leaves to 15 cm long; [introd. in Ont. and Que.] . . . . .
. . . . *C. bushianum* Aellen
7   Seeds mostly about 1.5 mm broad; leaves at most about 6 cm long;
[introd. in the Atlantic Provinces] . . . . *C. macrocalycium* Aellen

C. ambrosioides L.   Mexican-tea, Wormseed
Tropical American; introd. in waste and cult. ground of N. America, as in Alta. (Fort Saskatchewan; Groh and Frankton 1949b; CAN; DAO), Ont. (N to Carleton Co.), SW Que. (Montreal; MT), and N.S. (Boivin 1966b).
Var. *anthelminticum* (L.) Gray (at least the lower leaves laciniate-pinnatifid rather than re-

pand-toothed to entire) is known from Alta. (Fort Saskatchewan; CAN) and s Ont. (Niagara Falls and Fort Erie, Welland Co.).

C. bonus-henricus L.   Good King Henry
Eurasian; introd. into waste places in N. America, as in Ont. (N to Renfrew and Carleton counties; according to Boivin 1968, reports from Alta. and Sask. are based upon other species; the report from Man. by Shimek 1927, requires confirmation), Que. (N to the mouth of the York R., Gaspé Pen.; GH), N.B. (Bathurst; Chatham; Newcastle), P.E.I. (Brackley Point, Queens Co.; CAN), and N.S. (Annapolis and Sydney; CAN).

C. botrys L.   Jerusalem-oak, Feather-geranium.   Herbe à printemps
Eurasian; introd. along roadsides and in waste and cult. grounds of N. America, as in B.C. (N to Kamloops; CAN), Ont. (N to Cobalt, 47°25'N, and Ottawa), sw Que. (N to L. St. Peter, where very common; Raymond 1950b; see Que. map by C. Rousseau 1968: map 26, p. 65), N.B. (Fredericton, where taken by Fowler in 1878; NBM), P.E.I. (McSwain and Bain 1891), and N.S. (Pictou; CAN; also reported from Pennant by Lindsay 1878).

C. capitatum (L.) Aschers.   Strawberry-Blite, Indian-paint
/ST/X/E/   (T)   Light soils, clearings, burns, and waste places from N-cent. Alaska–Yukon (see Hultén 1944: map 485, p. 783) and the Mackenzie R. Delta to Great Bear L., Great Slave L., Sask. (N to Prince Albert), Man. (N to Churchill), Ont. (N to Fort Severn, Hudson Bay, ca. 56°N), Que. (N to Rupert House, SE James Bay at 51°29'N, L. St. John, and the Gaspé Pen.), N.B., and N.S. (not known from P.E.I.; the report from Nfld. by Reeks 1873, requires confirmation), s to Calif., N.Mex., Minn., Pa., and N.J.; Europe; introd. in Siberia. [Blitum L.]. MAP: Hultén 1968b:393.

[C. chenopodioides (L.) Aellen]
[Hitchcock et al. (1964) assign this species the range "B.C. to Sask., s. to Calif., Nev., and Colo.; Europe." They also note that many reports of C. rubrum L. from N. America are referable here. Further studies are necessary to clarify the situation for Canada. (Blitum L.; incl. C. macrospermum Hook. f.).]

[C. foggii Wahl]
[According to Wahl (1952), this species is a noteworthy development of the western C. pratericola Rydb. (C. leptophyllum var. oblongifolium Wats.). He reports it from s Ont. (Leeds Co.; also referring a collection from Lambton Co. here) and sw Que. (Pontiac Co.). The taxon should probably be merged with C. leptophyllum, from which it differs chiefly in leaf characters that probably intergrade.]

C. fremontii Wats.
/T/WW/   (T)   Fresh to saline or alkaline habitats and waste ground, the aggregate species from s B.C. (N to Kamloops; introd. at Carcross, the Yukon) to s Alta. (Milk River; CAN), Sask. (N to Saskatoon; Breitung 1957a), and s Man. (N to Brandon), s to Baja Calif., N Mexico, and Tex.
1   Leaves lanceolate, usually not at all hastate, mostly thin and often only sparsely farinose beneath; [C. atrovirens Rydb.; B.C.–Alta.: Hitchcock et al. 1964] . . . .
. . . . var. atrovirens (Rydb.) Fosberg
1   Leaves mostly rather broadly triangular and distinctly hastate-lobed at base, commonly greyish-farinose beneath.
  2   Plants low and spreading, to about 4 dm tall, densely farinose throughout; [C. incanum (Wats.) Heller; reported from the Cypress Hills region of SE Alta. and sw Sask. by Wahl 1952, but not listed by Breitung 1957a; perhaps merely an ecological variant] . . . . var. incanum Wats.
  2   Plants taller and more erect, to about 1 m tall, less densely farinose; [B.C. to sw Man.; according to Boivin 1968, the report from the Yukon by Hultén 1950, is based upon C. rubrum] . . . . var. fremontii

C. glaucum L.   Oak-leaved Goosefoot
Eurasian; waste places, roadsides, cult. land, alkaline flats, and brackish shores (ranges of Canadian taxa outlined below, var. *salinum* possibly native in N. America). MAP and synonymy: *see* below.
1   Leaves obtuse, undulate-dentate with obtuse teeth; flower-clusters mostly bractless;
    [range of the species] ....var. *glaucum*
1   Leaves acutish, serrate- or sinuate-dentate with acute, often involute teeth; flower-
    clusters nearly all bracted; [*C. salinum* Standl.; incl. ssp. *salinum* var. *pulchrum*
    Aellen; cent. Alaska (Tanana Hot Springs); Dist. Mackenzie (N to Norman Wells) and
    B.C. to Alta. (N to Fort Saskatchewan), Man. (N to Churchill), Ont. (near Ottawa; W
    James Bay watershed N to Attawapiskat, ca. 53°N), and Que. (E coast of James Bay
    N to Fort George, 53°50′N; waste heaps around cobalt mines in Timiskaming Co.);
    MAP: Hultén 1968*b*:394] ....var. *salinum* (Standl.) Boivin

[*C. hians* Standl.]
[Wahl (1952) assigns this taxon a range from B.C., Alta., and Sask. to Calif., Ariz., and N.Mex.
It should probably be merged with some other closely related species such as *C. leptophyllum*
or *C. fremontii*.]

C. hybridum L.   Maple-leaved Goosefoot
/ST/X/EA/   (T)   Thickets, shores, clearings, and waste places from cent. Yukon (Dawson;
CAN) and SW Dist. Mackenzie (J.W. Thieret, Can. Field-Nat. 75(3):115. 1961) to B.C.–Alta.,
Sask. (N to Prince Albert), Man. (N to Churchill), Ont. (N to the N shore of L. Superior), Que. (N
to the Gaspé Pen.), N.B. (Fredericton; GH), and N.S. (Springhill Junction, Cumberland Co.;
GH; not listed by Roland 1947; the report from P.E.I. by McSwain and Bain 1891, requires confirmation), S to Calif., N.Mex., Mo., and Va.; Eurasia. MAPS: Hultén 1968*b*:393 (ssp. *gig.*); Meusel, Jaeger, and Weinert 1965:132.
    The N. American plant has been separated as var. *gigantospermum* (Aellen) Rouleau
(*C. gig.* Aellen) and var. *standleyanum* (Aellen) Fern. (*C. stand.* Aellen), chiefly on the basis of
the size and degree of sculpturing of the seed. The two varieties, however, appear to represent merely the extremes of these characters in a completely intergrading series.

C. leptophyllum (Moq.) Wats.
/sT/WW/   (T)   Sandy or dry soil, the aggregate species from B.C. (N to Chilcotin, W of Williams Lake; Eastham 1947) to Alta. (N to L. Athabasca), Sask. (N to Prince Albert), and Man. (N
to Miniota, about 50 mi NW of Brandon; introd. at Churchill), S to Baja Calif., Mexico, and Tex.
MAP and synonymy: *see* below.
    Because of the rather weedy nature of this plant, its precise native range is difficult to es-
tablish. Reports from the Yukon (Hultén 1944; Porsild 1951*a*), Great Bear L., Ont. (John Macoun 1886; "Long Lake", presumably Longlac, N of L. Superior), and the sandy coast of the
Atlantic from Maine to Va. (Fernald *in* Gray 1950) are probably based upon the introd. plant. It
is also known from S Ont. (Essex, Lambton, Welland, and York counties) and N.S. (Steele's
Pond, Halifax Co.; ACAD), where also probably introd.
1   Leaves greenish, lightly farinose, mostly 1-nerved; [*C. subglabrum* (Wats.) Nels.;
    reported from Man. by Boivin 1966*b*, and from Swift Current and from near
    Saskatoon, Sask., by Wahl 1952] ....var. *subglabrum* Wats.
1   Leaves usually white-farinose beneath.
    2   At least the larger leaves 3-nerved and often over 4 mm broad; [*C. oblongifolium*
        (Wats.) Rydb.; *C. pratericola* Rydb. and its var. *oblong.* (Wats.) Wahl and ssp.
        desiccatum (Nels.) Aellen; S Alta. to S Man.] ....var. *oblongifolium* Wats.
    2   Leaves 1-nerved and mostly less than 4 mm broad; [*C. album* var. *lept.* Moq.; B.C.
        to Man.; introd. elsewhere; MAP (aggregate species): Hultén 1968*b*:396] ....
        ....var. *leptophyllum*

C. murale L.   Nettle-leaf Goosefoot
Eurasian; waste places of N. America, as in SW B.C. (ballast at Nanaimo, Vancouver Is., where
taken by John Macoun in 1887; CAN), S Ont. (reported from Chatham, Kent Co., by Groh and

Frankton 1949*b*, and from Guelph, Wellington Co., by Montgomery 1957), Que. (ballast at York, Gaspé Pen.; GH), and N.B. (James, in 1854, locality not given; GH).

C. polyspermum L.
Eurasian; introd. in waste and cult. ground in N. America, as in Sask. (a garden-weed at Wallwort, ca. 52°30′N; CAN; DAO), Ont. (N to Batchawana Bay, E end of L. Superior; Hosie 1938), Que. (N to Bellerive, Labelle Co., and Quebec City), and N.B. (St. Andrews, Charlotte Co.). [Incl. vars. *acutifolium* (Sm.) Gaud. and *obtusifolium* Gaud.].

C. rubrum L.   Coast-Blite
/sT/X/EA/   (T)   Salt-marshes and saline or alkaline soils from s Yukon–Dist. Mackenzie and B.C. to Alta. (N to Heart L. at 59°41′N; Raup 1935), Sask. (N to Wallwort, ca. 52°30′N; CAN), Man. (N to Swan River, N of Duck Mt.), Ont. (Prescott), Que. (N to Amos, 48°34′N; DAO), St-Pierre and Miquelon (Rouleau 1956; reported from Nfld. by Hooker 1838, and Fernald *in* Gray 1950), N.B. (Charlotte, Northumberland, St. John, and Restigouche counties; GH; NBM), P.E.I. (Charlottetown and Emerald; D.S. Erskine 1960), and N.S. (Sable Is.; Pictou), s to s Calif., Ariz., N.Mex., Nebr., Mo., N.Y., and N.J.; Eurasia. MAP: Hultén 1968*b*:394.
    Much of our material has been separated as var. *humile* (Hook.) Wats. (*C. humile* Hook., the type from "Marshes of the Saskatchawan"; stem prostrate, much branched at base, at most about 2.5 dm tall, rather than erect and to about 8 dm tall; leaves entire or variously few-toothed rather than prominently undulate-serrate; seeds averaging about 0.9 mm broad rather than 0.7 mm).

C. strictum Roth
Asiatic; known from dry sandy places in B.C. (Boivin 1968), Sask. (Boivin 1966*b*), s Man. (Grande Clarière; Winnipeg; Otterburne), Ont. (Ottawa; DAO), and sw Que. (Gatineau and Vaudreuil counties; DAO, detd. Wahl). [Incl. *C. glaucophyllum* Aellen].

C. urbicum L.
Eurasian; local in waste places in N. America, as in sw B.C. (Victoria and Nanaimo, Vancouver Is.; CAN), Ont. (N to Haileybury and Ottawa), Que. (Montreal dist.; St-Armand, Missisquoi Co.), N.B. (Kent, St. John, York, and Westmorland counties), and N.S. (ballast at Pictou; CAN).

C. vulvaria L.   Stinking Goosefoot
Eurasian; local in waste places of N. America, as in Ont. (Cambridge, Waterloo Co.; CAN; reported from Perth, Lanark Co., by Montgomery 1957) and E Que. (ballast at York, Gaspé Pen.; GH).

CORISPERMUM L.   [2245]   Bugseed, Tickseed

1   Spike dense, to about 8 mm thick, the axis covered by the strongly overlapping bracts; lower bracts lanceolate, commonly about 1 cm long, their bases mostly broader than and concealing the fruits; median and upper bracts ovate, about 5 mm long; fruit to 4.5 mm long, the wing about 0.5 mm broad; plant commonly more or less villous with branching hairs; (B.C. to Que.) . . . . *C. hyssopifolium*
1   Spike interrupted and very slender, the axis plainly visible, the bracts not strongly overlapping; lower bracts subulate, about 1 cm long, their bases not concealing the fruit; upper bracts lanceolate, shorter, the uppermost ones scarcely surpassing the subtended fruits; fruit to 3 mm long, narrowly winged; plant glabrous or sparingly villous with branching hairs; (s ?B.C. and s Alta. to w Ont.) . . . . *C. nitidum*

C. hyssopifolium L.   Bugseed
/ST/X/EA/   (T)   Sandy beaches, sand-hills, and sandy prairies, the aggregate species from cent. Alaska (?introd.; *see* Hultén 1944: map 492, p. 783) and Great Slave L. (Raup 1936) to B.C.–Alta., Sask. (N to North Battleford, 52°47′N), s Man., Ont. (sandy shores of Lake of the Woods; L. Erie (Norfolk and Welland counties); L. Huron (Lambton, Huron, and Simcoe coun-

ties); shore of L. Nipissing at North Bay; introd. on railway ballast and in waste-heaps along the N shore of L. Superior and at Cobalt), and Que. (sandy lake shore at Pontiac, Pontiac Co.; introd. on railway ballast at Taschereau, 48°40'N, and l'Annonciation, Labelle Co.), s to Mexico, Okla., and Ind. (adventive E to N.Y.); Eurasia. MAP and synonymy: see below.

1 Fruit distinctly winged, to 4.5 mm long; [*C. marginale* Rydb.; *C. simplicissimum* Lunell; range of the species; MAP (aggregate species): Hultén 1968*b*:400] . . . .
. . . . var. *hyssopifolium*
1 Fruit scarcely winged, to 3 mm long; [*C. emarginatum* Rydb. (*C. orientale* var. *emarg.* (Rydb.) Macbr); *C. villosum* Rydb.; ?B.C. (Boivin 1966*b*), s Alta. (Moss 1959), s Sask. (Beverley, Cadillac, and Webb; Breitung 1957*a*), and s Man. (Miami, about 40 mi s of Portage la Prairie; Matlock Beach, s end of L. Winnipeg; Gimli, w shore of L. Winnipeg about 45 mi N of Winnipeg), and reported eastwards to Que. by Boivin 1966*b*] . . . . var. *emarginatum* (Rydb.) Boivin

C. nitidum Kit.
/T/WW/EA/ (T) Dry sands and sandy prairies from s ?B.C. (reported from Lytton, about 65 mi sw of Kamloops, by Carter and Newcombe 1921) to Alta. (N to riverbank sand dunes near Jasper; CAN; collection also in CAN from sand dunes along the highway by the shore of L. Athabasca, where probably introd.), Sask. (sandy prairie at Pike Lake, sw of Saskatoon; CAN), and s Man. (Grande Clarière; St. Lazare, about 75 mi NW of Brandon; introd. on railway ballast at Sioux Lookout, Ont., about 175 mi NW of Thunder Bay, and in a gravel pit near Thunder Bay), s to Ariz., Tex., and Mo.; Eurasia.

Because of the sandy open habitats and weedy nature of our species of *Corispermum,* their precise native areas in N. America are difficult to define. Indeed, they are considered by some authors to be entirely introd. from Eurasia.

CYCLOLOMA Moq. [2224]

C. atriplicifolium (Spreng.) Coult. Winged Pigweed
/T/EE/ (T) Sandy beaches, clearings, blowouts, roadsides, and waste places from SE Sask. (Baildon, SE of Moose Jaw; Breitung 1957*a*) to s Man. (N to Shilo, about 10 mi E of Brandon), Ont. (shores of L. Erie and L. Ont.; introd. northwards to the Ottawa dist. and on the grounds of the St-Hubert airport near Montreal, Que.), s to Ark., N Mexico, Tex., and Ill.

EUROTIA Adans. [2232]

E. lanata (Pursh) Moq. Winter-fat, White or Winter Sage
/sT/WW/ (Ch) Dry prairies and plains (often saline or alkaline) and foothills: an isolated area in s Yukon (mountain slopes by Kluane L. at ca. 61°N; CAN); the main area from E Wash. to s Alta. (N to Lethbridge and Walsh; CAN), s Sask. (N to near Moose Jaw; CAN), and sw Man. (Virden; WIN), s to s Calif. and Tex. [*Diotis* Pursh; *E. ceratoides sensu* Hooker 1838, not (L.) Ledeb.; *E. cerat.* var. *lan.* (Pursh) Ktze.]. MAPS: Hultén 1968*b*:400; J.A. Neilson, Can. Field-Nat. 82(2): fig. 1, p. 115. 1968.

KOCHIA Roth [2240]

K. scoparia (L.) Schrad. Summer-cypress, Red Belvedere. Petits soldats
Eurasian; escaped from or persisting in old gardens in N. America, as in s B.C. (N to Kamloops), s Alta. (N to Calgary; CAN), Sask. (N to Saskatoon), s Man. (N to Erikson, about 45 mi N of Brandon), Ont. (N to the Ottawa dist.), Que. (N to Gaspé Basin, E Que.; Groh 1947), and N.S. (Boivin 1966*b*). [*Chenopodium* L.; the commonly cult. phase with a purple-red autumnal coloration may be distinguished as f. *trichophylla* Stapf].

MONOLEPIS Schrad. [2225]

M. nuttalliana (R. & S.) Greene Povertyweed
/ST/WW/ (T) A weedy species, partly native and partly introd., of saline and alkaline soils,

waste places, and roadsides from N-cent. Alaska–Yukon (*see* Hultén 1944: map 488, p. 783) to Great Bear L., Alta. (N to Fort Saskatchewan), Sask. (N to Prince Albert), and Man. (presumably native southwards; introd. in railway ballast and waste places N to Churchill), S to S Calif., Mexico, Tex., and Mo.; introd. eastwards as in S Ont. (as a seed impurity at Guelph; OAC), SW Que. (Montreal; Groh and Frankton 1949*b*), N.S. (railway ballast near Bridgewater, Lunenburg Co.; ACAD), and New Eng. [*Blitum* Schultes; *B. (M.) chenopodioides* Nutt., not L. nor Lam.]. MAP: Hultén 1968*b*:396.

POLYCNEMUM L. [2214]

P. arvense L.
Eurasian; this species was found in Ont. in 1940 by H.A. Senn (Can. Field-Nat. 55(2):17. 1941; *P. majus;* growing in colonies over a distance of about 2 mi along the boundary between Renfrew and Lanark counties). Senn writes, "In waste land, particularly an old, almost unused road allowance, the plant flourished in shallow soil underlain by limestone, being most abundant in depressions and in old wheel tracks. The most vigorous specimens however, made a solid mat for almost a quarter mile down the crushed limestone ridge in the centre of the moderately travelled road . . . . The whole colony is well-established and must have been in existence for many years but the adjacent cultivated fields do not appear to have been invaded." Collections in DAO and MT appear to be the only confirmable records of the occurrence of the plant as an adventive in N. America. However, Roland (1947) reports *P. verrucosum* as, "Collected by A.H. McKay near Halifax and sent to J. Macoun for identification. This specimen is in the National Herbarium at Ottawa and is dated Oct. 1896 . . . ." The present writer was unable to locate this N.S. collection in CAN, either under *Polycnemum* or under other genera with which it may have been confused. [Incl. var. *simplex* Wallr. (*P. majus* A. Br.) and var. *brachyphyllum* Neilr. (*P. verrucosum* Lang)].

SALICORNIA L. [2257] Samphire, Glasswort, Saltwort

1   Matted perennial with freely branching rhizomes and prostrate stems to 1 m long; flowering stems erect, numerous, to 3 dm tall, often brownish purple, the joints to 2 cm long; flowering spike to 4 cm long, its joints about 2.5 mm long and about as thick; (SE Alaska–B.C.) . . . . *S. virginica*
1   Annuals, mostly erect.
   2   Scales below spike mucronate-pointed, conspicuous when dry; spike to 6 mm thick, the joints to 3.5 mm long; (?N.S.) . . . . *[S. bigelovii]*
   2   Scales blunt or rounded, inconspicuous; spike at most 5 mm thick; (transcontinental) . . . . *S. europaea*

[S. bigelovii Torr.] Dwarf Saltwort
[N.S. is included in the range assigned this annual species of salt marshes of the E U.S.A. by Gleason (1958), probably on the basis of the report of *S. virginica* L. from N.S. by Lindsay (1878; Halifax), this taken up by John Macoun (1886) under the name *S. mucronata* Bigel. (*S. virginica* Moq., not L.), a synonym of *S. bigelovii* antedated by the name *S. mucronata* Lag. *S. virginica* L. (not Moq.), however, is a perennial species known along the Atlantic coast only from N.H. to S.C.]

S. europaea L. Glasswort, Samphire, Chickenclaws. Corail
/sT/X/EA/ (T) Saline shores, coastal salt-marshes, and (ssp. *rubra*) inland salt springs and wet alkaline flats, the aggregate species from S Alaska (*see* Hultén 1944: map 493, p. 784), S Yukon (Porsild 1951*a*), and S Dist. Mackenzie (Wood Buffalo National Park; CAN) to B.C.–Alta., Sask. (Old Wives L. and Round Valley L.; ssp. *rubra,* CAN), Man. (ssp. *rubra* N to Dawson Bay, L. Winnipegosis; ssp. *europaea* along the Hudson Bay coast N to Churchill), the coasts of James Bay (Ont. and Que.), E Que. (St. Lawrence R. estuary from l'Islet Co. to the Côte-Nord, Anticosti Is., and Gaspé Pen.), Nfld., N.B., P.E.I., and N.S., S to Calif., Nev., Kans., Ill., N.Y., and Ga.; Eurasia. MAPS and synonymy: *see* below.

1 Joints of the spike as thick as or thicker than long; seed about 1.2 mm long;
  [*S. rubra* Nels.; *S. europaea* var. *prono* (Lunell) Boivin; Alaska–B.C. to Man.] . . . .
  . . . . ssp. *rubra* (Nels.) Breitung
1 Joints of spike distinctly longer than thick; seeds to 2 mm long . . . . ssp. *europaea*
  2 Spikes at most 3 mm thick.
    3 Stem erect, often much branched; spikes to 1 dm long; [*S. herbacea* L.;
      E Que. to Nfld. and N.S.; MAPS (aggregate species): Meusel, Jaeger, and
      Weinert 1965:135; Hultén 1968*b*:401] . . . . var. *europaea*
    3 Stem ascending or depressed, the lower branches prostrate; spikes at most
      about 3 cm long; [*S. prostrata* Pall.; *S. pusilla* Woods; cent. Ont. (coast of
      James Bay) to Nfld. and N.S.] . . . . var. *prostrata* (Pall.) Fern.
  2 Spikes to 5 mm thick (and 1 dm long); stem simple or sparingly branched, weakly
    ascending or reclining; [var. *pachystachya* (Koch) Fern.; *S. herbacea* vars.
    pachystachya Koch and *simplex* Pursh; James Bay, Que.; N.B., P.E.I., and Nfld.] . . . . .
    . . . . var. *simplex* (Pursh) Fern.

S. virginica L. Perennial Saltwort, Leadgrass
/T/D (coastal)/ (Grh) Coastal salt marshes and beaches: Pacific coast from the south-
ernmost Alaska Panhandle (*see* Hultén 1944: map 494, p. 784) through w B.C. to Baja Calif.;
Atlantic and Gulf coasts from Mass. to Tex. [*S. ambigua* Michx.; *S. ?perennis* Mill. of Europe;
S. pacifica Standl., the name to be used for the western plant if it finally proves separable
from the eastern one]. MAP: Hultén 1968*b*:401.

SALSOLA L. [2269]

S. kali L. Saltwort. Soude. Var. *tenuifolia* the Russian Thistle or Chardon de Russie
/T/EE/EA/ (T) Sandy seashores from Que. (St. Lawrence R. estuary from l'Islet Co. to the
Côte-Nord and Gaspé Pen.) to Nfld., s ?Labrador (Fernald *in* Gray 1950; possibly referable to
the Côte-Nord, E Que.), N.B., P.E.I., and N.S., s along the Atlantic coast to Ga.; Eurasia.
  The Russian Thistle, var. *tenuifolia* Tausch, is introd. on sandy shores, along roadsides, and
in cult. fields and waste places (a noxious weed in the West), as in B.C. (N to Pouce Coupe,
ca. 55°45′N), Alta. (N to Beaverlodge, 55°13′N), Sask. (N to McKague, ca. 52°45′N), Man.
(N to Churchill), Ont. (N to Longlac, N of L. Superior), Que. (N to Kamouraska Co.), N.B., P.E.I.,
and N.S.
1 Lower leaves semicylindric; upper leaves to about 1.5 cm long, stiff, dilated at base,
  strongly spine-tipped.
  2 Plant pubescent; [E Que. to s ?Labrador, Nfld., and N.S.] . . . . var. *kali*
  2 Plant subglabrous; [sw Nfld.; also reported from s Ont. by Soper 1949] . . . .
    . . . . var. *caroliniana* (Walt.) Nutt.
1 Principal leaves filiform, to about 7 cm long and 1 mm broad, only weakly spine-
  tipped; [*S. pestifer* Nels.; *S. tragus* Rchb., not L.; introd. from B.C. to Que.
  and N.S.] . . . . var. *tenuifolia* Tausch

SARCOBATUS Nees [2259]

S. vermiculatus (Hook.) Torr. Greasewood
/T/WW/ (N) Saline or alkaline soils in the drier regions of s B.C. (Okanagan dist.; Henry
1915), s Alta. (N to Red Deer), and s Sask. (N to Swift Current), s to Calif. and Tex. [*Batis*
Hook.].

[SPINACIA L.] [2228]

[*S. oleracea* L.] Spinach
[A casual waif in waste ground and on dumps in N. America, as in Alaska (Tanacross; Hultén
1950), s Yukon (CAN), Alta. (N to Fort Smith on the Dist. Mackenzie boundary; W.J. Cody,
Can. Field-Nat. 70(3):111. 1956), and Man. (Fort Garry; CAN; WIN).]

SUAEDA Forsk.   [2261]   Sea-Blite

1   Perennial from a stout taproot, to 6 dm tall, more or less shrubby below; sepals
    subequal, only slightly cucullate (hooded) at tip and not at all keeled, about 1.5 mm
    long; leaves nearly terete, mostly 1 or 2 cm long, acute to rounded at tip, those of
    the inflorescence not greatly reduced; (?Alta.) . . . . [*S. intermedia*]
1   Annuals with slender taproots, herbaceous; sepals all more or less cucullate; leaves
    more or less flattened, those of the inflorescence markedly reduced.
    2   Sepals subequal, rather uniformly rounded or obscurely keeled on the back and
        thus not conspicuously cucullate; seed to 1.5 mm broad; leaves commonly 1 or
        2 cm long (but up to 5 cm); (essentially transcontinental in saline areas) . . . *S. maritima*
    2   Sepals unequal, one or more of them often conspicuously cucullate-keeled; seed
        about 1 mm broad.
        3   Floral bracts linear, to 5 mm long, usually only slightly if at all broader than
            the lower leaves (these to 3 cm long and 1.5 mm broad, acute or acuminate);
            (s Yukon) . . . . *S. occidentalis*
        3   Floral bracts broadly lanceolate to ovate, 2 or 3 mm long, usually broader
            than the much longer lower leaves; (var. *americana;* transcontinental) . . . .
            . . . . *S. maritima*

[S. intermedia Wats.]
[Alta. is included in the area of this taxon by Hitchcock et al. (1964), perhaps accepting the
range assigned to *Dondia fruticosa* (L.) Druce by P.C. Standley (N. Am. Flora 21:90. 1916).
The basis may be a collection in CAN from Milk River, s Alta., where taken by John Macoun in
1895 and distributed as *S. torreyana* Wats. The generally accepted range is from Wash. to
s Calif. and N Mexico. (*Dondia* Heller; *S. (D.) fruticosa* of American auth., perhaps not the Eurasian *Chenopodium fruticosum* L., basionym).]

S. maritima (L.) Dumort.
/aST/(X)/EA/   (T)   Coastal shores and salt marshes and inland on alkaline flats and around
salt springs, the aggregate species from s Alaska–Yukon and the coast of Dist. Mackenzie
(Coronation Gulf) to Great Bear L., northernmost Alta., Sask. (N to Tisdale, 52°51′N), Man.
(N to Churchill), Ont. (N to w James Bay at ca. 52°N), Que. (E James Bay N to ca. 53°N; St.
Lawrence R. estuary from l'Islet Co. to the Côte-Nord, Anticosti Is., and Gaspé Pen.), N.B.,
P.E.I., and N.S., s to Calif., Tex., and Fla.; Eurasia. MAPS and synonymy: *see* below.
1   Seeds about 2 mm broad; mature sepals subequal, rounded or obscurely keeled on
    the back; [*Chenopodium* L.; *Dondia* Druce; *Salsola* Poir.; incl. *Suaeda fernaldii*
    Standl. and *S. richii* Fern.; *S. linearis* var. *ramosa* Wats. at least in part; range of the
    species; MAP: Porsild 1966: map 54, p. 73] . . . . var. *maritima*
1   Seeds about 1.5 cm broad; mature sepals unequal, the upper 1 or 2 strongly keeled;
    [*Salsola salsa* var. *americana* Pers.; *Suaeda (Dondia) amer.* (Pers.) Fern.; *Salsola
    (Suaeda) depressa* Pursh; *Chenopodium (Suaeda) calceoliforme* Hook.; the Yukon
    (Boivin 1966b), sw Dist. Mackenzie (Fort Smith, 60°03′N), and Dist. Keewatin (Boivin
    1966b); Ont. (w James Bay N to ca. 52°N), Que. (E James Bay N to ca. 53°N; St.
    Lawrence R. estuary from Isle-Verte, Temiscouata Co., to the Mingan Is. of the Côte-
    Nord, Anticosti Is., and the Gaspé Pen.), N.B., P.E.I. (Cape Aylesbury, Prince Co.),
    and N.S.; MAP: Hultén 1968b:402 (*S. depressa*)] . . . . var. *americana* (Pers.) Boivin

S. occidentalis Wats.
/sT/W/   (T)   Saline or alkaline marshes and flats, the generally accepted range being from
Wash. to Nev., Wyo., and Colo.; Hultén (1950) reports a collection from an alkali flat near Carcross, s Yukon (Anderson and Brown, no. 10,349; Herb. Hultén, detd. P. Aellen). MAP: Hultén
1968b:402.

SUCKLEYA Gray   [2230]

S. suckleyana (Torr.) Rydb.   Poison Suckleya
/T/WW/   (T)   Streambanks from E Mont., S Alta. (N to near Bow L., 51°40′N; also known from near Brooks, Etzikom, and the Cypress Hills), and S Sask. (Tuxford and Moose Jaw; Breitung 1957*a*) to Colo. and S.Dak. [*Obione* Torr.; *S. petiolaris* Gray].

AMARANTHACEAE (Amaranth Family)

AMARANTHUS L.   [2299]   Amaranth, Water-hemp.   Amarante or Acnide

(Ref.: Sauer 1955; P.C. Standley, N. Am. Flora 21:101–23. 1917)
Herbs with simple alternate entire or undulate-margined leaves. Flowers small, unisexual, apetalous, subtended by up to 3 often coloured bracts in axillary or terminal spiked clusters.
Calyx of commonly 5 distinct sepals (or pistillate flowers with fewer or no sepals). Stamens 5
or fewer, opposite the sepals. Pistil 1. Stigmas commonly 3, sessile or nearly so. Ovary superior. Fruit a 1-seeded utricle.

1   Plants dioecious (unisexual).
  2   Sepals of the pistillate flowers regularly present, at least 1 of them about 2 mm
    long and with its midvein excurrent as a conspicuous spine (as also the relatively
    heavy midvein of the bracts); outer sepals of staminate flowers with a heavy
    midvein, distinctly surpassing the inner ones; utricle circumscissile at the middle;
    (introd.).
    3   Pistillate flowers with 1 or 2 sepals (the longer one about 2 mm long, the
      shorter one vestigial); bracts to 2 mm long; inflorescence a single elongate
      terminal spike or a panicle of numerous short spikes; utricle to 1.5 mm long;
      leaves oval to rhombic-oblong . . . . [A. tamariscinus]
    3   Pistillate flowers with 5 sepals, the 3 outer ones 3 or 4 mm long; bracts mostly
      4–6 mm long; inflorescence a terminal spike to 5 dm long, lateral spikes
      shorter or none; utricle to 2 mm long; leaves rhombic-lanceolate to -ovate . . . .
      . . . . A. palmeri
  2   Sepals of the pistillate flowers usually none (occasionally 1 or vestigial ones less
    than 1 mm long and lacking a visible midvein); outer sepals of the staminate
    flowers lacking a heavy midvein and not appreciably longer than the inner ones;
    bracts to 2 mm long; utricle indehiscent or bursting irregularly.
    4   Seed 2 or 3 mm long; utricle to 4 mm long; midrib of bracts scarcely
      excurrent; leaves mostly linear to narrowly lanceolate . . . . [A. cannabinus]
    4   Seed about 1 mm long; utricle not over 2 mm long; midrib of bracts markedly
      excurrent; leaves lanceolate to ovate; (?Man. to Ont. and sw Que.) . . . .
      . . . . [A. tuberculatus]
1   Plants monoecious (the staminate and pistillate flowers intermingled or in separate
  inflorescences on the same plant).
  5   Flowers chiefly in elongate terminal or panicled spikes (much smaller axillary
    panicles or clusters may also occur); (introd.).
    6   Leaf-axils mostly bearing a pair of rigid sharp-pointed spines to about 2.5 mm
      long; pistillate flowers with 5 sepals; utricle indehiscent or bursting irregularly,
      to 2 mm long; leaves lance-ovate to ovate . . . . A. spinosus
    6   Leaf-axils unarmed.
      7   Utricle indehiscent, very rugose when dry, to 1.5 mm long; pistillate sepals
        3, shorter than the utricle . . . . [A. viridis]
      7   Utricle circumscissile at the middle, to 2 mm long; pistillate sepals 5.
        8   Bracts subulate, rigid, to 8 mm long, usually twice as long as the
          utricle; sepals 3 or 4 mm long at maturity and considerably surpassing
          the utricle . . . . A. retroflexus
        8   Bracts thin, short-awned, not rigid, equalling or somewhat surpassing
          the utricle; sepals shorter than to slightly surpassing the utricle . . . .
          . . . . A. hybridus
  5   Flowers all or chiefly in small axillary clusters (sometimes also forming a small
    terminal panicle).
    9   Utricle indehiscent, smooth, to 2.2 mm long; sepals of pistillate flowers 2
      (rarely 3); stems prostrate to erect; (introd.) . . . . A. lividus
    9   Utricle circumscissile at the middle.

10 Sepals of the pistillate flowers usually 5 (sometimes 4), unequal; stamens 3 or 4; utricle to 2.5 mm long; seeds averaging about 1.5 mm long; bracts lance-acicular, to 3 mm long; stems whitish or purplish, prostrate or decumbent; (B.C. to Que.) . . . .*A. graecizans*
10 Sepals of the pistillate flowers usually 3; utricle less than 2 mm long; seeds averaging at most 1 mm long.
   11 Stems prostrate; sepals of the pistillate flowers very unequal, one of them about equalling the lance-linear subtending bract, the others much reduced or even wanting; stamens usually 1 or 2; leaf-blades commonly not over 1.5 cm long; (s Alta. and sw Sask.) . . . . . .*A. californicus*
   11 Stems commonly erect or ascending; sepals of the pistillate flowers about equal and similar to those of the staminate flowers; bracts lance-spinulose, rigid, to 3 mm long and about twice as long as the flowers; early leaves often as much as 8 cm long; (B.C. to N.S.) . . . .*A. albus*

A. albus L.   Tumbleweed
/T/X/EA/   (T)   A usually weedy species of disturbed or waste ground from s B.C. (Nanaimo and Summerland; Groh and Frankton 1948) to Alta. (near Medicine Hat; CAN), Sask. (common; Breitung 1957a), Man. (N to Benito, NW of Duck Mt.), Ont. (N to Cochrane, 49°03′N), Que. (N to the Quebec City dist.), N.B. (St. Andrews; Sackville), P.E.I. (Charlottetown; D.S. Erskine 1960), and N.S., s to Mexico and S. America; Eurasia. [*A. graecizans sensu* Roland 1947 (and other auth., at least in part), not L., a relevant collection from Hants Co., N.S., in ACAD].

A. californicus (Moq.) Wats.
/T/W/   (T)   More or less alkaline moist flats and lake shores from E Wash. to s Alta. (Cypress Hills, Calgary, Herronton, and Manyberries, where introd., according to Boivin 1966b; not listed by Moss 1959) and sw Sask. (introd. according to Boivin 1968; not listed by Breitung 1957a), s to s Calif., Nev., and Mont. [*Mengea* Moq.; *A. carneus* Greene].

[*A. cannabinus* (L.) Sauer]   Tidemarsh Water-hemp
[This species is noted by Sauer (1955; *see* his map, fig. 3, p. 14) as confined to brackish or saline shores, marshes, and tidal flats of the E U.S.A. Reports from Ont. and Que. by John Macoun (1886; *Acnida rusocarpa*) are all or mostly referable to *A. tuberculatus* (relevant collections from most of the cited localities in CAN and GH, detd. Sauer). (*Acnida* L.; *A. rusocarpa* Michx.).]

A. graecizans L.   Tumbleweed
/T/WW/EA/   (T)   A weedy species of disturbed or waste ground from B.C. (N to Quesnel) to Alta. (N to Spirit River, 55°47′N), Sask. (N to Carlton and Hudson Bay Junction, both ca. 52°50′N), and Man. (N to St. Lazare, about 75 mi NW of Brandon), s to Calif., Tex., and Kans.; introd. farther eastwards, as in Ont. (N to the Ottawa dist.) and Que. (railway ballast at New Carlisle, Gaspé Pen.), and perhaps much of the above-noted area, the precise native area difficult to delimit because of the weedy nature of the species; Mexico; W.I.; Eurasia. [*A. angustifolius* Lam.; *A. blitoides* Wats.]. MAP: Hultén 1968b:403.

A. hybridus L.   Pigweed, Wild Beet, Green or Purple Amaranth
Tropical and subtropical America; introd. northwards in waste places, along streets, and in cult. fields.
1 Bractlets of the pistillate flowers to 6 mm long, with a very long terminal mucro, the longest ones mostly twice as long as the perianth; panicle usually greenish [green amaranth; *A. chlorostachys* Willd.; *A. hypochondriacus* L.; s Man. (Winnipeg dist.), Ont. (N to the Ottawa dist.), and sw Que. (Montreal dist.)] . . . . .var. *hybridus*
1 Bractlets of the pistillate flowers to 4 mm long, with a short mucro, less than twice as long as the perianth; panicle usually reddish or purplish; [purple amaranth; *A. cruentus* L.; *A. paniculatus* L.; ?B.C. (Boivin 1966b; *A. paniculatus* reported by Henry 1915, as introd. at Sicamous), Alta. (N to Fort Saskatchewan), s Ont. (N to

Wentworth and York counties), and Que. (N to Les Eboulements, Charlevoix Co.; Bernard Boivin, Ann. ACFAS 6:108. 1940)] . . . . .var. *cruentus* (L.) Moq.

A. lividus L.
Tropical American; introd. in waste ground farther northwards, as in Ont. (Elgin, Huron, and Waterloo counties; Montgomery 1957) and sw Que. (Masson; Montreal; Quebec City).

A. palmeri Wats.
Native from Calif. and Kans. to Mexico and Tex.; introd. in Mo. and the E U.S.A., and in s Ont. (St. Thomas, Elgin Co.; TRT, detd. Mulligan; reported from Lambton Co. by Gaiser and Moore 1966). The native area is outlined in a MAP by Sauer (1955: fig. 8, p. 33).

A. retroflexus L.   Green Amaranth, Pigweed, Redroot
Tropical American; a very common weed of waste places and cult. ground from sw Dist. Mackenzie (N to Fort Simpson, 62°51′N; CAN) and B.C.–Alta.–Sask. to Man. (N to Churchill), Ont. (N to New Liskeard, 47°31′N), Que. (N to the Mingan Is. of the Côte-Nord; Saint-Cyr 1887), N.B., P.E.I., and N.S. MAPS and synonymy: *see* below.
1   Plant scurfy-villous for some distance below the inflorescence with flattened crisped multicellular hairs; leaves usually hairy beneath at least along the veins; sepals of pistillate flowers to 4 mm long, generally surpassing the mature fruit, broadly rounded to retuse at summit, with or without a short terminal bristle, their midveins conspicuously greenish; stamens usually 5 (sometimes 4); [range of the species; MAPS (aggregate species): Hultén 1968*b*:403; Meusel, Jaeger, and Weinert 1965:135] . . . .
. . . . .var. *retroflexus*
1   Plant glabrous to puberulent or sparingly pubescent (but not villous) below the inflorescence; leaves glabrous or nearly so; sepals of pistillate flowers usually 2 or 3 mm long, shorter than to about equalling the mature fruit, acute or obtuse to sometimes broadly rounded at apex, with a short terminal bristle, their midveins usually not conspicuously greenish; stamens usually 3 (sometimes 4); [*A. powellii* Wats.; B.C. to Sask. (Boivin 1966*b*); s Ont. (near Forest, Lambton Co.; OAC, detd. Sauer); P.E.I. (Boivin 1966*b*)] . . . . .var. *powellii* (Wats.) Boivin

A. spinosus L.   Thorny Amaranth
Asiatic; introd. in waste places of N. America, as in s Man. (Red R. Valley; Lowe 1943) and s Ont. (Swansea, near Toronto; CAN; reported from Lambton Co. by Dodge 1915, and from St. Thomas, Elgin Co., by Groh 1947).

[A. tamariscinus Nutt.]
[Sauer (1955) assigns this taxon a range along shores of lakes, ponds, and rivers (spreading to neighbouring fields, gardens, roadsides, and damp waste places) from N.Dak., Wisc., and Ind. to N.Mex., Tex., La., and Tenn., his map (fig. 7, p. 29) indicating no Canadian stations. A collection in CAN from along the Souris R., s Man., has been placed here by Uline and Bray, and Soper (1949) lists it for s Ont., perhaps on the basis of the inclusion of *Montelia tam.* in the synonymy of *Acnida rusocarpa* by John Macoun (1886; see *A. cannabinus*). The admission of this species to our flora awaits further study. (*Acnida* Wood).]

A. tuberculatus (Moq.) Sauer
/T/EE/   (T)   River-banks, low grounds, and disturbed soil from ?Man. (Boivin 1966*b*) to Ont. (N to Carleton, Russell, and Stormont counties) and sw Que. (Hull; CAN; GH; concerning reports from P.E.I., see D.S. Erskine 1960), s to Colo., Mo., La., and Tenn. [*Acnida* Moq.; *A. altissima* Riddell and its vars. *prostrata* (U. & B.) Fern. and *subnuda* (Wats.) Fern.]. MAP: Sauer 1955: fig. 5, p. 23.

[A. viridus L.]
[Tropical America; reported as introd. in Mass. by Fernald *in* Gray (1950); a collection in MT from sw Que. (Mt. Royal, Montreal; Cléonique-Joseph, no. 11,423) has been placed here but appears referable to *A. lividus*.]

NYCTAGINACEAE (Four-o'clock Family)

Herbs with opposite, entire or shallowly undulate-dentate, sessile or petioled leaves. Flowers perfect, in terminal heads or panicled clusters, each cluster subtended by a calyx-like involucre of about 5 separate or united bracts. Corolla none. Calyx 5-lobed, petaloid, greenish white, yellow, orangish, pink, or purple. Stamens mostly 4 or 5, hypogynous. Fruit an achene enclosed in the thickened, sometimes corky, often ridged or winged base of the calyx.

1 Flowers sessile in heads, the heads subtended by usually 5 distinct bracts; fruits broadly winged; leaf-blades mostly elliptic to ovate, rhombic-ovate, or nearly deltoid, usually less than 6 cm long; stems decumbent-based to prostrate or trailing; plants (including the perianth) glandular-puberulent; (B.C. and Alta.) . . . .*Abronia*
1 Flowers mostly pedicelled in cymose-paniculate inflorescences, the flowers or flower-clusters subtended by a 5-lobed saucer-shaped involucre that becomes enlarged and veiny in fruit; perianth glabrous to very pubescent; fruits merely ribbed or ridged; leaf-blades linear to broadly ovate or deltoid, essentially glabrous or their margins ciliate; stems erect or ascending, glabrous or pubescent in lines; plants perennial from a fleshy root, essentially glabrous to copiously glandular-pubescent in the inflorescence . . . .*Mirabilis*

ABRONIA Juss.   [2352]   Sand-Verbena

1 Stems prostrate or reclining but the ends of the branches ascending, the branches to 6 dm long; involucral bracts mostly narrowly to broadly lanceolate, to about 1 cm long; perianth greenish white, the tube to about 12 mm long, the limb to 5 mm broad; fruit averaging about 2 cm long, the thin papery strongly veined wings broadest near the middle; glandular-puberulent to subglabrous annual, mostly of sandy inland habitats; (s Alta.) . . . .*A. micrantha*
1 Stems trailing, to 1 m long, the tips appressed to the ground; fruit less than 1.5 cm long; glandular-puberulent perennials of western coastal sands.
  2 Involucral bracts narrowly lanceolate, 5 or 6 mm long; perianth-limb reddish purple, about 5 mm broad, the greenish to pink tube to 8 mm long; fruits with prominent thin wings at least as broad as the body and often prolonged above (the pressed fruit commonly obcordate in outline) . . . . [*A. umbellata*]
  2 Involucral bracts broadly elliptic to ovate-lanceolate, to 8 mm long; perianth-limb bright yellow or orangish, to 7 mm broad, the greenish-yellow tube to 1 cm long; fruits with thick keel-like wings narrower than the body, broadest slightly above midlength (the pressed fruit commonly rhombic-obovate in outline); (w B.C.) . . . .*A. latifolia*

A. latifolia Eschsch.   Yellow Sand-Verbena
/t/W/   (Grh)   Coastal sands from w B.C. (Queen Charlotte Is.; Vancouver Is.; Stubb's Is.) to s Calif. MAP: S.S. Tillett, Brittonia 19(4): fig. 4 (the Queen Charlotte Is. station reported by Calder and Taylor 1968, should be indicated), p. 304. 1967.

A. micrantha Torr.   Sand-puffs
/T/WW/   (T)   Sandy soil from E Mont. to s Alta. (near Milk River, where taken by John Macoun in 1895; CAN) and ?Sask. (the inclusion of Sask. in the range assigned *Trip. mic.* by Rydberg 1922 and 1932, requires confirmation; not listed by Breitung 1957a), s to Nev., N.Mex., and S.Dak. [*Tripterocalyx* Hook.].

[*A. umbellata* Lam.]   Bearded Sand-Verbena
[Native in the w U.S.A. (Wash. to Baja Calif.); the report from sw B.C. by John Macoun (1886; Vancouver Is.) is based upon *A. latifolia* (relevant collections in CAN, revised by Boivin, the probable basis of the report of var. *acutalata* (Standl.) Hitchc. (*A. acut.* Standl.) from Vancouver Is. by S.S. Tillett, Brittonia 19(4):323 and MAP, fig. 4, p. 304. 1967.]

MIRABILIS L. [2347] Four-o'clock, Umbrella-wort

1 Plant often copiously glandular-stipitate (especially about the upper nodes and the usually contracted inflorescence); leaves linear to lanceolate or oblong, tapering or broadly cuneate at the sessile or subsessile base; fruit with thickened obtuse ribs; (s Alta. to sw Man.; introd. in Ont.) . . . . *M. hirsuta*

1 Plant essentially glabrous, the branches of the finally very open, dichotomously forking inflorescence minutely appressed-pubescent but not stipitate-glandular; leaves narrowly to broadly ovate, commonly shallowly undulate-dentate, all except the uppermost ones distinctly petioled below the broadly cuneate to subcordate or cordate base; fruit with acutish ribs; (s B.C. to s Man.; introd. in Ont. and Que.) . . . .
. . . . *M. nyctaginea*

M. hirsuta (Pursh) MacM.

/T/WW/ (Grt) Dry plains and foothills, the aggregate species from Mont. and s Alta. (N to near Drumheller, 51°28′N; CAN) to Sask. (N to Saskatoon; reported N to Carlton House Fort, about 30 mi sw of Prince Albert, by Hooker 1838) and Man. (N to Millwood, about 90 mi NW of Brandon; CAN), s to Ariz., Mexico, Tex., and Mo.; introd. eastwards along roads and railways, as in Ont. (N to Frontenac, Lanark, and Grenville counties).

1 Leaves linear-lanceolate to rather broadly ovate; stem densely hirsute or pilose below; [*Oxybaphus* Sweet; *Allionia* Pursh; *A. pilosa* (Nutt.) Rydb.; range of the species] . . . . var. *hirsuta*

1 Leaves linear to linear-lanceolate; stem essentially glabrous below the inflorescence; [*Allionia (Oxybaphus) lin.* Pursh; *A. decumbens* (Nutt.) Spreng.; *A. lanceolata* Rydb.; *A. montanensis* Osterh.; *Calymenia (O.) angustifolia* Nutt.; s Alta. (Fort Macleod, Medicine Hat, and Belly River; CAN; not listed by Moss 1959), sw Sask. (Crane Lake and Cypress Hills; CAN; not listed by Breitung 1957a), and s-cent. Man. (Boivin 1966b)] . . . . var. *linearis* (Pursh) Boivin

M. nyctaginea (Michx.) MacM.

/T/(X)/ (Grt) Dry plains and ravines from s B.C. (Keremeos, about 20 mi sw of Penticton; CAN) to s Alta. (Bow Island and Medicine Hat; CAN), s Sask. (N to Swift Current and Mortlach), s Man. (N to Victoria Beach, about 55 mi NE of Winnipeg), and Wisc., s to Mexico, Tex., La., and Ala.; introd. eastwards along roads and railways, as in Ont. (N to the Ottawa dist.) and sw Que. (Groh and Frankton 1949b). [*Allionia* Michx.; *Oxybaphus* Sweet; *A. ovata* Pursh].

PHYTOLACCACEAE (Pokeweed Family)

PHYTOLACCA L.   [2380]   Pokeweed

Tall coarse glabrous perennial to about 3 m tall, branched above, with alternate, entire, narrowly oblong to ovate, petioled leaves to about 3 dm long. Flowers usually perfect, hypogynous, in peduncled racemes to about 2 dm long, these at first terminal, later lateral and opposite the leaves. Corolla none. Calyx with 5 greenish-white or pinkish sepals. Ovary superior, consisting of up to 12 carpels united in a ring, in fruit forming a dark-purple flattened berry about 1 cm broad. (s Ont. and sw Que.).

P. americana L.   Poke, Scoke, Pigeonberry
/T/EE/   (Grt)   Damp woods, fields, and rich low grounds from s Ont. (N to Grey, Simcoe, Northumberland, Leeds, and Grenville counties; *see* s Ont. map by Soper 1956: fig. 5, p. 78, who notes that a report from the Ottawa dist. by Dore is believed to represent an accidental or intentional introduction, the plant now extinct there) to sw Que. (Missisquoi, Shefford, and St. John counties; CAN; MT), N.Y., and New Eng., s to Tex. and Fla.; introd. in Europe. [*P. decandra* L.]. MAP: J.D. Sauer, Ann. Mo. Bot. Gard. 39(2): fig. 1, p. 115. 1952.

AIZOACEAE (Carpetweed Family)

MOLLUGO L.   [2387]

Low annual with repeatedly forking, commonly prostrate and mat-forming stems. Leaves narrowly to broadly oblanceolate, to about 3 cm long, tapering to an obscure petiole, in whorls of up to 8 at the nodes. Flowers perfect, slender-pedicelled, 2–5 from each node. Corolla none. Sepals 5, white inside, greenish outside, about 2 mm long. Stamens usually 3. Ovary superior. Fruit a many-seeded ovoid capsule about 3 mm long.

M. verticillata L.   Carpetweed.   Mollugine
Tropical American; sandy riverbanks, roadsides, and cult. grounds northwards, as in s B.C. (Agassiz, Mission, and Sicamous; Eastham 1947), Ont. (N to Ingolf, near the Man. boundary at ca. 49°50′N), Que. (N to the Dartmouth R., Gaspé Pen.; MT), N.B., and N.S. (not known from P.E.I.; reported from Nfld. by Reeks 1873, but not listed by Rouleau 1956).

PORTULACACEAE (Purslane Family)

(Ref.: P.A. Rydberg and Percy Wilson, N. Am. Flora. 21:279–336. 1932)

Herbs with simple, usually entire, opposite or alternate leaves. Flowers perfect. Sepals or calyx-lobes usually 2 (up to 8 in *Lewisia*), usually unequal. Petals mostly 5 (sometimes as few as 2 or as many as 15). Stamens often the same number as the petals and opposite them (sometimes fewer or more numerous). Pistil 1. Style commonly 3-parted. Ovary usually superior (partially inferior in *Portulaca*). Fruit a 1-locular capsule, circumscissile (*Lewisia* and *Portulaca*) or 2–3-valvate from the top.

1 Petioles of old leaves marcescent as spiny projections or weak, usually curved bristles on the caudex or branches; leaves linear, fleshy and nearly terete, alternate (or apparently opposite), entire, commonly 1 or 2 cm long; sepals 2, about 3 mm long, deciduous; flowers few to many in scaly bracted cymes, the petals soon withering; stamens 15 or more; ovary superior; capsule dehiscent by 3 valves, many-seeded; glabrous perennials, mat-forming by the freely branching caudex; (B.C.) . . . .*Talinum*
1 Petioles not persistent; leaves commonly broader or at least with usually flattened blades, entire; sepals persistent, sometimes more than 2.
  2 Ovary partially inferior, the lower half of the circumscissile, 1-locular, several-seeded capsule adherent to the calyx-tube; flowers yellow, small, axillary and in small terminal clusters, sessile, the 2 sepals usually 3 or 4 mm long, the yellow petals slightly smaller; stamens 6 to many; leaves succulent, spatulate to obovate, alternate or subopposite, to 3 cm long, somewhat involucrate at the stem-tips; glabrous annual with usually several prostrate stems to 3 dm long; (*P. oleracea*; introd., transcontinental) . . . .*Portulaca*
  2 Ovary superior (free from the calyx), usually 2–3-valved from the top (circumscissile in *Lewisia*); perennials with other than yellow flowers.
    3 Flowers in dense, short, somewhat scorpioid umbels or panicles on leafless to few-bracted peduncles; sepals 2, scarious-margined, to 4 mm long, much larger than the 4 unequal, quickly withering, white to pinkish petals; stamens 3; stigmas 2; capsule flattened, fully dehiscent by 2 valves, several-seeded; leaves glabrous, oblanceolate to oblong-spatulate, to 5(7) cm long, chiefly basal and forming rosettes; caudices thick and much branched, the branches forming mats to 1.5 dm broad; (s ?B.C.). . . . .*[Spraguea]*
    3 Flowers solitary or in usually open racemes or cymes; sepals 2 or more, usually not scarious; petals mostly 5 or more, generally rather showy; stamens often more than 3; stigmas 3 (or up to 8 in *Lewisia*).
      4 Flowers in leafy-bracted racemes, the lower bracts scarcely reduced; sepals unequal, in fruit to 12 mm long; petals about equalling the sepals, usually deep crimson-purple to (rarely) white; stamens 5 or more; stigmas 3; capsule 3-valved, with 15 or more black and shining seeds; leaves linear to oblanceolate, alternate, to 7 cm long, usually coarsely but sparsely ciliate, otherwise glabrous; stems low and spreading to erect, simple to branched from the base, glabrous or ciliate along the angles, to 3(4) dm long; annual; (sw B.C.) . . . .*Calandrinia*
      4 Flowers usually solitary or in minutely bracted or bractless racemes or cymes; petals white and obscurely colour-veined (usually thus in *Montia*) to white, pink, or deep rose and commonly veined with deeper colour (rarely purplish).
        5 Leaves thick and fleshy, essentially all in a basal rosette (those of the flowering scapes much reduced or bract-like); sepals 2 or more; petals and stamens each often more than 5; stigmas often more than 3; capsule circumscissile near base and sometimes dehiscing upward by 3–5 valves, usually many-seeded; (mts. of B.C.; *L. pygmaea* also in sw Alta.) . . . .*Lewisia*

5 Leaves cauline (basal leaves also sometimes present); sepals 2; petals and stamens each usually 5 (sometimes fewer); stigmas 3; capsule dehiscent downward by 3 valves, with at most 6 seeds.

6 Stems unbranched, erect or ascending from the axils of the leaves of a basal rosette, each bearing usually a single pair of opposite or subopposite, sessile or petioled leaves below the usually solitary raceme; slenderly taprooted annuals or perennials with rhizomes or runners, a heavy taproot, or a fleshy corm . . . . *Claytonia*

6 Stems sparingly to much branched, repent to ascending or erect, bearing several alternate or opposite leaves and lacking well-developed basal rosettes, the inflorescences borne from the leaf-axils or terminating the main branches, or both; slenderly taprooted annuals or rhizomatous or stoloniferous perennials (but never with fleshy thickened taproots or corms) . . . . *Montia*

CALANDRINIA HBK. [2407]

C. ciliata (R. & P.) DC. Red Maids
/t/W/ (T) Gravelly to heavy soils (the plant often weedy in nature) from sw B.C. (Vancouver Is. and adjacent islands; CAN; V) to s Calif. and Ariz.; S. America. [*Talinum* R. & P.; incl. var. *menziesii* (Hook.) Macbr. (*Talinum men.* Hook.; *C. caulescens* var. *men.* (Hook.) Gray)].

CLAYTONIA L. [2414] Spring-beauty

(Ref.: Davis 1966; Swanson 1966)
1 Plants perennial from deep-seated, fleshy, mostly subglobose corms (solid bulbs), the few basal leaves with their petioles largely subterranean.

2 Leaf-blades gradually narrowed to a distinct petiole, linear to linear-oblanceolate, more than 8 times as long as broad; (Ont. and s Que.) . . . . *C. virginica*

2 Leaf-blades sessile or abruptly narrowed to the petiole, mostly relatively broader; (Alaska–Yukon–B.C. to Sask.; Ont. to Nfld. and N.S.) . . . . *C. caroliniana*

1 Plants annual and with a slender taproot, or perennial and with a heavy taproot or tangled fleshy rhizomes or stolons; (western species).

3 Stem-leaves usually fused on one or both margins and forming a horizontal orbicular disk to 5 cm broad surrounding the stem; basal leaves linear-spatulate to rhombic-obovate, to 3 cm broad; racemes lax, often half the total height of the plant, the slender pedicels usually recurving, only the lowest one usually subtended by a bract; sepals to 4 mm long (in fruit to 5.5 mm), the white or pinkish petals to nearly twice as long; slenderly taprooted annual; (B.C.) . . . . *C. perfoliata*

3 Stem-leaves distinct (or, in *C. spathulata,* often fused on one side but for less than half their length and erect-ascending).

4 Slenderly taprooted annual; sepals 1 or 2 mm long; petals usually less than 5 mm long; raceme to 2 dm long, the pedicels to 1 cm long, usually recurved, only the lowest ones usually bracted; basal leaves linear to linear-spatulate, obscurely petioled, to about 6 cm long and 1.5 mm broad; stem-leaves narrowly lanceolate to narrowly ovate, often fused on one side below the middle; (sw B.C.) . . . . *C. spathulata*

4 Perennials (or *C. sibirica* often annual) with fleshy taproots (*C. sarmentosa* also with slender creeping bud-bearing stolons); sepals usually over 2 mm long; basal leaves often broader in outline, their petioles well differentiated from the blade; stem-leaves distinct to the sessile or short-petioled base.

5 Roots on older plants usually much over 5 mm thick, the crown seldom branching; basal leaves usually numerous, very fleshy and forming a distinct rosette; at least the lowest flowers usually bracted.

6 Basal leaves linear to lanceolate or oblanceolate, attenuate, sessile;

inflorescence 2–5-flowered; sepals to 1 cm long; petals to 2 cm long;
(?Alaska) . . . . [*C. eschscholtzii*]
  6 Basal leaves spatulate to obovate, petioled; inflorescence 2–9-
      flowered; sepals to 7 mm long; petals to 12 mm long.
      7 Stem-leaves linear to oblanceolate; (Alaska; sw Dist. Mackenzie;
         mts. of B.C. and sw Alta.) . . . . *C. megarhiza*
      7 Stem-leaves obovate to suborbicular; (Aleutian Is.) . . . . *C. arctica*
5 Roots usually not over 5 mm thick, the crown often branching at or below
  the surface of the soil; basal leaves usually neither very fleshy nor
  numerous nor forming a distinct rosette.
    8 Flowers usually solitary (sometimes 2 or 3); sepals 5 or 6 mm long;
      petals purple, to 1.5 cm long; basal leaves linear to linear-oblanceolate,
      their petioles conspicuously broadened and scarious along the basal
      third; (Alaska–Yukon) . . . . *C. scammaniana*
    8 Flowers few to many; petals white or pink; basal leaves only moderately
      or not at all broadened at base.
      9 Sepals to 6 mm long; petals to 1 cm long; inflorescence few–many-
         flowered, to 3 dm long, sometimes branching, with or without (var.
         cordifolia) a bract at the base of each pedicel; stem-leaves to 5 cm
         broad; plant often annual, to 4.5 dm tall, the leaf-bases thickened
         on the crown and often functioning as bulblets; (Alaska–B.C.) . . . .
         . . . . *C. sibirica*
      9 Sepals 2 or 3 mm long; petals to 13 mm long; inflorescence 2–6-
         flowered, usually a simple bractless raceme; stem-leaves to 7 mm
         broad; plant stricly perennial, to 2.5 dm tall, with a taproot and
         slender creeping bud-bearing stolons; (Alaska–Yukon–B.C.) . . . .
         . . . . *C. sarmentosa*

C. arctica Adams
/Ss/W/eA/ (Grt) Wet grassy tundra of the Aleutian Is. (*see* Hultén 1944: map 497, p. 784);
Siberia and Kamchatka. MAP: Hultén 1968*b*:407.

C. caroliniana Michx.
/ST/(X)/ (Gst) Rich woods, alluvial thickets, and moist slopes (up to alpine habitats in the
West; ranges of Canadian taxa outlined below), the western phases s to s Calif. and N.Mex.,
the typical form of the East s to N Ill., Tenn., and N.C. MAP and synonymy: *see* below.
1 Stem-leaves distinctly petioled; petals white to pink, with pink veins; [incl. the broad-
  leaved extremes, f. *latifolia* and f. *ovata* Louis-Marie; Ont. (N to about 10 mi NW of
  Thunder Bay and the Ottawa dist.), Que. (N to Duparquet, West Abitibi Co., the
  Gaspé Pen., and the Côte-Nord near Sept-Iles; *see* Que. map by Doyon and Lavoie
  1966: fig. 27, p. 821), w Nfld. (GH), N.B., P.E.I., and N.S.; MAP: Braun 1937: fig. 26,
  p. 202] . . . . var. *caroliniana*
1 Stem-leaves sessile.
    2 Petals entirely white (suffused with yellow at base) or only the veins sometimes
      pinkish, to 1.5 cm long; [*C. tuberosa* Pallas; cent. Alaska and extreme w-cent.
      Yukon (*see* Hultén 1944: map 504, p. 784) and N B.C. (Boivin 1966*b*)] . . . .
      . . . . var. *tuberosa* (Pall.) Boivin
    2 Petals pink or white with pink veins, to 1 cm long; [*C. lanceolata* Pursh; *C.
      chrysantha* Greene; *C. carol.* of Sask. reports, not Michx.; B.C. (N to Cariboo,
      52°51′N), mts. of sw Alta. (N to Jasper), and sw Sask. (Cypress Hills)] . . . .
      . . . . var. *lanceolata* (Pursh) Wats.

[*C. eschscholtzii* Cham.]
[According to Hultén (1944), reports of this species of Siberia and Kamchatka from Alaska (as
by P.A. Rydberg, N. Am. Flora 21:302. 1932, and A.E. Porsild, Rhodora 41(486):220. 1939)
probably refer to *C. acutifolia* ssp. *graminifolia* Hult., this included in the following treatment
of *C. megarhiza*.]

C. megarhiza (Gray) Parry
/ST/W/eA/ (Grt) Grassy tundra, gravelly soil, and talus slopes near or above timberline from cent. Alaska (N to the Seward Pen.; *see* Hultén 1944: map 496, p. 784; *C. acut.* ssp. *gram.*) through the mts. of B.C. and SW Alta. (N to Banff) to Nev., Utah, and N.Mex.; isolated in W Dist. Mackenzie (A.E. Porsild, Nat. Mus. Can. Bull. 101:18. 1945); E Siberia. [*C. arctica* var. *meg.* Gray; incl. *C. acutifolia* Pallas and its ssp. *graminifolia* Hult.]. MAP: combine the maps by Hultén 1968*b*:404 and 405 (*C. acut.* ssp. *gram.*).

C. perfoliata Donn
/T/WW/ (T) Open to shady moist sandy woods at low to moderate elevations from S B.C. (N to Clinton; John Macoun 1883) to Baja Calif., Ariz., and Wyo.; introd. at Unalaska, Alaska (Hultén 1944). [*Montia* Howell; *Limnia* Haw., *C. (L.; M.) parviflora* Dougl., not *Naiocrene "parviflora"* Rydb., which is *C. (M.) parvifolia* Moc.; *C. parviflora* var. *depressa* Gray]. MAP: Hultén 1968*b*:409.

C. sarmentosa Mey.
/aSs/W/eA/ (Grt) Moist grassy places from Alaska (N to the N coast; type from St. Lawrence Is,; *see* Hultén 1944: map 501, p. 784) and S Yukon (CAN) to N B.C. (S to the Cassiar dist. at ca. 58°30'N; CAN); E Siberia and Kamchatka. [*Montia* Bong.]. MAPS: Porsild 1966: map 56, p. 73; Hultén 1968*b*:408.

C. scammaniana Hult.
/Ss/W/ (Grt) Known only from Alaska (*see* Hultén 1944: map 502, p. 784; type from Porcupine Dome) and the Yukon (Mayo dist.; Porsild 1951*a*). [Perhaps best merged with *C. sarmentosa*]. MAPS: Hultén 1968*b*:408; Olav Gjaerevoll, K. Nor. Vidensk. Selsk. Skr. (1963, No. 4): fig. 4, p. 17. 1963.

C. sibirica L.
/sT/W/eA/ (T (Hs)) Dry to moist soils from the Aleutian Is. and S Alaska (*see* Hultén 1944: map 503, p. 784) through B.C. to S Calif. and Utah; E Asia (Bering Is. and Commander Is.). [*Montia* Howell; *Limnia* Haw.; *C. (Montia) alsinoides* Sims and its vars. *heterophylla* T. & G. and *rosea* DC.; *M. heter.* (T. & G.) Jeps.; *C. asarifolia* Bong.; *C. unalaschkensis* Fisch.]. MAPS: Hultén 1968*b*:407.

Some of the B.C. material is referable to var *cordifolia* (Wats.) Davis (*C. (Limnia; Montia) cord.* Wats; pedicels bractless or sometimes the lowest one subtended by a bract, rather than most of the pedicels subtended by a bract; collections from Vancouver Is., Sandon, Nelson, Monashee Pass, and Kootenay L. have been placed here).

C. spathulata Dougl.
/t/W/ (T) Dry to moist soil from SW B.C. (Vancouver Is. and adjacent islands) to S Calif. [*Limnia* Heller; *Montia* Howell; *C. exigua* T. & G.].

C. *virginica* L.
/T/EE/ (Gst (Grt)) Rich woods from Minn. to Ont. (N to the Ottawa dist.), Que. (N to the Montreal dist.; reports from N.S. require confirmation), and S New Eng., S to Tex., La., and Ga. [*C. media* Small].

LEWISIA Pursh [2422]

1 Flowering stems to 3 dm tall, bearing a many-flowered, small-bracted terminal panicle and generally several longer alternate bracts below the panicle, at least the upper bracts and the sepals glandular-dentate; sepals 2, to 3 mm long; petals commonly 8 or 9, white with pink to purplish veins, to about 1 cm long; stamens 5 or 6; seeds rarely more than 5; leaves narrowly spatulate to linear-oblanceolate, to about 1 dm long and 8 mm broad; (B.C.) . . . . *L. columbiana*
1 Flowering stems rarely to 1 dm tall, bearing a solitary terminal flower and a single

opposite pair or a whorl of bracts at the base of the peduncle; stamens and seeds each often more than 5; leaves typically linear or linear-clavate, subterete, less than 8 cm long.

   2   Sepals 2, green to red, typically glandular-serrate and strongly veined, to 5 mm long; petals usually about 7, white or greenish white to deep pink or sometimes lavender, often glandular-setose, 6–17 mm long; stamens at most 12; flowering stems sometimes to 1 dm tall, bearing a single pair of opposite, linear, more or less united bracts at or below midlength; (B.C. and sw Alta.) . . . .*L. pygmaea*

   2   Sepals commonly about 7 or 8, whitish to deep pink or rose, entire or erose, unequal, 1–2.5 cm long; petals usually about 15, pale to deep pink or rose (sometimes nearly white), mostly about 1 or 2 cm long; stamens 30 or more; flowering stems rarely over 3 cm tall, bearing a whorl of 5 or 6 (or even 8) linear scarious bracts at the base of the peduncle; (s B.C.) . . . .*L. rediviva*

L. columbiana (Howell) Robins.
/T/W/   (Grt)   Exposed gravel banks and rocky slopes from s B.C. (collection in CAN from 5,500 ft elevation on Mt. Arrowsmith, Vancouver Is., where taken by John Macoun in 1887; collection from Manning Provincial Park, se of Hope, in the park museum herbarium) to N Calif. and Idaho. [*Calandrinia* and *Oreobroma* Howell].

L. pygmaea (Gray) Robins.
/sT/W/   (Grt)   Gravelly and rocky slopes to above timberline from s Yukon (St. Elias Mts.; CAN), B.C. (N to McCallum Mt., near Atlin at ca. 59°30′N; CAN), and sw Alta. (Waterton Lakes; Breitung 1957*b*) to s Calif. and N.Mex. [*Calandrinia* and *Talinum* Gray; *Oreobroma* Howell]. MAP: Hultén 1968*b*:410.

L. rediviva Pursh   Bitter-root
/T/W/   (Grt)   Dry plains and slopes at low to moderate elevations from s B.C. (chiefly in the Dry Interior; N to Ashcroft, about 40 mi w of Kamloops) to s Calif. and Colo.

MONTIA L.   [2416]   Miner's Lettuce

(Ref.: Swanson 1966)
1   Stem-leaves usually several opposite pairs, rather narrowly oblong to rhombic-ovate, the lower leaves not forming a rosette.

   2   Perennial with slender rhizomes and freely rooting, sparingly bracted stolons, both of these producing bulblet-like offsets; racemes terminal and axillary, lax, the flowers on pedicels to 1.5(2.5) cm long, often replaced by bulbils, only the lowest pedicel bracted; sepals 2 or 3 mm long, the white or pinkish separate petals more than twice as long; leaves to 5 cm long; (Alaska–B.C.–?Alta.) . . . .
. . . .*M. chamissoi*

   2   Annual with slender, weak, decumbent to ascending, rather freely branching stems tending to root at the nodes; flowers in lax leafy-bracted racemes, on pedicels to 1(2) cm long, rarely replaced by bulbils; sepals usually less than 1.5 mm long, the white petals less than twice as long, united about half their length; leaves to about 1.5 cm long; (transcontinental) . . . .*M. fontana*

1   Stem-leaves alternate, usually several; at least the lower pedicels usually subtended by a bract.

   3   Leaf-blades mostly oblanceolate to rhombic or rotund, usually over 3 mm broad; sepals 2 or 3 mm long, unequal; stamens 5; plants with a poorly developed rosette-like cluster of early-deciduous basal leaves, the flowering stems to 2(3) dm tall.

      4   Perennial, sparingly to much branched near the base, from a slender rhizome, tending to spread by slender stolons and often forming large patches; flowers subtended by scaly bracts; petals to 1.5 cm long, white with pink veins; leaves mostly oblanceolate to narrowly obovate, those of the stem sessile or obscurely petioled; (s Alaska–Yukon–B.C.–sw Alta.) . . . .*M. parvifolia*

4 Annual, much branched above, slenderly taprooted; stem-leaves usually not greatly reduced even in the inflorescence; petals 3 or 4 mm long, white or pale pink; leaves lanceolate to ovate, rhombic, or subrotund, all except the uppermost ones long-petioled; (SW B.C.) . . . . *M. diffusa*

3 Leaf-blades narrowly linear to linear-spatulate, to 2(3) mm broad; petals white, about equalling the calyx (or wanting in *M. howellii*); stamens 3 (often 2 in *M. howellii*); basal rosettes wanting.

5 Sepals about 1 mm long; flowers clustered in the axils of scarious bracts opposite the leaves, the bracts often fused with the base of the leaves and concealing the very short floral rachis; leaves to 2 cm long and 1.5(2) mm broad, much surpassing the flowers; stems to 6 cm long, freely branching, creeping and often rooting at the lower nodes; (SW B.C.) . . . . *M. howellii*

5 Sepals at least 2 mm long; flowers on slender, often recurved pedicels in elongate racemes, bractless or the lower ones much surpassing their subtending bracts; stems not nodally rooting, sparingly to much branched above the base, the branches ascending to erect.

6 Sepals about 2 mm long; pedicels mostly less than 5 mm long; seeds about 1 mm long; leaves commonly less than 2 cm long and about 0.5 mm broad; stems less than 1 dm long; (SW B.C.) . . . . *M. dichotoma*

6 Sepals to 4 mm long (in fruit to 6); pedicels to 2 cm long; seeds usually over 1.5 mm long; leaves to about 5 cm long and 1(3) mm broad; stems to 2 dm long; (B.C. to SW Sask.) . . . . *M. linearis*

M. chamissoi (Ledeb.) Robins. & Fern.
/ST/W/ (Hpr) Wet to boggy places at low to moderate elevations from the Aleutian Is. and s-cent Alaska (type from Unalaska; *see* Hultén 1944: map 498, p. 784, *Claytonia cham.*) through B.C. and s ?Alta. (Hultén 1944; the inclusion of Man. in the range given by Hitchcock et al. 1964, is undoubtedly erroneous) to s Calif. and N.Mex.; isolated in the "driftless area" of Iowa. [*Claytonia* Ledeb.; *C. aquatica* Nutt.; *C. (Crunocallis) chamissonis* Eschsch.; *C. stolonifera* Mey.]. MAP: Hultén 1968b:409 (*Clay cham.*).

M. dichotoma (Nutt.) Howell
/t/W/ (T) Generally in moist lowlands from SW B.C. (Vancouver Is. and Mayne Is.; CAN) to N Calif., Idaho, and w Mont. [*Claytonia* Nutt.; *Montiastrum* Rydb.].

M. diffusa (Nutt.) Greene
/t/W/ (T) Mostly in moist woods from SW B.C. (Vancouver Is.: Alberni and Cameron Lake; Eastham 1947) to w Calif. [*Claytonia* Nutt.].

M. fontana L. Water-Blinks
/aST/X/GEA/ (T (Hel; HH)) Fresh or brackish shores, springy slopes, and ditches (sometimes floating), the aggregate species from the Aleutian Is., N-cent. Alaska, and the coast of the Yukon to cent. Victoria Is., E Dist. Keewatin, Baffin Is. (N to the Arctic Circle), and northernmost Ungava–Labrador, s in the West through B.C. to Calif., Nev., and Idaho, farther eastwards s to NE Man. (Churchill), cent. Ont. (w James Bay s to 53°16′N), Que. (s to E James Bay at 52°12′N and the St. Lawrence R. estuary from Rimouski Co. to the Côte-Nord, Gaspé Pen., and Magdalen Is.), Nfld., N.B. (Chatham; Petitcodiac; Shediac), P.E.I. (Summerside, Prince Co.; GH), N.S. (Cumberland, Halifax, and Inverness counties), and Maine; s half of w Greenland with an isolated station at ca. 81°N, E Greenland N to the Arctic Circle; Iceland; Eurasia. MAPS and synonymy: *see* below (the key based upon that by D.M. Moore, Bot. Not. 116(1): 16–30. 1963).

1 Seeds smooth and shining, lacking tubercles; [var. *lamprosperma* (Cham.) Fenzl (*M. lamprosperma* Cham.); *M. rivularis* of American auth. in part and perhaps in part of Gmel.; transcontinental; MAPS: Porsild 1957: map 131 (*M. lamp.*), p. 177; Hultén 1968b:410, and 1958: map 239 (*M. lamp.* and *M. riv.*), p. 259] . . . . ssp. *fontana*

1 Seeds more or less covered with tubercles.

2 Seeds with 7–11 rows of acute slender tubercles around the keel, the lateral cells elongated and lacking tubercles; [*Claytonia (M.) hallii* Gray; *M. fontana* var. *tenerrima* (Gray) Fern. & Wieg.; *M. rivularis* of American auth. in part and perhaps in part of Gmel.; s B.C. (Vancouver Is. and adjacent islands; *M. fontana* also reported from Kootenay by Henry 1915] . . . . ssp. *amporitana* Sennen
2 Seeds with a variable and patchy development of low (occasionally more elongated) tubercles on the keel; [Vancouver Is., B.C.; Moore, loc. cit.] . . . .
. . . . ssp. *variabilis* Walt.

M. howellii Wats.
/t/W/ (T) Moist lowlands from sw B.C. (Vancouver Is. and Mayne Is.; CAN) to NW Calif. [*Claytonia* Piper; *Montiastrum* Rydb.].

M. linearis (Dougl.) Greene
/T/W/ (T) Moist to dry sandy places in lowland valleys and foothills from B.C. (N to near Babine at ca. 55°N), Alta. (Twin Butte), and sw Sask. (Cypress Hills) to s Calif. and Utah. [*Claytonia* Dougl.; *Montiastrum* Rydb.].

M. parvifolia (Moc.) Greene
/ST/WW/ (Hsr) Low to moderately high elevations, the aggregate species from cent. Alaska and sw Yukon through B.C. and the mts. of sw Alta. (Waterton Lakes; Breitung 1957*b*) to Calif. and Utah; an isolated station in N Man. (near Gillam, about 160 mi s of Churchill; CAN). MAPS and synonymy: *see* below.
1 Basal leaves mostly less than 5 mm broad; petals 7–12 mm long; seeds to 1.2 mm long; [*Claytonia* Moc.; *Naiocrene* Rydb.; *C. filicaulis* Dougl.; incl. the reduced extreme, *C. bostockii* Porsild; range of the species; MAPS: combine the maps by Hultén 1968*b*:406 (*C. parv.* and *C. bost.*); the map for *C. bostockii* by Porsild 1966: map 55, p. 73, applies here; *see* J. McNeill and J.N. Findlay, Can. J. Bot. 49(5):713–15. 1971] . . . . var. *parvifolia*
1 Basal leaves well over 5 mm broad; petals 1–1.5 cm long; seeds to 1.5 mm long; [*Claytonia (Montia; Naiocrene) flagellaris* Bong., the type from Sitka, Alaska; SE Alaska through B.C. to Oreg.] . . . . var. *flagellaris* (Bong.) Hitchc.

PORTULACA L.   [2421]   Purslane.   Pourpier

1 Leaves linear, subterete; flowers white or various brilliant shades of yellow or red, to 4 cm broad, solitary at the ends of the branches; stem spreading or ascending, long-hairy at the nodes . . . . *P. grandiflora*
1 Leaves spatulate to obovate; flat; flowers pale yellow, at most 1 cm broad, solitary or in small terminal glomerules; stem prostrate, usually purplish red, glabrous . . . .
. . . . *P. oleracea*

P. grandiflora Hook.   Portulaca (of gardens)
S. American; persisting in flower-gardens or borders and occasionally escaping, as in s Ont. (reported from Lambton Co. by Gaiser and Moore 1966, and from Wentworth Co. by F.H. Montgomery, Can. Field-Nat. 62(3):94. 1948).

P. oleracea L.   Common Portulaca
Eurasian; a common weed of cult. and waste ground of N. America, as in B.C. (N to Kam-loops), Alta. (N to Fort Vermilion, 58°24′N), Sask. (Breitung 1957*a*), Man. (N to Victoria Beach, about 55 mi NE of Winnipeg), Ont. (N to Sandy L. at ca. 53°N, 93°W), Que. (N to L. Timiskaming and Ste-Anne-de-la-Pocatière, Kamouraska Co.; RIM), N.B., P.E.I., and N.S.

[SPRAGUEA Torr.]   [2408]

[S. umbellata Torr.]
[The inclusion of B.C. in the range assigned this species of the w U.S.A. (Wash. and Mont. to

Baja Calif.) by Jepson (1951; taken up by Hitchcock et al. 1964) requires confirmation. (*Calyptridium* Greene; *S. multiceps* Howell).]

TALINUM Adans.   [2406]   Fame-flower

1   Flowers white (perhaps sometimes yellowish or pinkish), rarely more than 9 in flat-topped cymes mostly 2 or 3 cm long; peduncles mostly not over 5 cm long; capsule about 3 mm long; leaves less than 1.5 cm long, their marcescent midribs usually more bristly than spiny, usually curved, rarely as much as 3 mm long; plants forming mats usually less than 5 cm broad; (s B.C.) . . . . *T. okanoganense*

1   Flowers pale to deep red, up to 25 in diffuse ascending cymes to 1.5 dm long; peduncles to 1.5 dm long; capsules to 5 mm long; leaves to 2.5 cm long, the rigid basal portions of their midribs forming somewhat spiny projections covering the stem; (sw B.C.) . . . . *T. spinescens*

T. okanoganense English
/T/W/   (Ch)   Exposed slopes and ledges in the lower mountains of s B.C. (apparently known only from Baldy Mt., near Kamloops) and Wash. (*T. wayae* Eastw.).

T. spinescens Torr.
/T/W/   (Ch)   Rocky outcrops and badlands in sw B.C. (known only from a mountain near Stump L., Vancouver Is., at 3,400 ft elevation, where taken by Dawson in 1888 and again by McEvoy in 1891; CAN) and Wash.

CARYOPHYLLACEAE (Pink Family)

Herbs with simple, entire, chiefly opposite (whorled in *Spergula*), commonly sessile leaves, the stems usually distinctly swollen at the nodes. Flowers usually perfect and 5-merous (sometimes 4-merous), commonly arranged in dichotomously branching cymes. Sepals distinct or united. Petals distinct (lacking in *Paronychia* and *Scleranthus* and occasionally in species of other genera). Stamens commonly 8 or 10. Pistil 1. Styles and stigmas 2, 3, or 5. Ovary essentially superior. Fruit commonly a capsule. (Including Alsinaceae, Corrigiolaceae, and Illecebraceae).

1   Leaves whorled, filiform, to 5 cm long, rather fleshy, subtended by minute scarious stipules; petals white, entire, about equalling the sepals; styles and capsule-valves 5; (introd.) . . . . *Spergula*
1   Leaves alternate or opposite.
   2   Fruit a utricle (indehiscent, 1-seeded, and bladdery).
     3   Leaves alternate, oblanceolate, rarely as much as 3 cm long, subsessile; stipules white, denticulate, about 1 mm long; flowers very small, closely packed in axillary and terminal cymose-paniculate clusters; calyx greenish or red, about 1 mm long, the lobes about equalling the tube; petals 5, white or pink-tinged, about equalling the calyx; styles 3; glabrous and glaucous annual or biennial, the usually numerous decumbent-based stems to 2.5 dm long; (introd.) . . . . *Corrigiola*
     3   Leaves opposite; styles 1 or 2.
       4   Calyx-lobes usually about equalling the tube, not at all hooded or spinose at tip; petals none; flowers green, sessile or subsessile in the upper leaf-axils; styles 2; leaves linear-subulate, connate at base, usually less than 2 cm long, exstipulate; low, spreading, glabrous to crisp-puberulent annual; (introd.) . . . . *Scleranthus*
       4   Calyx-lobes distinct nearly to base, often somewhat hooded and spinose at tip; style 1, 2-cleft; leaves stipulate.
         5   Sepals very unequal (the 3 outer ones much the largest, to 5 mm long), each with a terminal spine nearly as long as the body; petals 5, scale-like, scarcely half as long as the sepals; leaves acicular (needle-shaped), rather crowded, mostly not over 1 cm long, their subtending stipules not much shorter; prostrate matted perennial, the stems to 3 dm long, finely pubescent to somewhat tomentose, usually clothed at base with marcescent leaves and stipules; (s ?B.C.) . . . . [*Cardionema*]
         5   Sepals more nearly equal, with awns shorter than the body; petals none or merely minute teeth or bristle-like staminodia.
           6   Sepals usually more or less hooded or corrugated and spine-tipped (flat and blunt in *P. canadensis*); inflorescence usually open or diffuse (flowers usually solitary and terminal in *P. sessiliflora*); leaves with conspicuous hyaline stipules . . . . *Paronychia*
           6   Sepals not hooded, blunt; flowers crowded in axillary clusters; leaves less than 1 cm long, ovate-lanceolate, glabrous or with ciliate margins, with inconspicuous connate ciliate stipules; annual or biennial (rarely perennial) with a taproot, usually under 2 dm tall; (introd.) . . . . *Herniaria*
   2   Fruit a few- to many-seeded capsule; petals usually present.
     7   Sepals united into a distinct basal tube; petals with basal claws; leaves lacking stipules.
       8   Calyx subtended by 1–3 pairs of involucral bracts; styles 2; (introd.).
         9   Calyx 5-ribbed, 4 or 5 mm long; petals pink to purple, 5 or 6 mm long; leaves linear-subulate, at most about 1 cm long; stems decumbent at base; (garden-escape in B.C. and s Ont.) . . . . *Tunica*
         9   Calyx many-nerved, at least 12 mm long; petals to over 2.5 cm long . . . .
      . . . . *Dianthus*

  8 Calyx naked at base, not subtended by involucral bracts.

    10 Styles normally 5; capsule opening by 5 or 10 teeth.

      11 Calyx-lobes green and leaf-like, at least 2 cm long, much overtopping the unappendaged petals and the capsule, the petal-blades unappendaged at base; styles opposite the purplish-red petals; leaves linear to narrowly lanceolate; plant silky-pubescent; (introd.) . . . . *Agrostemma*

      11 Calyx-lobes not prolonged; petals with or without appendages at base of blade, alternate with the styles . . . . *Lychnis*

    10 Styles 2 or 3; capsule with 3, 4, or 6 valves.

      12 Styles normally 3; capsule opening by 3 or 6 teeth; calyx 10-nerved; corolla crowned, each petal with a pair of linear to roundish appendages at the juncture of the claw and the blade . . . . *Silene*

      12 Styles 2; capsule opening by 4 teeth or valves; calyx 5-nerved or angled, or only obscurely nerved; (introd.).

        13 Calyx subcylindric to ovoid, terete or 5-angled, obscurely nerved, not scarious; flowers at least 2 cm long; petals appendaged or unappendaged *(S. vaccaria)*; capsule opening by 4 apical teeth; seeds minutely reticulate or tuberculate . . . . *Saponaria*

        13 Calyx turbinate (top-shaped) or campanulate, scarious between the 5 green nerves; flowers at most 1 cm long; petals unappendaged; capsule deeply 4-valved; seeds tuberculate . . . . *Gypsophila*

  7 Sepals distinct or nearly so; petals lacking claws.

    14 Leaves subtended by broad scarious stipules; petals entire, white or pink; styles and capsule-valves 3; leaves linear or filiform; (chiefly saline sandy areas). . . . . *Spergularia*

    14 Leaves lacking stipules; petals mostly white.

      15 Styles normally 3, opposite 3 of the usually 5 sepals.

        16 Petals deeply notched or 2-cleft; capsule opening by 6 valves; leaves linear to ovate . . . . *Stellaria*

        16 Petals entire or merely shallowly 2-lobed.

          17 Inflorescence cymose; capsule ovoid or ellipsoid, opening by 3 or 6 valves; petals entire (sometimes barely notched, rarely wanting); leaves linear-filiform to dilated . . . . *Arenaria*

          17 Inflorescence umbellate; capsule ovoid-cylindric, often curved, opening by 6 apical teeth; flowers in peduncled umbels, their pedicels reflexed; petals denticulate; leaves oblong; peduncle and upper part of stem glandular; (introd.) . . . . *Holosteum*

      15 Styles usually 5 (sometimes 4 in *Sagina;* 3 or 4 in *Cerastium cerastoides*).

        18 Capsule cylindrical, often curved, opening by 10 apical teeth (or 6 or 8 in *C. cerastoides*); petals more or less deeply 2-cleft; styles opposite the sepals . . . . *Cerastium*

        18 Capsule ellipsoid to ovoid; styles alternating with the sepals.

          19 Petals entire, shorter or longer than the sepals or sometimes wanting; flowers small, terminating the stem and branches; capsule 4–5-valved to base; leaves filiform or subulate . . . . *Sagina*

          19 Petals deeply notched, much surpassing the sepals; flowers large, in open leafy terminal cymes; capsule opening by five 2-cleft valves; pedicels viscid, deflexed in fruit; leaves lanceolate to cordate-ovate; stems angled, minutely glandular-pilose; (introd.) . . . . *Myosoton*

AGROSTEMMA L.   [2488]   Corn-Cockle

A. githago L.   Purple Cockle.   Nielle des blés
Eurasian; introd. in grainfields and along roadsides of N. America, as in Alaska (Sitka; Fairbanks) and ?all the provinces (reported from Nfld. by Waghorne 1895, but not listed by Rouleau 1956). [*Lychnis* Scop.]. MAP: Hultén 1968*b*:439.

ARENARIA L.   [2443]   Sandwort.   Sabline

(Ref.: Bassett Maguire, Am. Midl. Nat. 46: 493–511. 1951)
1   Leaves relatively broad (mostly lanceolate to oblong or ovate) and rather uniformly distributed along the stem.
  2   Plants markedly fleshy and succulent (brittle when dried), yellowish green; petals and stamens inserted on a conspicuous 10-lobed disk, the petals (and sepals) to about 7 mm long; capsule broadly ovoid to globose, leathery, to 12 mm thick, dehiscing by as many entire valves (3–5) as there are styles; seeds to 4.5 mm long, pyriform (pear-shaped), with a nearly basal hilum; leaves lanceolate to oblong or ovate, to 4.5 cm long; stems much branched deep in the sand, strongly stoloniferous and rooting at the nodes, the leafy branches of the season procumbent and commonly forking; (transcontinental) . . . .*A. peploides*
  2   Plants less markedly fleshy; seeds rarely over 1.5 mm long, mostly reniform, with a marginal hilum.
    3   Capsule 3-locular, with much-inflated lobes, separating at maturity into 3 portions, broadly ovoid to globose, to about 12 mm long and thick; seeds pyriform; sepals to 7 mm long, the petals about as long or slightly longer; flowers mostly solitary and terminal at the summit of the stem or the ends of the branches; leaves oval or ovate, to about 2 cm long and sometimes over 1 cm broad; stems trailing or decumbent, often matted, glandular-pubescent; (Alaska to w Dist. Mackenzie) . . . .*A. physodes*
    3   Capsule 1-locular, dehiscing by twice as many valves as there are styles (the primary valves deeply split); seeds reniform; sepals rarely over 5 mm long.
      4   Stems mat-forming (very loosely to densely tufted); leaves rarely as much as 1 cm long, oblanceolate to obovate.
        5   Plant very densely tufted; petals none (but the corolla-disk bearing a crown of large scales that are emarginate or 2-lobed and nearly petaloid); sepals to 4 mm long; flowers solitary and terminal, subsessile or on pedicels at most 7 mm long and only slightly surpassing the leaves; seed solitary, reddish, obscurely papillate, to 1.4 mm broad; leaves densely crowded and overlapping, commonly acutish, glabrous, the old ones persisting; (Alaska) . . . .*A. chamissonis*
        5   Plant usually loosely tufted; petals present and disk-scales inconspicuous; sepals to 5 mm long; seeds less than 1 mm long; leaves acutish to blunt.
          6   Stems creeping and stoloniferous (mostly subterranean); leaves nerveless or obscurely 1-nerved, glabrous or often with a few short marginal cilia at or near the base, slightly fleshy; flowers mostly solitary, on pedicels to 3 cm long; petals about as long as or somewhat surpassing the nerveless or obscurely 1-nerved sepals; seeds reddish brown and shining, obscurely rugulose; (transcontinental) . . . .*A. humifusa*
          6   Stems not stoloniferous, the hairy prostrate shoots ascending at the ends when flowering; leaves evidently nerved, usually with conspicuous cilia at least on the lower half; flowers solitary or few in cymes; petals normally much surpassing the strongly 1–3-ribbed sepals; seeds black and markedly papillate; (E Greenland) . . . . .*A. ciliata*
      4   Stems not mat-forming, ascending.

  7 Leaves less than 1 cm long; stem and branches minutely ashy-pubescent; petals shorter than the sepals; seeds grey-black, dull, strongly rugose, about 0.6 mm long; annual; (introd.) . . . . *A. serpyllifolia*

  7 Leaves to over 7 cm long; seeds only slightly rugose, shining, mostly at least 1 mm long; perennials with filiform rhizomes; (transcontinental).

    8 Leaves essentially glabrous, lance-acuminate, broadest toward base and tapering with nearly straight margins to summit, to about 7 cm long; sepals acuminate, commonly 4 or 5 mm long, slightly surpassing the petals; capsule-valves strongly divergent after dehiscence; seeds reddish brown, to 1.6 mm long . . . . *A. macrophylla*

    8 Leaves typically minutely pubescent, broadest near the middle, rarely over 3.5 cm long; sepals obtuse, 2 or 3 mm long, the petals to over twice as long; capsule-valves only slightly divergent after anthesis; seeds black, at most 1.3 mm long . . . . *A. lateriflora*

1 Leaves filiform or linear, the majority in basal tufts, those of the stem relatively few and more or less reduced; cushion-like or mat-forming caespitose perennials (or *A. stricta* sometimes annual).

 9 Stems, pedicels, and calyces typically glabrous (pedicels and at least the upper part of the stem more or less glandular-puberulent in var. *puberulenta,* the western phase of *A. stricta*).

  10 Capsule-valves 2-cleft, the capsule dehiscing by twice as many teeth or half-valves (commonly 6) as there are styles, shorter or longer than the calyx; sepals obtuse, broadly scarious-margined, conspicuously thickened on the back at base, to 6 mm long, the petals about 1/3 longer; flowers usually several to many in congested or open cymes; leaves to 8 cm long, acute, only the basal ones with fascicles of smaller leaves in their axils; flowering stems to 4(5) dm tall; (s Alta. and sw Sask.) . . . . *A. congesta*

  10 Capsule-valves entire (or only slightly split at apex), the capsule dehiscing by as many valves (usually 3, sometimes 4 or 5) as there are styles.

   11 Petals to about twice as long as the sepals (except in *A. stricta* var. *dawsonensis*); flowers solitary to many.

    12 Sepals to 5 mm long, obtuse, scarious-margined, obscurely nerved; capsule not much surpassing the calyx; leaves soft, obtuse, to 1.5 cm long; (Que. to Labrador, Nfld., and N.S.) . . . . *A. groenlandica*

    12 Sepals to 3.5 mm long, acute, slightly scarious-margined, distinctly 3-nerved; capsule to half again as long as the calyx; leaves firm, acute, to 18 mm long, the principal ones mostly with axillary fascicles of smaller leaves; (transcontinental) . . . . *A. stricta*

   11 Petals shorter than or only slightly surpassing the usually acute, 1-nerved or obscurely 3-nerved sepals (sometimes vestigial or wanting); flowers often solitary, at most 5; capsule about equalling or only slightly surpassing the calyx; (transcontinental).

    13 Leaves to 2 cm long, bluntish, not fleshy; flowers up to 5, on pedicels to 6 cm long; sepals to 4 mm long, not spreading in anthesis; stems to 3 dm tall, erect; (*var uliginosa*) . . . . *A. stricta*

    13 Leaves less than 1 cm long, fleshy, the primary ones mostly with fascicles of reduced leaves in their axils; flower solitary, on a pedicel to 1.5 cm long; sepals about 3 mm long, usually spreading in anthesis; stems low and depressed, more or less trailing and covered with marcescent leaves, the flowering branches to 3 cm long . . . . *A. rossii*

 9 Stems (at least above), pedicels, and usually the calyces typically more or less glandular-pubescent or -pilose.

  14 Leaves to over 1 dm long, 1-nerved, acute to acuminate, finely ciliate, rather soft, usually glaucous; flowers usually few in small open cymes; sepals 1-nerved, obtusish to abruptly acute, broadly scarious-margined and with a faint midrib, thickened and cartilaginous at base, to about 6 mm long; petals

commonly about twice as long as the sepals; capsule to twice as long as the sepals, dehiscing by 6 apical teeth; seeds to 2.5 mm long; (Alaska to Dist. Mackenzie; B.C. and sw Alta.) . . . . *A. capillaris*

14 Leaves less than 2 cm long; capsule dehiscing by 3 entire valves; seeds less than 2 mm long.

    15 Flowering stems brittle and tending to shatter readily at the nodes, copiously glandular, usually bearing 7 or more flowers (rarely as few as 2 or 3), to 1 dm tall, the sterile stems trailing and forming mats as much as 3 dm broad; leaves to about 1 cm long, 3-nerved, acerose, the primary stem-leaves mostly with fascicles of reduced leaves in their axils; sepals mostly 3-nerved, acuminate to pungent (with a rigid sharp point), to 6 mm long, longer than the capsule but often considerably surpassed by the petals; seeds about 1.5 mm long, prominently long-papillate in concentric rows; (mts. of s B.C. and sw Alta.) . . . . *A. nuttallii*

    15 Flowering stems neither markedly brittle nor shattering, bearing mostly not more than 5 (commonly only 1 or 2) flowers; sepals mostly obtuse or at least blunt (acute in *A. rubella* and sometimes in *A. sajanensis*); seeds mostly less than 1.5 mm long.

        16 Sepals 1-nerved (with only a faintly marked midnerve), obtuse, to 8 mm long, the petals and capsule each to about 1 cm long; seeds prominently rugose-tuberculate marginally; leaves 1-nerved (with a faint midrib), obtuse, soft and rather fleshy, glabrous or with a few marginal cilia toward base; stems loosely to densely tufted, to about 12 cm tall, usually 1-flowered; (Alaska to sw Dist. Mackenzie) . . . . *A. arctica*

        16 Sepals 3(5)-nerved.

            17 Sepals acute or acuminate, with firm subulate tips, to 5 mm long, about equalling the petals, the capsule exserted up to 1/3 of its length; seeds rugose, to about 0.8 mm long; leaves firm, linear-subulate, to 1.5 cm long, with 3 essentially equal strong ribs; flowering stems to 2 dm tall, with up to 7 flowers, the sterile stems loosely or densely tufted, forming mats to 1.5 dm broad; (transcontinental) . . . . *A. rubella*

            17 Sepals obtuse or at least blunt (if attenuate in *A. sajanensis,* with soft scarious tips).

                18 Leaves, especially the basal ones, very acute and often sharply pointed, 1-nerved, to 1.5 cm long; sepals to 6.5 mm long, the petals to about twice as long; capsule more or less exserted, its seeds rugose and marginally papillate; flowering stems to 2 dm tall, with up to 5 flowers . . . . [*A. laricifolia*]

                18 Leaves abruptly acute or obtuse; flowering stems mostly not over 1.5 dm tall, 1(2,3)-flowered.

                    19 Leaves more or less distinctly 3-nerved, nearly flat, to 12 mm long, conspicuously ciliate with relatively long hairs; sepals to 7 mm long, the petals and capsule both to over twice as long; seeds rugose and dorsally papillate; (Alaska to w Dist. Mackenzie) . . . . *A. macrocarpa*

                    19 Leaves essentially 1-nerved (only the midnerve distinct), more or less short-ciliate; sepals to 5 or 6 mm long; seeds smooth or obscurely rugose or papillate.

                        20 Petals and capsule both about equalling the sepals; leaves to 13 mm long, commonly subtending fascicles of reduced leaves in their axils; (transcontinental in arctic, subarctic, and alpine regions) . . . . *A. sajanensis*

                        20 Petals and capsule both to about twice as long as the sepals; leaves to 8 mm long; (Alaska–Yukon–Dist. Mackenzie– B.C.–Alta.) . . . . *A. obtusiloba*

A. arctica Stev.   Arctic Sandwort
/aSs/W/A/   (Ch)   Sandy and gravelly river bars, lake shores, hummocky tundra, and talus slopes from the coasts of Alaska–Yukon (*see* Hultén 1944: map 536, p. 787; *Min. arct.*) and the Mackenzie R. Delta region to the Aleutian Is., Great Bear L., and s Dist. Mackenzie; NE ?Europe; Asia. [*Minuartia* Aschers. & Graebn.; *Alsine* Fenzl; incl. vars. *breviscapa* Regel and ?*grandiflora* Hook.]. MAP: Hultén 1968*b*:430.

A. capillaris Poir.
/aST/W/EA/   (Ch)   Dry plains to subalpine rocky slopes from N-cent. Alaska–Yukon (*see* Hultén 1944: map 544, p. 788), the Mackenzie R. Delta, and Great Bear L. (W.J. Cody, Can. Field-Nat. 70(3):112. 1956) through the mts. of B.C. and SW Alta. (N to Banff) to Oreg., N Nev., and Mont.; Eurasia. [*A. formosa* of American auth. in part, not Fisch.; *A. nardifolia sensu* A.E. Porsild, Rhodora 41(486):222. 1939, not Ledeb.]. MAP: Hultén 1968*b*:435.

The plant of B.C.–Alta. may be distinguished, at least in part, as var *americana* (Maguire) Davis, differing from the more northern typical form in its shorter sepals and glandular (rather than glabrous) inflorescence and upper part of stem. MAP: on the above-noted map by Hultén.

A. chamissonis Maguire
/aS/W/eA/   (Ch)   Coast of W Alaska (Seward Pen. N to Cape Lisburne at ca. 69°N; *see* Hultén 1944: map 545, p. 788, *A. dicran.*); E Siberia (St. Lawrence Bay). [*Cherleria (A.; Stellaria) dicranoides* C. & S., not *A. dicran.* HBK.]. MAP: Hultén 1968*b*:436.

A. ciliata L.
/AST/–/GE/   (Ch)   Coasts of E Greenland (between ca. 69° and 83°N; ssp. *pseudofrigida* Ostenf. & Dahl), Iceland, Spitsbergen, and N Europe, with several subspecies in central Europe. [Incl. *A. pseudofrigida* (Ostenf. & Dahl) Jus.]. MAPS: Hultén 1958: maps 65 and 66, p. 85; Gelting 1934: fig. 39, p. 269.

A. congesta Nutt.
/T/W/   (Ch)   Dry plains, slopes, and rocky ridges from Wash. to S Alta. (Cypress Hills and Sweetgrass Hills; CAN) and SW Sask. (Cypress Hills; CAN), S to Calif. and Colo. [*A. subcongesta* (Wats.) Rydb. in part].

The Canadian plant may apparently be distinguished as var. *lithophila* (Rydb.) Maguire (*A. lithophila* Rydb.; *A. glabrescens sensu* Henry 1915, perhaps not *A. fendleri* var. *glab.* Wats.; var. *expansa* Maguire; cyme more open than in the typical phase, the pedicels obvious and often longer than the calyces). The report of *A. congesta* var. *subcongesta* Wats. from S Yukon by J.M. Macoun (1895) is based upon *A. capillaris,* the relevant collection in CAN.

A. groenlandica (Retz.) Spreng.   Greenland-Sandwort
/aST/E/G/   (Ch)   Granitic ledges, sands, and rocky slopes from Que. (coast of E Hudson Bay N to near Ungava Bay at ca. 60°N; Mt. St-Urbain and Cap-à-l'Aigle, Charlevoix Co.; Côte-Nord; Gaspé Pen.; Magdalen Is.; reported from Anticosti Is. by Verrill 1865), Labrador (N to ca. 59°N), S Nfld., and N.S. (Halifax; ACAD; NSAC) to E Maine, and in the mts. to N.Y. and New Eng.; concerning a report from Man., *see* Scoggan (1957); an isolated station in the mts. of Brazil; W Greenland N to ca. 69°N, E Greenland N to ca. 62°N. [*Stellaria (Alsine; Alsinopsis; Minuartia; Sabulina) gr.* Retz., the type from Greenland; *St. labradorica* Schrank]. MAPS: Eric Hultén, Sven. Bot. Tidskr. 58(2): fig. 2 (N. American area), p. 433, and fig. 3 (total area), p. 434. 1964; Böcher 1954: fig. 6 (top), p. 31; Fernald 1918*a*: map 7 (incomplete), pl. 17. *See* R.E. Weaver, Jr. (Bull. Torrey Bot. Club 97(1):40–52. 1970).

A. humifusa Wahl.
/AST/X/GE/   (Ch)   Moist calcareous gravels and rock crevices from N Alaska, cent. Yukon, and the coast of Dist. Mackenzie to S Ellesmere Is., Baffin Is., and northernmost Ungava–Labrador, S to Great Slave L. (Raup 1936), S Dist. Keewatin, NE Man. (Churchill), N Ont. (Severn R. at ca. 55°45′N; Cape Henrietta Maria, NW James Bay), Que. (S to SE James Bay, L. Mistassini, and the Gaspé Pen.), S Labrador, and W Nfld., and through B.C. to the mts. of SW Alta.

(N to the Banff dist.); w Greenland N to ca. 78°N; Spitsbergen; N Scandinavia. [*A. ciliata* var. *hum.* (Wahl.) Hartm.; *A. cylindrocarpa* Fern.; incl. *A. longipedunculata* Hult.]. MAPS: Hultén 1968*b*:436, and 1958: map 169, p. 189 (noting several other total-area maps not listed here); Porsild 1957: map 147, p. 179; Raymond 1950*b*: fig. 10, p. 18; Raup 1947: pl. 23; Nicholas Polunin, Nature 152:452. 1943.

[A. laricifolia L.]
[M.L. Fernald (Rhodora 21(241):16. 1919) writes that "There is doubt as to just what Linnaeus had as *Ar. laricifolia* and a further doubt as to whether our American plant is identical with the European." Hultén (1968*b*) refers Alaskan reports to a new species under the genus *Minuartia, M. yukonensis* Hult. Many reports from Canada appear referable to closely related species such as *A. arctica, A. obtusiloba,* and *A. sajanensis.* Further studies are needed to clarify the problem. (*Alsinopsis* Heller). The MAP by Meusel, Jaeger, and Weinert (1965:149) indicates the species as confined to Europe.]

A. lateriflora L.   Grove-Sandwort
/ST/X/EA/   (Hpr)   Woodlands, meadows, and gravelly or turfy shores from the Aleutian Is. and N Alaska–Yukon to the Mackenzie R. Delta, Great Bear L., Alta. (N to L. Athabasca), Sask. (N to Prince Albert), Man. (N to Churchill), Ont. (N to Fort Severn, Hudson Bay, ca. 56°N), Que. (N to E James Bay at ca. 53°50′N, the Côte-Nord, Anticosti Is., and Gaspé Pen.), Labrador (N to the Hamilton R. basin), Nfld., N.B., P.E.I., and N.S., s to Calif., N.Mex., Mo., and Md.; Eurasia. [*Moehringia* Fenzl; *A. buxifolia* Poir.; *Stellaria ?biflora sensu* Pursh 1814, not L.; incl. vars. *angustifolia* (Regel) St. John and *taylorae* St. John, phases with relatively narrow leaves, those of the former more or less puberulent at least on the margins and midrib beneath, those of the latter glabrous or glabrate]. MAP *(M. lat.)*: Hultén 1968*b*:437.

A. macrocarpa Pursh
/aSs/W/EA/   (Ch)   Coasts and tundra from the N coasts of Alaska–Yukon to w Dist. Mackenzie (ca. 64°N), s to the Aleutian Is. and s Alaska (type locality); Novaya Zemlya; N Asia. [*Minuartia* Ostenf.; *A. crilloniana* Drew]. MAPS: Hultén 1944: map 540, p. 788, and 1968*b*: p. 429 (*Min. mac.*); Porsild 1966: map 57, p. 74.

A. macrophylla Hook.
/ST/(X)/A/   (Hpr)   Local on sandy or rocky shores and wooded slopes: s B.C. (N to Yale, lower Fraser Valley); Great Slave L.; N Sask. (s to ca. 56°N); shores of L. Superior in Ont. and Wisc.; Que. (Knob Lake dist. N to s Ungava Bay; Rimouski Co.; Gaspé Pen.); Labrador between ca. 55°30′ and 57°30′N; in the western U.S.A. s to s Calif. and N.Mex., in the East s to New Eng.; Asia (Altai Mts.). [*Moehringia* Torr.]. MAPS: *Atlas of Canada* 1957: map 18, sheet 38; Fernald 1925: map 31 (incomplete northwards), p. 259.

A. nuttallii Pax
/T/W/   (Ch)   Dry plains and gravelly benches or talus to alpine slopes from s B.C. (Vancouver Is.; Cheam, near Chilliwack; South Kootenay Pass) and sw Alta. (Crowsnest Pass; Waterton Lakes) to N Calif., Utah, and Wyo. [*A. pungens* Nutt., not Clem.; *Alsinopsis occidentalis* Heller].

A. obtusiloba (Rydb.) Fern.
/aST/W/   (Ch)   Gravel bars, talus slopes, and subalpine to alpine meadows (ranges of Canadian taxa outlined below), s to Oreg. and N.Mex. MAPS and synonymy: *see* below.
  The closely related *A. marcescens* Fern. is also keyed out below following the treatment by M.L. Fernald (Rhodora 21(241):13. 1919). If finally merged with *A. obtusiloba,* the distribution of this species would be disjunct rather than western. Hitchcock et al. (1964) refer w U.S.A. reports of *A. laricifolia* and *A. sajanensis* to *A. obtusiloba* (*see* discussions under those species).
1   Calyx glabrous; seeds smooth or obscurely pebbled; leaves glabrous-margined,
    deep green, loosely imbricated; [*A. laricifolia* var. *mar.* (Fern.) Boivin; serpentine and
    magnesian limestone ledges and gravels of w Nfld. (type from the Blomidon Mts.;

also known from Bonne Bay) and E Que. (Mt. Albert, Gaspé Pen.); Haystack Mt., N
Vt. (P.W. Cook, Rhodora 61(724):123. 1959); MAP: Hultén 1968b:430 (on *Minuartia
obtusiloba* map)] . . . . [*A. marcescens* Fern.]
1 Calyx glandular; seeds distinctly rugose or papillate; leaves minutely ciliate, pale
  green, very densely imbricated . . . . *A. obtusiloba*
  2 Petals roseate; [type from the Seward Pen., Alaska; merged with *A. arctica* by
    Hultén 1944] . . . . f. *rosea* Porsild
  2 Petals white; [*Minuartia* House; *Alsinopsis* Rydb.; *Arenaria biflora* Wats., not L.;
    A. biflora var. *obtusa* (Torr.) Wats. (*A. obtusa* Torr.); Alaska–Yukon–NW Dist.
    Mackenzie–B.C. and mts. of SW Alta.; MAPS: Hultén 1968b:430 *(Min. ob.)*; Porsild
    1966: map 58, p. 74; Fernald 1925: map 11 (generalized), p. 253] . . . . f. *obtusiloba*

A. peploides L.   Seabeach-Sandwort
/aST/X/GEA/   (Grh (Hpr))   Sandy seabeaches, the aggregate species from the Aleutian Is.
and coasts of Alaska–Yukon–Dist. Mackenzie–Dist. Keewatin to Banks Is., Victoria Is., N Baffin
Is., and northernmost Ungava–Labrador, S to NE Man. (Churchill), W and E James Bay, E Que.
(St. Lawrence R. estuary from I'Islet Co. to the Côte-Nord, Anticosti Is., and Gaspé Pen.),
Nfld., N.B., P.E.I., and N.S., S along the Pacific coast through coastal B.C. to NW Oreg. and
along the Atlantic coast to Md. and ?Va.; W Greenland N to ca. 78°N, E Greenland N to ca.
75°N; Iceland; Spitsbergen; Eurasia. MAPS and synonymy: *see below.*
1 Flowers in broad leafy terminal cymes; braches 1 or 2 mm thick.
  2 Branches freely forking; leaves mostly less than 2 cm long; sepals 4 or 5 mm
    long; seeds dark brown, minutely rugose; [*Alsine* Crantz; *Ammodenia* Rupr.;
    Halianthus Fries; *Hon(c)kenya* Ehrh.; *Merckia* Don; transcontinental; MAPS
    (aggregate species): Meusel 1943: fig. 7c (incomplete northwards); Meusel,
    Jaeger, and Weinert 1965:150; Hultén 1968b:434 *(Hon. pep.)*] . . . . var. *peploides*
  2 Branches simple or subsimple; leaves to over 4 cm long; sepals to 7 mm long;
    seeds light brown, smooth; [Aleutian Is. (type, as first collection cited, from Atka
    Is.) and Nfld.; M.L. Fernald, Rhodora 11(126):114. 1909] . . . . var. *maxima* Fern.
1 Flowers few, terminal and axillary, not in distinct cymes.
  3 Branches flaccid, scarcely fleshy, 1 or 2 mm thick; leaves mostly not over 1.5 cm
    long; pedicels slender; capsules to 8 mm thick; [*A. diffusa* (Hornem.) Wormsk.;
    transcontinental, largely replacing other forms northwards; MAP: Porsild 1957:
    map 146, p. 179] . . . . var. *diffusa* Hornem.
  3 Branches stiff, very fleshy or leathery, to over 4 mm thick; leaves to over 3 cm
    long; capsules to 12 mm thick.
    4 Leaves elliptic or oblong, narrowed at base; seeds lustrous; [var. *oblongifolia*
      (T. & G.) Wats.; *Honckenya (Ammodenia) ob.* T. & G.; *Arenaria sitchensis*
      Dietr.; Aleutian Is. and coastal Alaska–B.C.; MAP: Hultén 1968b:434] . . . .
      . . . . var. *major* Hook.
    4 Leaves oblong or oblong-ovate, scarcely narrowed at base; seeds distinctly
      papillate and only slightly lustrous; [*Adenarium maritimum* Raf.; *Holosteum
      succulentum* Nutt., not L.; E Que. to Nfld. and N.S.] . . . . var. *robusta* Fern.

A. physodes Fisch.
/aSs/W/eA/   (Grh)   Near water on sandy or gravelly banks nearly throughout Alaska–Yukon (*see* Hultén 1944: map 548, p. 788; *Mer. phy.*) and in NW Dist. Mackenzie (between Aklavik
and the coast); Siberia and Kamchatka. [*Merckia* Fisch.; *Wilhelmsia* McNeill; *Stellaria (A.)
ovalifolia* Hook.]. MAP: Hultén 1968b:437 *(Wil. phy.)*.

A. rossii R. Br.
/AST/X/GEeA/   (Ch)   Turfy, gravelly, or sandy calcareous soils, the aggregate species
from the coasts of Alaska–Yukon–Dist. Mackenzie–Dist. Keewatin to Banks Is., Melville Is.
(type locality), and northernmost Ellesmere Is., S in the West through the mts. of B.C. and SW
Alta. to Wash., ?Oreg., Idaho, and Colo., farther eastwards S to Great Bear L., NE Man. (Churchill, where taken by Eva Beckett in 1950; Schofield 1959), Southampton Is., S Baffin Is., and

Akpatok Is., N Ungava Bay, Que.; W Greenland at ca. 70° and 82°30'N, E Greenland between ca. 73° and 77°N; Spitsbergen; Kamchatka. MAPS and synonymy: *see* below.

1 Petals conspicuously surpassing the sepals, these mostly not over 2.5 mm long, obtusish, usually 1-nerved; pedicels to 2 cm long; leaves fleshy, subulate, obtuse; plant densely pulvinate or tufted; [incl. the large-petaled extreme, var. *daethiana* Polunin; transcontinental in the Arctic (type from Melville Is.); Greenland; MAPS (the occurrence at Churchill, NE Man., should be indicated on most): Porsild 1957: map 149, p. 179; Hultén 1968b:433, and 1958: map 160, p. 179; Böcher 1954: fig. 47 (top), p. 177; Raup 1947: pl. 23] . . . . ssp. *rossii*

1 Petals commonly shorter than the sepals or often lacking; sepals to 3.5 mm long, acute or acutish; pedicels often longer; leaves less fleshy; plant generally more loosely tufted.

2 Sepals commonly 3-nerved; petals sometimes equalling the sepals; [*A. (Minuartia) elegans* C. & S.; *A. rossii* var. *corollina* Fenzl; Alaska–Yukon–w Dist. Mackenzie] . . . . ssp. *elegans* (C. & S.) Maguire

2 Sepals often 1-nerved (sometimes weakly 3-nerved) . . . .
. . . . ssp. *columbiana* (Raup) Maguire

3 Petals present; [mts. of B.C. (type from Robb L.) and SW Alta.] . . . . var. *columbiana*

3 Petals obsolete or wanting; [s Yukon and mts. of w Alta.] . . . . . var. *apetala* Maguire

A. rubella (Wahl.) Sm.
/AST/X/GEA/ (Ch) Dry gravelly, sandy, or rocky places (often calcareous or magnesian) from the E Aleutian Is. and coasts of Alaska–Yukon–Dist. Mackenzie–Dist Keewatin throughout the Canadian Arctic Archipelago to northernmost Ellesmere Is. and northernmost Ungava–Labrador, s in the West through the mts. of B.C. and SW Alta. to Calif. and N.Mex., farther eastwards s to L. Athabasca (Alta. and Sask.), NE Man. (Churchill; reported s to York Factory by John Macoun 1883), Ont. (s to w James Bay at 54°52'N; the report from the Bruce Pen., L. Huron, by Krotkov 1940, is perhaps based upon *A. stricta*), James Bay (South Twin Is.), Que. (s to Cape Jones, NE James Bay, 54°37'N, Rimouski Co., the Shickshock Mts. of the Gaspé Pen., and the Côte-Nord; not known from Anticosti Is.), Nfld., and the mts. of N Vt.; circumgreenlandic; Iceland; Eurasia. [*Alsine* Wahl.; *Minuartia* Graebn.; *Ar. hirta* Wormsk.; *Ar. (Alsinopsis; Min.; Sabulina) propinqua* Rich.; *Ar. (Alsinopsis; Min.) quadrivalvis* R. Br.; *A. juniperina* Pursh, not L.; *A. verna* vars. *rubella* (Wahl.) Wats., *propinqua* (Rich.) Fern., and *pubescens* Fern.]. MAPS: Hultén 1968b:433 *(Min. rub.)*; Porsild 1957: map 148, p. 179; Meusel 1943: fig. 6b *(A. verna;* incomplete for N. America); Meusel, Jaeger, and Weinert 1965:149 *(A. verna)*; Raup 1947: pl. 23 *(A. verna* var. *pub.)*.

Forma *epilis* (Fern.) Polunin *(A. verna* var. *pro.* f. *ep.* Fern; plant glabrous rather than more or less glandular-pilose) is known from E Que. (type from the Gaspé Pen.), Nfld. (Rouleau 1956), Labrador (Ramah and Rowsell Harbour), and Iceland. Forma *plena* Calder (flowers "double", the petals numerous rather than 5) is known only from the type locality on Baffin Is.

A. sajanensis Willd.
/aST/X/GEA/ (Ch) Gravelly or rocky places (usually calcareous) from the coasts of Alaska–Yukon–Dist. Mackenzie–Dist. Keewatin to s Banks Is., Victoria Is., N-cent. Baffin Is., and northernmost Ungava–Labrador, s in the West through the mts. of B.C. and SW Alta. to ?Ariz., farther eastwards s to Great Bear L., s Dist. Keewatin, cent. Que. (s to ca. 55°N), and cent. Labrador (s to ca. 57°N); isolated on Mt. Albert, Gaspé Pen., E Que.; W and E Greenland N to ca. 78°N; Iceland; Eurasia. [*Alsinopsis* Cockerell; *Minuartia* House; *Ar. biflora* Wats., not L.; *Stellaria (Alsine; Alsinella; Cerastium; Sabulina) biflora* L., not *Ar. biflora* L.]. MAPS: Porsild 1957: map 151, p. 179; Raup 1947: pl. 24.

Further studies may radically alter the range outlined above. Hitchcock et al. (1964), for example, refer citations from the W U.S.A. (and, presumably, N to Alaska) to *A. obtusiloba,* this (and *A. arctica* and *A. sajanensis*) merged with *A. laricifolia* var. *occulta* by Boivin (1968).

A. serpyllifolia L. Thyme-leaved Sandwort
Eurasian; introd. along roadsides and in dry sterile fields and waste places of N. America, as in s B.C. (N to Lillooet and Revelstoke), s Sask. (near Tisdale, 52°51'N; Breitung 1957a), Ont.

(N to Thunder Bay and the Ottawa dist.), Que. (N to the Gaspé Pen.), N.B., P.E.I., and N.S. (reports from Labrador by John Macoun 1883, and other authors probably refer to some other species).

Some of the material from our area appears referable to var. *tenuior* Mert. & Koch (leaves relatively narrow, the panicle irregular, the fruiting calyx 2 or 3 mm long, rather than leaves ovate, the cymes borne in a nearly regular, dichotomously branching panicle, the fruiting calyx 3 or 4 mm long).

A. stricta Michx.
/aST/X/GEA/ (Ch) Plains, ledges, mossy tundra, etc., the aggregate species from N-cent. Alaska and cent. Yukon to Great Bear L., cent. Dist. Keewatin, N Baffin Is., northernmost Que., Labrador (Ramah, 58°54'N), and Nfld., s to Oreg., Tex., Ark., Ky., and S.C.; w and E Greenland between ca. 68° and 75°N; Iceland; Spitsbergen; Eurasia. MAPS and synonymy: *see* below.
1 Plants more or less glandular-puberulent on the calyces, pedicels, and upper part of stem; [ssp. *macra* (Nels. & Macbr.) Maguire (*A. macra* Nels. & Macbr.); *A tenella* Nutt., not Kit.; mts. of s B.C. and sw ?Alta.] . . . . var. *puberulenta* (Peck) Hitchc.
1 Plants completely glabrous.
    2 Sepals appearing virtually nerveless when fresh, obscurely 3-nerved when dried, about equalling the petals; stems 1–3(5)-flowered; taproot well developed, the plant forming loose soft tussocks; [*A. uliginosa* Schleich. and its f. *albina* Polunin; *Spergula (Alsine; Minuartia) stricta* Sw., not *Arenaria stricta* Michx.; N-cent. Alaska and cent. Yukon to Great Bear L., cent. Dist. Keewatin, N Baffin Is., Ungava (N to Sugluk, 62°08'N, and Akpatok Is., N Ungava Bay), and N Labrador (reported from Ramah, 58°54'N, by Fernald and Sornborger 1899), s to s Yukon, N Man. (Churchill; Gillam, about 165 mi s of Churchill), cent. Ont. (s to w James Bay at 54°22'N), and cent. Que. (s to E James Bay near Cape Jones, ca. 54°30'N, and Knob L., 54°48'N); w Greenland between ca. 68° and 73°N, E Greenland between ca. 70° and 75°N; Iceland; Spitsbergen; Eurasia; MAP: Porsild 1957: map 150 (*A. ulig.*), p. 179] . . . . var. *uliginosa* (Schleich.) Boivin
    2 Sepals distinctly 3-nerved even when fresh; stems many-flowered; taproot weakly developed, the plant not tussock-forming.
        3 Petals shorter than or at most about equalling the sepals; capsule exserted; [*A. (Alsinopsis; Minuartia; Sabulina) dawsonensis* Britt., the type from Dawson, the Yukon; *A. (Sabulina) litorea* Fern.; *A. ?juniperina* of early reports from Labrador and Nfld., not L.; N-cent. Alaska–Yukon to Great Bear L., L. Athabasca (Alta. and Sask.), Man. (N to Churchill), northernmost Ont., Que. (N to E Hudson Bay at ca. 57°N, the Koksoak R. at ca. 58°N, L. Mistassini, the Côte-Nord, Anticosti Is., and the Gaspé Pen.), and Nfld., s to B.C., Alta., Minn., s Ont., and E Que. (Rimouski Co.); MAPS: Raup 1947: pl. 23 (*A. daw.;* the occurrence at Churchill, NE Man., should be indicated); Hultén 1968b:432 (*Min. daw.*)] . . . . var. *dawsonensis* (Britt.) Scoggan
        3 Petals conspicuously surpassing the sepals; capsule not exserted; [*Spergula* Sw.; *Minuartia* Hiern.; *Alsinopsis* and *Sabulina* Small; *Alsine michauxii* Fenzl; s Ont. (N to the Ottawa dist.) and sw Que. (Pontiac and Missisquoi counties); MAP (*Min. str.*): Hultén 1968b:431] . . . . var. *stricta*

[CARDIONEMA DC.] [2480]

[*C. ramosissima* (Weinm.) Nels. & Macbr.]
[The report of this species of sandy beaches of the Pacific coast (Wash. to Mexico and Chile) from the coast of s B.C. by Lloyd (1924) requires confirmation. (*Loeflingia* Weinm.; *Pentacaena* H. & A.).]

CERASTIUM L.   [2430]   Mouse-ear Chickweed

(Ref.: Hultén 1956; M.L. Fernald and K.M. Wiegand, Rhodora 22(263):169–79. 1920)
1 Styles 3 (sometimes 4); capsules opening by 6 (sometimes 8) teeth; petals to 1 cm
   long, deeply bifid (cleft into 2 lobes); sepals 5 or 6 mm long; leaves linear to narrowly
   oblong or oblanceolate, usually glabrous and less than 1.5 cm long and 4 mm broad;
   stems usually less than 1.5 dm tall, with numerous very leafy prostrate or trailing
   matted branches, these and the stems glabrous or short-pilose in lines; (s Baffin Is.–
   Que.–Labrador–NW Nfld.) . . . .*C. cerastoides*
1 Styles usually 5; capsule usually opening by 10 teeth; median internodes of the
   flowering stems usually pubescent all around (or *C. regelii* often nearly or quite
   glabrous).
   2 Stems lax and weak, viscid-pilose; fruiting pedicels hooked at tip, filiform, to over
      5 cm long; petals narrowly obovate, cleft nearly to middle, longer than the sepals;
      capsule curved, to nearly 3 times as long as the calyx; leaves thin, oblong-
      lanceolate to narrowly obovate, acute or acutish, to about 8 cm long; annual,
      lacking persistent sterile basal leafy offshoots; (Alaska–B.C. to Que.) . . . . . .*C. nutans*
   2 Stems firm; fruiting pedicels straight or curved but scarcely hooked (reflexed in
      C. fischerianum).
      3 Petals narrow, shorter than or barely surpassing the sepals; (introd.).
         4 Stamens mostly 5 (sometimes 10); petals only shallowly notched; fruiting
            pedicels up to 4 times longer than the sepals; bracts of the finally loose
            and open cyme scarious-tipped; leaves thick, elliptic to broadly ovate,
            obtuse, minutely white-hispid; plant glandular-viscid, usually annual . . . .
            . . . .*C. semidecandrum*
         4 Stamens 10; petals cleft nearly to the middle.
            5 Flowers in loose cymes; bracts of cyme herbaceous or narrowly
               scarious-tipped; lower pedicels up to 4 times as long as the mature
               sepals; sepals naked above the scarious apex; leaves ovate, oblong, or
               elliptical, acute or obtuse, minutely apiculate; plant dark green and
               often suffused with dark purple, hirsute throughout (rarely also
               glandular in the upper half), commonly more or less perennial and with
               sterile basal leafy branches or offshoots . . . .*C. vulgatum*
            5 Flowers in compact clusters; bracts of cyme herbaceous; pedicels
               mostly shorter than the mature sepals; hairs near the tip of the sepals
               surpassing the narrowly scarious apex; leaves ovate or elliptical to
               obovate, rounded or obtuse at tip; plant often yellowish green,
               spreading-hirsute and glandular-viscid above; annual, lacking sterile
               basal offshoots . . . .*C. viscosum*
      3 Petals relatively broad, distinctly surpassing the sepals (commonly 2 or 3
         times as long); perennials with matted leafy basal branches or offshoots, or
         stoloniferous rhizomes.
         6 Plants densely white-tomentose; (introd.).
            7 Leaves linear-lanceolate, to about 2 cm long and 3 mm broad . . . .
               . . . .*C. tomentosum*
            7 Leaves lanceolate, to about 3 cm long and 6 mm broad . . . . .*C. biebersteinii*
         6 Plants not densely white-tomentose; native perennials.
            8 Leaves linear-subulate to narrowly ovate; petals usually about twice as
               long as the sepals.
               9 Stems several to many from slender stoloniferous rhizomes, almost
                  unbranched, to about 6 dm tall and up to 3 mm thick at base, they
                  and the leaves copiously puberulent; leaves narrowly to broadly
                  lanceolate, long-acuminate, to over 1 dm long and about 1.5 cm
                  broad; sepals to 11 mm long; capsule to 2 cm long, its teeth often
                  strongly recurved; (Alaska–Yukon) . . . .*C. maximum*
               9 Stems trailing and matted, producing depressed, sterile, leafy
                  offshoots at base, they and the leaves variously pubescent; leaves

linear-subulate to lanceolate or ovate, obtusish to acute, usually less than 3.5 cm long; sepals to 8.5 mm long, equalled to much surpassed by the capsule; (transcontinental) . . . .*C. arvense*

8 Leaves generally shorter and relatively broader; bracts of inflorescence herbaceous or only the upper ones more or less scarious-margined; petals not more than twice as long as the sepals; (chiefly arctic and subarctic regions).

10 Leaves glabrous except for the often softly ciliate margins, obovate to subrotund, more or less shining, somewhat fleshy, rarely over 12 mm long; petals 2 or 3 times as long as the glandular sepals; (plant often sterile); (essentially transcontinental) . . . .*C. regelii*

10 Leaves more or less pubescent in addition to the often ciliate margins.

11 Tips of the leaves of the sterile basal offshoots with shiny inflated woolly weak multicellular hairs often mingled with other types of hairs, the entire plant more or less viscid and clammy; calyx usually truncate at base; (N Sask. to Baffin Is., Labrador, and Nfld.) . . . .*C. alpinum*

11 Leaves lacking shiny inflated weak multicellular hairs, the hairs stiffer and shorter, often thickened at base, yellowish green to light brown, at most few-celled; calyx usually rounded at base.

12 Plant relatively tall, the coarse stem and pedicels yellowish-hirsute; inflorescence subumbellate, the pedicels reflexed in fruit; (Alaska–B.C.) . . . .*C. fischerianum*

12 Plant lower, the stem more delicate; pedicels not reflexed in fruit.

13 Flowers long-pedicelled and rather numerous in dichotomously branched cymes, they and the pedicels with short glandular or viscid hairs; petals usually only slightly surpassing the sepals; leaves lance-ovate; (transcontinental) . . . .*C. beeringianum*

13 Flowers often solitary, the lateral short-pedicelled ones mostly not opening; pedicels lanate or hirsute; petals about twice as long as the sepals; plant not viscid; (NE Canada) . . . .*C. arcticum*

C. alpinum L.

/AST/EE/GE/ (Ch) Rocky, sandy, or gravelly places, the species confined in N. America to Canada (ranges of taxa outlined below); circumgreenlandic; Iceland; Spitsbergen; Europe. MAPS and synonymy: see below.

1 Pubescence of leaves evenly distributed; [var. *legitimum* Lindbl.; N Europe] . . . .
. . . .[ssp. *alpinum*]

1 Tips of leaves of basal shoots with a brush of white entangled woolly hairs . . . .
. . . . .ssp. *lanatum* (Lam.) Aschers. & Graebn.

2 Pubescence of leaves relatively short and more or less strigose; [coast of E Dist. Mackenzie (type from Bathurst Inlet, as the first locality cited) to Southampton Is., S Baffin Is., and N Labrador, S to N Sask. (G.W. Argus, Can. Field-Nat. 80(3):136. 1966), S James Bay and N Nfld.] . . . . .var. *strigosum* Hult.

2 Pubescence of leaves long, wooly and entangled.

3 Leaf-margins bearing coarse broad-based hairs; [S Baffin Is. and Greenland (type from W Greenland)] . . . . .var. *robustum* Hult.

3 Leaf-margins bearing only soft slender hairs; [*C. lanatum* Lam.; *C. villosum* Baumg., not Muhl.; coast of Dist. Mackenzie to northernmost Ellesmere Is., S to NE Man. (Churchill), S James Bay, S Labrador, and Nfld.; circumgreenlandic; MAPS: Hultén 1956: fig. 4 (the aggregate ssp. *lanatum*), p. 431; Porsild 1957: map 138 (aggregate species), p. 178; Meusel, Jaeger, and Weinert 1965:145 (aggregate species)] . . . . .var. *lanatum*

C. arcticum Lange
/AST/EE/GE/ (Ch) Rocky, sandy, or gravelly places, the species confined in N. America to Canada (ranges of taxa outlined below); circumgreenlandic; Iceland; Spitsbergen; the Faeroes; Scotland; N Scandinavia; Novaya Zemlya. MAPS and synonymy: *see* below.
1 Leaves subglabrous or slightly hirsute (but lacking long woolly hairs) in addition to
    the marginal ciliation of relatively short hairs; [Baffin Is., N Ungava–Labrador, and
    Greenland (type from w Greenland); MAPS: Hultén 1956: fig. 15, p. 450, and 1958: map
    13 (dots only, the area within the bounding line representing that of the aggregate
    species), p. 33; Porsild 1957: map 140 (aggregate species; incomplete southwards
    according to Hultén's interpretation of the *C. alpinum-arcticum* complex), p. 178] . . . . . .
    . . . . .var. *arcticum*
1 Leaves more or less strongly lanate; marginal cilia often coarser and broader-based.
    2 Plant with long, relatively loosely tufted, erect stems; [*C. alpinum* var. *procerum*
        Lange; known only from Greenland, the type locality] . . . .var. *procerum* (Lange) Hult.
    2 Plant low-growing, densely tufted.
        3 Plant yellowish green, the pubescence pale; inflorescence usually consisting
            of a solitary long-pedicelled flower; [*C. alpinum* var. *glabratum* Hook.; Melville
            Is. to northernmost Ellesmere Is., s to NE Man. (Churchill), N James Bay, E
            Que. (Mingan Is.), and s Labrador; Greenland; MAP: Hultén 1956: fig. 20, p. 455] . . .
            . . . . .var. *vestitum* Hult.
        3 Plant dark green, the pubescence sordid; inflorescence with thick branches;
            [N Banks Is. to northernmost Ellesmere Is., s to cent. Dist. Keewatin
            (Chesterfield Inlet), Hudson Strait (Nottingham Is.), and s Baffin Is., with an
            isolated station at Cape Henrietta Maria, NW James Bay, Ont.; Greenland; MAP:
            Hultén 1956: fig. 22, p. 458] . . . . .var. *sordidum* Hult.

C. arvense L.   Field Chickweed
/ST/X/GEA/ (Ch) Rocks, gravels, and turfs (chiefly calcareous; often becoming weedy in grasslands), the aggregate species from s-cent. Alaska–Yukon and the Mackenzie R. Delta to Great Bear L., Alta. (N to L. Athabasca), Sask. (N to Prince Albert), Man. (N to Gillam, about 165 mi s of Churchill), Ont. (N to the N shore of L. Superior), Que. (N to Ungava Bay and the Côte-Nord), Nfld., N.B., P.E.I., and N.S., s to Calif., N.Mex., and Ga.; w Greenland near the Arctic Circle; Eurasia. MAPS and synonymy: *see* below.
1 Internodes of stem bearing gland-tipped short hairs intermixed with glandless ones;
    [*C. occidentale* Greene; *C. strictum* L.; Alaska and St. Paul Is., N.S. (Fernald *in* Gray
    1950); Man. (Scoggan 1957)] . . . . .var. *viscidulum* Gremli
1 Internodes of stem clothed with long reflexed eglandular hairs.
    2 Leaves mostly lanceolate, to over 6 cm long, often somewhat rounded at base;
        [s Ont.] . . . . .var. *villosum* (Muhl.) Hollick & Britt.
        3 Leaves permanently greyish-pilose; [*C. villosum* Muhl., not Baumg.; incl.
            C. velutinum Raf.; Bruce and Wentworth counties, s Ont.] . . . . .f. *villosum*
        3 Leaves glabrate above; [*C. oblongifolium* Torr.; *C. pubescens* Goldie; s Ont.:
            Lambton and Essex counties] . . . . .f. *oblongifolium* (Torr.) Pennell
    2 Leaves linear to lanceolate, to about 3.5 cm long, tapering to base; [incl. vars.
        ophiticola Raymond and *purpurascens* Boivin; *C. graminifolium* Rydb.;
        *C. alsophilum, C. angustatum, C. campestre, C. confertum, C. effusum, C.
        nitidum, C. scopulorum, C. subulatum,* and *C. vestitum* Greene; *C. pensylvanicum*
        Hornem.; transcontinental; MAPS (aggregate species): Meusel, Jaeger, and
        Weinert 1965:124; Hultén 1968*b*:425] . . . . .var. *arvense*

C. beeringianum C. & S.
/AST/X/EA/ (Ch) Rocky, sandy, or gravelly places, the aggregate species from the Aleutian Is. and coasts of Alaska–Yukon–Dist. Mackenzie to Banks Is., northernmost Baffin Is., and northernmost Que., s in the West through B.C.–Alta. to Calif., Ariz., and Colo., farther eastwards s to L. Athabasca (Alta. and Sask.), Southampton Is., E Que. (Rimouski Co.; Côte-Nord; Gaspé Pen.), s Labrador, and Nfld.; an isolated station along the NW shore of L. Superior, Ont.; Novaya Zemlya; Asia. MAPS and synonymy: *see* below.

1   Plant tawny or purplish, strongly matted and more or less decumbent; seeds about
     1.3 mm broad; [*C. terrae-novae* Fern. and its f. *waghornei* Fern. & Wieg.; Dist.
     Mackenzie (Great Bear L.); N Alta. (L. Athabasca); Dist. Keewatin (Kazan R.); E Que.,
     Labrador, and Nfld. (type from the Blomidon Mts.); MAP: Hultén 1956: fig. 28
     (crosses), p. 478] . . . . ssp. *terrae-novae* (Fern. & Wieg.) Hult.
1   Plant greyish green, erect or nearly so; seeds mostly less than 1 mm broad.
     2   Pedicels bearing very fine and short glandular hairs; flowers small, the petals only
          slightly surpassing the sepals; lower internodes of stem obscurely retrorse-hairy;
          leaves more or less glabrous; [*C. beer.* var. *capillare* Fern. & Wieg.; *C. earlei*
          Rydb.; *C. alpinum sensu* Henry 1915, not L.; mts. of S B.C. and SW Alta.; MAP:
          Hultén 1956: fig. 28 (open rings), p. 478] . . . . ssp. *earlei* (Rydb.) Hult.
     2   Pedicels bearing long glandular hairs; lower stem-internodes conspicuously
          retrorse-hairy . . . . ssp. *beeringianum*
          3   Flowers large, the petals about double the length of the sepals;
               [*C. scammaniae* Polunin; *C. fischerianum* of Canadian reports in part, not
               Ser.; Aleutian Is.–Alaska–Yukon–NW Dist. Mackenzie; MAP: Hultén 1968b:422] . . . . .
               . . . . var. *grandiflorum* Hult.
          3   Flowers small, the petals only slightly surpassing the sepals.
               4   Leaves more or less glabrous; [Dist. Mackenzie (Coronation Gulf); Prince
                    Patrick Is.; Prince Charles Is.; Southampton Is.; Baffin Is.; E Dist. Keewatin
                    (Rankin Inlet)] . . . . var. *glabratum* Hult.
               4   Leaves conspicuously hirsute; [*C. ?aleuticum* Hult.; *C. pilosum* Greene, not
                    Ledeb.; transcontinental in arctic and subarctic regions; type from
                    Kotzebue Sound, Alaska; MAPS: Hultén 1968b:421, and 1956: fig. 28 (dots),
                    p. 478; Porsild 1957: map 139 (aggregate species), p. 178]. A hybrid with
                    C. fischerianum is apparently reported from Alaska by Hultén (1968b) . . . .
                    . . . . var. *beeringianum*

C. biebersteinii DC.
Asiatic; a local garden-escape in N. America, as in Ont. (Michipicoten, NW shore of L. Supe-
rior; TRT) and N.S. (farm ravine near Kentville, Kings Co.; ACAD; reported from Wedgeport,
Yarmouth Co., by W.L. Klawe, Can. Field-Nat. 69(3):129. 1955).

C. cerastoides (L.) Britt.
/aST/E/GEA/   (Ch)   Wet rocks and mossy places from S Baffin Is. and northernmost Ungava–Labrador to E Que. (Shickshock Mts. of the Gaspé Pen.) and NW Nfld.; W Greenland N to
ca. 72°N, E Greenland N to ca. 75°N; Iceland; Jan Mayen; the Faeroes; Eurasia. [*Stellaria* L.;
Provencheria Boivin; *C. trigynum* L.]. MAPS: Hultén 1958: map 30, p. 49; Porsild 1957: map
142, p. 178; Böcher 1954: fig. 28 (top), p. 111; Meusel, Jaeger, and Weinert 1965:144.

C. fischerianum Ser.
/sT/W/eA/   (Ch)   Rocky, sandy, and gravelly places of the Aleutian Is.–S Alaska (*see* Hultén 1944: map 527, p. 787) and W-cent. B.C. (Queen Charlotte Is.); coastal E Asia. [*C. rigidum*
Ledeb.; *C. unalaschkense* Takeda]. MAPS: Hultén 1956: fig. 29, p. 487, and 1968b:424.

C. maximum L.   Great Chickweed
/Ss/W/EA/   (Ch)   Moist thickets and grassy places of Alaska–Yukon (N to ca. 70°N; *see* the
N Alaska map by Wiggins and Thomas 1962:380, and Hultén 1944: map 529, p. 787, who notes
that a report from Dist. Mackenzie is referable to *C. alpinum*); NE Europe; N Asia. [*C. grande*
Greene]. MAP: Hultén 1968b:421.

C. nutans Raf.
/sT/X/   (T)   Calcareous rocks, wooded slopes, alluvia, etc., from S Alaska (Franklin; CAN),
SW Dist. Mackenzie (near the SW end of Great Slave L.; CAN), and B.C. to L. Athabasca (Alta.
and Sask.), Man. (N to Gillam, about 165 mi S of Churchill), Ont. (N to Big Trout L. at ca.
53°45′N, 90°W), and SW Que. (N to the Montreal dist.; the inclusion of N.S. in the range by

Gleason 1958, requires confirmation), s to Ariz., Tex., and Fla. [Incl. vars. *brachypodum* Engelm. (*C. bra.* (Engelm.) Robins.) and *occidentale* Boivin and *C. longepedunculatum* Muhl.].

C. regelii Ostenf.

/Aa/(X)/GEA/ (Ch) Wet meadows, low calcareous tundra, and shores from Banks Is. to northernmost Ellesmere Is., s to the coasts of Dist. Mackenzie–Dist. Keewatin and w Baffin Is. near the Arctic Circle; N coast of Greenland and E Greenland s to ca. 69°30'N; Spitsbergen; Franz Josef Land; arctic coast of Asia. [*C. alpinum* f. *pulvinata* Simmons; incl. *C. jenisejense* Hult.]. MAPS: Hultén 1968b:423, 1958: map 1, p. 21, and 1956: fig. 25, p. 469; Porsild 1957: map 141, p. 178; *Atlas of Canada* 1957: map 4, sheet 38; Gelting 1934: fig. 7 (the w Greenland dot should probably be deleted), p. 43.

C. semidecandrum L.

Eurasian; introd. along roadsides and in sandy fields and cult. land of N. America, as in sw B.C. (Vancouver Is. and Vancouver) and s Ont. (Point Edward, Lambton Co.; OAC).

C. tomentosum L.   Dusty Miller, Snow-in-Summer

European; escaped from or persisting in old gardens and cemeteries of N. America, as in B.C. (Victoria; Queen Charlotte Is.; Kamloops), Man. (Boivin 1966b), s Ont. (Lambton and Brant counties), Que. (Ste-Anne-de-la-Pocatière, Kamouraska Co.; Tadoussac, Saguenay Co.), P.E.I. (dumps at Souris, Kings Co.; ACAD), and N.S. (Kentville, Kings Co.; Black Point, Victoria Co.).

C. viscosum L.

Eurasian; waste places, fields, and roadsides of N. America, the exact distribution uncertain through confusion with *C. vulgatum* and several other supposedly distinct taxa. Boivin (1966b) reports it only from B.C. (Vancouver Is., Triangle Is., Vancouver, Douglas, Agassiz, Manning Park, and Cranbrook; CAN; V) and Fernald *in* Gray (1950) reports it only from Nfld. (Burgeo; GH). Collections and reports from elsewhere in our area require confirmation.

Many botanists consider the name *C. viscosum* L. too ambiguous to be maintained. M. Mizushima (Sci. Rep. Tohoku Univ. Fourth Ser. (Biol.) 29:277–94. 1963) refers the taxon in part to *C. holosteoides* ssp. *triviale* (Link) Möschl. (*C. triviale* Link), this now generally accepted as part of the *C. vulgatum* complex. The names *C. caespitosum* Gilib. and *C. glomeratum* Thuill. have also been used but are themselves apparently often considered referable to that complex.

C. vulgatum L.   Common Mouse-ear Chickweed

Eurasian; a common weed of waste places, cult. fields, and roadsides of N. America, known from Alaska–Yukon, all the provinces, and Greenland. [Evidently incl. *C. caespitosum* Gilib., *C. fontanum* Baumg., *C. holosteoides* Fries, and *C. triviale* Link, at least in part; *see* discussion under *C. viscosum*]. MAP (*C. fontanum* ssp. *triviale*): Hultén 1968b:425.

CORRIGIOLA L.   [2469]

C. litoralis L.   Strapwort

European; Eastham (1947) reports as follows concerning a B.C. occurrence of this species: "A few plants of this annual have appeared for three successive years just outside the Government Fumigation Station for nursery stock, Vancouver. Possibly introd. as seed in soil adhering to roots of imported nursery stock."

DIANTHUS L.   [2502]   Pink, Carnation.   Oeillet

1   Flowers in dense terminal clusters or cymes, the slender subtending bracts about equalling the calyx; petals shallowly toothed; stems to about 8 dm tall; (introd.).
2   Leaves narrowly to broadly linear, to 8 mm broad, copiously short-pubescent; flowers few in small terminal clusters; petals pink or roseate, dotted with white,

the elliptic-oblanceolate limb not much surpassing the densely pubescent lance-subulate long-pointed bracts; calyx about 40-nerved; stem stiff, slender, simple or usually branched from base, pubescent below the nodes; annual or biennial . . . .*D. armeria*

2 Leaves lanceolate to oblanceolate, to over 1.5 cm broad, glabrous except for short-ciliate margins (or sometimes sparingly strigose beneath); flower-clusters in a broad dense terminal cyme; petals whitish to pink or dark red, the broad limb much surpassing the ciliate awn-pointed bracts; calyx 20–25 nerved; stem stout, simple or branched only above, glabrous (or long-pilose below the inflorescence and nodes); tufted perennial . . . .*D. barbatus*
1 Flowers all or nearly all solitary and long-pedicelled at the tips of the branches, 1–several on a stem, the subtending bracts usually at most half as long as the calyx (about equalling the calyx in the Alaskan *D. repens*); leaves linear or linear-lanceolate.
  3 Petals deeply lacerate-fringed; corolla-limb to over 3.5 cm broad; bracts subtending calyx at most 1/3 as long as the calyx; glabrous tufted perennials; (introd.).
    4 Flowers white to pink or red, with a striate or darker centre, the limb of the petals fringed to about one-third its depth; leaves glaucous, to over 8 cm long, longer than the internodes of the stem; stem to about 3 dm tall, decumbent or erect . . . .*D. plumarius*
    4 Flowers white with greyish or spotted centre, the limb of the petals fringed more than half its depth; leaves green, at most about 5 cm long, mostly shorter than the internodes; stem rarely over 1.5 dm tall, erect . . . .*D. arenarius*
  3 Petals merely toothed or ciliate; corolla-limb at most about 2.5 cm broad.
    5 Bracts subtending calyx nearly or quite equalling the calyx, lanceolate, to nearly 1.5 cm long, usually a single opposite pair; flowers purple; leaves to 2.5 cm long, they and the stiffish angled stems (to about 1.5 dm tall) glabrous; tufted perennial; (Alaska) . . . .*D. repens*
    5 Bracts subtending calyx at most about half as long as the calyx; (introd.).
      6 Petals glabrous, roseate; leaves glabrous . . . .*D. sylvestris*
      6 Petals bearded.
        7 Leaves short-hispid on margins and midrib, those of the stem mostly less than 3 cm long and shorter than the internodes; lower leaves oblanceolate, on elongate sterile trailing basal offshoots; flowers white to dark rose or purple, usually spotted and often with a V-shaped pattern in the throat, subtended by 2 (sometimes 4) bracts, the corolla-limb less than 2 cm broad; minutely scabrous-puberulent, loosely mat-forming perennial rarely over 4 dm tall . . . .*D. deltoides*
        7 Leaves glabrous, those of the stem to about 8 cm long, longer than the internodes, the basal ones early deciduous; flowers rose-lilac with purplish centre, subtended by 4 or 6 bracts, the corolla-limb to about 2.5 cm broad; glabrous or closely pubescent biennial or short-lived perennial to 7 or 8 dm tall . . . .*D. chinensis*

D. arenarius L.   Finland Pink
Eurasian; reported as established as a garden-escape in the Ottawa dist., Ont., by Gillett (1958; *D. ser.*). [*D. plumarius* var. *aren.* (L.) Neilr.; *D. serotinus* Waldst. & Kit.].

D. armeria L.   Deptford Pink
Eurasian; a garden-escape in N. America, as in s B.C. (Victoria; CAN; reported from Grand Forks, about 35 mi w of Trail, by Groh and Frankton 1949*b*), Ont. (N to the Ottawa dist.), Que. (N to the Montreal dist.), P.E.I. (DAO), and N.S.

D. barbatus L.   Sweet William
Eurasian; a garden-escape in N. America, as in s B.C. (Ainsworth Hot Springs, Kootenay L.; Deroche, near Vancouver), Alta. (Waterton), Man. (Morden; East Mossy Portage at the N end

of L. Winnipegosis), Ont. (N to L. Abitibi at ca. 48°30'N), Que. (N to Nominingue, Labelle Co., Bic, Rimouski Co., and the Gaspé Pen.; reported from Sheldrake, Saguenay Co. of the Côte-Nord, by Saint-Cyr 1887), and N.S. (Wolfville, Kings Co.).

D. chinensis L.   China Pink
Asiatic; reported as inclined to persist in sandy ground at Point Edward, Lambton Co., s Ont., by Dodge (1915).

D. deltoides L.   Maiden-Pink
Eurasian; a garden-escape in N. America, as in s B.C. (Vancouver Is.; Saltspring Is.; Abbotsford, near Vancouver), Ont. (N to the Ottawa dist.), Que. (N to L. Timiskaming at 47°28'N), P.E.I. (Panmure Is., Queens Co.), and N.S.

D. plumarius L.   Cottage Pink
Eurasian; a garden-escape in N. America, as in s Ont. (occasionally persisting after being thrown out of gardens; Montgomery 1957) and N.S. (in a meadow near Cape Blomidon, Kings Co.; ACAD).

D. repens Willd.   Northern Pink
/Ss/W/EA/   (Ch)   Known in N. America only from Alaska and NW Yukon (reported N to Cape Lisburne at ca. 69°N; see Hultén 1944: map 560, p. 789, who notes that reports from Greenland require confirmation); N Eurasia. [D. alpinus var. repens (Willd.) Regel]. MAP: Hultén 1968b:448.

D. sylvestris Wulfen   Wood Pink
European; reported as introd. in Alta. by Boivin (1966b; Fort Saskatchewan, where perhaps a garden-escape).

GYPSOPHILA L.   [2497]

1   Stems trailing or prostrate, the flowering stems at most about 1.5 dm tall; leaves linear, glabrous; panicle with few and relatively large flowers; perennial; (introd. in B.C.) . . . . .G. repens
1   Stems erect or ascending, often taller; (introd.).
  2   Leaves ovate-oblong, somewhat fleshy, the lower ones commonly about twice as long as broad; flowers pink to pale purple, commonly at least 7 mm broad, in loose panicled cymes; glabrous perennial to over 1 m tall; (a garden-escape in Alta.) . . . . .G. pacifica
  2   Leaves narrowly linear to lance-acuminate, several times longer than broad.
    3   Leaves linear-filiform, to about 2 cm long and 1 mm broad, attenuate at each end; flowers in very loose cymes (appearing as if solitary in the leaf-axils); very diffusely branched annual with capillary stems to about 2.5 dm tall; (introd. in Ont. and Que.) . . . . .G. muralis
    3   Leaves linear-lanceolate to lanceolate, to over 8 cm long; plants glaucous.
      4   Pedicels to 3.5 cm long; calyx to 5 mm long; lower leaves spatulate, the upper ones lance-acuminate, short-connate at base; slender-based annual or short-lived perennial to about 6 dm tall; (introd., widespread) . . . .G. elegans
      4   Pedicels at most about 12 mm long; calyx at most 3 mm long; leaves lance-acuminate, attenuate at base; hard-based perennials to over 1 m tall.
        5   Leaves linear-lanceolate, 1-nerved; pedicels usually glabrous; flowers white; (introd., widespread) . . . . .G. paniculata
        5   Leaves broader, 3 (–5)-nerved; pedicels glandular-pubescent; flowers white or roseate; (introd. in Alta.) . . . . .G. acutifolia

G. acutifolia Fisch.
European; introd. in Alta. (Calgary, where perhaps a garden-escape; Boivin 1966b).

G. elegans Bieb.
Eurasian; a garden-escape to roadsides and waste places in N. America, as in Alaska (Fairbanks; Hultén 1950), Alta. (Edmonton; Fort Saskatchewan), Sask. (Boivin 1966b), s Ont. (Guelph; OAC), Que. (Mt. Royal, Montreal), and s Labrador (Goose Bay, 53°19′N).

G. muralis L.
Eurasian; a garden-escape to roadsides, fields, and waste places of N. America, as in Ont. (Ottawa dist.; Gillett 1958) and sw Que. (N to Soulanges and Chateauguay counties).

G. pacifica Komarov
Asiatic; reported as a garden-escape in Alta. by Moss (1959; *G. perfoliata* var. *latifolia* Maxim.).

G. paniculata L.   Baby's-breath
Eurasian; a garden-escape to sandy roadsides, fields, and waste places of N. America, as in s B.C. (N to Cache Creek, about 25 mi w of Kamloops), Alta. (Calgary; Edmonton), Sask. (Breitung 1957a), Man. (N to Rossburn, about 70 mi NW of Brandon), s Ont. (near Forest, Lambton Co.; Thunder Bay), Que. (N to railway ballast at Rimouski; Ernest Lepage, Nat. can. (Que.) 89(2):78. 1962), and N.B. (St. Stephen, Charlotte Co.; CAN).

G. repens L.
European; introd. at the "Natural Bridge" near Field, SE B.C., where taken by the present writer in 1964, this apparently the first record for N. America.

HERNIARIA L.   [2476]

H. glabra L.   Rupturewort
Eurasian; an occasional escape from rock-gardens and cemeteries of N. America and reported from Ottawa, Ont., by Boivin (1966b).

HOLOSTEUM L.   [2431]   Jagged Chickweed

H. umbellatum L.
Eurasian; introd. in fields and cult. ground and along roadsides of N. America, as in sw B.C. (Saanichton, Vancouver Is.; Eastham 1947) and s ?Ont. (Kettle Point, Lambton Co.; R. Campbell, Can. Rec. Sci. 6(6):342–51. 1895).

LYCHNIS L.   [2491]   Campion.   Lychnide

(Ref.: Bassett Maguire, Rhodora 52(622):233–45. 1950)
1   Plant densely grey-tomentose throughout, to about 8 dm tall; leaves lanceolate to
    oblanceolate, the basal ones to 1 dm long; flowers few, red-purple, 2 or 3 cm long,
    on stiff ascending peduncles, the slightly emarginate blades of the petals with a pair
    of rigid acute lanceolate basal appendages to 4 mm long; calyx-lobes twisted; (introd.) . . .
    . . . . *L. coronaria*
1   Plants green, more or less pubescent (or glabrous in *L. alpina*) but not densely
    tomentose; blades of petals unappendaged or the appendages commonly less than
    0.5 mm long (at most 1 mm).
    2   Stems glabrous; leaves chiefly in a very dense basal rosette, linear to spatulate,
        subcoriaceous, at most about 6 cm long, the stem with usually not more than 7
        pairs of smaller leaves; flowers normally pink or roseate, numerous in a dense to
        loose corymbiform cyme, the deeply notched petals to 1 cm long; capsule
        stipitate, 4 or 5 mm long, dehiscent by 5 teeth; (Que., Labrador, and Nfld.) . . . *L. alpina*
    2   Stems pubescent at least above or in the inflorescence; leaves not predominantly
        in a dense basal rosette (or if so, the inflorescence usually few-flowered);
        capsule sessile.

3 Inflorescence a dense terminal capitate or subcapitate cluster of numerous roseate to scarlet flowers to about 2 cm long; petals deeply notched; leaves numerous, cordate-ovate, often bearing smaller ones in their axils; perennial with a loosely long-villous stem; (introd.) . . . . *L. chalcedonica*

3 Inflorescence loose to very open, or a single terminal flower.

    4 Flowers rather numerous (except in depauperate individuals); pubescence consisting of hairs lacking purple cross-walls.

        5 Petals deeply 4-cleft at summit into irregular linear lobes, pink to rose-purple, to 2 cm long; calyx about 1 cm long, strongly 10-nerved; capsule about 6 mm long, opening by 5 teeth; cyme open-paniculate; stem-leaves narrowly lanceolate, remote; basal leaves spatulate; stem sparingly pilose; (introd.) . . . . *L. flos-cuculi*

        5 Petals more or less deeply 2-cleft, the lobes entire; capsule opening by 10 teeth; stems rather densely and coarsely pubescent.

            6 Inflorescence wand-like, the flowers on stout appressed-erect pedicels; petals white or purplish, included or barely exserted, the blade narrower than the claw; fruiting calyx not inflated; leaves linear to narrowly oblanceolate; viscid-puberulent perennial from a stout caudex; (B.C. to Man.) . . . . *L. drummondii*

            6 Inflorescence open and more or less branched; petals with broad exserted notched blades; flowers unisexual, the plants commonly dioecious; fruiting calyx more or less inflated; leaves lanceolate to oval; annuals, biennials, or short-lived perennials; (introd.).

                7 Flowers white to pink, opening in the evening, odorous; calyx-teeth lance-linear, attenuate; capsule with erect or slightly spreading teeth at the narrow mouth . . . . *L. alba*

                7 Flowers pink to red, opening in the morning, inodorous; calyx-teeth broadly lanceolate; capsule with teeth recurved at the broad mouth . . . . *L. dioica*

    4 Flowers often solitary at the tip of the stem, or this sometimes bearing up to 4 or 5 additional flowers in the upper axils; petals 2-cleft; calyx prominently striped or nerved; leaves chiefly basal, linear-oblong to oblanceolate, the stem with at most 4 pairs of smaller lanceolate leaves; pubescence commonly consisting of multicellular hairs with purple cross-walls.

        8 Seeds at least 1.5 mm broad, narrowly to broadly winged; calyx in anthesis markedly inflated; (transcontinental in arctic and subarctic regions).

            9 Seeds broad-winged; petals lilac to dark purple, little exserted; calyx much inflated and papery; flower solitary, nodding during anthesis, the pedicel erect only when the capsule is mature . . . *L. apetala*

            9 Seeds narrow-winged; petals conspicuously exserted; flowers solitary or up to 5 or 6 on a stem, more erect . . . . *L. furcata*

        8 Seeds not over 1 mm broad, wingless; calyx in anthesis scarcely or only slightly inflated.

          10 Fruiting calyx closely investing the capsule, cylindric, green-nerved, copiously glandular-viscid; flowers numerous, on long appressed-ascending pedicels; petals white or purplish; stem stiffly erect; (B.C. to Man.) . . . . *L. drummondii*

          10 Fruiting calyx somewhat inflated, urceolate or campanulate; flowers few or solitary; petals white or pale pink; (arctic and subarctic regions) . . . . *L. triflora*

L. alba Mill.   White Cockle or Campion, Evening-Lychnis

Eurasian; introd. in fields and waste places and along roadsides in N. America, as in Alaska (Boivin 1966*b*; *L. loveae*) and B.C. (N to Dawson Creek, ca. 55°20′N), Alta. (N to Widewater, S of Lesser Slave L. at 55°22′N), Sask. (N to Saskatoon), Man. (N to Churchill), Ont. (N to Big

Trout L. at ca. 53°45'N, 90°W), Que. (N to the Gaspé Pen.), Nfld., N.B., P.E.I., and N.S.; Greenland. [*Melandrium* Garcke; *Silene* Krause; *M. dioicum* ssp. *album* (Mill.) D. Löve; *L. vespertina* Sibth.].

Löve and Bernard (1959) believe that the N. American plant is actually a hybrid between *L. alba* and *L. doioca* (× *L. loveae* Boivin, the type from Lethbridge, Alta.), "which due to its wide range of tolerance has spread more easily over this continent than the woodland ssp. *rubrum* or the open-habitat ssp. *album* would have done . . . ."

L. alpina L.   Alpine Campion
/aST/E/GE/   (Ch (Hs))   Gravelly or rocky barrens and ravines of Que. (E James Bay–Hudson Bay between ca. 52°30' and 55°30'N; Larch and Koksoak rivers at ca. 57°N to S Ungava Bay; Côte-Nord at Brest, Saguenay Co.; serpentine tableland and ravines of Mt-Albert, Gaspé Pen.), Labrador (entire coast), and Nfld.; W and E Greenland N to ca. 73°N; Iceland; Europe. [*Viscaria* Don; incl. var. *americana* Fern.].   MAPS: Porsild 1957 (1964 revision): map 338 *(V. alp.)*, p. 203; Hultén 1958: map 49 *(V. alp.* and var. *amer.)*, p. 69; Raymond 1950b: fig. 8 (the Asiatic area representing reports from the Altai Mts. of Mongolia should be deleted), p. 16; Meusel, Jaeger, and Weinert 1965:136.

The N. American plant has been rather arbitrarily separated as var. *americana* Fern.; its forma *albiflora* (Lange) Fern. (*Viscaria alpina* f. *alb.* Lange, the type from Greenland; flowers white rather than roseate) is known from E Que. (Côte-Nord; Gaspé Pen.) and Greenland.

L. apetala L.
/AST/X/GEA/   (Hs)   Moist tundra or gravels and mossy brooksides from the Aleutian Is. and coasts of Alaska–Yukon–Dist. Mackenzie–Dist. Keewatin nearly throughout the Canadian Arctic Archipelago to northernmost Ellesmere Is., Baffin Is., and northernmost Ungava–Labrador, S in the West through the mts. of B.C. and SW Alta. to E Utah and Colo., farther eastwards S to Great Bear L., SE Dist. Keewatin, NE Man. (Churchill; an early report from York Factory requires confirmation), cent. Ont. (W James Bay–Hudson Bay between ca. 54°30' and 56°30'N), James Bay (Bear Is., 54°20'N), and N Que. (S to Cape Jones, NE James Bay, and S Ungava Bay); W and E Greenland N of ca. 69°N; Spitsbergen; N Eurasia. [*Melandrium* Fenzl; *Silene* Chowdhuri; *Wahlbergella* Fries; incl. vars. *arctica* (Fries) Cody, *attenuata* (Farr) Hitchc. (*L. (M) att.* Farr), *glabra* Regel, *glandulosa-pubescens* Hook., *macropetala* C. & S., *montana* (Wats.) Hitchc. (*L. mont.* Wats.), and *nutans* Boivin, these all minor phases of a completely intergrading series].   MAPS: Hultén 1968b:445 *(M. apet.)*; Porsild 1957: map 153 *(M. apet.* ssp. *arct.)*, p. 180, and 1966: map 59 *(M. apet.* ssp. *att.)*, p. 74; Raup 1947: pl. 24.

L. chalcedonica L.   Scarlet Lychnis, Maltese-cross
Asiatic; persisting in old gardens or escaped to roadsides, thickets, and waste places in N. America, as in S B.C. (Abbotsford, near Vancouver; V), Sask. (Boivin 1966b), S Man. (near Otterburne, about 30 mi S of Winnipeg), Ont. (near Thunder Bay; Norfolk, Wellington, York, and Russell counties), Que. (N to Labelle and Kamouraska counties), N.B. (MTMG; locality not stated), P.E.I. (Tracadie Beach, Queens Co.), and N.S. (Noel L., Hants Co.; ACAD; CAN; not listed by Roland 1947).

L. coronaria (L.) Desr.   Rose-Campion, Mullein-Pink
European; a garden-escape to roadsides, riverbanks, and waste places in N. America, as in S B.C. (Vancouver Is.; Saltspring Is.; Vancouver), Ont. (N to Upsala, about 70 mi NW of Thunder Bay), and SW Que. (Hemmingford, Huntingdon Co.; Laprairie, near Montreal). [*Agrostemma* L.].

L. dioica L.   Red Campion
Eurasian; introd. along roadsides and in waste places of N. America, as in B.C. (N to Prince George, ca. 54°N), Ont. (Norfolk, Wellington, York, and Carleton counties; not listed by Gillett 1958), Que. (N to Baie-St-Paul, Charlevoix Co.), SE Nfld., and N.S. (Digby, Annapolis, and Kings counties). [*Melandrium* Coss. & Germ.; *Silene* Clairv.; *M. (L.) rubrum* (Weig.) Garcke; *L. diurna* Sibth.].

L. drummondii (Hook.) Wats.
/sT/WW/ (Hs) Dry plains and foothills to alpine talus from ?Dist. Mackenzie (Boivin 1966*b*) and B.C. (N to Hudson Hope, ca. 56°N) to Alta. (N to Peace Point in Wood Buffalo National Park, 59°07′N), Sask. (N to L. Athabasca), and S Man. (N to Millwood, about 85 mi NW of Brandon), S to Nev., Ariz., Colo., and Nebr. [*Silene* Hook.; *Melandrium* Porsild; *Wahlbergella* Rydb.; *L. pudica* Boivin; *L. (W.) striata* Rydb.]. The type locality of *Silene drummondii,* as the first region cited by Hooker, is "Plains of the Saskatchewan".

L. flos-cuculi L. Ragged-Robin, Cuckoo-flower
European; introd. in fields and meadows of N. America, as in Ont. (Morrison Is., Stormont Co.; DAO; reported from Cambridge (Galt), Waterloo Co., by R. Campbell, Can. Rec. Sci. 6(6):342–51. 1895), Que. (N to the Laurentide Provincial Park, N of Quebec City; *see* Que. map by C. Rousseau 1968: map 43, p. 75), Nfld. (Holyrood, Avalon Pen.; DAO), N.B. (Campbellton; CAN; DAO), and N.S. (Yarmouth, Kings, and Colchester counties).

L. furcata (Raf.) Fern.
/AST/X/GEA/ (Hs) Sandy, gravelly, or rocky places from the coasts of Alaska–Yukon–Dist. Mackenzie–Dist. Keewatin nearly throughout the Canadian Arctic Archipelago to Ellesmere Is. (N to ca. 82°N), Baffin Is., and northernmost Ungava–Labrador, S to SE Alaska (isolated in the mts. of the Banff dist., SW Alta.), Great Bear L., NE Man. (Churchill; an early report from York Factory requires confirmation), northernmost Ont. (near the mouth of the Black Duck R., Hudson Bay, at ca. 56°45′N; CAN), Que. (S to Cape Jones, NE James Bay, and S Ungava Bay), and Labrador (S to ca. 57°N; reported S to Hopedale, 55°27′N); W and E Greenland N of the Arctic Circle; Spitsbergen; N Eurasia. [*Silene* and *Viscago* Raf.; *L. (Melandrium; Wahlbergella) affinis* Vahl; *L. apetala* var. *elatior* Regel; *L. brachycalyx* Raup; *L. gillettii* Boivin; *L. (M.) taylorae* Robins.; *M. tay.* var. *glabrum* Hult.; *M. (L.) macrospermum* Porsild; *M. soczavianum* Schischkin]. MAPS: Porsild 1957: map 154 *(M. aff.),* p. 180; combine the maps by Hultén 1968*b*:445 *(M. macro.),* p. 446 *(M. affine),* and p. 447 *(M. tay.).*

L. triflora R. Br.
/aSs/X/G/ (Hs) Calcareous clays and gravels and stony barrens, the ranges of taxa outlined below, together with MAPS and synonymy.
1 Stems usually not over 1.5 dm tall, more or less densely short-pilose; calyx to 12 mm long; seeds pebbled-tuberculate on the back; [*Melandrium* Vahl; *L. soerensensis* Boivin; isolated in N-cent. Alaska; Banks Is. to northernmost Ellesmere Is., S to Baffin Is. at ca. 70°N; W Greenland S to the Arctic Circle, E Greenland S to ca. 70°N; MAPS *(Mel. tri.)*: Hultén 1968*b*:446; Porsild 1957: map 155, p. 180] . . . . ssp. *triflora*
1 Stems to 3 dm tall, villous or merely puberulent; calyx to 10 mm long; seeds low-tuberculate on the back; [var. *dawsonii* Rob., the type from about 100 mi NE of Dease L. in N B.C.; *L. daw.* (Rob.) And.; incl. *Melandrium (L.) ostenfeldii* Porsild and *M. (L.) taimyrense* Tolm.; cent. Alaska–Yukon to Dist. Mackenzie (Mackenzie R. Delta; Great Bear L.; Great Slave L.), N Banks Is., Prince Patrick Is., Axel Heiberg Is., Ellesmere Is. N of ca. 80°N (also reported from cent. Baffin Is. by Polunin 1940), and the mts. of northernmost B.C.; MAPS (combine the areas of the following): Porsild 1957: map 155 *(L. triflora;* excluding the Greenland area) and map 156 *(M. ostenf.),* p. 180; Porsild 1966: map 60 *(M. ostenf.)* and map 61 *(M. taim.),* p. 74; Hultén 1968*b*:447 *(M. taim)*] . . . . .
. . . . .ssp. *dawsonii* (Robins.) Maguire

MYOSOTON Moench   [2429]

M. aquaticum (L.) Moench   Giant Chickweed
European; introd. along shores and in meadows and alluvial thickets of N. America, as in SW B.C. (Nanaimo, Vancouver Is.; Aldergrove, near Vancouver), Ont. (N to Carleton Co.), and SW Que. (S Gatineau and S Papineau counties). [*Cerastium* L.; *Alsine* Britt.; *Stellaria* Scop.].

PARONYCHIA Mill [2473] Whitlow-wort

(Ref.: E.L. Core, Am. Midl. Nat. 26:369–97. 1941)
1 Annuals with a slender taproot, to over 2.5 dm tall, the slender stems forking to
  bushy-branched, the inflorescence thus diffuse.
  2 Stems glabrous; leaves thin, elliptic to oval, to 3 cm long; calyx to 1.5 mm long,
    1-nerved; (s Ont.) . . . . .P. canadensis
  2 Stems puberulent; leaves firm, oblanceolate to narrowly elliptic-lanceolate, to
    2 cm long; calyx 2 or 3 mm long, 1–3-nerved; (introd. in s Ont. and sw Que.) . . . .
    . . . . .P. fastigiata
1 Caespitose perennials to about 1 dm tall; leaves firm, linear or linear-subulate,
  spinulose-tipped, rarely over 8 mm long; sepals to over 2.5 mm long.
  3 Flowers solitary in the leaf-axils, the leaves commonly 5 or 6 mm long and
    scarcely surpassing the bracts; sepals spinulose-tipped; (s Alta., s Sask., and
    s ?Man.) . . . . .P. sessiliflora
  3 Flowers more or less clustered in dichotomously branching cymes; leaves to
    about 8 mm long, much longer than the bracts . . . .[P. jamesii]

P. canadensis (L.) Wood   Forked Chickweed
/t/EE/   (T)   Rocky or sandy woods and openings from Minn. to s Ont. (Amherstburg and
Leamington, Essex Co.; CAN; GH; reported from Norfolk Co. by John Macoun 1866; reports
from Nfld. by Reeks 1871 and 1873, require clarification) and s N.H., s to Kans., Ark., Tenn.,
and Ga. [*Queria* L.; *Anychia* Ell.; *A. dichotoma* Michx.].

P. fastigiata (Raf.) Fern.   Forked Chickweed
A native of the E U.S.A.; in Canada, known from s Ont. (near Caistorville, Haldimand Co.,
where taken by Putnam in scrubby woods on hard clay in 1969; W.J. Cody, Can. Field-Nat.
84(1):59. 1970) and sw Que. (along a railway at Val-Royal, near Montreal, where taken by G.
and P.H. Du Boulay in 1962; C. Rousseau 1968). [*Anychia* Raf.].

[*P. jamesii* T. & G.]
[Reports of this species of the w U.S.A. (Wyo., S.Dak., Colo., and Nebr.) from SE B.C. by Ulke
(1935; near Wilmer, Columbia Valley), from Alta. by Rydberg (1922; *P. diffusa*), and from Man.
by Jackson et al. (1922; *P. depressa,* this report taken up by Lowe 1943) require confirmation.
A so-named collection in WIN from Grand Beach, s Man., is based upon *Suaeda maritima* var.
americana. The report from Sask. by Fraser and Russell (1944) is referred to *P. sessiliflora* by
Breitung (1957a). (Incl. *P. depressa* Nutt. (*P. jamesii* var. *dep.* (Nutt.) T. & G.) and *P. diffusa*
Nels.).]

P. sessiliflora Nutt.
/T/WW/   (Ch)   Dry prairies, hills, and ridges from Alta. (N to the Red Deer Valley; CAN; reported N to between Edmonton and Carlton, Sask., by John Macoun 1883) and s Sask. (N to
Saskatchewan Landing, 50°39′N; concerning reports from Man., see Scoggan 1957) to Utah
and Tex.

SAGINA L. [2433] Pearlwort

1 Middle and upper leaves strongly reduced and scale-like, mostly subtending dense
  axillary bulb-like clusters of tiny leaves that propagate vegetatively, the stems and
  branches strongly moniliform; sepals and petals each 5, the petals usually about
  twice as long as the sepals; stamens 10; seeds dark brown or blackish, strongly
  pebbled-rugose, to 0.7 mm long; basal leaves to 3 cm long; tufted perennial,
  glabrous or atypically glandular-pubescent; (Alta. to Nfld. and N.S.) . . . . .S. nodosa
1 Middle and upper leaves less strongly reduced, without or a few pairs with axillary
  fascicles (but the fascicles not bulb-like and the stems thus not moniliform); petals
  shorter than or only slightly longer than the sepals; seeds yellow- to red-brown,
  obscurely rugose or only marginally pebbled.

2 Plants annual (*S. maxima* sometimes perennial), lacking a persistent basal
rosette (basal leaves usually withered at anthesis); stems erect or ascending, not
nodally rooting, their leaves lacking axillary fascicles of smaller leaves; pedicels
permanently straight; sepals 5 (rarely 4), mostly longer than the petals; stamens
3–10; seeds to 0.3 mm long.
   3 Pedicels and calyces usually weakly glandular-pubescent; petals 5; (Alaska–
w B.C.) . . . . *S. maxima*
   3 Plant usually completely glabrous; petals often rudimentary or none; (introd.) . . . . .
. . . . *S. decumbens*
2 Plants perennial or biennial (but apparently sometimes flowering in the first
season), glabrous throughout or rarely and atypically glandular-pubescent
above, with a usually persistent rosette of basal leaves, the stems and branches
prostrate to ascending, often rooting at the nodes and mat-forming; at least
some of the stem-leaves usually subtending axillary fascicles of reduced leaves.
   4 Seeds lustrous as though freshly varnished, about 0.5 mm long; sepals and
petals each 5, the sepals appressed to the capsule, to 3.5 mm long; basal
leaves to 3 cm long and up to 2 mm broad; (Alaska–w B.C.) . . . . *S. maxima*
   4 Seeds dull; sepals usually not over 3 mm long.
      5 Pedicels not hooked at summit; seeds dull, to about 0.7 mm long; stems
less than 4 cm tall, rarely rooting at the nodes; (transcontinental in arctic
and subarctic regions) . . . . *S. nivalis*
      5 Pedicels hooked at summit after flowering, later sometimes becoming
straight; seeds about 0.3 mm long.
         6 Flowers commonly solitary at the ends of the stems, 5(6)-parted;
stamens normally 10; pedicels usually recurving or hooked even in fruit;
sepals oval to oblong, to 3 mm long, appressed to the capsule, this to
about 5 mm long; leaves to 1.5 cm long, the stem-leaves rarely with
axillary clusters of reduced leaves; stems ascending, nodally rooting
only near base, usually less than 5 cm long; (B.C. and Alta.; Que., N.B.,
Labrador, and Nfld.) . . . . *S. saginoides*
         6 Flowers both terminal and axillary, 4(5)-parted, on pedicels to 2.5 cm
long; stamens 4, sometimes 5; pedicels nearly straight in fruit; sepals
oval to suborbicular, less than 2.5 mm long, tending to spread in fruit;
capsule less than 4 mm long; leaves to 2.5 cm long, several of the
stem-leaves usually subtending clusters of reduced leaves; stems
prostrate to ascending, often freely rooting at the nodes, to 1.5 dm
long; (chiefly coastal rocks of Alaska–B.C. and from E Que. to S
Labrador and Nfld.) . . . . *S. procumbens*

S. decumbens (Ell.) T. & G.
/T/(X)/ (T) Fernald *in* Gray (1950) assigns this species a range confined to the E U.S.A.
(moist or dryish sandy fields, paths, and open spots in woods from E Kans. to Ky. and S Vt., S
to Tex. and Fla.). It is known in Canada from B.C. (Victoria; Prince Rupert), Alta (E of the
Hand Hills, where taken by John Macoun in 1879; CAN), sw Sask. (Farewell Creek, Cypress
Hills, where taken by Macoun in 1895; CAN), Ont. (Ottawa), sw Que. (introd. along moist paths
at Montreal; CAN; MT), and N.B. (St. John). It is possible that it is entirely introd. in our area.
[*Spergula* Ell.].

[*S. maritima* Don]
[European; the report of this species (not keyed out above) from sw B.C. by J.M. Macoun
(1913; Longford L., Vancouver Is., as *S. stricta* var. *maritima* (Don) Fries; presumed basis of
the report of "*Stellaria stricta* var. *maritima* Fries" from that locality by Carter and Newcombe
1921) requires confirmation. (*S. stricta* Fries).]

S. maxima Gray
/aST/W/eA/ (T (Hs)) Mostly on moist sands or rocks from the Aleutian Is. and S Alaska
(*see* Hultén 1944: map 530, p. 787; *S. crass.*) through coastal B.C. to N Calif.; E Asia. [Incl. var.

crassicaulis (Wats.) Hara (*S. crass.* Wats.), *S. litoralis* Hult., and *S. ?occidentalis* Wats.]. MAP: combine the maps by Hultén 1968b:427 (*S. crass.*) and p. 428 (*S. occid.*).

S. nivalis (Lindbl.) Fries
/ASs/X/GEA/   (Ch)   Moist sands, gravels, and clays, the aggregate species along the Aleutian Is. and coasts of Alaska–Yukon (*see* Hultén 1944: map 531, p. 787; *S. intermedia*), farther eastwards through the area given below for var. *caespitosa* (not known from the U.S.A.); Greenland; Eurasia. MAPS and synonymy: *see* below.
1   Flowers normally 4-parted; sepals about 2 mm long; stamens 4 (rarely 5);
    [*S. intermedia* Fenzl; *S. micrantha* (Bunge) Fern.; *Spergula nivalis* Lindbl.;
    transcontinental; MAPS (*Sag. int.*): Hultén 1968b:427; Porsild 1957: map 145, p. 179] . . . . .
    . . . . var. *nivalis*
1   Flowers normally 5-parted; sepals to 3 mm long; stamens 10; [*Spergula (Arenaria; Sagina) caesp.* Vahl; cent. Dist. Keewatin to s-cent. Baffin Is. and northernmost
    Ungava–Labrador, s to N Man. (Baralzon L. at 60°00'N), NE James Bay (Cape Jones,
    54°37'N, and Stromness Is., 53°52'N), N Ungava (s to ca. 58°N), and N Labrador (s
    to Hebron, 58°13'N; Hustich & Pettersson 1943); W Greenland N to ca. 75°N, E
    Greenland at ca. 72°N; Iceland; Jan Mayen; N Scandinavia; MAPS (*S. caesp.*): Porsild
    1957: map 143, p. 178; Hultén 1958: map 161, p. 181; Gams, Phyton 5: 113. 1953] . . . .
    . . . . var. *caespitosa* (Vahl) Boivin

S. nodosa (L.) Fenzl
/aST/(X)/GEA/   (Hs (Ch))   Damp rocky, gravelly, or peaty places, the aggregate species from Great Bear L. to cent. Dist. Keewatin, s Baffin Is., Que. (N to Ungava Bay and the Côte-Nord), Nfld., N.B., P.E.I., and N.S., s to L. Athabasca (Alta. and Sask.), s Man., Ont. (s to the N shore of L. Superior and W James Bay), N Minn., and E Maine; SW Greenland at ca. 61°N, E Greenland near the Arctic Circle; Iceland; Eurasia. MAPS and synonymy: *see* below.
1   Upper part of stem minutely glandular-pubescent; [Que. (E James Bay at 52°37'N;
    Anticosti Is.), E Nfld. (Notre Dame Bay), St-Pierre and Miquelon (Boivin 1966b), N.B.
    (Charlotte Co.), and N.S. (Digby, Annapolis, Shelburne, Queens, and Lunenburg
    counties)] . . . . var. *pubescens* Mert. & Koch
1   Plant essentially glabrous . . . . var. *nodosa*
    2   Flowers none, the leaves bearing bulblets in their axils; [type from Lake Harbour,
        Baffin Is.] . . . . f. *bulbillosa* Polunin
    2   Flowers present; [*Spergula* L.; range of the species; MAPS (aggregate species):
        Porsild 1957: map 144, p. 178; Hultén 1958: map 105, p. 125, and 1968b:428;
        Meusel, Jaeger, and Weinert 1965:147] . . . . f. *nodosa*

S. procumbens L.   Birdseye
/aST/(X)/GEA/   (Ch (Hsr; T))   Fresh to brackish or saline sands and rocks, the aggregate species from s Alaska (Haines and Unalaska; CAN; ?introd.) and B.C. (introd. according to Calder and Taylor 1968) to N Calif., farther eastwards from Minn. to Que. (St. Lawrence R. estuary from Temiscouata Co. to the Côte-Nord, Anticosti Is., and Gaspé Pen.), Labrador (reported N to Hebron, 58°13'N, by Fernald and Sornborger 1899), Nfld., N.B., P.E.I., and N.S., s to Ohio and Del.; reported as a weed in lawns and rock-gardens of s Ont. by Soper (1949; Niagara, Welland Co.); southernmost Greenland; Iceland; Eurasia. MAPS and ranges of taxa: *see* below.
1   Capsule to over 3 mm long; sepals to about 2.5 mm long; leaves to about 2 cm long;
    [range of the species; MAPS (aggregate species): Hultén 1958: map 106, p. 125;
    Meusel, Jaeger, and Weinert 1965:146] . . . . var. *procumbens*
1   Capsule barely 2 mm long; sepals at most 1.5 mm long; leaves less than 1 cm long;
    plant very dwarf; [E Que. (Côte-Nord; Anticosti Is.; Gaspé Pen.), Labrador (N to
    Turnavik, 55°16'N; GH), and Nfld.] . . . . var. *compacta* Lange

S. saginoides (L.) Karst.   Arctic Pearlwort
/aST/(X)/GEA/   (CH (Hs))   Damp sandy, gravelly, or rocky places: Alaska (N to the Seward Pen.) and s Yukon through B.C. and the mts. of SW Alta. to Calif. and Mexico; E-cent. Dist.

Keewatin (coast of Hudson Bay near Chesterfield Inlet) to Southampton Is., Que. (Akpatok Is., Ungava Bay; SE coast of Hudson Bay at ca. 56°N; alpine ravines of Mt-Albert, Gaspé Pen.; reported from Anticosti Is. by Schmitt 1904), Labrador (northernmost tip at Cape Chidley), Nfld. (Boivin 1966*b*), and N.B. (Boivin 1966*b*); W and E Greenland N to ca. 69°N; Iceland; Eurasia. [*Spergula* L.; *Sag. linnaei* Presl; incl. var. *hesperia* Fern.]. MAPS: Hultén 1968*b*:426; Porsild 1957 (1964 revision): map 337 *(S. linn.)*, p. 203; Raup 1947: pl. 23 *(S. linn.)*.

SAPONARIA L. [2503]

1 Petals unappendaged, pale red; calyx ovoid, 5-ribbed, much inflated and wing-
  angled in fruit; leaves lanceolate to ovate-lanceolate, glabrous and glaucous,
  clasping at base or the lower ones connate; annual . . . .*S. vaccaria*
1 Petals crowned with a pair of linear appendages 1 or 2 mm long at juncture of the
  claw and blade; calyx terete, lightly nerved; leaves oval-lanceolate; perennial.
    2 Petals pink or whitish, notched at summit, the blade to 1.5 cm long; leaves to
      about 1 dm long, usually glabrous; stem stout and sparingly branched, to about
      8 dm tall . . . .*S. officinalis*
    2 Petals bright pink, small; leaves mostly less than 2.5 cm long, pubescent, their
      margins ciliate; stem slender, trailing and much branched . . . .[*S. ocymoides*]

[S. ocymoides L.]   Rock Soapwort
[This European species is represented from our area by a collection in DAO from Ont. ("local escape from rockery", Central Experimental Farm, Ottawa). It evidently does not become established in N. America.]

S. officinalis L.   Bouncing-Bet, Soapwort.   Herbe à savon
Eurasian; freely naturalized along ditches, banks, river shores, etc., in N. American, as in B.C. (Vancouver Is.; Lytton; Armstrong), Alta. (N to Fort Saskatchewan), Sask.–Man. (Boivin 1968), Ont. (N to Thunder Bay and Renfrew Co.), Que. (N to L. Nominingue, Labelle Co., and Grosse-Ile, about 30 mi NE of Quebec City), Nfld., N.B., P.E.I., and N.S. Much of our material consists of the "double-flowered" phase in which the reproductive organs are replaced by extra petals.

S. vaccaria L.   Cowherb, Cow-Cockle.   Saponaire des vaches
Eurasian; waste places and cult. ground of N. America, as in S Alaska (Juneau; Sitka), cent. Yukon (Dawson; CAN), B.C. (N to Kamloops), Alta. (N to Banff), Sask. (Cypress Hills; CAN), Man. (N to Churchill), Ont. (N to Rainy L. at ca. 48°35'N), Que. (N to Rimouski Co. and the SW Gaspé Pen. at Matapédia), N.B. (Campbellton; CAN), and N.S. (Kings, Hants, Lunenburg, and Halifax counties). [*Vaccaria* Britt.; *V. pyramidata* Medic.; *V. segetalis* (Neck.) Garcke; *V. vulgaris* Host]. MAP: Hultén 1968*b*:448 *(V. pyram.)*.
  Forma *grohii* Boivin (flowers white rather than pale red; type from Morden, S Man.) is reported from Sask. and Man. by Boivin (1966*b*).

SCLERANTHUS L. [2483] Knawel

1 Sepals acute, with narrow scarious margins, suberect in fruit; calyx glabrous, the
  tube rather deeply 10-furrowed in fruit; bracts usually surpassing the flowers; annual
  or biennial with a slender taproot . . . .*S. annuus*
1 Sepals blunt, with broad white margins, incurved in fruit; calyx-tube pubescent,
  shallowly 10-furrowed in fruit; bracts shorter than the flowers; perennial, somewhat
  woody at base (usually more robust and more glaucous than *S. annuus* and
  becoming reddish) . . . .*S. perennis*

S. annuus L.   Annual Knawel
Eurasian; introd. along roadsides and in waste places of N. America, as in B.C. (Agassiz; Kootenay L.; Creston), ?Alta. (Boivin 1966*b*), Sask. (Wolseley and Waseca; Breitung 1957*a*), Ont. (Middlesex, Waterloo, Wellington, and York counties), Que. (N to L. St. John and Rimouski, Rimouski Co.), N.B., P.E.I., and N.S.

S. perennis L.   Perennial Knawel
Eurasian; reported as introd. in Que. by Boivin (1966*b*; Baie-St-Paul, Charlevoix Co., about 60 mi NE of Quebec City).

SILENE L.   [2490]   Catchfly, Campion

(Ref.: Hitchcock and Maguire 1947)
1   Calyx glabrous (or the lobes merely ciliate) or only minutely puberulent at the base (copiously crisp-puberulent throughout in *S. stellata*).
  2   Dwarf moss-like cushion-forming plant at most about 6 cm tall; leaves linear, to about 1.5 cm long, densely crowded and imbricate, their dried remnants marcescent-persisting for many years; petals lilac or pinkish, notched or entire; calyx about 5 mm long, the capsule barely exserted; plant glabrous or the leaves ciliate at base to scabrous; (transcontinental) . . . .*S. acaulis*
  2   Tall plants, not cushion-forming.
    3   Leaves mostly in whorls of 4, linear- to ovate-lanceolate, long-acuminate, minutely puberulent beneath, glabrous to scabrous above; inflorescence paniculate; petals white, with fringed margin and woolly base; calyx obscurely nerved; corolla about 2 cm broad; (s ?Ont.) . . . .[*S. stellata*]
    3   Leaves opposite (sometimes with smaller leaves in their axils); inflorescence cymose or cymose-paniculate.
      4   Petals white (rarely pinkish), 2-cleft; stem not glutinous; perennials (or *S. cserei* biennial); (introd.).
        5   Calyx much inflated, to 2 cm long in fruit, its summit free of the short-stalked included capsule, its 20 nerves connected their entire length by a network of veinlets; inflorescence open . . . .*S. cucubalus*
        5   Calyx uninflated at maturity, at most 12 mm long, 20-nerved at base, its 10-nerved summit appressed to the subsessile exserted capsule, the veinlets hardly forming a network; inflorescence simple and elongate or with 2 erect slender branches . . . .*S. cserei*
      4   Petals pink, roseate, or purplish; calyx tight over the capsule, the 5–10 prominent straight ribs not evidently net-forming; annuals or biennials.
        6   Stem slender, the upper part usually with dark glutinous bands below the nodes, its slender branches and those of the panicle usually ascending; stem-leaves mostly linear to lanceolate or oblanceolate, to 6 cm long, their margins ciliate near the base; calyx at most 8 mm long, its short teeth often purple; capsule subsessile; petals more or less emarginate, their basal appendages less than 0.5 mm long; flowers slender-pedicelled, white to pink; (B.C. to w Ont.; introd. eastwards) . . . .*S. antirrhina*
        6   Stem relatively stout, lacking glutinous bands; leaves ovate-lanceolate to oblong-oblanceolate, glaucous and glabrous, the upper ones clasping, the lower ones to about 5 cm long; calyx to over 1.5 cm long; capsule long-stipitate within the calyx; petals subentire or minutely toothed, their linear basal appendages to 3 mm long; flowers short-pedicelled, pink to rose or lavender; (introd.) . . . .*S. armeria*
1   Calyx copiously puberulent or pubescent to pilose or pilose-hirsute (sometimes nearly glabrous in *S. douglasii*).
  7   Annuals with erect simple or branched stems, these, the peduncles, and the calyces conspicuously hirsute with multicellular hairs, the inflorescence also often glandular-pubescent; styles 3; capsules 3-locular; seeds about 1 mm long; basal leaves broadly petioled, the upper ones becoming reduced and sessile; (introd.).
    8   Calyx with about 30 prominent nerves, much inflated in fruit and up to 3 cm long; petals white to pink or purplish, the blades retuse but usually not 2-lobed . . . .*S. conoidea*

8 Calyx usually 10-nerved or -ribbed (if more than 10-nerved, the veins very indistinct and much branched).

   9 Inflorescence cymose, the opposite branches at each node about equally developed (but often much reduced in number and length); calyx greatly inflated in fruit and becoming up to 3 cm long; petals white to pinkish, the claw to 2.5 cm long, the blade to 1 cm long, 2-cleft less than half its length; leaves elliptic-oblanceolate to narrowly ovate, to over 12 cm long and 4 cm broad; stems to over 1 m tall . . . .*S. noctiflora*

   9 Inflorescence falsely racemose (one branch of each opposite pair at the nodes suppressed, the flowers thus solitary at the nodes); calyx to about 1.5 cm long; basal leaves lanceolate to oblanceolate or spatulate, mostly not over 1 cm broad.

      10 Blade of petal to 5 mm long, somewhat twisted, entire or shallowly notched at summit, white to pink, lavender, or purplish, the linear appendages at its base about 1 mm long, its claw to 6 mm long; stems to 4 or 5 dm tall . . . . : . . . . *S. gallica*

      10 Blade of petal to 9 mm long, 2-lobed to somewhat below midlength, white to reddish, its basal appendages about 0.2 mm long, its claw to 1.5 cm long; stems to over 1 m tall . . . .*S. dichotoma*

7 Perennials with tufted basal leaves or a usually much-branched woody caudex or slender rhizomes; styles commonly 3 (but sometimes 4 or even 5).

  11 Petals less than 1 cm long and at most only slightly surpassing the calyx, white; at least the lower flowers usually subtended by scarcely reduced leafy bracts; capsules 1-locular, their seeds less than 1 mm long; leaves mostly cauline, linear-lanceolate to narrowly obovate, mostly not over 6 cm long and 1.5 cm broad (but up to about 1 dm long and 3 cm broad); plant pubescent and also often glandular; (Alaska–B.C. to Man.) . . . . *S. menziesii*

  11 Petals mostly more than 1 cm long and conspicuously surpassing the calyx.

      12 Blades of petals at least 2 cm long, deep red to crimson, mostly 2-cleft; fruiting calyx to 2.5 cm long; flowers few, subtended by scarcely reduced foliage-leaves; basal leaves spatulate; stem-leaves oblanceolate, glaucous or merely ciliate, thin; stems slender and weak, villous at least above, to 6 dm tall; (s ?Ont.) . . . .[*S. virginica*]

      12 Blades of petals less than 1 cm long; flowers subtended by greatly reduced bracteal leaves; plants caespitose and mat-forming, with a usually branched woody caudex.

         13 Flowering stems numerous, decumbent, finely and densely crisp-pubescent throughout with nonglandular, usually retrorse hairs; petals creamy white, greenish, pink, or purplish-tinged, the appendages at the base of their blades about 1 (sometimes up to 3) mm long; ovary-stalk 3 or 4 mm long; capsule 1-locular; seeds about 1.3 mm long; leaves mostly matted at the base of the stems and on the new shoots, narrowly lanceolate to broadly oblanceolate, mostly not over 5 or 6 cm long and 7 or 8 mm broad; (B.C. and Alta.) . . . .*S. douglasii*

         13 Flowering stems pubescent and also more or less glandular (at least in the inflorescence).

            14 Ovary-stalk about 3 mm long, finely pubescent; hairs of calyx sometimes with purple cross-walls; petals white or greenish, often purple-tinged, 2-cleft nearly to the middle, each margin with a prominent lateral lobe, the blade sometimes nearly equally 4-lobed; capsule 1-locular, the seeds to 1.5 mm long; leaves mostly basal, linear-oblanceolate or spatulate, petioled, to 8 cm long and 1 cm broad, those of the stem usually 2 or 3 pairs, sessile; (mts. of B.C.–sw Alta.) . . . .*S. parryi*

            14 Ovary-stalk to 7 mm long; stem-leaves up to 6 pairs (or even 12 in *S. scouleri*).

               15 Capsules 3-locular (sometimes 4-locular) nearly or quite to

summit; seeds about 0.8 mm long; ovary-stalk puberulent; leaves mostly in basal tufts, oblanceolate, nearly or quite sessile, commonly not over 4 or 5 cm long and 6 mm broad; (Alaska–Yukon–Dist. Mackenzie–B.C.) . . . . *S. repens*

15 Capsules 1-locular except at the 3–4-locular base; seeds to 1.5 mm long; ovary-stalk puberulent to woolly; basal leaves rather long-petioled, oblanceolate, to about 1.5 dm long and 3 cm broad, the stem-leaves reduced gradually upward and mostly sessile; (SW B.C. and SW ?Alta.) . . . . *S. scouleri*

S. acaulis L.   Moss-Campion
/AST/X/GEA/   (Ch)   Gravelly, rocky, or turfy barrens and cliffs, the aggregate species from the coasts of Alaska–Yukon–Dist. Mackenzie–Dist. Keewatin nearly throughout the Canadian Arctic Archipelago to northernmost Ellesmere Is. and northernmost Ungava–Labrador, s in the West through B.C. and the mts. of SW Alta. to Oreg., Nev., Ariz., and N.Mex., farther eastwards s to Great Slave L., s Dist. Keewatin (the report from between York Factory and Churchill, NE Man., by Rae 1850, requires confirmation; reported from Sask. by Boivin 1966b; not known from Ont.), Que. (s to E James Bay at 52°37′N, the Côte-Nord, and Gaspé Pen.; not known from Anticosti Is.), Nfld., N.S. (St. Paul Is.; CAN; GH), and mts. of N.H.; circumgreenlandic; Iceland; Spitsbergen; Eurasia. MAPS and synonymy: *see* below.

1 Capsule commonly about twice as long as the calyx, on a peduncle about equalling it in length; [Eurasia; ?N. America; MAPS (aggregate species): Hultén 1968b:440, and 1958: map 180, p. 199; Meusel, Jaeger, and Weinert 1965:137] . . . .[var. *acaulis*]

1 Capsule barely exserted from the calyx, typically subsessile or short-peduncled.

  2 Calyx usually not over 6 mm long; petals mostly obovate and emarginate; [f. *sub. Williams*; Alaska–Yukon–W Dist. Mackenzie and mts. of B.C. and SW Alta.; MAP: Hultén 1968b:441] . . . . var. *subacaulescens* (Williams) Fern. & St. John

  2 Calyx to 10 mm long; petals oblong-oblanceolate, rounded or only slightly emarginate; [ssp. *arctica* Löve & Löve; transcontinental; MAPS: Hultén 1968b:440 (this taxon included in the typical form); Porsild 1957: map 152, p. 179; Raup 1947: pl. 24] . . . . var. *exscapa* (All.) DC.

S. antirrhina L.   Sleepy Catchfly
/sT/X/   (T)   Sandy soil of dry open woods, fields, and waste places from s B.C. (N to Kamloops) to L. Athabasca (Alta. and Sask.), Man. (N to Grand Rapids, near the NW end of L. Winnipeg), Ont. (N to Ingolf, near the Man. boundary at ca. 49°50′N, and Thunder Bay), Que. (N to Pontiac and Papineau counties), and N.B. (St. Leonard, Madawaska Co.; probably introd.), s to Mexico and S. America; introd. in Europe. [Incl. var. *depauperata* Rydb.].

Forma *apetala* Farw. (petals wanting) is known from Ont. (Havilland Bay, SE shore of L. Superior; CAN).

S. armeria L.   None-so-pretty, Sweet-William-Catchfly
European; persisting in old gardens or escaped to fields and roadsides in N. America, as in s B.C. (Vancouver Is. and adjacent mainland), Ont. (N to the Ottawa dist.), Que. (N to Rupert House, James Bay, ca. 51°30′N; J.M. Macoun 1895), Nfld. (near gardens at Deer L.; Waghorne 1898), N.B., and N.S.

S. conoidea L.
Eurasian; reported from Alta. by Boivin (1966b; Lacombe), apparently the first record from Canada.

S. cserei Baumg.
European; introd. along railways and roadsides and in waste places of N. America, as in B.C. (N to Prince George, ca. 54°N), Alta. (Moss 1959), Sask. (Cypress Hills; Swift Current; Mortlach; Wilcox), Man. (Virden; Brokenhead; Winnipeg), Ont. (N to Quetico Provincial Park, about 100 mi W of Thunder Bay, and the Moose R. s of James Bay at ca. 51°N), and Que. (Boivin 1966b).

S. cucubalus Wibel   Bladder-Campion.   Pétards or Péteux
Eurasian; a common weed of roadsides, fields, and shores of N. America, as in B.C. (N to Prince George, ca. 54°N), Alta. (N to Beaverlodge, 55°13'N), Sask. (Breitung 1957a), Man. (N to Duck Mt.), Ont. (N to Albany, SW James Bay, 52°11'N), Que. (N to the Côte-Nord, Anticosti Is., and Gaspé Pen.), Labrador (N to Makkovik, ca. 55°N; Hustich and Pettersson 1943), Nfld., N.B., P.E.I., and N.S. [S. inflata Sm.; S. vulgaris (Moench) Garcke; Cucubalus (S.) latifolius Mill., not S. latifolia Poir.; C. behen L., not S. behen L.].

S. dichotoma Ehrh.   Forking Catchfly
Eurasian; introd. in fields and waste places of N. America, as in S B.C. (Bonnington, Kootenay L., and between Kaslo and Robson; Eastham 1947), Ont. (Huron, Grey, Middlesex, and Dufferin counties), Que. (Shawinigan, St-Maurice Co.), and N.S. (Wolfville, Kings Co.; Groh 1946).

S. douglasii Hook.
/T/W/   (Hp)   Plains to montane slopes from S B.C. (N to near Kamloops) and SW Alta. (N to Banff) to Calif., Nev., and Utah. [S. lyallii Wats.; S. multicaulis Nutt.]. MAP: Hultén 1968b:442.

S. gallica L.
European; introd. along roadsides and in waste places of N. America, as in SW B.C. (Vancouver Is.; Mayne Is.; Aldergrove, near Vancouver), Ont. (Owen Sound, Grey Co.), N.B. (Sackville; ACAD), and N.S. (Digby, Annapolis, and Halifax counties). [Incl. S. anglica L.].

S. menziesii Hook.
/ST/WW/   (Hpr)   Damp thickets, shores, and clearings (ranges of Canadian taxa outlined below), S to S Calif. and N N.Mex. MAPS and synonymy: see below.
1 Seeds black, smooth and shining; calyx finely nerved; plant pubescent and
   sometimes also more or less viscid with glandular hairs; [S. obovata Porsild; S. stellarioides Nutt.; Anotites debilis, A. picta, A. tenerrima, and A. teretiuscula Greene; S Alaska-cent. Yukon (see Hultén 1944: map 551, p. 789) to Great Slave L., Sask. (N to Waskesiu Lake, ca. 54°N), and Man. (N to The Pas); MAP: Hultén 1968b:443] . . . .
   . . . . var. menziesii
1 Seeds brown, strongly tuberculate; calyx prominently nerved; plant viscid with
   glandular hairs; [S. williamsii Britt., the type from Dawson, the Yukon; Alaska–Yukon; MAPS: Hultén 1944: map 553 (S. will.), p. 789, and 1968b:443] . . . .
   . . . . var. williamsii (Britt.) Boivin

S. noctiflora L.   Night-flowering Catchfly, Sticky Cockle
European; often a troublesome weed in cult. ground and waste places of N. America (sometimes confused with Lychnis alba), as in Alaska (Juneau, Fairbanks, and Nome; Hultén 1944), B.C. (N to Queen Charlotte Is.; Calder and Taylor 1968), Alta. (Moss 1959), Sask. (Breitung 1957a), Man. (N to Churchill), Ont. (N to Kapuskasing, 49°24'N), Que. (N to L. Mistassini, Anticosti Is., and the Gaspé Pen.; reported from Rupert House, SE James Bay, by J.M. Macoun 1895), Nfld., N.B., P.E.I., and N.S. [Melandrium Fries]. MAP: Hultén 1968b:444 (Mel. noct.).

[The European S. nocturna L. is reported from Ont. by John Macoun (1886; "Observed growing at Fort Erie, Ont., in 1881. Not detected since."). It differs from S. noctiflora in its taller stem (to 6 dm, usually branched; rather than to 4 dm, simple or with a few basal branches), raceme-like (rather than dichotomously branched) inflorescence, and smaller calyces (to 13 mm long rather than 3 cm).]

S. parryi (Wats.) Hitchc. & Maguire
/T/W/   (Hs)   Montane slopes from S B.C. (N to the Marble Mts. NW of Clinton and Griffin L., near Kamloops) and SW Alta. (N to Banff) to cent. Idaho and N Wyo. [Lychnis Wats.; Wahlbergella Rydb.; L. elata Wats.; S. douglasii (scouleri) var. macounii (Wats.) Robins. (S. macounii Wats.); S. tetonensis Nels.].

S. repens Patrin
/ST/W/EA/   (Hs)   Dry sandy or gravelly places from N-cent. Alaska–Yukon (see Hultén

1944: map 552, p. 789) and NW Dist. Mackenzie through the mts. of B.C. to Mont. and Wyo.; NE Europe; Asia. MAP and synonymy: *see* below.
1   Stems usually much branched, averaging over 2.5 dm tall; inflorescence seldom congested; [Eurasia; MAP (aggregate species): Hultén 1968*b*:442] . . . . [ssp. *repens*]
1   Stems mostly simple, averaging less than 2.5 dm tall.
   2   Calyx greenish yellow to pink, moderately puberulent; inflorescence seldom congested; [?B.C.] . . . . [ssp *australe* Hitchc. & Maguire]
   2   Calyx reddish purple, densely long-pubescent; inflorescence usually congested; [*S. purpurata* Greene, the type from the Porcupine R., Alaska; *S. scouleri* var. *?costata* Williams; Alaska–Yukon–w Dist. Mackenzie and mts. of B.C.] . . . .
   . . . . ssp. *purpurata* (Greene) Hitchc. & Maguire

S. scouleri Hook.
/t/W/   (Hs)   Sandy and gravelly places from SW B.C. (Vancouver Is. and adjacent islands) and SW ?Alta. (Boivin 1966*b*) to cent. Calif., Ariz., and N.Mex.
    Var. *pacifica* (Eastw.) Hitchc. (*S. pacifica* Eastw.; leaves relatively broad and fleshy; petal-claw usually ciliate rather than eciliate, the blade seldom with lateral teeth rather than commonly with a small lateral tooth on each side below the level of the sinus) is reported from B.C. by Hitchcock et al. (1964).

[S. stellata (L.) Ait. f.]   Starry Campion, Widow's-frill
[The report of this species of the E U.S.A. (N to Minn. and Mass.) from S Ont. by John Macoun (1883; ''Dry stony places on the Niagara River.'') requires confirmation. A collection in OAC from dry woods in Victoria Park, Cambridge (Galt), S Ont., has been referred to var. *scabrella* Nieuwl. (pedicels and calyces densely crisp-puberulent rather than subglabrous). If correctly identified, it may represent a casual introduction.]

[S. virginica L.]
[Open woods, clearings, and slopes from Minn. to S Ont. (where probably now extinct; collection in CAN from islands in the Detroit R., where taken by Maclagen in 1873, the identification verified by Hitchcock and Maguire; reported from Port Franks, Lambton Co., by Dodge 1915) and W N.Y. (?extinct), S to Okla., Ark., Ala., and Ga. (*S. ?pensylvanica sensu* Hooker 1830, as to the S Ont. plant, not Michx.)]

[S. nivea (Nutt.) Otth]   Snowy Campion
[This species of the E U.S.A. (S.Dak. and Minn. to Pa., S to Mo. and Va.; not keyed out above) is reported as introd. in Que. by Lionel Cinq-Mars et al. (Nat. can. (Que.) 98(2):194. 1971; river shore near a summer camp, Quebec City), where perhaps not established.]

[S. sibirica (L.) Pers.]
[This Russian species (not keyed out above) is represented by collections in CAN and DAO from a cult. field at Bladworth, Sask., where taken by Garratt in 1954 (detd. Frankton) and probably a mere waif. It is reported from other Sask. localities (Duck Lake; Bethune; Nokomis) by Boivin (1968). Its fascicled linear-lanceolate leaves import a striking resemblance to *Galium boreale*. The inflorescence is a dense to interrupted thyrse consisting of many-flowered whorls. The calyces are 4 or 5 mm long.]

SPERGULA L.   [2449]   Spurrey

S. arvensis L.   Corn-Spurrey, Stickwort.   Grippe
Eurasian; a common weed of cult. fields and waste places in N. America. MAP and synonymy: *see* below.
1   Seeds minutely white-papillate; plant bright green, scarcely or not at all viscid; [introd. in S Alaska, S Yukon, S Dist. Mackenzie, B.C., Alta., Ont. (N to near Thunder Bay), Que. (N to L. St. John, the Côte-Nord, Gaspé Pen., and Magdalen Is.), Nfld., N.B., P.E.I., and N.S.; SW Greenland; MAP (aggregate species): Hultén 1968*b*:438] . . . .
   . . . . var. *arvensis*

1 Seeds obscurely reticulate, not papillate; plant dull green and very viscid or
   subglabrous; [*S. sativa* Boenn.; reported by Frankton 1955, from B.C., Alta., and
   Que., and a collection in CAN from St. Andrews, N.B., has been placed here] . . . .
   . . . . .var. *sativa* (Boenn.) Reichenb.

SPERGULARIA J. & C. Presl   [2450]   Sand-Spurrey

(Ref.: R.P. Rossbach 1940)
1 Leaves commonly with clusters of smaller leaves in their axils (sometimes not in
   S. macrotheca), mucronate; stipules lance-acuminate, much longer than broad;
   sepals usually densely glandular-pubescent; stamens commonly 10 (when less in
   S. rubra, aborted ones often present); pedicels glandular-pubescent.
   2 Seeds dark brown, strongly reticulate-sculptured and minutely dark-papillate,
     wingless, to 0.6 mm long; capsules to 5 mm long, equalling the calyx; sepals
     usually less than 5 mm long; petals less than 4 mm long; stipules to 5 mm long;
     leaves scarcely fleshy, to 2.5 mm long and 1.2 mm broad; annual or short-lived
     perennial; (introd. in s Alaska–B.C. and from Ont. to Nfld. and N.S.) . . . .*S. rubra*
   2 Seeds dark reddish brown, smooth or smoothish and never papillate, to 0.9 mm
     long, usually surrounded by a narrow white or brownish wing or by a narrower
     opaque brown rim; capsules to 1 cm long, shorter than to 2 mm longer than the
     calyx; sepals to 1 cm long; petals to 8 mm long; stipules to about 1 cm long;
     leaves fleshy, to 5 cm long and 3 mm broad; perennial with a branched caudex;
     (sw B.C.) . . . .*S. macrotheca*
1 Leaves not clustered (or occasionally some of the nodes with 1 or 2 additional
   smaller leaves); stipules about as broad as long or broader; capsules often
   somewhat exserted; annuals.
   3 Seeds silvery black, usually sculptured and sometimes with scattered small black
     papillae, wingless, to 0.5 mm long; sepals to about 3.5 mm long; petals less than
     3 mm long; stamens up to 7; pedicels glandular-pubescent; stipules 1 or 2 mm
     long; leaves glandular-pubescent, short-mucronate, to 2.5 cm long and 1 mm
     broad; (introd. in B.C.–Alta.) . . . .*S. diandra*
   3 Seeds dull brown or reddish brown, usually not markedly sculptured; stamens at
     most 5; leaves to over 4 cm long and about 2 mm broad; (transcontinental).
     4 Stipules mostly broader than long, less than 3 mm long; sepals glabrous, less
       than 4 mm long; petals less than 3 mm long; pedicels rarely somewhat
       glandular-pubescent; seeds often with an erose or friable wing, to 1.4 mm
       long, smoothish; leaves blunt . . . .*S. canadensis*
     4 Stipules mostly slightly longer than broad, to 4 mm long; sepals to 5 mm long;
       petals to 4 mm long; pedicels usually glandular-pubescent; seeds wingless,
       less than 1 mm long; leaves abruptly mucronate . . . .*S. marina*

S. canadensis (Pers.) Don
/sT/D (coastal)/   (T)   Brackish or saline coastal muds and sands (often inundated at high
tide): s Alaska (*see* Hultén 1944: map 549, p. 788) through coastal B.C. to N Calif.; coasts of w
and E James Bay (Dutilly, Lepage, and Duman 1954 and 1958); Que. (St. Lawrence R. estuary
from l'Islet and Charlevoix counties to the Côte-Nord, Anticosti Is., and Gaspé Pen.) to Nfld.,
N.B., P.E.I., N.S., and Long Is. MAPS and synonymy: *see* below.
1 Plant prostrate or decumbent, usually completely glabrous (pedicels rarely sparsely
   glandular-pubescent); sepals blunt, less than 3.5 mm long; [*Arenaria canadensis*
   Pers., the type from the mouth of the St. Lawrence R., Que.; *Tissa* Britt.; *Buda (S.)*
   borealis Wats.; *S. media* of Canadian reports in part, not *Arenaria media* L.; range of
   the species; MAPS: Hultén 1968b:438; R.P. Rossbach 1940: map 6 (incomplete
   northwards), p. 81] . . . . .var. *canadensis*
1 Plant erect or strongly ascending, glabrous or glandular-pubescent throughout;
   sepals acutish, to about 4.5 mm long; [s B.C.: Vancouver Is. and adjacent islands
   and mainland; MAPS: on the above-noted maps by Hultén and Rossbach] . . . .
   . . . . .var. *occidentalis* Rossbach

S. diandra (Guss.) Boiss.
European; locally introd. along the Atlantic (Mass.; Ga.) and Pacific (Wash. and Oreg.; inland in Idaho) coasts and reported from B.C. by Eastham (1947; Kamloops) and from SE Alta. by Moss (1959). [Arenaria Guss.; merged with S. marina by Boivin 1968].

S. macrotheca (Hornem.) Heynh.
/t/W/ (Hp) Coastal sands and salt marshes from SW B.C. (near Victoria, Vancouver Is.; CAN) to Baja Calif. (and inland in Calif.). [Arenaria Hornem.; Buda Ktze.]. MAP: R.P. Rossbach 1940: map 1, p. 81.

S. marina (L.) Griseb.
/sT/(X)/EA/ (T) Brackish or saline coastal muds and sands and alkaline or salt spring areas inland, the aggregate species from B.C. to S Dist. Mackenzie (Wood Buffalo National Park; also on the Alta. side), Sask. (N to Long L. at ca. 54°N; CAN), Man. (N to Churchill), Ont. (known only from W James Bay at ca. 51°45′N), Que. (St. Lawrence R. estuary from l'Islet Co. to Anticosti Is. and the Gaspé Pen.), Nfld. (Rouleau 1956), N.B., P.E.I., and N.S., S to Baja Calif., Tex., and N Fla.; S. America; Iceland; Eurasia. MAPS and synonymy: see below.
1 Seeds glandular-papillate; [Buda Dum.; Tissa Britt.; Arenaria (S.) rubra var. mar. L.; S. salina J. & C. Presl; S. sparsiflora (Greene) Nels.; range of the species; MAP: R.P. Rossbach 1940: map 7, p. 81] . . . . var. marina
1 Seeds not papillate; [S. lei. (Kindb.) Fern. & Wieg.; S B.C.–Alta.–Sask. (R.P. Rossbach 1940); Que. (Cacouna, Temiscouata Co.; Carleton, Gaspé Pen.; Magdalen Is.), Nfld., N.B., P.E.I., and N.S.; MAP: R.P. Rossbach 1940: map 8, p. 81] . . . . var. leiosperma (Kindb.) Gurke

S. rubra (L.) J. & C. Presl
European; introd. in fresh or brackish sandy sterile soils of S Alaska (Middleton Is.; CAN), B.C. (Vancouver Is. and Haines Road at ca. 59°30′N; CAN), Ont. (Barry's Bay, Renfrew Co.; OAC), Que. (Megantic, Temiscouata, and Rimouski counties and the Gaspé Pen.), Nfld., N.B., P.E.I., and N.S. [Arenaria L.; Buda Dum.; Lepigonum Wahl.; Tissa Britt.]. MAP: Hultén 1968b:439.

STELLARIA L.   [2429]   Chickweed, Starwort

1 Principal leaf-blades linear to lanceolate or narrowly elliptic, usually many times longer than broad (mostly at least more than 4 times; sometimes only 3 or 4 in S. calycantha), all sessile, glabrous or merely basally ciliate; flowers sometimes solitary in the leaf-axils and at the stem-tip but more commonly rather numerous in open, usually scarious-bracted cymes; perennials with 4-angled stems, these rarely if ever nodally rooting.
  2 Stems pubescent in lines; pedicels and axis of the leafy-bracted cyme puberulent; flowers to 2 cm broad; capsule inflated, globose, its seeds wrinkled on one side, strongly tuberculate on the back; leaves lance-attenuate, firm, scabrous-margined, to about 8 cm long; (introd.) . . . . [S. holostea]
  2 Stems, pedicels, and floral-axes usually glabrous or nearly so (stem sometimes slightly puberulent above or very rarely pubescent near base); flowers mostly smaller; capsule nearly always ovoid.
    3 Leaves rigid, mostly keeled below, linear to lance-attenuate, to about 4.5 cm long, they and the stem glabrous or essentially so; capsule usually exserted; seeds smoothish or low-pebbled; (transcontinental) . . . . S. longipes
    3 Leaves soft or firm but not rigid or keeled (the northwestern S. alaskana and S. ruscifolia may be sought here; see note under S. longipes).
      4 Flowers pedicelled in the axils of leaves or leaf-like bracts; sepals to 4.5 mm long at anthesis; petals shorter than the sepals or wanting; capsule usually about twice as long as the calyx; leaves lanceolate to ovate; (transcontinental) . . . . S. calycantha
      4 Flowers in well-developed cymes with small scarious bracts; petals surpassing the sepals.

     5 Sepals almost nerveless, eciliate, to 4.5 mm long; seeds nearly smooth; leaves linear, acutish at both ends, to about 5 cm long, their margins (as also often the angles near the top of the stem) minutely scabrous; (transcontinental) . . . .*S. longifolia*

     5 Sepals firm, strongly nerved; seeds pebbled in concentric rows; cymes terminal or terminal and axillary; leaf-margins smooth; (introd.).

         6 Sepals lance-attenuate, to 8 mm long; pedicels ascending or erect; leaves linear-lanceolate, glabrous throughout . . . .*S. palustris*

         6 Sepals lanceolate, acute, at most 5.5 mm long, often prominently ciliolate; pedicels spreading or reflexed; leaves lanceolate, marginally ciliate toward base . . . .*S. graminea*

1 Principal leaf-blades (usually the middle ones; the basal in *S. nitens*) rather broadly lanceolate or elliptic to oblong or ovate (mostly averaging not more than about 4 times longer than broad); upper and lower leaves (except in *S. nitens*) usually much reduced or even bract-like, but still relatively broad in comparison with their length.

    7 Some of the leaves (at least those toward or at the base of the stem) with petioles often nearly as long as or longer than the blade; petals shorter than the sepals or wanting; annuals.

       8 Stems decumbent and nodally rooting, to 5 dm long, they, the pedicels, and the petioles pubescent with multicellular hairs in rather broad longitudinal lines; leaves to over 2.5 cm long, usually somewhat ciliate; cymes leafy-bracted; sepals about 5 mm long, hairy and more or less glandular, shorter than the capsule; (introd.) . . . .*S. media*

       8 Stems erect, almost filiform, to 2 dm tall, not nodally rooting, they, the pedicels, and the petioles glabrous or rather uniformly crisp-pubescent; leaves to about 1 cm long, the stem-leaves sessile, narrower but slightly longer than the long-petioled basal leaves; bracts membranous and much reduced; sepals 3 or 4 mm long, glabrous, hyaline-margined, 3-nerved, about equalling or slightly surpassing the capsule; (s B.C.) . . . .*S. nitens*

    7 Leaves all sessile or subsessile, or the lower ones short-petioled, the petiole much shorter than the blade; sepals usually glabrous (often basally ciliate in *S. pubera*).

       9 Plants puberulent or copiously glandular-pubescent on the pedicels and at least the upper part of the stem; flowers in leafy cymes; sepals to 6 mm long, the petals somewhat longer; capsule shorter than the calyx; perennials with erect or ascending flowering stems.

        10 Stems and pedicels puberulent, the stems 4-angled, tough-based; principal leaves elliptic to elliptic-oblong, to about 1 dm long and 4 cm broad; sepals often basally ciliate; petals sometimes 2-cleft half their length, sometimes nearly to base; (s ?Ont.) . . . .[*S. pubera*]

        10 Stems and pedicels rather densely glandular-pubescent, the stems slightly angled, from slender branching rhizomes; principal leaves ovate, to 3 cm long and 1.5 cm broad; sepals glabrous; petals 2-cleft rarely more than half their length; (mts. of sw Alta.) . . . .*S. americana*

       9 Plants glabrous and non-glandular (or the leaves and angles of the stem at most scabrous-margined or the leaves merely basally ciliate); leaves commonly not over 2 cm long; capsules about equalling or commonly distinctly surpassing the calyx.

        11 Flowers numerous in open scaly-bracted cymes, the pedicels to 3 cm long; sepals 2 or 3 mm long; petals rudimentary or none; principal leaves narrowly oblong-ovate, thin, mostly not over 2 cm long and 5 mm broad (but rarely to 3 cm long), their margins often crisped and sometimes basally ciliate; stems scarcely angled, slender, to 2(3) dm tall; perennial with very slender rhizomes; (Alaska–B.C.–sw Alta.) . . . .*S. umbellata*

        11 Flowers solitary in the axils of foliage-leaves and at the stem-tips or few in

scaly-bracted or leafy-bracted cymes; stems usually matted, often trailing and freely rooting at the nodes.
12 Flowers few in scarious-bracted sessile or short-stalked cymes (the cymes lateral by prolongation of the main axis); sepals to 3.5 mm long, acute; petals about equalling the sepals (reportedly sometimes rudimentary or wanting), deeply 2-cleft nearly to base in narrow segments; capsule slightly surpassing the calyx, the seeds strongly papillate-rugose; principal leaves oblanceolate to oblong, to about 2 cm long and 5 mm broad, some of the lower ones usually distinctly short-petioled; stems strongly 4-angled; annual; (Que. to Nfld. and N.S.; introd. in B.C.) . . . .*S. alsine*
12 Flowers solitary in the leaf-axils (an additional one usually present at the stem-tip; occasionally a few in leafy-bracted cymes); seeds finely and very lightly rugose; stems weakly angled; perennials.
    13 Petals none; pedicels slender, to over 2 cm long; leaves acute or slightly acuminate, sessile or the lower ones short-petioled; (SW B.C. and SW Alta.).
        14 Leaves usually glabrous (the margins minutely hyaline-crisped, rarely ciliate at base), slightly acuminate, to 3 cm long, to 4 times as long as broad; sepals to 3.5(4) mm long, prominently 3-ribbed, scarious-margined, acute; capsule to nearly twice as long as the calyx . . . .*S. crispa*
        14 Leaves always ciliate at base, acute, mostly not over 1 cm long nor twice as long as broad, their margins not at all crisped; sepals to 2.5 mm long, obscurely 3-nerved, very slightly if at all scarious-margined, more or less obtuse; capsule equalling or only slightly surpassing the calyx . . . .*S. obtusa*
    13 Petals present, slightly longer than the acutish to more or less obtuse sepals; leaves glabrous (lacking basal ciliation), acutish to obtuse, all sessile, mostly 3 or 4 times as long as broad; (essentially transcontinental).
        15 Leaves narrowly oblong, thin and only slightly fleshy, acutish, the larger ones commonly 1.5(2) cm long; sepals to 4 mm long; capsule exserted 1 or 2 mm, its seeds distinctly rugose-tuberculate in concentric rows; (moist fresh soil) . . . . . .*S. crassifolia*
        15 Leaves elliptic or oval, fleshy (often drying thin), obtusish, the larger ones commonly about 1 cm long (but up to over 1.5 cm); sepals to 5 mm long; capsule included or barely exserted, its seeds very lightly reticulate but nearly smooth; (saline coastal marshes and meadows) . . . .*S. humifusa*

S. alsine Grimm
/T/EE/EA/ (T (Hs)) Borders of streams and brooks and other wet places from Que. (Pont-Rouge, near Quebec City; MT; CAN) to Nfld., N.B., P.E.I., and N.S., s to Pa. and Md. (reported from Ga.); introd. in the W U.S.A. and possibly in W Canada (but most reports probably refer to other species, e.g., from Blenkinsop Bay, B.C., by John Macoun 1886, to *S. humifusa,* and from Churchill, Man., by Scoggan 1957, to *S. crassifolia,* the relevant collections in CAN; reports from Alaska are referred by Hultén 1944, to *S. calycantha*); Eurasia. MAPS and synonymy: *see* below.
1 Leaves broadly ovate, to 3/5 as broad as long; [N.S. (Iona, Victoria Co.; M.L. Fernald, Rhodora 52(622):251. 1950), St-Pierre and Miquelon, and Nfld.] . . . .
   . . . . .f. *ovalifolia* (Peterm.) Fern.
1 Leaves mostly less than 1/2 as broad as long.
    2 Leaves firm, lanceolate, to 12 mm long; stem to about 1 dm long; (St-Pierre and Miquelon; Fernald, loc. cit.] . . . . .f. *alpina* (Schur.) Fern.
    2 Leaves flaccid, elliptic-lanceolate to oblong, to 2 cm long; stems prolonged-

trailing; [*S. uliginosa* Murr.; range of the species; MAPS (aggregate species): Hultén 1958: map 146, p. 165; Meusel, Jaeger, and Weinert 1965:144] . . . . f. *alsine*

S. americana (Porter) Standl.
/T/W/ (Hpr) Talus slopes at higher elevations in the mountains of SW Alta. (Waterton Lakes; Breitung 1957*b*) and Mont. [*S. dichotoma* var. *amer.* Porter; *Alsine* Rydb.].

S. calycantha (Ledeb.) Bong.
/aST/X/GEA/ (Hpr) Moist to wet or shaded places, the aggregate species from the Aleutian Is. and N-cent. Alaska–Yukon (*see* Hultén 1944: maps 508a, b, p. 785) to the Mackenzie R. Delta, Great Bear L., Great Slave L., L. Athabasca (Alta. and Sask.), S Dist. Keewatin, northernmost Man.–Ont., Que. (N to Ungava Bay, L. Mistassini, and the Côte-Nord), Labrador (N to Hebron, 58°13′N), Nfld, N.B., P.E.I., and N.S., S to Calif., Utah, Wyo., Mich., Pa., and New Eng.; W Greenland N to ca. 70°N, E Greenland N to near the Arctic Circle; Iceland; N Europe; E Asia. MAPS and synonymy: *see* below.
1 Calyx at anthesis less than 3 mm long; capsule to 5 mm long; fruiting pedicels rarely reflexed; leaves lanceolate to ovate, usually not over 2.5 cm long; [*Alsine* Rydb.; *Arenaria* Ledeb.; incl. var. *latifolia* Boivin and ssp. *interior* Hult.; *S. (Alsine) borealis* Bigel.; transcontinental; MAPS: Hultén 1968*b*:414 and 415 (ssp. *int.*), and 1958: map 178 (*S. calycantha* and its ssp. *int.*), p. 197; Raup 1947: pl. 23 (aggregate species)] . . . . . .
. . . . var. *calycantha*
1 Calyx at anthesis usually over 3 mm long; capsule to 7.5 mm long; fruiting pedicels usually abruptly reflexed from the base; leaves narrowly to broadly lanceolate, the main ones mostly well over 2.5 cm long (to nearly 1 dm).
   2 Flowers few in leafy-bracted cymes (or only 1 terminal, the others in the leaf-axils); [incl. vars. *floribunda, isophylla,* and *laurentiana* Fern., the first two originally published as varieties of *S. borealis; S. borealis* var. *bong.* Fern.; *S. longifolia* Bong., not Muhl.; *Spergulastrum (Micropetalum) lanceolatum* Michx.; transcontinental; type from Sitka, Alaska; MAP: Hultén 1968*b*:415 (ssp. *iso.*), and 1958: map 178 (vars. *iso., flor.,* and *laur.*), p. 197] . . . . var. *bongardiana* Fern.
   2 Flowers several in small terminal bracted cymes, the upper leaves considerably reduced; [*S. sitchana* Steud. (type from Sitka, Alaska; *S. bor.* var. *sit.* (Steud.) Fern.); *S. brachipetala* Bong.; *S. (Alsine) alpestris* Fries (*S. bor.* var. *alp.* (Fries) Gray; Aleutian Is.–Alaska–B.C.–W Alta.; MAP (*S. sit.*): Hultén 1968*b*:416] . . . .
. . . . var. *sitchana* (Steud.) Fern.

S. crassifolia Ehrh.
/aST/X/EA/ (Hpr) Wet meadows, streambanks, etc., from the Aleutian Is. and coasts of Alaska–Yukon–W Dist. Mackenzie to Victoria Is., cent. Dist. Keewatin, Southampton Is., Prince Charles Is. in Foxe Basin at ca. 57°10′N, S Baffin Is., and northernmost Ungava–Labrador, S in the West through B.C. (Anahim L., ca. 52°30′N; CAN) and Alta.–Sask.–Man. to Idaho, Mont., Colo., N.Dak., and Minn., farther eastwards S to W and E James Bay, E Que. (S to Bic, Rimouski Co.), Nfld., N.B., P.E.I., and N.S. (St. Paul Is.; John Macoun 1883); Iceland; Eurasia. [*Alsine* Britt.]. MAPS: Porsild 1957: map 137, p. 178; Hultén 1968*b*:413.
   Forma *gemmificans* Norman (producing gemma-like buds in the leaf-axils) apparently occurs nearly throughout the range.

S. crispa C. & S.
/sT/W/ (Hpr) Moist lowlands or lower montane woods from the Aleutian Is. and S Alaska (*see* Hultén 1944: map 511, p. 785; type from Unalaska) to S Yukon (White River; CAN), S through B.C. and SW Alta. (Waterton Lakes) to Calif. and Wyo. [*Alsine* Holz.]. MAP: Hultén 1968*b*:412.

S. graminea L.   Common Stitchwort
Eurasian; introd. in grasslands of N. America, as in B.C. (N to Queen Charlotte Is.; Calder and Taylor 1968; the report from Waskesiu Lake, Sask., by Breitung 1957*a,* may refer to *S. longifolia*), ?Man. (reported from Morden and Roseisle by Lowe 1943; the citations from

Churchill and The Pas by Scoggan 1957, are based upon *S. longifolia,* relevant collections in CAN), Ont. (N to L. Abitibi at ca. 48°50′N), Que. (N to the Matamek R., Côte-Nord; GH; reported from Fort George, James Bay, by J.M. Macoun 1895), ?Labrador (Boivin 1966*b*), Nfld. (CAN), N.B., P.E.I., and N.S. [*Micropetalum* Pers.; *Spergulastrum* Michx.].

[*S. holostea* L.]
[European; locally spread from cult. to roadsides and rocky woods in the E U.S.A.; the collection forming the basis of the report from Starrs Point, Kings Co., N.S., by D.S. Erskine (Rhodora 53(635):268. 1951) was later referred by him to *Cerastium arvense.* The report from s Que. by Lionel Cinq-Mars et al. (Nat. can. (Que.) 98(2):195. 1971; Verchères, near Montreal) requires confirmation.].

S. humifusa Rottb.
/AST/X/GEA/ (Ch (Hpr)) Brackish or saline shores and wet meadows from the Aleutian Is. and coasts of Alaska–Yukon–Dist. Mackenzie–Dist. Keewatin nearly throughout the Canadian Arctic Archipelago to Ellesmere Is. (N to 81°25′N) and northernmost Ungava–Labrador, s along the Pacific coast to Oreg., the coasts of Hudson Bay to w and E James Bay, and the Atlantic coast from E Que. (St. Lawrence R. estuary from l'Islet Co. to the Côte-Nord, Anticosti Is., Gaspé Pen., and Magdalen Is.) to Nfld., N.B., P.E.I., N.S., and Maine; w and E Greenland N to ca. 69°N; Iceland; Spitsbergen; Eurasia. [Incl. vars. *oblongifolia* Fenzl and *suberecta* Boivin; *Arenaria thymifolia* Pursh, not Sibth. & Sm.]. MAPS: Porsild 1957: map 136, p. 177; Hultén 1968*b*:413.

S. longifolia Muhl.
/ST/X/EA/ (Hpr (Ch)) Damp thickets, meadows, and shores from cent. Alaska–Yukon (*see* Hultén 1944: map 515, p. 785) and NW Dist. Mackenzie to Great Slave L., L. Athabasca (Alta. and Sask.), Man. (N to Churchill), Ont. (N to Fort Severn, Hudson Bay, ca. 56°N), Que. (N to E James Bay at 52°37′N and the Côte-Nord), s Labrador (Goose Bay, 53°19′N), Nfld., N.B., P.E.I., and N.S., s to Calif., N.Mex., La., and S.C.; Eurasia. [*Alsine* Britt.; var. *atrata* Moore (*S. atr.* (Moore) Boivin) and its f. *eciliata* Boivin]. MAPS: Hultén 1968*b*:414; Meusel, Jaeger, and Weinert 1965:143.

S. longipes Goldie
/AST/X/GEA/ (Hpr (Ch)) Gravelly or turfy tundra, meadows, and rocky places, the aggregate species from the coasts of Alaska–Yukon–Dist. Mackenzie–Dist. Keewatin nearly throughout the Canadian Arctic Archipelago to northernmost Ellesmere Is. and northernmost Ungava–Labrador, s in the West through B.C. and the mts. of sw Alta. to Calif. and N.Mex., farther eastwards s to s Sask.–Man., Minn., N Ind., Ont. (N to the shores of L. Superior, L. Erie, and L. Ontario; type from "woods near Lake Ontario"), Que., Nfld., N.B., N.S., and w N.Y.; nearly circumgreenlandic; Eurasia. MAPS and synonymy: *see* below.
   The following key, based upon that by Eric Hultén (Bot. Not. (1943):253. 1943), includes several closely related species (?microspecies) of the complex. *See,* also, A.E. Porsild (Nat. Mus. Can. Bull. 186:1–35. 1963), T.W. Böcher (Bot. Tidsskr. 48:401–20. 1951), and Hultén (1944:646–60).
1 Sepals marginally ciliate; leaves shining, distinctly keeled, linear to narrowly
   lanceolate or narrowly elliptic.
   2 Flowers in the axils of green leafy bracts lacking scarious margins; sepals more
     or less pubescent on the back; [*Alsine* Rydb.; transcontinental, the type from
     near Great Bear L.; MAPS: Porsild, loc. cit., fig. 6, p. 23, and 1957: map 135,
     p. 177; Hultén, loc. cit., fig. 8 (incomplete), p. 267, and 1968*b*:419; Böcher, loc.
     cit., fig. 4 (incomplete), p. 416] . . . . [*S. laeta* Richards.]
   2 Flowers in the axils of scarious bracts or scarious-margined leaves.
     3 Sepals glabrous or nearly so on the back; [*Alsine* Rydb.; *S. longipes* var. *ed.*
       (R. Br.) Wats.; *S. longipes* f. *humilis* (Fenzl) Ostenf. at least in part;
       S. ciliatosepala Trautv.; *S. nitida* Hook.; transcontinental, the type from
       Melville Is.; MAPS: Porsild, loc. cit., fig. 7, p. 31, and 1957: map 134 *(S. cil.),*

p. 177; Hultén, loc. cit., fig. 4 (*S. cil.;* incomplete), p. 258, and 1968*b*:420;
Böcher, loc. cit., fig. 5 (*S. cil.;* incomplete), p. 417; Raup 1947: pl. 23] . . . .
. . . . [*S. edwardsii* R. Br.]

3 Sepals densely pubescent on the back especially toward the tip; [Alaska–
Yukon; cent. Ellesmere Is. to N Baffin Is.; Greenland; MAP: Böcher, loc. cit.,
fig. 4, p. 416] . . . . [*S. laxmannii* Fisch.]

1 Sepals non-ciliate and glabrous.
4 Leaves dull, flat, coriaceous or fleshy, elliptic to ovate-lanceolate or ovate; entire
plant glabrous.
5 Pedicels arising from the axils of a pair of scarcely reduced leaves; petals
surpassing the sepals; [ssp. *aleutica* Hult., the type from Unalaska Is.,
Aleutian Is.; also known from the Pribilof Is. and SE Alaska; MAPS: Hultén 1944:
map 519, p. 786, and 1968*b*:417 (ssp. *al.*)] . . . .[*S. ruscifolia* Pallas]
5 Pedicels arising from a pair of scarious bracts; petals not surpassing the
sepals; [cent. Alaska and SW Yukon; type from Rapids, Alaska; MAPS: Olav
Gjaerevoll, K. Nor. Vidensk. Selsk. Skr. (1963, No. 4): fig. 5, p. 19. 1963; Hultén
1968*b*:418, and 1944: map 507 (incomplete), p. 785] . . . .[*S. alaskana* Hult.]
4 Leaves shining, keeled, scarcely coriaceous but sometimes rather fleshy, linear
to lanceolate or narrowly elliptic.
6 Flowers solitary (rarely 2 on a peduncle) in the axils of green leafy bracts
lacking scarious margins; [incl. var. *altocaulis* Hult. and ssp. *atlantica* Hult.;
S. hultenii Boivin; transcontinental; type from Glacier Bay, Alaska; MAPS:
Porsild, loc. cit., fig. 5, p. 23, and 1957: map 133, p. 177; Hultén, loc. cit.,
fig. 9, p. 267, and 1968*b*:418] . . . . [*S. monantha* Hult.]
6 Flowers commonly in well-developed cymes, the peduncles subtended by
small scarious bracts.
7 Plant of low and matted growth; flower usually solitary (rarely a second
lateral one); capsules (very rarely developed) pale and with reflexed teeth;
[Prince Patrick Is. to northernmost Ellesmere Is., S to Coronation Gulf,
E-cent. Dist. Keewatin, Labrador, and N Nfld.; Greenland; MAPS: Porsild,
loc. cit., fig. 2, p. 10, and 1957: map 132, p. 177; Hultén, loc. cit., fig. 3,
p. 258, and 1958: map 7, p. 27 (both incomplete southwards); Böcher, loc.
cit., fig. 5, p. 417; Savile 1961: map E, p. 928] . . . . [*S. crassipes* Hult.]
7 Plant mostly high-grown.
8 Stems strongly pubescent especially on the internodes; leaves usually
more or less villous; [*Alsine* Rydb.; *S. longipes* var. *sub.* (Greene)
Polunin; S Yukon–B.C. and SW Alta. (lectotype from near Banff) to E
Hudson Bay–James Bay; MAP: Porsild, loc. cit., fig. 4, p. 17] . . . .
. . . . [*S. subvestita* Greene]
8 Stems and leaves glabrous or essentially so.
9 Inflorescence many-flowered, with characteristically stiff and
strongly ascending branches, the terminal flowers commonly
approximate; petals scarcely surpassing the sepals; [*Alsine*
strictiflora Rydb.; SW Yukon–NW Dist. Mackenzie–B.C. to L.
Superior, Ont., and James Bay, Que.; the lectotype is from Great
Bear L.; MAP: Porsild, loc. cit., fig. 3, p. 17] . . . .[*S. stricta* Richards.]
9 Inflorescence commonly few-flowered, the branches spreading;
petals surpassing the sepals.
10 Capsule stramineous, its valves reflexed and outwardly
somewhat rolled at maturity; [known only from the type locality,
L. Athabasca, Sask.; MAP: Porsild, loc. cit., fig. 2, p. 10] . . . .
. . . .[*S. arenicola* Raup]
10 Capsule black and shining, its valves not reflexed; [*Alsine*
Coville; transcontinental; type from near L. Ontario, Ont.; MAPS:
Porsild, loc. cit., fig. 1, p. 10; Hultén, loc. cit., fig. 2 (dots for
Eurasia and probably Greenland should be deleted according to
Porsild), p. 255, and 1968*b*:419] . . . . *S. longipes*

S. media (L.) Cyrillo   Common Chickweed.   Mouron des oiseaux
Eurasian; a common weed of dooryards, cult. ground, waste places, and other disturbed areas in N. America; known from Alaska (N to ca. 68°N), the Yukon, Dist. Mackenzie, and all the provinces (in Man., N to Churchill; in Labrador, N to Hebron, 58°13′N); also introd. in Greenland. [*Alsine* L.; incl. var. *procera* Klett & Richter]. MAP: Hultén 1968*b*:412.

Var. *glaberrima* Beck (plant glabrous throughout rather than the stems pubescent in lines, the calyces usually pilose or villous) is known from E Que. (Anticosti Is.; MT).

S. *nitens* Nutt.
/t/W/   (T)   Gravelly plains, grassy hillsides, and streambanks from S B.C. (Vancouver Is. and adjacent islands; Agassiz; Kamloops) to Baja Calif. and Utah. [*Alsine* Greene; S. *praecox* Nels.].

S. *obtusa* Engelm.
/T/W/   (Hpr)   Damp meadows and streams from S ?Alaska (Boivin 1966*b*) through B.C. and SW Alta. (Waterton Lakes and near Blairmore; CAN) to Calif. and Colo. [*Alsine* Rose].

S. palustris Retz.
Eurasian; introd. in moist grasslands and along shores in N. America, as in ?Ont. (reported from Renison, on the Moose R. S of James Bay at ca. 51°N, by Ilmari Hustich, Acta Geogr. 13(2):46. 1955) and Que. (near Quebec City in Montmagny and Montmorency counties; CAN; GH; *see* B.L. Robinson, Rhodora 6(65):90. 1904). [Incl. S. *glauca* With. and S. *dilleniana* Moench, not Leers].

[S. pubera Michx.]   Great or Star-Chickweed
[A species of the E U.S.A. (Ill. and N.J. to Ala. and Fla.), to which collections in OAC and TRT from S Ont. (Lucan, Middlesex Co.; Guelph, Wellington Co.) have been referred, the basis of the listing for S Ont. by Soper (1949). It is not listed by Boivin (1966*b*) and the above collections may prove referable to some other species.]

S. *umbellata* Turcz.
/ST/W/eA/   (Hpr)   Moist meadows and montane forests of Alaska (Eagle Summit, cent. Alaska, and the Wrangell Mts. at 61°37′N; CAN) through B.C. (Prince George; Manning Provincial Park, SE of Hope) and SW Alta. (Waterton Lakes; Breitung 1957*b*) to Calif. and Colo.; Siberia. [S. *gonomischa* and S. *weberi* Boivin; *Alsine baicalensis* Cov., not *A. umbellata* Lam.; *Larbrea uliginosa* Hook.]. MAPS: Hultén 1968*b*:417; Olav Gjaerevoll, K. Nor. Vidensk. Selsk. Skr. (1963, No. 4): fig. 7, p. 23. 1963.

TUNICA Scop.   [2498]

T. saxifraga (L.) Scop.
European; a garden-escape locally to roadsides and waste places in N. America, as in B.C. (Prince George, ca. 54°N; Groh 1946) and S Ont. (roadsides at London, where taken by Burgess in 1886; GH).

CERATOPHYLLACEAE (Hornwort Family)

CERATOPHYLLUM L. [2516] Hornwort, Coon-tail. Cornifle

Aquatic herbs with freely branched stems and whorled sessile leaves, these palmately thrice-dissected into narrow divisions. Flowers minute, solitary in the axils, sessile, unisexual, lacking a perianth but each subtended by an 8–12-cleft calyx-like involucre. Fruit a spiny achene.

1 Achenes wingless, with only 2 basal spines, smoothish, rarely over 5 mm long; style at most 6 mm long; leaf-segments conspicuously sharp-toothed on one side; (B.C. to N.S.) . . . . C. demersum
1 Achenes to 7 mm long, vertically winged by the confluent bases of the several lateral spines, the surface elsewhere rather conspicuously tuberculate; style to 1 cm long; leaf-segments subentire; (Ont. to N.S.) . . . . C. echinatum

C. demersum L.
/ST/X/ (HH) Quiet waters from Alaska (N to near the Arctic Circle), S Dist. Mackenzie (E of Great Slave L.; J.W. Thieret, Can. Field-Nat. 76(4):207. 1962), and Alta. (Wood Buffalo National Park at 59°14′N) to Sask. (N to Heart Lake, 54°24′N; Breitung 1957a), Man. (N to Oxford L., on the Hayes R. NE of L. Winnipeg at ca. 55°N; CAN), Ont. (N to Cochrane, 49°03′N), Que. (N to the Montreal dist.), N.B., P.E.I., and N.S., S to Baja Calif., Mexico, Tex., Fla., and Central America. MAPS: Hultén 1968b:451; N.C. Fassett, Comun. Inst. Trop. Invest. Ci. Univ. El Salvador 2: map 1 (incomplete northwards), p. 43. 1953.

C. echinatum Gray
/T/EE/ (HH) Quiet waters from N Mich. (N to Isle Royale, close to Thunder Bay, Ont., and to be searched for in that region) and S ?Ont. (Norfolk Co.; Landon 1960) to Que. (Fernald *in* Gray 1950; reported N to the region S of L. St. John by Y. Desmarais, Nat. can. (Que.) 80(6/7): 167. 1953), N.B. (Grand Manan, Charlotte Co.; GH; CAN), and N.S. (Boivin 1966b), S to Mexico, Tex., and Fla. [*C. demersum* var. *echin.* Gray]. MAP: Fassett, loc. cit., map 2, p. 44.

NYMPHAEACEAE (Water-lily Family)

Aquatic herbs with submersed, floating, or emersed leaves, these usually essentially entire (submersed leaves palmately dissected in *Cabomba*). Flowers perfect. Sepals and petals each 3–many (scarcely differentiated from one another in *Nelumbo* and *Nuphar*). Stamens 3–many. Carpels 2–many, commonly united into a compound ovary (free in *Brasenia* and *Cabomba*), the mature fruit somewhat berry-like, leathery and indehiscent or finally breaking irregularly.

1 Leaves principally submersed and palmately dissected into narrowly linear segments, opposite or whorled on the stem; floating leaves few, entire, narrowly elliptic, centrally peltate, at most about 2 cm long; flowers cream-colour, less than 2 cm broad; sepals and petals each 3; stamens 3–6; carpels 2–6, free; (introd. in s Ont.) . . . . *Cabomba*
1 Leaves principally floating or emersed, essentially entire; flowers larger; stamens more numerous.
  2 Leaves centrally peltate, lacking a sinus.
    3 Flowers dull purple, usually less than 3 cm broad; sepals and petals each 3 (sometimes 4), the petals somewhat the shorter; stamens 12–18; carpels 4–18, free; leaves elliptic, flat, cauline, floating on the surface, at most about 1 dm long; (B.C. to N.S.) . . . . *Brasenia*
    3 Flowers pale yellow, to about 2.5 dm broad; sepals and petals numerous, scarcely differentiated; stamens numerous; carpels numerous, sunken in small pits on the truncate summit of the receptacle; leaves circular, with raised margins, normally raised above the surface of the water on long petioles arising from the thick rhizome, to about 6 dm broad; (s Ont.) . . . . *Nelumbo*
  2 Leaves ovate- to rotund-cordate, the petiole attached at the apex of a basal sinus; petals and stamens each numerous; carpels numerous, united into a compound ovary.
    4 Petals conspicuous, white to roseate, they and the 4 green or purplish sepals spreading widely before the final closing of the flower; petioles and peduncles with 4 large air-passages . . . . *Nymphaea*
    4 Petals small and stamen-like; sepals 5 or more, yellow or tinged with red or green, concave, the flower subglobose; petioles and peduncles with numerous minute air-passages . . . . *Nuphar*

BRASENIA Schreb. [2510]

B. schreberi Gmel.   Water-shield, Purple Wen-dock
/T/X/A/ (HH) Ponds and slow streams from the Alaska Panhandle (*see* Hultén 1944: map 561, p. 789) and B.C. to SE Man. (Whiteshell Forest Reserve; Boivin 1968; not known from Alta. or Sask.), Ont. (N to Lake of the Woods and Schreiber, N shore of L. Superior), Que. (N to New Richmond, s Gaspé Pen.; MT), N.B., and N.S. (not known from P.E.I.), s to Calif., Tex., and Fla.; Cuba; Central America; Europe (fossil); Asia; SW Africa; Australia. [*B. peltata* Pursh; *Hydropeltis (B.) purpurea* Michx.]. MAP: Hultén 1968*b*:449.

CABOMBA Aubl. [2509]

C. caroliniana Gray   Fanwort
Native in the E U.S.A. from E Mo., s Ill., and Va. to Tex. and Fla.; natzd. northwards to Ohio, N.Y., and Mass. (Fernald *in* Gray 1950) and in s Ont. (Wellington Co.; F.H. Montgomery, Can. Field-Nat. 62(2):92. 1948.

NELUMBO Adams. [2508]   Sacred Bean

N. lutea (Willd.) Pers.   Water-Chinquapin, Yellow Nelumbo
/t/EE/ (Hel) Ponds, quiet steams, and estuaries from Iowa to Minn., s Ont. (Essex, Kent,

Lambton, Norfolk, Haldimand, and Welland counties; *see* s Ont. map by Soper 1962: fig. 9, p. 17), N.Y., and s New Eng., s to Tex. and Fla.; W.I. [*Nelumbium* Willd.; *Cyamus* Bart.].

NUPHAR Sm.　[2514]　Yellow Pond- or Water-lily, Cow-lily

1　Anthers longer than the filaments; stigmatic disk green or greenish; flowers to over
　　1 dm broad when laid open; leaf-blades to 3 or 4 dm long.
　　2　Petioles flattened on the upper side and narrowly winged; leaves floating or some
　　　　submersed, the sinus narrow; (transcontinental) . . . . *N. variegatum*
　　2　Petioles terete or oval in cross-section, not winged; leaves erect and raised
　　　　above the surface of the water, the sinus broadly triangular; (s Ont.) . . . . . . *N. advena*
1　Anthers shorter than the filaments; leaves normally all floating (sometimes partially
　　or wholly raised above the water).
　　3　Sepals usually about 9 (at least 7, at most 12), the inner ones to 6 cm long, bright
　　　　yellow to reddish-tinged, the outer ones shorter, leathery and more greenish, the
　　　　flower to over 1 dm broad when laid open; anthers reddish or purplish; stigmatic
　　　　disk 13–25-rayed; leaf-blades to over 4 dm long; (B.C.; reported from Alta.) . . . .
　　　　. . . . . *N. polysepalum*
　　3　Sepals commonly 5 or 6, at most about 3 cm long; anthers commonly yellow;
　　　　stigmatic disk red (often bordered with yellow) or crimson.
　　　　4　Anthers not over 3 mm long; flowers at most 3 cm broad when laid open; fruit
　　　　　　naked at base, the stigmatic disk 6–10-rayed; leaf-blades rarely over 1 dm
　　　　　　long; (Man. to Nfld. and N.S.) . . . . *N. microphyllum*
　　　　4　Anthers to 6 mm long; flowers to about 6 cm broad when laid open; fruit
　　　　　　clothed at base by the persistent sepals and petals, the stigmatic disk 8–15-
　　　　　　rayed; leaf-blades to over 2 dm long; (Ont. to Nfld. and N.S.). . . . × *N. rubrodiscum*

N. advena (Ait.) Ait. f.
/t/EE/　(HH)　Ponds and quiet steams from Nebr. to Ohio., s Ont. (Essex, Lambton, Kent, Bruce, Middlesex, Waterloo, Wellington, York, and Welland counties), Pa., N.Y., and New Eng., s to E Mexico, Tex., and Fla. [*Nymphaea* Ait.; *Nymphozanthus* Fern.].

N. microphyllum (Pers.) Fern.
/sT/EE/　(HH)　Ponds and quiet waters from Man. (N to Cranberry Portage, about 45 mi SE of Flin Flon; WIN; the report from Sask. by Rydberg 1932, requires confirmation) to Ont. (N to Geraldton, about 140 mi NE of Thunder Bay), Que. (N to the E James Bay watershed at 53°31′N, L. St. John, Anticosti Is., and the Gaspé Pen.), Nfld. (near Salmonier; GH), N.B., and N.S. (not known from P.E.I.), s to Minn., Pa., and N.J. [*Nymphaea* Pers.; *Nymphozanthus* Fern.; *Nymphaea (Nuphar) lutea* var. *kalmiana* Michx.; *Nymphaea (Nuphar) kalmiana* (Michx.) Sims; *Nymphaea lutea* of Canadian reports, not L.; *Nymphaea (Nuphar) minima* of Canadian reports, not *Nym. lut.* var. *min.* Willd.; *Nymphaea (Nymphozanthus) pumila* of Canadian reports, not *Nym. lutea* var. *pum.* Timm].

N. polysepalum Engelm.　Rocky Mountain Cow-lily
/ST/WW/　(HH)　Ponds and quiet waters from N Alaska–Yukon–w Dist. Mackenzie (CAN) through B.C. (CAN; V; the inclusion of Alta. in the range by Hitchcock et al. 1964, requires clarification) to N Calif., Colo., and S.Dak. [*Nymphaea* Greene; *Nymphozanthus* Fern.]. MAP: Hultén 1968b:450.

× N. rubrodiscum Morong
This taxon, commonly considered to be a fertile hybrid between *N. microphyllum* and *N. variegatum,* occurs nearly throughout the range of *N. microphyllum:* Ont. (N to L. Abitibi and L. Kapuskasing), Que. (N to near L. St. John, Anticosti Is., and the Gaspé Pen.), Nfld., N.B., and N.S. [*Nymphaea* Greene; *Nymphozanthus* Fern.; *Nuphar advena* vars. ?*minor* Morong and *hybrida* Peck; *Nymphaea fletcheri* Lawson].

N. variegatum Durand   Bullhead-lily.   Pied-de-cheval
/ST/X/   (HH)   Ponds and quiet waters from s-cent. Yukon and B.C. (near Coal River, ca. 59°N; CAN) to NW Dist. Mackenzie, Great Bear L., Great Slave L., L. Athabasca (Alta. and Sask.), Man. (N to Reindeer L. at 57°37′N; CAN), Ont. (N to the W James Bay watershed between 54° and 55°N), Que. (N to the Wiachouan R. E of Hudson Bay at 56°10′N, L. Marymac at ca. 57°N, L. St. John, the Côte-Nord, Anticosti Is., and Gaspé Pen.), Labrador (N to the Hamilton R. basin), Nfld., N.B., P.E.I., and N.S., s to N Idaho–Mont., Nebr., Ohio, and Del. [*Nymphaea* Mill.; *Nymphozanthus* Fern.; *Nuphar americana* Provancher; *Nymphaea advena* var. *var.* (Durand) Fern.; *Nymphaea (Nuphar; Nymphozanthus) advena* of Canadian reports other than from s Ont., not Ait.]. MAP: Hultén 1968*b*:450.

NYMPHAEA L.   [2513]   Water-lily.   Lis d'eau

1   Leaves elliptic to ovate or obovate, to 12 cm long and about three-fourths as broad, mottled when young; flowers at most about 8 cm broad, inodorous; sepals rarely over 3.5 cm long; stigmas less than 10; (ssp. *leibergii;* widespread but localized) . . . .
. . . . *N. tetragona*
1   Leaves rotund; sepals to 8 cm long; stigmas at least 10.
   2   Leaves mostly not over about 2 dm broad, commonly purple beneath, the petioles not striped; petals narrowly elliptic, subacute; flowers very fragrant, rarely over 12 cm broad; (Man. to Nfld. and N.S.) . . . . *N. odorata*
   2   Leaves 2 or 3 dm broad, usually green beneath, the petioles usually striped; petals spatulate or oblanceolate, rounded at apex; flowers scarcely fragrant, to over 2 dm broad; (Ont. and s Que.) . . . . *N. tuberosa*

N. odorata Ait.   Fragrant Water-lily, Pond-lily.   Nénuphar blanc
/T/EE/   (HH)   Ponds and quiet waters from Man. (N to the Minago R. near Hill L., N of L. Winnipeg) to Ont. (N to Lake of the Woods and the N shore of L. Superior), Que. (N to about 90 mi N of Hull and the Gaspé Pen. near Mt-Louis and New Carlisle), Nfld., N.B., P.E.I., and N.S., s to Tex. and Fla.; introd. in the W U.S.A. [*Castalia* Greene; *N. minor* (Sims) DC.; *N. rosea* (Pursh) Raf.].

N. tetragona Georgi   Pygmy Water-lily
/ST/(X)/EA/   (HH)   Ponds and quiet waters, very local: Alaska (N to Fairbanks, ca. 55°N); s Dist. Mackenzie (N to Great Slave L.) and northernmost Alta. (Fort Smith, 60°N; W.J. Cody, Can. Field-Nat. 70(3):112. 1956); B.C. (N to Aleza and Hansard lakes, both ca. 54°N) to N Wash.-Idaho; cent. Sask. (near Cumberland L. at ca. 54°N) to Man. (Drunken L., off the Minago R. N of L. Winnipeg; Rennie, SE of Winnipeg), Ont. (N to the Severn R., Hudson Bay, at ca. 56°N and W James Bay at ca. 53°N; s to the Rainy R. region and the N shore of L. Superior), N Minn., N Mich. (Isle Royale, L. Superior), Que. (Duparquet, ca. 48°30′N; Bic and Rimouski, Rimouski Co.; L. Memphramagog, Stanstead Co.), N Maine, and R.I.; N Europe; Asia. [*Castalia* Lawson; *C. (N.) pygmaea* Salisb.]. MAPS: Hultén 1968*b*:449; Marcel Raymond and Pierre Dansereau, Mém. Jardin Bot. Montréal 41: fig. 1, p. 4, and fig. 2 (N. American stations), p. 6. 1953.
    The N. American plant may be separated as ssp. *leibergii* (Morong) Porsild (*N. (Castalia) leib.* Morong), said by A.E. Porsild (Can. Field-Nat. 53(4):48–50. 1939) to differ from the Eurasian plant in its obtuse (rather than acute) petals, its somewhat less acute sepals, and its more open, straightish-margined leaf-sinuses.

N. tuberosa Paine   Magnolia Water-lily
/T/EE/   (HH)   Ponds and quiet waters from Nebr. to Minn., Ont. (N to English River, about 100 mi NW of Thunder Bay, and the North Bay and Ottawa districts), and SW Que. (N to s Argenteuil Co. and the Montreal dist.), s to Ark., Ill., Ohio, and Md. [*Castalia* Greene; incl. var. *maxima* Conard; *N. reniformis* of auth., not Walt.].

[N. alba L.]   European White Water-lily
[European; this species (not keyed out above) is reported by D.S. Erskine (1960) as established in several ponds in P.E.I. following distribution from the Experimental Farm at Charlottetown. It has white to roseate flowers to about 12 cm broad and roundish leaves to about 3 dm broad.]

RANUNCULACEAE (Crowfoot Family)

Herbs (or *Clematis* a slightly woody vine) with simple or compound, commonly alternate or basal leaves (stem-leaves opposite or whorled in *Anemone, Anemonella,* and *Clematis*). Flowers perfect or unisexual, hypogynous, regular (except in *Aconitum* and *Delphinium*). Sepals 3–15, in some genera petaloid. Petals 2–15 or none. Stamens usually numerous. Pistils 1 to many, distinct (except in *Nigella*). Ovary superior. Fruit an achene, follicle, or berry. (Incl. Paeoniaceae).

1 Flowers spurred.
 2 Sepals 5, spurless; petals 5, large, each of them prolonged backwards into a long straight or hooked spur; fruit a several-seeded follicle (dehiscing by the ventral suture); leaves 2–3-ternately compound, the leaflets lobed; perennials . . . . . .*Aquilegia*
 2 Sepals spurred.
  3 Flowers regular, each of the 5 minute yellowish-green sepals prolonged backwards into a short spur; petals 5, spurless; fruit an achene (indehiscent); leaves all basal, linear-spatulate, entire, the 1-flowered scapes to about 1.5 dm tall; (s B.C. to s Ont.) . . . .*Myosurus*
  3 Flowers irregular, only the upper large petaloid sepal prolonged backwards into a spur; petals 2 or 4, 2 of them with long spurs enclosed in the sepal-spur; flowers in terminal racemes; fruit a several-seeded follicle; leaves cauline, palmately divided or cut; stems taller; (western or introd. species) . . . .*Delphinium*
1 Flowers spurless.
 4 Flowers irregular, blue-violet or purplish (rarely white), the upper petaloid sepal helmet-shaped, to over 2.5 cm high, long-beaked, enclosing the 2 small spur-like upper petals; fruit a follicle; leaves palmate-pinnately divided into numerous linear-oblong segments; (western or introd. species) . . . .*Aconitum*
 4 Flowers regular.
  5 Sepals small and inconspicuous, usually early deciduous; petals none or small and stamen-like.
   6 Leaves deeply palmately cleft to below the middle into usually 5 or 7 broad toothed lobes (but not into separate leaflets), cordate-rotund in outline, to over 2 dm broad, the basal ones long-petioled, the smaller cauline ones short-petioled to sessile; petals none.
    7 Flower solitary at the top of the stem; fruit a raspberry-like head of dark-red or crimson 1–2-seeded berries; basal leaf solitary, the pubescent stem 2-leaved near the top, to about 5 dm tall, from a thick and knotted yellow rhizome; (s Ont.) . . . .*Hydrastis*
    7 Flowers numerous in a terminal compound corymbose inflorescence; fruit a cluster of papery achenes 3 or 4 mm long, these strongly nerved on the 4 angles and beaked by the hooked style; basal leaves commonly 2 or 3, the usually 2 stem-leaves distant; stem usually glabrous below, somewhat crisp-puberulent above at least in the inflorescence, to about 1 m tall, from widely spreading rhizomes; (s B.C.) . . . .*Trautvetteria*
   6 Leaves 2–3-ternately compound (sometimes ternate-pinnate in *Cimicifuga*); sepals 4 or 5.
    8 Flowers white, greenish, or purplish, in large branched corymbs or panicles (in simple racemes only in *T. alpinum*), commonly unisexual; petals none; fruit an achene . . . .*Thalictrum*
    8 Flowers white (sometimes pinkish), in a simple or branched raceme; petals none or spatulate and stamen-like.
     9 Raceme simple, at anthesis less than 1 dm long and less than twice as long as thick; fruit berry-like, indehiscent . . . .*Actaea*
     9 Raceme slender and elongate, at anthesis over 1 dm long, often

branched and somewhat paniculate; fruit a usually solitary follicle
(sometimes 2, rarely 3); (s B.C.; s Ont.) . . . . *Cimicifuga*
5   Sepals or petals (when present) conspicuous.
     10 Stem-leaves opposite or whorled; petals none or represented by
          staminodia; fruit an achene; perennials.
          11 Leaves 3-foliolate or pinnately compound; stems climbing by bending
               of the leaf-stalks (except in *C. hirsutissima* and *C. recta*); sepals
               normally 4; mature styles to about 9 cm long, plumose (except in
               C. viticella) . . . . *Clematis*
          11 Leaves deeply incised or parted but not into distinct leaflets; sepals
               commonly 5 or more; stems not climbing; petals wanting . . . . *Anemone*
     10 Stem-leaves alternate or leaves all basal.
          12 Leaves alternate, partly or wholly cauline.
               13 Fruit an achene (1-seeded).
                    14 Petals 6 or more, orange, red, or bright scarlet, lacking
                         nectariferous pits or scales at base; sepals 5, green, shorter than
                         the petals; stem-leaves subsessile, deeply 3-pinnatifid into linear
                         acute segments; (introd.) . . . . *Adonis*
                    14 Petals commonly 5, white or yellow, with a nectar-pit at base;
                         sepals greenish or yellow, smaller or larger than the petals and
                         mostly soon deciduous; leaves various . . . . *Ranunculus*
               13 Fruit a few- to several-seeded capsule or follicle; plants glabrous.
                    15 Fruit capsule-like, many-seeded, globular, dehiscing at the top,
                         where terminated by the 5 long beaks of the very incompletely
                         separated follicles; flowers bluish, about 4 cm broad, closely
                         subtended by an involucre of dissected leaves; petals
                         represented by staminodia; stem-leaves deeply 2–3-pinnatifid
                         into capillary segments; (introd.) . . . . *Nigella*
                    15 Fruit a head of few- to many-seeded follicles.
                         16 Leaves subentire to coarsely crenate or dentate, oblong-
                              ovate to broadly cordate or reniform; petaloid sepals 5 or
                              more, white, pinkish, yellow, or orange; (wet habitats) . . . . . *Caltha*
                         16 Principal leaves divided nearly or quite to base; flowers
                              commonly solitary or paired at the top of the stem.
                              17 Principal leaves palmately divided into usually 5 rather
                                   deeply 3-lobed and coarsely toothed segments, long-
                                   petioled, the 1 or 2 stem-leaves short-petioled to sessile;
                                   flower usually solitary, showy, the petaloid sepals to 2 cm
                                   long; stem rather weak, to about 5 dm tall; (Aleutian Is.
                                   and mts. of B.C. and sw Alta.; *T. europaeus* introd.
                                   in N.B.) . . . . *Trollius*
                              17 Principal leaves 2-ternately compound, the leaflets
                                   toothed or lobed, rather long-stalked.
                                   18 Petals none; sepals white and petaloid; follicles to 1.5
                                        cm long; flowers often 2 (sometimes 3); stem-leaves
                                        sessile or very short-petioled (the long stalks being
                                        those of the leaflets); stem slender, erect or
                                        ascending, to 3 dm tall . . . . *Isopyrum*
                                   18 Petals 5, brownish-red-purple, rather fleshy, oval,
                                        deciduous, about equalling the greenish leathery
                                        unequal sepals; follicles leathery, to 5 cm long; flowers
                                        usually solitary; stem-leaves long-petioled; stem rather
                                        stout, more or less decumbent-based, to 4 dm tall,
                                        from thickened roots; plant glabrous and somewhat
                                        glaucous; (?B.C.) . . . . [*Paeonia*]
          12 Leaves all basal (except for more or less reduced leaves subtending
               the flowers).

19 Fruit a several-seeded follicle; flowers solitary; leaves 3-foliolate, the leaflets sessile or nearly so.
  20 Flowers white or greenish white, at most about 1.5 cm broad, solitary or up to 5; petals narrow, shorter than the sepals; follicles on stipes about equalling the body-length; leaves evergreen, lustrous, ternately or ternate-pinnately divided into broad segments; rhizomes filiform, bright yellow . . . . *Coptis*
  20 Flowers yellow, 3 or 4 cm broad, solitary; petals represented by scale-like nectaries; follicles much longer than their stipes; scape stoutish, to about 2 dm tall; leaflets deeply palmately divided into linear-oblong, abruptly mucronate, entire segments; perennial by tubers; (garden-escape) . . . . *Eranthis*
19 Fruit an achene.
  21 Petals present, yellow or sometimes white; sepals mostly 5 and soon deciduous . . . . *Ranunculus*
  21 Petals none, the 5–12 petaloid sepals white to bluish or pink-purple, to 1.5 cm long; stems scapose.
    22 Leaves 2–3-ternately compound, the leaflets 3-toothed near apex; achenes glabrous, strongly 8–10-ribbed; plant glabrous, from a cluster of tuberous-thickened roots; (s Ont.) . . . .
    . . . . *Anemonella*
    22 Leaves reniform in outline, deeply 3-lobed, thickish and evergreen, their lobes entire, their petioles (and the scapes) densely long-hairy; achenes pubescent, not strongly ribbed; elongate rhizomes present; (SE Man. to N.B. and N.S.) . . . *Hepatica*

ACONITUM L.   [2540]   Aconite, Monkshood, Wolfbane

(Ref.: Munz 1945)
1 Leaf-blades not divided to the very base (an intermediate band of continuous tissue several mm broad separating the relatively broad primary segments from the point of attachment to the petiole).
  2 Flowers purple-lilac, pubescent, their helmets to about 2 cm high, conic-cylindric (usually at least twice as high as long along the basal margin); carpels glabrous; lower leaves to 2 dm broad; leaf-blades 5–7-parted, the divisions 3-cleft to about half their length, then deeply laciniate-serrate; (introd.) . . . . [*A. lycoctonum*]
  2 Flowers blue or purple, villous, their relatively broad helmets conic-rounded above, to 2.5 cm high; carpels usually somewhat pubescent; leaves usually less than 1.5 cm broad; leaf-blades 3–5-parted, the divisions then laciniately toothed or cleft; (s B.C.; ?Alaska (see *A. maximum*)) . . . . *A. columbianum*
1 Leaf-blades divided to the very base (the primary segments distinctly stalked at the point of attachment to the petiole).
  3 Helmet low, hemispheric, somewhat crescentic in outline, slanting gradually in front; lateral sepals usually broader than long; flowers deep blue; leaves few, with few linear segments, their petioles mostly as long as the blades; plants usually less than 6 dm tall; (Alaska–B.C.–w Alta.) . . . . *A. delphinifolium*
  3 Helmet taller, more arched, not crescentic, more vertical in front; lateral sepals usually not as broad as long; leaves usually many, the cauline ones rather short-petioled; plants usually over 6 dm tall; (introd.).
    4 Anther-filaments glabrous; flowers blue or violet.
      5 Leaf-segments linear, to 3 mm broad; inflorescence dense, subsimple; seeds smooth on the faces . . . . [*A. napellus*]
      5 Leaf-segments averaging broader; inflorescence paniculate; seeds with undulating horizontal membranous plates on the faces . . . . *A. variegatum*
    4 Anther-filaments pilose.

6 Leaf-segments linear, to 3 mm broad (if broader, then the flowers mostly deep blue, not over 3 cm high, and the helmet not gaping); inflorescence dense, unbranched; plant fertile . . . . [*A. napellus*]

6 Leaf-segments lanceolate, to 5 mm broad; flowers frequently white with purple margins, to 4 cm high; helmet gaping; inflorescence branched; plant sterile . . . . *A. bicolor*

A. bicolor Schultes

European; persisting in old gardens or escaping to roadsides, fields, and borders of thickets in N. America. Reported from Ont. to Nfld., N.B., and N.S. by Boivin (1966*b*) and probable basis, in part, of the report of *A. napellus* from the same area by Fernald *in* Gray (1950).

According to Munz (1945), "*Aconitum bicolor* is supposed to be a hybrid between some form of *A. napellus* and *A. variegatum,* having leaves like the former and flowers near the latter. It is said always to be sterile."

A. columbianum Nutt.

/T/WW/ (Gst) Moist woods and streambanks up to subalpine meadows from B.C. (N to near Kamloops; CAN; reported N to the Skeena Valley, ca. 54°N, by Henry 1915; concerning reports from Alaska, see *A. maximum*) to Calif., N.Mex., Colo., and S.Dak. [*A. insigne* Greene].

A. delphinifolium DC.

/aST/W/eA/ (Grt) Moist meadows, thickets, and woods (ranges of Canadian taxa outlined below; not known from the U.S.A.); E Asia. MAPS and synonymy: *see* below.

1 Petal-spur hooked at apex; flowers relatively small and numerous; plant relatively tall; [*A. napellus* var. *del.* (DC.) Seringe; *A. semigaleatum* Rchb.; incl. the robust extreme, ssp. *chamissonianum* (Rchb.) Hult. (*A. cham.* Rchb.); Aleutian Is.–Alaska–Yukon (type from Sledge Is., off the coast of the Yukon; *see* Hultén 1944: map 575a, p. 791) and the Mackenzie R. Delta to B.C. (S to Queen Charlotte Is., Prince Rupert, Smithers, Hazelton, and Burns Lake) and the mts of SW Alta. (N to Jasper); MAPS: combine the maps by Hultén 1968*b*:459 and 460 (ssp. *cham.*); Raup 1947: pl. 24 (aggregate species)] . . . . var. *delphinifolium*

1 Petal-spur scarcely hooked at apex; flowers relatively large, solitary or few; plant rarely over 3 dm tall . . . . var. *paradoxum* Reichenb.

2 Flowers white; [known only from Little Diomede Is., Alaska, the type locality of *A. del.* var. *alb.* Porsild] . . . . f. *albiflorum* (Porsild) Boivin

2 Flowers deep blue; [*A. par.* Rchb.; coast of NW Alaska; MAPS: Hultén 1944: map 575c, p. 791, and 1968*b*:460] . . . . f. *paradoxum*

[A. lycoctonum L.] Wolfbane Monkshood

[European; reported from Que. by Boivin (1966*b*; Montreal). Tutin et al. (1964), however, note that the name is ambiguous, placing it in the synonymy of *A. septentrionale* Koelle.]

A. maximum Pallas

/sT/W/eA/ (Grt) Subalpine meadows and thickets of the Aleutian Is. and SW Alaska; E Asia. MAPS: Hultén 1944: map 576, p. 791, and 1968*b*:461.

The inclusion of Alaska in the range of *A. columbianum* by Hitchcock et al. (1964) is probably based upon *A. maximum* (if, indeed, the two species are actually distinct; *see* key under *A. columbianum*), these authors characterizing the corolla-helmet of *A. columbianum* as "with scarcely any beak, to gradually or abruptly narrowed into a conspicuous, descending to porrect beak". According to Hultén (1944), an 1885 report by Lawson of *A. fischeri* Rchb. from Alaska is to be discounted, it being restricted to Asia. The citation may refer either to *A. maximum* or *A. delphinifolium.*

[A. napellus L.] Aconite Monkshood

[European; reports from our area probably refer largely to *A. bicolor* or *A. variegatum.*]

A. variegatum L.   Manchurian Monkshood
European; a garden-escape in N. America (in Canada, known from Ont., Que., and N.S.).

ACTAEA L.   [2537]   Baneberry, Necklaceweed

1 Mature pedicels stout and nearly or quite as thick as the axis of the inflorescence, usually red; fruit white, capped by a broad sessile red or purple stigma; leaflets commonly glabrous; (Ont. to N.S.) . . . . *A. pachypoda*
1 Mature pedicels filiform; fruit typically red (white in f. *neglecta*), the capping stigma relatively small and inconspicuous; leaflets commonly pubescent on the veins beneath; (transcontinental) . . . . *A. rubra*

A. pachypoda Ell.   White Baneberry, Doll's-eyes
/T/EE/   (Grh)   Rich woods and thickets from Ont. (N to the SE shore of L. Superior and Renfrew and Carleton counties; concerning reports from Man., *see* Scoggan 1957) to Que. (N to Ville-Marie, 47°20′N, and the S Gaspé Pen. at Tracadigash Mt., Carleton), N.B., P.E.I., and N.S. (CAN; ACAD), S to Okla., La., and Ga. [*A. "brachypoda"* Ell.; *A. alba* Bigel., not (L.) Mill.].
Forma *rubrocarpa* (Killip) Fern. (*A. alba* f. *rub.* Killip; fruits red rather than white) is known from S Ont., SW Que., and N.B. A hybrid with *A. rubra* (× *A. ludovicii* Boivin) is known from Que. (type from La Trappe, near Oka; collection in RIM from St-Donat, Rimouski Co.).

A. rubra (Ait.) Willd.   Red Baneberry.   Pain de couleuvre
/ST/X/   (Grh)   Rich woods and thickets from N-cent. Alaska–Yukon (*see* Hultén 1944: maps 570a, b, p. 790) and W Dist. Mackenzie (N to Norman Wells, ca. 65°N; W.J. Cody, Can. Field-Nat. 74(2):87. 1960) to Great Slave L., L. Athabasca (Alta. and Sask.), Man. (N to York Factory, Hudson Bay, ca. 57°N), Ont. (N to Fort Severn, Hudson Bay, ca. 56°N), Que. (N to the Larch R. at ca. 57°45′N, the Côte-Nord, Anticosti Is., and Gaspé Pen.), Labrador (N to the Hamilton R. basin), Nfld., N.B., P.E.I., and N.S., S to Calif., Ariz., N.Mex., S.Dak., Ohio, and N.J. [Incl. var. *gigantea* Gates; *A. spicata (brachypetala)* var. *rubra* Ait.; *A. americana* var. *rubra* (Ait.) Pursh; *A. arguta* Nutt. and its var. *pauciflora* Gates; *A. asplenifolia* and *A. caudata* Greene]. MAPS: Hultén 1968b:456; Porsild 1966: map 63, p. 74; Raup 1947: pl. 24.
Forma *neglecta* (Gillman) Robins. (*A. negl.* Gill.; *A. eburnea* Rydb.; fruits white rather than red) occurs nearly throughout the range. A collection in TRT from Toronto, Ont., has been referred to var. *dissecta* Britt. (leaflets decompound and incised rather than merely more or less deeply sharp-toothed).

ADONIS L.   [2549]

A. annua L.   Pheasant's-eye
Eurasian; an occasional garden-escape in N. America, as in S Man. (Edwin, near Winnipeg; Herb. Man. Prov. Mus.; reported from Shoal Lake, near the Ont. boundary, by Lowe 1943) and S Ont. (?Guelph; OAC). The report from Cape Charles, Labrador, by Hooker (1829) undoubtedly refers to some other plant, possibly the habitally similar *Matricaria ambigua*.

ANEMONE L.   [2541]   Anemone, Wind-flower

1 Styles plumose, 2–3.5 cm long at maturity; flower solitary, very showy, the white to blue or purple sepals to 4 cm long; leaves deeply dissected into linear segments 1 or 2(3) mm broad, long-petioled in basal tufts; plants usually spreading-hirsute-villous (*A. patens* sometimes nearly glabrous), from a usually branched caudex.
  2 Sepals white or purplish-tinged; achenes about 4 mm long; leaves ternately divided into 3 primary leaflets, these 2-pinnately (sometimes 3-pinnately) divided into relatively short entire ultimate segments; involucral leaves mostly petioled; (mts. of B.C.–Alta.) . . . . *A. occidentalis*
  2 Sepals usually blue to purplish (rarely white); achenes about 3 mm long; leaves ternately divided into 3 primary leaflets, but the leaflets less finely (and scarcely

pinnately) dissected into mostly relatively long entire ultimate segments; involucral leaves nearly or quite sessile; (B.C. to w Ont.) . . . .*A. patens*
1 Styles usually not plumose, less than 5 mm long at maturity; flowers solitary or few; sepals at most 2.5 cm long, mostly white or yellow, frequently roseate or tinged with blue or purple; leaves variously dissected.
   3 Principal leaves twice-ternately (rarely quinate-ternately) divided into numerous linear-oblong segments (the segments themselves commonly deeply lobed); perianth-segments 4–9; stems from a simple or branched caudex, lacking slender creeping rhizomes; plants more or less silky-villous (or in age sometimes nearly glabrous).
     4 Achenes glabrous, with a style about 1 mm long, in a dense depressed-globose head; perianth-lobes white (sometimes tinged with blue on the back), to about 1.5 cm long; peduncles often 2 or more; (Alaska–Yukon–Dist. Mackenzie–B.C.) . . . .*A. narcissiflora*
     4 Achenes densely woolly or villous, in short-cylindric to globose heads; perianth-segments mostly not over 1 cm long.
       5 Plants copiously silky-villous, usually over 2 dm tall; flowers yellowish or greenish to red or purplish externally, commonly at least 2; styles to 1.5 mm long; (transcontinental) . . . .*A. multifida*
       5 Plants sparsely silky-hirsute to glabrate, rarely over 2 dm tall; flowers white, bluish, or blue, mostly solitary; styles commonly over 1.5 mm long; (western species).
         6 Sepals white or sometimes tinged with blue externally; anther-filaments and styles yellowish; achenes copiously white-woolly; leaves abundantly lobed, the lobes linear and acute; (Alaska–Yukon–Dist. Mackenzie and mts. of B.C.–sw Alta.) . . . .*A. drummondii*
         6 Sepals blue on both sides; anther-filaments blue; styles wine-red; achenes sparingly white-woolly; leaves with fewer and shorter, abruptly blunt lobes; (Alaska–Yukon) . . . .[*A. multiceps*]
   3 Leaves less finely divided, the 3 or 5 principal segments broader.
     7 Achenes long-woolly and forming dense heads; perianth-segments 4–9.
       8 Involucral leaves 2 or 3, sessile, with narrow blunt lobes; flower usually solitary, its 4–7 sepals white within, bluish and silky outside at base; slender creeping rhizomes present; (transcontinental) . . . .*A. parviflora*
       8 Involucral leaves petioled, their lobes and divisions acute or acutish; flowers mostly 2 or more; creeping rhizomes absent.
         9 Peduncles mostly naked; styles crimson, about 0.5 mm long, densely pilose; anthers about 1 mm long; fruiting head slender-cylindric, to 4 cm long; plant densely ashy-pubescent; (B.C. to Que.) . . . . . .*A. cylindrica*
         9 Peduncles themselves mostly with secondary involucral leaves; styles pale or merely crimson-tipped, to 1.5 mm long, short-pubescent; plants greener.
          10 Anthers at most 1.2 mm long; fruiting heads cylindric, less than 12 mm thick; mature styles upwardly curved; basal leaves sparingly pubescent, their divisions cuneate; (transcontinental) . . . .*A. riparia*
          10 Anthers at least 1.2 mm long; fruiting heads ovoid, at least 12 mm thick; mature styles strongly divergent; basal leaves more hairy, their divisions often broader and less cuneate at base . . . .[*A. virginiana*]
     7 Achenes glabrous to densely short-hirsute (but not woolly); stems from slender creeping rhizomes.
      11 Stem-leaves (involucral) on petioles to about 4 cm long, parted into 3 distinct toothed or incised leaflets; achenes finely pubescent, the styles to 2 mm long; perianth-segments 4–9; peduncles solitary; plants glabrous (or the leaves sparsely appressed-pubescent), to about 3 dm tall.
       12 Veins and veinlets of the petaloid sepals forming a conspicuous network below the usually free tips, the sepals white or pinkish

           (occasionally reddish purple or almost blue); rhizome subligneous,
           continuous, lacking scaly teeth; (introd.) . . . . *A. nemorosa*
     12 Veins and veinlets of the petaloid sepals free or only very slightly net-
        forming; rhizomes scaly; (B.C. to N.S.) . . . . *A. quinquefolia*
  11 Stem-leaves (involucral) nearly or quite sessile.
     13 Involucral leaves compound, divided into 3 separate toothed to deeply
        incised cuneate-lanceolate leaflets; perianth-segments usually 5,
        yellow; peduncles occasionally more than 1; achenes downy, with a
        short glabrous beak; (introd. in sw Que.) . . . . [*A. ranunculoides*]
     13 Involucral leaves simple, toothed to deeply divided but not separated
        into distinct leaflets.
        14 Stem-leaves merely coarsely toothed or with a few rather deep
           incisions, ovate, to 7 cm long; peduncle solitary; perianth-
           segments white, to 2.5 cm long; achenes more or less short-hirsute
           toward base . . . . [*A. deltoidea*]
        14 Stem-leaves deeply incised into 3 principal coarsely toothed to
           deeply incised segments; achenes glabrous or nearly so;
           (transcontinental).
           15 Flowers yellow, solitary, the peduncle subtended by 2 involucral
              leaves, these deeply 3–5-parted; perianth-segments 4–7;
              achenes ovate-oblong, wingless, reflexed . . . . *A. richardsonii*
           15 Flowers white, often 2 or more, the primary peduncle naked and
              subtended by an involucre of 3 cuneate-obovate, deeply 2–3-
              parted, coarsely toothed divisions, the other peduncles with 2
              similar but smaller involucral leaves; perianth-segments 5;
              achenes obovate to rotund, broadly wing-margined, in a globose
              head . . . . *A. canadensis*

A. canadensis L.   Canada Anemone
/sT/X/   (Grh) Moist thickets, meadows, and shores from sw Dist. Mackenzie and B.C.–Alta.
to Sask. (N to Prince Albert), Man. (N to the Churchill R. at ca. 57°25′N and York Factory, ca.
57°N), Ont. (N to w James Bay at ca. 53°30′N), Que. (N to E James Bay at ca. 53°N, Anticosti
Is., and the Gaspé Pen.), N.B., P.E.I., and N.S., s to N.Mex., Mo., Ohio, and N.J.
[*A. aconitifolia* Michx.; *A. pensylvanica* L.; *A. dichotoma* of Canadian reports, not L.].
    Forma *dicksonii* Boivin (the petaloid sepals very numerous, more or less erose at summit) is
known from the type locality, Wetaskiwin, Alta.

A. cylindrica Gray   Thimbleweed, Long-headed Anemone
/T/X/   (Hs) Dry open soil, prairies, and slopes from B.C. (N to Hudson Hope, ca. 56°N) to
Alta. (N to Peace Point, 59°07′N), Sask. (N to Prince Albert), Man. (N to Grand Rapids, near
the NW end of L. Winnipeg), Ont. (N to the Ottawa dist.), and sw Que. (N to L. St. Peter near
Sorel, Richelieu Co.), s to Ariz., N.Mex., Kans., Mo., and N.J.

[*A. deltoidea* Hook.]
[Reports of this species of the w U.S.A. (Wash. to N Calif.) from Salmon R., Coast Range,
B.C., by John Macoun (1883) and from Dease L., N B.C., ca. 58°30′N, by Raup (1934; this sta-
tion indicated on the maps by Hultén 1968*b*:462, and 1944: map 577, p. 791) are referable to
A. richardsonii and *A. parviflora,* respectively, the relevant collections in CAN.]

A. drummondii Wats.
/aST/W/   (Hs) Alpine and subalpine slopes and dry rocky ledges, the aggregate species
from the coasts of Alaska–Yukon (*see* Hultén 1944: map 578, p. 791) and NW Dist. Mackenzie
through B.C. and the mts. of sw Alta. (N to Jasper) to Calif., Idaho, and Mont. MAPS and synonymy: *see* below.
1   Leaf-segments mostly 1–1.5(2) mm broad; styles to 4 mm long; [*A. ?baldensis sensu*
     John Macoun 1883, not L., as to the Mt. Selwyn, B.C., plant, "but the specimens
     were lost"; reported from the Cascade Mts. of s B.C. by Hitchcock et al. 1964; MAPS

(aggregate species): Porsild 1966: map 64, p. 74; Hultén 1968*b*:466 (incl.
A. multiceps), and 1958: map 60, p. 79; Meusel, Jaeger, and Weinert 1965:160] . . . .
. . . . var. *drummondii*
1   Leaf-segments mostly 1.5–2.5 mm broad; styles to 2.5(3) mm long; [*A. lith.* Rydb.;
    range of the species; MAPS: G. Boraiah and M. Heimburger, Can. J. Bot. 42(7): fig. 22
    (*A. lith.*, indicating Canadian stations only in s B.C. and sw Alta.), p. 907. 1964; the
    more northern stations shown in the above-noted maps for the typical form
    presumably apply here] . . . . var. *lithophila* (Rydb.) Hitchc.

[A. multiceps (Greene) Standl.]
[The map by Hultén 1944: map 579, p. 791, indicates stations for this species in N-cent.
Alaska (Norton Sound and Seward Pen. on the west coast; near the Alaska–Yukon boundary;
type from the Porcupine R.) and A.E. Porsild (Rhodora 41(486):227. 1939) reports it from
w Yukon, the type locality of the identical *A. cairnesiana* Greene. As shown in the above
genus-key, it is scarcely separable from *A. drummondii,* with which it is merged by Hultén
(1968*b*). (*Pulsatilla* Greene).]

A. multifida Poir.
/ST/X/   (Hs)   Turfy tundra and dryish slaty or calcereous gravels and ledges, the aggregate species from N-cent. Alaska–Yukon to Great Bear L., Great Slave L., L. Athabasca (Alta.
and Sask.), Man. (N to Churchill), northernmost Ont., Que. (N to SE Hudson Bay at ca. 56°N,
Anticosti Is., and the Gaspé Pen.; isolated stations at Wager Bay, NE Dist. Keewatin, and the
Hudson Strait coast of NW Ungava), Nfld., and N.B. (CAN; NBM; not known from P.E.I. or
N.S.), s to N Calif., Nev., N.Mex., NE Nebr., Minn., and Maine; S. America. MAPS and synonymy:
see below.
1   Stems usually several-flowered, to about 7 dm tall; ultimate leaf-segments usually
    well over 3 mm broad; sepals to 1.7 cm long; [B.C. to E Que.] . . . . . var. *richardsiana* Fern.
    2   Sepals white or yellowish white; [var. *sansonii* f. *galactiflora* Boivin; type from
        banks of the Grand R., Gaspé Co., E Que.] . . . . f. *leucantha* Fern.
    2   Sepals bright red; [var. *sansonii* Boivin; type from banks of the Grand R., Gaspé
        Co., E Que.] . . . . f. *richardsiana*
1   Stems usually 1–3-flowered, to about 3 dm tall; ultimate leaf-segments usually less
    than 3 mm broad; sepals to about 1 cm long . . . . var. *multifida*
    3   Sepals about 15, bright red; [type from banks of the Grand R., Gaspé Co., E Que.,
        the only known locality] . . . . f. *polysepala* Fern.
    3   Sepals 5.
        4   Sepals bright red; [*A. sang.* Pursh; s Dist. Mackenzie–Alta. to E Que.] . . . .
            . . . . f. *sanguinea* (Pursh) Fern.
        4   Sepals yellowish white within, yellowish, greenish, or purplish outside; [var.
            globosa T. & G. (*A. globosa* (T. & G.) Nutt.); var. *hirsuta* Hitchc.; vars.
            nowasadii and *saxicola* Boivin; var. *?tetonensis* (Porter) Hitchc. (*A. tetonensis*
            Porter); *A. hudsoniana* Rich.; transcontinental; MAPS (*A. mult.*, aggregate
            species): G. Boraiah and M. Heimburger, Can. J. Bot. 42(7): fig. 11, p. 899.
            1964; also fig. 13 (var. *sax.*), p. 901, and fig. 20 (var. *tet.*), p. 907; Hultén
            1968*b*:465] . . . . f. *multifida*

A. narcissiflora L.
/ST/W/EA/   (Hs)   Meadows, tundra, and stony slopes from the Aleutian Is., N-cent.
Alaska–Yukon (*see* Hultén 1944: maps 581a, b, c, and d, pp. 791–92), and w Dist. Mackenzie
(N to the Mackenzie R. Delta region) to cent. B.C. (s to Queen Charlotte Is; the report from
NW Alta. by Hultén 1944, requires confirmation); related types in Wyo., Colo., and Iowa; Eur-
asia. MAPS: Raup 1947: pl. 24 (aggregate species); combine the maps for the four phases by
Hultén 1968*b*:463–65.
    According to Hultén, the typical phase is restricted to Europe, being represented in N.
America and Asia by several subspecies that are fairly distinct in isolation but freely inter-
grade when they meet. These are the villous-leaved extreme, ssp. *villosissima* (DC.) Hult. (var.
vill. DC., the type from Unalaska, Alaska), the moderately villous but generally fewer-flowered

ssp. *alaskana* Hult. (flowers 1 or 2(3); type from Kodiak, Alaska; s to Queen Charlotte Is., B.C.), and two sparingly pubescent phases that are nearly always 1-flowered: ssp. *sibirica* (L.) Hult. (*A. sibirica* L.; *A. zephyra* of Alaskan reports, not Nels.; coastal w Alaska) and ssp. *interior* Hult. (Alaska–Yukon–w Dist. Mackenzie; type from Keno, the Yukon), the latter differing from ssp. *sibirica* in its fewer and relatively narrow leaf-segments and its rhomboid petals that are very broad in the middle.

A. nemorosa L.   European Wood Anemone
Eurasian; the only indisputable evidence of this plant growing in N. America other than under active cultivation appears to be a collection in GH from St. John's, Nfld., where stated to be natzd. in a cemetery (Agnes Ayre, in 1932). It is also reported from Bonne Bay, Nfld., by Waghorne (1898), probably through confusion with some other species. MAP: Meusel, Jaeger, and Weinert 1965:159 (the dots indicating stations in E Que. are probably based upon *A. quinquefolia*).

A. occidentalis Wats.   Western Pasque-flower
/T/W/   (Hs)   Meadows and slopes at middle to high elevations from B.C. (N to Bess Pass near the Alta. boundary at ca. 53°N; CAN) and sw Alta. (N to Jasper National Park; according to Hultén 1944, the report from Alaska by John Macoun 1883, refers to *A. drummondii*) to N Calif., N Idaho, and Mont. [*Pulsatilla* Freyn; *A. alpina* Hook.]. MAP: Meusel, Jaeger, and Weinert 1965:161.

A. parviflora Michx.
/aST/X/eA/   (Grh)   Lowland to alpine meadows, calcareous ledges, and along streams from the coasts of Alaska–Yukon–Dist. Mackenzie to s Banks Is., Victoria Is., cent. Dist. Keewatin, and northernmost Ungava–Labrador, s in the West through B.C. and sw Alta. to Oreg., Idaho, and Colo., farther eastwards s to L. Athabasca (Alta. and Sask.), Man. (s to the Hayes R. about 100 mi sw of York Factory; isolated in N.Dak.), Ont. (coasts of Hudson Bay–James Bay; N shore of L. Superior), Que. (s to s James Bay, Rimouski Co., the Côte-Nord, Anticosti Is., and Gaspé Pen.; type probably from between Hudson Bay and L. Mistassini), Nfld., and N.B. (Restigouche R.; NBM; not known from P.E.I. or N.S., or the E U.S.A.); E Asia. [*A. borealis* Rich.; *A. cuneifolia* Juss.; *A. deltoidea sensu* Raup 1934, not Hook.; *A. narcissiflora sensu* Brunet (1865) and Reeks (1873), not L.; incl. var. *grandiflora* Ulbr.]. MAPS: Hultén 1968b:463; Porsild 1957: map 159, p. 180; Raup 1947: pl. 24.

A. patens L.   Pasque-flower, Prairie-smoke, Lion's-beard, "Prairie-Crocus"
/aST/WW/EA/   (Hs)   Prairies to exposed slopes from N Alaska and the coasts of the Yukon and NW Dist. Mackenzie to s Banks Is., Great Bear L., Great Slave L., L. Athabasca (Alta. and Sask.), Man. (N to Cross Lake, NE of L. Winnipeg at ca. 54°30′N; provincial floral emblem), and w Ont. (Kenora dist.; OAC), s to Wash., Utah, Tex., Mo., and N Mich.; E Europe; Asia. [*Pulsatilla* Miller; var. *multifida* Pritzel; var. *hirsutissima* (Britt.) Hitchc. (*P. (A.) hirsut.* Britt.), not *Clematis hirsut.* Pursh; var. *nuttalliana* (DC.) Gray (*A. (P.) nutt.* DC.); var. *wolfgangiana* (Bess.) Koch (*A. wolf.* Bess.) and its f. *stevensonis* Boivin; *A. (P.) ludoviciana* Nutt.]. MAPS: Hultén 1968b:466 (*P. pat.*); Porsild 1957: map 161, p. 181 (*P. ludov.*); Meusel, Jaeger, and Weinert 1965:161; A. Löve 1954: fig. 3, p. 221; Meusel 1943: fig. 63c.
Attempts to distinguish the N. American plant from the Eurasian one under one or other of the above names on the basis of somewhat more finely dissected leaves appear unwarranted.

A. quinquefolia L.   American Wood-Anemone
/T/X/   (Grh)   Moist woods, thickets, and open hillsides, the aggregate species from B.C. (N to the Dean R. N of Bella Coola at ca. 52°N; CAN) to Alta. (*A. nemorosa* reported N to Dunvegan, 55°54′N, by John Macoun 1883), Sask. (near Somme, 52°35′N; Breitung 1957a), Man. (N to 17 mi N of The Pas), Ont. (N to the Attawapiskat R. at ca. 53°N; CAN), Que. (N to the Harricanaw R. s of James Bay at ca. 50°N), N.B., and N.S. (not known from P.E.I.), s to N Calif., Alta.–Sask.–Man., Iowa, Ky., and N.C.
1   Stamens in essentially a single series, usually fewer than 35; sepals mostly less than
    1 cm long, usually white (to rose-tinged or bluish); rhizome short, to 4 mm thick;

[*A. lyallii* Britt.; *A. nemorosa sensu* John Macoun 1883, as to the B.C. plant, not L.; B.C., the type of *A. lyallii* from the lower Fraser R.] . . . . var. *lyallii* (Britt.) Robins.
1   Stamens in 2 or more series, mostly 35 or more; sepals to over 2 cm long; rhizome elongate, to 7 mm thick.
 2   Middle leaflet of the involucral leaves entire or bluntly few-toothed; lateral leaflets entire or slightly cleft, with at most 7 blunt marginal teeth; sepals commonly bluish or bluish purple; achene-beak straight; [*A. oregana* Gray; ?Vancouver Is.] . . . . .
  . . . . [var. *oregana* (Gray) Robins.]
 2   Middle leaflet of the involucral leaves usually sharp-toothed; lateral leaflets commonly cleft nearly or quite to base, with up to 12 teeth on the outer margin; sepals white or roseate; anther-filaments whitish; achene-beak falcate.
  3   Stems spreading-villous above the middle; [*A. ?nemorosa sensu* John Macoun 1883, as to the Dunvegan, Alta., plant, not L.; Alta. to N.B.] . . . . . var. *interior* Fern.
  3   Stem essentially glabrous; [incl. the 2-leaved var. *bifolia* Farw. (*A. nem.* var. *bif.* (Farw.) Boivin), occasionally associated with the 3-leaved type; *A. nemorosa* var. *quin.* (L.) Pursh; *A. nem. sensu* John Macoun 1883, as to the N.B. plant, not L.; Ont. to N.B. and N.S.] . . . . var. *quinquefolia*

[*A. ranunculoides* L.]   Yellow Wood-Anemone
[Eurasian; reported by F. Joseph-Adonis, f.m. (Ann. ACFAS 9:107. 1943) as introd. at the foot of Mt. St-Gregoire, about 20 mi SE of Montreal, Que., where probably not persistent.]

A. richardsonii Hook.
/aST/X/GeA/   (Grh)   Moist thickets and sheltered slopes from the Aleutian Is. and coasts of Alaska–Yukon–Dist. Mackenzie to S Victoria Is. and northernmost Que. (Hudson Strait and Ungava Bay), S in the West to S B.C.–Alta., farther eastwards S to Great Slave L., N Sask. (L. Athabasca), NE Man. (Churchill and York Factory; not known from Ont.), and cent. Que. (S to SE Hudson Bay at ca. 55°N); two stations in w Greenland at ca. 65° and 66°40′N; NE Asia. [*A. deltoidea sensu* John Macoun 1883, not Hook.; *A. ?racunculoides sensu* Richardson 1823, not L.]. MAPS: Hultén 1968b:462; Porsild 1957: map 160, p. 180; T.W. Böcher, J. Ecology 39(2): fig. 6, p. 387. 1951, and Tidsskr. Groenland (April, 1962):135. 1962; Raup 1947: pl. 24.

A. riparia Fern.   Riverbank Anemone
/sT/X/   (Hs)   Gravelly shores, thickets, and calcareous or slaty ledges from B.C. (N to Prince Rupert and Prince George, both ca. 54°N) to Alta. (N to Lesser Slave L.), Sask. (N to Nipawin, 53°22′N), Man. (N to The Pas), Ont. (N to w James Bay at ca. 53°N), Que. (N to L. St. John, Anticosti Is., and the Gaspé Pen.), Nfld., N.B., and N.S. (not known from P.E.I.), S to Minn., Ill., and New Eng. [*A. cylindrica sensu* Fowler 1885, not Gray; as treated here, incl. *A. virginiana* of Canadian reports, not L.; *A. virg.* var. *rip.* (Fern.) Boivin].

 Forma *inconspicua* Fern. (the sepaloid petals relatively thick, greenish and commonly about 1 cm long, rather than milk-white and to about 2 cm long) is known from E Que. (Temiscouata Co. and the Gaspé Pen.; type from Percé) and N.B. (Woodstock; GH). Forma *rhodantha* Fern. (the petaloid sepals bright red) is known from the type locality along the Grand R., Gaspé Pen., E Que.

[*A. virginiana* L.]   Thimbleweed
[According to Fernald *in* Gray (1950), this species is confined to the E U.S.A. (N to Minn. and Maine). Boivin (1966b), however, assigns it a transcontinental range in Canada and includes *A. riparia* as a variety of it. The complex requires further study.]

ANEMONELLA Spach   [2541]

A. thalictroides (L.) Spach   Rue-Anemone
/T/EE/   (Grt)   Open woods from Minn. to S Ont. (N to L. Ontario in Leeds Co.) and SW Maine, S to Okla. and NW Fla. [*Anemone thal.* L. and its var. *uniflora* Pursh; *Syndesmon* Hoffmgg.; *Thalictrum* Eames & Boivin; *T. anemonoides* Michx.]. MAP: J.H. Soper, W.G. Dore, and G. Boraiah, Can. Field-Nat. 77(4): fig. 1, p. 221. 1963.

AQUILEGIA L. [2538] Columbine. Ancolie

1 Spurred petals yellow or yellowish white; flowers usually 2 or more, ascending or nodding; stems leafy.
    2 Spurs strongly incurved or even hooked at tip, shorter than the petal-blade, rarely to 1 cm long; sepals blue or blue-purple, to about 1.5 cm long, the whole flower usually less than 2.5 cm long; beak of mature follicle less than 1/3 the length of the body; (Alaska–B.C. to James Bay) . . . .*A. brevistyla*
    2 Spurs slightly incurved or nearly straight, mostly longer than the petal-blades, to over 1.5 cm long, the whole flower usually over 2.5 cm long; beak of mature follicle more than 1/3 the length of the body; (B.C. and Alta.).
        3 Sepals yellow (sometimes pinkish); petal-blades usually over 6 mm long (up to 13 mm); spurs more or less incurved . . . .*A. flavescens*
        3 Sepals pale to deep red; petal-blades usually not over 5 mm long; spur nearly straight . . . .*A. formosa*
1 Spurred petals various shades of red, scarlet, blue, or purple (sometimes yellow within; sometimes entirely white in *A. vulgaris*).
    4 Stem scapose (leaves usually all basal), mostly less than 1.5 dm tall; leaves rarely much over 1 cm broad, 2-ternate, the leathery leaflets greatly crowded, deeply cleft into 3 or 4 lobes; flower solitary, erect; sepals usually deep blue or more or less purplish, the petals similarly coloured but commonly lighter, their blades to 2.5 cm long, longer than the spurs; (mts. of sw Alta.) . . . .*A. jonesii*
    4 Stem leafy, to over 7 dm tall; leaves several cm broad, 2–3-ternate, the leaflets relatively thin and not crowded; flowers usually at least 2.
        5 Spurs with strongly recurved or even hooked tips, short and stout; flowers white, pink, blue, or purple, mostly ascending; follicle-beaks to 1 cm long . . . .
        . . . .*A. vulgaris*
        5 Spurs slender or stout, straight or slightly recurving, their tips merely oblique; flowers scarlet or bright red (petals yellow within), mostly nodding; follicle-beaks to 2 cm long; (E Sask. to Nfld. and N.S.) . . . .*A. canadensis*

A. brevistyla Hook.
/ST/WW/ (Hs) Rock-crevices, meadows, and open woods from cent. Alaska–Yukon (*see* Hultén 1944: map 571, p. 790) and the Mackenzie R. Delta region to Great Bear L., Great Slave L., L. Athabasca (Alta. and Sask.), Man. (N to the Churchill R. at ca. 57°25′N; CAN), and cent. Ont. (N to the Fawn R. at ca. 55°N; CAN; concerning a James Bay, Que., report by Raymond, *see* Hultén 1950), s to B.C. (reported from Telegraph Trail by Henry 1915), s Alta., S.Dak., and Minn. [*A. canadensis* var. *hybrida* Hook.]. MAPS: Hultén 1968b:457; Raup 1947: pl. 24.

A. canadensis L. Wild Columbine. Glands or Gants de Notre-Dame
/T/EE/ (Hs) Rocky woods and open slopes, the aggregate species from SE Sask. (Qu'Appelle Valley, Thunderhill, and Canora; Breitung 1957a) to s Man. (N to Porcupine Mt.), Ont. (N to Sandy L. at ca. 53°N, 93°W; CAN), Que. (N to Bic Mt., Rimouski Co.; CAN), Nfld. (Rouleau 1956), N.B., and N.S. (not known from P.E.I.), s to Tex. and Fla.
1 Sepals less than 1.5 cm long.
    2 Spurs slender; sepals to 8 mm broad; follicles soon divergent at summit; [Ont. to Nfld. and N.S.] . . . . .var. *canadensis*
    2 Spurs stout; sepals slightly narrower; follicles erect; [var. *hybrida* of auth., not Hook.; *A. eminens* and *A. latiuscula* Greene; E Sask. to w Ont.] . . . .
    . . . . .var. *eminens* (Greene) Boivin
1 Sepals to 2 cm long; spurs stout; follicles erect; [*A. coccinea* Small; Ont.] . . . .
    . . . . .var. *coccinea* (Small) Munz

A. flavescens Wats. Yellow Columbine
/T/W/ (Hs) Moist meadows and slopes at moderate to high elevations from B.C. (N to Bess Pass, on the Alta. boundary at ca. 53°N; CAN) and sw Alta. (N to Jasper) to Oreg., Utah,

and Colo. [*A. formosa (caerulea)* var. *flav.* (Wats.) Hook. f.; *A. chrysantha sensu* J.M. Macoun 1894, not Gray].

Var. *miniata* Macbr. & Pays. (the sepals more or less pinkish rather than yellow, the petal-blades at most about 6 mm long rather than to 13 mm), apparently transitional to *A. formosa* and perhaps a hybrid between it and *A. flavescens,* is reported from B.C. and SW Alta. by Boivin (1966*b*; CAN, detd. Boivin).

A. formosa Fisch.   Sitka Columbine
/ST/W/   (Hs)   Open woods and rocky slopes (chiefly coastal) from S Alaska (*see* Hultén 1944: map 572, p. 791) and S Yukon (Porsild 1951a) through B.C. and SW Alta. (N to Jasper) to Baja Calif. and Utah; E ?Asia (the type locality was given as Kamchatka but Hultén 1944, states that the plant does not occur in Asia). [*A. canadensis* var. *form.* (Fisch.) Wats.; *A. columbiana* Rydb.; *A. truncata* F. & M.; incl. vars. *communis* and *megalantha* Boivin]. MAP: Hultén 1968*b*:457.

A. jonesii Parry
/T/W/   (Hs)   Usually subalpine on talus slopes or in rock-crevices from SW Alta. (Sheep Mt., Waterton Lakes; J.M. Macoun 1895; CAN) to NW Wyo.

A. vulgaris L.   European Columbine.   Gants de Notre-Dame
Eurasian; persisting in old gardens or escaping to roadsides, fields, and borders of woods in N. America, as in SW B.C. (Vancouver Is.; Rosedale, E of Chilliwack), Ont., Que., Nfld., N.B., P.E.I., and N.S.

CALTHA L.   [2524]   Marsh-Marigold.   Populage

1   Perianth-segments bright yellow or orange; follicles rarely more than 12; flowering-stems usually with 2 or more reduced short-petioled leaves; basal leaves long-petioled, broadly cordate to reniform; (transcontinental) . . . . *C. palustris*
1   Perianth-segments usually white or greenish white (sometimes pinkish).
  2   Flowering stems leafy, floating or creeping and rooting at the nodes; leaves ovate-reniform, thin, subentire, mostly less than 5 cm broad; perianth-segments white or pinkish, less than 1 cm long; follicles numerous in a globose head, to 5 mm long; (E B.C. to NW Ont.) . . . . *C. natans*
  2   Flowering stems erect, leafless or with 1 (sometimes 2) leaves subtending the peduncles; perianth-segments to over 1.5 cm long; follicles commonly fewer, longer; (western species).
    3   Leaves broadly cordate to reniform, usually about as broad as or broader than long, the sinus often closed by overlapping of the lobes, the margins commonly broadly but shallowly crenate; stems commonly 2-flowered; (B.C.) . . . . .
       . . . . *C. biflora*
    3   Leaves oblong-ovate to subrotund above a cordate base, longer than broad, the sinuses usually shallower and more open, the margins more dentate than crenate, the teeth often callous-tipped; flowers commonly solitary (rarely 2 or 3); (B.C. and Alta.) . . . . *C. leptosepala*

C. biflora DC.
/T/W/   (Hs)   Wet places (chiefly alpine or subalpine) from the southernmost Alaska Panhandle (*see* Hultén 1944: map 563, p. 790) through B.C. (type from Banks Is., S of Prince Rupert; Queen Charlotte Is.; Prince Rupert; Mt. Queest, NE of Kamloops; Tsi-Tsutl Mts., ca. 54°N) to Calif. and Colo. [*C. leptosepala* var. *bif.* (DC.) Lawson; *C. howellii* and *C. macounii* Greene; *C. palustris* var. *minima* Regel; incl. the robust extreme, var. *rotundifolia* (Huth) Hitchc. (*C. rot.* (Huth) Greene)]. MAP: Hultén 1968*b*:452.

C. leptosepala DC.   Elkslip
/sT/W/   (Hr)   Wet alpine and subalpine places from S Alaska (*see* Hultén 1944: map 564, p.

790; type from Prince William Sound) and s Yukon (Porsild 1951a) through B.C. and sw Alta. (N to the Jasper dist.; CAN) to Oreg., Nev., Utah, and Colo. [*C. chelidonii* Greene]. MAP: Hultén 1968b:452.

C. natans Pallas   Floating Marsh-Marigold
/ST/WW/EA/   (HH)   Ponds or muddy shores from N-cent. Alaska and cent. Yukon to Great Slave L., s Dist. Keewatin, and northernmost Ont., s to B.C. (s to the Peace River region), Alta. (s to Fort Saskatchewan), cent. Sask. (Windrum L. at ca. 56°N; Amisk L., near Flin Flon), Man. (s to Sasaginnigak L., about 125 mi NE of Winnipeg), and N Minn.; NE Europe; N Asia. MAP: Hultén 1968b:453.

C. palustris L.   King-cup, Cowslip.   Souci d'eau
/aST/X/EA/   (Hs (Hel))   Swampy ground and shallow water (ranges of Canadian taxa outlined below), s to Oreg., Nebr., and S.C.; Iceland; Eurasia. MAPS and synonymy: see below.
1   Flowers 1 (2, 3) on a stem, to about 2.5 cm broad; basal leaves rather finely toothed, usually more or less reniform, to about 6 cm long, their sinuses mostly open; stems often decumbent or prostrate and rooting at the nodes; [var. ?*sibirica* Regel; *C. asarifolia* DC.; Aleutian Is. and coastal s Alaska (see Hultén 1944: map 566b, p. 790) and coastal B.C.; MAP: Hultén 1968b:454] . . . . ssp. *asarifolia* (DC.) Hult.
1   Flowers usually several on a stem, to 3.5 cm broad; basal leaves broadly cordate to reniform, shallowly but rather coarsely crenate-dentate, their sinuses narrow and often overlapping; stems stout, erect or somewhat decumbent-based . . . . . . ssp. *palustris*
  2   Flowers usually less than 2.5 cm broad; follicles sometimes only about 5 mm long; basal leaves relatively small; [*C. arctica* R. Br.; *C. confinis* Greene; coasts of Alaska, the Yukon, Dist. Mackenzie, Banks Is., Victoria Is., Melville Is. (type locality), and N Dist. Keewatin, with stations in the interior at Great Bear L., Great Slave L., and cent. Dist. Keewatin; MAPS: Hultén 1968b:453; Porsild 1957: map 157, p. 180] . . . . var. *arctica* (R. Br.) Huth
  2   Flowers to over 3.5 cm broad; follicles at least 1 cm long; basal leaves to over 1 dm long; [Aleutian Is.–interior Alaska–s Yukon–s Dist. Mackenzie–Alta. to Sask. (N to Windrum L. at ca. 56°N), Man. (N to Churchill), northernmost Ont., Que. (N to Richmond Gulf, SE Hudson Bay, the Côte-Nord, Anticosti Is., and the Gaspé Pen.), Nfld., N.B., P.E.I., and N.S.; MAP (aggregate species): Meusel, Jaeger, and Weinert 1965:155] . . . . var. *palustris*

CIMICIFUGA L.   [2537]   Bugbane, Rattletop

1   Leaves mostly 2-ternate, the usually 9 leaflets broadly cordate-ovate, to 1.5 dm long, usually primarily 3-lobed and again irregularly lobed and serrate-dentate; follicle oblong, to 12 mm long, usually single in the upper flowers but often 2 or rarely 3 in the lower flowers of the racemes; seeds flat, vertical, roughened with small scales; (mts. of s B.C.) . . . . *C. elata*
1   Leaves 2-ternate or ternate-pinnate, the commonly more than 9 leaflets narrowly to broadly oblong or ovate, broadly obtuse to subcordate at base, mostly less than 1 dm long; follicle ovoid or globose-ovoid, to 9 mm long, usually single in all of the flowers (occasionally 2, rarely 3); seeds compressed, horizontal, obscurely roughened on the sides; (s Ont.) . . . . *C. racemosa*

C. elata Nutt.   Tall Bugbane
/T/W/   (Grh)   Moist shady woods from sw B.C. (collection in CAN from above 6,500 ft on Mt. Cheam, near Chilliwack, where taken by Gowan in 1895, and from along the Chilliwack R. at about 200 ft elevation, where taken by J.M. Macoun in 1901) to NW Oreg.

C. racemosa (L.) Nutt.   Black Snakeroot, Black Cohosh
/t/EE/   (Grh)   Rich woods from s Ont. (Elgin, Norfolk, Haldimand, Welland, Lincoln, Wentworth, and Waterloo counties; see s Ont. map by Soper 1962: fig. 27, p. 43) to w Mass., s to Mo., Tenn., and Ga. [*Actaea* L.; *C. serpentaria* Pursh].

CLEMATIS L.   [2542]   Clematis.   Clématite

1   Styles short, not plumose; peduncles 1–3-flowered; flowers roseate to blue or
    purplish blue, to about 5 cm broad, their obovate pointed petaloid sepals reflexed;
    leaflets commonly 3 (sometimes only 1 or up to 7); woody vine; (garden-escape
    in s Ont.) . . . . *C. viticella*
1   Styles plumose, to about 9 cm long.
   2   Flowers numerous in compound cymose panicles, mostly unisexual, the thin,
       white or whitish, spreading or ascending petaloid sepals at most about 12 mm
       long; petals represented by staminodia; mature plumose styles to about 3 cm
       long.
      3   Leaflets 3 (rarely 5 on the lowest leaves), entire to coarsely and irregularly
          incised or often deeply cleft; strongly climbing vine; (SE Man. to N.S.) . . . .
          . . . . *C. virginiana*
      3   Leaflets 5, 7, or 9.
         4   Leaflets entire, thin, up to 9 in number; plant scarcely climbing; (introd.
             in Ont.) . . . .*C. recta*
         4   Leaflets mostly coarsely toothed, firm, 5 or 7; strongly climbing vine; (B.C.
             to Man.) . . . .*C. ligusticifolia*
   2   Flowers solitary or sometimes several in leafy corymbs, the petaloid sepals to
       over 2.5 cm long (to about 6 cm).
      5   Plant not viny, sparsely villous to cobwebby or woolly nearly throughout, the
          herbaceous stems erect or slightly decumbent at base, simple, to 4(6) dm tall,
          bearing a single nodding flower on a terminal peduncle; calyx urceolate-
          campanulate, its petaloid sepals brownish purple, leathery, greyish-woolly-
          villous outside, mostly 2 or 3 cm long, united at base but with free and usually
          recurving tips; leaves sessile or short-petioled, to over 1 dm long, 2–4-pinnate
          into linear to narrowly lanceolate segments, the lower leaves reduced to small
          entire bracts; (s ?B.C.) . . . . *[C. hirsutissima]*
      5   Plants viny and strongly climbing; peduncles axillary, the flowers solitary or
          sometimes several in leafy corymbs.
         6   Leaflets 3; flower solitary, the thin, blue to purplish-blue or reddish-purple,
             purple-veined, distinct sepals to 6 cm long, spreading or ascending; outer
             stamens commonly altered into petaloid staminodia; styles to about 5 cm
             long; (B.C. to Sask.; Ont. to N.B.) . . . .*C. verticillaris*
         6   Leaflets 5, 7 or 9; sepals rarely over 2.5 cm long; staminodia none;
             (introd.).
            7   Sepals purplish, thick and leathery, united below into an urn-shaped
                tube; styles at most 5 cm long; anthers villous, prolonged into a sterile
                tip; leaflets rarely more than 7, entire or 2–3-lobed or deeply cleft . . . .
                . . . .*C. viorna*
            7   Sepals yellow or green, thin, distinct, spreading or ascending; styles to
                about 9 cm long; anthers glabrous, blunt; leaflets up to 9, typically
                sharply and coarsely toothed . . . .*C. orientalis*

[C. alpina (L.) Miller]
[European; reported from Keremeos, s B.C., by Boivin (1966b), where probably not persistent.
The taxon is not keyed out above but resembles *C. verticillaris* in the outer stamens being
modified into petaloid staminodia, differing in its 2-ternate leaves (leaflets 6 rather than 3).
(*Atragene* L.).]

[C. hirsutissima Pursh]   Vase-flower or -vine, Sugar-bowls
[The inclusion of B.C. in the range of this species of the w U.S.A. (N to Wash. and Mont.) by
Abrams (1944) and Hitchcock et al. (1964) requires confirmation. *C. douglasii* is listed by
John Macoun (1883) and Henry (1915) merely as a species to be expected and searched for
in that province. (*Viorna* Heller; *C. douglasii* Hook.).]

C. ligusticifolia Nutt.   White Virgin's-bower, Pipe-stems, Traveler's Joy
/T/WW/   (N (vine))   Climbing over bushes, especially along creek bottoms, from B.C. (N to Cache Creek and Kamloops) to S Alta. (Waterton Lakes to Medicine Hat), Sask. (N to near Saskatoon), and S Man. (N to Dropmore, NW of Riding Mt.), S to S Calif., N.Mex., and S.Dak. (adv. farther eastwards). [Incl. var. *brevifolia* Nutt.].

C. orientalis L.
Asiatic; the known Canadian stations are noted below.
1   Sepals pubescent within; leaflets coarsely toothed or lobed; [introd. in S Ont.: along the Welland Canal at Port Colborne, Welland Co.; limestone quarry near Beamsville, Lincoln Co.; persisting and covering most of an old quarry at Rockwood, Wellington Co.] . . . . var. *orientalis*
1   Sepals glabrous; leaflets commonly merely toothed; [*C. tangutica* (Maxim.) Korsh.; introd. from S B.C. (Saltspring Is., near Vancouver Is.; Ootsa Lake, 53°54′N) to Sask. (Boivin 1966*b*)] . . . . var. *tangutica* Maxim.

C. recta L.
Asiatic; known from a dump at Ottawa, Ont., where taken by Minshall in 1933 (DAO), and from Guelph, Wellington Co. [*C. erecta* L.].

C. verticillaris DC.   Purple Clematis or Virgin's-bower
/T/X/   (Mc (vine))   Rocky (often calcareous) slopes and open woods (ranges of Canadian taxa outlined below), S to Oreg., Mont., Wyo., Iowa, Ohio, and Md. MAP and synonymy: *see* below.
1   Leaflets commonly deeply and coarsely lobed; sepals merely acute or abruptly short-acuminate; [incl. var. *grandiflora* Boivin; *Atragene americana* Sims; Ont. (N to Thunder Bay, Hearst, and Renison, S of James Bay at ca. 51°N; concerning reports from Man., *see* Scoggan 1957), Que. (N to the Harricanaw R., Baie-St-Paul, Charlevoix Co., and the banks of the Grand R. and cliffs of Tracadigash Mt. near Carleton, Gaspé Pen.; not known from Anticosti Is. or Magdalen Is.), and N.B. (Charlotte Co. and the St. John R. valley); MAP: Meusel, Jaeger, and Weinert 1965:163] . . . . var. *verticillaris*
1   Leaflets commonly entire (occasionally with 1 or 2, rarely 3, distinct lobes toward base); sepals attenuate at tip; [*Atragene (C.) columbiana* Nutt.; *A. (C.) occidentalis* Hornem.; B.C. (N to Cassiar, ca. 58°30′N), Alta. (N to near Edmonton), and SW Sask. (Cypress Hills); MAP: on the above-noted map by Meusel, Jaeger and Weinert] . . . .
. . . . var. *columbiana* (Nutt.) Gray

C. viorna L.   Leather-flower, Vase-vine
A native of the E U.S.A. (N to Iowa and Pa.), reported from S Ont. by Stroud (1941; introd. in a meadow at Guelph, Wellington Co.).

C. virginiana L.   Virgin's-bower.   Herbe aux gueux
/T/EE/   (Mc (vine))   Low grounds, thickets, and borders of woods from SE Man. (Roseau R., SE of Winnipeg; CAN; WIN) to Ont. (N to New Liskeard, 47°31′N), Que. (N to the Gaspé Pen.; GH; CAN), N.B., P.E.I., and N.S., S to E Kans., La., and Ga. [*C. "virginica"*, erroneous orthographic variant].
   Forma *missouriensis* (Rydb.) Fern. (leaves permanently and densely pilose beneath rather than glabrous or sparingly pilose) is reported from Ont., Que., and N.S. by M.L. Fernald (Rhodora 39(464):310. 1937).

C. viticella L.   Italian Clematis
Eurasian; a garden-escape to thickets in N. America, as in S Ont. (Simcoe, Norfolk Co.; near Garnet, Haldimand Co.; OAC) and SW Que. (Boivin 1966*b*).

COPTIS Salisb. [2534] Goldthread. Coptide

1   Leaves "fern"-like, mostly divided into at least 5 leaflets, the leaflets themselves pinnately compound or deeply pinnatifid; scapes usually bearing 2 or 3 flowers on pedicels to 4 cm long, to 2.5 dm tall and usually surpassing the leaves; sepals filiform-lanceolate; petals narrowly tongue-shaped; follicles to 9 mm long; (S Alaska–B.C.) . . . . *C. asplenifolia*
1   Leaves divided into 3 merely toothed to deeply incised leaflets.
  2   Leaflets long-stalked, broadly ovate to cordate-ovate or -rotund, to 6 (or even 7) cm long, deeply incised to near or below the middle into 3 major lobes, the lobes themselves usually somewhat lobed; scapes with up to 5 flowers, to 2 dm tall, about equalling the leaves; sepals linear-lanceolate; petals narrowly tongue-shaped; (S ?B.C.) . . . . [*C. occidentalis*]
  2   Leaflets cuneate- to rhombic-obovate, to about 2.5 cm long, sharply toothed and very obscurely 3-lobed; scapes 1-flowered; petals fleshy, hollowed and nectariferous at the tip; (transcontinental) . . . . *C. trifolia*

C. asplenifolia Salisb.
/sT/W/ (Hrr) Moist woods and bogs in S Alaska (*see* Hultén 1944: map 568, p. 790), coastal B.C. (S to Vancouver Is. and the adjacent mainland; type from S Alaska or B.C.), and N Wash. (Hitchcock et al. 1969). [Incl. var. *biternatum* Huth]. MAPS: Hultén 1968b:455; *Atlas of Canada* 1957: map 10, sheet 38; J.G. Packer, Nat. can. (Que.) 98(2): fig. 4, p. 134. 1971.

[*C. occidentalis* (Nutt.) T. & G.] Western Goldthread
[The inclusion of S B.C. in the range of this species of the W U.S.A. (NE Wash. to NW Mont.) by Hitchcock et al. (1964) requires confirmation. (*Chrysocoptis* Nutt.).]

C. trifolia (L.) Salisb. Goldthread, Canker-root. Tisavoyane or Savoyane
/aST/X/GeA/ (Hrr (Ch)) Mossy coniferous forests and swamps, the aggregate species from the Aleutian Is. and Alaska (N to the Seward Pen.; *see* Hultén 1944: map 569, p. 790; not yet reported from the Yukon but known from very close to its boundary in SE Alaska) to Great Bear L., L. Athabasca (Alta. and Sask.), S Dist. Keewatin, S Baffin Is. (Frobisher Bay; Polunin 1940), Que. (N to Ungava Bay at ca. 59°N), Labrador (N to Nain, ca. 56°30′N), Nfld., N.B., P.E.I., and N.S., S to S B.C., N Iowa, Tenn., and N.C.; W and E Greenland N to near the Arctic Circle; E Asia. MAP and synonymy: *see* below.
1   Leaflets sessile or very short-stalked; sepals to 4 mm broad, obtusish; petals mostly as long as broad; follicles mostly not over 5 mm long; [*Helleborus* L.; Alaska–B.C. and E Asia; MAP (aggregate species): Hultén 1968b:455] . . . . ssp. *trifolia*
1   Leaflets short-stalked; sepals to 3 mm broad, acutish; petals broader than long; follicles to 9 mm long; [*Anemone (C.) gr.* Oeder, the type from Greenland; transcontinental, ?except Alaska–B.C.] . . . . ssp. *groenlandica* (Oeder) Hult.

DELPHINIUM L. [2539] Delphinium, Larkspur

(Ref.: Ewan 1945)
1   Annuals; flowers various shades of pink, blue, or purple (atypically white); petals 2, united; spur slender, straight or nearly so; follicle 1; leaves rather uniformly distributed along the stem, dissected to base into numerous filiform or narrowly linear segments 1 or 2 mm broad; (introd.).
  2   Follicle pubescent, to about 2 cm long; flowers numerous in elongate racemes, the lower bracts palmately divided; stem and inflorescence copiously puberulent . . . . . .
        . . . . *D. ajacis*
  2   Follicle glabrous, less than 1.5 cm long; flowers relatively few, in short corymbiform racemes, the bracts simple or subsimple; stem essentially glabrous up to the inflorescence, the flowers and their pedicels puberulent . . . . . [*D. consolida*]
1   Perennials, chiefly from solitary or clustered, fusiform to globose, fleshy roots, tubers, or corms, less frequently from freely branching and more or less fibrous

roots or from a short thick tough rhizome; petals 4, distinct, usually coloured like the sepals but lighter (often whitish or pale blue); spur slender or stout; follicles (and pistils) usually 3.

3 Stems hollow, to 3 m tall, usually glabrous up to the inflorescence; leaves gradually reduced toward the top of the stem, the principal ones deeply divided into 5 or 7 main relatively broad divisions that are variously toothed or moderately lobed but not dissected; racemes more or less open, the pedicels usually longer than the spurs of the flowers; (Alaska–B.C. to Sask.) . . . . . . *D. glaucum*

3 Stems solid or only slightly hollow, commonly puberulent or pubescent at least above and often also glandular near or in the inflorescence, rarely as much as 1 m tall.

    4 Leaves rather uniformly distributed along the stem, this commonly not over 6 or 7 dm tall (but up to 8 or 10), often more or less glandular-pubescent above and in the inflorescence; (B.C.).

        5 Leaves to 6 cm broad, strongly dimorphic, the middle ones closely overlapping, more finely divided (segments linear) and much shorter-petioled than the more distantly spaced long-petioled lower ones (with cuneate-obovate main segments); calyx to about 1 cm long, bluish purple (often streaked with lighter areas), the spur to over 1.5 cm long and considerably longer than its sepal-blade; follicles less than 1.5 cm long, finely puberulent and usually glandular; seeds very conspicuously white-winged on the angles; racemes mostly spike-like, often branching, the pedicels mostly strongly ascending and shorter than the spurs; plant from a small cluster of somewhat thickened fleshy roots; (B.C.) . . . . *D. burkei*

        5 Leaves not noticeably dimorphic (segments of middle and lower leaves of about the same shape), usually rather uniformly spaced and not overlapping; calyx mostly longer; raceme more open, at least the lower pedicels much longer than the flowers; follicles to 1.5 cm long; seeds only slightly wing-margined; plant perennial from small, usually clustered, fusiform to globose tubers or roots.

            6 Calyx less than 1.5 cm long, deep bluish-purple, usually with a median greenish pubescent band, the sepals only slightly spreading, the flower therefore somewhat cup-shaped; spur little if any longer than the sepal-blade; follicles glabrous to finely crisp-puberulent; racemes spike-like and closely flowered usually to below the middle, only the lowermost pedicels much longer than the flowers; leaves all long-petioled, to 1 dm broad, 3 or 4 times dissected into linear to narrowly lanceolate segments; plant crisp-puberulent and eglandular (sometimes glabrous below); (?B.C.) . . . . [*D. nuttallii*]

            6 Calyx to over 1.5 cm long, deep blue, the sepals widely spreading; spur to half again as long as its sepal-blade; follicles densely pubescent (rarely glabrous); racemes usually open and loose, most of the pedicels equalling to much longer than the flowers; upper leaves sessile or short-petioled, the lower leaves long-petioled, to 7 cm broad, mostly 2 or 3 times dissected into rather few oblong (sometimes linear) segments; plant glabrous to conspicuously pubescent with straight to crisped eglandular hairs (or the pubescence sometimes slightly glandular in the inflorescence); (B.C.) . . . . *D. menziesii*

    4 Leaves mostly basal or sub-basal.

        7 Flowers more or less white, greenish, or faintly tinged with blue, at most about 2 cm long (including spur), on short, erect, often closely appressed pedicels in a usually dense raceme, the bracts obsolete; seeds wingless, strongly scaly- or spinulose-rugose; leaves thinly pubescent on both surfaces, minutely ciliate, to 7 or 8 cm broad; stems copiously felty-villous with dingy curled hairs throughout or glabrate toward base (sometimes with glistening, tangled, often glandular hairs on the rachis and pedicels), to over 1.5 m tall; (SE Man.) . . . . *D. virescens*

7 Flowers various shades of blue or purple (sometimes nearly white in
   D. nuttallianum).

   8 Calyx rarely over 12 mm long, usually glandular-villous, the slender
     spur to over 1.5 cm long, the sepals flared or cupped forward; follicles
     less than 2 cm long, glandular-villous (rarely glabrate), the brownish-
     purple seeds narrowly white-margined on the angles; racemes spike-
     like, most of the nearly erect to moderately spreading pedicels shorter
     than the flowers (the lower ones occasionally somewhat longer);
     principal leaves to 6(8) cm broad, mostly twice-divided into narrowly to
     broadly cuneate-obovate primary segments, these with oblong lobes;
     plant usually finely crisp-puberulent or slightly glandular-puberulent
     except often near the base, or glabrous throughout, from a small
     cluster of somewhat fleshy tuberous roots; (?B.C.–Alta.) . . . .
     . . . . [*D. depauperatum*]

   8 Calyx to about 2.5 cm long, the sepals flaring, the lowest pair usually
     noticeably the largest; racemes usually more open, the spreading-
     ascending pedicels mostly much longer than the flowers; capsules to
     over 2 cm long, their slate-grey to blackish seeds wing-margined
     toward tip.

     9 Lower petals notched over 1/5 the length of the blade, often white
       or pale blue and strongly darker-veined; upper petals merely bluish-
       tinged; sepals from nearly white or pale greyish-blue to deep
       purplish-blue; follicles glabrous or pubescent; stems glabrous to
       copiously crisp-puberulent or soft-spreading-pubescent, glandular
       or eglandular; root-system varying from single or clustered, fusiform
       to globose tubers (usually in moister areas) to a more slender and
       fibrous freely branched system (usually in drier areas); (B.C. and SW
       Alta.) . . . . *D. nuttallianum*

     9 Lower petals notched less than 1/5 the length of the blade, deep
       blue; upper petals light blue or purple-lined; sepals deep purplish-
       blue; follicles usually finely puberulent (rarely glabrous); stems
       subglabrous to rather copiously spreading-puberulent and usually
       somewhat yellowish-glandular, from a rather extensive system of
       branching, fibrous to slightly fleshy roots; (B.C. to SW Sask.) . . . *D. bicolor*

D. ajacis L.   Rocket-Larkspur
European; a garden-escape in N. America, as in SW B.C. (Vancouver Is. and Mayne Is.), S
Man. (N to Dauphin, N of Riding Mt.), S Ont. (N to L. Scugog in Victoria and Durham counties;
J.M. Macoun 1894), SW Que. (R. Campbell, Can. Rec. Sci. 6(6):342–51. 1895; Dundee Twp.),
and N.S. [*Consolida ambigua* (L.) Ball & Heywood].

D. bicolor Nutt.
/T/WW/   (Hs)   Grasslands and wooded or open rocky slopes from S B.C. (N to Kamloops
and Revelstoke) to S Alta. (N to Banff) and S Sask. (N to Piapot, 50°00'N; Breitung 1957a), S to
Mont., Wyo., and S.Dak. [Incl. var. *montanense* Rydb.; *D. azureum sensu* John Macoun 1883,
at least as to the Cypress Hills plant, not Michx., and *D. variegatum sensu* John Macoun
1886, not T. & G., the relevant collections in CAN].

   Forma *devriesii* Boivin (flowers white rather than bluish purple) is reported from B.C.
(Stump L., near Kamloops) and Alta. (type from near Elkwater Lake Provincial Park) by Boivin
(1967a). Forma *helleri* (Rydb.) Ewan (pedicels more or less arched-spreading rather than
straightish) is reported from B.C. by Ewan (1945).

D. burkei Greene
/t/W/   (Grt)   Wet meadows and springy places in woods from S B.C. (Cascade, Trail, and
near the mouth of the Kootenay R.; CAN) to Oreg. and Idaho. [*D. simplex* Dougl.].

[D. consolida L.]   Forking Larkspur
[Eurasian; a garden-escape to fields and waste places in N. America, as in s Ont. (Lambton, Norfolk, Welland, Wentworth, and York counties; CAN; TRT; reported from Belleville, Hastings Co., and Prescott, Grenville Co., by John Macoun 1883, but the relevant Belleville collection in CAN is annotated by Ewan as referable to some other unidentified species). Most or all of our other material may actually be *D. ajacis*. (*Consolida regalis* Gray).]

[D. depauperatum Nutt.]
[Reports of this species of the w U.S.A. (Wash. to Calif. and Nev.) from B.C. and/or Alta. by Ewan (1945), Ulke (1935), and Rydberg (1922; *D. cyan.*) require confirmation. It seems scarcely separable from *D. nuttallianum*. (*D. cyanoreios* Piper).]

[D. elatum L.]   Bee Larkspur
[This Eurasian species (not keyed out above) is reported from the Cypress Hills (?Alta. or ?Sask.) by Boivin (1968; "probably represents a planting in the wild.")]

D. glaucum Wats.
/aST/W/   (Hs)   Meadows and streambanks (often alpine or subalpine) from Alaska (N to the Seward Pen.; *see* Hultén 1944: map 574, p. 791), the Yukon (N to Herschel Is., off the N coast), and the Mackenzie R. Delta to Great Slave L. and cent. Sask. (N to Meadow Lake, 54°08'N; the writer is unaware of the basis for the extension of the range eastwards to Que. by Boivin 1966b), s to Calif. and Nev. [*D. scopulorum* var. *gl.* (Wats.) Gray; *D. brownii* Rydb. and its f. *pallidiflorum* Boivin; *D. canmorense, D. ?elongatum,* and *D. ?ramosum* Rydb.]. MAPS: Hultén 1968b:459; Raup 1947: pl. 24.

D. menziesii DC.
/t/W/   (Grt)   Plains, open hillsides, and clearings from sw B.C. (Vancouver Is.; Chilliwack; Manning Provincial Park, SE of Hope; reports from Alta. and Sask. by John Macoun 1886, probably refer to some other species; according to Hultén 1944, reports from Alaska refer to *D. brachycentrum* or *D. glaucum*) to Calif.
   The closely related *D. brachycentrum* Ledeb. of Alaska–N Yukon–E Asia may be distinguished as follows:
1   Leaves short-pubescent beneath with straightish hairs; stem from small fusiform to
   globose tubers . . . .*D. menziesii*
1   Leaves cobwebby-villous beneath with curly hairs; stem from a somewhat woody
   rootstock . . . .*D. brachycentrum* Ledeb.
   2   Flowers deep blue; [*D. blaisdellii* Eastw.; *D. alatum, D. nutans,* and *D. ruthiae*
      Nels.; Alaska–Yukon–E Asia; MAP: Hultén 1968b:458] . . . . .f. *brachycentrum*
   2   Flowers creamy white; [type from Mt. McKinley Park, Alaska] . . . . . .f. *pallidum* Lepage

D. nuttallianum Pritzel
/T/WW/   (Hs)   Lowland to montane valleys and slopes from B.C. (N to Dease L. at ca. 58°30'N; CAN, detd. Porsild) and the mts. of sw Alta. (N to the Banff dist.) to N Calif., Ariz., Colo., and Nebr. [*D. bicolor* f. *mccallae* Ewan; *D. nelsonii* Greene; *D. variegatum sensu* John Macoun 1883, not T. & G., the relevant collection in CAN].

[D. nuttallii Gray]
[Reports of this species of the w U.S.A. (Wash. and Oreg.) from B.C. by Abrams (1944) and from "Oregon to Alaska; Banff" by Henry (1915; *D. col.*) probably refer chiefly or wholly to *D. brachycentrum* and *D. menziesii*. (*D. columbianum* Greene).]

D. virescens Nutt.   Plains Larkspur
/T/(X)/   (Hs)   Prairies, barren ground, and dry open woods from s Man. (reported from the Netley Marsh at the s end of L. Winnipeg by Jackson et al. 1922, and from Headingly, near Winnipeg, by Lowe 1943; *see* L.M. Perry, Rhodora 39(457):21. 1937) to Wisc., s to Ariz., Colo., Tex., Okla., and Mo. [*D. albescens* Rydb.; *D. azureum* var. *laxiflorum* Huth]. MAP: Ewan 1945: fig. 51, p. 237.

ERANTHIS Salisb.   [2528]

E. hyemalis (L.) Salisb.   Winter Aconite
European; cult. and inclined to persist in N. America, as in s Ont. (Lambton Co.; Gaiser and Moore 1966); also reported from Nfld. by Rouleau (1956), where probably not established. [*Helleborus* L.].

HEPATICA Mill.   [2541]   Hepatica, Liverleaf.   Trinitaire

1   Leaf-lobes acute or acutish, usually longer than broad; involucral bracts lanceolate
    to narrowly oval, acute or obtusish; (Ont. and Que.) . . . .*H. acutiloba*
1   Leaf-lobes blunt or rounded, usually broader than long; involucral bracts broadly
    elliptic to broadly oval, rounded at tip; (Man. to N.S.) . . . .*H. americana*

H. acutiloba DC.
/T/EE/   (Hr)   Rich woods from Minn. to Ont. (N to the Ottawa dist.), Que. (N to St-Joachim, about 25 mi NE of Quebec City; Dominique Doyon and L.-R. Cayouette, Nat. can. (Que.) 96: 751. 1969), and W Maine, S to Mo., Ala., and Ga. [*Anemone* Lawson; *H. nobilis* var. *acuta* (Pursh) Steyerm.; see J.A. Steyermark and C.S. Steyermark, Rhodora 62(740):223–32. 1960]. MAPS: Hultén 1958: map 243 *(A. acut)*, p. 263; Meusel, Jaeger, and Weinert 1965:160.
    Forma *diversiloba* Raymond (leaves entire or sometimes with a second small lobe rather than with 3 large lobes) is known from the type locality, St-Armand, Missisquoi Co., SW Que.

H. americana (DC.) Ker
/T/EE/   (Hr)   Dryish rich woods from S Man. (*H. triloba* reported from about 30 mi SW of Portage la Prairie by Lowe 1943; early reports of *A. hepatica* from along the Winnipeg R. noted by John Macoun 1883) to Ont. (N to the Kaministikwia R. near Thunder Bay, Timmins, and the Ottawa dist.), Que. (N to Ville-Marie, Timiskaming Co., and Rimouski, Rimouski Co.), N.B. (St. Stephen, Charlotte Co.; CAN; the report of *H. triloba* from P.E.I. by McSwain and Bain 1891, is not accepted by D.S. Erskine 1960, the species probably now being extinct there if the report proves valid), and N.S. (Roland 1947), S to Mo., Ala., and N Fla. [*H. triloba* var. *amer.* DC.; *Anemone* Hult.; *A. (H.) hepatica* of Canadian reports, not L.; *H. nobilis* var. *obtusa* (Pursh) Steyerm.; see the above-noted paper by Steyermark and Steyermark]. MAPS: Hultén 1958: map 243 *(A. amer.)*, p. 263; Meusel, Jaeger, and Weinert 1965:160.

HYDRASTIS Ellis   [2522]   Orangeroot, Yellow Puccoon

H. canadensis L.   Golden-seal
/t/EE/   (Grh)   Rich woods from Nebr. to Minn., S Ont. (Essex, Lambton, Norfolk, Welland, Huron, and Leeds counties), and Vt., S to E Kans. (extinct), Ark., Ala., and Ga.

ISOPYRUM L.   [2532]

1   Lobes of leaflets tipped with a short glandular point; petaloid sepals usually less
    than 1 cm long; stamens at most about 5 mm long; mature follicles less than 7 mm
    long; roots often bearing numerous small tuber-like thickenings; plant weakly
    rhizomatous; (S Ont.) . . . .*I. biternatum*
1   Lobes of leaves with a shallow glandular notch at apex; sepals to about 1.5 cm long;
    stamens to 8 mm long; mature follicles to 1.5 cm long; roots not thickened; plant
    strongly rhizomatous; (Queen Charlotte Is.) . . . .*I. savilei*

I. biternatum (Raf.) T. & G.
/t/EE/   (Hsr)   Rich woods and thickets from Minn. to S Ont. (Lambton, Middlesex, Elgin, and Norfold counties; see S Ont. map by Soper 1962: fig. 9, p. 17), S to Tex., Mo., Ala., and NW Fla. [*Enemion* Raf.].

I. savilei Calder & Taylor
/T/W/ (Hsr) Moist shady rocks, crevices, and talus slopes from low to fairly high eleva-
tions of w-cent. B.C. (Queen Charlotte Is.; type from Moresby Is.). MAP: J.A. Calder and R.L.
Taylor, Madroño 17(3): fig. 3, p. 74. 1963.

MYOSURUS L.   [2543]   Mousetail

M. minimus L.
/T/X/EA/ (T) Damp or wet clayey calcareous or alkaline soils (ranges of Canadian taxa
outlined below), s to s Calif., Tex., and Fla.; Europe; w Asia; Australia. MAP and synonymy: *see*
below.
1 Achene-beak to 1.5 mm long, straight or somewhat spreading to recurved, the
  achene with a broad low keel and usually 2 marginal ridges; sepals to 2.5 mm long,
  1-nerved (rarely with a pair of faint lateral nerves); stamens usually 5; spike usually
  not over 1 cm long; scape to about 1 dm tall; [*M. aristatus* Benth.; *M. apetalus* of
  Canadian reports, not Gay; B.C. (Lytton; Spences Bridge), Alta. (Manyberries), and s
  Sask. (Wood Mountain; Chaplin; Bulrush L.)] . . . . .var. *aristatus* (Benth.) Boivin
1 Achene-beak rarely over 0.5 mm long, straight, the achene prominently acutish-
  keeled on the back; sepals to 3(4) mm long, lightly 3(5)-nerved; stamens 5 or 10;
  spike to 5 cm long; scape to 1.5 dm tall; [var. *?interior* Boivin; var. *lepturus* Gray
  (*M. lept.* (Gray) Howell); ssp. *montanus* Campbell; *M. major* and *M. tenellus* Greene;
  M. shortii Raf.; B.C. (N to the Tsitsutl Mts., ca. 54°N; CAN), Alta. (Waterton Lakes;
  Purple Springs, near Fort Macleod; Magrath; Medicine Hat; Milk River Ridge, 40 mi s
  of Lethbridge), Sask. (N to Sutherland, near Saskatoon), Man. (Melita; Deloraine;
  Short Creek; Crystal City; Morden), and s Ont. (Ferry Point, Prince Edward Co.;
  Belleville, Hastings Co.); MAP (aggregate species): Meusel, Jaeger, and Weinert
  1965:168] . . . . var. *minimus*

NIGELLA L.   [2530]

N. damascena L.   Love-in-a-mist, Fennel-flower
Eurasian; a garden-escape to roadsides and waste places in N. America, as in s Ont. (Huron,
Wellington, and Peel counties) and sw Que. (Boivin 1966*b*).

[PAEONIA L.]   [2523]   Peony

[P. brownii Dougl.]
[Reports of this species of the w U.S.A. (Wash. to Calif., Nev., and Utah) from Vancouver Is.,
B.C. (as by John Macoun 1883; this tentatively accepted by Henry 1915) probably derive from
the fact that the type locality is Mt. Hood, near Vancouver, Wash.]

RANUNCULUS L.   [2546]   Buttercup, Crowfoot.   Renoncule

(Ref.: Drew 1936; Benson 1948)
1 Petals white (*R. testiculatus,* introd. in s B.C., may be sought here from dried
  specimens but its petals are possibly yellowish in life); sepals spreading, promptly
  deciduous; receptacle to 2 mm long; achene-beak minute or at most 1 mm long.
  2 Sepals 3 or 4, to 1 cm long and 5 mm broad; petals 5 or more, to 13 mm long;
    achenes to 4 mm long, with a slight transverse constriction near the middle, their
    beaks to 1 mm long, recurved at tip; receptacle depressed-globose, about 4 mm
    thick in fruit; leaves entire and narrowly oblong or 3-lobed with oblong segments;
    plant subaquatic, glabrous, the rhizomatous hollow stem to 6 mm thick, giving
    rise to flowering branches and basal leaves at each node; (transcontinental in
    arctic and subarctic regions) . . . .*R. pallasii*
  2 Sepals 5; petals 5, usually 2 or 3 times as long as the sepals; achenes to 2.5 mm
    long, with several more or less distinct transverse ridges, their beaks rarely as
    much as 0.5 mm long (to 1 mm in *R. longirostris*); receptacle subglobose or

pyriform, usually less than 2 mm thick in fruit; plants aquatic (or sometimes on shore mud), glabrous or sparingly pubescent, the branching stems floating and usually bearing finely dissected submersed leaves (except in *R. hederaceus*), floating broad-bladed leaves also sometimes present.

3 Floating leaves present, these small, reniform in outline, shallowly to deeply 3(5)-lobed but not filiform-dissected; receptacle (and entire plant) glabrous; achenes at most 15, glabrous.

    4 Leaves all floating, shallowly 3-lobed (the lateral lobes again commonly shallowly notched); petals to 2.5 mm long; achenes usually more than 6, to 1.5 mm long, their beaks 0.1 mm long; (SE Nfld.) . . . . *R. hederaceus*

    4 Leaves of 2 kinds, the floating reniform ones deeply 3-parted (the lateral lobes again shallowly 2-lobed), the submersed leaves dissected into filiform segments; petals to 6 mm long; achenes rarely more than 6, to 2.5 mm long, their beaks to 0.3 mm long; (SW B.C.) . . . . *R. lobbii*

3 Leaves usually all submersed and filiform-dissected (floating leaves with dilated blades often present in typical *R. aquatilis* of Eurasia and its var. *hispidulus* of Alaska–B.C. to Dist. Mackenzie); petals to over 9 mm long; receptacle usually minutely hispid; achenes mostly more than 15.

    5 Style persistent after flowering, the achene-beak to about 1 mm long; achenes commonly 15–25 (sometimes only about 7); leaves suborbicular or reniform in outline, tending to hold their shape out of water, to about 2 cm long and broad; (S Alta. to S Que.) . . . . *R. longirostris*

    5 Style largely deciduous after flowering, the achene-beak rarely as much as 0.5 mm long; (essentially transcontinental).

        6 Pedicels recurved from the base at fruiting time; leaves usually 1–2-trichotomous and sessile (the first divisions arising within the usually dilated stipular leaf-base), suborbicular, tending to hold their shape out of water, much shorter than the internodes; achenes usually more than 30, their beaks to 0.5 mm long . . . . *R. circinatus*

        6 Pedicels not recurved at fruiting time; leaves usually repeatedly trichotomous and petioled (the first divisions mostly arising well above the non-dilated stipular leaf-base), usually collapsing out of water, to about 4 cm long and 5 cm broad and often about equalling the internodes; achenes rarely more than 25, glabrous or pubescent, their beaks to 0.3 mm long . . . . *R. aquatilis*

1 Petals yellow or yellowish (sometimes whitish in age; possibly white or pinkish from the first in *R. testiculatus*), the basal nectar-pit often covered by a scale on the claw; achenes smooth or variously sculptured (irregularly transversely wrinkled or ridged centrally in *R. sceleratus*).

7 Achenes with 3 or 4 longitudinal nerves or striations on each face (the nerves sometimes forked), thin-walled and usually fragile; leaves ovate to cordate-rotund or reniform, all basal (but the scapes often scaly-bracted, to 3 dm tall).

    8 Scapes and leaves arising from the nodes of slender elongate stolons; scapes often branched, each usually pubescent peduncle terminated by a flower; petals longer than the sepals, commonly 5 (but up to 15); achenes to 1.5 cm long, up to about 150 in a cylindroid head to over 1 cm long, their beaks about 0.3 mm long; receptacle hairy; leaves chiefly ovate to cordate-rotund, shallowly crenate but unlobed, rarely over 3 cm long and 2 cm broad; plant glabrous or sparsely hirsute; (transcontinental) . . . . *R. cymbalaria*

    8 Scapes and leaves arising from a nonstoloniferous caudex about 1 cm long, the glabrous scapes unbranched and terminated by a single flower; petals at least 7 (up to 15), shorter than the sepals; achenes at most about 30 in a convex cluster, to 2.5 mm long, the beak about 1 mm long; receptacle glabrous; leaves reniform (appearing orbicular by overlapping of the lobes), deeply 3-parted to below the middle or nearly to base, then crenately toothed or lobed, to about 4 cm long and 7 cm broad; plant glabrous; (S Alaska–B.C.) . . . .
. . . . *R. cooleyae*

7 Achenes not longitudinally nerved.
  9 Basal leaves entire to merely slightly lobed; plants glabrous or nearly so.
    10 Leaves all basal, thick, oblong or ovate to subrotund, to about 2 cm long, tapering to petioles about 1 cm long; scapes to 1 dm tall; sepals 5, green tinged with red or purple, not petaloid, persistent in fruit; petals at least 7, to 1.5 cm long; receptacle to 2 mm long; achenes to 2 mm long and with a straight beak about as long; (Aleutian Is.–Alaska) . . . . *R. kamchaticus*
    10 Leaves both cauline and basal; sepals more or less yellowish and petaloid, promptly deciduous.
      11 Sepals 3; petals at least 7, to 1.5 cm long; receptacle hairy; achenes pubescent, to 4 mm long, beakless, commonly abortive; leaf-blades cordate-ovate, to 5 cm long; roots forming tubers that separate annually and regenerate new plants; (introd.) . . . .*R. ficaria*
      11 Sepals and petals each commonly 5; receptacle and achenes glabrous, the latter beaked; leaf-blades lanceolate to oblanceolate, oval, or ovate-oblong, tapering to base; plants of damp or wet habitats.
        12 Stems erect or decumbent, nonstoloniferous, from slender or slightly tuberous-thickened roots; basal leaves lanceolate, to about 12 cm long and 3 cm broad; sepals to 5 mm long; petals to 1 cm long; achenes to 2.5 mm long, up to about 50 in a subglobose head to 8 mm thick, their beaks to 0.9 mm long; (Vancouver Is.) . . . .
        . . . . *R. alismaefolius*
        12 Stems stoloniferous and rooting at the nodes.
          13 Sepals about 6 mm long; petals to 1 cm long and 3 mm broad; achenes to 2.5 mm long, the straight or recurved beak to 1.5 mm long; fruiting head to 7 mm long; leaf-blades lanceolate, to about 1.5 dm long and 3 cm broad, entire or shallowly and distantly serrate, the dilated petioles sheathing; (s ?Ont.) . . . . . . [*R. ambigens*]
          13 Sepals at most 4 mm long; achenes at most 2 mm long, beakless or very short-beaked.
            14 Stems quill-like, to 5 mm thick at base, erect, ascending, or trailing; sepals at least 3 mm long; petals to 7 mm long and about as broad; fruiting-heads at least 3.5 mm long; leaf-blades to about 5 cm long and 12 mm broad; (introd. in ᴇ Canada) . . . .*R. flammula*
            14 Stems filiform, creeping and matted, rooting at the nodes; sepals less than 3 mm long; petals at most 5 mm long and 3 mm broad; fruiting-heads not over 3 mm long; leaves filiform or linear or with lanceolate or oval blades to 3 cm long and 6 mm broad; (transcontinental) . . . .*R. reptans*
  9 Basal leaves mostly distinctly toothed, lobed, or divided (if sometimes essentially entire, the stem-leaves (wanting in *R. testiculatus*) then deeply lobed or cleft and unlike the basal leaves).
    15 Sepals 3 (occasionally 4 or 5 in *R. hyperboreus*); achenes glabrous, up to 20 in a subglobose or globose cluster; receptacle glabrous; stems very slender and extensively creeping, the deeply 3-lobed reniform leaves and the peduncles arising from the rooting nodes; plants glabrous; (transcontinental in arctic and subarctic regions).
      16 Leaves commonly about 1 cm broad, the primary ovate or obovate lobes entire or more or less notched; sepals to 3 mm long; petals 3, to about 4 mm long; achenes to about 1.5 mm long, not constricted, nearly beakless . . . .*R. hyperboreus*
      16 Leaves to over 5 cm broad, the primary fan-shaped segments 3–7-lobed; sepals to 7 mm long; petals 5 or more, to 6 mm long; achenes 4 or 5 mm long, constricted near the middle, with slender hooked beaks to 2 mm long . . . .*R. lapponicus*
    15 Sepals 5 (rarely more).

    17 Plants aquatic, the weak stems floating (or sometimes creeping on mud); achenes glabrous.

        18 Leaves all alike, reniform, to about 2.5 cm long and 3 cm broad, 3-lobed (the lateral lobes again more shallowly 2-lobed, the 5 major lobes entire or toothed); sepals and petals each 3 or 4 mm long; achenes about 1 mm long, their stout beaks 0.2 mm long; fruiting head to 7 mm long and 5.5 mm thick, the receptacle glabrous or sparsely short-hairy; (the Yukon–Alta.) . . . .*R. natans*

        18 Leaves dimorphic, the submersed ones more finely dissected than the floating ones; receptacle hairy; (essentially transcontinental).

            19 Submersed leaves 3-ternately dissected into linear-filiform segments to about 1 dm long; sepals to 8 mm long; petals to 1.5 cm long; fruiting heads usually at least 8 mm long; mature achenes corky-thickened toward base, to 2.5 mm long, their beaks to 1.5 mm long . . . .*R. flabellaris*

            19 Submersed leaves suborbicular, with up to 5 cuneate or linear-cleft segments usually less than 3 cm long; sepals not over 6 mm long; petals not over 7 mm long; fruiting heads about 5 mm long; achenes not noticeably corky-thickened, less than 2 mm long, their beaks at most 0.7 mm long . . . .*R. gmelinii*

    17 Plants not strictly aquatic, the mostly stouter stems commonly erect or merely decumbent; (*R. sceleratus* often grows in shallow water, its submersed leaves then commonly more dissected than the aerial ones).

        20 Achenes barely mucronate (the beak only 0.1 mm long), glabrous, corky-thickened toward base and on margins, about 1 mm long, rather strongly flattened, very numerous in a cylindroid head to 1 cm long and 6 mm thick; sepals glabrous or pilose, they and the petals each 2 or 3 mm long or the petals sometimes to 5 mm long; receptacle glabrous or slightly hairy; plant fleshy and glabrous (rarely somewhat hirsute), only the uppermost leaves sessile; (transcontinental) . . . .*R. sceleratus*

        20 Achenes distinctly beaked (sometimes nearly beakless in *R. abortivus*), not corky-thickened; stem-leaves more generally sessile; plants scarcely fleshy.

            21 Basal leaves (or most of them) entire or merely crenate or somewhat 3–5-lobed (but the lobes usually obtuse or rounded and entire, rarely crenate; *R. inamoenus* may be sought here), usually less than 5 cm broad; achenes only moderately flattened, at most 2 mm long and about twice as broad as thick, their margins inconspicuous and scarcely keeled, their beaks slender and commonly curved or recurved; receptacle in fruit usually at least 4 times the length in flower; sepals often tinged on the back with lavender or purple; nectary-scale attached to the petal laterally and forming a pocket; perennials . . . .*GROUP 1*

            21 Basal leaves more copiously and usually more deeply dissected, the lobes themselves toothed or lobed (often sharply so) . . . .*GROUP 2* (p. 740)

GROUP 1

1 Sepals densely reddish-brown-pilose dorsally; achenes glabrous (sometimes sparsely brown-hispid in *R. sulphureus*); stems mostly 1-flowered and usually less than 2.5 dm tall, usually bearing not more than 3 leaves; basal leaves commonly 2 or 3 cm broad; plants mostly glabrous or glabrate; (arctic and subarctic regions).

    2 Receptacle pubescent with reddish-brown hairs; body of achene about 2 mm long, the slender straightish beak about 1 mm long; petals yellow, to 13 mm long

and 12 mm broad; basal leaves broadly ovate to fan-shaped, crenately and rather shallowly 5–9-lobed; stems commonly 1-flowered; (transcontinental) . . . .
. . . .*R. sulphureus*

2   Receptacle glabrous; basal leaves mostly more deeply cleft.

     3   Petals roseate to purple (or reported to be sometimes white), to over 1.5 cm long and broad; sepals marcescent-persistent in fruit, to 13 mm long and 8 mm broad; achenes to 4 mm long, somewhat inflated and stomach-shaped, their beaks 2 or 3 mm long; stems often bearing 2 or 3 flowers; (NW Alaska; Greenland) . . . .*R. glacialis*

     3   Petals yellow, to 12 mm long and broad; sepals deciduous during or soon after anthesis, to 8 mm long and 5 mm broad; achenes about 1.5 mm long, not inflated, obovoid, their beaks 1 or 2 mm long; stems usually 1-flowered; (transcontinental) . . . .*R. nivalis*

1   Sepals glabrous or pubescent with white or whitish hairs; flowers usually 2 or more.

    4   Fruiting head commonly 1 or 2 cm thick and with up to about 150 usually finely pubescent achenes; achene-beaks to 0.6 mm long; petals to 1.5 cm long; sepals to 5 mm long, slightly pubescent dorsally; receptacle glabrous; basal leaves entire or with 3 or 5 rounded lobes at apex (rarely deeply 3-cleft); stems mostly less than 2 dm tall; plants glabrous; (S B.C. to S Sask.) . . . .*R. glaberrimus*

    4   Fruiting head at most about 6 mm thick, with rarely more than 50 glabrous achenes; petals less than 1 cm long.

      5   Sepals copiously pilose, shorter than the petals (these to 8 mm long); receptacle long-hairy; achene-beaks 0.3 mm long; basal leaf-blades crenate, to 5 cm long and 4 cm broad; stems to about 2 dm tall; plants more or less pilose-hirsute; (B.C. to S Ont.) . . . .*R. rhomboideus*

      5   Sepals glabrous or sparsely pubescent, equalling or surpassing the petals (these at most 5 mm long).

        6   Stems subscapose (leaves all basal or sub-basal), less than 2 dm tall, with rarely more than 3 flowers; basal leaves usually less than 2 cm broad; sepals sparingly pilose, they and the petals 4 or 5 mm long; achene-beaks slender and recurved, to 0.7 mm long; receptacle loosely villous; stem and pedicels more or less villous, the mature pedicels less than 1 dm long; (Baffin Is., James Bay–Hudson Bay, Que., and Labrador) . . . .*R. allenii*

        6   Stems relatively leafy, to about 5 dm tall, usually bearing several or many flowers; achene-beaks slender, commonly not over 0.3 mm long (or sometimes obsolete in *R. abortivus*).

          7   Stem from a dense cluster of fusiform-thickened roots, bearing up to about 25 flowers; basal leaves at most about 2.5 cm broad, coarsely dentate with less than 20 marginal teeth (some of them sometimes with 3 cuneate- to rhombic-obovate deep lobes, or stalked dentate or cleft leaflets as in the lower stem-leaves); sepals glabrous, to about 3.5 mm long; petals linear to narrowly oblong; achenes dull; receptacle essentially glabrous; mature pedicels less than 1 dm long; plant more or less villous . . . .[*R. micranthus*]

          7   Stem from fibrous roots; basal leaves commonly much broader, usually more finely toothed (some of them sometimes with 3 obovate, toothed, simple or lobed leaflets); sepals glabrous or pubescent, to 5 mm long; petals oblong to oval; achenes lustrous; receptacle sparingly villous or sometimes glabrous; mature pedicels to 4 or 5 dm long; (transcontinental) . . . .*R. abortivus*

GROUP 2 (see p. 739)

1   Achenes only moderately flattened (rarely more than about twice as broad as thick), at most about 2.5 mm long, their margins inconspicuous and scarcely keeled, their slender beaks commonly curved or recurved; receptacle in fruit usually at least 4

times the length in flower; flowers usually not more than 2 or 3 on each plant (up to
about 10 in *R. inamoenus* and *R. pedatifidus*); basal leaves rarely over 4 cm long and
broad, mostly ternately cleft or divided into 3 broad primary segments.
2 Achenes rather densely woolly, bearing the seed in the basal portion and bulged
   on one side into 2 blister-like vesicles, then narrowed into a lanceolate, laterally
   compressed, somewhat setose-tipped, straight beak to 4 mm long; fruiting head
   cylindric, to 1.5 cm long; sepals green, to 6 mm long, persistent in fruit; petals to
   8 mm long, their nectary-scales attached basally; leaves all basal, 1–2-ternate
   into linear divisions; annual, more or less finely tomentose throughout; (introd. in
   s B.C.) . . . . *R. testiculatus*
2 Achenes not woolly; sepals often tinged dorsally with lavender or purple, usually
   deciduous shortly after anthesis; nectary-scales attached to the petals laterally
   and forming a pocket; perennials, usually nearly or quite glabrous (*R. inamoenus*
   and *R. pedatifidus* often somewhat hirsute or pilose).
   3 Petals to about 1 cm long, distinctly longer than the sepals (*R. gelidus* may
      sometimes be sought here); basal leaf-blades to 3 or 4 cm long and broad.
      4 Fruiting head to about 1.5 cm long, the glabrous achenes with straightish
         beaks; receptacle glabrous; basal leaf-blades rounded to truncate at base,
         3-cleft or -divided, the middle lobe entire or again 3-lobed, the lateral lobes
         asymmetrically cleft or divided into up to 7 segments; plant glabrous, the
         stems to about 1.5 dm tall, with rarely more than 3 flowers; (mts. of B.C.
         and Alta.) . . . . *R. eschscholtzii*
      4 Fruiting head at most about 1 cm long, the very finely canescent or
         glabrate achenes commonly with more or less recurved beaks; plants
         often somewhat pubescent, commonly taller and with more flowers.
         5 Petals at most 8 mm long and 4 mm broad; sepals glabrous or thinly
            appressed-pubescent; achenes densely canescent to glabrate, their
            beaks straight or recurved; receptacle glabrous or minutely hispid;
            basal leaf-blades cuneate to truncate at base, some of them usually
            3-cleft or -divided (or all of them often merely crenate); (s B.C. to
            sw Sask.) . . . . *R. inamoenus*
         5 Petals to 11 or 12 mm long; sepals pilose-tomentose; achene-beak
            recurved; basal leaf-blades cordate at base.
            6 Receptacle usually glabrous, to 3.5 mm long in fruit; achenes to 3
               mm long, up to about 30 in a broadly ovoid head; petals to 11 mm
               long and 10 mm broad; basal leaf-blades markedly broader than
               long, from merely crenately toothed to 3–5-divided and again lobed
               and toothed; stems and petioles glabrous or very sparingly hirsute . . . . .
               . . . . [*R. auricomus*]
            6 Receptacle canescent, to 9 mm long in fruit; achenes very finely
               canescent or glabrate, to 2 mm long, up to over 70 in a cylindroid
               head; petals to 12 mm long and 8 mm broad; basal leaf-blades only
               slightly broader than long, nearly always pedately parted or divided
               into 5–7 linear lobes some of which are again lobed; (trans-
               continental) . . . . *R. pedatifidus*
   3 Petals shorter than or at most only about 1 mm longer than the sepals;
      achenes glabrous; leaves palmately 3-lobed or -cleft, the lateral lobes
      commonly again lobed or cleft; plants nearly or quite glabrous.
      7 Receptacle pubescent; head of achenes to 9 mm long; sepals often
         purple-tinged; stems rarely over 2 dm tall.
         8 Achenes to 2.5 mm long, their stout hooked beaks about 0.5 mm long;
            sepals promptly deciduous; basal leaves mostly deeply cordate at base,
            orbicular to reniform in outline, from 3-lobed nearly to base (and with
            the primary lobes less deeply 2–3-lobed) to more deeply dissected into
            7–13 oblong segments; pedicels crisp-puberulent, the plant otherwise
            essentially glabrous; (mts. of B.C. and Alta.) . . . . *R. gelidus*

        8   Achenes to about 1.5 mm long, their recurved beaks to 1 mm long; sepals tardily deciduous; basal leaves broadly cuneate at base, obovate to rotund-obovate in outline, 3-lobed or the lateral lobes again 2-lobed or with additional teeth; stem and pedicels glabrous or more or less pilose; (transcontinental in arctic regions) . . . . *R. sabinei*

    7 Receptacle glabrous.

        9   Achenes about 1 mm long, their beaks straight; sepals and petals each usually less than 4 mm long; flowers usually 1 (sometimes 2); basal leaves to about 1.5 cm long and broad, often not cordate at base; (transcontinental in arctic, subarctic, and alpine regions) . . . . . *R. pygmaeus*

        9   Achenes longer, their beaks recurved; sepals and petals commonly over 4 mm long; basal leaves deeply cordate at base; (mts. of B.C. and Alta.).

           10 Achenes to 2.5 mm long; sepals elliptic to rotund; petals obovate; stems with rarely more than 3 flowers; leaves to about 3 cm long and broad . . . . *R. gelidus*

           10 Achenes about 1.5 mm long; sepals and petals generally somewhat narrower in outline; stems with up to 5 flowers; leaves rarely over 2 cm long and broad . . . . *R. verecundus*

1   Achenes very strongly flattened, at least twice as broad as thick, their margins usually distinctly keeled, their beaks usually relatively stout and rather broad-based; receptacle in fruit commonly not more than 3 times the length in flower; nectary-scale free laterally for usually at least 2/3 of its length, not forming a pocket (except in *R. recurvatus*); sepals usually not tinged with lavender or purple; flowers usually relatively numerous; plants commonly rather copiously hispid or hirsute (sometimes sparingly so or even nearly or quite glabrate in *R. acris, R. macounii,* and *R. uncinatus*).

   11 Achenes rough-papillate or short-bristly (papillae prolonged into short stout spines in *R. muricatus*), their margins moderately to strongly thickened; plants chiefly annual, perhaps sometimes perennial; (introd.).

      12 Achenes elliptic-obovate, mostly at least 4 mm long, commonly 5 (but up to about 20) on a subglobose hirsute receptacle, their faces bearing short stout spines but the strongly thickened margins not spiny; achene-beak to 2.5 mm long; basal leaves cordate or reniform, to about 6 cm long, shallowly to deeply 3-lobed, the primary segments themselves crenate to moderately lobed; stems to over 4 dm tall; plant glabrous to sparsely hirsute . . . . [*R. muricatus*]

      12 Achenes nearly circular in outline, 2 or 3 mm long, papillate or bristly (but not spiny), their beaks at most 1 mm long.

         13 Achenes merely papillate (or some of them glabrous), their strongly thickened margins subglabrous, up to 25 in a head to 8 mm thick; receptacle long-hairy, ovoid, to 2 mm long in fruit; sepals greenish yellow, reflexed, to 5 mm long; petals 5, to 9 mm long; basal leaf-blades pinnately compound (terminal leaflet long-stalked), the 3 leaflets parted and lobed into deltoid ultimate segments; plant sparingly to copiously hirsute; (introd. in Ont. and N.B.) . . . . *R. sardous*

         13 Achenes covered with bristle-like hooked hairs on the faces and strongly thickened margins, rarely more than 10 in a head to 5 mm thick; receptacle glabrous, globose, 0.6 mm long in fruit; sepals yellow, spreading, 1.5 mm long; petals none or up to 5, about 1.5 mm long; basal leaf-blades deeply 3-parted and again lobed, the ultimate lobes acute; plant finely pilose; (introd. on Vancouver Is.) . . . . [*R. hebecarpus*]

   11 Achenes glabrous or more or less pubescent (but neither papillate, bristly, nor spiny), usually distinctly longer than broad; plants chiefly perennial (*R. pensylvanicus* annual or perennial).

      14 Petals rarely over 4 or 5 mm long, shorter than or barely surpassing the sepals, these reflexed.

15 Receptacle glabrous; fruiting head globose, about 5 mm long and thick; achenes glabrous or hispidulous, to 3 mm long, the slender recurved beaks to 2 mm long, hooked at tip; basal leaves palmately parted into 3 broad principal segments (or sometimes separate leaflets); (B.C. and Alta.) . . . .*R. uncinatus*

15 Receptacle more or less short-hairy; achenes glabrous, their beaks relatively stout and broad-based.

  16 Achenes in a globose head to about 7 mm long and thick, to 2 mm long, their recurved beaks to 1.4 mm long, strongly hooked at tip; petals pale yellow, the nectary-scale forming a pocket at least basally; basal leaves palmately cleft to deeply parted into 3 broad, toothed or shallowly lobed, principal segments (but not into distinct leaflets); stem more or less bulbous at base; (Ont. to Nfld. and N.S.) . . . .*R. recurvatus*

  16 Achenes in an ovoid or cylindroid head distinctly longer than thick, to 2.5 or 3 mm long, their beaks straight or gradually bent toward tip; nectary-scale not forming a pocket; basal leaves pinnately parted into 3 or 5 usually separate stalked leaflets, the leaflets again usually deeply incised into relatively narrow ultimate segments; stems not bulbous at base; (transcontinental).

    17 Stems reclining or prostrate to suberect, often rooting at least at the lower nodes; petals deep yellow, to over 5 mm long; sepals to 7 mm long, often purple-tinged; achenes to 3 mm long, in a head to 12 mm long and 7 mm thick, their beaks to 1.2 mm long . . . .*R. macounii*

    17 Stems erect, not rooting at the nodes; petals pale yellow, 2 or 3 mm long; sepals yellowish, 4 or 5 mm long; achenes to 2.5 mm long, in a head to 14 mm long and 9 mm thick, their beaks 0.9 mm long . . . .*R. pensylvanicus*

14 Petals to over 1.5 cm long and conspicuously surpassing the sepals; fruiting heads ovoid to globose, usually as thick as or thicker than long.

  18 Stems from a corm-like bulbous base to 7 mm long and 13 mm thick; sepals reflexed at the middle; achenes in a globose head to 7 mm long and thick, to 2.8 mm long, glabrous, their stout recurved beaks to 0.4 mm long; receptacle pubescent; basal leaves pinnately parted into 3 separate leaflets, the leaflets themselves deeply 3-parted and again toothed or lobed; (introd. in B.C. and from Ont. to Nfld. and N.S.) . . . .*R. bulbosus*

  18 Stems usually not bulbous-based (but often somewhat so in *R. hispidus*).

    19 Basal leaves simple, deeply palmately or pedately parted into 3 principal toothed or lobed segments (but not separate leaflets); receptacle glabrous.

      20 Basal leaves pentagonal in outline, pedately parted nearly or quite to base into 3 sessile divisions (but appearing 5-parted by the forking of the lateral ones; the 5 principal divisions again deeply lobed or toothed); sepals spreading; achenes to 2.5 mm long, commonly 25 or more, their stout recurved beaks about 0.6 mm long; (introd., transcontinental) . . . .*R. acris*

      20 Basal leaves suborbicular to reniform in outline, palmately parted to below the middle into 3 broad segments, these again rather shallowly lobed and toothed; sepals usually reflexed; achenes rarely more than 15, to 3.5 mm long, usually more or less hispid (sometimes glabrous), with slender, straight or slightly recurving beaks to 2 mm long; (B.C. and Alta.) . . . .*R. occidentalis*

    19 Basal leaves mostly compound and pinnately parted into 3 or more separate lobed or incised leaflets (at least the terminal leaflet usually long-stalked); receptacle usually more or less villous or hispidulous (rarely glabrous in *R. repens*); achenes glabrous, commonly more than 15.

      21 Basal leaves with mostly 5 or 7 leaflets (the whole leaf usually longer

than broad); achenes to about 3 mm long, their beaks slender and
straight; stems not rooting at the lower nodes.

  22 Sepals reflexed; achene-beaks about 3 mm long; basal leaves to
over 1 dm long, their ultimate lobes acute or obtuse; stems
coarse, to over 1 m tall; roots 1 or 2 mm thick; (SE Alaska–B.C.) . . . . .
. . . .*R. orthorhynchus*

  22 Sepals spreading; achene-beaks less than 2.5 mm long; basal
leaves rarely over 5 cm long, their ultimate lobes blunt or
rounded; stems slender, to about 3 dm tall; roots of two types,
some filiform, others tuberous-thickened and fusiform, to 5 mm
thick; (SE Man. and S Ont.) . . . .*R. fascicularis*

21 Basal leaves with mostly 3 (sometimes 5) deeply incised and
toothed leaflets, the ultimate lobes mostly acute; sepals spreading.

  23 Achenes to 2.5 mm long, their stout beaks at most 1 mm long,
strongly recurved; stigma nearly covering one side of the short
style and persistent in fruit; fruiting head subglobose, to 1 cm
thick; some branches commonly trailing or repent; stems
prostrate to suberect, some commonly stoloniferous and rooting
at least at the lower nodes; (introd., transcontinental) . . . . .*R. repens*

  23 Achenes to 3.5 mm long, their beaks relatively slender and
straight, to 2 or 3 mm long; stigmas terminating the long style
and usually finally deciduous; stems suberect.

    24 Stems coarse, to over 1 m tall, some of them stoloniferous
and rooting at the nodes; roots coarse but not tuberous-
thickened; basal leaves to 2 dm broad; stipules usually
conspicuous, rounded at the summit; achenes to 4.5 mm
long, their thin edges with a pair of prominent lateral keels,
their beaks to 3 mm long; fruiting head to 1.5 cm thick;
(S Man. to P.E.I.) . . . .*R. septentrionalis*

    24 Stems relatively slender, commonly not over 3 dm tall, neither
stoloniferous nor rooting at the nodes, often somewhat
bulbous at base; roots usually fleshy, to 2.5 mm thick; basal
leaves to about 1 dm broad; stipules inconspicuous, tapering
to the petiole; achenes to 3.5 mm long, their lateral keels
obscure, their beaks to 2 mm long; fruiting head to about 1
cm thick; (S Ont.) . . . .*R. hispidus*

R. abortivus L. Kidney-leaf Buttercup
/ST/X/ (Hs) Moist woodlands, thickets, streambanks, and subalpine meadows from
S Alaska, S-cent. Yukon, and S Dist. Mackenzie to N Alta. (Wood Buffalo National Park), Sask.
(N to McKague, 52°37′N; CAN), Man. (N to the Pas; CAN), Ont. (N to Fort Severn, Hudson Bay,
ca. 56°N), Que. (N to S Ungava Bay and the Côte-Nord), Labrador (N to L. Petitsikapau at ca.
55°N, 67°W), Nfld., N.B., P.E.I., and N.S., s to Wash., Idaho, Colo., Tex., and N Fla.; Cuba.
[Incl. var. *eucyclus* Fern. (*see* N.C. Fassett, Am. Midl. Nat. 27:522. 1942) and var. *sylvaticus*
Lawson]. MAP: Hultén 1968*b*:479.

    Much of our material, particularly northwards, may be distinguished as var. *acrolasius* Fern.
(peduncles and upper stem-internodes minutely pilose rather than the plant essentially
glabrous).

R. acris L. Common Buttercup. Bouton d'or
Eurasian; a common weed of moist or wet places of S Alaska, S Dist. Mackenzie, and all the
provinces (in Labrador, N to the Hamilton R. basin). MAPS and synonymy: *see* below.
1 Pubescence appressed; basal leaves often cleft less than halfway to base; [*R.
?grandis* Honda; W Aleutian Is., where considered native by Hultén; MAPS: Hultén
1944: map 586, p. 792, and 1968*b*:485 (*R. gr.* var. *austrokurilensis*); Meusel, Jaeger,
and Weinert 1965:164 (*R. gr.*)] . . . . .var. *frigidus* Regel
1 Pubescence spreading.

2　Basal leaves cleft nearly to base . . . . .var. *acris*
　　3　Petals mostly 5; [*R. acer* L.; *R. mccallai* Davis; transcontinental; MAP
　　　　(aggregate species): Hultén 1968*b*:485] . . . . .f. *acris*
　　3　Petals more numerous; [Otterburne, S Man.; Löve and Bernard 1959] . . . .
　　　　. . . . . .f. *pleniflorus* Hiit.
2　Basal leaves mostly cleft less than halfway to base . . . . .var. *latisectus* Beck
　　4　Petals mostly 5; [var. *stevenii* of Canadian reports, not Lange; essentially
　　　　transcontinental but not yet known from Sask., N.B., or Nfld.] . . . . .f. *latisectus*
　　4　Petals more numerous; [var. *stevenii* f. *mult.* Boivin, the type from Kentville,
　　　　Kings Co., N.S.] . . . . .f. *multiplicipetalus* Boivin

R. alismaefolius Geyer
/T/W/　(Hs)　Swampy ground, streambanks, and alpine meadows from SW B.C. (Vancouver
Is.; CAN) to Calif. and Colo. [*R. bolanderi* Greene]. MAP: Benson 1962: fig. 5-12, p. 177.

R. allenii Robins.
/aST/E/　(Hs)　Wet gravels and flood-plains of alpine brooks: SE Baffin Is.; islands in James
Bay–Hudson Bay (North Twin Is.; Long Is.); Que. (coasts of James Bay–Hudson Bay N to ca.
56°N; Akpatok Is., Ungava Bay; Knob Lake dist. at ca. 55°N, 56°W; Shickshock Mts. of the
Gaspé Pen., the type from Mt. Albert); Labrador (between ca. 57° and 60°10′N). MAP: Porsild
1957: map 174, p. 182.

[*R. ambigens* Wats.]　Water-plantain-Spearwort
[Reports of this species of the E U.S.A. (N to Minn. and Maine) from S Ont. by Soper (1949),
Fernald *in* Gray (1950), and Benson (1962; indicated by a dot on his map, fig. 2-8, p. 31) are
possibly based upon the citation from Port Colborne, Welland Co., by John Macoun (1886;
this being a correction of his 1883 report of *R. alismaefolius* from S Ont.). The Port Colborne
collection, said to be deposited in MTMG, was not found there by the present writer.]

R. aquatilis L.　White Water-Crowfoot
/aST/X/GEA/　(HH)　Fresh, brackish, or calcareous ponds and slow streams, the aggregate species from the Aleutian Is., N Alaska, S Yukon, and NW Dist. Mackenzie to Great Bear
L., Great Slave L., L. Athabasca (Alta. and Sask.), E-cent. Dist. Keewatin, northernmost Baffin
Is. (an isolated station in northernmost Ellesmere Is.), northernmost Ungava–Labrador, Nfld.,
N.B., P.E.I., and N.S.; S to Baja Calif., Mexico, Tex., Kans., Pa., and Del.; W Greenland N to ca.
77°N, E Greenland N to 74°28′N; Iceland; Eurasia. MAPS and synonymy: *see* below.
1　Floating dilated leaves nearly always present, to about 1.5 cm long and 2 cm broad,
　　deeply 3-lobed, the lateral lobes again notched or 2-lobed; submersed leaves
　　dissected into capillary segments; receptacle hirsute, the hairs tufted.
　　2　Petals commonly over 1 cm long; stamens about 30; achenes often more than 25,
　　　　glabrous or hispidulous, to 2 mm long; submersed dissected leaves longer than
　　　　the stem-internodes; [Eurasia] . . . .[var. *aquatilis*]
　　2　Petals about 5 mm long; stamens commonly less than 25; achenes usually less
　　　　than 25, glabrous, to 1.5 mm long; submersed leaves usually shorter than the
　　　　internodes; [*R. trichophyllus* var. *hisp.* (E. Drew) W. Drew; *R. (Batrachium)*
　　　　grayanus Freyn; Aleutian Is. and SW Alaska (*see* Hultén 1944: map 608b, p. 794);
　　　　Dist. Mackenzie (Great Bear L.); S B.C. (Vancouver Is.; Chilliwack); MAP: Hultén
　　　　1968*b*:469] . . . . .var. *hispidulus* E. Drew
1　Floating dilated leaves wanting, the submersed leaves dissected into capillary
　　segments, usually shorter than the internodes (except often in var. *capillaceus*);
　　petals to 8 mm long; achenes usually less than 25, glabrous or subglabrate.
　　3　Receptacle glabrous or the sparse hairs not tufted; petals about 5 mm long;
　　　　stamens at least 10; achenes mostly at least 1.5 mm long; [*R. trich.* var. *calv.*
　　　　Drew; Ont. to Nfld. and N.S.] . . . . .var. *calvescens* (Drew) Benson
　　3　Receptacle minutely hirsute, the hairs tufted; (transcontinental).
　　　　4　Stamens rarely more than 8; petals to 6 mm long; achenes about 1 mm long;
　　　　　　stems to 1 mm thick; [var. *confervoides* (Fries) Robins. (*Batrachium con.*

Fries); *R. trich.* var. *erad.* (Laest.) Drew; the common phase northwards; MAPS: Hultén 1968b:470 *(R. conf.)*; Porsild 1957: map 162, p. 181] . . . .
. . . . var. *eradicatus* Laest.

4   Stamens 10–25; petals to 8 mm long; achenes to 1.5 mm long; stems to 2(2.5) mm thick; [incl. vars. *brachypus* H. & A., *codyanus* Boivin, and *lalondei* Benson; *R. cap.* Thuill.; *R. (Batrachium) trichophyllus* Chaix; *B. drouetii* (Schultz) Nym.; *B. flaccidum* (Pers.) Rupr.; the common phase southwards; MAPS: Hultén 1968b:469 *(R. trich.)*; Meusel, Jaeger, and Weinert 1965:163 (aggregate species, incomplete northwards; the N. American area is largely applicable here)] . . . . var. *capillaceus* (Thuill.) DC.

[R. auricomus L.]
[Reports of this European species from E Greenland (*see* MAPS by Böcher 1938: fig. 40, p. 89, and Hultén 1958: map 11 (var. *glab.*), p. 31) all appear to be based upon var. *glabratus* Lynge (achenes glabrous rather than densely pubescent), which is relegated to synonymy under *R. affinis* (*R. pedatifidus* var. *leiocarpus* of the present treatment) by Tutin et al. (1964).]

R. bulbosus L.   Bulbous Buttercup or Crowfoot
European; introd. in pastures, fields, and waste places in N. America, as in S B.C. (Revelstoke; CAN), S Ont. (N to Simcoe and Hastings counties), Que. (Ste-Anne-de-la-Pocatière, Kamouraska Co.; Groh 1947; DAO), Nfld., ?P.E.I. (McSwain and Bain 1891; no recent collections), and N.S. [*R. tuberosus* Hornem., not Lapeyr.].
   Var. *valdepubens* (Jord.) Briq. (plant densely hoary-villous rather than moderately silky-villous to glabrate) is known from S Ont. (Hepworth, Bruce Co.; TRT).

R. circinatus Sibth.   White Water-Crowfoot
/aST/X/E/   (HH)   Calcareous or brackish ponds and quiet waters from S Victoria Is., SW Yukon, and the Mackenzie R. Delta to Great Slave L., L. Athabasca, NE Dist. Keewatin (Melville Pen.), Prince Charles Is. (in Foxe Basin, W coast of cent. Baffin Is.), Southampton Is., northernmost Ont., Que. (N to NE James Bay and the Gaspé Pen.), Nfld., and N.S. (not known from N.B. or P.E.I.), S to Mexico, Tex., S.Dak., Minn., and Mass.; Europe. [*R. subrigidus* Drew]. MAP: Porsild 1957: map 163 *(R. sub.),* p. 181.

R. cooleyae Vasey & Rose
/sT/W/   (Hr)   Damp slopes and rock crevices from S Alaska (type from Juneau; *see* Hultén 1944: map 590, p. 792) through W B.C. (chiefly in the Cascades) to Wash. [*Arcteranthis* Greene]. MAPS: *Atlas of Canada* 1957: map 10, sheet 38; Hultén 1968b:474.

R. cymbalaria Pursh   Seaside Crowfoot
/aST/X/GEA/   (Hsr)   Saline or brackish shores and marshes and salt springs and alkaline flats inland, the aggregate species from N Alaska, cent. Yukon, and the Mackenzie R. Delta to Victoria Is., northernmost Alta., Sask. (N to Prince Albert), Man. (N to Churchill), northernmost Ont., Que. (N to E Hudson Bay at ca. 57°N, the Côte-Nord, Anticosti Is., and Gaspé Pen.), Nfld., N.B., P.E.I., and N.S., S to N.Mex., Tex., Ark., Ill., and N.J.; S. America; W Greenland between ca. 65° and 67°N (?introd.); N Europe (?introd.); Asia. MAPS and synonymy: *see* below.
1   Leaf-blades ovate to reniform, to over 2 cm long; sepals and petals to 5 mm long; fruiting heads to over 8 mm long . . . . var. *cymbalaria*
   2   Plant glabrous throughout; [*Cyrtorhyncha* Britt.; *Halerpestes* Greene; *Oxygraphis* Prantl; incl. var. *americanus* DC. and the reduced extreme, var. *alpinus* Hook.; transcontinental; MAPS: Porsild 1957: map 168, p. 181; Hultén, 1968b:475, and 1958: map 245, p. 265; H.K. Svenson, Rhodora 29(342): fig. 1 (incomplete northwards), p. 112. 1927] . . . . f. *cymbalaria*
   2   Peduncles and/or petioles pilose; [Alta. (type from Banff); Man. to N.B. and N.S.] . . . .
. . . . f. *hebecaulis* Fern.
1   Leaf-blades cordate-ovate (rarely reniform), to about 4 cm long; sepals and petals to 8 mm long; fruiting heads to 12 mm long; [B.C., Alta. (Hitchcock et al. 1964), Sask. (Moose Jaw), and Man. (Brandon)] . . . . var. *saximontanus* Fern.

R. eschscholtzii Schlecht.
/ST/W/eA/ (Hr (Hs)) Turfy tundra, alpine meadows, and talus slopes (ranges of Canadian taxa outlined below), s to Calif., Ariz., and N.Mex.; E Asia. MAPS and synonymy: *see* below.

1 Ultimate leaf-lobes and sinuses mostly rounded, the middle lobe of the basal leaves entire to shallowly 3-lobed; [*R. nivalis (hyperboreus)* var. *esch.* (Schlecht.) Wats.; *R. ?schlectendalii* Hook.; Aleutian Is.–Alaska (N to ca. 65°N; *see* Hultén 1944: map 592, p. 793; type from Unalaska), the Yukon (Porsild 1951a), Dist. Mackenzie (Mackenzie R. Delta; Great Bear L.; Brintnell L.), B.C., and sw ?Alta.; MAPS (aggregate species): Hultén 1968b:475; Raup 1947: pl. 25] . . . . var. *eschscholtzii*
1 Ultimate leaf-lobes and sinuses mostly acute, the middle lobe of the basal leaves often deeply lobed (to entire); [*R. suks.* Gray; *R. eximius* Greene; *R. saxicola* Rydb.; var. *hultenianus* Benson; mts. of B.C. (Burgess Pass and Yoho; Eastham 1947) and sw Alta. (Spray R.; Benson 1948)] . . . . var. *suksdorfii* (Gray) Benson

R. fascicularis Muhl. Early Buttercup or Crowfoot
/T/EE/ (Hs) Open woods or exposed hillsides and ledges (often calcareous) from SE Man. (Falcon Lake, near the Ont. boundary; DAO) to s Ont. (N to Great Cloche Is., N L. Huron; Fernald 1935) and s N.H., s to Tex., La., and Miss.

The report from Cumberland House, E Sask., ca. 54°N, by Benson (1948) is based upon an early but undated collection in CAN by Richardson, bearing the ambiguous designation "New York and Cumberland House". This was probably intended as a general statement of the range and undoubtedly included Richardson's concept of some more western species, perhaps *R. macounii*. The reports from Churchill, Man., by H.E. McClure (Ecol. Monogr. 13(1):10. 1943) and from Nfld. by Waghorne (1898) also require clarification.

R. ficaria L. Lesser Celandine, Pilewort. Ficaire
Eurasian; an old garden-plant of N. America, occasionally spreading to open woods and waste places, as in sw B.C. (Nanaimo, Vancouver Is.; Benson 1948), s Ont. (Wellington Co.; Stroud 1941), sw Que. (Montreal dist.; MT, verified by Benson), and Nfld. (Rouleau 1956).

Some or all of our material is referable to var. *bulbifera* Marsden-Jones (leaves bearing small bulblets in their axils).

R. flabellaris Raf. Yellow Water-Crowfoot or -Buttercup
/T/X/ (HH) Quiet waters and muddy shores from s B.C. (N to the Bonaparte R. w of Kamloops; Henry 1915) to s Alta. (Red Deer; Benson 1948; CAN; not known from Sask.), s Man. (Portage la Prairie and Boissevain; CAN), Ont. (N to the Ottawa dist.), Que. (N to about 25 mi s of Rimouski, Rimouski Co.), N.B. (St. John R. in Sunbury Co.; ACAD; reports from P.E.I. require confirmation; not known from N.S.), and Maine, s to N Calif., Utah, Kans., La., and N.C. [*R. delphinifolius* Torr.; *R. multifidus* Pursh, not Forsk.].

Forma *riparius* Fern. (*R. del.* var. *terrestris* Farw., not *R. mult.* var. *terr.* Gray; stem shortened, the more or less reduced leaves thicker and less dissected than those of the typical submersed phase) occurs throughout the range. It is merely an expression of the stranded or shore habitat and such leaves may occur on aerial parts of otherwise submersed plants with finely dissected leaves.

R. flammula L. Spearwort
Eurasian; Canadian distribution, MAP, and synonymy: *see* below.

1 Lower leaves oblanceolate to ovate-oblong, their blades to about 5 cm long and 12 mm broad; [SE Nfld.: Quiddy Viddy, Avalon Pen., where considered native by Fernald *in* Gray 1950, but more likely introd.; *see* note under *Luzula campestris*] . . . .
. . . . var. *angustifolius* Wallr.
1 Leaves all linear-lanceolate to lanceolate, their blades mostly not over 3 cm long and 6 mm broad; [introd. in B.C. (Vancouver Is.), ?Ont. (Soper 1949), w N.S. (Tusket, Yarmouth Co.; Uniacke, Hants Co.), St-Pierre and Miquelon, and SE Nfld. (Avalon Pen.); MAP (aggregate species): Hultén 1958: map 147, p. 167]. It is possible that the Vancouver Is. plant belongs to the taxon generally known as *R. flam.* var.

unalaschensis (Bess.) Ledeb. (*R. unal.* Bess.), generally considered to be a hybrid
between *R. flammula* and *R. reptans* . . . . var. *flammula*

R. gelidus Kar. & Kir.
/aST/W/eA/ (Hs) Moist tundra, alpine meadows, and talus slopes from the coasts of
Alaska–Yukon and the Richardson Mts. of NW Dist. Mackenzie (Porsild 1943) through the mts.
of B.C. (Marble Range, NW of Clinton; Benson 1948) and SW Alta. (Jasper dist.; CAN) to Mont.
and Colo.; E Asia. [*R. drummondii* Greene; *R. grayii* Britt.; *R. hookeri* Regel, not Schlecht.].
MAPS: Hultén 1968*b*:477 (ssp. *grayii*); Porsild 1966: map 65, p. 75; Benson 1962: fig. 2-20, p. 46.

R. glaberrimus Hook.   Sagebrush Buttercup
/T/WW/ (Hs) Sandy plains, valleys, and open woodlands to alpine meadows (ranges of Canadian taxa outlined below), S to N Calif., N.Mex., and Nebr.
1   Basal leaf-blades usually ovate to obovate (sometimes broader than long),
    commonly shallowly lobed; stem-leaves often entire; [B.C.: N to 150 Mile House,
    ca. 52°N] . . . . var. *glaberrimus*
1   Basal leaf-blades oblanceolate to elliptic, usually entire; stem-leaves entire to
    3-lobed, the middle lobe much the largest; [*R. ellipticus* Greene; B.C., Alta.
    (Waterton Lakes; Red Rock Canyon), and S Sask. (Bienfait; Consul; Cadillac; Swift
    Current; Mortlach)] . . . . var. *ellipticus* Greene

R. glacialis L.
/ASs/D/GEA/ (Hs) Wet tundra, gravels, snow-patches, and streambanks (ranges of
Alaska–Greenland taxa outlined below; not known elsewhere in N. America); Iceland; Spitsbergen; Europe; E Asia. MAPS and synonymy: *see* below.
1   Stems suberect, glabrous or glabrate; primary divisions of the basal leaves stalked,
    their lobes usually obtuse; stem-leaves glabrous; [*Beckwithia* Löve & Löve; not
    Ficaria (Oxygraphis) glacialis Fisch., which is *R. kamchaticus* DC.; E Greenland
    between the Arctic Circle and ca. 80°N; MAPS: Hultén 1958: map 73, p. 93; Meusel,
    Jaeger, and Weinert 1965:167; Böcher 1938: fig. 43, p. 92; Löve & Löve 1956*b*: fig. 7,
    p. 143] . . . . var. *glacialis*
1   Stems erect, densely brown-hairy above and near the nodes; primary divisions of
    basal leaves usually sessile, their lobes often acutish; stem-leaves often copiously
    rusty-hairy; [*R. c(h)amissonis* Schlecht.; NW Alaska; MAPS: Benson 1962: fig. 9-8, p.
    300; Hultén 1968*b*:473; also on the above-noted maps by Hultén and Meusel, Jaeger,
    and Weinert] . . . . var. *chamissonis* (Schlecht.) Benson

R. gmelinii DC.   Small Yellow Water-Crowfoot or -Buttercup
/aST/X/EA/ (HH) Cool ponds, shallow streams, shores, and wet meadows, the aggregate
species from the coasts of Alaska–Yukon–Dist. Mackenzie to Prince Patrick Is. (N of Banks
Is.), S Dist. Keewatin, Southampton Is., Que. (N to SE Hudson Bay at ca. 55°30'N, Anticosti Is.,
and the Gaspé Pen.), Nfld., N.B., P.E.I., and N.S., S to Oreg., N.Mex., S.Dak., Iowa, Mich., and
Maine; NE Europe; Asia. MAPS and synonymy: *see* below.
1   Sepals at least 4 mm long; petals to 7 mm long and 6 mm broad; leaves deeply 3-
    parted, the divisions again 2 or 3 times forked or sometimes dissected into ribbon-
    like divisions; plant glabrous or essentially so; [var. *purshii* (Rich.) Hara; *R. purshii*
    Rich. and its var. *hookeri* Don (type material from "Slave Lake, Cumberland House",
    either in Dist. Mackenzie, Alta., or Sask.), var. *prolificus* Fern., var. *repens* Hook.
    (neither *R. repens* L. nor *R. multifidus* var. *repens* Hook.), and var. *terrestris* Ledeb.;
    R. fistulosus Pursh; transcontinental; MAPS: Hultén 1968*b*:471 (ssp. *purshii*); Porsild
    1966: map 66 *(R. purshii)*, p. 75; Raup 1947: pl. 24 (var. *purshii*); Benson 1962: fig.
    9-13, p. 306] . . . . var. *hookeri* (Don) Benson
1   Sepals less than 4 mm long; petals 4 or 5 mm long; stems to about 1 mm thick.
    2   Leaf-segments relatively broad, the leaf usually 3-parted and again once or twice
        lobed into usually broad, rounded or obtuse segments (but sometimes
        dissected); plant markedly pubescent; [*R. limosus* Nutt.; *R. multifidus* var. *lim.*
        (Nutt.) Lawson; S Dist. Mackenzie (J.W. Thieret, Can. Field-Nat. 75(3):116. 1961)

Ranunculus

and B.C. to Man.; MAP: Benson 1962: fig. 9-12 (the S Dist. Mackenzie station should be indicated), p. 305] . . . . var. *limosus* (Nutt.) Hara
2 Leaf-segments narrow, the leaf 3-parted, the primary segments then usually finely dissected into linear acute divisions; plant sparsely to moderately pubescent; [var. *yukonensis* (Britt.) Benson (*R. yuk.* Britt.); *R. purshii* var. *gmel.* (DC.) Don; Alaska to Prince Patrick Is., S to S Yukon, northernmost Alta., SE Dist. Keewatin, Southampton Is., and NE ?Man.; MAPS: Hultén 1968b:470; Porsild 1957: map 166, p. 181; Benson 1962: fig. 9-12 (indicating a NE Man. station not shown on Porsild's map), p. 305] . . . . var. *gmelinii*

[R. hebecarpus H. & A.]
[This species of the W U.S.A. (Wash. to Baja Calif. and Ariz.) is reported as introd. in SW B.C. by John Macoun (1890; in ballast on wharves at Nanaimo, Vancouver Is.) but the relevant collection by Macoun has not been located and no other report from our area has been found.]

R. hederaceus L.
/T/E/E/ (HH) Shallow pools and wet sandy depressions of SE Nfld. (several localities on the Avalon Pen.; GH; CAN) and along the Atlantic Coastal Plain from SE Pa. and Md. to S.C.; W Europe (where now partly extinct; considered a relic-species in N. America by Benson 1948). [*Batrachium* Gray]. MAP: Hultén 1958: map 137, p. 157 (noting the possibility of the species being introd. in N. America).

R. hispidus Michx.   Bristly Buttercup
/t/EE/ (Hs) Moist meadows and rich moist woods (ranges of Canadian taxa outlined below), S to Nebr., Ark., and Ga. MAP and synonymy: see below.
1 Principal leaves completely 3-parted, their lateral leaflets 2–3-cleft; body of achene at least 3 mm long, the dorsal keel to 0.5 mm broad; [*R. repens* var. *hisp.* (Michx.) Chapm.; *R. hirtipes* Greene; S Ont. (collections in CAN, all verified by Benson, from Essex, Elgin, Welland, Waterloo, and Peel counties, and in OAC from Norfolk, Lincoln, Wentworth, and Dufferin counties, and in TRT from Middlesex, Brant, and York counties; reported from Lambton Co. by Dodge 1914); MAP: Benson 1962: fig. 2-17, p. 42] . . . . var. *hispidus*
1 Principal leaves usually not completely parted, their lateral segments shallowly 2-lobed or merely deeply toothed; body of achene not over 2.5 mm long, the dorsal keel about 0.2 mm broad; [var. *marilandicus* of auth., perhaps not *R. marilandicus* Poir.; *R. cardiopetalus* Greene; S Ont. (collections in CAN, detd. Benson, from Niagara Falls, Welland Co., and Toronto, York Co.; collection in OAC from Port Ryerse, Norfolk Co.; reported from Lambton Co.); MAP: on the above-noted map by Benson] . . . . var. *falsus* Fern.

R. hyperboreus Rottb.
/AST/X/GEA/ (HH (Hsr)) Shallow fresh or brackish waters from the Aleutian Is. and coasts of Alaska–Yukon–Dist. Mackenzie–Dist. Keewatin throughout the Canadian Arctic Archipelago to northernmost Ellesmere Is. and northernmost Ungava–Labrador, S in the West through B.C.–Alta. to Mont., farther eastwards S to NE Man. (Churchill; not known from Sask.), N Ont. (known only from NW James Bay at and near Cape Henrietta Maria; Dutilly, Lepage, and Duman 1954), Que. (S to NE James Bay and the Côte-Nord), S Labrador, and Nfld.; circumgreenlandic; Iceland; Spitsbergen; N Eurasia. [Incl. the high-arctic dwarf extreme, ssp. *arnellii* Scheutz (ssp. *samojedorum* (Rupr.) Hult.)]. MAPS: combine the maps by Hultén 1968b:471 and 472 (ssp. *arn.*); Porsild 1957: map 165, p. 181; Raup 1947: pl. 25.
Var. *turquetilianus* Polunin (leaves with relatively narrow segments, somewhat resembling those of *R. gmelinii* var. *hookeri*) is known from the type locality, Chesterfield, E Dist. Keewatin.

R. inamoenus Greene
/T/W/ (Hs) Moist banks, slopes, and alpine meadows from S B.C. (Fraser and Yoho valleys; Crowsnest Pass) to S Alta. (N to Jasper) and SW Sask. (Cypress Hills; Breitung 1957a), S to Wash., Idaho, Nev., Ariz., and Colo. [Incl. var. *elatior* Boivin and *R. alpeophilus* Nels.].

R. kamchaticus DC.
/Ss/W/A/ (Hr) Wet ground near sea level to high elevations in the mountains in the Aleu-tian Is. and Alaska (NW coast between Seward Pen. and N of Cape Lisburne at ca. 69°N); Asia. [*Ficaria (Oxygraphis) glacialis* Fisch., not *R. glacialis* L.]. MAPS *(Oxy. glac.)*: Hultén 1968*b*:486, and 1944: map 585, p. 792.

R. lapponicus L.   Lapland Buttercup
/aST/X/GEA/ (Hrr) Damp mossy woods and sphagnum bogs from the coasts of Alaska–Yukon–Dist. Mackenzie to Great Bear L., Great Slave L., L. Athabasca (Alta. and Sask.), S-cent. Dist. Keewatin, northernmost Que. (Hudson Strait), Baffin Is. N to near the Arctic Circle), and Labrador (N to Rigolet, 54°10'N; reported N to Nain, 56°33'N), S to cent. B.C. (S to McLeod L. at ca. 54°20'N), Alta. (S to Red Deer, 52°16'N; CAN), Sask. (S to Langham, 52°22'N; Breitung 1957*a*), Man. (S to Duck Mt.), N Minn., Ont. (mouth of the Black Duck R., Hudson Bay, at ca. 56°45'N; W James Bay; shores of L. Nipigon and L. Superior; Ellen L.; Cochrane; Kapuskasing), Que. (S to SE James Bay, Watson L. at 49°19'N, the Laurentide Park N of Montreal, and Cap-à-l'Orignal, near Bic, Rimouski Co.), and N Maine; S half of W Green-land; Spitsbergen; N Eurasia. [*Coptidium* Gand.]. MAPS: Hultén 1968*b*:473; Porsild 1957: map 167, p. 181; Raup 1947: pl. 25.

R. lobbii (Hiern) Gray
/t/W/ (T) Shallow pools near sea level from SW B.C. (near Victoria, Vancouver Is.; CAN) to Calif. [*Batrachium* Howell; *R. hydrocharis* f. *lobbii* Hiern; *R. aquatilis (hederaceus)* var. *lobbii* (Hiern) Wats.; *R. hed. sensu* John Macoun 1883, not L.].

R. longirostris Godr.   White Water-Crowfoot
/T/(X)/ (HH) Shallow ponds and quiet waters from SW Alta. (Jasper; CAN) to SW Sask. (Cy-press Hills and Crane Lake; Breitung 1957*a*), S ?Man. (Benson 1948), Ont. (N to Manitoulin Is., N L. Huron, and the Ottawa dist.; tentatively reported from Albany, SW James Bay, by Dutilly, Lepage, and Duman 1954), and SW Que. (N to near Sorel, at the SW end of L. St. Peter), S to Wash., Ariz., N.Mex., Tex., Kans., Pa., and Del. [*Batrachium* Schultz; *R. aquatilis* var. *long.* (Godr.) Lawson].

R. macounii Britt.
/ST/X/ (Hs) Alluvial thickets, low woods, and damp meadows from cent. Alaska–Yukon and NW Dist. Mackenzie to Great Slave L., northernmost Alta. (Wood Buffalo National Park N to ca. 59°30'N), Sask. (N to L. Athabasca), Man. (N to Northern Indian L. at ca. 57°30'N), Ont. (N to Fort Severn, Hudson Bay, ca. 56°N), Que. (N to E James Bay at ca. 54°N, Anticosti Is., and the Gaspé Pen.; not known from the Maritime Provinces), Labrador (Hamilton R. basin), and Nfld., S to Calif., N.Mex., Kans., Mich., and S Que. [*R. pacificus* (Hult.) Benson].
Var. *oreganus* (Gray) Davis (*R. oreg.* (Gray) Howell; plant essentially glabrous rather than moderately to densely hirsute) is reported from S B.C. by Boivin (1966*b*).

[*R. micranthus* Nutt.]
[The report of this species of the E U.S.A. (N to Ill. and Mass.) from Quesnel, B.C., by John Ma-coun (1883; *R. abort.* var. *mic.*) is based upon *R. abortivus* var. *acrolasius* (relevant collection in CAN), to which Ont. and N.S. reports by Macoun (1883; 1886) may also refer. (*R. abortivus* var. *mic.* (Nutt.) Gray).]

[*R. muricatus* L.]
[European; the report from N.B. by John Macoun (1886; "On ballast heaps at St. John") is based upon *R. sardous,* relevant collections in CAN and NBM.]

R. natans Mey.
/T/W/A/ (HH) Cold ponds and muddy banks from W-cent. Yukon and SW Alta. to Idaho and Colo.; Asia.
1   Receptacle sparingly hairy; leaves to 2.5 cm long and 3 cm broad, their major lobes

toothed, the sinus closed or very narrow; [*R. hyperboreus* var. *natans* (Mey.) Regel; Asia only, reports from w Canada referring to the following or some other species] . . . . . .
. . . . [var. *natans*]
1   Receptacle glabrous; leaves usually not over 1.5 cm long and 2.5 cm broad, their major lobes entire, the acute sinus not closed; [*R. intertextus* Greene; *R. hyp.* var. *int.* (Greene) Boivin; w-cent. Yukon (Boivin 1966*b*); ?B.C. (reports from the Bonaparte R., Griffin L., near Kamloops, and the Gold Range by John Macoun 1890, require confirmation); sw Alta. (Nordegg; Benson 1948)] . . . .
. . . . var. *intertextus* (Greene) Benson

R. nivalis L.
/AS/X/GEA/   (Hs)   Moist ground (often near melting snowbeds or on mossy brook-margins) from the Aleutian Is. and coasts of Alaska–Yukon–Dist. Mackenzie–Dist. Keewatin nearly throughout the Canadian Arctic Archipelago to northernmost Ellesmere Is. at ca. 80°N and northernmost Ungava–Labrador, s to SE Alaska, N B.C. (Tagish L. at 59°35′N), Great Bear L., s Baffin Is., Que. (coast of Hudson Bay s to ca. 56°N), and Labrador (s to ca. 59°N; reported s to Hopedale, 55°27′N, by Delabarre 1902); w and E Greenland between the Arctic Circle and ca. 78°N; Spitsbergen; N Eurasia. MAPS: Hultén 1968*b*:476; Porsild 1957: map 169, p. 182; Raup 1947: pl. 25.
Forma *subglobosus* Polunin (mature fruiting receptacle subglobose rather than distinctly longer than broad) is known from the Hudson Strait coast of N Que. (Wakeham Bay; type from Wolstenholme).

R. occidentalis Nutt.   Western Buttercup
/aST/W/   (Hs)   Moist to well-drained soil, the aggregate species from the Aleutian Is., s Alaska, and the coasts of the Yukon (Herschel Is. and King Point; Benson 1948, as *R. turneri*) and NW Dist. Mackenzie through B.C. and sw Alta. (Moose Pass and Mt. Robson, both ca. 53°10′N; Benson 1948, var. *brevistylis*) to Calif. MAPS and synonymy: *see* below.
1   Stamens usually 6; petals 8 or more; [*R. hex.* Benson, the type from Queen Charlotte Is., B.C., the only known locality; MAP: Benson 1962: fig. 9-5, p. 295] . . . .
. . . . var. *hexasepalus* Benson
1   Stamens 5; petals usually 6.
    2   Sepals spreading; [*R. turneri* Greene, the type from the Porcupine R., near the Alaska–Yukon boundary; also known from the coast of the Yukon and NW Dist. Mackenzie; MAP: Hultén 1944: map 609, p. 794] . . . . var. *turneri* (Greene) Benson
    2   Sepals rather sharply reflexed at the middle.
        3   Stems to 5 mm thick toward base, erect; basal leaves to 4.5 cm long and 7 cm broad; plant hirsute to nearly glabrous; [*R. recurvatus* var. *nelsonii* DC., the type from Unalaska; *R. nelsonii* (DC.) Gray; Aleutian Is.–sw Alaska–?B.C. (collection in CAN, detd. Benson, from Bradfield Inlet, ca. 56°N, but Benson 1948, gives the range only as Aleutian Is.–Alaska; reports of *R. nelsonii* from Vancouver Is. and Queen Charlotte Is., B.C., by John Macoun 1883, were later (1888) referred by him to other entities); MAPS: Hultén 1968*b*:484; Benson 1962: fig. 9-5, p. 295] . . . . var. *nelsonii* (DC.) Benson
        3   Stems more slender.
            4   Basal leaves to 3 cm long and 6 cm broad; stems erect; plant soft-pubescent to nearly glabrous; [ssp. *insularis* Hult.; *R. nelsonii* ssp. *insul.* Hult.; Aleutian Is., s Alaska (type from Yes Bay), s Yukon, B.C. (s to the Tsitsutl Mts. at ca. 54°N), and Alta. (s to Mt Robson, w of Jasper); MAPS: Benson 1962: fig. 9-5, p. 295; combine the maps by Hultén 1968*b*:483 and 484 (ssp. *insul.*)] . . . . var. *brevistylis* Greene
            4   Basal leaves to 3.5 cm long and 4.5 cm broad; stems somewhat decumbent-based; plant hirsute; [var. *robustus* Gray; *R. californicus sensu* John Macoun 1883, not Benth.; B.C. (N to Queen Charlotte Is. according to Benson 1948, but only s Vancouver Is. indicated on the MAP by Benson 1962: fig. 9-4, p. 294] . . . . var. *occidentalis*

R. orthorhynchus Hook.
/T/W/ (Hs) Moist ground and streambanks to alpine meadows and slopes (ranges of Canadian taxa outlined below), s to Calif., Utah, and Wyo. MAP and synonymy: *see* below.
1 Stems and sepals glabrous; leaf-segments relatively broad; petals yellow; [*R. alaskanus* Standl.; s Alaska Panhandle (Hultén 1944: map 601, p. 794; type from Yes Bay) and NW B.C. (Bradfield Inlet, ca. 56°N; Graham Is., Queen Charlotte Is.; MAP: Hultén 1968b:483]. . . . . .var. *alaschensis* Benson
1 Stems and sepals sparsely to copiously hirsute; segments of stem-leaves linear; [B.C.].
  2 Petals uniformly yellow, usually less than twice as long as broad; achene-beaks usually less than 3.5 mm long; [*R. platyphyllus* (Gray) Piper; s ?Alaska (*see* Benson 1948) and B.C. (Nelson; Trail; ?Vancouver Is., ?Queen Charlotte Is.)] . . . .
  . . . . .var. *platyphyllus* Gray
  2 Petals yellow but tinged with red or purple, usually over twice as long as broad; achene-beaks to 4 mm long; [B.C.: Vancouver Is.; Port John, King Is.; Somas Falls; Burrard Inlet; 4-Mile House] . . . . .var. *orthorhynchus*

R. pallasii Schlecht.
/aS/X/EA/ (Hsr (HH)) Wet brackish meadows and shallow water along or near the coasts of Alaska–Yukon–Dist. Mackenzie (type from Alaska), E-cent. Dist. Keewatin, NE Man. (Churchill), N Ont. (James Bay–Hudson Bay between ca. 54°22′N and 56°N), Que. (Hudson Strait s to Fort George, E James Bay, 53°50′N), southernmost Baffin Is., and Labrador (s to ca. 55°N); Spitsbergen; NE Europe; N Asia. MAPS: Hultén 1968b:472; Porsild 1957: map 164, p. 181.

R. pedatifidus Sm.
/AST/X/GEA/ (Hs) Moist meadows and turfy tundra at low elevations to alpine meadows and slopes, the aggregate species from the coasts of Alaska–Yukon–Dist. Mackenzie–Dist. Keewatin to N Ellesmere Is. at ca. 80°N and northernmost Ungava–Labrador, s in the West through B.C.–Alta.–SW Sask. to Ariz. and N.Mex., farther eastwards s to L. Athabasca, NE Man. (Churchill), northernmost Ont. (Hudson Bay coast near the Man. boundary and at Cape Henrietta Maria), Que. (s to E James Bay, the Knob Lake dist. at ca. 55°N, and the Shickshock Mts. of the Gaspé Pen.), and N Nfld.; W Greenland between ca. 66° and 79°N, E Greenland between ca. 68° and 75°N; Spitsbergen; Eurasia. MAPS and synonymy (together with a distinguishing key to the scarcely separable *R. eastwoodianus* Benson of Alaska–Yukon): *see* below.
1 Basal leaves uncleft (merely crenate to shallowly lobed and toothed), to 6 cm long and nearly as broad, cordate-based, pilose; petals to 1.5 cm long, their basal nectary-scales conspicuously ciliate toward summit with hairs to 1 mm long (the surrounding petal-surface often with similar hairs); achenes finely canescent; [*R. cardiophyllus* Hook., the type "From Canada to lat. 55°"; *R. affinis* var. *card.* (Hook.) Gray; B.C. (N to near Cassiar at ca. 58°30′N), Alta. (L. Athabasca), and SW Sask. (Cypress Hills)] . . . .*R. pedatifidus* var. *cardiophyllus* (Hook.) Britt.
1 Basal leaves pedately divided into 5–7 linear divisions (some of which are themselves usually lobed), to about 3.5 cm long and 4 cm broad, cordate in outline, pilose to glabrous; petals to 1 cm long, their basal nectary-scales glabrous.
  2 Margins of nectary-scales not prolonged . . . .*R. pedatifidus*
    3 Leaves to 2.5 cm broad, finely twice or more dissected into narrowly linear segments at most 2.5 mm broad; stem slender and delicate, to 2 dm tall; achenes usually finely canescent; [the MAP by Benson 1962: fig. 2-11, p. 34, indicates a station at Nome, Alaska; also reported from Axel Heiberg Is. by Boivin 1967a] . . . . .var. *pedatifidus*
    3 Leaves to 3(4) cm broad, usually divided into 5–7 linear segments to 4 mm broad (some of these again lobed); stem more robust, to 4 dm tall; achenes glabrous; [*R. affinis* R. Br. and its var. *leiocarpa* Trautv.; *R. apetalus* Farr. (*R. ped.* var. *card.* f. *apet.* (Farr) Boivin); *R. arcticus* Rich.; *R. auricomus* var. *glabratus* Lynge; *R. verticillatus* Eastw.; *R. vicinalis* Greene; transcontinental;

MAPS: Porsild 1957: map 171, p. 182; Benson 1962: fig. 2-11 (var. *affinis*), p. 34;
Hultén 1968*b*:480 (ssp. *affinis*)] . . . . var. *leiocarpus* (Trautv.) Fern.
2   Margins of nectary-scales prolonged into 2 flaps attached most of their length to
the petal-blade, each flap 4 or 5 mm long; achenes glabrous; plant glabrous or
the stem and leaves with a few long hairs; [Alaska (type from Skagway) and the
Yukon (Gold Run Creek)] . . . . [*R. eastwoodianus* Benson]

R. pensylvanicus L. f.   Bristly Crowfoot
/ sT /X/   (T)   Moist meadows and wet ground from B.C. (N to Kamloops; CAN) to SW Dist.
Mackenzie (reported from a pasture on the Experimental Farm at Fort Simpson, ca. 62°N, by
W.J. Cody, Can. Field-Nat. 75(2):62. 1961, where probably introd.; reported by Hultén 1944,
as introd. in Alaska N to Fairbanks), Alta. (N to Pine Lake at 59°34'N), Sask. (N to the Methy R.
at ca. 56°30'N; CAN, detd. Benson), Man. (N to York Factory, Hudson Bay, ca. 57°N), Ont. (N
to Moosonee, S James Bay, 51°16'N), Que. (N to E James Bay at 52°16'N, L. St. John, the
Côte-Nord, Anticosti Is., and Gaspé Pen.), S Labrador (Hamilton R. basin), Nfld., N.B., P.E.I.,
and N.S., S to Wash., Ariz., N.Mex., Nebr., Ohio, Pa., and Del.; (reports from Burma and China
by Benson 1948, may refer to some other species). [*R. ?canadensis* Jacq.; *R. hispidus sensu*
John Macoun 1890, not Michx., as to the Donald and Kamloops, B.C., plant (relevant collections in CAN) and perhaps his other B.C. and Alta. citations]. MAPS: Hultén 1968*b*:480; Benson
1962: fig. 2-3, p. 25.

R. pygmaeus Wahl.   Dwarf Buttercup
/ AST /X/ GEA /   (Hs)   Moist places, streambanks, and alpine meadows, the aggregate species from the coasts of Alaska–Yukon–Dist. Mackenzie–Dist. Keewatin to Ellesmere Is. at ca.
79°N and northernmost Ungava–Labrador, S in the West through B.C. and the mts. of SW
Alta. to Mont., Wyo., and Colo., farther eastwards S to S Dist. Keewatin, Coats Is., and Que. (S
to E Hudson Bay at ca. 55°20'N; isolated in the Shickshock Mts. of the Gaspé Pen.); W Greenland N to ca. 80°N, E Greenland N to ca. 77°N; Iceland; Spitsbergen; N Eurasia. MAPS and synonymy: *see* below.
1   Fruiting-heads usually less than 5 mm long; basal leaves deeply 3-lobed, the middle
lobe commonly entire, the lateral lobes themselves 2–3-lobed; [transcontinental;
MAPS (aggregate species): Hultén 1968*b*:478; Porsild 1957: map 172, p. 182; W.J.
Cody, Nat. can. (Que.) 98(2): fig. 2, p. 146. 1971] . . . . var. *pygmaeus*
1   Fruiting-heads at least 5 mm long; basal leaves more deeply divided or compound,
the divisions sometimes stalked, the middle division or segment again usually
3-lobed, the lateral ones 2–4-lobed; [var. *petiolulatus* Fern.; reported by Fernald *in*
Gray 1950, from NE Labrador and E Que. (Mt. Albert, Gaspé Pen.); type from
W Greenland] . . . . var. *langeanus* Nathorst

R. recurvatus Poir.
/ T / EE /   (Hs)   Damp or swampy ground and rich woods from Ont. (N to New Liskeard,
47°31'N; reports from Man. require confirmation) to Que. (N to the S Gaspé Pen.; GH; the report from L. Mistassini by John Macoun 1886, as well as early reports from Labrador, may refer to *R. macounii*), Nfld., N.B., P.E.I., and N.S., S to E Tex., Miss., and Fla.
   Var. *adpressipilis* Weatherby (stems appressed-short-pubescent rather than villous-hirsute)
is reported from SW Que. by Boivin (1966*b*).

R. repens L.   Creeping Buttercup.   Bassinet
Eurasian; a common weed of wet to dry open soil in N. America; (ranges of Canadian taxa outlined below).
1   Flowers "double", the petals more than 10; [a garden-escape reported from Craig,
Alaska, by Benson 1948] . . . . var. *pleniflorus* Fern.
1   Flowers normal, the petals usually 5 (but varying to as many as 10).
2   Trailing branches wanting; stem and petioles essentially glabrous; [E Que.
(Temiscouata Co. and the Gaspé Pen.), Nfld., N.B. (St. Andrews, Charlotte Co.),
and N.S. (Margaree, Inverness Co., Cape Breton Is.)] . . . . var. *erectus* DC.

2 Trailing branches or stolons present.
  3 Stem and petioles essentially glabrous; [s Alaska to s B.C.; Ont. to SE
    Labrador (Cartwright, 53°42′N), Nfld., and N.S.] . . . . var. *glabratus* DC.
  3 Stem and petioles distinctly hirsute.
    4 Pubescence spreading; [Que. to SE Labrador (N to Square Island Harbour,
      ca. 52°45′N), Nfld., and N.S.] . . . . var. *villosus* Lamotte
    4 Pubescence appressed-ascending; [transcontinental, but not known from
      Sask. nor definitely from Man.; MAP: Hultén 1968*b*:481] . . . . var. *repens*

R. reptans L.   Creeping Spearwort
/aST/X/GEA/   (Hsr (HH))   Damp sandy, gravelly, or muddy shores and shallow water, the
aggregate species from the Aleutian Is. and N Alaska–Yukon–w Dist. Mackenzie to Great Bear
L., N Dist. Keewatin, Ont. (N to the Severn R. at ca. 55°50′N), Que. (N to the Larch R. at ca.
56°45′N, L. St. John, the Côte-Nord, Anticosti Is., and Gaspé Pen.), Labrador (N to Saglek,
ca. 58°20′N), Nfld., N.B., and N.S. (not known from P.E.I.), s to Calif., Colo., Minn., and Mass.;
w Greenland N to ca. 71°N, E Greenland N to ca. 66°N; Iceland; N Eurasia. MAPS and synonymy: *see* below.
1 Leaves linear and essentially bladeless or with linear-lanceolate blades; [*R. flammula*
  vars. *reptans* (L.) Mey., *filiformis* (Michx.) DC. (*R. fil.* Michx.), and *intermedia* Hook. in
  part; range of the species; MAPS: Hultén 1958: map 148, p. 167, and 1968*b*:474;
  Meusel, Jaeger, and Weinert 1965:167] . . . . var. *reptans*
1 Leaves with well-developed lanceolate to oval blades to about 6 mm broad; [*R.
  filiformis* var. *ovalis* Bigel.; *R. flammula* vars. *ovalis* (Bigel.) Benson, *erectus* Vict. &
  Rousseau, *intermedia* Hook. in part, and *?unalaschensis* (Bess.) Ledeb. (× *R. ?unal.*
  Bess.; *see* under *R. flammula*); sw Dist. Mackenzie–B.C.–Alta. to Sask. (N to
  Saskatoon), Man. (N to Oxford L. on the Hayes R., ca. 55°N), Ont. (N to Hearst,
  49°42′N, and the Attawapiskat R. at 52°06′N), Que. (N to the Côte-Nord, Anticosti
  Is., and the Gaspé Pen.), Nfld., and N.S.; MAP: on the above-noted 1958 map
  (somewhat incomplete) by Hultén] . . . . var. *ovalis* (Bigel.) T. & G.

R. rhomboideus Goldie   Prairie-Buttercup or -Crowfoot
/T/(X)/   (Hs)   Prairies, sandy fields, rock outcrops, and dry open woods from B.C. (N to Hudson Hope, ca. 56°N; CAN), southernmost w Dist. Mackenzie (near Fort Smith, ca. 60°N; W.J.
Cody, Can. Field-Nat. 70(3):113. 1956), and northernmost Alta. (Wood Buffalo National Park
at 59°34′N) to Sask. (reported N to Carlton House, about 35 mi sw of Prince Albert, by John
Macoun 1883), Man. (N to Norway House, off the NE end of L. Winnipeg), Ont. (N to the Kenora dist. and the type locality near L. Simcoe in Ontario Co.), and sw ?Que. (the report of an
early collection by Holmes near Montreal by John Macoun 1883, requires confirmation), s to
Nebr., Ill., and Mass. [*R. brevicaulis* Hook.; *R. ovalis* of Canadian reports, not Raf.].

R. sabinei R. Br.
/Aa/X/G/   (Hs)   Moist gravelly, clayey, or turfy places along the coast from the coasts of
Alaska, Dist. Mackenzie, and Dist. Keewatin (not known from the Yukon) to Melville Is. (type
locality) and northernmost Ellesmere Is.; N and w Greenland s to ca. 76°N. MAPS: Hultén
1968*b*:478 (*R. pygmaeus* ssp. *sab.*); Porsild 1957: map 173, p. 182; Savile 1961: map G, p. 929;
Tomachev 1932: fig. 5 (very incomplete for N. America and erroneously indicating the occurrence in N Asia), p. 51.
  Early reports from Labrador probably refer largely to *R. pygmaeus.* A collection from N Que.
by F. Johansen (Can. Field-Nat. 48(8):129. 1934; Eric Cove, near Wolstenholme, Hudson
Strait) appears to Polunin (1940) to portray characters intermediate between those of *R. nivalis* and *R. pygmaeus,* possibly resulting from hybridization between them.

R. sardous Crantz
Eurasian; introd. along roadsides and in waste places of N. America, as in Ont. (Kincardine,
Bruce Co.) and N.B. (wharf-ballast at St. John, where taken by Hay in 1881 and 1884; CAN;
NBM). [*R. hirsutus* Curtis; *R. parvulus* L.; *R. muricatus sensu* John Macoun 1886, not L., the
relevant collection being the above-noted N.B. one].

R. sceleratus L.   Cursed Crowfoot
/ST/X/EA/   (T (Hel))   Brackish or fresh pools and wet ground (ranges of Canadian taxa outlined below), S to Calif., N.Mex., La., and Fla.; Eurasia. MAP and synonymy: *see* below.
1   Lower leaves with relatively long fan-shaped divisions much narrowed at base and
    cleft into numerous oblong to lanceolate lobes; median leaves with numerous linear
    to lanceolate lobes; [not *R. multifidus* Pursh, which is *R. flabellaris* Raf.; cent.
    Alaska–S Yukon–NW Dist. Mackenzie (N to Aklavik, 68°13'N) and B.C.–Alta. to Great
    Bear L., Great Slave L., Sask. (N to Prince Albert), Man. (N to Churchill), Ont. (N to
    Fort Severn, Hudson Bay, ca. 56°N), Que. (N to E James Bay at 53°44'N, Charlevoix
    Co., and Magdalen Is.), and NE N.B. (Dalhousie); MAP: Hultén 1968*b*:479] . . . .
    . . . . var. *multifidus* Nutt.
1   Principal leaf-blades 3–5-parted into cuneate divisions with oblong or roundish lobes
    or crenate teeth; upper leaves obovate, entire or only slightly toothed . . . . var. *sceleratus*
    2   Aquatic, the floating leaves with petioles to over 5 dm long; [Man. (Whitewater L.
        N of Turtle Mt.; Whiteshell Forest Reserve E of Winnipeg); probably throughout
        the range of f. *sceleratus*] . . . . f. *natans* Glück
    2   Terrestrial, the relatively short-petioled leaves emersed; [essentially the range of
        var. *multifidus* but also known from N.S. (Halifax Co. and Cape Breton Is.; E.C.
        Smith and W.B. Schofield, Rhodora 54(645):226. 1952) and reported from P.E.I.
        by Herbert Groh, Sci. Agric. 7: 394. 1927; reports from Labrador may refer to the
        Côte-Nord, E Que.] . . . . f. *sceleratus*

R. septentrionalis Poir.
/sT/EE/   (Hsr)   Damp or swampy ground from S Man. (N to Gimli, about 45 mi N of Winnipeg) to Ont. (N to Moose Factory, S of James Bay at ca. 51°15'N), Que. (N to SE James Bay at
ca. 52°30'N and the Gaspé Pen.; the report from Anticosti Is. by John Macoun 1890, is based
upon *R. macounii*, the relevant collection in CAN), N.B., and P.E.I. (CAN; not known from
N.S.), S to Tex., Ky., and Va. [*R. octopetalus* Greene; *R. repens* var. *nitidus* (Muhl.) Chapm.,
not *R. nitidus* Walt.]. MAP: Benson 1962: fig. 2-14, p. 38.
    Var. *caricetorum* (Greene) Fern. (*R. car.* Greene; pubescence of the stem more or less re-
flexed and usually very dense rather than spreading to erect-appressed and sometimes nearly
lacking) is reported from S Ont. by Montgomery (1945; Cambridge (Galt), Waterloo Co.).

R. sulphureus Soland.
/ASs/X/GEA/   (Hs)   Moist turfy or gravelly tundra from the Aleutian Is. and coasts of
Alaska and Dist. Mackenzie (not known from the Yukon) nearly throughout the Canadian Arctic Archipelago to northernmost Ellesmere Is., S to S Alaska, Dist. Keewatin, Southampton Is.,
Coats Is., N Que. (S to Ungava Bay), and northernmost Labrador; W and E Greenland N of the
Arctic Circle; Spitsbergen; N Eurasia. [*R. nivalis* var. *sul.* (Sol.) Wahl.]. MAPS: Hultén
1968*b*:476; Porsild 1957: map 170, p. 182, and 1955: fig. 6, p. 39; *Atlas of Canada* 1957: map
1, sheet 38.
    Var. *intercedens* Hult. (the basal leaves deeply cleft into 3 distinct coarsely toothed lobes
rather than merely coarsely toothed but uncleft) is known from the Aleutian Is. MAP: Hultén
1968*b*:477.

R. testiculatus Crantz
Eurasian; spreading rapidly throughout the NW U.S.A. according to Hitchcock et al. (1964)
and reported from Kamloops, B.C., by Boivin (1966*b*). [*Ceratocephalus* Roth].

R. uncinatus Don
/sT/W/   (Hs)   Moist soil (ranges of Canadian taxa outlined below), S to Calif. and N.Mex.
MAP and synonymy: *see* below.
1   Achenes glabrous; plant glabrous to sparingly hirsute; [*R. douglasii* Howell; *R.
    tenellus* Nutt., not Viviani; S ?Alaska (Benson 1948, but no collections cited), SW Dist.
    Mackenzie (near Fort Smith, ca. 60°N; W.J. Cody, Can. Field-Nat. 70(3):114. 1956),
    B.C. (N to Queen Charlotte Is.), and N Alta. (Wood Buffalo National Park at 58°42'N)] . . . .
    . . . . var. *uncinatus*

1   Achenes minutely hispid; plant usually more or less densely hirsute; [*R. bongardii* Greene; *R. greenei* Howell; *R. occidentalis* vars. *lyallii* Gray and *parviflorus* Torr.; *R. lyallii* (Gray) Rydb.; Aleutian Is. (Attu), s Alaska (*see* Hultén 1944: map 588, p. 792; *R. bong.*), B.C., and w Alta. (20 mi NW of Edson; Crowsnest Pass; Waterton Lakes); MAP *(R. bong.)*: Hultén 1968*b*:482] . . . . .var. *parviflorus* (Torr.) Benson

R. verecundus Robins.
/T/W/   (Hs)   Wet slopes from near sea level to alpine meadows from s ?Alaska (Benson 1948; *see* Hultén 1968*a* and 1944: map 610, p. 794) through B.C. and the mts. of sw Alta. (N to Sawback Mt., near Banff; Benson 1948) to Wash., Idaho, and Mont.

THALICTRUM L.   [2548]   Meadow-rue.   Pigamon

(Ref.: Bernard Boivin 1944, and Can. Field-Nat. 62(6):167–70. 1948)
1   Achenes very strongly flattened, semi-obovate and very asymmetrical (obliquely ''half-moon''-shaped, one of the margins straight), on stipes to 3 mm long; flowers perfect, with 5 perianth-segments; stigmas included; anthers at most 1 mm long, their filaments clavate; pedicels all subtended by a small but compound leaf-like bract; leaflets mostly 3-lobed, the lobes commonly coarsely crenate; stem simple, or branched above; (Alaska–B.C. to Ont.) . . . .*T. sparsiflorum*
1   Achenes more or less inflated, more symmetrical, sessile or on stipes at most about 1.5 mm long; flowers usually unisexual at least in part, rarely with more than 4 perianth-segments; stigmas exserted beyond the perianth-segments; anthers commonly longer; most or all of the pedicels bractless or subtended by minute simple bracts.
  2   Inflorescence a simple raceme terminating the unbranched stem, the latter slender and scapose (rarely with a solitary leaf), commonly less than 2.5 dm tall; flowers perfect, with 5 perianth-segments; anthers to 2.3 mm long; achenes less than 4 mm long, subsessile; leaflets coriaceous, shining, fan-shaped, 3–5-lobed, mostly less than 1 cm long; (B.C.; Que. to Labrador and Nfld.) . . . .*T. alpinum*
  2   Inflorescence a panicle or corymb (if sometimes raceme-like, the pedicels mostly arising 2 or 3 together); stem often branched.
    3   Leaflets entire or with 3 (sometimes 5) entire lobes; anthers less than 3 mm long, their filaments white or yellowish; stem from a short thick crown.
      4   Leaflets bearing sessile or short-stalked glands beneath, coriaceous and with more or less revolute margins; anthers to 2.8 mm long, their filaments to 5.5 mm long, soon drooping, capillary or only slightly widened toward the anther, this to about 3 mm long; achene-stipes to 0.4 mm long; (s Ont.) . . . .*T. revolutum*
      4   Leaflets glabrous or pubescent beneath with flexuous hairs.
        5   Anthers at least 1.5 mm long, soon drooping and becoming entangled; fruiting head subhemispherical, the lowermost achenes barely deflexed, their stipes at most 0.3 mm long; inflorescence narrowly pyramidal, acute at summit; achenes commonly brownish-hairy; (B.C. to w James Bay) . . . .*T. dasycarpum*
        5   Anthers less than 1.5 mm long, their filaments rigid and conspicuously broadened toward summit; fruiting head subglobose, the lowermost achenes reflexed, their stipes to 1 mm long; inflorescence commonly broader, rounded at summit; achenes glabrous or pubescent; (w Ont. to Labrador, Nfld., and N.S.) . . . .*T. pubescens*
    3   Leaflets with up to 5 (sometimes 7) crenate lobes; anthers to 4 mm long, their filaments usually more or less purplish, sometimes yellowish, filiform and commonly entangling in age.
      6   Stem from a short thick crown; leaves below inflorescence 1 or none; leaf subtending lowest flowering branch on a petiole to about 8 cm long (many times longer than the green and herbaceous basal stipular dilation);

flowers vernal, appearing with the leaves, the fruits dropping in late spring or early summer; body of achene about 4 mm long, the stipe to 0.4 mm long; stigmas at most 2.5 mm long; anther-filaments less than 6 mm long; (Ont. and Que.) . . . . *T. dioicum*

6 Stem from a cord-like subhorizontal rhizome; leaves below the inflorescence 1 or more; leaf subtending the lowest flowering branch sessile or with a short petiole at most about 3 cm long; stipules firm, brownish; flowers mostly appearing in summer after the leaves, forming fruit in summer or autumn.

   7 Achenes distinctly compressed, thin-walled and with relatively narrow ribs separated by shallow rounded grooves, on stipes to 1.5 mm long, the body to about 1 cm long, fusiform or lanceolate; stigmas to over 4 mm long; anther-filaments to about 8 mm long; leaflets glabrous or minutely glandular-puberulent beneath; (B.C. to Sask.) . . . . . . *T. occidentale*

   7 Achenes turgid and scarcely compressed, their stipes at most 0.3 mm long; anther-filaments commonly 4 or 5 mm long; leaflets glabrous.

      8 Body of achene to about 6 mm long; stigmas to about 5 mm long; fruiting pedicels rather stiff, to about 2 cm long; leaflets with a relatively obscure network of veins; (Ont. to N.S.) . . . . *T. confine*

      8 Body of achene rarely over 4 mm long; stigmas commonly not over 2 mm long; fruiting pedicels relatively slender, commonly less than 1 cm long; leaflets generally firmer, strongly net-veined beneath; (B.C. to Que.) . . . . *T. venulosum*

T. alpinum L.   Alpine Meadow-Rue
/aST/D/GEA/ (Hr) Peaty or boggy ground, wet calcareous gravels and ledges, and alpine meadows: N Alaska, S-cent. Yukon, and W-cent. Dist. Mackenzie (N to Norman Wells, ca. 65°20′N) through the mts. of B.C. to Calif. and N.Mex.; Que. (S Ungava Bay watershed; Côte-Nord; Anticosti Is.; Shickshock Mts. and river-ledges of the Gaspé Pen.), N Labrador (S to ca. 57°N), and Nfld.; W Greenland N to ca. 71°N, E Greenland N to 73°38′N; Iceland; Eurasia. [Incl. vars. *gaspense, microspermum, nesioticum,* and *pudicum* Greene]. MAPS: Hultén 1958: map 220, p. 239 (noting 3 earlier total-area maps); Meusel, Jaeger, and Weinert 1965:157.

T. confine Fern.
/ST/EE/ (Hs) Rocky or gravelly calcareous shores, talus, and alluvium from Ont. (N to the Severn R. at ca. 54°30′N; type, as first collection cited, from Ottawa) to Que. (N to the E James Bay watershed at ca. 52°30′N, the Côte-Nord, Anticosti Is., and Gaspé Pen.), N.B. (York, Carleton, and Restigouche counties), P.E.I. (Campbellton, Prince Co.; ACAD), and N.S. (E.C. Smith and J.S. Erskine, Rhodora 56(671):248. 1954; Grand Lake, Halifax Co.), S to NE Minn., N Mich., N.Y., and Vt. [*T. venulosum* var. *con.* (Fern.) Boivin; *T. purpurascens* var. *monoicum* DC.; *T. dioicum* as to N.B. reports by John Macoun 1883, and Fowler 1885, not L. (relevant collections in CAN and NBM; reports from the Gaspé Pen., E Que., by Macoun and from Anticosti Is., E Que., by Verrill (1865), Schmidt (1904), and B. Billings (Ann. Bot. Soc. Can. 1:58. 1861) may also refer here); *T. occidentale* as to N.B. reports by C.H. Bissell (Rhodora 2(23):233. 1900; also the Man. report) and J.M. Macoun (1901), not Gray (relevant collections in CAN, GH, and NBM)].

T. dasycarpum Fisch. & Lall.   Purple Meadow-Rue
/sT/(X)/ (Hs) Meadows, swampy ground, and damp thickets, the aggregate species from S B.C. (Creston and Kootenay L.; CAN) to Alta. (N to Fort Saskatchewan; CAN), Sask. (N to Prince Albert), Man. (N to Hill L., about 25 mi N of L. Winnipeg), Ont. (N to the Nipigon R. N of L. Superior and the W James Bay watershed at ca. 52°N), and W-cent. Que. (Boivin 1966b), S to Wash., Ariz., N.Mex., Tex., La., and Ohio.
1 Leaflets more or less finely pubescent beneath; anthers to 2.5 mm long, their filaments to about 4 mm long; mature achenes ovoid; [*T. purpurascens* var. *das.* (F. & L.) Trel.; range of the species] . . . . var. *dasycarpum*

1　Leaflets glabrous; anthers to 3.2 mm long, their filaments to 7 mm long; mature
　achenes lanceolate; [*T. hypoglaucum* Rydb.; B.C.–Alta.] . . . .
　. . . . . var. *hypoglaucum* (Rydb.) Boivin

T. dioicum L.　Early Meadow-Rue, Quicksilver-weed
/T/EE/　(Hs)　Rich rocky woods, ravines, and alluvium from Minn. to Ont. (N to Matheson,
48°32′N; CAN; the report from Renison, s of James Bay at ca. 51°N, by Hustich 1955, requires confirmation; reports from Sask. and Man. are largely based upon *T. venulosum*), Que.,
(N to the Montreal dist.), and ?St-Pierre and Miquelon (Rouleau 1956), s to N.Dak., Mo., Ala.,
and Ga. [Incl. vars. *adiantinum, huronense,* and *langfordii* Greene].

T. occidentale Gray　Western Meadow-rue
/T/W/　(Hs)　Meadows, thickets, and swamps from SE Alaska (*see* Hultén 1944: map 613, p.
795), s Yukon (CAN), SW Dist. Mackenzie, and B.C.–Alta. to Sask. (Candle Lake, 53°50′N;
CAN), s to Utah, Wyo., and Colo. [Incl. vars. *macounii* Boivin and *palouense* St. John; *T. breitungii* Boivin; *T. heterophyllum* Nutt.; *T. propinquum* Greene; *T. fendleri sensu* J.M. Macoun
1894, not Engelm.]. MAP: Porsild 1966: map 67, p. 75.

　The European *T. minus* L. is reported as a garden-escape in s Ont. by Gaiser and Moore
(1966; Lambton Co.) and there is a collection in OAC from a roadside at Grand Bend, Huron
Co., s Ont. Its ssp. *kemense* (Fries) Hult. (*T. kemense* Fries; *T. hultenii* Boivin) is native in the
E Aleutian Is. (*see* Hultén 1944: map 612, p. 795) and Alaska (MAP: Hultén 1968b:488). Hultén
separates it from *T. occidentale* on the basis of its perfect rather than unisexual flowers, its
sessile rather than short-stipitate achenes, and its slightly dilated rather than filiform anther-
filaments.

T. pubescens Pursh
/T/EE/　(Hs)　Meadows, thickets, and swamps, the aggregate species from Ont. (N to
Hearst, 49°42′N) to Que. (N to Swampy L. at 55°15′N, the Côte-Nord, Anticosti Is., and Gaspé
Pen.), s Labrador (N to the Hamilton R. basin), Nfld., N.B., P.E.I., and N.S., s to Tenn. and Ga.
1　Inflorescence paniculate; anthers usually about 1 mm long, their filaments to about 5
　mm long; stigmas mostly less than 2 mm long; [*T. corynellum* DC.; *T. glaucodeum*
　Greene; *T. polygamum* Muhl.; *T. tortuosum* Greene, not Jord.; *T. cornuti* and *T.*
　purpurascens of Canadian reports in part, not L.; essentially the range of the
　species but not known from Labrador] . . . . var. *pubescens*
1　Inflorescence corymbose; anthers mostly somewhat longer, their filaments to 8 mm
　long; stigmas to 3.5 mm long; [*T. polygamum* var. *heb.* Fern.; *T. labradoricum,*
　T. leucocrinum, T. terrae-novae, and *T. zibellinum* Greene; range of the species] . . . .
　. . . . . var. *hebecarpum* (Fern.) Boivin

T. revolutum DC.　Skunk- or Wax-leaved Meadow-Rue
/t/EE/　(Hs)　Dry open woods, thickets, prairies, and meadows from s Ont. (Essex, Lambton, Kent, Norfolk, Haldimand, Welland, Middlesex, and Wellington counties) to Mass., s to
Mo., Ala., and N Fla. [*T. purpurascens* var. *ceriferum* Aust.].

T. sparsiflorum Turcz.
/ST/WW/A/　(Hs)　Damp thickets and streambanks from N-cent. Alaska–Yukon, SW Dist.
Mackenzie (CAN), and B.C.–Alta. to Sask. (N to Windrum L. at ca. 56°N; CAN), Man. (N to
York Factory, Hudson Bay, 57°N), and Ont. (Albany, w James Bay, 52°11′N), s to s Calif.,
Utah, and Colo.; Asia. [Incl. var. *viridius* Boivin]. MAP: Hultén 1968b:487.

　Our plant may be separated from the Asiatic one as var. *richardsonii* (Gray) Boivin (*T. rich.*
Gray; *T. ?clavatum sensu* Hooker 1829, not DC.; anther-filaments to 4.5 rather than 6 mm
long; mature achenes to 10 mm long and 2.5(3) mm broad rather than to about 8 mm long
and 2 mm broad, broadly rounded rather than tapering to apex, the stipe to 3 rather than 1.5
mm long).

T. venulosum Trel.

/ST/X/ (Hs) Open woods, thickets, prairies, and shores from the Yukon (Boivin 1966*b*) to Great Bear L., Great Slave L., N Alta. (Wood Buffalo National Park), Sask. (N to Prince Albert), Man. (N to York Factory, Hudson Bay, 57°N), Ont. (N to Fort Severn, Hudson Bay, ca. 56°N), and Que. (Renfrew and Labelle counties; ?introd.), s to Oreg., Idaho, Wyo., S.Dak., Minn., and N Wisc. [*T. columbianum* Rydb.; *T. campestre, T. fissum,* and *T. lunellii* Greene; *T. turneri* Boivin].

TRAUTVETTERIA Fisch. & Mey.   [2545]   False Bugbane

T. caroliniensis (Walt.) Vail   Tassel-Rue

/t/D/eA/ (Grh) Moist woods, plains, and streambanks: s B.C. (Vancouver Is.; lower Fraser Valley; Columbia L., sw of Creston) to Calif. and N.Mex.; Mo. to sw Pa. and Fla.; Japan. [*Hydrastis* Walt.; *Cimicifuga (T.; Actaea) palmata* Michx.].

The B.C. plant may be rather arbitrarily distinguished as var. *occidentalis* (Gray) Hitchc. (*T. palmata* f. *occ. Gray; T. grandis* Nutt.; *T. saniculifolia* Greene; the leaves somewhat firmer and the stamens perhaps averaging slightly longer than those of the typical phase).

TROLLIUS L.   [2525]   Globe-flower

1 Petaloid sepals greenish white to cream-colour, widely spreading, at most 9; petals (more or less staminoid) much shorter than the functional stamens; (s B.C. and sw Alta.). . . . .*T. laxus*
1 Petaloid sepals lemon- to golden-yellow, very concave, incurved; petals (more or less staminoid) about equalling the functional stamens.
  2 Petaloid sepals up to 15 in number; stem to 7 dm tall; (introd.) . . . .[*T. europaeus*]
  2 Petaloid sepals at most about 9; stem to 3 or 4 dm tall; (Aleutian Is.) . . . .*T. riederianus*

[T. europaeus L.]
[European; reported as introd. in s N.B. by Boivin (1966*b*; Lakewood, near St. John), where, however, probably not established.]

T. laxus Salisb.

/T/D/ (Hs) Swampy ground and wet slopes to alpine meadows: s B.C. (N to Rogers Pass in the Selkirks) and the mts. of sw Alta. (N to Jasper) to Wash. and Colo.; Mich. to Conn. (formerly to Maine), s to Pa. [*T. americanus* DC.; incl. var. *albiflorus* Gray (*T. alb.* (Gray) Rydb.)]. MAP: the N. American area for the genus *Trollius* in the map by Meusel, Jaeger, and Weinert 1965: 155, is applicable here.

T. riederianus Fisch. & Mey.

/sT/W/A/ (Hs) Moist meadows of the w Aleutian Is. (Kiska Is.; *see* Hultén 1944: map 567, p. 790); Asia. MAP: Hultén 1968*b*:454.

BERBERIDACEAE (Barberry Family)

Herbs or shrubs with alternate or basal, simple to deeply lobed or compound leaves with dilated bases or stipules. Flowers regular, perfect, hypogynous. Sepals 4 or 6, often early deciduous and in some genera petaloid. Petals and stamens as many as or more than the sepals, the petals sometimes reduced to nectaries. Ovary superior. Fruit a berry or capsule.

1 Shrubs with yellow racemose flowers and yellowish bark and wood; sepals and petals each 6, the sepals subtended by 3 scaly bracts . . . . *Berberis*
1 Perennial herbs.
  2 Leaves distributed along the stem.
    3 Flowers several in panicles to about 6 cm long, yellowish green or purplish, about 1 cm broad; petaloid sepals, petals, and stamens each 6 (the short-clawed petals thick and gland-like); ovary soon bursting and exposing the 2 blue drupe-like seeds; leaves sessile, 3-ternate (simulating 3 biternate leaves), the obovate-oblong leaflets 2–5-lobed above the middle; (s Man. to N.S.) . . . .
       . . . . *Caulophyllum*
    3 Flower solitary, white, to about 5 cm broad; sepals 6; petals 6–9; stamens twice as many as the petals; fruit a large yellow pulpy berry to about 5 cm long; leaves an opposite pair below the flower (solitary on sterile plants), very deeply palmately 5–9-lobed into toothed or lobed segments, peltate on long petioles; (Ont. to N.S.) . . . . *Podophyllum*
  2 Leaves all basal.
    4 Flower solitary, white, 2 or 3 cm broad; sepals usually 4; petals and stamens usually 8; fruit a pear-shaped capsule 2 or 3 cm long, the upper part opening like a hinged lid; leaves deeply divided into 2 obliquely semi-ovate lobed segments, their petioles to about 5 dm long and finally much surpassing the naked scape; (s Ont.) . . . . *Jeffersonia*
    4 Flowers in spikes or panicles, small; (s B.C.).
      5 Flowers in a short dense spike; perianth wanting; stamens at least 9; fruit dry and indehiscent, broadly moon-shaped, 1-seeded; leaves 1-ternate, the 3 leaflets sessile, fan-shaped, sinuate-dentate, to over 1.5 dm broad, commonly broader than long; (sw B.C.) . . . . *Achlys*
      5 Flowers in an open panicle; sepals, petals, and stamens each 6; fruit a several-seeded follicle; leaves mostly 2-ternate or pinnate-ternate, the leaflets slender-stalked, ovate to roundish, 3-lobed at apex, cordate at base, to 3 or 4 cm long, seldom broader than long; (?Vancouver Is.) . . . .
       . . . . [*Vancouveria*]

ACHLYS DC.   [2561]

A. triphylla (Sm.) DC.   Vanilla-leaf, Deer-foot
/t/W/   (Grh)   Deep woods and open areas (particularly along streambanks) from sw B.C. (Vancouver Is. and adjacent islands; Bute Inlet; Chilliwack R.; Hope) to nw Calif. [*Leontice* Sm.]. MAP: I. Fukuda, Taxon 16(4): fig. 8, p. 311. 1967.

BERBERIS L.   [2566]   Barberry

1 Leaves simple, deciduous, spatulate to obovate, clustered in the axils of simple or 3-branched spines; berries scarlet to red; (introd.).
  2 Leaves entire; spines usually simple; flowers solitary at the nodes or in clusters of up to 4; berries dryish . . . . *B. thunbergii*
  2 Leaves closely bristle-toothed; spines triple or branched; flowers commonly 10 or more in racemes to about 6 cm long; berries juicy . . . . *B. vulgaris*
1 Leaves pinnately compound, the leaflets prickle- or spine-toothed, coriaceous and evergreen, narrowly to broadly ovate, mostly over 3 cm long; branches unarmed; berries blue-glaucous; (s B.C. and s Alta.).

3   Leaflets commonly more than 9, more or less palmately veined, mostly over 4 cm
    long; bud-scales subcoriaceous, commonly over 2 cm long (up to 4 cm),
    persistent; anther-filaments not 2-toothed at apex; berry to 11 mm long; plant
    strongly rhizomatous; (s B.C.). . . . .*B. nervosa*
3   Leaflets mostly not more than 9 (sometimes 11), pinnately veined; bud-scales
    less than 1 cm long, usually deciduous; anther-filaments 2-toothed at apex; berry
    to 14 mm long; (s B.C. and sw Alta.) . . . . *B. aquifolium*

B. aquifolium Pursh   Oregon-Grape
/T/W/   (N (evergreen))   Woods to sagebrush slopes (ranges of Canadian taxa outlined below), s to Oreg. and Idaho.
1   Leaflets frequently as many as 9, mostly averaging at least twice as long as broad,
    with mostly less than 30 spinulose teeth, usually rather glossy above, glossy to dull
    (but not papillose) beneath; stems stiffly erect to trailing and stoloniferous; [*Mahonia*
    Nutt.; *Odostemon* Rydb.; *M. aquifolium* var. *nutkana* DC.; *B. (O.) nut.* (DC.) Kearney;
    s B.C. (N to Revelstoke and Salmon Arm) and sw Alta. (Waterton Lakes); introd.
    along roadsides and spreading in cemeteries in s Ont. (Toronto; Guelph; Puslinch;
    Owen Sound) and in sw Que. (Montreal)] . . . . .var. *aquifolium*
1   Leaflets mostly not more than 7, averaging less than twice as long as broad, with up
    to 40 or more spinulose teeth, glossy or somewhat dull above, dull and somewhat
    glaucous (with minute papillae) beneath; stems always more or less procumbent and
    long-stoloniferous; [*B. (Odostemon) repens* Lindl.; *B. (O.) brevipes* Greene; *B. nana*
    Greene; B.C. (N to Stuart L. at ca. 54°30′N) and sw Alta. (Waterton Lakes)] . . . .
    . . . . .var. *repens* (Lindl.) Scoggan

B. nervosa Pursh
/t/W/   (N (evergreen))   West of the Cascades, usually in light woods, from sw B.C. (Vancouver Is. and adjacent islands and mainland; CAN; V) to cent. Calif. [*Mahonia* Nutt.; *Odoste-
mon* Rydb.; *B. ?pinnata sensu* Hooker 1829, not Lag.].

B. thunbergii DC.   Japanese Barberry
Asiatic; spread from cult. to pastures and fields in N. America, as in Ont. (N to the Ottawa
dist.), N.B. (Hampton, Kings Co.), P.E.I. (Upton, Queens Co.; ACAD), and N.S. (Roland 1947).
    A hybrid with *B. vulgaris* (× *B. ottawensis* Schneid.) is reported from Ont. by Gillett (1958;
Ottawa, the type locality), where perhaps known only under cultivation.

B. vulgaris L.   Common Barberry.   Épine-vinette
Eurasian; formerly abundantly natzd. in thickets, pastures, and fencerows in N. America but
subjected to an intense programme of eradication because of its role as host to the fungus
causing stem rust of cereals. It is known from s B.C. (Ladner; Okanagan), s Man. (near Brandon and Winnipeg), Ont. (N to Grey, Renfrew, and Carleton counties; *see* s Ont. maps by
Montgomery 1957: fig. 7, p. 10, and Soper and Heimburger 1961:65), Que. (N to Ste-Anne-de-
la-Pocatière, Kamouraska Co.), Nfld., N.B. (Shediac, Westmorland Co.; DAO), P.E.I., and N.S.
    The horticultural f. *atropurpurea* Regel (leaves deep purple rather than green) is reported
from s Ont. by Boivin (1966*b*).

CAULOPHYLLUM Michx.   [2565]   Blue Cohosh

C. thalictroides (L.) Michx.   Papoose-root
/T/EE/eA/   (Grh)   Rich woods from se Man. (N to Selkirk, about 20 mi NE of Winnipeg) to
Ont. (N to the e shore of L. Superior at Batchawana), Que. (N to the sw Gaspé Pen. at Mata-
pédia; *see* Que. map by Doyon and Lavoie 1966: fig. 24, p. 820), N.B. (St. John R. valley in
York and Victoria counties; not known from P.E.I.), and N.S. (Kings, Colchester, Pictou, and
Inverness counties), s to Mo., Tenn., and S.C.; e Asia. [*Leontice* L.; incl. var. *giganteum*
Farw.]. MAP: W.G. Dore, Ontario Naturalist 2(1): map 1, p. 6. 1964.

JEFFERSONIA Bart.   [2559]

J. diphylla (L.) Pers.   Twinleaf
/t/EE/   (Grh)   Rich woods from NE Iowa to Wisc., S Ont. (N to S Lennox-Addington Co. and the N shore of L. Ontario in Prince Edward Co.; *see* S Ont. map by Soper 1962: fig. 10, p. 18), and N.Y., S to Ala. and Md. [*Podophyllum* L.].

PODOPHYLLUM L.   [2558]

P. peltatum L.   May-apple, Mandrake.   Pomme de mai
/T/EE/   (Grh)   Rich woods, thickets, and pastures from Minn. to S Ont. (N to Stormont Co.), SW Que. (N to L. St. Peter in St-Maurice Co.), and N.S. (collections in DAO from Wolfville, Kings Co., and Spryfield, Halifax Co.; not listed by Roland 1947; not known from N.B. or P.E.I.), S to Tex. and Fla. (elsewhere spread from cult.).

[VANCOUVERIA Morr. & Dec.]   [2564]

[V. hexandra (Hook.) Morr. & Dec.]   Inside-out-flower
[Early reports of this species of the w U.S.A. (Wash. to NW Calif.) from Vancouver Is., B.C. (*see* John Macoun 1883:30) probably reflect a misinterpretation of locality in the name *Vancouveria*. The genus actually honours Captain Vancouver. No B.C. collections have been seen except one in Herb. V from a garden in Victoria. The MAP by W.T. Stearn (J. Linn. Soc. Lond., Bot. 51(340): map 1, p. 429. 1938) indicates no Canadian stations. (*Epimedium* Hook.).]

MENISPERMACEAE (Moonseed Family)

MENISPERMUM L.   [2567]   Moonseed

Twining vine with simple, alternate, palmately veined and shallowly lobed, long-petioled, broadly ovate to subrotund leaves peltate near the margin. Flowers small, regular, unisexual, hypogynous, in axillary racemes or panicles, white or whitish. Sepals and petals 4–8. Stamens 12–24. Fruit a subglobose blue-black glaucous drupe to 1 cm long, the terminal stigmatic scar far to one side at maturity (the superior ovary becoming strongly incurved, the stone crescent- or ring-shaped). (SE Man. to S Que.).

M. canadense L.   Yellow Parilla.   Raisin de couleuvre
/T/EE/   (Ch (vine))   Rich thickets and streambanks from SE Man. (N to East Selkirk, about 20 mi NE of Winnipeg) to Ont. (N to the Ottawa dist.), SW Que. (N to L. St. Peter in St-Maurice Co.; not known from the Maritime Provinces; a puzzling report from Nfld. by Waghorne 1898), and W New Eng., S to Okla., Ark., Ala., and Ga.

MAGNOLIACEAE (Magnolia Family)

Trees with alternate, entire or lobed leaves. Flowers large, regular, perfect, hypogynous, the calyx and corolla scarcely differentiated. Sepals 3. Petals 6. Stamens and pistils each numerous. Ovary superior.

1   Leaves squarish in outline, mostly 4-lobed, retuse at the very broad summit, to about 1.5 dm long and broad; petals greenish yellow, blotched with orange inside at base, 4 or 5 cm long; fruit consisting of narrow elongate leathery indehiscent 1–2-seeded samaras to 4 cm long in a cone-like head; tree to about 40 m tall; (s Ont.) . . . *Liriodendron*
1   Leaves entire or with 2 small basal lobes, elliptic to broadly oblong, abruptly acuminate, acute to broadly rounded at base, minutely pubescent beneath, to about 2 dm long; petals glaucous-green, tinged with yellow, to about 8 cm long; fruit consisting of leathery dehiscent follicles in a cone-like head, the seeds persistent on slender threads; slender tree to about 30 m tall; (s Ont.) . . . . *Magnolia*

LIRIODENDRON L.   [2654]   Tulip-tree

L. tulipifera L.   Tulip-Poplar
/t/EE/   (Mg)   Rich soil from E Wisc. to s Mich., s Ont. (N to Huron, Wentworth, and Welland counties; *see* s Ont. maps and discussion by Fox and Soper 1952: fig. 2, p. 69, and P.F. Maycock, Can. J. Bot. 41(3): fig. 12, p. 426. 1963), and Vt., s to La. and Fla. MAPS: Hosie 1969:212; Fowells 1965:256; Gleason and Cronquist 1964: fig. 14.7, p. 161; *Atlas of Canada* 1957: map 12, sheet 38; Canada Department of Northern Affairs and Natural Resources 1956: 194; Preston 1961:234; Meusel 1943: fig. 41f; Hough 1947:215; Munns 1938: map 127, p. 131; Fernald 1918b: map 11, pl. 12, and 1929: map 2, p. 1488; Little 1971: map 137-E.

MAGNOLIA L.   [2651]   Magnolia

M. acuminata L.   Cucumber-tree
/t/EE/   (Ms)   Rich woods from s Ill. to s Ont. (evidently native in Lambton, Norfolk, Welland, and Lincoln counties and planted elsewhere; *see* s Ont. map and discussion by Fox and Soper 1952: fig. 2, p. 69) and w N.Y., s to Ark., Ala., and Ga. MAPS: Hosie 1969:210; Canada Department of Northern Affairs and Natural Resources 1956:192; Preston 1961:232; Hough 1947:205; Munns 1938: map 126, p. 130; Little 1971: map 141-E.

ANNONACEAE (Custard-apple Family)

ASIMINA Adans.   [2673]   North American Pawpaw

Shrub or small tree to about 12 m tall, the young shoots and expanding leaves rusty-downy. Leaves alternate, entire, narrowly ovate to ovate-oblong, to about 3 dm long. Flowers regular, perfect, hypogynous, dull purple, 3 or 4 cm broad, on villous pedicels. Sepals 3, soon deciduous. Petals 6, the outer 3 spreading, larger than the nearly erect inner ones. Stamens numerous. Ovary superior. Fruit thick-cylindric, pulpy, green, finally dark brown, to about 1.5 dm long. (s Ont.).

A. triloba (L.) Dunal   Pawpaw
/t/EE/   (Ms)   Rich woods and alluvium from SE Nebr. to Mich., S Ont. (Essex, Kent, Lambton, Elgin, Middlesex, Norfolk, Oxford, Haldimand, Welland, and Lincoln counties; *see* s Ont. maps and discussion by Fox and Soper 1952: fig. 3, p. 72, Soper and Heimburger 1961:8, and W.M. Bowden and Bert Miller, Can. Field-Nat. 65(1): fig. 1, p. 28. 1951 (reporting a fossil occurrence in the Don Valley near Toronto)), w N.Y., and N.J., S to Tex. and Fla. [*Anona (Annona) tri.* L.]. MAPS: Hosie 1969:214; Canada Department of Northern Affairs and Natural Resources 1956:196; Hough 1947:217.

LAURACEAE (Laurel Family)

Aromatic trees or shrubs with simple alternate exstipulate entire or lobed leaves. Flowers perfect or unisexual, more or less perigynous. Perianth 6-parted, the segments all alike. Fertile stamens 9. Style 1. Ovary more or less inferior. Fruit a red or blue drupe to about 1 cm long.

1 Flowers yellow, appearing before the leaves, subsessile in dense clusters from the previous year's nodes; pistillate flowers with up to 18 staminodia of 2 forms; drupe red; leaves mostly obovate or obovate-oblong, entire and unlobed; shrub to about 5 m tall; (s Ont.) . . . .*Lindera*
1 Flowers greenish yellow, in loose peduncled racemes among the young leaves, the peduncles and pedicels finally red and up to 1 dm long, the fruiting pedicels very strongly clavate near summit; pistillate flowers with 6 short staminodia opposite the perianth-segments; drupe blue; leaves variable, from ovate and unlobed to asymmetrically 2-lobed or more symmetrically 3-lobed (sometimes 5-lobed), otherwise with entire margins; tree to about 40 m tall; (s Ont.) . . . .*Sassafras*

LINDERA Thunb.   [2821]   Wild Allspice, Feverbush

L. benzoin (L.) Blume   Spicebush, Benjamin-bush
/t/EE/   (Mc)   Damp woods and along streams from Ill. to s Mich., s Ont. (N to Grey, York, Hastings, and Prince Edward counties; *see* s Ont. maps and discussion by Fox and Soper 1952: fig. 5, p. 75, and Soper and Heimburger 1961:10), and sw Maine, s to Tex. and Fla. [*Laurus* L.; *L. pseudo-benzoin* Michx.; *L. (Benzoin) aestivalis* L. in part; *B. odoriferum* Nees].

SASSAFRAS Nees   [2795]   Sassafras

S. albidum (Nutt.) Nees   White Sassafras
/t/EE/   (Ms)   Woods and thickets from Kans. to Iowa, Ill., s Ont. (N to Peel and York counties; *see* s Ont. maps and discussion by Fox and Soper 1952: fig. 4, p. 73, and Soper and Heimburger 1961:9), and sw Maine, s to Tex. and Fla. [*Laurus* Nutt.; *S. officinale* var. *alb.* (Nutt.) Blake]. MAPS: Hosie 1969:216; Fowells 1965:654; Preston 1961:238; Canada Department of Northern Affairs and Natural Resources 1956:198; Hough 1947:223 *(S. sass.)*; Munns 1938: map 129 *(S. var.)*, p. 133; Little 1971: map 191-E.

Some or all of the s Ont. material is referable to var. *molle* (Raf.) Fern. (*S. officinale* Nees & Eberm.; *Laurus (S.) sassafras* L.; *S. triloba* Raf.; *S. variifolium* (Salisb.) Ktze.; leaves densely pubescent when young rather than essentially glabrous from the first).

PAPAVERACEAE (Poppy Family)

Herbs with acrid, milky or coloured juice (watery in *Eschscholzia*). Leaves simple or compound, usually alternate (opposite in *Meconella*; solitary and basal in *Sanguinaria* and some species of *Papaver*). Peduncles mostly 1-flowered. Flowers regular, perfect, hypogynous. Sepals 2 or 3, soon falling. Petals usually 4, sometimes 6, 8, or even 12. Stamens usually numerous. Ovary superior. Fruit a many-seeded capsule.

1   Leaf solitary, basal, cordate-rotund, palmately veined and lobed or undulate, to over
    2.5 dm broad, long-petioled; petals 8 or more, white, early deciduous; stigma
    capitate, 2-lobed; capsule fusiform, 2-valved, to 5 cm long; scape 1-flowered, from a
    thick prostrate rhizome with red-orange juice; (SE Man. to N.S.) . . . .*Sanguinaria*
1   Leaves cauline (and also often in a basal tuft).
    2   Leaves entire, to about 4 cm long, those of the stem opposite, linear to elliptic, to
        about 4 cm long, the basal ones long-petioled, their spatulate-obovate blades
        less than 2 cm long; sepals often reddish; petals commonly 6 (sometimes 5,
        rarely 4), white, to 4 mm long; capsule linear, often twisted, to about 2 cm long;
        slender glabrous and glaucous annual to about 1.5 dm tall; (SW B.C.) . . . . . .*Meconella*
    2   Leaves toothed to deeply dissected, those of the stem mostly alternate.
        3   Petals none, the 2 sepals cream-colour; capsule narrowly ovoid, 2-locular,
            with 2 or 3 seeds in each locule; flowers numerous in elongate terminal
            panicles; leaf-blades cordate-rotund, deeply lobed, whitened beneath, to
            3 dm long; stems to 2.5 m tall; (introd.) . . . .[*Macleaya*]
        3   Petals present but deciduous, usually 4 (rarely 6).
            4   Plant spiny throughout, the deeply sinuate-lobed leaves thistle-like, the
                upper ones involucrate; capsule opening above middle by 3–6 valves;
                stigma 4–6-radiate; juice orange-yellow; (introd.) . . . .*Argemone*
            4   Plant not spiny.
                5   Capsule ovoid to globose, opening by pores under the margin of the
                    5–15-rayed broad disk of fused stigmas; flowers large, white, red,
                    scarlet, or purple (yellow only in *P. pygmaeum* and *P. radicatum*); juice
                    milky or pale yellow . . . .*Papaver*
                5   Capsule dehiscing to base between the mature valves; flowers yellow
                    or orange.
                    6   Leaves 3-ternately dissected into linear or linear-oblong segments,
                        narrowly fan-shaped in outline; flowers to 7.5 cm broad; stigma 4–6-
                        lobed; capsule very slender, to 1 dm long; juice watery; (introd.) . . . .
                        . . . .*Eschscholzia*
                    6   Leaves pinnately divided or lobed; juice orange-yellow.
                        7   Ovary and thick-fusiform to ovoid capsule bristly-hirsute, the
                            latter 2 or 3 cm long; seeds conspicuously crested; style about 1
                            cm long; flowers about 5 cm broad; leaves divided nearly or
                            quite to base into 5–7 obtusely lobed segments, pale beneath,
                            subglabrous, a single opposite pair on the stem and several
                            basal ones; plant hirsute on upper parts; (s Ont.) . . . . . .*Stylophorum*
                        7   Ovary and slender capsule not pubescent; stigma sessile or
                            subsessile, 2-lobed; leaves glaucous, the cauline ones more
                            numerous, alternate; (introd.).
                            8   Flowers several in peduncled umbels, about 2 cm broad;
                                capsule 1-locular, smooth, to 5 cm long; seeds crested;
                                leaves long-petioled (petioles hairy toward base), divided
                                nearly or quite to base into 5–9 segments; stem very brittle . . . . . .
                                . . . .*Chelidonium*
                            8   Flower solitary, terminal or axillary, about 5 cm broad;
                                capsule 2-locular, scabrous, to 2 dm long; seeds crestless;

leaves thick and firm, those of the stem cordate-clasping,
sinuate-lobed and toothed, the basal ones deeply pinnatifid . . . . .
. . . . [*Glaucium*]

ARGEMONE L.   [2852]   Prickly Poppy, Devil's-fig

1   Flowers white (rarely pinkish or purplish), to 1 dm broad; leaves not blotched . . . .
. . . . [*A. intermedia*]
1   Flowers orange, yellow, or cream-colour, to about 6 cm broad; leaves commonly
blotched with paler green . . . . *A. mexicana*

[A. intermedia Sweet]
[Native in the U.S.A. from Idaho to Ill., s to N.Mex., Tex., Okla., and Mo. According to Breitung (1957a), the report from Prince, near Battleford, Sask., by Fraser and Russell (1944) may
be based upon a casual garden-escape that may prove referable to *A. platyceras* Link & Otto,
more common in cultivation.]

A. mexicana L.
Native in the sw U.S.A. and Tropical America; a casual garden-escape elsewhere, as in sw
B.C. (Victoria, Vancouver Is.; Carter and Newcombe 1921), s Man. (Kenville, near Swan
River), and Ont. (N to the Ottawa dist.; Gillett 1958; also reported from Sarnia, Lambton Co.,
by Dodge 1915, and from Wellington Co. by Stroud 1941).
    The cream-flowered phase may be distinguished as var. *ochroleuca* (Sw.) Lindl. It is re-
ported from the Ottawa dist., Ont., by Gillett (1958).

CHELIDONIUM L.   [2845]

C. majus L.   Celandine, Swallowwort.   Grande Éclaire or Herbe aux verrues
Eurasian; often abundant in rich damp soils about towns in N. America, as in sw B.C. (Nanaimo, Vancouver Is.; CAN), Ont. (N to the Ottawa dist.), Que. (N to Ste-Anne-de-la-Pocatière,
Kamouraska Co.; RIM), N.B., P.E.I. (Charlottetown; DAO), and N.S.; w Greenland (Polunin
1959).

ESCHSCHOLZIA Cham.   [2840]

E. californica Cham.   California Poppy
Native in the w U.S.A. (Wash. to Calif.); a garden-escape elsewhere, as in sw B.C. (Vancouver
Is.), N Alta. (Slave R. at 59°31′N; CAN), Man. (Dauphin; DAO), P.E.I. (Souris, Kings Co.;
ACAD), and N.S. (Cheticamp, Inverness Co.; ACAD). [*E. recta* Greene].

[GLAUCIUM Mill.]   [2848]   Sea-Poppy

[G. flavum Crantz]   Yellow Horn-Poppy
[Eurasian; reported from wharf-ballast at St. John, N.B., by G.U. Hay, J. Vroom, and R. Chalmers (Nat. Hist. Soc. N.B., Bull. 3:32. 1884), where probably not established and evidently not
collected in Canada since that date. (*G. luteum* Crantz; *Chelidonium (G.) glaucium* L.).]

[MACLEAYA R. Br.]   [2846]

[M. cordata (Willd.) R. Br.]   Plume-Poppy, Tree-Celandine
[Asiatic; a garden-escape in N. America, known from s Ont. (Simcoe, Norfolk Co.) and sw
Que. (Philipsburg, Missisquoi Co.), where, however, scarcely established. (*Bocconia* Willd.).]

MECONELLA Nutt.   [2835]

M. oregana Nutt.
/t/W/   (T)   Open damp or springy ground w of the Cascades from sw B.C. (Victoria, Vancouver Is.; CAN) to Calif. [*Platystigma* Brew. & Wats.].

PAPAVER L.   [2853]   Poppy.   Pavot

1   Capsules more or less villous or hispid with yellowish or brownish hairs; flowers
    commonly yellow (rarely roseate or nearly white), solitary on leafless scapes usually
    less than 3 dm tall; leaves deeply dissected; native perennials.
    2   Leaves glabrous or sparingly setose-hispid, at most 3 or 4 cm long; scapes to
        about 6 cm tall, sparingly or moderately setose; (mts. of B.C. and sw Alta.) . . . .
        . . . .*P. pygmaeum*
    2   Leaves copiously pubescent or hirsute on both sides, mostly longer; scapes
        taller, densely hispid; (transcontinental in arctic and subarctic regions) . . . .
        . . . .*P. radicatum*
1   Capsules glabrous; flowers various shades of red or purple (rarely white, never
    yellow), borne on more or less leafy, usually branching stems; (introd.).
    3   Stem-leaves cordate-clasping, coarsely toothed or shallowly lobed; flowers
        white, red, or purple; capsule broadly ovoid to subglobose; stigmatic rays 8–
        12; plant glabrous and glaucous . . . . *P. somniferum*
    3   Stem-leaves not clasping, the leaves deeply pinnatifid; flowers usually scarlet;
        plant bristly-hirsute.
        4   Capsule clavate (obconic or slightly obovoid); stigmatic rays at most 9;
            annual . . . .*P. dubium*
        4   Capsule broadly obovoid to subglobose, its summit bearing up to 15 rays.
            5   Flowers to about 1.5 dm broad, the 4 (sometimes 6) obovate petals
                scarlet with a black spot at base; capsule to about 2.5 cm long;
                peduncles with coarse appressed white hairs; leaves regularly
                pinnatifid; perennial . . . .[*P. orientale*]
            5   Flowers rarely over 1 dm broad, the orbicular petals brick-red to scarlet
                or deep purple (atypically white or white with red margins), sometimes
                with a dark spot at base; capsule less than 2.5 cm long; peduncles with
                spreading shaggy hairs; leaves irregularly pinnatifid; annual . . . . . .*P. rhoeas*

P. dubium L.
European; introd. (largely in cereal crops) in cult. fields and waste ground of N. America, as in
N.B. (reported from St. Stephen, Charlotte Co., by G.U. Hay, J. Vroom, and R. Chalmers, Nat.
Hist. Soc. N.B., Bull. 3:32. 1884, and from Buctouche, Kent Co., by Fowler 1885) and N.S.
(Boivin 1967*a*).

[P. orientale L.]   Oriental Poppy
[Eurasian; reported from Nfld. by Rouleau (1956), where presumably a garden-escape but
scarcely established.]

P. pygmaeum Rydb.
/T/W/   (Hr)   Talus slopes and higher mts. of se B.C. (South Kootenay Pass on the B.C.–
Alta. boundary, where taken by Dawson in 1881; CAN), sw Alta. (Waterton Lakes, where taken
by John Macoun in 1881; CAN), and nw Mont. [*P. pyrenaicum sensu* J.M. Macoun 1895, not
L., based upon the above-noted collections in CAN; *P. ?alpinum sensu* Henry 1915, not L.].
MAP: D. Löve, Brittonia 21(1): fig. 2, p. 2. 1969.

P. radicatum Rottb.   Arctic Poppy
/AST/X/GEA/   (Hr (Ch))   Sandy or gravelly soils, the collective species (including N. American members of the complex keyed out below) from the coasts of Alaska–Yukon–Dist. Mackenzie–Dist. Keewatin throughout the Canadian Arctic Archipelago to northernmost Elles-

mere Is. and northernmost Ungava–Labrador, s to n B.C. (Summit Pass, 58°31′N; CAN; isolated in the mts. of w Alta.), Great Bear L., Southampton Is., n Que. (s to s Ungava Bay), and n Labrador (s to ca. 57°N); circumgreenlandic; Iceland; Spitsbergen; n Eurasia.

P. radicatum Rottb., described from material taken by Rottböll in Greenland, Iceland, and Norway, is a very polymorphic species from which many "microspecies" have been separated. The following treatment is based upon those by Hultén (1945), D. Löve and N.J. Freedman (Bot. Not. (1956) vol. 109 (Fasc. 2):173–88. 1956), G. Knaben (Opera Bot. 2(3):1–96. 1959), Polunin (1959), A. Löve (Taxon 11(4):132–38. 1962), D. Löve (McGill Univ. Mus., Publ. 2(2):17–39. 1962), and Olav Gjaerevoll (K. Nor. Vidensk. Selsk. Skr. (1963, No. 4):1–97. 1963). It indicates the relationship of several of the more or less separable members of the complex with *P. radicatum* and the Rocky Mountain *P. pygmaeum* and attempts to place in the proper synonymy other "microspecies" reported from Alaska–Canada.

1 Leaves glabrous or sparingly setose-hispid, at most 3 or 4 cm long; capsules to 1.5 cm long.
  2 Capsule, sepals, and upper part of scape conspicuously beset with sharp, appressed-ascending, straight bristles; petals orange-yellow, about 1 cm long; leaves glabrous to sparingly setose-hispid (at least most of their teeth bristle-tipped), deeply dissected into oblong or ovate segments; scapes to about 6 cm tall; [mts. of B.C. and sw Alta.] . . . . *P. pygmaeum*
  2 Capsule, sepals, and upper part of scape copiously shaggy-villous with reddish-brown flexuous hairs; petals typically white to light yellow (turning green on drying), to 1.5 cm long; leaves nearly or quite glabrous, entire or merely 3-lobed; scapes to over 1 dm tall; [known only from Alaska, the type locality; MAPS: Hultén 1968*b*:490, and 1945: map 620, p. 967] . . . . *P. walpolei* Porsild
    3 Petals yellow . . . . var. *walpolei*
    3 Petals white with a yellow basal spot . . . . var. *sulphureomaculata* Hult.
1 Leaves hispid or hirsute on both sides, often longer.
  4 Capsules slenderly oblong-clavate, broadest near the summit (the stigmatic disk as broad as the capsule, with 3 or 4(5) rays), tapering at base, to about 2 cm long, up to 6 times as long as thick; petals yellow, commonly somewhat crenate-dentate toward apex, to 3.5 cm long; lobes of leaves acute or acutish; scapes hispid, rarely over 2 dm tall; [*P. hultenii* Knaben; Alaska–Yukon (*see* Hultén 1945: map 617a, p. 967) and w Dist. Mackenzie; MAP (aggregate species): Porsild 1966: map 69A (not indicating the station on the Coppermine R., nw Dist. Mackenzie, the type locality of *P. hultenii*), p. 75] . . . . *P. macounii* Greene
    5 Leaves, petioles, and peduncles rather copiously pubescent; [type from St. Paul Is., Alaska; MAP: Hultén 1968*b*:491] . . . . var. *macounii*
    5 Leaves, petioles, and peduncles subglabrous or sparingly pubescent, the leaves distinctly ashy green beneath; [*P. keelei* Porsild; *P. microcarpum sensu* Porsild 1943, in part, not DC.; type from Nome, Alaska] . . . . var. *discolor* Hult.
  4 Capsules ovoid or obovoid to subglobose, broadest at or slightly above the middle (the stigmatic disk rarely as broad as the capsule, with usually at least 5 rays), rounded at base; petals mostly entire or nearly so.
    6 Petals white, tinged with salmon or rose, or uniformly roseate, to about 12 mm long; capsule to 12 mm long; petioles coarse-hispid with ascending hairs; scapes to 12 cm tall; [s Alaska and Asia; reports from the Yukon are not accepted by Gjaerevoll, loc. cit.; MAPS: Hultén 1968*b*:491, and 1945: map 616, p. 967] . . . . *P. alboroseum* Hult.
    6 Petals mostly pale to deep yellow and longer.
      7 Scapes sparsely hispid, to about 4 dm tall; leaves bright green (but not glaucous), at least some of their lobes themselves shallowly pinnatifid toward tip; capsules mostly at least 2 cm long; [Alaska–Yukon; reports from elsewhere in Canada (as by John Macoun 1883 and 1886, and Macoun and Holm 1921) refer to other entities; reported as a garden-escape in Alta. by Moss 1959; MAPS: Hultén 1968*b*:494, and 1945: map 618, p. 967; Wiggins and Thomas 1962:385] . . . . *P. nudicaule* L.

7 Scapes densely hispid at least near the flower, usually not over 2 dm tall; leaf-lobes usually entire; capsules mostly not over 1.5 cm long.

   8 Petioles long-ciliate marginally, coarsely and densely hispid on the back toward base, the basal sheaths light brown, numerous on a long caudex; petals with only a slight tendency to turn green on drying, withering, or after bruising; [MAP: Hultén 1968*b*:492] . . . . . *P. alaskanum* Hult.

     9 Flowers to 6 cm broad; larger leaves 5–7-lobed; plant relatively tall; [type from St. Paul Is., Alaska] . . . . var. *macranthum* Hult.

     9 Flowers smaller; leaves 3–5-lobed (or some of them entire); plant usually smaller; [incl. the depauperate extreme, var. *latilobum* Hult.; *P. alpinum* of Alaskan reports in part, not L.; *P. microcarpum sensu* Porsild 1943, in part, not DC.; Aleutian Is. and s Alaska–Yukon, the type from Unalaska; MAP: Hultén 1945: map 615, p. 967] . . . . var. *alaskanum*

   8 Petioles short-ciliate marginally, glabrous or nearly so on the back toward base, the basal sheaths dark greyish-brown, less numerous on a shorter caudex; petals often turning partly greenish . . . . *P. radicatum*

     10 Petals white; [retained here as a variety rather than a mere form, its rarity, in the opinion of E.C. Abbe, Rhodora 38(448):151. 1936, supporting the probability that, on a genetical basis, it "would seem to be a case of sporadic, recessive mutation, rather than due to the segregation of individuals out of a population carrying factors for both white and yellow . . . ."; collections in CAN from Banff Park, Alta., and from Cornwallis Is.; type from Greenland] . . . . var. *albiflorum* Lange

     10 Petals sulphur-yellow; [incl. subspecies *labradoricum* Fedde, *lapponicum* Tolm., *occidentale* Lundstr., and *porsildii* (Knaben) Löve (three of these treated as subspecies of *P. lapponicum* (Tolm.) Nordh. by Knaben); incl. *P. cornwallisensis*, *P. freedmanianum*, *P. kluanensis*, *P. nigroflavum,* and *P. scammanianum* D. Löve, *P. dahlianum* Nordh., *P. denalii* Gjaerevoll, and *P. mcconnellii* Hult.; *P. alpinum* of reports from Alaska–Canada in part, not L.; transcontinental in arctic, subarctic, and alpine regions, the type from Greenland; MAPS: Porsild 1957: map 175, p. 182 (collective species); D. Löve 1962: map 4 (incl. the areas of several of the microspecies here reduced to synonymy), p. 33; Hultén 1968*b*:493 (*P. lapp.* ssp. *occ.* and ssp. *pors.*)] . . . . var. *radicatum*

P. rhoeas L. Corn-Poppy. Coquelicot
Eurasian; a garden-escape to rubbish-heaps and disturbed places in N. America, as in sw B.C. (Vancouver Is.; Eastham 1947), Sask. (Boivin 1966*b*), s Man. (N to the Winnipeg dist.), Ont. (reported N to a grain-field near Ottawa by John Macoun 1883; not listed by Gillett 1958), Que. (Oka and Montreal), N.B. (Kent and Kings counties), and N.S. (Hants, Halifax, Cumberland, Pictou, and Cape Breton counties). MAP: Hultén 1968*b*:489.

P. somniferum L. Common or Opium Poppy
Eurasian; introd. with grain or a garden-escape to roadsides and waste places in N. America, as in s B.C. (Vancouver Is.; New Westminster; Sicamous), N Alta. (Slave R. at 59°31′N; CAN), Sask., s Man. (Sandy Lake, about 50 mi N of Brandon; CAN), Ont. (N to the Ottawa dist.), Que. (N to the Gaspé Pen.; CAN), Nfld. (Bard Harbour; GH), N.B. (John Macoun 1883), and N.S.

SANGUINARIA L. [2841]

S. canadensis L. Bloodroot. Sang-dragon or Sanguinaire
/T/EE/ (Grh) Rich woods from SE Man. (N to Woodhaven, near Winnipeg) to Ont. (N to near Thunder Bay and Timmins), Que. (N to Rimouski, Rimouski Co., and the sw Gaspé Pen.

at the mouth of the Matapédia R.; *see* Que. map by Doyon and Lavoie 1966: fig. 26, p. 821), N.B., and N.S. (reported from P.E.I. by McSwain and Bain 1891, where apparently now extinct), s to E Tex. and N Fla.

Forma *multiplex* (Wilson) Weath. (petals very numerous, the flowers "double") is reported from sw Que. by S.D. Hicks (Trail and Landscapes 5(2):51–53. 1971; Gatineau Park, N of Hull).

STYLOPHORUM Nutt.   [2843]   Celandine-Poppy

S. diphyllum (Michx.) Nutt.   Wood-Poppy
/t/EE/   (Hs)   Rich woods and bluffs from Wisc. to s Ont. (near London, Middlesex Co., where taken by Elliot and Dearness in 1887; CAN; now probably extinct) and w Pa., s to Mo., Tenn., and w Va. [*Chelidonium* Michx.].

FUMARIACEAE (Fumitory Family)

Delicate herbs with decompound or dissected, chiefly alternate (basal in *Dicentra*) leaves and watery juice. Flowers in racemes or panicles, hypogynous, irregular, the corolla either bilateral or zygomorphic. Sepals 2, small and scale-like, soon deciduous. Petals 4 (in 2 pairs), 1 or 2 of the outer ones spurred or saccate at base. Stamens in 2 sets of 3 each opposite the larger petals, each set with a median 2-celled and two lateral 1-celled anthers. Ovary superior. Fruit a 1-locular capsule. (Often included in the Papaveraceae).

1 Corolla bilaterally symmetrical, the 2 outer petals spurred or more or less saccate at base; capsules several-seeded.
    2 Petals white, pink, or purplish, united into a subcordate-ovate, persistent, finally spongy corolla; seeds not crested; flowers in panicles; delicate biennial vine climbing the second year by the upper part of the leaf-rachises, the uppermost leaflets of the 3-pinnate alternate leaves greatly reduced; (Man. to N.S.; introd. in B.C.) . . . .*Adlumia*
    2 Petals only slightly cohering; corolla usually deciduous; seeds crested; flowers in racemes or panicles; non-climbing perennials, the leaves all basal . . . .*Dicentra*
1 Corolla zygomorphic, deciduous, only 1 of the outer petals spurred or saccate; flowers in racemes; stems leafy, the leaves alternate.
    3 Fruit a slender dehiscent capsule, the several seeds crested or with an aril; biennials or perennials . . . .*Corydalis*
    3 Fruit subglobose, indehiscent, 1-seeded, the seed crestless; annuals; (introd.) . . . .
    . . . .*Fumaria*

ADLUMIA Raf.   [2857]

A. fungosa (Ait.) Greene   Climbing Fumitory, Mountain-fringe
/T/EE/ (Hs (vine)) Wet or recently burned woods or rocky slopes from SE Man. (Victoria Beach, S L. Winnipeg; West Hawk L., near the Ont. boundary) to Ont. (N to Quetico Park, about 100 mi W of Thunder Bay, and Haileybury, 47°27'N), Que. (N to St-Fabien, Rimouski Co.; Herb. Hugh Scoggan), N.B. (Hampstead, Queens Co.; St. Stephen, Charlotte Co.), and N.S. (Halifax; ACAD; not known from P.E.I.), S to Tenn. and N.C.; introd. elsewhere, as in B.C. (Boivin 1966*b*) and N Alta. (reported by Groh 1949, as freely escaping from a garden at Fort Vermilion, 58°24'N). [*Corydalis* Vent.; *Fumaria* Ait.; *F. recta* Michx.; *A. cirrhosa* Raf.].

CORYDALIS Medic.   [2858] Corydalis.   Corydale

1 Flowers yellow; capsules loosely spreading or drooping, usually less than 2 cm long; seeds at least 2 mm long; stems diffuse or lax.
    2 Corolla pale yellow, at most 8 mm long, the 2 outer petals with 3–4-toothed dorsal wings; seeds minutely reticulate; (S Ont.) . . . .*C. flavula*
    2 Corolla golden yellow, about 1.5 cm long, the 2 outer petals keeled but scarcely winged; seeds obscurely reticulate; (Alaska–B.C. to Que.) . . . .*C. aurea*
1 Flowers typically pink to roseate or purplish.
    3 Stems less than 2 dm tall, the 2 or 3 principal leaves borne near the base (those subtending the flowers at most 7 mm long); leaves to about 2.5 cm long and 3 cm broad, ternately divided into 3 principal segments, these 2–3-cleft or -lobed (rarely 1 segment entire); flowers 2 or 3, to 2 cm long (including the spur, which is up to 1.5 cm long); (Alaska–Dist. Mackenzie–N B.C.) . . . .*C. pauciflora*
    3 Stems to over 8 dm tall, leafy throughout; leaves pinnately decompound, larger; flowers more numerous.
        4 Corolla 2 or 3 cm long, somewhat deeper pink at tip; spur over 1 cm long, narrowed to tip, longer than its petal-blade; stigma longer than broad; capsules obovoid, to 1.5 cm long and 4 mm broad; seeds about 4 mm long; racemes mostly with more than 15 flowers, sometimes only the terminal

raceme developing; leaves usually 3, near or above the middle of the stem, the lowest one often several dm long, the ultimate segments averaging mostly over 5 mm broad (up to 2.5 cm); perennial, the hollow stem from thick rhizomes; (sw B.C.) . . . . *C. scouleri*

4 Corolla to 1.5 cm long, yellow-tipped; spur less than 5 mm long, broadly round-tipped, shorter than its petal-blade; stigma broader than long; capsules linear-cylindric, to about 5 cm long and 2 mm broad; seeds about 1.5 mm long; racemes with rarely more than 10 flowers, the terminal and axillary ones usually forming a loose panicle; leaves several or numerous, the basal ones long-petioled, the upper ones greatly reduced and becoming sessile, the ultimate segments averaging mostly less than 5 mm broad; glaucous biennial; (transcontinental) . . . . *C. sempervirens*

C. aurea Willd. Golden Corydalis
/ST/X/ (T (Hs)) Moist to dry sandy or rocky places (largely introd. northwards) from cent. Alaska–Yukon (*see* Hultén 1945: map 621, p. 967) to Great Bear L., Great Slave L., L. Athabasca (Alta. and Sask.), Man. (N to Indian L. on the Churchill R. at ca. 57°N), Ont. (N to Big Trout L. at ca. 54°N, 90°W), and Que. (N to L. St. John and the Gaspé Pen.; not known from the Atlantic Provinces), s to Calif., Mexico, Tex., Mo., Ohio, and Vt. [*Capnodes* Ktze.; *Fumaria* Edwards; *Neckera* Millsp.; *Odoptera* Raf.]. MAPS: Hultén 1968*b*:495; G.B. Ownbey, Ann. Mo. Bot. Gard. 34(3): map 11, p. 232. 1947.

Var. *occidentalis* Engelm. (*C. (Capnoides) montana* Englem.; capsules ascending or only slightly spreading rather than loosely spreading to drooping, the seeds with thinnish rather than rounded margins, the racemes mostly equalling or surpassing the leaves rather than mostly considerably shorter than the leaves) is reported from N to Stuart L., B.C., ca. 54°30'N, and from the Hand Hills, s Alta., by John Macoun (1883), and from N to Telegraph Creek, B.C., ca. 58°N, by J.M. Macoun (1894), but the map by Ownbey (loc. cit., map 12, p. 236) confines the range to the U.S.A.

C. flavula (Raf.) DC. Yellow-Harlequin, Yellow Fumewort
/t/EE/ (Hs) Shores, moist woods, and open slopes from Minn. to s Ont. (Pelee Is. and Pelee Point, Essex Co.; Point Abino, Welland Co.) and Conn., s to E Kans., La., Tenn., and Va. [*Fumaria* Raf.; *Capnodes* Ktze.]. MAP: G.B. Ownbey, Ann. Mo. Bot. Gard. 34(3): map 5, p. 216. 1947.

C. pauciflora (Steph.) Pers.
/aST/W/A/ (Grt) Heaths, meadows, snow beds, and moist spruce forests at low to moderate elevations from the N coast of Alaska to N Yukon, sw Dist. Mackenzie, and cent. B.C. (s to near Hudson Hope at ca. 56°N); Asia. [*Fumaria* Steph.]. MAPS: Porsild 1966: map 68, p. 75; Hultén 1968*b*:495; Raup 1947: pl. 25; G.B. Ownbey, Ann. Mo. Bot. Gard. 34(3): map 3, p. 208. 1947.

Forma *albiflora* (Porsild) Boivin (flowers white rather than bluish violet) is known from the type locality of var. *alb.* Porsild, Mile 95 of the Canol Road, s Yukon.

C. scouleri Hook.
/t/W/ (Grh) Moist, usually shady places w of the Cascades from sw B.C. (Vancouver Is. and adjacent mainland) to N Oreg. [*Capnodes* Ktze.]. MAP: G.B. Ownbey, Ann. Mo. Bot. Gard. 34(3): map 1, p. 200. 1947.

C. sempervirens (L.) Pers. Pale Corydalis, Rock-Harlequin
/ST/X/ (Hs (?T)) Rocky places (particularly recent burns and clearings) from cent. Alaska–Yukon (*see* Hultén 1945: map 623, p. 967) to NW Dist. Mackenzie, Great Bear L., Great Slave L., L. Athabasca (Alta. and Sask.), Man. (N to Nejanilini L. at 59°22'N and Churchill), Ont. (N to the Fawn R. at ca. 54°N, 90°W), Que. (N to s Ungava Bay, the Côte-Nord, and Gaspé Pen.), Labrador (N to the Hamilton R. basin), Nfld., N.B., P.E.I., and N.S., s to s B.C., N Mont., Minn., and N Ga. [*Fumaria* L.; *Capnoides* Borckh.; *Neckera* Neck.; *Cory. glauca* Pursh].

MAPS: Hultén 1968b:496; G.B. Ownbey, Ann. Mo. Bot. Gard. 34(3): map 4, p. 212. 1947; Braun 1937: fig. 25, p. 199.
The white-flowered f. *candida* Lakela is reported from N Sask. by Boivin (1966b).

DICENTRA Bernh. [2856]

1 Flowers solitary and terminal on scapes usually not over 8 cm tall; corolla white to pinkish, cordate, the spur very short and rounded; upper half of the outer petals slender, widely spreading and slightly recurved; inner petals usually purplish-tipped, not crested; plant from a cluster of small fusiform fleshy roots; (s B.C.) . . . . *D. uniflora*
1 Flowers commonly several; outer petals with merely divergent tips commonly 3 or 4 mm long; inner petals more or less wing-crested near tip; scapes to over 3 dm tall.
　2 Corolla not cordate, white or pale pink; outer petals each with a divergent spur to about 1 cm long; inner flowers racemose; plant from a short erect rootstock covered with numerous small grain-like tubers; (Ont. to N.B. and N.S.) . . . *D. cucullaria*
　2 Corolla cordate, the spurs of the outer petals broadly rounded and not over 4 mm long.
　　3 Plants from subterranean shoots bearing scattered yellow tubers (resembling peas or grains of corn); flowers greenish white and pink-tinged, racemose, about 1 cm long; (Ont. and Que.) . . . . *D. canadensis*
　　3 Plants from slender rather brittle horizontal rhizomes, deep pink or pinkish purple, paniculate, about 1.5 cm long; (sw B.C.) . . . . *D. formosa*

D. canadensis (Goldie) Walp. Squirrel-corn, Bleeding-heart. Cœur-saignants
/T/EE/ (Gst (Grt)) Rich woods from Minn. to Ont. (N to the Ottawa dist.), Que. (N to Portneuf and Montmorency counties; *see* Que. map by Dominique Doyon and Victorin Lavoie, Nat. can. (Que.) 93(1):6. 1966), and New Eng., s to Mo., Tenn., and N.C. [*Corydalis canadensis* Goldie, the type from near Montreal, Que.; *Bicuculla* Millsp.; *Dielytra (Diclytra)* DC.]. MAP: K.R. Stern, Brittonia 13(1): fig. 28, p. 41. 1961.

D. cucullaria (L.) Bernh. Dutchman's-breeches
/T/D/ (Gb (Gst)) Rich woods, var. *occidentalis* in Wash., Oreg., and Idaho, the typical phase from Ont. to N.B. and N.S., s to E Kans., Mo., Ala., and Ga.
1 Ultimate leaf-segments relatively broad, averaging slightly over 2 (up to 5) mm broad; [*Bicuculla (D.) occid.* Rydb.; W U.S.A. only (Wash., Oreg., and Idaho), but to be looked for in s B.C.; a very interesting range, completely disjunct from the eastern area, the plants of the two regions distinguished by intergrading leaf characteristics that would otherwise be considered of little taxonomic value] . . . .
. . . . [var. *occidentalis* (Rydb.) Peck]
1 Ultimate leaf-segments averaging 1 or 2 (but up to 3) mm broad . . . . var. *cucullaria*
　2 Sepals deep purple; petals pink, deep orange at the flexure; [Que.: St-Jean, on the Richelieu R. s of Montreal; Marcel Raymond, Rhodora 51(602):30. 1949] . . . .
. . . . f. *purpuritincta* Eames
　2 Sepals and petals white to pale pink; [*Bicuculla (Bikukulla)* Millsp.; *Corydalis* Pers.; *Dielytra ("Diclytra")* DC.; *Fumaria* L.; Ont. (N to the Ottawa dist.), Que. (N to L. St. John and the Gaspé Pen.; *see* Que. map by Dominique Doyan and Victorin Lavoie, Nat. can. (Que.) 93(1):5. 1966), N.B., ?P.E.I. (early reports; probably now extinct), and N.S.] . . . . f. *cucullaria*

D. formosa (Andr.) Walp. Bleeding-heart
/t/W/ (Grh) Moist woods from s B.C. (Vancouver Is. and adjacent islands and mainland N to Yale in the lower Fraser Valley and E to Manning Provincial Park, SE of Hope; a collection in CAN from Keno, Mayo dist., the Yukon, is believed by Hultén 1945, to have probably been taken from introd. plants) to cent. Calif. [*Fumaria* Andr.; *Bikukulla* Cov.; *Corydalis* Pursh; *Dielytra* DC.; *F. (Diel.) ?eximia* Ker]. MAP: K.R. Stern, Brittonia 13(1): fig. 23, p. 29. 1961.

D. uniflora Kell.   Steer's-head
/T/W/   (Grt)   On well-drained soil from the foothills to subalpine slopes from s B.C. (Armstrong; Phoenix; Rossland; Manning Provincial Park, se of Hope) to Calif., Utah, and Wyo. [*Bicuculla* Howell]. MAP: K.R. Stern, Brittonia 13(1): fig. 23, p. 29. 1961.

FUMARIA L.   [2861]   Fumitory, Earth-smoke

1   Corolla to 13 mm long, pink, the tips and wings blackish red; upper petal broad but not compressed; lower petal with narrow erect margins, not spatulate; sepals oval, to 5 mm long and 2.5 mm broad; leaf-lobes oblong or cuneiform . . . .*F. martinii*
1   Corolla rarely as much as 9 mm long; upper petal dorsally compressed; lower petal distinctly spatulate; sepals to 3.5 mm long and 1.5 mm broad; leaf-lobes narrower in outline.
   2   Corolla to 8 (sometimes 9) mm long, pink, the tip and wings blackish red; sepals ovate-lanceolate to ovate, to 3.5 mm long and 1.5 mm broad; fruit obscurely keeled; leaf-lobes flat, lanceolate or linear-oblong . . . .*F. officinalis*
   2   Corolla 5 or 6 mm long, white or pinkish, the tips of the lateral petals blackish red; sepals broadly ovate, at most 1.5 mm long and less than 1 mm broad; fruit distinctly keeled; leaf-lobes channelled, subulate or linear . . . .[*F. parviflora*]

F. martinii Clav.
European; reported as introd. in sw B.C. (presumable Vancouver Is.) by Boivin (1966*b*).

F. officinalis L.   Common Fumitory.   Fummeterre
Eurasian; somewhat local and casual in cult. and waste ground of N. America, as in sw B.C. (White Rock, near New Westminster; Eastham 1947), Alta. (Boivin 1966*b*), Sask. (Lewvan; Breitung 1957*a*), Man. (n to Miniota, about 50 mi nw of Brandon), Ont. (n to the n shore of L. Huron), Que. (n to the n Gaspé Pen. at Mont-Louis), Nfld., N.B., P.E.I., and N.S.

[F. parviflora Lam.]
[Eurasian; John Macoun (1886) reports this species from waste heaps at Bedford, Pictou, and North Sydney, N.S., but the relevant collection in CAN from North Sydney proves to be *F. officinalis,* to which his other N.S. citations may also refer.]

CAPPARIDACEAE (Caper Family)

Annual herbs with alternate palmately compound leaves, the leaflets entire or finely serrulate. Flowers regular, hypogynous, in terminal bracted racemes. Sepals and petals each 4. Stamens 6 or more. Ovary superior. Fruit a 1-locular capsule.

1 Petals entire, white or roseate; stamens 6; capsule long-stipitate . . . . *Cleome*
1 Petals notched at apex, whitish; stamens commonly at least 11; capsule subsessile; leaflets 3, elliptic or oblong, to about 5 cm long; plants clammy-viscid; (B.C. to sw Que.) . . . . *Polanisia*

CLEOME L.   [3082]

1 Leaflets 3, entire, narrowly lanceolate, usually less than 6 cm long, the petioles unarmed; petal-blade much longer than the claw; capsule to 5 cm long, the stipe at most about 2 mm long and about equalling the pedicel; stem glabrous or glabrate; (B.C. to s Man.; introd. eastwards) . . . . *C. serrulata*
1 Leaflets 5 or 7, often finely serrulate, oblanceolate, to about 1 dm long, the petioles with a pair of short spines at base; petal-blade about equalling the claw; capsule to 1 dm long, the stipe about the same length and nearly twice as long as the pedicel; stem viscid-pubescent; (introd. in s Ont.) . . . . *C. spinosa*

C. serrulata Pursh   Stinking-clover, Spider-flower, Rocky Mountain Bee-plant
/T/WW/   (T)   Prairies, damp sands, and waste places from s B.C. (N to Kamloops and near Golden) to s Alta. (Crowsnest Pass to Medicine Hat), Sask. (N to Saskatoon; CAN), and s Man. (N to Plumas, about 45 mi NW of Portage la Prairie), s to Calif., N.Mex., and Ill.; introd. elsewhere, as in s Ont. (in a poultry yard at Guelph; OAC) and sw Que. (Oka; MT). [*Atalanta* Nutt.; *Peritoma* (*C.*) *integrifolia* Nutt.].

Forma *albiflora* Cock. (petals white rather than roseate) is reported from Sask. by Boivin (1966b). *C. lutea* Hook. (similar to *C. serrulata* but the petals yellow rather than typically pink to purplish) occurs from Wash. and Mont. to Calif., Tex., and Nebr., and is to be searched for in our West.

C. spinosa Jacq.   Spider-flower
Native of Tropical America; a garden-escape in N. America to waste ground or alluvium, as in s Ont. (Guelph, Wellington Co., Niagara Falls, Welland Co., and Cartwright, Ontario Co.; OAC; TRT).

POLANISIA Raf.   [3090]

P. dodecandra (L.) DC.   Clammyweed
/T/(X)/   (T)   Sandy or gravelly soils and alluvia (ranges of Canadian taxa outlined below), s to Calif., Mexico, Tex., Tenn., and Md. MAPS and synonymy: see below.
1 Longest petals rarely to 8 mm long (usually not over 6.5 mm); longest stamens usually not over 1 cm long (but up to 14 mm), scarcely surpassing the petals; [*P. graveolens* Raf.; *Cleome dodecandra* L. and its var. *canadensis* L.; s Sask. (Cypress Hills; Old Wives Lakes), s Man. (Aweme, about 20 mi SE of Brandon), s Ont. (N to the N shore of L. Ontario), and sw Que. (N to Montreal); MAP: H.H. Iltis, Brittonia 10(2):45. 1958] . . . . var. *dodecandra*
1 Longest petals commonly over 8 mm long; longest stamens commonly over 12 mm long (up to 3 cm), usually much surpassing the petals; [*P.* (*Jacksonia*) tr. T. & G.; s B.C., s Alta. (Calgary; Medicine Hat), s Sask. (Gull Lake, Island L., Long L., Mortlach, Maple Creek, Katepwa, and Saskatchewan Landing; Breitung 1957a), and s Man. (near Carberry); MAP: H.H. Iltis, Brittonia 10(2):46. 1958] . . . var. *trachysperma* (T. & G.) Iltis

CRUCIFERAE (Mustard Family)

Annual or perennial herbs with simple or compound, alternate or opposite leaves. Flowers in terminal racemes or corymbs, usually regular, hypogynous. Sepals and petals each 4. Stamens 6 (4 long, 2 short) or rarely only 4 or 2. Ovary superior. Fruit a specialized capsule or pod (a short silicle or a long silique), usually dehiscent by 2 valves, the 2 locules usually separated by a thin papery septum stretched between the marginal placentae, the septum persistent on the pedicel after separation of the valves and often indicated externally by a median nerve on the face of each valve (but the septum sometimes wanting and the pod then 1-locular). (Brassicaceae).

1   Fruit a silicle (type of pod rarely more than 3 times as long as broad, excluding the
     beak, if present), the seed-bearing body oblong or elliptic to obovoid, cuneate-
     obcordate, orbicular, or even reniform in outline.
  2   Leaves (at least the lower stem-leaves and the rosette-leaves when present)
       more or less pinnatifid, lyrate-pinnatifid, or even pinnately parted . . . . *GROUP 1*
  2   Leaves entire to coarsely toothed or even moderately lobed or lyrate but rarely
       distinctly pinnatifid (*Bunias* may be sought here) . . . . *GROUP 2* (p. 779)
1   Fruit a silique (a type of pod rarely less than 4 times as long as broad), linear to
     narrowly oblong or narrowly elliptic in outline.
  3   Leaves (at least the lower stem-leaves and the rosette-leaves when present)
       more or less pinnatifid, lyrate-pinnatifid, or even pinnately parted (palmately 3–5-
       foliolate in *Dentaria*) . . . . *GROUP 3* (p. 783)
  3   Leaves entire to coarsely toothed or even moderately lobed or lyrate but rarely
       distinctly pinnatifid . . . . *GROUP 4* (p. 786)

GROUP 1

1   Petals creamy to yellow (sometimes cream-white in *Eruca*); pubescence (when
     present) consisting mostly or entirely of simple hairs.
  2   Beak of fruit broad and flat, half as long to nearly as long as the 1–3-nerved
       valves; fruit indehiscent or tardily dehiscent, lance-ovoid, somewhat 4-angled in
       section, to 2.5 cm long (including the beak) and 5 mm thick, erect on stout
       ascending pedicels; seeds 2-rowed; petals to 2 cm long, with reddish-purple
       veins; leaves to 1.5 dm long, not clasping, chiefly basal and rosulate, sinuate-
       pinnatifid; stem to about 1 m tall; plants more or less pilose with simple hairs;
       annual; (introd.) . . . . *Eruca*
  2   Beak of fruit represented by the usually slender terete style (this stout and
       conical in *Rapistrum perenne* and only about 1 mm long).
    3   Pods 2-jointed, obovoid, the upper joint ovoid to subglobose, usually
         1-seeded and strongly several-ribbed, indehiscent, the lower joint cylindrical,
         finally dehiscent, usually 1-seeded (but its seeds often none or 2 or 3);
         pedicels strongly ascending; petals to about 1 cm long, yellow with darker
         veins; leaves narrowly to broadly oblanceolate, the principal ones mostly in a
         basal rosette; plants more or less hirsute with stiff simple hairs; (introd.) . . . .
         . . . . *Rapistrum*
    3   Pods rather slenderly oblong or elliptic, not jointed, the valves 1-nerved.
      4   Racemes glandular-warty; pods 1–4-seeded, obliquely ovoid, indehiscent,
           to 1 cm long and with up to 4 seeds, they and the stem sparingly rugose-
           warty; petals 3 or 4 mm long; leaves lyrate-pinnatifid toward base,
           sparingly pubescent with chiefly 2-forked hairs, not clasping; stems to 1 m
           tall; biennial or perennial; (introd.) . . . . *Bunias*
      4   Racemes nonglandular; fruits smooth; leaves commonly more or less
           auriculate-clasping; plants glabrous or more or less pubescent with simple
           hairs . . . . *Rorippa*
1   Petals white (sometimes tinged with purple in *Coronopus* and *Smelowskia*; yellow
     only in *Lepidium perfoliatum*; sometimes lacking).

5   Pods indehiscent or only tardily dehiscent, less than 3 mm long, usually as broad as or broader than long, slightly angustiseptate (compressed at right angles to the narrow internal septum), the strongly reticulate or rough-wrinkled walls of its 1-seeded valves much hardened; racemes compact, often arising opposite the leaves; petals to about 1 mm long; stems depressed, often matted; plants glabrous, scurfy-pubescent, or somewhat hirsute with simple hairs; annuals; (introd.) . . . . *Coronopus*

5   Pods dehiscent, their thin walls smooth or reticulate but not very rough; racemes terminal (axillary ones also often present); stems erect or strongly ascending.

   6   Pods broadly ovate to obcordate or even rotund in outline, usually retuse or notched at summit, very strongly flattened (angustiseptate), the valves usually strongly keeled or even more or less wing-margined (especially the two apical lobes); basal leaves usually forming definite rosettes.

      7   Pods 2-seeded, broadly elliptic-ovate to broadly obovate, glabrous or pubescent, the style present or wanting; pedicels erect to widely divergent, rarely much longer than the pods (except in *L. latifolium*); stamens 2 or 6 (rarely 4) . . . . *Lepidium*

      7   Pods normally with 4 or more seeds; pedicels widely divergent, to over twice the length of the pods; stamens 6; annuals.

         8   Pods inverted-triangular, broadest at the subtruncate or retuse summit, to 1 cm long; seeds numerous; pedicels to about 1.5 cm long; stem-leaves usually several, strongly sagittate-clasping; stems to 6 dm tall; plant more or less hirsute with simple and branched hairs; (introd.) . . . . *Capsella*

         8   Pods oblong-obovate to suborbicular, broadest near the middle, notched at summit, to 3.5 mm long, 4-seeded; pedicels rarely over 8 mm long; leaves all in a basal rosette or sometimes a few near the base of the stem; plant glabrous, to about 2.5 dm tall; (introd. in s B.C.) . . . . *Teesdalia*

   6   Pods elliptic-ovate to -obovate, not notched at the obtuse summit, less strongly flattened, the valves not wing-margined and rarely distinctly keeled; basal leaves not forming distinct rosettes; stems rarely over 2 dm tall, their leaves not clasping.

      9   Plant annual, from a slender taproot, glabrous or the basal leaves stellate-pubescent, the stems filiform; racemes lax, often more than half the entire height of the plant, the spreading pedicels to 1 cm long; sepals barely 1 mm long, the petals shorter or slightly longer; pods to 4 mm long; (transcontinental) . . . . *Hutchinsia*

      9   Plant perennial, the stems terminating a usually several-branched caudex clothed with marcescent leaves; raceme more compact, the pedicels ascending; sepals to 3.5 mm long; petals 4 or 5 mm long, sometimes purple-tinged; pods to 6 mm long; plant more or less greyish throughout with a mixture of soft fine branched hairs and longer stiffer hairs; (*S. ovalis*; mts. of B.C.) . . . . *Smelowskia*

GROUP 2 (see p. 778)

1   Petals creamy to yellow (sometimes fading or drying whitish).

   2   Stem-leaves sagittate- or auriculate-clasping at base, entire or more or less crenulate or sinuate-dentate; pods indehiscent (or tardily dehiscent in *Camelina*), their walls hardened; (introd.).

      3   Plants glabrous and more or less glaucous (or sparsely hirsute below with simple hairs); pods 1-seeded, on upwardly enlarged pedicels somewhat shorter than the pods.

         4   Pods broadly winged toward the truncate or rounded apex, obovate (samara-like and somewhat resembling those of the ash, *Fraxinus*),

strongly compressed (angustiseptate), to about 2 cm long, becoming dark purple-brown at maturity, the pedicels becoming reflexed; petals about 3.5 mm long; stem-leaves lanceolate to elliptic, mostly entire and glabrous, gradually reduced upward; rosette-leaves long-petioled, to over 1 dm long, more or less crenulate, soft-ciliate to sparsely short-pilose; biennial or perennial to over 1 m tall . . . . *Isatis*

    4 Pods wingless, cuneate-lyrate, to 8 mm long, with 1 seed in the basal half and 2 opposite rounded empty locules below the beak; petals about 1 mm long; pedicels appressed-ascending; stem-leaves oblong, obtuse, the upper ones not much reduced; stiff-stemmed annual . . . . *[Myagrum]*

  3 Plants more or less hirsute with stalked stellate and branched hairs (simple hairs also sometimes present; *Camelina sativa* often subglabrous); fruits with usually 2 or more seeds, inflated but slightly compressed (latiseptate; compressed parallel to the broad internal septum); annuals; (introd.).

    5 Pods depressed-globose, about 2 mm long and slightly broader, indehiscent, their walls strongly reticulate-pitted; seeds usually 2; style about 1 mm long; pedicels ascending, to about 1 cm long; petals about 2 mm long. . . . . *Neslia*

    5 Pods obovate, very narrowly wing-margined or keeled, relatively thin-walled, tardily dehiscent, mostly 5 mm long or more, their valves obscurely to moderately reticulate when dry; seeds usually several in 2 rows; style to 2.5 mm long; pedicels spreading-ascending, to 2 cm long; petals commonly 4 or 5 mm long . . . . *Camelina*

 2 Stem-leaves scarcely clasping (leaves often all in a basal rosette in *Draba*).

  6 Pods with a narrow apical sinus to 4 mm deep and a slightly cordate base, much inflated, to over 12 mm long and often broader than long, their walls thin and papery; style slender, to 9 mm long; seeds 4–6; petals to 12 mm long; rosette-leaves numerous, broadly oblanceolate to obovate or somewhat rhombic, entire or few-toothed, marcescent, to about 8 cm long, the stem-leaves reduced and mostly oblanceolate; stems somewhat decumbent-based, to about 1.5 dm tall; plant perennial, from a thick root, silvery-stellate, the hairs not closely appressed; (s B.C. and sw Alta.; ?Sask.) . . . . *Physaria*

  6 Pods rounded at apex or *(Alyssum)* very shallowly emarginate.

    7 Pods 2-jointed, obovoid, the upper joint ovoid to subglobose, usually 1-seeded and strongly several-ribbed, indehiscent, the lower joint cylindrical, finally dehiscent, usually 1-seeded (but seeds often 0 or 2 or 3); pedicels strongly ascending; petals to about 1 cm long, yellow with darker veins; leaves narrowly to broadly oblanceolate; plants more or less hirsute with simple hairs; (introd.) . . . . *Rapistrum*

    7 Pods not transversely jointed, dehiscent, the valves nerveless or 1-nerved; seeds 2-rowed; plants mostly closely and finely appressed-stellate-pubescent.

      8 Pods very strongly flattened (latiseptate), ovate-elliptic to rotund, with 2 or 4 seeds, usually shallowly notched at summit, the valves nerveless, the style to about 1 mm long; leaves narrowly oblanceolate to narrowly obovate, entire, not rosette-forming; annuals or biennials . . . . *Alyssum*

      8 Pods not strongly flattened (subterete to somewhat latiseptate), not notched at the obtuse to rounded apex, the seeds usually more than 4; rosette-leaves present (in *Draba,* leaves sometimes all in a basal rosette); perennials (sometimes biennials), the stems commonly from a simple or branching caudex.

        9 Pods broadly ovate to elliptic-oblong or rotund, their valves nerveless, their slender styles commonly about as long as or longer than the body; plants usually silvery with a dense, closely appressed, stellate pubescence; (chiefly western; *L. arctica* transcontinental) . . . . *Lesquerella*

        9 Pods relatively narrow, narrowly ovate to elliptic or oval, their valves commonly 1-nerved at least below; styles rudimentary or well developed but much shorter than the body; plants more or less pubescent with usually stalked branched hairs, with or without long simple hairs (sometimes essentially glabrous) . . . . *Draba*

1 Petals white to pink or purple (yellowish only in *Lepidium perfoliatum*).

  10 Stem-leaves strongly sagittate- or cordate-clasping; pubescence consisting of simple hairs.

    11 Pods 1-locular and 1-seeded, indehiscent, broadly oval or obovate to orbicular, strongly flattened, to 8 mm long, often very convex on one side, broadly winged all around, the wing radiately green-nerved; pedicels almost filiform, recurved, to 7 mm long; style to about 0.5 mm long; sepals about 1 mm long, often purplish, white-margined; petals narrow, about equalling the sepals; leaves narrowly lanceolate to oblanceolate, entire or the lower ones dentate to shallowly runcinate, to 5 cm long, the basal ones often deciduous by anthesis; stems to 8 dm tall, hirsute below with simple hairs, becoming glabrous above; annual; (sw B.C.) . . . . *Thysanocarpus*

    11 Pods 2-locular, with 2 or more seeds, on ascending to divergent (but rarely recurved) pedicels.

      12 Pods typically strongly inflated and only slightly compressed, orbicular or depressed-cordate to reniform in outline, not wing-margined, slightly or not at all notched at summit; seeds commonly 2, sometimes 4; sepals about 2 mm long, the petals about twice as long; pedicels slender, mostly about 1 cm long; puberulent to hoary-pubescent rhizomatous perennials; (introd.) . . . . *Cardaria*

      12 Pods strongly compressed at right angles to the narrow septum (angustiseptate) and usually distinctly notched at the wing-margined apex; annuals or perennials.

        13 Pods 2-seeded (or 1 of the seeds abortive), to 5 or 6 mm long; petals at most 2.5 mm long, often vestigial or wanting; plants commonly more or less pubescent . . . . *Lepidium*

        13 Pods with 4 or more 1-rowed seeds, to over 1 cm long; petals to over 4 mm long; plants glabrous . . . . *Thlaspi*

  10 Stem-leaves scarcely clasping, or leaves all or nearly all basal or sub-basal.

    14 Leaves all basal or sub-basal.

      15 Flowers solitary on leafless scapes to 13 cm tall; sepals and petals each about 2 mm long; pods oblong-oval to suborbicular, strongly compressed parallel to the broad internal septum (latiseptate), to 12 mm long, tipped by a very short style, not notched; seeds several, about 5 mm long, broadly winged all around (the wing commonly about half the width of the seed-bearing body); leaves ovate, entire or 2-lobed at base, to 1.5 cm long, slender-petioled; glabrous annual; (sw B.C.) . . . . *Idahoa*

      15 Flowers 2 or more in terminal racemes; seeds much smaller, wingless or very narrowly wing-margined.

        16 Plants more or less pubescent with simple, stellate, or branched hairs (or these admixed), rarely essentially glabrous, often perennial from simple or branched crowns and often marcescent-leafy at base; styles often well developed; pods subterete or more or less compressed (latiseptate), not notched at summit; petals commonly to 4 or 5 mm long . . . . *Draba*

        16 Plants glabrous, annual; petals about 1 mm long, about twice as long as the minute sepals; style none, the sessile stigma tipping the more or less compressed (angustiseptate) pod.

          17 Leaves linear, entire, subterete in cross-section, to about 5 cm long; flowers 2–8, on mostly strongly ascending pedicels; pods elliptic to oval, slightly compressed, not notched at summit, about 2.5 mm

long, several-seeded; plants to about 1 dm tall, usually submersed; (transcontinental) . . . .*Subularia*

17 Leaves oblanceolate to oval or obovate, entire to rather deeply lobed, to 5 cm long (including the long petiole); flowers commonly more than 10, on divergent pedicels; pods oblong-obovate to suborbicular, strongly compressed, notched at summit, to 3.5 mm long; seeds 4; plants to about 2.5 dm tall; (introd. in s B.C.) . . . .*Teesdalia*

14 Leaves cauline (basal rosettes also sometimes present).

  18 Pods inflated or slightly flattened but not strongly so.

    19 Plants glabrous or nearly so.

      20 Pods 2-jointed, to 2.5 cm long, the upper, ovoid, usually 1-seeded joint larger than the narrowly campanulate lower joint (1-seeded or empty), separating from it (but neither joint dehiscent); petals white to purple, to 7 mm long; leaves oblong-lanceolate to -obovate, deeply crenate to sinuate-dentate, to about 7 cm long; stems and lower branches often decumbent-based; subglabrous succulent annual of sandy shores; *(C. edentula)* . . . .*Cakile*

      20 Pods not jointed, broadly oblong to subglobose, less than 1 cm long.

        21 Stems coarse, erect, to over 1 m tall; basal leaves oblong to oblong-ovate, to 4 dm long (including the long petiole), crenate; stem-leaves lanceolate, the reduced upper ones crenate, the lower ones often pinnatifid; petals white; valves of pods nerveless; style very short; perennial, with a thick taproot (horseradish); *(A. lapathifolia;* introd., widespread) . . . .*Armoracia*

        21 Stems slender, usually several, decumbent (sometimes erect), commonly less than 3 dm long; leaves fleshy, the blades of the lower ones ovate or cordate-oblong to reniform, to about 2 cm long, entire to sinuate, the petioles several times longer, the stem-leaves narrower and entire; petals white, pinkish, or purplish; valves of pods strongly nerved; styles mostly relatively long, biennials or perennials . . . .*Cochlearia*

    19 Plants distinctly pubescent with branched or stellate hairs (simple hairs also often present); pods rather broadly oblong or elliptic-oblong.

      22 Plant annual, from a taproot, stellate-canescent, to over 1 m tall; leaves oblanceolate, entire, to 5 cm long, the lower stem-leaves usually deciduous with the basal leaves by anthesis; pods to 7 mm long and about as broad, tardily dehiscent; seeds wing-margined; (introd.) . . . .*Berteroa*

      22 Plants perennial, the stems from a simple or branched crown, usually less than 2 dm tall; leaves entire or remotely dentate, the lower ones persistent and forming rosettes; seeds sometimes wing-margined . . . .*Draba*

  18 Pods strongly flattened.

    23 Pods to over 4 cm long and 2 cm broad, oblong to rotund, long-stipitate within the calyx (the stipe to over 1 cm long), compressed (latiseptate), not apically notched, the valves thin and papery, the slender style to 0.8 mm long; seeds usually about 5, reniform, to 1 cm broad, winged; petals purple, to about 2 cm long; leaves finely to coarsely serrate; sparingly pubescent annuals or biennials; (introd.) . . . .
. . . .*Lunaria*

    23 Pods not over 6 mm long, sessile within the calyx, often apically notched, the style relatively short or none; seeds relatively small, wingless; petals commonly white (sometimes reddish or purplish), 1 or 2 mm long (sometimes wanting).

      24 Pods strongly compressed parallel to the broad septum (latiseptate; or pods 1-locular in *Athysanus*), indehiscent or tardily dehiscent, 1-

seeded, wingless, to about 3.5 mm long, slender-pedicelled; annuals to 3.5 dm tall.

  25 Pods 1-locular, suborbicular, slightly notched at apex, on gently recurved pedicels to 4 mm long in elongate, open, more or less 1-sided racemes, the nerveless valves copiously hirsute (at least marginally) with hooked hairs, the style to 0.3 mm long; petals white (sometimes wanting), 1 or 2 mm long; leaves oblanceolate to obovate, entire or remotely toothed, to about 3 cm long and 1 cm broad; plant hirsute with 2–4-rayed stalked trichomes and some simple hairs; (s B.C.) . . . . *Athysanus*

  25 Pods 2-locular (but 1-seeded), oval-elliptic, not notched at summit, on divergent pedicels to 1 cm long in rather crowded racemes, the 1-nerved valves sparsely hairy, the style to 0.5 mm long; petals white or bluish-tinged, to 4 mm long; leaves linear-oblanceolate, to 4 cm long and 4 mm broad; plant greyish-strigillose with malphigian pubescence (appressed, 2-pronged hairs); (introd.) . . . . *Lobularia*

24 Pods strongly compressed at right angles to the narrow internal septum (angustiseptate), dehiscent, on divergent to ascending pedicels, glabrous or pubescent with short straight hairs.

  26 Stems filiform, procumbent or weakly ascending, to 1.5 (rarely 2) dm long; racemes lax, often more than half the entire height of the plant, the spreading pedicels to 1 cm long; sepals barely 1 mm long, the petals shorter or slightly longer; pods to 4 mm long, elliptic to elliptic-obovate, usually with 4 or more seeds, wingless, not notched at summit, the style to 0.2 mm long; annual from a slender taproot, glabrous or the basal leaves stellate-pubescent; (transcontinental but local) . . . . *Hutchinsia*

  26 Stems stouter and firm; racemes mostly more compact; pods broadly ovate to oval, obovate, or rotund, notched at the usually winged summit (except in *Lepidium latifolium*); seeds 1 or 2.

    27 Petals unlike, the 2 lower (outer) ones much larger than the 2 upper ones; flowers showy, white to roseate, crimson, or purple; slender style projecting from between the 2 apical points of the 1–2-seeded pods; leaves elliptic-oblanceolate or oblanceolate, to about 1 dm long, entire or with a few irregular obtuse teeth; annuals; (introd.) . . . . [*Iberis*]

    27 Petals all alike (sometimes lacking), usually white, sometimes greenish, reddish, or purplish; pods 2-seeded, the style lacking or usually not projecting beyond the terminal sinus-lobes . . . . *Lepidium*

GROUP 3 (*see* p. 778)

1 Petals pale to deep yellow (sometimes fading or drying whitish; sometimes tinged with lavender or purple, or purple-veined, in *Raphanus* and *Rorippa crystallina*).

  2 Plants more or less pubescent with forked or stellate hairs, with or without longer simple or glandular hairs; fruits linear-clavate to -cylindric, subterete (or often somewhat 4-angled because of the prominent midnerves of the valves); seeds usually 1-rowed in each locule (but those of *D. pinnata* 2-rowed at least near the middle of the pod); flowers small, the sepals to 2.5 mm long, the petals shorter than the sepals or up to 3.5 mm long; racemes bractless; annuals from a taproot . . . . .
. . . . *Descurainia*

  2 Plants glabrous or moderately pubescent with simple hairs.

    3 Racemes bracted nearly or quite throughout, the lower pedicels subtended by leafy bracts, the upper bracts gradually reduced; stems retrorsely strigose-pilose, to 8 dm tall; pedicels ascending, less than 1 cm long; petals pale

yellow, to 7 mm long, twice as long as the sepals; pods to about 4 cm long and 2 mm thick, tardily dehiscent, 4-angled owing to the prominent midnerve on each valve (lateral nerves delicate and forming a reticulum); seeds 1-rowed in each locule; style to 3 mm long; leaves 1-pinnatifid into oblong lobes with rounded sinuses; annual; (introd.) . . . . *Erucastrum*

3   Racemes bractless except sometimes at base; pubescence of stem spreading (sometimes retrorse in *Sisymbrium loeselii*) and relatively stiff, or the plant glabrous.

    4   Pods tipped with a beak-like indehiscent stout style 1/6 to nearly as long as the seed-bearing body, often over 4 mm thick (at most 2.5 mm thick in some species of *Brassica*), indehiscent or tardily dehiscent; petals to over 1.5 cm long; taprooted annuals (sometimes biennial); (introd.).

        5   Fruits with a short, sterile, rather stipe-like basal segment markedly distinct from the seed-bearing portion, more or less deeply grooved lengthwise, indehiscent but finally sometimes breaking across the corky-pithy layer between the seeds; petals to 2 cm long, often purplish-tinged or at least with violet veins; leaves strongly lyrate (with a large terminal segment and much smaller lateral lobes); plants more or less rough-hairy . . . . *Raphanus*

        5   Fruits lacking a sterile differentiated basal segment, indehiscent or tardily dehiscent, nearly terete or somewhat quadrangular, the valves 1- or 3-nerved.

            6   Seeds 2-rowed in each locule; pods to 2.5 cm long (including the broad flat beak, this half to nearly as long as the valves) and 5 mm thick; sepals to 1 cm long; petals to 2 cm long, yellowish (sometimes white), with reddish-purple veins; leaves sinuate-pinnatifid, neither markedly lyrate nor clasping . . . . *Eruca*

            6   Seeds 1-rowed in each locule; pods often longer and sometimes not over 2.5 mm thick; sepals to 6 mm long; petals rarely over 1.5 cm long; leaves strongly lyrate, sometimes auriculate-clasping . . . . . *Brassica*

    4   Pods tipped with a short style or the stigma sometimes subsessile (but the conical beak to 4 mm long in *Diplotaxis*), rarely over 2.5 mm thick, dehiscent (tardily so in *Barbarea* and perhaps in *Diplotaxis*).

        7   Leaves linear, to 9 cm long and 4 mm broad, entire or toothed, the basal ones usually with linear entire lobes, commonly deciduous by anthesis; sepals to 5 mm long, yellowish; petals to 1 cm long; pods to 5 cm long and 1 mm thick, nearly terete, the valves with an obscure midnerve and often a pair of faint lateral nerves; seeds 1-rowed in each locule; style obsolete; glabrous and somewhat glaucous rhizomatous perennial, often with a large branched caudex; (s B.C. and sw Alta.) . . . .
. . . . *Schoenocrambe*

        7   Leaves broader in outline, their segments mostly also broader and usually toothed or lobed (or those of the upper leaves of *Sisymbrium altissimum* linear), the basal ones usually persistent; valves of pods strongly 1-nerved (an additional pair of faint lateral nerves also often present).

            8   Stem-leaves rather strongly auriculate-clasping; pods tardily dehiscent, their seeds 1-rowed in each locule, the valves nerved, the style 0.5–3 mm long; plants glabrous or sparingly hirsute . . . *Barbarea*

            8   Stem-leaves not clasping.

                9   Pods terminated by a slender-conical indehiscent beak to about 3.5 mm long, the seeds 2-rowed in each locule, the valves nerved; (introd.) . . . . *Diplotaxis*

                9   Pods dehiscent to tip, lacking a rather long indehiscent beak.

                    10 Seeds 1-rowed in each locule; valves of pods nerved; plants more or less hirsute; (introd.) . . . . *Sisymbrium*

        10 Seeds irregularly 2-rowed in each locule (except in
            R. sylvestris); valves of pods nerveless; plants usually glabrous . . .
. . . . *Rorippa*

1   Petals white or purple-tinged to purple (*Rorippa crystallina* may key out here).
   11 Leaves palmately parted or palmately compound (the segments or leaflets
      themselves also often palmately cleft), a single opposite or subopposite pair
      (sometimes a whorl of 3) above the middle of the stem; flowers large and showy,
      white or purple; pods rarely maturing or up to about 5 cm long, their wingless
      seeds 1-rowed; stems from a fleshy, toothed or jointed rhizome; (Ont. to N.S.) . . . .
      . . . . *Dentaria*
   11 Leaves mostly pinnately lobed, parted, or compound (if sometimes palmately
      cleft or divided in *Cardamine,* often several on a stem and distinctly alternate).
      12 Seeds 2-rowed in each locule; pedicels slender, ascending to somewhat
         reflexed; valves of pods nerveless; glabrous, aquatic or subaquatic perennials,
         the weak stems floating or prostrate on the mud, freely rooting at the nodes.
         13 Pods ovoid, 1-locular, to 8 mm long, the style to 4 mm long; submersed
            leaves 1–3-pinnately dissected into numerous capillary divisions; emersed
            leaves oblong, entire, serrate, or pinnatifid; (*A. aquatica*; Ont. and Que.) . . . . . .
            . . . . *Armoracia*
         13 Pods linear, commonly about 1.5 cm long (up to 2.5 cm), usually
            upcurved, the stout style about 1 mm long; principal leaves usually with a
            large ovate or cordate terminal leaflet and 1–5 pairs of narrower lateral
            leaflets; (introd.) . . . . *Nasturtium*
      12 Seeds 1-rowed in each locule.
         14 Pods stipitate within the calyx or with a rather broad basal segment distinct
            from the seed-bearing body; petals to 2 cm broad; annuals or biennials.
          15 Pods narrowly linear, about 1 mm thick, completely dehiscent, on
            strongly divergent to reflexed pedicels to 5 mm long, the seeds
            numerous, the valves 1-nerved, the slender style to about 3 mm long;
            petals white, their blades linear to narrowly spatulate, strongly
            ascending to erect; leaves rather fleshy, the basal ones deltoid-
            lanceolate to ovate, sharply and deeply lobed, to 4.5 dm long (including
            the long petiole), the stem-leaves from nearly entire to subpinnatifid;
            plants glabrous and glaucous, to over 2 m tall, the stem often hollow;
            (dry regions of s B.C.). . . . . *Thelypodium*
          15 Pods lanceolate, lightly several-grooved, to 6 cm long and 1 cm thick,
            narrowed to a broad sterile basal segment distinct from the indehiscent
            seed-bearing body and terminated by a sharp conical beak up to half
            as long as the body, corky-thickened between the seeds, on spreading
            to strongly ascending pedicels to 2.5 cm long; seeds usually not more
            than 3; petals commonly purplish but varying to white or yellow with
            purplish veins, their blades obovate to rotund, horizontally spreading;
            basal leaves strongly lyrate-pinnatifid, with a large, toothed, ovate to
            rotund terminal segment and a few pairs of more slender lateral
            segments, the upper leaves reduced and merely toothed; plants
            sparsely hispid with simple, often pustular-based hairs, the stem to
            about 1 m tall; (*R. sativus*; introd.) . . . . *Raphanus*
        14 Pods neither stipitate within the calyx nor with a differentiated sterile basal
          segment, tipped with a short style or the stigma subsessile; seeds usually
          numerous; plants usually more or less pubescent (sometimes nearly or
          quite glabrous in *Cardamine*).
         16 Plants copiously greyish-pubescent with a mixture of long, soft, simple
            and forking hairs and shorter freely branched hairs, to 2 dm tall,
            perennial by a simple to much-branched and usually matted caudex
            covered with marcescent leaf-bases; pods linear to broadly obovate;
            (Alaska–B.C.–Alta.) . . . . *Smelowskia*

16 Plants glabrous or pubescent with simple hairs only, not from a
marcescent-leafy caudex; pods linear.
  17 Plants annual or biennial, taprooted, strongly pilose or hirsute, to
over 1 m tall; calyx to 9 mm long, more or less pilose; petals with a
narrow claw about equalling the calyx, the lanceolate blade
somewhat crisped, white with purple veins to rose-purple bordered
with white, 2 or 3 mm long; pods to over 1 dm long, subterete, the
valves 1-nerved their whole length; stigma sessile; (?B.C.) . . . .
. . . . [*Caulanthus*]
  17 Plants usually perennial from rhizomes or tuberous bases
(sometimes annual or biennial), glabrous or sparingly pubescent;
petals commonly rather showy, not crisped, white to pink or
roseate; pods less than 5 cm long, slightly compressed (latiseptate),
the valves very indistinctly 1-nerved only near the base; style
evident . . . . *Cardamine*

GROUP 4 (*see* p. 778)

1 Petals creamy to yellow (sometimes fading or drying whitish; *Arabis glabra* and
sometimes *Parrya arctica* may key out here; petals purple in *Erysimum pallasii*).
  2 Stem-leaves strongly cordate-clasping, mostly oblong-lanceolate, strongly
ascending; basal leaves oblanceolate to obovate, narrowed gradually to the
subpetiolar base, to about 9 cm long, they and the stem-leaves entire or nearly
so; sepals to 8 mm long; petals creamy to lemon-yellow, to 12 mm long; pods to
over 1 dm long, to 2 mm thick, erect on ascending pedicels to 1.5 cm long;
glabrous, glaucous annual to about 8 dm tall; (introd.) . . . . *Conringia*
  2 Stem-leaves not clasping.
    3 Plants glabrous and somewhat glaucous; leaves linear, to 9 cm long and 4
mm broad, entire or toothed (the basal ones usually with linear lobes but
mostly deciduous by anthesis); petals to 1 cm long; pods to 5 cm long and 1
mm thick, nearly terete; seeds 1-rowed in each locule; rhizomatous perennial
to 7 dm tall, often with a large branched caudex; (s B.C. and sw Alta.) . . . .
. . . . *Schoenocrambe*
    3 Plants pubescent with forked or branched hairs, longer simple hairs also
sometimes present; leaves often partly or mostly in a basal rosette; seeds 2-
rowed in each locule; plants chiefly perennial (sometimes annual or biennial).
      4 Plant pubescent with appressed, 2-pronged (malphigian) hairs oriented
with the axis of the stem or leaf (3–4-rayed appressed hairs also often
present on the leaves and branches); petals pale yellow to deep orange or
even reddish (purple in *E. pallasii*); pods to about 1 dm long, the seeds 1-
rowed in each locule; stems usually erect and mostly over 2 dm tall,
usually from a simple caudex . . . . *Erysimum*
      4 Plants pubescent with mostly stellate or branched stalked hairs, with or
without simple hairs; petals creamy to yellow; pods mostly less than 1.5 cm
long, the seeds 2-rowed in each locule; stems often decumbent-based,
mostly from a branched caudex . . . . *Draba*
1 Petals white to pink or purple (creamy in *Arabis glabra*).
  5 Plants pubescent with stellate, branched, or dentritic (branching along an erect
or ascending central axis) hairs, longer simple hairs also often present; pods
sessile within the calyx.
    6 Pods terminated by 2 long divergent horns, to about 1 dm long, spreading
and having the appearance of branches; flowers about 1.5 cm long, white,
pink, or violet, solitary and sessile in the upper axils; leaves linear to narrowly
lanceolate, to about 9 cm long, entire or remotely denticulate; perennial;
(garden-escape) . . . . *Matthiola*
    6 Pods not terminated by 2 horns.

7 Petals over 1.5 cm long (up to 2.5 cm), commonly purple, sometimes rose or pink to white; stem-leaves strongly sagittate-clasping, shallowly serrate-dentate, to 2 dm long, lanceolate to rather narrowly ovate, the lower ones long-petioled but not forming definite rosettes; pods to 14 cm long, the 1-rowed seeds wingless, the valves strongly 1-nerved and often with a pair of faint lateral nerves; biennial or perennial to over 1 m tall; (common garden-escape) . . . . *Hesperis*
7 Petals mostly less than 1.5 cm long; stem-leaves mostly not clasping (sagittate-clasping in many species of *Arabis* and our 2 species of *Halimolobos*).
  8 Stems often abundantly branched and diffuse; basal leaves not forming definite rosettes; pods to about 7 cm long, their 1-rowed seeds wingless; annuals; (garden-escapes) . . . . [*Malcolmia*]
  8 Stems simple or branching but not diffuse; basal leaves usually forming distinct rosettes.
    9 Pods moderately to rather strongly compressed parallel to the septum (latiseptate); plants mostly perennial, from a simple to much-branched crown.
      10 Pods commonly not over 1 cm long (sometimes to 1.5 cm, rarely to 2 cm), usually less than 8 times as long as broad; seeds 2-rowed in each locule, wingless; petals to 7 mm long; stem-leaves not sagittate-clasping; stems sometimes scapose . . . . *Draba*
      10 Pods usually averaging over 2 cm long (except in *A. nuttallii*), to over 1 dm long, usually at least 8 times as long as broad, their wingless or narrowly wing-margined seeds 1–2-rowed in each locule; stem-leaves often sagittate-clasping, the stems never scapose . . . . *Arabis*
    9 Pods terete, subterete, or slightly 4-angled in cross-section, slightly if at all compressed, commonly more than 15 times as long as broad, their seeds wingless; petals to about 5 mm long.
      11 Stem-leaves (at least the middle and upper ones) sagittate-clasping, to 3 or 4 cm long; seeds 2-rowed in each locule, the glabrous pods to 4 cm long; petals white, or their veins strongly pinkish or lavender . . . . *Halilolobos*
      11 Stem-leaves not clasping; seeds 1-rowed or only obscurely 2-rowed in each locule (distinctly 2-rowed in *Braya purpurascens*).
        12 Pods glabrous, scarcely torulose; styles to 0.4 mm long; petals white; simple to rather freely branched annual to 4 dm tall, the basal leaves sparsely to thickly hirsute with simple and forked hairs, the stems pubescent near the base with mostly simple spreading hairs; (*A. thaliana*; introd. in s B.C. and s Ont.) . . . . *Arabidopsis*
        12 Pods often stellate-pubescent (sometimes glabrous); petals white or their veins strongly pink or purplish; perennials, usually developing a branched caudex.
          13 Pods very slightly torulose, finely stellate-pubescent, linear, to about 2 cm long but less than 1.5 mm broad, the style scarcely 0.5 mm long; pedicels to 2 cm long; rosette-leaves to 1 dm long and 2 cm broad, entire to few-toothed or even shallowly lyrate; stems leafy; (*H. whitedii*; s ?B.C.) . . . . *Halimolobos*
          13 Pods plane to strongly torulose, glabrous or stellate-pubescent, linear to narrowly oblong and up to 2.5 mm broad, the style very short or to about 1 mm long, the septum consisting of characteristic transversely

elongated thick-walled cells; pedicels usually less than 1 cm long; rosette-leaves entire to shallowly toothed; stems leafy or scapose . . . . *Braya*

5 Plants glabrous or the pubescence consisting of simple hairs (*Halimolobos mollis* may key out here but its seeds are 2-rowed); seeds 1-rowed in each locule (sometimes 2-rowed in *Braya*; internal septum lacking in *Aphragmus*).

14 Plants scapose or subscapose, mostly not over 1.5 dm tall, the leaves all or nearly all in basal rosettes or rarely more than 2 or 3 near the base of the stem; petals white to purple (rarely creamy in *Parrya arctica*); leaves entire to coarsely toothed; perennials from usually branching caudices; (chiefly arctic, subarctic, and alpine regions).

15 Seeds to 4 or 5 mm long (only 2 or 3 in each locule), with a membranous wing about 1 mm wide; fruiting pedicels often over 1 cm long; petals in one species to about 1.5 cm long; scapes to 1.5(3) dm tall . . . . *Parrya*

15 Seeds small, wingless; pedicels rarely over 1 cm long; petals at most 8 mm long; plants commonly less than 1 dm tall.

16 Pods to 3.5 cm long and 1.5 mm broad, the valves very lightly nerved on the lower half, the style to 3 mm long; seeds 1-rowed in each locule; leaves more or less rhombic-elliptic to -ovate, to about 3 cm long and 1 cm broad; plant glabrous, with slender and somewhat rhizome-like branches; *(C. bellidifolia)* . . . . *Cardamine*

16 Pods to about 1 cm long and 2.5 mm broad, the valves usually rather strongly 1-nerved, the style to 1 mm long, the septum consisting of characteristic transversely elongated thick-walled cells; seeds in 1 or 2 rows in each locule; leaves to about 3 mm broad; plants subglabrous to copiously pilose . . . . *Braya*

14 Plants leafy-stemmed (basal rosettes also often present).

17 Stem-leaves auriculate-clasping; pods dehiscent, their valves 1-nerved (sometimes only near the base in *Arabis*).

18 Stem-leaves sharply and often doubly serrate, tapering to each end (the lower ones to auriculate-clasping winged petioles), narrowly ovate to ovate-oblong; rosette-leaves rounded or cordate at base, slender-petioled; pods to 4 cm long, on short, horizontally spreading to somewhat ascending pedicels, their seeds 1-rowed in each locule; petals whitish to pink-purple, to about 1.5 cm long; essentially glabrous perennial to about 9 dm tall . . . . *[Iodanthus]*

18 Stem-leaves entire or merely sinuate-dentate, lanceolate to oblong-lanceolate, broad-based (or the lower ones tapering to winged petioles in *Halimolobos*); rosette-leaves lanceolate to oblanceolate, tapering to winged petioles.

19 Plants annual, glabrous and glaucous, to about 1.5 dm tall; petals white, to 3 mm long; pods to about 1.5 cm long and 0.8 mm thick, nearly terete, their seeds 1-rowed; stem-leaves to 1.5 cm long, the rosette-leaves somewhat smaller and short-petioled; *(A. salsuginea;* B.C. to w Ont.) . . . . *Arabidopsis*

19 Plants perennial, commonly taller, from a simple or branching caudex; petals white to reddish or purple, to over 1 cm long; pods rather strongly compressed (latiseptate), mostly longer (to over 1 dm long), their wingless or narrowly wing-margined seeds in 1 or 2 rows in each locule; rosette-leaves longer than the stem-leaves, tapering to relatively long margined petioles . . . . *Arabis*

17 Stem-leaves not clasping.

20 Pods indehiscent, torulose and finally breaking between the 1-seeded shelly-walled segments, to 4.5 cm long, upcurved on stout, spreading to somewhat ascending pedicels to 4 mm long, terminated by a beak to 2 cm long, the valves strongly 1-nerved, the style lacking; petals purple-red, to about 1 cm long, the spreading blade narrowly oblong;

leaves lanceolate to oblanceolate or elliptic-oblong, all but the
uppermost ones petioled, the blades to 8 cm long, rather deeply
sinuate-dentate; stipitate-glandular and often sparsely hirsute-pilose
annual to 5 dm tall; (introd. in s B.C.) . . . . *Chorispora*
20 Pods dehiscent.
   21 Pods lacking a partitioning septum, compressed, to 12 mm long and
      3 mm broad, with up to 10 seeds; flowers white, small; leaves long-
      petioled, entire, the lanceolate to ovate blades commonly less than
      1 cm long; plant to about 5 cm tall; (Aleutian Is. to the Yukon) . . . .
      . . . . *Aphragmus*
   21 Pods with an internal septum.
      22 Leaves lanceolate to oblanceolate or rather narrowly obovate,
         sessile or the lower ones tapering gradually to winged petioles,
         entire or remotely dentate, those of the rosettes persisting
         through the growing season; petals white to purplish; pods more
         or less compressed parallel to the broad septum (latiseptate),
         the style wanting or very short; perennials.
         23 Plant glabrous; leaves entire, slightly fleshy; petals to 4 mm
            long; pods often purplish, to about 2 cm long and 2.5 mm
            broad; seeds wingless, 1-rowed in each locule; plants to
            about 4.5 dm tall; (transcontinental in arctic and subarctic
            regions) . . . . *Eutrema*
         23 Plants usually more or less pubescent, the basal leaves
            sometimes distinctly toothed; petals to over 1 cm long; pods
            mostly over 2 cm long; seeds wingless or narrowly wing-
            margined, in 1 or 2 rows in each locule . . . . *Arabis*
      22 Leaves relatively broad, deltoid to cordate-rotund or even
         reniform, mostly over 3 cm broad, usually coarsely sinuate-
         crenate; petals white; pods subterete or slightly 4-angled, their
         wingless seeds 1-rowed in each locule; plants subglabrous or
         the stems sparsely pubescent toward base.
         24 Perennial to 6 dm tall, with elongate slender rhizomes; petals
            to 12 mm long; pods to 3.5 cm long and 4 mm broad, with a
            stylar beak to 2 (or even 6) mm long, on pedicels to 2 cm
            long, the valves very indistinctly 1-nerved near base; (*C.*
            cordifolia; mts. of s B.C.) . . . . *Cardamine*
         24 Taprooted biennial to about 1 m tall, garlic-scented; petals to
            6 mm long; pods to 6 cm long, on pedicels to 6 mm long, the
            style short and stout, the valves 3-nerved; rosette-leaves
            often withered by anthesis; (introd. in sw B.C., Ont., and Que.) . . .
            . . . . *Alliaria*

ALLIARIA Ehrh. [2914]

A. officinalis Andrz.   Garlic-Mustard
Eurasian; introd. near habitations, along roadsides, and in open woods in N. America, as in
sw B.C. (Vancouver Is.), Ont. (N to the Ottawa dist.), and Que. (N to Quebec City). [*Sisymbrium (A.) alliaria* L.].

ALYSSUM L. [3006] Alyssum

1 Capsule 2-seeded, with a single winged seed in each locule, stellate-pubescent or
   glabrate; (introd.) . . . . *A. murale*
1 Capsule 4-seeded, with 2 winged seeds in each locule.
   2 Capsules glabrous, the style nearly 1 mm long; sepals deciduous shortly after
      anthesis; leaves narrowly oblanceolate; (introd.) . . . . *A. desertorum*
   2 Capsules copiously stellate-pubescent.

   3 Sepals deciduous shortly after anthesis; petals golden yellow; leaves lanceolate to obovate; (introd.) . . . .[*A. montanum*]

   3 Sepals persistent; petals yellow or whitish.

      4 Pods to 4 mm long, tipped by a style scarcely 0.5 mm long; leaves linear-spatulate; stems to 3 dm tall; (introd.) . . . . *A. alyssoides*

      4 Pods to about 3 mm long, tipped by a style to slightly over 1 mm long; leaves spatulate-obovate; stems to about 2 dm tall; (Alaska to sw Dist. Mackenzie) . . . .*A. americanum*

A. alyssoides L.

Eurasian; introd. into grassland, roadsides, and waste places of N. America, as in s B.C. (N to Nicola, sw of Kamloops), s Alta. (Waterton Lakes; Breitung 1957*b*), Ont. (N to the Missinaibi R. at 49°37′N near Mattice; CAN), Que. (N to St-Onésime, Kamouraska Co.; DAO), and Nfld. (Rouleau 1956). [*A. calycinum* L.].

A. americanum Greene

/ST/W/A/ (Ch) Gravel banks of Alaska–Yukon between ca. 61° and 69°N (type from the Porcupine R. of Alaska–Yukon) and sw Dist. Mackenzie (Fort Simpson, ca. 62°N; CAN); Asia. MAPS: Porsild 1966: map 70, p. 75; Hultén 1968*b*:552.

A. desertorum Stapf

Eurasian; introd. in dry soils of sw Alta. (G.A. Mulligan, Can. J. Bot. 42(11):1509. 1964; near Pincher Creek), s Sask. (Indian Head and Mortlach; Breitung 1957*a*), and s Man. (Edwin, about 10 mi sw of Portage la Prairie; Herb. Man. Prov. Mus., Winnipeg). [*A. alyssoides sensu* Scoggan 1957, not L.].

[A. montanum L.]

[Eurasian; a collection in CAN from s Ont. (Seville, Elgin Co.; L.E. James in 1910) lacks data as to whether it was taken in a garden or as an escape.]

A. murale Waldst. & Kit.

Eurasian; a garden-escape in B.C. (Boivin 1966*b*) and in s Ont. (Port Franks, Lambton Co.; Rondeau Provincial Park, Kent Co.).

APHRAGMUS Andrz. [2911]

A. eschscholtzianus Andrz.

/Ss/W/ (Ch) Solifluction (frost-disturbed) soils of the Aleutian Is. (type locality), Alaska (N to the Seward Pen.), and sw Yukon. [*Braya* B. & H.; *Oreas involucrata* C. & S.]. MAPS: Hultén 1968*b*:500, and 1945: map 627, p. 968.

ARABIDOPSIS Heynh. [2999]

1 Stem-leaves auriculate-clasping, to 1.5 cm long; basal leaves few, entire, short-petioled, usually smaller than the stem-leaves; plant glabrous and glaucous, rarely over 1.5 dm tall; (B.C. to w ?Ont.). . . . .*A. salsuginea*

1 Stem-leaves nearly sessile but not auriculate-clasping, to 2 cm long, the upper ones often glabrous; basal leaves more numerous than the stem-leaves, remotely serrulate, thickly hirsute with simple and forking hairs, to 4 cm long, narrowed to slender petioles; stems pubescent near base with mostly simple spreading hairs, glabrous above, to 4 dm tall; (introd. in B.C. and s Ont.) . . . .*A. thaliana*

A. salsuginea (Pall.) Busch

/aST/WW/EA/ (T) Saline shores and alkaline or saline flats and prairies from southernmost Yukon (CAN) and the coast of Dist. Mackenzie (Anderson R. Delta, Liverpool Bay, and Kendall Is.; (CAN) to Great Bear L., Great Slave L., and northernmost Alta. (Wood Buffalo

National Park at ca. 59°45′N), s to sw B.C. ("Alkali spots on range land, Windermere, Columbia Valley"; Eastham 1947, as *A. glauca*), Sask. (near Saskatoon and Parkbeg; CAN; reported from Nokomis by Herbert Groh, Can. Field-Nat. 55(4):54. 1941), s Man. (Winnipeg dist. and Cartwright, E of Turtle Mt.; DAO), and w ?Ont. (Thunder Bay; Groh, loc. cit.), and in the U.S.A. to Colo.; E Europe; Asia. [*Sisymbrium* Pall.; *Thellungiella* Schulz; *S. (A.) glaucum* Nutt.; *Turritis diffusa* Hook.]. MAP: Hultén 1968b:502 *(Thell. sal.)*.

A. thaliana (L.) Heynh.   Mouse-ear-Cress, Thale Cress
Eurasian; introd. along roadsides and in dry fields and waste places of N. America, as in B.C. (N to Hazelton, ca. 54°N) and s Ont. (Essex, Kent, Elgin, Norfolk, Welland, Halton, Bruce, and Carleton counties). [*Arabis* L.; *Sisymbrium* Gay].

ARABIS L.   [3001]   Rock-Cress.   Arabette

(Ref.: Hopkins 1937; Rollins 1941)
1   Mature fruiting-pedicels deflexed, the pods pendent or strictly reflexed, glabrous (atypically pubescent in *A. holboellii*).
  2   Stem-leaves oblong-lanceolate to elliptic, to 2.5 cm broad, minutely dentate, tapering to a sessile non-clasping base, the lowest ones villous-hirsute; basal leaves soon deciduous; stem sparsely hirsute at base; petals creamy white, to 5 mm long; pods at least 2.5 mm broad; seeds broadly winged; (s Ont. and sw Que.) . . . .*A. canadensis*
  2   Stem-leaves linear to narrowly oblong or lanceolate, less than 1 cm broad, entire, sessile or auriculate-clasping, minutely stellate-pubescent or short-hirsute (or the upper ones sometimes glabrous); basal leaves persistent; petals white, pink, or purple; pods at most 2.5 mm broad; seeds narrowly winged; (Alaska–B.C. to Que.) . . . .*A. holboellii*
1   Mature fruiting-pedicels erect to wide-spreading or somewhat decurved, but not markedly deflexed.
  3   Fruiting pedicels nearly erect and rather closely appressed to the stem (*A. microphylla* may key out here); pods glabrous; stem-leaves auriculate- or sagittate-clasping at base.
    4   Basal leaves glabrous (except for the ciliate petiolar base) or rather sparsely pubescent with minute appressed 2–3-pronged hairs; petals to 1 cm long; pods strongly flattened.
      5   Seeds 1-rowed or imperfectly 2-rowed, orbicular, about 2 mm long and broad, the narrow wing less than 0.5 mm broad; pods to about 6 cm long; petals roseate or purplish; basal leaves to about 3 cm long; stems rarely over 2.5 dm tall, their leaves sessile or slightly auriculate-clasping, to 2 cm long; (mts. of B.C. and Alta.) . . . .*A. lyallii*
      5   Seeds 2-rowed, winged at the apex and on 1 side with a wing to 1 mm broad, narrowly winged or wingless on the other side, oblong or slightly broader, usually about 2 mm long and 1 mm broad; pods to 9 cm long; petals white or pinkish; basal leaves to about 9 cm long; stems to about 8 dm tall, glabrous throughout or sparsely appressed-pubescent at base, their glabrous leaves sagittate-clasping, to 7 cm long; (transcontinental) . . . .*A. drummondii*
    4   Basal leaves (and at least the base of the stem) copiously pubescent with coarse simple or branching hairs.
      6   Pods nearly terete in cross-section, to 1.3 mm thick, the wingless or very narrowly winged seeds 1-rowed or irregularly 2-rowed; petals yellowish, to 7 mm long; basal leaves usually coarsely pubescent with forked or dendritic hairs; stem glabrous and glaucous above, densely spreading-hirsute below; (introd. from B.C. to Que.) . . . .*A. glabra*
      6   Pods strongly flattened, to 5 cm long and 1 mm broad, the seeds 1-rowed, broadly winged above; petals white to pale yellow (rarely pinkish), to 9 mm

long; basal leaves more or less short-hirsute to villous-hirsute on both
surfaces; stem pubescent at least at base; (B.C. to N.S.) . . . .*A. hirsuta*

3 Fruiting pedicels not closely appressed to the stem; pods erect to horizontally
spreading or somewhat decurved.

   7 Stem-leaves tapering to a non-clasping base; petals white, pinkish, or
lavender-tinged; pods glabrous; seeds wingless, less than 1 mm broad; stems
rarely over 3.5 dm tall, hirsute below or essentially glabrous throughout.

      8 Leaves all entire, hirsute on both surfaces to glabrous, those of the stem
oblong to somewhat elliptic, at most 1.5 cm long; basal leaves to 4 cm
long and 1 cm broad; petals to 8 mm long; sepals to 4 mm long; pods to
about 3 cm long and 1.5 mm broad, their seeds 1-rowed; (mts. of B.C. and
Alta.) . . . .*A. nuttallii*

      8 Leaves (at least the basal ones) commonly shallowly dentate to lyrate-
pinnatifid; sepals usually less than 3 mm long.

         9 Pods to 3 cm long and 2 mm broad, their seeds 2-rowed; petals to 5
mm long; basal leaves usually shallowly dentate with up to 3 pairs of
teeth (sometimes entire); (N Sask. to Labrador) . . . .*A. arenicola*

         9 Pods to 4.5 cm long and less than 1.5 mm broad, their seeds 1-rowed;
petals to 8 mm long; basal leaves usually dentate to lyrate-pinnatifid;
(B.C. to W Que.) . . . .*A. lyrata*

   7 Stem-leaves distinctly auriculate-clasping at base; seeds essentially 1-rowed
(2-rowed when young in *A. divaricarpa*).

   10 Leaves and stems glabrous (except for the pilose leaves of the soon
disappearing first year's rosette in *A. laevigata*); pods glabrous, to about
1 dm long, recurving in maturity; plants biennial, from a simple or
branched taproot, the stems simple or branched from the base or above.

      11 Plant glaucous, the stem to 1 m tall, its lower leaves subentire to
serrate-dentate; pilose leaves of the first year's rosette soon withering;
pods to 2.5 mm broad, the valves faintly 1-nerved at base, rarely up to
the middle; petals white, to 5 mm long, equalling or slightly surpassing
the sepals; (Ont. and Que.) . . . .*A. laevigata*

      11 Plant green, the stem to about 5 dm tall, its lower leaves sharply
serrate-dentate to strongly laciniate or rarely lyrate-pinnatifid; glabrous
leaves of the first year's rosette persistent; pods to 2 mm broad, the
valves 1-nerved up to the middle or often 2/3 their length; petals
creamy- or yellowish-white, to 8 mm long, twice as long as the sepals;
(S ?Ont.) . . . .[*A. missouriensis*]

   10 Leaves (at least the basal ones) and stems (at least toward base, except
sometimes in *A. divaricarpa*) conspicuously pubescent.

      12 Pods finely stellate-pubescent (rarely glabrous), to 4 cm long and 1.25
mm broad, the valves nerveless or faintly nerved at base; seeds
wingless, oblong, averaging 1 mm long and 0.5 mm broad; petals white
to creamy, to 3 or 4 mm long; basal leaves mostly dentate, finely
stellate beneath, strigose above, to 1.5 dm long and 6 cm broad; stem-
leaves similarly pubescent or glabrous above, to 6 cm long; biennial
from a simple taproot, the stems to about 7 dm tall, simple or branched
from the base (rarely from the top); (S Ont.) . . . .*A. perstellata*

      12 Pods glabrous; seeds narrowly to rather broadly winged, orbicular.

         13 Plants biennial (rarely perennial), the erect stems usually solitary
(sometimes 2 or more) from a taproot, to about 9 dm tall, sparingly
appressed-pubescent at base with forking hairs or glabrous
throughout, their leaves mostly glabrous (very rarely the extreme
lowermost ones sparingly stellate-pubescent); basal leaves to 6 cm
long and 1 cm broad, finely and evenly pubescent on both surfaces
with minute stellate hairs, usually more or less dentate; petals pink
or purplish (rarely white), to 8 mm long; pods to 9 cm long and 3

mm broad, the valves prominently nerved 2/3 of their length or
more; (transcontinental) . . . . *A. divaricarpa*

13 Plants perennial, the stems usually few to numerous from a
branching caudex (sometimes solitary from a simple caudex in *A.
sparsiflora*), usually simple (occasionally branched above), erect or
somewhat decumbent at base.

14 Leaves fleshy, to over 1 dm long and 2.5 cm broad, stellate-
pubescent on both surfaces with 2–3-pronged hairs; petals white
to deep cream-colour; pods ascending or spreading-ascending,
to 7 cm long and 2 mm broad, their valves nerveless or faintly
nerved only at the very base.

15 Petals to 9 mm long; leaves greenish, moderately pubescent
with relatively coarse hairs, with up to 6 coarse teeth on each
margin; (s Dist. Keewatin and N Man. to Labrador and Nfld.) . . . . .
. . . . *A. alpina*

15 Petals to about 1.5 cm long; leaves densely whitish-felty-
tomentose (the hairs more stellate), with only 2 or 3 small
teeth on each margin; (introd.) . . . . *A. caucasica*

14 Leaves scarcely fleshy, at most 1 cm broad, entire or remotely
and shallowly dentate; petals commonly pink to reddish purple
(white in *A. sparsiflora* var. *columbiana*); (mts. of B.C.; *A.
lemmonii* also in the mts. of Alta.).

16 Basal leaves (and sometimes the lower stem-leaves) felted
with a dense coat of very minute branching hairs, to 2 cm
long, obtuse; petals to 6 mm long; pods to 4 (rarely 5) cm
long and 3.5 mm broad, slightly ascending to somewhat
pendent; stems to 2(4) dm tall . . . . *A. lemmonii*

16 Basal leaves (and sometimes the lower stem-leaves) with a
looser coarser pubescence of stalked 2–3-pronged hairs,
with or without an admixture of long simple hairs, usually
acute; pods narrower and mostly longer.

17 Pods erect to obliquely ascending, to 6 cm long and 1.5
mm broad, the valves faintly nerved toward base; seeds
about 1 mm broad; petals pale rose to purplish, to 6 mm
long; basal leaves to 2 cm long; stems to 5(7) dm tall . . . .
. . . . *A. microphylla*

17 Pods spreading-ascending to somewhat reflexed, to over
1 dm long and 2 mm broad, the valves nerved below the
middle; seeds to 2 mm broad; petals white, to nearly 1.5
cm long; basal leaves to 1 dm long; stems to 9 dm tall . . . .
. . . . *A. sparsiflora*

A. alpina L.

/aST/EE/GEA/ (Hsr (Ch)) Damp calcareous rocks and gravels, springy slopes, and wet
meadows (often subalpine) from sw-cent. Dist. Keewatin (Dubawnt L.; CAN) and NE Man.
(Churchill; Schofield 1959) to Southampton Is., cent. Baffin Is., and northernmost Ungava–
Labrador, s to N Ont. (Hawley L. in the Hudson Bay Lowlands at ca. 54°N; CAN), s Hudson
Bay (Long Is. and the Belcher Is., ca. 56°30′N), Que. (Hudson Bay coast s to ca. 55°N; Côte-
Nord; Gaspé Pen.; not known from the Maritime Provinces), and w Nfld.; w and E Greenland N
to ca. 75°N; Iceland; Spitsbergen; Eurasia. [*A. stricta sensu* Pursh 1814, and probably most
other Labrador reports, not Huds.]. MAPS: Hultén 1958: map 31, p. 51 (noting 3 other but very
erroneous total-area maps), and 1937b: map 5, p. 127; Porsild 1957: map 196, p. 185; *Atlas of
Canada* 1957: map 5, sheet 38; Hopkins 1937: map 3 (very incomplete), p. 85; Fernald 1924:
map 3, p. 560, and 1925: map 2, p. 248.

Forma *phyllopetala* Fern. (the firm petals greenish white and coarsely veined rather than
whiter and delicately veined) is known from the type locality, St. John Bay, w Nfld.

A. arenicola (Richards.) Gelert

/AST/(X)/G/ (Hs (Ch)) Dryish calcareous sands, gravels, and clays in Canada and Greenland (ranges of taxa outlined below, together with MAPS and synonymy).

1 Rosette-leaves and stem essentially glabrous; [*Eutrema* Rich.; *Parrya* Hook.; *Sisymbrium (A.) humifusum* Vahl; Sask. (L. Athabasca); coast of E Dist. Keewatin and Southampton Is. to cent. Baffin Is. and northernmost Ungava–Labrador, S to N Man. (S to York Factory), N Ont. (S to S Hudson Bay), the Belcher Is. in S Hudson Bay, and Labrador (S to ca. 57°N); W Greenland N to ca. 78°N, E Greenland between ca. 70°–72°N; MAPS (aggregate species): Porsild 1957: map 197 (the dot for S Victoria Is. should probably be deleted according to Porsild 1955), p. 185; Böcher 1954: fig. 32 (map 3), p. 134] . . . . var. *arenicola*

1 Rosette-leaves and base of stem pubescent with simple and forking hairs; [*A. humifusa* var. *pub.* Wats.; *Arabis petraea (Cardaminopsis* Hiit.) *sensu* John Macoun 1883, as to the York Factory, Man., plant, not (L.) Lam., and probably *sensu* John Rae 1850; essentially the range of the typical form but also known from Alaska, E-cent. Dist. Mackenzie, and an isolated station on Ellesmere Is. at ca. 80°N, and probably absent from Greenland; MAPS: Hultén 1968*b*:544; the above-noted maps by Porsild and Böcher evidently apply here except as to Greenland; W.J. Cody, Nat. can. (Que.) 98(2): fig. 22 (also indicating the area of var. *arenicola*), p. 152. 1971] . . . . var. *pubescens* (Wats.) Gelert

A. canadensis L. Sicklepod

/T/EE/ (Hs) Rich woods, thickets, and rocky banks from Nebr. to Minn., S Ont. (N to Waterloo and Victoria counties), SW Que. (reported from Breckenridge, S Gatineau Co., by Bernard Boivin, Can. Field-Nat. 65(1):16. 1951, and from Mt. Royal, Montreal, by R. Campbell, Can. Rec. Sci. 6(6):342–51. 1895), and cent. Maine, S to Tex. and Ga. [*Erysimum* Ktze.; *A. falcata* Michx.].

A. caucasica Schlecht. Wall Rock-Cress

Eurasian; cult. in borders and rock-gardens in N. America and occasionally spreading, as in S Ont. (common on rocky cliffs at Brockville, Leeds Co.; G.A. Mulligan, Can. J. Bot. 42(11):1511. 1964) and Que. (collection in DAO taken from a large tuft growing along the shore of the St. Lawrence R. near Notre-Dame-du-Portage, Kamouraska Co.); also reported from Nfld. by Rouleau (1956; lacking information as to whether or not escaped). [*A. alpina* ssp. *cau.* (Schlecht.) Briq.; *A. albida* Stev.]. MAP: Hultén 1958: map 31, p. 51.

A. divaricarpa Nels.

/ST/X/ (Hs) Ledges, gravels, sands, and dry hillsides, the aggregate species from N-cent. Alaska, cent. Yukon, and NW Dist. Mackenzie to Great Bear L., Great Slave L., L. Athabasca (Alta. and Sask.), Man. (N to Gillam, about 165 mi S of Churchill), Ont. (N to L. Nipigon; CAN), Que. (N to the Côte-Nord, Antiscosti Is., and Gaspé Pen.), and N.B. (Eel River, Restigouche Co.; not known from P.E.I. or N.S.), S to Calif., Colo., Nebr., Mich., and Vt. MAPS and synonymy: *see* below.

1 Pods less than 1.5 mm broad; [Sask. (Pilot Butte; Mortlach; Prince Albert), Man. (Brandon), and E Que. (type from Bic, Rimouski Co.); MAP: Hopkins 1937: map 17 (the Brandon station should be indicated), p. 133] . . . . var. *stenocarpa* Hopkins

1 Pods to 3 mm broad.

   2 Pods frequently slightly falcate, more or less spreading to slightly ascending or descending at a variety of angles, the inflorescence rather untidy in appearance; [*A. dacotica* Greene; *A. bourgovii* Rydb. (*Turritis patula* Graham); *A. div.* var. *pinetorum sensu* Bernard Boivin, Can. Field-Nat. 65(1):16. 1951, not *A. pinetorum* Tidestr.; essentially throughout the range of var. *divaricarpa*] . . . . var. *dacotica* (Greene) Boivin

   2 Pods straightish and more uniformly disposed in the inflorescence.

      3 Pedicels and upper part of stem rather copiously pubescent; [*A. interposita* and *A. acutina* Greene; B.C.: Chilcotin and Lytton; Herb. V] . . . . var. *interposita* (Greene) Rollins

3 Pedicels and upper part of stem essentially glabrous; [incl. vars. *deschamplainii* and *hemicylindrica* Boivin; *Turritis (A.) brachycarpa* T. & G.; *A. drummondii* var. *br.* (T. & G.) Gray; *A. brevisiliqua* Rydb.; *A. pratincola* Greene; *A. confinis* Wats. in part; *A. lyallii sensu* John Macoun 1886, as to the Cypress Hills, Sask., plant, not Wats.; transcontinental; MAPS (all but the first of the aggregate species): Hopkins 1937: map 16, p. 131; N.C. Fassett, Ann. Mo. Bot. Gard. 28(3): map 31, p. 365. 1941; Porsild 1966: map 71, p. 75; Hultén 1968b:548] . . . . var. *divaricarpa*

A. drummondii Gray

/ST/X/ (HS) Ledges, gravels, and thickets from s Alaska, cent. Yukon, and the Mackenzie R. Delta to Great Bear L., Great Slave L., N Alta. (L. Athabasca), Sask. (N to ca. 53°N), Man. (N to Kasmere L. at 59°34′N), Ont. (N to the N shore of L. Superior and the Ottawa dist.), Que. (N to the Côte-Nord, Anticosti Is., and Gaspé Pen.), Labrador (N to the Hamilton R. basin), Nfld., N.B., and N.S. (not known from P.E.I.), s to Calif., Colo., Iowa, Ohio, and Del. [*Erysimum* Ktze.; *Turritis* Lunell; *T. stricta* Grah., not *A. str.* Huds.; *A. albertina* and *A. oxyphylla* Greene; *A. confinis* Wats. in part]. MAPS: Hultén 1968b:548; Porsild 1966: map 72, p. 75; Raup 1947: pl. 26; N.C. Fassett, Ann. Mo. Bot. Gard. 28(3): map 32, p. 365. 1941; Hopkins 1937: map 18, p. 138.

The broad-podded extreme, var *connexa* (Greene) Fern. (*A. connexa* Greene; pods to 3.3 mm broad rather than at most 2.3 mm), occurs at widely separated locations throughout the range but seems scarcely worthy of recognition. Rollins (1941) notes that in one stand of the species in Colorado, nearly the complete range of pod-width was observed.

A. glabra (L.) Bernh. Tower-Mustard. Tourette

Eurasian; possibly native in the U.S.A. but apparently introd. in fields and thickets and on cliffs and ledges from s Alaska–Yukon–Dist. Mackenzie–B.C.–Alta. to Sask. (N to Bjorkdale, 52°43′N), Man. (N to Gillam, about 165 mi s of Churchill), Ont. (N to the Kaministikwia R. w of Thunder Bay and Matheson, 48°32′N), Que. (N to Bic, Rimouski Co.), and ?N.B. (Nat. Hist. Soc. N.B., Bull 11:48. 1893; *A. perfoliata*). [*Turritis* L.; *A. perfoliata* Lam.]. MAPS: Hultén 1968b:543 (*T. gl.*); Meusel, Jaeger, and Weinert 1965:190.

A. hirsuta (L.) Scop.

/ST/X/ (Hs) Cliffs, ledges, gravels, fields, and waste places, the aggregate species from the Aleutian Is. and cent. Alaska–Yukon–w Dist. Mackenzie to L. Athabasca (Alta. and Sask.), Man. (N to Gillam, about 165 mi s of Churchill), northernmost Ont., Que. (N to Anticosti Is. and the Gaspé Pen.), N.B., and N.S. (not known from P.E.I.), s to Calif., N.Mex., Kans., Mo., and N Ga. MAPS and synonymy: *see* below.

1 Pods rather plump and moniliform, 1-nerved to tip, the style at most 0.5 mm long; seeds narrowly winged only at the apex; stem-leaves distant, rather strongly dentate with up to 7 teeth; [*Turritis* L.; *A. sagittata sensu* Richardson 1823, not DC.; Eurasia; MAP (aggregate species): Meusel, Jaeger, and Weinert 1965:189] . . . . [var. *hirsuta*]
1 Pods less markedly moniliform, 1-nerved at most to the middle, the style to 0.9 mm long; seeds winged all around (very broadly so at apex); stem-leaves entire or with usually not more than 1 or 2 teeth.
    2 Petals mostly not over 5 mm long, white to cream-colour; outer sepals only moderately saccate; pods strictly erect; stem-leaves rather crowded; basal leaves rather copiously hirsute; stems commonly hirsute throughout.
        3 Stem spreading-hirsute with mostly simple hairs, its leaves hirsute; [var. *minshallii* Boivin; *A. pycnocarpa* Hopkins (the type from Nouvelle, Bonaventure Co., E Que.) and its var. *reducta* Hopkins; *A. ?borealis* Andrz.; *A. ovata* of auth. in part, perhaps not *Turritis ovata* Pursh, basionym; transcontinental; MAPS: Hultén 1968b:547; Hopkins 1937: map 9 (incomplete north-wards), p. 114; Porsild 1966: map 73, p. 76] . . . . . var. *pycnocarpa* (Hopkins) Rollins
        3 Stem appressed-pubescent or strigose with chiefly 2-forked hairs, its leaves essentially glabrous; [*A. pycnocarpa* var. *ad.* Hopkins; s Ont. (Essex, Huron, and Kent counties); MAP: Hopkins 1937: map 12, p. 117] . . . .
        . . . . var. *adpressipilis* (Hopkins) Rollins

    2 Petals to 9 mm long, white or pinkish; outer sepals markedly saccate; pods often
somewhat divergent; stem-leaves mostly remote; basal leaves sparsely hirsute to
nearly glabrous.

        4 Pods about 1 mm broad, the stigma nearly entire; stem-leaves usually entire;
upper part of stem glabrous; [*A. pycnocarpa* var. *gl.* (T. & G.) Hopkins;
A. rupestris Nutt.; s B.C. and sw Alta. (the inclusion of Sask. in the range of
A. rupestris by Rydberg 1922, requires confirmation); MAPS: Hopkins 1937:
map 10, p. 116; Rollins 1941: map 1, p. 321] . . . . var. *glabrata* T. & G.

        4 Pods to 2 mm broad, the stigma noticeably notched at apex; stem-leaves
usually dentate; upper part of stem hirsute; [*A. eschscholtziana* Andrz., the
type from Unalaska, Alaska; Aleutian Is.–s Alaska–w B.C.; MAPS: Hultén
1968b:547; Rollins 1941: map 1, p. 321] . . . . . . var. *eschscholtziana* (Andrz.) Rollins

A. holboellii Hornem.
/aST/X/G/   (Hs)   Calcareous cliffs and gravels and dry prairies and slopes up to fairly high
elevations (ranges of Canadian taxa outlined below), s to Calif., Colo., Nebr., Mich., and E
Que.; w and E Greenland N to ca. 71°N. MAPS and synonymy: *see* below.
    For a study of the *A. holboellii* complex, *see* T.W. Böcher (Sven. Bot. Tidskr. 48(1):31–44.
1954). The report of the closely related *A. puberula* Nutt. from B.C. by T.M.C. Taylor (1966b)
requires confirmation.

1 Stem-leaves not auricled at base; basal leaves less than 3 mm broad; stems
commonly less than 2 dm tall, pubescent below with coarse, simple or branched,
often spreading hairs; pedicels arched downward, not strictly reflexed and
straightish; [*A. pendulocarpa* Nels.; *A. canescens sensu* John Macoun 1890, as to
the Yale, B.C., plant, not Nutt. (which is the more southern *A. cobrensis* Jones; the
other B.C. citations by Macoun, at least for Lytton and the Nicola Valley, are based
upon var. *retrofracta*); s B.C. and sw ?Alta.; MAP: Rollins 1941: map 22, p. 442; the
map of the area of *A. pendulocarpa* by Hopkins 1937: map 31, p. 184, applies to
other varieties] . . . . var. *pendulocarpa* (Nels.) Rollins

1 Stem-leaves auricled at base and thus sagittate-clasping; basal leaves commonly
over 3 mm broad; stems often over 2 dm tall.

    2 Pedicels gently curved downward, the pods pendulous and usually somewhat
curved inward; basal leaves densely pubescent with coarse branching hairs;
[*A. pinetorum* Tidestr.; s B.C. to sw Sask.; MAP: Rollins 1941: map 20, p. 442] . . . .
. . . . var. *pinetorum* (Tidestr.) Rollins

    2 Pedicels abruptly bent near base, straight or at least not uniformly curved, the
pods strictly reflexed to somewhat spreading but not loosely pendulous;
pubescence of basal leaves fine.

        3 Lower part of stem hirsute with long, spreading, simple and forked hairs;
rosette-leaves mostly less than 5 cm long; stem-leaves less than 2.5 cm long
and 5 mm broad; petals to 7 mm long; sepals less than 1 mm broad; pods to 6
cm long and 1.5 mm broad, 2-nerved to or above the middle; [*A. collinsii*
Fern., the type from Bic, Rimouski Co., E Que.; *A. retrofracta* var. *coll.* (Fern.)
Boivin; the Yukon–Dist. Mackenzie (Boivin 1966b); B.C. to Rimouski Co.,
E Que.; MAP: Rollins 1941: map 22 (requiring considerable expansion
northwards and eastwards), p. 442] . . . . var. *collinsii* (Fern.) Rollins

        3 Lower part of stem finely and minutely hoary-stellate; rosette-leaves to 8 cm
long; stem-leaves to 4 cm long and 9 mm broad; petals to 1 cm long; sepals at
least 1 mm broad; pods to 8 cm long and 2.5 mm broad.

            4 Stem-leaves revolute-margined, the upper ones finely pubescent; sepals
rather persistently pubescent; pods strongly reflexed, acuminate, the
valves nerved to or above the middle; [*A. (Turritis) retrofracta* Graham (the
type from NW Canada) and its var. *multicaulis* Boivin; cent. Alaska–B.C. to
Man. (N to about 150 mi s of Churchill) and Ont. (N to Big Trout L. at ca.
54°N); E Que. (near Baie-St-Paul, Charlevoix Co.); MAPS (w area): Hopkins
1937: map 30, p. 180; Rollins 1941: map 21, p. 442] . . . .
. . . . var. *retrofracta* (Graham) Rydb.

4   Stem-leaves usually flat, the upper ones glabrous; sepals soon glabrate; pods slightly reflexed, blunt, the valves prominently 1-nerved only at base; [cent. Alaska–Yukon to B.C. (Marble Mts. NW of Clinton; Mt. Selwyn, ca. 55°N) and mts. of SW Alta. (region of Banff); E Que. (Bic, Rimouski Co.; L. Matane, Matane Co.; Cap-des-Rosiers, Gaspé Co.); Greenland N to ca. 71°N (type from near Jakobshavn); MAPS: Rollins 1941: map 20 (W area), p. 442; Hopkins 1937: map 29 (E area), p. 171; the area of the aggregate species is shown in maps by Raup 1947: pl. 26, T.W. Böcher, Biol. Skr. 6: fig. 19, p. 50. 1951, and Hultén 1968b:549] . . . . var. *holboellii*

A. laevigata (Muhl.) Poir.   Smooth Rock-Cress
/T/EE/   (Hs)   Rich woods, slopes, and shady (chiefly calcareous) ledges from ?N.Dak. to Minn., S Ont. (N to Bruce, Peel, Prince Edward, and Dundas counties), and SW Que. (N to Missisquoi and Rouville counties), S to Okla. and Ga. [*Turritis* Muhl.].
    Reports N to near Ottawa, Ont., and Quebec City, Que., by John Macoun (1883) and from Nfld. by Waghorne (1898) probably refer to some other species.

A. lemmonii Wats.
/sT/W/   (Hs (Ch))   Alpine meadows, cliffs, and talus slopes (ranges of Canadian taxa outlined below), S to Calif. and Colo. MAPS and synonymy: *see* below.
1   Pods usually not over 2 mm broad; stems usually several and not over 2 dm tall; [*A. canescens* var. *latifolia* Wats.; *A. oreocallis* Greene; SW Yukon (Mt. Archibald, near Mi. 1022 of the Alcan Highway) and mts. of B.C. and SW Alta. (Waterton Lakes to Bow Pass, about 25 mi NW of Lake Louise); MAPS: Rollins 1941: map 9, p. 358: Hultén 1968b:546 (aggregate species); Porsild 1966: map 74 (aggregate species), p. 76] . . . . var. *lemmonii*
1   Pods over 2 mm broad; stems few, usually over 2 dm tall; [*A. drepanoloba* Greene; SW Alta. (Crowsnest Pass; Waterton Lakes; Banff); MAP: Rollins 1941: map 11, p. 396] . . . .
    . . . . var. *drepanoloba* (Greene) Rollins

A. lyallii Wats.
/sT/W/   (Hs (Ch))   Subalpine to alpine ridges, cliffs, and drier meadows from SW Yukon through the mts. of B.C. and SW Alta. (N to Banff) to Calif., Utah, and Wyo. [*A. drummondii* var. *alpina* Wats.; *A. oreophila* Rydb.]. MAPS: Hultén 1968b:546; Rollins 1941: map 3 (incomplete northwards), p. 321.

A. lyrata L.
/ST/X/eA/   (Hs)   Ledges, cliffs, gravels, and sands (ranges of Canadian taxa outlined below), S to Wash., Mont., Minn., Mo., Tenn., N Ga., and N.C.; E Asia. MAPS and synonymy: *see* below.
1   Stems and rosette-leaves essentially glabrous; style short or obsolete; [vars. *glabra* (DC.) Hopkins and *occidentalis* Wats. (*A. occ.* (Wats.) Nels.); *A.* (*Cardaminopsis*) *petraea* and its var. *ambigua* (DC.) Regel (*A. ambigua* DC.) of Alaska–Canada reports, not *Cardamine pet.* L., basionym; Aleutian Is.–N Alaska–cent. Yukon–Dist. Mackenzie–B.C. to Sask. (between Prince Albert and L. Athabasca); Ont. (SE shore of L. Superior); Que. (Richmond Gulf, Hudson Bay, ca. 56°10′N); MAPS: Hultén 1968b:545; combine the maps by Hopkins 1939: map 6 (var. *kam.*), p. 92, and map 7 (var. *glabra*), p. 93; Raup 1947: pl. 26 (W area); Rollins 1941: map 5 (W area), p. 358] .
    . . . . var. *kamchatica* Fisch.
1   Stems hirsute below with simple or 2-forked hairs; rosette-leaves hirsute below and often above; style about 1 mm long . . . . var. *lyrata*
    2   Pods to 2 cm long; styles less than 0.5 mm long; petals relatively small; [Ottawa, Ont.] . . . . f. *parvisiliqua* Hopkins
    2   Pods to 4.5 cm long; styles to 1.25 mm long; petals to 8 mm long; [*Cardaminopsis* Hiit.; *A. petraea sensu* John Macoun 1883, as to the Ont. plant, not *Cardamine pet.* L.; Alaska (Hyder), SW Yukon, SW Dist. Mackenzie, L. Athabasca (Alta. and Sask.), Man. (Cowan, NE of Duck Mt.; reported from Carberry by Shimek 1927),

and Ont. (N to Schreiber, N shore of L. Superior); MAPS: Meusel, Jaeger, and Weinert 1965:188 (aggregate species); Hopkins 1937: map 5, p. 90] . . . . f. *lyrata*

A. microphylla Nutt.
/T/W/ (Hs (Ch)) Subalpine to alpine slopes and meadows from S B.C. (Lillooet; Nicola; Manning Provincial Park, SE of Hope; near Cranbrook) to Oreg., Mont., and Wyo. [*A. macounii* Wats.; *A. mic.* var. *mac.* (Wats.) Rollins]. MAP: Rollins 1941: map 16, p. 396.

[*A. missouriensis* Greene]
[The listing of this species of the E U.S.A. (N to Mich. and Maine; *see* Hopkins 1937: map 24 (*A. viridis*), p. 157) for S Ont. by Soper (1949) requires confirmation, perhaps being based upon the closely related *A. laevigata* (*A. viridis* Harger).]

A. nuttallii Robins.
/T/W/ (Hs) Moist grassy flats or thickets from S B.C. (Vancouver Is. and the mainland N to Nicola and Vernon) and SW Alta. (Crowsnest Pass; Waterton Lakes; Porcupine Hills) to Wash., Nev., Utah, and Wyo.; introd. at Whitehorse, S Yukon, and in NE ?Man. (reported from Churchill in the undated supplement to Lowe's 1943 checklist). MAPS: Hultén 1968b:545; Rollins 1941: map 6, p. 358.

A. perstellata E.L. Br.
/t/EE/ (Hs) Wooded hillsides and calcareous ledges from S.Dak. to Minn., S Ont. (Pelee Point and Middle Sister Is., Essex Co.), and N.Y., S to Kans., Ark., and Va.
    The Ont. plant is referable to var. *shortii* Fern. (*A. shortii* (Fern.) Gl.; *A. dentata* (Torr.) T. & G., not Clairv.; petals white to creamy, 2 or 3 mm long, rather than roseate and 3 or 4 mm long; fruiting pedicels to 4 mm long rather than to 10 mm; stem-leaves to 6 cm long rather than to 3 cm; stems relatively tall).

A. sparsiflora Nutt.
/sT/W/ (Hs) Dry hillsides from southernmost Yukon (Atlin; Rollins 1941; var. *columbiana*) through B.C. (Fort St. James, ca. 54°30′N; Vancouver Is.; North Thompson and Fraser valleys; Manning Provincial Park, SE of Hope) and ?Alta. (Hitchcock et al. 1964) to Calif., Utah, and Wyo.
    Our material is referable to var. *columbiana* (Macoun) Rollins (*A. col.* Macoun, the type from between Yale and Spences Bridge, Fraser Valley, B.C.; *A. ?breweri sensu* Carter and Newcombe 1921, not Wats.; petals white and at most 8 mm long rather than pink to purplish and usually over 8 mm long). Boivin (1966b) evidently includes this phase in var. *subvillosa* (Wats.) Rollins (the petals as in the typical form but the pedicels conspiciously hirsute (as in var. *columbiana*) rather than sparsely hairy to glabrous).

ARMORACIA Gaertn., Mey., & Scherb. [2965]

1 Basal leaves repeatedly pinnately dissected into filiform segments; emersed leaves (if present) finely to coarsely dentate; fruit ovoid, 1-locular, to 8 mm long, the style to 4 mm long, tipped by a 2-lobed stigma; stem submersed or prostrate; (Ont. and Que.) . . . . *A. aquatica*
1 Basal leaves coarsely and irregularly crenate, the blades to 3 dm long, cordate at base; stem-leaves smaller, the lower ones often pinnatifid; fruit subglobose or globose-obovoid, 2-locular, to 6 mm long, the short style tipped by a broad depressed stigma; stem erect; (introd.) . . . . *A. rusticana*

A. aquatica (Eat.) Wieg. Lake-Cress
/T/EE/ (HH) Lakes and quiet streams from Ont. (N to the Ottawa dist.; the report N to Batchawana Bay at the E end of L. Superior by Hosie 1938, is based upon *Bidens beckii*, the relevant collection in CAN) and SW Que. (N to Hull, Oka, Montreal, and Yamaska) to La. and Fla. [*Cochlearia* Eat.; *Neobeckia* Greene; *Radicula* Robins.; *Rorippa* Palmer & Steyerm.; *Nasturtium lacustre* Gray; *N. natans* var. *americanum* Gray; *Ror. amer.* (Gray) Britt.].

Forma *capillifolia* Vict. & Rousseau (aerial leaves similar to the much-dissected submersed leaves rather than entire or merely serrate or pinnatifid) is known from sw Que. (Oka; type from Boucherville, Chambly Co.).

A. rusticana (Lam.) Gaertn., Mey., & Scherb.   Horseradish.   Raifort
Eurasian; persisting in gardens or spreading to moist places in N. America, as in sw-cent. Yukon (Hultén 1945), sw-cent. Dist. ?Mackenzie (*see Rorippa crystallina*), s B.C. (Chilliwack; Deadman R., near Kamloops; Golden), Alta. (Fort Saskatchewan), Sask. (Breitung 1957a), Man. (N to Flin Flon), Ont. (N to Ottawa), Que. (N to the Gaspé Pen.), N.B., P.E.I., and N.S. [*Cochlearia* Lam.; *C. (A.; Nasturtium; Radicula; Rorippa) armoracia* L.; *A. lapathifolia* Gilib.]. MAP: Hultén 1968b:511.

ATHYSANUS Greene   [2993]

A. pusillus (Hook.) Greene
/t/W/   (T)   Dry, often grassy places from s B.C. (Vancouver Is.; Crawford Bay, Kootenay L.; Skagit and Columbia valleys) to s Calif. and Idaho. [*Thysanocarpus* Hook.].

BARBAREA R. Br.   [2961]   Winter-Cress

1   Basal leaves with up to 10 pairs of ovate, shallowly sinuate, lateral lobes; stem-leaves with up to 8 pairs of linear to oblong, mostly entire lobes; fruits mostly at least 4 cm long, on pedicels commonly over 1 mm thick, their beaks to 2.5 mm long; petals bright yellow, to 8 mm long; (introd.) . . . . *B. verna*
1   Basal leaves simple or rarely with more than 4 pairs of lateral lobes; fruits usually less than 3.5 cm long, on pedicels less than 1 mm thick.
  2   Beak of fruit stout, rarely over 1 mm long; petals pale yellow, at most 5 mm long; uppermost leaves lyrate-pinnatifid; middle and lower leaves with up to 6 or more pairs of small lateral lobes; (transcontinental) . . . . *B. orthoceras*
  2   Beak of fruit relatively slender, to 3 mm long; petals bright yellow, to 8 mm long; upper leaves merely coarsely dentate to angulate or lobed; lower leaves with at most about 4 pairs of small lateral lobes; (introd.) . . . . *B. vulgaris*

B. orthoceras Ledeb.
/aST/X/GEA/   (Hs)   Streambanks, swampy ground, and wet rocks from the Aleutian Is. and cent. Alaska–Yukon to Great Bear L., Great Slave L., L. Athabasca (Alta. and Sask.), northernmost Man.–Ont., Que. (N to s Ungava Bay, L. Mistassini, the Côte-Nord, and Gaspé Pen.), Labrador (N to L. Petitsikapau at ca. 55°N, 67°W), Nfld., and N.B. (Campbellton and Grand Manan; CAN; the report from P.E.I. by Hurst 1952, is based upon *B. vulgaris*, the relevant collection in DAO; not known from N.S.), s to s Calif., Ariz., Minn., and N.H.; southernmost Greenland; Eurasia. [*Campe* Heller; *B. (C.) americana* Rydb.; *B. planisiliqua* Mey.; *B. stricta* of Canadian reports in part, not Andrz.; incl. the completely intergrading var. *dolichocarpa* Fern., the pedicels and fruits more or less spreading rather than essentially erect]. MAPS: Hultén 1968b:506; Meusel, Jaeger, and Weinert 1965:187.

B. verna (Mill.) Aschers.   Early Winter-Cress, Belle-Isle Cress
Eurasian; a field-weed in N. America, as in sw B.C. (Vancouver Is.; Vancouver) and St-Pierre and Miquelon (GH); the report from Iona, P.E.I., by Hurst (1952) is thought by D.S. Erskine (1960) to refer to *B. vulgaris*.

B. vulgaris R. Br.   Common Winter-Cress, Yellow Rocket.   Cresson d'hiver or Herbe de Sainte-Barbe.
Eurasian; a very common weed of cult. fields, roadsides, and waste places in N. America and known from all the provinces with the exception of Sask., from where it has evidently not yet been reported; s Greenland.
1   Pedicels ascending to erect, the fruits closely overlapping in a dense raceme.

    2 Fruit (excluding beak) to about 3 cm long . . . . var. *vulgaris*
        3 Petals 4; [var. *longisiliquosa* Carion.; *B. (Campe) stricta* of auth. in part, not
            Andrz.; transcontinental, introd.] . . . . f. *vulgaris*
        3 Petals numerous, by transition from the stamens; [introd. at Wolfe Cove near
            Quebec City, Que.] . . . . f. *plena* Fern.
    2 Fruit (excluding beak) at most 1.5 cm long; [introd. on Anticosti Is., E Que.] . . . .
    . . . . var. *sylvestris* Fries
1 Pedicels spreading, the raceme lax and open.
    4 Fruit (excluding beak) to about 3 cm long; [introd. from Ont. to St-Pierre and
        Miquelon and N.S.] . . . . var. *arcuata* (Opiz) Fries
    4 Fruit (excluding beak) at most 1.5 cm long; [introd. on Anticosti Is., E Que.] . . . .
    . . . . var. *brachycarpa* Rouy & Foucaud

BERTEROA DC. [3015]

B. incana (L.) DC. Hoary Alyssum
Eurasian; introd. in fields and waste places of N. America, as in S B.C. (N to Spences Bridge),
S Alta. (Groh 1944a; High River, 50°35′N), S Sask. (Balgonie and Mortlach; Breitung 1957a), S
Man. (N to Ethelbert, E of Duck Mt.), Ont. (N to Renfrew and Carleton counties), Que. (N to
Cap-à-l'Aigle, Charlevoix Co., and the Gaspé Pen. near Métis), N.B. (near Buctouche, Kent
Co.), and N.S. (Annapolis and Kings counties). [*Alyssum* L.].

BRASSICA L. [2949] Mustard, Turnip. Moutarde or Navette

1 Beak of pod rather strongly flattened and 2-edged, 3-nerved, commonly more than
    half as long as the strongly 3-nerved (sometimes 5-nerved) valves and usually
    containing 1 seed in an indehiscent locule at its base (the dehiscent body of the pod
    with up to 8 or more seeds); petals to 1.5 cm long; stem-leaves not clasping, at least
    the lower ones petioled; stems hispid-hirsute below, often glabrous above; (*Sinapis*
    L.; introd.).
    2 Pods to 4 cm long and 4.5 mm broad, conspicuously bristly-hirsute, their sabre-
        like beaks from 2/3 as long as to nearly twice as long as the valves; seeds at most
        8, about 3 mm long; pedicels spreading horizontally or only slightly ascending;
        leaves all petioled, most of them lyrate-pinnatifid into up to 7 sinuate-toothed
        segments (only the reduced upper leaves often merely sinuate-lobed) . . . . *B. hirta*
    2 Pods to 5 cm long and 3 mm broad, not at all bristly, usually glabrous (or the
        beak stiffly hairy), the beak at most 2/3 as long as the valves; seeds often more
        than 8, about 2 mm long; pedicels strongly ascending (but not appressed);
        middle and upper leaves sessile and usually merely sinuate-dentate, the lower
        leaves lyrate-pinnatifid and on hispid petioles . . . . *B. kaber*
1 Beak of pod more or less terete, usually seedless and at most about half as long as
    the valves, these 1-nerved or sometimes with a less distinct pair of lateral nerves;
    (true *Brassica* L.; introd.).
    3 Upper leaves petioled or sessile but neither auricled nor clasping; beak of pod
        rarely more than 1/4 as long as the valves; petals to 8 or 9 mm long.
        4 Petals bright yellow; flowering pedicels usually shorter than the sepals;
            fruiting pedicels stout and erect, to 6 mm long; pods usually tightly
            appressed-ascending, to 2.5 cm long and 1.5 mm broad, their midnerves as
            prominent as the sutures; basal leaves lyrate-pinnatifid into a large terminal
            segment and a few small lateral ones; upper leaves sinuate-serrate; plant
            commonly sparingly to densely hirsute-hispid at least near the base . . . . . . *B. nigra*
        4 Petals pale yellow; flowering pedicels longer than the sepals; fruiting pedicels
            spreading-ascending, to 1.5 cm long; pods spreading-ascending, to 4 cm long
            and 3 mm broad, their midnerves much less prominent than the sutures; basal
            leaves lyrate-pinnatifid; upper leaves entire or dentate; plant nearly or quite
            glabrous and somewhat glaucous . . . . *B. juncea*

3 Upper leaves sessile, commonly broadened to a rounded or deeply cordate, more or less clasping and auricled base (if narrowed, their margins convex, the base thus not petiolar).

5 All leaves glabrous and glaucous; middle and upper stem-leaves never more than 1/3 clasping; upper leaves entire; basal leaves roundish with sinuate margins (occasionally lyrate-pinnatifid with a few small basal lobes); buds overtopping the open flowers; petals lemon-yellow, to 2.5 cm long; all stamens erect; pods to 1 dm long, subterete, the beak to 1 cm long; seeds to 4 mm thick; stem becoming woody and covered with conspicuous leaf-scars below; taproot not tuberous . . . . *B. oleracea*

5 Lowest leaves always somewhat bristly, usually more or less lyrate-pinnatifid; middle and upper stem-leaves cordate-based and at least 1/2 clasping; leaf-scars less conspicuous; filaments of outer stamens curved at base; pods more or less flattened; taproot stout and often tuberous.

6 Open flowers overtopping the buds, their bright-yellow petals to 1 cm long; pods to 6.5 cm long, the beak to 1/2 as long as the body; lowest leaves grass-green, bristly . . . . *B. rapa*

6 Open flowers slightly overtopped by the buds, their pale yellow or buff petals to 14 mm long; pods to over 1 dm long, the beak about 1/4 as long as the body; leaves all glaucous, the lowest ones sparsely bristly . . . . . *B. napus*

B. hirta Moench   White Mustard.   Moutarde blanche
Eurasian; introd. or esc. from cult. in N. America (as a source of mustard and as salad), as in the Yukon (Dawson; Porsild 1951a), B.C. (N to Kamloops), Alta. (Beaverlodge), Sask. (Cuworth; Melville; Saskatoon), Man. (near Otterburne), Ont. (N to Ottawa), Que. (N to Quebec City), N.B., P.E.I., and N.S.; s Greenland. [*Sinapis (B.) alba* L.]. MAP: Hultén 1968b:504 *(S. alba)*.

B. juncea (L.) Czern.   Chinese or Leaf-Mustard
Asiatic; introd. or esc. from cult. in N. America (as a source of oil from the seeds), as in s Alaska (Hultén 1945), cent. Dist. Mackenzie (Indin L., 64°17′N; W.J. Cody, Can. Field-Nat. 70(3):115. 1956), and in all the provinces. [*Sinapis* L.]. MAP: Hultén 1968b:504.

According to G. Berggren (Sven. Bot. Tidskr. 56(1):66. 1962), artificial hybridization between *B. campestris* (probably *B. rapa* of the present treatment; n = 10) and *B. nigra* (n = 8) results in plants identical with or very similar to *B. juncea* (n = 18). The crossing of *B. campestris* with *B. oleracea* (n = 9) produced apparent *B. napus* (n = 19) and the cross between *B. nigra* and *B. oleracea* resulted in apparent *B. carinata* (n = 17). He suggests that the high-chromosome species have originated by such hybridization between low-chromosome species.

B. kaber (DC.) Wheeler   Charlock.   Moutarde d'été
Eurasian; a common weed of fields and waste places in N. America, as in Alaska–Yukon–Dist. Mackenzie and all the provinces. MAP (*Sinapis arvensis*; aggregate species): Hultén 1968b:503.

1 Pods to about 2.5 cm long, on pedicels to 3 mm long, their beaks at most 12 mm long; [*Sinapis* DC.; *S. arvensis* var. *brevirostris* (Spach) Schulz; not yet definitely known from our area but to be searched for] . . . . [var. *kaber*]

1 Pods to about 5 cm long, on pedicels to about 7 mm long, their beaks to about 1.5 cm long.

2 Pod-beak glabrous; [*Sinapis or.* L.; *S. (B.) arvensis* var. *or.* (L.) Koch & Ziz; reported from Otterburne and Matlock, s Man., by Löve and Bernard 1959] . . . .
. . . . var. *orientalis* (L.) Scoggan

2 Pod-beak hispid.

3 Pods 3 or 4 mm thick, scarcely torulose; [*Sinapis arvensis* L. and its var. *pinnatifida* Stokes; *B. arv.* (L.) Rabenh., not L. (which is *Moricandia arv.* (L.) DC.); *B. sinapistrum* Boiss.; transcontinental, the common phase in N. America] . . . . var. *pinnatifida* (Stokes) Wheeler

3   Pods not over 2 mm thick, strongly torulose; [*S. schk.* Rchb.; *S. arvensis* var. *schk.* (Rchb.) Hagenb.; range of var. *pinnatifida* but less common] . . . . var. *schkuhriana* (Reichenb.) Wheeler

B. napus L.   Turnip, Winter Rape.   Navette
Eurasian; persisting after cult. in N. America and occasionally spreading to waste ground, as in s Alaska (Hultén 1945), sw Dist. Mackenzie (W.J. Cody, Can. Field-Nat. 77(2):118. 1963), B.C.–Alta.–Sask.–Man. (Boivin 1968), Ont. (N to sw James Bay), Que. (N to Duparquet, ca. 48°30′N), Labrador (N to the Hamilton R. basin), Nfld., N.B., P.E.I., and N.S.; s Greenland. [*B. campestris* and *B. rapa* of auth., not L.; incl. *B. napobrassica* (L.) Mill., Rutabaga or Swedish Turnip]. MAP: Hultén 1968b:505.

B. nigra (L.) Koch   Black Mustard.   Moutarde noire
European; introd. in cult. fields and waste places of N. America, as in s B.C. (Vancouver Is. and Revelstoke; CAN), Sask. (Saskatoon; Boivin 1969; reports from Man. probably refer to *B. kaber*), Ont. (N to Ottawa; John Macoun 1883), Que. (N to Matane, NW Gaspé Pen.), Nfld., N.B., P.E.I., and N.S. [*Sinapis* L.].

B. oleracea L.   Wild Cabbage (cult. races: Cabbage, Kale, Cauliflower, Broccoli, Brussels Sprouts, Kohlrabi).   Chou
European; occasionally esc. from cult. in N. America, as in s Ont. (Soper 1949), Que. (N to Rivière-du-Loup, Temiscouata Co.), Nfld. (Corner Brook; MT), and P.E.I. (D.S. Erskine 1960); cult. in s Greenland.

B. rapa L.   Bird's Rape.   Navette
Eurasian; cult. in N. America and spreading to waste places, as in Alaska (N to the Seward Pen.), s Dist. Mackenzie (W.J. Cody, Can. Field-Nat. 70(3):115. 1956; Yellowknife), and probably in all the provinces (but often confused with *B. napus*); s Greenland. [*B. campestris* L. in part]. MAP: Hultén 1968b:505.

BRAYA Sternb. & Hoppe   [3021]

(Ref.: *see* the following for further discussion of this very critical genus: Hultén 1945; Porsild 1943 and 1957; Polunin 1959; Joergensen, Soerensen, and Westergaard 1958; M.L. Fernald, Rhodora 20(240):201–03. 1918; E.C. Abbe, Rhodora 50(589):1–15. 1948; L.H. Jordal, Rhodora 54(638):36–38. 1952; R.C. Rollins, Rhodora 55(652):109–16. 1953; T.W. Böcher, Medd. Gronl. 147(7):24–33. 1950, 124(7):1–29. 1956, and Biol. Skr. 14(7):39–71. 1966)
1   Flowering stems leafy, the basal leaves entire or more or less toothed; pods linear, about 1 mm broad, their seeds 1-rowed or obscurely 2-rowed . . . . *B. humilis*
1   Flowering stems scapose; leaves entire; pods plump, 2 or 3 mm broad, their seeds distinctly 2-rowed.
    2   Scapes stiffly erect-ascending; pods 3–5 times as long as broad, soft-pubescent or glabrate . . . . *B. purpurascens*
    2   Scapes decumbent; pods at most about twice as long as broad, densely pilose . . . . *B. thorild-wulfii*

B. humilis (C.A. Mey.) Robins.
/AST/X/GA/   (Hs (Ch))   Calcareous gravelly or clayey barrens, the aggregate species from the coasts of Alaska–Yukon–Dist. Mackenzie to s Banks Is. and cent. Victoria Is. (an isolated station on w Ellesmere Is. at ca. 80°N), s in the West through the mts. of B.C. and sw Alta. to Colo. (ssp. *ventosa*; CAN), farther eastwards s to Great Slave L., N Man. (Churchill; York Factory; Gillam, about 165 mi s of Churchill), Ont. (sw James Bay N to s Hudson Bay at ca. 56°45′N; Big Trout L. at ca. 53°45′N, 90°W; N shore of L. Superior), N Mich. (Isle Royale, N L. Superior), E Que. (Anticosti Is.), Nfld., and the mts. of N Vt.; w Greenland near the Arctic Circle, E Greenland N of ca. 72°N; Asia. MAPS and synonymy: *see* below.
1   Pods to about 2 cm long, the styles about 0.5 mm thick.

2 Stems to about 2 dm tall; pods to 2 cm long, their styles less than 1 mm long; [*Sisymbrium* Mey.; *Torularia* Schulz; *Pilosella (B.) richardsonii* Rydb.; *S. arabidoides* Hook., at least in part; incl. ssp. *arctica* (Böcher) Rollins; western part of the N. American range; MAPS: Böcher, loc. cit. 1950:30 (aggregate species, as *Torularia hum.*) and loc. cit., 1966: fig. 21 (agg. sp.), p. 69; Porsild 1957: map 200 (ssp. *arct.*), p. 185; combine the maps by Hultén 1968*b*:553 (ssp. *rich.*) and p. 554 (ssp. *arct.*)] . . . . var. *humilis*

2 Stems to about 6 cm tall; pods to about 1.5 cm long, their styles about 1 mm long; [*B. novae-angliae* ssp. *abbei* Böcher, the type from Table Mt., Nfld., the only known locality; *B. ?fernaldii* Abbe; *B. ?longii* Fern.] . . . . var. *abbei* (Böcher) Boivin

1 Pods to about 2.5 cm long, with slender styles about 1 mm long; receptacle distinctly enlarged.

    3 Pods glabrous; style at most 0.25 mm thick; [*Pilosella (Arabidopsis; Braya) novae-angliae* Rydb.; *B. humilis* var. *nov.* (Rydb.) Fern.; L. Superior region, Ont.] . . . .
. . . . var. *leiocarpa* (Trautv.) Fern.

    3 Pods sparingly pubescent; style somewhat thicker.

        4 Mature fruiting pedicels to about 4 mm long; rosette-leaves often coarsely toothed or moderately lobed; [*B. novae-angliae* var. *laur.* Böcher, the type from Anticosti Is., E Que.] . . . . var. *laurentiana* (Böcher) Boivin

        4 Mature fruiting pedicels to 6 mm long; rosette-leaves entire or with a few teeth; [*B. novae-angliae* var. *interior* Böcher, the type from Churchill, Man.; Dist. Mackenzie and Alta.; N Man. and N Ont.] . . . . var. *interior* (Böcher) Boivin

B. purpurascens (R. Br.) Bunge
/Aa/X/GEA/ (Hr (Ch)) Calcareous gravelly and clayey barrens from the coasts of Alaska, Dist. Mackenzie, and Dist. Keewatin (not known from the Yukon) throughout the Canadian Arctic Archipelago (type from Melville Is.) to northernmost Ellesmere Is., s to w-cent. Dist. Mackenzie, Southampton Is., Coats Is., and northernmost Ungava–Labrador; w and E Greenland N of ca. 70°N; Iceland; Spitsbergen; N Eurasia. [*Platypetalum* R. Br.; incl. *P. dubium* R. Br.]. MAPS: Porsild 1957: map 201, p. 186; Hultén 1968*b*:554 (his maps for *B. bartlettiana, B. henryae,* and *B. pilosa* also probably apply here); Fernald 1925: map 58 (incomplete northwards), p. 325.

Several other species of this very critical genus that have been reported from our area may probably be included here. These are *B. americana* (Hook.) Fern. (*B. alpina* var. *amer.* Hook.; *B. humilis* var. *amer.* (Hook.) Boivin), *B. bartlettiana* Jordal, *B. glabella Rich., B. henryae* Raup, *B. intermedia* Soer., *B. linearis* Rouy, *B. pilosa* Hook., and possibly *B. fernaldii* Abbe and *B. longii* Fern., these treated as varieties of *B. purpurascens* by Boivin (1966*b*).

B. thorild-wulfii Ostenf.
/A/(X)/G/ (Hr (Ch)) Calcareous gravelly barrens of the N Canadian Arctic Archipelago (Prince Patrick Is.; Melville Is.; Ellesmere Is. at ca. 80°N) and w and E Greenland N of ca. 77°N (type from Greenland). [*B. purpurascens* var. *th.* (Ost.) Boivin]. MAPS: Porsild 1957: map 202, p. 186; Savile 1961: map J, p. 929; Böcher, loc. cit., 1966: fig. 21, p. 69.

BUNIAS L. [3046]

B. orientalis L.
Eurasian; introd. in meadows and waste places of N. America, as in s B.C. (Botanie and Lytton; Eastham 1947), Que. (Montreal dist.; Grosse-Ile, Montmagny Co.), sw N.B. (Grand Manan), and N.S. (Boivin 1966*b*).

CAKILE Mill. [2920] Sea-Rocket. Caquillier

1 Fruits slightly to much constricted at the joint; leaves commonly spatulate and sinuately toothed (varying to pinnately lobed or nearly entire); (coastal sands of the Pacific and Atlantic oceans and the Great Lakes) . . . . *C. edentula*

1   Fruits usually expanded at the joints into projecting wings; at least the lower leaves
    usually distinctly pinnatifid; (introd. in sw B.C.) . . . .*C. maritima*

C. edentula (Bigel.) Hook.
/sT/D (coastal)/E/   (T)   Coastal sands: s Alaska through w B.C. to Calif.; shores of Lakes
Michigan, Huron, Erie, and Ontario; E Que. (St. Lawrence R. estuary from l'Islet Co. to the
Côte-Nord, Anticosti Is., and Gaspé Pen.) to s Labrador (Forteau, 51°27'N), Nfld., N.B., P.E.I.,
and N.S., s to S.C.; Iceland; the Azores; N Norway and N Russia. MAPS and synonymy: *see*
below.
1   Upper joint of fruit flattened-ovoid, to about 13 mm long and 6.5 mm broad, at least
    1/3 as broad as long; [*Bunias* Bigel.; *C. maritima* var. *americana* (Nutt.) T. & G. (*C.
    amer.* Nutt.); *C. maritima* of Canadian reports other than by Boivin 1966*b*, not Scop.;
    C. ed. var. *californica* (Heller) Fern. (*C. calif.* Heller); Pacific and Atlantic coasts (the
    report from Churchill, Man., by Lowe 1943, is based upon *Chrysanthemum arcticum,*
    the relevant collection in Herb. Man. Prov. Mus., Winnipeg, Man.); MAPS (aggregate
    species): Hultén 1968*b*:503; Meusel, Jaeger, and Weinert 1965:177; A. Löve and D.
    Löve, Iceland Univ. Inst. Appl. Sci. Dept. Agric. Repts. Ser. B2: fig. 8, p. 10. 1947] . . . .
    . . . . .var. *edentula*
1   Upper joint of fruit lance-ovoid, to about 2 cm long and 4 mm broad, not over 1/3 as
    broad as long; [s Ont.: shores of Lakes Erie, Huron, and Ontario] . . . . .var. *lacustris* Fern.

C. maritima Scop.
European; introd. on coastal rubbish in N. America and reported from sw B.C. by Boivin
(1966*b*).

CAMELINA Crantz   [2987]   False Flax

1   Seeds about 1 mm long and 0.7 mm broad, oblong or narrowly oval, only slightly
    compressed, brownish red, at first honeycomb-reticulate, becoming warty; fruits less
    than 5 mm thick, their walls remaining thin, obscurely reticulate, the valves with an
    indistinct midrib; pedicels seldom over 1.5 cm long; stem and leaves harsh with long
    simple and branching hairs exceeding the short stellate pubescence . . . . .*C. microcarpa*
1   Seeds commonly over 2 mm long, light orange, minutely tuberculate; fruits to 7 mm
    thick, their walls soon hardening, moderately reticulate when dry, the valves with a
    prominent midrib; pedicels often over 1.5 cm long; stem and leaves glabrate or
    sparingly pubescent with stellate hairs and short simple hairs.
    2   Seeds narrowly oval to ellipsoid and twisted-conical; cotyledons incumbent
        (tangential to the radicle or embryo-root) . . . .*C. sativa*
    2   Seeds mitiform (concave on one face and somewhat resembling a baseball
        catcher's glove in shape); cotyledons accumbent (radial to the radicle) . . . . .*C. parodii*

C. microcarpa Andrz.
Eurasian; introd. along roadsides and in fields and waste places of N. America, as in B.C. (N to
Dawson Creek, ca. 55°45'N), Alta. (Moss 1959), Sask. (Breitung 1957*a*), Man. (N to Swan
River, N of Duck Mt.), Ont. (N to Moosonee, sw James Bay, 51°16'N), Que. (N to the sw Gaspé
Pen. at Matapédia), Nfld., N.B., P.E.I., and N.S.

C. parodii Ibarra & LaPorte
Eurasian; introd. in waste and cult. fields of N. America, as in s Alta. (Aden), s Sask. (Delisle;
?Swift Current), and s Man. (Arborg; Winnipeg). [*C. dentata* of most or all Canadian reports,
not (Willd.) Pers.].

C. sativa (L.) Crantz
Eurasian; introd. along roadsides and in cult. fields and waste places in N. America, as in s
Alaska (Sitka), s Dist. Mackenzie (N to Fort Simpson, ca. 62°N; W.J. Cody, Can. Field-Nat.
75(2):63. 1961), and all the provinces. [*Myagrum* L.]. MAP: Hultén 1968*b*:519.

CAPSELLA Medic.   [2986]   Shepherd's-purse.   Tabouret

1 Lateral margins of fruit straight or slightly convex; petals white, to over 2 mm long, distinctly surpassing the sepals . . . . *C. bursa-pastoris*
1 Lateral margins of fruit concave; petals usually red-tinged, rarely over 1.5 mm long, at most only slightly surpassing the sepals . . . . *C. rubella*

C. bursa-pastoris (L.) Medic.
Eurasian; a common weed of roadsides, fields, and waste places in N. America, known in our area from N-cent. Alaska, cent. Yukon, NW Dist. Mackenzie, and all the provinces (in Sask. N to L. Athabasca; in Ont., N to S Hudson Bay; in Labrador, N to Nain, 56°33′N); S Greenland. [*Thlaspi* L.; *Bursa* Britt.]. MAP: Hultén 1968*b*:518.
   Var. *bifida* Crépin (the pods with an apical notch about 1 mm deep rather than subtruncate or merely somewhat emarginate at summit) is known from Nfld. (Burgeo and Birchy Cove; GH).

C. rubella Reut.
Eurasian; introd in waste places of N. America (but much less common than the preceding species), as in the Aleutian Is. and Alaska (Hultén 1945), E Que. (Côte-Nord and Gaspé Pen.), Labrador (N to Nain, 56°33′N; GH), Nfld. (GH), and N.B. (St. John; GH). MAP: Hultén 1968*b*:518.

CARDAMINE L.   [2966]   Bitter Cress

(Ref.: Detling 1937; 1936 (*Dentaria,* an alternative genus for several species))
1 Leaves all simple, entire to coarsely few-toothed or lobed but scarcely pinnatifid; (perennials).
   2 Plant glabrous, the numerous scapose stems mostly less than 1.5 dm tall, from a taproot and often a slender-branched caudex; leaves all or nearly all long-petioled in dense basal tufts, their ovate blades entire or with 1 or 2 lateral teeth, to 1.5 cm long; petals white or pink, to 5 mm long; pods to 3.5 cm long, crowded and erect on pedicels to 1 cm long, the main axis scarcely elongating; (transcontinental in arctic, subarctic, and alpine regions) . . . . *C. bellidifolia*
   2 Plants leafy-stemmed and taller; leaves mostly larger and usually shallowly sinuate or with a few very coarse teeth; floral axis greatly elongating in fruit.
      3 Leaves all petioled, up to about 8 on a stem, broadly cordate-ovate to reniform, subentire to rather shallowly sinuate-lobed; petals white, to 12 mm long; pods to 4 cm long, on pedicels to about 3 cm long; stems from a running rootstock, to 6 dm tall; (S B.C.) . . . . *C. cordifolia*
      3 Upper stem-leaves sessile at the broadly cuneate to rounded base, the stem-leaves lanceolate to broadly ovate, entire to coarsely few-toothed, the basal leaves long-petioled, oblong to cordate-rotund or reniform; pods to about 3 cm long; stems from a short thick tuberous base.
         4 Petals normally pink-purple, to 2 cm long; lowest fruiting pedicels to 4 cm long; stem more or less spreading-hirsute, with mostly not more than 5 leaves, these all sessile except sometimes the lower 1 or 2; (Ont.) . . . .
             . . . . *C. douglassii*
         4 Petals normally white, to about 1.5 cm long; lowest fruiting pedicels to about 2.5 cm long; stem glabrous (or sometimes retrorse-hirsute at the very base), with up to 14 leaves, the lower 2–5 leaves petioled; (SE Man. to S Que.) . . . . *C. bulbosa*
1 At least some of the principal leaves usually deeply pinnatifid or pinnately compound (sometimes palmately compound; uppermost leaves often simple; at least some of the lowermost leaves of *C. breweri* usually simple).
   5 Petals commonly about 1 cm long (at least 8 mm and up to about 15 mm); perennials.
      6 Leaflets numerous (usually at least 9), pinnately arranged, those of the lower leaves ovate to roundish or reniform and stalked, those of the upper leaves

linear to oblong, entire or obscurely toothed; style at most 2 mm long; pods to about 3 cm long and 2 mm broad; stems to about 5 dm tall, from a short rhizome; (transcontinental) . . . . *C. pratensis*

6   Leaflets 3 or 5 (sometimes 7 on the basal leaves); (B.C.).

     7   Stems to 8 dm tall, from slender extensively creeping rhizomes; leaflets of the stem-leaves narrowly to broadly ovate, to 7 cm long, with 3–5(7) coarse teeth or angulate lobes; sepals to 3 mm long; petals white to pinkish; style to 4 mm long; pods to 4 cm long and 2 mm broad . . . . *C. angulata*

     7   Stems to about 3 dm tall, from short slender rhizomes commonly not over 3 cm long; leaflets of the stem-leaves mostly narrowly oblong and entire or nearly so; sepals to 5 mm long, often purplish; petals pink to reddish or purplish; style to 6 mm long; pods to about 5 cm long and 1.5 mm broad . . . . . .
. . . . *C. pulcherrima*

5   Petals at most about 8 mm long; style to 2 mm long; at least the lower stem-leaves pinnately parted or divided, the terminal lobe usually much the largest.

     8   Radical leaves usually simple (at least in part, or some of them with a pair of relatively small lateral leaflets; *C. purpurea* may sometimes key out here), broadly cordate to reniform, subentire or sinuate; stem-leaves mostly pinnately 5-foliolate (or the upper ones 3-foliolate); petals white, to 7 mm long; pods to 3 cm long and 1.5 mm broad; stems to 6 dm tall; rhizomatous perennial; (B.C.) . . . . *C. breweri*

     8   Radical leaves pinnately compound (as also at least the principal stem-leaves).

         9   Perennials; petals mostly to 7 or 8 mm long (at most 5 mm in *C. occidentalis*).

             10 Petals at most 5 mm long, white; inflorescence elongate; pods to 3 cm long; basal leaves numerous in a rosette, with 5 or 7 oval to cordate-oval, entire or shallowly sinuate leaflets, the terminal leaflet to 2 cm long; lateral leaflets of the stem-leaves linear to ovate-lanceolate, the terminal leaflet more nearly ovate to cuneate; plant glabrous or sparingly hirsute but finally glabrate, to about 4 dm tall, from a short slender rhizome; (B.C.) . . . . *C. occidentalis*

             10 Petals to 7 or 8 mm long; inflorescence often subumbellate; plants rarely over 2 dm tall; (western arctic and subarctic regions).

                 11 Leaflets all linear or linear-lanceolate, entire, acute, the terminal leaflet of the solitary radical leaf to 4 cm long; petals white; pods to 4 cm long; plant glabrous, from a slender horizontal rhizome . . . .
. . . . *C. digitata*

                 11 Leaflets ovate to orbicular or reniform, commonly less than 1.5 cm long, the terminal leaflet the largest and often 3-toothed or -lobed toward the apex.

                     12 Leaves and stem glabrous, the stem to 2 dm tall, with up to 5 leaves, from slender horizontal rhizomes; petals white; pods to 4 cm long . . . . *C. minuta*

                     12 Leaves and upper part of stem pubescent, the stem to 1.5 dm tall and bearing up to 3 leaves, from a tough rhizome; petals white to violet-purple; pods usually less than 2.5 cm long . . . .
. . . . *C. purpurea*

         9   Annuals or biennials, fibrous-rooted or a slender taproot also present; petals 3 or 4 mm long, white; pods to 3 cm long.

             13 Leaflets of the stem-leaves linear to narrowly oblanceolate, commonly not over 1 or 2 mm broad, slender-stalked, their bases not decurrent along the rachis, the terminal leaflet only slightly broader than the lateral ones; leaflets of the basal leaves oblong to obovate or rotund; petioles eciliate; petals to 3.5 mm long; stem glabrous throughout; (transcontinental) . . . . *C. parviflora*

13 Leaflets of the stem-leaves mostly oblanceolate to obovate, ovate, or
   rotund, often more than 2 mm broad, slender-stalked.
   14 Stems usually glabrous, stiffly ascending, to 3 dm tall; leaflets of the
      stem-leaves slender-stalked, their bases not decurrent along the
      rachis; petioles hirsute-ciliate; petals to 2 mm long (sometimes
      wanting); stamens 4; styles about 0.5 mm long; (introd.) . . . . . .*C. hirsuta*
   14 Stems hispid or hirsute at least toward the base; stamens mostly 6
      (sometimes 4 in *C. oligosperma*).
      15 Petioles of the stem-leaves eciliate; leaflets of the stem-leaves
         commonly with oblique bases decurrent along the rachis (or
         some of the stem-leaves simple and uncleft or merely pinnatifid);
         petals to 4 mm long; style to 2 mm long; (transcontinental) . . . .
         . . . . *C. pensylvanica*
      15 Petioles of the stem-leaves conspicuously hirsute-ciliate; leaflets
         slender-stalked, their bases not decurrent along the rachis.
         16 Fruiting pedicels to 13 mm long; style to 1 mm long; (introd.
            in Que. and Nfld.) . . . . *C. flexuosa*
         16 Fruiting pedicels rarely over 6 mm long; style scarcely 0.5 mm
            long; (B.C. and w Alta.) . . . . *C. oligosperma*

C. angulata Hook.
/T/W/ (Grh) Wet ground, streambanks, and moist woods on the w side of the Cascades
from the southernmost Alaska Panhandle through B.C. to N Calif. MAP: Hultén 1968*b*:513.

C. bellidifolia L.
/AST/X/GEA/ (Ch (Hr)) Mossy tundra, snow-patches, cold ravines, and wet mossy rocks
from the coasts of Alaska–Yukon–Dist. Mackenzie to northernmost Ellesmere Is. and northernmost Ungava–Labrador, s in the West through the mts. of B.C. and sw Alta. to N Calif., farther eastwards s to s Dist. Keewatin, Que. (s to SE Hudson Bay at ca. 56°30′N, Mollie T. Lake
at 55°03′N, 67°10′W, and the Shickshock Mts. of the Gaspé Pen.), and Labrador (s to ca.
56°N), and the mts. of Maine and N.H.; circumgreenlandic; Iceland; Spitsbergen; Eurasia.
MAPS: Hultén 1968*b*:512; Porsild 1957: map 180, p. 183; Böcher 1954: fig. 47 (bottom), p. 177;
Raup 1947: pl. 26; Tolmachev 1952: map 20 (very incomplete for N. America); Meusel, Jaeger,
and Weinert 1965:187; Meusel 1943: fig. 7a (very incomplete for N. America).
   Forma *laxa* (Lange) Polunin (plant relatively loose in habit, the stems to over 1.5 dm long,
the branches elongated below the surface of the moss-cover) occurs throughout the range.
Var. *pinnatifida* Hult. (some of the leaves distinctly pinnatifid) is reported from the type locality, Cape Beaufort, Alaska, by Hultén (1968*a*).

C. breweri Wats.
/T/W/ (Gst) Wet places chiefly w of the Cascades from s ?Alaska (*see* below) through
B.C. to Calif. and Wyo.
1 Terminal leaflet of the stem-leaves cuneate to truncate or rounded at base; sepals to
   2.5 mm long; petals to 7 mm long; [sw B.C. (Langley, near Vancouver; CAN; the
   report of *C. pratensis* var. *occidentalis* Wats. (*C. occid.* (Wats.) Howell) from B.C. by
   John Macoun 1890, is referred here by J.M. Macoun 1894); reports from Alaska
   probably refer to *Barbarea orthoceras*] . . . . var. *breweri*
1 Terminal leaflet of at least the lower compound stem-leaves cordate at base; sepals
   to 2 mm long; petals to 6 mm long; [*C. orbicularis* Greene; Alaska southwards
   according to Hitchcock et al. 1964, but *Barbarea orthoceras* may be the Alaskan
   species concerned] . . . . [var. *orbicularis* (Greene) Detling]

C. bulbosa (Schreb.) BSP. Spring-Cress
/T/EE/ (Gst) Meadows, wet woods, and streambanks from SE Man. (Otterburne, about 30
mi s of Winnipeg; Löve and Bernard 1959) to Ont. (N to the Ottawa dist.; a collection in TRT
from the Pigeon R. near Thunder Bay may also belong here), Que. (N to Gatineau, Vaudreuil,

Deux-Montagnes, and Chateauguay counties; reports from N.S. by John Macoun 1883, may refer to *C. pensylvanica*), and Vt., s to E S.Dak., Tex., and Fla. [*Arabis* Schreb.; *C. rhomboidea* DC.; *C. rotundifolia sensu* John Macoun 1883, not Michx., according to Macoun 1890].

C. cordifolia Gray
/T/W/ (Grh) Mountain streambanks to alpine meadows from s B.C. (Horsethief Creek in the Purcell Range; Ulke 1935; *C. lyallii* reported from the Cascades by Henry 1915, and from near Princeton by J.M. Macoun, Ottawa Naturalist 21(8):158. 1907) to N Calif., Nev., and Idaho.

The B.C. plant is evidently var. *lyallii* (Wats.) Nels. & Macbr. (*C. lyallii* Wats.; petals at most 9 mm long rather than to 12 mm).

C. digitata Richards.
/aS/WW/eA/ (Grh) Moist turfy or hummocky tundra from the coasts of Alaska–Yukon–Dist. Mackenzie to N Banks Is., Victoria Is., and cent. Dist. Keewatin, s to N-cent. Alaska–Yukon, Great Bear L., and SE Dist. Keewatin near the Man. boundary; E Asia. [*C. hyperborea* Schulz; *C. richardsonii* Hult.]. MAPS: Hultén 1968*b*:516 (*C. hyp.*); Porsild 1957: map 182, p. 183; *Atlas of Canada* 1957: map 17, sheet 38; Tolmachev 1952: map 15 (*C. hyp.*); W.J. Cody, Nat. can. (Que.) 98(2): fig. 5, p. 148. 1971.

C. douglassii (Torr.) Britt.
/T/EE/ (Gst) Rich moist woods and wet ground from Wisc. to Ont. (N to the Ottawa dist.; Gillett 1958; the report from Churchill, Man., by Lowe 1943, may refer to *C. pratensis* var. *palustris*) and Conn., s to Mo., Tenn., and Va. [*Arabis* Torr.; *C. rhomboidea (bulbosa)* var. *purpurea* Torr.].

C. flexuosa With.
European; known in Canada from Que. (Peribonka R., N of L. St. John; CAN) and Nfld., where considered to be at least partly indigenous by M.L. Fernald (Rhodora 35(416):267. 1933), who, however, notes that it was possibly introd. in a park at St. John's, Nfld. Collections from along a railway track at Whitbourne, Nfld. (Robinson and Schrenk in 1894; CAN; GH) are undoubtedly from introd. plants, as is probably the case with all Canadian material (*see* discussion under *Luzula campestris*). The reports from Shannonville and Island Portage, Ont., by John Macoun (1890) are based upon *C. parviflora* var. *arenicola* (relevant collections in CAN). [*C. scutata* ssp. *flex.* (With.) Hara; *C. sylvatica* Link]. MAP: Hultén 1958: map 125 (together with the scarcely separable *C. regeliana* Miquel of the w Aleutian Is. and Asia), p. 145.

C. hirsuta L.
Eurasian; introd. along roadsides and in lawns and old fields in N. America, as in B.C. (N to Revelstoke; CAN), Ont. (Point Pelee, Essex Co.; Wasaga Beach, Simcoe Co.; Ottawa dist.), and ?Que. (Rouleau 1947). [*C. ?virginica sensu* Pursh 1814, not L., which is the southern *Sibara virg.* (L.) Rollins].

C. minuta Willd.
/aS/W/eA/ (Grh) Wet places of N Alaska (s to the Seward Pen. at ca. 64°N and St. Lawrence Is., Bering Strait) and NW Dist. Mackenzie (Richardson Mts. near the Yukon boundary at 67°33′N; G.A. Mulligan, Can. J. Bot. 43(6):662. 1965); E Asia. [*C. blaisdellii* Eastw.; *C. microphylla* Adams, not J. & C. Presl nor *Dentaria mic.* Willd.]. MAPS: Hultén 1968*b*:516 (*C. mic.*); Tomachev 1952: map 16.

C. occidentalis (Wats.) Howell
/T/W/ (Grh) Wet ground and streambanks from ?Alaska (Hitchcock et al. 1964) and B.C. (N to Queen Charlotte Is.; G.A. Mulligan, Can. J. Bot. 43(6):662. 1965) to Oreg. [*C. pratensis* var. *occ.* Wats.].

C. oligosperma Nutt.

/ST/W/eA/ (Grh) Wet places (ranges of Canadian taxa outlined below), s to s Calif. and Mont.; E Siberia. MAPS and synonymy: *see* below.

1 Raceme open, its rachis usually well over 3 cm long; [*C. hirsuta* var. *parviflora* Nutt.; B.C., the N limits uncertain through gradual intergradation with the following taxon] . . . . .
. . . . var. *oligosperma*

1 Raceme subumbellate, the rachis usually only 1 or 2 cm long; [*C. sylvatica* var. *kamt.* Regel, the type from St. Paul Is., Alaska; *C. hirsuta* var. *acuminata* Nutt. (*C. acum.* (Nutt.) Rydb.); *C. intermedia* Holm; *C. ?neglecta* and *C. umbellata* Greene; Aleutian Is.–Alaska–s Yukon (*see* Hultén 1945: map 643 *(C. umb.),* p. 969) and mts. of B.C. and sw Alta. (Banff; Jasper; a mt. at 53°54'N); MAPS *(C. umb.):* Hultén 1968*b*:514; Porsild 1966: map 76, p. 76; Tolmachev 1952: map 18; W.J. Cody, Nat. can. (Que.) 98(2): fig. 7, p. 148. 1971] . . . . var. *kamtschatica* (Regel) Detling

C. parviflora L.

/sT/X/EA/ (Hs) Ledges, sandy soil, and dry woods from B.C. (N to Fort Nelson, 58°48'N; CAN) and sw Dist. Mackenzie (Yellowknife; W.J. Cody, Can. Field-Nat. 70(3):115. 1956) to Alta. (Crowsnest L.; CAN), Man. (N to Flin Flon; not known from Sask.), Ont. (N to Schreiber, N shore of L. Superior; TRT), Que. (N to St-Denis, Kamouraska Co.; QSA), Nfld. (Bonavista North; ACAD), N.B. (Grand Manan, Charlotte Co.; CAN; GH), and N.S. (Digby, Kings, Halifax, Cumberland, and Victoria counties; not known from P.E.I.), s to Oreg., Minn., Tex., and N Fla.; Eurasia. MAP: Meusel, Jaeger, and Weinert 1965:187.

The N. American plant has been distinguished as var. *arenicola* (Britt.) Schulz (*C. aren.* Britt.; petals to 3.5 mm long rather than 2.5 mm; pods to 3 cm long rather than 2 cm; stem-leaves with rarely more than 6 pairs of linear to oblanceolate leaflets rather than with up to 8 pairs of linear ones).

C. pensylvanica Muhl.

/sT/X/ (Hs) Low wet places from s Alaska (Hultén 1950; ?introd.; *see* Hultén 1945:834), s-cent. Yukon, and sw Dist. Mackenzie to L. Athabasca, Man. (N to the Cochrane R. at 58°38'N), Ont. (N to Fort Severn, Hudson Bay, ca. 56°N), Que. (N to E James Bay at 53°34'N, L. St. John, and the Côte-Nord), s Labrador, Nfld., N.B., P.E.I., and N.S., s to N Calif., Tex., Ark., and Fla. [*C. scutata* Thunb., the correct name through priority according to Boivin 1966*b*; *C. flexuosa* ssp. *regeliana* f. *sitchensis* Schulz; incl. *C. multifolia* and *C. polyphylla* Rydb.]. MAP: Hultén 1968*b*:513.

Collections in GH from Nfld. (Harry's Brook) and N.S. (Baddeck, Victoria Co.) have been referred to var. *brittoniana* Farw. (at least some of the stem-leaves entire).

C. pratensis L. Cuckoo-flower, Lady's-smock

/AST/X/GEA/ (Hs) Wet calcareous meadows and peaty barrens, the aggregate species from the coasts of Alaska–Yukon–Dist. Mackenzie–Dist. Keewatin to northernmost Ellesmere Is. and northernmost Ungava–Labrador, s to s Alaska–Yukon–Dist. Mackenzie, L. Athabasca, Man. (s to Sasaginnigak L., about 125 mi NE of Winnipeg), Ont. (s to w James Bay at ca. 53°30'N), James Bay (South Twin Is. at ca. 53°N), Que. (s to E James Bay at ca. 53°50'N, L. Mistassini, and the Gaspé Pen. at New Richmond), Nfld., and s Labrador (var. *pratensis* introd. in the East s to Ohio and Mass.; not known from P.E.I.); w and E Greenland N to ca. 78°N; Iceland; Spitsbergen; Eurasia. MAPS and synonymy: *see* below.

1 Lateral leaflets of the basal leaves ovate to reniform; leaflets thin, their veins not imbedded.
   2 Terminal leaflet of basal leaves shallowly 3–9-toothed; lateral leaflets of middle and upper leaves subsessile; petals white or pink; stems to about 5 dm tall; [Eurasian; introd. in Ont. (N to near Ottawa), Que. (N to near Quebec City), Nfld., St-Pierre and Miquelon, N.B., and N.S.; MAPS (aggregate species): Porsild 1957: map 181 (the open circles evidently include var. *palustris*), p. 183; Raup 1947: pl. 26; Meusel 1943: fig. 30b; Meusel, Jaeger, and Weinert 1965:187; B. Lovkvist, Symb. Bot. Ups. 14(2): map 1, pl. 1. 1956] . . . . var. *pratensis*

2 Terminal leaflet of the basal leaves entire or obscurely toothed; lateral leaflets of middle and upper leaves short-stalked; petals white or lilac; stems lower; [*C. palustris* (Wimm. & Grab.) Peterm.; range uncertain through confusion with the other varieties, but essentially that of var. *angustifolia*] . . . . var. *palustris* Wimm. & Grab.

1 Lateral leaflets of the basal leaves linear to elliptic or oblong; leaflets thick, their veins imbedded; stems to about 2.5 dm tall; petals white or lilac; [*C. nymanii* Gand.; transcontinental, the type from Southampton Is.; MAPS: Porsild 1957: map 181 (dots), p. 183; Lovkvist, loc. cit., map 3 *(C. nym.)*, pl. 3; Hultén 1968*b*:514] . . . . var. *angustifolia* Hook.

C. pulcherrima Greene

/t/W/ (Grh) Moist woods from SW B.C. (Vancouver Is. and adjacent islands and mainland E to the lower Fraser Valley), W of the Cascades to N Calif.

Some of the B.C. material is referable to var. *tenella* (Pursh) Hitchc. (*Dentaria ten.* Pursh; *C. nuttallii* Greene; basal leaves mostly simple or, if deeply lobed, the lobes nearly or quite entire, rather than basal leaves usually palmately compound, the 3–5(7) leaflets generally pinnately lobed or dissected).

C. purpurea C. & S.

/Ss/W/eA/ (Hr) Wet hillsides to subalpine slopes of Alaska (N to Cape Lisburne) and W Yukon (N to ca. 65°N); E Siberia. MAPS: Hultén 1968*b*:517; Tolmachev 1952: map 17; W.J. Cody, Nat. can. (Que.) 98(2): fig. 30, p. 155. 1971.

Plants with white (rather than violet-purple) petals may be distinguished as var. *albiflos* Hultén (1968*a*).

CARDARIA Desv. [2883]

1 Fruits essentially glabrous, tipped by a slender style about 1 mm long; sepals glabrous; stem-leaves sessile or sagittate-clasping; plant more or less hoary with short appressed simple hairs; (widespread weed) . . . . *C. draba*

1 Fruits subglobose, pubescent, nearly equalled by the slender style; sepals pubescent; stem-leaves clasping by a cordate or sagittate base; plant minutely pubescent; (var. *elongata* Rollins; introd. from B.C. to S Man.) . . . . *C. pubescens*

C. draba (L.) Desv. Heart-pod, Hoary Cress

Eurasian; introd. along roadsides and in fields and waste places of N. America, as in S B.C. (N to 8 mi S of Kamloops), Alta. (N to Fort Saskatchewan), Sask. (N to Saskatoon), Man. (Brandon; Birtle; Sinclair; Deloraine), Ont. (N to the Ottawa dist.), Que. (Cap-à-l'Aigle, Charlevoix Co.), and N.S. (Yarmouth; GH). [*Lepidium* L.]. MAP: G.A. Mulligan and Clarence Frankton, Can. J. Bot. 40(11): fig. 8 (Canadian stations), p. 1423. 1962.

Some of the Canadian material is referable to ssp. *chalapensis* (L.) Schulz (*Lepidium (C.) chal.* L.; *Physolepidion (C.; L.) repens* Schrenk; pods strongly flattened, ovate, somewhat tapering at base as well as at apex, rather than only slightly flattened and deltoid to subcordate at base). MAP: Mulligan and Frankton, loc. cit., fig. 9 (Canadian stations), p. 1423.

C. pubescens (Mey.) Jarm. Globe-pod, Hoary Cress

Eurasian; introd. in fields and waste places of N. America, as in B.C. (N to Dawson Creek, ca. 55°40′N), Alta. (N to Grande Prairie, 55°12′N), Sask. (N to Sutherland, near Saskatoon), and S Man. (Oak Bluff, near Winnipeg). [*Hymenophysa* Mey.]. MAP: G.A. Mulligan and Clarence Frankton, Can. J. Bot. 40(11): fig. 10, p. 1423. 1962).

R.C. Rollins (Rhodora 42:306. 1940) distinguishes the N. American phase as var. *elongata* Rollins (pods smaller than those of the typical form but the raceme elongating to about 1 dm rather than remaining compact and subcorymbose).

[CAULANTHUS Wats.]   [2869]

[C. pilosus Wats.]
[The inclusion of B.C. in the range assigned this species of the w U.S.A. (Wash. to Calif. and Utah) by Rydberg (1922) requires confirmation. (*Streptanthus* Jeps.).]

CHORISPORA R. Br.   [3051]

C. tenella (Pall.) DC.
Eurasian; introd. in dry waste places of w N. America, as in s B.C. (Okanagan; CAN; reported from Kaleden, near Penticton, by Groh 1947). [*Raphanus* Pall.].

COCHLEARIA L.   [2907]   Scurvygrass.   Cuillerée

1   Rosette-leaves ovate to oblong or obovate, usually more or less cuneate or rounded (never cordate) at base; stem-leaves mostly sessile, the upper ones clasping the stem; flowers to nearly 1.5 cm broad; style to 2.2 mm long; pods ovoid-oblong, to 1.5 cm long, much compressed laterally . . . . [*C. anglica*]
1   Rosette-leaves truncate to cordate at base; flowers at most 1 cm broad; style less than 1 mm long; pods to about 8 mm long, little compressed laterally.
  2   Fruits compressed-ovoid to -subglobose, with a slender style to 0.8 mm long; (E Que., s Labrador, and Nfld.).
    3   Fruiting pedicels at most about 8 mm long; mature fruiting valves distinctly reticulate; stem-leaves oblanceolate to narrowly obovate, sharply 2–8-toothed near the middle . . . . [*C. tridactylites*]
    3   Fruiting pedicels to about 2 cm long; mature fruiting valves only obscurely reticulate; stem-leaves oblanceolate to suborbicular, entire or coarsely 2–4-toothed . . . . [*C. cyclocarpa*]
  2   Fruits generally ellipsoid-oblong and tapering at both ends, the style at most about 0.5 mm long or the stigma subsessile.
    4   Stem-leaves triangular-hastate and 3–7-lobed or the uppermost ones sometimes oblong-lanceolate, mostly petioled; mature fruits rarely over 5 mm long; stems ascending, to about 2 dm long . . . . [*C. danica*]
    4   Stem-leaves oblanceolate to oblong, subentire or shallowly and distantly toothed or sinuate, only the lowest ones short-petioled; mature fruits to about 8 mm long; stems often depressed or prostrate, to about 5 dm long; (transcontinental in arctic and subarctic coastal regions) . . . . *C. officinalis*

[C. anglica L.]
[Reports of this European species from B.C. by John Macoun (1883) and Henry (1915) probably refer to *C. officinalis*.]

[C. cyclocarpa Blake]
[The type of this obscure species is from Nfld. ("wet conglomerate limestone and calcareous sandstone cliffs and ledges, Cow Head; S.F. Blake, Rhodora 16(189):135. 1914) and collections in CAN and GH from the Côte-Nord and Anticosti Is., E Que., have been placed here. However, it seems scarcely separable from *C. officinalis*.]

[C. danica L.]
[The report of this European species from St-Pierre and Miquelon by Rouleau (1956) requires confirmation, perhaps being based upon *C. officinalis*.]

C. officinalis L.
/AST/X/GEA/   (Hs (bien. or T))   Moist coastal sands, marshes, and muddy areas from the coasts of Alaska–Yukon–Dist. Mackenzie–Dist. Keewatin to northernmost Ellesmere Is. and northernmost Ungava-Labrador, s along the Pacific coast to Vancouver Is. and ?Wash., along

the Hudson Bay–James Bay coasts of Man.–Ont.–Que. to ca. 53°N, and along the Atlantic coast to E Que. (Côte-Nord and Anticosti Is.), S Labrador, and Nfld.; nearly circum-greenlandic; Iceland; Spitsbergen; N Eurasia. [Incl. vars. *groenlandica* (L.) Gel. (*C. gr.* L.) and *sessilifolia* (Rollins) Hult. (*C. sess.* Rollins), ssp. *oblongifolia* (DC.) Hult. (*C. oblongifolia* DC.), ssp. *arctica* (Schlecht.) Hult. (*C. arct.* Schl.), and *C. fenestrata* R. Br.; *Draba corymbosa* R. Br.]. MAPS: Porsild 1957: map 177, p. 183; Meusel, Jaeger, and Weinert 1965:181; Meusel 1943: fig. 7b (incomplete for N. America); combine the maps by Hultén 1968b:499 (ssp. *arct.*) and p. 500 (ssp. *obl.*).

This is a very plastic species, concerning which Hultén (1958) states, "The form of the leaves and pods which provides the differences separating the races is very variable and offers no good bases for distinguishing different taxa." However, L.H. Saunte (Hereditas 41(3/4):513. 1955) found that plants referred by him to *C. officinalis* always had a 2n chromosome-count of 24, whereas all plants from Greenland and Iceland were on the diploid-level with a 2n count of 14 (he also reports 2n counts of 48 and 42 for *C. anglica* and *C. danica,* respectively).

[C. tridactylites Banks]
[This obscure species, scarcely separable from *C. officinalis,* was described from type material collected in Labrador (reported N to 52°10′N by Brunet 1865) and collections from Nfld. and E Que. (Côte-Nord, Anticosti Is., and Magdalen Is.) have been referred to it.]

CONRINGIA Adans.   [3055]

C. orientalis (L.) Dumort.   Hare's-ear-Mustard
Eurasian; introd. in waste places of N. America, as in Alaska (St. Paul Is.; Hultén 1945) and all the provinces (in Man., N to Churchill). [*Brassica or.* L., not *Sinapis or.* L. nor *Sisymbrium or.* L.; *Erysimum or.* (L.) Cr., not Mill.; *Iodanthus pinnatifidus sensu* Soper 1949, at least in part, not (Michx.) Steud., a relevant collection from Vineland, S Ont., in TRT].

CORONOPUS Trew   [2884]   Swine-Cress, Wart-Cress

1   Fruit notched at both ends, 1 or 2 mm long, shorter than its pedicel, reticulate-pitted; style none; petals shorter than the sepals or more usually none; fertile stamens 2 (rarely 4); leaves to about 3 cm long, very deeply 1–2-pinnatifid; plant thinly pubescent . . . .*C. didymus*
1   Fruit notched only at base, to 2.5 mm long, longer than its pedicel, reticulate-pitted or strongly and irregularly ridged or tuberculate, narrowed at summit into the short pointed style; petals surpassing the sepals; fertile stamens usually 6; leaves to about 5 cm long; plant glabrous . . . .*C. squamatus*

C. didymus (L.) Sm.   Lesser Swine-Cress
?European or ?S. American; introd. in waste places and cult. fields of N. America, as in B.C. (Nanaimo, Vancouver Is.), SW ?Alta. (Banff; Groh and Frankton 1949b), Que. (York, Gaspé Pen.; GH; CAN), Nfld. (St. John's), N.B. (Gloucester and St. John counties), and N.S. (Yarmouth, Digby, Annapolis, Halifax, and Victoria counties). [*Lepidium* L.; *Carara* Britt.; *Senebiera* Pers.; *S. pinnatifida* DC.].

C. squamatus (Forsk.) Aschers.
European; occasional on wharf-ballast in N. America, as in Ont. (Toronto; Groh and Frankton 1949b), E Que. (Gaspé Basin; MTMG), N.B. (St. John; CAN), and N.S. (Pictou; Roland 1947). [*C. procumbens* Gilib.; *Cochlearia (Carara; Senebiera) coronopus* L.].

DENTARIA L.   [2967]   Toothwort, Pepperroot

1   Rhizome prominently toothed, elongate and continuous, the annual segments scarcely distinguishable; leaflets coarsely blunt-toothed, the central one of the

subopposite pair of stem-leaves broadly elliptic to ovate, to about 1 dm long and 4.5 cm broad, that of the basal leaves to 8.5 cm long and 6.5 cm broad; petals white; fruit rarely maturing; (Ont. to N.S.) . . . . *D. diphylla*
1 Rhizome constricted at intervals representing a single year's growth, the segments easily separable.
  2 Rhizome prominently toothed; stem-leaves 2 or 3, subopposite or distinctly alternate, sharply toothed, the central leaflet or its middle segment lanceolate to narrowly ovate, to 6 cm long and 3.5 cm broad; basal leaves sharply toothed or sometimes deeply incised, usually to about 5 cm long and 3 cm broad; petals white or purplish; fruit rarely maturing; (Ont. and s Que.) . . . . *D. maxima*
  2 Rhizome toothless or nearly so, consisting of fusiform, easily separable tubers; leaves subopposite; larger leaflets or segments of stem-leaves at most 3.5 cm broad; fruits lance-subulate, to about 5 cm long (including the long beak).
    3 Rachis of inflorescence more or less hirsute; stem usually with 3 subverticillate leaves above the middle, these deeply 3-parted or 3-foliolate into linear to oblanceolate or oblong, nearly entire to laciniately toothed segments, the segments themselves sometimes 2–3-cleft to base; basal leaves similar but usually absent at anthesis; petals white or purplish; (Ont. and s Que.) . . . . *D. laciniata*
    3 Rachis of inflorescence glabrous; stem-leaves 2 (rarely 3), subopposite, their narrowly oblong segments entire or toothed; basal leaves with 3 ovate to rhombic-ovate, crenate, dentate, or lobed leaflets; petals pink or purplish; (s ?Ont.) . . . . [*D. heterophylla*]

D. diphylla Michx.   Snicroûte or Carcajou
/T/EE/   (Grh)   Rich woods from Ont. (N to New Liskeard, 47°31′N; CAN) to Que. (N to L. St. John and the Gaspé Pen. along the Cap Chat R.; *see* Que. map by Dominique Doyon, Nat. can. (Que.) 93(3):162. 1966), N.B. (St. John, Kings, Kent, and Restigouche counties; not known from P.E.I.), and N.S., s to Mich., Ky., and S.C. MAP: F.H. Montgomery, Rhodora 57(678): fig. 3, p. 165. 1955.

An apparent hybrid between this species and *D. laciniata* (× *D. anomala* Eames) is known from s Ont. (Georgetown, Halton Co.; TRT). *See* Wiegand and Eames (1926) for arguments that *D. maxima* is also a hybrid of this parentage.

[*D. heterophylla* Nutt.]
[This species of the E U.S.A. (N to Ohio and N.J.) is reported from s Ont. by F.H. Montgomery (1945; Waterloo Co.) but is not indicated for that locality in his later map (Rhodora 57(678): fig. 2, p. 165. 1955). It reaches the s shore of L. Erie in Ohio but may now be extinct on the Ont. side.]

D. laciniata Muhl.   Cutleaf Toothwort
/T/EE/   (Gst)   Rich damp or wet woods and calcareous rocky banks from Nebr. to Minn., Ont. (N to the Ottawa dist.), and s Que. (N to Grondines, about 45 mi W of Quebec City; *see* Que. map by Dominique Doyon, Nat. can. (Que.) 93(3):168. 1966), s to E Kans., La., Ala., and Fla. MAP: F.H. Montgomery, Rhodora 57(678): fig. 4, p. 165. 1955.

Forma *albiflora* Louis-Marie (flowers white rather than purplish; type from near Ste-Anne-de-Bellevue, near Montreal, Que.) occurs throughout the range.

D. maxima Nutt.
/T/EE/   (Grh)   Streambanks and calcareous wooded slopes from Wisc. to Ont. (N to the Ottawa dist.), SW Que. (N to near Quebec City; *see* Que. map by Dominique Doyon, Nat. can. (Que.) 93(3):166. 1966), and N.B. (near Fredericton; DAO), s to Tenn., W.Va., and Pa. MAP: F.H. Montgomery, Rhodora 57(678): fig. 5, p. 165. 1955.

Forma *albiflora* Louis-Marie (flowers white rather than purplish; type from Ste-Geneviève, Que.) occurs throughout the range. Forma *aphylla* Louis-Marie (leaves wanting) is known from the type locality, La Trappe, near Oka, Que. *See* note under *D. diphylla*.

Cruciferae

DESCURAINIA Webb & Berthelot   [2997]   Tansy-Mustard

(Ref.: Detling 1939)
1   Capsules narrowly clavate, rounded at tip, to 2 cm long, on spreading-ascending
    pedicels to about 1.5 cm long, their seeds 2-ranked (at least near the middle of the
    pod), their septa usually nerveless; plant green, more or less pubescent and often
    glandular; (B.C. to Que.) . . . . D. pinnata
1   Capsules linear-cylindric, their seeds 1-ranked.
    2   Racemes condensed near top, the flowers surpassed by a dense subumbellate
        cluster of young fruits crowning an elongated raceme of older ones (giving a top-
        heavy and often tousled appearance); plant subglabrous to somewhat
        puberulent, the racemes and top of stem sometimes glandular; (western arctic,
        subarctic, and alpine regions) . . . . D. sophioides
    2   Racemes uniformly elongated.
        3   Fruits to about 3 cm long, rounded at tip, usually arching, on spreading-
            ascending pedicels to over 1 cm long, their septa with 2 or 3 nerves; plant
            stellate-pubescent, nonglandular; (introd.) . . . . D. sophia
        3   Fruits at most about 1 cm long, pointed at tip, straight, on strongly ascending
            pedicels at most 8 mm long, their septa 1-nerved; plant hoary-canescent and
            sometimes glandular; (transcontinental) . . . . D. richardsonii

D. pinnata (Walt.) Britt.   Moutarde tanaisie
/sT/X/   (T (Hs))   Dry sands and waste places (often weedy), the aggregate species from SW
Dist. Mackenzie (N to Fort Simpson, ca. 62°N; CAN) and B.C. to Alta. (N to Fort Vermillion,
58°24'N; Groh 1949), Sask. (N to Saskatoon), Man. (N to Ste. Lazare, about 75 mi NW of Brandon), Ont. (N to the N shore of L. Superior and the Ottawa dist.), and Que. (N to the N shore of
the Gaspé Pen. at La Madeleine and Ste-Anne-des-Monts; GH; CAN), S to Calif., Mexico, Tex.,
and Fla. MAPS and synonymy: see below.
1   Fruiting pedicels very widely divergent (to nearly horizontal); pods to 9 mm long;
    plants moderately stipitate-glandular especially in the inflorescence; [Erysimum
    (Sophia) pinnatum Walt.; Sisymbrium canescens Nutt.; SE U.S.A. only, reports from
    Canada referring to the following taxa] . . . . [var. pinnata]
1   Fruiting pedicels commonly spreading about 45° (up to about 70°).
    2   Plants stipitate-glandular especially in the inflorescence; pods to 10(12) mm long;
        petals 2 or 3 mm long; [Sisymbrium (Sophia) brachycarpon Rich., the type from
        NW Canada; S. canescens var. br. (Rich.) Wats.; S Dist. Mackenzie–Alta. to E
        Que.; MAP: combine the maps by Detling 1939: map 1 (N area), p. 489, and map 6
        (S area), p. 502] . . . . var. brachycarpa (Richards.) Fern.
    2   Plants nonglandular (or occasionally glandular above in var. filipes).
        3   Pods to 12 mm long, usually about equalling or slightly longer than their
            pedicels, the seeds always 2-rowed; [Sophia (D.; Sisymbrium) intermedia
            Rydb.; B.C. (N to Fort Fraser, ca. 54°N) and S Alta. (Kananaskis; Pincher
            Creek; Medicine Hat); MAP: Detling 1939: map 6, p. 502] . . . .
            . . . . var. intermedia (Rydb.) Hitchc.
        3   Pods to about 2 cm long, mostly shorter than their pedicels, the seeds often
            1-rowed; [Sisymbrium incisum (brachycarpon) var. fil. Gray; Sis.
            longipedicellatum Fourn.; Sophia fil. (Gray) Heller; Sop. gracilis Rydb.; B.C. (N
            to Hudson Hope at ca. 56°N and possibly N to Telegraph Creek, a branch of
            the Stikine R. at ca. 57°45'N); Alta. (N to Edmonton); Sask. (reported from the
            Touchwood Hills by J.F. Macbride, Rhodora 17(199):141. 1915, and from Swift
            Current and Val Marie by Fraser and Russell 1944); reported from Ont. and
            Que. by Boivin 1966b; MAPS: Hultén 1968b:542; the map by Detling 1939: map
            6, p. 502, indicates a Canadian occurrence only in S B.C.] . . . .
            . . . . var. filipes (Gray) Peck

D. richardsonii (Sweet) Schulz   Moutarde tanaisie grise
/ST/X/   (T (Hs))   Calcareous gravels, prairies, roadsides, and waste places (apparently

Diplotaxis

largely introd. northwards), the aggregate species from cent. Alaska–Yukon–Dist. Mackenzie to Great Bear L., Great Slave L., N Alta. (Wood Buffalo National Park), Sask. (N to Prince Albert), Man. (N to Churchill), Ont. (N to the N shore of L. Superior and Moosonee, SW James Bay, 51°16′N), Que. (N to the Côte-Nord, Anticosti Is., and Gaspé Pen.), and S Labrador (Hamilton R. basin; not known from the Atlantic Provinces), S to Mont., Idaho, Colo., N.Mex., Kans., Minn., and Maine. MAPS and synonymy: see below.

1 Pedicels and pods ascending to rather widely spreading; plant densely stipitate-glandular (especially in the inflorescence) and more or less densely pubescent with mixed simple and stellate hairs (but not canescent); [*Sophia viscosa* Rydb.; B.C. (Rossland and Lytton; Eastham 1947) and SW Alta. (Lake Louise; Laggan); MAP: Detling 1939: map 2, p. 490] . . . . var. *viscosa* (Rydb.) Peck
1 Pedicels and pods erect and closely appressed to the rachis of the raceme; plants typically nonglandular.
  2 Plant green, subglabrous or only moderately stellate-pubescent; [incl. var. *procera* (Greene) Breitung (*Sophia procera* Greene), the report of which from Waterton Lakes, SW Alta., by Breitung 1957b, is referred to *D. pinnata* var. *filipes* by Boivin 1968; the ?Yukon (Whitehorse) and ?Sask. (Maple Creek); see Boivin 1968; MAP: Detling 1939: map 2 (ssp. *procera*; incomplete northwards), p. 490] . . . .
      . . . . var. *macrosperma* Schulz
  2 Plant greyish-stellate-canescent; [*Sisymbrium rich.* Sweet; *S. canescens* var. *major* Hook. and var. *hartwegianum* (*S. incisum* var. *hart.*) of auth., not *S. hart.* Fourn.; transcontinental; MAPS: combine the maps by Detling 1939: map 1 (N limits; incomplete northwards and eastwards), p. 489, and map 2 (S limits), p. 490; Hultén 1968b:542 (aggregate species)] . . . . var. *richardsonii*

D. sophia (L.) Webb Sagesse des chirurgiens
Eurasian; introd. along roadsides and in waste places of N. America, as from cent. Alaska–Yukon–Dist. Mackenzie and B.C.–Alta. to Sask. (N to Tisdale, 52°51′N), Man. (N to Churchill), Ont. (N to Longlac, N of L. Superior at 49°47′N), Que. (N to the Gaspé Pen. at Mont-Louis and Amqui), Nfld., N.B., P.E.I., and N.S.; SW Greenland. [*Sisymbrium* L.; *Sophia* Britt.; *Sophia multifida* Gilib.]. MAP: Hultén 1968b:541.

D. sophioides (Fisch.) Schulz
/aS/WW/A/ (T (Hs)) Damp soils (usually disturbed, as on landslides; often weedy on waste land) from the coasts of Alaska–Yukon–Dist. Mackenzie to Banks Is. and Victoria Is., S to S Alaska–Yukon, Great Slave L., and NE Man. (between Churchill and the Hayes R. about 20 mi SW of York Factory); Siberia and Kamchatka. [*Sisymbrium sophioides* Fisch., the type material from "York Factory in Hudson's Bay, to the shores of the Arctic sea, westward of the Mackenzie River"; *Sophia* Heller]. MAPS: Hultén 1968b:541; Porsild 1957: map 179, p. 183; Detling 1939: map 1, p. 489.

DIPLOTAXIS DC. [2946] Wall-Rocket

1 Petals white or pale lilac, with pink or purplish veins, to 11 mm long; fruits nonstipitate, on hirsute pedicels at most 1 cm long, the conical beak to 4 mm long; sepals hirsute on back; leaves all usually pinnately lobed or divided, the lobes with coarse and irregular whitish horny-tipped teeth; scabrous annual or biennial, the leaves of the first season nearly all confined to a basal rosette . . . . *D. erucoides*
1 Petals yellow (sometimes drying purplish); fruits on essentially glabrous pedicels to about 3.5 cm long, their slender beaks at most 2 mm long; sepals essentially glabrous.
  2 Fruits nonstipitate, much longer than their pedicels; petals less than 1 cm long; sepals about 4 mm long; leaves coarsely toothed to pinnatifid; annual or biennial, the leaves of the first season nearly all confined to a basal rosette, the stem somewhat hirsute at base . . . . *D. muralis*
  2 Fruits stipitate (the stipes 1 or 2 mm long), at least the lower ones not much longer than their pedicels; petals to 1.5 cm long; sepals to 8 mm long; leaves

deeply pinnately parted; perennial, the leafy stem somewhat woody at base; plant glabrous or nearly so . . . . *D. tenuifolia*

D. erucoides (L.) DC.
European; apparently known definitely in N. America only from the tip of the Gaspé Pen., E Que. (ballast near fish-houses at York, mouth of the York R., where taken by Collins et al. in 1904 and Williams et al. in 1905; GH; noted by M.L. Fernald, Rhodora 53(625):22. 1951, as "abundant and coloring the area"). [*Sinapis* L.; *Brassica* Boiss.]. Concerning other reports from N. America (one from Mont. referable to *Erucastrum gallicum*), *see* S.F. Blake (Rhodora 55(657):291–92. 1953).

D. muralis (L.) DC.   Wall-Rocket or -Mustard, Stinkweed
European; introd. along roadsides and in waste places of N. America, as in SW B.C. (Nanaimo, Vancouver Is.; CAN), S Alta. (Waterton Lakes; Calgary; Red Deer), Sask. (Saskatoon; Fernwood; Bjorkdale), S Man. (Grandview; Winnipegosis), S Ont. (N to Wellington and Lanark counties), Que. (N to York, E Gaspé Pen.; GH), N.B., P.E.I., and N.S. [*Sisymbrium* L.; *Brassica* Boiss.].

D. tenuifolia (L.) DC.
European; introd. along roadsides and in waste places of N. America, as in S Ont. (N to Wellington, York, and Frontenac counties; OAC), SW Que. (N to the Montreal dist.; MT; CAN), N.B. (Carleton and Westmorland counties), and N.S. (Pictou; CAN); also reported from Alta. by Groh and Frankton (1949*b*). [*Sisymbrium* L.; *Brassica* Fries].

DRABA L.   [2989]   Draba.   Drave

(Ref.: Fernald 1934; C.L. Hitchcock 1941)
1 Flowering stem commonly bearing 3 or more leaves above the basal rosette, often over 1 dm tall; leaves more or less pubescent, often distinctly toothed (vigorous individuals of scapose species listed under the contrasting lead 1 may often key out here).
  2 Petals pale to deep yellow (sometimes drying whitish or pinkish).
    3 Style very short or obsolete; pods plane; leaves to 4 cm long; stem to 4 dm tall, glabrous above and in the inflorescence; annuals or biennials.
      4 Pods to 13 mm long and 3 mm broad, glabrous or puberulent, on filiform pedicels to about 3 cm long (commonly 2 or 3 times as long as the pods); leaves and lower part of stem pubescent with mixed simple and 2-forked hairs; (B.C. to Que.) . . . . *D. nemorosa*
      4 Pods to about 2 cm long but less than 3 mm broad, glabrous, on slender pedicels shorter than or rarely more than twice as long as the pods; leaves pubescent with simple or 1–2-forked hairs; stems glabrous above, sometimes hirsute with simple or forked hairs below; (mts. of B.C. and Alta.) . . . . *D. stenoloba*
    3 Style to 1.5 mm long or more; pedicels rarely more than twice the length of the pods; perennials.
      5 Pods glabrous, oblong-lanceolate to oval or oblong, to 2 cm long and 1 cm broad; basal leaves to over 1.5 dm long; plant usually rather uniformly pubescent with short simple or (mostly) 1–2-forked hairs, succulent and loosely branched, from a thick taproot; (Alaska–B.C.) . . . . *D. hyperborea*
      5 Pods copiously pubescent with simple and branched hairs, lanceolate to narrowly oblong, usually twisted, to 2 cm long and 4 mm broad; plants more or less canescent with mixed simple, branched, and stellate hairs, from a simple or branched caudex; (essentially transcontinental) . . . . . *D. aurea*
  2 Petals white; pedicels rarely more than twice as long as the pods.
    6 Plant annual, to 1.5 dm tall, the larger ones with depressed or diffuse filiform branches, hispid below, glabrous above and on the rachis and pedicels; leaves entire or nearly so, bristly-ciliate, their lower surfaces with stellate and

forking hairs, the stem-leaves rarely more than 4; pods glabrous or minutely hispid, linear or narrowly oblong, plane, to about 2 cm long, the raceme short and subumbelliform; style very short or obsolete; petals dimorphic, some of them to over 3.5 mm long, others smaller or some flowers apetalous; (s Alta. to s Ont.) . . . . *D. reptans*

6 Plants perennial or biennial, with a simple or branched caudex; stem-leaves often more numerous; mature raceme usually elongate; petals uniform.

    7 Biennial, the many stem-leaves (to over 50) merging gradually with those of the first year's rosette; scape, rachis, and pedicels hirsute with simple or forking hairs; pods to about 1.5 cm long, glabrous or pubescent; (NE Man. to Labrador, Nfld., N.B., and P.E.I.) . . . . *D. incana*

    7 Perennial (or *D. praealta* often biennial), with relatively few stem-leaves.

        8 Pubescence of leaves consisting chiefly of relatively long, simple or irregularly forking dendritic hairs (*D. hirta* var. *laurentiana* may key out here; leaves glabrous except for sparse marginal ciliation in *D. norvegica* var. *sornborgeri*); style very short or obsolete; (w Dist. Mackenzie to Labrador, Nfld., and N.S.) . . . . *D. norvegica*

        8 Pubescence of leaves consisting of a pannose coat of minute, regularly stellate or pectinately branched hairs (simple or 2-forked hairs also sometimes present).

            9 Pods typically glabrous or nearly so, plane or strongly twisted, to 1.5 cm long; raceme usually bractless; (transcontinental) . . . . *D. glabella*

            9 Pods copiously pubescent.

                10 Stem-leaves to 1.5 cm broad, usually distinctly toothed, uniformly pubescent with mostly 4–6-rayed stellate hairs; basal leaves to 4 cm long; pods to about 1.5 cm long and 5 mm broad, usually twisted, soft-stellate (sometimes glabrate); styles to 1 mm long; (mts. of B.C. and Alta.) . . . . *D. borealis*

                10 Stem-leaves narrower, entire or nearly so; basal leaves to 3 cm long; pods to about 1.5 cm long but at most 3 mm broad.

                    11 Style obsolete or nearly so (at most 0.25 mm long, the stigma subsessile); pods plane, soft-pubescent with short forked or simple hairs; leaves with rather numerous simple or 2-forked hairs in addition to the rather dense coat of short-stalked stellate hairs; (mts. of B.C.–Alta.) . . . . *D. praealta*

                    11 Style to over 0.5 mm long; pods densely coated with minute short-stalked stellate or dendritic hairs, simple hairs wanting; (essentially transcontinental).

                        12 Pods mostly plane, spreading to erect-ascending; pubescence of leaves consisting entirely of a thick coat of minute hairs pectinately branched along the vertical axis; stems to about 2.5 dm tall, with rarely more than 5 leaves . . . . *D. cinerea*

                        12 Pods often strongly twisted, closely appressed; upper leaves often with a dense coat of minute, soft, stellate or many-branched hairs only, the lower leaves sometimes with a few simple cilia (especially toward base); stems to 3.5 dm tall, with up to 10 leaves . . . . *D. lanceolata*

1 Flowering stem scapose (the entire or sparingly toothed leaves rarely over 3 cm long, all in a basal rosette or at most 1 or 2 (sometimes 3 in *D. longipes*) near the base of the scape or a single leafy bract subtending the lowest flower), commonly not over 1 or 2 dm tall, the perennial base (except in the annual *D. verna*) usually bearing remnants of old leaves (depauperate individuals of leafy-stemmed species may often key out here); pods usually plane (or more or less twisted in *D. ventosa*).

  13 Leaves usually glabrous or essentially so on both surfaces or merely ciliate-margined with usually simple hairs (sometimes with elongate, coarse, simple or branched hairs beneath, but these usually marginal or confined to the midrib and

few; *D. fladnizensis* may sometimes key out here); pedicels usually glabrous; scapes to about 2 dm tall, glabrous or with a few simple or branched hairs near base to strigose-stellate or densely hirsute throughout.

14 Pods usually coarsely pubescent with simple or branched hairs (sometimes glabrous), to 7 mm long and 3.5 mm broad, with up to 12 seeds about 2 mm long, the style to 1 mm long; petals yellow, to 6 mm long; leaves linear to linear-oblanceolate, to about 1.5 cm long and 3 mm broad, their margins often considerably crisped, their usually very prominent midribs marcescent-persistent at the base of the scape; (mts. of s B.C. and sw Alta.) . . . . .*D. densifolia*

14 Pods glabrous, to 12 mm long and 3 mm broad, with up to 60 seeds about 1 mm long, the style wanting or less than 0.2 mm long; petals yellow but fading to white, often purple-tinged, 2 or 3 mm long; leaves mostly narrowly oblanceolate, to 2.5 cm long, little persistent; (transcontinental in arctic, subarctic, and alpine regions) . . . .*D. crassifolia*

13 Leaves distinctly pubescent at least beneath.

15 Petals pale yellow to deep yellow (sometimes drying whitish; perhaps white in life in *D. oligosperma* but drying yellow); pods usually shorter than or about equalling their pedicels (rarely much longer).

16 Pedicels glabrous or essentially so (*D. incerta* may sometimes key out here); leaves linear to linear-oblong, to 3 mm broad; (western species).

17 Leaves to 1.5 cm long, densely and regularly long-ciliate, otherwise glabrous or with some forked hairs beneath; pods glabrous; scapes normally glabrous, to 1.5 dm tall; (N Alaska–Yukon–w Dist. Mackenzie) . . . .*D. pilosa*

17 Leaves mostly not over 1 cm long, covered (at least beneath and often as a marginal ciliation) with long doubly-pectinate appressed hairs; pods pubescent with simple and forked, usually retrorsely appressed hairs; scapes pubescent throughout or glabrous above, to 1 dm tall; (B.C. and Alta.). . . . .*D. oligosperma*

16 Pedicels (and scapes) usually copiously pubescent.

18 Leaves at most 1.5 mm broad, linear to narrowly spatulate, less than 1.5 cm long, covered beneath and as a marginal ciliation with elongate, tangled, branched, stalked hairs, the upper surface with simple and forked hairs, the midrib prominent, strongly marcescent-persistent; pods normally hispidulous with simple or branched hairs, to 5 mm long, their styles 0.5 mm long or more; stems commonly less than 6 cm tall, they and the pedicels hirsute with long freely branched hairs; (mts. of B.C. and Alta.) . . . .*D. paysonii*

18 Leaves mostly at least 2 mm broad.

19 Leaves linear-oblanceolate, to 3.5 mm broad, pubescent beneath with ascending, irregularly branched hairs (these in part usually doubly pectinate), their margins ciliate with simple to pectinately branched hairs; pods pubescent (sometimes glabrate) with short stiff simple or branched hairs, their styles to 1 mm long; (mts. of B.C. and Alta.) . . . .*D. incerta*

19 Leaves pubescent or ciliate with simple to branched or stellate (but never doubly pectinate) hairs, to over 4 mm broad.

20 Style obsolete or rudimentary, the stigma sessile or nearly so; pods beset with simple or 2-forked hairs, to 9 mm long and 4 mm broad; leaves to 1.5 cm long and 6 mm broad, pubescent especially beneath and marginally ciliate with simple hairs especially toward the base, strongly marcescent; scapes to 1 dm tall, their pubescence (and that of the pedicels) consisting chiefly of branched or stellate hairs; plant densely tufted to somewhat pulvinate (cushion-like); (arctic regions) . . . . .*D. oblongata*

20 Style distinct, to over 0.5 mm long.

21 Pods glabrous or sparsely hispidulous with short forked hairs, to 11 mm long and 4 mm broad, the style to 0.7 mm long; leaves to over 2 cm long, conspicuously ciliate with mostly simple hairs to about 1 mm long, otherwise glabrate or more or less pubescent with simple or forking hairs on one or both surfaces, not strongly marcescent; plant to over 2 dm tall, the caudex branching to form few to many crowded crowns; (transcontinental in arctic, subarctic, and alpine regions) . . . .*D. alpina*

21 Pods typically densely and softly pubescent with simple to 4-rayed or several-branched hairs; leaves to 12 mm long, densely short-hispid with mostly simple hairs, strongly marcescent; scapes rarely over 4 cm tall; (mts. of B.C.) . . . .*D. ventosa*

15 Petals white or cream-colour (presumably so in *D. peasei* of E Que., the flowers yet unknown).

22 Petals 2-cleft nearly to middle; pods glabrous, to 1 cm long; style very short or obsolete; mature pedicels to 3 cm long, they and the filiform scapes (up to 3 dm tall) essentially glabrous; plant annual; (introd. in B.C., Ont., and Que.) . . . .*D. verna*

22 Petals rounded or merely emarginate at summit; pedicels shorter than or only slightly longer than the pods; plants perennial, with freely branching caudices; (chiefly arctic, subarctic, and alpine regions).

23 Pods typically pubescent (sometimes glabrate in *D. norvegica*).

24 Pod-pubescence consisting of simple or branched hairs; style very short or obsolete; scape (at least below), pedicels, and leaves hispid with simple or variously branched hairs; leaves thin, soon wilting (if persistent, remaining merely as marcescent shreds); (W Dist. Mackenzie to Labrador, Nfld., and N.S.) . . . .*D. norvegica*

24 Pod-pubescence consisting of a felt-like coat of stellate hairs; style to 1 mm long; scape, pedicels, and leaves canescent-pannose with minute stellate hairs, simple elongate hairs wanting or very sparse; midribs of leaves becoming firm and prominent beneath, persisting as crowded subulate remains; (E Que.) . . . .*D. peasei*

23 Pods typically glabrous or nearly so; midribs of leaves becoming firm and prominent beneath, persisting as crowded subulate remains.

25 Leaf-pubescence a pale glaucous felt-like coat of minute stellate hairs; scape and pedicels sparsely stellate-pubescent; style to 0.4 mm long; (transcontinental in arctic, subarctic, and alpine regions) . . . .*D. nivalis*

25 Leaf-pubescence a mixture of simple or variously branched hairs; scape glabrous or pubescent near base with simple or forked hairs (rarely pubescent throughout).

26 Inflorescence capitate, scarcely elongating in fruit; pods broadly oval, to about 5 mm long and 3 mm broad; leaves conspicuously marcescent; plant commonly 4 or 5 cm tall; (arctic regions) . . . .*D. subcapitata*

26 Inflorescence elongating in fruit; pods ovate-lanceolate or elliptic, to 1 cm long.

27 Leaves pubescent beneath with 1–2-forked hairs (or sometimes merely marginally ciliate); style obsolete or nearly so; scapes rarely over 6 cm tall, from a simple or branched caudex; (var. *fladnizensis*; mts. of B.C. and SW Alta.) . . . .*D. fladnizensis*

27 Leaves sparingly pubescent beneath with mostly several-forked hairs (or even stellate in *D. flad.* var. *het.*); style to over 0.5 mm long; caudex much branched.

28 Pods oblong to narrowly oblong-ovate, to 1 cm long and 3(4) mm broad, on pedicels to 6 mm long; style to 0.5 mm long; petals to about 4 mm long; ciliation of leaves stiff, consisting mostly only of simple hairs, commonly extending from base to apex; scapes to about 1 dm tall, leafless (very rarely with a single leaf); (var. *heterotricha*; transcontinental in arctic, subarctic, and alpine regions) . . . . *D. fladnizensis*

28 Pods linear-lanceolate to broadly lanceolate, to 1.5 cm long and 2.5 mm broad, on pedicels to 1.5 cm long; style to 1 mm long; petals to 6 mm long; ciliation of leaves relatively weak, the cilia mostly simple or 1–2-forked, often confined to near the base of the leaf; scapes to about 2 dm tall, sometimes bearing up to 3 leaves; (mts. of B.C.) . . . . *D. longipes*

D. alpina L.

/AST/X/GEA/ (Ch (Hr)) Moist tundra and wet gravelly barrens, the aggregate species from the coasts of Alaska–Yukon–Dist. Mackenzie–Dist. Keewatin throughout the Canadian Arctic Archipelago to northernmost Ellesmere Is., s to cent. Alaska–Dist. Mackenzie, NE Man. (Churchill), N Ont. (w James Bay at 54°25′N), Que. (s along the Hudson Bay coast to ca. 56°N), and northernmost Labrador; circumgreenlandic; Iceland; Spitsbergen; Eurasia. MAPS and synonymy (together with distinguishing keys to 3 other scapose species of NW N. America): *see* below.

1 Habit stoloniferous, the branches of the caudex mostly prostrate and leafy, the flowering stems normally leafless; leaves glabrous or more or less pubescent on both surfaces with simple and branched hairs; petals yellow; style to 1 mm long; [*Lepidium* Pall.; incl. *D. ogilviensis* Hult.; the Yukon (Ogilvie Mts., about 120 mi NW of Dawson; A.E. Porsild, Can. Field-Nat. 78(2):96. 1964); E Greenland at ca. 70°N; E Europe; Asia; MAPS: Hultén 1968b:538 *(D. ogil.),* and 1958: map 90, p. 109] . . . . *D. sibirica* (Pall.) Thell.

1 Habit tufted, the branches of the caudex ascending.
  2 Petals white (or yellowish white), to 6 mm long; style to nearly 2 mm long; pubescence including short stellate hairs in addition to longer simple and branched hairs; [*D. glacialis* of auth., not Adams; Alaska–Yukon; MAPS: Hultén 1968b:525, and 1945: map 653, p. 970] . . . . *D. eschscholtzii* Pohle
  2 Petals yellow; style less than 1 mm long.
    3 Pedicels very slender and nearly twice as long as the pods; leaves minutely stellate-canescent, with a few simple cilia near the base; [*D. palanderiana* Kjellm.; *D. chamissonis* of auth., perhaps not G. Don; Alaska–Yukon–w Dist. Mackenzie; MAPS: Hultén 1968b:524, and 1945: map 649, p. 970; Porsild 1966: map 80 *(D. pal.),* p. 76] . . . . *D. caesia* Adams
    3 Pedicels stouter, rarely longer than the pods; leaves pubescent with mixed simple and forking hairs on one or both surfaces (or glabrate), conspicuously ciliate with mostly simple hairs; [transcontinental] . . . . *D. alpina*
      4 Pods conspicuously pubescent; petals pale yellow or creamy white; leaf-pubescence consisting of simple and variously branched hairs; scapes less than 1 dm tall; [*D. bellii* Holm, this considered by Polunin 1959, as probably identical with *D. oblongata; D. alpina* vars. *bellii* (Holm) Schulz, *gracilis* Ekm., and *pohlei* Schulz; *D. macrocarpa* Adams; N part of the range of var. *alpina* (s to cent. Alaska, the coasts of the Yukon–Dist. Mackenzie–Dist. Keewatin, northernmost Ungava (Digges Is.; Akpatok Is.), s Baffin Is., and w and E Greenland s to ca. 70°N); MAPS *(D. bellii):* Porsild 1957: map 186, p. 184; *Atlas of Canada* 1957: map 15, sheet 38; Tolmatchev 1932: fig. 6 *(D. mac.),* p. 52] . . . . var. *nana* Hook.
      4 Pods glabrous or nearly so; petals yellow; leaves copiously ciliate with rather stiff hairs to about 1 mm long, otherwise glabrate or sparingly

pubescent on one or both surfaces with simple or variously branched hairs; scape to about 2 dm tall; [incl. vars. *gracilescens* Simmons, *hydeana* Boivin, and *inflatisiliqua* Polunin; *D. ?algida* Adams; *D. ?pauciflora* R. Br.; transcontinental; MAPS: Hultén 1968*b*:529 (aggregate species); Porsild 1957: map 185, p. 184] . . . . var. *alpina*

D. aurea Vahl

/aST/X/G/ (Ch (Hs)) Dry gravelly or forested slopes and alpine meadows from cent. Alaska–Yukon and NW Dist. Mackenzie to Great Bear L., Great Slave L., NW Sask. (L. Athabasca), NE Man. (Churchill), Ont. (coasts of Hudson Bay–James Bay; N shore of L. Superior), islands in James Bay, Que. (James Bay N to Hudson Bay at ca. 56°10'N; Mingan Is. of the Côte-Nord), and N Labrador (S to ca. 57°N), and in the Rocky Mts. of the West through B.C. and SW Alta. to Ariz. and N.Mex.; S half of W and E Greenland (type from Greenland). [*D. aureiformis* Rydb.; *D. luteola* Greene and its var. *minganensis* Vict. (*D. ming.* (Vict.) Fern.); *D. borealis sensu* M.L. Fernald, Rhodora 7:267. 1905, not DC.]. MAPS: Hultén 1968*b*:536; Porsild 1966: map 77, p. 76; Fernald 1934: map 8 (E area; incomplete northwards), p. 299.

Var. *leiocarpa* (Pays. & St. John) Hitchc. (*D. aureiformis* var. *lei.* Pays. & St. John; pods glabrous rather than copiously pubescent with mixed simple and forked hairs) is reported from the Marble Mts. NW of Clinton, B.C., by C.L. Hitchcock (1941) and tentatively from Alta. by Boivin (1966*b*).

D. borealis DC.

/aST/W/eA/ (Ch (Hs)) Grassy alpine slopes and ledges from the Aleutian Is. and N coast of Alaska (type from St. Paul Is., Bering Sea) to SE Yukon (Porsild 1951*a*) and the mts. of B.C. (S to Dawson Creek, ca. 55°40'N; Raup 1934) and SW Alta. (Columbia Icefield, about 50 mi SE of Jasper; CAN); E Asia. [*D. incana* var. *bor.* (DC.) T. & G.; *D. mccallai* Rydb. (*D. henneana* var. *mccallai* (Rydb.) Schulz); *D. unalashkiana* DC.; incl. the robust extreme, *D. maxima* Hult.]. MAP: combine the maps by Hultén 1968*b*:534 and 535 (*D. max.*).

D. cinerea Adams

/ASs/X/GEA/ (Ch) Dryish tundra and talus slopes to alpine ledges from the coasts of Alaska–Yukon–Dist. Mackenzie–Dist. Keewatin nearly throughout the Canadian Arctic Archipelago to northernmost Ellesmere Is., S to cent. B.C. (Mt. Selwyn, ca. 56°N; not known from Alta.), N Sask. (Hasbala L., 59°55'N; L. Athabasca), Southampton Is., N Ont. (Cape Henrietta Maria, NW James Bay; Dutilly, Lepage, and Duman 1954), and Que. (Akpatok Is., Ungava Bay; L. Mistassini); W and E Greenland between ca. 65° and 79°N; Spitsbergen; N Eurasia. [*D. arctica* Vahl; incl. *D. groenlandica*, *D. ostenfeldii*, and *D. ovibovina* Ekm.]. MAPS: Hultén 1968*b*:537; combine the maps by Porsild 1957: map 194 and map 195 (*D. groenl.*), p. 185; Raup 1947: pl. 25; combine the maps by G.A. Mulligan, Can. J. Bot. 49(1): fig. 6, p. 91, and fig. 7 (*D. groenl.*), p. 92. 1971.

D. crassifolia Graham

/aST/X/GE/ (Ch (Hr)) Turfy banks and cold ravines from Alaska (N to ca. ?70°N; *see* N Alaska map by Wiggins and Thomas 1962: p. 387, and Hultén 1968*a*) to the Yukon (near Mayo) and the Mackenzie R. Delta, S in the West through the mts. of B.C. and SW Alta. to Calif., Ariz., and Colo., farther eastwards known from S-cent. Dist. Keewatin, S Baffin Is., northernmost Que. (Wakeham Bay, Hudson Strait), and N Labrador (S to ca. 57°N); W and E Greenland between ca. 64° and 75°N; N Scandinavia. [*D. albertina* Greene; *D. fernaldiana* Polunin; *D. crassifolia* was described from material cult. from seed collected by Drummond in the Rocky Mts. between 52° and 57°N]. MAPS: Hultén 1968*b*:522, and 1958: map 184, p. 183 (both maps indicating an extremely isolated station in the vicinity of Ignace, Ont., about 125 mi NW of Thunder Bay, but said by Hultén (1958) to represent a collection from L. Agnes, S Ont.; the relevant collection has not been seen but was probably made at L. Agnes, Banff National Park, Alta.); Porsild 1958: map 184, p. 183; Böcher 1954: fig. 29, p. 115.

D. densifolia Nutt.

/aSs/W/eA/ (Ch) Talus slopes and alpine ledges of the Aleutian Is., Alaska (N to ca.

65°N), the Yukon (N to ca. 65°N), and SW Dist. Mackenzie (CAN), S through the mts. of B.C. and SW Alta. (near Coleman, near the E end of Crowsnest Pass; CAN) to N Calif., Utah, and Wyo.; NE Siberia. [Incl. *D. aleutica* Ekm. and *D. stenopetala* Trautv.]. MAPS: Porsild 1966: map 83 (*D. sten.*; *see* discussion), p. 77; combine the maps by Hultén 1968*b*:530 and 531 (*D. al.* and *D. sten.*).

D. fladnizensis Wulfen
/AST/X/GEA/ (Ch (Hr)) Turfy tundra and cold ravines to the highest alpine summits, the aggregate species from the coasts of Alaska–Yukon–Dist. Mackenzie–Dist. Keewatin through-out the Canadian Arctic Archipelago to northernmost Ellesmere Is. and northernmost Un-gava–Labrador, S in the West through the mts. of B.C. and SW Alta. (N to Jasper; V) to Utah and Colo., farther eastwards S to NE Man. (Churchill), Que. (coast of Hudson Bay S to NE James Bay at ca. 54°N), and Labrador (S to ca. 55°30'N); W Greenland N to ca. 79°N, E Green-land between ca. 68° and 78°N; Spitsbergen; N Eurasia. MAPS and synonymy: *see* below.
1 Leaves ciliate with simple hairs, otherwise glabrous or more or less pubescent with mixed simple and 1–2-forked hairs; [incl. *D. lapponica* Willd. and *D. pseudopilosa* Pohle; Aleutian Is.–cent. Alaska (*see* Hultén 1945: map 655, p. 970); B.C. (Limestone Mt. near Clinton, in the Cariboo Dist. at ca. 52°N; Omineca Mts. at ca. 56°N; Mt. Selwyn, ca. 56°N); SW Alta. (Banff; Jasper); also reported from Baffin Is. and E Greenland by Hultén 1945, but this probably referable to the following taxon; MAPS: Hultén 1968*b*:527, and 1958: map 207, p. 227; Meusel, Jaeger, and Weinert 1965:185; Böcher 1954: fig. 47 (top; aggregate species), p. 177] . . . . var. *fladnizensis*
1 Leaves ciliate with a mixture of simple and forked hairs as well as pubescent on both sides with a mixture of simple or several-forked hairs; [*D. lactea* Adams; *D. androsacea* Wahl., not Willd.; incl. the glabrous extreme, *D. allenii* Fern.; transcontinental; MAPS: Raup 1947: pl. 25; Hultén 1968*b*:527 (*D. lactea*), and 1958: map 208 (*D. lactea* and *D. allenii*), p. 227; Porsild 1957: map 189 (*D. lactea*), p. 184; Meusel, Jaeger, and Weinert 1965:185]. Because of the intermediate character of the leaf-pubescence of var. *heterotricha* (*D. lactea* Adams) between that of *D. fladnizensis* and *D. nivalis* Lilj., Hultén (1958) notes the possibility that it may perhaps be a hybrid-series between these last-named species, a complete series of transitional forms being known . . . . var. *heterotricha* (Lindbl.) Ball

D. glabella Pursh
/AST/X/GEA/ (Ch (Hs)) Moist rocky or grassy places, the aggregate species from the coasts of Alaska–Yukon–Dist. Mackenzie–Dist. Keewatin to Ellesmere Is. at 81°25'N (G.R. Brassard and R.E. Beschel, Can. Field-Nat. 82(2):112. 1968) and northernmost Ungava–Lab-rador, S to N B.C., Great Slave L., NE Man. (S to Gillam, about 165 mi S of Churchill), Ont. (coast of Hudson Bay S to James Bay at ca. 54°40'N; near Thunder Bay and Schreiber, N shore of L. Superior), Que. (S to SE James Bay at ca. 52°15'N, the Côte-Nord, Anticosti Is., and Gaspé Pen.), Nfld., N.B. (Restigouche, Gloucester, and Kings counties), N.S. (Boivin 1966*b*; not known from P.E.I.), and N.Y. (L. Champlain); W Greenland between ca. 65° and 78°N, E Greenland between ca. 69° and 77°N; Eurasia. MAPS and synonymy (together with dis-tinguishing keys to the closely related *D. arabisans* Michx., *D. laurentiana* Fern., and *D. pyc-nosperma* Fern. & Knowlt., here included in the *D. glabella* complex): *see* below.
1 Pods plump, their seeds overlapping and often turned oblique to the septum; stem-leaves 1–4, sparingly hirsute with simple, 2-forked, and stellate hairs, or glabrate; rosette-leaves finely and closely stellate-pannose, to 5 cm long and 1.5 cm broad; flowering stems loosely to densely stellate-pubescent, often with an admixture of simple and forking hairs; [*D. hirta* var. *pyc.* (Fern. & Knowlt.) Boivin; E Que. (type from Cap Blanc, near Percé, Gaspé Co.), NW Nfld. (Highlands of St. John), and N.S. (along the Salmon R., Victoria Co., Cape Breton Is.); MAP: Fernald 1934: map 16 (the Cape Breton Is. station should be indicated), p. 330] . . . [*D. pycnosperma* Fern. & Knowlt.]
1 Pods strongly flattened, their seeds not overlapping, lying flat against the septum; stem-leaves often more numerous, stellate-pubescent to glabrate.
2 At least the lower stem-internodes abundantly hirsute with elongate simple hairs

overtopping the stellate pubescence; rosette-leaves thick and firm, to about 4 cm long and 1 cm broad, often with an admixture of elongate, simple and forking hairs in addition to the stellate pubescence; [*D. hirta* var. *laur.* (Fern.) Boivin; E Que. (Mingan Is.; Anticosti Is.; Mt. St-Pierre, Gaspé Co.) and N Nfld. (type from Grassy Is., St. John Bay); MAP: Fernald 1934: map 15 (the Gaspé and Anticosti Is. stations should be indicated), p. 328] . . . . [*D. laurentiana* Fern.]

2 Stems closely stellate-pannose (often glabrate at summit), sparsely or not at all hirsute below; rosette-leaves commonly softer and larger, closely stellate-pannose (sometimes glabrate).

3 Style 0.5–1 mm long; pods scarcely veiny, usually strongly twisted (sometimes plane), the lowest ones on pedicels to 1.5(2.5) cm long; stem-leaves attenuate to a petiolar base . . . . [*D. arabisans* Michx.]

4 Pods distinctly stellate-pubescent; [Pigeon Bay, near Thunder Bay, Ont.; F.K. Butters and E.C. Abbe, Rhodora 55(652):153. 1953] . . . . [var. *superiorensis* Butters & Abbe]

4 Pods glabrous or essentially so.

5 Pods elliptic-ovate, to 8 mm long and 4 mm broad; scapes rarely over 1.5 dm tall; [*D. canadensis* Brunet, the type from Cap Tourmente, NE of Quebec City, Que.; E Que. (Montmorency and Rimouski counties) and Nfld. (Bonne Bay)] . . . . [var. *canadensis* (Brunet) Fern. & Knowlt.]

5 Pods narrowly lanceolate to narrowly elliptic or ovate, to 1.5 cm long but rarely over 3 mm broad; [*D. arabis* Pers.; *D. incana* vars. *arabisans* (Michx.) Wats and *glabriuscula* Gray; *D. megasperma* var. *?leiocarpa* Schulz; Ont. (N to L. Nipigon) to Que. (N to Anticosti Is.) and Nfld.; MAP: Fernald 1934: map 21, p. 354] . . . . [var. *arabisans*]

3 Style at most 0.5 mm long; pods distinctly veiny, plane or only slightly twisted, glabrous or minutely hirsute, the lowest ones on pedicels mostly not over 6 mm long; stem-leaves rounded or subclasping at base . . . .*D. glabella*

6 Pods lanceolate, acute or subacute, to 3 mm broad; seeds to 1 mm long.

7 Stem-leaves at most 5; longer racemes mostly with less than 20 flowers; [*D. daurica* DC.; *D. henneana* Schlecht.; *D. longii* Schwein.; *D. ?ramosissima* (*Alyssum dentatum* Nutt.) *sensu* Saint-Cyr 1886, not Desv.; *D. stylaris* Fern. & Knowlt.; *D. hirta* of Canadian reports in large part, not L. (which is *Braya hirta* (L.) Fern. (*B. alpina* Sternb. & Hoppe)); transcontinental, the type from Hudson Bay; MAPS: Porsild 1957: map 193, p. 185 (aggregate species); Raup 1947: pl. 25 (aggregate species); Fernald 1934: map 17 (E area; incomplete for James Bay–Hudson Bay), p. 334; Hultén 1968b:532 (as *D. hirta*)] .var. *glabella*

7 Stem-leaves commonly more numerous (up to 8); longer racemes with up to 35 pods; [*D. arabisans* var. *orth.* Fern. & Knowlt.; NE Man. (Churchill) and Que. (SE Hudson Bay at ca. 56°15′N; Mingan Is.; Temiscouata Co. to Gaspé Co. (type from Bic, Rimouski Co.); MAP: Fernald 1934: map 18 (E area), p. 336] . . . . .var. *orthocarpa* (Fern. & Knowlt.) Fern.

6 Pods elliptic to oblong-ovate, obtuse, to 5 mm broad; seeds to 1.3 mm long.

8 Stem-leaves at most 4; [*D. hirta* var. *br.* Rupr.; reported by Polunin 1940, from Melville Pen. and N Baffin Is., S to E Dist. ?Keewatin, ?Southampton Is., and northernmost Que. (Hudson Strait and Ungava Bay) and reported from an island in E James Bay at 54°11′N by Dutilly, Lepage, and Duman 1958; Greenland] . . . . . . var. *brachycarpa* (Rupr.) Fern.

8 Stem-leaves at least 5 (up to about 15); [*D. megasperma* Fern. & Knowlt., the type from Paspébiac, Bonaventure Co., E Que.; cent. Ont. (near Schreiber, N shore of L. Superior); E Que., N.B. (Belledune Point, Gloucester Co.), S Labrador (Forteau, 51°28′N), and Nfld.; MAP: Fernald 1934: map 20 (E area), p. 337]. The report of the Eurasian *Arabis*

petraea (L.) Lam. from Minister's Face, N.B., by Fowler 1885, and John Macoun 1886, may belong here. M.L. Fernald and C.H. Knowlton (Rhodora 7(76):67. 1905) refer it to var. *orthocarpa,* the occurrence of which in N.B., however, requires confirmation . . . .
. . . . var. *megasperma* (Fern. & Knowlt.) Fern.

D. hyperborea (L.) Desv.
/ST/W/eA/ (Hs) Coastal cliffs of the Aleutian Is., s Alaska (an isolated station also on Little Diomede Is. off the Seward Pen. at ca. 65°N), and w B.C. (Queen Charlotte Is.; Vancouver Is. and adjacent islands and mainland N to Skedans, ca. 52°N); E Asia (Kurile Is.). [*Alyssum hyp.* L., described from plants grown from seed collected on Bird Is., Shumigan Is., Alaska; *D. (Nesodraba) grandis* Langsd; *Cochlearia (D.) spathulata* Schlecht.; *C. (N.) siliquosa* Schlecht.; incl. var. *sil.* f. *megalocarpa* (Greene) Schulz (*N. meg.* Greene)]. MAP: Hultén 1968*b*:538.

D. incana L.
/aST/EE/GE/ (Hs) Turfy or gravelly barren ground, cliffs, and ledges (ranges of Canadian taxa outlined below; known in the U.S.A. only from islands and shores of L. Superior in Mich.); w Greenland N to ca. 70°N, E Greenland N to 66°18′N; Iceland; Europe; (reports from the mts. of cent. Asia refer to other species): MAPS and synonymy: *see* below.
1   Pods glabrous; [var. *contorta* Lilj.; Ont. (N to near the mouth of the Black Duck R., Hudson Bay, at ca. 56°50′N; isolated on Passage Is. and the Gull Is., N L. Superior; the report from Red Rock on the Nipigon R. by John Macoun 1886, is based upon *D. lanceolata* (relevant collection in CAN), as also, probably, reports from B.C. and Alta.) to James Bay (Charlton Is.; Akimiski Is.; South Twin Is.), Que. (s James Bay to SE Hudson Bay at ca. 56°20′N; Côte-Nord; Anticosti Is.; Gaspé Pen.; Magdalen Is.; Chimo, s Ungava Bay), Labrador (N to 59°07′N), and Nfld.; w Greenland N to ca. 70°N, E Greenland N to 66°18′N; Iceland; Europe; MAPS (aggregate species): Hultén 1958: map 23, p. 43; Fernald 1934: map 10 (incomplete northwards), p. 315] . . . .
. . . . var. *incana*
1   Pods pubescent; [var. *conica* Schulz; *D. confusa* Ehrh; essentially the range of var. *incana* but also known from Man. (Churchill; York Factory; *D. incana* reported from Wilkins Point, L. Winnipegosis, by John Macoun 1883), NE N.B. (collection in GH from Miscou Is., Gloucester Co.; reports from Nashwaaksis by Macoun 1883, and Fowler 1885, are based upon *D. lanceolata,* relevant collections in CAN), and P.E.I. (North Point, Prince Co.; PEI), and apparently absent from Labrador and Greenland] . . . .
. . . . var. *confusa* (Ehrh.) Lilj.

D. incerta Payson
/ST/W/ (Ch (Hr)) Montane rocky slopes from E Alaska (N to ca. 79°30′N), s Yukon, NW Dist. Mackenzie, and Great Bear L. through the mts. of B.C. and sw Alta. (N to ca. 54°N) to Wash., Idaho, and Wyo. [*D. glacialis* of American auth., not Adams]. MAPS: Hultén 1968*b*:525; Porsild 1966: map 78, p. 76.

D. lanceolata Royle
/aST/X/GA/ (Ch (Hs)) Calcareous cliffs and dry places from Alaska (N to ca. 70°N; *see* N Alaska map by Wiggins and Thomas 1962:387) to cent. Yukon, the coast of Dist. Mackenzie (Mackenzie R. Delta; Coronation Gulf), Great Slave L., L. Athabasca (Alta. and Sask.; reports from Churchill, Man., by Scoggan 1957 and 1959, are based upon *D. aurea,* the relevant collections in CAN), Ont. (N to the N shore of L. Superior), James Bay (South Twin Is.), Que. (NE James Bay near Cape Jones; King Mt., N of Hull; L. Mistassini; Larch R. at ca. 57°35′N; Kamouraska and Rimouski counties; Gaspé Pen.), and N.B. (near Fredericton; CAN), s to Nev., Utah, Colo., Wisc., Mich., and N New Eng.; w Greenland between ca. 65° and 71°N; Asia. [*D. ?cana* Rydb.; *D. stylaris* of American auth. in part, not Gay; *D. incana sensu* John Macoun 1886, as to the Red Rock, L. Superior, Ont., plant, not L., the relevant collection in CAN; *D. incana* var. *confusa sensu* John Macoun 1883, and Fowler 1885, as to the Nashwaaksis, N.B., plant, not (Ehrh.) Lilj., the relevant collection in CAN]. MAPS: Hultén 1968*b*:536;

Raup 1947: pl. 25; T.W. Böcher, Medd. Gronl. 147(9): fig. 11, p. 28. 1952; G.A. Mulligan, Can. J. Bot. 49(1): fig. 5 (Canadian area; as *D. cana*), p. 91. 1971.

According to Mulligan, our species should be known as *D. cana* Rydb., *D. lancelolata sensu* Fernald (1934) and many authors not being *D. lanceolata* Royle.

D. longipes Raup

/aSs/W/ (Ch) Moist tundra and near snowbeds in the mts. of Alaska–Yukon–Dist. Macken-zie (N to the arctic coasts) and B.C. (S to Mt. Selwyn, ca. 56°N, the type locality). MAPS: Hultén 1968*b*:533; Porsild 1957 (1964 revision): map 339, p. 203; Raup 1947: pl. 25.

D. nemorosa L.

/ST/X/EA/ (T) Open flats and slopes up to moderate elevations from cent. Alaska–Yu-kon–Dist. Mackenzie to Sask. (N to L. Athabasca), Man. (N to Churchill), Ont. (N to Sandy L. at ca. 53°N, 90°W), and SW Que. (S Gatineau Co.; Montreal), S to N Calif., Colo., Minn., and Mich. (probably introd. in the E and N parts of the Canadian range); Eurasia. [Var. *hebecarpa* Lindbl.; *D. dictyota* Greene; *D. nemoralis* Ehrh.]. MAPS: Meusel, Jaeger, and Weinert 1965:185; Hultén 1937: fig. 14, p. 129, and 1968*b*:537.

Var. *leiocarpa* Lindbl. (pods essentially glabrous rather than minutely strigose-hispid) oc-curs throughout the range, largely replacing the typical phase northwards.

D. nivalis Lilj.

/AST/X/GEA/ (Ch (Hr)) Dry calcareous gravels and cliffs, the aggregate species from the coasts of Alaska–Yukon–Dist. Keewatin to northernmost Ellesmere Is. and northernmost Un-gava–Labrador, S in the West through the mts. of B.C. and SW Alta. (chiefly var. *elongata*) to Oreg., Idaho, Wyo., and Colo., farther eastwards S to Great Bear L., NE Man. (Churchill), N Ont. (Cape Henrietta Maria, NW James Bay), Que. (coasts of Hudson Bay–James Bay S to ca. 53°N; Knob Lake, 54°48′N; Shickshock Mts. of the Gaspé Pen.; not known from the Maritime Provinces), and Nfld.; nearly circumgreenlandic; Iceland; Spitsbergen; N Eurasia. MAPS and synonymy: *see* below.

1 Stellate hairs sessile or nearly so, spreading, many-rayed; leaves and stems stellate throughout, simple hairs rarely present.

  2 Stems leafless or rarely with one leaf; [*D. stellata* of Canadian reports, not Jacq.; *D. stellata* var. *nivalis* (Lilj.) Regel; *D. ?laevipes* Adams; transcontinental; MAPS: Hultén 1968*b*:523; Porsild 1957: map 188, p. 184; *Atlas of Canada* 1957: map 2, sheet 38; Fernald 1934: map 6 (SE area), p. 297, and 1925: map 68 (incomplete), p. 339] . . . . var. *nivalis*

  2 Stems bearing up to 4 leaves; [*D. kamt.* (Ledeb.) Busch; *D. lonchocarpa* ssp. *kamt.* (Lebed.) Calder & Taylor; reported from S Alaska and Mt. Arrowsmith, Vancouver Is., B.C., by C.L. Hitchcock 1941; MAP: Hultén 1968*b*:533 (*D. kamt.*)] . . . . var. *kamtschatica* (Ledeb.) Pohle

1 Stellate hairs usually stalked, 4–many-rayed; leaves usually with a few simple hairs.

  3 Stem-leaves 1 or 2, to 5 mm broad, sparingly pubescent; pods to 2 cm long; [var. *?glabrescens* (Kurtz) Schulz; var. *?glabriuscula* Pohle; Alaska, the type of *D. lonchocarpa* var. *den.* Schulz from Muir Glacier] . . . . var. *denudata* (Schulz) Hitchc.

  3 Stem-leaves 1 or none, to 3 mm broad, densely pubescent; pods mostly somewhat shorter.

    4 Plant glabrous except for a few stellae on the leaf-margins; [Cougar Valley in the Selkirk Mts. of B.C.; C.L. Hitchcock 1941] . . . . var. *canadica* Schulz

    4 Plant more pubescent, at least the leaves stellate on both surfaces; [*D. lonchocarpa* Rydb. and its var. *dasycarpa* Schulz; *D. ?macounii* Schulz; Alaska–Yukon–B.C.–SW Alta.; MAPS: Hultén 1968*b*:523 (*D. lonch.*); Raup 1947: pl. 25] . . . . var. *elongata* Wats.

D. norvegica Gunn.

/AST/D/GE/ (Ch) Moist gravels, cliffs, and ledges (known in N. America only from Canada, the ranges of Canadian taxa outlined below, together with MAPS and synonymy and a dis-tinguishing key to the scarcely separable *D. arctogena* Ekm.); Greenland; Europe.

1 Stems bearing at most 1 leaf; rosette-leaves entire, their pubescence dense
   (consisting mainly of simple hairs covering the blades); pods usually with many
   stellate hairs; inflorescence usually only slightly elongating; [Axel Heiberg Is.,
   Ellesmere Is., and Melville Pen.; type from Greenland] . . . .[*D. arctogena* Ekman]
1 Stems with sometimes up to 3 leaves; rosette-leaves often more or less dentate,
   their pubescence usually not dense (the surface of some with many stellate hairs,
   other leaves merely with ciliated margins); pods typically glabrous or promptly
   glabrate; inflorescence commonly elongating . . . .*D. norvegica*
   2 Leaves glabrous except for sparsely ciliate margins, thin, conspicuously veiny on
      drying, the whole plant otherwise glabrous except for the sparsely pilose sepals;
      pedicels to 1 cm long, the lower ones nearly equalling the oblong-lanceolate
      pods; [*D. sornborgeri* Fern., the type from Ramah, Labrador, 58°54′N; ?Baffin Is.;
      MAP: Fernald 1934: map 11, p. 320] . . . . .var. *sornborgeri* (Fern.) Boivin
   2 Leaves conspicuously hispid with simple and 2–several-forked hairs; stems
      hirsute at least toward base; pedicels mostly much shorter than the pods.
      3 Stem-leaves narrowly lanceolate, to 6 mm broad; sepals to about 2 mm long
         and 1 mm broad; petals to 1.5 mm broad; pods linear to linear-lanceolate, to
         2.5 mm broad; lowest pedicels to 1 cm long; [var. *laxa* of E Que. reports, not
         D. laxa Lindbl.; *D. clivicola* Fern., the type from Mt. Mattaouisse, Matane Co.,
         E Que.; also known from Mts. Logan and Pembroke, Matane Co. (*see* Fernald
         1934: MAP 14, p. 327) and E N.S. (Inverness and Victoria counties, Cape
         Breton Is.), and reported from Reed Mt., Que., ca. 52°N, 68°W, by P. Landry,
         Nat. can. (Que.) 89(10):288. 1962] . . . . .var. *clivicola* (Fern.) Boivin
      3 Stem-leaves ovate, to 1 cm broad; sepals to about 2.5 mm long and 1.5 mm
         broad; petals 2 or 3 mm broad; pods oblong-lanceolate or oblong, to over 3.5
         mm broad; pedicels rarely over 5 mm long.
         4 Pods permanently hispid; flowering stems hispid to summit; [E James Bay
            (Dutilly, Lepage, and Duman 1958); Cape Chidley, northernmost Labrador
            (Polunin 1940); SW Nfld.; Greenland] . . . . .var. *hebecarpa* (Lindbl.) Schulz
         4 Pods glabrous or promptly glabrate.
            5 Stem-leaves usually 6 or more; fruiting stems to over 2.5 dm tall; [E
               Que. (Blanc-Sablon, Strait of Belle-Isle) and NW Nfld. (type from Burnt
               Cove); MAP: Fernald 1934: map 13, p. 324] . . . . .var. *pleiophylla* Fern.
            5 Stem-leaves at most 5; fruiting stems to about 2 dm tall; [*D. hirta* var.
               nor. (Gunn.) Lilj.; *D. rupestris* R. Br. and its var. *leiocarpa* Schulz (most
               or all reports of *D. rupestris* from E Que. are based upon var. *clivicola*);
               an isolated station in W Dist. Mackenzie at ca. 63°N (DAO); South-
               ampton Is. and S Baffin Is. to James Bay, Que., S Labrador, and NW
               Nfld.; MAPS: Porsild 1957: map 192, p. 184; Hultén 1958: map 14, p. 33;
               W.J. Cody, Nat. can. (Que.) 98(2): fig. 4, p. 146. 1971] . . . . . . .var. *norvegica*

D. oblongata R. Br.
/Aa/(X)/GEA/ (Ch) Tundra and rocky slopes of the Canadian Arctic Archipelago (Ellesmere Is. at ca. 80°N S to S Banks Is. and Baffin Is. at ca. 70°N) and the coast of Dist. Keewatin
(N tip of Melville Pen.); W and E Greenland S to ca. 73°N; Eurasia. [Incl. *D. adamsii* Ledeb., *D.
gredinii* Ekm., and *D. micropetala* Hook.]. MAPS: Porsild 1957: map 191, p. 184; Hultén
1968b:528 (*D. mic.*).

D. oligosperma Hook.
/ST/W/ (Ch) Tundra and rocky slopes from S Alaska–Yukon (N to ca. 63°N) to the Macken-
zie R. Delta (type locality) and Great Bear L., S through the mts. of N and SE B.C. and SW Alta.
(N to the Jasper dist.) to N Calif. and Colo. [*D. andina* (Nutt.) Nels.]. MAPS: Hultén 1968b:522;
Porsild 1966: map 79, p. 76.

D. paysonii Macbr.
/S/W/ (Ch) Subalpine to alpine cliffs and ledges from S B.C. (N to the Marble Mts. NW of

Clinton; an isolated station in E-cent. Alaska; several other localities cited by C.L. Hitchcock 1941) and sw Alta. (N to Jasper) to N Calif., Nev., Utah, and Wyo. MAP: G.A. Mulligan, Can. J. Bot. 49(1): fig. 8, p. 1457. 1971.

The Canadian plant is referable to var. *treleasii* (Schulz) Hitchc. (*D. barbata* var. *trel.* Schulz, the type from Sheep Mt., Waterton Lakes, sw Alta.; pods at most 5 mm long, their styles less than 1 mm long, rather than pods to 8 mm long, the style about 1 mm long).

D. peasei Fern.
/T/E/ (Ch) Known only from the type station, limestone talus slopes of Mont-St-Alban, Cap-des-Rosiers, at the E tip of the Gaspé Pen., E Que. [*D. oligosperma sensu* A.S. Pease, Rhodora 31(363):55. 1929, not Hook., the relevant collection, in GH, being the type of *D. peasei*].

D. pilosa Adams
/a/W/eA/ (Ch) Dryish places along the coasts of NW Alaska (s to the Seward Pen.), the Yukon (Herschel Is.; CAN), and NW Dist. Mackenzie (near the mouth of the Mackenzie R.); arctic Asia. [*D. alpina* var. *pil.* (Adams) Regel]. MAPS: Hultén 1968b:526; Tolmachev 1952: map 11 (incomplete).

D. praealta Greene
/ST/W/ (Hs) Moist montane woods to subalpine ridges from cent. Alaska–Yukon to Great Bear L. and Great Slave L., s through the mts. of B.C. and sw Alta. (N to the Jasper dist.; type from Banff) to Oreg., Nev., and Wyo. [*D. columbiana* Rydb.]. MAPS: Hultén 1968b:535; Porsild 1966: map 81, p. 77.

D. reptans (Lam.) Fern.
/T/X/ (T) Sandy places, ledges, and foothills, the aggregate species from Wash. to s Alta.–Sask.–Man., Minn., Mich., s Ont., Pa., and Conn., s to s Calif., N.Mex., Tex., and Ga.
1 Pods glabrous; [*Arabis* Lam.; *D. caroliniana* Walt.; s Ont.: Essex, Lambton, Hastings, and Frontenac counties] . . . . var. *reptans*
1 Pods minutely hispid; [*D. micrantha* Nutt.; *D. coloradensis* Rydb.; s Alta. (Boivin 1966b), SE Sask. (gravel pit near Weyburn, about 75 mi SE of Regina, where probably introd.; A.J. Breitung, Am. Midl. Nat. 61(2):511. 1959), and s Man. (collection in WIN from sandy soil near Melita, about 60 mi sw of Brandon; collection in CAN from railway cinders at Gimli, about 45 mi N of Winnipeg, where undoubtedly introd.; collections in DAO from sandy soil at Birds Hill, near Winnipeg, and from Aweme, about 20 mi SE of Brandon; reported from Elva and Tilston by Lowe 1943)] . . . .
. . . . var. *micrantha* (Nutt.) Fern.

D. stenoloba Ledeb.
/ST/W/ (T (Hs)) Moist banks, meadows, and dry slopes to near timberline, the aggregate species from the E Aleutian Is., cent. Alaska–Yukon, and w Dist. Mackenzie (Porsild and Cody 1968) through the mts. of B.C. and sw Alta. (N to Lake Louise) to Calif. and Colo. MAPS and synonymy: see below.
1 Base of stem with chiefly several-rayed hairs, the hairs of the leaves mostly about 4-rayed; [*D. acinacis* St. John; *D. macouniana* Rydb.; *D. oligantha* Greene; *D. hirta* var. *siliquosa* C. & S.; Aleutian Is.–Alaska–southernmost Yukon (see Hultén 1945: map 669, p. 972; type from Unalaska, Alaska) and mts. of B.C. and sw Alta.; MAPS (aggregate species): Porsild 1966: map 82, p. 77; Hultén 1968b:532] . . . . . . var. *stenoloba*
1 Base of stem glabrous or it and the leaves with mostly simple or forked hairs; [*D. nitida* Greene and its var. *nana* Schulz (see Porsild 1951a); SE Yukon and mts. of s B.C. and sw Alta. (Lake Louise, near Banff)] . . . . var. *nana* (Schulz) C.L. Hitchc.

D. subcapitata Simmons
/Aa/(X)/GEA/ (Ch) Dry calcareous tundra and gravels nearly throughout the Canadian Arctic Archipelago from s Banks Is. to northernmost Ellesmere Is. (type locality), s to s Vic-

toria Is., s Southampton Is., and se Baffin Is.; w and e Greenland s to ca. 68°N; Spitsbergen; arctic Asia. MAPS: Hultén 1968b:528, and 1958: map 3, p. 23; Porsild 1957: map 190, p. 184; Tolmachev 1952: map 14 (the N Alaska–Dist. Mackenzie area should be deleted).

D. ventosa Gray
/aST/W/ (Ch) Ridges and slopes to high elevations from the coast of Alaska (Seward Pen. and NE coast at Icy Reef; CAN; *see* Hultén 1945: map 654 *(D. exal.),* p. 970, the Icy Reef station not indicated on his below-noted 1968b map), northernmost Yukon (Herschel Is.; CAN), and SW Dist. Mackenzie (Brintnell L., ca. 62°N; CAN) through the mts. of B.C. (Mt. Waddington; Mt. Chris Spencer; Manning Provincial Park; reported from ?Alta. by Boivin 1966b) to Wash. and Utah.

This is a very poorly understood species but our plant appears to be referable to var. *ruaxes* (Pays. & St. John) Hitchc. (*D. ruaxes* Pays & St. John; *D. sphaeroides* var. *cusickii* (Rob.) Hitchc. (*D. cus.* Rob.); incl. *D. exalata* Ekm.; pubescence less entangled than that of the typical phase, including many simple or merely forked (rather than irregularly 4–many-branched) hairs). MAPS: Hultén 1968b:524 (N area; *D. exal.*); G.A. Mulligan, Can. J. Bot. 49(8): fig. 7, p. 1457. 1971.

D. verna L. Whitlow-grass
Eurasian; introd. in open dry places of N. America, as in s B.C. (Vancouver Is.; Greenwood, about 40 mi W of Trail), s Ont. (Essex, Norfolk, Lincoln, and Wentworth counties), and Que. (near Quebec City, where taken by Bell in 1865; CAN). [*Erophila* Chev.; *E. vulgaris* DC.].

Most or all of the Canadian material appears referable to var. *boerhaavii* Van Hall (var. *aestivalis* Lej.; *Erophila boer.* (Van Hall) Dum.; pods relatively broad in outline, at most about 6 mm long but up to 4 mm broad and with relatively few seeds, rather than to 1 cm long but at most about 2.5 mm broad and with up to about 60 seeds).

ERUCA Mill. [2944]

E. sativa Mill. Garden-Rocket. Roquette
Eurasian; introd. in waste and cult. grounds of N. America, as in Alta. (Lacombe), Sask. (Bradwell; Carnduff; Grenfell; Indian Head; Regina; Seemans), Man. (Groh and Frankton 1949b; no locality cited), Ont. (N to Renfrew and Carleton counties), and SW Que. (Montreal). [*Brassica (E.) eruca* L.; *E. vesicaria* of auth., not (L.) Cav.].

ERUCASTRUM Presl [2947]

1 Basal lobes of the upper stem-leaves not clasping; inflorescence bracted in the
   lower part; flowers yellowish white; sepals erect; fruit not stalked above the
   sepal-scars . . . . *E. gallicum*
1 Basal lobes of the upper stem-leaves downwardly directed and clasping the stem;
   inflorescence bractless; flowers bright yellow; sepals spreading; fruit distinctly
   stalked above the sepal-scars . . . . [*E. nasturtiifolium*]

E. gallicum (Willd.) Schulz Dog-Mustard. Moutarde des chiens
Eurasian; introd. in fields and waste places of N. America, as in B.C. (Kamloops; Eastham 1947), Alta. (N to Brownvale, 56°08′N), Sask. (Breitung 1957a), Man. (N to Thanout L. at 59°23′N), Ont. (N to Longlac, N of L. Superior, 49°47′N), Que. (N to the Gaspé Pen. at Cap Chat; CAN), Nfld., N.B., P.E.I. (Charlottetown), and N.S. [*Sisymbrium* Willd.; *E. pollichii* Schimper & Spenner].

[*E. nasturtiifolium* (Poir.) Schulz]
[European; the indication (by triangles) of stations in Man. in the MAP by Meusel, Jaeger, and Weinert (1965:175) requires confirmation. (*Sinapis* Poir.).]

ERYSIMUM L.   [3004]   Wallflower, Treacle-Mustard.   Vélar

(Ref.: G.B. Rossbach 1958)
1   Petals small, yellow, at most 13 mm long and 5 mm broad; style short and stout, the
    pod-beak about 1 mm long; seeds at most 2 mm long and 1 mm broad; leaves linear
    to lanceolate or oblanceolate, entire to remotely sinuate-denticulate (or the basal
    ones sometimes repand-lobed).
    2   Pubescence of leaves consisting chiefly of 2-pronged appressed hairs.
        3   Pods glabrous or remotely strigose, distinctly torulose, to 8 (sometimes 10)
            cm long, on strongly divergent pedicels, these equally thick throughout
            (usually about as thick as the fruit and not noticeably dilated at summit);
            basal leaves usually somewhat sinuate-dentate or even repand-lobed; green
            or somewhat greyish-canescent, freely branched annual; (introd. in s Ont. and
            sw Que.) . . . . .E. repandum
        3   Pods greyish-canescent, non-torulose, to 6 cm long, on strongly ascending to
            erect pedicels, these enlarged toward tip; leaves entire or remotely and
            obscurely sinuate-dentate; perennial, usually distinctly greyish-canescent,
            simple or branched (usually only above); (transcontinental) . . . . . .E. inconspicuum
    2   Pubescence of leaves consisting chiefly of 3–4-pronged appressed hairs; petals
        yellow; pods to about 3 cm long, their beaks about 1 mm long; leaves lanceolate,
        entire to remotely dentate; (introd.).
        4   Hairs on upper leaf-surfaces chiefly 3-pronged; petals pale yellow, to 5 mm
            long; pods divergent on filiform pedicels at least 8 mm long; seeds about
            1 mm long; annual, rarely over 1 m tall . . . . .E. cheiranthoides
        4   Hairs on upper leaf-surfaces chiefly 4-pronged; petals sulphur-yellow, to 8 mm
            long; pods appressed, on pedicels about 5 mm long; seeds to 1.3 mm long;
            biennial or short-lived perennial, commonly over 1 m tall . . . . .E. hieracifolium
1   Petals larger, mostly over 1.5 cm long; pods to over 1 dm long; seeds usually at least
    2 mm long and 1 mm broad (except in E. asperum).
    5   Petals purple (rarely pale yellow), to about 2 cm long; calyx to 8 mm long; stigma
        subsessile, the pod-beak very short; pods on spreading-ascending pedicels to
        about 1.5 cm long; leaves linear to oblanceolate, entire or remotely dentate;
        fruiting-stem to about 1.5 dm tall (or in late-flowering plants, scarcely
        elongating); (arctic regions and mts. of w Alta.) . . . . .E. pallasii
    5   Petals yellow or orange; style elongate, the pod-beak commonly over 2 mm long.
        6   Pods very rigidly divaricate, equally or subequally tetragonal and little
            compressed, their flat surfaces with very protrusive keels prominent as 4 dark,
            less pubescent stripes; seeds about 1.5 mm long; leaves narrowly
            oblanceolate, some or all dentate, their hairs 2-pronged; (s B.C. to s Man.;
            introd. in s Ont. and sw Que.) . . . . .E. asperum
        6   Pods ascending (occasionally becoming arched-divaricate), subequally
            tetragonal to strongly compressed, their flat surfaces less strongly keeled and
            not markedly striped.
            7   Leaves entire or essentially so, the hairs of their upper surface 2-pronged;
                petals yellow; seeds very elongate (to 2.3 mm long but only to about
                0.7 mm broad); (Alaska–Yukon) . . . . .E. angustatum
            7   Leaves mostly distinctly denticulate to runcinate-dentate, the hairs of their
                upper surfaces 2–3 (or more)-pronged; seeds to about 2 mm long and
                1 mm broad.
                8   Fresh petals usually orange (also shades of yellow, brick-red, and
                    orange-brown), drying purplish; pods relatively strongly keeled on the
                    flat surfaces; leaves usually denticulate or dentate, some or all of the
                    hairs on their upper surfaces 3 (or more)-pronged, 2-pronged hairs also
                    frequently present; (s B.C.) . . . . .E. capitatum
                8   Petals always yellow; pods with very narrow, scarcely protrusive keels

on the flat surfaces, moniliform and often slightly torulose, purplish; leaves runcinate-dentate, their hairs 2–3-pronged; (?Vancouver Is.) . . . . [*E. torulosum*]

E. angustatum Rydb.
/Ss/W/ (Hs) Dry slopes of E-cent. Alaska and the Yukon (N to near Dawson, the type locality, ca. 64°N). [*E. asperum* var. *ang.* (Rydb.) Boivin, not *Cheiranthus ang.* Greene]. MAPS: Hultén 1968*b*:552; W.J. Cody, Nat. can. (Que.) 98(2): fig. 21, p. 152. 1971.

E. asperum (Nutt.) DC.   Western Wallflower, Prairie-Rocket
/T/WW/ (Hs) Dry prairies and sand-hills from S B.C. (N to Kamloops; CAN) to S Alta. (Dunmore and Medicine Hat; CAN), Sask. (N to near Prince Albert), and S Man. (N to Millwood, about 90 mi NW of Brandon), S to N Calif., N.Mex., Okla., Kans., and Minn.; introd. eastwards along railways to Ont. (reported from Point Edward, Lambton Co., by Dodge 1915, and from the Ottawa dist. by Gillett 1958) and SW Que. (Hull and Montreal; reports from E Que. by St. John 1922, and Fernald 1925, and from Nfld. by Waghorne 1898, and the report of *E. lanceolatum* R. Br. from E Que. by Verrill 1865, are based upon *E. inconspicuum* var. *coarctatum,* relevant collections in GH). [*Cheiranthus asper* Nutt.; *E. (Cheiranthus; Cheirinia) elatum* Nutt.].

E. capitatum (Dougl.) Greene
/t/X/ (Hs) Dry prairies and hills from S B.C. (Strathcona Park, Vancouver Is., and Trail; CAN, detd. Rossbach) to Idaho and Ohio, S to Mexico and Tex. [*Cheiranthus* Dougl.; *E. asperum* var. *cap.* (Dougl.) Boivin].

E. cheiranthoides L.   Wormseed-Mustard.   Herbe au chantre
Eurasian; introd. along roadsides and in fields and waste places of N. America, as in Alaska–Yukon–Dist. Mackenzie (N to ca. 69°N) and all the provinces. [Incl. ssp. *altum* Ahti; *Cheirinia* Link]. MAP: combine the maps by Hultén 1968*b*:550 and 551 (ssp. *altum,* this perhaps native in N. America; *see* Hultén 1968*a*).

E. hieracifolium L.
European; introd. along roadsides and in waste places in Canada (no U.S.A. reports have been seen), as in S Sask. (Stoughton), Ont. (N to Renfrew and Carleton counties; *see* S Ont. map by Montgomery 1957: fig. 8, p. 13), SW Que. (about 40 mi N of Shawinigan, Laviolette Co.), and N.S. (Heatherdale, Victoria Co., Cape Breton Is.). *See* G.A. Mulligan and Clarence Frankton, Can. J. Bot. 45(5):755–56. 1967.

E. inconspicuum (Wats.) MacM.
/ST/X/ (Hs) Dry open soil (ranges of Canadian taxa outlined below), S to Oreg., Nev., Colo., S.Dak., Minn., and Ont. (adv. S to Kans. and Mo. and E to N.S. and New Eng. according to Fernald *in* Gray 1950, but the entire range treated as native by G.B. Rossbach 1958). MAP and synonymy: see below.
1 Leaves usually cinereous and not crowded; stems commonly solitary or, if more than one, usually strict; petals mostly pale yellow and under 1 cm long, usually not over 2 mm broad; [*E. asperum* var. *inc.* Wats.; *Cheirinia inc.* (Wats.) Rydb.; *E. lanceolatum* R. Br., not C. & S.; *E. parviflorum* Nutt., not Pers.; Alaska–Yukon (*see* Hultén 1945: map 681, p. 973) and coast of Dist. Mackenzie to B.C., Alta., Sask. (N to Moose Jaw), Man. (N to The Pas), and Ont. (N to L. Nipigon and the N shore of L. Superior); reports from farther eastwards are referable to the following taxon according to G.B. Rossbach 1958; MAP (aggregate species): Hultén 1968*b* 551] . . . . var. *inconspicuum*
1 Leaves usually greener and more crowded; stems often more than 1, spreading-ascending; petals usually rich yellow and usually at least 1 cm long and 2 mm broad; [*E. coarctatum* Fern., the type from the Mingan Is. of the Côte-Nord, E Que.; Que. (L. St. John; Bic, Rimouski Co.; Gaspé Pen.; Anticosti Is.; Côte-Nord), Nfld., N.B. (St. Leonard, Madawaska Co.; CAN), and N.S. (Springhill Junction, Cumberland Co.; GH)] . . . . var. *coarctatum* (Fern.) Rossbach

E. pallasii (Pursh) Fern.
/AST/X/GA/ (Hs) Calcareous tundra (common near animal burrows or below bird cliffs) and slopes to fairly high elevations from the coasts of Alaska–Yukon–Dist. Mackenzie to northernmost Ellesmere Is., s to s Alaska–Yukon, Great Bear L., and n Baffin Is.; isolated in the mts. of sw Alta. (Byng Pass; Laggan; Jasper); n and nw Greenland s to ca. 78°30′N; arctic Asia. [*Cheiranthus* Pursh; *Hesperis* Seem.; *Cheirinia* Rydb.; *Cheiranthus (E.; H.) pygmaeus* Adams; *H. hookeri* Ledeb.]. MAPS: Hultén 1968*b*:550; Porsild 1957: map 199, p. 185; A.I. Tolmatchev, Sven. Bot. Tidskr. 20:61. 1926.

Forma *humilum* (Tolm.) Polunin, the late-flowering nearly stemless phase, is reported from n Baffin Is. by Polunin (1940). The high-grown extreme, var. *bracteosum* Rossbach (the stem to over 1.5 dm tall to the base of the raceme, the leaves copiously and deeply dentate rather than entire or shallowly dentate, many of the pedicels subtended by a bract or small leaf rather than only the lowest ones), is reported from the type locality, Teller, w Alaska, by G.B. Rossbach (1958).

E. repandum L.
European; locally introd. in waste places of N. America, as in s Ont. (Essex, Kent, and Lambton counties; DAO; GH; OAC) and Que. (Rouleau 1947).

[*E. torulosum* Piper]
[The report of this species of Wash.–Oreg. from sw B.C. by Carter and Newcombe (1921; Mt. Arrowsmith, Vancouver Is.) requires confirmation. (*E. arenicola* var. *tor.* (Piper) Hitchc.).]

EUTREMA R. Br. [2913]

E. edwardsii R. Br.
/AS/X/GEA/ (Hs) Turfy tundra, solifluction areas, and moist slopes from the coasts of Alaska–Yukon–Dist. Mackenzie–Dist. Keewatin nearly throughout the Canadian Arctic Archipelago (type from Melville Is.) to northernmost Ellesmere Is. and northernmost Ungava–Labrador, s to n B.C. (Summit Pass; V; reported from Alta. by Boivin 1966*b*), Great Bear L., NE Man. (Churchill), and n Que. (Hudson Bay coast s to ca. 60°N); w and E Greenland s to ca. 70°N; Spitsbergen; arctic and alpine Eurasia. MAPS: Hultén 1968*b*:501; Porsild 1957: map 178, p. 183; *Atlas of Canada* 1957: map 1, sheet 38; Polunin 1960: fig. 46, p. 185; Fernald 1925: map 65, p. 337, and 1929: map 21, p. 1498.

HALIMOLOBOS Tausch [3079]

1   Stem-leaves linear-lanceolate to narrowly oblanceolate, narrowed to a sessile or short-petioled base but not auriculate-clasping, to 5 cm long; petals to 7 mm long; pods finely stellate-pubescent, to about 2 cm long, their seeds 1-rowed; (?B.C.) . . . .
. . . . [*H. whitedii*]
1   Stem-leaves lanceolate to oblong, to 4 cm long, auriculate-clasping at base; petals to 4 mm long; pods glabrous, to 4 cm long, their seeds 2-rowed.
    2   Lower stem-leaves mostly entire; stems usually several from a caudex, glabrous above or rarely sparsely hirsute with simple hairs; (Alaska, the Yukon, nw Dist. Mackenzie, Baffin Is., and Greenland) . . . .*H. mollis*
    2   Lower stem-leaves dentate; stems single from the caudex, pubescent above with appressed multiple-branched hairs; (SE Alta. and sw Sask.) . . . .*H. virgata*

H. mollis (Hook.) Rollins
/AS/(X)/G/ (Hs) Dry calcareous slopes (common in manured areas) from Alaska (N to ca. 67°N) and the coasts of the Yukon–Dist. Mackenzie (E to Coronation Gulf) to s Alaska, s-cent. Yukon, and Great Bear L.; isolated on E Baffin Is. at ca. 70°N; w Greenland between ca. 65° and 73°N, with isolated stations at ca. 79°N. [*Turritis* Hook., the type from "Shores of the Arctic Sea, between long. 107° and 130°"; *Arabidopsis mollis* Schulz, not *Arabis mollis* Stev.; *Arabis hookeri* Lange]. MAPS: Hultén 1968*b*:543; Porsild 1957: map 198, p. 185; T.W.

Böcher, J. Ecol. 39(2): fig. 8 (Alta. stations referable to *H. virgata*), p. 390. 1951; Hopkins 1937: map 15 (*Arabis hookeri*; very incomplete), p. 126.

H. virgata (Nutt.) Schulz
/T/W/   (Hs)   Plains and foothills from s Alta. (Rosedale; Medicine Hat; Cypress Hills) and sw Sask. (Cypress Hills; Wood Mountain; the inclusion of the Yukon in the range given by Hitchcock et al. 1964, is perhaps based upon *H. mollis*) to Utah and Colo. [*Sisymbrium* Nutt.; *Arabidopsis* Rydb.; *A. (Pilosella) stenocarpa* Rydb.; reports of *H. mollis* from Alta. and Sask. are probably referable here].

[H. whitedii (Piper) Rollins]
[The reports of this species of Wash. from B.C. by J.M. Macoun (Ottawa Naturalist 23(7):121. 1909; near Sidley, w of Midway) and Eastham (1947; Osoyoos, about 25 mi w of Midway) require confirmation. (*Arabis* Piper).]

HESPERIS L.   [3041]   Rocket

H. matronalis L.   Dame's-Violet.   Julienne des Dames
Eurasian; a garden-escape to roadsides, thickets, and open woods in N. America, as in s Alaska (Hultén 1945) and all the provinces (in Man., N to The Pas; in Que., N to the Gaspé Pen.). MAP: Hultén 1968b:556.

HUTCHINSIA R. Br.   [2985]

H. procumbens (L.) Desv.
/ST/(X)/EA/   (T)   Damp calcareous, saline, or alkaline ledges, gravels, and flats from s B.C. (Vancouver Is., Spences Bridge, and Kamloops; CAN; V; the inclusion of Alta. in the range given by Fernald *in* Gray 1950, requires confirmation) to Calif. and Colo., farther eastwards known from s Sask. (shores of saline lakes at Parkbeg and Fox Valley, both ca. 50°30'N), NE Man. (Schofield 1959; Churchill, where "Forming thick colonies among stones and on gravel, damp area of beach above tide level, and on the margin of the coastal salt marshes . . ."), s Labrador (Dead Islands, 52°48'N, where taken by Allen in 1882; GH), and Nfld. (GH; CAN; the report from Que. by Rouleau 1947, requires confirmation); Chile; Eurasia; N Africa; Australia. [*Lepidium* L.; *Hymenolobus* Nutt.; *Capsella* Fries; *C. divaricata* Walp.; *C. elliptica* Mey.].

[IBERIS L.]   [2892]   Candytuft

1   Leaves obtuse, mostly with a few or several large irregular obtuse teeth; flowers
    white or purplish, in a globular cluster soon elongating into a distinct raceme; plant
    sparingly pubescent . . . . [*I. amara*]
1   Leaves acute, essentially entire; flowers roseate to purplish (varying to nearly white),
    the cluster remaining about as broad as long; plant essentially glabrous . . . . [*I. umbellata*]

[I. amara L.]   Rocket Candytuft
[Eurasian; a garden-escape in N. America but scarcely established, as in s Alaska (Hultén 1945), Ont. (Ottawa), sw Que. (Aylmer), and N.S. (Halifax; Yarmouth).]

[I. umbellata L.]   Globe Candytuft
[European; a garden-escape in N. America but scarcely established, as in Ont. (Norfolk, Ontario, and Carleton counties), sw Que. (Gatineau, Gatineau Co.; Côteau-du-Lac, Soulanges Co.), P.E.I., and N.S. (Boivin 1966b).]

IDAHOA Nels. & Macbr.   [2972A (*Platyspermum*)]

I. scapigera (Hook.) Nels. & Macbr.
/t/W/   (T)   Dry to moist soil and rocky places from sw B.C. (Mt. Douglas, Mt. Finlayson, and Observatory Hill, Vancouver Is.; CAN; V) to Calif., Nev., and Idaho. [*Platyspermum* Hook.].

[IODANTHUS T. & G.]   [2963]

[I. pinnatifidus (Michx.) Steud.]   Purple Rocket
[Native along streams and on alluvial soil in the E U.S.A. (N to Minn. and Pa.) and reported from SW Que. by John Macoun (1883; Montebello, Papineau Co., as *Thel. pinn.*, where probably introd. if correctly identified). The report from S Ont. by Soper (1949) is probably based upon a collection in TRT from Vineland, Lincoln Co., actually referable to *Conringia orientalis*. The report from Man. by Lowe (1943; Pipestone) is referable to *Raphanus sativus*, the relevant collection in WIN. (*Hesperis* Michx.; *Thelypodium* Wats.).]

ISATIS L.   [2931]   Woad

I. tinctoria L.   Dyer's Woad, Asp-of-Jerusalem
European; still cult. to some extent in N. America as the source (after moistening the leaves and allowing them to ferment) of the blue dye used by the ancient Britons to paint their bodies; escaped to roadsides and waste places in SW B.C. (Vancouver Is.; Herb. V), Ont. (Toronto and near Guelph; Montgomery 1957), SW Que. (Luskville, Pontiac Co.; DAO), and Nfld. (Ship Cove; GH).

LEPIDIUM L.   [2883]   Pepperwort, Peppergrass

(Ref.: C.L. Hitchcock 1936; Mulligan 1961)
1   Pedicels (and pods) strongly appressed-ascending; pods about 3 mm long, slightly longer than the pedicels; style less than half as long as the deep notch at summit of fruit; leaves deeply dissected into linear segments; (introd. in S Ont.) . . . . [L. aucheri]
1   Pedicels spreading or spreading-ascending (if sometimes rather strongly appressed-ascending in *L. sativum*, fruits 5 or 6 mm long).
  2   Stem-leaves (at least the middle and upper ones) sagittate- or deeply cordate-clasping at the sessile base, entire or slightly toothed, markedly different from the lower leaves; stamens usually 6; (introd.).
    3   Middle and upper stem-leaves deeply cordate-clasping, ovate to suborbicular in outline; basal leaves deeply 2–3-pinnatifid, the lower stem-leaves usually similar; petals pale yellow, less than 2 mm long, slightly surpassing the sepals; pods rhombic-ovate, about 4 mm long, glabrous or sometimes slightly pubescent, barely winged at apex, the sinus about 0.2 mm deep, the style about as long; pedicels usually somewhat longer than the pods; annual, glabrous and glaucous above, usually somewhat puberulent or pubescent below . . . . *L. perfoliatum*
    3   Middle and upper stem-leaves sagittate-clasping, lanceolate to oblong-lanceolate; basal leaves entire to lyrate-pinnatifid; petals white, to 2.5 mm long; pods 5 or 6 mm long; pedicels about equalling or shorter than the pods.
      4   Annual or biennial with usually a single erect stem to about 6 dm tall; anthers yellow; pods covered with small white vesicles that become scale-like when dry, the style included to slightly exserted from the shallow apical notch; (widespread) . . . . *L. campestre*
      4   Perennial with numerous ascending stems to 4.5 dm tall, from a stout woody rootstock; anthers violet to purple; pods essentially glabrous, with few or no vesicles, the style mostly exserted from the shallow apical notch; (introd. in SW B.C.) . . . . *L. heterophyllum*
  2   Stem-leaves not clasping.
    5   Pods 5 or 6 mm long and longer than the pedicels, about 4 mm broad, glabrous, the style about half as long as the apical notch; petals white or reddish, to twice as long as the sepals; basal leaves 2-pinnatifid; glabrous and somewhat glaucous annual to 7 dm tall; (introd.) . . . . *L. sativum*
    5   Pods mostly less than 4 mm long; pedicels mostly equalling or longer than the pods (shorter than the pods in *L. strictum*); petals (when present) white.

6 Pods barely or not at all notched at summit, sparingly short-hirsute or glabrate, tipped by the broad subsessile stigma, broadly ovate to nearly orbicular, to about 2 mm long, much shorter than their pedicels; stamens 6; petals up to twice as long as the sepals; leaves thickish and rugose, those of the stem narrowly ovate, entire or minutely toothed, the principal ones to 1 dm long and 2 cm broad, tapering to a sessile or subsessile base; basal leaves long-petioled, their blades to 3 dm long and 8 cm broad, toothed or pinnately lobed (with a large terminal lobe and 2 or more smaller lateral lobes); essentially glabrous, glaucous, rhizomatous perennial to 2 m tall; (introd.) . . . .*L. latifolium*

6 Pods distinctly notched or emarginate at summit (apically 2-toothed); petals often vestigial or wanting; stamens 2 (sometimes 4); basal leaves 1–2-pinnatifid, the stem-leaves usually less divided, the upper ones often entire; annuals (sometimes biennials) rarely more than 4 dm tall.

  7 Sepals persistent until the pod is well developed; pedicels shorter than the fruits, slightly flattened and very narrowly wing-margined; petals vestigial or lacking; pods plainly reticulate, glabrous or sparsely ciliate, the sinus about 0.4 mm deep; basal leaves 2-pinnatifid; (sw ?B.C.) . . . .
. . . .[*L. strictum*]

  7 Sepals usually deciduous at (or shortly after) anthesis; pedicels usually equalling or shorter than the fruits.

    8 Apical teeth of pod acute, typically very short and widely divergent, the sinus broadly and shallowly U-shaped; pods finely reticulate; pedicels distinctly flattened; petals rudimentary or none; stamens usually 4; basal leaves 1-pinnatifid into acute linear segments; (introd. in sw B.C.) . . . .[*L. oxycarpum*]

    8 Apical lobes of pod rounded to acute or obtuse tips, the sinus relatively narrow.

      9 Pods pubescent at least along the margins; petals at most 3/4 as long as the sepals or wanting.

        10 Pods commonly hispid-pubescent over both faces (rarely glabrous); pedicels distinctly flattened; plant short-hirsute throughout; (sw ?B.C.) . . . .[*L. lasiocarpum*]

        10 Pods pubescent only near the margins (over both faces only in *L. densiflorum* var. *pubicarpum*); pedicels usually nearly terete or only slightly flattened; plants sparsely to densely puberulent or pubescent.

          11 Inflorescence congested into numerous axillary racemes as well as terminal ones; pods to 3 mm long and 2 mm broad, with acute apical teeth; (se B.C. to Ont.; introd. eastwards) . . . .*L. ramosissimum*

          11 Inflorescence consisting of a single raceme or of sparingly branched racemes; pods to 3.5 mm long and 3 mm broad, with obtuse or rounded apical teeth; (varieties in B.C. and Alta.) . . . .*L. densiflorum*

      9 Pods typically glabrous; pedicels nearly terete or only slightly flattened.

        12 Petals commonly equalling or longer than the sepals; pods oval to orbicular, to 4 mm long and 4 mm broad; lower and middle leaves irregularly toothed or incised to pinnatifid, the divisions often again dissected; (B.C.; Ont. to Nfld. and N.S.) . . . . .
. . . .*L. virginicum*

        12 Petals none or rudimentary; pods mostly smaller.

          13 Pods oblong-obovate to broadly obcordate, broadest above the middle, to 3.5 mm long and 3 mm broad, rounded or abruptly curved into the obtuse apical teeth;

> petals present; lower leaves coarsely toothed to
> pinnatifid; (varieties apparently native in B.C. and Alta.;
> probably introd. elsewhere in Canada) . . . . *L. densiflorum*
>
> 13 Pods ovate or obovate, broadest near or below the
> middle, to 2.5 mm long and 2 mm broad, narrowed into
> the acute apical teeth; petals wanting; lower leaves
> deeply 2-pinnatifid; (introd.) . . . . *L. ruderale*

[L. aucheri Boiss.]
[Asiatic; apparently recorded for N. America only from s Ont. (Montgomery 1957, as *L. spinosum;* Toronto, where taken in a ball park by Scott in 1906 as a casual waif; TRT; not listed by Mulligan 1961).]

L. campestre (L.) R. Br.   Cow-Cress.   Cresson des champs
Eurasian; introd. along roadsides and in fields and waste places of N. America, as in B.C. (N to Queen Charlotte Is.), s Alta. (near Pincher Creek), Ont. (N to Longlac, N of L. Superior at 49°47'N), Que. (N to the Gaspé Pen.), Nfld., N.B., P.E.I., and N.S. [*Thlaspi* L.]. MAP: Mulligan 1961: fig. 12, p. 82.

L. densiflorum Schrad.
/T/WW/   (Hs (bien. or T))   Native in the western provinces according to Mulligan (1961) but the plant so weedy in nature and so rapidly spreading into all types of disturbed habitats northwards and eastwards (as well as in most other parts of the world) as to negate attempts to define its native range. Native or introd., the aggregate species ranges from s Alaska, s-cent. Yukon (N to Watson L.), and Great Slave L. through B.C.–Alta.–Sask. to Man. (N to Churchill), Ont. (N to s James Bay), Que. (N to Anticosti Is. and the Gaspé Pen.), Labrador (N to the Hamilton R. basin), Nfld., N.B., P.E.I., and N.S., s (apparently native) to Calif., Ariz., and Colo., farther eastwards (apparently largely or wholly introd.) through most of the E U.S.A. MAPS and synonymy: *see* below.
1   Pods averaging about 2.5 mm long, suborbicular (broadest at or only slightly above the middle); pedicels scarcely flattened; stem-leaves mostly toothed; [*L. apetalum* of auth., not Willd.; *L. neglectum* Thell.; transcontinental, largely introd.; MAPS: Meusel, Jaeger and Weinert 1965:178 (aggregate species); Mulligan 1961: fig. 13, p. 85; Hultén 1968b:497 (aggregate species)] . . . . var. *densiflorum*
1   Pods averaging about 3 mm long, broadly obovate (broadest somewhat above the middle); pedicels usually noticeably flattened; at least the middle and upper stem-leaves commonly entire or nearly so; [native].
  2   Pods glabrous; [*L. densiflorum* var. *bourgeauanum* of auth., possibly not *L. bourg.* Thell.; B.C., Alta. (type from Lethbridge), and w Sask.; MAP: Mulligan 1961: fig. 13, p. 85] . . . . var. *macrocarpum* Mulligan
  2   Pods pubescent.
    3   Pods pubescent on both surfaces; [*L. pubicarpum* Nels.; s B.C.; MAP: Mulligan 1961: fig. 13, p. 85] . . . . var. *pubicarpum* (Nels.) Thell.
    3   Pods pubescent only on the margins; [*L. elongatum* Rydb.; *L. simile* Heller; s Alaska–s Yukon–B.C.; MAP: Mulligan 1961: fig. 13, p. 85] . . . .
. . . . var. *elongatum* (Rydb.) Thell.

L. heterophyllum Benth.
European; apparently introd. in N. America only in sw B.C. (Mulligan 1961; listing several Vancouver Is. localities, these indicated on his MAP, fig. 12, p. 82). [*L. smithii* Hook.].

[L. lasiocarpum Nutt.]
[The report of this species from sw B.C. by Henry (1915; Victoria, Vancouver Is.) requires confirmation, probably being referable to some other taxon. It is not listed by Mulligan (1961).]

L. latifolium L.   Grande passerage
Eurasian; introd. along beaches and tidal shores and in waste places in N. America, as in s

Cruciferae

Alta. (Mulligan 1961; Lethbridge; CAN) and Que. (Groh 1944a; railway yards at Quebec City; MT; DAO). MAP: Mulligan 1961: fig. 12, p. 82.

[L. oxycarpum T. & G.]
[This species of the W U.S.A. (chiefly Calif., N to ?Oreg.) is known in Canada from an 1893 collection by Macoun in SW B.C. (Cadboro Bay, Vancouver Is., this locality indicated in the MAP by Mulligan 1961: fig. 12, p. 82; CAN), where perhaps introd. along saline shores but not taken since and apparently extinct if actually once native there. (L. ?strictum sensu Henry 1915, not (Wats.) Rattan, this also reported from the Gulf Is. adjacent to Vancouver Is. by Henry).]

L. perfoliatum L.
Eurasian; introd. along roadsides and in fields and waste places of N. America, as in S B.C. (Osoyoos; Kelowna; Cranbrook), S Alta. (Lethbridge), S Sask. (Swift Current), S Ont. (SE York Co.), and ?Que. (Rouleau 1947). MAP: Mulligan 1961: fig. 12, p. 82.

L. ramosissimum Nels.
/T/WW/ (Hs (bien. or T)) As in the case of L. densiflorum (from which it is doubtfully distinct), this species is considered native in the Prairie Provinces by Mulligan (1961) but is so weedy in habit and spreads so rapidly into disturbed areas that it is impossible to define its native range. Native or introd., it ranges from SE B.C. to cent. Alta. (isolated stations on Great Bear L. and Great Slave L., where doubtless introd.), cent. Sask., Man. (N to Churchill), Ont. (N to the N shore of L. Superior), and E Que. (Fernald in Gray 1950). [Var. robustum Thell.; L. ?bourgeauanum Thell.; L. fletcheri Rydb.]. MAP: Mulligan 1961: fig. 13, p. 85.

L. ruderale L. Cresson puant
Eurasian; introd. along roadsides and in fields and waste places of N. America, as in Sask. (Regina), S Man. (near Brandon and Winnipeg), S Ont. (N to Prince Edward Co.), SW Que. (Montreal dist.), N.B., and N.S. MAPS: Mulligan 1961: fig. 12, p. 82; Meusel, Jaeger, and Weinert 1965:177.

L. sativum L. Garden-Cress. Cresson alénois
Asiatic; introd. along roadsides and in waste places of N. America, as in cent. Yukon (Dawson; CAN), Dist. Mackenzie (Norman Wells, 65°17′N; DAO), S B.C. (Vancouver Is.; Vancouver; Nelson), Alta. (N to Brownvale, 56°08′N), Sask. (N to near Saskatoon), S Man. (near Winnipeg; Bourgeau, in Palliser 1863), Ont. (N to the N shore of L. Superior; Groh and Frankton 1949b), Que. (N to the Côte-Nord and Gaspé Pen.), N.B., P.E.I., and N.S.; SW Greenland. MAPS: Mulligan 1961: fig. 12, p. 82; Hultén 1968b:497.

[L. strictum (Wats.) Rattan]
[Concerning the report of this S. American species from SW B.C. by Henry (1915), see L. oxycarpum. (L. oxycarpum var. str. Wats.).]

L. virginicum L. Poor-man's-pepper
/T/X/ (Hs (bien. or T)) Dry open soil, roadsides, and waste places, the typical phase native in the E U.S.A. (introd. in the W U.S.A., in E Canada from Ont. to Nfld. and N.S., and in Europe), the only native area in Canada being that of the other varieties keyed out below (SW B.C.). Native or introd., the aggregate species ranges from SW B.C. (introd. in SE Alaska; not known from Alta.–Sask.–Man.) to Mont., S.Dak., Ont. (N to the Ottawa dist.), SW Que. (N to L. St. Peter), Nfld. (St. John's), N.B., P.E.I., and N.S., S to N Calif., N.Mex., Tex., and Fla. MAPS and synonymy: see below.
1 Cotyledons accumbent (an edge of each against the radicle); pods usually longer than broad; [L. texanum Buckl. in part; introd. from Ont. to Nfld. and N.S.; MAPS (aggregate species): Mulligan 1961: fig. 12, p. 82; Hultén 1968b:498] . . . . . var. virginicum
1 Cotyledons oblique to the radicle or incumbent (the back of one against the radicle); (SW B.C.: Vancouver Is. and adjacent islands and mainland, where apparently native).

836

2 Pedicels and upper portion of stem glabrous; [*L. medium* Greene; *L. intermedium* Gray, not Richard] . . . . .var. *medium* (Greene) C.L. Hitchc.
2 Pedicels and upper portion of stem pubescent.
  3 Basal leaves pinnate, the pinnae deeply lobed, the hairs crisped; pods sometimes ciliate; [*L. menziesii* DC.] . . . . .var. *menziesii* (DC.) C.L. Hitchc.
  3 Basal leaves less divided, the pubescence usually not crisped; pods glabrous; [*L. intermedium* var. *pub.* Greene] . . . . .var. *pubescens* (Greene) C.L. Hitchc.

LESQUERELLA S. Wats. [2983] Bladder-pod

(Ref.: Payson 1921)
1 Pods to 9 mm long, typically globose, glabrous or with a few stellate hairs, on straight or slightly arched-recurving pedicels; stem-leaves 1–few; basal leaves spatulate or oblanceolate, tapering gradually to the petioles, often prostrate on the ground, varying greatly in length, to 2 cm broad; stems 1–many, prostrate to ascending, to 3 dm long; (transcontinental, chiefly in arctic and alpine habitats) . . . .
. . . .*L. arctica*
1 Pods at most about 6 mm long, usually copiously stellate-pubescent.
  2 Pedicels generally recurved or arched-recurved to reflexed in fruit, rarely straight and ascending, not sigmoid; pods oblong-rotund to globose, 3 or 4 mm long, with commonly 8 or more seeds; stem-leaves few to numerous; basal leaves to 1 dm long, narrowly to broadly lanceolate, gradually tapering to the petioles; stems decumbent to nearly erect, to 4 dm long; (s Alta. to s Man.) . . . .*L. ludoviciana*
  2 Pedicels usually spreading to erect, often sigmoid (S-shaped); basal leaves oblanceolate to obovate, rather abruptly narrowed to the petiole.
    3 Pods globose to subglobose, not flattened along the margins or near the tip, 3 or 4 mm long, with at most 8 seeds; stem-leaves numerous, usually linear to linear-oblanceolate; basal leaves to 12 cm long; stems erect or somewhat decumbent-based, to 4 (sometimes 5) dm tall; (s B.C.) . . . .*L. douglasii*
    3 Pods more elongate, usually elliptic-oblong or ovate in outline, usually noticeably flattened along the margins at the tip, to 6 mm long; stem-leaves at most about 5, similar to or slightly narrower in outline than the basal leaves; stems prostrate to erect, usually not over 1.5 dm long.
      4 Basal leaf-blades linear to oblanceolate or narrowly obovate, to 4 cm long and rarely over 4 mm broad; petals to 7 mm long; (s Alta. and s Sask.) . . . .
. . . .*L. alpina*
      4 Basal leaf-blades oblanceolate to ovate, obovate, or subrotund, to 8 cm long and over 2 cm broad; petals to 1 cm long; (s ?B.C.) . . . . . .[*L. occidentalis*]

L. alpina (Nutt.) S. Wats.
/T/WW/ (Ch (Hs)) Drier lowlands, foothills, and mountain ridges from Mont. to s Alta. (Manyberries; Milk River; Belly R.; Sweetgrass Hills) and sw Sask. (Cypress Hills; Val Marie; Swift Current; Wood Mountain), s to Idaho, Colo., and S.Dak. [*Vesicaria* Nutt.; *L. nodosa* Greene; *L. spathulata* Rydb.].

L. arctica (Wormsk.) S. Wats.
/AST/X/GA/ (Ch (Hs)) Calcareous barrens and slopes, the aggregate species from the coasts of Alaska–Dist. Mackenzie–Dist. Keewatin (in the Yukon, N to ca. 67°N) to Banks Is., Melville Is., and N Ellesmere Is. (N to ca. 80°N), s to s Alaska–Yukon–Dist. Mackenzie (isolated in the mts. of B.C. and sw Alta. and at Churchill, NE Man.), Southampton Is., Coats Is., and N Labrador (Ramah, 58°54′N); isolated in E Que. and w Nfld.; w and E Greenland N of the Arctic Circle; arctic Asia. MAPS and synonymy: *see* below.
1 Pods completely glabrous, to 9 mm long; sepals subacute; rosette-leaves spatulate or oblanceolate, broad-petioled; [*Alyssum* Wormsk.; *Vesicaria* Rich.; incl. var *scammanae* Rollins and *L. calderi* Mulligan & Porsild; transcontinental, the type from Greenland; replaced in E Que. and Nfld. by the following taxon; MAPS (aggregate species, except that by Porsild): Hultén 1968*b*:517; Porsild 1957: map 183, p. 183;

Böcher 1938: fig. 51, p. 109, and 1954: fig. 33, (map 1), p. 135; Fernald 1918a: map 4, pl. 16, 1925: map 55, p. 323, and 1929: map 12, p. 1492; Tolmachev 1932:55] . . . .
. . . . var. *arctica*
1   Pods often somewhat scurfy, sometimes glabrous, at most 7 mm long; sepals obtuse; rosette-leaves narrowly oblanceolate, slender-petioled; [*L. purshii* (Wats.) Fern.; Alaska–Yukon–W Dist. Mackenzie and mts. of B.C. and sw Alta.; Anticosti Is., E Que., the type locality; W Nfld.; MAP: Porsild 1957: map 183, p. 183] . . . var. *purshii* Wats.

L. douglasii S. Wats.
/T/W/   (Hs)   Dry open or wooded places from s B.C. (Vancouver Is. and adjacent islands E to Cranbrook, N to Kelowna and Windermere) to N Oreg. and Idaho. [*Vesicaria ludoviciana sensu* John Macoun 1883, as to the B.C. plant, not (Nutt.) DC., the relevant collection in CAN].

L. ludoviciana (Nutt.) S. Wats.
/T/WW/   (Ch (Hs))   Dry plains and foothills from E Mont. and s Alta. (N to Calgary; CAN) to s Sask. (N to near Saskatoon; CAN) and s Man. (N to Steeprock, about 100 mi N of Portage la Prairie), s to Utah, Colo., Kans., Minn., and Ill. [*Alyssum* Nutt.; *Vesicaria* DC.; *Myagrum (L.) argenteum* Pursh].
    Much or all of the Canadian material is referable to var. *arenosa* (Rich.) Wats. (*Vesicaria (L.) aren.* Rich.; *L. macounii, L. rosea,* and *L. versicolor* Greene; *L. ?prostrata sensu* Rydberg 1922, as to the Sask. report, not Nels.).

[*L. occidentalis* S. Wats.]
[The report of this species of the W U.S.A. (N to NE Oreg. and Idaho) from the Osoyoos Valley of s B.C. by J.M. Macoun (1899) is probably based upon *L. douglasii,* this taken in 1905 by Macoun at the same locality (the 1898 collection by Green cited by Macoun was not located).]

LOBULARIA Desv.   [3013]

L. maritima (L.) Desv.   Sweet Alyssum
European; much used as an ornamental edging plant in N. America and inclined to escape to lawns, etc., as in sw B.C. (near a wharf at Victoria, Vancouver Is.; CAN; J.M. Macoun 1897), s Ont. (Lambton, Wellington, York, and Welland counties), and sw Que. (Boivin 1966b). [*Clypeola* L.; *Alyssum* Lam.; *Koniga* R. Br.].

LUNARIA L.   [2969]

1   Fruit broadly elliptic to rotund, to 5 cm long and about two-thirds as broad, rounded at both ends; seeds orbicular; leaves coarsely serrate, the uppermost ones subsessile . . . .*L. annua*
1   Fruit oblong, to about 8 cm long and 2.5 cm broad, acutish at both ends; seeds reniform; leaves all distinctly petioled, finely and sharply serrate . . . .[*L. rediviva*]

L. annua L.   Honesty
European; a garden escape to roadsides and waste places in N. America, as in s B.C. (Vancouver Is.; Revelstoke), s Man. (Benito, N of Duck Mt.), Ont. (Wellington, Welland, and Bruce counties), sw Que. (Montreal dist.), and N.S. (Annapolis Co.; NSPM). [*L. biennis* Moench].

[*L. rediviva* L.]   Perennial Honesty
[Eurasian; an occasional garden-escape in N. America, as in s Ont. (Meaford, Grey Co.; MT; reported from Niagara, Lincoln Co., by Groh and Frankton 1949b), but scarcely established.]

[MALCOLMIA R. Br.]   [3032]

1   Principal leaves oblanceolate, remotely dentate, rather copiously pubescent with

small, freely branched hairs; petals pinkish, to about 8 mm long; pods rigidly
spreading-ascending, scarcely constricted between the seeds . . . . [*M. africana*]
1   Principal leaves obovate-oblong, entire or nearly so, thinly pubescent with closely
appressed, chiefly 2-pronged hairs attached near the middle; petals white to lilac,
red, or blue-violet, commonly over 1 cm long; pods flexuous, spreading or
downwardly curved, constricted between the seeds . . . . [*M. maritima*]

[M. africana (L.) R. Br.]   African Stock
[Native in the Mediterranean region; reported by Fraser and Russell (1944) as escaped but
not established at Swift Current, Sask. (*Hesperis* L.).]

[M. maritima (L.) R. Br.]   "Virginia Stock"
[Reported by Montgomery (1957) as taken as a garden-escape at Blackstock, about 50 mi
NE of Toronto, Ont., by Scott in 1897, presumably as a casual escape and not established.
(*Cheiranthus* L.).]

MATTHIOLA R. Br.   [3042]   Stock

M. bicornis (Sibth. & Sm.) DC.   Evening Stock
Asiatic; an occasional garden-escape in N. America, as in Sask. (Boivin 1966*b*) and Ont. (reported from Lambton Co. by Dodge 1915, as "Plentiful in one place growing in sand on Lake
Huron shore near summer cottages." and presumably from North Bay by Montgomery 1957,
as *M. "biennis"*). [*Cheiranthus* Sibth. & Sm.].

[MYAGRUM L.]   [2922]

[M. perfoliatum L.]
[Eurasian; an occasional garden-escape in N. America but scarcely established, as in SW Que.
(near Quebec City; CAN; reported from near Rigaud, Vaudreuil Co., by Groh and Frankton
1948).]

NASTURTIUM R. Br.   [2965]   Watercress.   Cresson

N. officinale R. Br.
Eurasian; (ranges in Alaska–Canada outlined below, together with MAPS and synonymy).
1   Pods less than 2 cm long but up to 2.5 mm broad, beakless or with a thick style at
most 1 mm long; seeds distinctly 2-rowed, with about 25 pits on each face;
lowermost pedicels generally not over 1.5 cm long; [*Sisymbrium (N.; Radicula;
Rorippa) nasturtium-aquaticum* L.; introd. in SW B.C. (Comox, Vancouver Is.) and S
Alta. (Boivin 1966*b*); MAPS: Hultén 1968*b*:507 (aggregate species, as *Ror. nast.*); P.S.
Green, Rhodora 64(757): fig. 3, p. 36. 1962]. According to Green, this is a diploid
taxon, reports of which from E Canada refer to the following tetraploid phase. A
purported hybrid between the two phases (× *Rorippa sterilis* Airy-Shaw) is reported
from Alta. and N.S. by Boivin (1966*b*) . . . . var. *officinale*
1   Pods to about 2.5 cm long but not over 1.5 mm broad, the style often over 1 mm
long; seeds more or less 1-rowed, with about 100 pits on each face; lowermost
pedicels to over 2 cm long; [*N. (Rorippa) mic.* Boenn.; *N. fontanum* var. *longisiliquum*
Irmsch.; introd. in Alaska (Manly Hot Springs), B.C. (N to Atlin, ca. 59°N), Alta.
(Banff; Pincher Creek), Man. (Awene, 12 mi SE of Brandon), Ont. (N to the Ottawa
dist.), Que. (N to the Gaspé Pen. at Percé), Nfld., N.B., P.E.I., and N.S.; MAP: Green,
loc. cit., fig. 8 (*Ror. mic.*; incomplete northwards), p. 36] . . . .
. . . . var. *microphyllum* (Boenn.) Thell.

NESLIA Desv.   [2988]

N. paniculata (L.) Desv.   Ball-Mustard
Eurasian; introd. in grainfields and waste places of N. America, as in S Alaska–Yukon–Dist.

Mackenzie and all the provinces (in Man., N to Churchill). [*Myagrum* L.]. MAP: Hultén 1968b:519.

PARRYA R. Br. [3053]

1 Petals purple (rarely white or creamy white), usually less than 1 cm long; anthers short, ovate; pods commonly 2 or 3 cm long and 3 or 4 mm broad, their margins not markedly sinuate, the stigma more or less sessile; leaves 2 or 3 cm long, entire or rarely short-toothed, short-petioled; scape usually less than 1.5 dm tall, glabrous; (N Yukon to Southampton Is.) . . . . *P. arctica*
1 Petals rose-purple or white, to about 1.5 cm long; anthers linear-oblong, to about 2 mm long; pods to about 5 cm long and 6 mm broad, strongly sinuate, the style to 3 mm long; leaves to about 1 dm long, entire to distinctly serrate, relatively long-petioled; scape to 2(3) dm tall, more or less glandular-hispidulous; (Alaska to Victoria Is. and N B.C.) . . . . *P. nudicaulis*

P. arctica R. Br.

/Aa/(X)/ (Ch (Hr)) Wet calcareous clayey and gravelly barrens from Prince Patrick Is. to Cornwallis Is. and Somerset Is., S to N Yukon at ca. 73°N, Great Bear L., the coast of Dist. Mackenzie, and N Southampton Is. (type from Melville Is.). MAPS: Porsild 1957: map 203, p. 186, and 1955: fig. 11, p. 44; *Atlas of Canada* 1957: map 15, sheet 38; W.J. Cody, Nat. can. (Que.) 98(2): fig. 23, p. 152. 1971.

The report from Cape Chidley, northernmost Ungava–Labrador, by John Macoun (*in* Robert Bell, Geol. Surv. Canada, Rep. of Progress 1882–84:39DD. 1885) is based upon *Arabis alpina* (the relevant collection in CAN; his reports from Hopedale and Nain, Labrador, may also belong here). Forma *albiflora* Boivin (flowers white rather than purple) is known from King William Is. and the type locality, Cambridge Bay, S Victoria Is.

P. nudicaulis (L.) Regel

/aSs/W/EA/ (Ch (Hr)) Moist places, sandy slopes, and alpine meadows from the coasts of Alaska–Yukon–W Dist. Mackenzie and SW Victoria Is. to the mts. of northernmost W B.C. (Father Mt., ca. 59°30'N, where taken by Tyrrell in 1898; CAN); arctic E Europe (Kanin Pen.; an old report from Spitsbergen); arctic Asia and mts. of cent. Asia. [*Cardamine* L.; *Arabis* DC.; *C. articulata* Pursh; *P. macrocarpa* R. Br.; incl. the narrow-leaved extreme, ssp. *interior* Hult. and its var. *grandiflora* Hult.]. MAPS: combine the maps by Hultén 1968b:557 and 558 (ssp. *int.*); Porsild 1957: map 204, p. 186.

Some of our material is referable to the completely glabrous phase, ssp. *septentrionalis* Hult. (MAP: Hultén 1968b:558).

PHYSARIA Gray [2982]

P. didymocarpa (Hook.) Gray Twin-pod

/T/W/ (Ch (Hs)) Scablands, shale banks, talus slopes and gravelly places from SE B.C. (Kootenay; Columbia Valley; Windermere; Big Bend, N of Revelstoke) and SW Alta. (N to 15 mi N of Jasper; reports from Sask. require confirmation) to Wash., Idaho, and Wyo. [*Vesicaria did.* Hook., the type a Drummond collection from "Rocky Mountains, between lat. 52° and 57°", presumably in Alta.; *P. macrantha* Blank.]. MAP: G.A. Mulligan, Can. J. Bot. 46(6): fig. 1, p. 736. 1968.

RAPHANUS L. [2950] Radish. Radis

1 Petals commonly pale yellow with violet veins (turning whitish); fruit to about 6 mm thick, strongly constricted between the usually 4 or more seeds and finally breaking between them, prominently several-grooved lengthwise, the beak relatively slender . . . . .
. . . . *R. raphanistrum*

1   Petals commonly pale purple; fruit to 1 cm thick, not constricted between the
    usually 2 or 3 seeds and usually not breaking between them, lightly grooved
    lengthwise, the beak conical . . . .*R. sativus*

R. raphanistrum L.   Wild Radish, Jointed Charlock.   Rave sauvage
Eurasian; a weed of grainfields, waste places, etc., in N. America, the Canadian distribution of
various colour-phases noted below.
1   Petals white.
    2   Petals with violet veins; [B.C. (Vancouver Is.), N.S. (Hantsport, Hants Co.), and
        P.E.I. (Souris, Kings Co.)] . . . . f. *albus* (Schuebler & Martens) Hayek
    2   Petals with pale or greenish veins; [Montague, P.E.I.; D.S. Erskine 1960] . . . .
        . . . . f. *candidus* (Opiz) Beck
1   Petals not white, at least when fresh.
    3   Petals uniformly purple-violet; [Ont. (Ottawa dist.; Gillett 1958) and N.S. (Halifax;
        NSPM)] . . . . f. *purpureus* (Reichenb.) Domin
    3   Petals yellow, at least when fresh (fading to white).
        4   Petals with yellow veins; [Grand Manan Is., Charlotte Co., sw N.B.; A.R.
            Hodgdon and R.B. Pike, Rhodora 64(758):101. 1962] . . . .
            . . . . f. *sulphureus* (Babey) Hayek
        4   Petals with violet veins; [*Raphanistrum innocuum* Moench; B.C. (N to Queen
            Charlotte Is.), Alta. (Moss 1959), Sask. (N to Tisdale, 52°51′N), Ont. (N to the
            Ottawa dist.), Que. (N to Taschereau, 48°40′N, and the Gaspé Pen.), Nfld.,
            N.B., P.E.I., and N.S.; s Greenland] . . . . f. *raphanistrum*

R. sativus L.   Radish.   Radis
Eurasian; persisting in gardens or escaping to waste places in N. America, as in Alaska (Fair-
banks), B.C. (Vancouver Is.; Agassiz; Chilliwack), s Man. (Brandon; Pipestone), Ont. (N to
Carleton Co.), Que. (N to Ste-Flavie, Rimouski Co.), Nfld., N.B., P.E.I., and N.S.; s Greenland.
[*R. raphanistrum* var. *sat.* (L.) Beck]. MAP: Hultén 1968*b*:506.

RAPISTRUM Crantz   [2956]

1   Upper joint of pod strongly ribbed, gradually narrowed into a broad conical beak
    about 1 mm long; petals bright yellow with darker veins; pedicels up to twice as long
    as the usually 1-seeded lower joint of the pod; lower leaves with about 6 pairs of
    lateral lobes and a terminal lobe somewhat larger than the adjacent lateral pair, the
    coarse teeth distinctly callous-tipped; biennial or perennial with 1 to several
    branching stems from a stout taproot; (introd. in se Sask.) . . . .*R. perenne*
1   Upper joint of pod abruptly or gradually narrowed to the slender persistent style, this
    up to 5 mm long and usually at least half as long as the joint; petals lemon-yellow
    with darker veins; lower leaves with a large terminal lobe and about 3 pairs of much
    smaller lateral ones, their teeth less strongly callous-tipped; more or less glaucous
    annual (rarely biennial) with a simple or branched stem from a slender taproot;
    (introd. in Ont. and s Que.) . . . .*R. rugosum*

R. perenne (L.) All.
European; apparently introd. in N. America only in waste places of se Sask. (Broadview and
Grenfell; CAN and SASK, respectively; *see* Herbert Groh, Sci. Agric. 13:726. 1933; inadver-
tently reported under *Raphanistrum* by Breitung 1957*a*). [*Myagrum* L.].

R. rugosum (L.) All.
Native in the Mediterranean region; local in waste places of N. America, as in Ont. (in a dump
at Ottawa; gravel pit at Cambridge, Waterloo Co.) and Que. (Montreal dist.; reported from
Métis, sw Gaspé Pen., by R.T. Clausen, Rhodora 42(498):202. 1940). [*Myagrum* L.; incl. ssp.
linnaeanum Rouy & Fouc., the upper joint of the fruit only slightly ribbed rather than strongly
rugose].

RORIPPA Scop.   [2965]   Yellow Cress

1   Principal stem-leaves merely rather coarsely serrate or shallowly lobed; fruiting
    pedicels to over 1.5 cm long.
    2   Pods narrowly cylindric, at least 1.5 cm long, their seeds to 2 mm long; styles
        about 1 mm long; pedicels horizontally spreading to somewhat ascending; sepals
        to 5 mm long; petals to 8 mm long, whitish, sometimes tinged below with light
        lavender; basal leaves tufted on short shoots, lanceolate to ovate, shallowly and
        coarsely dentate, cuneate at base, they and the oblanceolate, toothed or lobed
        lower stem-leaves petioled; upper stem-leaves sessile, entire to sparingly
        toothed; stems erect to decumbent; (s ?Dist. Mackenzie) . . . . [R. crystallina]
    2   Pods ellipsoid or ovoid to subglobose, at most 6 mm long; seeds about 1 mm
        long; petals yellow; stems stoloniferous, creeping and rooting at the nodes;
        (introd.).
        3   Fruits broadly ellipsoid to subglobose, at most 3 mm long (the style about the
            same length), on slightly ascending pedicels; petals little surpassing the
            sepals; leaves narrowly oblanceolate, nearly entire to rather shallowly and
            irregularly toothed, the lower ones petioled and auricled at base, the upper
            ones sessile and cordate-clasping . . . . R. austriaca
        3   Fruits ovoid, to 6 mm long (the style at most 2 mm long), on horizontally
            spreading or deflexed pedicels; petals about twice as long as the sepals;
            leaves elliptic to broadly oblanceolate, entire, toothed, or lobed, chiefly
            sessile (the lower short-petioled ones sometimes deeply pectinate), usually
            none of the leaves distinctly auricled . . . . R. amphibia
1   At least the lower stem-leaves typically pinnatifid nearly or quite to base (except for
    an often broad terminal segment).
    4   Petals mostly 3 or 4 mm long; rhizomatous perennials.
        5   Pods ovate to oblong, to 7 mm long and 2.5 mm broad, pubescent; sepals
            tending to persist well into the fruiting stage; plant finely pubescent or
            papillate nearly throughout; (introd. in NW Dist. Mackenzie) . . . . R. calycina
        5   Pods narrower, mostly to about 1.5 cm long and 1.5 mm broad; sepals usually
            deciduous shortly after anthesis; plants mostly glabrous or nearly so, at least
            above.
            6   Fruits linear-cylindric, to about 2.5 cm long; leaves thin, deeply pinnately
                parted into linear to lanceolate toothed or incised segments; (introd.) . . . .
                . . . . R. sylvestris
            6   Fruits thick-cylindric to lanceolate, curving, at most 1.5 cm long; leaves
                firm, regularly sinuate- to pectinate-pinnatifid, the linear-oblong to oblong
                lobes essentially entire; (Alta. and Sask.) . . . . R. sinuata
    4   Petals 1 or 2 mm long; annuals or biennials, lacking rhizomes.
        7   Pedicels to 12 mm long, usually at least as long as the pods; pods ovate to
            oblong, commonly not over 8 mm long (but up to 12 mm), 2 or 3 mm broad;
            stems mostly erect, to 1 m tall; (transcontinental) . . . . R. islandica
        7   Pedicels commonly not over 4 mm long (but up to 7 mm), usually markedly
            shorter than the fruits; stems commonly somewhat spreading to decumbent,
            rarely over 4 dm tall.
            8   Pods usually curved, linear, to 1.5 cm long and 1.5 mm broad; plant
                glabrous to sparingly short-strigose; (Alaska–Yukon–B.C.) . . . . . . R. curvisiliqua
            8   Pods straightish, oblong-lanceolate to oval, to 8 mm long and 2.5 mm
                broad; plant glabrous; (B.C. and Alta.) . . . . R. obtusa

R. amphibia (L.) Bess.
Eurasian; introd. in quiet waters and along shores (sometimes even along dry roadsides) in N.
America, as in sw Que. (between Montreal and L. St. Peter; see sw Que. map by Frère Marie-
Victorin, Contrib. Inst. Bot. Univ. Montréal 17: fig. 1, p. 4. 1930; the report from Fort William
(Thunder Bay), Ont., by John Macoun 1883, is based upon R. islandica var. hispida, the rele-
vant collection in CAN; Macoun's other Ont. reports and his Gaspé Pen., Que., report may
also refer to R. isl.). [Sisymbrium L.; Nasturtium R. Br.].

Some of the Que. material is referable to f. *variifolia* (DC.) Hayek (the first leaves of the season (usually submerged) deeply pinnatifid or even pectinate, with linear segments, rather than entire or merely irregularly sinuate-toothed). Some collections from the Montreal dist. have been named × *R. prostrata* (Berg.) Schinz & Thell. (*R. amphibia* × *R. sylvestris;* × *R. ?subglobosa* Barb.).

R. austriaca (Crantz) Bess.
Eurasian; introd. in wet meadows and along muddy shores in N. America, as in Alta. (Fort Saskatchewan; Herbert Groh, Can. Field-Nat. 55(4):55. 1941), Sask. (Greenstreet, 53°28′N; Herbert Groh, Sci. Agric. 13:725. 1933; detd. Rollins), and s Man. (Pilot Mound, about 60 mi sw of Portage la Prairie; DAO). [*Nasturtium* Crantz].

R. calycina (Engelm.) Rydb.
Native in the w U.S.A. (Wash. to Nebr., s to Calif. and N.Mex.); reported as probably a chance introduction by man from NW Dist. Mackenzie by G.A. Mulligan and A.E. Porsild (Can. J. Bot. 44(8):1105. 1966; delta of the Anderson R. at 69°42′N, 129°W). [*Nasturtium* Englem.; *Radicula* Greene]. MAP: Hultén 1968b:511.

[R. crystallina Rollins]
[For a discussion of this puzzling species, known only from the type locality along the Yellowknife Highway near Great Slave L., s Dist. Mackenzie, *see* R.C. Rollins (Rhodora 64(760):324–27. 1962). It may actually represent a chance introduction by man of horseradish (*Armoracia rusticana*), known in the same latitudes from the Yukon.]

R. curvisiliqua (Hook.) Bess.
/t/W/ (T (Hs)) Moist soil from s B.C. and Alta. to Baja Calif. and Colo. MAP and synonymy: *see* below.
1 Sepals to 2 mm long, early deciduous; petals to 2 mm long; leaves usually not lyrate; stem to 5 dm tall; [*Sisymbrium* Hook.; *Nasturtium* Nutt.; *Radicula* Greene; *N. curv. var. nuttallii* Wats.; *Radicula (Ror.) nutt.* (Wats.) Greene; apparently native in s B.C. from Vancouver Is. to Flathead, N to Yale; introd. in interior Alaska (Park and Rapids; E. Scamman, Rhodora 42(501):327. 1940), sw Yukon (Haines Road; Hultén 1950), and N B.C. (Haines Road at ca. 59°30′N; CAN). MAP (aggregate species): Hultén 1968b:510] . . . . .var. *curvisiliqua*
1 Sepals mostly less than 1.5 mm long, often persistent into the fruiting stage; petals rarely over 1.5 mm long; leaves largely lyrate; stem diffusely branched, rarely over 2 dm tall; [*Nasturtium (Rad.; Ror.) lyr.* Nutt.; *Rad. (Ror.) ?curvipes* Greene; *N. (Ror.) indicum sensu* J.M. Macoun 1913, not *Rad. indica* L., the relevant collection in CAN; introd. in s Alaska (Juneau; CAN) and sw B.C. (wharf-ballast at Nanaimo, Vancouver Is.; CAN; distributed as *Radicula indica*); *R. curvipes* reported from Alta. (Craigmyle; Crowsnest; Milk River) and Sask. (Caron; Rosedale) by Boivin 1968] . . . . .var. *lyrata* (Nutt.) Peck

R. islandica (Oeder) Borbas
/aST/X/GEA/ (Hs (bien. or T)) Shores, wet ground, and waste places (perhaps both native and introd.), the aggregate species from the Aleutian Is. and N Alaska–Yukon–w Dist. Mackenzie to Great Bear L., E-cent. Dist. Mackenzie (Thelon Game Sanctuary), NE Man. (Churchill), northernmost Ont., Que. (N to SE Hudson Bay at ca. 56°N, s Ungava Bay, the Knob Lake dist., and the Côte-Nord), Labrador (N to the Hamilton R. basin), Nfld., N.B., P.E.I., and N.S., s to Calif., N.Mex., Tex., and Fla.; W.I.; w Greenland at ca. 61° and 69°N; Iceland; Eurasia (introd. in many other parts of the world). MAPS and synonymy: *see* below.
1 Pods with usually 4 locules (sometimes 3 or up to 6; dehiscing by as many valves), to about 12 mm long and 5 mm broad; surface of seeds distinctly honeycomb-reticulate; anthers mostly over 3 times as long as broad; [f. *tetrapoma* (Busch) Boivin; *Camelina (R.; Tetrapoma) barb.* DC.; *R. hispida* var. *barb.* (DC.) Hult.; incl. the intergrading var. *occidentalis* (Wats.) Butt. & Abbe (*Nasturtium terrestre* var. *occ.* Wats.); *R. (Radicula) clavata* Rydb.; *R. pacifica* Howell); Alaska–Yukon and Asia;

MAPS: Hultén 1968*b*: 509 (*R. hisp.* var. *barb.*); Porsild 1966: map 84 *(R. barb.),* p. 77] . . . . .
. . . . var. *barbaraefolia* (DC.) Scoggan

1 Pods with rarely more than 2 locules, at most about 4 mm broad; surface of seeds
minutely pebbled; anthers less than twice as long as broad.
  2 Leaves relatively thin, the upper (like the lower) pinnatifid; pods mostly 3 or 4 mm
  long; plant essentially glabrous; [*Sisymbrium* Oeder; *S. amphibium* var. *palustre*
  L.; *S. (R.; Nasturtium; Radicula) pal.* (L.) Bess., not *N. pal.* Crantz; *N. (Rad.)*
  terrestre R. Br.; SE Man. (Otterburne; Löve and Bernard 1959), Ont. (N to Winisk,
  55°12′N), N.B. (Bathurst), P.E.I. (D.S. Erskine 1960), and N.S. (Halifax,
  Colchester, and Cape Breton counties); MAP: Hultén 1968*b*:508] . . . . var. *islandica*
  2 Leaves firmer, the upper ones merely dentate to cleft or shallowly lobed; plant
  relatively stout.
    3 Pods less than 6 mm long, short-ellipsoid to subglobose; plant more or less
    hirsute; [*Brachilobus (R.; Radicula) hisp.* Desv.; *Rad. (Nasturtium) palustris*
    var. *hisp.* (Desv.) Rob.; *N. terrestre* var. *hisp.* (Desv.) F. & M.; *Ror. hisp. (isl.)*
    var. *glabrata* Lunell; transcontinental; MAP: Hultén 1968*b*:509 *(Ror. hisp.)*] . . . .
    . . . . var. *hispida* (Desv.) Butt. & Abbe
    3 Pods to 9 mm long, slenderly ellipsoid or subcylindric; plant essentially
    glabrous . . . . var. *fernaldiana* Butt. & Abbe
      4 Stems long-creeping and rooting at the nodes, bearing clusters of mostly
      subentire leaves; [Otterburne, SE Man.; Löve and Bernard 1959]. . . . .
      . . . . f. *reptabunda* Fern.
      4 Stems erect or strongly ascending, at least the lower leaves usually
      pinnatifid; [var. *microcarpa* (Regel) Fern.; *R. williamsii* Britt.;
      transcontinental; MAPS: Raup 1947: pl. 26 (var. *mic.*); Hultén 1968*b*:508] . . . . . .
      . . . . f. *fernaldiana*

R. obtusa (Nutt.) Britt.
/T/(X)/ (T) Moist, usually sandy soil from S B.C. (N to Kamloops; CAN; reported as probably introd. at Juneau, SE Alaska, by Hultén 1950) to S Alta. (Crowsnest Pass and Milk River; a
collection in CAN from L. Mamawi at 58°35′N has also been placed here by Raup, but the
plant may have been introd. there), Mich., and SW Que., S to Calif., Tex., Mo., and W.Va.
[*Nasturtium* Nutt.; *Radicula* Greene; *Ror. ?tenerrima* Greene]. MAP: Hultén 1968*b*:510.
    The plant of SW Que. is referable to var. *integra* (Rydb.) Vict. (*R. int.* Rydb.; leaves merely
dentate rather than pinnately parted or divided). It is known from two localities in the Montreal dist. (*see* SW Que. map by Frère Marie-Victorin, Contrib. Inst. Bot. Univ. Montréal 17: fig.
7, p. 11. 1930).

R. sinuata (Nutt.) Hitchc.
/T/WW/ (Grh) Sandy or rocky shores, moist ground, and roadsides from SE ?B.C. (*Nast. tr.*
reported from the Flathead R. by John Macoun 1886) to S Alta. (Nobleford; Hand Hills; Medicine Hat; Cypress Hills), and S Sask. (Kabri, Kindersley, and Tessier; Breitung 1957a; concerning a report from Churchill, Man., *see* Scoggan 1957; reported from St. Thomas, Elgin
Co., S Ont., by Groh and Frankton 1947*b*, where perhaps introd.), S to Calif. and Tex. [*Nasturtium* Nutt.; *N. trachycarpum* Gray; *R. columbiae sensu* Fraser and Russell 1944, not (Suksd.)
Howell].

R. *sylvestris* (L.) Bess.   Creeping Yellow Cress
European; introd. in meadows and along shores and roadsides in N. America, as in S B.C. (N
to Prince Rupert and Smithers), S Alta. (Olds; Banff), Sask. (Regina and Leader; Breitung
1957a), S Man. (Morden), Ont. (N to the Ottawa dist.), Que. (N to the Côte-Nord and Anticosti
Is.; MT), Nfld., N.B., P.E.I. (near Charlottetown; MT), and N.S. [*Sisymbrium* L.; *Nasturtium* R.
Br.; *Radicula* Druce; incl. var. *stenocarpa* (Godr.) Vict.].

SCHOENOCRAMBE Greene   [2867]

S. linifolia (Nutt.) Greene   Rush Mustard
/T/W/   (Grh (Ch))   Sagebrush plains to lower montane slopes from s B.C. (Dry Interior N to Kamloops; introd. in dry pastureland at Fort Saskatchewan, Alta.) to Nev. and N.Mex. [*Sisymbrium* Nutt.].

SISYMBRIUM L.   [2917]

1   Upper leaves with filiform or elongate-linear entire segments, sessile or nearly so; lower leaves with linear-lanceolate serrate segments, petioled; petals pale yellow, about 7 mm long; fruits about 1 dm long, on short divergent pedicels to 1 cm long; stem sparingly spreading-hirsute at base; (introd.) . . . .*S. altissimum*
1   All the leaves with lanceolate to ovate or triangular segments and usually more or less petioled; (introd.).
   2   Fruits 1 or 2 cm long, on stout erect pedicels mostly 2 or 3 cm long closely appressed to the main axis; petals pale yellow, to 4 mm long; stem hirsute at least at base . . . .*S. officinale*
   2   Fruits to 6 cm long, spreading-ascending on divergent pedicels.
      3   Style of fruit commonly 1 or 2 mm long; petals golden yellow, about twice as long as the sepals; fruits and their clavate pedicels so curved and twisted as to appear irregularly crowded . . . .[*S. austriacum*]
      3   Style of fruit at most 0.5 mm long.
         4   Petals pale yellow, 3 or 4 mm long, little surpassing the sepals; young fruits projecting beyond the corolla; mature fruits to 6 cm long; segments of lower leaves oblong to ovate; stem glabrous or appressed-strigose with recurving hairs . . . .[*S. irio*]
         4   Petals golden yellow, about 6 mm long, about twice as long as the sepals; young fruits scarcely or not at all projecting beyond the corolla; mature fruits rarely over 3.5 cm long; segments of lower leaves ovate or triangular; stem usually retrorse-hispid . . . .*S. loeselii*

S. altissimum L.   Tumble-Mustard.   Moutarde roulante
Eurasian; introd. in fields and waste places of N. America, as in s Alaska–Yukon–Dist. Mackenzie and all the provinces (in Man., N to Churchill). [*Norta* Britt.; *S. sinapistrum* Crantz]. MAP: Hultén 1968*b*:502.

[S. austriacum Jacq.]
[European; collections in CAN and MT from Montreal, Que., originally placed here, have been referred to *S. loeselii* by Boivin; the report of *S. acutangulum* from New Westminster, B.C., by John Macoun (1883) requires confirmation. (*S. acutangulum* DC.).]

[S. irio L.]
[European; the report of this species from Sauble Beach, Bruce Pen., s Ont., by Krotkov (1940) is referred to *Erucastrum gallicum* by Groh (1947; relevant collection in TRT).]

S. loeselii L.
Eurasian; introd. in old fields and waste places of N. America, as in s B.C. (N to Kamloops), Alta. (N to Fort Saskatchewan), Sask. (N to Saskatoon), Man. (N to Churchill), Ont. (N to Thunder Bay; also known from Lambton and Huron counties), and Que. (Montreal). [*S. austriacum sensu* Raymond 1950*b*, not Jacq., relevant collections in CAN and MT].

S. officinale (L.) Scop.   Hedge-Mustard.   Herbe au chantre
Eurasian; introd. in fields and waste places of N. America, as in SE Alaska, s B.C., s Alta. (Moss 1959; not known from Sask.), Man. (Boivin 1966*b*), Ont. (N to Ottawa), Que. (N to the

Gaspé Pen.), ?Nfld. (Rouleau 1956, perhaps taking up the report by Reeks 1873), N.B., P.E.I., and N.S. [*Erysimum* L.]. MAP: Hultén 1968b:501.

Some of our material is referable to var. *leiocarpum* DC. (pods essentially glabrous rather than minutely pubescent or tomentose).

SMELOWSKIA C.A. Meyer [2996]

(Ref.: Drury and Rollins 1952)
1 Caudex usually simple and usually more than 5 mm thick (or with slender stolon-like offshoots); stems branched from near the base, becoming decumbent in fruit; pedicels widely divergent or recurved.
   2 Petals lavender to deep purple, to 6 mm long; sepals usually purple, to 3 mm long; pods linear to oblong or broadly obovate, to nearly 2 cm long and 6 mm broad; basal leaves palmately 3–5-lobed, the lobes short; caudex about 5 mm long; stem 2 or 3 cm long; (Alaska–Yukon–Dist. Mackenzie) . . . .*S. borealis*
   2 Petals white or creamy, about 3 mm long; sepals yellow-brown, 1 or 2 mm long; pods narrowly obovate or pear-shaped, to 6 mm long and 2 or 3 mm broad; basal leaves pinnately cut to midrib into about 9 lobes; caudex and stem each to about 1.5 dm long; (Alaska) . . . .*S. pyriformis*
1 Caudex usually branched and relatively slender; stems usually simple, each arising from a separate caudex-branch; pedicels widely divergent to ascending; petals white, cream, or lavender.
   3 Mature pods linear to narrowly oblong, tapering at both ends, to 13 mm long and 2.5 mm broad; sepals early deciduous; petals to 8 mm long; fruiting inflorescence to 1 dm long; basal leaves strongly ciliate at base with long stiff hairs; (Alaska–W Dist. Mackenzie and mts. of B.C. and SW Alta.) . . . .*S. calycina*
   3 Mature pods oblong to ovate, to 6 mm long and 3 mm broad; sepals persistent until the fruits are well developed; petals to 5 mm long; fruiting inflorescence to 5 cm long; basal leaves not ciliate; (mts. of S ?B.C.) . . . .[*S. ovalis*]

S. borealis (Greene) Drury & Rollins
/aS/W/ (Hs (Ch)) Limestone scree and rubble in Alaska (N to ca. 69°N), the Yukon (N to near the Arctic Circle), and W-cent. Dist. Mackenzie. MAPS and synonymy: *see* below.
1 Calyx promptly deciduous; styles less than 0.5 mm long; rachis and pedicels white-villous; [Alaska, the type from the Richardson Mts.; MAP: Drury and Rollins 1952: fig. 2, p. 93] . . . . .var. *jordalii* Drury & Rollins
1 Calyx persistent; style over 0.5 mm long.
   2 Pubescence predominantly white-villous; pods oblong, the valves rigid; petals to 6 mm long; [Alaska, the type from Sable Mt., Mt. McKinley Park; MAP: on the above-noted map by Drury and Rollins] . . . . .var. *villosa* Drury & Rollins
   2 Pubescence sparse to dense but not predominantly white-villous; pods ovate to obovate; petals to 4.5 mm long.
      3 Pods membranaceous, inflated; leaves densely pubescent but scarcely ashy; [*Acroschizocarpus kol.* Gombocz; Alaska, the type from the head of the Savage R.; MAP: on the above-noted map by Drury and Rollins] . . . . .var. *koliana* (Gombocz) Drury & Rollins
      3 Pods rigid, uninflated; leaves ashy-pubescent; [*Melanidion* Greene; *Ermania* Hult.; *E. parryoides sensu* Hultén 1945 (according to Hultén 1950), not Cham.; the Yukon (?type of *M. boreale* from Runt Creek) and W Dist. Mackenzie; MAPS: Hultén 1968b:540; Porsild 1966: map 85, p. 77; also on the above-noted map by Drury and Rollins] . . . . .var. *borealis*

S. calycina (Steph.) Mey.
/aST/W/A/ (Hs (Ch)) Subalpine to alpine gravels and talus slopes from N Alaska (N to ca. 69°N) and NW Dist. Mackenzie (Richardson Mts.; not known from the Yukon) through the mts. of S B.C. (Mt. Cheam, near Chilliwack) and SW Alta. (N to Banff) to Nev., Utah, and Colo.; Asia. MAPS and synonymy: *see* below.

1   Sepals persistent; [*Lepidium* Steph.; cent. Siberia] . . . . [var. *calycina*]
1   Sepals early deciduous.
   2   Basal leaves entire or shallowly lobed at tip; stem-leaves entire or shallowly
      3-lobed.
      3   Basal leaf-blades oval to obovate, longer than their petioles; pedicels
         commonly divergent at an angle greater than 60°; [*Hutchinsia cal.* var. *integ.*
         Seeman; Alaska (type from Cape Mulgrave) and Siberia; MAPS: Hultén
         1968b:539; Drury and Rollins 1952: fig. 2, p. 93] . . . var. *integrifolia* (Seeman) Rollins
      3   Basal leaf-blades linear to narrowly spatulate, shorter than their petioles;
         pedicels divergent at an angle of less than 60°; [Alaska, the type from the
         Kokrines Mts.; MAP: on the above-noted map by Drury and Rollins] . . . .
         . . . . var. *porsildii* Drury & Rollins
   2   Basal leaves (at least some of them) and stem-leaves pinnately lobed.
      4   Pedicels divergent at an angle of at least 50°; pods broadest above the
         middle; stem-leaves 2 or 3, few-lobed (or some nearly entire); [Alaska (type
         from Lake Schrader) and NW Dist. Mackenzie; MAPS: on the above-noted map
         by Drury and Rollins; Hultén 1968b:539] . . . . var. *media* Drury & Rollins
      4   Pedicels divergent at an angle of less than 50°; pods broadest at the middle,
         tapering equally toward base and apex; stem-leaves up to 7, many-lobed;
         [*Hutchinsia cal.* var. *amer.* Regel & Herder; *S. amer.* (R. & H.) Rydb.; *S. lin-*
         eariloba and *S. lobata* Rydb.; mts. of S B.C. and SW Alta.; MAP: on the above-
         noted map by Drury and Rollins]. . . var. *americana* (Regel & Herder) Drury & Rollins

[S. ovalis Jones]
[Drury and Rollins (1952) assign this species a range from Wash. to Calif. but their MAP (fig. 2, p. 93) indicates a station in southernmost B.C. (presumably in the Skagit Valley of the Cascade Mts. E of Chilliwack), where confirmatory material should be searched for.]

S. pyriformis Drury & Rollins
/S/W/   (Hs (Ch))   Known only from the type station, limestone talus of Farewell Mt., Kuskokwim R. basin, Alaska, W of Mt. McKinley at ca. 63°N. MAPS: Drury and Rollins 1952: fig. 2, p. 93; Hultén 1968b:540.

SUBULARIA L.   [2881]

S. aquatica L.   Awlwort
/aST/X/GEA/   (T)   Shallow waters or sandy shores of lakes and slow streams from the Aleutian Is. and Alaska (N to the Seward Pen.) to S-cent. Yukon, Great Bear L., S Dist. Keewatin, Que. (N to S Ungava Bay, the Côte-Nord, and Gaspé Pen.), Labrador (N to Indian Harbour, 54°25′N), Nfld., and N.S. (not known from N.B. or P.E.I.), S to N Calif., Wyo., Great Slave L., cent. Sask. (Amisk Lake, 54°35′N), S Man., Ont. (Eagle L., near Kenora; St. Ignace Is., near Thunder Bay; Port Sandfield, Lake Muskoka), N N.Y., and N New Eng.; southernmost Greenland and E Greenland near the Arctic Circle; Iceland; Eurasia. [Incl. ssp. *americana* Mulligan & Calder]. MAPS: Hultén 1968b:496, and 1958: map 197, p. 217; G.A. Mulligan and J.A. Calder, Rhodora 66(766): fig. 1, p. 128. 1964; Böcher 1938: fig. 51, p. 109; Meusel 1943: fig. 26a.

TEESDALIA R. Br.   [2882]

T. nudicaulis (L.) R. Br.   Shepherd-Cress
European; introd., usually in sandy soil, in W N. America and known from SW B.C. (Thetis Lake Park, Vancouver Is.; Locarno Park, Vancouver; Vancouver airport; Hope). [*Lepidium* L.].

THELYPODIUM Endl.   [2868]

T. laciniatum (Hook.) Endl.
/t/W/   (Hs)   Dry sandy places from S B.C. (Dry Interior at Ashnola, Keremeos, Summerland, Penticton, Vaseaux L., and Osoyoos) to Calif., Nev., and Idaho. [*Macropodium* Hook.].

THLASPI L.   [2903]   Penny-Cress.   Cents

1   Fruit broadly oblong to suborbicular, 1 or 2 cm long, its very broad wing with an
    apical notch 2 or 3 mm deep; seeds blackish, with concentric ridges; stem-leaves
    entire or remotely dentate, oblong-lanceolate, sagittate-clasping by acutish auricles;
    (introd.) . . . . *T. arvense*
1   Fruit narrower in outline, to about 7 mm long, entire at the apex or with a notch less
    than 1 mm deep; seeds brownish, smooth.
    2   Pods obovate, to 5 mm broad, winged above the middle (the wing very narrow
        toward base), with an evident apical notch; stem-leaves ovate or ovate-oblong, to
        3 cm long, the auricles at their bases rounded; plant annual or overwintering, to
        about 3 dm tall; (introd.) . . . . *T. perfoliatum*
    2   Pods cuneate-oblanceolate, mostly less than 3 mm broad, acute to rounded or
        truncate at apex (or even with a very shallow emargination); stem-leaves
        lanceolate, commonly less than 1 cm long, truncate at base or some of them with
        acutish basal auricles; plant perennial, the stems from a many-branched caudex,
        to about 2 dm tall; (Alaska–Yukon–Dist. Mackenzie and mts. of B.C.–Alta.) . . . .
        . . . . *T. fendleri*

T. arvense L.   Field Penny-Cress, Frenchweed.   Cennes
Eurasian; introd. in fields and waste places of N. America, as in Alaska–Yukon–Dist. Mackenzie and all the provices (in Alaska and Dist. Mackenzie N to ca. 65°N; in Labrador, N to
54°10′N); s Greenland. MAP: Hultén 1968b:499.

T. fendleri Gray
/aST/W/   (Hs (Ch))   Lower valleys to alpine slopes (ranges of Canadian taxa outlined below), s to Calif. and N.Mex. MAPS and synonymy: *see* below.
1   Stem-leaves usually not more than 5, much reduced, rarely as much as 1.5 cm long
    and usually less than half the length of the internodes; [*T. glaucum* var. *hesperium*
    Payson; *T. hesperium* (Pays.) Jones; *T. ?arcticum* Porsild; *T. alpestre* of American
    auth., not L.; *T. montanum sensu* Hooker 1830, not L.; NE Alaska–Yukon–NW Dist.
    Mackenzie (*see* the MAPS for *T. arct.* by Porsild 1966: map 86, p. 77, and Hultén
    1968b:498); reported from B.C. by Hitchcock et al. 1964] . . . var. *hesperium* (Pays.) Hitchc.
1   Stem-leaves mostly larger and more numerous, usually over half the length of the
    internodes.
    2   Stems rarely over 1 dm tall; sepals and basal leaves often purplish; inflorescence
        relatively compact even in fruit; [*T. purpurascens* Rydb.; mts. from Wyo. to Ariz.
        and N.Mex.] . . . . [var. *fendleri*]
    2   Stems mostly over 1 dm tall; sepals and basal leaves rarely purplish;
        inflorescence more elongate; [*T. alpestre* var. *glaucum* Nels.; *T. glaucum* Nels.;
        B.C. and Alta.] . . . . var. *glaucum* (Nels.) Hitchc.

T. perfoliatum L.
Eurasian; locally introd. in fields and waste places of N. America, as in s Ont. (in a dump at Toronto; TRT; the report from near Hamilton, Ont., by John Macoun 1890, is based upon a collection in CAN referable to some other undetermined species) and reported from sw Que. by
Rouleau (1947).

THYSANOCARPUS Hook.   [2993]

T. curvipes Hook.
/t/W/   (T)   Dry hills and open woodlands from sw B.C. (several localities on Vancouver Is.;
CAN; V) to Calif. and Idaho.

RESEDACEAE (Mignonette Family)

RESEDA L.   [3125]   Mignonette

Herbs with alternate entire or deeply pinnatifid leaves with only glands for stipules. Flowers perfect, hypogynous, somewhat irregular, small, in dense terminal racemes. Sepals and yellow, greenish-white, or greenish-yellow petals each 4 or 6, the petals irregularly incised or deeply cleft, in 2 or 3 pairs of different sizes. Stamens 8 or more. Ovary superior. Fruit a 1-locular, 3–6-lobed and 3–6-horned capsule opening at the top before the seeds are full grown. (Introduced species).

1   Sepals and petals each 4; petals yellow, the lower one coarsely crenate or shallowly lobed, the smaller lateral pair and the large upper one cleft into broad lobes; sepals triangular-ovate; raceme spike-like; capsules globose; leaves narrowly lanceolate to oblanceolate, entire . . . . R. luteola
1   Sepals and petals each 6, the petals in 3 pairs of different sizes, the uppermost pair the largest, the lowermost pair the smallest; upper petals with 2 broad appendages and a slender intermediate one; lower petals with 3 narrow appendages; sepals linear-oblong; capsules oblong; raceme relatively open, the flowers rather long-pedicelled; leaves deeply pinnatifid.
  2   Flowers greenish white; the whole leaf regularly pinnatifid into several linear-oblong acute segments . . . . R. alba
  2   Flowers greenish yellow; terminal half of leaf deeply and irregularly pinnatifid into a few linear to oblanceolate segments, the basal half entire, linear-cuneate . . . R. lutea

R. alba L.   White Mignonette
Eurasian; locally introd. in fields and waste places of N. America, as in sw B.C. (Victoria, Vancouver Is.), Sask. (Brock, about 60 mi sw of Saskatoon; Trevarga), Man. (Brandon), s Ont. (Guelph, Wellington Co.; Niagara Falls, Welland Co.), and sw Que. (Boivin 1966b).

R. lutea L.   Yellow Mignonette
Eurasian; locally introd. in fields and waste places of N. America, as in s B.C. (Victoria, Vancouver Is.; Sicamous), Sask. (Grenfell, Spy Hill, and Swift Current; Breitung 1957a), s Man. (Beulah; Birtle; Boissevain; Shoal Lake), and s Ont. (Huron and Grey counties).

R. luteola L.   Dyer's Rocket
Eurasian; occasionally introd. in waste places of N. America, as in N.S. (waste ground near Halifax, where taken by D. Erskine in 1955; CAN).

SARRACENIACEAE (Pitcher-plant Family)

SARRACENIA L. [3130] Pitcher-plant

Plant insectivorous, the basal hollow horn-shaped leaves retaining water in which insects drown, broadly winged on the inner side and with a broad erect terminal hood. Flowers perfect, hypogynous, to about 7 cm broad, solitary and nodding at the top of a naked scape to about 5 dm tall. Sepals 5, deep red-purple, persistent. Petals 5, usually dark purple-red, incurved, deciduous. Style 1, extended above into a 5-rayed umbrella-shaped top. Ovary superior. Fruit a 5-locular capsule.

S. purpurea L. Pitcher-plant. Petits cochons or Herbe-crapaud
/ST/X/ (Hr (Ch)) Sphagnous bogs and peaty barrens, the aggregate species from Great Bear L. and NE B.C. (near Fort Nelson at ca. 58°45′N) to L. Athabasca (Alta. and Sask.), Man. (N to Bear L. at ca. 55°N), Ont. (N to the Fawn R. at 54°40′N), Que. (N to E James Bay at 53°43′N, the Côte-Nord, and Gaspé Pen.), Labrador (N to the Hamilton R. basin), Nfld. (provincial floral emblem), N.B., P.E.I., and N.S., S to S-cent. Sask., Minn., N Ill., Ohio, and Del. MAPS and synonymy: *see* below.
1 Stigmatic disk distinctly incised or even 5-lobed; [type from L. Albanel, Que., at ca. 51°30′N] . . . . f. *incisa* Rousseau & Rouleau
1 Stigmatic-disk merely 5-angled.
 2 Stamens and pistils modified into petal-like organs to form a rosulate flower; [f. *klawei* Boivin; type from Wedgeport, Yarmouth Co., N.S.] . . . . f. *plena* Erskine
 2 Stamens and pistils normal.
  3 Sepals, petals, and stigmatic-disk yellowish or yellow-green; leaves pale green; [*S. heterophylla* Eat.; Ont. (reported from a bog near Ottawa by John Macoun 1883; reported from Algonquin Park, Renfrew Co., by J.M. Macoun 1901), Nfld. (*see* the below-noted map by Case), and N.S. (Cape Breton Is. and Annapolis, Queens, Cumberland, and Halifax counties)] . . . .
   . . . . var. *heterophylla* (Eat.) Fern.
  3 Sepals deep red-purple; petals and stigmatic-disk red; leaves more or less suffused with red or purple; [incl. the reduced extremes, vars. *ripicola* Boivin and *terrae-novae* La Pylaie; range of the species; MAPS (the first two incomplete northwards): F.W. Case, Jr., Rhodora 58(692): fig. 1, p. 204. 1956; E.T. Wherry, Bartonia 15: fig. 1, p. 6. 1933; V.J. Krajina, Syesis 1: fig. 2 (noting an additional 1935 map by Wherry and the first record of the plant in B.C.), p. 123. 1968] . . . . f. *purpurea*

DROSERACEAE (Sundew Family)

DROSERA L.   [3136]   Sundew

Low insectivorous scapose herbs of damp or wet soil, the leaves all in a basal rosette, bearing long reddish gland-tipped hairs that exude a clear viscid liquid to which small insects stick. Flowers small, usually white or pinkish, regular, perfect, hypogynous, 5-merous, borne along the upper side of a nodding raceme-like cyme terminating the naked scape. Stamens 5. Styles commonly 3. Ovary superior. Fruit a 1-locular capsule.

(Ref.: Wynne 1944)
1   Leaf-blades rotund, usually broader than long, the petioles hairy; seeds spindle-shaped, chaff-like, the loose finely longitudinally striate outer coat prolonged at both ends; (transcontinental) . . . . *D. rotundifolia*
1   Leaf-blades linear to spatulate or narrowly obovate, much longer than broad, the petioles smooth.
   2   Leaf-blades narrowly linear, to 6 cm long; seeds rhomboidal, the close outer coat densely shallow-pitted; (transcontinental) . . . . *D. linearis*
   2   Leaf-blades spatulate to narrowly obovate, mostly less than 2.5 cm long.
      3   Stipules nearly free from the bases of the petioles; seeds ellipsoid-obovoid, reddish brown, densely papillose; (B.C.; Ont. to Labrador, Nfld., and N.S.) . . . .
. . . . *D. intermedia*
      3   Stipules adnate to the petioles except at tip; seeds spindle-shaped, blackish, the loosely honeycomb-reticulate outer coat prolonged at both ends; (transcontinental) . . . . *D. anglica*

D. anglica Huds.
/ST/X/EA/   (Hr (Hel))   Peaty or boggy places (often calcareous) from Alaska (N to near the Arctic Circle) to s-cent. Yukon, Great Bear L., L. Athabasca (Alta. and Sask.), ?Man. (Porcupine Mt.; John Macoun 1886), Ont. (N to Hawley L. at 54°34′N), Que. (N to the Wiachouan R. SE of Hudson Bay at ca. 56°10′N, L. Mistassini, the Côte-Nord, and Gaspé Pen.), SE Labrador (Hamilton R. basin), and Nfld. (not known from the Maritime Provinces), s to N Calif., Nev., Idaho, Wisc., Mich., and s Ont.; Hawaii; Eurasia. MAPS: Hultén 1968b:559; Wynne 1944: fig. 2, p. 167; Meusel, Jaeger, and Weinert 1965:195.
   See C.E. Wood, Jr., (Rhodora 57(676):105–30. 1955) concerning the possible origin of this species through hybridization between *D. linearis* and *D. rotundifolia*. A hybrid with *D. rotundifolia* (× *D. obovata* Mert. & Koch) is reported from Nfld. by Fernald (1933).

D. intermedia Hayne
/sT/X/EA/   (Hr)   Wet acid peats and sands, the main area from Minn. to Ont. (N shore of L. Superior southwards; an isolated station at Fort Severn, Hudson Bay, ca. 56°N), Que. (N to E James Bay at 53°50′N, the Côte-Nord, and Gaspé Pen.), SE Labrador (Hamilton R. basin), Nfld., N.B., P.E.I., and N.S., s to E Tex. and Fla.; isolated stations in B.C. (35 mi N of Prince George at ca. 54°N and Liard Hot Springs, ca. 59°N; reports from Sask. and Man. require confirmation); Europe; Asia Minor. MAPS: Hultén 1958: map 38, p. 57; Wynne 1944: fig. 3 (incomplete northwards), p. 167; Meusel, Jaeger, and Weinert 1965:195.
   Forma *natans* Heuser (occurring in very wet places, the leaves becoming scattered along the prolonged caudex) is reported from Nfld. by Rouleau (1956). A purported hybrid with *D. rotundifolia* is reported from N.S. by Fernald (1921; type from Lower Argyle, Yarmouth Co.).

D. linearis Goldie
/T/X/   (Hr (Hel))   Marly bogs and wet calcareous shores from B.C. (Boivin 1966b; also tentatively reporting it from Alta.) to Sask. (Prince Albert, the probable basis of the dot for that region in the 1958 map by Hultén for *D. intermedia*; CAN), s Man. (Scoggan 1957), Ont. (N to Sandy L. at ca. 53°N, 93°W), Que. (N to L. Mistassini, Anticosti Is., and the Gaspé Pen.), and Nfld. (not known from the Maritime Provinces), s to Minn., Mich., s Ont., and Maine. MAP: Wynne 1944: fig. 5 (incomplete), p. 167.

D. rotundifolia L.   Round-leaved Sundew

/aST/X/GEA/   (Hr (Hel))   Peaty acid swamps and bogs, the aggregate species from the Aleutian Is. and Alaska (N to near the Arctic Circle) to cent. Yukon, the Mackenzie R. Delta, Great Bear L., Great Slave L., L. Athabasca (Alta. and Sask.), northernmost Ont., Que. (N to Ungava Bay and the Côte-Nord), Labrador (N to Cape Harrigan, 55°50′N), Nfld., N.B., P.E.I., and N.S., s to Calif., Nev., Mont., Minn., Ala., and N Fla.; southernmost Greenland; Iceland; Eurasia. MAPS: *see* below.

1   Inflorescence commonly capitate and few-flowered; petals greenish or crimson;
     carpels (and sometimes other floral parts) modified into gland-bearing leaves; [Que.
     (E James Bay at ca. 52°10′N; Côte-Nord; Gaspé Pen., the type from the mouth of the
     Grand R.) and N.B. (Grand Manan Is. and Wolf Is., Charlotte Co.)] . . . . . var. *comosa* Fern.
1   Inflorescence commonly elongate and bearing up to 15 or more flowers; petals white
     (rarely pink) . . . . var. *rotundifolia*
     2   Scape stiffly erect, rarely over 4 cm tall and only slightly surpassing the leaves,
         1–3(4)-flowered; [Que., Labrador, Nfld., and N.S. (Cape Breton Is.)] . . . .
         . . . . f. *breviscapa* (Regel) Domin
     2   Scape to about 3 dm tall, filiform, much surpassing the leaves, bearing up to
         about 25 flowers; [transcontinental; MAPS (aggregate species): Hultén 1968*b*:559;
         Wynne 1944: fig. 1 (incomplete northwards), p. 167; Meusel, Jaeger, and Weinert
         1965:195] . . . . f. *rotundifolia*

PODOSTEMACEAE (Riverweed Family)

PODOSTEMUM Michx.   [3156]   Riverweed

Immersed aquatic, the stem attached to stones by fleshy disks, to about 1 dm long. Leaves alternate, overlapping in 2 vertical ranks, usually rigid, olive-green, linear and entire or more commonly forking into numerous filiform or linear lobes. Flowers perfect, lacking a perianth, solitary in sessile obovoid axillary spathes. Stamens 2. Stigmas 2, subulate. Ovary superior. Fruit a strongly 8–10-ribbed 2-locular capsule. (Podostemataceae).

P. ceratophyllum Michx.   Threadfoot
/T/EE/   (HH)   Attached (by fleshy disks or processes replacing roots) to rocks in streams from Ont. (N to Renfrew and Carleton counties) to Que. (N to Hull, St-Eustache, and Montreal), N.B. (near Woodstock, Carleton Co.; CAN; not known from P.E.I.), and N.S. (Quarryville, Northumberland Co.; ACAD), s to Ark. and Ga. MAP: Raymond 1950*b*: fig. 37 (with a dot for a reputed station in Minn.), p. 105.

CRASSULACEAE (Orpine Family)

(Ref.: N.L. Britton and J.N. Rose, N. Am. Flora 22(1):7–74. 1905)
Usually succulent herbs with simple leaves. Flowers small, regular, usually perfect, from nearly hypogynous to perigynous, solitary in the leaf-axils or in terminal cymes. Sepals (or calyx-lobes), petals, and pistils each usually 3–5 (up to 16 in *Sempervivum*; petals usually none in *Penthorum*), the stamens as many or twice as many. Ovary more or less inferior. Fruit a cluster of follicles.

1   Small aquatic or subaquatic annuals with filiform stems at most about 1 dm tall; flowers solitary in the leaf-axils, sessile or short-pedicelled, greenish white, 3–4-merous; stamens 3 or 4; leaves opposite, connate at base, linear to linear-oblong, usually less than 7 mm long; (Alaska–Dist. Mackenzie–B.C.; Ont. to Nfld. and N.S.) . . . . *Tillaea*
1   Stems taller; flowers in terminal cymes; stamens usually twice as many as the sepals.
    2   Plant not succulent; flowers greenish, 1-sided along the strongly stipitate-glandular branches of the terminal cyme; petals usually none; sepals or calyx-lobes usually 5; leaves lanceolate to narrowly elliptic, finely serrate, acute at both ends, to about 1 dm long; stem about 1 m tall, decumbent at base, stoloniferous; (SE Man. to N.B.) . . . . *Penthorum*
    2   Plants succulent; petals conspicuous.
       3   Flowers 4–5-merous; stamens 8 or 10; stem-leaves alternate, opposite, or whorled . . . . *Sedum*
       3   Flowers commonly 12–16-merous; stamens 12–many; flowers pink-purple, about 2 cm broad, their sepals (and pedicels) very pubescent; stem-leaves alternate, pubescent, the leaves of the dense basal rosette glabrous except for ciliate margins; (introd.) . . . . *Sempervivum*

PENTHORUM L. [3173]

P. sedoides L. Ditch-Stonecrop
/T/EE/ (Hpr) Wet low grounds from Nebr. to Minn., SE Man. (near Otterburne, about 30 mi S of Winnipeg; banks of the Red R. at St. Vital, E of Winnipeg), Ont. (N to near Ottawa), Que. (N to near Quebec City; CAN; reported N to Rivière-du-Loup, about 105 mi E of Quebec City, by John Macoun, Can. J., n.s. 15(94, 95). 1877), and N.B. (Sunbury, York, and Kings counties; not known from P.E.I. or N.S.; reports from Nfld. by Reeks 1873, and Waghorne 1895, require confirmation), S to Tex. and Fla. [Genus assigned to the Saxifragaceae by some authors].

SEDUM [3161] Stonecrop, Orpine. Orpin

1   Plants not mat-forming, the stems erect or ascending, sterile creeping stems or offshoots wanting.
    2   Annuals or biennials (or plants occasionally perennial) with fibrous roots; leaves alternate, linear-oblong to ovate or obovate, entire.
       3   Plant glabrous, rarely over 12 cm tall; leaves to 6 mm long, 2-spurred at base; petals 5, bright yellow, narrowly to broadly lanceolate, acute or acuminate; stamens 10; (Greenland) . . . . *S. annuum*
       3   Plants typically glandular-pubescent at least in the inflorescence, often taller; leaves to over 1 cm long, not spurred at base or only slightly spurred.
          4   Petals 6 or more (the stamens twice as many), lanceolate, acuminate, white with a pink or green median dorsal stripe; (introd.) . . . . *S. hispanicum*
          4   Petals 5 (the stamens usually 10, rarely 5), rather broadly ovate, acutish, pale pink to purplish; (E Que.; Greenland) . . . . *S. villosum*
    2   Glabrous perennials, the stems from a thick fleshy rootstock or from fleshy carrot-like tubers, coarse and succulent, to over 4 dm tall; leaves broadly oblanceolate to broadly obovate.

5 Stems commonly less than 1.5 dm tall (but up to 4 dm), from scaly short branches of a thick fleshy rootstock, the root suckering; leaves pale and more or less glaucous, spirally arranged to whorled, entire or serrulate, to 2(4) cm long; flowers in small head-like cymes, mostly unisexual and the plant dioecious (the staminate flowers yellow or yellowish, the pistillate ones usually deep purple or sometimes greenish purple); sepals 1 or 2 mm long; petals 2 or 3 mm long; (Alaska, w Dist. Mackenzie, B.C., and w Alta. (var. *integrifolium*); Baffin Is. to N.B., N.S., and Nfld.) . . . . *S. roseum*

5 Stems often taller, from fleshy carrot-like tubers; flowers perfect, in compact to rather open, often somewhat paniculate cymes or corymbs; (introd.).
   6 Petals roseate to deep purple; leaves mostly several-toothed, the upper ones alternate; stem to 8 dm tall . . . . *S. purpureum*
   6 Petals greenish·yellow or pale pink; leaves mostly opposite; stems at most about 5 dm tall.
      7 Petals greenish yellow; leaves ovate-lanceolate to ovate, regularly dentate . . . . *S. telephium*
      7 Petals pale pink; leaves oblanceolate or obovate to suborbicular, essentially entire . . . . [*S. alboroseum*]

1 Plants commonly mat-forming, the leaves mostly along the creeping, freely rooting, sterile stems or crowded on sterile basal offshoots; flowering stems erect or ascending, usually not over 2 dm tall, their leaves often narrower in outline than those of the sterile stems and generally deciduous by late anthesis; glabrous perennials (or the leaves sometimes more or less papillate-rugose).
  8 Leaves of the flowering stems mostly opposite or in whorls of 3; petals to 9 mm long.
    9 Petals yellow; leaves entire, fleshy.
     10 Plants with short stout rootstocks, producing long prostrate barren shoots that root at the tip; leaves in whorls of 3, flat, broadly lanceolate, acute, spurred at base, to 3 cm long; follicles ascending; (introd.) . . . . *S. sarmentosum*
     10 Plants without thickened rootstocks, the prostrate stems freely rooting and producing erect flowering stems at the nodes; leaves opposite or subopposite, subterete, oval to broadly obovate or suborbicular, finely papillose, mostly less than 1 cm long; follicles united at base for about 2 mm and then strongly divergent; (B.C.) . . . . *S. divergens*
    9 Petals white to roseate; follicles erect or only slightly divergent; (introd.).
     11 Leaves entire, usually 1 or 2 cm long, those on the lower part of the flowering stem often in whorls of 3; petals usually white . . . . *S. ternatum*
     11 At least the larger leaves coarsely dentate, to about 3 cm long, those of the flowering stems opposite or the upper ones alternate; petals usually roseate . . . . *S. spurium*
  8 Leaves of the flowering stems alternate, the stems mostly not over 2 dm tall; petals yellow (sometimes aging or drying pinkish or reddish).
   12 Leaves at most about 1 cm long, entire, broadly spurred at base; (introd.).
    13 Leaves tightly overlapping, narrowly ovate, blunt, to 6 mm long; flowering stems to about 1 dm tall; petals to 1 cm long; follicles divergent, 4 or 5 mm long . . . . *S. acre*
    13 Leaves not tightly overlapping, linear to narrowly oblanceolate, apiculate, to 1 cm long; flowering stems to 3 dm tall; petals to 6 mm long; follicles suberect, papillose, 6 or 7 mm long . . . . *S. rupestre*
   12 Leaves to 2 or 3 cm long.
    14 Leaves linear or narrowly linear-lanceolate, entire, strongly keeled or nerved above, acuminate and attenuate-subulate at the papillose-roughened tip, not very fleshy, those of the flowering stems often mostly deciduous by anthesis (or the upper ones often marcescent-persistent and bearing bulbil-like tufts in their axils), those of the sterile offshoots often marcescent-persistent (sometimes only the thickened midribs persistent); mature follicles widely divergent (even nearly horizontal); some

(occasionally all) of the flowers transformed into bulbil-like tufts; (s
B.C.–Alta.) . . . . *S. stenopetalum*
  14 Leaves mostly spatulate or oblanceolate to obovate (often linear or linear-
    lanceolate in *S. lanceolatum,* but then very fleshy and blunt), not strongly
    keeled; bulbil-like tufts rarely (if ever) present; follicles usually more erect.
    15 Leaves distinctly toothed at least above the middle; plants with short
      stout rootstocks; (introd.).
      16 Flowering stems arising from creeping stems with many prominent
        sterile offshoots; flowers to about 2 cm broad; stamens about 2/3 as
        long as the lanceolate petals . . . . *S. hybridum*
      16 Flowering stems arising from a thick knotted rootstock, the stems
        neither creeping nor with many sterile offshoots at anthesis; flowers
        less than 1.5 cm long; stamens nearly as long as the linear-
        lanceolate petals . . . . *S. aizoön*
    15 Leaves entire; sepals subequal; yellow petals often aging pinkish or
    reddish.
      17 Leaves linear to linear-lanceolate (broadest below the middle),
        terete or subterete in section, smooth or finely papillate; sepals
        triangular-lanceolate, usually less than 4 mm long; (Alaska–B.C. to
        Sask.) . . . . *S. lanceolatum*
      17 Leaves spatulate-oblanceolate to obovate (broadest above the
        middle), glaucous, flattened but very succulent; sepals to 4 or 5 mm
        long; (B.C.).
        18 Petals to 13 mm long, united at base for usually 2 or 3 mm,
          narrowly lanceolate and long-acuminate; follicles erect . . . .
          . . . . *S. oreganum*
        18 Petals mostly not over 1 cm long, nearly or quite distinct,
          narrowly oblong-lanceolate but not long-acuminate; follicles
          more or less divergent . . . . *S. spathulifolium*

S. acre L. Mossy Stonecrop, Wallpepper
Eurasian; spreading from rock-gardens to walls and dry rocky flats in N. America, as in s B.C.
(Vancouver Is.; Sechelt, near Vancouver; Nakusp, about 65 mi E of Vernon), Alta. (near Edmonton), Ont. (N to Ottawa), Que. (N to the Gaspé Pen.), St-Pierre and Miquelon, N.B., P.E.I.
(Souris, Kings Co.; ACAD), and N.S. MAPS: Hultén 1958: map 87 (indicating stations in s Nfld.;
listed only for St-Pierre and Miquelon by Rouleau 1956), p. 107; Meusel, Jaeger, and Weinert
1965:197.

S. aizoön L.
Asiatic; a local garden-escape in N. America, as in Alta. (Ma-Me-O Beach, near Edmonton;
Boivin 1966*b*) and Sask. (Breitung 1957*a*; Saskatoon).

[S. alboroseum Baker]
[Reported as a garden-escape in Nfld. by Fernald *in* Gray (1950), where, however, probably
not established].

S. annuum L.
/aST/–/GE/ (T (Hs)) Dry acidic rocks and sands from low to fairly high elevations: W
Greenland N to near the Arctic Circle, E Greenland N to ca. 69°N; Iceland; Europe. MAPS: Hultén 1958: map 72, p. 91; Meusel, Jaeger, and Weinert 1965:197; Böcher 1938: fig. 33 (Greenland distribution), p. 111.

S. divergens Wats.
/sT/W/ (Ch) Subalpine to alpine rocky ledges, ridges, and talus slopes from B.C. (N to
Telegraph Creek on the Stikine R. at ca. 58°N; V) to Mt. Hood, Oreg.

S. hispanicum L.

Eurasian; apparently recorded as an established garden-escape in N. America only from about 11 mi sw of Ottawa, Ont. (where forming several dense stands on shattered sandstone in an old quarry) and from sw Que. (Bromptonville, Richmond Co.).

S. hybridum L.

Eurasian; a garden-escape in Alta. (Fort Saskatchewan), s Man. (Pointe du Bois, about 75 mi NE of Winnipeg), and Que. (St-Sauveur-des-Monts, Terrebonne Co.).

S. lanceolatum Torr.

/ST/WW/ (Ch) Cliffs and gravelly or rocky places from low to subalpine elevations (ranges of Canadian taxa outlined below), s to Calif., N.Mex., Colo., and Nebr. MAP and synonymy: *see* below.

1 Leaves mostly smooth, closely tufted and overlapping (even on the flowering stem), to 3 cm long, not scarious when dried; inflorescence tending to become loose, with the branches slightly divergent and recurved; [*S. nesioticum* Jones; B.C. coast: Hitchcock et al. 1964] . . . . var. *nesioticum* (Jones) C.L. Hitchc.

1 Leaves mostly finely papillate, generally not overlapping on the flowering stem, seldom over 2 cm long, mostly scarious when dried; inflorescence usually compact.

  2 Leaves of the flowering stem relatively broad in outline, usually less than 1 cm long and incurved; [*S. rup.* Jones; B.C.: Hitchcock et al. 1964] . . . .
     . . . . var. *rupicolum* (Jones) C.L. Hitchc.

  2 Leaves of the flowering stem mostly linear or linear-lanceolate, generally over 1 cm long, usually not strongly incurved; [*S. stenopetalum* (*S. douglasii* Hook.) of auth., not Pursh; *S. subalpinum* Blank.; SE Alaska–s Yukon (the map given by Hultén 1945: map 693, p. 974, for *S. stenopetalum* is applicable here), B.C., Alta. (Moss 1959, as *S. sten.*: Cypress Hills and elsewhere), and s Sask. (Breitung 1957a, as *S. sten.*: Cypress Hills; Swift Current); MAP (aggregate species): Hultén 1968b:560] . . . . var. *lanceolatum*

S. oreganum Nutt.

/sT/W/ (Ch) Rocky ledges, gravelly ridges, and talus slopes from SE Alaska–B.C. (N to ca. 60°N) to N Calif. (chiefly w of the Cascade Mts.). [*Gormania* Britt.; *S. ?obtusatum sensu* John Macoun 1883, and Henry 1915, not Gray]. MAP: Hultén 1968b:560.

S. purpureum (L.) Schultes   Live-forever.   Vit-toujours

Eurasian; a garden-escape to roadsides, banks, and open woods in N. America, as in Ont. (N to Moose Factory, sw James Bay, 51°15'N; Dutilly and Lepage 1947), Que. (N to the Gaspé Pen. at Métis and Percé), Nfld. (Fernald *in* Gray 1950), N.B., P.E.I., and N.S. [*S. telephium* var. *purp.* L.; *S. purpurascens* and *S. fabaria* Koch].

S. roseum (L.) Scop.   Roseroot

/aST/D/GEA/ (Ch) Moist cliffs, talus, and alpine ridges (ranges of Canadian taxa outlined below), s in the West to Calif. and Colo. and in the East to Pa. and Roan Mt., Va., with isolated stations in SE Minn.; w Greenland N to ca. 69°N, E Greenland N to ca. 75°N; Iceland; Spitsbergen; Eurasia. MAPS and synonymy: *see* below.

1 Petals of the pistillate flowers yellow; anther-filaments yellow; anthers (?always) purple; leaves to 4 cm long, often rather coarsely toothed; [*Rhodiola rosea* L.; *S. rosea,* the original spelling; *S. rhodiola* DC.; *S. ?elongatum* Ledeb.; *S. heterodonton* Hook.; Seward Pen., Alaska; moist rocky ledges and cliffs (usually near the sea) from northernmost Ungava–Labrador to s-cent. Baffin Is., s along the coast to E Que. (Côte-Nord; reported from Anticosti Is. by Verrill 1865), Nfld., N.B. (Charlotte, St. John, and Northumberland counties), and N.S. (Shelburne, Digby, Annapolis, Kings, Cumberland, Halifax, Victoria, and Inverness counties; not known from P.E.I.); w Greenland N to ca. 69°N, E Greenland N to ca. 75°N; Iceland; Spitsbergen; Eurasia; MAPS: Hultén 1958: map 33, p. 53; Porsild 1957: map 205 *(Rhodiola rosea),* p. 186] . . . . . .
   . . . . ssp. *roseum*

1   Petals of the pistillate flowers usually purplish black (those of the staminate flowers yellow or yellowish); leaves commonly less than 2.5 cm long, entire or minutely serrate . . . . ssp. *integrifolium* (Raf.) Hult.

    2   Anther-filaments yellow; [*Rhodiola borealis* Borisova; *S. ?elongatum* Ledeb.; included here are intermediate forms reported by Hultén 1945, from westernmost Alaska and Asia, in the area of overlap of the following taxa].

    2   Anther-filaments purplish black; anthers yellow.

        3   Leaves green or only slightly glaucous; [*Rhodiola integ.* Raf.; *S. atropurpureum* Turcz.; *S. rhodioloides* Raf.; *S. ?rhodanthum* Gray; Aleutian Is.–Alaska–Yukon–w Dist. Mackenzie and mts. of B.C. and sw Alta.; Asia; MAPS: Hultén 1968*b*:561, and 1958: map 34, p. 53; Raup 1947: pl. 26] . . . . var. *integrifolium*

        3   Leaves strongly glaucous; plant relatively high-grown; [*S. frigidum* Rydb., the type from the Aleutian Is.; *Rhodiola (S.) alaskana* Rose; *S. roseum* var. *aleuticum* Frod.; reported from coastal Alaska (Alaska Pen. and the Bering Sea coast) by Hultén 1945, who suggests that it is a minor race freely intermingling with the more inland var. *integrifolium*] . . . . var. *frigidum* (Rydb.) Hult.

S. rupestre L.
European; a garden-escape to roadsides and waste places of N. America, as in s Que. (reported from Ste-Clotilde, Chateauguay Co., by Lionel Cinq-Mars et al., Nat. can. (Que.) 98(2):196. 1971) and P.E.I. (a dump on sand dunes at Souris, Kings Co.; ACAD). [Incl. *S. forsteranum* Sm. and *S. reflexum* L.]

S. sarmentosum Bunge
Asiatic; a garden-escape to roadsides and waste places of N. America, as in s Ont. (Boivin 1966*b*; reported from Collins Creek, Frontenac Co., by R.E. Beschel, Blue Bill 16(2):24. 1969).

S. spathulifolium Hook.
/t/W/   (Ch)   Coastal cliffs and ledges and gravels of the foothills w of the Cascade Mts. from s B.C. (Vancouver Is. and adjacent islands and mainland N to the mouth of the Bella Coola R. at ca. 52°N, E to the lower Fraser Valley near Hope) to N Calif. [Incl. *S. pruinosum* Britt.]. MAP: R.T. Clausen and C.H. Uhl, Madroño 7(6): fig. 2, p. 170. 1944.

S. spurium Bieb.
Eurasian; a garden-escape to sandy roadsides, banks, and old fields in N. America, as in Ont. (reported from Collins Creek, Frontenac Co., by R.E. Beschel, Blue Bill 16(2):24. 1969; reported from Ottawa and Waubaushene, near the SE end of Georgian Bay, L. Huron, by W.J. Cody, Can. Field-Nat. 81(4):273. 1967), SE Nfld. (near St. John's; GH; CAN), and N.S. [*S. stoloniferum sensu* Fernald 1921, Groh 1947, and Roland 1947, not Gmel., relevant collections in CAN and GH].

S. stenopetalum Pursh
/T/W/   (Ch)   Grasslands and sagebrush plains or ponderosa-pine forest (occasionally to subalpine ridges) from s B.C. (N limits uncertain through confusion with other species, particularly *S. lanceolatum*) and sw Alta. (N to Banff; CAN; the report from s Sask. by Breitung 1957*a*, is based upon *S. lanceolatum*) to Oreg. and Mont. [*S. douglasii* Hook.].

S. telephium L.   Live-forever.   Vit-toujours
Eurasian; a garden-escape to roadsides, banks, and open woods in N. America, as in B.C. (Boivin 1966*b*), Man. (sandy soil near a cemetery at The Pas), Ont. (N to New Liskeard, 47°31′N), Que. (N to Anticosti Is. and the Gaspé Pen.), Nfld., N.B., and N.S.

S. ternatum Michx.
A native of the E U.S.A. (N to Mich. and N.Y.); a garden-escape to damp roadsides and cool

rocks farther northwards, as in s Ont. (roadside at Rockway, Lincoln Co., where taken by Soper in 1952, validating reports from s Ont. by John Macoun 1883; CAN). MAP (E U.S.A.): Cain 1944: fig. 62, p. 460.

S. villosum L.
/aST/E/GE/   (Ch)   Moist turfy, rocky, or clayey places: E Que. (three localities along the St. Lawrence R. in E Saguenay Co. of the Côte-Nord, where reported by M.L. Fernald, Rhodora 34(402):120. 1932, as extending for a distance of 42 mi along the coast; CAN); W and E Greenland N to ca. 70°N; Iceland; the Faeroes; Europe. MAPS: Hultén 1958: map 94, p. 113; Meusel, Jaeger, and Weinert 1965:196.

SEMPERVIVUM L.   [3162]   Houseleek

S. tectorum L.   Hens-and-chickens
Eurasian; a garden-escape or persisting from old plantings in N. America, as in s Ont. (Wellington Co.; F.H. Montgomery, Can. Field-Nat. 62(2):94. 1948).

TILLAEA L.   [3168]

T. aquatica L.   Pigmyweed
/ST/(X)/EA/   (T)   Pond-margins and fresh to tidal shores, the known distribution very localized, probably because of the inconspicuous nature of the plant: coast of s Alaska; N shore of Great Slave L.; s B.C. (N to Kamloops) to Oreg., Utah, and Wyo.; cent. Ont. (Minnitaki L., near Sioux Lookout at ca. 50°N); SW Minn.; Mexico, Tex., and La.; Que. (E James Bay at Fort George, 53°50′N; St. Lawrence R. estuary between L. St. Peter and St-Vallier, Bellechasse Co.; Grindstone Is., Magdalen Is.) to Nfld. (Placentia Bay), N.B., P.E.I. (Queens Co.), and N.S., s along or near the coast to Md.; Iceland (reports from Spitsbergen now discredited); Eurasia. [*Crassula* Schönl.; *Tillaeastrum* Britt.; *Tillaea simplex* Nutt.; *T. vaillantii* of Canadian reports, not Willd.]. MAPS: Hultén 1958: map 248 *(Crass. aq.)*, p. 267; W.J. Cody, Rhodora 56(665): fig. 1, p. 98. 1954; Meusel, Jaeger, and Weinert 1965:196; Fassett 1928: fig. 2 (incomplete), pl. 13.

Hultén's map indicates a northernmost station for this species on Ellesmere Is. at ca. 69°N which, if validated by further collections, would rank it as high-arctic rather than subarctic.

SAXIFRAGACEAE (Saxifrage Family)

Herbs or shrubs with simple, opposite or alternate (sometimes all basal in *Parnassia* and *Saxifraga*), usually exstipulate leaves. Flowers commonly perfect, regular or slightly irregular, more or less perigynous to epigynous. Sepals (or calyx-lobes) and petals usually 5 (sometimes 3 or 4), the stamens usually as many or twice as many (at least 20 in *Philadelphus*), they and the petals inserted on the calyx. Pistils usually 2. Ovary more or less inferior. Fruit commonly a capsule or follicle (a berry in *Ribes*). (Including Grossulariaceae, Hydrangeaceae, and Parnassiaceae).

1 Shrubs, the stems and branches woody.
    2 Leaves alternate; stamens and petals each 5, the petals smaller than the sepals; fruit a berry commonly about 5 mm thick; flowers in clusters or racemes, each subtended by a small bract; plants unarmed or bristly or prickly . . . . *Ribes*
    2 Leaves opposite; petals white; fruit a capsule; unarmed plants to about 3 m tall.
        3 Flowers numerous in flattish- or convex-topped corymbs, all fertile or some of the marginal ones sterile; fertile flowers with minute sepals, small petals about 3 mm long, and 8 or 10 stamens; sterile flowers consisting only of a large white or coloured calyx of 3 or 4 sepals; capsule 2-locular below; leaves ovate to ovate-oblong, sharply serrate; (introd.) . . . . [*Hydrangea*]
        3 Flowers solitary at the ends of the twigs or in terminal cymes or leafy-bracted false racemes; petals to 2 or 3 cm long; stamens at least 20; capsule usually 4-locular; leaves narrowly or broadly elliptic to ovate, obscurely and often remotely toothed (sometimes entire on old branches) . . . . *Philadelphus*
1 Herbs; fruit a capsule (in *Leptarrhena* and often in *Saxifraga*, nearly or quite separated into 2 distinct follicles).
    4 Flowering stems scapose, naked or bracteate (lower bracts sometimes leaf-like but greatly reduced and sessile, the foliage-leaves borne in a basal rosette and mostly petioled; 2 or 3 short-petioled but reduced leaves sometimes present below the middle of the stem in *Heuchera*).
        5 Flower solitary on a naked or 1-leaved scape, with 5 palmately-cleft gland-tipped staminodia alternating with the 5 true stamens; capsule 1-locular, opening by 4 valves; stigmas 4, nearly sessile; leaves all or mostly in a basal rosette, entire; plants completely glabrous . . . . *Parnassia*
        5 Flowers in terminal racemes or panicles (sometimes solitary in *Saxifraga*), lacking staminodia; rosette-leaves toothed or lobed (sometimes entire in *Saxifraga*); plants more or less pubescent at least in the inflorescence.
            6 Petals very deeply pectinate-fringed or apically 3(5)-lobed, longer than the sepals; stamens usually 5 (10 in *M. nuda*); the 2 valves of the capsule widely spreading upon dehiscing and "nesting" the shining, obscurely reticulate, black or blackish seeds; leaves ovate-cordate to reniform . . . . *Mitella*
            6 Petals entire.
                7 Stamens 10; flowers usually panicled (sometimes solitary in *Saxifraga*).
                    8 Ovary 1-locular, with parietal placentation (the seeds developed on the inside wall near the base); capsule dehiscing into 2 unequal, thin-walled valves, the larger up to twice as long as the smaller; seeds nearly black, shining and almost smooth; petals white; leaves cordate-ovate to -rotund in outline . . . . *Tiarella*
                    8 Ovary 2-locular, the placentation axile (seeds developing along the central axis); fruit often follicular, the subequal carpels more or less distinct at least in age; leaves all simple.
                        9 Carpels distinct almost to base, the fruit consisting of 2 separate follicles; seeds light brown, to 3.5 mm long, the empty tail-like ends of the seed-coat 2 or 3 times as long as the rest of the seed; petals white, to twice as long as the sepals (these about 1 mm long); leaves leathery, glabrous, elliptic to narrowly obovate or ovate-oblong, moderately crenate-serrate, bright green

above, pale green beneath, to about 1.5 dm long, narrowed to a short broad petiole less than half as long as the blade; flowering stem more or less glandular-pubescent, the 1–3 reduced leaves cordate-clasping (the upper ones bract-like); (B.C. and sw Alta.) . . . .
. . . . *Leptarrhena*

9 Carpels usually fused or adnate to the calyx for at least 1/5 their length, the resulting follicles united at base or the fruit a capsule; seeds smooth or variously sculptured, but lacking tails . . . . .
. . . . *Saxifraga*

7 Stamens 5 (1 or more often rudimentary in *Heuchera*), opposite the calyx-lobes; ovary 1-locular and with usually 2 parietal or sub-basal placentae (the longitudinally striate seeds developing on the inside wall), the fruit consisting of 2 essentially equal valves; leaves cordate-rotund or reniform, long-petioled (short-petioled and reduced leaves sometimes present below the middle of the stem in *Heuchera*).

10 Flowers up to 10 or 12 in a simple, loose, finely glandular-pubescent raceme, on pedicels to 5 mm long, their subtending bracts more or less minutely laciniate; petals white, 4 or 5 mm long, longer than the sepals, the oblanceolate to rhombic blade about equalling the claw; calyx turbinate-obconic, basally adnate to the ovary for up to half its length, the free tubular portion about equalling the 5 erect to slightly spreading lobes; leaves to 4 cm broad, rather leathery, shallowly and broadly double-crenate, stiffly ciliate (the cilia on either side of each tooth curving toward the apex of the tooth), otherwise usually glabrous; (s Alta.) . . . . *Conimitella*

10 Flowers in congested to open and diffuse panicles, the petals variously coloured, shorter to longer than the sepals; calyx never turbinate-obconic, from shallowly saucer-shaped to tubular-campanulate, adnate almost to the top of the ovary but with a short to well-developed free hypanthium (often more or less oblique at summit); leaves usually pubescent at least beneath . . . . *Heuchera*

4 Flowering stems distinctly leafy, at least their lower leaves petioled and not greatly reduced; fruit a capsule (sometimes follicular in *Saxifraga*, the 2 carpels separate to near base).

11 Stems prostrate, soft, the flowering branches ascending from the leafy rooting nodes; leaves succulent, oval or ovate to rotund or reniform, coarsely crenate, to about 2 cm long; flowers apetalous, greenish yellow and inconspicuous, solitary in the leaf-axils or in leafy-bracted cymose clusters; stamens 4 or 8; seeds smooth; plants glabrous or pubescent . . . . . *Chrysosplenium*

11 Stems mostly erect; flowers petaliferous, in racemes or panicles (or sometimes solitary in *Saxifraga*); plants nearly always more or less pubescent and often glandular at least in the inflorescence.

12 Petals deeply fringed laterally or lobed toward apex; ovary 1-locular and with usually 2 parietal or sub-basal placentae (the seeds developing on the inside wall), maturing into a capsule; inflorescence a raceme; leaves cordate-ovate to reniform.

13 Calyx (including the part adnate to the ovary) usually not over 4 mm long (to 6 mm long in *M. stauropetala*, but the petals then merely 3-lobed), campanulate; petals 3-lobed to pectinately filiform-dissected; stamens 5 or 10; the 2 valves of the capsule widely spreading upon dehiscing and "nesting" the shining, obscurely reticulate, black or blackish seeds; stem-leaves opposite or alternate . . . . *Mitella*

13 Calyx (including the part adnate to the ovary) to 8 mm long in anthesis, to 11 mm long in fruit, cup-shaped and not at all or barely flared at the summit; seeds brown, more or less wrinkled-warty lengthwise; stem-leaves alternate; (B.C.).

14 Stamens 5, opposite the lobes of the greenish-yellow calyx; petals

white, 3–7-lobed at apex; basal leaves reniform, coarsely and doubly crenate; petioles and lower part of stem from strongly short-hirsute-glandular to both hirsute and puberulent . . . . *Elmera*

14 Stamens 10; calyx green; petals greenish white to reddish (often colouring in age), pinnately fringed; basal leaves mostly cordate-deltoid or -ovate, with up to 7 shallow lobes, their margins singly or doubly crenate-dentate; petioles and lower part of stem very strongly hirsute . . . . *Tellima*

12 Petals entire; stem-leaves usually alternate (all or mostly opposite in *Saxifraga nathorstii* and *S. oppositifolia*).

15 Inflorescence a simple raceme (*Suksdorfia violacea* may be sought here); ovary 1-locular and with usually 2 parietal or sub-basal placentae (the seeds developing on the inside wall).

16 Stamens 3 (2 long, 1 short), opposite the 3 larger calyx-lobes; calyx greenish purple to chocolate-colour, irregular, the tubular oblique-based hypanthium to 9 mm long, the 3 larger (upper) lobes to 5 mm long; petals chocolate-colour, usually (?always) 4; capsules slender and slender beaked, to 14 mm long, becoming longer than the calyx and protruding sidewise in the slit between the 2 smaller (lower) lobes; seeds finely spinulose-striate; raceme to 3 dm long; basal leaves broadly cordate-ovate, to 1 dm long and about as broad; plant hirsute throughout and more or less glandular at least in the inflorescence; (B.C.) . . . . *Tolmiea*

16 Stamens 10; calyx regular, shallowly 5-lobed; petals white to pink or purplish-tinged; capsules short-beaked; seeds from only slightly wrinkled to minutely warty, spinulose, or irregularly reticulate; racemes shorter; basal leaves narrowly to broadly reniform, usually deeply palmately cleft nearly to base into almost separate entire or lobed leaflets or segments; (w Canada) . . . . *Lithophragma*

15 Inflorescence a dense to very open panicle (flowers sometimes solitary in *Saxifraga*).

17 Ovary 1-locular, with parietal placentation (the seeds developed on the inside wall near the base); capsule dehiscing into 2 unequal thin-walled valves, the larger valve to twice as long as the smaller; seeds nearly black, shining and almost smooth; stamens 10; petals white; leaves simple or compound, cordate-ovate to -rotund in outline . . .
. . . . *Tiarella*

17 Ovary 2-locular, the placentation axile (the seeds developing along the central axis).

18 Petioles of stem-leaves reduced up the stem to increasingly dilated sheathing stipules (upper leaves bladeless apart from the broad entire stipules); basal leaves cordate-rotund to reniform, from very coarsely crenate to divided nearly to base (usually withered by flowering time in *S. violacea*); calyx campanulate; petals white or purplish-violet; stamens 5; seeds finely to prominently warty; (B.C. and sw Alta.) . . . . *Suksdorfia*

18 Petioles of stem-leaves not noticeably dilated upwardly, the blades obvious but becoming shorter-petioled to sessile; basal leaves toothed to moderately lobed (cleft not more than half their length; entire and sessile in *Saxifraga nathorstii* and *S. oppositifolia*).

19 Stamens 5; calyx turbinate or campanulate; petals whitish or pinkish; seeds minutely tuberculate; leaf-blades cordate-ovate to reniform; stems more or less brown-hairy; (B.C.) . . . .
. . . . *Boykinia*

19 Stamens 10.

20 Petals reddish purple, 2 or 3 mm long; calyx turbinate-campanulate, usually reddish, to 13 mm long; styles partially connate; fruit a capsule; seeds brown and shining; stem-leaves only 1 or 2; leaf-blades reniform, doubly crenate to shallowly lobed and doubly crenate-dentate, slender-petioled, to about 5 cm broad; plant usually less than 1.5 dm tall, usually glandular-pubescent throughout, the upper stem and inflorescence often light to deep reddish-purple; (B.C. and sw Alta.) . . . . *Telesonix*

20 Petals usually white to greenish or yellow (often dotted with yellow, orange, red, or purple; petals rose-lilac to purple in *S. nathorstii* and *S. oppositifolia*); calyx saucer-shaped to conic or campanulate, green to purplish-black; styles free above the ovule-bearing portion of the ovary; fruit often follicular; seeds smooth or variously sculptured; basal leaves oblanceolate or spatulate to cordate-ovate or reniform, entire to toothed or deeply lobed, subsessile to slender-petioled; plants usually glandular-hairy, sometimes glabrous . . . . *Saxifraga*

BOYKINIA Nutt. [3185]

1 Leaves eciliate, deeply lobed to nearly halfway to the narrow sinus, the lobes acute; inflorescence an open loose panicle of somewhat secund cymes; calyx 4 or 5 mm long; petals 5 or 6 mm long; stem sparingly pilose toward base with long reddish or brownish hairs; (B.C.) . . . . *B. elata*

1 Leaves prominently ciliate with stout hairs tipped with dark glands, shallowly lobed, the lobes rounded; panicle congested and spike-like or racemose; calyx to about 1 cm long; petals about 1 cm long; stem copiously hirsute with brownish-stalked, dark-purple glands; (Alaska–Yukon–NW Dist. Mackenzie) . . . . *B. richardsonii*

B. elata (Nutt.) Greene
/t/W/ (Hs) Moist woods and streambanks from sw B.C. (Vancouver Is. and adjacent mainland; CAN; V) s along the coast and w slopes of the Cascades to N Calif. [*Saxifraga* Nutt.; *B. nuttallii* Macoun; *B. (Therophon) occidentalis* T. & G.; *B. vancouverense* Rydb.; *T. (B.) circinnatum* Rosend. & Rydb., at least in part].

B. richardsonii (Hook.) Gray
/aS/W/ (Hs) Subalpine forests, tundra meadows, and along streams in Alaska (s to ca. 62°N), the Yukon (s to ca. 65°N), and NW Dist. Mackenzie (type from between the Mackenzie and Coppermine rivers). [*Saxifraga* Hook.; *Therofon* Ktze.]. MAP: Hultén 1968*b*:562.

CHRYSOSPLENIUM L. [3199] Golden Carpet, Golden Saxifrage. Dorine

1 Leaves mostly opposite (the uppermost ones usually alternate); flowers usually solitary in the leaf-axils; sepals and stamens each usually 8; plants glabrous.
  2 Leaves coarsely crenate with few, very broad teeth; flowers subsessile; (Ont. to N.S.) . . . . *C. americanum*
  2 Leaves crenate-dentate with numerous (up to 20) teeth; flowers short-pedicelled in the upper axils; (?B.C.) . . . . [*C. glechomaefolium*]
1 Leaves alternate, with up to 11 broad crenate teeth; flowers few in leafy false cymes terminating the branches.
  3 Petioles and stem with curly rust-coloured hairs; leaves thickish, markedly paler beneath, mostly basal and terminal on the flowering stems; sepals and follicles tinged with purple; stamens 8; (Alaska–Yukon–Dist. Mackenzie) . . . . *C. wrightii*
  3 Petioles and stem glabrous or with a few light-coloured (rarely brownish) hairs;

leaves thin, yellowish green on both sides, more uniformly distributed on the
flowering stems; sepals and follicles green; stamens 4 or 8; (transcontinental) . . . .
. . . . *C. alternifolium*

C. alternifolium L.
/AST/X/GEA/ (Hsr) Cool wet places from the Aleutian Is. and coasts of Alaska–Yukon–
Dist. Mackenzie–Dist. Keewatin to Banks Is., northernmost Ellesmere Is., Baffin Is., and northernmost Ungava–Labrador, s to Wash. (isolated in the mts. of Colo. and in Iowa), B.C.–Alta.,
Sask. (s to McKague, 52°37′N), Man. (s to Riding Mt.), Ont. (s to the w James Bay watershed
at 54°22′N), Que. (s to ca. 55°N), and Labrador (s to ca. 55°N); E Greenland at ca. 75°N;
Spitsbergen; Eurasia. [Incl. vars. *sibiricum* Ser. and *tetrandrum* Lund (*C. tet.* (Lund) Fries), *C.
iowense* Rydb., *C. pacificum* Hult., and *C. rosendahlii* Packer]. MAPS (all as *C. tetr.*): Hultén
1968*b*:587; Porsild 1957: map 222, p. 188; Raup 1947: pl. 27; Meusel, Jaeger, and Weinert
1965:206; J.G. Packer, Can. J. Bot. 41(1): fig. 11, p. 97. 1963.
   For further discussion, *see* C.O. Rosendahl (Rhodora 49(578):25–35. 1947), H. Hara (Rhodora 51(609):191–92. 1949), Hultén (1945:949–50), and Porsild (1955:142–44).

C. americanum Schwein.   Water-mat, Water-carpet
/T/EE/ (Hpr) Cool wet places from Minn. to Ont. (N to Agawa Bay, E shore of L. Superior
at ca. 47°20′N, and the Ottawa dist.; reports from Man. by Lowe 1943, probably refer to *C. alternifolium*), Que. (N to the Gaspé Pen.), N.B., P.E.I., and N.S., s to Iowa, Ind., Ohio, and Ga.
[*C. oppositifolium sensu* Pursh 1814, not L.]. MAP: Meusel, Jaeger, and Weinert 1965:206.

[*C. glechomaefolium* Nutt.]
[The presumed report of this species of the w U.S.A. (Wash. to Calif.) from B.C. by Henry
(1915; "West of the Cascades; B.C. to Oregon."; this taken up in the range given by Hitchcock et al. 1961) requires confirmation. (*C. oppositifolium* var. *scouleri* Hook.; *C. scoul.*
(Hook.) Rose).]

C. wrightii Franch. & Savat.
/Ss/W/eA/ (Hsr) Rocky slopes and solifluction areas of the Aleutian Is., Alaska (N to ca.
69°N), the Yukon (N to ca. 68°N), and w Dist. Mackenzie (Porsild and Cody 1968); E Siberia
and Kamchatka. [*C. beringianum* Rose]. MAPS: Hultén 1968*b*:587; Meusel, Jaeger, and Weinert 1965:206.

CONIMITELLA Rydb.   [3198b]

C. williamsii (Eat.) Rydb.
/t/W/ (Hr) Moist cliffs and rocky slopes from sw Alta. (Crowsnest Forest Reserve, where
taken by Cram in 1920; CAN) and E Mont. to Idaho and Wyo. [*Heuchera* Eat.; *Lithophragma*
Greene; *Tellima nudicaulis* Greene].

ELMERA Rydb.   [3198a]

E. racemosa (Wats.) Rydb.
/T/W/ (Hs) Rock crevices, ledges, and talus slopes from sw B.C. (known only from mts. in
the Skagit Valley near Chilliwack; CAN; Henry 1915) to Wash. [*Heuchera* Wats.; *Tellima*
Greene].

HEUCHERA L.   [3195]   Alumroot

(Ref.: Rosendahl, Butters, and Lakela 1936; J.K. Small and P.A. Rydberg, N. Am. Flora 22:97–
117. 1905)
1 Panicle large, open and diffuse, with linear bracts and filiform branches and
   pedicels; calyx not strongly oblique at summit; stamens long-exserted; styles
   slender, to 3 mm long.

2 Leaf-blades mostly with rounded lobes; petioles usually glabrous; stems glabrous or short-pubescent below; petals whitish, greenish, pinkish, or reddish purple, shorter than the sepals (var. *brevipetala*); hypanthium (together with sepals) to 4 mm long; plant to 1 m tall; (s Ont.) . . . . *H. americana*

2 Leaf-blades with acutish lobes; petals whitish, longer than the sepals; hypanthium (together with sepals) to 3 mm long; plants to 6 dm tall.

   3 Petioles glabrous (occasionally glandular-pubescent); stipules ciliate; leaf-blades (as measured from the basal sinus) nearly always broader than long, sparingly glandular-pubescent beneath but otherwise usually glabrous; stems glabrous or occasionally glandular-puberulent at base; calyx glandular-pubescent; seeds brown, 3 or 4 times as long as broad; (Alaska, B.C., and sw Alta.) . . . . *H. glabra*

   3 Petioles and lower part of stems usually strongly villous; stipules pectinate-villous with marginal hairs to 3 mm long; leaf-blades often longer than broad, commonly more or less strigose beneath (and sometimes above); stems usually strongly villous below; calyx usually villous; seeds nearly black, less than twice as long as broad; (sw B.C.) . . . . *H. micrantha*

1 Panicle remaining narrow and thyrsoid, the branches and pedicels scarcely elongating; styles relatively stout.

   4 Calyx at anthesis mostly 2 or 3 mm long, regular, turbinate at the adnate base, the hypanthium flared and somewhat saucer-shaped, lined with a thin glandular disk that more or less covers the almost completely inferior ovary; petals white or yellowish, broadly elliptic to ovate, spreading, much longer than the spreading sepals; stamens very short, incurved; styles less than 0.5 mm long; leaves essentially glabrous above, more or less puberulent beneath especially along the veins; plant to 6 dm tall; (Cypress Hills of se Alta. and sw ?Sask.) . . . . *H. parvifolia*

   4 Calyx at anthesis usually well over 3 mm long (to over 1 cm long at maturity), often strongly oblique at summit, generally campanulate at base, the hypanthium cup-shaped and not much shorter than the erect lobes, not gland-lined or if so, the disk not covering the top of the incompletely inferior ovary; petals narrow, shorter or only slightly longer than the sepals or wanting.

      5 Stamens more or less exserted; styles 1.5 mm long or more; calyx strongly oblique at summit and gibbous at base (the hypanthium to 4 mm long on one side and scarcely half as long on the other); petals spatulate, clawed, purplish, gland-margined, equalling or slightly surpassing the sepals; panicle becoming more or less open; plants to 7 dm tall; (sw Dist. Mackenzie and n B.C. to w Ont.) . . . . *H. richardsonii*

      5 Stamens shorter than the calyx-lobes; styles at most 0.5 mm long; hypanthium slightly to considerably oblique; petals cream-colour or greenish yellow, shorter than the sepals (or wanting); plants to about 1 m tall.

         6 Petioles and lower parts of stem densely villous with brownish (when dried), mostly eglandular hairs 2–5 mm long; panicle contracted and dense; sepals bright green; filaments often more than twice as long as the dehisced anthers; (B.C.) . . . . *H. chlorantha*

         6 Petioles and lower parts of stem glabrous to glandular-pubescent or somewhat glandular-villous (the hairs, if as much as 2 mm long, whitish when dried and usually glandular); panicle becoming more or less open; sepals cream to yellow (occasionally red-tinged); filaments mostly less than twice as long as the dehisced anthers; (B.C. and sw Alta.) . . . . *H. cylindrica*

H. americana L.   Rock-Geranium
/t/EE/   (Hr)   Rich woods and shaded calcareous slopes and rocks from Mich. to s Ont. (Essex Co.: Pelee Point, Pelee Is., Malden, and Amherstburg) and Conn., s to Okla., Ala., and Ga. [Incl. var. *brevipetala* R., B., & L.]. MAP: C.O. Rosendahl, F.K. Butters, and Olga Lakela, Minn. Stud. Pl. Sci. 2: fig. 5, p. 125. 1936.

H. chlorantha Piper
/T/W/ (Hr) Gravelly prairies and wooded hillsides from w B.C. (N to Queen Charlotte Is. and Hazelton) s along the Cascade Mts. to Oreg. MAP: Calder and Savile 1959: map 1, p. 55.

Calder and Savile report a hybrid with *H. cylindrica* var. *orbicularis* from near Lillooet, s B.C., and one with *H. micrantha* var. *diversifolia* (× *H. easthamii* Calder & Savile) from the type station near Hazelton, B.C., ca. 55°15′N.

H. cylindrica Dougl.
/T/W/ (Hr) Rocky soil, cliffs, and talus slopes (ranges of Canadian taxa outlined below), s to N Calif., Nev., and Wyo. MAPS and synonymy: *see* below.

1 Leaves rarely much over 2.5 cm broad, mostly rounded or moderately cordate at base, they and the lower part of the stem finely glandular-pubescent (varying to hirsute); [var. *ovalifolia* (Nutt.) Wheelock (*H. oval*. Nutt.); *H. alpina* (Wats.) Blank.; *H. ovalifolia* var. *alp*. (Wats.) Rosend.; *H. hallii sensu* John Macoun 1883, not Gray, according to Macoun 1886; mts. of B.C. (N to Kamloops) and sw Alta. (Crowsnest Pass; Kananaskis; Castle Mt., NW of Banff)] . . . . var. *alpina* Wats.

1 Leaves often over 2.5 cm broad, usually cordate-based and with a definite sinus.

  2 Petioles glabrous to minutely glandular-puberulent, with or without longer hairs at most 1 mm long; [*H. glabella* T. & G.; incl. vars. *orbicularis* (R., B., & L.) Calder & Savile and *septentrionalis* R., B., & L., these transitional to the following taxon; B.C. (N to Cariboo, Chilcotin, and Kamloops) and sw Alta. (N to Banff); MAP: J.K. Calder & D.B.O. Savile, Brittonia 11(2): map 2 (vars. *glabella* and *orbicularis*), p. 55. 1959] . . . . var. *glabella* (T. & G.) Wheelock

  2 Petioles occasionally glandular-puberulent, generally with short glandular hairs mixed with long, usually gland-tipped hairs to 3 mm long; [*H. columbiana* and *H. suksdorfii* Rydb.; *H. saxicola* Nels.; the common phase in B.C. (N to Queen Charlotte Is. and Smithers, ca. 54°45′N) and Alta. (Waterton Lakes; Banff); MAP: on the above-noted map by Calder and Savile] . . . . var. *cylindrica*

H. glabra Willd.
/sT/W/ (Hr) Grassy hillsides and rocky ravines to alpine ledges and slopes from the E Aleutian Is. and s Alaska (*see* Hultén 1945: map 726, p. 977) through B.C. and the mts. of sw Alta. (Boivin 1966*b*) to Oreg.

A hybrid with *H. micrantha* var. *diversifolia* is reported from sw B.C. by Boivin (1966*b*; Mt. Joan, Vancouver Is.).

H. micrantha Dougl.
/t/W/ (Hr) Gravelly banks and rock crevices at low to subalpine elevations from sw B.C. (Vancouver Is. and adjacent islands and mainland; CAN; V; the report N to Queen Charlotte Is. by John Macoun 1883, probably refers to *H. glabra,* this and *H. chlorantha* listed for Queen Charlotte Is. by Calder and Taylor 1968) to N Calif. and Idaho.

The B.C. plant may be distinguished as var. *diversifolia* (Rydb.) R., B., & L. (*H. div.* Rydb.; *H. barbarossa* Presl; *H. longipetala* Moc.; incl. f. *acuta* R., B., & L.; leaves relatively deeply lobed and often longer than broad rather than more shallowly lobed and mostly at least as broad as long, the petioles and lower part of the stem usually strongly villous rather than often subglabrous or merely puberulent).

H. parvifolia Nutt.
/T/W/ (Hr) Gravelly montane slopes and talus from s ?B.C. (Trail; Henry 1915) through s Alta. to the Cypress Hills of SE Alta. and sw ?Sask. ("On dry gravel ridges west of Fort Walsh, on the top of the Cypress Hills"; CAN; this collection may actually have been taken in SE Alta.), s to Ariz. and N.Mex.

Our material may be distinguished as var. *dissecta* Jones (*H. flabellifolia* Rydb.; leaves cleft as far as midway to base rather than mostly not over 1/3 their length).

H. richardsonii R. Br.
/sT/WW/ (Hr) Dry sandy prairies and gravelly or rocky shores and slopes (ranges of Canadian taxa outlined below), s to Colo., S.Dak., Wisc., and Ind. MAP and synonymy: *see* below.
1 Scape and petioles moderately hispid with glandular hairs averaging less than 1.5 mm long; leaves to about 6 cm broad; [*H. hispida* of Canadian reports, not Pursh; SW Dist. Mackenzie (N to Fort Simpson, ca. 62°N; CAN) and B.C. to Alta. (N to L. Athabasca), Sask. (N to Prince Albert; collection in CAN from Nistoassini L., probably farther north), Man. (N to Norway House, off the NE end of L. Winnipeg), and w Ont. (near Sioux Lookout, about 175 mi NW of Thunder Bay; Quetico Provincial Park, about 100 mi w of Thunder Bay; NW shore of L. Superior; Sandy L. at ca. 53°N, 93°W); MAP: Rosendahl, Butters, and Lakela 1936: fig. 5 (somewhat incomplete northwards), p. 125] . . . . var. *richardsonii*
1 Scape and petioles densely hispid with glandular hairs to 3.5 mm long; leaves to about 8 cm broad; [Alta. to w Ont.] . . . . var. *hispidior* Rosend., Butt., & Lak.

[HYDRANGEA L.] [3247] Hydrangea

[H. arborescens L.] Wild Hydrangea
[Native in the E U.S.A. N to N.Y.; known from s N.B. (Chamcook L., near St. Stephen, Charlotte Co., where persisting near an old habitation; CAN), and doubtless so in other parts of our area.]

LEPTARRHENA R. Br. [3179]

L. pyrolifolia (Don) R. Br.
/ST/W/ (Hs) Streambanks and wet meadows to moist alpine and subalpine slopes from the Aleutian Is. and s-cent. Alaska–Yukon (N to ca. 63°30′N) through B.C. and the mts. of SW Alta. (N to near Jasper) to Oreg., Idaho, and Mont. [*Saxifraga* Don; *S. (L.) amplexifolia* R. Br.]. MAP: Hultén 1968*b*:562.

LITHOPHRAGMA Nutt. [3197]

(Ref.: R.L. Taylor 1965)
1 Calyx elongate-obconical, to 6 mm long at anthesis and 1 cm long in fruit; petals usually 3-lobed; seeds irregularly reticulate and longitudinally ridged; flowers up to 11 in number; plant often canescent; (s B.C. and SW Alta.) . . . .*L. parviflora*
1 Calyx campanulate; petals usually 5-lobed.
  2 Basal leaves glabrous or very sparingly pubescent, often bearing bulblets in their axils; flowers rarely more than 5; seeds muricate; (s B.C. to SW Sask.) . . . .*L. glabra*
  2 Basal leaves usually hirsute on both surfaces, nonbulbiferous; flowers up to 10; seeds irregularly reticulate or slightly warty to nearly smooth except for some wrinkling; (s B.C.) . . . .*L. tenella*

L. glabra Nutt. Prairie-star
/T/WW/ (Hs) Grasslands, sagebrush plains, and woodlands from B.C.–Alta. (ranges given below) to Calif., Colo., and S.Dak. MAP and synonymy: *see* below.
1 Stem-leaves not bulbiferous; [*Tellima* Steud.; B.C. (N to Telegraph Creek, ca. 58°N; CAN); MAP: R.L. Taylor 1965: fig. 21, p. 69] . . . . var. *glabra*
1 Stem-leaves bearing bulblets in their axils; [*L. (Tellima) bulb.* Rydb.; *L. tenella* var. *ramulosa* Suksd.; s B.C. (N to Merritt, about 25 mi s of Kamloops), SW Alta. (Waterton Lakes), and SW Sask. (Cypress Hills; Robsart)] . . . . var. *bulbifera* (Rydb.) Jeps.

L. parviflora (Hook.) Nutt. Fringe-cup, Prairie-star
/T/WW/ (Hs) Prairies and grassland to lower montane forest from s B.C. (N to Kamloops) and the mts. of SW Alta. (N to Banff) to N Calif., Colo., and S.Dak. [*Tellima* Hook.; incl. var. *micrantha* T. & G.]. MAP: R.L. Taylor 1965: fig. 23, p. 75.

L. tenella Nutt.   Prairie-star

/t/W/ (Hs) Dry plains, hills, and pine forest from SE B.C. (reported from Princeton, Penticton, and Osoyoos by R.L. Taylor 1965; the reports from elsewhere in B.C. by J.M. Macoun (1895: N to Telegraph Creek, ca. 58°N; excluding the Lytton plant, the relevant collection in CAN proving referable to *L. parviflora*) refer to *L. glabra,* relevant collections in CAN; Macoun's report from the Cypress Hills of Alta.–Sask. is also based upon *L. glabra*) to Nev., Ariz., and Colo. [Incl. var. *thompsonii* (Hoover) Hitchc. (*L. thompsonii* Hoover); *Tellima* Walp.]. MAP: R.L. Taylor 1965: fig. 24, p. 80.

MITELLA L.   [3198]   Mitrewort, Bishop's-cap.   Mitrelle

(Ref.: J.K. Small and P.A. Rydberg, N. Am. Flora 22:91–96. 1905)
1 Stems bearing up to 3 more or less reduced but distinct leaves.
 2 Stem-leaves a single opposite sessile pair; basal leaves long-petioled, 3–5-lobed and dentate, with scattered hairs on both sides; petals white, deeply fringed laterally; stamens 10; ovary largely superior; (Ont and Que.) . . . .*M. diphylla*
 2 Stem-leaves 1–3, alternate, petioled; stamens 5, opposite the calyx-lobes; ovary at least half inferior; plants more or less densely glandular-puberulent throughout.
  3 Raceme blossoming from the top downward; calyx 5 or 6 mm broad; petals greenish but often purplish-based, the fringe consisting of about 8 lateral segments; style about 1 mm long; (B.C.) . . . .*M. caulescens*
  3 Raceme blossoming from the bottom upward; calyx to about 3 mm broad; petals white, tinged with pink or purple, the fringe consisting of mostly 3 (sometimes 4 or 5) apical segments; style nearly obsolete . . . . [*M. diversifolia*]
1 Stems usually leafless or merely membranous-bracted.
 4 Stamens 10; ovary mostly superior; style about 0.5 mm long; petals greenish yellow; scape to about 2 dm tall, finely glandular-puberulent; leaves sparingly hirsute at least above; (transcontinental) . . . .*M. nuda*
 4 Stamens 5; ovary at least half inferior.
  5 Stamens alternate with the calyx-lobes (opposite the petals); anthers cordate-reniform, much broader than long; stigmas nearly sessile; petals greenish; scapes glandular-puberulent to subglabrous; leaves coarsely hirsute on both surfaces to subglabrous; (Alaska–B.C. to SW Alta.) . . . .*M. pentandra*
  5 Stamens opposite the calyx-lobes (alternate with the petals); anthers usually at least as long as broad.
   6 Calyx saucer-shaped, considerably broader than long, the triangular lobes spreading-recurved; anthers cordate; styles to 0.3 mm long; stigmas 2-lobed; petals usually greenish yellow.
    7 Leaf-blades to 8 cm broad, always shorter (as measured from the basal sinus) than broad, slightly if at all white-hirsute; pedicels to 2 mm long in anthesis, to 5 mm long in fruit; scapes (below inflorescence) glabrous or sparingly brownish cobwebby-pilose; (B.C. and SW Alta.) . . . . . .
    . . . .*M. breweri*
    7 Leaf-blades mostly not over 3.5 cm broad, always longer (as measured from the basal sinus) than broad, usually copiously coarse-hirsute above; pedicels rarely as much as 2 mm long; scapes coarsely hirsute below . . . .*M. ovalis*
   6 Calyx cup-shaped to campanulate, usually distinctly longer than broad, the ovate to oblong lobes often erect or with only the tips spreading; anthers ovate to oblong; stigmas broadly flattened, subsessile; petals usually whitish or tinged with pink to purple.
    8 Leaf-blades cordate-triangular to -ovate, about as long (measured from the basal sinus) as broad, with 5 (sometimes 7) angled lobes, the terminal lobe often acute; petals 3–5-lobed at summit; flowering stems often with 1 or 2 leaves . . . .*M. diversifolia*

8 Leaf-blades cordate-ovate to reniform, always shorter (as measured from the basal sinus) than broad, shallowly rounded-lobed, the terminal lobe not acute; petals 3-lobed; flowering stems rarely with any true leaves.

9 Racemes strongly 1-sided, with up to about 45 flowers; calyx about 5 mm long, the lobes with a simple central vein and branched lateral veins; petals to 4 mm long, the usually filiform terminal lobes widely spreading to ascending . . . . [*M. stauropetala*]

9 Racemes scarcely 1-sided, with rarely more than 20 flowers; calyx to 3.5 mm long, the lobes with a branched central vein and usually simple lateral veins; petals usually not over 2.5 mm long, the narrow (but not filiform) terminal lobes ascending to erect; (B.C. and sw Alta.) . . . . *M. trifida*

M. breweri Gray
/T/W/ (Hrr) Moist valleys and open or wooded slopes up to timberline from s B.C. (N to Revelstoke) and the mts. of sw Alta. (Waterton Lakes; Simpson Pass, on the B.C. boundary sw of Banff) to cent. Calif., Idaho, and Mont. [*Pectiantia* Rydb.; incl. f. *denticulata* Rosend.].

M. caulescens Nutt.
/t/W/ (Hpr) Meadows and swampy woods or open places from sw B.C. (Vancouver Is. and adjacent mainland E to the Chilliwack R.; CAN) to N Calif., Idaho, and Mont. [*Mitellastra* Howell].

M. diphylla L.   Coolwort
/T/EE/ (Hsr) Rocky moist woods from Minn. to Ont. (N to Algonquin Park, Renfrew Co., and the Ottawa dist.; the report from Man. by Burman 1909, requires confirmation) and Que. (N to L. Nominingue, Labelle Co., and St-Joachim, NE of Quebec City; *see* Que. map by Doyon and Lavoie 1966: fig. 12, p. 817; reported N to Rivière-du-Loup, Temiscouata Co., by John Macoun 1883; the report from Nfld. by Waghorne 1895, requires confirmation), s to Mo., Miss., Tenn., and S.C.

[M. diversifolia Greene]
[The report of this species of the w U.S.A. (Wash. to NW Calif.) from s B.C. by J.M. Macoun (1906; Trail, Columbia Valley) is based upon *M. trifida,* the relevant collection in CAN.]

M. nuda L.
/ST/X/A/ (Hrr) Cool or mossy woods and swampy places from SE ?Alaska (*see* Hultén 1945: map 729, p. 977), s Yukon, and sw Dist. Mackenzie to L. Athabasca (Alta. and Sask.), s Dist. Keewatin, northernmost Ont., cent. Que. (N to SE Hudson Bay at ca. 56°N, the Knob Lake dist., and the Côte-Nord), Labrador (N to Attikamagen L. at ca. 55°N and the Hamilton R. basin), Nfld., N.B., P.E.I., and N.S., s to Mont., N.Dak., Minn., and Pa.; Asia. [*M. cordifolia* and *M. reniformis* Lam.; *M. prostrata* Michx.]. MAPS: Hultén 1968b:586; *Atlas of Canada* 1957: map 8, sheet 38; A.E. Porsild and Howard Crum, Nat. Mus. Can. Bull. 171: fig. 2, p. 146. 1961.

M. ovalis Greene
/t/W/ (Hrr) Deep moist woods from sw B.C. (Vancouver Is.: Mt. Arrowsmith, Nanaimo, and Goldstream; CAN; V) w of the Cascades to N Calif.

M. pentandra Hook.
/sT/W/ (Hrr) Moist woods to wet montane meadows along the coast from s Alaska–Yukon (N to ca. 62°N) through B.C. and the mts. of sw Alta. (N to Banff) to N Calif. and Colo. [*Pectiantia* Rydb.; incl. f. *maxima* Rosend.]. MAP: Hultén 1968b:586.

[M. stauropetala Piper]
[This species of the w U.S.A. (N to Oreg. and Mont.) is not yet known from Canada but should be searched for in s B.C.–Alta. (*Ozomelis* Rydb.).]

M. trifida Graham
/T/W/ (Hrr) Moist forest to montane slopes from B.C. (N to Mt. Selwyn, ca. 56°N) and the mts. of SW Alta. (N to the Banff dist.; reported N to the Smoky R. at ca. 56°N by John Macoun 1883) to Calif., Idaho, and Mont. [*M. violacea* Rydb.].

PARNASSIA L. [3203] Grass-of-Parnassus, Bog-stars

1 Petals pectinately fringed on the lower half with numerous long slender cellular-warty filaments; staminodia (sterile stamens) with 7–9 short thick marginal segments and a larger terminal segment; leaves mostly reniform and broader than long (but sometimes more nearly cordate or truncate to slightly cuneate at base and somewhat longer than broad); scape with a solitary cordate and more or less clasping leaf-like bract borne slightly below to considerably above the middle; (B.C. and Alta.) . . . .*P. fimbriata*
1 Petals not fringed; marginal segments of staminodia filament-like.
  2 Staminodia cleft into up to 15 or more slender divisions; petals with up to 9 principal veins; leaves rounded or cordate at base, a solitary sessile one usually borne near or below the middle of the scape; (transcontinental) . . . .*P. palustris*
  2 Staminodia cleft into not more than 7 slender divisions; leaves tapering, rounded, or subcordate at base.
    3 Petals shorter than to about equalling the ascending calyx-lobes, 3-veined; leaves all basal, deltoid- or rhombic-ovate; (transcontinental) . . . .*P. kotzebuei*
    3 Petals surpassing the calyx-lobes, with at least 5 veins.
      4 Petals less than twice as long as the ascending calyx-lobes; staminodia with up to 7 unequal slender segments; scape usually bearing a sessile leaf below or near the middle; (essentially transcontinental) . . . .*P. parviflora*
      4 Petals 3 or more times as long as the calyx-lobes, these reflexed at maturity; staminodia cleft nearly to base into 3 stout lance-subulate segments; scape naked or with a sessile leaf near the base; (Sask. to Nfld. and N.B.) . . . .*P. glauca*

P. fimbriata Konig
/sT/W/ (Hs) Bogs, wet meadows, and streambanks up to alpine elevations from S-cent. Alaska–Yukon–w Dist. Mackenzie (N to ca. 63°30′N) through B.C. and the mts. of SW Alta. (N to Jasper) to Calif. and N.Mex. MAPS: Hultén 1968*b*:588; Raup 1947: pl. 27.

P. glauca Raf.
/T/EE/ (Hs) Wet calcareous soils and cold bogs from Sask. (N to Prince Albert; Breitung 1957*a*) to Man. (reported N to Flin Flon by Lowe 1943), Ont. (N to Renison, S of James Bay at ca. 51°N; Hustich 1955), Que. (N to Anticosti Is. and the Gaspé Pen.), Nfld., and N.B. (Victoria, Restigouche, and Gloucester counties; not known from P.E.I. or N.S.), S to S.Dak., Ill., Ohio, and New Eng. [*P. americana* Muhl.; *P. caroliniana* of Canadian reports, not Michx.].

P. kotzebuei Cham.
/aST/X/GeA/ (Hr) Wet calcareous rocks and swampy places from the coasts of Alaska–Yukon–Dist. Mackenzie–Dist. Keewatin to southernmost Baffin Is. and northernmost Ungava–Labrador, S in the West through B.C. and SW Alta. to Wash., Nev., and Wyo., farther eastwards S to Great Slave L., N Sask. (S to L. Athabasca), cent. Man. (S to the Hargrave R. about 30 mi N of L. Winnipeg), cent. Ont. (S to the Kapiskau R. at ca. 52°30′N), islands in James Bay, Que. (S to NE James Bay at Cape Jones, 54°37′N, the Knob Lake dist., the Côte-Nord, and Gaspé Pen.), Labrador (S to Forteau, 51°28′N), and Nfld.; W Greenland at ca. 61° and 70°N; NE Siberia. MAPS: Hultén 1968*b*:589; Porsild 1957: map 223, p. 188; Raup 1947: pl. 27; Fernald 1925: map 3, p. 248.

P. palustris L.
/ST/X/EA/ (Hs) Wet meadows and thickets, the aggregate species from the Aleutian Is.

and N Alaska–Yukon–Dist. Mackenzie to Great Bear L., Great Slave L., L. Athabasca (Alta. and Sask.), S Dist. Keewatin, northernmost Ont., Que. (N to S Ungava Bay and the Gaspé Pen.), Labrador (N to the Fraser R. at ca. 57°N), and Nfld. (not known from the Maritime Provinces), S to Calif., Wyo., N.Dak., and N Mich.; Iceland; Eurasia. MAPS and synonymy: see below.

1 Staminodia mostly with 5–7(9) segments; petals only slightly surpassing the calyx-lobes; leaves rounded or subcordate at base, the stem-leaf scarcely clasping; [*P. montanensis* Fern. & Rydb.; the Yukon (N to near Mayo), W Dist. Mackenzie (N to Great Slave L. and Fort Norman), (B.C. (S to the Carbon R. at ca. 54°N), the mts. of SW Alta., and L. Athabasca, Sask.] . . . . var. *montanensis* (Fern. & Rydb.) Hitchc.

1 Staminodia with mostly 9–17 segments; petals commonly about twice the length of the calyx-lobes; leaves cordate-based, the stem-leaf often clasping.

  2 Petals mostly with 7–11 veins, usually withering-persistent; staminodia with slender claw-like bases; [incl. var. *tenuis* Wahl.; *P. multiseta sensu* M.L. Fernald, Rhodora 28(335):211. 1926, not *P. pal.* var. *mult.* Ledeb.; *P. obtusiflora* of Canadian reports, not Rupr.; transcontinental; MAPS: Hultén 1968b:589; Raup 1947: pl. 27; A. Löve 1950: fig. 10 (*P. obtus.*), p. 41] . . . . var. *neogaea* Fern.

  2 Petals mostly with (11)13 veins, soon deciduous; staminodia (and petals) with short broad claws; [W Alaska (see Hultén 1945); Eurasia; MAP (aggregate species): Meusel, Jaeger, and Weinert 1965:207] . . . . var. *palustris*

P. parviflora DC.

/ST/X/ (Hr) Bogs and wet meadows from B.C. (N to Liard Hotsprings, 59°25′N; CAN; concerning reports from SE Alaska, see Hultén 1945; the report from Great Bear L. by Porsild 1943, is based upon *P. palustris* var. *montanensis,* the relevant collection in CAN) to Alta. (N to Mayerthorpe, ca. 54°N; reported N to the Peace R. at ca. 56°N by John Macoun 1883; not known from Sask.; the report from Man. by Scoggan 1957, is based upon *P. kotzebuei,* the relevant collection in CAN), Ont. (N to the Severn and Fawn rivers at ca. 55°N), Que. (N to Rupert House, SE James Bay, 51°29′N, the Côte-Nord, Anticosti Is., and Gaspé Pen.), Labrador (N to Nachvak, ca. 59°N; Delabarre 1902), Nfld., P.E.I. (Cape Wolfe, Prince Co.), and N.S. (Inverness Co., Cape Breton Is.; not known from N.B.), S to N Idaho, Mont., S.Dak., Wisc., S Ont., and Que. (S to the Quebec City dist.). [*P. palustris* var. *parv.* (DC.) Boivin].

PHILADELPHUS L. [3208] Mock-orange, Syringa

1 Flowers solitary or 2 or 3(4) in terminal cymose clusters, scentless; leaves entire or obscurely denticulate; (introd.) . . . . [*P. inodorus*]

1 Flowers up to 11 in racemose clusters; leaves entire to dentate (often strongly but remotely serrate-dentate on vigorous new shoots).

  2 Leaves of the flowering shoots commonly entire or merely denticulate; second-year twigs with tardily exfoliating bark; flowers fragrant; (B.C. and SW Alta.) . . . *P. lewisii*

  2 Leaves of the flowering shoots mostly dentate; second-year twigs with freely exfoliating bark; flowers scentless; (introd.) . . . . *P. coronarius*

P. coronarius L.

Eurasian; occasionally spread from cult. in N. America to roadside thickets, as in S Ont. (riverbanks at London, Middlesex Co.) and SW Que. (Montreal; Rock Forest, Sherbrooke Co.).

[*P. inodorus* L.]

[Native in the E U.S.A. (N to Tenn. and Va.) and spreading from cult. northwards; reported from S Ont. by Stroud (1941; Wellington Co.), but probably not established there. (Incl. var. *grandiflorus* (Willd.) Gray).]

P. lewisii Pursh

/T/W/ (N) In gullies and on rocky slopes, cliffs, and hillsides from S B.C. (N to Shuswap L., NE of Kamloops; CAN) and SW Alta. (Waterton Lakes; Breitung 1957b) to Oreg., Idaho, and Mont. [*P. columbianus* Koehne; *P. gordonianus* Lindl.; *P. trichothecus* Hu].

RIBES L.   [3249]
Currant.   Gadellier
Gooseberry.   Groseillier

(Ref.: F.V. Coville and N.L. Britton, N. Am. Flora 22(3):193–225. 1908)
1   Plants with spines or prickles at the nodes (also often along the internodes and on
     the berry); leaves not resin-dotted beneath.
     2   Pedicels jointed near summit just below the ovary (or berry); free part of
         hypanthium shallowly cup- or saucer-shaped; stamens about equalling the
         pinkish or purplish petals; racemes 3–15-flowered; berries usually glandular-
         bristly, somewhat palatable; leaves cordate or subcordate at base, mostly deeply
         5-cleft to at least half their length. (Currants).
         3   Leaves copiously pubescent and more or less glandular, mostly less than 2.5
             cm broad; berries reddish; pedicels stout, usually less than twice as long as
             the bracts; (s B.C.) . . . . R. montigenum
         3   Leaves glabrous or only sparingly pubescent, never glandular, to over 5 cm
             broad; berries deep purple; pedicels slender, often at least twice as long as
             the bracts; (transcontinental) . . . . R. lacustre
     2   Pedicels not jointed near ovary; free part of hypanthium tubular or campanulate
         (rarely cup-shaped; never saucer-shaped); flowers solitary or in racemose
         clusters of up to 5. (Gooseberries).
         4   Styles completely glabrous; (s B.C.).
             5   Calyx greenish or only slightly red-tinged; stamens much shorter than the
                 extended sepals; anthers white, smooth on the back; petals white; berry
                 covered with bristles 2–4 mm long; leaves to about 5 cm broad, thickly
                 puberulent (especially beneath) and often also somewhat glandular;
                 branches copiously greyish-hairy and abundantly glandular-bristly . . . .
                 . . . . R. watsonianum
             5   Calyx crimson at least on the inner surface of the lobes; stamens about
                 equalling the extended sepals; anthers reddish or purple, warty or
                 papillate on the back; petals white or pinkish; berry stipitate-glandular;
                 leaves commonly not over 2.5 cm broad, sparingly pubescent or glabrous
                 above, paler and usually pubescent as well as glandular beneath;
                 branches finely pubescent . . . . R. lobbii
         4   Styles hairy toward base.
             6   Berry (and ovary) covered with few to many subulate prickles (at least the
                 largest of these not gland-tipped), on elongate pedicels; berry purplish-red
                 to -black; peduncles elongate; calyx-lobes shorter than the tube,
                 surpassing the stamens; leaves rounded or subcordate at base, soft-
                 pubescent, deeply 3–5-lobed to about half their length; (Ont. and Que.) . . . .
                 . . . . R. cynosbati
             6   Berry (and ovary) usually glabrous (or pubescent and often glandular, but
                 not prickly, in R. grossularia and R. setosum); inflorescence usually more
                 compact; calyx-lobes usually at least as long as the tube.
                 7   Stamens usually about as long as the petals, never as long as the
                     extended calyx-lobes and not conspicuously exserted even with the
                     calyx-lobes reflexed; petals white or pinkish; leaves usually pubescent
                     at least beneath, and also usually glandular-puberulent beneath except
                     in old age.
                     8   Hypanthium narrowly tubular, 2–4 times as long as broad, usually
                         longer than the white or pinkish calyx-lobes, the whole flower
                         usually well over 1 cm long with the lobes extended; anthers usually
                         over 1 mm long; leaves rather deeply 3(5)-lobed.
                         9   Calyx glabrous externally; flowers to 13 mm long, the
                             hypanthium to 5 mm long; berries deep purplish-black; nodal
                             spines to 2 cm long; (Alta to James Bay) . . . . R. setosum

        9 Calyx more or less finely pilose externally; flowers to about 1.5 cm long, the hypanthium to 6 mm long; berries reddish but drying blue-black, palatable; (s ?B.C.) . . . . [*R. cognatum*]

    8 Hypanthium flared and more or less campanulate, about as broad at the top as long; flowers usually less than 1 cm long with the calyx-lobes extended; calyx glabrous externally; anthers barely 1 mm long; berries deep blue-purple; leaves (3)5-lobed to about half their length.

        10 Branches rather stout, yellowish, puberulent and densely bristly when young and usually remaining so in age; leaves more or less pubescent and usually also strongly glandular-puberulent at least beneath; calyx-lobes about equalling the hypanthium; styles united for about half their length; flowers to about 7 mm long; berry palatable; (transcontinental) . . . . *R. oxyacanthoides*

        10 Branches rather slender, finely puberulent, rarely at all bristly when young; leaves usually finely pubescent (but not glandular) on both surfaces, sometimes glabrous above; calyx-lobes about half again as long as the hypanthium; styles united to near tip; flowers to over 1 cm long; berry ?palatable; (B.C.) . . . . . . *R. irriguum*

7 Stamens about equalling to surpassing the extended calyx-lobes; berry palatable (but sour in some species); pubescence of the leaves (when present) rarely including glands; branches usually unarmed except for the nodal spines.

    11 Berry more or less pubescent and glandular-bristly (rarely glabrate), yellowish to red; ovary villous; calyx pilose externally, the lobes about as long as the hypanthium and slightly surpassing the stamens; leaves pubescent or glabrate, mostly cordate or subcordate at base, 3–5-lobed; (introd.) . . . . *R. grossularia*

    11 Berry (and ovary) glabrous; calyx usually glabrous externally (sometimes copiously pubescent in *R. divaricatum*).

        12 Calyx-lobes white or slightly greenish, rarely pinkish-tinged, to 8 mm long and usually at least twice as long as the hypanthium, sharply reflexed in anthesis; petals white; stamens surpassing the extended calyx-lobes by up to 3 mm, the anthers hairy; styles united well over half their length; berry blue-black; leaves finely pubescent at least beneath, 3–5-lobed to about half their length . . . . [*R. niveum*]

        12 Calyx-lobes greenish to pinkish or purplish, spreading to reflexed; anthers glabrous; styles united at most only slightly over half their length; berry reddish purple to purplish black; leaves finely pubescent beneath or glabrous.

            13 Calyx-lobes usually purplish, to 7 mm long and up to 3 times as long as the hypanthium, the stamens surpassing the extended lobes by 1 or 2 mm; petals white to red; leaves rounded to truncate or slightly cordate at base, mostly 3-lobed to about half their length, the lower segments again often shallowly cleft into 2 unequal lobes; (sw B.C.) . . . . *R. divaricatum*

            13 Calyx-lobes usually greenish or only slightly purple-tinged, at most twice as long as the hypanthium; petals white or pinkish; leaves 3–5-lobed to about half their length.

               14 Stamens about equalling the extended calyx-lobes, these slightly shorter than the hypanthium; berries reddish purple; leaves usually cordate (sometimes rounded) at base, glabrous (except for the soft ciliation) or occasionally sparingly pubescent and with minute sessile

or stalked glands; petioles mostly slightly pubescent and with a few longer slender stipitate-glandular hairs; (var. *inerme*; B.C. and sw Alta.) . . . . *R. divaricatum*

14 Stamens often slightly surpassing the extended calyx-lobes, these slightly longer than the hypanthium; berries purple to purplish black or black; leaves without surface glands; petioles bearing long plumose trichomes; (varieties; Alta. to Nfld. and N.S.) . . . . *R. oxyacanthoides*

1 Plants lacking spines or prickles; flowers mostly more than 5 in usually elongate racemes, their pedicels jointed just below the ovary (the mature fruit readily dropping); stamens shorter than the extended calyx-lobes, at most only slightly longer than the petals. (Currants).

15 Leaves copiously sprinkled beneath with yellow or amber-coloured resin-dots (these sometimes few or wanting in *R. laxiflorum*); berry purplish black to black.

16 Berry glandular-bristly; free hypanthium shallowly bowl-shaped, about 1 mm long, broader than long; bracts of the erect or ascending raceme 1 or 2 mm long, the pedicels to 1 cm long; calyx greenish white and pinkish-tinged to deep red or purple, the spreading lobes to 3 mm long; petals red to purplish; leaves commonly 5-lobed nearly halfway to base, deeply cordate, glabrous above, paler beneath (where more or less crisp-puberulent and usually with a sprinkling of yellow resin-dots and more numerous, very short-stalked glands); (B.C. and sw Alta.) . . . . *R. laxiflorum*

16 Berry not glandular-bristly; petals white or whitish.

17 Hypanthium broadly tubular-campanulate, somewhat longer than broad; berries glabrous; bracts usually longer than the pedicels; petals white; calyx greenish white, essentially glabrous, its reflexed lobes about as long as the hypanthium; racemes spreading or drooping; leaves 3-lobed nearly halfway to base, the lower segments also often rather shallowly cleft; (Alta. to N.S.) . . . . *R. americanum*

17 Hypanthium saucer-shaped or very shallowly cup-shaped, as broad as or broader than long; berries (and ovary) usually sprinkled with yellowish sessile resin-dots.

18 Racemes drooping, their bracts small and inconspicuous; hypanthium cup-shaped, pubescent, the dull-white to green or purplish-green sepals ascending at anthesis and recurved at about the middle; petals reddish; leaves 3–5-lobed to about the middle, broadly truncate to cordate at base, sparingly pubescent; (garden-escape) . . . . *R. nigrum*

18 Racemes spreading or ascending to nearly erect; hypanthium saucer-shaped, the sepals spreading from the base; petals white; berry with a disagreeable taste.

19 Bracts conspicuous (the lower ones often leaf-like and usually surpassing the pedicels), gradually reduced upward, but even the upper ones usually with a greenish, often somewhat expanded tip; mature berry usually strongly glaucous with a dense bloom; calyx usually greenish to brownish-purple; racemes to 3 dm long; leaves 5–7-lobed mostly to below the middle, cordate, sparingly pubescent to glabrous (except for the resin-dots); (se Alaska–B.C.) . . . .
. . . . *R. bracteosum*

19 Bracts very narrowly linear-lanceolate, all shorter than the pedicels and soon deciduous; mature berry less glaucous; calyx white; racemes usually not over 1 dm long; leaves primarily 3-lobed less than halfway to base, the lower segments obscurely lobed; (Alaska–B.C. to w Que.) . . . . *R. hudsonianum*

15 Leaves not copiously resin-dotted beneath (a few dots occasionally present in *R. aureum* and *R. howellii*); ovary (and berry) lacking sessile resin-dots (but sometimes bearing stalked glands).

20 Calyx golden yellow; flowers glabrous, in spreading to reflexed racemes; petals yellow to orange or reddish; free part of hypanthium cylindric, much longer than broad, the short calyx-lobes spreading; berry red to purple or black (atypically yellow), glabrous; bracts foliaceous, mostly longer than the pedicels; leaves thick, pale green, cordate at base, primarily 3-lobed less than halfway to base, the lobes usually entire except for up to 5 rounded teeth but the lower lobes sometimes again shallowly cleft.

  21 Hypanthium over 1 cm long, about twice as long as the sepals; (introd.) . . . . [R. odoratum]

  21 Hypanthium less than 1 cm long and usually less than twice as long as the sepals; (s B.C. to s Sask.) . . . . R. aureum

20 Calyx not yellow; flowers usually glandular or pubescent or both.

  22 Free part of hypanthium nearly cylindric or tubular-campanulate, longer than broad.

    23 Anthers not gland-tipped; hypanthium tubular-campanulate, to 5 mm long, only slightly longer than the spreading-ascending, pale- to deep-rose lobes; petals white to pale rose; racemes stiffly ascending to erect; berries glaucous-black, more or less stipitate-glandular; leaves deltoid-ovate to cordate-orbicular or reniform, mostly 5-lobed with deltoid to rounded lobes, much paler and more densely hairy beneath than above; (B.C.) . . . . R. sanguineum

    23 Anthers tipped with a small cup-like gland; styles usually connate almost to the stigmas; flowers white or pinkish to green; berry more or less glandular-bristly, unpalatable; leaves usually copiously pubescent and more or less stipitate-glandular on both surfaces, shallowly 3–5-lobed much less than half their length (sometimes almost equally coarsely crenate-dentate in R. cereum), the lobes rounded; (B.C. and sw Alta.).

      24 Hypanthium nearly cylindric, twice as long as the spreading-recurved lobes; bracts usually more or less flabellate, broadly rounded to truncate at base, several-lobed or very prominently toothed; flowers in clusters of up to 8 at the ends of the spreading peduncles; petals to 2 mm long; berry dull to bright red; leaves broadly cuneate-flabellate to almost reniform . . . . R. cereum

      24 Hypanthium tubular-campanulate, about equalling the spreading-ascending lobes; bracts oblanceolate, entire or minutely erose; flowers up to 12 or more in erect to somewhat drooping racemes; petals to 4 mm long; berry bluish to black; leaves orbicular-reniform . . . . R. viscosissimum

  22 Free part of hypanthium saucer-shaped or very shallowly cup-shaped, broader than long.

    25 Ovary (and berry) pubescent or stipitate-glandular or both; leaves 3–5-lobed, deeply cordate at base.

      26 Racemes drooping, the bracts to 5 mm long, mostly equalling the pedicels; anther-filaments much broadened at base, borne on a low disk projecting upward in the centre of the flower; petals pink; berry glaucous-black, sparingly low-glandular-stipitate and slightly pubescent; leaves glabrous above, puberulent at least on the veins and often resin-dotted beneath; (s B.C.) . . . . R. howellii

      26 Racemes ascending, the bracts much shorter than the pedicels; anther-filaments neither flattened nor borne on a projecting disk; petals whitish to pink; berry red, covered with stipitate glands to 1.2 mm long; leaves glabrous above, puberulent on the veins beneath, lacking resin-dots; bruised plant and berries with a skunk-like fetid odour; (transcontinental) . . . . R. glandulosum

    25 Ovary (and red berry) glabrous; racemes ascending to drooping; petals scarcely 1 mm long.

27 Leaves cuneate-obovate, unequally 3-lobed at apex; (introd. in s
Man.) . . . .*R. diacanthum*
27 Leaves broadly rounded to truncate or shallowly cordate at base,
3–5-lobed.
   28 Calyx greenish yellow; petals creamy to pinkish or yellowish-red;
   anthers dumbbell-shaped, the sacs separated by almost the
   width of the filament; pedicels nonglandular; terminal lobe of leaf
   ovate; stem usually erect; berry palatable; (garden-escape) . . . .
   . . . .*R. sylvestre*
   28 Calyx deep purplish or purplish-tinged; petals reddish purple;
   anthers broadly cordate and retuse, the sacs only slightly
   separated; berry sour; stem often decumbent and rooting at the
   lower nodes; (transcontinental) . . . .*R. triste*

R. americanum Mill.   Wild Black Currant
/T/X/ (N) Moist thickets and woods from Mont. to Alta. (N to Lac la Biche, 54°48'N; W.J.
Cody, Can. Field-Nat. 70(3):117. 1956), Sask. (N to Tisdale, 52°51'N), Man. (N to Hill L., N of L.
Winnipeg), Ont. (N to Renison, s of James Bay at ca. 51°N; Hustich 1955), Que. (N to L. Tim-
iskaming at ca. 47°30'N), N.B. (St. John, Kings, and Northumberland counties), and N.S. (col-
lection in NSPM from Windsor, Hants Co., and reported from Truro, Colchester Co., by G.G.
Campbell (Proc. N.S. Inst. Sci. 6:213. 1886) but not listed by Roland 1947; not known from
P.E.I.; reports from Nfld. by Waghorne 1898, and from Anticosti Is., E Que., by Verrill 1865, are
probably referable to *R. triste*), s to N.Mex., Nebr., Mo., and Del. [*R. floridum* l'Hér.; *R. recurva-
tum* Michx.].

R. aureum Pursh   Golden Currant
/T/WW/ (N) Streambanks and wet grasslands to dry plains and open or wooded slopes
from s B.C. (near Princeton; Eastham 1947), s Alta. (Milk River and Medicine Hat; introd. at
Fort Saskatchewan), and sw Sask. (near the E end of the Cypress Hills; Breitung 1957a, also
reporting it as introd. at Mortlach), s to N.Mex. and S.Dak.; introd. elsewhere, as in s Ont. and
sw Que. [*Chrysobotrya* Rydb.].

R. bracteosum Dougl.   Stinking Currant
/sT/W/ (N) Streambanks and moist woods from s Alaska (*see* Hultén 1945: map 736, p.
978) through B.C. w of the Cascades to NW Calif. MAP: Hultén 1968b:591.

R. cereum Dougl.   Squaw-Currant
/T/WW/ (N) Rocky places (common on the E slope of the Cascades) from interior B.C. (N
to Kamloops) and the mts. of sw Alta. (Banff; CAN) to s Calif., N.Mex., and Nebr.

[R. cognatum Greene]   Umatilla Gooseberry
[This species of the w U.S.A. (Wash., Oreg., and Idaho) is reported as possibly reaching s
B.C. by Hitchcock et al. (1961) and should be searched for there.]

R. cynosbati L.   Prickly Gooseberry
/T/EE/ (N) Moist rocky woods from N Minn. to Ont. (N to Algonquin Park, Renfrew Co.,
and the Ottawa dist.; *see* s Ont. map by Soper and Heimburger 1961:72) and Que. (N to Mont-
morency Falls, E of Quebec City; CAN; reports from farther N in Que. and from N.B. by John
Macoun 1883, may be based upon *R. oxyacanthoides*; not known from P.E.I. or N.S.), s to
Mo., Ala., and N.C. [*Grossularia* Mill.].
   Var *atrox* Fern. (internodes of the fruiting stems densely prickly with dark stiff bristles) is
known from the type locality near Little Current, Manitoulin Is., N L. Huron, Ont. Forma *inerme*
Redh. (nodal spines wanting rather than to 1 cm long in the typical phase) is known from s
Ont. (Lambton Co.; OAC) and sw Que. (Chateauguay Co.; GH).

R. diacanthum Pallas   Siberian Currant
Asiatic; the first record of this plant in N. America is the report from Brandon, s Man., by G.A.

Stevenson (Can. Field-Nat. 79(3):175. 1965; noting occasional plants in woodland near the Experimental Farm, where first observed in 1947).

R. divaricatum Dougl.   Straggly Gooseberry
/T/W/   (N)   Open woods, prairies, and moist hillsides, the aggregate species from s B.C. and sw Alta. to Calif. and N.Mex.

1   Calyx-lobes usually rather strongly purple-tinged, to 7 mm long, at least twice as long as the hypanthium, the stamens surpassing the extended lobes by 1 or 2 mm; petals white or red, to 2.5 mm long, rarely half as long as the calyx-lobes; [sw B.C.: Vancouver Is. and adjacent islands and mainland]. A purported hybrid with *R. lobbii* is reported from Mt. Tolmie, Vancouver Is., by Henry (1915) . . . . var. *divaricatum*

1   Calyx-lobes usually greenish or merely tinged with red or purple, to 4(5) mm long, less than twice as long as the hypanthium, the stamens scarcely exserted; petals white or pinkish, to 1.5(2) mm long, up to 3/5 as long as the calyx-lobes; [*R. (Grossularia) inerme* Rydb.; s B.C. (Rossland; Flathead) and sw Alta. (Waterton Lakes; Breitung 1957*b*)] . . . . var. *inerme* (Rydb.) McMinn

R. glandulosum Grauer   Skunk-Currant
/ST/X/   (N)   Moist woods, clearings, and rocky slopes from cent. Alaska–Yukon to Great Slave L. (a report from Great Bear L. requires confirmation), northernmost Sask. (Hasbala L. at ca. 60°N), Man. (N to Nueltin L. at 59°48′N), Ont. (N to Fort Severn, Hudson Bay, ca. 56°N), Que. (N to Ungava Bay, the Côte-Nord, Anticosti Is., and Gaspé Pen.), Labrador (N to ca. 58°N; DAO), Nfld., N.B., P.E.I., and N.S., s to B.C.–Alta., Minn., Ohio, and N.C. [*R. prostratum* l'Hér.; *R. trifidum* Michx.; *R. rigens* Michx., not Kirschn.; *R. ?alpinum* of Canadian reports, not L.; *R. ?laxiflorum sensu* Richardson 1823, not Pursh]. MAPS: Hultén 1968*b*:592; Raup 1947: pl. 28 (the occurrence in Man. should be indicated); M.L. Fernald, Rhodora 13(151): map 6 (*R. pro.*; E Canada), facing p. 137. 1911.

R. grossularia L.   Gooseberry (of Europe)
European; persisting in old gardens or spreading to thickets and roadsides in N. America, as in Que. (Marie-Victorin 1935), Nfld. (Rouleau 1956), and ?N.S. (Cochran 1829). [*R. uva-crispa* L.].

R. howellii Greene
/T/W/   (N)   Subalpine streambanks, meadowland thickets, and open ridges and talus from s B.C. (Grouse Mt., Vancouver; Garibaldi, N of Vancouver, Mt. Cheam, near Chilliwack, and Manning Park, SE of Hope; CAN; V) to N Oreg. and Idaho. [*R. acerifolium* Howell, not Koch].

R. hudsonianum Richards.
/ST/(X)/   (N)   Wet woods and rocky slopes from N-cent. Alaska, cent. Yukon, and NW Dist. Mackenzie to Great Bear L., Great Slave L., L. Athabasca (Alta. and Sask.; type from ca. 67°N in Alta.), Man. (N to Churchill), northernmost Ont., and W Que. (coast of Hudson Bay at ca. 56°30′N; L. Mistassini), s to N Calif., Utah, Wyo., Iowa, Mich., and s Ont. [*R. ?nigrum sensu* Richardson 1823, not L.]. MAPS: Hultén 1968*b*:591; Raup 1947: pl. 27; Raymond 1950*b*: fig. 5, p. 12.

   Some of our western material (Alta. westwards) is referable to var. *petiolare* (Dougl.) Jancz. (f. *?glabrum* Thieret; *R. pet.* Dougl.; plant nearly or quite glabrous or lightly pubescent on the calyces, young stems, petioles, and veins of the lower leaf-surfaces rather than rather copiously hairy nearly throughout).

R. irriguum Dougl.   Idaho Gooseberry
/T/W/   (N)   Moist to dry ravines and open to wooded hillsides from B.C. (N to Lac la Hache and Kamloops) to N Oreg. and W Mont. [*Grossularia* Cov. & Britt.; *R. oxyacanthoides* var. *irr.* (Dougl.) Jancz.].

R. lacustre (Pers.) Poir.   Bristly or Swamp Black Currant
/ST/X/   (N)   Moist woods and swamps to subalpine ridges from cent. Alaska–Yukon to Great Slave L., L. Athabasca (Alta. and Sask.), Man. (N to Churchill), northernmost Ont., Que.

(N to SE Hudson Bay at ca. 56°30'N, L. Mistassini, the Côte-Nord, Anticosti Is., and Gaspé Pen.), Labrador (N to the Hamilton R. basin), Nfld., N.B., P.E.I., and N.S., S to Calif., Colo., Minn., N.Y., and Tenn. [*R. oxyacanthoides* var. *lac.* Pers., the type from L. Mistassini, Que.; *Limnobotrya* Rydb.; *R. (L.) echinatum* Dougl.; *R. grossularioides* Michx.; incl. var. *parvulum* Gray (*L. parv.* (Gray) Rydb.)]. MAPS: Hultén 1968*b*:590; Raup 1947: pl. 27.

Forma *subblandum* Boivin (ovary and fruit glabrous rather than bristly) is known from the type locality, Sidley, W of Midway, S B.C.

R. laxiflorum Pursh   Trailing Black Currant
/sT/W/eA/   (N)   Wet coastal woods to montane slopes from S Alaska (N to ca. 63°N) and southernmost Yukon through B.C. and the mts. of SW Alta. (N to the Jasper dist.) to Calif. and Idaho; E Asia. [*R. affine* Dougl.; incl. var. *japonicum* Jancz., the Asiatic phase]. MAP: Hultén 1968*b*:592.

R. lobbii Gray
/T/W/   (N)   Lowland valleys and streambanks to open or wooded montane slopes from SW B.C. (Vancouver Is. and adjacent islands; collections from several localities in CAN and V) to NW Calif.

R. montigenum McClatchie   Alpine Prickly Currant
/T/W/   (N)   Subalpine to alpine talus slopes, ridges, and rock crevices from S B.C. (New Westminster and Midway; CAN; reported from the Fraser Valley N of Boston Bar by John Macoun 1883) to S Calif. and N.Mex. [*Limnobotrya* Rydb.; *R. lacustre* vars. *lentum* Jones (*R. lentum* (Jones) Cov. & Rose) and *molle* Gray].

R. nigrum L.   Black Currant.   Cassis
Eurasian; cult. and occasionally escaping to thickets in N. America, as in S B.C. (Vancouver Is.; CAN), S Ont. (Guelph, Wellington Co.; OAC), Que. (Bic, Rimouski Co., and Métis, Gaspé Pen.; CAN; GH), Nfld., St-Pierre and Miquelon, N.B. (Petit Rocher, Gloucester Co.; CAN), P.E.I., and N.S. (Shelburne, Hants, and Lunenburg counties; CAN; NSPM; not listed by Roland 1947).

[R. niveum Lindl.]
[This is a species of the W U.S.A. (Wash. to Nev. and Idaho) that should be searched for in S B.C. However, collections from that region in CAN that were originally referred to it apparently belong to *R. divaricatum* or related species.]

[R. odoratum Wendland f.]   Missouri or Buffalo Currant
[Native in the U.S.A. from Minn. to Tex. and Ark. and a garden-escape elsewhere. A collection in OAC from near Tillsonburg, Norfolk Co., S Ont., has been placed here and it is reported from the Ottawa dist., Ont., by Gillett (1958) and from Lambton Co., S Ont., by Dodge (1915; "Abundant and spreading in sand of Pt. Edward."). There is also a collection in Herb. V from a garden near Vernon, S B.C., where perhaps established. However, it is so closely related to *R. aureum* as to require further studies on the relative occurrence of these species in Canada. (*Chrysobotrya* Rydb.; *R. aureum* of American auth. in part, not Pursh).]

R. oxyacanthoides L.   Canada Gooseberry.   Fausse-épine
/ST/X/   (N)   Swampy or rocky woods, thickets, and clearings (ranges of Canadian taxa outlined below), S to Mont., S.Dak., Minn., Ill., Ohio, and Pa. MAPS and synonymy: *see* below.
1   Fruiting branches very thickly bristly when young and usually remaining so and with 1–3(5) nodal spines to 1 cm long; leaves and floral bracts usually strongly glandular-puberulent at least beneath; stamens about equalling the petals; [*Grossularia* Mill.; S-cent. Yukon, Great Bear L., Great Slave L., and L. Athabasca (Alta. and Sask.), through B.C.–Alta.–Sask. to Man. (N to Churchill), Ont. (N to Fort Severn, Hudson Bay, ca. 56°N), and Que. (N to SE James Bay; type from the Hudson Bay region, perhaps in Que.); MAPS (aggregate species): Hultén 1968*b*:590; Raup 1947: pl. 27] . .
. . . . var. *oxyacanthoides*

1 Fruiting branches rarely bristly at least in the middle and upper internodes; nodal spines to 8 mm long; leaves and floral bracts not glandular; stamens distinctly surpassing the petals.

    2 Leaves densely soft-pubescent beneath, subtruncate to cordate at base; [*R. hirtellum* var. *calc.* Fern., the type from the Gaspé Pen., E Que.; S Man. (Max L., Turtle Mt.), Ont. (forms intermediate between vars. *calcicola* and *hirtellum* reported N to the W James Bay region by Dutilly, Lepage, and Duman 1954), Que. (similar intermediate forms reported N to the E James Bay region by Dutilly, Lepage, and Duman 1958), N.B. (Charlotte, Restigouche, and Gloucester counties), and N.S.] . . . . var. *calcicola* Fern.

    2 Leaves merely pilose on the nerves beneath.

        3 Leaves cuneate or cuneate-truncate at base; [*R. (Grossularia) hirt.* Michx., the type from Saguenay Co., E Que.; *R. rotundifolium sensu* John Macoun 1883, in part, perhaps not Michx.; Sask. (McKague), Man. (N to Berens River, about 165 mi N of Winnipeg), Ont. (N to Fort Severn, Hudson Bay, ca. 56°N), Que. (N to NE James Bay at 54°25′N, L. Mistassini, and the Côte-Nord), Nfld., N.B., P.E.I., and N.S.] . . . . var. *hirtellum* (Michx.) Scoggan

        3 Leaves broadly rounded to cordate at base; [*R. saxosum* Hook.; *R. hirt.* var. *sax.* (Hook.) Fern.; Alta. (Edmonton), S Sask. (Tisdale), Man. (N to Moosehorn), Que. (N to the Côte-Nord), Nfld., N.B., P.E.I., and N.S.] . . . . var. *saxosum* (Hook.) Cov.

R. sanguineum Pursh   Red or Blood-Currant
/T/W/   (N)   Moist to dryish valleys and open or wooded slopes from B.C. (N to Quesnel, ca. 53°N) to Calif. [*Calobotrya* Spach].

R. setosum Lindl.
/ST/(X)/   (N)   Rocky slopes from Mont. and Alta. (N to Edmonton; reported from Strathcona Park, Vancouver Is., SW B.C., by Eastham 1947, where probably introd.) to Sask. (Breitung 1957a; concerning reports from Man., see Scoggan 1957), Ont. (W James Bay watershed between the Moose and Kapiskau rivers; Dutilly, Lepage, and Duman 1954), and W-cent. Que. (E James Bay watershed N to ca. 54°N; Dutilly, Lepage, and Duman 1958), S to Wyo., Nebr., and Mich. [*Grossularia* Cov.].

R. sylvestre (Lam.) Mert. & Koch   European Red Currant
European; commonly cult. in N. America and spreading to open woods and thickets, as in SW B.C. (Vancouver Is.; Carter and Newcombe 1921), SE Man. (a clearing at Otterburne, about 30 mi S of Winnipeg; Löve and Bernard 1959), Ont. (N to Sheek Is., Stormont Co.; Dore and Gillett 1955), Que. (N to Bic, Rimouski Co.; GH), N.B., P.E.I. (Charlottetown; GH), and N.S. [*R. rubrum* L. in part; *R. rubrum* var. *sativum* Rchb. (*R. sat.* (Rchb.) Syme); *R. vulgare* Lam. and its var. *syl.* Lam.].

R. triste Pallas   Red Currant
/ST/X/eA/   (N)   Moist woods to montane rocky slopes from N Alaska–Yukon–Dist. Mackenzie (N to ca. 68°N) to Great Bear L., Great Slave L., L. Athabasca (Alta. and Sask.), northernmost Man.–Ont., Que. (N to S Ungava Bay and the Côte-Nord), S Labrador (Fernald *in* Gray 1950), Nfld., N.B., P.E.I., and N.S., S to Oreg., S.Dak., and Va.; E Asia. [*R. albinervium* Michx.; *R. propinquum* Turcz.; incl. var. *alaskanum* Berger]. MAPS: Hultén 1968b:593; Raymond 1950b: fig. 3, p. 11; Raup 1947: pl. 28.

    Forma *pyriforme* Lepage (berries obovate in outline rather than globose) is known from N Que. (Larch R. at 57°35′N; type from the Kaniapiskau R. at 57°32′N).

R. viscosissimum Pursh   Sticky Currant
/T/W/   (N)   Moist to dryish slopes up to near timberline from S B.C. (N to Lillooet and Sicamous) and SW Alta. (Waterton Lakes; Breitung 1957b) to Calif. and NW Colo.

R. watsonianum Koehne
/T/W/   (N)   Ravines and ridges in the Cascade Mts. of Wash. and Oreg. and reported by
Boivin (personal communication) from the Monashee Mts. of SE B.C.

SAXIFRAGA L.   [3189]   Saxifrage

(Ref.: J.K. Small and P.A. Rydberg, N. Am. Flora 22:126–57. 1905; *Saxifraga,* etc.)
1 Leaves entire or essentially so (apart from marginal ciliation, when present;
   S. pensylvanica may be sought here); hypanthium only slightly developed and
   scarcely enlarged at maturity . . . .*GROUP 1*
1 Leaves more or less toothed or lobed (merely remotely denticulate in
   S. pensylvanica and minutely serrulate in *S. aizoön*).
   2 Flowering stem leafy (*S. mertensiana* may sometimes be sought here); basal
      rosettes of leaves present or wanting . . . .*GROUP 2* (p. 881)
   2 Flowering stem scapose, usually leafless (but usually bracted), the foliage-leaves
      all or mostly in a basal rosette (*S. mertensiana* with up to 3 leaves just above the
      base); sepals cleft nearly to base or at least to the middle, the hypanthium usually
      poorly developed . . . .*GROUP 3* (p. 882)

GROUP 1

1 Flowering stems scapose, leafless or with at most 3 reduced bract-like leaves.
   2 Plant low and mat-forming (resembling *Diapensia lapponica*), with numerous
      sterile leafy branches; flowering stem to 8 cm tall, glabrous or pubescent with
      purple-tipped hairs, sometimes bearing 1–3 reduced leaves; leaves fleshy and
      more or less terete or revolute, mostly not over 1 cm long, oblanceolate or
      spatulate, glabrous or their bases sparingly long-ciliate, tapering to a petiolar
      base; flowers solitary or up to 4 in a loose cymose inflorescence (lower branches
      usually with 1–3 leaf-like bractlets); calyx saucer-shaped, often purplish-tinged,
      the spreading, oval to oblong-ovate lobes 2 or 3 mm long; petals white; follicles
      to 12 mm long, often purplish-mottled; (Alaska–B.C.) . . . .*S. tolmiei*
   2 Plant to over 3 dm tall, lacking sterile leafy branches, the flowering stems mostly
      solitary, leafless, from coarsely pilose to pubescent or subglabrous below, usually
      copiously glandular-pubescent with purple-tipped hairs above and in the
      inflorescence; leaves often bulbiferous in their axils, lanceolate to ovate or
      obovate, to about 1 dm long and 6 cm broad; flowers rather numerous in a
      compact cymose panicle; calyx broadly conic, the reflexed (sometimes merely
      spreading), oblong-lanceolate to deltoid lobes 1 or 2 mm long; follicles to 5 mm
      long, often reddish or purplish; (S B.C.) . . . .*S. integrifolia*
1 Flowering stems leafy.
   3 Leaves (at least the lower ones) opposite, thick and leathery, coarsely ciliate,
      oblanceolate to obovate, to 7 mm long; flowers normally rose-lilac to purple,
      solitary and terminal; plants loosely matted to densely caespitose, commonly less
      than 6 cm tall.
      4 Upper stem-leaves normally all opposite, the lower ones mostly 4-ranked;
         petals typically rose-lilac to deep purple, to 1 cm long; (transcontinental in
         arctic, subarctic, and alpine regions) . . . .*S. oppositifolia*
      4 Upper stem-leaves opposite or alternate, the lower ones mostly opposite,
         rarely 4-ranked on the fertile shoots; petals pale rose to purplish, to 12 mm
         long; (Greenland) . . . .[*S. nathorstii*]
   3 Leaves alternate, usually longer; stems erect or ascending; flowers usually yellow
      (white and usually strongly purple-spotted above the middle in *S. bronchialis*),
      usually rather numerous in cymose panicles.
      5 Leaves densely pectinate-fringed with whitish broad-based cilia to 0.5 mm
         long, usually about 2 mm long (but up to 4 mm) and 1 mm broad, soon
         becoming whitish, parchment-like, and translucent; flowers small, the petals

minute; capsules to 3 mm long; plant cushion-forming or very densely matted; (Alaska) . . . . *S. eschscholtzii*

5   Leaves not pectinate-fringed, larger; flowers, petals, and capsules larger.
   6   Plant with numerous slender whip-like naked stolons producing tiny rosettes at their rooting tips; leaves oblanceolate, acute, the lower ones (to 2 cm long and 4 mm broad) spinulose-tipped and pseudo-serrate with a marginal row of pale bristles, the narrower upper ones merely glandular-ciliate; flowers 1–3, the pale-yellow petals about twice as long as the densely black-glandular-stipitate sepals; (transcontinental) . . . .*S. flagellaris*
   6   Plants otherwise.
      7   Leaves spinulose-tipped at the acute apex, rigid, closely crowded and overlapping, linear-lanceolate to narrowly elliptic, strongly marcescent, bristly-ciliate, to about 1.5 cm long and 3 mm broad; calyx saucer-shaped, the spreading-ascending, oval to triangular lobes to 3 mm long; petals white, usually strongly purple-spotted above the middle; capsule usually purplish, to 5 mm long (exclusive of the slightly divergent beaks); (Alaska–B.C.–Alta.) . . . .*S. bronchialis*
      7   Leaves not spinulose-tipped; petals yellow, often orange-dotted toward base.
         8   Flowers usually several in terminal cymes; petals deep yellow, slightly longer than the ascending sepals; follicles about 5 mm long; pedicels and base of calyx minutely glandular-puberulent; leaves spreading-ascending, linear to linear-oblong, fleshy, blunt, glabrous or sparsely ciliate, sessile, usually crowded and overlapping; (transcontinental) . . . .*S. aizoides*
         8   Flowers usually solitary; petals pale yellow, much longer than the sepals; leaves erect-ascending.
            9   Flowering stems with up to about 15 rather crowded glabrous leaves to 3 cm long and 6 mm broad, rusty-woolly above and on the calyces; sepals more or less ciliate with reddish hairs, strongly reflexed in fruit; petals elliptic to oblong or obovate, clawless, to about 1.5 cm long; follicles to about 1.5 cm long; (essentially transcontinental in wet arctic, subarctic, and alpine regions) . . . .*S. hirculus*
            9   Flowering stems with normally not more than 3 leaves, with numerous dark-headed short glandular hairs at least above; leaves to 9 mm long and 3 mm broad, glabrous to glandular-hairy; sepals glabrous or minutely glandular-hairy, spreading-ascending; petals somewhat broader in outline, abruptly narrowed to a short claw, they and the follicles less than 1 cm long; (Aleutian Is. to w Dist. Mackenzie) . . . .*S. serpyllifolia*

GROUP 2 (see p. 880)

1   Leaves (at least the lower) with 3 apical cartilaginous-margined cuspidate teeth (otherwise entire except for marginal ciliation), very rigid, often reddish purple; hypanthium only slightly developed, scarcely enlarged at maturity, the sepals distinct nearly to base; flowers rather numerous; petals white or cream-colour (rarely pinkish-tinged), to 7 mm long; plants usually matted, the dead leaves more or less crowded on the numerous, and often trailing, basal shoots.
   2   Terminal teeth of leaves ending in a long rigid spine-like mucro; leaves cuneate-oblong or -oblanceolate, to 2 cm long, the marginal cilia weak and gland-tipped; petals spotted with orange or purplish dots; capsules to 8 mm long; (trans-continental) . . . .*S. tricuspidata*
   2   Terminal teeth with small mucros or none; leaves broadly obovate, to about 1 cm

long and about half as broad, the marginal cilia firmer and never gland-tipped; petals unspotted; capsules to about 6 mm long; (Queen Charlotte Is.) . . . . . . *S. taylori*

1 Leaves variously toothed or lobed, but not with 3 apical cuspidate teeth (often 3-toothed in *S. adscendens,* but the teeth then soft and not cartilaginous); hypanthium well developed, commonly enlarged at maturity and usually longer than the sepals.

   3 Leaves with a marginal limy encrustation (a lime-encrusted pore on the upper surface at the base of each appressed cartilaginous serrulation), those of the basal rosette flat, leathery, marcescent, oblong to spatulate or narrowly obovate, sessile, to 4 cm long; flowers rather numerous; petals white, usually red-dotted; (Dist. Mackenzie; Ont. to Labrador, Nfld., and N.S.) . . . .*S. aizoön*

   3 Leaves lacking a marginal limy encrustation, softer, coarsely toothed or lobed.

      4 Leaves sessile or subsessile; petals white, deciduous; plants often strongly glandular-pubescent, loosely to densely caespitose, with perennial, very leafy caudices and numerous basal offshoots covered with the overlapping remains of old leaves.

         5 Plant not strongly caespitose, usually single-stemmed from a basal rosette of 3(5)-toothed (rather than lobed) leaves, those of the often basally branched flowering stems usually more prominently toothed than the rosette-leaves; petals abruptly narrowed to a short but distinct claw; anther-filaments shorter than the sepals; (Alaska–Yukon–Dist. Mackenzie–B.C.–sw Alta.) . . . . *S. adscendens*

         5 Plant usually strongly caespitose; leaves usually lobed (rather than toothed), those of the simple flowering stems usually less deeply lobed than the rosette-leaves (sometimes entire); petals gradually narrowed to a broad base, scarcely clawed; filaments longer than the sepals; (transcontinental) . . . .*S. caespitosa*

      4 Leaves (at least the basal ones) slender-petioled, the lower ones rotund-cordate to reniform, rather deeply 3–7(9)-lobed; petals white, often with pinkish or purplish veins; plants perennial from a small rhizome, no caudex developed.

         6 Lowermost 1 or 2 (sometimes all) flowers replaced by clusters of small reddish-purple bulblets; upper stem-leaves (as well as the basal leaves) often bearing numerous pale rice-like bulblets in their axils; ovary scarcely 1/4 inferior at anthesis, the calyx-lobes up to 4 times as long as the adnate lower portion; stems rather stout, commonly at least 1 dm tall, rather thickly glandular-pubescent to greyish-glandular-pilose or rusty-lanate below; (transcontinental) . . . .*S. cernua*

         6 Flowers usually all normal, none of them replaced by clusters of bulblets; stem slender, its leaves not bearing axillary bulblets; plants more or less glandular-pubescent at least in the inflorescence.

            7 Basal leaves 3–5-lobed, rather fleshy, to about 2 cm broad, not bearing bulblets in their axils; petals to 6 mm long; capsules to 7 mm long; stems slender; (transcontinental) . . . .*S. rivularis*

            7 Basal leaves 5–8-lobed, thinner and often broader, frequently bearing bulblets in their axils; petals and capsules commonly longer; plants stouter; (Alaska–Yukon–Dist. Mackenzie) . . . .*S. sibirica*

GROUP 3 (*see* p. 880)

1 Leaves with narrow but distinct pale cartilaginous margins, the blade orbicular to reniform, crenate-dentate, rounded at apex, with long hairs on both surfaces, abruptly narrowed to a slender petiole at least twice the length of the blade; petals sometimes dotted with yellow or red, slightly unequal, spreading; anther-filaments spatulate; panicle open; (introd. in ?Nfld.) . . . .[*S. hirsuta*]

1 Leaves not cartilaginous-margined.

2 Leaves cordate-rotund to reniform, usually at least as broad as long, to over 5 cm broad, shorter than the petioles; sepals reflexed in age; anther-filaments clavate; panicle open; (B.C. and/or Alta.).

    3 Leaves with thin, membranous, mostly connate-sheathing stipules, the petioles and scape-like stem usually pilose; leaf-blades shallowly crenate-lobed (the lobes themselves often 3-toothed), usually sparsely hirsute at least beneath; bulblets generally replacing at least some of the flowers and also usually present in the axils of the leaves; petals white, to 5 mm long; capsules reflexed; stem commonly pilose and often glandular below, becoming pilose-pubescent and purplish-glandular above (at least the longer hairs multicellular); rhizomes short and thick, the plants tending to form large clumps; (s Alaska–B.C.–Alta.) . . . . *S. mertensiana*

    3 Leaves with narrow, non-sheathing stipular margins, mostly very coarsely simple-toothed or -lobed; bulblets lacking; capsules erect or nearly so; rhizomes elongate and slender.

        4 Petioles and scape (below as well as above) copiously pubescent with long curly multicellular hairs; leaves minutely soft-pubescent on both sides; flowers yellowish, in narrow and often spike-like panicles; (Alaska–Yukon) . . . . *S. spicata*

        4 Petioles, leaves, and lower part of scape glabrous or nearly so; flowers white, in more open panicles.

            5 Inflorescence glandular-puberulent to -pubescent, the hairs mostly 1–3-celled, the gland-tip often reddish purple; petals usually dissimilar (2 or 3 broader than the others but with the oblong to oval blade not more than 1.5 times as long as broad), often truncate to slightly cordate at base and narrowed abruptly to a slender claw; (B.C.) . . . . *S. odontoloma*

            5 Inflorescence usually somewhat pilose with often wavy or curly, several-celled hairs, not conspicuously glandular; petals mostly alike, the blades usually well over 1.5 times as long as broad, cuneate to rounded at base and narrowed gradually to a rather wide claw; (Alaska–B.C.–Alta.) . . . . *S. punctata*

2 Leaves narrower in outline, mostly lanceolate to obovate or fan-shaped, the blade usually much longer than broad and longer than the petiole.

    6 Leaves very large, to about 3 dm long, lanceolate to narrowly ovate or spatulate-oblong, more or less pubescent, remotely short-dentate (often appearing entire), tapering to short, broad, more or less clasping petioles; petals normally yellowish white to greenish yellow; anther-filaments filiform-subulate; panicle becoming much interrupted and lax, to 6 dm long; scape to 1.5 m tall, soft, stoutish, glandular-pilose to villous, especially above; (s Ont.) . . . . *S. pensylvanica*

    6 Leaves smaller and more distinctly toothed; petals usually white or creamy (sometimes pink in age; petals greenish purple in *S. hieracifolia*), often with 2 yellow basal spots; scapes lower.

        7 Petals dissimilar, the 3 upper ones lanceolate, with truncate or cordate bases, the 2 lower ones elliptic or spatulate and shorter (flowers often partly or wholly replaced by bulblet-like tufts of small leaves); anther-filaments subulate; seeds papillate-striate lengthwise; leaves narrowly spatulate or oblanceolate, toothed only above the middle (usually only near the apex), tapering to narrowly winged petioles.

            8 Plant sparingly glandular-pubescent to almost glabrous, the leaves ciliate toward base and often with long scattered hairs at least above, the hairs permanently pale; (transcontinental in arctic, subarctic, and alpine regions) . . . . *S. stellaris*

            8 Plant copiously pubescent with finally rust-coloured hairs; (s Alaska to w Dist. Mackenzie and mts. of B.C. and sw Alta.) . . . . *S. ferruginea*

7 Petals about equal in shape and length; seeds variously reticulate or wrinkled (but not uniformly papillose-striate except in *S. lyallii* and *S. ?davurica*).

9 Cymes permanently compact, aggregated into a terminal head or in several heads terminating the short branches of the inflorescence; anther-filaments subulate.

10 Petals greenish purple, about equalling the sepals; inflorescence consisting of several sessile or subsessile heads of cymes, each head subtended by a conspicuous bract (lower bracts more or less leaf-like); scape stout, glandular-pubescent, to 5 dm tall; (transcontinental in arctic and subarctic regions) . . . . *S. hieracifolia*

10 Petals about equalling or surpassing the sepals; inflorescence relatively open at maturity, at least the lower cymes short-peduncled.

11 Scape glabrous to glandular-pubescent at base and always rather copiously glandular-pubescent above with whitish hairs tipped with a yellowish to reddish gland; petals white or cream-colour; leaves mostly with thick, deltoid to rhombic-deltoid blades, ciliate, generally glabrous above but sparsely to moderately rusty-cobwebby or -pilose beneath; (s B.C. to sw Sask.) . . . . *S. rhomboidea*

11 Scape glandular-puberulent at least above; petals greenish-white to purplish; leaves broadly spatulate, glabrous or essentially so above at maturity; (transcontinental in arctic and subarctic regions) . . . . *S. nivalis*

9 Cymes open at maturity, the panicle with relatively long branches; petals white, often with a pair of yellow spots below the middle.

12 Leaves to about 1 dm long, ovate to oblong, toothed to below the middle, the broad petiole ciliate; sepals ascending; anther-filaments subulate; scape stout but soft, usually glandular-pubescent, to about 3.5 dm tall; (s Man. to Que. and N.B.) . . . . *S. virginiensis*

12 Leaves usually less than 6 cm long; sepals reflexed at maturity; anther-filaments clavate (except in some varieties of *S. occidentalis*); scape usually not over 2.5 dm tall.

13 Leaf-blades flabellate (narrowed with nearly straight margins to the petiole, this also gradually narrowed to base), coarsely few-toothed chiefly above the middle, the teeth directed forward, the blades glabrous or nearly so; calyces, follicles, and bracts purplish black to nearly black at maturity.

14 Inflorescence paniculate, the main axis prolonged, the relatively long branches bearing scattered capitate glands; petals white, oblong-oval, rounded to a short but distinct claw, with 2 yellow basal blotches; capsules to 12 mm long; (Alaska to sw Dist. Mackenzie and mts. of B.C. and sw Alta.) . . . . .
. . . . *S. lyallii*

14 Inflorescence corymbose, the main axis scarcely prolonged, the short branches bearing elongate, multicellular, viscid but not distinctly capitate hairs; petals white or purplish, unblotched; capsule to 9 mm long; (Alaska–Yukon–Dist. Mackenzie) . . . . *S. davurica*

13 Leaf-blades lanceolate to ovate or elliptic, toothed to near base, rather abruptly merging with the relatively broad petiole-summit; calyces, follicles, and bracts becoming purplish but scarcely blackish.

15 Petals markedly surpassing the sepals, white with 2 basal yellow spots and often tinged with pink or purple; leaf-blades glabrous above or nearly so, the smaller ones usually with at

least some reddish tomentum beneath; scapes usually more
or less reddish-glandular; (s B.C. to sw Sask.) . . . . . *S. occidentalis*
15 Petals white with generally 2 basal yellow spots, much
shorter than the sepals; leaf-blades pubescent on both
surfaces but becoming glabrate at least above; scapes
glandular-pubescent at least above; (Alaska–Yukon–Dist.
Mackenzie–n B.C.) . . . . *S. reflexa*

S. adscendens L.
/ST/W/E/ (Hs) Rock crevices, glacial moraines, and alpine gravelly meadows from Alaska
(n to ca. 65°N), s-cent. Yukon, and sw Dist. Mackenzie through the mts. of B.C. and sw Alta.
(n to Jasper) to Oreg., Utah, and Colo.; Europe. [*Muscaria* Small]. MAP (aggregate species):
Hultén 1958: map 229, p. 249; Meusel, Jaeger and Weinert 1965:201.

The N. American plant may be distinguished as var. *oregonensis* (Raf.) Breitung (*Ponista
oreg.* Raf.; *S. petraea sensu* Hooker 1832, not L.; the plant lower and with smaller flowers but
with relatively broader leaves than the typical phase). MAPS: Hulten 1968b:582; Porsild 1966:
map 87, p. 77.

S. aizoides L.   Yellow Mountain-Saxifrage
/AST/X/GEA/ (Ch) Moist calcareous clays, gravels, and rocky ledges from cent. Yukon
and Great Bear L. to Banks Is., s Ellesmere Is., Baffin Is., and northernmost Ungava–Labrador, s in the West to the mts. of se B.C. and sw Alta., farther eastwards s to Great Slave L., n
Man. (s to Lamprey, about 45 mi s of Churchill), cent. Ont. (s to Albany, sw James Bay,
52°11'N), Que. (s to e James Bay at ca. 53°N and the Gaspé Pen.), Labrador (s to ca. 57°N),
Nfld., and N.S. (Big Southwest Brook, Inverness Co.; ACAD; not known from N.B. or P.E.I.); w
Greenland n to ca. 78°N, e Greenland n to 75°18'N; Iceland; Spitsbergen; Europe; a few stations in nw Siberia. [*Leptasea* Haw.; *S. (L.) van-bruntiae* Small]. MAPS: Hultén 1968b:568, and
1958: map 26, p. 45; Porsild 1957: map 206, p. 186; Meusel, Jaeger, and Weinert 1965:205;
Raup 1947: pl. 27; A. Löve and D. Löve, Sven. Bot. Tidskr. 45(2): fig. 8, p. 378. 1951; Meusel
1943: fig. 12b.

S. aizoön Jacq.
/aST/(X)/GE/ (Ch) Calcareous gravels and ledges, an isolated station at the e end of
Great Slave L. (Fairchild Point, 62°43'N, where taken by Raup in 1927; CAN; GH; reported
from Mt. Selwyn and the Wicked R., B.C., ca. 56°N, by Raup 1934), the main area from north-
ernmost Baffin Is. to Ont. (L. Nipigon; n shore of L. Superior; Algonquin Park, Renfrew Co.),
Que. (se James Bay n to e Hudson Bay at ca. 56°30'N; s Ungava Bay; Knob Lake dist. at ca.
54°45'N; L. Mistassini; Rivière-du-Loup, Temiscouata Co.; Bic and Rimouski, Rimouski Co.;
Côte-Nord; Gaspé Pen.), Labrador (n to Komaktorvik Fjord, 59°17'N), Nfld., N.B. (near St.
John; NBM), and N.S. (Kings, Cumberland, Inverness, and Victoria counties; not known from
P.E.I.), and the mts. of n N.Y. and New Eng. (and shores of L. Superior in ne Minn. and n
Mich.): w Greenland n to ca. 74°30'N, e Greenland n to ca. 71°20'N; Iceland; Europe. MAPS
and synonymy: *see* below.
1 Seeds rugose-papillate, the papillae relatively long and crowded; capsule and calyx-
lobes subequal, the edges of the separated follicle-beaks thickish; [*Chondrosea*
Haw.; European, reports from Canada referring to the following taxa] . . . . . . [var. *aizoön*]
1 Seeds less rugose, their less crowded (sometimes obsolescent) papillae about half
the size of those of var. *aizoön*; capsule usually overtopping the calyx-lobes, the
edges of the separated follicle-beaks thinner; [N. America] . . . . var. *neogaea* Butters
2 Panicle few-flowered; [the reduced northern extreme; type from Manitounuk
Sound, se Hudson Bay, Ungava; also reported by F.K. Butters, Rhodora 46(543):
66. 1944, from Baffin Is., islands in James Bay and Hudson Bay, the Côte-Nord of
e Que., Labrador, Nfld., Greenland, and Iceland] . . . . f. *frigida* Butters
2 Panicle many-flowered; [*S. paniculata* ssp. *neo.* (Butters) D. Löve; *S. cotyledon
sensu* Bachelot de la Pylaie 1823, not L.; range of the species; MAPS: Porsild
1957: map 207, p. 186; the N. American part of the map by Meusel, Jaeger, and
Weinert 1965:204, for the European *S. paniculata* Mill. (*S. cotyledon* L.) is

applicable here]. The report of *S. aizoön* from Sask. by Hooker (1832) is evidently based upon a collection from "British N.W. America" by Richardson or Drummond (collection in CAN, bearing the annotation "(?) Saskatchewan"). It is not known from that province. The report from Flin Flon (and probably, also, from Riding Mt.), Man., by Lowe 1943, is based upon *S. tricuspidata* (relevant collection in WIN). The European *S. umbrosa* L., habitally similar to *S. aizoön* and also with white-cartilaginous-margined leaves, is reported by Rouleau (1956) as introd. in Nfld., but with no indication as to it being a garden-escape or persisting . . . .
. . . . f. *neogaea*

S. bronchialis L.

/aST/W/EA/ (Ch) Cliffs and talus at low to alpine elevations (ranges of Canadian taxa outlined below), s to Oreg. and N.Mex.; (the inclusion of Greenland in the range by Hitchcock et al. 1961, doubtless refers to *S. tricuspidata*); E Europe (the Urals); Asia. MAPS and synonymy: *see* below.

1 Petal-spots (at least the uppermost) deep red, the petals scarcely clawed; leaves to about 12 mm long, acute; [*S. (Leptasea) aust.* Wieg.; B.C. (N to near Prince Rupert) and SW Alta.; MAPS: J.A. Calder and D.B.O. Savile, Brittonia 11(4): fig. 7, p. 236, and fig. 8, p. 239. 1959] . . . . ssp. *austromontana* (Wieg.) Piper
1 Petal-spots yellow (or rarely the uppermost red-tinged), the petals distinctly clawed . . . . .
. . . . ssp. *funstonii* (Small) Hult.
   2 Leaves usually not over 5 mm long, obtuse or rounded at apex; [var. *minor* H. & A.; *S. (Leptasea) cher.* Don; Attu, W Aleutian Is.; MAPS: Hultén 1968b:570; Calder and Savile, loc. cit., fig. 9, p. 244] . . . . var. *cherlerioides* (Don) Engl.
   2 Leaves to 12 mm long, acute; [*Leptasea fun.* (Small) Fedde; *S. bron.* ssp. *fun.* var. *purpureomaculata* Hult.; *S. ?pseudo-burseriana* Fisch.; *S. ?nitida* Ledeb., not DC.; Alaska–Yukon–W Dist. Mackenzie–N B.C. (s to ca. 59°30′N); MAPS: Hultén 1968b:570; Calder and Savile, loc. cit., fig. 9, p. 244] . . . . var. *funstonii*

S. caespitosa L.

/AST/X/GEA/ (CH) Gravels, cliffs, and rocky slopes at low to alpine elevations, the aggregate species from the Aleutian Is. and coasts of Alaska and Dist. Mackenzie throughout the Canadian Arctic Archipelago to northernmost Ellesmere Is. and northernmost Ungava–Labrador, s in the West through the mts. of B.C. and W Alta. to Nev., Ariz., and N.Mex., farther eastwards s to s Canada as noted below; circumgreenlandic; Iceland; Spitsbergen; N Eurasia. MAPS and synonymy: *see* below.

1 Petals mostly not over 5 or 6 mm long and usually less than twice the length of the triangular to ovate calyx-lobes.
   2 Flower usually solitary at the tip of the stem; calyx purplish black; [*S. uniflora* R. Br., the type from Melville Is.; *S. groenlandica* var. *uni.* (R. Br.) Simmons; *S. venosa* Haw.; arctic part of the area; MAP: Porsild 1957: map 209, p. 187] . . . .
. . . . ssp. *uniflora* (R. Br.) Porsild
   2 Flowers mostly 3–5; calyx greenish purple; [*S. (Muscaria) sileniflora* Sternb. in part. (Engler and Irmscher, Pflanzenreich 4(117):375–77 (1958 reprint), list var. *drummondii* Engl. & Irmsch. and var. *delicatula* (Small) Engl. & Irmsch. (*M. (S.) del.* Small) under this species, merging *S. exarata* Hook. and *Muscaria emarginata*, *M. ?micropetala*, and *M. monticola* Small with var. *drummondii*, and *S. caespitosa* var. *minima* Blank. with var. *delicatula*. The key to *Muscaria* and the species descriptions by J.K. Small and P.A. Rydberg, N. Am. Flora 22:129–30. 1905, raise doubts as to the validity of some or all of these concepts); NW Dist. Mackenzie, SW Yukon, and the mts. of B.C. and SW Alta. (MAP: Porsild 1966: map 88, p. 77; *S. caesp.* ssp. *monticola* (Small) Porsild); s Ellesmere Is. and the Hudson Bay–James Bay region (MAP: Porsild 1957: map 210, p. 187; ssp. *exar.*)] . . . . . .
. . . . ssp. *exaratoides* (Simm.) Engl. & Irmsch.
1 Petals to 1 cm long and up to about 4 times the length of the oblong-lanceolate calyx-lobes.

3   Lower stem-leaves often bearing buds in their axils; [known from Wash., Oreg., and Mont., and a collection in Herb. V from the Telkwa Range of B.C. at ca. 54°N has been placed here] . . . . ssp. *subgemmifera* Engl. & Irmsch.

3   Leaves not bearing buds in their axils.

    4   Basal leaves (3)5–7(11)-lobed, the lobes obtusish to acutish or even mucronate; leaves sparingly to densely long-hairy with multicellular hairs; [*S. decipiens* Ehrh.; w Greenland N to ca. 70°N; MAP: Hultén 1958: map 77, p. 97] . . . . ssp. *decipiens* (Ehrh.) Engl. & Irmsch.

    4   Basal leaves 3–5-lobed, the lobes obtusish (rarely acutish); leaves sparingly to densely short-hairy; [f. *multiflora* Calder; *S. groenlandica* L.; *S. hypnoides* (*S. spathulata* Haw.) *sensu* J.M. Macoun 1903, not L.: ?Alaska; w Dist. Mackenzie to Devon Is., Que., Labrador, and Nfld.; MAPS: Porsild 1957: map 208, p. 186; Hultén 1968*b*:583, and 1958: map 78 (aggregate species), p. 97; A. Löve and D. Löve, Sven. Bot. Tidskr. 45(2): fig. 10 (aggregate species; the general area too broad for N. America), p. 382. 1951; Meusel, Jaeger, and Weinert 1965:203 (aggregate species)] . . . . ssp. *caespitosa*

S. cernua L.   Nodding Saxifrage

/AST/X/GEA/ (Hs) Moist ledges, sands, and gravels, the aggregate species from the coasts of Alaska–Yukon–Dist. Mackenzie–Dist. Keewatin to northernmost Ellesmere Is. and northernmost Ungava–Labrador, s in the West through the mts. of B.C. and sw Alta. to Wash., Nev., and Idaho, farther eastwards s to Great Bear L., s Dist. Keewatin, northernmost Ont. (isolated in Cook Co., NE Minn.), Southampton Is., N Que. (s to the Larch R. at 57°35′N), and N Labrador (s to ca. 57°N; the report from Nfld. by John Macoun (1883; taking up the report of *S. sibirica* L. from there by Pursh 1814) may be based upon *S. rivularis*); isolated on Mt. Logan of the Shickshock Mts., Gaspé Pen., E Que.; circumgreenlandic; Iceland; Spitsbergen; Eurasia. MAPS and synonymy: *see* below.

1   Upper stem-leaves broadly ovate to reniform, subcordate to cordate at base, scarcely differentiated from the floral bracts; [mts. of Alta.; Ellesmere Is., Baffin Is., Dist. Keewatin, Southampton Is., N Ungava–Labrador, SE Hudson Bay, and the Shickshock Mts. of the Gaspé Pen., E Que. (type from Tabletop Mt.)] . . . . f. *latibracteata* (Fern. & Weath.) Polunin

1   Upper stem-leaves mostly narrower, cuneate to truncate at base, the floral bracts abruptly differentiated.

    2   Stem branching; [s Baffin Is.; Polunin 1940] . . . . f. *ramosa* Gmel.

    2   Stem unbranched.

        3   Leaves deeply incised, with much narrower and more pointed segments than those of the typical form, the radical ones thus "star-shaped", the cauline ones more or less flabelliform; [var. *exilioides* Polunin, the type from Chesterfield, E Dist. Keewatin; also reported from Wolstenholme, northernmost Que., by Polunin 1940] . . . . f. *exilioides* (Polunin) Scoggan

        3   Leaves merely 5–7-lobed.

            4   Plant robust, with relatively numerous blackish bulblets in the leaf-axils; [E Dist. Keewatin and Southampton Is.; Polunin 1940] . . . . f. *bulbillosa* Engl. & Irmsch.

            4   Plant relatively weak and with fewer pale bulblets in the leaf-axils; [*Lobaria* Haw.; *S. sibirica sensu* Hooker 1832, in part, not L.; range of the species; MAPS (aggregate species): Hultén 1968*b*:575; Porsild 1957: map 211, p. 187] . . . . f. *cernua*

S. davurica Willd.

/aSs/W/A/ (Hr) Dry to wet places at low to moderate elevations in the Aleutian Is., Alaska–Yukon (N to ca. 70°N), and sw-cent. Dist. Mackenzie (near the Yukon boundary at ca. 65°N); Asia. [Incl. f. *grandipetala* Engl. & Irmsch. and *S. unalaschcensis* Sternb. (*S. flabellifolia* R. Br.)]. MAPS: combine the maps by Hultén 1968*b*:578 (ssp. *grand.*) and 579 (*S. unal.*); Porsild 1966: map 89 (ssp. *grand.*), p. 78; Meusel, Jaeger, and Weinert 1965:200 (*S. unal.*).

S. eschscholtzii Sternb.
/Ss/W/eA/ (Ch) Calcareous gravels, cliffs, and ledges in the mts. of Alaska (N to ca. 69°N); NE Siberia. [*S. (Leptasea) fimbriata* Don]. MAPS: Hultén 1968*b*:566, and 1945: map 702, p. 975.

S. ferruginea Graham
/sT/W/ (Hr) Wet rocks at low to high elevations from S Alaska–Yukon and the Mackenzie R. Delta (CAN) through B.C. and SW Alta. (Waterton Lakes) to N Calif., Idaho, and Mont. [*Hexaphoma* Raf.; *Spatularia* and *Hydatica* Small; *Sax. bongardii* Presl; *Spat. (Sax.) newcombei* Small; *Sax. leucanthemifolia* vars. *ferr.* (Grah.) T. & G. and *brunoniana* (Bong.) Engelm. (*S. stellaris* var. *br.* Bong.; *Spat. br.* (Bong.) Small); incl. vars. *cuneata, diffusa,* and *grandiflora* Johnson]. MAPS: Hultén 1968*b*:581, and 1958: map 92, p. 111.
    Some of our material is referable to var. *vreelandii* (Small) Engl. & Irmsch. (var. *macounii* Engl. & Irmsch.; *Spat. (Hyd.) vree.* Small; *Sax. nutkama (nootkana)* Howell; at least some of the flowers replaced by leafy bulblets).

S. flagellaris Willd.
/AST/X/GEA/ (Hsr (Ch)) Streambanks, gravelly and rocky places, and talus at low to high elevations, the aggregate species from northernmost Alaska, cent. Yukon, and NW Dist. Mackenzie (Richardson Mts.) throughout the Canadian Arctic Archipelago to northernmost Ellesmere Is. and Devon Is., S in the West through B.C. and the mts. of SW Alta. to Ariz. and N.Mex.; NW Greenland S to ca. 78°N, NE Greenland S to ca. 72°N; Spitsbergen; Eurasia. MAPS and synonymy: see below.
1 Hypanthium flat.
    2 Stolons lacking glands; stem-leaves considerably longer than the internodes and
       crowded at the base of the stem; [*Leptasea flag.* Small; Eurasia only, reports from
       Alaska–Canada referring to the following taxa; MAPS: Eric Hultén 1958: map 231,
       p. 251, and Sven. Bot. Tidskr. 58(1): fig. 4, p. 94. 1964] . . . . [ssp. *flagellaris*]
    2 Stolons more or less glandular; stem-leaves shorter and more evenly distributed;
       [incl. var. *stenosepala* Trautv.; *S. setigera* Pursh; Alaska to W Dist. Mackenzie and
       the mts. of B.C. and SW Alta.; MAPS: on the above-noted 1964 map by Hultén;
       Hultén 1968*b*:569] . . . . ssp. *setigera* (Pursh) Tolm.
1 Hypanthium turbinate (top-shaped), forming a more or less conical lump below the
    base of the calyx-lobes; [var. *plat.* Trautv.; Alaska to Ellesmere Is. and N Greenland;
    MAPS: Hultén, loc. cit., 1964: fig. 5, p. 95; 1958: map 231, p. 251; and 1968*b*:569] . . . .
    . . . . ssp. *platysepala* (Trautv.) Porsild

S. hieracifolia Waldst. & Kit.
/aSs/X/GEA/ (Hr) Moist places, solifluction areas, and alpine meadows from the coasts of Alaska–Yukon–NW Dist. Mackenzie to Melville Is., Devon Is., and N Baffin Is., S to S Alaska–Yukon–Dist. Keewatin; E Greenland between ca. 70° and 75°N; Spitsbergen; Eurasia. [*Micranthes* Haw.; *S. plantaginifolia* Hook.; *S. integrifolia sensu* A.E. Porsild, Rhodora 41:241. 1939, not Hook.]. MAPS: Hultén 1968*b*:580; Porsild 1957: map 214, p. 187.
    Some of the Alaskan material has been distinguished as var. *angusticapsula* Hult. (capsules relatively narrow; type from Eagle Summit, N-cent. Alaska). Other Alaskan material has been separated as var. *rufopilosa* Hult. (leaves rusty-pilose beneath rather than essentially glabrous; type from Wainwright, Alaska).

S. hirculus L.   Yellow Marsh-Saxifrage
/AST/X/GEA/ (Hs (Ch)) Bogs, wet meadows, and streambanks from the Aleutian Is. and coasts of Alaska–Yukon–Dist. Mackenzie–Dist. Keewatin throughout the Canadian Arctic Archipelago to northernmost Ellesmere Is. and northermost Que. (not known from Labrador), S to S Alaska–Yukon, Great Bear L., N Man. (S to York Factory, 57°N), cent. Ont. (W James Bay S to ca. 53°N), and Que. (S to the E James Bay watershed at 54°19′N); isolated in the mts. of ?Utah and Colo.; NW Greenland between ca. 77° and 79°N, NE Greenland between ca. 73°

and 76°N; Iceland; Spitsbergen; Eurasia. [*Leptasea* Small; *L. alaskana* Small; incl. *S. propinqua* R. Br.]. MAPS: Hultén 1968*b*:568; Porsild 1957: map 215, p. 187; Meusel, Jaeger, and Weinert 1965:201.

[*S. hirsuta* L.]
[M.L. Fernald (Rhodora 28:51. 1926) notes a report by Britton of a collection by Durand of the European *S. geum* L. in Nfld., the exact locality unknown. *S. aizoön* may be the species involved. According to Tutin et al. (1964), the original description of *S. geum* by Linnaeus (1753 (facsimile ed., 1957), not his later concept of the species as described by him in 1762) actually involves a hybrid between *S. hirsuta* and *S. umbrosa* (*see* note under *S. aizoön* f. *neogaea*). [*S. geum* L., 1762, not 1753]. MAPS: Hultén 1958: map 129, p. 149; Fernald 1918*b*: map 15, pl. 13, and 1929: map 44, p. 1505 (both as *S. geum*).]

S. integrifolia Hook.
/T/W/ (Hr) Grassy slopes and prairies to alpine meadows from s B.C. (Vancouver Is. and adjacent islands and mainland) to Calif. and Idaho.
1   Petals white, to 3(4.5) mm long, ovate, oval, or obovate, usually at least twice as
      long as broad.
    2   Leaf-blades mostly strongly ciliate-pilose, usually slightly to densely coarse-
          hirsute as well as rusty-cobwebby beneath, ovate-lanceolate to rhombic-ovate,
          rather gradually narrowed to broad petioles mostly shorter than the blade;
          [*Micranthes (S.) bidens* Small; sw B.C.: Vancouver Is. and adjacent islands] . . . .
          . . . . var. *integrifolia*
    2   Leaf-blades mostly glabrous except for weak marginal ciliation and sometimes a
          sparse rusty-cobwebby pubescence beneath, lanceolate to ovate or deltoid,
          abruptly narrowed to slender petioles often as long as or longer than the blade;
          [*S. claytoniaefolia* Canby; ?B.C.: Hitchcock et al. 1961] . . . .
          . . . . [var. *claytoniaefolia* (Canby) Rosend.]
1   Petals commonly yellowish or greenish-white (often tinged with purple or pink), less
      than 3 mm long, usually spatulate or obovate and more than twice as long as broad.
    3   Leaf-blades mostly rhombic-lanceolate, gradually narrowed to broad, often
          conspicuously ciliate-pilose petioles; stems mostly strongly hirsute at base and
          copiously glandular-pubescent above; inflorescence sometimes glomerulate;
          petals to 2.5 mm long; [*S. bracteosa* var. *lept.* Suksd.; s B.C.: Hitchcock et al.
          1961] . . . . var. *leptopetala* (Suksd.) Engl. & Irmsch.
    3   Leaf-blades mostly rhombic-ovate, abruptly narrowed to relatively slender, weakly
          ciliate to glabrous petioles; stems sparsely pilose to glabrous at base and usually
          only moderately glandular-pubescent above; inflorescence not glomerulate;
          petals much smaller; [*S. col.* Piper; s B.C.] . . . . var. *columbiana* (Piper) Hitchc.

S. lyallii Engl.
/ST/W/ (Hr (Ch)) Wet places, streambanks, and gravelly meadows from Alaska (N to ca. 67°N), the Yukon (N to ca. 63°N), and sw Dist. Mackenzie (Brintnell L., ca. 62°N) through B.C. and the mts. of sw Alta. (N to Jasper) to Wash., Idaho, and w Mont. [*Micranthes* Small; incl. vars. *hultenii* Calder & Savile and *laxa* Engl.; *S. dahurica sensu* Hooker 1832, in part, not Pallas nor *S. davurica* Willd.]. MAPS: Hultén 1968*b*:578; Porsild 1966: map 90, p. 78; Calder and Savile 1960: fig. 3, p. 416; *Atlas of Canada* 1957: map 9, sheet 38; Raup 1947: pl. 26; J.G. Packer, Nat. can. (Que.) 98(2): fig. 5, p. 134. 1971.

S. mertensiana Bong.
/sT/W/ (Hs) Wet places and along gravelly streams from s Alaska through the mts. of B.C. and sw Alta. to nw Calif. and Idaho. MAPS and synonymy (together with a distinguishing key to the scarcely separable *S. nudicaulis* of Alaska): *see* below.
1   Leaves to about 2.5 cm broad, with at most 9 coarse, triangular or ovate, usually
      acute or apiculate lobes; scapes rarely as much as 2 dm tall; [*Ochraria* Small; w
      Alaska, the type locality; MAPS: Hultén 1945: map 712, p. 975, and 1968*b*:576] . . . .
      . . . . *S. nudicaulis* Don

1 Leaves to about 1 dm broad, coarsely crenate-lobed and secondarily crenate-
dentate with obtuse or rounded teeth; scapes to 4 dm tall . . . . *S. mertensiana*
    2 Flowers all normal; [*Heterisia east.* Small; SE B.C.: Boivin 1966*b*] . . . .
    . . . . f. *eastwoodiae* (Small) Boivin
    2 At least some of the flowers replaced by pinkish bulbils; [*Heterisia* Small; *S.
    heteranthera* Hook.; s Alaska (type from Sitka Is.) and mts. (chiefly) of B.C. and
    SW Alta. (Waterton Lakes); MAP: Hultén 1968*b*:571] . . . . f. *mertensiana*

[S. nathorstii (Dusén) Hayek]
[This species, originally published as *S. oppositifolia* var. *nathorstii* Dusén, is known only from
NE Greenland (N to 75°18′N; type from E Greenland). According to Joergensen, Soerensen,
and Westergaard (1958), "*S. Nathorstii* takes up an intermediate position between *S. aizoides*
and *S. oppositifolia,* and several botanists have suggested it being a hybrid between these
two species."]

S. nivalis L.   Alpine Saxifrage
/AST/X/GEA/ (Hr) Dry rocky slopes and ledges, the aggregate species from the E Aleu-
tian Is. and coasts of Alaska–Yukon–Dist. Mackenzie–Dist. Keewatin through the Canadian
Arctic Archipelago to northernmost Ellesmere Is. and northernmost Ungava–Labrador, s to s
Alaska–Yukon (isolated in SE ?B.C.; a 1904 collection in CAN by John Macoun from Ottertail
Pass, on the B.C.–Alta. boundary at ca. 51°N, has been tentatively referred to var. *tenuis* by
Porsild), Great Bear L., s Dist. Keewatin, Que. (coast of Hudson Bay s to ca. 56°30′N; Ungava
Bay watershed s to ca. 57°30′N; Shickshock Mts. of the Gaspé Pen.), and N Labrador (s to ca.
58°N); circumgreenlandic; Iceland; Spitsbergen; Eurasia. MAPS and synonymy: *see* below.
1 Inflorescence relatively open and few-flowered, with slender branches and
  peduncles; follicles 5 or 6 mm long; lower leaf-surfaces (and petioles) with coarse
  rusty hairs; [*S. tenuis* (Wahl.) Sm.; *S. gaspensis* Fern.; incl. vars. *labradorica* Fern.
  and *rufopilosa* Hult.; essentially the range of the species but more southern; MAPS
  (S. tenuis): Porsild 1957: map 220, p. 188; Savile 1961: map I, fig. 2, p. 929] . . . .
  . . . . var. *tenuis* Wahl.
1 Inflorescence a terminal head of clustered cymules or occasionally a few of the
  heads on short branches; follicles 3 or 4 mm long; lower leaf-surfaces lacking coarse
  rusty hairs . . . . var. *nivalis*
    2 Leaves slender-petioled; [Richmond Gulf, SE Hudson Bay, Que.; Dutilly and
    Lepage 1951*b*] . . . . f. *longipetiolata* Engl. & Irmsch.
    2 Leaves tapering gradually to the subpetiolar or subsessile base; [*Micranthes
    Small; S. ?hieracifolia sensu* Waghorne 1895, not Waldst. & Kit.; transcontinental;
    MAPS (aggregate species): Hultén 1968*b*:579; Porsild 1957: map 216, p. 187;
    Meusel, Jaeger, and Weinert 1965:200; Raup 1947: pl. 26] . . . . f. *nivalis*

S. occidentalis Wats.
/T/W/ (Hs) Moist meadows to subalpine rocky slopes (ranges of Canadian taxa outlined
below), s to Oreg., Nev., and Wyo.
1 Inflorescence usually relatively small and compact, rounded to pyramidal, less than 5
  cm long at anthesis and 1 dm long in fruit, the branches ascendant to erect; anther-
  filaments clavate; [*Micranthes* Small; *S. (M.) saximontana* Nels.; *S. ?eriophora* Wats.;
  s B.C., SW Alta. (Waterton Lakes), and SW Sask. (Cypress Hills), the type, as first
  specimen cited, a Drummond collection from the Rocky Mts. of B.C.] . . . . var. *occidentalis*
1 Inflorescence open, its branches commonly spreading, often over 5 cm long at
  anthesis (to over 1 dm long in fruit).
    2 Inflorescence usually distinctly flat-topped; bracts and calyces often reddish-
    pilose-lanate; anther-filaments subulate or only slightly clavate; scapes and
    flowers often purple-tinged; [*Micranthes ruf.* Small, the type from Mt. Finlayson,
    Vancouver Is.; *S. ruf.* (Small) Macoun; SE ?Alaska (*see* Hultén 1945:937); mts. of
    s B.C.] . . . . var. *rufidula* (Small) Hitchc.
    2 Inflorescence usually pyramidal, the branches mostly ascending; bracts and

calyces seldom reddish-pilose; filaments clavate; plants often lacking any purple tinge; [*Micranthes (S.) allenii* and *M. (S.) lata* Small; s B.C.: reported from Lytton by Henry 1915, and from Carbonate Draw in the Selkirk Mts. by A.M. Johnson, Univ. Minn. Stud. Biol. Sci. 4:22. 1919] . . . . .var. *allenii* (Small) Hitchc.

S. odontoloma Piper

/T/W/ (Hr) Subalpine to alpine meadows and wet places from s B.C. (Vancouver Is. and the mainland N to ca. 50°N) to Calif. and N.Mex. [*S. (Micranthes) arguta* of auth., not Don]. MAP: Calder and Savile 1960: fig. 1, p. 412.

A hybrid with *S. lyallii* is reported from s B.C. (near Nelson; South Kootenay Pass) and sw Alta. (Crowsnest Pass; Waterton Lakes) by Calder and Savile (1960).

S. oppositifolia L.   Purple Mountain-Saxifrage

/AST/X/GEA/ (Ch) Tundra and moist calcareous gravels and wet cliffs from the Aleutian Is. and coasts of Alaska–Yukon–Dist. Mackenzie–Dist. Keewatin throughout the Canadian Arctic Archipelago to northernmost Ellesmere Is. and northernmost Ungava–Labrador, s in the West through the mts. of B.C. and sw Alta. (N to Jasper) to Oreg., Idaho, and Wyo., farther eastwards s to Great Bear L., s Dist. Keewatin, NE Man. (Churchill), James Bay (South Twin Is.; Solomon's Temple Is.), Que. (s to NE James Bay at Cape Jones, L. Mistassini, the Côte-Nord, Anticosti Is., and Gaspé Pen.), and Nfld. (not known from the Maritime Provinces), and the mts. of N Vt.; circumgreenlandic; Iceland; Spitsbergen; N Eurasia. MAPS and synonymy: *see* below.

1 Flowers white; [var. *alb.* Lange, the type from Greenland; also reported from the
   Kaumajet Mts., Labrador, at 57°47′N, by M.L. Fernald, Rhodora 38(449):165. 1936] . . . . . .
   . . . . .f. *albiflora* (Lange) Fern.
1 Flowers rose-lilac, becoming violet.
   2 Petals 8–10, the flowers "double"; [type from Resolute Bay, Cornwallis Is.] . . . .
      . . . . .f. *schofieldii* Boivin
   2 Petals 5.
      3 Stem elongate; [Que.: reported from L. Mistassini and from Great Whale R., SE
         Hudson Bay, by Dutilly and Lepage 1947 and 1951*b*, respectively] . . . .
         . . . . .f. *reptans* And. & Hess.
      3 Stem not abnormally elongate.
         4 Leaves at most about 3 mm long; peduncles usually not over 1 cm long;
            [var. *?smalliana* Engl. & Irmsch.; *S. (Antiphylla) ?pulvinata* Small; Alaska–
            Yukon–N B.C. and Ellesmere Is., Devon Is., and Baffin Is. (Polunin 1940);
            MAP (ssp. *smalliana*): Hultén 1968*b*:565] . . . . .f. *pulvinata* And. & Hess.
         4 Leaves to 5 mm long; peduncles to over 3 cm long; [*Antiphylla* Fourr.; *A.
            spathulata arctica* Haw., not *S. spath.* Haw.; transcontinental; MAPS: Hultén
            1968*b*:565; Porsild 1957: map 217, p. 188; Raup 1947: pl. 27; Meusel,
            Jaeger, and Weinert 1965:205; Wynne-Edwards 1937: map 2, p. 24;
            Fernald 1933: map 1, p. 7, and 1918*a*: map 1, pl. 15] . . . . .f. *oppositifolia*

S. pensylvanica L.   Swamp-Saxifrage, Wild-beet

/t/EE/ (Hr) Wet meadows, swamps, and boggy thickets from Minn. to s Ont. (Fort Erie and Long Beach, Welland Co.; John Macoun 1886; Zenkert 1934) and s Maine, s to Mo., Ill., and Va. [*Micranthes* Haw.]. MAPS: G.W. Burns, Am. Midl. Nat. 28(1): fig. 1, p. 129, and fig. 9A, p. 145. 1942.

S. punctata L.

/aST/WW/EA/ (Hr) Moist tundra and streambanks to alpine meadows, the aggregate species from the Aleutian Is. and coasts of Alaska–Yukon–Dist. Mackenzie to sw-cent. Dist Keewatin (Dubawnt L.; CAN), s through the mts. of B.C. and sw Alta. (N to Jasper) to Oreg.; NE Europe; Asia. MAPS and synonymy: *see* below.

1 Panicle-hairs mostly short, erect and tipped with prominent yellowish or reddish
   glands; petals always white.

    2 Leaves glabrous to sparingly pubescent; panicle-branches slender, the panicle usually open especially in fruit; [Asia only; the MAP of the area of the aggregate species by Raup 1947: pl. 26, refers to the following taxa] . . . . [ssp. *punctata*]

    2 Leaves distinctly pubescent; panicle-branches mostly stout, the panicle usually dense; [*S. (Micranthes) nelsoniana* Don, the type from Cape Newenham, Alaska; Alaska–Yukon–NW Dist. Mackenzie; MAPS: Calder and Savile 1960: fig. 4, p. 422; Hultén 1968*b*:572] . . . . ssp. *nelsoniana* (Don) Hult.

1 Panicle-hairs long and flexuous, eglandular or with small gland-tips; petals white or pink-tinged.

    3 Largest leaves with usually less than 12 teeth; capsules to 12 mm long; [B.C.: Queen Charlotte Is. (type from Moresby Is.) and the adjacent mainland; MAPS: on the above-noted map by Calder and Savile; Hultén 1968*b*:574] . . . .
. . . . ssp. *carlottae* Calder & Savile

    3 Largest leaves with up to 18 teeth; capsules at most 8 mm long.

        4 Panicle-hairs appressed; panicle open; plant slender; [*S. (Micranthes) aestivalis* of auth. in part, not Fisch. & Mey.; SW B.C.; MAP: on the above-noted map by Calder and Savile] . . . . ssp. *cascadensis* Calder & Savile

        4 Panicle-hairs ascending; panicle often congested; plant stoutish.

            5 Leaves thick and fleshy; capsules usually cleft less than 1/3 from summit; [Aleutian Is. (type from Carlisle Is.) and St. Paul Is., Alaska; MAPS: on the above-noted map by Calder and Savile; Hultén 1968*b*:572] . . . ssp. *insularis* Hult.

            5 Leaves thin; capsules usually more deeply cleft.

                6 Leaves to over 7 cm broad, essentially glabrous; capsules cleft to about 2/3 from summit; [*S. ?arguta* Don; *S. (Micranthes) ?aestivalis* Fisch. & Mey.; S Alaska, the type from Juneau; MAPS: on the above-noted map by Calder and Savile; Hultén 1968*b*:573] . . . . . . ssp. *pacifica* Hult.

                6 Leaves less than 4 cm broad, glabrous to sparingly pubescent; capsules cleft to 3/4 from summit; [cent. Yukon to the coast of Dist. Mackenzie and NW Dist. Keewatin, S to the mts. of B.C. (type from Azouzetta L.) and SW Alta.; MAPS: on the above-noted map by Calder and Savile; Hultén 1968*b*:573] . . . . ssp. *porsildiana* Calder & Savile

S. reflexa Hook.
/aSs/W/ (Hr) Dry places at low to alpine elevations from the coasts of Alaska–Yukon–NW Dist. Mackenzie (type from N Dist. Mackenzie between the Mackenzie and Coppermine rivers) to northernmost B.C. (CAN). [*Micranthes* Small; *M. yukonensis* Small]. MAPS: Hultén 1968*b*:580; Meusel, Jaeger, and Weinert 1965:200.

S. rhomboidea Greene
/T/W/ (Hr) Moist lowlands to subalpine meadows from B.C. (N to Mt. Selwyn, ca. 56°N; a collection in CAN from near Atlin, ca. 59°35'N, may also belong here), SW Alta. (N to Jasper), and SW Sask. (Cypress Hills; DAO) to Idaho, Utah, and Colo. [*Micranthes* Small; *M. (S.) crenatifolia* Small].

S. rivularis L. Alpine-brook-Saxifrage
/AST/X/GEA/ (Hs) Wet gravelly or mossy cliffs and streambanks from the Aleutian Is. and coasts of Alaska–Yukon–Dist. Mackenzie–Dist. Keewatin throughout the Canadian Arctic Archipelago to northernmost Ellesmere Is. and northernmost Ungava–Labrador, S in the West through the mts. of B.C. and SW Alta. to Mont., farther eastwards S to S Dist. Keewatin, NE Man. (Churchill), Que. (S to SE Hudson Bay at Cape Jones, S Ungava Bay, the Côte-Nord, and Shickshock Mts. of the Gaspé Pen.), S Labrador, and NW Nfld., and the mts. of N.H.; circumgreenlandic; Iceland; Spitsbergen; N Eurasia. [*Lobaria* Haw.; *S. petiolaris* R. Br.; *S. ?cymbalaria sensu* Torrey and Gray 1838–40, not L.; *S. ?sibirica sensu* Hooker 1832, not L., as to the Labrador and Nfld. plants; incl. the long-pedicelled extreme, var. *flexuosa* (Sternb.) Engl. & Irmsch. (*S. flex.* Sternb.), and the dwarf extreme, f. *hyperborea* (R. Br.) Hook. (*S. hyp.* R. Br.)]. MAPS: combine the maps by Hultén 1968*b*:577 (vars. *riv.* and *flex.*); Porsild 1957: map 218, p. 188; Böcher 1954: fig. 47 (bottom), p. 177; Raup 1947: pl. 27.

Forma *purpurascens* Lange (petals purplish red rather than white or merely purple-tinged; type from Greenland) is known from the Canadian Arctic Archipelago (Polunin 1940) and from Stromness Is., James Bay (Dutilly, Lepage, and Duman 1958).

S. serpyllifolia Pursh
/Ss/W/eA/ (Ch) Rock slides and dry places at low to moderate elevations in the Aleutian Is., Alaska (N to ca. 70°N), the Yukon, and W Dist. Mackenzie (N to ca. 64°30′N; CAN); NE Asia. [*Leptasea* Small]. MAPS: Hultén 1968*b*:567; Porsild 1966: map 91, p. 78.
Forma *purpurea* (Hult.) Boivin (var. *purp.* Hult.; petals purple rather than yellow) is known from the type locality, False Pass, Alaska.

S. sibirica L.
/aSs/W/A/ (Hs) Rocky slopes to alpine meadows of the Aleutian Is., Alaska–Yukon (N to the N coasts), and W Dist. Mackenzie (reports from B.C. require confirmation); N Asia. [Incl. *S. bracteata* Don, *S. cymbalaria* Cham., *S. laurentiana* Ser., and *S. radiata* Small; *S. exilis* Steph., not Pallas]. MAPS: combine the maps by Hultén 1968*b*:575 *(S. ex.)* and 576 *(S. br.)*; Raup 1947: pl. 26 *(S. rad.).*

S. spicata Don
/S/W/ (Hr) Moist rocky slopes along streams in Alaska (N to ca. 68°N; type from Sledge Is.) and W Yukon (a single station at ca. 64°N). [*Micranthes* Small; *S. (M.) galacifolia* Small]. MAPS: Hultén 1968*b*:574, and 1945: map 720, p. 976.

S. stellaris L.
/AST/X/GEA/ (Hr (Ch)) Mossy tundra, wet rocky slopes, and streambanks from the coasts of Alaska–Yukon–Dist. Mackenzie–Dist. Keewatin nearly throughout the Canadian Arctic Archipelago to N Ellesmere Is. and Baffin Is., S to the E Aleutian Is., S Alaska, Great Bear L., SE Dist. Keewatin, N Que. (S to NE Hudson Bay at ca. 60°45′N), N Labrador (S to Cutthroat Harbour, ca. 57°30′N), NW Nfld., and Mt. Katahdin, Maine; circumgreenlandic (but with large gaps in E Greenland); Iceland; Spitsbergen; Eurasia. [*Spatularia* Haw.]. MAPS: Hultén 1958: map 91, p. 111; Porsild 1957: map 219, p. 188; Böcher 1954: fig. 28 (top), p. 111; Meusel, Jaeger, and Weinert 1965:200; A. Löve and D. Löve, Sven. Bot. Tidskr. 45(2): fig. 5 (incomplete for N Labrador), p. 374. 1951.
The typical phase with normal flowers is known in N. America only from E Baffin Is. (a single station near the Arctic Circle) and N Labrador, as indicated in the above-noted maps. The transcontinental phase is var *comosa* Poir. (*S. foliolosa* R. Br.; flowers largely or wholly replaced by leafy bulblets). MAPS *(S. fol.)*: Hultén 1968*b*:581, and 1958: map 92, p. 111 (noting other total-area maps by Engler and Temesey); Porsild 1957: map 213, p. 187; Meusel, Jaeger, and Weinert 1965:200; Löve and Löve, loc. cit., fig. 6 (inaccurate for N. America), p. 375.

S. taylori Calder & Savile
/T/W/ (Ch) Known only from the Queen Charlotte Range, Queen Charlotte Is, W B.C. (type from Tasu Sound; Calder and Savile 1959, with MAP, fig. 8, p. 239).

S. tolmiei T. & G.
/sT/W/ (Ch) Rock-crevices and moist alpine slopes from the W Aleutian Is., the Alaska Panhandle, and W B.C. to cent. Calif., Idaho, and Mont. [*Leptasea* Small; incl. *S. aleutica* Hult.]. MAP: combine the maps by Hultén 1968*b*:567 and 566 *(S. al.).*

S. tricuspidata Rottb.
/AST/X/G/ (Ch) Dry sands, gravels, and rocks from the coasts of Alaska–Yukon–Dist. Mackenzie–Dist. Keewatin throughout the Canadian Arctic Archipelago to northernmost Ellesmere Is. and northernmost Ungava–Labrador, S to S B.C. (S to near Clinton at ca. 51°N), Alta. (S to near Jasper), Sask. (S to Lac la Ronge, 55°10′N), SE Man. (Lake of the Woods), cent. Ont. (English River, about 100 mi NW of Thunder Bay; shore of L. Superior 20 mi SW of Nipigon; Raft R.; coast of W James Bay N to Cape Henrietta Maria), N Mich. (Isle Royale, L. Superior), islands in James Bay, Que. (coasts of Hudson Bay–James Bay S to ca. 54°N; S Ungava

Bay watershed s to ca. 58°N), and N Labrador (s to ca. 59°N); w Greenland between ca. 65°
and 80°N, E Greenland between ca. 69° and 73°N. MAPS and synonymy: *see* below.
1 Most of the leaves entire; [*S. austromontana sensu* F. Harper, Can. Field-Nat.
   45(5):102. 1931, not Wieg.; range of the species] . . . . . .f. *subintegrifolia* (Abrom.) Polunin
1 Most or many of the leaves with 3 apical teeth.
   2 Petals strap-shaped, to 9 mm long but at most about 1.5 mm broad; [type from
      Chesterfield Inlet, Dist. Keewatin, the only known locality] . . . f. *ligulata* Savile & Calder
   2 Petals more or less elliptic, to 7 mm long and 3.5 mm broad.
      3 Anthers very small and seemingly abnormal; [Alaska; type from Kotzebue
         Sound] . . . . f. *micrantha* (Sternb.) Calder & Savile
      3 Anthers normal.
         4 Stems prostrate and lax, the plant sterile or with 1 or 2 subsessile flowers;
            [type from Committee Bay, Melville Pen.] . . . . f. *woodruffii* Calder
         4 Stems stiffly erect; flowers numerous, in panicles; [*Chondrosea* Haw.;
            Leptasea Haw.; *S. chamissoi* Sternb.; *S. vespertina* of B.C. reports, not
            Leptasea vesp. Small; transcontinental, the type from Greenland; MAPS:
            Hultén 1968*b*:571; Calder and Savile 1959: fig. 7, p. 236; Porsild 1957: map
            221, p. 188; Raup 1947: pl. 27; *Atlas of Canada* 1957: map 7, sheet 38; the
            maps by Porsild and Raup indicate a station in s Labrador at ca. 53°N
            requiring confirmation] . . . . .f. *tricuspidata*

S. virginiensis Michx. Early Saxifrage
/T/EE/ (Hr) Dry or wet sands, gravels, and rocks from E Man. (N to Tulabi L., NE of Lac du
Bonnet at ca. 50°30′N) to Ont. (N to Schreiber, N shore of L. Superior), Que. (N to Duparquet,
SE of L. Abitibi, and Bic, Rimouski Co.), and N.B. (York Co.; not known from P.E.I. or N.S.), s
to Mo., Tenn., and Ga. [*Micranthes* Small; *S. vernalis* Willd.]. MAP: Meusel, Jaeger, and Wei-
nert 1965:200.

SUKSDORFIA Gray [3187]

1 Petals white (or purple-tinged at base), spreading, to 4 mm long; hypanthium
   shallowly and broadly campanulate, to about 2.5 mm long, lined with a thick disk
   partly covering the ovary and bearing the stamens on its outer edge; calyx-lobes
   triangular-lanceolate, spreading; filaments about equalling the anthers; flowers
   rather numerous; basal leaves usually several, to 4 cm broad, ternately parted nearly
   to the petiole into 3 cuneate-obovate, entire to crenately lobed segments; stem to
   about 3.5 dm tall, bearing up to 9 upwardly reduced leaves . . . .*S. ranunculifolia*
1 Petals purplish violet (rarely white), suberect, to 9 mm long; hypanthium more
   narrowly campanulate, to about 7 mm long, the disk obsolete; calyx-lobes linear-
   lanceolate, suberect; anthers subsessile; flowers usually less than 10; basal leaves
   1–3, to 2.5 cm broad, coarsely crenate-lobed, usually withered by anthesis; stem to
   about 2 dm tall, bearing 3–5 upwardly reduced leaves . . . .*S. violacea*

S. ranunculifolia (Hook.) Engler
/T/W/ (Gst) Wet to dryish mossy rocks at low to subalpine elevations from B.C. (N to
Prince Rupert and Terrace) and SW Alta. (Waterton Lakes; Breitung 1957*b*) to N Calif., Idaho,
and Mont. [*Saxifraga* Hook.; *Boykinia* Greene; *Hemieva* Raf.].

S. violacea Gray
/T/W/ (Gst) Rock crevices, mossy banks, and shaded sandy places from s B.C. (N to Si-
camous, about 60 mi E of Kamloops) and SW Alta. (Waterton Lakes; Breitung 1957*b*) to Wash.,
N Idaho, and Mont. [*Hemieva* Wheelock].

TELESONIX Raf. [3189]

T. jamesii (Torr.) Raf.
/T/WW/ (Hs (Ch)) Moist rock outcrops and talus slopes from ?B.C. and the mts. of W Alta.

(Riche Miette, near Jasper) to Nev., Utah, Colo., and S.Dak. [*Saxifraga* Torr.; incl. var. *heucheriformis* (Rydb.) Bacig. (*T. (Boykinia) heuch.* Rydb.)].

TELLIMA R. Br.   [3197]

T. grandiflora (Pursh) Dougl.   Fringe-cup
/sT/W/   (Hsr)   Streambanks and woods at low to moderate elevations from the E Aleutian Is. and s Alaska through B.C. (E to the Selkirk Mts.) to Oreg. and Idaho. [*Mitella* Pursh; *T. odorata* Howell; *Tiarella alternifolia* Fisch.]. MAP: Hultén 1968*b*:585.

TIARELLA L.   [3193]   False Mitrewort, Foamflower

1   Leaves 3-foliolate, the lateral leaflets themselves commonly more or less deeply cleft (nearly to base in ssp. *laciniata*); inflorescence a narrow panicle; petals linear-subulate; stem bearing up to 4 leaves; (s Alaska, B.C., and w Alta.) . . . . *T. trifoliata*
1   Leaves simple, broadly cordate, shallowly to rather deeply palmately 3–5(7)-lobed.
   2   Inflorescence a simple raceme; petals oblanceolate to elliptic; stem scapiform or with a few scales (rarely with a single small leaf); (Ont. to N.S.) . . . . *T. cordifolia*
   2   Inflorescence a narrow panicle; petals linear-subulate; stem normally bearing up to 4 leaves, these relatively more deeply 3-lobed than the basal leaves; (ssp. *unifoliata*; s Alaska, B.C., and w Alta.) . . . . *T. trifoliata*

T. cordifolia L.   False Mitrewort, Foamflower
/T/EE/   (Hrr)   Rich woods from Mich. to Ont. (N to Batchawana Bay on the SE shore of L. Superior; Cache L. in Algonquin Park, Renfrew Co.), Que. (Ste-Rose-du-Dégelé, Temiscouata Co.), N.B., and N.S. (not known from P.E.I.), s to Tenn. and N.C. MAP: see below.
1   Carpel-valves subequal; [Aylmer, Elgin Co., s Ont.] . . . . f. *subaequalis* Lakela
1   Upper carpel-valve at most 3/4 the length of the lower one.
   2   Anthers (and pollen-grains) orange; [common throughout the range of f. *cordifolia*, the type from near Montreal, Que.] . . . . f. *allanthera* Vict. & Rousseau
   2   Anthers (and pollen-grains) yellow; [range of the species; MAP: O. Lakela, Am. J. Bot. 24(6): fig. 1, p. 346. 1937] . . . . f. *cordifolia*

T. trifoliata L.   Laceflower, Sugar-scoop
/sT/W/   (Hsr)   Moist woods, the aggregate species from SE Alaska through B.C. and SW Alta. to Calif., Idaho, and Mont. MAPS and synonymy: see below.
1   Leaves simple (very rarely some of the upper stem-leaves 3-foliolate), shallowly to rather deeply 3–5-lobed; [*T. (Petalosteira) unif.* Hook. and its f. *trisecta* Lakela; SE Alaska–B.C.–SW Alta. (Banff; Waterton Lakes); MAP: Hultén 1968*b*:584 (*T. uni.*)] . . . .
   . . . . ssp. *unifoliata* (Hook.) Kern.
1   Leaves 3-foliolate, the leaflets stalked . . . . ssp. *trifoliata*
   2   At least the lateral leaflets cleft nearly their full length and more or less laciniate into narrowly oblong ultimate segments; [*T. (Petalosteira) lac.* Hook.; B.C.: Vancouver Is. and adjacent islands] . . . . var. *laciniata* (Hook.) Wheelock
   2   Leaflets usually lobed not over half their length, their broad ultimate segments usually merely dentate; [*Blondia trif.* Raf., the type thought by Hultén 1945, to have probably been taken at Cape St. Elias, Alaska; *T. stenopetala* Presl; s Alaska–B.C.–Alta. (near Whitecourt, ca. 54°N); MAP: Hultén 1968*b*:583] . . . var. *trifoliata*

TOLMIEA T. & G.   [3196]

T. menziesii (Pursh) T. & G.   Youth-on-age
/T/W/   (Hsr)   Moist woods from SE Alaska through w B.C. (W of the Cascades; type probably from Banks Is., E of Queen Charlotte Is. according to Hultén 1945) to Calif. [*Tiarella* Pursh; *Heuchera* Hook.; *Leptaxis* Raf.]. MAP: Hultén 1968*b*:585.

HAMAMELIDACEAE (Witch-hazel Family)

Trees or shrubs with alternate simple leaves and deciduous stipules. Flowers perfect or unisexual or both, perigynous. Calyx small or rudimentary. Petals 4 and linear, or none. Stamens 4 or many. Ovary partly inferior. Fruit a capsule.

1 Leaves pinnately veined, wavy-toothed, obovate or oval to suborbicular, inequilateral at the broadly rounded or subcordate base; flowers few in axillary clusters, opening in the autumn, the definite calyx yellowish brown within; petals 4, bright yellow, linear; stamens 4; capsules distinct, each with 2 wingless bony seeds; tall shrub or small tree; (Ont. to N.S.) . . . . *Hamamelis*
1 Leaves palmately veined and deeply 5–7-lobed, glandular-serrate, smooth and shining, the lobes pointed; flowers commonly unisexual, the staminate ones in a conical cluster, their stamens numerous, the pistillate ones in globose heads; petals none; calyx rudimentary, dark red within; capsules fused at base into a globular prickly head 3 or 4 cm thick, each capsule with many small winged seeds; large tree; (cult. in s Ont.) . . . . *[Liquidambar]*

HAMAMELIS L.   [3309]

H. virginiana L.   Witch-hazel.   Café du diable
/T/EE/   (Mc)   Dry or moist woods from Minn. to Ont. (N to the Ottawa dist.; *see* s Ont. maps by Fox and Soper 1953: fig. 18, p. 16, and Soper and Heimburger 1961:11), Que. (N to the Quebec City dist.), N.B., and N.S. (not known from P.E.I.; the report from Nfld. by Waghorne 1895, is perhaps based upon a species of *Alnus*), s to Mo., Tenn., and Ga. MAPS: Hosie 1969:218; Canada Department of Northern Affairs and Natural Resources 1956:200; Preston 1961:240; Hough 1947:225; Munns 1938: map 130, p. 134.

Var. *parvifolia* Nutt. (leaves densely stellate-tomentose and whitened or more or less rust-coloured beneath, coriaceous and mostly less than 1 dm long, rather than glabrous or merely sparingly pilose on the nerves beneath, to about 1.5 dm long) is known from N.S. (Cumberland and Yarmouth counties).

[LIQUIDAMBAR L.]   [3298]

[*L. styraciflua* L.]   Sweet Gum
[Native in the E U.S.A., Mexico, and Central America; planted in s Ont. and noted here because of the persistence in a cemetery at Port Dover, Norfolk Co., of three large trees planted, according to the caretaker (1960), about 80 years ago. The native area is shown in MAPS by Fowells 1965:248, Preston 1961:240, and Braun 1935: fig. 1, p. 352.]

PLATANACEAE (Plane-tree Family)

PLATANUS L.   [3314]

Tree to about 50 m tall, with alternate, palmately 3–5-lobed, deeply serrate leaves and sheathing stipules. Flowers in globose unisexual heads. Sepals, petals, stamens, and pistils commonly each 3 or 4 (sometimes up to 8). Ovary superior. Fruit a cluster of 1–2-seeded beaked capsules in a globose head 3 or 4 cm thick.

P. occidentalis L.   Sycamore, Buttonwood, Plane-tree
/t/EE/   (Mg)   Rich soils from Nebr. to s Ont. (N to Grey, York, and Prince Edward counties; *see* s Ont. map by Fox and Soper 1952: fig. 6, p. 77) and s Maine, s to Tex., Miss., Ala., and N Fla. MAPS: Fowells 1965:489; Hosie 1969:220; Canada Department of Northern Affairs and Natural Resources 1956:202; Polunin 1960: fig. 54, p. 192; Hough 1947:229; Cain 1944: fig. 5, p. 98; Preston 1961:242; M.L. Fernald, Rhodora 33(386): map 6, p. 31. 1931; Munns 1938: map 132, p. 136; Little 1971: map 147-N.

ROSACEAE (Rose Family)

(Ref.: P.A. Rydberg, N. Am. Flora 22:239–533. 1908–18)
Herbs, shrubs, or trees with alternate, usually stipulate, often compound, usually toothed leaves. Flowers regular, perfect, perigynous or epigynous, the sepals and petals commonly 5, they and the usually numerous stamens inserted at or near the margin of the urn-shaped, cup-shaped, or saucer-shaped hypanthium (enlarged receptacle). Ovary superior to inferior. Fruit various. (Incl. Amygdalaceae and Malaceae).

1 Trees or shrubs (stems essentially herbaceous in certain species of *Rubus* and only semishrubby in *Dryas*).
  2 Leaves compound.
    3 Ovary actually or apparently inferior, the achenes or seeds enclosed in the enlarged fleshy hypanthium, this bearing the remains of the calyx at its summit.
      4 Flowers numerous, white, corymbose-paniculate, to about 1.5 cm broad; stipules adnate to the petiole only at base, soon deciduous; small tree or large shrub with thornless stems . . . . *Sorbus*
      4 Flowers solitary or few, roseate (sometimes white), larger; stipules usually adnate to the petiole for more than half their length, persistent; medium-sized shrubs with usually thorny or prickly stems . . . . *Rosa*
    3 Ovary superior, the fruit commonly subtended by the remains of the calyx.
      5 Fruit a cluster of several or many fleshy 1-seeded drupes on the enlarged spongy receptacle (raspberries, blackberries, etc.); petals white to pink or roseate; flowers in racemes; stems often prickly . . . . *Rubus*
      5 Fruit a cluster of dry achenes, the receptacle neither enlarged nor spongy; petals white or yellow; flowers solitary or cymose; stems not prickly . . . *Potentilla*
  2 Leaves simple.
    6 Leaves cuneate or flabelliform, simply or doubly 3-cleft from the summit, to about 2.5 cm long (including the wing-margined petiole).
      7 Freely and rigidly branched shrub commonly 1 or 2 m tall (but up to 4 m); leaves deciduous, stipulate, apically 3-cleft, commonly glandular, greenish above, greyish-tomentose beneath, usually more or less revolute, closely crowded on short lateral spurs terminated by solitary flowers; calyx strongly stipitate-glandular as well as tomentose or arachnoid, the lobes about equalling the hypanthium; petals yellow, to 9 mm long; fruit a short-stipitate finely puberulent rather cartilaginous achene to about 1.5 cm long, containing a solitary black pyriform seed to 8 mm long; (s B.C.) . . . *Purshia*
      7 Rhizomatous and stoloniferous, essentially glabrous, mat-forming, evergreen, semishrub with upright leafy flowering stems to about 1.5 dm tall; leaves exstipulate, usually 2-ternately dissected into linear lobes, mostly crowded in thick basal tufts, often marcescent; flowers in leafy-bracted racemes; calyx-lobes about twice as long as the hypanthium; petals white, to 3.5 mm long; fruit a several-seeded follicle with a stipe-like base, to about 5 mm long, slightly silky on the ventral suture; (mts. of B.C. and Alta.) . . . . *Luetkea*
    6 Leaves otherwise; petals usually white or pink-tinged (often creamy to orange-yellow in *Dryas*).
      8 Ovary actually or apparently inferior, the achenes or seeds enclosed in the enlarged fleshy hypanthium, this bearing the remains of the calyx at its summit.
        9 Stems armed with thorns.
          10 Thorns naked; leaves usually deciduous, often deeply incised or lobed as well as toothed; corymbs rather few-flowered, the flowers mostly over 1 cm broad; fruit yellow to red or nearly black, with 1–5 carpels and 1–5 bony seed-like nutlets . . . . *Crataegus*

          10 Thorns leafy; leaves evergreen, merely finely crenate-serrate, lanceolate to oblanceolate, usually acute, glabrous or slightly pubescent beneath, to about 5 cm long; corymbs many-flowered, the flowers less than 1 cm broad; fruit with 5 carpels and 5 nutlets; (introd. in sw B.C.) . . . . *Pyracantha*

    9 Stems unarmed; leaves deciduous, rarely incised.

        11 Leaves entire, green and glabrous or nearly so above, paler and more pubescent or even tomentose beneath, commonly not over 5 cm long; flowers pinkish, in cymose clusters terminating leafy lateral spurs; fruits black, with usually 2 nutlets; (introd.) . . . . *Cotoneaster*

        11 Leaves distinctly toothed at least toward summit.

            12 Fruit berry-like, apparently 10-locular and normally 10-seeded; inflorescence racemose (except in *A. bartramiana*) . . . . . *Amelanchier*

            12 Fruit berry-like or a pome, the 2–5-locules mostly 2-seeded; flowers solitary or in umbels or corymbs . . . . *Pyrus*

  8 Ovary superior, the fruit commonly subtended by the remains of the calyx.

    13 Fruit a 1-seeded, more or less fleshy drupe.

        14 Leaves entire, the blades narrowly oblong-lanceolate to -obovate, glabrous above, slightly paler and often pubescent beneath, to 12 cm long and 4 cm broad; flowers greenish white, in axillary, usually drooping racemes, imperfect (the pistillate flowers with the normal number of stamens but the filaments very short and the anthers small and probably never functional); petals 5 or 6 mm long, deciduous; pistils usually 5, developing into up to 5 thin-fleshed bluish-black drupes (but these often fewer through abortion); (s B.C.) . . . . *Osmaronia*

        14 Leaves toothed; flowers perfect; petals mostly longer; pistil 1, each flower producing a single drupe . . . . *Prunus*

    13 Fruit consisting of achenes, follicles, or capsular follicles.

      15 Fruit dehiscent (a follicle or capsule with 2 or more seeds).

        16 Leaves palmately 3–5-lobed and irregularly serrate; calyx usually finely stellate-pubescent; petals white; fruit a cluster of up to 5 more or less bladdery-inflated follicles to 1 cm long, these dehiscent on both sutures; stem to over 3 m tall, the bark exfoliating in long strips . . . . *Physocarpus*

        16 Leaves pinnately many-lobed or toothed; calyx not stellate; fruit consisting of up to 8 uninflated follicles less than 1 cm long, these dehiscent only ventrally; stem commonly lower, the bark not conspicuously exfoliating . . . . *Spiraea*

      15 Fruit a cluster of indehiscent, usually 1-seeded achenes.

        17 Flowers small and very numerous in a terminal diffuse pubescent panicle to over 1.5 dm long, whitish; petals and calyx-lobes each 5; achenes usually 5, hirsute, about 2 mm long; leaves narrowly to broadly ovate, greenish and more or less hirsute above, paler and strongly pilose or woolly beneath, rather shallowly lobed and also serrate, to over 7 cm long; stems to 3 m tall, the branches angled by the decurrent petioles; (B.C.) . . . . *Holodiscus*

        17 Flowers relatively large, solitary on naked or weakly bracted erect scapes commonly 1 or 2 dm tall; petals and calyx-lobes usually 8–10; achenes numerous, tipped with a long plumose style; leaves entire to crenate-serrate, thickish, usually revolute, greenish above, commonly white-tomentose beneath; prostrate semishrubs, the usually freely rooting branches often forming large patches . . . . *Dryas*

1 Herbs (*Sorbaria* sometimes more or less shrubby; *Rubus acaulis, R. chamaemorus,* and *R. pubescens* may key out here).

18 Leaves simple.
  19 Flowers solitary on long hairy peduncles, 5–6-merous; petaliferous white
     flowers showy, sterile; apetalous flowers recurving and maturing up to 10 dry
     seed-like drupes near the ground at the bottom of the concave receptacle;
     stamens numerous; leaves rotund-cordate, low-crenate; (Ont. to N.S.) . . . *Dalibarda*
  19 Flowers numerous in panicled corymbs, usually 4-merous, all apetalous,
     small, yellowish green; achenes 1–4, enclosed in the tube of the persistent
     calyx; stamens usually 4; leaves flabellate to reniform, palmately lobed and
     also serrate (rarely palmately compound) . . . . *Alchemilla*
18 Leaves compound (*Alchemilla alpina* may be sought here).
  20 Leaves 2–3-ternate-pinnate, the narrowly to broadly ovate leaflets sharply and
     somewhat doubly serrate, acuminate, to about 1.5 dm long; panicle to about
     3 dm long; flowers dioecious; petals white, those of the staminate flowers
     about 1 mm long, those of the pistillate flowers somewhat smaller; follicles
     about 2 mm long; (s Alaska–B.C.; introd. in Que. and N.S.) . . . . *Aruncus*
  20 Leaves once-compound.
    21 Leaves 3-foliolate.
      22 Fruit dehiscent, consisting of 5 separate pubescent follicles from each
        of the white or pinkish, loosely paniculate-corymbed flowers; petals
        linear to narrowly lanceolate, somewhat unequal, to over 2 cm long;
        leaves nearly sessile; leaflets lanceolate to ovate-oblong, sharply and
        irregularly serrate, tapering at both ends; (s Ont.) . . . . *Gillenia*
      22 Fruit consisting of achenes; at least the basal leaves long-petioled.
        23 Leaflets cleft into linear segments; stamens 5; petals white or
          purplish, about as long as the calyx-lobes, these lacking alternating
          bractlets; plant glandular-pubescent, to about 3 dm tall; (B.C. to
          s Man.) . . . . *Chamaerhodos*
        23 Leaflets at most moderately incised into broad teeth or lobes.
          24 Receptacle greatly enlarged and spongy or fleshy in fruit (the
            fruit a strawberry or strawberry-like); sepals alternating with
            foliaceous bractlets; leaves all or nearly all in a basal cluster;
            superficial runners normally developed.
            25 Petals yellow, 3-lobed at summit; receptacle spongy to fleshy
              but not juicy; (introd. in ?B.C.) . . . . [*Duchesnea*]
            25 Petals white or pinkish, entire; receptacle fleshy and juicy . . . .
              . . . . *Fragaria*
          24 Receptacle not greatly enlarged in fruit, dry.
            26 Flowers yellow, to about 2 cm broad, usually at least 2 on
             peduncles terminating a hairy scape; sepals usually lacking
             alternating bractlets; leaflets broadly cuneate-obovate, cut-
             toothed, pubescent; (Ont., Que., and N.B.) . . . . *Waldsteinia*
            26 Flowers borne at the ends of leafy stems or branches
             (*Sibbaldia* sometimes with nearly leafless scapes); sepals
             alternating with usually smaller bractlets.
             27 Stamens 5; achenes usually less than 10; petals yellow,
              much smaller than the sepals; leaflets obovate, 3-toothed
              at the truncate summit, they and their petioles pubescent;
              stems from a branching caudex; (transcontinental in
              arctic, subarctic, and alpine regions) . . . . *Sibbaldia*
             27 Stamens and achenes both numerous; petals white or
              yellow, often longer than the sepals . . . . *Potentilla*
    21 Leaves (at least the basal ones) pinnately compound with at least 5
      leaflets.
      28 Petals none; sepals 4, green or petaloid; inflorescence spicate or
        capitate; fruit an achene . . . . *Sanguisorba*
      28 Petals and sepals usually each 5 (6 or 7 in *Filipendula hexapetala*).

29 Fruit dehiscent, consisting of thin-walled follicles; flowers white, in dense terminal panicles; petals about 3 mm long; leaflets at least 13, lanceolate, finely serrate, long-acuminate; (introd.) . . . . *Sorbaria*
29 Fruit indehiscent, consisting of achenes (or in *Filipendula,* 2-seeded follicle-like bodies).

  30 Calyx turbinate (top-shaped), armed with hooked bristles at summit, indurated in fruit and enclosing 2 achenes; petals yellow . . . . *Agrimonia*
  30 Calyx saucer-shaped to hemispheric, unarmed, not enclosing the achenes.

   31 Styles persistent and elongating after anthesis, plumose or jointed (if jointed, the upper segment deciduous); sepals usually alternating with 5 small bractlets . . . . *Geum*
   31 Styles not elongating and usually deciduous.

    32 Sepals lacking alternating bractlets; fruit 2-seeded, follicle-like but indehiscent; flowers white or pink, in large panicles; stipules large, more or less reniform; (introd.) . . . . *Filipendula*
    32 Sepals with alternating bractlets; fruit a head of 1-seeded achenes; flowers mostly yellow (sometimes white; purplish in *P. atrosanguinea* and *P. palustris*), solitary or cymose; stipules relatively narrow . . . . *Potentilla*

AGRIMONIA L. [3376] Agrimony. Aigremoine

1 Hypanthium densely long-hirsute; floral-axis spreading-hirsute; leaves chiefly confined to the lower half of the stem (peduncles scapiform), the leaflets densely cinereous-villous and nonglandular beneath; (introd.) . . . . [*A. eupatoria*]
1 Hypanthium glabrous or glandular, or sparingly strigose only in the furrows between the glabrous ribs; (native species).

  2 Floral-axis nonglandular, densely short-pilose with upcurving or appressed-ascending hairs; hypanthium glandless, minutely strigose in the furrows, the hooked bristles ascending or connivent; larger leaves with up to 11 or 13 principal leaflets.

   3 Mature hypanthium less than 4 mm long; leaflets velvety-pubescent beneath, glandless; root fusiform-thickened; (s Ont. and sw ?Que.) . . . . *A. pubescens*
   3 Mature hypanthium 4 or 5 mm long; leaflets conspicuously gland-dotted beneath, otherwise glabrous except for the sparingly fine-pilose veins; root not fusiform-thickened; (transcontinental) . . . .*A. striata*

  2 Floral-axis minutely glandular and also often with remote long divergent hairs, with or without short incurved hairs; hypanthium glandular, lacking minute strigose hairs in the furrows, deflexed at maturity; leaflets conspicuously gland-dotted beneath, otherwise glabrous except for sparse pubescence on the veins; root not fusiform-thickened.

   4 Mature hypanthium about 3 mm long, the hooked bristles ascending or spreading; floral-axis densely short-pubescent with incurved hairs, with or without long spreading hairs; larger leaves with up to 23 principal leaflets; stem densely long-hirsute; (s Ont.) . . . . *A. parviflora*
   4 Mature hypanthium to 5 mm long, the hooked bristles spreading, the short outer ones often reflexed; floral-axis with remote long divergent hairs, lacking short incurved hairs; larger leaves with rarely more than 9 principal leaflets; stem sparingly spreading-hirsute; (B.C.; Ont. to N.S.) . . . . *A. gryposepala*

[A. eupatoria L.]
[Eurasian; locally introd. in waste places and old fields of the E U.S.A. but early reports from Canada refer chiefly to A. *striata* (relevant collections in several herbaria).]

A. gryposepala Wallr.
/T/(X)/ (Hpr) Thickets and borders of woods from s B.C. (Agassiz, about 50 mi E of Van-
couver, where taken by John Macoun in 1889 and distributed as *A. eupatoria*; CAN; reported
from the lower Fraser Valley, Tappen, Armstrong, and N of Hazelton at ca. 55°N by Eastham
1947, but a collection in CAN from N of Hazelton was distributed by Eastham as *A. striata*) to
Calif.; the main area from N.Dak. to Ont. (N to the Rainy River dist. SE of Kenora; CAN), SW
Que. (N to L. St. Peter), N.B., P.E.I., and N.S. (reports from Man., from farther N in Ont. and
Que., and from Nfld. all appear referable to *A. striata*), s to Kans., Mo., Tenn., and N.C. [*A. hirsuta* Bickn.].
   The very similar *A. odorata* Mill. of Europe is reported by D.S. Erskine (1960) as persisting in
abundance in a garden at Brackley Point, Queens Co., P.E.I.

A. parviflora Ait.
/t/EE/ (Hpr) Damp thickets and rocky slopes from Nebr. to Ohio, s Ont. (Amherstburg,
Leamington, and Sandwich, Essex Co.; CAN; reported from near London, Middlesex Co., by
John Macoun and John Gibson, Can. J., n.s. 15(93). 1877, and from Fort Erie, Welland Co., by
Zenkert 1934), N.Y., and Conn., s to E Tex. and Fla.

A. pubescens Wallr.
/T/EE/ (Hpr) Rich woods and shaded calcareous ledges from E Kans. to Mich., s Ont. (Essex, Kent, Lambton, and Waterloo counties), SW ?Que. (Boivin 1966b), N.Y., and Mass., s to
Okla. and Ga. [*A. bicknellii* (Kearney) Rydb.; *A. mollis* (T. & G.) Britt.]. MAP: Meusel, Jaeger,
and Weinert 1965:221.

A. striata Michx.
/T/X/ (Hpr) Thickets and borders of woods from B.C. (N to near Hazelton at ca. 55°N) to
Alta. (N to High Prairie, 55°26′N), Sask. (N to Meadow Lake, 54°08′N), Man. (N to Minitonas, N
of Duck Mt.), Ont. (N to the Nipigon R. N of L. Superior), Que. (N to the Gaspé Pen.), Nfld.,
N.B., P.E.I., and N.S., s to Ariz., N.Mex., Nebr., Iowa, Ohio, and N.J. [*A. brittoniana* Bickn.; *A.
eupatoria* of most early Canadian reports, not L., relevant collections in several herbaria].
MAP: Meusel, Jaeger, and Weinert 1965:221 (the occurrence in Nfld. should be indicated).

ALCHEMILLA L.   [3375]   Lady's-mantle

(Ref.: P.A. Rydberg, N. Am. Flora 22:377–80. 1908; Bradshaw, Dansereau and Valentine 1964;
Walters 1949; M.L. Fernald and K.M. Wiegand, Rhodora 14(168):229–34. 1912)
1 Leaves mostly basal, orbicular or reniform in outline, the principal ones long-
   petioled, those of the stem reduced and short-petioled or sessile; flowers borne in
   terminal cymes; stamens 4 (rarely 5), alternate with the sepals, the anthers introrse;
   perennials.
   2 Leaves palmately divided nearly or quite to base into 5 or 7 oblong-oblanceolate
      leaflets up to 2 cm long and 6 mm broad; leaflets sharply serrate at apex, green
      and glabrous above, densely silvery-silky beneath; (Greenland; introd. in
      St-Pierre and Miquelon) . . . . *A. alpina*
   2 Leaves simple, divided less than half-way to centre, green on both sides . . . *A. vulgaris*
1 Leaves well distributed along the stem, fan- or wedge-shaped, short-petioled, deeply
   3-lobed (the primary lobes themselves mostly 3–5-lobed), usually less than 1.5 cm
   long, subtended by cup-like, foliaceous, deeply 5–7-lobed stipules; flowers borne in
   small dense cymose clusters in the axils of the stipules on the side of the stem
   opposite the petiole; stamen 1 (rarely 2), opposite a sepal, the anthers extrorse;
   annuals, simple or freely branching from the base; (introd.).
   3 Lobes of stipules triangular-ovate, little longer than broad, about half as long as
      the basal undivided portion; fruit (including the adnate calyx) about 2.5 mm long,
      the calyx-lobes ascending so that the whole appears bottle-shaped; leaves to 1.5
      cm broad; plant greyish green, to 2 dm tall . . . . [*A. arvensis*]
   3 Lobes of stipules oblong, about twice as long as broad and nearly as long as the

basal undivided portion; fruit (including calyx) less than 2 mm long, the calyx-lobes convergent so that the whole appears ovoid; leaves to 6 mm broad; plant not greyish, to about 1 dm tall . . . . *A. occidentalis*

A. *alpina* L.   Alpine Lady's-mantle
/aST/–/GE/   (Hsr (Ch))   Grassy slopes, rock slides, crevices, and mountaintops of Green-land (W and E coasts N to ca. 70°N), Iceland, and Europe. Known in N. America only from Miquelon Is., St-Pierre and Miquelon, off the S coast of Nfld., where considered native by Fernald *in* Gray (1950). Hultén (1958), however, points out that, "As *A. alpina* often behaves as a weed in Central Europe it seems reasonable to assume that it is introduced on Miquelon." *See* discussion under *Luzula campestris*. MAPS: Hultén 1958: map 93, p. 113; Meusel, Jaeger and Weinert 1965:223; Böcher 1954: fig. 21 (top), p. 79, and 1938: fig. 59, p. 122.

[A. *arvensis* (L.) Scop.]
[Eurasian; the report of this species from N.S. by Lindsay (1878; Lucyfield and St. Paul's, Cape Breton Is.) requires confirmation. If correctly identified, it was probably a casual intro-duction and appears not to have been again taken there since that date. The report from B.C. by John Macoun (1883; near Victoria, Vancouver Is.) is based upon *A. occidentalis*, the rele-vant collection in CAN. (*Aphanes* L.).]

A. *occidentalis* Nutt.   Parsley-piert
?European (considered by some authors as a local native species in the W U.S.A. (Wash. to Calif., Idaho, and Mont.), but so weedy in nature and so closely related to the Eurasian *A. arvensis* as to argue against this concept); it is known from fields, waste places, and wooded slopes in B.C. (Queen Charlotte Is.; Vancouver Is. and adjacent islands; CAN; V); also introd. in the E U.S.A. [*Aphanes* Rydb.; *Aph. macrosepala* Rydb.; *Al. arvensis* var. *occ.* (Nutt.) Piper; *Al. microcarpa* Boiss. & Reut.].

A. *vulgaris* L.
/aST/E/GEA/   (Hsr)   Apparently both native (cool or wet rocks and brooksides at low to subalpine areas) and introd. (roadsides, fields, and thickets) in E N. America and Greenland (ranges of Canadian taxa outlined below), the collective species (including several "micro-species") keyed out below, together with maps and synonymy; Eurasia.
1   Petioles and stem subglabrous or with appressed hairs.
  2   Stem and petioles densely appressed-silky-hairy; leaves hairy above (the hairs beneath sometimes confined to the veins), usually 7–9-lobed, the lobes often about twice as broad as long (often overlapping and folded when pressed), the middle lobes with up to 15 broad but subacute, somewhat curved teeth; basal leaf-sinus open; flower-clusters dense; [A. *vulg.* vars. *glom.* (Bus.) Ahlf. and *comosa* (Brenner) Fern. & Wieg.; Ungava–Labrador N to ca. 59°30'N; Greenland N to ca. 70°15'N; MAPS: Hultén 1958: map 95, p. 115; G. Samuelsson, Acta Phytogeogr. Suec. 16: fig. 1, p. 15. 1943] . . . . [A. *glomerulans* Buser]
  2   Stem nearly glabrous or appressed-hairy only toward base; leaves glabrous above (and also beneath except along the veins), their middle lobes with up to 19 teeth; flower-clusters usually lax.
    3   Basal leaf-sinus open; sinuses between the leaf-lobes toothed to base, the teeth relatively broad, somewhat curved, the apical one conspicuously narrower and often shorter than the adjacent teeth; [A. *vulg.* var. *grandis* Blytt; A. ?*alpestris* Schmidt; Saguenay and Matane counties, E Que.; MAP: Hultén 1958: map 110, p. 129] . . . . [A. *glabra* Neygenf.]
    3   Basal leaf-sinus closed or nearly so; sinuses between the leaf-lobes ending in a narrow entire base; teeth of leaf-lobes subequal and relatively narrow, strongly curved toward apex; [A. *vulg.* var. *wich.* (Stef.) Boivin; A. *acutidens* of auth., perhaps not Buser; A. *acut.* var. *alpestriformis* Salmon; introd. in SE Greenland; MAPS: Hultén 1958: map 75, p. 95; Löve and Löve 1956b: fig. 23, p. 228; Samuelsson, loc. cit., fig 2, p. 17] . . . . [A. *wichurae* Stef.]

1 Petioles and at least the lower part of the stem more or less densely spreading-hairy.

    4 Leaves glabrous above, hairy on the veins beneath (and sometimes thinly so over the lower surface), with usually 9 rounded lobes (middle lobes with up to 15 curved teeth), the basal sinus wide; [A. pratensis and A. vulgaris of Canadian reports, perhaps not Opiz nor L., respectively; introd. at Yarmouth and Bridgetown, N.S.] . . . . [A. xanthochlora Rothm.]

    4 Leaves hairy above, at least in the folds along the veins.

        5 Pedicels spreading-hairy; leaves with (5)7–9 lobes, the middle lobes with 9–11(13) teeth.

            6 Basal leaf-sinus closed or nearly so; teeth subobtuse, nearly straight; plant silvery-silky; [A. anglica Rothm.; A. minor Huds. in part; Grosse-Ile, near Quebec City, Que., where probably introd.: Bradshaw, Dansereau, and Valentine 1964] . . . . [A. glaucescens Wallr.]

            6 Basal leaf-sinus wide (at least 60°); teeth acute, somewhat curved; pubescence less dense and silky; [A. filicaulis f. vest. Buser; A. minor Huds. in part; introd. in E Que. and S Labrador at the Strait of Belle Isle and in Nfld. and N.S. (Digby and Halifax counties); S Greenland; MAP: Hultén 1958: map 109, p. 128] . . . . [A. vestita (Buser) Raunk.]

        5 Pedicels glabrous (but the petioles and lower part of stem with some spreading hairs), the pubescence of the whole plant relatively sparse.

            7 Basal leaf-sinus closed or nearly so; leaves thickly hairy on both surfaces, usually 9-lobed, with up to 19 acute, somewhat curved teeth on the middle lobes; [A. pastoralis Buser; A. vulg. var. past. (Buser) Boivin; introd. in SE Nfld. (where a bad weed according to Fernald in Gray 1950) and in N.S. (St. Peters, Richmond Co.; DAO, annotated as an occasional garden-escape), and reported from Que. and Ont. by Boivin 1966b] . . . . [A. monticola Opiz]

            7 Basal leaf-sinus open, forming an angle of up to nearly 90°; leaves usually 7-lobed (with commonly not more than 11 or 13 teeth on the middle lobes), at least the summer leaves rather thinly hairy (the hairs often restricted to the folds above and the veins beneath).

                8 Stipules usually tinged purplish red; flowers often slightly hairy on the receptacle; teeth of leaves acute, somewhat curved toward apex; [A. vulgaris var. fil. (Buser) Fern. & Wieg.; A. minor ssp. fil. (Bus.) Lindb. f.; Que. (N to the George R. at ca. 57°N), Labrador (N to ca. 59°N according to Hultén's map), and Nfld., and reported from Ont. and N.S. by Boivin 1966b; MAPS: Hultén 1958: map 96, p. 115; Böcher 1954: fig. 21 (top), p. 79; Samuelsson, loc. cit., fig. 3, p. 19; Raymond 1950b: fig. 9, p. 17] . . . . [A. filicaulis Buser]

                8 Stipules untinged or brownish; receptacle glabrous; leaf-lobes short, with broad blunt teeth; [introd. in W Greenland; MAPS: Löve and Löve 1956b: fig. 22, p. 227; Samuelsson, loc. cit., fig. 3, p. 19] . . . . [A. subcrenata Buser]

AMELANCHIER Medic. [3343] Juneberry, Serviceberry, Shadbush.
Poirier or Petites Poires

(Ref.: Wiegand 1912; Nielsen 1939; Jones 1946)

1 Inflorescence with at most 4 flowers, 1 flower terminal, the others from leaf-axils; ovary subconical below the densely tomentose summit, the fruit longer than thick; leaves oblong-elliptic or somewhat obovate, acute to blunt, sharply and closely serrate, gradually tapering or cuneate to a petiole at most about 1 cm long; (Ont. to Labrador, Nfld., and N.S.) . . . . A. bartramiana

1 Inflorescence racemose, only the lowest pedicels subtended by leaves; summit of ovary low and rounded, the fruit usually about as broad as long; petioles mostly at least 1 cm long.

    2 Ovary glabrous at summit or soon so.

3   Stoloniferous or suckering shrub forming more or less circular loose colonies rarely over 2 m tall; leaves broadly elliptic to subrotund, acute (or obtuse and more or less mucronate), finely and evenly serrate nearly or quite to base, glabrous, dark green and shining above; fruiting raceme with glabrous rachis and pedicels, the pedicels to about 2.5 cm long; petals at most about 7 mm long; (N.S.) . . . . *A. lucida*
3   Mostly taller coarse shrubs or small trees with more strongly ascending branches.
  4   Racemes ascending; mature sepals erect or irregularly recurving; petals to 12 mm long.
    5   Leaves oblong to oblong-elliptic or narrowly oblong-obovate, rounded to barely mucronate or subacute at apex, rounded at base, with up to 11 teeth per cm, scarcely half-grown at anthesis and then copiously white-felted beneath, finally glabrate; calyces, rachis, and pedicels tomentose, the pedicels not much over 2 cm long; (Ont. to N.B. and N.S.) . . . . *A. canadensis*
    5   Leaves relatively broader, usually short-acuminate, commonly cordate at base, with about 6 teeth per cm, well-grown and glabrate or only sparsely pubescent at anthesis; calyces, rachis, and pedicels nearly or quite glabrous, the pedicels to about 3.5 cm long; (Ont. to Nfld. and N.S.) . . . . *A. intermedia*
  4   Racemes flexuous or nodding; mature sepals abruptly reflexed from the base; petals 1 to 2 cm long; leaves elliptic to ovate or slightly obovate, acuminate, rounded or cordate at base, with mostly 6–10 teeth per cm.
    6   Leaves small and folded at anthesis, then densely white-tomentose beneath, green above, retaining some pilosity beneath and on the petioles in maturity; racemes at most 5 cm long, the pedicels not much over 1.5 cm long; petals less than 1.5 cm long; fruit dry and insipid; (Ont. to N.B.) . . . . *A. arborea*
    6   Leaves half-grown at flowering time, usually reddish or purple-tinged, essentially glabrous; petioles glabrous; racemes to over 7 cm long, the pedicels to 5 cm long; petals to 2 cm long; fruit juicy and sweet; (Ont. to Nfld. and N.S.) . . . . *A. laevis*
2 Ovary densely tomentose at summit, the mature fruit retaining some of this pubescence; leaves oblong to broadly ovate, obovate, or subrotund, subtruncate at base, rounded or short-pointed at apex.
  7   Mature leaves of fertile branches rather closely serrate with mostly at least 6 teeth per cm.
    8   Leaves obtuse or merely mucronate, toothed along the upper 2/3 of the margin, densely white-tomentose beneath when young, soon glabrate, their lateral veins not prominent near the margins; racemes relatively compact, erect, the rachis and pedicels pubescent during anthesis; mature pedicels to about 1.5 cm long; sepals rarely over 3 mm long, soon reflexed from near the middle; (Ont. to Nfld. and N.S.) . . . . *A. stolonifera*
    8   Leaves rounded to acutish at apex, toothed to base, glabrous from the first, their lateral veins prominent beneath to tip; racemes loose and spreading, glabrous, the pedicels to 3.5 cm long; sepals at least 3 mm long, erect or somewhat spreading; (Que. to Nfld. and N.S.) . . . . *A. fernaldii*
  7   Mature leaves of fertile branches coarsely serrate-dentate with usually less than 6 teeth per cm.
    9   Leaves broadly elliptic to quadrate-rotund, mostly subtruncate to broadly truncate at apex, yellowish-tomentose beneath when young, soon glabrate; flowering racemes to about 3 cm long, the rachis silky, the pedicels not much over 1 cm long; petals less than 8 mm long; sepals about 3 mm long and nearly as broad; (cent. Alaska–B.C. to w Que.) . . . . *A. alnifolia*

9 Leaves usually rounded or acute at apex, elliptic to oblong, slightly
  obovate or subrotund; sepals to about 5 mm long.
    10 Veins of leaves forming a network short of the margins, many of them
      not entering the teeth, these extending nearly to the leaf-base; petals
      less than 1 cm long; racemes glabrous.
        11 Racemes strict, to about 5 cm long; pedicels rarely over 1.5 cm
          long, only the lowest one subtended by a leaf; sepals at least 3.5
          mm long; leaves short-acuminate or mucronate at apex, densely
          pubescent when expanding; (SE Man. and Ont.) . . . . *A. mucronata*
        11 Racemes loose and open, to 8 cm long; pedicels to 3 cm long, the
          lower 1, 2, or 3 subtended by large leaves; sepals at most 3.5 mm
          long; leaves rounded or subtruncate at apex, glabrous or nearly so
          from the first; (Ont. to Que. and N.B.) . . . . *A. gaspensis*
    10 Veins or their branches extending into the teeth of the leaves.
        12 Racemes densely silky-tomentose, erect, to about 5 cm long;
          pedicels less than 1.5 cm long; petals to about 1 cm long, broadly
          obovate, about half as broad as long; leaves densely tomentose
          beneath at anthesis, finally glabrate or with pubescent petioles,
          entire or toothed to slightly below the middle; colonial, stoloniferous
          or strongly suckering shrub to 8 m tall; (Ont. and Que.) . . . . . . *A. humilis*
        12 Racemes essentially glabrous, mostly loose and open, to 7 cm long;
          petals linear-lanceolate to broadly oblanceolate; plant
          nonstoloniferous and nonsuckering, or essentially so.
          13 Leaves rounded and short-acuminate or short-pointed at apex,
            sharply serrate, the sinuses narrow and acute; stronger veins
            commonly not more than 11 pairs, mostly forking at apex;
            mature sepals strongly reflexed from the base; petals to 1.5 cm
            long; (Ont. to Nfld. and N.S.) . . . . *A. wiegandii*
          13 Leaves rounded or merely subacute at apex, dentate, the
            sinuses usually more open; stronger veins commonly up to 15
            pairs; mature sepals recurving from near the middle; (Ont. and
            Que.).
            14 Leaves with 3 or 4 teeth per cm of margin, the primary upper
              veins curving forward, simple or forking, their branches
              entering the teeth; overwintering buds lustrous; petals
              broadly oblanceolate to obovate . . . . *A. huronensis*
            14 Leaves with mostly simple and straight primary upper veins,
              these running directly to the teeth; overwintering buds dull;
              petals linear to narrowly spatulate . . . . *A. sanguinea*

A. alnifolia Nutt.   Saskatoon-berry
/ST/(X)/ (Mc) Thickets and borders of woods, the aggregate species from cent. Alaska–Yukon to Great Bear L., L. Athabasca (Alta. and Sask.), Man. (N to Gillam, about 165 mi S of Churchill), Ont. (N to the Fawn R. at ca. 55°N, 88°W), and W Que. (known only from the Nottaway R. SE of James Bay at 50°21′N; Dutilly and Lepage 1963), S to Calif., N.Mex., Colo., Nebr., and Iowa. MAPS and synonymy: see below.
1 Petals usually less than 12 mm long; top of ovary usually copiously pubescent.
  2 Styles rarely less than 5; leaves usually strongly toothed along most of the upper
    half . . . . var. *alnifolia*
    3 Berries blue-purple; [*A. canadensis* var. *aln.* (Nutt.) T. & G.; *A. carrii* Rydb.;
      A. florida of Canadian reports E of B.C., not Lindl.; *Aronia ovalis* sensu
      Richardson 1823, and *Amel. ovalis* sensu Hooker 1832, not *Pyrus ovalis* Willd.,
      basionym, nor *Amel. ovalis* Medic. nor Borkh.; Alaska–B.C. to W Que.; MAPS:
      Hultén 1968b:599; Jones 1946: map 9 (the Yukon–B.C. to S Man.), p. 69; the
      maps for *A. florida* by Raup 1947: pl. 28, and Preston 1947:174, are largely
      applicable here] . . . . f. *alnifolia*

3   Berries white; [Alta. and Sask.] . . . . f. *alba* Nielsen
2   Styles 4; leaves subentire or with a few small teeth toward summit; [*A. florida* var.
     hump. Jones; B.C.] . . . . var. *humptulipensis* (Jones) Hitchc.
1   Petals usually well over 12 mm long.
     4   Top of ovary varying from glabrous to rather copiously hairy but usually not
          greyish-tomentose; petals to 2.5 cm long and 8.5 mm broad; calyx-lobes
          averaging at least 3 mm long; [*A. cusickii* Fern.; s B.C.; MAP: Jones 1946: map 11
          (*A. cusickii*), p. 79] . . . . var. *cusickii* (Fern.) Hitchc.
     4   Top of ovary concealed by a copious greyish tomentum; petals to about 1.5 cm
          long, less than 4 mm broad; calyx-lobes averaging less than 3 mm long; [*A. ovalis*
          var. *semi.* Hook.; *A. florida* Lindl.; *A. gormanii* Greene; *A. oxyodon* Koehne; s
          Alaska–B.C.; MAPS (*A. florida*): Jones 1946: map 10, p. 75; Hultén 1968*b*:599] . . . .
          . . . . var. *semiintegrifolia* (Hook.) Hitchc.

A. arborea (Michx. f.) Fern.
/T/EE/   (Mc)   Woods and thickets from Minn. to Ont. (N to Renfrew and Carleton counties),
Que. (N to Grosse-Ile, Montmagny Co.), and s N.B. (Charlotte and York counties), s to Okla.,
La., and N Fla. [*Mespilus* Michx. f.]. MAPS: Jones 1946: map 5, p. 37; Preston 1961:250 (in-
accurate northwards).

A. bartramiana (Tausch) Roemer
/ST/EE/   (N)   Thickets and peaty or boggy places from Ont. (N to Hawley L. at 54°34′N) to
Que. (N to the s Ungava Bay watershed at 57°42′N, L. Mistassini, and the Côte-Nord), Labrador (N to Turnavik, ca. 56°N), Nfld., N.B., P.E.I., and N.S., s to Minn., Mich., Pa., and Mass.
[*Pyrus* Tausch; *A. canadensis* var. *oligocarpa* (Michx.) T. & G.]. MAP: Jones 1946: map 1 (incomplete northwards), p. 22.
    Hybrids with the following species have been reported from Canada or are so-named on
herbarium sheets: with *A. fernaldii* (Que.: Magdalen Is. and Val-d'Or, Abitibi Co.; CAN); with *A.
gaspensis* (Que.: Rimouski, Rimouski Co.; CAN, detd. Wiegand); with *A. humilis* (× *A. quinti-
martii* Lalonde, the type from Rougemont, Rouville Co., sw Que.; also known from near Sherbrooke and from Val-Jalbert, L. St. John, Que.); with *A. laevis* (× *A. neglecta* Egglest.; Ont.:
reported from the SE shore of L. Superior by Hosie 1938; Que.: N to the Gaspé Pen.; Nfld.;
N.B.: Woodstock; P.E.I.: Queens Co.; N.S.: Digby and Colchester counties); with *A. stolonifera*
(Nfld. and P.E.I.; CAN); with *A. wiegandii* (Ont.: collection in CAN from Timmins; Que.: N to the
Gaspé Pen.).

A. canadensis (L.) Medic.
/T/EE/   (Ms)   Low ground, swamps, and thickets from Ont. (N to Algonquin Park, Renfrew
Co., and the Ottawa dist.) to Que. (N to the Montreal dist.), N.B. (Charlotte and Kent coun-
ties), P.E.I. (Kings Co.), and N.S., s to Ga.; introd. in Europe (Hultén 1958). [*Mespilus* L.;
Pyrus (A.) botryapium L. f.; incl. *A. oblongifolia* (T. & G.) Roemer]. MAPS (those by Hough and
Munns scarcely reflecting the present concept of the species): Jones 1946: map 6, p. 46;
Hough 1947: p. 243; Munns 1938: map 133, p. 137; M.L. Fernald and Harold St. John, Rho-
dora 23(269): map 8, pl. 130, facing p. 120. 1921.

A. fernaldii Wieg.
/T/EE/   (N)   Calcareous thickets, shores, and ravines from Que. (N to the E James Bay wa-
tershed at ca. 51°30′N, L. St. John, and the Côte-Nord; type from Magdalen Is.) to Nfld., N.B.
(Dalhousie, Restigouche Co.), and N.S. MAP: Jones 1946: map 8, p. 61.
    A purported hybrid with *A. gaspensis* is known from E Que. (Bic, Rimouski Co.; CAN; MT).

A. gaspensis (Wieg.) Fern. & Weath.
/T/EE/   (N)   Ledges and shores (chiefly calcareous) from N Minn. to Ont. (N to the Ekwan
R. at ca. 53°30′N), Que. (N to the E James Bay watershed at ca. 52°N and the type locality at
the mouth of the Bonaventure R., Gaspé Pen.), and N N.B. (Portage Is., Northumberland Co.).
[*A. sanguinea* var. *gaspensis* Wieg.]. MAP: Jones 1946: map 7, p. 54.

A purported hybrid with *A. wiegandii* is reported from Que. by Ernest Lepage (Nat. can. (Que.) 69(12):267. 1942; Trois-Pistoles, Temiscouata Co.).

A. humilis Wieg.
/T/EE/ (Mc) Rocky or sandy shores and ledges (often calcareous) from Minn. to Ont. (N to the W James Bay watershed at ca. 51°30'N and Big Trout L. at ca. 54°N, 90°W; CAN) and Que. (N to the E James Bay watershed at ca. 52°N and the Gaspé Pen.), S to S.Dak., Wisc., Ohio, and Vt. [Incl. var. *compacta* Nielsen; *A. spicata sensu* Jones 1946, in part, not (Lam.) Koch].

A. huronensis Wieg.
/T/EE/ (N) Thickets, cliffs, and shores from Minn. to Ont. (N to W James Bay at ca. 53°N) and Que. (N to Price, Matane Co., Gaspé Pen.; RIM, detd. Nielsen).
   Jones (1946) merges this species with *A. sanguinea*. A purported hybrid with *A. laevis* is reported from the SE shore of L. Superior, Ont., by Hosie (1938).

A. intermedia Spach
/T/EE/ (Mc) Thickets, shores, and swampy places from Minn. to Ont. (N to Stormont Co.; Dore and Gillett 1955), Que. (N to near Quebec City), Nfld., N.B. (Charlotte Co.), P.E.I. (Kings Co.), and N.S., S to N.C. [*A. canadensis sensu* Jones 1946, in part, not (L.) Medic.].

A. laevis Wieg.
/T/EE/ (Mc) Thickets and swampy places from Ont. (N to Matheson, 48°32'N) to Que. (N to the Gaspé Pen.), Nfld., N.B., P.E.I., and N.S., S to Iowa, Ohio, Del., and Ga. [*A. arborea* var. *cordifolia* (Ashe) Boivin; incl. var. *nitida* (Wieg.) Fern.; *A. canadensis sensu* Fowler 1885 (incl. var. *oblongifolia*) as to the Campbellton and Bass River collections, not (L.) Medic. (relevant collections in NBM) and *sensu* Saint-Cyr 1887 (*see* St. John 1922); *Prunus serotina sensu* Lindsay 1878, not Ehrh., at least in part, a relevant collection from Northwest Arm, Halifax, N.S., in NSPM]. MAP: Jones 1946: map 4, p. 32.

A. lucida Fern.
/T/E/ (Mc) Known only from boggy or rocky barrens and gravelly thickets of N.S. (Annapolis, Yarmouth, Shelburne, Lunenburg, and Halifax counties; type from Middleton, Annapolis Co.). [*A. stolonifera* var. *luc.* Fern.; *A. spicata sensu* Jones 1946, in part, not (Lam.) Koch].

A. mucronata Nielsen
/T/EE/ (Mc) Rocks (chiefly calcareous) from SE Man. (Fernald *in* Gray 1950) to N Minn. and Ont. (Mattice, on the Missinaibi R. SW of James Bay at ca. 49°30'N; CAN, detd. Nielsen). [*A. spicata sensu* Jones 1946, in part, not (Lam.) Koch].

A. sanguinea (Pursh) DC.   Petites poires
/T/EE/ (Mc) Open woods and rocky slopes from Ont. (N to Nikip L. at ca. 53°N, 92°W) to Que. (N to Aylmer, Pontiac Co., and the Montreal dist.), S to Iowa, Ohio, and N.C. [*Pyrus* Pursh; *A. spicata sensu* Jones 1946, in part, not (Lam.) Koch; incl. f. *grandiflora* Wieg. (*A. amabilis* Wieg.), considered by Jones 1946, to be a hybrid between *A. canadensis* and *A. laevis*]. MAP: Jones 1946: map 8, p. 61.

A. stolonifera Wieg.   Petites poires
/T/EE/ (N) Acid rocks and sands from Ont. (N to SW James Bay at 51°16'N) to Que. (N to E James Bay at ca. 51°30'N, L. St. John, Anticosti Is., and the Gaspé Pen.), Nfld., N.B., P.E.I., and N.S., S to Minn., Mich., and Va. [*A. spicata sensu* Jones 1946, in part, not (Lam.) Koch].

A. wiegandii Nielsen
/T/EE/ (Mc) Rocky or sandy places and streambanks from Ont. (Stokes Bay, Bruce Co.; CAN; a collection from Big Trout L., at ca. 54°N, 90°W, has also been placed here) to Que. (N to the Côte-Nord, Anticosti Is., and the Gaspé Pen.), Nfld., N.B., P.E.I., and N.S., S to Minn., Mich., N.Y., and N New Eng. [*A. interior sensu* Jones 1946, in part, not Nielsen].

ARUNCUS L. [3322]

A. sylvester Kostel.   Goat's-beard
/sT/W/EA/ (Hp) Moist woods and streambanks from s Alaska (*see* Hultén 1946: map 747, p. 1061) through B.C. (E to the Selkirk Mts.) to NW Calif.; Eurasia. Introd. in Que. (Knowlton, Brome Co.; Sweetsburg, Missisquoi Co.) and N.S. (Yarmouth Co.; NSPM). [*A. dioicus* (Walt.) Fern.; *Spiraea (A.) acuminata* Dougl.; *S. (Astilbe) aruncus* L.; *S. (Ar.) kamchatica* Maxim.; *Ar. vulgaris* Raf.]. MAPS: Hultén 1968*b*:595; Meusel, Jaeger, and Weinert 1965: 206 *(A. dioicus)*.

CHAMAERHODOS Bunge [3361]

C. erecta (L.) Bunge
/ST/WW/A/ (Hs) Arid plains and hills from s-cent. Yukon (*see* Hultén 1946: map 789, p. 1065), s Dist. Mackenzie (Porsild and Cody 1968), and B.C.–Alta. to Sask. (N to L. Athabasca) and SW Man. (N to Bield, NW of Riding Mt.), s to Colo., N.Dak., Minn., and N Mich.; Asia. [*Sibbaldia* L.; incl. var. *nuttallii* Pickering (*C. nuttallii* (Pick.) Rydb.), var. *parviflora* (Nutt.) Hitchc., and the villous as well as glandular var. *keweenawensis* Fern.]. MAPS: Hultén 1968*b*:624; Fernald 1935: map 10 (incomplete northwards), p. 214.

COTONEASTER Medic. [3333]

1   Leaves elliptic-ovate, broadly acute, persistently rather densely white-tomentose beneath; calyx-tube pubescent; fruit with 2 nutlets; (introd. from Alta. to Ont.) . . . .
. . . . *C. acutifolia*
1   Leaves ovate or oval to subrotund, broadly acute to rounded at summit, yellowish-tomentose beneath (becoming merely pubescent at maturity); calyx-tube glabrous externally; fruit with 3 or 4 nutlets; (introd. in Alta. and Man.) . . . . *C. melanocarpa*

C. acutifolia Turcz.
Asiatic; introd. in Alta. (Edmonton), Sask. (Saskatoon), Man. (Brandon, Fort Garry, and Pointe du Bois; G.A. Stevenson, Can. Field-Nat. 79(3):175. 1965), and Ont. (Boivin 1966*b*).

C. melanocarpa Lodd.
Eurasian; introd. in Alta. (Edmonton, where "Growing wild quite plentifully in poplar-birch woods along the eastern slope of the Great Ravine"; CAN, detd. Porsild) and s Man. (Brandon; Stevenson, loc. cit.).

CRATAEGUS L.   [3345]   Hawthorn, Red Haw.   Aubépine, Pommettes, or Cenellier

(Ref.: Sargent 1908; Palmer 1925, 1946; Kruschke 1965)
1   Veins of the larger leaves running both to the sinuses and the points of the lobes; leaves relatively deeply 3–7-lobed, the lobes few-toothed; stamens about 20; anthers red; nutlets 1 or 2; (introd.).
   2   Nutlet usually 1; fruit at most about 8 mm thick; leaves deeply lobed . . . . *C. monogyna*
   2   Nutlets 2; fruit commonly larger; leaves less deeply lobed . . . . [*C. oxyacantha*]
1   Veins of leaves running only to the points of the lobes or of the larger teeth.
   3   Nutlets pitted or deeply concave on the inner (ventral) face.
      4   Fruit purplish black; nutlets 3–5; stamens usually 10 or less (sometimes 20); anthers white or pale pink; leaves elliptic to oval or oblong-obovate, usually indented only above the middle; branchlets thornless or with thorns at most 2.5 cm long; (B.C. to SW Sask.; W Ont.) . . . . *C. douglasii*
      4   Fruit orange, scarlet, or red; thorns mostly at least 3 cm long.
         5   Nutlets 3–5, only slightly pitted, acute at both ends; stamens about 20; leaves with usually acuminate apex and lobes; (Ont., Que., and N.S.) . . . .
. . . . *C. brainerdii*
         5   Nutlets 2 or 3, more deeply pitted, rounded at both ends; leaves with pointed or rounded apex and lobes.

6   Leaves dull yellow-green above, usually with 3–5 pairs of shallow often asymmetric lobes; young branchlets tomentose; stamens about 20; (s Ont.) . . . . *C. calpodendron*

6   Leaves green above, commonly with 4 or 5 pairs of lobes; branchlets glabrous or rarely slightly villous when young; (Man. to N.S.) . . . .
. . . . *C. succulenta*

3   Nutlets smooth on inner face.

7   Leaves of flowering branches commonly broadest above the middle; (Ont. and Que.).

8   Leaves unlobed or only slightly lobed on vegetative shoots, their veins only slightly impressed above; leaf-blade commonly at least 4 times as long as the petiole; stamens about 10; fruit with thin dryish flesh and 1–3 nutlets . . . . . .
. . . . *C. crus-galli*

8   Leaves of flowering branchlets commonly more or less lobed, those of vegetative shoots more deeply cut, the veins usually conspicuously impressed above; leaf-blade often less than 4 times as long as the petiole; stamens usually about 20; mature fruit fleshy and edible, with usually 3–5 nutlets . . . . *C. punctata*

7   Leaves of flowering branches broadest at or below the middle; nutlets usually 3–5.

9   Petioles and base of leaves conspicuously glandular; flowers 3–7 in nearly simple corymbs; bracts of corymb copiously glandular; stamens about 10; anthers white or pale yellow (rarely pink); fruit with thin dry flesh; (s Ont. and N.S.) . . . . *C. intricata*

9   Petioles and leaves glandless or becoming nearly so; flowers few to many in usually compound cymes or corymbs.

10 Leaves of flowering branchlets mostly elliptic or rhombic, broadest near the middle, cuneate or abruptly narrowed at base.

11 Anthers typically pink or red; apex and lobes of leaves of flowering branchlets acuminate; leaves of vegetative shoots seldom as broad as long; (Ont., Que., and N.S.) . . . . *C. brainerdii*

11 Anthers commonly white or pale yellow; apex and lobes of leaves of flowering branchlets usually acute or obtuse; leaves of vegetative shoots sometimes broader than long; (B.C. to N.S.) . . . . . . *C. rotundifolia*

10 Leaves of flowering branchlets commonly broadest below the middle, broadly cuneate to rounded or subcordate at base.

12 Fruit bearing a relatively small calyx; nutlets 3–5; stamens usually not more than 10; young leaves appressed-strigose above; (Ont. to N.S.) . . . . *C. flabellata*

12 Fruit typically bearing a large prominent calyx.

13 Leaves rather densely short-hairy above and more or less tomentose beneath while young; petioles and midribs stout; corymbs tomentose; fruit pubescent at least when young; nutlets usually 5; stamens about 20, their anthers white or pale yellow (rarely pink); (s Ont.) . . . . *C. mollis*

13 Leaves and corymbs glabrous or pubescent; petioles and midribs slender; fruit glabrous; nutlets 3–5.

14 Leaves of flowering branchlets prevailingly oblong-ovate, broadest near middle; stamens 10 or less (atypically about 20); anthers pink or red; mature fruit mellow or juicy; nutlets 3–5; (Ont. to N.S.) . . . . *C. coccinea*

14 Leaves of flowering branchlets mostly ovate, rhombic, or deltoid, broadest below middle; stamens commonly about 20.

15 Fruit bright red, with thick mellow or succulent flesh and usually 5 nutlets; corymbs glabrous or sparsely villous; flowers usually over 2 cm broad; anthers roseate; leaves

of flowering branches broadly ovate or deltoid-ovate;
(s Ont. and sw Que.) . . . . *C. dilatata*
15 Fruit dull crimson or green, with thin dry or mealy flesh
and 3–5 nutlets; corymbs glabrous; flowers at most 2 cm
broad; anthers white, creamy white, or pink; (s Ont., sw
Que., and Nfld.) . . . . *C. pruinosa*

C. brainerdii Sarg.
/T/EE/ (Mc) Thickets and pastures, the aggregate species from s Ont. (N to the Ottawa
dist.), sw Que. (N to the Montreal dist.), and N.S. (Kings and Cape Breton counties; GH) to
Mich., N.Y., New Eng., and N.C.
1 Leaves prevailingly oval, obtuse or short-pointed, only obscurely lobed; [*C. affinis*
and *C. egglestonii* Sarg.; s Que. and N.S.] . . . . var. *egglestonii* (Sarg.) Robins.
1 Leaves elliptic to oblong-ovate, acuminate.
2 Leaves thinnish, relatively smooth above; stamens about 20; anthers pink; [Ont.
and Que.] . . . . var. *brainerdii*
2 Leaves firm, roughish above; stamens 10–20.
3 Pedicels sometimes sparsely villous; anthers pink; [*C. asperifolia*,
C. aquilonaris, and *C. picta* Sarg.; s Ont. and sw Que.] . . . .
. . . . var. *asperifolia* (Sarg.) Egglest.
3 Pedicels glabrous; anthers pink or pale yellow; [*C. balkwillii* and *C. scabrida*
Sarg.; s Ont., s Que. (C.S. Sargent, Rhodora 3(28):76. 1901), and N.S.
(Fernald *in* Gray 1950)] . . . . var. *scabrida* (Sarg.) Egglest.

C. calpodendron (Ehrh.) Medic.
/t/EE/ (Mc) Open woods and thickets from Minn. to s Ont. (Fernald *in* Gray 1950; Soper
1949), s to Mo., Ala., and Ga. [*Mespilus* Ehrh.; *C. pubifolia* and *C. structilis* Ashe; incl. var. *mi-crocarpa* (Chapm.) Palmer].

C. coccinea L.
/T/EE/ (Mc) Thickets, pastures, and streambanks from Minn. to Ont. (N to the Ottawa
dist.), Que. (N to Berthier-en-Bas, Montmagny Co.), and N.S. (*C. holmesiana* reported from
Cape Breton Is. by C.S. Sargent, Rhodora 3(28):76. 1901; not known from N.B. or P.E.I.), s to
Ill., Ind., and Pa. [*C. holmesiana* Ashe and its var. *villipes* Ashe; *C. chippewaensis, C. cocci-nata, C. confinis, C. confragosa, C. ellwangeriana, C. ?improvisa, C. lenta, C. lobulata, C. mi-randa, C. pedicellata, C. pringlei, C. robesoniana, C. sejuncta, C. spissiflora, C. tardipes,* and
C. vivida Sarg.; *C. ?cordata* and *C. ?glandulosa* Willd.].
C. *anomala* Sarg. (type from Caughnawaga, near Montreal, Que.), *C. aulica* Sarg. (type
from near Toronto, Ont.), *C. illecebrosa* Sarg. (reported from s Ont.), and *C. knieskerniana*
Sarg. (reported from sw Que.) are suspected by Gleason and Cronquist (1963) to be hybrids
between *C. coccinea* and *C. mollis, C. dilatata, C. coccinoides,* and *C. flabellata,* respectively.

C. crus-galli L. Cockspur-Thorn
/T/EE/ (Mc) Dry or rocky thickets and pastures from Minn. to s Ont. (Essex, Lambton,
Middlesex, Welland, and Grey counties) and sw Que. (N to the Montreal dist.; MT; reported N
to Beauport, near Quebec City, by John Macoun, Can. J., n.s. 15(94, 95). 1877), s to E Tex.
and S.C. [*C. arduennae* Sarg.; *C. fontanesiana* (Spach) Steud.; *C. tenax* Ashe; incl. var. *pyra-canthifolia* Ait.]. MAP: Hough 1947:245.
C. *disperma* and *C. pausiaca* Ashe (*C. punctata* var. *paus.* (Ashe) Palmer) are thought by
Gleason and Cronquist (1963) to be possible hybrids between *C. crus-galli* and *C. punctata.*

C. dilatata Sarg.
/T/EE/ (Mc) Thickets and hillsides from Ont. (N to the Ottawa dist.), Que. (N to the Mon-treal dist.), and ?N.B. (Boivin 1966b; not known from P.E.I. or N.S.) to New Eng. [*C. conspecta*
and *C. macounii* Sarg.].

C. douglasii Lindl.
/T/WW/ (Mc) Open woods and rocky banks, the aggregate species from s Alaska and B.C. to Alta. (N to Jasper), sw Sask. (Cypress Hills), s ?Man. (John Macoun 1886), and cent. Ont. (SE shore of L. Superior; Abitibi R.), s to Calif., S.Dak., and N Mich. MAPS and synonymy: *see* below.

1 Flowers mostly with 10 stamens; ovary often slightly hairy; leaves tending to be obovate in outline; [*C. brevispina* (Dougl.) Heller; *C. rivularis* Nutt.; range of the species; MAP: Hultén 1968*b*:600] . . . . var. *douglasii*
1 Flowers mostly with 20 stamens; ovary usually glabrous; leaves tending to be elliptic or oblong in outline; [s B.C.] . . . . var. *suksdorfii* Sarg.

C. flabellata (Spach) Koch
/T/EE/ (Mc) Thickets and open woods, the aggregate species from Ont. (N to the Ottawa dist.) to sw Que. (*C. crudelis* reported N to Montmorency Falls, near Quebec City, by C.S. Sargent, Rhodora 5(53):144. 1903; reported N to Ile-aux-Coudres, about 70 mi NE of Quebec City, by Marie-Victorin 1935), N.B. (Grand Manan Is., Charlotte Co.; not known from P.E.I.), and N.S. (Victoria Co.; ACAD; GH), s to N.Y. and New Eng.

1 Leaves of flowering branchlets mostly ovate, with 5 or 6 pairs of acuminate lateral lobes, short-pilose above and sometimes villous along the veins beneath while young.
2 Stamens 10 or fewer; fruit oblong or subglobose; [incl. *C. gravis, C. macrosperma, C. prona,* and *C. roanensis* Ashe, *C. basilica* and *C. iracunda* Beadle, and *C. acuminata, C. acutiloba, C. alnorum, C. beata, C. blandita, C. colorata, C. compta, C. congestiflora, C. crudelis, C. demissa, C. formosa* (a possible hybrid between *C. flabellata* and *C. pruinosa*), *C. genialis, C. glaucophylla, C. lemingtonensis, C. levis, C. matura, C. ornata, C. pallidula, C. pastorum, C. pentandra, C. promissa, C. rubicunda, C. sarniensis, C. splendida, C. stolonifera, C. streeterae,* and *C. suavis* Sarg.; *C. fluviatilis* Sarg. in part; Ont. to N.B. and N.S.] . . . . var. *flabellata*
2 Stamens about 20; fruit short-oblong or subglobose; [*C. grayana* Egglest.; Ont. and Que.] . . . . var. *grayana* (Egglest.) Palmer
1 Leaves of flowering branchlets mostly elliptic, with 4 or 5 pairs of acute lateral lobes, glabrous except for short strigose pubescence on the upper surface while young; stamens 10 or fewer; [*C. densiflora* Sarg., the type from near Montreal, Que.; s Ont., sw Que., and N.S. (Cape Breton Is.); perhaps a hybrid between *C. flabellata* and *C. rotundifolia*] . . . . var. *densiflora* (Sarg.) Kruschke

C. intricata Lange
/T/EE/ (Mc) Thickets and open woods from Mich. to s Ont. (reported from Wellington Co. by Stroud 1941, who, however, lists *C. coccinea* in synonymy; *C. foetida* reported from Welland Co. by Sargent 1908) and N.S. (Melanson, Kings Co.; ACAD; not known from Que., N.B., or P.E.I.), s to Mich. and Va. [*C. biltmoreana* Small; *C. boyntonii* Beadle; *C. foetida* Ashe].

C. mollis (T. & G.) Scheele
/t/EE/ (Mc) Thickets and open woods from Mich. to s Ont. (Essex, Lambton, and Lincoln counties), s to Okla. and Ala. [*C. coccinea* var. *mollis* T. & G.; *C. canadensis, C. sera,* and *C. submollis* Sarg.; *C. subvillosa* Schrad.].

C. monogyna Jacq. English Hawthorne
European; cult. in N. America and often spreading to roadsides and borders of woods, as in B.C. (Sidney, Vancouver Is.), Ont. (N to Wellington, Ontario, and Durham counties), Que. (Marie-Victorin 1935), Nfld. (Rouleau 1956), N.B., P.E.I., and N.S.

[C. oxyacantha L.]
[European; occasionally escaping from cult. in N. America, as in s ?Ont. (Cambridge, Waterloo Co.; W. Herriot, Ont. Nat. Sci. Bull. 7:30. 1912) and sw ?Que. (a collection in MT from St.

Helen's Is., Montreal, has been placed here). It is reported from B.C. by Carter and New-combe (1921; Vancouver Is.). However, several reports from E Canada (as by Fowler 1885; relevant collections in NBM and NSPM) are based upon *C. monogyna* and the above citations require confirmation.]

C. pruinosa (Wendl.) Koch
/T/EE/ (Mc) Thickets and rocky ground (ranges of Canadian taxa outlined below), s to Ark., Ky., and N.C.

   C. rotundata Sarg. and *C. silvestris* Sarg. (the type locality of each near London, Ont.) are considered by Gleason and Cronquist (1963) as possible hybrids between *C. pruinosa* and *C. rotundifolia* and *C. punctata,* respectively.

1   Leaves ovate or deltoid, with 3–5 pairs of deep, acuminate, sharp lobes; petioles half
    to nearly as long as the leaf-blades; nutlets 2 or 3; [*C. compacta, C. leiophylla, C.
    longipedunculata,* and *C. prominens* Sarg.; *C. leiophylla* reported from s Ont. by
    Fernald *in* Gray 1950] . . . . var. *rugosa* (Ashe) Kruschke
1   Leaves prevailingly ovate, unlobed or only shallowly lobed; petioles at most 2/3 as
    long as the leaf-blades.
    2   Stamens about 10; calyx nearly sessile on the fruit; [*C. dissona* and *C. exornata*
        Sarg.; s Ont.: Lincoln and Welland counties; Sargent 1908] . . . .
        . . . . var. *dissona* (Sarg.) Egglest.
    2   Stamens about 20; calyx of fruit somewhat elevated.
        3   Anthers pink or rarely creamy white; calyx-lobes lanceolate; [*C. latisepala*
            Ashe; *C. cognata* Sarg.; SE Canada: Fernald *in* Gray 1950] . . . .
            . . . . var. *latisepala* (Ashe) Egglest.
        3   Anthers white or yellowish; calyx-lobes rather broadly triangular; [*C.
            perjucunda* and *C. placiva* Sarg.; s Ont. (Kent and York counties), SW Que.
            (Mt. St. Hilaire), and Nfld.] . . . . var. *pruinosa*

C. punctata Jacq.
/T/EE/ (Mc) Thickets, pastures, and open rocky ground from Ont. (N to the Ottawa dist.) and Que. (N to Quebec City; MT) to Iowa, Ind., and Ky.

   C. nitidula Sarg. (reported from s Ont.) is thought by Gleason and Cronquist (1963) to be a possible hybrid between *C. punctata* and *C. rotundifolia.* They also consider *C. ardua* Sarg. (type from near Toronto, Ont.), *C. celsa* Sarg. (*C. florifera* and *C. virilis* Sarg.; type of *C. virilis* from near Toronto, Ont.), and *C. integriloba* Sarg. (type from Beauharnois, Que.) possible hybrids between *C. punctata* and *C. succulenta.*

1   Fruit dull red or orange-red; anthers red or yellow.
    2   Leaves glabrous or merely more or less pubescent along the veins beneath;
        [*C. tomentosa* var. *punctata* (Jacq.) Gray; incl. *C. inaudita, C. saundersiana,* and
        C. suborbiculata Sarg.; *C. ?elliptica* and *C. ?flava* Ait.; Ont. and Que.; MAP: Hough
        1947:247] . . . . f. *punctata*
    2   Leaves (and corymbs) densely greyish-pubescent; [var. *can.* Britt.; Ont.: Fernald *in*
        Gray 1950] . . . . f. *canescens* (Britt.) Kruschke
1   Fruit bright yellow; anthers usually yellow; [var. *aurea* Ait.; SW Que.] . . . .
    . . . . f. *aurea* (Ait.) Rehder

C. rotundifolia Moench
/T/(X)/ (Mc) Thickets, streambanks, and hillsides from B.C. (N to the Peace River dist.) to Alta. (Waterton Lakes; Edmonton; Cypress Hills), Sask. (N to Tisdale, 52°51′N), Man. (N to Grand Rapids, near the NW end of L. Winnipeg), Ont. (N to the Missinaibi R. at ca. 50°N), Que. (N to the Harricanaw R. at ca. 49°N and the Gaspé Pen.), N.B. (Woodstock, Carleton Co.; GH), P.E.I., and N.S., s to Idaho, Mont., N.Mex., Wisc., and New Eng. [Incl. *C. columbiana* Howell, *C. piperi* Britt., *C. chrysocarpa, C. dodgei,* and *C. margaretta* Ashe, and *C. aborigi-num, C. blanchardii, C. brunetiana, C. champlainensis, C. crassifolia, C. delosii, C. faxonii, C. fernaldii, C. flavida, C. irrasa, C. jackii, C. jonesiae, C. laurentiana* (thought by Gleason and Cronquist 1963, to be a possible hybrid between *C. rotundifolia* and *C. succulenta*), *C. minuti-flora,* and *C. praecoqua* Sarg.].

C. succulenta Link

/T/EE/ (Mc) Thickets, rocky pastures, and borders of woods, the aggregate species from s Man. (Portage la Prairie; Macgregor) to Ont. (N to Hearst, ca. 49°30'N; CAN), Que. (N to Quebec City), N.B. (Woodstock, Carleton Co.), P.E.I., and N.S., s to Iowa, N.Y., and New Eng.

1 Stamens about 20; anthers pink or rarely white; fruit glabrous, succulent when ripe; [incl. *C. conspicua, C. divida, C. gemmosa, C. glabrata, C. saeva,* and *C. venulosa* Sarg.; Ont. to N.B. and N.S.] . . . . var. *succulenta*

1 Stamens about 10.

  2 Fruit pubescent at the ends; corymbs villous; [*C. occidentalis* Britt.; *C. macracantha* var. *occ.* (Britt.) Egglest.; incl. *C. flammea* and *C. microsperma* Sarg.; *C. punctata sensu* Scoggan 1957, not Jacq.; s Man. and w Ont.] . . . .
    . . . . var. *occidentalis* (Britt.) Palmer

  2 Fruit glabrous; corymbs glabrous or only slightly villous.

    3 Thorns relatively numerous, to over 8 cm long; anthers white, pale yellow, or rarely pink; fruit to 1 cm thick; [*C. macracantha* Lodd.; incl. *C. armigera, C. debilis, C. delectabilis, C. dumicola, C. ferentaria, C. ferta, C. fertilis, C. fulgida, C. limulata, C. peramoena, C. praeclara, C. prinoides, C. rhombifolia, C. stenophylla,* and *C. victorinii* Sarg.; *C. tomentosa* var. *pyrifolia sensu* Fowler 1885, and John Macoun 1883, as to Fredericton, N.B., collections, not *C. pyrifolia* Ait.; *C. ?glandulosa* Moench; apparently throughout the range of the aggregate species] . . . . var. *macracantha* (Lodd.) Egglest.

    3 Thorns fewer and shorter; fruit to 8 mm thick; [*C. neofluvialis* Ashe; *C. pisifera* Sarg.; s Ont.: Fernald *in* Gray 1950] . . . . var. *neofluvialis* (Ashe) Palmer

DALIBARDA Kalm [3353] False Violet

D. repens L. Robin-run-away

/T/EE/ (Hrr) Moist woods from Mich. to Ont. (N to Georgian Bay, L. Huron, and the Ottawa dist.), Que. (N to St-Pascal, Kamouraska Co., and the Mingan Is. of the Côte-Nord), N.B., and N.S. (concerning a possible former occurrence in P.E.I., *see* D.S. Erskine 1960), s to Ohio and N.C. [*D. violaeoides* Michx.; *Rubus dalibarda* L.].

DRYAS L. [3368] Dryas, Mountain Avens

(Ref.: Porsild 1947; Hultén 1959)

1 Petals orange-yellow, ascending; sepals broadly ovate; anther-filaments hairy toward base; receptacle flattish; peduncles with up to 4 minute bracts; leaves elliptic to narrowly obovate, cuneate at base, coarsely dentate to apex; (Alaska–B.C. to Sask.; Ont.; Que.; w Nfld.) . . . . *D. drummondii*

1 Petals white or creamy, spreading; sepals lanceolate to linear-oblong; filaments glabrous; receptacle convex; peduncles bractless or with only 1 rudimentary bract; leaves lance-oblong to deltoid-ovate, truncate or cordate at base.

  2 Leaves coarsely incised-crenate to apex, strongly rugose above, the midvein prominent beneath, bearing sessile or stalked glands; (Alaska–Yukon–NW Dist. Mackenzie and mts. of B.C. and w Alta.; E Greenland) . . . . *D. octopetala*

  2 Leaves entire or merely with a few teeth in the lower half, scarcely rugose above, the midvein beneath neither prominent nor glandular; (transcontinental) . . . .
    . . . . *D. integrifolia*

D. drummondii Richards.

/ST/D/ (Ch) Calcareous cliffs, talus, and river-gravels (ranges of Canadian taxa outlined below), s in the West to Oreg., Idaho, and Mont., farther eastwards with isolated stations noted below. The type locality was given as "rivers in the Rocky Mountains and about Slave Lake". MAPS and synonymy: *see* below.

1 Calyx and hypanthium densely silky-appressed-pubescent, completely lacking stipitate glands; [Alaska (Glacier Bay) and the mts. of B.C. and sw Alta. (type from Pipestone Summit, Banff National Park)] . . . . var. *eglandulosa* Porsild

1 Calyx and hypanthium densely covered with black or purplish stipitate glands.
  2 Leaves canescent-tomentose and whitish above; [*D. tomentosa* Farr, the type
     from Emerald Lake, SE B.C.; SE Alaska–Yukon–W Dist. Mackenzie and the mts. of
     SE B.C. and SW Alta.] . . . . var. *tomentosa* (Farr) Williams
  2 Leaves dark green and essentially glabrous above; [Alaska to L. Athabasca,
     Sask., S in the foothills and mts. through B.C. and SW Alta.; W Ont. (Slate Is., L.
     Superior); Que. (L. Mistassini; Côte-Nord; Anticosti Is.; Gaspé Pen.) and W Nfld.;
     MAPS: Porsild 1947:183; Hultén 1968*b*:629, and 1959: fig. 8, p. 525; Raup 1947: pl.
     29; *Atlas of Canada* 1957: map 18, sheet 38; Meusel, Jaeger, and Weinert
     1965:220; Fernald 1918*b*: map 9 (incomplete), pl. 12]. A purported hybrid with *D.
     integrifolia* (× *D. wyssiana* Beauv. (× *D. lewinii* Rouleau)) is reported from the
     Mingan Is. of the Côte-Nord, E Que., and from Nlfd. by Rouleau 1956. However,
     Porsild has annotated a Mingan Is. collection, ''I can see no trace of *D.
     drummondii* in this.'' . . . . var. *drummondii*

D. integrifolia Vahl
/AST/X/GeA/ (Ch) Calcareous gravels, rocky barrens, cliffs, and talus, the aggregate species from the coasts of Alaska–Yukon–Dist. Mackenzie–Dist. Keewatin throughout the Canadian Arctic Archipelago to northernmost Ellesmere Is. and northernmost Ungava–Labrador, S
in the West through the mts. of E B.C. and SW Alta. to ?Mont., farther eastwards S to S Dist.
Mackenzie–Dist. Keewatin, NE Man. (Churchill; a Gardner collection in CAN, purportedly from
Flin Flon, probably originated from Churchill), N Ont. (S to W James Bay at 54°22′N; isolated
stations on the Slate Is., N L. Superior), islands in James Bay, Que. (S to E James Bay at
52°37′N, L. Mistassini, the Côte-Nord, Anticosti Is., and Gaspé Pen.), Labrador (S to Battle
Harbour, 52°17′N), Nfld., and SE N.B. (Albert Co.; P.R. Roberts, Rhodora 67(769):92. 1965;
R.P. Gorham, Acadian Naturalist 1(4):185. 1944); circumgreenlandic; NE Siberia. MAPS and synonymy: *see* below.
1 Leaf-bases cuneate-truncate, the blades linear-oblong, plane, essentially entire; [*D.
   sylv.* (Hult.) Porsild; Alaska (type from Circle) to Great Bear L. and Great Slave L.;
   MAPS: Porsild 1947:183 *(D. sylv.)*; Hultén 1968*b*:632, and 1959: fig. 12, p. 536] . . . .
   . . . . ssp. *sylvatica* Hult.
1 Leaf-bases cordate-truncate, the leaves with revolute margins.
  2 Leaves crenate to tip, oblong-ovate, thin, flat, about 3 times as long as broad; [*D.
     crenulata* Juz.; *D. babingtoniana* Porsild in part; considered by Hultén 1959, to be
     a hybrid between *D. integrifolia* and *D. octopetala*; Alaska–W Yukon–NW Dist.
     Mackenzie; Greenland; E Siberia; MAP: Porsild 1947:183 *(D. cren.)*] . . . .
     . . . . ssp. *crenulata* (Juz.) Scoggan
  2 Leaves entire or merely with a few teeth in the lower half.
    3 Leaves ovate-elliptic, at most twice as long as broad; flowers at most 2 cm
       broad; petals retuse; [*D. chamissonis* Spreng.; Alaska, the type from
       Kotzebue Sound; E Siberia; MAP: Porsild 1947:183 *(D. cham.)*] . . . .
       . . . . ssp. *chamissonis* (Spreng.) Scoggan
    3 Leaves lanceolate, about 3 times as long as broad; flowers mostly over 2 cm
       broad; petals not retuse . . . . ssp. *integrifolia* var. *integrifolia*
      4 Upper leaf-surfaces canescent-tomentose; [var. *can.* Simmons, the type
         from Ellesmere Is.; Alaska, NW Dist. Mackenzie, E Dist. Keewatin, Axel
         Heiberg Is., Baffin Is., Ellesmere Is., and Nfld.; MAP: Porsild 1947:183
         (somewhat incomplete)] . . . . f. *canescens* (Simmons) Fern.
      4 Upper leaf-surfaces glabrous or nearly so, dark green and shining.
        5 Leaves distinctly dentate; [var. *intermedia* Nathorst; *D. oct.* var. *integ.* f.
           inter. (Nathorst) Hartz; reported by Polunin 1940, from E Dist. Keewatin,
           Ellesmere Is., Baffin Is., and Southampton Is.] . . . .
           . . . . f. *intermedia* (Nathorst) Polunin
        5 Leaves entire or subentire; [*D. octopetala* var. *integ.* (Vahl) Hook.;
           D. integ. var. *subintegrifolia* Hult. in part; *D. tenella* Pursh;
           transcontinental; type from W Greenland; MAPS: Porsild 1957: map 235,
           p. 190, 1955: fig. 9, p. 39, and 1947:183; Hultén 1968*b*:631, and 1959:

fig. 12, p. 536; Böcher 1954: fig. 2 (map 1), p. 134; Savile 1961: map B,
p. 928; Raup 1947: pl. 29; *Atlas of Canada* 1957: maps 7 and 7a, sheet
38; Fernald 1925: map 57, p. 323, and 1918a: map 3, pl. 16] . . . . f. *integrifolia*

D. octopetala L.
/AST/W/GEA/ (Ch) Calcareous gravels, tundra, and alpine heaths, the aggregate species
from N Alaska, cent. Yukon, and the Mackenzie R. Delta to Banks Is., NW Victoria Is., and E
Melville Is., s through the mts. of B.C. and sw Alta. to Oreg., Idaho, and Colo.; E Greenland between ca. 68° and 79°N; Iceland; Spitsbergen; Eurasia. MAPS and synonymy: *see* below.
1 Upper leaf-surfaces lacking viscid sessile wart-like glands; the stipitate glands often
   present on the midrib (sometimes also on the lateral veins) of the lower leaf-surfaces
   bearing small lateral tufts of white hairs . . . . ssp. *octopetala*
   2 Lower leaf-surfaces bearing stalked capitate glands on the midrib; [*D. kamt.* Juz.;
      W Alaska; MAPS: Hultén 1968b:630, and 1959: fig. 10, p. 533] . . . .
      . . . . var. *kamtschatica* (Juz.) Hult.
   2 Lower leaf-surfaces lacking stalked capitate glands on the midrib; (incl. var.
      luteola Hult., with yellowish petals) . . . . var. *octopetala*
      3 Upper leaf-surfaces more or less densely silky-tomentose; [var. *argentea* Blytt;
         reported from Greenland by Boivin 1967a] . . . . f. *argentea* (Blytt) Hult.
      3 Upper leaf-surfaces glabrous or sparingly hirsute, dark green; [var. *?minor*
         Hook.; *D. chamaedrifolia* (Crantz) Gray; Alaska–Yukon–W Dist. Mackenzie–N
         B.C. (59°51'N); MAPS: Porsild 1947:183; Hultén 1968b:630, and 1959: fig. 9, p.
         529; Raup 1947: pl. 29; Meusel, Jaeger, and Weinert 1965:220] . . . . . . f. *octopetala*
1 Upper leaf-surfaces with punctiform, wart-like glands or excrescences especially on
   the lobes (and often on the petioles and stipules) or merely glandular-viscid along
   the leaf-folds.
   4 Stipitate glands on the veins of the lower leaf-surfaces bearing small lateral tufts
      of white or brown hairs . . . . ssp. *punctata* (Juz.) Hult.
      5 Leaves more or less densely white-tomentose beneath; [*D. punctata* Juz.; *D.
         oct.* var. *viscida* Hult.; Alaska–Yukon–NW Dist. Mackenzie and Banks Is.; MAPS:
         Porsild 1947:183 (*D. punctata*; a dot should be added for Banks Is.)] . . . .
         . . . . var. *punctata*
      5 Leaves essentially glabrous beneath (except for glands on the veins); [type
         from McKinley Park, Alaska] . . . . var. *glabrata* Hult.
   4 Stipitate glands on the veins of the lower leaf-surfaces naked.
      6 Leaves linear to oblong, broadest above the middle, to 5.5 cm long and 1.5
         cm broad, to 3.5 times longer than broad, incised up to halfway to the midrib,
         dark green and somewhat lustrous above, glabrate or thinly tomentose
         beneath; [*D. alaskensis* Porsild, the type from the Alaska Range, Alaska;
         Alaska–Yukon–NW Dist. Mackenzie; MAPS: Porsild 1947:183, and 1966: map 92,
         p. 78 (both as *D. alaskensis*); Hultén 1968b:631, and 1959: fig. 10, p. 533] . . . .
         . . . . ssp. *alaskensis* (Porsild) Hult.
      6 Leaves ovate, broadest near or below the middle, usually less than 3 cm long
         and at most about 12 mm broad, to 2.5 times longer than broad, less deeply
         incised, dull dark green above, densely white-tomentose beneath; [*D.
         hookeriana* Juz.; Alaska (Kenai Pen.), s ?Yukon, W Dist. Mackenzie (Porsild
         and Cody 1968), and the mts. of B.C. and sw Alta.; the type is from the Rocky
         Mountains, presumably of B.C. or Alta.; MAPS (only the last one indicating
         stations in Alaska–Yukon): Porsild 1947:183 (*D. hook.*); Hultén 1959: fig. 10, p.
         533; *Atlas of Canada* 1957: map 9 (*D. hook.*), sheet 38] . . . .
         . . . . ssp. *hookeriana* (Juz.) Hult.

[DUCHESNEA Smith]   [3355]

[*D. indica* (Andr.) Focke]   India Strawberry
[Asiatic; occasionally cult. and escaped to roadsides and waste places in N. America. The report from B.C. by Hitchcock et al. (1961) requires confirmation. (*Fragaria* Andr.).]

FILIPENDULA Mill.   [3374]

1   Leaves chiefly basal, glabrous or hirsute on the veins beneath, with 10 or more pairs of deeply toothed or incised lateral leaflets, these 1 or 2 cm long and commonly not over about 1 cm broad; sepals and petals each 6 or 7, the latter white or pale pink; achene-like follicles erect, pubescent . . . . *F. vulgaris*
1   Leaves both cauline and basal, with at most 5 pairs of broad lateral leaflets, these to over 5 cm long; sepals and petals each 4 or 5; achene-like follicles glabrous.
    2   Petals pink; follicles erect, to 8 mm long; leaves glabrous; lateral leaflets deeply 3–5-lobed; terminal leaflet deeply 7–9-parted . . . . *F. rubra*
    2   Petals white; follicles twisted about half a turn, tightly overlapping, to 4 mm long; leaves typically canescent-tomentose beneath; lateral leaflets merely coarsely toothed; terminal leaflet rather deeply 3–5-lobed . . . . *F. ulmaria*

F. rubra (Hill) Robins.   Queen-of-the-prairie
Native in the E U.S.A. (Iowa to Mich. and Pa., S to Ill., Ky., and Ga.); cult. and escaped elsewhere, as in S Ont. (Norfolk Co.; OAC), SW Que. (Iberville Co. and the Montreal dist), Nfld. (Rouleau 1956; ?escaped), and N.S. (Yarmouth and Guysborough counties). [*Ulmaria* Hill; *Spiraea lobata* Gronov.].

F. ulmaria (L.) Maxim.   Queen-of-the-meadow
Eurasian; a garden-escape to roadsides and thickets in N. America, as in S Ont. (Montgomery 1957), Que. (N to the Gaspé Pen.), Nfld. (GH), N.B., P.E.I., and N.S. [*Spiraea* L.].
  [According to Hultén (1946), reports of the similar *F. kamtschatica* (Pall.) Maxim. from the Aleutian Is. (as by P.A. Rydberg, N. Am. Flora 22:268. 1908) require confirmation, although it is known from Bering Is., U.S.S.R. It differs from *F. ulmaria* in its less distinctly pinnate leaves with minute lateral leaflets rather than with up to 5 pairs of relatively large ones alternating with very small ones and in its very flat follicles tapering to a distinctly stipitate base rather than spirally twisted follicles with semicordate bases.]

F. vulgaris Moench
Eurasian; a garden-escape to roadsides and waste places in N. America, as in S Ont. (Lambton and York counties), Nfld. (along an old railway track at St. John's; GH), and N.S. (waste ground at Yarmouth, Yarmouth Co.; GH). [*F. hexapetala* Gilib.; *Spiraea (F.) filipendula* L.].

FRAGARIA L.   [3354]   Strawberry.   Fraisier

(Ref.: Staudt 1962)
1   Terminal tooth of each leaflet commonly projecting beyond a line joining the tips of the two adjacent teeth; leaflets subsessile or with stalks up to 3 mm long, coarsely crenate-serrate most of their length, the upper surface bright yellow-green and usually very sparsely hairy, the lower surface pale green, finely pilose-silky and usually slightly glaucous but not prominently reticulate-veiny; achenes typically almost completely superficial on the receptacle (often in shallow pits in western varieties); calyx-lobes spreading or reflexed; petals commonly less than 1 cm long; inflorescence usually equalling or surpassing the leaves; (transcontinental) . . . . . *F. vesca*
1   Terminal tooth of each leaflet commonly shorter than the adjacent teeth; achenes set in shallow pits on the mature receptacle; calyx-lobes appressed about the young fruit; petals commonly over 1 cm long; inflorescence usually shorter than the leaves.
    2   Leaves thick and coriaceous, deep green, shining, rugose, and glabrous above, strongly reticulate and greyish-silky to somewhat tomentose beneath, coarsely crenate-serrate mostly above the middle (sometimes only across the summit), to about 4 cm long; leaflets distinctly stalked, the stalk of the terminal one to 1 cm long; petioles, peduncles, and stolons pubescent with silky, spreading to somewhat reflexed hairs; petals to 16 mm long; fruit usually at least 1.5 cm thick, rather strongly pilose-lanate with hairs as long as the ovaries; (Alaska–B.C.) . . . .
. . . .*F. chiloensis*

2 Leaves thinner, coarsely crenate-serrate most of their length, usually glaucous-bluish-green and glabrous above, sparingly to copiously silky-villous beneath, to over 7 cm long; petals to 13 mm long; fruit about 1 cm thick.

    3 Leaves and scapes from numerous erect crowns forming a branching caudex, superficial runners rarely developed; leaflets sessile, appressed-silky beneath, strigose or glabrate above, very sharply serrate, at most about 3 cm long; (E Que.). . . . . [*F. multicipita*]

    3 Crowns mostly single, terminating thick rhizomes, regularly developing superficial runners; leaflets short-stalked (the stalk of the terminal one to 7 mm long), to 1 dm long, their teeth commonly blunter; (transcontinental) . . . .
. . . .*F. virginiana*

F. chiloensis (L.) Dcne.

/sT/W/ (Hrr) Coasts of the Aleutian Is. and s Alaska (*see* Hultén 1946: map 764, p. 1062) through w B.C. to Calif. and S. America; Hawaii. [*F. vesca* var. *chil.* L.; *F. chilensis* Molina and its var. *scouleri* Wats.]. MAP: Hultén 1968b:606.

Plants with hairs of the stem and petioles appressed may be separated as ssp. *lucida* (Vilm.) Staudt (reported from Queen Charlotte Is., B.C., by Calder and Taylor 1968). Those with hairs of the stem and petioles spreading may be known as ssp. *pacifica* Staudt (Aleutian Is.–s Alaska–B.C.).

The garden strawberry, × *F. ananassa* Dcne. (*F. chiloensis* × *F. virginiana*), is reported from Nfld. by Rouleau (1956), where perhaps persisting in old gardens. It is now considered to be a hybrid-complex, one of whose nothomorphs, nm. *cuneifolia* (Nutt.) Staudt (*F. cun.* Nutt.; *F. latiuscula* Greene; *F. platypetala* and *F. suksdorfii* Rydb.; *F. ?grandiflora* Ehrh., not Crantz), is known from s B.C. (Vancouver Is.; Cascade; type of *F. lat.* from Chilliwack L.). It is also reported from sw Alta. by Breitung (1957b; Waterton Lakes, as *F. virginiana* var. *platypetala* (Rydb.) Hall).

[*F. multicipita* Fern.]

[Known only from the type locality on gravels and bars of the Ste-Anne-des-Monts R., Gaspé Co., E Que., where taken by Fernald and Collins in 1906 and now extinct. According to Gleason (1958), it is probably merely a runnerless phase of *F. virginiana* var. *terrae-novae* (included below in var. *glauca*). Staudt (1962) notes that a similar runnerless phase of *F. vesca* in Europe is perhaps best treated as a form, f. *eflagellaris* (Dcne.) Staudt, but makes no mention of *F. multicipita*.]

F. vesca L. Woodland Strawberry. Fraisier à vaches

/sT/X/EA/ (Hrr) Rocky woods and openings, the aggregate species from B.C.–Alta. to Great Slave L., Sask. (N to Waddy L. at ca. 56°10′N), Man. (N to Knee L. NE of L. Winnipeg at ca. 55°N), Ont. (N to James Bay), Que. (N to E James Bay, L. St. John, and the Côte-Nord), Nfld., N.B., ?P.E.I., and N.S., s to Calif., N.Mex., Nebr., Mo., Ill., and Va.; Eurasia. MAPS and synonymy: *see* below.

1 Leaflets rather thick, densely silky and slightly tomentulose beneath, silky but becoming glabrous above; flowers 2 or 3 cm broad; fruiting peduncles often shorter than the leaves; achenes in shallow pits on the ovoid or subconic mature receptacle; [*F. crinita* Rydb.; *F. californica* Newberry, not C. & S.; B.C. (N to Queen Charlotte Is.) and w Alta. (Boivin 1966b)] . . . . var. *crinita* (Rydb.) Hitchc.

1 Leaflets relatively thin, rather sparingly silky at least beneath when young but glabrate in age; fruiting peduncles often equalling or surpassing the leaves.

    2 Fruit usually hemispheric or subglobose, to 1.5 cm thick, the achenes almost completely superficial; flowers to 1.5 cm broad; mature calyx-lobes reflexed; pubescence of scape and petioles spreading; [a garden-escape in E Canada (but considered to be native in E Que. and Nfld. by Fernald *in* Gray 1950; *see* note under *Luzula campestris*); reported N to a railway clearing at Moosonee, s James Bay, Ont., by Dutilly, Lepage, and Duman 1954; MAPS (aggregate species): Hultén 1958: map 54, p. 73 (noting other total-area maps by Lippmaa, Staudt, and Saxer); Meusel 1943: fig. 31c; Meusel, Jaeger, and Weinert 1965:218] . . . . . . var. *vesca*

2 Fruit subconic or ovoid, usually with a distinct basal constriction or neck, to 1 cm
thick and 1.5 cm long.
  3 Mature calyx-lobes spreading or somewhat ascending; flowers to 2 cm broad;
achenes often in shallow pits; pubescence of scape, pedicels, and petioles
spreading or somewhat reflexed, the scape commonly with a unifoliate leafy
bract below the inflorescence . . . . var. *bracteata* (Heller) Davis
    4 Petals white; [*F. bracteata* Heller; *F. retrorsa* Greene; s B.C. and sw Alta.
(Waterton Lakes; Breitung 1957*b*)] . . . . f. *bracteata*
    4 Petals pink or roseate; [*F. helleri* Holz.; *F. vesca* var. *crinita* f. *helleri* (Holz.)
Boivin; Vancouver Is., B.C.] . . . . f. *helleri* (Holz.) Scoggan
  3 Mature calyx-lobes spreading or ascending; flowers to 1.5 cm broad; achenes
almost completely superficial; pubescence of scape spreading or slightly
ascending, that of the petioles and peduncles appressed-ascending, the
scape rarely with a leafy bract at summit . . . . var. *americana* Porter
    5 Berry red; [*F. americana* (Porter) Britt.; transcontinental; MAPS: on the
above-noted maps for var. *vesca*] . . . . f. *americana*
    5 Berry whitish or yellowish; [known from Norfolk Co., s Ont. (type from
Woodhouse Township), the probable basis of the report by Landon 1960,
under *F. virginiana* var. *illinoensis,* that, "The white fruited form is also
common"; a collection in ACAD from Glendyer, Inverness Co., N.S., has
been referred to *F. vesca* f. *alba* (Dcne.) Staudt but may finally prove to
belong here] . . . . f. *landonii* Boivin

F. virginiana Dcne.
/ST/X/ (Hrr (Ch)) Fields and borders of woods from cent. Alaska–Yukon (*see* Hultén 1946:
map 765, p. 1062; *F. glauca*) and NW Dist. Mackenzie to Great Bear L., Great Slave L., L. Atha-
basca (Alta. and Sask.), Man. (N to Churchill), northernmost Ont., Que. (N to NE James Bay,
the Côte-Nord, Anticosti Is., and Gaspé Pen.), Labrador (N to the Hamilton R. basin), Nfld.,
N.B., P.E.I., and N.S., s to Calif., Colo., Okla., Tenn., and Ga. [Incl. var. *illinoensis* (Prince)
Gray; *F. australis* Rydb.; *F. canadensis* Michx.]. MAP: Hultén 1968*b*:606.
  The typical form is largely replaced northwards by var. *glauca* Wats. (var. *terrae-novae*
(Rydb.) Fern. & Wieg.; *F. glauca* (Wats.) Rydb.; *F. pauciflora, F. terrae-novae,* and *F. yukonensis* Rydb.; hairs of stem and petioles appressed-ascending or sometimes nearly wanting
rather than widely spreading to slightly ascending, petals mostly not over 1 cm long rather
than to over 12 mm long; MAPS (NW area; *F. glauca*): Hultén 1968*b*:606; Raup 1947: pl. 28).

GEUM L. [3365] Avens. Benoîte

(Ref.: P.A. Rydberg, N. Am. Flora 22:401–14. 1913)
1 Style straight or flexuous, not obviously jointed; sepals ascending to erect; leaves
chiefly basal, those of the stem greatly reduced.
  2 Basal leaves pinnate with up to 17 variously incised and toothed, cuneate, larger
leaflets alternating with smaller bracts (never lyrate, the terminal leaflet about
equalling the lateral ones); style not plumose; petals yellow, orbicular, spreading
(or at least not erect or convergent); flower commonly solitary; stems commonly
less than 2.5 dm tall, from a large dark-brown woody caudex; (Alaska–B.C. to
Ellesmere Is.) . . . . *G. rossii*
  2 Basal leaves lyrate-pinnatifid (the terminal leaflet much the largest); style
plumose at least below the middle; flowers usually 2 or more.
    3 Basal leaves with a large round-reniform, lobed and doubly serrate, terminal
leaflet and a few greatly reduced small lateral leaflets usually less than 1 cm
long; flowers ascending, their spreading yellow or orange petals broadly
obovate to suborbicular; bractlets of the green calyx shorter than the sepals;
styles not over 1 cm long, the upper third not plumose.
      4 Terminal leaflet of basal leaves truncate at base or with a very open
shallow rounded sinus; petals to 1.5 cm long; plant essentially glabrous
except for ciliation on the leaf-margins and on the petioles; (N.S.) . . . . . *G. peckii*

4 Terminal leaflet of basal leaves with a deep, rather narrow sinus; petals to 1 cm long; plant more or less hirsute; (s Alaska–w B.C.) . . . . *G. calthifolium*

3 Basal leaves with 2 or more pairs of cuneate to obovate lateral leaflets increasing gradually in size toward the terminal leaflet; styles mostly over 2 cm long in fruit, plumose for most of their length.

  5 Plant glabrous, more or less woody at base; petals white, spreading; sepals spreading or reflexed, slightly surpassing the alternating bractlets; leaves crowded at the ends of the ascending to prostrate branches, with up to 7 cuneate or narrowly obovate leaflets to 1.5 cm long that are serrate toward tip; (Aleutian Is.) . . . . *G. pentaphyllum*

  5 Plants conspicuously pubescent, from a thick rootstock; sepals and the yellowish to purplish petals ascending to suberect; principal leaves in a basal rosette.

    6 Stem-leaves deeply 3-lobed, the middle lobe longer than the lateral pair; leaves densely pilose beneath with long soft yellowish hairs, their teeth terminated by a ''rope'' of twisted hairs to 5 mm long; flower usually solitary, erect; petals pale yellow; bractlets shorter than the sepals, to about 5 mm long; (Alaska to w Dist. Mackenzie) . . . . . . *G. glaciale*

    6 Stem-leaves pinnate; leaves finely pubescent beneath and also more or less pilose on the veins; flowers commonly at least 2 (up to 9 in a cyme), nodding; petals commonly purplish, sometimes yellowish; bractlets usually surpassing the sepals, to over 1.5 cm long; (B.C. to s Ont.) . . . . *G. triflorum*

1 Style distinctly jointed near or above the middle, the terminal portion deciduous from the finally hooked basal portion; stem-leaves less markedly reduced.

  7 Sepals purple or crimson, erect or ascending, to 1 cm long; petals erect, yellowish with purple blotches and veins; flowers nodding; style plumose at base and on the terminal deciduous portion; (transcontinental) . . . . *G. rivale*

  7 Sepals green or greenish, smaller, reflexed at anthesis; petals spreading, white or yellow; flowers ascending; style not plumose.

    8 Calyx lacking bractlets in the sinuses; fruiting head conspicuously stipitate above the calyx; achenes minutely appressed-puberulent; terminal segment of style glabrous; petals yellowish, about 2 mm long, not surpassing the sepals; some of the basal leaves simple and at most shallowly lobed; (s Ont.) . . . . *G. vernum*

    8 Calyx usually with bractlets in the sinuses; fruiting-head sessile in the calyx; terminal segment of style usually short-hispid.

      9 Petals golden yellow, about equalling the sepals.

        10 Style minutely glandular at base; denuded receptacle glabrous or merely short-hispid; peduncles slender; sepals broadly deltoid, at most 5 mm long; terminal leaflet of basal leaves suborbicular to reniform; upper stem-leaves simple, 3-lobed or -incised; (transcontinental) . . . . *G. macrophyllum*

        10 Style glandless; denuded receptacle long-hirsute; segments of leaves generally obovate to rhombic, broadly cuneate at base, serrate and rather shallowly incised, the upper stem-leaves (1)3–5-foliolate.

          11 Lanceolate sepals and petals 4 or 5 mm long; terminal portion of style minutely pubescent; stem-leaves with rhombic acuminate leaflets; (introd.) . . . . *G. urbanum*

          11 Lanceolate to lance-ovate sepals and broadly obovate to suborbicular petals to 1 cm long; terminal portion of style conspicuously hirsute; peduncles somewhat clavate at summit; leaflets mostly incised-serrate; (transcontinental) . . . . *G. aleppicum*

      9 Petals white, pale yellow, or greenish yellow (if yellow, much shorter than the sepals), narrowly elliptic to broadly obovate.

        12 Petals pale yellow or greenish yellow, to 4 mm long, much shorter than

the sepals; denuded receptacle densely hirsute; peduncles filiform, minutely pilose; basal and lower stem-leaves simple or with up to 7 leaflets, the segments or leaflets blunt at apex and with obtuse teeth; stem hirsute below . . . . [G. virginianum]

12 Petals white; basal and lower stem-leaves simple or with 3 (5) leaflets, the segments or leaflets serrate and more or less incised; (Ont. to N.S.).

13 Petals at least 5 mm long, about equalling the sepals; denuded receptacle densely white-villous; peduncles filiform . . . . . . G. canadense

13 Petals usually less than 5 mm long, much shorter than the sepals; denuded receptacle essentially glabrous; peduncles stout, copiously hirsute with spreading or reflexed hairs . . . . G. laciniatum

G. aleppicum Jacq.
/ST/X/EA/ (Hs) Marshy or damp woods, thickets, and meadows from s Alaska–Yukon–Dist. Mackenzie and B.C.–Alta. to Sask. (N to Waddy L. at ca. 56°N), Man. (N to York Factory, Hudson Bay, 57°N), Ont. (N to Fort Severn, Hudson Bay, ca. 56°N), Que. (N to the E James Bay watershed at 52°37'N and the Gaspé Pen.; reported from Anticosti Is. by Verrill 1865), Nfld., N.B., P.E.I., and N.S., s to Calif., N.Mex., Nebr., Pa., and N.J.; Eurasia. [Incl. vars. *cuneatum* Boivin and *strictum* (Ait.) Fern. (*G. strictum* Ait.); *G. ?urbanum sensu* Cochran 1829, not L.]. MAPS: Hultén 1968b:626 (ssp. *str.*); Porsild 1966: map 93, p. 78; Meusel, Jaeger, and Weinert 1965:220.

A hybrid with *G. rivale* (× *G. aurantiacum* Fries) is reported from B.C. and Alta. by Rydberg (1922).

G. calthifolium Menzies
/sT/W/eA/ (Hs) Wet meadows from the Aleutian Is. and s Alaska (*see* Hultén 1946: map 790, p. 1065) through coastal B.C. to Vancouver Is. (the type material taken within this w N. American area); s Kamchatka and Japan. [*Acomastylis* Bolle; *Parageum* Nakai & Hara; *Sieversia* Don; *S. radiata sensu* Hooker 1832, not *G. rad.* Michx.; *G. (S.) rotundifolium* F. & M., not Moench]. MAP: Hultén 1968b:627.

A hybrid with *G. rossii* (× *G. macranthum* (Kearney) Boivin; *S. mac.* Kearney; *A. humilis sensu* P.A. Rydberg, N. Am. Flora 22:412. 1913, in part, not *G. hum.* R. Br.; *G. schofieldii* Calder & Taylor) is known from the Aleutian Is., Alaska, and B.C. (Queen Charlotte Is.).

G. canadense Jacq.
/T/EE/ (Hs) Rich thickets and borders of woods, the aggregate species from N.Dak. to Minn., Ont. (N to Renfrew and Carleton counties), Que. (N to Kamouraska Co.), N.B., and N.S. (not known from P.E.I.; the report of *G. album* from Nfld. by Waghorne 1898, is probably based upon *G. aleppicum*), s to Tex., Okla., Ala., and S.C. MAP and synonymy: *see* below.

1 Stem-leaves mostly strigose-pilose above; peduncles often rather densely pilose; [*G. camporum* Rydb.; s Ont. (Lincoln Co.), Que. (Berthier-en-bas, Montmagny Co.; Ste-Anne-de-la-Pocatière, Kamouraska Co.), N.B. (Sussex, Kings Co.; ACAD), and N.S.] . . . . var. *camporum* (Rydb.) Fern. & Weath.

1 Stem-leaves mostly glabrous above; peduncles minutely pubescent or with remote long hairs . . . . var. *canadense*

2 Sepals and peduncles beset with stiff jointed gland-tipped hairs; [Que. (type from Montmorency Falls, near Quebec City) and N.B. (Woodstock, Carleton Co., where taken by John Macoun in 1899; CAN)] . . . . f. *glandulosum* Fern. & Weath.

2 Sepals and peduncles glandless; [*G. album* Gmel.; *G. meyerianum* Rydb.; range of the species; MAP: Meusel, Jaeger, and Weinert 1965:220] . . . . f. *canadense*

G. glaciale Adams
/aS/W/A/ (Hs) Stony slopes and dry heaths of N Alaska–Yukon (s to ca. 65°N; *see* Hultén 1946: map 791, p. 1065) and the Mackenzie R. Delta.; arctic Asia. [*Sieversia* R. Br.]. MAP: Hultén 1968b:628.

Rosaceae

G. laciniatum Murr.
/T/EE/ (Hs) Damp thickets, meadows, and roadsides from Ont. (N to Sudbury; Fernald 1935) to Que. (N to St-Roch-des-Aulnets, l'Islet Co.; Bernard Boivin, Nat. can. (Que.) 87(2):34. 1960), P.E.I. (York, Queens Co.; MT; not known from N.B.), and N.S., S to Kans., Mo., and N.C. [*G. virginianum* var. *murrayanum* Fern.; *G. virg. sensu* Fernald 1921, not L. (relevant collections from N.S. in GH) and probably *sensu* P.A. Rydberg, N. Am. Flora 22:402. 1913, as to the N.B. area].
   Some of our material is referable to var. *trichocarpum* Fern. (achenes hirsute at summit rather than glabrous).

G. macrophyllum Willd.
/ST/X/eA/ (Hs) Rich woods, damp thickets, and meadows (ranges of Canadian taxa outlined below), S to Baja Calif., Mexico, Minn., Mich., N.Y., and New Eng.; var. *sachalinense* Koidz. in Kamchatka and Japan. MAPS and synonymy: *see* below.
1   Upper stem-leaves 3-parted nearly to base into narrowly lanceolate, copiously
    incised lobes; terminal leaflet of the basal leaves rather deeply incised, the lobes
    serrate; [*G. perincisum* Rydb. (the type from Banff, Alta.) and its var. *intermedium*
    Boivin; *G. oregonense* (Schuetz) Rydb.; cent. Alaska–cent. Yukon (*see* Hultén 1946:
    map 792b, p. 1065) and B.C.–Alta. to Great Bear L., Great Slave L., Sask. (N to ca.
    56°N), Man. (N to Churchill), Ont. (N to Fort Severn, Hudson Bay, ca. 56°N), and
    Que. (N to the Koksoak R. S of Ungava Bay at ca. 57°45′N; *see* E Canada map by
    Dutilly, Lepage, and Duman 1953: fig. 14, p. 73); MAPS: Hultén 1968b:626; H.M. Raup
    1947: pl. 29, and Rhodora 33(392):175 (bottom). 1931]. A hybrid between *G.*
    perincisum var. *intermedium* and *G. rivale* (× *G. pervale* Boivin) is known from the
    type locality, the Cypress Hills of SW Sask. . . . . var. *perincisum* (Rydb.) Raup
1   Upper stem-leaves less deeply lobed, the lobes relatively broad; terminal leaflet of
    the basal leaves shallowly lobed, dentate.
    2   Upper stem-leaves deeply 3-parted, the lobes broadly oblanceolate to obovate;
        [Alaska–Yukon–B.C.; Boivin 1966b] . . . . var. *rydbergii* Farw.
    2   Upper stem-leaves merely 3-lobed, the lobes squarrish; [Aleutian Is.–S Alaska
        (*see* Hultén 1946: map 792a, p. 1065); the Yukon–B.C. (var. *rydbergii*); Ont. (N to
        the Kenora dist. and Moose Factory, near James Bay), Que. (N to E James Bay at
        52°37′N, and the Côte-Nord), Labrador (N to the Hamilton R. basin), Nfld., N.B.,
        P.E.I., and N.S.; MAPS: Hultén 1968b:625; H.M. Raup, Rhodora 33(392):175 (top;
        incomplete). 1931]. A hybrid with *G. rivale* (× *G. pulchrum* Fern.; type, as first
        collection cited, from Bic, Rimouski Co., E Que.) occurs locally nearly throughout
        the range. It has the habit and purple calyx-lobes of *G. rivale* but the calyx-lobes
        are spreading rather than erect, and it has the golden-yellow petals of *G. macro-*
        phyllum . . . . var. *macrophyllum*

G. peckii Pursh
/T/E/ (Hs) Damp slopes and gravels of N.S. (Digby, Cumberland, and Pictou counties; ACAD; CAN; not listed by Roland 1947) and cliffs and subalpine meadows of the White Mountains of N.H. [*Sieversia* R. Br.]

G. pentaphyllum (L.) Makino
/sT/W/eA/ (Hs) Wet places in the Aleutian Is. (*see* Hultén 1946: map 793, p. 1065); Kamchatka to Japan. [*Dryas* L.; *Sieversia* Greene; *D. (G.; S.) anemonoides* Pallas]. MAP: Hultén 1968b:628.

G. rivale L.   Water- or Purple Avens
/ST/X/EA/ (Hs) Swampy ground, wet meadows, and peaty slopes from B.C. (N to McLeod L. at ca. 55°N) to Alta. (N to near Briarville, 54°22′N), Sask. (N to Meadow Lake, 54°08′N), Man. (N to Duck Mt.), Ont. (N to Fort Severn, Hudson Bay, ca. 56°N), Que. (N to S Ungava Bay and the Côte-Nord), Labrador (N to Attikamagen L. at ca. 55°N), Nfld., N.B., P.E.I., and N.S., S to Wash., N.Mex., Mo., Ind., Pa., and N.J.; Iceland; Europe; W Asia. [Incl. var. *subalpinum* Neuman]. MAPS: Hultén 1958: map 42, p. 61; Meusel, Jaeger, and Weinert 1965:220.

G. rossii (R. Br.) Ser.
/ASs/(X)/eA/ (Hs) Dry to moist calcareous clays and tundra (often in solifluction areas) from the Aleutian Is., Alaska–Yukon, Great Bear L., and N B.C. (collection in V from ca. 57°35′N) to the mts. of Oreg., Nev., Ariz., and N.Mex., with isolated stations on Melville Is., Axel Heiberg Is., and Ellesmere Is. at ca. 80°N; NE Siberia and Kamchatka. [*Sieversia* R. Br.; *Acomastylis* Greene; *S. (A.) humilis* R. Br.]. MAPS: Hultén 1968*b*:627; Porsild 1957: map 237, p. 190.

G. triflorum Pursh Lion's-beard, Old Man's-whiskers, Purple Avens
/sT/WW/ (Hs) Prairies and plains to the lower foothills and subalpine ridges and talus (ranges of Canadian taxa outlined below), s to Calif., N.Mex., Nebr., Iowa, and Ill. (and, formerly, N.Y.).
1 Flowers commonly 3; terminal segment of style usually persistent; sepals lanceolate; principal leaflets usually not more than 15 in number, 2–3-cleft at apex less than halfway to base . . . . var. *triflorum*
  2 Calyx yellowish; [Cypress Hills, SW Sask.; Boivin 1967*b*] . . . . f. *pallidum* Fassett
  2 Calyx purplish; [*Sieversia* R. Br.; *Erythrocoma* Greene; *E. affinis* Greene; SW Dist. Mackenzie–B.C.–Alta. (N to L. Athabasca), Sask. (N to Prince Albert), Man. (N to Duck Mt.), and S Ont. (N to Great Cloche Is., N L. Huron; early reports from Labrador and Nfld. probably refer to *G. rivale*)] . . . . f. *triflorum*
1 Flowers commonly more numerous; terminal segment of style usually deciduous; sepals lance-ovate; principal leaflets up to 19 in number, more deeply cleft . . . .
. . . . var. *ciliatum* (Pursh) Fassett
  3 Calyx yellowish; [B.C.; Boivin 1966*b*] . . . . f. *flavulum* (Greene) Fassett
  3 Calyx purplish; [*G. (Sieversia) ciliatum* Pursh; B.C. (Anarchist Mt., near Osoyoos), SW Alta. (Banff; Waterton Lakes), and SW Sask. (Cypress Hills; Breitung 1957*a*)] . . . . . .
. . . . f. *ciliatum*

G. urbanum L. Wood Avens
Eurasian; reported as introd. in Ont. by Gillett (1958; Ottawa dist.). The report from N.S. by Cochran (1829) requires confirmation, possibly referring to *G. aleppicum* or *G. macrophyllum*.

G. vernum (Raf.) T. & G.
/t/EE/ (Hs) Rich woods and openings from Mich. to S Ont. (Amherstburg and Leamington, Essex Co.; CAN; GH; reported from Walpole Is., Lambton Co., by Dodge 1915) and N.Y., S to E Kans., Mo., Tenn., and Va. [*Stylipus* Raf.].

[*G. virginianum* L.]
[A native of the E U.S.A. (Ind. to Mass., S to Tenn. and S.C.). The reports from N.B. by John Macoun (1883) and Fowler (1885) are based upon *G. aleppicum* (relevant collection from Petitcodiac in NBM), as are, probably, most or all other reports from Canada. (*G. flavum* (Porter) Bickn.).]

GILLENIA Moench [3325] Indian-physic

G. trifoliata (L.) Moench Bowman's-root
/t/EE/ (Grh (Hp)) Rich woods from Mich. to S Ont. (Essex, Brant, Wentworth, and York counties; CAN; TRT) and N.Y., S to Ala. and Ga.; a garden-escape elsewhere, as in ?Alaska (Hultén 1946; Juneau) and ?Nfld. (Waghorne 1898; not listed by Rouleau 1956). [*Spiraea* L.; *Porteranthus* Britt.].

HOLODISCUS Maxim. [3332]

H. discolor (Pursh) Maxim. Ocean-spray
/T/W/ (N) Gravels, cliffs, and dry to moist open woods and lower mts. from S B.C. (Vancouver Is. and adjacent islands E to Creston, N to Lillooet and Sicamous) to S Calif., Idaho, and Mont. [*Spiraea* Pursh; *Sericotheca* Rydb.; *Sp. ariaefolia* Sm.].

LUETKEA Bong.   [3321]

L. pectinata (Pursh) Ktze.   Partridge-foot
/ST/W/   (Ch)   Moist or shaded, usually sandy soil from subalpine elevations to well above timberline from s-cent. Alaska–Yukon and NW Dist. Mackenzie (Porsild 1943) through the mts. of B.C. and SW Alta. (N to Jasper) to N Calif., Idaho, and Mont. [*Saxifraga* Pursh; *Eriogynia* Hook.; *Spiraea* T. & G.; *L. sibbaldioides* Bong.]. MAP: Hultén 1968b:595.

OSMARONIA Greene   [3392]

O. cerasiformis (T. & G.) Greene   Indian-Plum, Osoberry
/t/W/   (Mc)   Streambanks, moist to dryish open woods, and roadsides from SW B.C. (Vancouver Is.; Agassiz; Chilliwack R.; lower Fraser R. N to Yale) to N Calif. [*Nuttallia* T. & G.; incl. var. *lancifolia* Greene].

PHYSOCARPUS Maxim.   [3316]   Ninebark

1 Follicles commonly 2 (sometimes 1 or 3, rarely 4 or 5), copiously stellate-pubescent, united nearly two-thirds their length, flattened laterally and somewhat keeled, about 5 mm long; leaves glabrous or more or less stellate on both sides; (S B.C. and SW Alta.) . . . . *P. malvaceus*
1 Follicles commonly 5 (sometimes fewer), completely glabrous when mature, united only at the base, turgid, to 1 cm long; (S Alaska–B.C.–Alta.; Ont. to N.S.) . . . . *P. opulifolius*

P. malvaceus (Greene) Ktze.   Mallow-Ninebark
/T/W/   (N)   Rocky ravines, hillsides, and coniferous forest from SE B.C. (Grand Forks to Kootenay L. and Creston) and SW Alta. (Waterton Lakes; Breitung 1957b) to Oreg., Utah, and Wyo. [*Neillia* Greene; *Opulaster* Ktze.; *O. pauciflorus* (T. & G.) Heller].

P. opulifolius (L.) Maxim.   Ninebark
/T/X/   (Mc)   Swampy ground, streambanks, and moist woods, var. *tomentellus* from the SE Alaska Panhandle through B.C. and SW Alta. (Waterton Lakes; CAN) to S Calif. and N Idaho, the typical phase and var. *intermedius* from Minn. to Ont. (N to the Kaministikwia R. W of Thunder Bay and W James Bay at ca. 53°N) and Que. (N to E James Bay at 51°21′N and Bic, Rimouski Co.; Herb. Hugh Scoggan), S to Colo., Ark., Ill., Tenn., and S.C. MAPS and synonymy: *see* below.
1 Capsules permanently pubescent; [*Opulaster int.* Rydb.; S Ont. (Lambton, Bruce, and Welland counties)] . . . . var. *intermedius* (Rydb.) Robins.
1 Capsules essentially glabrous.
    2 Leaves sparingly pubescent or glabrous above, more or less densely stellate-pubescent or sometimes glabrous beneath, those of the sterile shoots often 5-lobed and scarcely longer than broad; caruncle of the seeds short and almost terminal; follicles not more than half longer than the sepals; [*Spiraea* (P., *Neillia; Opulaster) capitata* Pursh; *S. (Neillia) opulifolia* vars. *mollis* T. & G. and *tomentella* Ser.; SE Alaska, B.C., and SW Alta.; MAP: Hultén 1968b:593 (*P. cap.*)] . . . . var. *tomentellus* (Ser.) Boivin
    2 Leaves glabrous except sometimes along the veins and in their axils, those of sterile shoots 3-lobed and usually longer than broad; caruncle of the seeds lateral, about 1/3 as long as the seed; follicles usually twice as long as the sepals; [*Spiraea* L.; *Opulaster* Ktze.; *O. australis* Rydb.; Ont. and Que.; introd. in Man., N.B., and N.S.; MAP: Hultén 1968b:593 (broken line)] . . . . var. *opulifolius*

POTENTILLA L.   [3356]   Cinquefoil, Five-finger.   Potentille or Quinte-feuille

(Ref.: P.A. Rydberg, N. Am. Flora 22:293–355, 365–76. 1908)
1 Basal leaves (when present) or at least the lower stem-leaves typically with only 3 leaflets.

2 Petals white or dark purple; perennials.
  3 Petals dark purple; achenes glabrous; leaflets broadly oblong or obovate,
    silky-pubescent, usually short-stalked; (introd. in N.B.) . . . . *P. atrosanguinea*
  3 Petals white; achenes pubescent.
    4 Leaflets normally bright green and nearly glabrous, leathery, evergreen,
      narrowly cuneate-oblong, entire except for the coarsely 3-toothed
      (sometimes 5-toothed) apex; achenes densely hairy; styles basal; flowers
      rather numerous in stiff terminal cymes; (transcontinental) . . . . . . *P. tridentata*
    4 Leaflets pubescent, herbaceous, obovate to rotund, coarsely crenate-
      serrate to the middle or below; achenes sparsely pilose; styles terminal;
      flowers solitary or few on filiform branches; plant with elongate stolon-like
      leafy branches; (introd. in Nfld.) . . . . *P. sterilis*
2 Petals yellow; achenes glabrous; styles lateral or terminal.
  5 Cymes very leafy, many-flowered; petals shorter than or only slightly longer
    than the sepals; leaves mostly cauline; leaflets coarsely toothed.
    6 Flowers 4-merous; stem-leaves appearing 5-foliolate because of the large
      deeply incised stipules, sparingly pubescent or glabrate; (introd. in Nfld.) . . . . . .
      . . . . *P. erecta*
    6 Flowers 5-merous; stipules smaller; plants usually more pubescent.
      7 Petals about equalling the calyx-lobes; stamens commonly 20; achenes
        longitudinally ribbed, to 1.3 mm long; leaflets oblanceolate to obovate;
        (transcontinental) . . . . *P. norvegica*
      7 Petals about half as long as the calyx-lobes; stamens commonly 10 or
        15; achenes smooth, at most 0.8 mm long.
        8 Calyx mealy-glandular; basal portion of stem pubescent in part with
          multicellular, more or less moniliform, often glandular hairs; (s B.C.
          and s Alta.; reported from Sask.) . . . . *P. biennis*
        8 Calyx eglandular; basal portion of the stem soft-pubescent, often
          more or less woolly, eglandular, the hairs unicellular; (B.C. to
          w Ont.) . . . . *P. rivalis*
  5 Cymes not very leafy, generally rather few-flowered; petals much surpassing
    the sepals; (arctic, subarctic, and alpine regions).
    9 Leaflets more or less pilose (but not tomentose) or becoming glabrate,
      broadly obovate.
      10 Leaflets more or less regularly cleft about 2/3 of the distance to the
        midrib or farther; (mts. of n B.C.).
        11 Stems 1-flowered, to about 5 cm tall, forming cushions to 1.5 dm
          broad; leaflets to about 1 cm long, not divided to base, the
          segments mostly obtuse, the petioles and leaflets more or less
          sparsely hairy; petals less than 5 mm long . . . . *P. elegans*
        11 Stems bearing 1 or 2 flowers, to about 1.5 dm tall, tufted but
          scarcely cushion-forming; leaflets to 2 cm long, at least the terminal
          one cleft nearly to base into 3 narrow, usually acute, revolute-
          margined segments, the lateral leaflets cleft into 2 or 3 such
          segments, the segments usually glabrate above in age but
          permanently more or less silky beneath; petals to 1 cm long . . . . *P. biflora*
      10 Leaflets merely toothed (or the stem-leaves of *P. flabellifolia* often cleft
        to about halfway to the midrib).
        12 Leaflets cuneate-flabelliform, glabrate or short-pubescent, those of
          the stem often cleft to about halfway to the midrib; stems to over
          2.5 dm tall; cymes few-flowered; (mts. of s B.C. and s Alta.) . . . .
          . . . . *P. flabellifolia*
        12 Leaflets broadly cuneate-obovate, decidedly long-pubescent,
          coarsely crenate; (transcontinental in arctic, subarctic, and alpine
          regions) . . . . *P. hyparctica*
    9 Leaflets densely tomentose beneath, coarsely toothed.
      13 Leaflets coriaceous, silvery-whitish-tomentose and strongly ribbed

beneath, rotund-ovate; flowers to 3 cm broad; bractlets alternating with the calyx-lobes elliptic; plant relatively robust, to about 3 dm tall, usually several-flowered; (mts. of B.C. and Alta.) . . . . *P. villosa*

   13 Leaflets scarcely coriaceous, whitish-tomentose and not strongly ribbed beneath; flowers mostly smaller; plants less robust; (essentially transcontinental in arctic, subarctic, and alpine regions).

      14 Leaflets relatively narrow, often cuneate-oblanceolate; bractlets alternating with the calyx-lobes linear-oblong to ovate, bluntish; flowers usually solitary (sometimes 2, rarely 3), to slightly over 2 cm broad; stems usually less than 1 dm tall . . . . *P. vahliana*

      14 Leaflets broad, mostly obovate; bractlets linear to narrowly lanceolate, acute; flowers commonly several, rarely as much as 2 cm broad; stems to 4 dm tall . . . . *P. nivea*

1 Basal leaves (when present) or at least the lower stem-leaves with at least 5 leaflets.

  15 Lower (principal) leaves palmately compound.

    16 Flowers mostly solitary on long axillary peduncles; stem early or finally decumbent or prostrate and often rooting at the nodes, flagelliform; styles filiform; leaflets glabrous or more or less strigose beneath (but not tomentose), toothed above the middle; perennials.

      17 Flowers mostly 4-merous, to 2 cm broad, on peduncles often over 1 dm long; bractlets between the ovate sepals rather broadly lanceolate; leaves essentially glabrous; stem from a deep non-tuberous root, soon dichotomously branching above; (introd. in s Labrador, Nfld., and N.S.) . . . .
. . . . *P. anglica*

      17 Flowers 5-merous.

        18 Leaves essentially glabrous; stem from a deep non-tuberous root, rarely with more than a few short branches from the flowering nodes; flowers to 2 cm broad, on peduncles often over 1 dm long; bractlets between the ovate sepals rather broadly lanceolate; (introd. in s Ont., sw Que., and N.S.) . . . . *P. reptans*

        18 Leaves pubescent beneath; flowers at most 1.5 cm broad, on peduncles less than 1 dm long; bractlets between the lanceolate to lance-ovate sepals linear or linear-lanceolate; stems from tuberous-thickened rhizomes; (Ont. to Nfld. and N.S.) . . . . *P. canadensis*

    16 Flowers few to many in cymes (if sometimes solitary, plant usually with a short thick caudex).

      19 Leaves densely tomentose beneath (except in some phases of *P. gracilis*); perennials.

        20 Cymes very leafy, paniculately branched; leaflets of basal leaves linear-oblanceolate to narrowly wedge-oblong, very deeply toothed; stem freely and often diffusely branched; (introd., transcontinental) . . . .
. . . . *P. argentea*

        20 Cymes less leafy and simpler; stem simple or sparingly branched.

          21 Basal leaflets pectinately divided well over halfway to midrib into linear lobes; (B.C. to Man.; introd. in Ont. and Que.) . . . . *P. gracilis*

          21 Basal leaflets merely more or less deeply toothed with ovate teeth.

            22 Flowers at least 2 cm broad; sepals at least 5 mm long; stem to over 7 dm tall; anthers commonly about 1 mm long; (B.C. to Man.; introd. in Ont. and Que.) . . . . *P. gracilis*

            22 Flowers at most about 1 cm broad; sepals 4 or 5 mm long; stem commonly not over 3 dm tall; anthers less than 1 mm long; (B.C. to Man.) . . . . *P. concinna*

      19 Leaflets typically glabrous or more or less pubescent but not tomentose (some phases of *P. gracilis* may key out here).

        23 Petals shorter than the calyx; flowers commonly numerous in leafy cymes; styles thickened and somewhat glandular-warty at base; leaflets coarsely toothed; stems with few or no marcescent stipules at base.

24 Stamens 5; (var. *pentandra*; B.C. to Man.) . . . . *P. rivalis*
24 Stamens commonly at least 10; (introd.) . . . . *P. intermedia*
23 Petals surpassing the calyx.
  25 Stipules of stem-leaves peculiar, at least the lowest leaf subtended
    by a broadly dilated stipule united with the petiole to form an ovate
    or oblong structure to over 2.5 cm long, this entire or 2-toothed at
    apex; leaflets of basal leaves mostly 9, linear to oblong-lanceolate,
    with up to 5 small terminal teeth at the often truncate apex,
    otherwise entire; pedicels, calyces, and leaf-margins somewhat
    pubescent, the plant otherwise essentially glabrous; (Alaska) . . . .
    . . . . *P. stipularis*
  25 Stipules not as above; leaflets of basal leaves mostly 5, commonly
    broader in outline, their margins more or less copiously toothed.
    26 Flowers to 2.5 cm broad, numerous, pale yellow, on erect or
      strongly ascending pedicels in a stiffly erect nearly leafless
      cyme; styles thickened at base, shorter than the mature,
      strongly reticulate achenes; stamens mostly 30 (sometimes 25);
      leaflets with narrowly deltoid teeth, sparingly hirsute; stems with
      few or no marcescent stipules at base; (introd.) . . . . *P. recta*
    26 Plants lacking the above combination of characters.
      27 Petals deep yellow; stems from crowns bearing few, if any,
        marcescent stipules; leaflets grey-strigose, mostly 1 or 2 cm
        long; (introd. in s Ont.) . . . . *P. verna*
      27 Petals pale yellow; stems from crowns heavily covered with
        dark marcescent stipules; leaflets often longer.
        28 Petioles glabrous or nearly so; leaflets rather deeply
          toothed or cleft, the teeth or lobes often lanceolate, acute
          or barely obtusish; larger leaflets often relatively narrow,
          usually more or less oblong and to over 3 cm long;
          achenes finally weakly reticulate; (Alaska–B.C. to Sask.;
          N Labrador) . . . . *P. diversifolia*
        28 Petioles sparsely to copiously pilose; leaflets with mostly
          short roundish to oblong teeth; larger leaflets more or
          less obovate, usually less than 2 cm long; (eastern arctic
          and subarctic regions) . . . . *P. crantzii*
15 Lower leaves mostly distinctly pinnately compound.
  29 Flowers solitary on naked peduncles from the nodes of the slender runners;
    styles lateral; leaflets sharply serrate; perennials; (transcontinental).
    30 Leaflets tomentose beneath and also silvery-silky and shining with long
      appressed hairs; bractlets of calyx usually toothed or cleft; achenes corky,
      grooved near the summit . . . . *P. anserina*
    30 Leaflets glabrous or white-tomentose beneath with opaque hairs, the
      remainder of the plant essentially glabrous; bractlets of calyx mostly
      entire; achenes neither corky nor grooved . . . . *P. egedii*
  29 Flowers few to many in leafy cymes.
    31 Shrub to about 1 m tall, the pale outer bark shredding; stamens 25–30;
      achenes strongly whitish-hirsute; style lateral; leaflets entire, mostly 5 or 7,
      linear to oblanceolate or oblong, to about 3 cm long and 9 mm broad;
      (transcontinental) . . . . *P. fruticosa*
    31 Herbs; achenes glabrous; leaflets toothed to deeply incised.
      32 Petals and inner face of sepals dark purple; style lateral; leaflets 5 or 7,
        oblong-lanceolate to oblanceolate, to about 1 dm long, coarsely
        toothed; stem stout, from a decumbent woody rooting base; perennial;
        (transcontinental in wet habitats) . . . . *P. palustris*
      32 Petals yellow or whitish.
        33 Plants copiously glandular-villous with brownish hairs; style inserted

near or below the middle of the achene; leaflets (5)7–9(11), coarsely toothed to shallowly incised.

  34 Cymes narrow and strict (often much elongate); sepals mostly at least 6 mm long at anthesis; petals pale yellow, shorter than to as much as 2 mm longer than the sepals; plants mostly over 4 dm tall; (transcontinental) . . . . *P. arguta*

  34 Cymes usually open to diffuse (sometimes glomerate); sepals often less than 6 mm long; petals pale to deep yellow, about equalling the sepals; plants often less than 4 dm tall; (s B.C. and sw Alta.) . . . . *P. glandulosa*

33 Plants not glandular-villous; style inserted at or near the summit of the achene.

  35 Cymes very leafy, many-flowered; leaflets oblong to cuneate-obovate, coarsely crenate; annuals, biennials, or short-lived perennials from a taproot; (B.C. to Ont.).

    36 Achenes with a corky wedge-shaped protuberance on the inner edge nearly as large as the body; petals about equalling the sepals; lower leaves with 5–9(11) distant leaflets . . . . *P. paradoxa*

    36 Achenes lacking a corky protuberance; petals about half as long as the sepals; lower leaves with commonly 5 crowded leaflets (appearing subpalmate; upper leaves always 3-foliolate) . . . . *P. rivalis*

  35 Cymes less leafy and generally with fewer flowers; perennials.

    37 Style little (if any) longer than the mature achene; leaflets commonly tomentose beneath; (essentially transcontinental).

      38 Style scarcely thickened at the eglandular base; leaflets 5–7, greyish-tomentose beneath, smooth above, pectinately divided to near the midrib into linear acute revolute segments . . . . *P. multifida*

      38 Style thickened and glandular at base; leaflets mostly incised at least halfway to the midrib.

        39 Basal leaves with commonly 5 (sometimes 7) leaflets, they and the upper leaves silky-pubescent on both sides with yellowish-tinged hairs; stems generally less than 1 dm tall, silky-hirsute with yellowish hairs . . . . *P. pulchella*

        39 Basal leaves with usually 7 or more leaflets (commonly only 5 in var. *pectinata*); stems generally at least 2 dm tall . . . . *P. pensylvanica*

    37 Style filiform and considerably longer than the mature achene.

      40 Leaflets dissected at most only about halfway to the midrib, 5–11; pedicels permanently erect or ascending, straightish; stems to about 5 dm tall.

        41 Leaves sparingly to rather copiously strigose-hirsute but always greenish, often glabrate; petals to 11 mm long; (B.C. and Alta.) . . . . *P. drummondii*

        41 Leaves densely tomentose on both sides; petals commonly less than 1 cm long; (B.C. to w Ont.; introd. eastwards) . . . . *P. hippiana*

      40 Leaflets dissected nearly to the midrib; stems commonly less than 2 dm tall.

        42 Leaflets of basal leaves 5 (rarely 3), crowded, densely silky-white-tomentose beneath; flowers to 2.5 cm broad; petals dark yellow, overlapping; (transcontinental) . . . . *P. pulchella*

42 Leaflets of basal leaves mostly at least 9; flowers
smaller; petals paler yellow.
    43 Pedicels arcuate-spreading (at least in fruit); leaves
    appressed-strigose or glabrate; (Alta. to sw Man.) . . . . .
    . . . . *P. plattensis*
    43 Pedicels permanently erect or ascending,
    straightish; leaves mostly copiously silky-hirsute, at
    least beneath; (s B.C. and sw Alta.) . . . .*P. ovina*

P. anglica Laich.
European; introd. in thickets and peats of E N. America, as in s Labrador (Torrey and Gray 1840), SE Nfld. (Avalon Pen.; GH; CAN), and N.S. (Digby, Yarmouth, Inverness, Victoria, Richmond, and Cape Breton counties). [*P. nemoralis* Nestler; *P. procumbens* Sibth.]. MAPS: Hultén 1958: map 135, p. 155; Fernald 1929: map 28, p. 1502.

Fernald *in* Gray (1950) considers this species to be introd. in sw N.S. and E Pa. but native in s Labrador, SE Nfld., and Cape Breton Is., N.S. Hultén (1958), however, believes it more likely that the entire N. American population is introd. *See note under Luzula campestris.*

P. anserina L.   Silverweed.   Argentine or Richette
/aST/X/GEA/   (Hsr (Hrr; Ch))   Gravelly or sandy shores and flats from Alaska (near the Arctic Circle) and s-cent. Yukon–Dist. Mackenzie to Alta. (N to L. Athabasca), Sask. (N to Prince Albert), Man. (N to Churchill; Schofield 1959), northernmost Ont., Que. (N to E James Bay at ca. 53°45′N and the Côte-Nord), Nfld., N.B., P.E.I., and N.S., s to s Calif., N.Mex., Iowa, Ind., N.Y., and New Eng.; E Greenland N to ca. 65°N; Iceland; Eurasia. [*Argentina* Rydb.]. MAPS: Hultén 1968b:621; Meusel, Jaeger, and Weinert 1965:218.

Forma *sericea* (Hayne) Hayek (var. *ser.* Hayne; var. *concolor* Ser. (*Anserina con.* (Ser.) Rydb.); *A. argentea* Rydb., not *P. argentea* L.; *P. pratincola* Boivin; leaflets silvery-silky on both surfaces rather than green and essentially glabrous above) occurs in drier habitats throughout the area.

P. argentea L.   Silvery Cinquefoil
Eurasian; widely introd. in dry open ground in N. America, as in B.C. (N to Prince George), Sask. (N to Lac la Ronge, 55°10′N), Man. (N to Warren Landing, near the N end of L. Winnipeg), Ont. (N to Longlac, 49°47′N), Que. (N to the Gaspé Pen. at New Carlisle), Nfld., N.B., P.E.I., and N.S.

P. arguta Pursh   Tall Cinquefoil
/sT/X/   (Hs)   Dry prairies and rocky or alluvial soil from s-cent. Alaska–Yukon and s Dist. Mackenzie to L. Athabasca (Alta. and Sask.), Man. (N to Tod L. at ca. 56°45′N), Ont. (N to L. Nipigon), Que. (N to the Gaspé Pen.; reported from Saguenay Co. of the Côte-Nord by Saint-Cyr 1887, but not listed by St. John 1922), and N.B. (York, Carleton, Victoria, and Restigouche counties; not known from P.E.I. or N.S.), s to Oreg., Ariz., N.Mex., Okla., Mo., Ohio, and W.Va. [*Geum (Drymocallis) agrimonoides* Pursh; *D. (P.) corymbosa* Rydb.; incl. the generally smaller-dimensioned var. *convallaria* (Rydb.) Wolf (*P. con.* Rydb.)]. MAPS: Hultén 1968b:618; Porsild 1966: map 94, p. 78; Meusel, Jaeger, and Weinert 1965:215; Clausen, Keck, and Hiesey 1940: fig. 12, p. 38.

P. atrosanguinea Lodd.   Himalayan Cinquefoil
Asiatic; reported from N.B. by Boivin (1966b; Kouchibougouac, where introd. in a strawberry bed).

P. biennis Greene
/T/WW/   (Hs (bien. or T))   Sandy soil, shores, wet meadows, roadsides, and waste places from s B.C. (N to Clinton, about 50 mi NW of Kamloops; reported by Porsild 1951a, as introd. near Dawson, the Yukon) and sw Alta. (Cardston; CAN; reports from Sask. require confirmation) to Baja Calif., Colo., and S.Dak. [*Tridophyllum* Greene]. MAP: Hultén 1968b:609.

P. biflora Willd.
/aST/W/A/ (Ch (Hs)) Rocky ground and heaths from the coasts of Alaska–Yukon to w-cent. Dist. Mackenzie and N B.C. (S to Summit Pass, ca. 58°30′N); Asia. MAPS: Hultén 1968b:610; Porsild 1966: map 95, p. 78.

P. canadensis L.
/T/EE/ (Hsr) Dry to moist soil from Minn. to Ont. (N to the Ottawa dist.), Que. (N to the Montreal dist.; *P. simplex* reported N to Quebec City by John Macoun 1883), Nfld., N.B., P.E.I., and N.S., S to Okla., Mo., Tenn., and Ga. [*P. pumila* Poir.; incl. *P. simplex* Michx. and its var. *calvescens* Fern.].

P. concinna Richards.
/T/WW/ (Ch) Dry sandy or gravelly prairies and slopes, the aggregate species from SE B.C. and S Alta. (N to Alliance, 52°26′N; CAN) to S Sask. (N to Moose Jaw) and S Man. (N to St. Lazare, about 75 mi NW of Brandon), S to Nev., Utah, N.Mex., and S.Dak.
1 Leaves usually distinctly digitate, the leaflets mostly only 5; [Alta. to Man.].
    2 Leaflets mostly toothed not over halfway to the midrib; [*P. humifusa* Nutt.; type
        from "British America"] . . . . .var. *concinna*
    2 Leaflets dissected over halfway to the midrib; [*P. divisa* Rydb.; *P. nivea*
        (concinna) var. *dissecta* Wats., not *P. dissecta* Nutt. (which is *P. diversifolia*
        Lehm.) nor Pursh] . . . . .var. *divisa* Rydb.
1 Leaves distinctly pinnate, the leaflets often 7(9).
    3 Leaflets usually distinctly greyish-tomentose above; [*P. macounii* Rydb., the type
        from Crowsnest Pass, SE B.C.; also known from Banff and Waterton Lakes,
        SW Alta.] . . . . .var. *macounii* (Rydb.) Hitchc.
    3 Leaflets usually greenish above, often strongly hirsute or strigose but not
        tomentose; [*P. intermittens, P. rubripes,* and *P. saximontana* Rydb.; S Alta.] . . . .
        . . . . .var. *rubripes* (Rydb.) Hitchc.

P. crantzii (Crantz) Beck
/aST/EE/GEwA/ (Ch (Hs)) Calcareous barrens from northernmost Ungava–Labrador and SE Baffin Is. (an isolated station near the Arctic Circle) to James Bay (S to Akimiski Is. at ca. 53°N), Que. (S to the S Ungava Bay watershed and Greenly Is. of the Côte-Nord), S Labrador, and W Nfld.; W Greenland N to ca. 72°N, E Greenland N to 74°13′N; Iceland; Spitsbergen; Europe; W Asia. [*Fragaria* Crantz; *P. alpestris* Hall. f.; *P. maculata* Pourr. and its var. *firma* Lange; *P. opaca* La Pey.; *P. rubens* Rydb., not Vill.; *P. salisburgensis* Haenke]. MAPS: Hultén 1958: map 27, p. 47; Porsild 1957: map 225, p. 189; A. Löve 1950: fig. 12, p. 44.
    Var. *hirta* (Lange) Malte (*P. maculata* var. *hirta* Lange, the type from Greenland; *P. langeana* Rydb.; leaves pilose on both surfaces rather than only along the nerves beneath, the petioles more or less densely hirsute rather than essentially glabrous) is known from N Ungava–Labrador and Greenland.

P. diversifolia Lehm.
/aST/D/G/ (Hs (Ch)) Subalpine to alpine meadows, rocks, and slopes, the aggregate species from S-cent. Alaska–Yukon–W Dist. Mackenzie through the mts. of B.C.–Alta. and SW Sask. (Cypress Hills; Breitung 1957a) to Calif., Utah, and N.Mex.; var. *ranunculus* with isolated stations in N Labrador and Greenland (W Greenland N to ca. 67°N, E Greenland N to ca. 63°N). MAPS and synonymy: *see* below.
1 Stems from a long creeping rootstock; leaves glabrous or merely ciliate, glaucous;
    [*P. ranunculus* Lange, the type from Greenland; incl. *P. rubella* Soerensen; N
    Labrador (Okak, 57°35′N) and Greenland] . . . . .var. *ranunculus* (Lange) Boivin
1 Stems from short woody caudices.
    2 Leaves mostly distinctly digitate, the leaflets usually merely deeply toothed to
        shallowly dissected; [*P. dissecta* Nutt., not Pursh; *P. glaucophylla* Lehm.; S
        Alaska–Yukon–SW Dist. Mackenzie–B.C. to SW Sask.; MAPS: Raup 1947: pl. 28
        (var. *glaucophylla*); Clausen, Keck, and Hiesey 1940; fig. 48, p. 134; Hultén
        1968b:621] . . . . .var. *diversifolia*

2 Leaves distinctly pinnate, the leaflets more deeply dissected; [s B.C. and sw Alta.].
3 Leaves greyish, coarsely strigose, the ultimate segments mostly linear; [*P. multisecta* (Wats.) Rydb.] . . . . var. *multisecta* Wats.
3 Leaves greenish, glabrous to moderately strigose, the segments linear to oblong; [*P. perdissecta* Rydb.; *P. decurrens* (Wats.) Rydb.] . . . .
. . . . var. *perdissecta* (Rydb.) Hitchc.

P. drummondii Lehm.
/T/W/ (Hs) Subalpine to alpine wet meadows and open slopes from B.C. (N to Kimsquit, ca. 53°N; CAN; reported from Alaska by Boivin 1966b, but not listed by Hultén 1968b or 1946) and Alta. (N to the type locality N of the Smoky R. at ca. 56°N) to N Calif. [*P. cascadensis* Rydb.]. MAP: Clausen, Keck, and Hiesey 1940: fig. 69, p. 179.

P. egedii Wormsk.
/aST/X/GEA/ (Hsr (Hrr)) Coastal sands and wet brackish flats, the aggregate species from the Aleutian Is. and coasts of Alaska–Yukon–Dist. Mackenzie–Dist. Keewatin to Victoria Is., s Baffin Is., and northernmost Ungava–Labrador, s in the West through coastal B.C. to s Calif., farther eastwards s to Great Bear L., NE Man. (s to York Factory, Hudson Bay, 57°N), the Hudson Bay–James Bay coasts of Ont. and Que., E Que. (St. Lawrence R. estuary between Berthier-en-Bas, Montmagny Co., and the Côte-Nord, Anticosti Is., and Gaspé Pen.), Nfld., N.B., P.E.I., N.S., and Long Is.; w Greenland N to ca. 68°50′N, E Greenland N to near the Arctic Circle; Iceland; Eurasia. MAPS and synonymy: see below.
1 Leaves less than 1 dm long, with at most 9 narrowly obovate leaflets to 2 cm long, the leaflets essentially glabrous beneath; [*Argentina* Rydb.; *P. anserina* var. *egedii* (Wormsk.) T. & G.; *P. pacifica* Howell; Aleutian Is. and w-cent. Alaska (*see* Hultén 1946: map 779 *(P. pacifica),* p. 1064) through coastal B.C. to s Calif.; Manawanan Is., James Bay; Que. (coasts of James Bay and s Ungava Bay); Labrador N to ca. 55°N; Nfld.; w Greenland (type locality) N to ca. 68°50′N; MAPS: Hultén 1968b:622; Porsild 1957: map 226 (solid circles), p. 189; Meusel, Jaeger, and Weinert 1965:218] . . . var. *egedii*
1 Leaves to 5 dm long, with up to 31 obovate to oblong leaflets to 6 cm long, the leaflets densely tomentose beneath; [*P. anserina* vars. *groenl.* Tratt. (type from Greenland), *grandis* T. & G., and *rolandii* and *lanata* Boivin; *Argentina litoralis, A. pacifica,* and *A. subarctica* Rydb. (not *P. litoralis* nor *P. subarctica* Rydb., which are *P. pensylvanica* var. *pectinata* and *P. pulchella,* respectively); *P. yukonensis* Hult.; with the typical form, basis of reports of *P. anserina* from Labrador, relevant collections in several herbaria; transcontinental in arctic and subarctic regions; MAPS: Porsild 1957: map 226, p. 189; combine the maps by Hultén 1968b:622 and 623 (ssp. *grandis* and ssp. *yukonensis*)] . . . . var. *groenlandica* (Tratt.) Polunin

P. elegans C. & S.
/aSs/W/A/ (Ch (Hs)) Dry to moist places at low to moderate elevations from N Alaska, s-cent. Yukon, and w-cent. Dist. Mackenzie to N B.C. (s to near Cassiar at ca. 58°30′N; CAN); N Asia. MAP: Hultén 1968b:611.

P. erecta (L.) Räuschel
Eurasian; introd. in E Mass. and in mossy places of SE Nfld. (Quiddy Viddy, where considered native by Fernald *in* Gray 1950, but more likely introd.; GH; *see* Hultén 1958:134, and note under *Luzula campestris*). [*Tormentilla* L.; *P. tormentilla* Stokes]. MAP: Hultén 1958: map 116, p. 135.

P. flabellifolia Hook.
/T/W/ (Hs) Wet meadows and streambanks to alpine ridges and talus from s B.C. (N to Lillooet and Lytton; the inclusion of SE Alta. in the range by Hitchcock et al. 1961, requires confirmation) to Calif., Idaho, and Mont. [*P. ?gelida* of Canadian reports, not Mey.].

P. fruticosa L.　Shrubby Cinquefoil

/aST/X/EA/　(N)　Dry to moist ground at low to subalpine elevations, the aggregate species from the coasts of Alaska–Yukon–Dist. Mackenzie to Great Bear L., Great Slave L., L. Athabasca (Alta. and Sask.), Man. (N to York Factory, Hudson Bay, 57°N; the report from Churchill by Gardner 1937, is probably the result of confusion with collections from Flin Flon), northernmost Ont., Que. (N to SE Hudson Bay at ca. 56°50′N and the Côte-Nord), S Labrador, Nfld., N.B., and N.S. (cult. in P.E.I., where not considered native by D.S. Erskine 1960), S to Calif., N.Mex., S.Dak., Iowa, Pa., and N.J.; Eurasia. MAPS and synonymy: *see* below.

1　Leaflets lanceolate to oblanceolate or oblong, to about 3 cm long and 9 mm broad; flowers to 3 cm broad; calyx to 1.5 cm long, its bractlets lanceolate to narrowly oblong . . .
. . . . var. *fruticosa*

　　2　Leaves silky to subglabrous; [*Dasiphora* Rydb.; *Pentaphylloides* Schwarz; *Potentilla (Pentaphylloides) floribunda* Pursh; transcontinental; MAPS (aggregate species): Hultén 1968*b*:609; Raup 1947: pl. 29; Meusel, Jaeger, and Weinert 1965:214] . . . . f. *fruticosa*

　　2　Leaves densely white-villous on both surfaces; [Ont.: reported from Batchawana Bay, L. Superior, by Hosie 1938, and from Great Cloche Is., L. Huron, the type locality, by M.L. Fernald, Rhodora 37(440):292. 1935] . . . . f. *villosissima* Fern.

1　Leaflets linear to linear-lanceolate, strongly revolute, to about 1.5 cm long and 3 mm broad; flowers to 1.5 cm broad; calyx to 1 cm long, its bractlets narrowly linear; [S Labrador (N to the Hamilton R. basin), E Que. (Gaspé Pen.), and Nfld.] . . . .
. . . . var. *tenuifolia* Lehm.

P. glandulosa Lindl.

/T/W/　(Hs)　Dry open ground and slopes (ranges of Canadian taxa outlined below), S to N Baja Calif., Ariz., and Colo. MAPS and synonymy: *see* below.

1　Plants glandular almost throughout.

　　2　Inflorescence usually leafy-bracted; petals oblanceolate to narrowly obovate, about equalling or at most 0.5 mm longer than the sepals; [*Drymocallis* Rydb.; *D. albida* and *D. ?fissa* Rydb.; *P. (Drym.) oregana* Nutt.; *P. (Drym.) valida* Greene; *P. (Drym.) wrangelliana* Fisch. & Lall.; B.C. (N to Mile 155, Haines Road); MAPS: Meusel, Jaeger, and Weinert 1965:215; Clausen, Keck, and Hiesey 1940: fig. 13, p. 40] . . . . var. *glandulosa*

　　2　Inflorescence seldom leafy-bracted; petals oval to broadly obovate, to 1.5 mm longer than the sepals; [*P. (Drymocallis) pseudorupestris* Rydb.; SE B.C. and SW Alta. (Waterton Lakes)] . . . . var. *pseudorupestris* (Rydb.) Breitung

1　Plants with few if any glandular hairs; inflorescence leafy-bracted; [*Drymocallis pseudorupestris* var. *int.* Rydb.; SE B.C. and SW Alta.] . . . . . var. *intermedia* (Rydb.) Hitchc.

P. gracilis Dougl.

/ST/WW/　(Hs)　Moist, fresh to brackish meadows and prairies to subalpine meadows (ranges of Canadian taxa outlined below), S to Baja Calif., N.Mex., Nebr., and S.Dak. MAPS and synonymy: *see* below.

1　Leaflets dissected at least 2/3 of the way to the midrib, the segments usually linear and greyish- or whitish-pubescent beneath.

　　2　Leaflets white-tomentose beneath, subglabrous above; [*P. ?alaskana* Rydb.; *P. flabelliformis* Lehm. and its var. *?tenuior* Lehm.; *P. ctenophora* Rydb.; S Alaska (probably introd.) and B.C. to Man.; MAPS *(P. flab.)*: Clausen, Keck, and Hiesey 1940: fig. 47, p. 131; Hultén 1968*b*:620] . . . . var. *flabelliformis* (Lehm.) Nutt.

　　2　Leaflets silky (or silky and tomentose) beneath, silky above; [*P. elmeri* Rydb.; ?B.C.; *see* Hitchcock et al. 1961:145] . . . . [var. *elmeri* (Rydb.) Jeps.]

1　Leaflets dissected not over 2/3 of the way to the midrib, the segments usually relatively broad and often greenish (although generally pubescent) beneath.

　　3　Leaflets usually greyish beneath, finely and deeply serrate or lobed to nearly halfway to the midrib, the leaves often somewhat pinnate rather than distinctly digitate; [*P. camporum* and *P. filipes* Rydb.; *P. pulcherrima* Lehm., not Rydb. (*P. hippiana* var. *pul.* (Lehm.) Wats.); B.C. to Man. (collections from the NW shore

of L. Superior and Deep River, Ont., and Hull, Que., where probably introd., have also been placed here); MAP: Clausen, Keck, and Hiesey 1940: fig. 47 *(P. pulch.),* p. 131] . . . . var. *pulcherrima* (Lehm.) Fern.
3 Leaflets either greenish beneath or more coarsely and/or sharply serrate.
    4 Stems and petioles spreading-hirsute; [*P. permollis* Rydb.; B.C.: Hitchcock et al. 1961:145] . . . . var. *permollis* (Rydb.) Hitchc.
    4 Stems and petioles appressed-strigose or -silky.
        5 Leaves variously pubescent but not white-woolly beneath; [var. *fastigiata* (Nutt.) Wats. (*P. fastigiata* Nutt.); *P. nuttallii* Lehm. and its var. *glabrata* Lehm. (*P. glabrata* (Lehm.) Rydb.); *P. blaschkeana* Turcz.; *P. glomerata* and *P. jucunda* Nels.; *P. dichroa, P. grosseserrata* in part, and *P. viridescens* Rydb.; *P. chrysantha* Lehm., not Trev.; *P. rigida* Nutt., not Wall.; Alaska–Yukon–B.C. to Man. (collections from near Thunder Bay, Ont., and L. Timiskaming, Que., where probably introd., have also been placed here); MAP: Clausen, Keck, and Hiesey 1940: fig. 48 (ssp. *nutt.*), p. 134] . . . . var. *glabrata* (Lehm.) Hitchc.
        5 Leaves white-woolly beneath; [Alaska–Yukon–B.C. to Sask. (reports from ?Ont., Que., and P.E.I. by Boivin 1966*b*, probably refer to introductions of this typical form or its varieties); MAPS: Clausen, Keck, and Hiesey 1940: fig. 48, p. 134; Hultén 1968*b*:620] . . . . var. *gracilis*

P. hippiana Lehm.
/T/WW/ (Hs) Open grassland and pine forest at low to moderate elevations from B.C. (N to Pine Pass, 55°15′N; an 1888 Macoun report from Telegraph Creek, ca. 57°40′N, tentatively accepted by Hultén 1946; the report from near Summit, Alaska, by A.E. Porsild, Rhodora 41(486):246. 1939, is referred to *P. pensylvanica* by Boivin 1967*a*, the relevant collection in CAN) to S Alta. (N to Banff and Edmonton), Sask. (N to near Prince Albert), S Man. (N to Birtle, about 65 mi NW of Brandon), and W Ont. (Sibley Pen., NW shore of L. Superior near Thunder Bay; CAN), S to Ariz., N.Mex., and Nebr.; introd. farther eastwards, as in Ont. (pasture near Deep River, Renfrew Co.; T.C. Brayshaw, Can. Field-Nat. 78(3):153. 1964), Que. (St-Fulgence, Chicoutimi Co.; L.-R. Cayouette, Nat. can. (Que.) 93(6):889. 1966), and N.S. (field near Brooklyn Corner, Kings Co.; E.C. Smith and J.S. Erskine, Rhodora 56(671):248. 1954). [Incl. *P. effusa* Lehm. and its var. *filicaulis* Nutt.]. MAP: Hultén 1968*b*:619.

Var. *argyrea* (Rydb.) Boivin (*P. arg.* Rydb., the type from Moose Jaw, Sask.; leaves loosely tomentose and rather dull rather than silky and lustrous, the inflorescence relatively compact) is reported from Alta. (Boivin 1966*b*), Sask. (N to Saskatoon; Breitung 1957*a*), and Man. (Rydberg 1932).

P. hyparctica Malte
/AST/X/GEA/ (Ch (Hs)) Tundra and open rocky ground at low to fairly high elevations, the aggregate species from the Aleutian Is. and coasts of Alaska–Yukon–Dist. Mackenzie–Dist. Keewatin nearly throughout the Canadian Arctic Archipelago to Ellesmere Is. at ca. 80°N and northernmost Ungava–Labrador, S in the West to N B.C. (Summit Pass, 58°31′N; CAN) and the mts. of SW Alta. (N to Jasper; CAN), farther eastwards S to S Dist. Keewatin, N Man. (Churchill; CAN), James Bay (Bear Is., 54°20′N), and Que. (S along the coast of Hudson Bay to Cape Jones, 54°37′N and along Hudson Strait to Ungava Bay; isolated in the Shickshock Mts. of the Gaspé Pen.); W and E Greenland S to near the Arctic Circle; Spitsbergen; arctic Eurasia. MAPS and synonymy: *see* below.
1 Stems rarely over 1 dm tall, mostly 1-flowered; petioles of basal leaves scarcely elongating after flowering, their stiff pubescence horizontally spreading; leaflets permanently pilose on both faces, the terminal ones generally about twice as long as broad; bracts of calyx shorter than the calyx-lobes; [*P. robbinsiana* ssp. *hyp.* (Malte) D. Löve; *P. emarginata* Pursh (not Desf.) and its f. *tardinix* Polunin; *P. flabellifolia* var. *emarg.* (Pursh) Boivin; *P. groenlandica* R. Br.; *P. nana* Willd.; range of the species (type from Ellesmere Is.) but somewhat more northern than the following taxon; MAPS (aggregate species): Hultén 1968*b*:613; Porsild 1957: map 227, p. 189] . . . . var. *hyparctica*

1   Stems to over 2 dm tall, 1–several-flowered; petioles of basal leaves conspicuously
    elongating after flowering, their softer pubescence generally ascending; leaflets
    becoming more or less glabrous, the terminal ones often about as broad as long;
    bracts of calyx becoming about as long as the calyx-lobes; [*P. emarginata* var.
    elatior Abrom., the type from Greenland; *P. nana* and *P. fragiformis* of reports from E
    Que. and Labrador, not Willd.; range of the species] . . . . var. *elatior* (Abrom.) Fern.

P. intermedia L.

Eurasian; introd. along roadsides and in old fields of N. America, as in Ont. (N to Sault Ste.
Marie and Renfrew and Carleton counties), Que. (N to St-Simon, Rimouski Co.; RIM; CAN),
Nfld. (Humber dist.; MT), N.B. (Fredericton; Groh and Frankton 1949b), P.E.I. (New London;
Bideford; Plat River), and N.S. (Cumberland and Queens counties).

   This species is more or less intermediate in characters between *P. argentea* and *P. norvegica* and considered a hybrid of this parentage by some European botanists. Var. *canescens*
(Bess.) Rupr. (*P. canescens* Bess.; *P. inclinata* of auth., not Vill.; leaves greyish-silky beneath
with a thin tomentum rather than sparingly pilose and green on both sides) occurs throughout the Canadian range.

   The closely related *P. thuringiaca* Bernh. of Europe (leaves mostly 7–9 rather than mostly 5,
the style short rather than about equalling the mature achene) is known from Que. (Sillery,
near Quebec City; L.-R. Cayouette, Nat. can. (Que.) 93(6):894. 1966).

P. multifida L.

/ST/X/EA/   (Hs (Ch))   Rock crevices, ledges, and dry open soil from N Alaska, S Yukon,
and NW-cent. Dist. Mackenzie to Great Slave L., L. Athabasca (Alta. and Sask.), Man. (N to
Churchill), Ont. (NW shore of L. Superior near Thunder Bay; L. Nipigon; Sandy L. at ca. 53°N,
93°W; W James Bay N to ca. 53°N), islands in James Bay N to ca. 53°45′N, and N Que. (E
James Bay N to ca. 52°N; S Ungava Bay; Larch R. at ca. 57°45′N), S to S Alaska–Yukon (a collection in Herb. V from Chezacut, B.C., ca. 52°N, has also been placed here), L. Athabasca,
and S-cent. Man. (S to Gypsumville, about 125 mi N of Portage la Prairie); Spitsbergen; Eurasia. MAPS: Hultén 1968b:617; Porsild 1966: map 98, p. 79; Dutilly, Lepage, and Duman 1953:
fig. 15 (E Canada area; somewhat incomplete), p. 75.

P. nivea L.

/AST/X/GEA/   (Ch (Hs))   Dry calcareous rocks and slopes, the aggregate species from the
coasts of Alaska–Yukon–Dist. Mackenzie–Dist. Keewatin to Banks Is., Victoria Is., Baffin Is. (N
to ca. 70°N; an isolated station on Ellesmere Is. at ca. 80°N), and northernmost Ungava–Labrador, S in the West through the mts. of B.C. and SW Alta. to Nev., Utah, and Colo., farther
eastwards S to L. Athabasca (Alta. and Sask.), NE Man. (Churchill), N Ont. (Sutton R., SW Hudson Bay at ca. 55°10′N), Que. (coasts of James Bay–Hudson Bay to Ungava Bay; Knob Lake
dist. at ca. 54°48′N; L. Marymac at ca. 57°N; Bic, Rimouski Co.; Shickshock Mts. of the
Gaspé Pen.), Labrador (S to ca. 57°N; not known from the Maritime Provinces), and Nfld.;
nearly circumgreenlandic; Spitsbergen; Eurasia. MAPS and synonymy: *see* below.

1   Petioles floccose with curly hairs, lacking long straight hairs.
    2   Leaflets coarsely toothed but scarcely lobed . . . . ssp. *nivea*
        3   Leaves dark green and essentially glabrous above; [incl. vars. *?macrophylla*
            Ser., *pallidior* Sw., and *subviridis* Lehm.; transcontinental; MAPS: Porsild 1957:
            map 228, p. 189; Hultén 1968b:614, and 1945a: fig. 6 (incomplete for the
            Hudson Bay–James Bay region), p. 143; Raup 1947: pl. 28 (aggregate species)] . . .
            . . . . var. *nivea*
        3   Leaves more or less densely tomentose and long-silky-hairy above; [Alaska–
            Yukon–B.C.; reported from Vancouver Is. and Mt. Selwyn, B.C., and from E
            Que., Labrador, Nfld., and Greenland by Hultén 1946:1022] . . . .
            . . . . var. *tomentosa* Nilsson-Ehle
    2   Leaflets deeply cut into relatively narrow lobes and tending to be 5-parted; [var.
        subquinata Lange, the type from Greenland; vars. *?pentaphylla* and *?pinnatifida*
        Lehm.; var. *?quinquefolia* Rydb. (*P. quinq.* Rydb.); *P. ?furcata* Porsild; *P. nipharga*

Rydb. in part; essentially transcontinental; MAPS: Hultén 1945a: fig. 8, p. 146; the map for *P. furcata* by Porsild 1966: map 96, p. 78, is interpreted as applying here] . . . .
. . . . ssp. *subquinata* (Lange) Hult.
1   Petioles with all or part of their pubescence consisting of spreading hairs several times longer than the thickness of the petiole; leaflets coarsely toothed but scarcely lobed.
  4   Petioles 2 or 3 times longer than the blade, densely short-pubescent as well as long-hairy; [*P. hookeriana* Lehm.; *P. nipharga* Rydb. in part; western part of the area; MAPS: Porsild 1957: map 229, p. 189; Hultén 1968b:615, and 1945a: fig. 7 *(P. hook.),* p. 144] . . . . ssp. *hookeriana* (Lehm.) Hiitonen
  4   Petioles longer, their surfaces essentially glabrous beneath the long-hairy pubescence; [*P. chamissonis* Hult.; *P. nivea* var. *lapponica* C. & S.; essentially transcontinental; MAPS: Porsild 1957: map 230, p. 189; Hultén 1968b:616, 1945a: fig. 7 *(P. cham.),* p. 144, and 1958: map 8 *(P. cham.),* p. 27] . . . .
. . . . ssp. *chamissonis* (Hult.) Hiitonen

P. norvegica L.
/aST/X/GEA/   (Hs (bien. or T))   Moist ground and waste places (probably both native and introd.), the aggregate species from N-cent. Alaska–Yukon and NW Dist. Mackenzie to Great Bear L., Great Slave L., L. Athabasca (Alta. and Sask.), Man.–Ont., Que. (N to Ungava Bay and the Côte-Nord), Labrador (reported N to Nachvak, 59°07′N), Nfld., N.B., P.E.I., and N.S., s to Calif., Mexico, Tex., and N.C.; introd. in W Greenland at ca. 60° and 70°N; Iceland; Eurasia. MAPS and synonymy: *see* below.
1   Stem hirsute with stiff, mostly spreading hairs; leaflets more or less hirsute; [incl. var. *hirsuta* (Michx.) Lehm. (*P. hirsuta* Michx.); *P. monspeliensis* L.; transcontinental; MAPS: Hultén 1968b:614; Raup 1947: pl. 28 (aggregate species)] . . . . var. *norvegica*
1   Stem and leaflets essentially glabrous; [*P. labradorica* Lehm.; *P. flexuosa* Raf.; s Ont. (Bruce Pen. and Georgian Bay, L. Huron), Que. (E James Bay at 53°50′N; SE Hudson Bay at ca. 55°15′N; Bic, Rimouski Co.; Côte-Nord; Anticosti Is.; Gaspé Pen.), Labrador (reported N to Nachvak, 59°07′N; type from Labrador), Nfld., and N.B. (near Grand Falls, Victoria Co.; CAN)] . . . . var. *labradorica* (Lehm.) Fern.

P. ovina J.M. Macoun
/T/W/   (Ch)   Open ridges, barren slopes, and moist meadows from middle altitudes to above timberline in the mts. of SE ?B.C. (Sheep Mt., presumably the one in the Kootenay dist.; Henry 1915) and SW Alta. (N to the type locality, Silver City, a former settlement near Castle Mt., NW of Banff; the inclusion of Sask. in the range by Hitchcock et al. 1961, requires confirmation) to NE Calif. and Colo. [*P. diversifolia* var. *pinnatisecta* Wats.].

P. palustris (L.) Scop.   Marsh-Five-Finger.   Comaret or Argentine rouge
/aST/X/GEA/   (Grh (Hel; Ch))   Bogs, wet meadows, and margins of ponds and slow streams, the aggregate species from the Aleutian Is. and coasts of Alaska–Yukon–Dist. Mackenzie to Great Bear L., Great Slave L., L. Athabasca (Alta. and Sask.), E-cent. Dist. Keewatin (Chesterfield Inlet), northernmost Man.–Ont.–Ungava–Labrador, Nfld., N.B., P.E.I., and N.S., s to N Calif., Wyo., Iowa, Ohio, Pa., and N.J.; W Greenland N to 67°50′N, E Greenland N to 66°10′N; Iceland; Eurasia. MAPS and synonymy: *see* below.
1   Terminal leaflet not over twice as long as broad; flowers usually not more than 3 or 4 on a branch; [*Comarum angustifolium* var. *parvifolium* Raf.; the common form northwards] . . . . var. *parvifolia* (Raf.) Fern. & Long
1   Terminal leaflet at least twice as long as broad; flowers relatively numerous . . . .
. . . . var. *palustris*
  2   Plant densely villous with usually glandular hairs (especially on the petioles, peduncles, and calyces); [var. *villosa* (Pers.) Lehm.; frequent throughout the area] . . . . f. *glandulosa* Gunnarsson
  2   Plant glabrous or pubescent but nonglandular.
    3   Leaflets silvery-silky; [frequent throughout the area] . . . . . f. *subsericea* (Beck) Wolf

3 Leaflets green and glabrous or nearly so; [*Comarum palustre* L.; transcontinental; MAPS: Meusel, Jaeger, and Weinert 1965:213; Hultén 1968*b*:608] . . . . f. *palustris*

P. paradoxa Nutt.
/T/(X)/ (Hs (bien. or T)) Moist flats and shores from s B.C. (N to Spences Bridge) to s Alta. (N to Medicine Hat), Sask. (N to Nipawin, 53°22′N), Man. (N to The Pas), and s Ont. (Essex, Kent, Lincoln, Wentworth, and York counties), s to Mexico, N.Mex., Kans., La., Mo., Ohio, and w N.Y.; ?Asia. [*Tridophyllum* Greene; *P. supina* Michx., not L.].

P. pensylvanica L.
/ST/X/A/ (Hs (CH)) Dry prairies to montane ridges (ranges of Canadian taxa outlined below), s to Nev., N.Mex., Kans., Iowa, Minn., Mich., N.H., and Maine; Asia. MAP and synonymy: see below.
1 Leaflets essentially glabrous, scarcely paler beneath; [*P. sericea* var. *glabrata* Hook.; *P. glabrella* Rydb.; cent. Alaska–s Yukon–Alta. to SW James Bay, Ont.] . . . . var. *glabrata* (Hook.) Wats.
1 Leaflets tomentose beneath.
　2 Basal leaves with 5(7) leaflets, these greyish-tomentose beneath, nearly glabrous above; [*P. pect.* Raf.; *P. litoralis* Rydb.; Great Slave L., Dist. Mackenzie; L. Athabasca, Alta. and Sask.; Man. (The Pas; York Factory; Churchill) to Ont. (N to s James Bay), Que. (N to the Larch R. at ca. 57°30′N; CAN; RIM), Labrador (N to the Dead Is., 52°48′N; GH), Nfld., and N.S. (Cheticamp, Inverness Co., Cape Breton Is.; ACAD)] . . . . var. *pectinata* (Raf.) Lepage
　2 Basal leaves with 7–15 leaflets.
　　3 Leaves whitish-tomentose beneath, silvery-silky above; [*P. bipinnatifida* Dougl., the type from "Plains of the Saskatchewan"; Alta. (N to near Lesser Slave L.) to Sask. (N to Prince Albert) and s Man.] . . . . var. *bipinnatifida* (Dougl.) T. & G.
　　3 Leaves greyish-tomentose beneath, grey-green and often strigose above; [incl. vars. *arida* Boivin and *strigosa sensu* Pursh; *P. strigosa sensu* P.A. Rydberg, N. Am. Flora 22:351. 1908, perhaps not Pallas; *P. atrovirens, P. lasiodonta, P. platyloba,* and *P. pulcherrima* Rydb., not *P. pulch.* Lehm.; *P. virgulata* Nels.; Alaska–B.C. to Ont.; introd. in a railway clearing at Sorel, Que. (reports from James Bay, Ont. and Que., by Dutilly, Lepage, and Duman 1954 and 1958, are referable to var. *pectinata;* MAP (aggregate species): combine the maps by Hulten 1968*b*:619 (*P. pen.*) and 618 (*P. virg.*)] . . . . . . var. *pensylvanica*

P. plattensis Nutt.
/T/WW/ (Hs (Ch)) Moist meadows and prairies from s Alta. (Moss 1959; Boivin 1966*b*), s Sask. (N to near Moose Jaw; CAN), and sw Man. (Forrest, about 8 mi N of Brandon; Oak River; Napinka) to Calif., Utah, N.Mex., and S.Dak. [Incl. *P. breweri* Wats.].

P. pulchella R. Br.
/ASs/X/GEA/ (Ch (Hs)) Dry tundra and open sandy places (often in solifluction areas) from the w Aleutian Is. (Kiska Is.; A.E. Porsild, Can. Field-Nat. 58(4):131. 1944) and coasts of Alaska–Yukon–Dist. Mackenzie–Dist. Keewatin nearly throughout the Canadian Arctic Archipelago (type from Melville Is.) to northernmost Ellesmere Is. and northernmost Que. (Digges Is. and Akpatok Is., Hudson Strait), s to s Alaska–Yukon, Great Bear L., NE Man. (Churchill), N Ont. (s to the Sutton R., Hudson Bay, at ca. 55°15′N), islands of James Bay (s to Gasket Shoal, ca. 52°30′N), Que. (s to SE Hudson Bay at Cape Jones, 54°37′N), Labrador (Boivin 1966*b*), and Nfld. (type locality of *P. usticapensis*); w Greenland s to ca. 63°N, E Greenland s to ca. 69°N; Spitsbergen; arctic Lapland; arctic Asia. [*P. nivea* var. *pul.* (R. Br.) Durand; incl. var. *elatior* Lange (var. *gracilicaulis* Porsild; *P. subarctica* Rydb.), *P. rubricaulis* Lehm., and *P. usticapensis* Fern.]. MAPS: Hultén 1958: map 164, p. 183; combine the maps by Hultén 1968*b*:617 and 616 (*P. rub.*); Porsild 1955: fig. 21 (*P. rub.*), p. 151; combine the maps by Porsild 1957: map 213 (*P. pul.* var. *grac.*) and map 232 (*P. rub.*), p. 189.

P. recta L.

Eurasian; introd. along roadsides and in waste places of N. America, as in s B.C. (Vancouver Is.; Lytton to Spences Bridge; Monte Creek; Kelowna), Alta. (Boivin 1966b; var. *obscura*), Sask. (Mortlach; Swift Current), Man. (Birds Hill, near Winnipeg; WIN), Ont. (N to Kapuskasing, 49°24'N; Baldwin 1958), Que. (N to Ville Marie, Timiskaming Co., 47°20'N, and the Gaspé Pen. at Port Daniel), Nfld., N.B., P.E.I., and N.S. [*Hypargyrium* Fourr.; incl. *P. obscura* Nestler, *P. pilosa* Willd., and *P. sulphurea* Lam. & DC.].

P. reptans L.

Eurasian; introd. along roadsides and in lawns and waste places of N. America, as in Ont. (Lambton, Middlesex, Elgin, and Wellington counties), sw Que. (Montreal dist.; MT), and N.S. (Yarmouth, Hants, and Halifax counties).

P. rivalis Nutt.

/T/WW/ (Hs (bien. or T)) Swampy ground and damp soil (ranges of Canadian taxa outlined below), s to s Calif., N Mexico, N.Mex., Ark., and Ill.

1 Basal leaves distinctly pinnate (but the 2(3) pairs of lateral leaflets closely approximate), the upper leaves 3-foliolate (basal leaves sometimes 3-foliolate, but the terminal leaflet then 2-cleft); stamens about 10; [*Tridophyllum* Greene; s B.C. to s Alta., Sask. (N to Prince Albert), Man. (N to The Pas), and w Ont. (Boivin 1966b)] . . . . . .
. . . . var. *rivalis*

1 Basal leaves all digitate (the 3 or 5 leaflets all arising close together from the tip of the petiole).

2 Stamens about 10; leaves all 3-foliolate; [*P. millegrana* Engelm.; B.C. (N to Lytton), Alta. (N to Wood Buffalo National Park at 59°31'N), Sask. (N to Hudson Bay Junction, 52°52'N), Man. (N to The Pas), and Ont. (near Sault Ste. Marie and Chalk River)] . . . . var. *millegrana* (Engelm.) Wats.

2 Stamens 5; lower leaves 5-foliolate (sometimes 3-foliolate, but the terminal leaflet then 2-cleft); uppermost leaves 3-foliolate; [*P. pentandra* Engelm.; B.C. (N to Lac La Hache and Cariboo), s Alta. (Banff; Waterton Lakes; Kananaskis), Sask. (Yorkton; Touchwood), and Man. (Turtle Mt.; Brandon; East Selkirk)] . . . .
. . . . var. *pentandra* (Engelm.) Wats.

P. sterilis (L.) Garcke   Strawberry-leaved Cinquefoil

European; known in N. America only from thickets, clearings, and rocky slopes of SE Nfld. (Fernald 1933; GH), where considered native by Fernald but more likely introd. (see note under *Luzula campestris*). [*Fragaria* L.; *P. fragariastrum* Ehrh.]. MAP: Hultén 1958: map 131, p. 151.

P. stipularis L.

/aS/W/GA/ (Hs (Ch)) Meadows and sandy loams of N Alaska (collection in CAN, detd. Porsild, from Umiat, ca. 69°30'N, 152°W, where taken in 1961 by Raymond and Mildred Wood), E Greenland (at ca. 70° and 75°N), and N Asia. [Incl. var. *groenlandica* Soer.]. MAPS: Hultén 1968b:610; Gelting 1934: fig. 12 (not indicating the occurrence in Alaska), p. 113.

P. tridentata Ait.   Three-toothed Cinquefoil

/aST/EE/G/ (Ch) Dry sands, gravels, rocks, and peats from s Dist. Mackenzie (Taltson R. s of Great Slave L.; CAN; not known from B.C.) to L. Athabasca (Alta. and Sask.), Man. (N to the Cochrane R. at ca. 58°N), northernmost Ont., Que. (N to s Ungava Bay and the Côte-Nord), Labrador (N to Nachvak, 59°07'N), Nfld. (type locality), N.B., P.E.I., and N.S., s to N.Dak., Iowa, Minn., Mich., N.Y., and Ga.; w and E Greenland N to ca. 70°N. [*Sibbaldiopsis* Rydb.].

Forma *aurora* Graustein (petals pink rather than white) is known from E Que. (Bic, Rimouski Co.). Forma *hirsutifolia* Pease (leaves hirsute on both sides rather than essentially glabrous) is frequent throughout the range.

P. vahliana Lehm.
/AS/X/GeA/ (Ch (Hs)) Dry calcareous barrens from the coasts of Alaska–Yukon–Dist. Mackenzie–Dist. Keewatin throughout the Canadian Arctic Archipelago to northernmost Ellesmere Is. and Baffin Is., s to s Alaska–Yukon, Great Bear L., s Dist. Keewatin, Southampton Is., and northernmost w Ungava (Sugluk and Wolstenholme, Hudson Strait), and in the mts. of the West through B.C. and sw Alta. (N to Jasper) to Oreg., Mont., and Colo.; w Greenland (type locality) s to near the Arctic Circle; NE Asia (Wrangell Is. and islands in the Bering Sea). [*P. nivea* var. *vahl.* (Lehm.) Seem.; incl. *P. ledebouriana* Porsild and *P. uniflora* Ledeb.]. MAPS: Porsild 1957: map 233 (incomplete westwards), p. 190; combine the maps by Hultén 1968*b*:612 (*P. uniflora* and *P. vahl.*).

P. verna L.
European; reported by Fernald *in* Gray (1950) only from grassy roadsides in s Conn. but noted by Montgomery (1957) as occurring in a cemetery and in lawns at Toronto, Ont.

According to Tutin et al. (1968), the name *P. verna* L. is synonymous with *P. crantzii*, its application by European authors referring chiefly to the European *P. tabernaemontani* Aschers., to which our plant is also probably referable.

P. villosa Pallas
/ST/W/eA/ (Ch (Hs)) Rocky places from the Aleutian Is., Alaska (N to Cape Lisburne at ca. 69°N), and s Yukon (Porsild 1951*a*; CAN) through the mts. of B.C. and sw Alta. to Wash.; NE Asia. [*P. nivea* var. *villosa* (Pall.) Regel & Tiling; incl. the smaller-dimensioned extremes, vars. *parviflora* Hitchc. and *unifoliolosa* Hult.]. MAP: Hultén 1968*b*:611.

PRUNUS L.   [3396]   Plum, Cherry, etc.   Prunier, Cerisier, etc.

(Ref.: Groh and Senn 1940)
1 Flowers in elongate terminal racemes; petals white; fruit a cherry.
  2 Calyx-tube pubescent within; petals elliptic, at least 6 mm long; leaves oblong-obovate, finely sharp-serrate; (introd.) . . . .*P. padus*
  2 Calyx-tube glabrous within; petals roundish, less than 5 mm long.
    3 Leaves finely serrate with blunt incurved teeth, lance-oblong to oblong-ovate, firm; calyx-lobes acute, usually longer than broad, persistent in fruit; fruit dark red; (Ont. to N.S.) . . . .*P. serotina*
    3 Leaves finely sharp-serrate, ovate or obovate, thin; calyx-lobes blunt, often broader than long, conspicuously glandular-erose, soon deciduous; (transcontinental) . . . .*P. virginiana*
1 Flowers solitary or in small umbel-like clusters (in *P. mahaleb,* in short few-flowered racemes).
  4 Flowers (and fruits) sessile or nearly so, mostly solitary, in pairs, or clustered on the spurs; leaves serrate; (introd.).
    5 Leaves glabrous, broadly lanceolate to oblong-lanceolate, to over 2 dm long; flowers pink, to about 5 cm broad; fruit the common peach . . . .*P. persica*
    5 Leaves tomentose beneath, broadly oval to broadly obovate, at most about 7 cm long; flowers white or pink-tinged, about 2 cm broad; fruit a slightly pubescent cherry . . . .*P. tomentosa*
  4 Flowers (and fruits) distinctly pedicelled.
    6 Inflorescence a short 4–10-flowered raceme on a leafy-bracted peduncle; petals white, to 8 mm long; fruit a dark-red to black cherry usually about 6 mm thick; leaves broadly ovate to rotund, rounded or subcordate at base, finely serrate with rounded teeth; (introd.) . . . .*P. mahaleb*
    6 Inflorescence an umbel-like cluster or the flower solitary.
      7 Leaves entire or subentire toward base, the teeth not gland-tipped; flowers white, umbellate; fruit a cherry; low slender shrub; (Sask. to N.B.) . . . .*P. pumila*
      7 Leaves toothed nearly or quite to base; small trees or coarse shrubs.
        8 Plums; stone flattened or turgid, more or less 2-edged.

9 Flowers commonly solitary (sometimes 2 or 3), white or greenish-tinged; leaves oblanceolate to obovate, more or less pubescent beneath at least when young; (introd.).
    10 Branches conspicuously thorny; leaves at most about 4 cm long; flowers usually solitary; petals at most 8 mm long; pedicels glabrous; fruit blue-black; stone little flattened . . . . *P. spinosa*
    10 Branches unarmed or somewhat thorny; leaves to over 1 dm long; flowers 1, 2, or 3; petals to over 12 mm long; stone flattened . . . . *P. domestica*
9 Flowers 2–5 in umbels, white or roseate; petals to 1.5 cm long; fruit red to orange-red or yellow, 2 or 3 cm long; stone flattened; leaves lance-ovate to broadly ovate or obovate, slightly pubescent to glabrate beneath; twigs often somewhat spiny.
    11 Teeth of young leaves rounded and glandular, becoming callous-tipped; petioles usually with 2 apical glands; calyx-lobes glandular-serrate; petals often becoming roseate; (SE Man. to N.S.) . . . . *P. nigra*
    11 Teeth of leaves sharp and glandless, often double; petioles mostly lacking apical glands; calyx-lobes glandless or nearly so; petals white; (S Sask. to SW Que.) . . . . *P. americana*
8 Cherries; flowers normally white; stone more or less globose; teeth of young leaves gland-tipped.
    12 Flowers rarely over 1.5 cm broad, the clusters not subtended by leafy bracts from the same bud; fruit light red, about 6 mm thick; stone to 5 mm long; leaves thinnish, finely toothed, acute to acuminate, glabrous or soon glabrate; (transcontinental) . . . . *P. pensylvanica*
    12 Flowers to over 3 cm broad, the clusters subtended by leafy bracts from the same bud; fruit usually red to purplish-black, at least 1.5 cm long; stone about 1 cm long; leaves coarsely toothed, abruptly pointed; (introd.).
        13 Leaves to 1.5 dm long, somewhat drooping, soft, pubescent on the nerves beneath; inner bud-scales widely spreading or reflexed below the pedicels; calyx-tube constricted at summit, the lobes entire; petals obovate; stone ellipsoid; (sweet cherry) . . . . *P. avium*
        13 Leaves at most 1 dm long, more or less ascending, firm, glabrous; inner bud-scales erect; calyx-tube not constricted, the lobes serrate; petals roundish; stone subglobose; (sour cherry) . . . . *P. cerasus*

P. americana Marsh.   American Plum
/T/(X)/   (Ms)   Thickets and borders of woods from Mont. to S Sask. (Estevan and Roche Percee; Breitung 1957a), S Man. (N to Winnipeg), Ont. (N to Kakabeka Falls, about 20 mi W of Thunder Bay, and the Ottawa dist.), and Que. (N to the Montreal dist.; ?introd.), S to Ariz., Ark., and N Fla. [*P. hiemalis* Michx.; *Cerasus canadensis* Loisel., not Mill. nor Provancher]. MAPS: Canada Department of Northern Affairs and Natural Resources 1956:228; Hosie 1969:250; Preston 1961:264, and 1947:188; Hough 1947:271; Munns 1938: map 135, p. 139.
    [*P. maritima* Marsh. (the beach-plum of the E U.S.A.; Maine to E Pa. and Del.) is accredited to N.B. by Gleason and Cronquist (1963), this requiring confirmation. It resembles *P. americana* in the glandless leaf-teeth but has usually purplish-black (rather than typically red) fruits, the petals being at most 6 mm long rather than up to 1.5 cm.]

P. avium L.   Sweet Cherry.   Mazzard, Cerisier de France
Eurasian; persisting or spreading to roadside thickets and borders of woods in N. America, as in S Ont. (Kent, Lambton, Norfolk, Lincoln, and York counties), Que. (N to Les Eboulements, Charlevoix Co.; MT), and N.S. (Annapolis Valley).

Rosaceae

P. cerasus L.   Sour or Pie-Cherry
Asiatic; persisting or spreading to roadside thickets and borders of woods in N. America, as in
B.C. (Boivin 1966b), S Ont. (Lambton, Lincoln, Waterloo, and York counties), P.E.I. (Brackley
Point, Queens Co.; CAN; GH), and N.S. (Roland 1947).

P. domestica L.   Damson Plum.   Bullace, Prunier de l'Islet
Eurasian; persisting or spreading from cult. in Canada as indicated below. The species is
probably of hybrid origin.
1   Pedicels and young twigs sparingly pubescent or glabrous; petals tinged with green;
    fruit variously coloured, usually at least 4 cm long, its sharply angled stone
    commonly free from the flesh; usually a small tree, not thorny; [S Ont. (Montgomery
    1957), Que. (near Quebec City; John Macoun 1886), Nfld. (Rouleau 1956; ?escaped),
    and N.S. (Kings, Pictou, and Halifax counties)] . . . . var. *domestica*
1   Pedicels and young twigs densely pubescent; petals pure white; fruit usually purple
    to blue-black, rarely as much as 4 cm long, its bluntly angled stone adherent to the
    flesh; usually a shrub, often somewhat thorny; [*P. insititia* L.; × *P. dom.* nm. *inst.* (L.)
    Boivin; Ont. (Essex, Waterloo, Peel, and York counties), Que. (N to Ste-Anne-de-la-
    Pocatière, Kamouraska Co.), and N.S. (Kings, Queens, and Pictou counties)] . . . .
    . . . . ssp. *insititia* (L.) Poir.

P. mahaleb L.   Mahaleb or Perfumed Cherry
Eurasian; cult. in N. America and spreading to roadsides, rocky banks, and borders of woods,
as in S Ont. (Welland, Lincoln, Waterloo, and Wentworth counties).

P. nigra Ait.   Canada Plum.   Guignier or Prunier sauvage
/T/EE/   (Mc)   Thickets and borders of woods from SE Man. (N to near Winnipeg) to Ont. (N
to the NW shore of L. Superior and L. Timiskaming at ca. 47°30'N), Que. (N to Ville Marie, ca.
47°20'N, and the Quebec City dist.), N.B. (St. John; GH), and N.S. (Annapolis Valley; not
known from P.E.I.; reports from Nfld. require confirmation), S to Iowa, Va., and Ga. [*Cerasus*
Loisel.; *P. americana* var. *nigra* (Ait.) Waugh]. MAPS: Hosie 1969:248; Canada Department of
Northern Affairs and Natural Resources 1956:226; Hough 1947:269 (the Nfld. area should be
deleted); Groh and Senn 1940: fig. 2, p. 326.
   The form with roseate petals and sepals has been separated as f. *roseiflora* Rouleau (type
from Deux-Montagnes Co., Que.) but these organs often become roseate in age in the typical
form.

P. padus L.   European Bird-Cherry
Eurasian; occasionally cult. in N. America and spreading to roadsides and borders of woods,
as in Ont. (Wellington, York, and Carleton counties).

P. pensylvanica L. f.   Bird-, Pin-, or Fire-Cherry.   Cerises d'été or Petit Merisier
/sT/X/   (Ms)   Woods, thickets, clearings, and burned areas, the aggregate species from SW
Dist. Mackenzie (N to Fort Simpson, ca. 62°N; CAN) and B.C. to L. Athabasca (Alta. and
Sask.), Man. (N to the Cochrane R. at 58°13'N), Ont. (N to the Fawn R. at ca. 54°N, 89°W, and
W James Bay at ca. 53°N), Que. (N to the Swampy R. at 56°06'N, L. Mistassini, and the Côte-
Nord), Labrador (N to the Hamilton R. basin), Nfld., N.B., P.E.I., and N.S., S to Mont., Colo.,
S.Dak., Tenn., and N.C. MAPS and synonymy: see below.
1   Leaves gradually acuminate, finely serrate; fruit red, to 7 mm long; [*Cerasus* Loisel.;
    C. (Prunus) borealis Michx.; *C. canadensis* Prov., not Loisel. nor Mill.;
    transcontinental; MAPS (all except those by Hosie and Munns should be amended to
    include SW Dist. Mackenzie N to ca. 62°N): Hosie 1969:244; Canada Department of
    Northern Affairs and Natural Resources 1956:220; Hough 1947:267; Munns 1936:
    map 136, p. 140; Preston 1947:190, and 1961:262; the E Canada distribution is
    mapped in detail by Groh and Senn 1940: fig. 7, p. 334] . . . . var. *pensylvanica*
1   Leaves acute to rounded at apex, crenulate to serrate; fruit red to black, to 12 mm
    long; (western phases).

940

2 Plant more tree-like than shrubby (the main trunk as much as 2.5 dm thick), to 15 m tall, heavily pubescent (especially on the lower leaf-surfaces and on the calyces); [*Cerasus mollis* Dougl.; *P. emarginata* vars. *mollis* (Dougl.) Brew. and *villosa* Suksd.; *Cerasus erecta* Presl; B.C. N to the Tsitsutl Mts., ca. 54°N; John Macoun 1886; CAN] . . . . var. *mollis* (Dougl.) Boivin

2 Plant more shrubby than tree-like, to 4(8) m tall, from glabrous to rather heavily pubescent on the leaves; [*P. (Cerasus) emarginata* (Dougl.) Walpers; *P. corymbulosa* Rydb.; *P. (Cerasus) prunifolia* (Greene) Shafer; S B.C. and SW Alta. (Waterton Lakes; Breitung 1957b); MAPS (all as *P. emarginata*; none including Alta. in the range): Hosie 1969:246; Canada Department of Northern Affairs and Natural Resources 1956:224; Preston 1947:192, and 1961:262] . . . .
. . . . var. *saximontana* Rehd.

P. persica (L.) Batsch   Peach
Asiatic; occasionally spreading from cult. to roadsides and thickets in N. America, as in S Ont. (reported from islands of the Erie Archipelago, Essex Co., by Dodge 1914, and Core 1948; reported from Lincoln Co. by Groh and Senn 1940). [*Amygdalus* L.].

P. armenica L. (apricot) is reported from S Ont. by Gaiser and Moore (1966; Lambton Co.), presumably as an escape from cult.

P. pumilla L.   Sand-Cherry.   Cerisier de sable, Minel du Canada, or Ragouminier
/sT/(X)/   (Ch (N))   Sandy beaches, dunes, and calcareous shores and ledges (ranges of Canadian taxa outlined below), S to Wyo., Colo., Kans., Ind., and Va. MAPS and synonymy: see below.

1 Branches trailing and mat-forming; leaves narrowly oblanceolate to narrowly obovate, acutish to rounded at apex, rarely over 1/3 as broad as long; fruit about 1 cm thick, the stone commonly 5 or 6 mm thick, acute at both ends; [*P. (Cerasus) depressa* Pursh; *P. ?maritima sensu* Schmitt 1904, not Marsh.; *Cerasus pumila sensu* A. Michaux 1803, not *P. pumila* L.; Ont. (N to the Albany R. at 51°24'N), Que. (N to L. Mistassini, L. St. John, and Anticosti Is.), S Labrador (Hamilton R. basin), and rivers of N.B. (the report from Nfld. by Waghorne 1895, requires confirmation, as also early reports from P.E.I. by Bain 1890, and McSwain and Bain 1891); MAP: Groh and Senn 1940: fig. 4 (somewhat incomplete), p. 327] . . . . var. *depressa* (Pursh) Bean

1 Branches erect or strongly ascending; stone of fruit ellipsoid to subglobose, rounded at base.
  2 Leaves narrowly oblanceolate, acuminate, at most about 1/3 as broad as long, appressed-serrate, scarcely whitened beneath; stone about 7 mm broad; [*Cerasus (P.) canadensis* Mill., not Loisel. nor Prov.; Ont. (shores of the Great Lakes); MAP: Groh and Senn 1940: fig. 3, p. 327] . . . . var. *pumila*
  2 Leaves elliptic to narrowly obovate, short-acute to blunt, up to 3/5 as broad as long, distinctly whitened beneath.
    3 Leaves of fertile branches to 7 cm long and 3 cm broad, low-crenate; fruit about 1 cm thick; stone 5 or 6 mm thick; [var. *cuneata* (Raf.) Bailey; *P. cuneata* Raf.; *P. susquehanae* Willd.; S Man. (near Brandon and Otterburne) to Ont. (N to Matheson) and SW Que. (Pontiac and Gatineau counties); MAP: Groh and Senn 1940: fig. 5, p. 327] . . . . var. *susquehanae* (Willd.) Jaeg.
    3 Leaves of fertile branches mostly not over about 4 cm long and 2 cm broad, low-serrate; fruit about 1.5 cm thick, the stone about 7 mm thick; [*P. besseyi* Bailey; S Sask. (Welby and Hudson Bay Junction; Breitung 1957a) and S Man. (near Otterburne; Löve and Bernard 1959)] . . . . var. *besseyi* (Bailey) Gleason

P. serotina Ehrh.   Black or Rum-Cherry.   Cerisier d'automne
/T/EE/   (Ms)   Dry woods and fence-rows from N.Dak. to Minn., Ont. (N to Algonquin Provincial Park and the Ottawa dist.; reported N to the Kaministikwia R. near Thunder Bay by John Macoun 1886; reports from Man. require confirmation), Que. (the report from Lorette, near Quebec City at 46°47'N is substantiated by a slightly less northern locality in Lévis Co. at 46°43'N noted by Dominique Doyon and L.-R. Cayouette, Nat. can. (Que.) 96:751. 1969), S

N.B., and sw N.S. (reports from P.E.I. require confirmation), s to Mexico, Tex., and Fla. [*Cerasus* Loisel.]. MAPS: Fowells 1965:539; Hosie 1969:240; Canada Department of Northern Affairs and Natural Resources 1956:218; Groh and Senn 1940: fig. 8, p. 338; Preston 1961:260; Hough 1947:283; Munns 1938: map 38 (the sE Man. area should be deleted), p. 142; Little 1971: map 155-N.

P. spinosa L.   Sloe, Blackthorn
Eurasian; occasionally spreading from cult. in N. America, as in s Ont. (Pelee Is., Essex Co.; Cambridge, Waterloo Co.) and N.S. (Summerville and Wolfville, Kings Co.; Groh and Senn 1940).

P. tomentosa Thunb.   Manchu Cherry
Asiatic; apparently known as an escape from cult. in N. America only from s Ont. (banks of a stream in woods near Vineland, Lincoln Co.; OAC; reported from St. Thomas, Elgin Co., by Boivin 1966b).

P. virginiana L.   Choke-Cherry.   Cerisier à grappes
/sT/X/   (Mc)   Thickets, shores, rocky woods, and coastal bluffs (ranges of Canadian taxa outlined below), s to Calif., N.Mex., Kans., Mo.,Tenn., and N.C. MAPS and synonymy: see below.
1   Leaves generally pubescent over most or all of the lower surface; shrub or small tree
    to about 6 m tall; [f. *deamii* Jones; *Cerasus (Prunus; Padus) demissa* Nutt.; B.C. (N to
    Stuart L. at ca. 54°30′N) and Alta. (N to Waterways, 56°42′N); MAPS (both incomplete
    northwards): Benson 1962: fig. 9-10, p. 302; Preston 1947:194 (the Sask. area is
    evidently referable to the other varieties)] . . . . var. *demissa* (Nutt.) Torr.
1   Leaves generally glabrous beneath or merely pubescent in the vein-axils.
    2   Leaves thickish; shrub or small tree to about 6 m tall . . . var. *melanocarpa* (Nels.) Sarg.
        3   Fruit deep-blue-purple to nearly black; [*P. mel.* (Nels.) Rydb.; *Cerasus*
            demissa var. *mel.* Nels.; B.C. (N to Liard Hot Springs, ca. 59°20′N; Hultén
            1950), Alta., Sask., and Man. (N to Duck Mt.; J.L. Parker, personal
            communication); MAP: Benson 1962: fig. 9-10 (very incomplete for Canada),
            p. 302] . . . . f. *melanocarpa*
        3   Fruit yellow; [Sask.: near Yorkton and McKague; Breitung 1957a] . . . .
            . . . . f. *xanthocarpa* Sarg.
    2   Leaves relatively thin; large shrubs or small trees to about 15 m tall . . . . var. *virginiana*
        4   Fruit crimson to deep red; [*Cerasus* Michx.; *Padus* Mill.; *Prunus (Padus) nana*
            Du Roi; sw Dist. Mackenzie–B.C. to Alta., Sask. (N to Carswell L., 58°35′N),
            Man. (N to Gods L., ca. 55°N), Ont. (N to w James Bay at ca. 53°N), Que. (N to
            L. St. John and Anticosti Is.), Nfld., and N.S.; MAPS: Hosie 1969:242
            (aggregate species); Benson 1962: fig. 9-10, p. 302 (sE Sask. to Nfld. and N.S.;
            the "sw Dist. Mackenzie–B.C. to Alta." part of the above range may eventually
            prove referable to the other varieties); the following maps of the area of the
            aggregate species are all more or less inaccurate or incomplete: Canada
            Department of Northern Affairs and Natural Resources 1956:222; Munns 1938:
            map 137, p. 141; Hough 1947:281; Preston 1961:260; the detailed distribution
            from Ont. to N.S. is shown in a map by Groh and Senn 1940: fig. 9, p. 340] . . . .
            . . . . f. *virginiana*
        4   Fruit whitish to yellowish or amber-colour; [Fredericton, N.B.; C.E. Atwood,
            Rhodora 36(423):89. 1934] . . . . f. *leucocarpa* (Wats.) Haynie

[P. glandulosa Thunb.]   Dwarf Flowering Almond
[Asiatic; this species (not keyed out above) is reported from s Ont. by Gaiser and Moore (1966; Lambton Co.), where, however, scarcely established if actually spreading from cult. Its pink flowers are "double" (with extra petals), accounting for its widespread use as an ornamental. (Var. *sinensis* (Pers.) Koehne).]

PURSHIA DC.   [3372]

P. tridentata (Pursh) DC.   Antelope-brush or -bush
/t/W/   (N (Mc))   Grassland and sagebrush plains, dry rocky hillsides, and ponderosa-pine forest from SE B.C. (Dry Interior between Penticton and Kimberley S to the U.S.A. boundary) to Calif. and N.Mex. [*Tigarea* Pursh].

PYRACANTHA Roemer   [3333]

P. coccinea Roemer   Fire-Thorn
European; cult. for hedges in N. America and becoming established after spreading, as in SW B.C. (near Victoria and Nanaimo, Vancouver Is.; CAN; V). [*Mespilus (Cotoneaster) pyracantha* L.].

PYRUS L.   [3338]   Apple, Pear.   Pommier or Poirier

1   Petals less than 1 cm long, white or pink-tinged; fruit at most 1 cm thick; inflorescence cymose; leaves broadly oblanceolate to narrowly obovate or somewhat elliptic, glandular above along the midrib; shrubs with slender loosely ascending branches; (Ont. to Nfld. and N.S.) . . . .*P. arbutifolia*
1   Petals commonly at least 1 cm long (occasionally slightly shorter in *P. fusca*); fruit often over 3 cm thick (at most about 1 cm thick in *P. fusca*); leaves not glandular above along the midrib; small trees or coarse shrubs.
   2   Leaves entire, oblong or broadly ovate, often subcordate, blunt or very short-pointed, to about 1 dm long, tomentose beneath, becoming glabrous above; flowers solitary and terminating leafy shoots of the season, the petals white or light pink; sepals reflexed; fruit the yellow fuzzy pear-shaped quince; thornless small tree with blackish bark; (introd.) . . . .[*P. cydonia*]
   2   Leaves toothed; inflorescence a raceme or a simple or umbelliform cyme; small trees or coarse shrubs, the branchlets in some species often with thorny or spine-like spurs (reduced fruit-bearing branchlets).
      3   Fruit about 1 cm thick (and to about 1.5 cm long), yellow to purplish-red; styles united at base; leaves lanceolate to ovate-lanceolate or -oblong, gradually acute to acuminate, to 1 dm long, deep green and glabrous or pubescent above, paler and somewhat crisp-puberulent to lanate beneath; branches somewhat thorny, crisp-puberulent when young; (SE Alaska–B.C.) . .
. . . .*P. fusca*
      3   Fruit often 3 cm thick or more.
         4   Leaves involute in the bud (their margins rolled inward before expanding and covering the upper surface), elliptic to ovate-rotund, abruptly acuminate, crenate (never lobed), glabrous or soon glabrate; styles free to base; fruit the common pear with abundant grit-cells; twigs glabrous or glabrate; (introd.) . . . .*P. communis*
         4   Leaves plicate in the bud (plaited lengthwise) or with revolute downward-rolled margins covering the lower surface; styles united at base; fruit an apple or crab-apple, lacking grit-cells.
            5   Anthers red; flowers bright roseate, fading to nearly white; leaves plicate in the bud, at maturity broadly ovate, acute or acuminate, mostly rounded at base, sharply serrate and often more or less lobed or cleft, soon glabrate; (S Ont.) . . . .*P. coronaria*
            5   Anthers yellow; flowers white or pinkish; leaves revolute in the bud, never lobed; (introd.).
               6   Leaves crenate-serrate, oblong-ovate, rounded to cordate at base, more or less persistently tomentose beneath and on the petioles (as also on the young twigs); flowers pinkish white; calyx-lobes persistent, tomentose on the back; fruit an apple at least 3 cm thick . . . .
. . . .*P. malus*

6 Leaves sharply serrate, oblong-ovate to ovate-rotund, glabrous or slightly pubescent on the veins beneath, their petioles essentially glabrous; calyx glabrous or soon glabrate; fruit a crab-apple.

7 Calyx-lobes persistent; fruit about 2 cm thick; young twigs pubescent . . . . *P. prunifolia*

7 Calyx-lobes deciduous; fruit barely 1 cm thick; young twigs soon glabrate . . . . *P. baccata*

P. arbutifolia (L.) L. f.   Red Chokeberry
/T/EE/   (Mc)   Low woods, wet thickets, and swampy ground, the aggregate species from Ont. (N to Sandy L. at ca. 53°N, 92°W; CAN; the report of *P. melanocarpa* from St. Lazare, SW Man., by Lowe in his undated supplement to his 1943 checklist requires confirmation) to Que. (N to the Gaspé Pen. at Mal Baie, near Percé), Nfld., N.B., P.E.I., and N.S., S to E Tex. and Fla.

1 Plant glabrous or nearly so; fruit black; [*Aronia nigra* (Willd.) Britt.; *Mespilus arbutifolia* var. *melanocarpa* Michx.; *P. (Aronia; Sorbus) melan.* (Michx.) Willd.; Ont. (N to Sandy L., ca. 53°N) to N.B., P.E.I., and N.S.; reported from Nfld. by Rouleau 1956; MAP: Braun 1935: fig. 3 *(P. melan.)*, p. 355] . . . . var. *nigra* Willd.

1 Plant more or less pubescent in the inflorescence and on the lower leaf-surfaces.

2 Sepals nearly or quite glandless; mature fruit purple or purple-black, to 1 cm thick; pubescence usually rather sparse; [*Aronia atrop.* Britt.; *A. (Pyrus) floribunda* Spach; *A. prunifolia* (Marsh.) Rehd., not *P. prunifolia* Willd.; Ont. to S ?Labrador (Fernald *in* Gray 1950), Nfld., and N.S.]. A hybrid with *Sorbus decora* (× *P. arsenii* (Britt.) Arsène) is reported from the type locality, St-Pierre and Miquelon, by Brother Louis Arsène (Rhodora 29(345):177. 1927) and is also known from Moncton, N.B. . . . . var. *atropurpurea* (Britt.) Robins.

2 Sepals bearing stipitate glands; mature fruit red, rarely over 7 mm thick; young shoots, branches of the inflorescence, and lower leaf-surfaces copiously tomentose; [*Mespilus* L.; *Aronia* Ell.; S Ont. (Norfolk and Wellington counties), SW Que. (Wychwood), N.B., P.E.I., and N.S. (the report from Nfld. by Robinson and von Schrenk 1896, is based upon var. *atropurpurea*, the relevant collection in CAN]. A hybrid with *Sorbus (P.) americana* (× *P. hybrida* Moench) is reported from Nfld. by Rouleau (1956) and a collection in CAN from Moncton, N.B., has been referred to it . . . . var. *arbutifolia*

P. baccata L.   Siberian Crab
Asiatic; spread from cult. to thickets and clearings in N. America, as in S Ont. (banks of the St. Clair R., Lambton Co.; Dodge 1915; collections in CAN and TRT from along an old abandoned railway near Fort Erie, Welland Co., have also been placed here) and S Nfld. (Bell Is. and Rennie's R., near St. John's; GH).

P. communis L.   Common Pear
Eurasian; spreading from cult. or rejected cores to thickets, borders of woods, and clearings in N. America, as in SW B.C. (near Victoria, Vancouver Is.; CAN) and S Ont. (Niagara, Welland Co.; CAN; reported from Essex Co. by Dodge 1914, where "Several large trees, apparent escapes, along north shore of Lake Erie.").

P. coronaria L.   Wild Crab
/t/EE/   (Mc)   Low ground, thickets, and clearings from Minn. to S Ont. (N to S York Co.; see S Ont. map by Fox and Soper 1953: fig. 19, p. 19) and cent. N.Y., S to Kans., Tenn., and N.C. [*Malus* Mill.; *M. glaucescens* Rehd.; incl. var. *dasycalyx* (Rehd.) Fern., the calyx-tube sparingly pilose outside rather than glabrous, to which some of the S Ont. material is referable]. MAPS: Hosie 1969:232; Preston 1961:246; Hough 1947:231.

[*P. cydonia* L.]   Common Quince
[Asiatic; introd. in N. America but scarcely established outside of cultivation, as in S Ont. (streambank at Aylmer, Elgin Co.; OAC; reported from Essex Co. by Dodge 1914: "Several

fine looking trees in waste places along north shore of Lake Erie, but perhaps not escapes.''). (*Cydonia oblonga* Mill.; *C. vulgaris* Pers.).]

P. fusca Raf.   Oregon Crab-Apple
/sT/W/   (Mc (Ms))   Moist woods, streambanks, swamps, and bogs from s Alaska (*see* Hultén 1946: map 748, p. 1061; *Malus fusca*) through coastal B.C. to Calif. [*Malus* Schn.; *M. macounii* Greene; *P. diversifolia* Bong.; *P. (M.) rivularis* Dougl.]. MAP: Hultén 1968*b*:596.

P. malus L.   Apple.   Pommier
Eurasian; spread from cult. to roadsides, borders of woods, and clearings in N. America, as in ?B.C. (Henry 1915), s Man. (Brandon), Ont. (N to the E shore of L. Superior at Michipicoten; CAN), Que. (N to near Quebec City; CAN), Nfld. (Rouleau 1956), N.B., P.E.I., and N.S. [*Malus pumila* Mill.; *M. sylvestris* (L.) Mill.].

P. prunifolia Willd.   Chinese Apple, Crab-Apple
Asiatic; spread from cult. to roadsides and thickets in N. America, as in N.B. (Fernald *in* Gray 1950) and N.S. (steep river-terrace near Weymouth, Digby Co.; GH; CAN). [*Malus* Borkh.; not *P. (Aronia) prunifolia* Steud., which is *P. arbutifolia* var. *atropurpurea*].

ROSA L.   [3389]   Rose.   Rosier

(Ref.: P.A. Rydberg, N. Am. Flora 22:483–533. 1918)
1   Styles and stamens definitely exserted beyond the mouth of the ''hip'' (fruiting receptacle); flowers to about 8 cm broad; stipules entire or sparingly glandular-ciliate; branches commonly showing a strong tendency to climb, bearing rather remote prickles.
  2   Styles distinct, about twice as long as the stamens; flowers 1–3, white, pinkish, or salmon-yellow, very fragrant; leaflets 5 or 7, lustrous above, glabrous beneath; (introd.) . . . .*R. odorata*
  2   Styles united into a column not much longer than the long-filamented stamens; flowers several or many in a corymb, nearly scentless.
    3   Leaflets commonly 3 (rarely 5), lanceolate to oblong-ovate, acuminate, to 1 dm long; stipules entire or their margins merely ciliate; flowers several, to 8 cm broad, pink or roseate, fading to white; sepals over 1 cm long; (s Ont.) . . . .*R. setigera*
    3   Leaflets commonly 7 or 9, elliptic to obovate, obtuse or merely acute, to about 4 cm long; stipules deeply toothed; flowers abundant, to about 4 cm broad, commonly white; sepals less than 1 cm long; (introd.) . . . .*R. multiflora*
1   Styles scarcely or not at all exserted, distinct, much shorter than the stamens and forming a dense brush in the mouth of the fruiting receptacle; plants scarcely climbing.
  4   Flowers commonly ''double'' (having more than the normally single rank of petals), pink or pinkish purple; branches prickly, the infrastipular prickles usually with a broad flattened base; (introd.).
    5   Achenes lining inner wall of fruit as well as its base; flowers declined or nodding on long slender stipitate-glandular pedicels; leaflets commonly 5 (sometimes 3, rarely 7), sometimes pubescent above . . . .*R. centifolia*
    5   Achenes confined to bottom of fruit; flowers not declined; pedicels smooth; leaflets 5 or 7, pubescent, paler beneath . . . .*R. cinnamomea*
  4   Flowers commonly ''single'' (with the normal solitary rank of petals; *R. cinnamomea* may sometimes key out here).
    6   Outer sepals pinnatifid with several lateral lanceolate segments; styles somewhat exserted from the mouth of the fruiting receptacle; achenes lining inner wall as well as base of fruit; (introd.).
      7   Leaflets 5 or 7, oval or narrowly ovate, tomentose and glandular beneath; pedicels and backs of sepals strongly glandular-hispid; stem armed with broad-based subulate straight prickles to 1 cm long . . . .*R. tomentosa*

7 Leaflets finely pilose to glabrous beneath; prickles of stem hooked or recurving.
  8 Leaflets 5 or 7, ovate-elliptic, essentially glabrous, glandless on both faces (rarely slightly glandular on the midrib beneath), their sharp, often simple teeth glandless; pedicels smoth . . . . *R. canina*
  8 Leaflets glandular and more or less pilose beneath, their teeth doubled and gland-tipped; pedicels glandular-hispid.
    9 Leaflets 7 or 9, elliptic to suborbicular, glandular-scurfy on both faces, resinous-aromatic, all or mostly rounded at base; sepals subpersistent; styles pubescent . . . . *R. eglanteria*
    9 Leaflets 5 or 7, more nearly ovate, acuminate, nearly glandless above, not strongly fragrant, mostly narrowed to an acute base; sepals promptly deciduous; styles essentially glabrous . . . . [*R. micrantha*]
6 Outer and inner sepals entire or with a few linear appendages from near the base; styles mostly included.
  10 Young stems and branches tomentose beneath the very numerous prickles and bristles; leaflets 5, 7, or 9, dark green and rugose above; flowers rose-purple or white, to over 1 dm broad, on short bristly pedicels; (introd.) . . . . *R. rugosa*
  10 Stems and branches glabrous or essentially so; flowers smaller.
    11 Styles deciduous with the upper part of the fruiting receptacle, which falls off like a ring (also carrying the sepals with it, these at most 12 mm long); pistils (and achenes) rarely more than 12; petals to 1.5 cm long, pinkish to deep rose; flowers mostly solitary at the ends of the branches, the slender pedicels usually coarsely stipitate-glandular; leaflets 5–9, mostly doubly serrate; twigs armed with slender prickles to nearly unarmed; (s B.C.) . . . . *R. gymnocarpa*
    11 Styles (as well as the upper part of the fruiting receptacle) persistent; sepals often more than 12 mm long; pistils (and achenes) usually at least 15.
      12 Flowers solitary at the ends of the branches, yellow, white, or pink, the glabrous pedicel not subtended by a bract; leaflets 7–13, ovate to orbicular; stems very prickly and bristly; (introd.) . . . . . *R. spinosissima*
      12 Flowers solitary or in corymbs (when solitary, the pedicel bracted near base).
        13 Sepals finally deciduous, usually widely spreading or reflexed; hypanthium and pedicels more or less stipitate-glandular; achenes confined to base of fruit.
          14 New stems and branches very densely covered with spreading bristles up to the inflorescence, a few longer prickles also often present; leaflets 7 or 9, finely and sharply serrate; (Ont. to Nfld. and N.S.) . . . . *R. nitida*
          14 Middle and upper internodes of stem with few or no bristles; prickles or thorns confined chiefly to near the base of the stipules.
            15 Leaflets 5–9, finely serrate nearly to base, with up to 25 teeth on each margin above the middle, minutely pubescent beneath; stipules firm and trough-like; internodal prickles none or very few; (Ont. to N.S.) . . . . *R. palustris*
            15 Leaflets more coarsely toothed, with at most about 17 teeth on each margin above the middle.
              16 Leaflets 5–11, dark green and shining above; stipules broad and herbaceous; infrastipular prickles stout, flattened toward base, often decurved; internodal prickles commonly lacking; (Ont. to Nfld. and N.S.) . . . . *R. virginiana*

16 Leaflets 5–9, dull or only slightly shining above;
stipules firm and trough-like; infrastipular prickles
straight, slender, scarcely flattened; internodal
prickles commonly present; (Ont. to N.S.) . . . . . . *R. carolina*
13 Sepals persistent in fruit, erect to divergent after flowering;
hypanthium and pedicels usually glabrous; achenes commonly
lining the inner wall as well as the base of the fruit . . . . *GROUP A*

GROUP A

1 Flowers rather small (less than 5 cm broad; petals at most about 2 cm long), mostly
in small corymbiform cymes terminating the branches of the season; sepals
commonly not over 1.5 cm long, usually coarsely stipitate-glandular on the back;
leaflets 5–9, rather finely and closely serrate, puberulent beneath; infrastipular
prickles often present; (s B.C.) . . . . *R. pisocarpa*
1 Flowers mostly larger (normally more than 5 cm broad); petals commonly over 2 cm
long; sepals commonly over 1.5 cm long.
    2 Stems semiherbaceous and mostly dying back, bristly, to about 5 dm tall; leaflets
    mostly 9 or 11; flowers pink, fading to whitish, in terminal corymbs on suckers of
    the current season or solitary on branches of older wood; sepals ascending at
    maturity, beak-like at the summit of the fruit; (B.C. to Man.) . . . . *R. arkansana*
    2 Stems more woody, commonly taller; flowers usually more deeply roseate, on
    lateral branches; leaflets mostly 5 or 7 (sometimes 9).
        3 Stem and branches very bristly; infrastipular prickles not clearly differentiated
        from those of the internodes; leaflets often resinous-puberulent beneath, the
        leaf-rachis usually glandular; flowers solitary (rarely 2) on lateral branches of
        the season; sepals ascending at maturity, beak-like at the summit of the fruit;
        (Alaska–B.C. to Que.) . . . . *R. acicularis*
        3 Stem less bristly, the bristles scarcely (if at all) extending into the branches.
            4 Sepals ascending at maturity, beak-like at the summit of the fruit; flowers
            solitary or in few-flowered corymbs; stems unarmed or, when young,
            bearing slender weak deciduous prickles; (Dist. Mackenzie; Sask. to N.S.) . . . . .
            . . . . *R. blanda*
            4 Sepals ascending to widely spreading or reflexed at maturity; stems
            typically more or less bristly or prickly.
                5 Infrastipular prickles commonly present, clearly differentiated from the
                bristles (when present) of the stem-internodes.
                    6 Petals and sepals each to 4 cm long; sepals glabrous or sometimes
                    glandular-bristly on the back; flowers typically solitary at the ends of
                    the lateral branches of the season; infrastipular prickles typically
                    strongly flattened at the broad base; (Alaska–B.C.) . . . . *R. nutkana*
                    6 Petals to 2.5 cm long; sepals to about 1.5 cm long, glabrous to
                    puberulent or occasionally inconspicuously glandular (rarely
                    coarsely stipitate-glandular); flowers mostly in corymbiform cymes
                    terminating the lateral branches of the season; infrastipular prickles
                    usually smaller; (Alaska–B.C. to Ont.) . . . . *R. woodsii*
                5 Infrastipular prickles wanting or not clearly differentiated from those of
                the internodes; (E Que.).
                    7 Stipules at most about 2 cm long; sepals at most about 1.5 cm long . . . .
                    . . . . *R. williamsii*
                    7 Stipules to 3.5 cm long; sepals over 1.5 cm long . . . . . . *R. rousseauiorum*

R. acicularis Lindl. Prickly Rose
/ST/X/EA/ (N) Thickets and rocky slopes, the aggregate species from N Alaska–Yukon–
Dist. Mackenzie to Great Bear L., Great Slave L., L. Athabasca (Alta. and Sask.; provincial
floral emblem of Alta.), Man. (N to about 10 mi s of Churchill), northernmost Ont., Que. (N to E
James Bay at ca. 51°30′N, L. Mistassini, and Bic, Rimouski Co.), and N ?N.B. (a collection in

NBM from the Nipisiguit R. bears Fernald's verification but his 1950 manual does not include N.B. in the range; not known from P.E.I. or N.S.), s to Idaho, N N.Mex., S.Dak., Minn., and Vt.; Eurasia. MAPS and synonymy: see below.

1 Pedicels stipitate-glandular; [Eurasia and Alaska; see Hultén 1946:1056; MAP: W.H. Lewis, Brittonia 11(1): fig. 4, p. 12. 1959] . . . . var. *acicularis*
1 Pedicels glabrous . . . . var. *bourgeauiana* Crépin
    2 Petals more than 5 (up to 15), the flowers "double"; [*R. acic.* ssp. *sayii* f. *plena* Lewis, the type from Moose Range, Sask.] . . . . f. *plena* (Lewis) Scoggan
    2 Petals 5; [*R. bourg.* Crépin; *R. acic.* var. *cucurbiformis* Raup and ssp. *sayii* (Schw.) Lewis; *R. sayii* Schw.; *R. engelmannii* Wats.; *R. blanda sensu* Richardson 1823, not Ait.; *R. majalis sensu* Hooker 1832, not Borrer; Alaska–B.C. to ?N.B.; MAPS: W.H. Lewis, Brittonia 11(1): fig. 4 (ssp. *sayii*), p. 12. 1959; Raup 1947: pl. 29 (aggregate species); Hultén 1968*b*:634 (agg. sp.)] . . . . f. *bourgeauiana*

R. arkansana Porter

/T/WW/ (N) Dry prairies and open woods (ranges of Canadian taxa outlined below), s to Mont., N.Mex., Tex., and Mo.

1 Leaflets soft-pilose beneath; [*R. alcea, R. heliophila, R. pratincola,* and *R. suffulta* Greene; *R. stricta* of auth., not Borrer; Alta., Sask., and Man. (Boivin 1966*b*; *R. alcea*)] . . . . var. *suffulta* (Greene) Cock.
1 Leaflets glabrous.
    2 Flowers "double", with as many as 20 petals; [type from Woodrow, Sask.] . . . .
       . . . . f. *plena* Lewis
    2 Flowers with the usual 5 petals; [*R. blanda* var. *ark.* (Porter) Best; *R. lunellii* and *R. rydbergii* Greene; B.C. (Boivin 1966*b*), Alta. (N to Grande Prairie, Peace River dist.), Sask. (N to McKague, 52°37′N), and s Man. (N to Gypsumville, about 125 mi N of Portage la Prairie)] . . . . f. *arkansana*

R. blanda Ait.

/sT/(X)/ (N) Thickets and rocky slopes, the aggregate species with an isolated area in w Dist. Mackenzie (Wrigley, ca. 63°10′N, and Fort Liard, ca. 60°15′N; CAN, detd. Porsild; according to Boivin 1967*a*, reports from B.C. (as by John Macoun 1883, and Henry 1915) probably mostly refer to *R. nutkana*; not known from Alta.), the main area from E Sask. (W.H. Lewis, Brittonia 14(1):67. 1962) to Man. (N to Grand Rapids, near the NW end of L. Winnipeg), Ont. (N to W James Bay at ca. 51°30′N), Que. (N to E James Bay at ca. 51°30′N and the Mingan Is. of the Côte-Nord), N.B., and N.S. (P.E.I. reports require confirmation), s to Nebr., Mo., Ind., and Pa. MAP and synonymy: see below.

1 Sepals divergent or strongly reflexed . . . . var. *glabra* Crépin
    2 Flowers white; [*R. johannensis* f. *albinea* Fern.; known from the type locality, Woodstock, Carleton Co., N.B.] . . . . f. *albinea* (Fern.) Scoggan
    2 Flowers rose-pink; [*R. johannensis* Fern.; Dist. Mackenzie (Boivin 1966*b*); ?Ont., Que. (N to L. St. John, Anticosti Is., and the Gaspé Pen.), N.B. (banks of the St. John R. in Carleton and York counties), and N.S. (Brier Is., Digby Co.; ACAD); MAP: Frère Marie-Victorin, Contrib. Inst. Bot. Univ. Montréal 4: fig. 12 (incomplete northwards), p. 72. 1925] . . . . f. *glabra*
1 Sepals erect, forming a beak-like cap on the fruit . . . . var. *blanda*
    3 Flowers white; [Otterburne, Man., about 30 mi s of Winnipeg; Löve and Bernard 1959] . . . . f. *alba* (Schuette) Fern.
    3 Flowers rose-pink.
       4 Pedicels and hypanthia glandular-hispid; [Gaspé Pen., E Que.; E.W. Erlanson, Bot. Gaz. 96(2):237. 1934] . . . . f. *carpiohispida* (Schuette) Lewis
       4 Pedicels and hypanthia glabrous.
          5 Leaflets linear to linear-lanceolate, long-acuminate, their margins entire or merely undulate; [type from along the Gatineau R. about 22 mi N of Mont-Laurier, Labelle Co., Que.] . . . . f. *angustior* Vict. & Rolland-Germain
          5 Leaflets elliptic to oblong-obovate; [*R. fraxinifolia* var. *blanda* (Ait.) Ser.;

R. solanderi Tratt.; *R. subblanda* Rydb.; range of the species, the type from near Hudson Bay]. A hybrid with *R. woodsii* (× *R. dulcissima* Lunell) is indicated near Winnipeg, Man., on a map by W.H. Lewis (Brittonia 14(1): fig. 1, p. 67. 1962) . . . . f. *blanda*

R. canina L.   Dog-Rose
Eurasian; locally spead from cult. in N. America to thickets, dry banks, and open fields, as in B.C. (Boivin 1966b), s Ont. (London, Middlesex Co.; OAC), and N.S. (Kentville, Kings Co.; ACAD). [Incl. var. *dumetorum* Baker].

R. carolina L.
/T/EE/   (N)   Dry sandy or rocky places and open woods (ranges of Canadian taxa outlined below), s to Tex. and Fla.
1   Flowers to 7 cm broad; leaflets obovate or broadly oval, obtuse or subacute, sublustrous; [*R. humilis* var. *gr.* Baker; *R. obovata* Raf.; s Ont.: Grand Bend, Huron Co., and Hamilton, Wentworth Co.; GH] . . . . var. *grandiflora* (Baker) Rehd.
1   Flowers to about 5.5 cm broad; leaflets narrowly ovate-lanceolate to narrowly obovate, acute or obtuse, dull . . . . var. *carolina*
     2   Leaf-rachis stipitate-glandular; teeth of leaflets mostly gland-tipped; [*R. humilis* Marsh.; range of f. *carolina*] . . . . f. *glandulosa* (Crépin) Fern.
     2   Leaf-rachis glabrous; teeth of leaflets not gland-tipped; [Ont. (N to the Ottawa dist.), Que. (N to Magdalen Is.; CAN), N.B., P.E.I., N.S., and ?St-Pierre and Miquelon] . . . . f. *carolina*

R. centifolia L.   Cabbage-Rose
Asiatic; spread from cult. in N. America, as in s Ont. (Gaiser and Moore 1966; Lambton Co.), N.B. (Boivin 1966b), and P.E.I. (roadside near Southport, Queens Co.; D.S. Erskine 1960). [*R. gallica* var. *cent.* (L.) Regel; probably a hybrid between *R. gallica* and some other Old World species].

R. cinnamomea L.   Cinnamon-Rose
Eurasian; spread from cult. to roadsides and fields in N. America, as in Ont. (N to the Ottawa dist.), Que. (N to Portneuf, about 40 mi SW of Quebec City; MT), N.B. (Chatham, Richibucto, and Saskville; CAN), P.E.I. (Alberton, Prince Co.; MT), and N.S. (Annapolis, Digby, Yarmouth, and Pictou counties).

R. eglanteria L.   Sweet-Brier or Eglantine.   Eglantier or Cébreur
Eurasian; spread from cult. to thickets, clearings, and roadsides in N. America, as in B.C. (Victoria; New Westminster), Ont. (N to the Ottawa dist.), Que. (N to Bic, Rimouski Co.), Nfld. (Bay of Islands; GH), N.B., P.E.I., and N.S. [*R. rubiginosa* L.].

R. gymnocarpa Nutt.
/T/W/   (N)   Moist or dry woods and clearings at low to rather high elevations from s B.C. (N to Bella Coola and Revelstoke) and NW Mont. to Calif. [*R. apiculata* and *R. leucopsis* Greene].
    A purported hybrid with *R. nutkana* is reported from SW B.C. by Henry (1915; Crescent, near Vancouver).

[R. micrantha Borrer]
[European; very similar to *R. eglanteria* and perhaps best treated as a variety of that species (as already done under the name *R. rubiginosa* var. *mic.* (Borrer) Lindl.). The report from Victoria, B.C., by Henry (1915) is probably based upon *R. eglanteria,* an apparently relevant collection in CAN.]

R. multiflora Thunb.
Asiatic; spread from cult. to roadsides, borders of woods, and clearings in N. America, as in s Ont. (Lambton and Oxford counties; OAC; TRT).

R. nitida Willd.
/T/EE/ (N) Acid bogs, wet thickets, and margins of ponds and streams from Ont. (Constance Bay, near Ottawa; A.J. Breitung, Nat. can. (Que.) 79:186. 1952) to Que. (N to the Bell R. s of James Bay at 49°40′N and the Côte-Nord), Nfld., N.B., P.E.I., N.S., and s New Eng. MAP: Fernald 1918*b*: map 1, pl. 12.

Hybrids with *R. palustris* and with *R. virginiana* are reported from N.S. by M.L. Fernald (Rhodora 24:176. 1922; Hassett, Digby Co., and Cape Forchu, Yarmouth Co., respectively). W.H. Lewis (Rhodora 60(717):237. 1958) treats the former one (and, tentatively, the latter one) as *R. nitida* f. *spinosa* Lewis ("Floral stems armed with fine bristles and enlarged infrastipular thorns, often in pairs.", the typical form nearly or quite devoid of such thorns) and also accredits it to sw Que. (Magog, Stanstead Co.) and SE Nfld. (St. John's).

R. nutkana Presl
/sT/W/ (N) Woods and open places at low to moderate elevations from the Aleutian Is. and s Alaska through coastal B.C. to N Calif., Utah, and Colo. MAP and synonymy: *see* below.
1 Leaflets doubly serrate with gland-tipped teeth, distinctly glandular beneath; leaf-rachis distinctly stipitate-glandular; infrastipular prickles becoming much enlarged and conspicuously flattened toward base; [*R. muriculata* Greene; *R. ?blanda sensu* Henry 1915, and John Macoun 1883 (as to B.C. reports), not Ait.; *R. ?californica sensu* Hooker 1832, not C. & S.; *R. ?cinnamomea sensu* Hooker 1832, not L.; *R. fraxinifolia sensu* Hooker 1832, as to western reports, not Borkh. nor Lindl.; Aleutian Is.–s Alaska (*see* Hultén 1946: map 802, p. 1066) and B.C. (type from Nootka Sound, Vancouver Is.); MAP (aggregate species): Hultén 1968*b*:635] . . . . var. *nutkana*
1 Leaflets singly (rarely doubly) serrate, with usually eglandular teeth, their lower surfaces and the leaf-rachis glabrous or puberulent and sometimes also glandular; prickles seldom much enlarged and flattened toward base; [*R. macdougalii* Holz.; *R. spaldingii* Crépin; s B.C. (Vancouver Is.; CAN; reported from Elgin and Spences Bridge by Henry 1915)] . . . . var. *hispida* Fern.

R. odorata Sweet   Tea-Rose
Asiatic; a collection in Herb. PEI from near Southport, Queens Co., P.E.I., where growing along a roadside bank together with persisting plants of lilac, has been referred here by Erskine and Smith.

R. palustris Marsh.
/T/EE/ (N) Wet ground and shores from Minn. to Ont. (N to the SE shore of L. Superior and the Ottawa dist.), Que. (N to the mouth of the Bonaventure R., Gaspé Pen.; RIM), N.B. (Torreyburn, near St. John; ACAD; not known from P.E.I.), and N.S., s to Ark. and Fla. [*R. pensylvanica* Michx.; *R. carolina* of many auth. in part, incl. Linnaeus 1762, not 1753].

Forma *inermis* (Regel) Lewis (the floral stems lacking the bristles and prickles of those of the typical form) is reported from s Ont. by W.H. Lewis (Rhodora 60(717):239. 1958; Dorset, near Georgian Bay, L. Huron).

R. pisocarpa Gray
/t/W/ (N) Thickets, streambanks, and swampy places at low elevations from s B.C. (N to Lillooet, about 70 mi w of Kamloops) to N Calif.

R. rousseauiorum Boivin
/T/E/ (N) Wet ground and marshes of E Que. (type from Les Éboulements, Charlevoix Co.; also known from Bic, Rimouski Co., and the Gaspé Pen.). [Included in *R. blanda* by A.J. Breitung, Nat. can. (Que). 79:188. 1952].

Forma *chrysocarpa* Boivin (fruits orange-coloured rather than red) is known from Que. (type from Les Éboulements, Charlevoix Co.; also known from Fort Coulonge, Pontiac Co.).

R. rugosa Thunb.
Asiatic; introd. along roadsides and in sand dunes, seashore thickets, etc., in N. America, as in Ont. (N to the Ottawa dist.), Que. (St. Lawrence R. estuary between the Quebec City dist.

and the Gaspé Pen. at Matane and Grosses-Roches), Nfld. (Steady Brook, Humber dist.; MT), N.B., P.E.I., and N.S.

R. setigera Michx.   Climbing or Prairie-Rose
/t/EE/   (N)   Open woods, thickets, clearings, and banks from Nebr. to Mo., Ohio, s Ont. (reported from Essex Co. by John Macoun 1883, and Dodge 1914; reported from Lambton Co. by Gaiser and Moore 1966; the report from Anticosti Is., E Que., by Saint-Cyr 1887, is probably erroneous), and N.Y., s to Tex. and Fla.

Some of the Ont. material is referable to var. *tomentosa* T. & G. (*R. rubifolia* R. Br.; leaflets dull above, tomentose beneath, rather than lustrous above and glabrous or merely pilose on the nerves beneath).

R. spinosissima L.   Scotch or Burnet-Rose
Eurasian; spread from cult. to roadside thickets in N. America, as in Ont. (Timagami Forest Reserve; MT), Que. (N to Rimouski, Rimouski Co.; MT), N.B. (Kent Co.; NBM), P.E.I. (Queens Co.; ACAD), and N.S. (Tusket, Yarmouth Co.; GH).

The similar *R. hemisphaerica* Herrm. (sulphur rose) of E Asia (but the fruit red rather than blackish and the branches only armed with prickles rather than with both prickles and bristles) is reported as a garden-escape in s Ont. by Gaiser and Moore (1966; Lambton Co.).

R. tomentosa Sm.
European; apparently known in the wild state in N. America only from roadside thickets of P.E.I. (Southport, Queens Co.; GH). [Incl. var *globulosa* Rouy].

R. virginiana Mill.
/T/EE/   (N)   Shores, swamps, thickets, and clearings from s Ont. (N to Georgian Bay, L. Huron) to Que. (N to the Gaspé Pen.), Nfld., N.B., P.E.I., and N.S., s to Mo., Tenn., and Ala. [*R. lucida* Ehrh.; incl. the reduced extreme, f. *nanella* (Rydb.) Fern. (*R. nanella* Rydb.)].

R. williamsii Fern.
/T/E/   (N)   Known only from calcareous cliffs and sands of E Que. (type from Bic, Rimouski Co.; also known from La Madeleine, Gaspé Pen.). [Considered by E.W. Erlanson, Bot. Gaz. 96(2):229. 1934, to be perhaps a calciphile ecotype of *R. blanda*].

R. woodsii Lindl.
/ST/(X)/   (N)   Prairies, thickets, and clearings from cent. Alaska, s Yukon and sw Dist. Mackenzie to B.C.–Alta., Sask. (N to Tisdale, 52°51'N), Man. (N to Cross Lake, NE of L. Winnipeg), and Ont. (N to the w James Bay watershed at ca. 53°N; also reported from SE James Bay, Que., by Bernard Boivin, Nat. can. (Que.) 75(8/9/10):221. 1948, but not accredited to Que. in his 1966b paper), s to s Calif., N Mexico, Tex., Mo., and Minn. MAP and synonymy: *see* below.
1   Leaflets usually puberulent beneath, their teeth and those of the stipules gland-
      tipped; [*R. fendleri* Crépin; *R. parviflora sensu* John Macoun 1883, not Ehrh.; B.C. to
      w Ont.: Fernald *in* Gray 1950] . . . . var. *fendleri* (Crépin) Rydb.
1   Leaflets puberulent to glabrous, their teeth and those of the stipules not gland-
      tipped . . . . var. *woodsii*
      2   Ovary and fruit bristly; [var. *hispida* G.T. Turner, Can. Field-Nat. 63(1):17. 1949,
            not f. *hispida* W.H. Lewis, Rhodora 60(717):240. 1958; type from Fort
            Saskatchewan, Alta.] . . . . f. *hispida* (Turner) Boivin
      2   Ovary and fruit glabrous; [incl. the taller extreme with relatively large leaflets, var.
            ultramontana (Wats.) Jeps. (*R. californica* var. *ultra.* Wats.; *R. ultra.* (Wats.)
            Heller) and the prickly extreme, var. *terrens* (Lunell) Breitung (*R. terrens* Lunell);
            R. macounii of Canadian reports, perhaps not Greene; cent. Alaska and B.C.
            (Eastham 1947) to Man.; also reported from the James Bay region of Ont. and
            Que. by Bernard Boivin, Nat. can. (Que.) 75(8/9/10):221. 1948, but this eastward
            extension doubtful according to Boivin 1966b; MAP (aggregate species): Hultén
            1968b:634] . . . . f. *woodsii*

RUBUS L.   [3353]   Raspberry, Blackberry, Bramble.   Framboisier or Ronce

(Ref.: Bailey 1932, 1941–45, 1947, 1949b; Hodgdon and Steele 1966; P.A. Rydberg, N. Am. Flora 22:425–80. 1913)

1 Leaves simple, merely toothed or lobed (or some of them often 3-foliolate in
   R. lasiococcus and *R. nivalis*).
   2 Stems retrorse-prickly, pubescent, trailing and freely rooting at the nodes; leaves
      evergreen, cordate-ovate, usually glabrous, bright green and shining above,
      strongly toothed to prominently 3-lobed (or some of them even 3-foliolate),
      usually prickly beneath along the veins, to 6 cm long; stipules lanceolate to
      ovate, free or nearly so, to 1 cm long; flowers single or in pairs in the leaf-axils;
      petals ?white to pink or dull purple, narrowly elliptic-lanceolate, equalling to half
      again as long as the reflexed calyx-lobes (these to 9 mm long); drupelets red,
      large, not more than 5 or 6 of them maturing; (sw B.C.) . . . .*R. nivalis*
   2 Stems unarmed; leaves shallowly to deeply 3–7-lobed (or even 3-foliolate in
      R. lasiococcus).
      3 Flowers few to many in cymose clusters (rarely solitary) terminating leafy
         branches in the axils of stout woody stems to over 2 m tall; mature fruit red;
         stipules narrow, somewhat adnate to the petioles; leaves numerous, with
         (3)5(7) deep acutish to acuminate lobes.
         4 Petals white, to about 2 cm long; calyx-lobes copiously pubescent but
            usually glandless; fruit juicy; leaf-lobes merely acute or acutish, the
            terminal one about a third of the total length of the leaf; stem and
            branches more or less glandular but scarcely bristly; (B.C.–Alta.; Ont.) . . . .
            . . . .*R. parviflorus*
         4 Petals rose-purple, to 2.5 cm long; calyx-lobes, branches, and peduncles
            more or less bristly with dark stipitate glands; fruit dryish; leaf-lobes
            acuminate, the terminal one to over half the total length of the leaf; (Ont.
            to N.S.) . . . .*R. odoratus*
      3 Flowers borne singly or in pairs on erect stems or branches to 1 or 2 dm tall
         bearing usually 2 or 3 leaves, the teeth or lobes of the leaf mostly obtuse or
         rounded; stipules broad, free or nearly so; fruit consisting of relatively large
         drupelets; plants subherbaceous.
         5 Floral branches bearing 1 or 2 flowers, arising from slender horizontal
            sterile stems freely rooting at the nodes; flowers perfect; petals white, less
            than 1 cm long; mature fruit red, densely cottony; leaves shallowly to
            deeply 3-lobed (or some of them 3-foliolate), more or less crisp-puberulent
            to pilose; stipules about 5 mm long; (sw B.C.) . . . .*R. lasiococcus*
         5 Floral stems usually 1-flowered (rarely 2-flowered), arising directly from
            creeping scaly rhizomes; leaves thickish; petals to over 1.5 cm long.
            6 Petals erect, oblanceolate, pink or roseate; anther-filaments dilated;
               flowers perfect; fruit ?red; stipules to 1 cm long; leaves rather deeply
               3-lobed, pubescent at least on the veins beneath; (Alaska–Yukon–n
               B.C.) . . . .*R. stellatus*
            6 Petals ascending or spreading, obovate, white; anther-filaments not
               dilated; flowers unisexual; fruit red-tinged when young, then amber-
               colour, finally yellowish; leaves with (3)5(7) rather shallow lobes,
               sparingly hairy or glabrate on both sides; (transcontinental) . . . .
               . . . .*R. chamaemorus*
1 Leaves normally compound (a few, chiefly the upper ones, sometimes simple).
   7 Plants unarmed, subherbaceous, rarely over 4 dm tall, without succession of
      primocanes (first year's stems, usually lacking flowers) and floricanes (the
      flowering second year's development of the primocanes); (if plant nearly or quite
      unarmed but stems more or less woody and with definite succession of
      primocanes and floricanes, see the contrasting lead 7); stipules broad, free or
      nearly so; fruit red.

8   Leaves digitately 5-foliolate (occasionally 3-foliolate but the lower pair again
     divided nearly to base); leaflets doubly serrate-dentate or incised-dentate,
     subglabrous to more or less silky pilose, to 3 cm long; petals white; flowering
     stems bearing up to 3 or 4 leaves and a single flower on a slender terminal
     peduncle to 6(8) cm long, arising from the nodes of the whip-like creeping
     sterile stem; (mts. of B.C.–Alta.) . . . . *R. pedatus*
8   Leaves 3-foliolate.
   9   Stems tufted and erect, from a short branched perennial base, lacking
        prolonged runners; petals pink or roseate, to about 1.5 cm long.
      10 Petals relatively narrow, oblanceolate to narrowly obovate, distinctly
          clawed; calyx glabrous or sparingly hairy but not glandular; leaflets all
          rounded at apex; stems rarely over 1.5 dm tall, bearing a single flower
          (rarely 2); (transcontinental) . . . . *R. acaulis*
      10 Petals more broadly obovate (to about 9 mm broad), scarcely clawed;
          calyx pubescent and often glandular with yellowish glands; leaflets of
          at least the upper leaves usually acute; stems often taller and bearing
          up to 3 flowers; (mts. of B.C.–Alta.) . . . . *R. arcticus*
   9   Stems stoloniferous, trailing or loosely ascending, the flowering branches
        or stems to about 4 dm long; leaflets acute.
      11 Flowers greenish white, about 1 cm broad, short-pedicelled or
          subsessile in a compact, umbel-like, commonly 3–6-flowered cluster
          well hidden beneath the leaves; (s Greenland) . . . . *R. saxatilis*
      11 Flowers white to roseate, commonly 1–4 on slender, not closely
          contiguous pedicels.
        12 Petals roseate, to over 1.5 cm long and up to 7 mm broad; calyx-
            lobes to over 1 cm long; leaflets firm, more or less shining above;
            vegetative shoots rarely prolonged; (Alta. to Labrador, Nfld., and
            N.S.) . . . . *R. paracaulis*
        12 Petals white or pale pink, not over about 1 cm long and 3 mm
            broad; calyx-lobes less than 1 cm long; leaflets softer, opaque;
            elongate runners with rooting tips commonly developed;
            (transcontinental) . . . . *R. pubescens*
7 Plants usually weakly to strongly armed with prickles or bristles or both, mostly
   taller; stems more or less woody, with definite succession of primocane and
   floricane (except in *R. illecebrosus,* with annual fruiting canes); stipules linear or
   setaceous, more or less adnate to the petioles.
   13 Mature fruit usually red, scarlet, or purplish black (yellow to reddish in
      R. spectabilis), readily separating from the dry receptacle, this persistent on
      the pedicel; (raspberries).
      14 Flowers to over 4 cm broad, 1–few on short leafy branches; fruits to over
         2 cm long; inflorescence nonglandular, the whole plant essentially
         glabrous.
        15 Leaflets 3 (or the lateral ones occasionally divided nearly or quite to
           base into distinct leaflets), ovate, acute to acuminate; petals red to
           reddish-purple; fruit yellow to salmon-colour or reddish; plant
           commonly unarmed or the canes weakly bristly, the yellow or brown
           bark finally loosely exfoliating; (s Alaska–w B.C.) . . . . *R. spectabilis*
        15 Leaflets 5, 7, or 9, lance-attenuate, pinnately arranged; petals white;
           fruit red or scarlet, 2 or 3 cm thick, suggesting a strawberry; canes,
           petioles, and leaf-rachises rather sparingly armed with broad-based
           stout prickles to 3 or 4 mm long; bark green or greenish, not shredding;
           (garden-escape in N.S.) . . . . *R. illecebrosus*
      14 Flowers about 1 cm broad, the narrowly obovate, spreading-ascending,
         white petals shorter than to about equalling the sepals.
        16 Canes, pedicels, and calyces densely villous with long gland-tipped
           reddish hairs; calyx-lobes much surpassing the small petals, soon

becoming erect and covering the developing red fruit; leaflets 3, strongly white-tomentose beneath and with reddish veins; canes tip-rooting; (introd.). . . . . [*R. phoenicolasius*]

16 Canes smooth or minutely pubescent to bristly or prickly (but if glandular, the hairs pale and not crowded); calyx-lobes not much surpassing the petals, spreading or reflexed under the developing fruit.

    17 Canes erect, not tip-rooting, bristly to smoothish, with or without hooked prickles; leaves of primocanes, if 5-foliolate, pinnate; calyx often bristly, its lobes (excluding the caudate tips) about equalling the petals; fruit red, the drupelets not separated by bands of tomentum; (transcontinental) . . . . *R. idaeus*

    17 Canes and branches long-arching, finally tip-rooting, with hooked prickles but no bristles, very glaucous; leaves of primocanes, if 5-foliolate, digitate; calyx scarcely if ever bristly, its lobes much surpassing the petals; fruit purple-black, the immature drupelets separated by bands of white tomentum; (B.C.; Ont., Que., and N.B.) . . . .
. . . . *R. occidentalis*

13 Mature fruit black or blackish, usually falling with the fleshy receptacle or often drying without falling; (blackberries).

  18 Armature consisting of stiff or glandular bristles or slender, straight or barely curved, slightly reflexed prickles to 4 mm long, these numerous to almost wanting, mostly slender to the base but sometimes with an expanded base to 5 mm broad; shorter glandular hairs usually also present, especially in the inflorescence.

    19 Primocanes trailing to low-arching, rooting at the tip; (Ont. to N.S.) . . . .
. . . . *R. hispidus*

    19 Primocanes normally erect or ascending, not rooting at the tip.

      20 Armature consisting of a dense coat of soft pale bristles to 4 mm long; (Ont. to N.S.) . . . . *R. setosus*

      20 Armature sparser, consisting of stiff acicular prickles; (Ont. to ?Nfld. and N.S.) . . . . *R. vermontanus*

  18 Armature consisting entirely of stout, stiff, often hooked prickles with more or less expanded bases; bristles none but minute glandular hairs often present.

    21 Stems trailing or low-arching, normally rooting at the tip and also at some of the nodes; prickles of the primocanes distinctly hooked.

      22 Plants more or less completely unisexual (the pistillate flowers with distinctly rudimentary stamens, the staminate with small nonfunctional pistils); flowers up to 10 in corymbs; calyx villous-tomentose, usually stipitate-glandular and sometimes weakly prickly; petals white; fruits to 2.5 cm long; leaflets 3 (or the terminal leaflet itself frequently 3-lobed or occasionally completely divided into 3 separate leaflets); canes finally glabrate, slender, trailing and tip-rooting, abundantly armed with rather slender, slightly hooked, almost terete prickles; (B.C.) . . . . *R. ursinus*

      22 Plants with flowers all perfect.

        23 Young primocanes glaucous; some of the lower nodes of the inflorescence bearing 2 or 3 flowers or bearing a short branch with 2 or more flowers; (garden-escape) . . . . [*R. caesius*]

        23 Young primocanes not glaucous; lower nodes of the inflorescence 1-flowered.

          24 Leaflets laciniately lobed or divided into secondary leaflets that are themselves deeply and coarsely toothed to irregularly jagged-lobed or incised; leaves evergreen; flowers rather numerous in usually partially compound, more or less flat-topped and somewhat leafy racemes, the axis and pedicels strongly armed and copiously pubescent but

eglandular; petals generally pinkish; armature of canes and
branches copious and vicious, the stout prickles flattened
and recurved; (a garden-escape in B.C.) . . . .*R. laciniatus*
24 Leaves normally merely toothed or moderately lobed; (native
species).
25 Flowers few or several, mostly subtended by stipules or
the lowest one in the axil of an expanded petiolate leaf;
(Ont. to Nfld. and N.S.) . . . .*R. recurvicaulis*
25 Flowers mostly subtended by simple or 3-foliolate leaves
or the flower solitary and terminal.
26 Terminal leaflet of the 3-foliolate floricane leaves more
or less ovate, often coarsely or doubly serrate,
commonly sharply acute to long-acuminate; (Ont. to
N.B.) . . . . *R. flagellaris*
26 Terminal leaflet of the 3-foliolate floricane leaves
oblanceolate to oblong or obovate, narrowly to
broadly cuneate at base, obtuse to very abruptly short-
acuminate; (s Ont.) . . . . *R. enslenii*
21 Stems normally erect or ascending; prickles of the primocanes straight,
spreading, or barely reflexed (but not hooked).
27 Glandular hairs abundant on the pedicels and often elsewhere.
28 Terminal leaflet of the primocane-leaves narrowly ovate to
obovate-oblong, rarely more than 3/5 as broad as long; (Ont. to
N.S.) . . . . *R. allegheniensis*
28 Terminal leaflet of the primocane-leaves broadly ovate to
subrotund, 3/4 to fully as broad as long; (Ont. to Nfld. and N.S.) . . . . .
. . . . *R. pensilvanicus*
27 Glandular hairs wanting or sometimes a very few present on the
pedicels.
29 Leaves glabrous beneath or essentially so; (Ont. to Nfld. and N.S.) . . .
. . . . *R. canadensis*
29 Leaves soft-pubescent beneath.
30 Terminal leaflet of the primocane-leaves less than half as
broad as long; (s ?Ont.) . . . .[*R. argutus*]
30 Terminal leaflet of the primocane-leaves at least half as broad
as long.
31 Inflorescence corymbose-paniculate, with up to 20
flowers; fruit to about 2 cm long and 1.5 cm thick;
(garden-escape in s B.C.) . . . . *R. procerus*
31 Inflorescence a usually few-flowered raceme; fruit smaller;
(Ont. to Nfld. and N.S.) . . . . *R. pensilvanicus*

R. acaulis Michx.

/ST/X/ (Hpr) Peaty soil, moist woods, and tundra from N Alaska, N-cent. Yukon, and NW
Dist. Mackenzie to Great Bear L., L. Athabasca (Alta. and Sask.), and northernmost Man.–
Ont.–Que.–Labrador, s in the West through B.C.–Alta. to the mts. of Mont., Wyo., and Colo.,
farther eastwards s to N Minn., Ont. (s to L. Superior), Que. (s to s James Bay, L. Mistassini
(probable type locality), and the Gaspé Pen.; not known from the Maritime Provinces), and
Nfld. [*Manteia* Raf.; *R. arcticus* ssp. *ac.* (Michx.) Focke; *R. arct.* var. *grandiflorus* of American
auth., not Ledeb.; *R. castoreus sensu* M.L. Fernald, Rhodora 9(105):162. 1907, not Laest.; *R.
?pistillatus* Sm.]. MAPS: Hultén 1968b:603 (*R. arct.* ssp. *ac.*); Raup 1947: pl. 28.

Apparent hybrids with *R. arcticus* are reported from Alaska by Hultén (1946). *R. propinquus*
Rich., thought by P.A. Rydberg (N. Am. Flora 22:437. 1913) to be a probable hybrid with *R.
pubescens,* is known from Dist. Mackenzie, the type locality.

R. allegheniensis Porter

/T/EE/ (Hp) Thickets and clearings from Minn. to Ont. (N to the Ottawa dist.), Que. (N to

Montmagny Co.), N.B., P.E.I., and N.S., s to Mo., Tenn., and N.C. [Incl. *R. adenocaulis* Fern., *R. sativus* Brainerd, *R. biformispinus, R. glandicaulis, R. montpeleriensis, R. permixtus,* and *R. recurvans* Blanch., and *R. acadiensis, R. atwoodii, R. auroralis, R. nigrobaccus, R. nuperus, R. ortivus, R. particeps, R. pennus, R. perinvisus,* and *R. pugnax* Bailey].

R. arcticus L.
/ST/W/EA/ (Hpr) Peaty soil, thickets, and tundra from Alaska (N to ca. 68°N), the Yukon (N to ca. 65°N; *see* Hultén 1946: map 756, p. 1062), and the Mackenzie R. Delta to B.C. and the mts. of sw Alta. (reports from elsewhere in Canada refer largely or wholly to *R. acaulis* and *R. paracaulis*); Eurasia. MAP: Hultén 1968*b*:602.
    A hybrid with *R. stellatus* is reported from Alaska by Hultén (1946). Var. *pentaphylloides* Hult. (the lateral leaflets cleft nearly to base, the leaf thus appearing 5-foliolate rather than 3-foliolate) is reported from the type locality, near Klondike, the Yukon, by Hultén (1968*a*).

[R. argutus Link]
[The report of this species of the E U.S.A. (N to s III. and Mass.) from s Ont. by Montgomery (1945; taken up by Soper 1949) is based upon a collection in OAC from Cambridge (Galt), Waterloo Co. However, it is felt inadvisable to admit this member of such an extremely critical genus to our flora on the basis of a single collection.]

[R. caesius L.] European Dewberry
[Eurasian; locally spreading from cult. in the U.S.A. and a collection in OAC from Huron Co., s Ont. (where perhaps not established), has been placed here.]

R. canadensis L.
/T/EE/ (Hpr) Thickets and ravines from Ont. (N to L. Superior; John Macoun 1883) to Que. (N to Rimouski, Rimouski Co.), Nfld., N.B., P.E.I., and N.S., s to Tenn. and N Ga. [Incl. *R. amabilis, R. elegantulus,* and *R. multiformis* Blanch., *R. kennedyanus* Fern., *R. millspaughii* Britt., *R. randii* (Bailey) Rydb., and *R. amicalis, R. lepagei, R. quaesitus,* and *R. ulterior* Bailey; *R. ?trivialis sensu* Hooker 1832, in part, not Michx.].

R. chamaemorus L. Baked-apple-berry. Mûres blanches
/aST/X/GEA/ (Hp) Peat bogs from the Aleutian Is. and coasts of Alaska–Yukon–Dist. Mackenzie–Dist. Keewatin to Southampton Is., s Baffin Is., and northernmost Ungava–Labrador, s to sw B.C. (Vancouver Is. and Lulu Is.; V), Alta. (s to Lesser Slave L.), Sask. (s to Tisdale, 52°51′N), Man. (s to Duck Mt.), Ont. (s to the SE shore of L. Superior), Que. (s to the Laurentide Provincial Park N of Quebec City; Raymond 1950*b*), Nfld., N.B., P.E.I. (Prince Co.; D.S. Erskine 1960), N.S., and Long Is.; w Greenland N to near the Arctic Circle; Spitsbergen; N Eurasia. MAPS: Hultén 1968*b*:602; Porsild 1957: map 224, p. 188; *Atlas of Canada* 1957: map 3, sheet 38; Raup 1947: pl. 28; Raymond 1950*b*: fig. 16, p. 29; Meusel, Jaeger, and Weinert 1965:211.

R. enslenii Tratt.
/t/EE/ (Hpr) Thickets and open woods from Wisc. to s Ont. (Grand Bend, Huron Co.; MT), Ohio, and Pa., s through much of the E U.S.A. [*R. flagellaris* var. *humifusus* (T. & G.) Boivin; *R. baileyanus* Britt.].

R. flagellaris Willd.
/T/EE/ (Hpr) Thickets and dry fields from Minn. to Ont. (N to the Ottawa dist.), Que. (N to Lorette, near Quebec City; MT), and N.B. (Edmundston, Madawaska Co.; GH), s to Ark. and Ga. [Incl. *R. procumbens* Muhl., *R. roribaccus* (Bailey) Rydb., and *R. gordonii, R. jaysmithii, R. maltei,* and *R. tetricus* Bailey; *R. villosus* of Canadian reports in part, not Ait.].

R. hispidus L.
/T/EE/ (Hpr) Thickets, open woods, and clearings from Wisc. to Ont. (N to the Ottawa dist.), Que. (N to Bagotville, near L. St. John; MT), N.B., P.E.I., and N.S., s to III. and N.C. [Incl. *R. adjacens* Fern., *R. obovalis* Michx., *R. jacens* and *R. trifrons* Blanchard, and *R. emeritus,*

R. paganus, R. pudens, R. rowleei, R. russeus, R. segnis, R. signatis, and *R. vigoratus* Bailey; *R. obovatus* Ell., not Pers.]. MAPS: Braun 1935: fig. 3, p. 355, and 1937: fig. 23, p. 199.

R. idaeus L.   Red Raspberry
/ST/X/EA/   (Hp)   Thickets, open woods, and fields, the aggregate species from N-cent. Alaska–Yukon and NW Dist. Mackenzie to S Dist. Keewatin, Ont. (N to the Fawn R. at ca. 55°N, 88°W), Que. (N to Ungava Bay and the Côte-Nord), Labrador (N to ca. 56°30′N), Nfld., N.B., P.E.I., and N.S., S to Calif., N.Mex., N Mexico, Tenn., and N.C.; Eurasia. MAP and synonymy: *see* below.

1   Pedicels and calyces lacking glands or minute bristles; [introd.; MAP (aggregate
    species): Hultén 1968*b*:604] . . . . var. *idaeus*
    2   Prickles of new canes (primocanes) strong and relatively broad-based; [Ont. to
        Nfld. and N.S.] . . . . f. *idaeus*
    2   Prickles wanting, the canes smooth; [E Que. (Brion Is., Magdalen Is.) and N.S.
        (St. Paul Is.)] . . . . f. *inermis* Kaufmann
1   Pedicels and calyces bearing glands and minute bristles; primocanes usually bearing
    slender bristles and often also stipitate-glandular.
    3   Primocanes glabrous or glaucous beneath the prickles, becoming lustrous.
        4   Prickles mostly strong and relatively broad-based . . . .
            . . . . var. *aculeatissimus* Regel & Tiling
            5   Petals white; [*R. melanolasius* and *R. melanotrachys* Focke; *R.
                sachalinensis* Lévl. in part; evidently from Dist. Mackenzie and B.C. to
                Man. and in Asia; reported from Attawapiskat, W James Bay, Ont., by
                Dutilly, Lepage, and Duman 1954]. A hybrid with *R. spectabilis* is reported
                from Alaska by Boivin (1967*a*) . . . . f. *aculeatissimus*
            5   Petals pink; [the Yukon (type from Stewart Landing) and Sask. (Elbourne,
                N of Regina] . . . . f. *erythrochlamydeus* Boivin
        4   Prickles (when present) slender and narrow-based . . . .
            . . . . var. *strigosus* (Michx.) Maxim.
            6   Fruit amber-white; [*R. idaeus* f. *?succineus* Rehd.; N.S.: Kings Co.; W.B.
                Schofield and E.C. Smith, Can. Field-Nat. 67(2):93. 1953] . . . .
                . . . . f. *albus* (Bailey) Fern.
            6   Fruit red.
                7   Primocanes smooth, lacking bristles; [E Que. and Nfld.] . . . . . f. *tonsus* Fern.
                7   Primocanes bristly; [*R. (Batidaea) strigosus* Michx.; transcontinental] . . . . . .
                    . . . . f. *strigosus*
    3   Primocanes ashy-puberulent beneath the prickles.
        8   Many of the prickles stout and broad-based; [Grand Manan Is., SW N.B.] . . . .
            . . . . var. *heterolasius* Fern.
        8   Prickles all slender and bristleform.
            9   Leaves simple or with 3 barely separate rounded leaflets; [E Que., the type
                from Ruisseau à Rebours, Gaspé Co.] . . . . var. *eucyclus* Fern.
            9   Leaves compound.
                10   Leaves glabrous or subglabrous and greenish beneath; [*R.
                    sachalinensis* Lévl. in part; *Batidaea (R.) peramoena* and *B. (R.)
                    viburnifolia* Greene; Alaska–Yukon–B.C.] . . . var. *peramoenus* (Greene) Fern.
                10   Leaves densely white-tomentose beneath . . . . var. *canadensis* Fern.
                    11   Leaflets lanceolate to ovate, coarsely toothed and moderately
                        lobed; [*R. sachalinensis* Lévl. in part; *R. carolinianus* Rydb.; *R.
                        subarcticus* (Greene) Rydb.; transcontinental] . . . . f. *canadensis*
                    11   Leaflets narrowly lanceolate, long-attenuate, those of the
                        primocanes deeply cleft; [SE Nfld., the type from St. John's] . . . .
                        . . . . f. *caudatus* (Robins. & Schrenk) Fern.

R. illecebrosus Focke   Strawberry-Raspberry
Asiatic; persisting in old gardens or spreading to roadsides and waste places in N. America, as in N.S. (Annapolis Royal, Annapolis Co.; GH; CAN).

R. laciniatus Willd.   Evergreen Blackberry
?European; a common garden-escape in w B.C. (Queen Charlotte Is.; Vancouver Is. and adjacent islands and mainland).

R. lasiococcus Gray
/t/W/   (Hpr)   Thickets, woods, and clearings at low to moderate elevations from sw B.C. (Vancouver Is.; Skagit Valley; Yale dist.; Hope; Manning Provincial Park, se of Hope) to nw Calif.

R. nivalis Dougl.
/T/W/   (Hpr)   Open to deeply shaded slopes at low to fairly high elevations from sw B.C. (Vancouver Is.; J.M. Macoun 1913; CAN; V) to sw Oreg. and Idaho. [R. pacificus J.M. Macoun, not Hance].

R. occidentalis L.   Black Raspberry, Thimbleberry.   Mûrier
/sT/(X)/   (Hpr)   Thickets, ravines, and open woods, var. leucodermis from s Alaska (see Hultén 1946: map 759, p. 1062; R. leuc.) through B.C. to s Calif., Nev., and Utah, the typical form from Minn. to Ont. (n to the Ottawa dist.; the report from Man. by Shimek 1927, requires confirmation), Que. (n to Rimouski Co.; MT), and N.B. (Keswick Ridge, York Co.; NBM; reports from P.E.I. and Nfld. require confirmation; not known from N.S.), s to Okla., Ark., and Ga. MAP and synonymy: see below.
1   Terminal leaflet of the primocane leaves abruptly pointed; prickles of pedicels neither stout nor very broad-based, mostly straightish; primocanes usually glaucous-purple, their prickles few and scattered, mostly curved or hooked . . . . . . var. occidentalis
    2   Fruit purple-black; [Ont., Que., and N.B.] . . . . f. occidentalis
    2   Fruit yellowish or amber; [var. pallidus Bailey; Que.: Boivin 1966b] . . . .
        . . . . f. pallidus (Bailey) Robins.
1   Terminal leaflet of the primocane leaves relatively narrow and gradually long-pointed; prickles of the pedicels very stout and usually long and broad-based, mostly hooked; primocanes glaucous-grey, their prickles abundant and mostly straight; [R. leucodermis Dougl.; se Alaska (see Hultén 1946: map 759, p. 1062) and B.C.; MAP (R. leuc.): Hultén 1968b:605] . . . . var. leucodermis (Dougl.) Focke

R. odoratus L.   Purple-flowering Raspberry, Thimbleberry.   Calottes or Chapeaux rouges
/T/EE/   (Hp)   Thickets and borders of woods from Ont. (n to Renfrew and Carleton counties; CAN; DAO; reported from near Sault Ste. Marie by John Macoun 1883) to Que. (n to 23 mi n of Mont-Laurier, Labelle Co.; reported from Rivière-du-Loup, Temiscouata Co., by John Macoun 1883), N.B. (in old gardens at Chamcook, Charlotte Co., where probably introd.; not known from P.E.I.), and N.S. (Lunenberg and Inverness counties), s to Tenn. and Ga. [Rubacer Rydb.]. MAP: N.C. Fassett, Ann. Mo. Bot. Gard. 28(3): map 12, p. 353. 1941.
1   Pedicel-glands with stalks mostly over 1 mm long; leaves stipitate-glandular above, more or less velvety beneath; [var. malachopyllus Fern.; Ont. (Brockville, Leeds Co.) and N.S. (Belleville, Yarmouth Co.)] . . . . f. hypomalacus Fassett
1   Pedicel-glands mostly less than 1 mm long.
    2   Leaves stipitate-glandular above, more or less velvety beneath; [Ont.: Brockville, Leeds Co.] . . . . f. bifarius Fassett
    2   Leaves not glandular above, glabrous, glabrate, or sparingly appressed-pubescent beneath; [Ont.: Brockville, Leeds Co.] . . . . f. glabrifolius Fassett

R. paracaulis Bailey
/sT/(X)/   (Hpr)   Peaty places and moist woods from cent. Alta. (Whitecourt and Fort Saskatchewan; CAN) to Sask. (n to L. Athabasca; R. arcticus sensu Breitung 1957a, not L.), northernmost Man.–Ont., Que. (n to e James Bay at 53°50′N, the Côte-Nord, and Gaspé Pen.), Labrador (n to ca. 55°N), Nfld., N.B. (Campbellton, Restigouche Co.; CAN, detd. Porsild), and N.S. (St. Paul Is. and Kings and Inverness counties; not known from P.E.I. or the U.S.A.). [R. pubescens vars. par. (Bailey) Boivin and scius Bailey; R. arcticus sensu Fernald in Gray 1950, as to citations e of Alta., not L.; R. ?propinquus Rich.].

R. parviflorus Nutt.   Thimbleberry
/T/WW/   (Hp)   Thickets and borders of woods, the main area from SE Alaska through B.C. and SW Alta. to S Calif., N Mexico, and N.Mex., isolated areas in the Black Hills of S.Dak. and in the Great Lakes region of the U.S.A. and Ont. (N shore and islands of L. Superior; St. Joseph Is., N L. Huron; Bruce Pen., L. Huron). MAPS and synonymy: *see* below.
1   Glands of the pedicels all or nearly all sessile or subsessile or even wanting; leaves
     glabrous beneath; [*R. nutkanus* var. *scop.* Greene; SE B.C. (Kicking Horse Valley);
     MAPS: Fernald 1935: map 21, p. 283; N.C. Fassett, Ann. Mo. Bot. Gard. 28(3): map 18
     (dots), p. 355. 1941] . . . . f. *scopulorum* (Greene) Fassett
1   Glands of the pedicels all or nearly all long-stipitate.
     2   Leaves distinctly soft-pubescent beneath.
          3   Pedicel-glands very unequal, mostly dark-coloured, to 2 mm long; calyx not
               villous; [var. *hypomalacus* Fern.; SE Alaska–B.C.; S Alta. (Waterton Lakes;
               Cypress Hills); L. Superior and L. Huron, Ont.; MAPS: Fernald 1935: map 17, p.
               278; Fassett, loc. cit., map 14, p. 355] . . . . f. *hypomalacus* (Fern.) Fassett
          3   Pedicel-glands mostly subequal and short, often pale, rarely over 0.5 mm long
               (or a few scattered ones to about 1 mm long).
               4   Calyx not villous; [var. *bifarius* Fern. and its f. *lacera* (Ktze.) Fern. and f.
                    fraserianus (Henry) Fern.; B.C. (N to the Wicked R., near the Peace R. at
                    ca. 56°N; type from Vancouver Is.); L. Superior and L. Huron, Ont.; MAPS:
                    Fernald 1935: map 19, p. 280; Fassett, loc. cit., map 16, p. 355] . . . .
                    . . . . f. *bifarius* (Fern.) Fassett
               4   Calyx with long villous hairs hiding the glands; [L. Huron, Ont.] . . . .
                    . . . . f. *trichophorus* Fassett
     2   Leaves glabrous or soon glabrate beneath.
          5   Pedicel-glands very unequal, mostly dark-coloured, to 2 mm long; calyx not
               villous; [var. *heteradenius* Fern.; L. Superior and L. Huron, Ont.; MAPS: Fernald
               1935: map 18, p. 279; Fassett, loc. cit., map 15, p. 355] . . . .
               . . . . f. *heteradenius* (Fern.) Fassett
          5   Pedicel-glands mostly subequal and short, often pale, rarely over 0.5 mm long
               (or a few scattered ones to about 1 mm long).
               6   Calyx not villous; [var. *grandiflorus* Farw.; *R. nutkanus* Moc.; SE Alaska
                    (Wrangell; Juneau); B.C. (Peace R. at ca. 56°N; Donald; Emerald L.;
                    Carbonate, Selkirk Mts.); L. Superior and L. Huron (type from near
                    Meldrum Bay), Ont.; MAPS (as var. *grandiflorus*): Hultén 1968b:605; Fernald
                    1935: map 20, p. 282; Fassett, loc. cit., map 17, p. 355] . . . .
                    . . . . f. *glabrifolius* Fassett
               6   Calyx with villous hairs hiding the glands; [var. *genuinus sensu* Fernald
                    1935; *R. nutkanus* var. *nuttallii* T. & G.; L. Huron, Ont.; MAPS (as var.
                    genuinus): Fernald 1935: map 15, p. 277; Fassett, loc. cit., map 13, p. 355] . . . . .
                    . . . . f. *nuttallii* (T. & G.) Fassett

R. pedatus Sm.
/sT/W/eA/   (Hpr)   Moist woods at low elevations to near timberline from S Alaska–Yukon (*see* Hultén 1946: map 761, p. 1062) through B.C. and SW Alta. to Oreg., Idaho, and Mont.; E Asia. [*Comaropsis* DC.; *Dalibarda* Steph.]. MAP: Hultén 1968b:601.

R. pensilvanicus Poir.
/T/EE/   (Hpr)   Thickets, borders of woods, and clearings from Minn. to Ont. (N to the Ottawa dist.), Que. (N to Pontiac and Beauce counties), Nfld., ?N.B. (Boivin 1966b; not known from P.E.I.), and N.S., S to Okla., Ark., Tenn., and Ala. [Incl. *R. frondosus* Bigel., *R. ostryifolius* Rydb., *R. abbrevians, R. amnicola, R. andrewsianus, R. orarius,* and *R. pergratus* Blanchard, and *R. alumnus, R. attractus, R. bellobatus, R. breitungii, R. burnhamii, R. eriensis, R. facetus, R. perfoliosus,* and *R. victorinii* Bailey].

[R. phoenicolasius Maxim.]   Wine Raspberry
[Asiatic; a collection in Herb. V from Texada Is., near Vancouver Is., B.C., has been placed here but further material is desirable before accepting the species as one of our established adventives.]

R. procerus Muell.   Himalayan Blackberry
Eurasian; reported as an occasional garden-escape in s B.C. by Eastham (1947), from Queen Charlotte Is. by Calder and Taylor (1968), and there is a collection in CAN from Nanaimo, Vancouver Is., where taken by the writer in 1964. [R. ?fruticosus L.; R. thyrsanthus of auth., not Focke].

R. pubescens Raf.   Dwarf Raspberry.   Catherinettes
/ST/X/   (Hpr)   Thickets, open woods, and shores, the aggregate species from the Mackenzie R. Delta and n B.C. to Great Slave L., L. Athabasca (Alta. and Sask.), Man. (n to Gillam, about 165 mi s of Churchill), northernmost Ont., Que. (n to the Kaniapiscau R. at 57°27'N), Nfld., N.B., P.E.I., and N.S., s to Wash., n Colo., S.Dak., Pa., and N.J. MAPS and synonymy: see below.
1   Leaves copiously velvety-pilose beneath; [s Man. (Otterburne, about 30 mi s of
      Winnipeg; Löve and Bernard 1959), E Que. (Magdalen Is.; GH), N.B. (Wolf Is.,
      Charlotte Co.), and Nfld. (Fernald in Gray 1950)] . . . . var. pilosifolius Hill
1   Leaves glabrous or nearly so . . . . var. pubescens
      2   Flowers deep roseate; [Alta., Sask., Ont., and Que.] . . . . . . f. roseiflorus (Peck) House
      2   Flowers white.
            3   Flowers "double" with numerous petals; [type from La Bataille, near Montreal,
                  Que.] . . . . f. multiplex Raymond
            3   Flowers with the usual 5 petals; [R. americanus (Pers.) Britt.; R. mucronatus
                  Ser.; R. saxatilis var. canadensis Michx.; R. transmontanus Focke; R. triflorus
                  Rich.; transcontinental, the type from near Hudson Bay; MAPS (aggregate
                  species): Hultén, 1968b:601, and 1958: map 85, p. 105; Meusel, Jaeger, and
                  Weinert 1965:211] . . . . f. pubescens

R. recurvicaulis Blanchard
/T/EE/   (Hpr)   Thickets and open woods from Wisc. to Ont. (n to Constance Bay, about 30 mi w of Ottawa) to Que. (n to near Quebec City), St-Pierre and Miquelon, Nfld., N.B., and N.S. (not known from P.E.I.), s to Ind., W.Va., and Md. [Incl. R. arcuans Fern. & St. John, R. bracteoliferus Fern., R. brainerdii Rydb., R. severus Brainerd, R. arenicola, R. arundelanus, and R. plicatifolius Blanchard, and R. armatus, R. botruosus, R. complex, R. licens, R. mananensis, R. obsessus, R. oriens, R. problematicus, and R. provincialis Bailey].

R. saxatilis L.
/aST/–/GEA/   (Hpr)   Thickets and rocky places in SE Greenland (n to ca. 63°N), Iceland, and n Eurasia. MAP: Hultén 1958: map 85, p. 105.

R. setosus Bigel.
/T/EE/   (Hpr)   Damp thickets and swampy places from Wisc. to Ont. (n to Sudbury and Ottawa), Que. (n to near Quebec City), N.B. (Charlotte, St. John, and Westmorland counties; reports from P.E.I. require confirmation), and N.S. (Digby Co.), s to W.Va. and Md. [Incl. R. frondisentis Blanchard, R. nigricans Rydb., and R. gulosus, R. lawrencei, R. rotundior, R. textus, and R. univocis Bailey].

R. spectabilis Pursh   Salmonberry
/sT/W/eA/   (Hpr)   Moist woods and swampy places at low to medium elevations from the Aleutian Is. and s Alaska (see Hultén 1946: map 762, p. 1062) through coastal B.C. to n Calif.; E Asia. MAP: Hultén 1968b:604.
    A probable hybrid with R. (arcticus ssp.) stellatus (R. alaskensis Bailey, the type from s Alaska; R. pubescens var. al. (Bailey) Boivin) is known from the type region, Alaska, and is re-

ported from the ?Yukon and B.C. by Boivin (1966*b*), who considers the affinities of *R. alaskensis* to be with *R. pubescens* rather than with *R. (arcticus* ssp.) *stellatus.*

R. stellatus Smith
/ST/W/eA/ (Hpr) Peaty soil, thickets, and tundra from cent. Alaska–Yukon (*see* Hultén 1946: map 763, p. 1062; type probably from SE Alaska according to Hultén) to the Aleutian Is., S Alaska, and N B.C. (S to Dease L. at ca. 58°30′N); NE Asia. [*R. arcticus* ssp. *st.* (Sm.) Boivin]. MAP: Hultén 1968*b*:603 (*R. arct.* ssp. *st.*).

R. ursinus C. & S. Pacific Blackberry or Dewberry
/T/W/ (Hpr) Plains, woodlands, and clearings at low to middle elevations from B.C. (N to Queen Charlotte Is.; John Macoun 1883; Calder and Taylor 1968; reported E to the Columbia Valley by Macoun) to N Calif. and Idaho. [*R. helleri* Rydb.; *R. macropetalus* Dougl.; *R. vitifolius* ssp. *urs.* (C. & S.) Abrams].

R. vermontanus Blanchard
/T/EE/ (Hpr) Dry to moist thickets and clearings from Ont. (N to the Ottawa dist.) to Que. (N to Portneuf Co.), ?Nfld. (Boivin 1966*b*), N.B., P.E.I., and N.S., S to Minn., Mich., Pa., and New Eng. [Incl. *R. junceus* and *R. tardatus* Blanchard and *R. malus, R. navus, R. quebecensis,* and *R. weatherbyi* Bailey].

SANGUISORBA L. [3381] Burnet

(Ref.: P.A. Rydberg, N. Am. Flora 22:386–89. 1908)
1 Leaflets pectinate-pinnatifid nearly to midrib into narrowly linear segments, broadly obovate in outline, to about 2 cm long; flowers perfect; spikes oblong-cylindric to globose, to 3 (sometimes 4) cm long; sepals green with white-scarious margins; anther-filaments filiform; stigmas brush-like; achenes single from each flower; glabrous annuals or biennials with a taproot.
  2 Fruiting calyx with very narrow thick wings, more or less reticulate on the faces, the sepals not conspicuously thickened at base; stamens usually 2; (S B.C.) . . . .*S. occidentalis*
  2 Fruiting calyx with thin wings about 0.5 mm broad, not reticulate on the faces, the sepals tuberculose-thickened at base; stamens usually 4; (introd. in S Ont.) . . . .*S. annua*
1 Leaflets merely rather coarsely toothed; rhizomatous, essentially glabrous perennials (or stems of *S. minor* often sparsely pilose with multicellular hairs).
  3 Achenes 2 from each flower; mature calyx very rough between the wings, the sepals greenish or purple-tinged; stamens in the staminate (lower) flowers numerous and declined (middle flowers perfect, upper flowers pistillate); anther-filaments filiform; stigmas brush-like; spikes short-ovoid to globose, to about 2 cm long; leaflets ovate to orbicular, with up to 7 deep sharp teeth on each margin, rarely over 2 cm long; (introd.) . . . .*S. minor*
  3 Achene 1 from each flower; mature calyx not roughened between the wings; flowers perfect; stamens 4, not declined; stigmas merely warty-papillate.
    4 Stamens shorter than or at most about equalling the maroon to dull-violet or dark-purple sepals, the filaments filiform; spikes ellipsoid or short-cylindric, to about 3 cm long; leaflets commonly more than twice as long as broad; (Alaska–Yukon–Dist. Mackenzie–B.C.; introd. in N.S.) . . . .*S. officinalis*
    4 Stamens 2 or 3 times as long as the sepals, the filaments flattened and dilated above the middle.
      5 Flowers purplish, in oblong obtuse spikes to 7 cm long; leaflets ovate to oblong, to 6 cm long, usually less than twice as long as broad; (S Alaska–W B.C.) . . . .*S. menziesii*
      5 Flowers white to greenish (sometimes yellowish or slightly tinged with pink or purple); spikes to over 1 dm long, tapering to apex; (Alaska–Yukon– B.C.; Que. to Labrador and N.S.) . . . .*S. canadensis*

S. annua Nutt.   Prairie Burnet
Native in the U.S.A. from Kans. and Ark. to Tex.; a collection in OAC from s Ont. (Bruce Station, Bruce Pen., L. Huron; "heavy infestation in new seeding") has been placed here, as also other collections along the islands and shores of L. Huron; the report from B.C. by Boivin (1966b) is probably based upon collections in CAN finally referred to S. occidentalis. (Poterium Nutt.).

S. canadensis L.   Canada Burnet.   Herbe à pisser
/ST/D/eA/   (Hs)   Bogs, swamps, and streambanks (ranges of Canadian taxa outlined below), s in the West to Oreg. and Idaho, in the East to Ill., Ohio, and Del., and in the mts. to Ga.; E Asia. MAPS and synonymy: see below.
1   Leaflets lance-oblong to oblong-ovate, commonly over twice as long as broad; midrib of sepals thickened toward apex; [Poterium B. & H.; Que. (St. Lawrence R. from Montreal to the Côte-Nord, Anticosti Is., Gaspé Pen., and Magdalen Is.; St-Hyacinthe R. in St-Hyacinthe Co.; St. John R. in Dorchester Co.; Hubbard L. at ca. 54°45'N, 64°30'W), Labrador (N to Makkovik, 55°05'N), Nfld., St-Pierre and Miquelon, N.B. (near Bathurst, Gloucester Co.), and N.S. (St. Paul Is. and Kings, Inverness, Victoria, Richmond, and Cape Breton counties); MAP: Meusel, Jaeger, and Weinert 1965:221] . . . . ssp. canadensis
1   Leaflets ovate-oblong to ovate, mostly less than twice as long as broad; midrib of sepals not thickened; [var. lat. Hook.; S. lat. (Hook.) Cov.; S. (Poterium) sitchensis Mey.; S. stipulata Raf.; Aleutian Is.–cent. Alaska–cent. Yukon (see Hultén 1946: map 800, p. 1066) through B.C. (type from Observatory Inlet at ca. 55°N) to Oreg. and Idaho; reports from E Canada refer to the above taxon; MAPS: on the above-noted map by Meusel, Jaeger, and Weinert; Hultén 1968b:633 (S. stip.)]. Alaskan collections in CAN from Cape Vancouver and in GH from Nunivak Is. are noted by Hultén as probable hybrids with S. officinalis . . . . ssp. latifolia (Hook.) Calder & Taylor

S. menziesii Rydb.
/sT/W/   (Hs)   Coastal bogs and marshes from s Alaska (see Hultén 1946: map 798, p. 1066; type from Short Bay) through coastal B.C. (Queen Charlotte Is.; Prince Rupert; Ocean Falls; Calvert Is.; Vancouver Is.) to Wash. [According to Hultén 1968b, this taxon is possibly a hybrid between S. canadensis var. latifolia (S. stipulata Raf.) and S. officinalis]. MAP: Hultén 1968b:633.

S. minor Scop.   Small Burnet
Eurasian; a garden-escape to roadsides, fields, and waste places in N. America, as in s B.C. (Spences Bridge, where taken by John Macoun in 1889; CAN), s Ont. (Middlesex, Welland, Waterloo, Wellington, Halton, and Frontenac counties), ?Que. (garden at Ste-Anne-de-la-Pocatière, Kamouraska Co., where perhaps not an escape; QSA), N.B. (Boivin 1966b), and N.S. (near Windsor, Hants Co.; ACAD; CAN). [Poterium sanguisorba L.].

S. occidentalis Nutt.
/t/W/   (Hs (bien. or T))   Grassy flats (often semiwaste) from s B.C. (Vancouver Is.; near Ymir, s of Nelson; Okanagan) and w Mont. to s Calif. [Poteridium Rydb.; Poterium annuum sensu John Macoun 1890 (this taken up by Henry 1915, and Boivin 1966b), not Nutt., the relevant collection in CAN]. MAP: Meusel, Jaeger, and Weinert 1965:221.

S. officinalis L.   Burnet-Bloodwort, Great Burnet
/ST/W/EA/   (Hs)   Muskeg, swamps, and bogs from N Alaska–Yukon (N to ca. 68°N; see Hultén 1946: map 799, p. 1066) and NW Dist. Mackenzie (Porsild and Cody 1968) through coastal B.C. (Queen Charlotte Is.; Prince Rupert; Calvert Is.; Vancouver Is.) to N Calif.; introd. in N.S. (near Sherbrooke, Guysborough Co., a "long-established but not large station" in a meadow; J.S. Erskine 1953); Iceland; Eurasia. [Poterium Gray; S. microcephala Presl]. MAPS: Hultén 1968b:632; Meusel, Jaeger, and Weinert 1965:221 (S. mic.).

SIBBALDIA L.   [3359]

S. procumbens L.
/aST/X/GEA/   (Ch)   Moist gravelly tundra and subalpine to alpine meadows from the Aleutian Is., N Alaska, cent. Yukon, and NW Dist. Mackenzie to SE Baffin Is. and northernmost Ungava–Labrador, S in the West to S Calif., Utah, and Colo., farther eastwards S to SE Dist. Keewatin, James Bay (South Twin Is. at ca. 53°N), Que. (S to E James Bay at ca. 54°N, cent. Ungava at ca. 55°N, and the Shickshock Mts. of the Gaspé Pen.; not known from Sask., Man., Ont., or the Maritime Provinces), Nfld., and the White Mts. of N.H.; W and E Greenland N to ca. 72°N; Iceland; Spitsbergen; arctic and alpine Eurasia. [*Potentilla sibbaldia* Haller f.]. MAPS: Hultén 1968*b*:624, and 1958: map 217, p. 237; Porsild 1957: map 234, p. 190; Raup 1947: pl. 29; Böcher 1954: fig. 21 (top), p. 79; Raymond 1950*b*: fig. 25, p. 65; Meusel, Jaeger, and Weinert 1965:219.

SORBARIA A. Br.   [3323]

S. sorbifolia (L.) A. Br.   False Spiraea
Asiatic; a garden escape to thickets and waste places in N. America, as in Alta. (Peace River, 56°14′N; Groh and Frankton 1949*a*), Sask. (Clearwater L.; Breitung 1957*a*), Ont. (N to the N shore of L. Superior; W.J. Cody, Can. Field-Nat. 76(2):106. 1962), Que. (N to the Gaspé Pen.; ?cult.), Nfld. (Rouleau 1956; ?cult.), N.B., P.E.I., and N.S. [*Spiraea* L.].

SORBUS L.   [3338]   Mountain-Ash.   Sorbier

(Ref.: Jones 1939)
1   Fruits few, ellipsoid, to 1.5 cm thick; flowers to 1.5 cm broad; calyx 5 or 6 mm long at anthesis; leaflets at most 11, lanceolate to ovate-lanceolate, acuminate, broadest near base, sharply serrate nearly to base; (Aleutian Is.) . . . . *S. sambucifolia*
1   Fruits usually rather numerous, mostly globose, to 11 mm thick; flowers to 1 cm broad; calyx to 4 mm long at anthesis; leaflets often more numerous.
  2   Winter-buds copiously whitish-villous, scarcely glutinous; peduncles, pedicels, leaf-rachises, and petioles densely white-tomentose at least at flowering-time; leaflets oblong, acute or obtuse, dull green above, paler and usually permanently pubescent beneath; (introd.) . . . . *S. aucuparia*
  2   Winter-buds glabrous or sparingly pilose, usually more or less ciliate; peduncles, etc., glabrous or sparingly pilose; leaflets glabrous or soon glabrate (or the main veins beneath more or less persistently but sparingly pilose in *S. decora*).
    3   Leaflets 9 or 11, not glossy, oval or oblong (broadest near middle and less than 3 times as long as broad), obtuse or acutish, coarsely and sharply serrate to middle or below (occasionally subentire); winter-buds dull, their scales pilose dorsally with rusty hairs as well as marginally ciliate; pedicels rusty-pilose at anthesis; (Alaska, the Yukon, B.C., and Alta.) . . . . *S. sitchensis*
    3   Leaflets mostly 13 or 15; winter-buds glossy and glutinous; stipules soon deciduous.
      4   Lateral leaflets oval or oblong (broadest near the middle), abruptly acute and rarely more than 3 times as long as broad, not glossy, serrate to the middle or below; winter-buds with glabrous or sparsely pilose outer scales, the inner scales ciliate with whitish or rusty hairs; inflorescence flat-topped, to 1.5 dm broad; (Sask. to Labrador, Nfld., and N.S.) . . . . *S. decora*
      4   Lateral leaflets lanceolate to oblong-lanceolate (broadest below the middle), tapering rather gradually to the acute or acuminate apex and commonly more than 3 times as long as broad, more or less glossy above, often serrate nearly to base.
        5   Flowers to 6 mm broad; fruits to 6 mm thick; inflorescence flat-topped, to 1.5 dm broad; winter-buds usually completely glabrous; (Ont. to Nfld. and N.S.) . . . . *S. americana*

5 Flowers to 1 cm broad; fruits to 1 cm thick; winter-buds more or less
pilose and ciliate; (Alaska–B.C. to Sask.) . . . . *S. scopulina*

S. americana Marsh.   American Mountain-Ash.   Cormier
/T/EE/   (Ms)   Damp woods from Ont. (N to the Moose R. S of James Bay; Dutilly, Lepage,
and Duman 1954) to Que. (N to the Côte-Nord; the report N to Richmond Gulf, E Hudson Bay
at ca. 56°10′N, by Dutilly and Lepage 1951a, may refer to *S. decora*), Nfld., N.B., P.E.I., and
N.S., S to Ill., Mich., Tenn., and Ga. [*Pyrus* DC.; *Aucuparia* Nieuwl.; *S. (P.) microcarpa* Pursh].
MAPS (the last two very inaccurate, doubtless through confusion with *S. decora*): Canada Department of Northern Affairs and Natural Resources 1956:210; Preston 1961:248; Hough
1947:239; Hosie 1969:224.

S. aucuparia L.   European Mountain-Ash, Rowan-tree
Eurasian; spread from cult. to roadsides and borders of woods in N. America, as in Alaska
(Wrangell; Hultén 1946), B.C. (Queen Charlotte Is.; Vancouver Is.; Revelstoke), Sask. (Boivin
1966b), Ont. (N to the Ottawa dist.), Que. (N to Hull, Oka, and Montreal), Nfld. (Bay of Islands,
where taken by Waghorne in 1898; GH), P.E.I. (Brackley Point; Charlottetown), and N.S. (Pictou, Cumberland, Colchester, and Halifax counties). [*Pyrus* Gaertn.]. MAP: Hultén 1968b:597.

S. decora (Sarg.) Schneid.   Mountain-Ash
/aST/EE/G/   (Mc)   Rocky woods and shores (ranges of Canadian taxa outlined below), S
to Minn., Ind., Ohio, N.Y., and Mass.; S Greenland. MAPS and synonymy: see below.
1   Leaflets firm, rounded at tip to a short point, whitish beneath; cyme to about 1.5 dm
broad; [*S. (Pyrus) americana* var. *decora* Sarg.; *P. dec.* (Sarg.) Hyl.; *P. sambucifolia*
sensu Waghorne 1895, and Robinson and von Schrenk 1896, not C. & S. (relevant
collections from Whitbourne, Nfld., in CAN and GH), and probably *sensu* Lindsay
1878; reports of the European *S. aucuparia* L. from Labrador by von Schrank 1818,
Meyer 1830, and Schlechtendal 1836, probably refer to this or the following taxon;
S. scopulina sensu Jackson et al. 1922, and Lowe 1943, not Greene; Sask. (N to
Little Bear L. at ca. 54°N; Breitung 1957a), Man. (N to Bear L. at ca. 56°N), Ont. (N to
Big Trout L. at ca. 54°N), Que. (N to Ungava Bay at ca. 58°30′N), S Labrador, Nfld.,
N.B., P.E.I. (Charlottetown; Jones 1939), and N.S.; MAPS (aggregate species;
incomplete northwards): Hosie 1969:226; Canada Department of Northern Affairs
and Natural Resources 1956:208] . . . . var. *decora*
1   Leaflets relatively thin, tapering from near middle to the acuminate tip, merely paler
green beneath; cyme usually less than 1 dm broad; [*S. americana* var. *gr.* Schn., the
type from Greenland; *S. gr.* (Schn.) Löve & Löve; *S. amer. sensu* J.M. Macoun 1895,
not Marsh.; *S. scopulina sensu* R.H. Wetmore, Rhodora 25(289):9. 1923, and Hough
1947, not Greene; *Pyrus (S.) sambucifolia* of early E Canadian reports in part, not C.
& S.; Que. (N to Ungava Bay and the Gaspé Pen.), Labrador (N to Anatolak,
56°33′N), and Nfld.; W Greenland N to 63°10′N, E Greenland N to 60°10′N] . . . .
. . . . var. *groenlandica* (Schneid.) Jones

S. sambucifolia (C. & S.) Roemer
/sT/W/eA/   (Mc)   Rocky slopes of the westernmost Aleutian Is. (*see* Hultén 1946: map 749,
p. 1061); E Asia. [*Pyrus* C. & S.]. MAP: Hultén 1968b:598.

S. scopulina Greene
/ST/WW/   (Mc)   Foothills to alpine elevations from cent. Alaska–Yukon and SW Dist. Mac-
kenzie to B.C.–Alta. and Sask. (Cypress Hills and L. Athabasca; Breitung 1957a, referring here
Raup's report of *S. sitchensis* from L. Athabasca), S to N Calif., N.Mex., and S.Dak. [*Pyrus*
Longyear; *S. alaskana* and *S. andersonii* Jones; *S. angustifolia* Rydb.; *S. dumosa* and *S. sit-
chensis sensu* Raup 1936, not Greene nor Roemer, respectively]. MAP: Hultén 1968b:597.
   Var. *cascadensis* (Jones) Hitchc. (*S. cascadensis* Jones; leaflets rarely if ever more than 11
rather than mostly 13 in number, the stipules relatively persistent) is reported from B.C. by
Hitchcock et al. 1961.

S. sitchensis Roemer

/sT/W/ (Mc) Woods up to subalpine elevations (ranges of Canadian taxa outlined below), s to N Calif., Idaho, and Mont. MAPS and synonymy: *see* below.

1 Leaflets toothed usually at least the whole length of the upper half; [*Pyrus* Piper; *P. ?americana sensu* Richardson 1823, not *S. amer.* Marsh.; *S. tillingii* Gandg.; s Alaska–Yukon (*see* Hultén 1946: map 751, p. 1061; type from Sitka, Alaska) to B.C. (Mt. Selwyn, ca. 56°N; Queen Charlotte Is.; Vancouver Is.; Manning Provincial Park, sw of Princeton) and w Alta. (Lake Louise; Jasper; Lesser Slave L.); MAPS (aggregate species): Hultén 1968*b*:598; Preston 1961:172] . . . . var. *sitchensis*

1 Leaflets toothed mostly only above the middle, sometimes nearly entire; [*S. sambucifolia* var. *grayii* Wenzig; *Pyrus (S.) occidentalis* Wats.; B.C.: Skagit and Chilliwack rivers; CAN; reported from the Cascade Mts. by Henry 1915, and from Vancouver Is. by Carter and Newcombe 1921] . . . . var. *grayii* (Wenzig) Hitchc.

SPIRAEA L. [3319] Spiraea. Spirée

(Ref.: P.A. Rydberg, N. Am. Flora 22:245–52. 1908)

1 Leaves typically densely tomentose-felted beneath, lanceolate to oblong, elliptic, or oval; inflorescence typically a spire-like panicle of short, densely flowered, spike-like racemes; sepals finally reflexed; petals pink to roseate.
  2 Follicles shining, glabrous or merely sparsely ciliate along the suture; (SE Alaska–B.C.) . . . . *S. douglasii*
  2 Follicles typically densely short-tomentose; (Ont. to N.S.) . . . . *S. tomentosa*
1 Leaves not densely tomentose-felted beneath.
  3 Panicle elongate, cylindric or thyrsoid to open-pyramidal, distinctly longer than broad and tapering to the summit; petals white but often tinged with lavender or pink; leaves moderately puberulent to glabrate.
    4 Sepals soon reflexed; follicles glabrous to somewhat pubescent; branches of inflorescence more or less puberulent; (B.C.) . . . . *S. pyramidata*
    4 Sepals merely spreading; follicles glabrous and shining; branches of inflorescence glabrous to thinly pubescent; (Alta. to Nfld. and N.S.) . . . . *S. alba*
  3 Panicle flat-topped, often as broad as or broader than long.
    5 Petals pink to red; sepals erect or spreading; follicles glabrous or sparsely ciliate along the suture; inflorescence and lower leaf-surfaces often puberulent; (s B.C. and sw Alta.) . . . . *S. densiflora*
    5 Petals white or with only a pale-pinkish or lavender tinge.
      6 Sepals finally reflexed; follicles (and whole inflorescence) puberulent; leaves minutely puberulent or glabrate; (N B.C.) . . . . *S. beauverdiana*
      6 Sepals erect or spreading; follicles glabrous or sparsely ciliate along the suture; whole plant glabrous or merely ciliolate along the margins of the leaves and bracts; (B.C. to Sask.) . . . . *S. betulifolia*

S. alba Du Roi Meadow-sweet

/sT/EE/ (N) Wet meadows, swampy ground, and shores (ranges of Canadian taxa outlined below), s to N.Dak., Mo., Ill., Ohio, and Del. MAP and synonymy: *see* below.

1 Inflorescence thinly pubescent; sepals usually obtuse; leaves usually at least 3 times as long as broad; twigs dull brown or yellow-brown; [*S. salicifolia* of Canadian reports in part, not L.; Alta. (Moss 1959), Sask. (N to near Prince Albert), Man. (N to Norway House, off the NE end of L. Winnipeg), Ont. (N to Sandy L. at ca. 53°N, 93°W), and Que. (N to Amos, 48°34′N); MAP: Braun 1935: fig. 3 (incomplete northwards), p. 355] . . . . var. *alba*

1 Inflorescence glabrous or sparingly villous; sepals usually acute; leaves usually less than 3 times as long as broad; twigs red-brown or purple-brown; [var. *septentrionalis* Fern.; *S. salicifolia* var. *lat.* Ait. (*S. lat.* (Ait.) Borkh.); Man. (Boivin 1966*b*), Ont. (N to Renison, s of James Bay at ca. 51°N; Hustich 1955), Que. (N to the George R., Ungava Bay, at 58°15′N, L. Mistassini, and the Côte-Nord; the report from s

Labrador by Fernald *in* Gray 1950, may refer to the Côte-Nord, Que.), Nfld., N.B., P.E.I., and N.S.; introd. with cranberry plants from the East at Ucluelet, Vancouver Is., B.C., whence reported by J.M. Macoun 1913, as *S. salicifolia*] . . . . var. *latifolia* (Ait.) Ahles

S. beauverdiana Schneid.
/aST/W/eA/ (N) Meadows, tundra bogs, thickets, and woods up to alpine elevations from Alaska–Yukon–NW Dist. Mackenzie (N to near the N coasts) to N B.C. (S to ca. 59°N; CAN); E Asia. [*S. stevenii* (Schn.) Rydb.; *S. betulifolia* of Alaska–Yukon reports, not Pall.; *S. chamaedrifolia sensu* Hooker 1832, not L.]. MAP: Hultén 1968*b*:594.

S. betulifolia Pallas
/T/WW/A/ (N) Streambanks, wooded valleys, and rocky hillsides from B.C. (N to near Fort St. John at 56°10′N) to Alta. (N to Beaverlodge, 55°10′N) and SW Sask. (Breitung 1957*a*; Cypress Hills), S to Oreg., Wyo., and S.Dak.; Asia. [Incl. var. *lucida* (Dougl.) Hitchc. (*S. luc.* Dougl.)].

S. densiflora Nutt.
/T/W/ (N) Rocky or wooded slopes up to high elevations from S B.C. (N to Revelstoke and Glacier) and SW Alta. (Waterton Lakes; Breitung 1957*b*, *S. helleri*) to Calif. and Mont. [*S. betulifolia* var. *rosea* Gray; *S. helleri* Rydb.; *S. ?arbuscula* Greene].
Var. *splendens* (Baum.) Hitchc. (*S. spl.* Baum.; plant distinctly puberulent rather than essentially glabrous) is reported from Alta. by Boivin (1966*b*).

S. douglasii Hook.   Western Hardhack
/T/W/ (N) Bogs, swamps, and moist meadows at low to subalpine elevations (ranges of Canadian taxa outlined below), S to N Calif. and Idaho. MAP and synonymy: *see* below.
1 Leaves greyish-tomentose beneath . . . . var. *douglasii*
  2 Flowers white; [type from Vancouver Is., B.C.] . . . . f. *alba*
  2 Flowers pink to deep rose; [B.C.: N to Queen Charlotte Is.] . . . . f. *douglasii*
1 Leaves glabrous or pubescent (but not greyish-tomentose) beneath . . . .
  . . . . var. *menziesii* (Hook.) Presl
  3 Flowers white; [type from Sicamous, B.C.] . . . . f. *pseudosalicifolia* Boivin
  3 Flowers pink to deep rose; [*S. menziesii* Hook.; *S. subvillosa* Rydb.; S Alaska
    Panhandle (*see* Hultén 1946: map 745 (*S. men.), p. 1061) and W B.C.; MAP: Hultén
    1968*b*:594] . . . . f. *menziesii*

S. pyramidata Greene
/T/W/ (N) Streambanks and moist to dry slopes from B.C. (N to Hazelton, ca. 54°50′N) to N Oreg. and Idaho. [Intermediate in characters between *S. betulifolia* and *S. douglasii* and possibly a hybrid of this parentage].

S. tomentosa L.   Hardhack, Steeple-bush.   Thé du Canada
/T/EE/ (N) Sterile meadows and pastures (ranges of Canadian taxa outlined below), S to N Miss. and N.C. MAPS and synonymy: *see* below.
1 Inflorescence an open panicle of relatively distant groups of rather loosely clustered
  flowers; follicles with relatively thin pubescence, becoming glabrate; [*S. rosea* Raf.;
  Man. and Ont.: Fernald *in* Gray 1950] . . . . var. *rosea* (Raf.) Fern.
1 Inflorescence a spire-like panicle of short densely flowered spike-like racemes;
  follicles densely and permanently short-tomentose . . . . var. *tomentosa*
  2 Flowers white; [Charlotte Co., N.B.; Fowler 1885] . . . . f. *albiflora* Macbr.
  2 Flowers roseate; [Ont. (N to the N shore of L. Superior and Matheson, 48°32′N),
    Que. (N to St-Pascal, Kamouraska Co.), N.B., P.E.I., and N.S.; (concerning
    reports from Man.; *see* Scoggan 1957; reports from Nfld. by Reeks 1873, and
    Waghorne 1895, require confirmation); MAPS (aggregate species): Braun 1935:
    fig. 3, p. 355, and 1937: fig. 24, p. 199] . . . . f. *tomentosa*

WALDSTEINIA Willd.   [3363]

W. fragarioides (Michx.) Tratt.   Barren Strawberry
/T/EE/   (Hrr)   Woods, thickets, and clearings from Minn. to Ont. (N to Renfrew and Carleton counties), Que. (N to the mouth of the Chaudière R. near Quebec City; L.-R. Cayouette, Ann. ACFAS 23:97. 1957), and N.B. (Eel River, Carleton Co., where taken by Hay in 1884; NBM; apparently now extinct in that province; not known from P.E.I. or N.S.), S to Mo., Tenn., and Ga. [*Dalibarda* Michx.; *Comaropsis* Nestler].

LEGUMINOSAE (Pulse or Pea Family)

Chiefly herbs, sometimes shrubs or trees, with alternate, stipulate, usually compound leaves (upper leaves sometimes simple; leaves nearly all simple only in *Astragalus spatulatus* and *Cercis,* reduced to spine-tipped petioles in *Ulex*). Flowers mostly perfect, hypogynous to slightly perigynous, usually more or less zygomorphic or papilionaceous, the upper petal (banner or standard) enclosing the smaller lower ones in the bud, the 2 lateral petals (wings) oblique and overlapping the 2 lowest ones, these connivent and forming the keel, which usually encloses the stamens and pistils. Stamens commonly 10 (9 in *Petalostemum*), mostly diadelphous (9 united by their filaments into a tube, 1 free nearly or quite to base), sometimes monadelphous (all united into a tube at least at base), more rarely all free to base. Ovary superior. Fruit a bilaterally symmetrical, unilocular, commonly several-seeded pod (legume), this sometimes articulated into 1 or more 1-seeded articles and then known as a loment. (Incl. Caesalpinaceae, Fabaceae, and Mimosaceae).

1   Trees or shrubs; corolla imperfectly papilionaceous; flowers solitary in the leaf-axils, clustered near the ends of the branch-tips; stamens 10.
   2   Leaves simple or reduced to rigid spine-tipped petioles.
     3   Leaves reduced to rigid spine-tipped petioles on greenish, prominently angled, spiny branches, the spines branching; calyx yellow, hairy, 2-lobed nearly to base, the lobes essentially entire; corolla yellow, to 2 cm long, its keel hairy; stamens monadelphous and dimorphic (the anthers alternately globose and linear); pods hairy, about 12 mm long; (introd. in s B.C.) . . . . *Ulex*
     3   Leaves with expanded green entire blades; plants unarmed; calyx green or purplish, glabrous; corollas and pods glabrous.
       4   Leaves long-petioled, mostly broadly rotund-cordate and short-acuminate, to about 12 cm long and usually somewhat broader; flowers pink to purplish-red (atypically white), about 12 mm long, long-pedicelled in umbel-like clusters along the branches of the previous year; calyx 5-toothed; stamens all free; tree to about 12 m tall; (s Ont.) . . . . [*Cercis*]
       4   Leaves subsessile, oblong-lanceolate, acute or mucronate, to about 3 cm long; flowers yellow, to about 1.5 cm long, short-pedicelled, solitary in the leaf-axils but clustered near the tips of the striate branches to form spike-like false racemes; calyx shallowly 2-lipped (the upper lip deeply 2-cleft, the lower one shortly 3-toothed); stamens monadelphous, dimorphic (the anthers alternately large and small); shrub to about 7 dm tall; (introd.) . . . .
. . . . *Genista*
   2   Leaves compound.
     5   Leaflets 3 (but the upper leaves simple in *C. scoparius*), obovate, about 1 cm long; calyx 2-lipped nearly to middle, the upper lip 2-lobed, the lower lip shallowly 3-toothed; stamens monadelphous, dimorphic (the filaments alternately long and with minute anthers, short and with linear anthers); shrubs to about 3.5 dm tall, the yellow or purplish-tipped flowers to 2.5 cm long, solitary or paired in the upper leaf-axils to form a large terminal raceme; (introd.) . . . . *Cytisus*
     5   Leaflets more than 3, pinnately arranged; stamens not dimorphic.
       6   Leaves mostly 2-pinnate (smaller leaves often 1-pinnate in *Gleditsia*); stamens distinct, their filaments all free to base; flowers regular (the narrow petals equal in size and shape), unisexual, the staminate and pistillate flowers borne on the same or on different plants; trees to over 30 m tall; (introd.).
         7   Stems thornless; leaves unequally 2-pinnate, the ovate, abruptly acuminate leaflets to 3 cm broad; flowers greenish white, softly pubescent, about 1 cm long, long-pedicelled in terminal panicles; calyx 5-cleft above an elongate tube; pods to 2.5 dm long and 4 cm broad, with thick woody valves; (possibly native in s Ont.) . . . . *Gymnocladus*

7 Stem and branches thorny; leaves 1–2-pinnate, the oblong-lanceolate, obtuse or mucronate leaflets at most 1 cm broad; flowers greenish yellow, inconspicuous, short-pedicelled, the staminate ones in dense racemes to 1 dm long, the pistillate racemes looser; calyx short, 3–5-lobed, the lobes spreading; pods to 4.5 dm long, usually twisted, rather papery in texture, the seeds separated by a sweet pulp; (possibly native in s Ont.) . . . . *Gleditsia*

6 Leaves 1-pinnate; stamens united into a tube at base.

8 Flowers reduced to only the standard, blue, violet, or purple, small, in dense spike-like racemes; stamens monadelphous at the very base, otherwise distinct; pods at most 8 mm long . . . . *Amorpha*

8 Flowers normal, distinctly papilionaceous; stamens diadelphous; (introd.).

9 Flowers yellow, solitary in the leaf-axils; leaflets about 5 pairs, oval or obovate, to about 2.5 cm long; plants spiny . . . . *Caragana*

9 Flowers white to pink or rose-purple, in axillary racemes; leaflets up to 25 pairs, elliptic to suborbicular; plants unarmed or spiny or thorny . . . . *Robinia*

1 Plants herbaceous (or the stems merely woody-based or from a more or less woody crown or caudex); flowers usually more or less papilionaceous (nearly regular in *Cassia*); stamens mostly diadelphous (monadelphous in *Anthyllis, Lupinus, Onobrychis,* and often in *Desmodium, Psoralea,* and *Tephrosia;* the tenth stamen lacking in *Petalostemum;* stamens all distinct in *Baptisia, Cassia,* and *Thermopsis*); leaves once-compound (pinnate, palmate, or 3-foliolate, never 2-pinnate).

10 Leaves evenly 1-pinnate, the terminal leaflet sometimes wanting but usually represented by a tendril, the plant thus climbing (leaves completely reduced to tendrils in *Lathyrus aphaca;* tendrils wanting in *L. littoralis* and *Vicia faba*).

11 Flowers nearly regular (not papilionaceous, the usually yellow, only slightly unequal petals spreading); stamens all free to base; sepals 5, distinct nearly or quite to base; leaflets 5 or more pairs; (s Ont.) . . . . *Cassia*

11 Flowers more or less distinctly papilionaceous (the petals differentiated into a standard, lateral wings, and a basal keel); stamens diadelphous.

12 Stipules mostly larger than the leaflets, these oval to oblong, to about 5 cm long, glaucous; calyx-lobes more or less leaf-like; flowers white or coloured; wings of corolla somewhat adherent to the keel; style bearded down one side; pods many-seeded; (introd.) . . . . [*Pisum*]

12 Stipules usually smaller than the leaflets (nearly as large or larger in *Lathyrus japonicus, L. littoralis,* and *L. polyphyllus*); calyx-lobes not leaf-like.

13 Calyx-lobes several times longer than the tube; flowers small, bluish white, 1–3 on short axillary peduncles; wings of corolla somewhat adherent to the keel; style bearded down one side; pods 1–2-seeded; leaflets 4–7 pairs, linear-oblong; (introd.) . . . . [*Lens*]

13 Calyx-lobes shorter than to at most about twice as long as the tube.

14 Leaves not terminated by a tendril, with up to 25 pairs of narrowly oblong leaflets; corolla pale yellow, often spotted, the wing-petals free from the keel; pods to 2 dm long, with thickened margins; erect annual to 3 m tall; (introd.) . . . . [*Sesbania*]

14 Leaves terminated by a tendril (except in *Vicia faba*); corolla often purple, the wing-petals adhering to the middle of the keel; pods smaller.

15 Style filiform, bearded in a tuft or ring at apex below the stigma; wings of corolla adherent to middle of keel; stem often terete . . . *Vicia*

15 Style upwardly dilated and flattened, bearded along the inner side; wings free or nearly so; stem usually angled or winged . . . . *Lathyrus*

10 Leaves odd-pinnate (terminal leaflet present), palmate, or 3-foliolate (but leaves nearly all simple in *Astragalus spatulatus* and the upper ones sometimes reduced to a single leaflet in *Coronilla scorpioides, Lotus purshianus,* and *Oxytropis mertensiana*).

    16 Leaves mostly with more than 3 leaflets (leaves nearly all simple in *Astragalus spatulatus;* leaflets 3 in *A. gilviflorus*) . . . . *GROUP 1*

    16 Leaves mostly with only 3 leaflets (terminal leaves sometimes reduced to a single leaflet in *Coronilla scorpioides* and *Lotus purshianus; Trifolium macrocephalum* usually with at least 5 leaflets) . . . . *GROUP 2* (p. 971)

GROUP 1

1 Flowers in heads or capitate umbels, or solitary; plants neither twining nor climbing.

  2 Flowers usually solitary, white to purplish, long-peduncled, at most 1 cm long; stem-leaves distinctly petioled; leaflets 9–15, rhombic-elliptic, sharply serrate, about 1.5 cm long; pods inflated, the 1 or 2 seeds to about 1 cm broad; stamens diadelphous; (introd.) . . . . *Cicer*

  2 Flowers 2 or more, to 1.5 cm long; stem-leaves apparently sessile; leaflets entire.

    3 Stamens monadelphous, the free tips of the filaments dilated; heads short-peduncled, subtended by 3-cleft bracts; flowers yellow to crimson; pods nearly or quite indehiscent; leaflets 5–11, oblanceolate to oblong; plant appressed-pubescent; (introd.) . . . . *Anthyllis*

    3 Stamens diadelphous; heads long-peduncled, ebracteate; pods to 4 cm long; plants nearly or quite glabrous.

      4 Flowers roseate, up to 15 in a head, their keels tipped with purple; pods indehiscent, 3–7-jointed, each of the 4-angled articles about 6 mm long; leaves with up to 21 oblong to obovate glabrous leaflets 1 or 2 cm long; stipules dilated; (*C. varia;* introd.) . . . . *Coronilla*

      4 Flowers yellow (often tinged with pink, orange, red, or purple), solitary or up to 15 in a head; pods usually dehiscent, not jointed; free tips of alternate anther-filaments usually considerably dilated; leaves with rarely more than 9 ovate-lanceolate to elliptic, oblong, or obovate leaflets less than 2 cm long . . . . *Lotus*

1 Flowers in terminal or axillary spikes or racemes; leaflets entire.

  5 Leaves palmately compound; anthers alternately oblong and roundish; plants neither twining nor climbing; (chiefly B.C. to Man.).

    6 Leaflets 5; stamens diadelphous (sometimes monadelphous); calyx with a long tube about equalling or longer than the longest lobe; flowers blue . . . . *Psoralea*

    6 Leaflets commonly 7 or more; stamens monadelphous; calyx very deeply 2-lipped, the upper lip 2-toothed, the lower lip entire or shallowly 3-lobed; flowers white or yellow to roseate or purplish blue . . . . *Lupinus*

  5 Leaves pinnately compound; anthers uniform in shape.

    7 Leaflets gland-dotted; pods indehiscent or nearly so; plants neither twining nor climbing.

      8 Flowers white, roseate, or purplish, small, obscurely papilionaceous, the corolla reduced to the standard only; stamens 9, monadelphous toward base, 5 of them fertile, the 4 alternating ones modified into petaloid staminodia; pod unarmed, enclosed by the persistent calyx . . . . . *Petalostemum*

      8 Flowers pale yellow, about 1.5 cm long, distinctly papilionaceous; stamens 10, diadelphous for about half their length, the anthers all fertile; pod densely beset with hooked prickles; (B.C. to Ont.) . . . . *Glycyrrhiza*

    7 Leaflets not gland-dotted; stamens 10, usually more or less diadelphous.

      9 Stem twining; calyx very irregular, the lowest lobe elongate, the upper pair of lobes very short, the lateral pair nearly obsolete; flowers brown-purple or mauve, to 13 mm long, the keel-petals strongly curved and horseshoe-

shaped; pod about 1 dm long; leaflets usually 5 or 7, lanceolate to ovate, acute or acuminate, to 6 cm long; rootstocks with numerous tuberous enlargements; (Ont. to N.B. and N.S.) . . . . *Apios*

9 Stem not twining; calyx regular or only slightly oblique, its lobes subequal in size and shape.

  10 Racemes commonly terminal (if sometimes lateral, the peduncle inserted on the side of the stem opposite a leaf), compact, villous, to about 8 cm long; flowers to 2 cm long, the suborbicular standard yellow, the wings pink or pale purple; pods heavily shaggy-villous, to 5 cm long; leaflets 9–27, elliptic to narrowly oblong, to about 3 cm long; plant copiously villous; (s Ont.) . . . . *Tephrosia*

  10 Racemes or spikes peduncled in the leaf-axils.

    11 Pods transversely jointed, the readily disarticulating articles indehiscent; flowers whitish to pale yellow or pink to deep purple, to over 2 cm long; leaflets 7–23, lanceolate to narrowly ovate, to about 3 cm long . . . . *Hedysarum*

    11 Pods not jointed.

      12 Pod short-spiny on the nerves and dorsal suture, broadly oval, to 8 mm long, strongly reticulate, 1–2-seeded; flowers roseate, to 2 cm long; calyx-lobes about 4 mm long, much longer than the tube; stamens monadelphous; leaflets 11–25, oblanceolate to oblong, to about 2 cm long; (introd. in B.C., s Ont., and Que.) . . . . *Onobrychis*

      12 Pod not spiny, linear to ovoid or subglobose; seeds more numerous.

        13 Stamens monadelphous; pods linear, terete; flowers white to purplish-blue, about 1 cm long; bracts setaceous, mostly persistent; leaflets narrowly oblanceolate, to 4 or 5 cm long; plant glabrous or nearly so, to about 1 m tall; (introd. in s Ont.) . . . . [*Galega*]

        13 Stamens diadelphous.

          14 Flowering stems leafless; corolla-keel abruptly narrowed into a slender, straight or curved, cusp-like point . . . . *Oxytropis*

          14 Flowering stems mostly leafy; keel rounded or obtuse (rarely subacute) at apex.

            15 Calyx subtended by a pair of readily deciduous bractlets barely 1 mm long, white-strigose, the tube to 4.5 mm long, the subequal triangular teeth to 2 mm long; flowers on pedicels 3–5 mm long, up to about 15 in loose axillary racemes less than 1 dm long in fruit, dull brick- or tomato-red (drying lavender-brown), the subequal petals to 1.5 cm long, the lateral ones not cohering by their edges; pods membranous, inflated, to 3 cm long and 1.5 cm broad, on stipes up to twice as long as the calyces; leaflets up to 25, to 2 cm long, glabrous above, sparsely strigose beneath; stem to 9 dm tall, from extensive woody rootstocks; (introd. in s Sask.) . . . . *Sphaerophysa*

            15 Calyx usually lacking bractlets; pedicels often less than 3 mm long; lateral petals cohering lightly by their edges; pods sessile or stipitate, of various textures; stems often lower . . . . *Astragalus*

GROUP 2 (see p. 970)

1 Leaflets serrulate; flowers in heads, spikes, or racemes; stamens diadelphous; pods usually indehiscent; plants neither twining nor climbing.

2 Pods becoming strongly curved or spirally coiled (sometimes nearly straight in *M. falcata*), firm-walled, free from the petals and stamens; flowers short-pedicelled, mostly yellow (purplish only in *M. sativa*); terminal leaflet stalked; (introd.) . . . .
. . . . *Medicago*

2 Pods straight or nearly so.
  3 Pod papery, usually shorter than the persistent calyx; petals white or yellow to purple, adherent to the stamen-column and more or less persistent in fruit; terminal leaflet commonly sessile or nearly so . . . . *Trifolium*
  3 Pod firm, free from the usually deciduous corolla; terminal leaflet stalked; (introd.).
    4 Pods short-pointed, otherwise beakless; flowers in lax racemes, white or yellow . . . . *Melilotus*
    4 Pods long-breaked; flowers in racemose heads, blue-and-white or pink-and-white . . . . *Trigonella*

1 Leaflets entire (or those of *Strophostyles* sometimes with 1 or 2 broad shallow lobes).
  5 Stems more or less twining; at least the terminal leaflet long-stalked; stamens diadelphous.
    6 Calyx-lobes 5, the upper pair smallest but distinct; keel-petals spirally coiled at summit; style coiled, bearded on one side; (introd.) . . . . [*Phaseolus*]
    6 Calyx-lobes 4 by fusion of the upper pair; keel-petals not coiled, straight or merely upwardly curved.
      7 Keel-petals nearly straight; calyx-teeth subequal; style beardless; flowers racemose or paniculate, the upper petaliferous ones less than 1.5 cm long and producing several-seeded pods to 4 cm long, the lower apetaliferous ones producing fleshy, chiefly 1-seeded, often subterranean pods; stems very slender; (E Sask. to N.S.) . . . . *Amphicarpa*
      7 Keel-petals strongly curved upward; lowest calyx-tooth the longest; style bearded; flowers all petaliferous; pods to nearly 1 dm long.
        8 Flowers to 2.5 cm long, in elongate fascicled racemes to 3 dm long; keel-petals curved near middle; style bearded at summit; leaflets broadly rhombic-ovate; (introd.) . . . . [*Dolichos*]
        8 Flowers less than 1.5 cm long, in capitate racemes; keel-petals curved above middle; style bearded down 1 side; leaflets ovate or ovate-oblong, commonly with 1 or 2 broad shallow lobes; (S Ont. and SW Que.) . . .
. . . . *Strophostyles*
  5 Stems not twining.
    9 Stamens distinct, their filaments free nearly or quite to base.
     10 Pods flat, linear to linear-oblong, straight to strongly curved, sessile to rather long-stipitate within the calyx, to over 8 cm long; corolla yellow, commonly over 1.5 cm long; stipules linear-lanceolate to subrotund, often leaflet-like, persistent . . . . *Thermopsis*
     10 Pods plump or inflated, to 3 or 4 cm long, nearly straight, long-stipitate within the calyx; corolla white or yellow, to 1.5 cm long; stipules setaceous, soon deciduous; (S Ont.) . . . . *Baptisia*
    9 Stamens mostly diadelphous (one of the 10 stamens free; monadelphous in 3 species of *Desmodium* and sometimes in *Psoralea*).
     11 Flowers creamy or yellow.
      12 Calyx-tube campanulate, the broad lower lip with 3 short triangular teeth, the narrowly triangular upper lip deeply cleft; flowers not more than 5; leaves sessile (the upper ones sometimes simple), glabrous, the terminal leaflet elliptic-oval, to 3 cm long, the lateral leaflets (when present) rotund or oblate, much smaller; stems to about 4 dm tall; (*C. scorpioides*; introd. in N.B. and N.S.) . . . . *Coronilla*
      12 Calyx-tube very short, the densely hairy sepals nearly or quite distinct; flowers more numerous; leaves petioled, 3-foliolate, more or less

pubescent, the leaflets to 4.5 cm long; stems to over 1 m tall; (*L. hirta* and *L. capitata*; s Ont. and s Que.) . . . . *Lespedeza*
11 Flowers white, pink, blue, or purple.
  13 Flowers solitary and subsessile in the leaf-axils or solitary (rarely 2) on axillary peduncles, cream or yellow, usually tinged with red or purple; annuals; (*L. denticulatus, L. micranthus,* and *L. purshianus*) . . . . *Lotus*
  13 Flowers in capitate or elongate racemes or spikes; leaves petioled.
    14 Leaflets gland-dotted (the glands often obscured by the dense appressed-silvery-silky pubescence in *P. argophylla*); flowers white or dark blue (the banner yellowish green in *P. physodes*), to about 12 mm long, sessile or short-pedicelled; pods indehiscent; (western species) . . . . *Psoralea*
    14 Leaflets not gland-dotted.
      15 Pods jointed, the 1-seeded articles indehiscent; calyx 2-lipped, the upper lip entire or shallowly cleft, the lower lip usually deeply 2-cleft; (eastern species) . . . . *Desmodium*
      15 Pods not jointed.
        16 Calyx nearly regular, 5-toothed; flowers in dense or interrupted spikes or racemes, often cleistogamous; pods oval to elliptic, 1-seeded, indehiscent; perennials; (s Ont.) . . . . *Lespedeza*
        16 Calyx 2-lipped, the 2 upper teeth united to or above the middle; flowers inconspicuous, in clusters on the continuous rachis; pods 2–4-seeded, dehiscent; annual; (introd.) . . . . [*Glycine*]

AMORPHA L. [3707]

1 Leaflets conspicuously gland-dotted beneath, to about 1 cm long; petioles to 5 mm long; racemes solitary at the tips of the branches; plant essentially glabrous, less than 1 m tall; (s Man.) . . . . *A. nana*
1 Leaflets not gland-dotted; racemes paniculate-clustered.
  2 Plant densely white-villous, rarely as much as 1 m tall; pods white-villous, long-beaked, about 4 mm long; petioles 1 or 2 mm long; leaflets subsessile, to 1.5 cm long; (s Man. to w Ont.) . . . . *A. canescens*
  2 Plant sparingly pubescent or glabrate, to over 2 m tall; pods strongly resinous-dotted, often curved, to 8 mm long; leaves long-petioled; leaflets distinctly stalked, to about 4 cm long; (s Man.; introd. in Ont. and Que.) . . . . *A. fruticosa*

A. canescens Nutt. Leadplant
/T/WW/ (N) Dry sandy prairies and hillsides from s Man. (N to Brokenhead, about 30 mi NE of Winnipeg; reports from Sask. require confirmation) and w Ont. (Boivin 1966b; a s Ont. collection in TRT from Guelph, Wellington Co., probably represents a casual waif) to N.Mex., Tex., Ark., and Ind.

A. fruticosa L. False Indigo, Indigo-bush
/T/EE/ (N (Mc)) Dry prairies, grassy slopes, and thickets (ranges of Canadian taxa outlined below), s to N Mexico, Tex., La., and N Fla. MAP and synonymy: *see* below.
1 Leaflets mostly elliptic-obovate (broadest above the middle), to 4 times as long as broad, narrowed to base; pubescence appressed; [*A. ang.* (Pursh) Boynton; *A. fragrans* Sweet; SE Man. (N to Selkirk, about 20 mi NE of Winnipeg; concerning an early report from Sask., *see* Breitung 1957a); introd. in SW Que. (Vaudreuil, near Montreal). MAP: Fassett 1939:49] . . . . var. *angustifolia* Pursh
1 Leaflets mostly broadly elliptic (broadest near the middle), rarely over twice as long as broad, about equally rounded at both ends; pubescence spreading; [E U.S.A. only; a garden-escape in E Canada, as in Que. (Montreal; Grosse-Ile, Montmagny Co.) and s Ont. (Guelph, Wellington Co., and Burlington Beach, Wentworth Co.; TRT)] . . . . var. *fruticosa*

A. nana Nutt.   Fragrant False Indigo
/T/WW/   (N)   Dry prairies from s Man. (N to Oak Point, about 50 mi NW of Winnipeg; reports from Sask. require confirmation, perhaps (as in the case of *A. canescens*) being based upon early Bourgeau collections in the old "District of Assiniboia" before the establishment of the present-day boundaries) to Kans. and Iowa. [*A. microphylla* Pursh].

AMPHICARPA Ell.   [3860]

A. bracteata (L.) Fern.   Hog-Peanut
/T/(X)/   (Hpr)   Damp woodlands (ranges of Canadian taxa outlined below), s to Mont., Tex., La., and Fla. MAPS and synonymy: *see* below.
1   Pubescence pale; stem capillary, retrorse-appressed-pubescent or sparingly hirsute; leaflets minutely strigose on both surfaces, mostly not over 6 cm long; flowers usually white to pale lilac; bracts to 2.5 mm long, mostly surpassed by the pedicels; aerial pods glabrous or strigose on the sides, to 3 cm long, the sutures ascending-pubescent below the middle, the stylar beak to 3 mm long; [*Glycine* L.; *G. (A.) monoica* L.; *A. chamaecaulis* Boivin & Raymond; E Sask. (D. Löve, Can. J. Bot. 37(4):565. 1959; not listed by Breitung 1957a), s Man. (N to Brandon, Portage la Prairie, and Winnipeg), Ont. (N to the Kaministikwia R. w of Thunder Bay and near Ottawa), Que. (N to L. Timiskaming at ca. 47°20′N and Ste-Anne-de-Beaupré, Montmorency Co.), N.B., and N.S.; MAP: Fassett 1939:125] . . . . var. *bracteata*
1   Pubescence sordid or tawny; stem stouter, densely villous-hirsute with mostly reflexed hairs (as also the petioles); leaflets more coarsely pubescent, to 1 dm long; flowers often deeper purple; bracts longer; aerial pods villous-hirsute, to 4 cm long, the sutures retrorse-pubescent below the middle, the stylar beak to 5 mm long; [*Glycine comosa* L.; *A. pitcheri* T. & G.; s Man. (near Portage la Prairie according to Fassett's map), s Ont. (N to Stormont Co.; Dore and Gillett 1955), and Que. (N to near Quebec City; Fassett's map); MAP: Fassett 1939:130] . . . . var. *comosa* (L.) Fern.

ANTHYLLIS L.   [3691]

A. vulneraria L.   Lady's-fingers
European; locally introd. into clover fields and waste places in N. America, as in s Ont. (Oxford, Waterloo, and Wellington counties), E Que. (slaty banks of the Restigouche R. near Matapédia, Gaspé Pen.; CAN; MT), and N.B. (Newcastle, Northumberland Co.; NSPM; MT). [Incl. var. *maritima* Koch].

APIOS Medic.   [3874]

A. americana Medic.   Groundnut.   Patates en chapelet
/T/EE/   (Gst)   Rich thickets from Ont. (N to the Ottawa dist.) to Que. (N to St-Vallier, E of Quebec City), N.B., and N.S., s to Colo., Tex., La., and Fla. [*Glycine (A.) apios* L.; *A. tuberosa* Moench). MAP: Fassett 1939:127 (the dot indicating a station in P.E.I. should apparently be deleted)].

ASTRAGALUS L.   [3766]   Milk-Vetch, Locoweed, Rattlepod

(Ref.: Barneby 1964; P.A. Rydberg, N. Am. Flora 24:251–462. 1929)
1   Pods glabrous or nearly so at least at maturity.
  2   Pods sessile within the calyx-tube or on a short stipe rarely over 1 mm long . . . .
      . . . .*GROUP 1*
  2   Pods stipitate within the calyx-tube, the stipe about equalling to much exceeding the calyx; flowers white to yellowish (sometimes pink-tinged), the keel often purple-tipped; pubescence (when present) consisting of basifixed hairs . . . .
      . . . .*GROUP 2* (p. 975)
1   Pods distinctly pubescent.

3   Pods sessile within the calyx-tube or on a short stipe at most 1 mm long and much shorter than the tube (*A. bourgovii, A. lentiginosus,* and *A. robbinsii* may sometimes key out here) . . . . *GROUP 3* (p. 976)

3   Pods stipitate within the calyx-tube (the stipe often equalling or surpassing the calyx), usually arcuate-spreading to pendulous or reflexed (ascending in *A. bourgovii* and sometimes in *A. robbinsii*), 1-locular (the lower septum mostly not prominently intruded) . . . . *GROUP 4* (p. 980)

GROUP 1

1   Pubescence dolabriform (the hairs closely appressed and 2-branched, attached between the middle and one end; *A. miser* may sometimes key out here); flowers white or ochroleucous, to 18 mm long, up to about 150 in a crowded raceme, the peduncles mostly about equalling the leaves; calyx to 9 mm long, the minutely strigose to glabrous tube about twice as long as the linear-lanceolate teeth; pods completely 2-locular, erect, cartilaginous-woody, to 2 cm long and 5 mm broad; leaflets ovate-lanceolate to oblong, up to 14 pairs, to 4 cm long and 18 mm broad; stems erect or decumbent, to 8 dm tall; plant greenish- to greyish-strigillose but becoming glabrate; (B.C. to Que.) . . . . *A. canadensis*

1   Pubescence (when present) consisting of simple basifixed hairs; flowers white (the keel usually purplish-tipped), usually less than 35 in a raceme.

  2   Pods very fleshy (the walls at least 2 mm thick, hard and bony when dry), indehiscent, subglobose, nearly terete, almost completely 2-locular, to 2.5 cm long; flowers to 2.5 cm long, up to 20 in a raceme shorter than to about equalling the subtending leaf; calyx more or less black-strigose, the tube to 2/3 the corolla-length, the lanceolate teeth to 1/3 the tube-length; leaflets rather fleshy, elliptic to oblong-oblanceolate, up to 10 pairs, to 2 cm long, minutely strigillose beneath; stems prostrate to ascending; (SE B.C. to S Man.) . . . . *A. crassicarpus*

  2   Pods not fleshy, dehiscent, the thin walls membranous to chartaceous or cartilaginous.

    3   Leaflets 11–19, to 1.5 cm long; corolla to 18 mm long, the calyx about half as long; pods to 2 or 3 cm long, usually somewhat arcuate, 2-locular for most of their length by the intrusion of the lower suture but prolonged into a sterile, unilocular, compressed and flattened beak; plant glabrous to strigose, the stems to 4 dm long; (S B.C.). . . . . *A. lentiginosus*

    3   Leaflets at most 11, to 3 cm long; corolla not over 14 mm long, the calyx about half as long; pods 1-locular.

      4   Pods pendulous, laterally compressed, linear to linear-oblanceolate, to 3 cm long and 4 mm broad; flowers up to 10 in a loose raceme surpassing the subtending leaf; leaflets linear to oblong or oval; (var. *serotinus*; S B.C. and SW Alta.) . . . . *A. miser*

      4   Pods erect-ascending, inflated-ovoid, to 2 cm long and 1.5 cm thick; flowers usually more numerous in a rather crowded raceme scarcely surpassing the subtending leaf; leaflets oblong or elliptic; (S Man. and S Ont.) . . . . *A. neglectus*

GROUP 2 (see p. 974)

1   Pods linear, partly to nearly completely 2-locular, coriaceous, pendulous, short-beaked, the straight or slightly curved body to over 2.5 cm long and about 5 mm broad; racemes at first rather dense (with up to 50 nodding, white or pinkish flowers), elongating in fruit to about the length of the peduncle (this usually shorter than the subtending leaf); calyx about 1 cm long (including teeth about half the tube-length); leaflets up to 15 pairs, to 3.5 cm long and 1 cm broad.

  2   Plant copiously greyish-villous; calyx black-hairy; flowers to 2.5 cm long; pods nearly completely 2-locular (deeply cordate in cross-section); (Alta. and Sask.) . . . . . .
. . . . *A. drummondii*

    2 Plant strigose or glabrate; calyx long-white-strigose; flowers about 1.5 cm long; pods triangular-compressed, with concave sides, only partially 2-locular (the septum very narrow); (Sask.) . . . .*A. racemosus*

1 Pods usually broader in outline (if linear, the calyx at most 6 or 7 mm long), completely 1-locular or the lower suture sometimes intruded as a very narrow partition.

    3 Calyx to 14 mm long (the tube and linear-lanceolate teeth subequal), glabrous or very sparsely blackish-strigillose; flowers creamy white to dirty yellow, spreading, to about 2 cm long, up to 15 in a rather loose raceme about equalling the subtending leaf; pods coriaceous, ascending, obcompressed, the lunate body to 3 cm long and nearly 1 cm thick, sometimes more or less purplish-mottled; stipe stout, about equalling the calyx, jointed to the fruit; leaflets up to 12 pairs, to 2 cm long and 1 cm broad; plant glabrous to sparsely strigillose-puberulent; (s B.C.) . . . .*A. beckwithii*

    3 Calyx usually not over 6 mm long; pods papery, chartaceous, or membranous, spreading, drooping, or reflexed, often more or less compressed laterally.

        4 Pods asymmetrical and more or less falcate-lunate, pendulous, strongly compressed, to 3 cm long and 5 mm broad, membranous; flowers whitish with a purple keel to purplish overall; pedicels at most about 2 mm long; peduncles mostly equalling or surpassing the leaves; leaflets narrowly lanceolate to oblong-elliptic; (B.C. to sw Man.; Que.) . . . .*A. aboriginum*

        4 Pods nearly symmetrical, straight or only slightly curved; flowers yellowish white or pinkish-tinged, spreading or drooping.

            5 Calyx-teeth linear-lanceolate, to about 2 mm long and about equalling the black-(white-)strigillose tube; flowers to 9 mm long (the keel usually somewhat purple-tipped), up to 20 in a very loose raceme usually much longer than the peduncle, their pedicels to 3 mm long; peduncles mostly shorter than the leaves; pods to 1.5 cm long, linear-elliptic, often finely mottled, very strongly compressed, the stipe up to twice the length of the calyx; leaflets up to 6 or 7 pairs, linear to oblong-elliptic, glabrous or sparingly strigose beneath or on both sides, to 2 cm long and 5 mm broad; (B.C. to Man.) . . . .*A. tenellus*

            5 Calyx-lobes broadly ovate or depressed-triangular, to barely 1 mm long; pods usually longer and not mottled; flowers to about 1.5 cm long, more uniformly yellowish white.

                6 Pods strongly compressed, greenish, linear to narrowly oblong-elliptic, to 3.5 cm long and 6 mm broad, the stipe to 1.5 cm long; calyx to 6 mm long, black-(white-)strigillose; flowers up to 30 in a lax raceme nearly equalling the peduncle in fruit, their pedicels to 6 mm long; peduncles usually much surpassing the subtending leaves; leaflets linear to linear-oblanceolate, up to 12 pairs, to 2 cm long and 2 mm broad; plant strigillose; (s B.C.) . . . .*A. filipes*

                6 Pods inflated and nearly terete, ellipsoid, to 3 cm long and 1 cm broad, the stipe not more than twice as long as the calyx; calyx to 5 mm long, nearly glabrous except for ciliation of the lobes; flowers up to 40 in a rather loose raceme, their pedicels to 1 cm long; peduncles usually shorter than the subtending leaves; leaflets broader in outline, up to 8 pairs, to 5 cm long and 1.5 cm broad; plant glabrous or the leaves (usually) sparsely pilose beneath; (B.C. to E Que.) . . . .*A. americanus*

GROUP 3 (*see* p. 975)

1 Pubescence consisting chiefly of dolabriform hairs (closely appressed and 2-branched, attached between the middle and one end; *A. miser* may sometimes key out here).

    2 Leaflets tipped with a short pale spine 2 or 3 mm long, mostly 5 (sometimes 7), subulate, rigid, about 1 cm long and 0.5 mm broad, greyish-strigose; flowers

   sessile or very short-peduncled; corolla yellowish white with a purple tinge, to 7
   mm long; calyx-tube and its subulate-filiform teeth each about 2 mm long; pods
   elliptic, 1-locular, laterally compressed, coriaceous, indehiscent, to 7 mm long;
   stems diffusely spreading and intricately branched from a densely caespitose
   caudex; (s Alta. and sw Sask.) . . . . *A. kentrophyta*
2 Leaflets not spinulose-tipped.
   3 Leaves simple (or some of them with 3, rarely 5, leaflets), linear-oblanceolate,
      silky-canescent, to about 4 cm long and 3 mm broad, clustered at the ends of
      the densely caespitose caudices; scapes to about 6 cm tall, with up to
      7 flowers; corolla bluish purple, to 9 mm long; pods oblong, gradually acute,
      1-locular, erect, sessile, white-strigose, to 12 mm long; (s Alta. and s Sask.) . . . . . .
      . . . . *A. spatulatus*
   3 Leaves compound.
      4 Leaflets usually 3, appressed-silky on both surfaces, narrowly
         oblanceolate, 1 or 2 cm long; racemes mostly with only 1 or 2 flowers,
         subsessile in the leaf-axils at the ends of the branching caudex; corolla
         yellow (the keel often purple-tipped), 2 or 3 cm long; calyx-tube to 1.5 cm
         long, the teeth 3 or 4 mm long; pods broadly ovoid, 1-locular, coriaceous,
         indehiscent, silky-villous, to 1 cm long; plant densely caespitose, nearly
         stemless, usually less than 5 cm tall; (s Alta. to sw Man.) . . . . *A. gilviflorus*
      4 Leaflets at least 5, pinnately arranged.
         5 Corolla greenish white or ochroleucous to cream-colour or sulphur-
            yellow (sometimes slightly tinged with lavender or purple).
            6 Leaves with rarely more than 6 pairs of leaflets, the leaflets
               commonly less than 2 cm long; pods 1-locular, to about 3.5 cm long
               and 8 mm broad; racemes of earlier (normal) flowers consisting of
               up to 17 rather crowded flowers to 17 mm long on a peduncle to
               about 1 dm long; later flowers cleistogamous, subsessile or short-
               peduncled in the leaf-axils; plant silvery-pubescent, to about 1 dm
               tall; (B.C. to sw Man.) . . . . *A. lotiflorus*
            6 Leaves with up to 17 pairs of leaflets, these to 3.5 cm long; pods
               2-locular, to about 2 cm long and 5 mm broad; flowers all normal, in
               dense, many-flowered racemes on peduncles to 2 dm long; plants
               greyish-strigulose, to over 8 dm tall; (varieties; B.C.) . . . . . . *A. canadensis*
         5 Corolla purplish.
            7 Leaflets up to 12 pairs, narrowly oblong, to 2.5 cm long; flowers
               pale purple (sometimes creamy or whitish), to 18 mm long,
               numerous in dense racemes, the peduncles often much shorter
               than the leaves; pods partially 2-locular, membranous, to 12 mm
               long, densely white-strigose; plant cinereous-pubescent to glabrate;
               (B.C. to Man.; introd. in w Ont.) . . . . *A. adsurgens*
            7 Leaflets rarely more than 7 pairs, elliptic to oblong-elliptic, to 1.5 cm
               long; flowers rose-purple (petals sometimes yellow at base), to 2.5
               cm long, up to 9 in a raceme; peduncles to about 1 dm long and
               about equalling the subtending leaves; pods 1-locular, coriaceous,
               to 2.5 cm long, strigose; plant low, caespitose, silvery-pubescent;
               (Alta. to sw Man.) . . . . *A. missouriensis*
1 Pubescence (when present) consisting of simple basifixed hairs.
   8 Pods densely greyish-woolly or silky-villous, 1-locular, coriaceous,
      obcompressed, straight or more or less lunate, to 2.5 cm long; flowers dull white
      or yellowish white to very pale lavender (the keel purple-tipped), 2 or 3 cm long,
      up to 10 in racemes that are subsessile or on peduncles sometimes surpassing
      their subtending leaves; calyx to 2/3 the corolla-length, the linear-lanceolate
      teeth to half the length of the tube; leaflets up to 9 pairs, elliptic to obovate or
      suborbicular, acute to rounded at apex, to 2 cm long; whole plant greyish-woolly;
      (B.C. to sw Sask.) . . . . *A. purshii*
   8 Pods less heavily pubescent (usually merely more or less strigose).

9 Pods mostly spreading-ascending to erect.
  10 Corolla whitish or ochroleucous (often drying yellowish); racemes with up to about 30 flowers; pods 2-locular at least in the lower half, pubescent with white, black, or mixed white and black hairs, to about 1.5 cm long; leaflets to about 3.5 cm long; plants more or less strigillose with appressed to somewhat ascending hairs less than 1 mm long.
    11 Stems to 7 dm tall; leaflets commonly more than 17; peduncles to about 1 dm long, usually much shorter than the leaves; racemes at most about 5 cm long in fruit; calyx to 9 mm long; pods ascending or spreading, with up to 14 seeds; (introd. in Alta. and Man.) .... *A. cicer*
    11 Stems to 4(5) dm tall; leaflets at most 15; peduncles to about 2 dm long, the longest ones greatly surpassing their subtending leaves; racemes elongating to over 1 dm in fruit; calyx less than 7 mm long; pods erect, with usually not more than 8 seeds; (Alaska–Yukon) .... *A. williamsii*
  10 Corolla pink or pale lavender to purple; racemes with usually not more than 15 flowers; pods rarely over 12 mm long; leaflets at most 9 pairs, mostly less than 2 cm long; stems to about 4 dm tall.
    12 Pods completely 2-locular (deeply cordate in cross-section), coriaceous, densely pubescent above the glabrate base with straight or curly, white, silky hairs; calyx to about 12 mm long; corolla usually purplish or the wings whitish, to about 2 cm long, the banner only slightly upturned; peduncles either longer or shorter than the leaves; (B.C. to Man.; w James Bay) .... *A. agrestis*
    12 Pods 1-locular, membranous or chartaceous; calyx to 7 mm long; corolla-banner strongly upturned.
      13 Calyx to 7 mm long, strigose with black or mixed black and white hairs; corolla reddish lilac to pink-purple, the banner strongly ascending; all but the uppermost peduncles usually surpassing their subtending leaves; (N Alta.; cent. Man.; NW Nfld.) .... *A. bodinii*
      13 Calyx to about 4 mm long, densely strigose with white or mixed white and black hairs; corolla pink to magenta-purple, the erect banner prominently purple-veined; peduncles rarely surpassing their subtending leaves; (s B.C.) .... *A. microcystis*
9 Pods mostly horizontally spreading to strongly deflexed.
  14 Flowers to over 2 cm long, uniformly yellowish white, up to 30 in a compact to rather loose raceme; calyx-tube black-strigose, to 6 mm long, the teeth to 3 mm long; pedicels to 5 mm long; peduncles about equalling their subtending leaves; pods fleshy and nearly solid (drying woody), oblong-ovoid, nearly terete, 1-locular, to 2 cm long and 7 mm thick, abruptly narrowed to a sharply upcurved beak about 5 mm long; leaflets up to 8 pairs, linear, to 6 cm long and about 1.5 mm broad; plant greyish-strigillose; (s Alta. to s Man.) .... *A. pectinatus*
  14 Flowers to about 12 mm long, white to purple-tinged or dark purple (often white in *A. vexilliflexus,* but the keel then purple-tipped); pods membranous or chartaceous, sometimes becoming leathery but scarcely woody; leaflets mostly broader in outline (if sometimes linear, not over 3 cm long).
    15 Flowers at most 5 in a short loose raceme with an axis about 1 cm long, white with a purple-tipped keel, to 12 mm long; calyx-tube to about 3.5 mm long, the teeth to 2.5 mm long; pods pendulous, 1-locular, somewhat obcompressed, to about 1.5 cm long and 4 mm broad, slightly curved; peduncles filiform, mostly about half the length of their subtending leaves; leaflets mostly lance-elliptic, to 1.5 cm long, up to 13 pairs; lower stipules connate; plant bright green and thinly strigillose, delicate and diffuse, the stems arising at intervals from a subterranean rhizome .... [*A. leptaleus*]

15 Flowers usually more numerous in a longer raceme; stipules often all
free to base; stems arising close together from the root-crown or
caudex.

  16 Pods nearly completely 2-locular (broadly cordate in cross-section),
reflexed, to 8 mm long and 3.5 mm broad, their papery valves
greenish or minutely ashy-tomentose; flowers to 9 mm long, white
or purple-tinged or -veined, commonly drying yellowish, up to 35 in
a loose raceme; calyx to 5.5 mm long, the teeth about as long as to
considerably longer than the tube; peduncles to 6.5 cm long,
usually shorter than their subtending leaves; leaflets linear to linear-
elliptic or narrowly oblong, to 1.5(2) cm long, up to 10 pairs; plant
greyish-strigose to woolly or silky . . . .[A. lyallii]

  16 Pods 1-locular or only slightly 2-locular; calyx-teeth rarely over half
the length of the calyx-tube.

    17 Racemes at most loosely 10-flowered, on peduncles shorter than
or only slightly surpassing their subtending leaves; pods laterally
compressed.

      18 Pods linear to linear-oblanceolate, to 3 cm long and 4 mm
broad; flowers to 12 mm long, mostly white, the banner and
wings bluish-veined, the keel usually purple-tipped; calyx to
4(6) mm long, the triangular teeth about 1/2 the length of the
tube; leaflets linear to oblong or oval, to 3 cm long, up to 8
pairs, more or less ashy or silvery; (SE B.C. and SW Alta.) . . . .
. . . . .A. miser

      18 Pods narrowly oblong-elliptic, to 11 mm long and 3 mm
broad; flowers to 8(10) mm long, ochroleucous and with a
purple keel to rather uniformly deep lavender-purple; calyx to
about 4 mm long, the linear-lanceolate teeth about 2/3 the
length of the tube; leaflets linear- to oblong-elliptic, to 12 mm
long, up to 6 pairs; plant greyish-strigillose and often matted;
(SE B.C. to SW Sask.) . . . . .A. vexilliflexus

    17 Racemes usually more than 10-flowered, on peduncles often up
to about twice the length of their subtending leaves.

      19 Pods to 2 cm long, spreading to moderately reflexed (or the
lower ones strongly reflexed), 1-locular (neither suture
intruded), subterete, acute at each end, straight or slightly
arcuate, somewhat leathery, partially filled with spongy
filaments that dry to fibrous material attached to the walls;
calyx to about 5 mm long, strigillose with white and black
hairs; stems erect to decumbent-based from a branched
caudex; (SE B.C. to S Man.). . . . . .A. flexuosus

      19 Pod rarely over 10 or 11 mm long, reflexed, strongly
compressed, 1-locular but the lower suture conspicuously
intruded; flowers to about 8 mm long.

        20 Pods fleshy but becoming leathery and transversely
rugose-reticulate, to about 8 mm long, when dry filled
with fibrous material; calyx less than 3.5 mm long,
strigillose with white (rarely a few black) hairs; banner of
corolla strongly upturned; stems often rather deeply
buried and rhizome-like at base; (Sask.) . . . . .A. gracilis

        20 Pods rather firmly papery, to about 12 mm long; calyx to
over 5 mm long, strigillose with black or mixed black and
whitish (rarely all white) hairs; banner of corolla only
slightly upturned; stems from a superficial, usually
branched caudex; (transcontinental) . . . . .A. eucosmus

GROUP 4 (see p. 975)

1 Flowers lilac to blue or purple; pods membranous, their stipes shorter than or only slightly surpassing the calyx-teeth.

　　2 Pods ascending, blackish-strigillose, to 1.5 cm long and 3 mm broad; flowers blue-purple, to 1 cm long; calyx-tube about 3 mm long, its teeth about as long; racemes loosely 5–10-flowered, the peduncles usually at least twice as long as their subtending leaves; leaflets to 1(2) cm long, 5–9 pairs; plant very finely strigillose; (S B.C. and SW Alta.). . . . .*A. bourgovii*

　　2 Pods mostly arcuate-spreading to pendulous or strongly deflexed.

　　　　3 Calyx strongly gibbous at base, to 9 mm long, the slender teeth about equalling the tube; flowers usually purplish (occasionally pale lavender to nearly white), mostly drooping, to 1.5 cm long, up to about 150 in racemes on peduncles up to twice the length of the subtending leaves; pods strongly obcompressed (nearly twice as thick as wide), with a groove on either side of the ventral (upper) suture, white-puberulent (sometimes glabrate), to about 2 cm long and 2 mm broad, the stipe about equalling the calyx-tube; leaflets to 2.5 cm long and 8 mm broad, up to 13 pairs; plant greenish, sparingly soft-strigillose; (Alta. to Man.) . . . .*A. bisulcatus*

　　　　3 Calyx nearly symmetrical at base, usually black-strigillose (sometimes with an admixture of white hairs), the tube about 3 mm long, the teeth about half as long; flowers mostly ascending (the lower ones often drooping), to about 12 mm long, mostly less than 25 in a raceme, the peduncles less than twice as long as their subtending leaves; pods more or less laterally compressed.

　　　　　　4 Flowering stems erect to decumbent-based; flowers violet to purple; calyx to 8 mm long; leaflets to 2.5 cm long, ashy-strigillose on both surfaces, usually not more than 6 pairs; (B.C. and Alta.; E Que., S Labrador, and Nfld.) . . . .*A. robbinsii*

　　　　　　4 Flowering stems depressed, branching at base and forming an intricate mat; flowers purple, or lilac with a purple keel; calyx usually less than 6 mm long; pods to 1.5 cm long; leaflets to 1.5 cm long, up to 11 pairs; plant sparsely to densely strigillose or silky but usually greenish; (transcontinental) . . . .*A. alpinus*

1 Flowers white or greenish white to ochroleucous or greenish yellow (*A. robbinsii* may sometimes be sought here); pod-stipe usually surpassing the calyx-teeth (but not in *A. robbinsii*).

　　5 Calyx-teeth broad and short, at most about 1.5 mm long and not over 1/4 the length of the tube; pods to over 3 cm long.

　　　　6 Pods strongly curved at maturity, laterally compressed; racemes closely to laxly flowered; pedicels at most 3 mm long.

　　　　　　7 Flowers ochroleucous, to about 2 cm long; calyx gibbous at base, to over 1 cm long, the lance-ovate teeth barely 1 mm long; pods membranous, reflexed, to 3.5 cm long and 5 mm broad, coiled in a half to a full circle at maturity, the stipe at least twice as long as the calyx; racemes with up to 40 flowers, on peduncles about equalling to twice as long as their subtending leaves; leaflets to about 1.5 cm long and 7 mm broad, up to 8 pairs; plant minutely greyish-strigillose; (S ?B.C.) . . . .[*A. curvicarpus*]

　　　　　　7 Flowers white to greenish white (the wings often pale purple, the keel usually purple-tipped), less than 1.5 cm long; calyx nearly symmetrical at base, to 7 mm long, the upper 2 teeth noticeably broader than the other 3; pods fleshy, drying leathery-cartilaginous, pendulous, curving to a half circle and often purple-mottled at maturity, to 3 cm long and 9 mm broad, the stipe to 2 cm long; racemes with up to 30 flowers, on peduncles about equalling their subtending leaves; leaflets to 3 cm long and 4 mm broad, up to 10 pairs; plant sparsely to densely silvery-strigillose; (S B.C.) . . . .
. . . .*A. sclerocarpus*

6 Pods permanently straight or nearly so, pendulous or spreading, membranous; calyx-teeth barely 1 mm long; pedicels to 1 cm long; plants greenish.

    8 Flowers cream-colour, to 13 mm long, spreading or spreading-ascending on pedicels to 6 mm long, up to 30 in lax racemes much elongating in fruit and nearly equalling the peduncles, these usually much surpassing their subtending leaves; calyx to 6 mm long, black-strigillose (sometimes with an admixture of white hairs); pods strongly laterally compressed, to 3.5 cm long and 6 mm broad, the stipe to 1.5 cm long; leaflets linear to linear-oblanceolate, to 2 cm long and 2 mm broad, up to 12 pairs; plant strigillose; (s B.C.) . . . . *A. filipes*

    8 Flowers ochroleucous, to 1.5 cm long, mostly reflexed on pedicels to 1 cm long, up to about 40 in loose racemes on peduncles usually shorter than their subtending leaves; calyx to 5 mm long, nearly glabrous except for ciliation of the teeth; pods nearly terete, to 3 cm long and 1 cm thick, the stipe to twice as long as the calyx; leaflets to 5 cm long and 1.5 cm broad, up to 8 pairs; plant glabrous or very sparingly pilose; (Alaska–Yukon–Dist. Mackenzie–N B.C.) . . . . *A. umbellatus*

5 Calyx-teeth subulate or linear to linear-lanceolate or lance-deltoid, usually at least 1/3 as long as the tube; flowers to about 1.5 cm long; pods pendulous, somewhat compressed; all but the shortest upper peduncles usually surpassing the leaves.

    9 Pods nearly symmetrical, straight or only slightly incurved, to about 2.5 cm long and 3.5 mm broad, the valves becoming leathery and impressed-reticulate, the stipe to about 1.5 cm long; flowers mostly reflexed; calyx to 1 cm long, white-strigose (or sometimes with some black hairs); corolla-banner only slightly upturned, considerably shorter than the wings; leaves with up to 10(12) pairs of linear to oblanceolate or oblong leaflets; plant finely crisp-puberulent or -strigulose; (s B.C.) . . . . *A. collinus*

    9 Pods rather strongly asymmetrical, falcate-lunate or semiovate, their valves membranous or chartaceous; flowers at first ascending or horizontally spreading, later reflexed; calyx rarely over 8 mm long; corolla-banner strongly upturned, considerably longer than the wings.

        10 Leaves with at most 7 pairs of linear-lanceolate to oblong-elliptic leaflets; calyx usually black-hairy; pods to 3 cm long and 4 mm broad, on stipes to 8 mm long; (B.C. to Man.; Que.) . . . . *A. aboriginum*

        10 Leaves with up to 17(19) pairs of elliptic to oval or oblong leaflets; calyx usually white-hairy; pods to about 4 cm long and 2 cm broad, more or less bladdery-inflated, on stipes to over 1.5 cm long; (introd. on Vancouver Is.) . . . . [*A. trichopodus*]

A. aboriginum Richards.
/aST/D/EA/ (Ch (Hp)) Streambanks, plains, and foothills to subalpine rocks and ledges (ranges of Canadian taxa (as "variants"; *see* Barneby 1964) outlined below), s in the West to Oreg. and Nev., farther eastwards confined to Canada; Eurasia. MAPS and synonymy: *see* below.
1 Leaflets elliptic.
  2 Leaflets hairy above.
    3 The hairs curly or spreading.
      4 Pods glabrous; [var. *fastigiorum* Jones in part; sw Alta.; an intergradient with Variant f also reported from s Yukon by Barneby] . . . . Variant a
      4 Pods hairy; [*A. (Atelophragma) aboriginum* Rich., the type of *A. "aboriginorum"* from Carlton House, Sask.; *A. scrupulicola* Fern. and Weath.; Rocky Mountains of B.C. N to ca. 56°N; s-cent. Sask.; Mont-St-Pierre, Gaspé Pen., E Que.] . . . . Variant aa
    3 The hairs straightish and more or less appressed.
      5 Pods glabrous; [s B.C. and sw Alta.] . . . . Variant b

          5 Pods hairy; [sw Alta.] . . . . Variant bb
    2 Leaflets glabrous above.
        6 The hairs beneath curly or spreading.
            7 Pods glabrous; [*A. (Atelophragma) forwoodii* Wats. in part; Fort Saskatch-
               ewan, Alta.] . . . . Variant c
            7 Pods hairy; [such a plant as yet unknown] . . . . [Variant cc]
        6 The hairs beneath straightish and appressed.
            8 Pods glabrous; [var. *fastigiorum* Jones in part; *A. forwoodii* Wats. in part;
               A. vaginatus Rich., not Pallas; *A. glabriusculus* var. *major* Gray; Alta. to
               Sask.; sw Que.] . . . . Variant d
            8 Pods hairy; [Fort Saskatchewan, Alta.] . . . . Variant dd
1 Leaflets linear or nearly so.
    9 Leaflets hairy above.
        10 The hairs curly or spreading.
            11 Pods glabrous; [known only from the upper Yukon Valley, the Yukon] . . . .
                . . . . Variant e
            11 Pods hairy; [B.C. to s Man.] . . . . Variant ee
        10 The hairs straightish and more or less appressed.
            12 Pods glabrous; [the type of *Atelophragma (Astrag.) lineare* Rydb. is
                intermediate between this variant and Barneby's "Behringian variant" of
                Alaska–Yukon; the Yukon and mts. of sw Alta.; Cypress Hills of sw
                Sask.] . . . . Variant f
            12 Pods hairy; [Bow R., w Alta.] . . . . Variant ff
    9 Leaflets glabrous above.
        13 The hairs beneath curly or spreading.
            14 Pods glabrous; [known only from near Whitehorse, the Yukon] . . . . . . Variant g
            14 Pods hairy; [known only from NE B.C.] . . . . Variant gg
        13 The hairs beneath straightish and subappressed.
            15 Pods glabrous; [*Phaca (Astragalus; Atelophragma; Homalobus;
                Tragacantha) glabriuscula* Hook.; *A. abor.* var. *glab.* (Hook.) Rydb.; Bow
                Valley, Alta.; the report from Taylor Flats, cent. B.C., by Raup 1934,
                probably refers to some other variant] . . . . Variant h
            15 Pods hairy; [*A. abor.* var. *muirei* Hult.; *Atelophragma herriotii* Rydb.;
                Alaska–B.C. to sw Man.] . . . . Variant hh

NOTE: Barneby's "Mackenzie variant" is another glabrous-podded form, the leaflets being
mostly elliptic but sometimes hairy, sometimes glabrate above. He does not characterize the
leaflet-hairs as to straightness. Specimens would presumably key out as above into Variants
a, b, c, or d. However, the Mackenzie variant is distinguished by its larger flowers, with a calyx-tube 4 or 5 mm long (rather than not over 3.9 mm). The range is from Alaska to Victoria Is.
and Great Bear L. Reports of *A. richardsonii* Sheld. (*A. abor.* var. *rich.* (Sheld.) Boivin) from
Alaska–Canada are mostly referable here. *A. lepagei* Hult. (*A. abor.* var. *lep.* (Hult.) Boivin) is
intermediate between the Mackenzie and Behringian variants (*see* under Variant f).

A. adsurgens Pallas
/ST/WW/ (Ch (Hp)) Dry prairies and hillsides, the aggregate species from cent. Alaska–
Yukon and NW Dist. Mackenzie to Great Slave, Alta. (N to Wood Buffalo National Park), Sask.
(N to Prince Albert), and Man. (N to Gillam, about 165 mi s of Churchill, where perhaps introd.
in a gravel pit; there is also a collection in TRT from railway ballast at Thunder Bay, Ont.), s to
N.Mex., Kans., and w Minn. MAPS and synonymy: *see* below.
1 Banner of corolla 3 or 4 times as long as the calyx-tube; [E Asia only; reports from
   Canada refer chiefly to var. *robustior*] . . . . [var. *adsurgens*]
1 Banner less than 3 times as long as the calyx-tube.
    2 Pods stipitate (the stipe over 0.5 mm long); calyx-teeth mostly not over 1 mm
       long (rarely to about 2 mm); [*A. tananaicus* Hult.; *A. vicifolius* Hult. (basionym),
       not DC., the type from Rapids Lodge, Alaska (*see* Hultén 1947: map 823 (*A. vic.*),

p. 1192); Alaska and s Yukon; MAPS: Barneby 1964: map 77, p. 613; Porsild 1966: map 103 *(A. tan.),* p. 79; Hultén 1968*b*:652] . . . . var. *tananaicus* (Hult.) Barneby
2 Pods sessile or nearly so (stipe not over 0.5 mm long and usually as thick as long); calyx-teeth to about 4 mm long . . . . var. *robustior* Hook.
   3 Flowers white or ochroleucous; pubescence of leaves relatively silvery; [*A. chandonnetii* Lunell; Alta. to Man.: Boivin 1966*b*] . . . f. *chandonnetii* (Lunell) Boivin
   3 Flowers blue-purple; [*A. striatus* Nutt.; *A. hypoglottis* var. *robustus* Hook.; the Yukon–B.C. to w Ont.; MAPS: Barneby 1964: map 77, p. 613; Porsild 1966: map 102 *(A. str.),* p. 79; Hultén 1968*b*:651] . . . . f. *robustior*

A. agrestis Dougl.
/ST/WW/ (Ch (Hs)) Moist plains to alpine meadows and slopes from cent. Yukon–w Dist. Mackenzie to B.C.–Alta., Sask. (N to Prince Albert), Man. (N to the Churchill R. at ca. 57°15'N and York Factory, Hudson Bay, 57°N), and NE Ont. (w James Bay), s to N Calif., N.Mex., Kans., Iowa, and Minn. [*A. goniatus* Nutt.; *A. tarletonensis* Rydb.; *A. dasyglottis* Fisch. (*A. hypoglottis (danicus)* var. *dasy.* (Fisch.) Ledeb.), not Pallas; closely related to the Eurasian *A. danicus* Retz.]. MAPS: Hultén 1968*b*:652; Barneby 1964: map 78, p. 620; Meusel, Jaeger, and Weinert 1965:243 (the N. American area outlined for *A. danicus* applies here).
    Forma *virgultulus* (Sheld.) Scoggan (*A. virg.* Sheld.; flowers white or cream-colour rather than purplish) occurs throughout the range.

A. alpinus L.
/aST/X/GEA/ (Ch (Hpr)) Shores, meadows, turfy hillsides, ledges (often calcareous), and talus at low to high elevations, the aggregate species from the coasts of Alaska–Yukon–Dist. Mackenzie–Dist. Keewatin to Prince Patrick Is., N Baffin Is., and northernmost Ungava–Labrador, s in the West to Nev. and N.Mex., farther eastwards s to S.Dak., N Wisc., s Sask.–Man., Ont. (s to the E shore of L. Superior), Que. (s to the E James Bay watershed at ca. 53°N and Gerin Mt., 55°04'N), Labrador (s to ca. 53°N), and Nfld.; E Greenland at ca. 72°N (?introd.); Eurasia. MAPS and synonymy (together with the distinguishing characters of the closely related *A. nutzotinensis* Rousseau of Alaska–Yukon–N B.C.): *see* below.
1 Pods jointed to a stipe to about 1 cm long, strongly compressed laterally, not grooved dorsally, commonly sickle-shaped and incurved through at least half a circle, to nearly 5 cm long and 7 or 8 mm broad, truly 1-locular (valves not inflexed); [*A. falciferus* Hult.; *Gynophoraria falcata* Rydb., not *A. falcatus* Lam.; Alaska, sw Yukon (type from Kluane L.), and N B.C. near the Yukon boundary; MAPS: Hultén 1968*b*:651; Barneby 1964: map 39, p. 377] . . . . *A. nutzotinensis* Rousseau
1 Pods persistent on stipes 3.5 mm long, broadly obcordate in cross-section, grooved dorsally, straight or lunate-incurved up to 90°, to about 1.5 cm long and 4 mm broad, the valves inflexed as a very narrow septum . . . . *A. alpinus*
  2 Hairs of the pod usually appressed, averaging less than 0.4 mm long . . . . var. *brunetianus* Fern.
    3 Flowers white; [*A. labradoricus* f. *alb.* Rousseau, the type from Berthier, Montmagny Co., Que.] . . . . f. *albinus* (Rousseau) Boivin
    3 Flowers pale lilac to purplish; [*A. brun.* (Fern.) Rousseau; *A. (Atelophragma) labradoricus* DC.; *A. secundus* Michx., not DC.; Que., Nfld., and N.B. (but reported as transcontinental by Boivin 1966*b*); MAPS: Barneby 1964: map 2, p. 107; combine the maps by J. Rousseau 1933: fig. 6, p. 23, and fig. 7 *(A. brun.),* p. 26] . . . . f. *brunetianus*
  2 Hairs of the pod loosely ascending, averaging over 0.4 mm long . . . . var. *alpinus*
    4 Calyces and pods nearly or quite glabrous; [type from along the Larch R., Ungava, at 57°41'N] . . . . f. *lepageanus* Rousseau
    4 Calyces and pods copiously black (rarely white)-strigose; [incl. f. *parvulus* Rousseau, var. *alaskanus* (Hult.) Lepage and its f. *albovestitus* Lepage, and ssp. *arcticus* (Hult.) Bunge (*A. arcticus* Bunge); *Atelophragma* and *Tium* Rydb.; *Tragacantha* Ktze.; *Phaca* Piper; *P. andina* Nutt.; *P. astragalina* DC.; transcontinental; MAPS: Barneby 1964: map 2, p. 106; J. Rousseau 1933: fig. 6

(*A. alp.* and *A. brun.*; incomplete), p. 23; Porsild 1957: map 240 (aggregate species), p. 190; Raup 1947: pl. 29 (aggregate species); Fassett 1939:71 (aggregate species); combine the maps by Hultén 1968*b*:649 and 650 (ssp. *arcticus*)] . . . . f. *alpinus*

A. americanus (Hook.) Jones
/ST/(X)/ (Hpr) Meadows and streambanks from cent. Alaska–Yukon–w Dist. Mackenzie to Great Slave L., Alta. (N to Wood Buffalo National Park), Sask. (N to Hasbala L. at ca. 60°N), Man. (N to the Hayes R. about 100 mi SW of York Factory), and cent. Ont. (Fawn R. at ca. 54°10′N, 88°W; Severn R. at ca. 55°45′N, 88°W), S to S B.C., Mont., N Colo., and the Black Hills of S.Dak.; isolated in E Que. (along the Rimouski R. in Rimouski Co.; Gaspé Pen.). [*Phaca* Rydb.; *P. (A.) frigida* var. *am.* Hook.; *A. gaspensis* Rousseau]. MAPS: Hultén 1968*b*:647; Barneby 1964: map 1, p. 96; Meusel, Jaeger, and Weinert 1965:242.

A. beckwithii T. & G.
/t/W/ (Ch (Hs)) Grassy, rocky, and clayey soils, mostly in the lower foothills, from S B.C. (Dry Interior N to Kamloops) to Oreg., Nev., and Utah. [*Phaca* Piper; *Tragacantha* Ktze.]. MAP: Barneby 1964: map 106, p. 782.

The B.C. plant is referable to var *weiserensis* Jones (*Phacomene pontina* Rydb.; flowers averaging slightly larger than those of the typical form but the leaflets rarely over 17 in number rather than up to 25).

A. bisulcatus (Hook.) Gray
/T/WW/ (Hp) Prairies, gravelly hillsides, and clayey alluvial soils from Alta. (N to Peace River Landing) to S Sask. (N to Yorkton) and S Man. (N to Roblin, S of Duck Mt.), S to Mont., N.Mex., Colo., and Nebr. [*Phaca* Hook., the type from "plains of the Saskatchewan"; *Diholcus* Rydb.; *Tragacantha* Ktze.]. MAP: Barneby 1964: map 45, p. 411.

Forma *albiflorus* Boivin (flowers white rather than purplish) is known from Sask. (type from Saskatchewan Landing, N of Swift Current; Boivin 1966*b*).

A. bodinii Sheldon
/ST/D/ (Ch (Hpr)) Moist gravelly banks, gravel bars, and wet meadows in two main areas as presently known, one from cent. Alaska, S-cent. Yukon, and the Mackenzie R. Delta to Great Slave L. and N Alta. (S to McMurray, 56°44′N), the other in Wyo., Utah, Colo., and W Nebr., with isolated stations in cent. Man. (Pipestone L. and Cross L., N of L. Winnipeg) and NW Nfld. (type of *A. stragalus* from Pistolet Bay). [*Phaca* Rydb.; *P. (A.; Homalobus) debilis* Nutt.; *A. stragalus* Fern.; *A. (P.) yukonis* Jones; *H. retusus* Rydb., not Willd.; *A. neglectus sensu* Raup 1936, not (T. & G.) Sheld.]. MAPS: Barneby 1964: map 39, p. 376; Hultén 1968*b*:655.

The closely related *A. polaris* (Seem.) Benth. of Alaska may be distinguished from *A. bodinii* as follows:

1   Pods to 12 mm long, little inflated, with at most 10 seeds; racemes loose, with up to
    15 flowers, sometimes to nearly 1 dm long in fruit; stems to 4 dm long . . . . *A. bodinii*
1   Pods to over 1.5 cm long (to 4 cm), greatly inflated, with up to 17 seeds; racemes
    dense and subumbellate, with rarely more than 6 flowers, the axis less than 1.5 cm
    long in fruit; stems to about 1 dm long; [*Oxytropis polaris* Seem., the type from
    Eschscholtz Bay, Alaska; *Homalobus (A.) amblyodon* Rydb.; Alaska; MAPS: Barneby
    1964: map 39, p. 377; Hultén 1968*b*:650, and 1947: maps 820 and 814
    (*A. amblyodon;* combine these two maps), p. 1192] . . . . *A. polaris* (Seem.) Benth.

A. bourgovii Gray
/T/W/ (Ch (Hp)) Gravel bars, streambanks, and alpine slopes, chiefly on limestone, from SE B.C. (N to near the Alta. boundary 32 mi W of Banff) and SW Alta. (N to Jasper National Park; type from "Rocky Mountains on the British Boundary", probably in Alta.) to Idaho and Mont. [*Homalobus* Rydb.; *Tragacantha* Ktze.]. MAP: Barneby 1964: map 36, p. 354.

A. canadensis L.

/sT/X/ (Hp (Grh)) Shores and rich thickets, the aggregate species from extreme SW Dist. Mackenzie (CAN) and B.C. to Alta. (N to Waterways, 56°42′N), Sask. (N to Prince Albert), Man. (N to Cross Lake, NE of L. Winnipeg; the report from York Factory by Hooker 1831, may refer to *A. americanus*), Ont. (N to the S James Bay watershed at ca. 51°30′N), and Que. (N to Baie-St-Paul, Charlevoix Co.; Abbé Alexandre Gagnon, G.W. Corrivault, and A. Morin, Ann. ACFAS 6:107. 1940; the report from N.B. by John Macoun and John Gibson, Can. J., n.s. 15(93). 1877, requires confirmation), S to Calif., Colo., Tex., Ark., and Va. MAPS and synonymy: *see* below.

1 Pod terete, not grooved dorsally, it and the ovary usually glabrous; [*A. carolinianus* L.; SW Dist. Mackenzie–B.C. to Que.; MAPS: Barneby 1964: map 76, p. 605; Fassett 1939:73 (incomplete northwards)] . . . . var. *canadensis*
1 Pod grooved dorsally, it and the ovary usually pubescent; [S B.C.].
  2 Calyx white-hairy, its teeth to 2 mm long, the upper pair much broader and shorter than the lower three; plants usually more or less silvery-pubescent; [*A. brevidens* (Gandg.) Rydb.; S B.C.: Hitchcock et al. 1961; MAP: Barneby 1964: map 75, p. 602] . . . . var. *brevidens* (Gandg.) Barneby
  2 Calyx pubescent with an admixture of white and black hairs, its subequal teeth to 3 mm long; plants greenish (not silvery-pubescent); [*A. mortonii* Nutt.; B.C. (N to Quesnel, ca. 52°30′N: Eastham 1947); MAP: Barneby 1964: map 75, p. 602] . . . . var. *mortonii* (Nutt.) Wats.

A. cicer L.

European; introd. in SW Alta. (Boivin 1966*b*) and S Man. (Brandon, where taken as a weed in a clover field by G.A. Stevenson in 1958, its first-noted occurrence in Canada; CAN; DAO; a 1946 collection in Wash. and a possible occurrence in Nev. also noted by Barneby 1964). [*Cystium* Stev.].

A. collinus (Hook.) Don

/t/W/ (Ch (Hp)) Grasslands and sagebrush plains from S B.C. (Dry Interior from Kamloops S to Osoyoos and Vernon) to Oreg. and Idaho. [*Phaca* Hook.; *Homalobus* Rydb.; *Tragacantha* Ktze.; *A. cyrtoides* Gray; *A. gibbsii sensu* John Macoun 1883, not Kellogg, the relevant collection in CAN]. MAP: Barneby 1964: map 28, p. 296.

A. crassicarpus Nutt.

/T/WW/ (Ch (Hp)) Prairies and foothills from SE B.C. (Crowsnest Pass; V) to Alta. (N to Red Deer, 52°16′N), Sask. (N to McKague, 52°37′N), S Man. (N to Duck Mt.), and Minn., S to Ariz., N.Mex., Tex., Mo., and Tenn. [*Geoprumnon* Rydb.; *A. carnosus* Pursh; *A. (Tragacantha) caryocarpus* Ker; *A. (G.) succulentus* Rich.]. MAPS: Barneby 1964: map 101, p. 757; N.C. Fassett 1939:66, and Ann. Mo. Bot. Gard. 28(3): map 25, p. 361. 1941.

Var. *paysonii* (Kelso) Barneby (*A. succ.* var. *pay.* Kelso; flowers whitish rather than purplish-tinged to purple) is indicated as the common phase in Alta. on the above-noted map by Barneby.

[*A. curvicarpus* (Sheld.) Macbr.]

[The report of this species of the W U.S.A. (N to Wash. and Idaho) from S B.C. by Henry (1915; Summerland; as *A. speirocarpus* var. *falciformis* Gray) requires confirmation. The MAP by Barneby (1964: map 28, p. 296) indicates no Canadian stations.]

A. drummondii Hook.

/T/WW/ (Hp (Ch; Grh)) Dry hillsides and prairies from Alta. (N to Edmonton) and Sask. (N to Cochin, 53°05′N; Breitung 1957*a*; type locality given as "Eagle and Red-Deer Hills of the Saskatchewan") to Idaho, Utah, and N.Mex. [*Tium* Rydb.; *Tragacantha* Ktze.; the report of *Tium drum.* from Angusville, Man., by Lowe 1943, is based upon *Oxytropis deflexa* var. *sericea,* the relevant collection in WIN]. MAP: Barneby 1964: map 58, p. 492.

A. eucosmus Robins.

/aST/X/ (Ch (Hp)) Moist meadows, calcareous gravels and ledges, and montane woods from the coasts of Alaska–Yukon–Dist. Mackenzie to s Baffin Is. and northernmost Ungava–Labrador, s in the West through N B.C. (s to the Peace R. at ca. 56°N) and Alta. to N Utah and Colo., farther eastwards s to Sask. (s to the Saskatoon dist.), NE Man. (known from Churchill s to Gillam, about 165 mi s of Churchill), N Ont. (s to the James Bay watershed at ca. 53°N), Que. (s to NE James Bay at ca. 54°30′N, the Côte-Nord, Cabano, Temiscouata Co., and the Gaspé Pen.; not known from Anticosti Is.), N.B. (Restigouche and Carleton counties; CAN; GH; not known from P.E.I. or N.S.), and N Maine. MAPS and synonymy: see below.

1   Flowers white; [Ha-Ha Bay, Nfld., the type locality] . . . . f. *albinus* Fern.
1   Flowers deep purple
    2   Pods white-hairy.
        3   Calyx-tube essentially glabrous or sparingly white-strigose; [var. *facinorum* Fern., the type from near Grand Falls on the Exploits R., Nfld.] . . . . f. *facinorum* (Fern.) Boivin
        3   Calyx-tube black-strigose or with an admixture of white hairs; [type from Alaska; also reported from Cape Jones, E James Bay, Que., by Dutilly, Lepage, and Duman 1958] . . . . f. *leucocarpus* Lepage
    2   Pods black-hairy; [var. *terrae-novae* Fern. and its f. *caespitosus* and f. *villosus* Rousseau; *A. oroboides* var. *americanus* Gray, basionym, based in turn upon *Phaca (A.; Atelophragma) elegans* Hook.; *P. elegans* var. *minor* Hook.; *A. sealei* Lepage; *Atel. atratum* Rydb., not *Astragalus atratus* Wats.; transcontinental; MAPS: Barneby 1964: map 4, p. 118; Hultén 1968b:648 (also ssp. *sealei*); Porsild 1957: map 241, p. 191; J. Rousseau 1933: fig. 11 (incomplete), p. 42; the map for the closely related *A. norvegicus* Grauer of Eurasia by Meusel, Jaeger, and Weinert 1965:242, apparently applies here in its N. American area] . . . . . . f. *eucosmus*

A. filipes Torr.
/t/W/ (Hp) Sagebrush plains and lower foothills from s B.C. (Dry Interior sw of Kamloops between Spences Bridge and Nicola; CAN) and Idaho to Baja Calif. [*Homalobus* Heller; *Tragacantha* Ktze.; *A. (H.) stenophyllus* of B.C. reports, not T. & G.]. MAP: Barneby 1964: map 31, p. 321.

A. flexuosus (Hook.) Don
/T/WW/ (Ch (Hp)) Prairies, sandy fields and roadsides, gravelly and rocky hillsides, etc., from SE B.C. (?introd. at Cranbrook; see Barneby 1964) to Alta. (N to Edmonton), Sask. (N to Prince Albert), Man. (N to Dropmore, about 100 mi NW of Brandon), and Minn., s to N.Mex. and Kans. [*Phaca flexuosa* Hook., the type locality given as "Red River and Assiniboin, lat. 50°"; *Homalobus* and *Pisophaca* Rydb.; *Tragacantha* Ktze.; *Phaca (Pisophaca) elongata* Hook.]. MAP: Barneby 1964: map 14, p. 204.

A. gilviflorus Sheldon
/T/WW/ (Ch) Dry prairies and foothills from s Alta. (Waterton Lakes; Fort MacLeod; Lethbridge; Manyberries; Medicine Hat) to s Sask. (Indian Head; Moose Jaw) and sw Man. (Turtle Mt.; WIN; reported from Reston and Lyleton by Lowe 1943), s to Colo. and Nebr. [*A. triphyllus* Pursh; *Phaca (Orophaca) caespitosa* Nutt., not *A. caesp.* Pall. nor Gray nor *Homalobus caesp.* Nutt.]. MAP: Barneby 1964: map 163, p. 1152.

A. gracilis Nutt.
/T/WW/ (Hp) Sandy bluffs, barren hilltops, dunes, and prairie ravines, the main area from Mont. to N.Dak., s to N.Mex. and Okla., with a isolated station in Sask. (Saskatchewan R. between Prince Albert and Rosthern; Barneby 1964). MAP: Barneby 1964: map 17, p. 220.

A. kentrophyta Gray
/T/W/ (Ch) Dry prairies and lower foothills from s Alta. (Belly R.; Milk R.; Medicine Hat; Cypress Hills) and sw Sask. (Stinking L., N of the Cypress Hills, where taken by John Macoun in 1880; CAN; reported from Webb, near Swift Current, by Breitung 1957a) to Ariz. and N.Mex. [*Kentrophyta (A.) montana* Nutt., not *A. montanus* L.]. MAP: Barneby 1964: map 37, p. 361.

A. lentiginosus Dougl.
/T/W/   (Ch)   Sagebrush plains and salt flats to barren subalpine slopes from s B.C. (Dry Interior at Spences Bridge, Kamloops, and in the Nicola Valley; CAN; reported from the Columbia Valley by John Macoun 1883) and Mont. to Calif. and Utah. [*Cystium* Rydb.; *Tragacantha* Ktze.] The MAPS for the typical form and varieties by Barneby (1964: map 127, p. 918; map 128, p. 924; map 129, p. 930; map 130, p. 934; map 131, p. 937; and map 132, p. 950) indicate no Canadian stations.

[*A. leptaleus* Gray]
[According to Barneby (1964), the report of this species of the w U.S.A. (Mont. and Idaho to Colo.) from Canada by M.E. Jones in a 1923 monograph of the genus (presumably the basis of the Alta. report noted by Hitchcock et al. 1961) is based on old collections of *A. bodinii*. [*Phaca* Rydb.; *A. (P.) pauciflorus* (Nutt.) Gray, not Pallas nor Hook.]. The MAP by Barneby (1964: map 3, p. 112) indicates no Canadian stations.]

A. lotiflorus Hook.
/T/WW/   (Hp (Ch))   Plains and sandy prairies from s B.C. (Dry Interior at Spences Bridge and near Kamloops) to s Alta. (Medicine Hat and Milk River; CAN), Sask. (N to Saskatoon; Breitung 1957a), and sw Man. (Treesbank and Wawanesa, both about 20 mi se of Brandon; CAN; the report from Carberry by Lowe 1943, is based upon *A. missouriensis,* the relevant collection in WIN), s to Mont., N.Mex., Tex., Mo., and Iowa. [*Batidophaca* Rydb.; *Phaca* T. & G.; *P. cretacea* Buckl.; *A. elatiocarpus* Sheldon]. MAP: Barneby 1964: map 139, p. 996.

The European *A. falcatus* Lam. is reported from s Man. by Boivin (1967a; Brandon, where presumably introd. but not so-indicated by Boivin). It resembles both *A. lotiflorus* and *A. canadensis* in its dolabriform pubescence. It has the strongly caulescent habit, numerous leaflets, and 2-locular capsules characteristic of *A. canadensis* but the stipules at the lower nodes are not connate opposite the petioles as in that species.

[*A. lyallii* Gray]
[The type locality of this species of the w U.S.A. (Wash., Oreg., and Idaho) was given as "Upper Yakima River, on the boundary between British Columbia and Washington Territory" but this is a misrepresentation of the course of that river and the species is not indicated as extending N of cent. Wash. in the MAP by Barneby (1964: map 156, p. 1104).]

A. microcystis Gray
/t/W/   (Ch (Hp))   Plains, foothills, and ponderosa-pine forest from se B.C. (Waneta, near the Wash. boundary se of Trail; Boivin 1966b; the report from Portage la Loche, Sask., 56°38′N, by John Macoun 1883, requires clarification, possibly being based upon an 1872 collection in CAN from "West of the North Saskatchewan River" (presumably Alta.) referred by Boivin to *A. bodinii* var. *yukonis*) to Wash. and Mont. [*Phaca* Rydb.]. MAP: Barneby 1964: map 36, p. 354.

A. miser Dougl.
/T/WW/   (Ch (Hp))   Grasslands, moist meadows, and dry ridges at low to alpine elevations, the aggregate species from B.C. (N to near Quesnel, ca. 53°N; Eastham 1947) and sw Alta. (N to near Jasper) to Nev., Utah, Colo., and S.Dak. MAPS and synonymy: *see* below.
1 Pubescence dolabriform (the hairs appressed and 2-pronged, attached some
    distance from one end); [*Homalobus (A.) decumbens* Nutt.; the report from Spences
    Bridge, B.C., by Henry 1915, probably refers to one of the following varieties, no
    Canadian stations being indicated on the MAP by Barneby 1964: map 21, p. 243] . . . .
    . . . . [var. *decumbens* (Nutt.) Cronq.]
1 Pubescence consisting of basifixed hairs; [s B.C. and sw Alta.].
    2 Leaflets commonly glabrous or glabrate above (if pubescent above, the relatively
        small flowers with a keel at most 8 mm long); pods either glabrous or puberulent;
        [*A. (Homalobus; Phaca; Tragacantha) serotinus* Gray; *A. campestris* var. *ser.*
        (Gray) Jones; *A. (Homalobus) palliseri* Gray; MAP: Barneby 1964: map 20, p. 239] . . . . .
        . . . . var. *serotinus* (Gray) Barneby

2 Leaflets equally silvery- or cinereous-pubescent on both surfaces; corolla-keel usually over 8 mm long; pods pubescent; [*Homalobus* Rydb.; MAP: Barneby 1964: map 20, p. 239] . . . . var. *miser*

A. missouriensis Nutt.
/T/WW/ (Ch (Hp)) Dry prairies and E foothills of the Rocky Mts. from S Alta. (N to Alliance, 52°26′N; CAN) to Sask. (N to Saskatoon), SW Man. (N to Miniota, about 50 mi NW of Brandon), and Minn., S to N.Mex. and Tex. [*Tragacantha* Ktze.; *Xylophacos* Rydb.; *A. melanocarpus* Nutt.]. MAP: Barneby 1964: map 94, p. 714.

A. neglectus (T. & G.) Sheldon
/T/EE/ (Hp (Ch)) Calcareous gravels, cliffs, and talus from Minn. to S Man. (reported from Aweme, about 20 mi SE of Brandon, by N. Criddle, Can. Field-Nat. 41(3):51. 1927, and from Kleefeld, S of Winnipeg, by Löve and Bernard 1959; the report from McMurray, N Alta., by Raup 1936, is based upon *A. bodinii,* the relevant collection in CAN) and Ont. (N to the Ottawa dist.; Gillett 1958; reports of *A. cooperi* from Que. by John Macoun 1883, require clarification), S to Iowa, Wisc., Mich., Ohio, and N.Y. [*Phaca* T. & G.; *A. cooperi* Gray]. MAPS: Barneby 1964: map 74, p. 594; Fassett 1939:66.

A. pectinatus Dougl.
/T/WW/ (Ch (Hp)) Prairies (often strongly alkaline) and E slopes of the Rocky Mts. from S Alta. (Fort MacLeod; Milk River; Grassy L.; Medicine Hat) to S Sask. (N to Moose Jaw) and S Man. (N to Gypsumville, about 125 mi N of Portage la Prairie; ?introd.), S to Mont., Utah, Colo., and Kans. The type locality is presumably in Sask., being given for *Phaca pect.* (Dougl.) Hook. as "Pastures of the Saskatchewan, Drummond; and on the Red-Deer and Eagle Hills bordering on that river. Douglas." [*Phaca* Hook.; *Cnemidophacos* and *Ctenophyllum* Rydb.; *Cnem. ?flavus sensu* Fraser and Russell 1944, not (Nutt.) Rydb.]. MAP: Barneby 1964: map 48, p. 425.

A. purshii Dougl.
/T/WW/ (Ch (Hp)) Dry prairies, sagebrush plains, foothills, and lower montane slopes, the aggregate species from S B.C.–Alta.–Sask. to N Calif., N.Mex., and S.Dak. MAPS and synonymy: *see* below.
1 Flowers reddish purple; pods usually arcuate; [*A. (Phaca; Tragacantha; Xylophacos) glar.* Dougl.; S B.C. (Lytton, Oliver, Merritt, Penticton, and Osoyoos; Herb. V); MAP: Barneby 1964: map 87, p. 680] . . . . var. *glareosus* (Dougl.) Barneby
1 Flowers ochroleucous or very pale lavender (the keel merely purple-tipped); [*Phaca* Piper; *Tragacantha* Ktze.; *Xylophacos* Rydb.; S Alta. (Medicine Hat and Cypress Hills; CAN) and SW Sask. (Cypress Hills and Climax); MAP: Barneby 1964: map 86, p. 675] . . . .
. . . . var. *purshii*

A. racemosus Pursh
/T/WW/ (Hp) Ravines, barren slopes, and alluvial bottomlands from S Sask. (locally abundant near Moose Jaw and on the headwaters of the Qu'Appelle R.; reported from Saskatoon by Breitung 1957a) and N.Dak. to Utah, N.Mex., Tex., and Okla. [*Tium* Rydb.]. MAP: Barneby 1964: map 46, p. 417.

A. robbinsii (Oakes) Gray
/ST/D/ (Ch (Hp)) Meadows, streambanks, and calcareous ledges, cliffs, and talus (ranges of Canadian taxa outlined below), S in the West to Nev., Idaho, and Colo., farther eastwards with a widely disjunct area comprising SE Labrador (Forteau, 51°28′N), NW Nfld. (Highlands of St. John), E Que. (Côte-Nord at the mouth of the Blanc Sablon R. opposite Forteau, Labrador), N.S. (Cap d'Or, Cumberland Co.; W.B. Schofield, Rhodora 57(683):308. 1955), and Vt. MAPS and synonymy: *see* below.
1 Leaves densely greyish-pubescent beneath with hairs to 0.8 mm long; pod-stipe to 3 mm long; pod-septum to 2 mm broad; [*Atelophragma (Astrag.) harringtonii* Rydb., the type from Good News Bay, Alaska; known only from S Alaska; MAPS: Barneby 1964:

map 5, p. 126; Hultén 1968*b*:653, and 1947: map 817 *(A. harr.)*, p. 1192] . . . .
. . . . var. *harringtonii* (Rydb.) Barneby
1   Leaves thinly pubescent beneath with hairs mostly not over 0.6 mm long.
   2   Pod-stipe to 6.5 mm long; pod-body to 2.5 cm long; pod-septum 1(1.5) mm
       broad; petals pale purple, or whitish with a purple-tipped keel; [*Phaca elegans*
       var. *minor* Hook., the type a Drummond collection probably from NW Canada; *A.*
       minor (Hook.) Jones; *A. eucosmus* f. *minor* (Hook.) Rousseau; *A. blakei* Egglest.;
       A. (Atelophragma) macounii Rydb.; *Atelophragma (A.) collieri* Rydb.: Alaska–
       Yukon–Dist. Mackenzie (Great Bear L.) and B.C.–SW Alta.; MAPS: Hultén
       1968*b*:653; Barneby 1964: map 5 (as var. *blakei,* but this merged with var. *minor*
       in the text), p. 126] . . . . var. *minor* (Hook.) Barneby
   2   Pod-stipe at most 3(3.5) mm long; pod-body less than 2 cm long.
      3   Petals lilac to purplish; calyx to 6.5 mm long, its teeth to 2.5 mm long; pod-
          septum to 0.8 mm broad; pod-beak to 2 mm long; [*Atelophragma (A.) fernaldii*
          Rydb. (*A. eucosmus* var. *fern.* (Rydb.) Boivin), the type from S Labrador; also
          known from E Que. and Nfld.; MAP: Barneby 1964: map 5, p. 126] . . . .
          . . . . var. *fernaldii* (Rydb.) Barneby
      3   Petals uniformly white; calyx to 5 mm long, its teeth less than 2 mm long; pod-
          septum about 0.3 mm broad; pod-beak not over 1 mm long; [*Phaca robbinsii*
          Oakes, the type from Burlington, Vt., where now extinct; reported from
          "Acadia" by Macoun and Gibson 1877, and from Cape d'Or, Cumberland Co.,
          N.S., by W.B. Schofield, Rhodora 57(683):308. 1955, but no Canadian stations
          are indicated on the map by Barneby 1964: map 5, p. 126] . . . . var. *robbinsii*

A. sclerocarpus Gray

/t/W/   (Ch (Hp))   Dunes and sandy barrens of S B.C. (known only from the Okanagan Valley; collection in V from Okanagan L.; three other stations indicated in the map by Barneby), E Wash., and N Oreg. [*Tragacantha* Ktze.; *Phaca (Homalobus) podocarpa* Hook., not *A. podocarpus* Mey.; *A. ?sinuatus (whitedii) sensu* Boivin 1967*a*, probably not Piper]. MAP: Barneby 1964: map 30, p. 314.

A. spatulatus Sheldon

/T/WW/   (Ch)   Dry prairies and hillsides from Mont. to SE Alta. (Cypress Hills) and SW Sask. (Cypress Hills, Eatonia, and Govenlock; Breitung 1957*a*), S to Utah, Colo., and W Nebr. [*Homalobus (A.) caespitosus* Nutt., not *A. caesp.* Pallas]. MAP: Barneby 1964: map 26, p. 285.

A. tenellus Pursh

/sT/WW/   (Ch (Hp))   Prairies, shores, foothills, and lower montane slopes from S-cent. Yukon (*see* Hultén 1947: map 821, p. 1192), NW Dist. Mackenzie, and B.C.–Alta. to Sask. (N to Saskatoon) and Man. (N to Gillam, about 165 mi S of Churchill; gravel pit, ?introd.), S to Nev., N.Mex., and Minn. [*Homalobus* Britt.; *Tragacantha* Ktze.; *Ervum (A.; Homalobus) multiflorum* Pursh; *H. stipitatus* Rydb.; *Phaca nigrescens* Hook.]. MAPS: Hultén 1968*b*:654; Barneby 1964: map 34, p. 346.

[A. trichopodus (Nutt.) Gray]

[A native of Calif. and Baja Calif. (*see* Barneby 1964: map 112, p. 822); introd. elsewhere in W N. America, as in SW B.C. (Nanaimo, Vancouver Is., where taken by John Macoun in 1893 and reported as *A. leucopsis* by J.M. Macoun 1894, with the note, "The seed was doubtless brought from California in ballast."; CAN). It was apparently a mere waif at Nanaimo and no other Canadian collections have been made since that time.

The B.C. plant is referable to var. *lonchus* (Jones) Barneby (*A. leucopsis* (T. & G.) Torr. var. *lonchus* Jones; *Phaca canescens* Nutt., not H. & A.; pods pubescent rather than nearly always glabrous).]

A. umbellatus Bunge

/aSs/W/EA/   (Hpr)   Meadows, stony slopes, and solifluction areas at low to moderate elevations from the coasts of Alaska–Yukon–Dist. Mackenzie (E to Coronation Gulf) to the Aleutian Is., s Alaska–Yukon–w Dist. Mackenzie, and northernmost w B.C. (s to ca. 59°30'N); Eurasia. [*Phaca frigida* var. *littoralis* Hook. (*A. (Phaca) litt.* (Hook.) Cov. & Standl.); *A. frig.* var. *dawsonensis* Rousseau]. MAPS: Hultén 1968*b*:647; Barneby 1964: map 1 (top), p. 97; Raup 1947: pl. 29 (*A. frig.* var. *litt.*).

A. vexilliflexus Sheldon
/T/W/ (Ch (Hp)) Sagebrush plains, prairies, streambanks, and open forest from SE B.C. (near the Alta. boundary), s Alta. (N to Banff), and s Sask. (Cypress Hills and Rock Glen; Breitung 1957*a*) to Idaho, Wyo., and w S.Dak. [*Homalobus* Rydb.; *A. pauciflorus* Hook., not (Nutt.) Gray nor Pallas]. MAP: Barneby 1964: map 35, p. 351.

A. williamsii Rydb.
/Ss/W/ (Ch (Hpr)) Gravel bars, streambanks, and open woods of Alaska (N to ca. 67°30'N), the Yukon (N to ca. 65°N; type from Big Salmon R.), and northernmost w ?B.C. (Hultén's maps indicate a station on or very close to the B.C.–Yukon boundary). [*Atelophragma* Rydb.; *Astrag. gormanii* Wight]. MAPS: Hultén 1968*b*:654, and 1947: map 824, p. 1192; Barneby 1964: map 5, p. 127.

BAPTISIA Vent. [3618] False Indigo

1 Corolla yellow, to about 1.5 cm long; racemes very numerous, terminating the branchlets; pods long-exserted, their bodies to 1.5 cm long; leaflets cuneate-obovate, to about 4 cm long; (s Ont.) . . . . *B. tinctoria*
1 Corolla white; racemes solitary or few; (s ?Ont.).
  2 Pods erect, brown, linear-cylindric, mostly 2 or 3 cm long, on stipes scarcely surpassing the calyces; flowers less than 2 cm long; leaflets oblanceolate to oblong, to about 4 cm long, on slender stalks . . . . [*B. alba*]
  2 Pods drooping, blackish, ellipsoid-ovoid, to about 4 cm long, long-exserted on stipes about twice as long as the calyces; flowers to 2.5 cm long, the standard sometimes purple-tinged; leaflets oblanceolate to narrowly obovate from a cuneate base, to about 5 cm long, on stouter stalks . . . . [*B. leucantha*]

[B. alba (L.) R. Br.]
[The report of this species of the E U.S.A. (Tenn. and Va. to Fla.) from s Ont. by John Macoun and J. Gibson (Can. J., n.s. 15(93). 1877; shore of L. Erie) requires clarification. [*Crotalaria* L.]. The MAP by M.M. Larisey (Ann. Mo. Bot. Gard. 27(2): fig. 4, p. 128. 1940) indicates no Canadian stations.]

[B. leucantha T. & G.]
[This U.S.A. species (Nebr. to Ohio, s to Tex. and Miss.) is reported from s Ont. by John Macoun (1883, citing *B. alba* in synonymy; "In rich alluvial soil. Shore of Lake Erie. (Goldie.). This species has not been detected since the time of Goldie."). Soper (1962) notes that it is occasionally planted in gardens and may escape, his s Ont. map (fig. 12a, p. 20) indicating the location in Norfolk Co. of "A single immature specimen which appears to be this species . . . ." However, the MAPS by M.M. Larisey (Ann. Mo. Bot. Gard. 27(2): fig. 5, p. 130. 1940) and Fassett (1939:28) indicate no Canadian stations and both of the above s Ont. reports require confirmation. The species is probably now extinct in Canada even if Goldie's collection is finally located for validation.]

B. tinctoria (L.) R. Br. Wild Indigo, Rattleweed
/t/EE/ (Hp) Dry open woods and clearings from Minn. to s Ont. (Essex, Lambton, Norfolk, and Wentworth counties; *see* s Ont. map by Soper 1962: fig. 12, p. 20), N.Y., Vt., and Maine, s to La. and Fla. [*Sophora* L.; *Podalyria* Willd.; incl. the coarser extreme of a completely intergrading series, var. *crebra* Fern.; *B. ?australis sensu* Soper 1962, probably not (L.) R. Br.]. MAP: M.M. Larisey, Ann. Mo. Bot. Gard. 27(2): fig. 6, p. 132. 1940.

CARAGANA Lam.   [3761]   Pea-shrub

1   Leaves with 4–6 pairs of bright-green leaflets; pods to about 5 cm long . . . *C. arborescens*
1   Leaves with 2 pairs of dull-green membranous leaflets; pods to about 3.5 cm long . . . . . .
. . . . *C. frutex*

C. arborescens Lam.   Siberian Pea-shrub
Asiatic; commonly cult. as a hedge or windbreak, particularly in the Prairie Provinces, and oc-
casionally spreading to open woods and clearings, as in Alta. (Grande Prairie; Groh and
Frankton 1949*b*), Sask. (Breitung 1957*a*), and Man. (N to Herb Lake, about 75 mi NE of The
Pas); reported from Que., ?B.C., and the ?Yukon by Boivin (1966*b*).

C. frutex (L.) Koch   Russian Pea-shrub
Eurasian; reported as escaped from cult. in s Ont. by Gaiser and Moore (1966; Lambton Co.),
apparently the first such record for N. America. [*Robinia* L.].

CASSIA L.   [3536]   Senna

1   Leaflets up to 18 pairs, mostly not over 2 cm long, touch-sensitive and therefore
    dorsally opposed and overlapping when collected and dried; stipules persistent;
    racemes at most 6-flowered, mostly supra-axillary (the peduncle arising above the
    leaf-axil); anthers all perfect; pods mostly less than 5 cm long; annual; (s ?Ont.) . . . .
    . . . . [*C. fasciculata*]
1   Leaflets usually not more than 9 pairs, to about 5 cm long; stipules deciduous;
    racemes usually more abundantly flowered, axillary; the 3 upper anthers imperfect;
    pods to 12 cm long; root-perennial; (s Ont.) . . . . *C. hebecarpa*

[C. fasciculata Michx.]   Partridge-Pea, Golden Cassia
[The inclusion of s Ont. in the range of this species of the E U.S.A. (N to Minn., Ohio, N.Y.,
and Mass.) by Fernald *in* Gray (1950) requires confirmation. The MAP of the area by Fassett
(1939:28) indicates no Canadian stations.]

C. hebecarpa Fern.   Wild Senna
/t/EE/   (Hp)   Alluvial soils, dry slopes, and thickets from Wisc. to s Ont. (Essex, Kent, Middlesex, and Welland counties; *see* s Ont. map by Soper 1956: map 9d, p. 81) and New Eng., s
to Tenn. and N.C. [*C. marilandica* of Ont. reports, not L.]. MAP: the map for *C. marilandica* by
Fassett (1939:26) is applicable here.

[CERCIS L.]   [3526]   Judas-tree

[C. canadensis L.]   Redbud
[This tree of the E U.S.A. (N to Wisc., Mich., Pa., N.Y., and Conn.) is known in the apparently
native state in Canada only through an 1892 collection by John Macoun on Pelee Is., L. Erie,
Essex Co., s Ont. The relevant report by J.M. Macoun (1897) notes that, "One tree of this species was pointed out to Prof. Macoun in 1892. An old resident remembered having seen this
tree in his boyhood, but knew of no other on the island. It grows close beside the lake, and is
doubtless indigenous." It is planted elsewhere in Ont. as far N as Ottawa (CAN) but, according to Fox and Soper (1953; *see* discussion and s Ont. map 21, p. 23; *see*, also, Soper 1956),
is now extinct at the Pelee Is. station. MAPS: Hosie 1969:256; Canada Department of Northern
Affairs and Natural Resources 1956:230; Preston 1961:272; Hough 1947:285; Milton Hopkins,
Rhodora 44(522): map 1, p. 197. 1942; Munns 1938: map 139, p. 143; M.L. Fernald, Rhodora
33(386): map 7, p. 31. 1931.]

CICER L.   [3851]

C. arietinum L.   Chick-Pea
Asiatic; an occasional garden-escape to rubbish heaps and waste places in N. America, as in
B.C. (Spences Bridge; CAN), Sask. (Boivin 1966b), s Man. (Winnipeg, Selkirk, St. Eustace,
and Erickson), and s Ont. (Wingham, Huron Co.; CAN).

CORONILLA L.   [3774]   Crown-Vetch

1   Leaflets 3 (or the terminal leaf reduced to a single leaflet), the terminal one broadly
    elliptic to oval, to 3 cm long, the lateral ones oblate or rotund, much smaller; flowers
    yellow, rarely more than 5 in an umbel . . . . *C. scorpioides*
1   Leaflets 11 or more, oblong to obovate, 1 or 2 cm long; flowers pink, commonly 10 or
    more in an umbel . . . . *C. varia*

C. scorpioides (L.) Koch
European; reported as occurring in a garden (?introd.) in sw N.B. by G.V. Hay, J. Vroom, and
R. Chalmers (Nat. Hist. Soc. N.B., Bull. 3:33. 1884; St. Stephen, Charlotte Co.; CAN) and as in-
trod. on ballast heaps in N.S. by John Macoun (1886; Pictou). [*Ornithopus* L.; *Astrolobium*
DC.].

C. varia L.
European; persisting about old habitations or spreading to roadsides and waste places in N.
America, as in sw B.C. (about 45 mi E of Vancouver; CAN), Man. (Brandon), s Ont. (Brant, Lincoln, and York counties), sw Que. (St. Andrews, Argenteuil Co.), and N.S. (Kings and Victoria
counties).

CYTISUS L.   [3682]   Broom

1   Flowers light yellow, about 1 cm long, up to 10 in compact racemes on short lateral
    shoots; upper calyx-lip deeply 2-lobed, the lower lip shallowly 3-toothed; pods
    reddish-hairy; leaves all 3-foliolate; plant villous-pubescent to glabrate; (introd. in
    s ?B.C.) . . . . [*C. monspessulanus*]
1   Flowers bright yellow or purplish-tinged, to 2.5 cm long, solitary (sometimes 2 or 3)
    on short axillary peduncles; upper and lower calyx-lobes about equally 2-toothed
    and 3-toothed, respectively; pods glabrous except along the villous margins; leaves
    becoming simple near the ends of the strongly angled branches; plant glabrous or
    pubescent; (introd. in B.C., P.E.I., and N.S.) . . . . *C. scoparius*

[C. monspessulanus L.]
[European; an occasional garden-escape in w N. America, the report of it as such in B.C. by
Hitchcock et al. (1961) requiring confirmation.]

C. scoparius (L.) Link   Scotch Broom
European; a garden-escape to sandy roadsides, barrens, and open woods in N. America, as in
B.C. (Queen Charlotte Is.; Vancouver Is. and adjacent islands and mainland), P.E.I. (a large
colony at some distance from its original site in a cemetery at Georgetown, Kings Co.), and
N.S. (Sable Is., Boularderie Is., and Kings, Yarmouth, and Shelburne counties). [*Spartium* L.;
Sarothamnus Wimm.].

DESMODIUM Desv.   [3807]   Tick-trefoil, Tick-clover

1   Stamens monadelphous; calyx-lobes less than half as long as the tube; pod-stipe
    more than 3 times as long as the calyx and much surpassing the persistent remains
    of the stamens; pod-articles (sections of the pod) straight or slightly concave on the
    glabrous dorsal suture; stipules bristle-form; leaflets ovate to rhombic-ovate.
    2   Corolla white, to 6 mm long; pod-stipe to about 1 cm long, finely pubescent;

inflorescence consisting of short, mostly axillary racemes; leaves scattered along
the low slender stem; stipules deciduous; (s ?Ont.) . . . . [*D. pauciflorum*]
  2 Corolla roseate to purple, to 8 mm long; pod-stipe glabrous at maturity.
      3 Flowering stem leafless, arising from the base; terminal leaflet distinctly
           longer than broad, acute or short-acuminate; pedicels to over 2 cm long; pod-
           stipe about 1 cm long; stipules deciduous; (Ont. and s Que.) . . . . *D. nudiflorum*
      3 Flowering stem arising from a whorl of leaves; terminal leaflet nearly as broad
           as long, long-acuminate; pedicels less than 1 cm long; pod-stipe rarely over
           6 mm long; stipules persistent; (Ont. to N.S.) . . . . *D. glutinosum*
1 Stamens diadelphous; calyx-lobes more than half as long as the tube; pod-stipe
rarely more than twice as long as the calyx and shorter than the remains of the
stamens; pod-articles more or less convex on both of the pubescent sutures.
  4 Stipules conspicuous, ovate, attenuate at apex; (s Ont.).
      5 Stems prostrate, trailing, slender; terminal leaflets broadly obovate to
           suborbicular, appressed- to spreading-pilose on both surfaces; corolla purple;
           racemes simple or little branched . . . . *D. rotundifolium*
      5 Stems erect, stout; leaflets ovate, pubescent beneath with hooked hairs;
           racemes panicled.
         6 Flowers white, on pedicels to over 2 cm long, in a wand-like terminal
            inflorescence; pod-articles oval to orbicular, at most 7 mm long; leaflets
            firm, strongly reticulate; stipules usually ascending . . . . [*D. illinoense*]
         6 Flowers pinkish, becoming green, on pedicels less than 1.5 cm long, in
            axillary and terminal inflorescences; pod-articles usually semirhombic, to
            13 mm long; leaflets thin; stipules usually reflexed at maturity . . . . *D. canescens*
  4 Stipules linear to narrowly ovate; racemes panicled.
      7 Leaves sessile or on petioles not over 3 mm long; leaflets linear-oblong;
           flowers pinkish to lavender; pod-articles about 5 mm long, broadly curved
           above, rounded beneath; (s Ont.; ?extinct) . . . . [*D. sessilifolium*]
      7 Leaves distinctly petioled; leaflets broader.
         8 Lower margin of pod-articles abruptly curved near middle, the articles
            (usually 4 or more) somewhat triangular or semirhombic; (s Ont.).
            9 Leaflets ovate, sharply acuminate; stipules to 2 cm long, usually
               persistent; panicle sparingly branched; pod-stipe to 5 mm long . . . .
               . . . . *D. cuspidatum*
            9 Leaflets narrowly to rather broadly lanceolate, blunt; stipules at most 6
               mm long, often deciduous; panicle diffuse; pod-stipe about 3 mm long . . . . .
               . . . . *D. paniculatum*
         8 Lower margin of pod-articles broadly rounded, nearly semicircular.
           10 Flowers to over 1 cm long; pods with up to 5 articles, each to about 6
             or 7 mm long; (s Man. to N.S.) . . . . *D. canadense*
           10 Flowers about 5 mm long; pods with at most 3 articles, these not over
             5.5 mm long; (s Ont.).
             11 Stem, petioles, and leaves essentially glabrous; leaflets at most 3.5
               cm long, the lateral ones about as long as the petiole . . . .
               . . . . *D. marilandicum*
             11 Stem, petioles, and leaves pubescent; lateral leaflets distinctly
               longer than the petiole.
               12 Terminal leaflet to 7 cm long; stipules early deciduous; stem and
                 petioles finely pubescent with hooked hairs . . . . [*D. rigidum*]
               12 Terminal leaflet at most 3 cm long; stipules mostly persistent;
                 stem and petioles with long pilosity in addition to shorter hooked
                 pubescence . . . . *D. ciliare*

D. canadense (L.) DC.
/T/EE/ (Hp) Open woods and clearings from s Man. (N to the Winnipeg dist.; WIN; the re-
port N to Norway House by Hooker 1833, requires clarification, as do reports from Sask.) to
Ont. (N to Renfrew and Carleton counties), Que. (N to L. Timiskaming at ca. 47°30′N and the

Gaspé Pen. near Matapédia), N.B., and N.S. (Colchester and Pictou counties; ACAD; CAN; not known from P.E.I.), s to Okla., Ohio, and Va. [*Hedysarum* L.; *Meibomia* Ktze.]. MAP: Fassett 1939:98 (the occurrence in s Man. should be indicated).

D. canescens (L.) DC.
/t/EE/ (Hp) Dry sandy fields and woods from Nebr. to s Ont. (Pelee Is., Pelee Pt., Malden, and Amherstburg, Essex Co.; Chatham and Rondeau Provincial Park, Kent Co.; CAN; TRT) and Mass., s to E Tex. and Fla. [*Hedysarum* L.; *Meibomia* Ktze.]. MAP: Fassett 1939:96.

D. ciliare (Muhl.) DC.
/T/EE/ (Hp) Dry sandy woods and clearings from Mich. to s Ont. (Lincoln Co. and Georgian Bay, L. Huron; CAN), N.Y., and New Eng., s to Mexico, Tex., and Fla. [*Hedysarum* Muhl.; *Meibomia* Blake; *D. obtusum* of auth., not (Muhl.) DC.].

D. cuspidatum (Muhl.) Loud.
/T/EE/ (Hp) Rich woods and banks from Mich. to s Ont. (Lambton, Elgin, Middlesex, Norfolk, Waterloo, Welland, Lincoln, Wentworth, Northumberland, and Hastings counties), N.H., and Vt., s to E Tex., Ark., and Fla. [*Hedysarum* Muhl.; *Meibomia* Ktze.; *D. bracteosum* (Michx.) DC.; *D. grandiflorum* (Walt.) DC., not of auth. generally]. MAP: Fassett 1939:96 *(D. bract.).*
Var. *longifolium* (T. & G.) Schub., the pubescent extreme, is reported from s Ont. by Landon (1960; Norfolk Co.).

D. glutinosum (Muhl.) Wood
/T/EE/ (Hp) Dry or rocky woods from Minn. to Ont. (N to the Ottawa dist.; Gillett 1958; reports of *D. acuminatum* from Sask. are excluded by Breitung 1957a), Que. (N to St-Joachim, NE of Quebec City; see Que. map by Doyon and Lavoie 1966: fig. 15, p. 818), N.B. (St. Croix, York Co., and Woodstock, Carleton Co.; CAN; NBM; not known from P.E.I.), and N.S. (Kings and Hants counties), s to Mexico, Tex., La., Tenn., and Fla. [*Hedysarum* Muhl.; *Meibomia* Ktze.; *D. acuminatum* (Michx.) DC.; *D. grandiflorum* of auth., not (Walt.) DC.]. MAPS: Fassett 1939:91 (*D. acum.*; the s Sask. area should be deleted); D. Isley, Brittonia 7(3): fig. 11G, p. 189. 1950.
Forma *chandonnetii* (Lunell) Schub. (the leaves scattered along the stem rather than whorled near the base) is reported from s Ont. by Gaiser and Moore (1966; Lambton Co.) and from SW Que. by Boivin (1966b).

[D. illinoense Gray]
[Prairies and dry soils from Nebr. to s Ont. (Komoka, near London, Middlesex Co., where taken by Dearness in 1888; CAN; probably now extinct in Canada), s to Tex., Okla., and Mo. [*Meibomia* Ktze.]. MAP: Fassett 1939:96 (the s Ont. station should be indicated).]

D. marilandicum (L.) DC.
/t/EE/ (Hp) Dry open woods from Mich. to s Ont. (Essex, Lambton, Norfolk, and Waterloo counties) and New Eng., s to E Tex., Tenn., and S.C. [*Hedysarum* L.; *Meibomia* Ktze.].

D. nudiflorum (L.) DC.
/T/EE/ (Hp) Rich or dry woods from Minn. to Ont. (N to Carleton Co.), Que. (N to Argenteuil Co. and the Montreal dist.; reported N to Quebec City by John Macoun 1883) and Maine, s to E Tex., La., Miss., and N Fla. [*Hedysarum* L.; *Meibomia* Ktze.]. MAPS: Fassett 1939:91; D. Isley, Brittonia 7(3): fig. 11P, p. 189. 1950.

D. paniculatum (L.) DC.
/t/EE/ (Hp) Dry woods and clearings from Nebr. to s Ont. (N to York Co.; TRT; collections from farther north, commonly distributed as *D. dillenii,* require further study), SW ?Que. (*D. dillenii* reported N to the Montreal dist. by Marie-Victorin 1935), and N.H., s to Tex. and Fla. [*Hedysarum* L.; *Meibomia* Ktze.; *D. dillenii* of Canadian reports in part, not Darl., this, according to B.G. Schubert, Rhodora 52(618):154. 1950, being a mixture of two different elements, *D. glabellum* (Michx.) DC. and *D. perplexum* Schub., neither of which occurs in Canada].

[D. pauciflorum (Nutt.) DC.]
[Reports of this species of the E U.S.A. (N to Iowa and N.Y.) from Ont. (as by John Macoun 1883, John Macoun and J. Gibson, Can. J., n.s. 15(93). 1877, Stroud 1941, and Soper 1949) and Que. (as by W.T. Macoun, Ottawa Naturalist 16(6):137. 1902) probably refer largely to *D. paniculatum*. The MAP by D. Isley (Brittonia 7(3): fig. 11P, p. 189. 1950) shows no Canadian stations. (*Hedysarum* Nutt.; *Meibomia* Ktze.).]

[D. rigidum (Ell.) DC.]
[The report of this species of the E U.S.A. (N to Mich. and Mass.) from S Ont. by Dodge (1915; Lambton Co.; this taken up by Soper 1949) requires confirmation, as also the identity of collections in TRT from Lincoln and Welland counties that have been placed here. (*Hedysarum* Ell.; *Meibomia* Ktze.).]

D. rotundifolium (Michx.) T. & G.
/t/EE/ (Hp) Dry woods from Mich. to S Ont. (Lambton, Middlesex, Norfolk, Waterloo, and Welland counties; John Macoun 1883; J.M. Macoun 1896; Dodge 1915; Montgomery 1945; MT; OAC), N.Y., and Vt., S to Tex. and Fla. [*Hedysarum* Michx.; *Meibomia* Ktze.; *M. michauxii* Vail].

[D. sessilifolium (Torr.) T. & G.]
[Dry sandy soils from Mich. to S Ont. (Sandwich, Essex Co., where taken by John Macoun in 1901 as apparently the only Canadian record and now probably extinct; CAN) and Mass., S to E Tex., La., and S.C. (*Hedysarum* Torr.; *Meibomia* Ktze.).]

[DOLICHOS L.] [3910]

[D. lablab L.] Hyacinth-Bean
[Asiatic; often cult. for ornament and tending to escape in N. America, as in S Ont. (Soper 1949), where, however, scarcely established.]

[GALEGA L.] [3715]

[G. officinalis L.] Goat's-Rue
[Eurasian; there is a collection in TRT from a moist waste meadow near Toronto, Ont., where taken by J. Gibson in 1953 but scarcely established. No other reports of its escaping from cult. in N. America have been found.]

GENISTA L. [3675]

G. tinctoria L. Dyer's Greenweed
Eurasian; introd. in dry sterile soils of N. America, as in SW Que. (Oka, near Montreal; Ayers Cliff, Stanstead Co.).

GLEDITSIA L. [3544]

G. triacanthos L. Honey-Locust
/t/EE/ (Mg) Rich woods from S.Dak. to S Ont. (apparently native on Middle Sister Is. and Pelee Is. and at Pelee Pt. and Amherstburg, all along the shore of L. Erie in Essex Co.; probably introd. farther northwards as far as Ottawa; *see* S Ont. maps and discussion by Fox and Soper 1953: map 22, p. 24, and Soper 1956: map 9b, p. 81; also planted elsewhere and reported from N.S. by Boivin 1966*b*, where undoubtedly introd.) and N.Y., S to Tex. and Fla. MAPS: Hosie 1969:252; Canada Department of Northern Affairs and Natural Resources 1956:232; Fowells 1965:198; Preston 1961:276; Hough 1947:289; Fassett 1939:21; Munns 1938: map 142, p. 146; Little 1971: maps 132-W and 132-E.

[GLYCINE L.] [3874]

[G. max (L.) Merr.] Soy-Bean
[Asiatic; an occasional garden-escape to rubbish heaps, old fields, and roadsides in N. America, as in s Ont. (railway ballast at Point Edward, Lambton Co.; OAC) and Que. (reported from near a grain elevator at Quebec City by Lionel Cinq-Mars et al., Nat. can. (Que.) 98(2):195. 1971), where, however, scarcely established. (*Phaseolus* L.; *G. soja* (L.) Sieb. & Zucc.).]

GLYCYRRHIZA L. [3769] Licorice

G. lepidota Nutt. Wild Licorice
/T/WW/ (Grh) Prairies, meadows, shores, and waste places from SE B.C. (Kootenay L.; Cranbrook; Crowsnest Pass) to Alta. (N to McMurray, 56°44′N), Sask. (N to Hudson Bay Junction, 52°52′N; the report N to L. Athabasca by John Macoun 1883, is probably erroneous, perhaps based upon Alta. material from the Athabasca R.), Man. (N to Roblin, s of Duck Mt.), and w Ont. (reported from sand-hills at the mouth of the Rainy R., Lake of the Woods, by Macoun 1883; known also from Waterloo and Welland counties, s Ont., where probably introd.), s to s Calif., Mexico, Tex., and w Mo. MAP: Fassett 1939:79.

Var. *glutinosa* (Nutt.) Wats. (*G. glut.* Nutt.; stipitate glands present throughout the inflorescence and often also on the petioles, leaf-rachises, and stems rather than confined to the calyx) is reported from the upper Columbia Valley, s B.C., by Macoun (1883).

GYMNOCLADUS Lam. [3545]

G. dioica (L.) Koch Kentucky Coffee-tree. Chicot or Gros Févier
/t/EE/ (Mg) Alluvial flats, streambanks, and rich woods from S.Dak. to s Ont. (apparently native in Essex, Kent, and Lambton counties of the sw Niagara Pen.; *see* s Ont. maps and discussion by Fox and Soper 1953: map 23, p. 23, and Soper 1956: map 9c, p. 81; probably also native in Norfolk Co. according to Landon 1960; planted and natzd. elsewhere as far N as Ottawa and in sw Que. as far N as Montreal) and N.Y., s to Okla., Mo., and Tenn. [*Guilandina* L.; *Gym. canadensis* Lam.]. MAPS: Hosie 1969:254; Canada Department of Northern Affairs and Natural Resources 1956:234; Preston 1961:274; Hough 1947:287; Fassett 1939:21; Munns 1938: map 141, p. 145.

HEDYSARUM L. [3778] Sainfoin

(Ref.: Rollins 1940)
1 Corolla pale yellow to nearly white, to 18 mm long, the basal lobes of its wings about equalling the wing-claw; calyx to 4 mm long, the teeth all shorter than the tube (the upper 2 broader and shorter than the lower 3); fruit glabrous, consisting of up to 4 more or less obovate segments (articles) to 1 cm broad, these lightly and irregularly reticulate except along the narrowly winged margins; (mts. of B.C. and Alta.) . . . .
. . . .*H. sulphurescens*
1 Corolla carmine or magenta to reddish purple or purple; calyx usually longer; (transcontinental).
  2 Fruits usually pubescent, with at most 4 segments, these to 13 mm broad and with wing-margins to 2 mm broad; flowers to over 2 cm long (rarely less than 18 mm); leaflets conspicuously veined, usually pubescent above; (?B.C. and ?Alta.). . . . . . .
. . . . [*H.occidentale*]
  2 Fruits with up to 6 segments, these rarely over 7 mm broad, the wing at most 1 mm broad; (transcontinental).
    3 Calyx-teeth distinctly unequal, all shorter than the tube, the lower 3 lanceolate, to about 2 mm long, the upper 2 shorter and broader; corolla reddish purple, typically not over 1.5 cm long, the basal lobes of its wings about equalling the wing-claw; segments of fruit narrowly wing-margined, more or less oval or ovate-elliptic, not noticeably cross-corrugated, the reticulation more or less quadrate; leaflets conspicuously veined . . . . . .*H. alpinum*

3 Calyx-teeth subequal, linear or linear-lanceolate, to 6 mm long, at least the lower ones usually longer than the tube; corolla carmine, magenta, or purple, to slightly over 2 cm long, the basal lobes of its wings scarcely 1/3 as long as the wing-claw; segments of fruit not at all wing-margined, roundish, plainly cross-corrugated, the reticulation laterally elongated; leaflets rather obscurely veined . . . . *H. boreale*

H. alpinum L.
/aST/X/EA/ (Hp) Calcareous sands, gravels, rocky slopes, and tundra, the aggregate species from the coasts of Alaska–Yukon–Dist. Mackenzie–Dist. Keewatin to Banks Is., Victoria Is., northernmost Ont., Que. (N to S Ungava Bay, Anticosti Is., and the Gaspé Pen.; a large gap from S Ungava Bay to the Côte-Nord), Nfld., and N.B. (St. John R. system; not known from P.E.I. or N.S.), S to cent. B.C. (Mt. Selwyn, ca. 56°N), SW Alta. (near Jasper), N Mont., Wyo., S.Dak., S Sask.–Man., cent. Ont. (S to the N shore of L. Superior), Maine, and the mts. of N Vt.; Eurasia. MAPS and synonymy: *see* below.
1 Pods pubescent on both surfaces; [*H. philoscia* Nels.; S-cent. Alta. (Fort Saskatchewan) to Sask. (Rollins 1940; not listed by Breitung 1957a), Man. (Hargrave R. N of L. Winnipeg; Grand Rapids, near the NW end of L. Winnipeg), and Ont. (Kapuskasing, 49°24′N; CAN)] . . . . var. *philoscia* (Nels.) Rollins
1 Pods glabrous or very sparingly pubescent along the margins.
  2 Flowers to 15 mm long; half-keel (longitudinally) 3 or 4 mm broad . . . .
    . . . . var. *americanum* Michx.
    3 Flowers white; [E Que. (Mt-Commis, Rimouski Co.) and Nfld.] . . . .
      . . . . f. *albiflorum* (Standl.) Fern.
    3 Flowers pink to reddish-purple; [*H. americanum* (Michx.) Britt.; *H. auriculatum* Eastw.; *Astragalus mistassinicus* Rousseau; range of the species; MAPS: Raup 1947: pl. 30; Hultén 1968b:668] . . . . f. *americanum*
  2 Flowers to 18 mm long; half-keel to 5.5 mm broad; [incl. var. *grandiflorum* Rollins, *H. hedysaroides* (L.) Schinz. & Thell., *H. arcticum* Fedtsch., *H. obscurum* L., and *H. truncatum* Eastw.; Alaska–northernmost Yukon–NW Dist. Mackenzie–E Banks Is.–E Victoria Is. and mts. of B.C. (Mt. Selwyn, ca. 56°N) and SW Alta. (Maligne L., near Jasper); var. *grandiflorum* reported from S Labrador and N and W Nfld. by Rollins 1940; MAPS (W area): Hultén 1968b:668 (*H. hed.*); Porsild 1957: map 252, p. 192]. A hybrid with *H. (mack.) boreale* var. *mackenzii* is reported from Herschel Is., off the coast of the Yukon, by Macoun and Holm (1921) . . . . var. *alpinum*

H. boreale Nutt.
/aST/X/A/ (Hp) Calcareous gravels and rocky slopes, the aggregate species from the coasts of Alaska–Yukon–Dist. Mackenzie–Dist. Keewatin to Banks Is., Victoria Is., northernmost Ont., Que. (E James Bay N to ca. 55°N; Swampy Bay R. at ca. 57°N, 69°W; Anticosti Is.; not known from the Maritime Provinces), and W Nfld., S in the West through B.C.–Alta.–Sask. to Oreg., Ariz., and N.Mex., farther eastwards S to N-cent. Man. (S to Gillam, about 165 mi S of Churchill) and N-cent. Ont. (coasts of Hudson Bay–James Bay S to ca. 53°N); N Asia. MAPS and synonymy: *see* below.
   In addition to the following forms, one in which the flowers are replaced by clusters of small scales has been distinguished as *H. boreale* var. *mackenzii* f. *proliferum* (Dore) Boivin (*H. mackenzii* f. *proliferum* W.G. Dore, Can. Field-Nat. 73(3):151. 1959; known only from the type locality along the Tanana R., Alaska).
1 Racemes usually compact, to 4(6) cm long, with up to 15(20) flowers to about 2 cm long; fruits with up to 6(8) segments; leaves usually glabrous to sparingly strigose above; plant generally unbranched . . . . var. *mackenzii* (Richards.) Hitchc.
  2 Flowers purple; [*H. mackenzii* Rich. and its var. *fraseri* Boivin; transcontinental, the type from "Point Lake to the Arctic Sea"; MAPS (*H. mack.*): Hultén 1968b:667; Porsild 1957: map 253, p. 192; Raup 1947: pl. 30; Meusel, Jaeger, and Weinert 1965:247] . . . . f. *mackenzii*
  2 Flowers white; [*H. mackenzii* f. *niveum* Boivin; known from the Yukon (type from Pine Creek) and Churchill, Man.] . . . . f. *niveum* Boivin

1 Racemes often as much as 1.5 dm long, the flowers often more numerous, typically carmine, magenta, or purple, to 17 mm long; fruits with usually not more than 5 segments; plant usually branched.

   3 Plant usually greenish, the leaves only sparsely hairy, often glabrous above; [*H. pabulare* Nels.; incl. *H. dasycarpum* Turcz.; B.C.–Alta.] . . . . var. *boreale*

   3 Plant greyish-hairy, the leaves pubescent on both surfaces (but intergrading in this character with var. *boreale*) . . . . var. *cinerascens* (Rydb.) Rollins

      4 Flowers carmine, magenta, or purple; [*H. cinerascens* Rydb.; *H. canescens* Nutt., not L.; s Alta. and s Sask.] . . . . f. *cinerascens*

      4 Flowers white; [type from Eastend, sw Sask.] . . . . f. *album* Boivin

[H. occidentale Greene]
[This species of the higher mts. of the w U.S.A. (Wash. to Mont., Wyo., and Colo.) is reported from Alta. by Rydberg (1922; as *H. lancifolium*) and a collection in Herb. V from Strathcona Park, Vancouver Is., sw B.C., has been placed here by G.N. Jones. It may possibly have been introd. at the latter location. Further collections may eventually establish it as a member of our native flora. (*H. lancifolium* Rydb.).]

H. sulphurescens Rydb.
/T/W (Hp) Open forested areas E of the Cascade Mts. from SE B.C. (Golden, Field, and Yoho s to near Creston and Cranbrook) and sw Alta. (N to Banff and Laggan) to Wash., Mont., and Wyo. [*H. boreale* var. *albiflorum* Macoun (*H. alb.* (Macoun) Fedtsch.)].

LATHYRUS L.   [3854]   Vetchling, Wild Pea.   Gesse

(Ref.: C.L. Hitchcock 1952)

1 Leaflets none, the leaves reduced to tendrils, these and the 1-flowered peduncles subtended by a pair of broadly sagittate-ovate leaf-like stipules up to 4 cm long; flowers lemon-yellow, mostly solitary, long-peduncled, about 1 cm long; calyx-lobes about twice as long as the tube; glabrous annual; (introd.) . . . . [*L. aphaca*]

1 Leaflets 1 or more pairs; flowers usually 2 or more; calyx-lobes seldom as much as twice as long as the tube.

   2 Leaflets a single pair, the leaf-rachis terminated by simple or forking tendrils; (introd.).

      3 Flowers bright yellow, to 2 cm long; pods to 3 cm long and 7 mm broad; leaflets lanceolate to linear-oblong, to 4 cm long; stipules sagittate-lanceolate to -ovate, each with 2 prolonged basal lobes; stem wingless; subglabrous to rather densely villous-hirsute rhizomatous perennial . . . . *L. pratensis*

      3 Flowers purplish or bluish-purple to roseate or white; stipules semisagittate, each with a single prolonged basal lobe.

         4 Stem and filiform petioles wingless; leaflets oblong, at most about 3.5 cm long; flowers about 1.5 cm long, up to 6 per raceme, fragrant; pods to 4 cm long and 4 mm broad; glabrous perennial with freely tuberiferous rhizomes . . . . *L. tuberosus*

         4 Stem and petioles commonly distinctly winged; rhizomes not tuberiferous.

            5 Peduncles bearing up to about 10 flowers; perennials.

               6 Flowers about 2.5 cm long; largest (lowest) calyx-tooth about equalling the tube; leaflets lanceolate to oval, mostly less than 1 dm long; pods with a smooth dorsal suture, to 1 dm long and 1 cm broad . . . . *L. latifolius*

               6 Flowers about 1.5 cm long; calyx-teeth all considerably shorter than the tube; leaflets narrowly lanceolate, mostly at least 1 dm long; pods with toothed ridges on the dorsal suture, to 6 cm long and 6 mm broad . . . . *L. sylvestris*

            5 Peduncles 1–3(5)-flowered; annuals.

               7 Leaflets elliptic to oval or oblong, to about 5 cm long; flowers very

fragrant, variously coloured, to 3 cm long; pod to 6 cm long, rough-
hairy, 4–10-seeded . . . . [*L. odoratus*]

7   Leaflets linear to lanceolate or narrowly elliptic; flowers not
fragrant; plants (including pods) glabrous.
   8   Calyx-teeth shorter than the tube; flowers 1–3, rose-purple, to
3 cm long; pods linear, to 1 dm long and 9 mm broad, rather
leathery, with at least 6 seeds; leaflets to 1 dm long . . . . . *L. tingitanus*
   8   Calyx-teeth equalling to nearly twice as long as the tube; flowers
at most about 2 cm long.
      9   Pods obliquely oblong, to about 4 cm long and 1.5 cm broad,
with rarely more than 4 seeds; flowers solitary, white, pink, or
blue, to about 2 cm long; leaflets to 1 dm long; stems to
1 m long . . . . *L. sativus*
      9   Pods linear, at most 5 mm broad, with usually more than 4
seeds; flowers about 1 cm long, bluish or purplish; leaflets to
5 or 6 cm long.
         10 Plant glabrous; peduncles 1-flowered . . . . *L. sphaericus*
         10 Plant usually sparingly pubescent; peduncles 1–3-
flowered . . . . [*L. pusillus*]
2   Leaflets at least 4 on some of the leaves; rhizomatous perennials.
  11 Tendrils lacking (usually represented only by a terminal simple bristle); calyx-
teeth subequal, the largest one at most about as long as the tube; stems not
winged; (B.C.).
    12 Plant densely villous, occurring on coastal sand dunes; leaflets 2–4 pairs,
to about 2 cm long; stipules usually equalling the leaflets; peduncles with
up to 6(10) pink to red or purple flowers to 18 mm long; calyx to 11 mm
long; pods to 3 cm long and 1 cm broad, hairy, with rarely more than 5
seeds; stems to 6 dm long, prostrate to erect but not climbing . . . . . . *L. littoralis*
    12 Plant glabrous to sparsely crisp-puberulent; leaflets 1 or 2(3) pairs, to 1.5
dm long; stipules to about 1/3 the length of the leaflets; pods to 4 cm long
and 7 mm broad, glabrous, with up to 12 seeds . . . . *L. bijugatus*
  11 Tendrils present, either simple or forking.
    13 Stipules obliquely hastate- to sagittate-ovate (with 2 basal lobes), from
only slightly shorter than to longer than the rather fleshy 3–6 pairs of
leaflets; flowers light blue to reddish-purple, to 3 cm long; calyx to 1.5 cm
long, the 3 lowest teeth all usually longer than the tube; pods usually
pubescent; stem wingless; (transcontinental) . . . . *L. japonicus*
    13 Stipules narrower, strongly oblique (with 1 basal lobe), mostly smaller than
the usually scarcely fleshy leaflets.
      14 Flowers ochroleucous, to about 1.5 cm long; leaflets 2–4 pairs, elliptic or
ovate, to about 5 cm long; stipules semicordate, about half as large as
the leaflets; stem wingless; plant glabrous; (B.C. to Que.) . . . *L. ochroleucus*
      14 Flowers various shades of pink, red, blue, or purple (the wings and keel
often paler, sometimes white or whitish), to over 2 cm long.
         15 Leaflets alternate, up to 8 pairs, elliptic to broadly lanceolate, to
about 6 cm long and 2(4) cm broad; stipules sagittate-ovate, usually
well over half as long as the leaflets, not constricted near the
middle; calyx to 13 mm long, its teeth usually pubescent, the plant
otherwise nearly or quite glabrous; stem wingless; (?B.C.) . . . .
. . . . [*L. polyphyllus*]
         15 Leaflets opposite, mostly averaging not more than 5 pairs (if more
than 5, other characters not as in *L. polyphyllus*).
           16 Inflorescence with up to 19 flowers, mostly surpassed by the
subtending leaves, these with 5 or 6 pairs of elliptic to ovate
leaflets; stipules linear-lanceolate; stem 4-angled but not
winged; plant copiously short-pubescent; (B.C. to w Ont.;
E Que.) . . . . *L. venosus*

16 Inflorescence with rarely more than 9 flowers, usually nearly equalling to overtopping the subtending leaves.

    17 Stem distinctly winged (except in vars. *myrtifolius* and *retusus*); calyx to 12 mm long, glabrous to uniformly pubescent, its teeth very unequal, the longest one about equalling the tube; corolla-keel about equalling the wing-petals; plant glabrous to densely pubescent; (trans-continental) . . . .*L. palustris*

    17 Stem angled but not winged; corolla-keel 1–4 mm shorter than the wing-petals; (B.C.).

        18 Calyx to 18 mm long, its teeth glabrous or merely ciliate, distinctly unequal, at least the lowest one usually longer than the tube; leaflets rather thick and fleshy, from linear and up to 8 cm long to ovate or ovate-elliptic and to 4 or 5 cm long; plant usually glabrous (except for the ciliation of the calyx-teeth and occasional pubescence on the stipules); (?B.C.) . . . .[*L. pauciflorus*]

        18 Calyx to 12 mm long, generally somewhat pubescent, its teeth subequal, the longest (lowest) one rarely over 3/4 the length of the tube; leaflets linear to lance-elliptic or -ovate, to 12 cm long; plant sparsely to rather densely soft-pubescent; (B.C.) . . . .*L. nevadensis*

[L. aphaca L.]   Pea-vine
[Eurasian; reported by Hitchcock et al. (1961) as fairly well established in the w U.S.A. It is known in Canada only through an 1883 collection by John Macoun in N.S. (wharf-ballast at Pictou, Pictou Co.; CAN).]

L. bijugatus White
/t/W/   (Grh)   Open or forested foothills from se B.C. (Kootenay Valley 11 mi s of Elko, se of Cranbrook; Boivin 1966*b*) to e Wash., Idaho, and ?Mont.

L. japonicus Willd.   Beach-Pea.   Pois de mer
/aST/X/GEA/   (Grh (Gst; Hpr))   Gravelly or sandy coasts and shores, the aggregate species from the Aleutian Is. and coasts of Alaska–Yukon–w Dist. Mackenzie (CAN) s along coastal B.C. to n Calif., with inland stations in Man. (shores of lakes Manitoba and Winnipeg and of Hudson Bay n to Churchill), Ont. (L. Nipigon, L. Simcoe, and the Great Lakes; also the U.S.A. shores of the last), and the James Bay–Hudson Bay coasts of Ont.–Que. n to ca. 56°N, then along the Atlantic coast from e Que. (St. Lawrence R. estuary from near Quebec City to the Côte-Nord, Anticosti Is., and Gaspé Pen.; isolated on L. St. John and on L. St. Peter in Nicolet Co.) to Labrador (n to Nain, 56°10′N), Nfld., N.B., P.E.I., N.S., and N.J. (isolated at L. Oneida, N.Y.); s Greenland; Iceland; Eurasia. maps and synonymy: *see* below.

1 Tendrils mostly simple; leaflets relatively thin, mostly less than 4 cm long, not strongly glaucous; stem slender.

    2 Plant essentially glabrous; [*L. maritimus* var. *thunbergianus* Miquel; *L. pisiformis* Houtt., not L.; transcontinental; maps (aggregate species): Meusel 1943: fig. 7f; Meusel, Jaeger, and Weinert 1965:252] . . . . .var. *japonicus*

    2 Plant densely pilose on the calyces, pedicels, peduncles, and lower leaf-surfaces . . . . .var. *aleuticus* (Greene) Fern.

        3 Flowers reddish- to bluish-purple; [*L. maritimus* var. *al.* Greene (*L. al.* (Greene) Pobed.) and var. *pubescens* Hartm.; *Pisum maritimum* L. in small part; transcontinental; map (*L. mar.* ssp. *pub.*; incl. var. *pellitus*): Hultén 1968*b*:673] . . . . .f. *aleuticus*

        3 Flowers white; [type from along the Northwest R., Hamilton R. basin, s-cent. Labrador] . . . . .f. *albinus* Fern.

1 Tendrils mostly forking; leaflets thick, glaucous, to about 7 cm long; stem relatively thick.

4 Plant essentially glabrous.
  5 Corolla to over 1.5 cm long; pods to over 6.5 cm long . . . . . . var. *glaber* (Ser.) Fern.
    6 Leaflets elliptic or obovate, to 4 cm broad; [*Pisum maritimum* var. *glabrum*
       Ser.; *L. maritimus* Bigel. (not L.) and its var. *glaber* (Ser.) Eames; Alaska–
       B.C.; Man. to s Labrador and Nfld.; MAPS: C.L. Hitchcock 1952: map 6, p.
       98; Fassett 1939:118; the map for *L. maritimus* by Hultén 1968*b*:672, is
       applicable here] . . . . f. *glaber*
    6 Leaflets elliptic-lanceolate, acute, to 1 cm broad; [Nfld.] . . . .
      . . . . f. *acutifolius* (Bab.) Fern.
  5 Corolla less than 1.5 cm long; pods less than 5 cm long; [shores of L.
    Winnipeg, Man., L. Erie, Ont., and the type locality, L. Nipissing, Ont.] . . . .
    . . . . var. *parviflorus* Fassett
4 Plant densely pilose on the calyces, pedicels, peduncles, and lower leaf-surfaces . . . .
  . . . . var. *pellitus* Fern.
  7 Flowers reddish- to bluish-purple; [Ont. to Nfld. and N.S. (type from St. Paul
    Is.); MAPS: C.L. Hitchcok 1952: map 6, p. 98; Fassett 1939:116] . . . . f. *pellitus*
  7 Flowers white; [Labrador; Boivin 1966*b*] . . . . f. *candidus* Fern.

L. latifolius L.
European; a garden-escape to roadsides, thickets, and waste places in N. America, as in sw B.C. (Vancouver Is.; Vancouver), Ont. (N to Manitoulin Is., N L. Huron), and Que. (N to the Gaspé Pen.).

L. littoralis (Nutt.) Endl.
/t/W/ (Grh) Sand dunes along the Pacific coast from w B.C. (Queen Charlotte Is.; Vancouver Is.; Stubbs Is.) to N Calif. [*Astrophia* Nutt.].

L. nevadensis Wats.
/T/W/ (Grh) Thickets and woods from B.C. (Vancouver Is. and adjacent islands and mainland N to Williams Lake, ca. 52°N) to Calif. and Idaho.
    The B.C. plant is referable to ssp. *lanceolatus* (Howell) Hitchc. var. *pilosellus* (Peck) Hitchc. (*L. rigidus* var. *pil.* Peck; *L. nuttallii* Wats.; *L. pauciflorus sensu* J.M. Macoun 1913, not Fern., relevant collections in CAN; flowers averaging less than 17 mm long rather than over 17 mm, tendrils usually well developed and branching rather than usually unbranched or even bristle-like). *L. pauciflorus* is reported in B.C. N to the Nass R. at ca. 54°N by Eastham (1947), which would extend the N limit in B.C. beyond that given above if the report proves referable here.

L. ochroleucus Hook.
/sT/X/ (Grh (Hpr)) Moist woods, thickets, and clearings from w Dist. Mackenzie (N to Wrigley, ca. 63°10'N) and B.C. to L. Athabasca (Alta. and Sask.), Man. (N to Gillam, about 165 mi s of Churchill), Ont. (N to Sachigo L., ca. 53°50'N, 93°W), and Que. (N to the Nottaway R. SE of James Bay at 51°19'N; RIM; not known from the Atlantic Provinces), s to Wash. (?Oreg.), Wyo., S.Dak., Ohio, Pa., and Vt. The type, as first collection cited, is from Hudson Bay (?Man.). MAPS (both somewhat incomplete northwards): C.L. Hitchcock 1952: map 7, p. 99; Fassett 1939:118.

[*L. odoratus* L.] Sweet Pea
[European; an occasional garden-escape to waste places in N. America but scarcely established, as in Man. (Brandon) and s Ont. (Port Dover, Norfolk Co.; OAC; reported from the Ottawa dist. by Gillett 1958).]

L. palustris L. Vetchling
/ST/X/EA/ (Grh (Hpr)) Meadows and damp thickets, the aggregate species from the Aleutian Is., Alaska (N to near the Arctic Circle), sw Yukon (Hultén's 1968*b* map), and B.C.–Alta. to Sask. (N to ca. 53°10'N; Fassett's map), Man. (N to Churchill), northernmost Ont., Que. (N to the E James Bay watershed at ca. 53°50'N, L. St. John, the Côte-Nord, Anticosti Is., and

Gaspé Pen.), Nfld., N.B., P.E.I., and N.S., s to N Calif., N.Dak., Mo., Tenn., and N.C.; Eurasia. MAPS and synonymy: *see* below.

1 Stem to 3 mm thick below the lowest peduncle, winged; leaflets lanceolate to oblanceolate or elliptic, mostly 2–5 pairs; flowers to 2.5 cm long.

    2 Plant essentially glabrous; [s B.C.; s Man. to s Nfld. and N.S.; MAPS: Fassett 1939:121 (var. *genuinus*); C.L. Hitchcock 1952: map 10 (aggregate species), p. 100; Meusel, Jaeger, and Weinert 1965:252 (aggregate species)] . . . . . var. *palustris*

    2 Plant finely pubescent; [*L. macranthus* (White) Rydb.; s Alaska–B.C.; s Man. to Nfld. and N.S.; MAP: Fassett 1939:124] . . . . var. *macranthus* (White) Fern.

1 Stem not over 1.5 mm thick below the lowest peduncle; flowers less than 2 cm long.

    3 Stem winged; leaflets 2–5 pairs, linear to narrowly oblong; peduncles 2–5-flowered.

        4 Plant essentially glabrous; [transcontinental; MAP (incomplete northwards): Fassett 1939:119] . . . . var. *linearifolius* Ser.

        4 Plant distinctly pubescent; [*L. pilosus* Cham.; transcontinental; MAPS: Hultén 1968b:673; Fassett 1939:126; C.L. Hitchcock 1952: map 10, p. 100] . . . .
        . . . . var. *pilosus* (Cham.) Ledeb.

    3 Stem wingless or nearly so.

        5 Plant glabrous; leaflets 2 or 3 pairs, broadly lanceolate to ovate; raceme with up to 9 flowers; [*L. myrtifolius* Muhl.; *L. ?stipulaceus sensu* Hooker 1831, possibly not Le Conte; Ont. to N.B. and N.S.; MAPS (both somewhat incomplete northwards): Fassett 1939:124; C.L. Hitchcock 1952: map 10, p. 100] . . . . var. *myrtifolius* (Muhl.) Gray

        5 Plant minutely pilose; leaflets up to 5 pairs, cuneate-elliptic, broadest near the retuse summit; flowers commonly about 4; [known only from the type locality, Sable Is., N.S., and from St-Pierre and Miquelon] . . . . var. *retusus* Fern.

[*L. pauciflorus* Fern.]
[Reports of this species of the w U.S.A. (N to Wash. and Idaho) from sw B.C. by J.M. Macoun (1913) are based upon *L. nevadensis* ssp. *lanceolatus* var. *pilosellus* (relevant collections in CAN), to which B.C. reports by Eastham (1947) may also refer.]

[*L. polyphyllus* Nutt.]
[The inclusion of B.C. in the range of this species of the w U.S.A. (Wash. to Calif.) by Abrams (1944; taken up by Eastham 1947) and Jepson (1951) requires clarification.]

L. pratensis L.　Yellow Vetchling
Eurasian; a garden-escape to roadsides, fencerows, meadows, and shores in N. America, as in B.C. (Victoria; Kaslo), Ont. (N to the s James Bay watershed at 51°15′N), Que. (N to the Gaspé Pen. at Percé), Nfld. (it is very doubtful that this species is possibly native in Nfld. as suggested by Fernald *in* Gray 1950; *see* note under *Luzula campestris*), N.B., P.E.I., and N.S.

[*L. pusillus* Ell.]
[The tentative report of this species of the E U.S.A. (N to Kans., Mo., and N.C.) from B.C. by Boivin (1967a) is probably based upon a collection in Herb. V from Vancouver Is., the identity of which requires clarification.]

L. sativus L.
Eurasian; rarely introd. about seaports in the U.S.A.; in Canada, known from Sask. (Boivin 1966b), s Ont. (field at Guelph, Wellington Co.; OAC), and Que. (Ste-Anne-de-la-Pocatière, Kamouraska Co.; QSA).

L. sphaericus Retz.
Eurasian; reported by Hitchcock et al. (1961) as occasionally escaping and becoming fairly well established in Oreg. and by Boivin (1966b) as introd. in sw B.C. (Duncan, Vancouver Is.).

L. sylvestris L.   Everlasting or Perennial Pea
Eurasian; a garden-escape to roadsides and waste places in N. America, as in sw B.C. (Denman Is.; Langley Prairie), Ont. (N to the Ottawa dist.), Que. (N to the Gaspé Pen. at Escuminac, Bonaventure Co.), N.B., P.E.I., and N.S.

L. tingitanus L.   Tangier Pea
European; reported by Hitchcock et al. (1961) as often grown as an ornamental and occasionally escaping and becoming established in Oreg. and Calif., and reported from sw B.C. by Boivin (1966*b*; Yarrow, near Vancouver).

L. tuberosus L.   Tuberous Vetchling
Eurasian; a garden-escape to fields, meadows, and roadsides in N. America, as in s Man. (near Winnipeg; CAN), Ont. (N to the Ottawa dist.), and sw Que. (Boivin 1966*b*).

L. venosus Muhl.
/T/(X)/   (Grh (Hpr))   Rich woods, thickets, streambanks, and sandy places from the SE Alaska Panhandle and B.C. to Alta. (Red Deer; CAN), Sask. (N to Prince Albert), Man. (N to The Pas), and w Ont. (N to the Kaministikwia R. near Thunder Bay; an isolated station on the banks of the Petit-Cascapédia R., Gaspé Pen., E Que., the type locality of *L. rollandii*), s to E Tex., La., and Ga. MAP (aggregate species): C.L. Hitchcock 1952: map 7, p. 99.

Our plant is referable to var. *intonsus* Butt. & St. John (*L. rollandii* Vict. & Rousseau; plant copiously short-hirsute rather than essentially glabrous; stipules linear-lanceolate, to about 2 cm long and 5 mm broad, rather than narrowly ovate and to about 3.5 cm long and 1 cm broad).

[LENS Mill.]   [3468]

[L. culinaris Medic.]   Lentil
[Eurasian; an occasional garden-escape to waste places and rubbish heaps in N. America but scarcely persistent, as in Ont. (N to Sault Ste. Marie; Montgomery 1957), Que. (Boivin 1966*b*), and Nfld. (Rouleau 1956; ?escaped).]

LESPEDEZA Michx.   [3820]   Bush-Clover

(Ref.: Clewell 1966)
1   Stems trailing, prostrate or reclining (*L. violacea* may sometimes be sought here); leaves oval, oblong, or obovate; flowers of two kinds, the larger ones purplish, petaliferous, on elongate filiform peduncles, the smaller (mostly apetalous) ones in sessile or subsessile axillary clusters; (s ?Ont.).
   2   Stems soft-downy with dense spreading pubescence . . . . [*L. procumbens*]
   2   Stems glabrate or minutely appressed-pubescent . . . . [*L. repens*]
1   Stems erect or ascending; (s Ont.; *L. capitata* var. *vulgaris* also in sw ?Que.).
   3   Terminal leaflet linear or linear-oblong, mostly at least 4 times as long as broad; stem wand-like or with few erect branches: flowers purple, on very crowded short peduncles; (s Ont.; ?extinct) . . . . [*L. virginica*]
   3   Terminal leaflet broader in outline.
      4   Flowers purplish, of two kinds; (s Ont.).
         5   Peduncles mostly very short; racemes bearing up to 10 flowers, these to 7 mm long; calyx to 4.5 mm long; stipules to 4 mm long . . . .*L. intermedia*
         5   Peduncles mostly surpassing their subtending leaves; racemes rarely with as many as 8 flowers, these to 9 mm long; calyx to 6 mm long; stipules to 6 mm long . . . .*L. violacea*
      4   Flowers yellowish or creamy, with a purple blotch, uniform.
         6   Peduncles much surpassing their subtending leaves; flowers less than 1 cm long, in spike-like racemes; calyx commonly not much longer than the pod; (s Ont.) . . . .*L. hirta*

6 Peduncles shorter than the subtending leaves; flowers to 12 mm long, in very dense subglobose heads; calyx greatly surpassing the pod; (s Ont. and sw ?Que.) . . . . *L. capitata*

L. capitata Michx.

/T/EE/ (Hp) Dry open soils, prairies, and sand dunes (ranges of Canadian taxa outlined below), s to Tex. and Fla.

1 Leaflets silvery-silky beneath, greyish and lustrous above; [var. *sericea* H. & A.; s Ont. (N to York and Frontenac counties); MAPS (aggregate species): Clewell 1966: fig. 3, p. 375; Fassett 1939:98] . . . . var. *capitata*
1 Leaflets dull.
  2 Leaflets narrowly obovate or oblong, velvety-pilose; [*L. velutina* Bickn.; *L. bicknellii* House; s Ont.: Lambton, Norfolk, Waterloo, and York counties] . . . .
    . . . . var. *velutina* (Bickn.) Fern.
  2 Leaflets mostly broader, green above, opaque beneath; [Ont.: N to Shirleys Bay, w of Ottawa, this possibly the basis of the report from sw Que. by Fernald *in* Gray 1950, Shirleys Bay being in Ont., not Que.] . . . . var. *vulgaris* T. & G.

L. hirta (L.) Hornem.

/t/EE/ (Hp) Dry soils from Ont. (N to Huron, Wellington, York, Hastings, Leeds, and Grenville counties; *see* s Ont. map by Soper 1962: fig. 14, p. 23) to Maine, s to E Tex. and Ga. [*Hedysarum* L.; *L. polystachya* Michx.]. MAP: Clewell 1966: fig. 4, p. 375.

L. intermedia (Wats.) Britt.

/T/EE/ (Hp) Dry open woods and thickets from E Kans. to Wisc., Mich., s Ont. (N to Huron, Waterloo, Peel, and Leeds counties; *see* s Ont. map by Soper 1962: fig. 15, p. 24), N.Y., and Maine, s to Tex. and Fla. [*L. stuvei* var. *int.* Wats., not *L. int.* Nakai; *L. frutescens* of auth., not (L.) Britt.]. MAP: Clewell 1966: fig. 6, p. 375.

[L. procumbens Michx.]

[The listing of this species of the E U.S.A. (N to Kans. and N.H.) for s Ont. by Soper (1949) requires clarification. No Canadian stations are indicated in the MAPS by Clewell (1966: fig. 8, p. 384) and Fassett (1939:107).]

[L. repens (L.) Bart.]

[The listing of this species of the E U.S.A. (N to Kans., Wisc., Ohio, and Conn.) for s Ont. by Soper (1949) is probably based upon its report from there by John Macoun (1883; this based in part upon the citation of a Douglas collection of *L. prostrata* from "Upper Canada" by Hooker 1831). Macoun, however, notes that the Ont. reports probably refer to *L. reticulata (L. virginica).* No Canadian stations are indicated in the MAPS by Clewell (1966: fig. 9, p. 384) and Fassett (1939:107). (*Hedysarum* L.; *L. prostrata* Pursh).]

L. violacea (L.) Pers.

/t/EE/ (Hp) Dry woods, thickets, and openings from E Kans. to Wisc., Mich., s Ont. (Niagara Gorge, Welland Co.; CAN; TRT; reported from Waterloo Co. by Montgomery 1945, and from Wentworth Co. by John Macoun and J. Gibson, Can. J., n.s. 15(93). 1877), Ohio, N.Y., and N.H., s to Tex. and Fla. [*Hedysarum* L.; *L. prairea* (Mack. & Bush) Britt.]. MAPS: Clewell 1966: fig. 12, p. 391; Fassett 1939:107 (the occurrence in s Ont. should be indicated).

[L. virginica (L.) Britt.]

[This species of the E U.S.A. (N to Kans., Mich., and N.H.) is known from Canada only through an 1892 collection in CAN by John Macoun at Leamington, Essex Co., s Ont. It has apparently not been found in Canada since that date. The MAPS by Clewell (1966: fig. 13, p. 391) and Fassett (1939:107) indicate no Canadian stations. (*Medicago* L.; *L. reticulata* (Muhl.) Pers., not Wats.).]

LOTUS L.   [3698]   Deer-Vetch

(Ref.: Zandstra and Grant 1968; Ottley 1923)
1   Stipules membranous, rounded to acuminate at apex, 3–10(15) mm long; flowers to
    1.5 cm long, subsessile (their pedicels barely 1 mm long), 3–12 in head-like umbels
    on axillary peduncles shorter than to several times surpassing their subtending
    leaves; calyx to 8 mm long, its narrowly triangular teeth to 1/3 as long as the tube;
    pods to 6 cm long and 2 mm broad; leaflets elliptic to oblong or obovate; glabrous or
    very sparsely strigose perennials with hollow, sprawling to erect stems; (B.C.).
    2   Corolla with a yellow banner and keel and cream-colour wings; the upper two
        calyx-teeth united for at least 3/4 of their length; peduncles naked or with a
        usually lanceolate, membranous, simple bract just below the inflorescence;
        leaflets 5–9 . . . .*L. pinnatus*
    2   Corolla strongly tinged with pink or purple, the keel purple-tipped; the upper two
        calyx-teeth usually not united for over 1/2 their length; peduncles with a usually
        3-foliolate bract just below the inflorescence (or the bract occasionally simple or
        sometimes 5(7)-foliolate); leaflets commonly 5 (3–6) . . . .*L. formosissimus*
1   Stipules gland-like, blackish; flowers yellow but often tinged with orange or red.
    3   Leaflets typically 5 (the lower pair (except in *L. nevadensis*) adjacent to the
        reduced glandular stipules and simulating foliaceous stipules).
        4   Pods falcate, scarcely twice as long as the calyx, indehiscent, with at most 3
            seeds; calyx to 6 mm long; peduncles to 3 cm long; leaves mostly on petioles
            2–4 mm long, the leaflets to 1.5 cm long; plant hirsute-strigose to villous,
            usually greyish; (s ?B.C.). . . . .[*L. nevadensis*]
        4   Pods nearly straight, many times longer than the calyx, dehiscent by 2 valves,
            many-seeded, to about 3 cm long; plants glabrous or pubescent; (introd.).
            5   Flowers to 18 mm long, usually in umbels of 5–12; leaflets broadly ovate.
                6   Calyx at anthesis with spreading hairs, its teeth spreading in the bud,
                    the 2 upper ones separated by an acute sinus; flowers to 12 mm long,
                    up to 12 in a head; peduncles to 1.5 dm long; petioles to 1 cm long;
                    leaflets to 2 cm long; stems hollow, to over 6 dm long, from a slender
                    rootstock producing numerous stolons . . . .*L. pedunculatus*
                6   Calyx at anthesis glabrous or with straight erect hairs, its teeth erect in
                    the bud, the 2 upper ones separated by an obtuse sinus; flowers to 1.5
                    cm long, rarely over 6 in a head; peduncles to 8 cm long, stout; leaves
                    nearly or quite sessile (the lowest pair of leaflets simulating stipules);
                    leaflets to 1 cm long; stem solid, to about 4 dm long, from a stout,
                    scarcely stoloniferous rootstock . . . .*L. corniculatus*
            5   Flowers to 10 mm long, solitary or in umbels of 2–4.
                7   Flowers (2)3 or 4, yellow or bluish when dry; leaflets of the cauline
                    leaves linear-lanceolate, acute . . . .*L. tenuis*
                7   Flowers 1 or 2(3), reddish when dry; leaflets of the cauline leaves
                    obovate, obtuse or rounded at apex . . . .*L. krylovii*
    3   Leaflets 2, 3, 4, or 6 (sometimes 5 in *L. micranthus*), the lowest ones well
        separated from the glandular stipules; flowers solitary (rarely 2) and subsessile in
        the leaf-axils or on axillary peduncles to about 3 cm long, at most 8 mm long;
        annuals.
        8   Flowers subsessile in the leaf-axils, to 8 mm long; leaflets (2)3 or 4, to 18 mm
            long and 8 mm broad, usually 2 on either side of the tip of the flattened
            rachis, 1 or 2 below these; calyx to 5 mm long, its linear teeth nearly twice as
            long as the usually brownish-mottled, soft-pilose to subglabrous tube; pods to
            1.5 cm long and 4 mm broad, sparsely soft-appressed-pubescent, not
            constricted between the 2–4 seeds; plant finely appressed-puberulent; (B.C.) . . . . .
            . . . .*L. denticulatus*
        8   Flowers on peduncles to 2 or 3 cm long; leaf-rachis not flattened; pods often
            longer but at most 2.5 mm broad, usually somewhat constricted between the
            4–8 seeds.

9   Leaflets mostly 3, to 3 cm long and 1.5 cm broad; flowers to 8 mm long, the peduncle to 3 cm long and usually with a small simple bract just below the flower; calyx to 6 mm long, its linear teeth mostly more than twice as long as the tube; pods only slightly constricted between the seeds; plant sparsely to densely villous; (sw B.C. to s Man.) . . . . *L. purshianus*

9   Leaflets mostly 5, to 12 mm long and 4 mm broad; flowers to 5 mm long, the peduncles to 2 cm long, with a 2–3-foliolate bract just below the flower; calyx about 2 mm long, its linear-lanceolate teeth usually shorter than the tube; pods more noticeably constricted between the seeds; plant glabrous to sparsely short-pubescent; (s B.C.) . . . . *L. micranthus*

L. corniculatus L.   Birdsfoot-Trefoil

Eurasian; introd. along roadsides and in fields and waste places of N. America, as in B.C. (N to Dawson Creek, ca. 55°45′N), Alta. (N to Beaverlodge, 55°10′N), Man. (Brandon; Gilbert Plains), Ont. (N to Grey and Prince Edward counties), Que. (N to Bic, Rimouski Co.), Nfld., N.B. (Charlotte and St. John counties), and N.S. (Kings and Halifax counties). [Incl. var. *ciliatus* Koch]. MAP (Canadian area): combine the maps by Zandstra and Grant 1968: fig. 14 (E Canada) and fig. 15 (w Canada), p. 573.

L. denticulatus (Drew) Greene

/T/W/   (T)   Usually in sandy soil from B.C. (N to Smithers, ca. 54°45′N) to N Calif. [*Hosackia* Drew; *H. (L.) subpinnata sensu* John Macoun 1890, not (Lag.) T. & G., relevant collections in CAN]. MAP (Canadian area): Zandstra and Grant 1968: fig. 13, p. 572.

L. formosissimus Greene

/t/W/   (Hp)   Usually on moist soil at low to moderate elevations from sw B.C. (Vancouver Is. and adjacent islands) to Calif. [*Hosackia gracilis* Benth.] MAP (Canadian area): Zandstra and Grant 1968: fig. 10, p. 572.

L. krylovii Schischk. & Serg.

Eurasian; apparently known in N. America only through two collections at White L., Oliver, B.C., s of Penticton, this location shown on the MAP of the Canadian area by Zandstra and Grant 1968: fig. 17, p. 573.

L. micranthus Benth.

/t/W/   (T)   Sandy coastal flats to montane slopes from sw B.C. (Vancouver Is. and adjacent islands and mainland N to Armstrong, about 15 mi N of Vernon) to Calif. [*Hosackia parviflora* Benth.]. MAP (Canadian area): Zandstra and Grant 1968: fig. 11, p. 572.

[L. nevadensis (Wats.) Greene]

[The reports of this species of the w U.S.A. (Wash. to Calif., Nev., and Idaho) from s B.C. by John Macoun (1883; 1886: Spences Bridge and Thompson R.; both as *Hosackia decumbens*; this taken up by Henry 1915, and Hitchcock et al. 1961) require clarification. (*Hosackia decumbens* var. *nev.* Wats.; incl. *H. (Syrmatium) dec.* Benth. (*L. douglasii* Greene), not *L. dec.* Poir.).]

L. pedunculatus Cav.

Eurasian; apparently known in N. America only from moist waste places and old fields in Canada, as in s B.C. (*L. ulig.* reported by Eastham 1947, as introd. as a forage crop and apparently well established along roadside ditches at New Westminster and vicinity; collection from near Hatzie in V), Sask. (Boivin 1966*b*), s Ont. (near Hamilton, Wentworth Co.; Montgomery 1957), E Que. (w Gaspé Pen.), N.B. (near St. Stephen, Charlotte Co., where taken by Pickett in 1894; CAN), and N.S. (Boivin 1966*b*). [*L. uliginosus* Schk.]. MAPS (Canadian area): Zandstra and Grant 1968: fig. 16 (E Canada) and fig. 17 (w Canada; the occurrence in Sask. should be indicated), p. 573.

L. pinnatus Hook.
/t/W/ (Hp) Moist places from sw B.C. (Nanaimo and vicinity, Vancouver Is.; CAN; reported from Victoria by Henry 1915; the citation by John Macoun 1883, of a Douglas collection of *Hosackia bicolor* from "On the Columbia, near its source in British Columbia" is based upon the citation of that collection by Hooker 1831, from "between Fort-Vancouver and the Grand Rapids of the Columbia", this region lying along the w Wash.–Oreg. boundary) to cent. Calif. [*Hosackia bicolor* Dougl.]. MAP (Canadian area): Zandstra and Grant 1968: fig. 10, p. 572.

L. purshianus (Benth.) Clem. & Clem. Prairie-Trefoil
/T/WW/ (T) Chiefly in sandy or rocky open or wooded areas from sw B.C. (Vancouver Is. and adjacent islands; V; not known from Alta.), s Sask. (Gainsborough, Carievale, and Broomhead; Breitung 1957a), and s Man. (N to near the s end of L. Manitoba) to Calif., Mexico, Tex., and Ark.; (introd. eastwards to N.Y. and Va.). [*Hosackia* Benth.; *Trigonella (Acmispon; H.; L.) americana* Nutt., not *L. amer.* Vell.; *H. (L.) unifoliata* Hook.]. MAP (Canadian area): Zandstra and Grant 1968: fig. 12, p. 572.

L. tenuis Waldst. & Kit.
Eurasian; introd. in saline, alkaline, and poorly-drained clayey soils of w N. America, as in sw B.C. (Vancouver Is., near Lillooet, and between Lytton and Spences Bridge; CAN) and s Ont. (N to Bruce and Simcoe counties). [*L. corniculatus* var. *tenuifolius* L.]. MAPS (Canadian area): combine the maps by Zandstra and Grant 1968: fig. 16 (E Canada) and fig. 17 (w Canada), p. 573.

LUPINUS L. [3672] Lupine

(Ref.: Phillips 1955; Dunn and Gillett 1966)
1 Annuals, the stem from a slender taproot, usually freely branched or even bushy and rarely over 4.5 dm tall; leaflets rarely over 4 cm long.
  2 Flowers white or pale yellow (often pink-tinged), distinctly whorled, to about 1.5 cm long, densely ciliate near the claws of the wings and keel; pods 2-seeded, less than 2 cm long, sparsely to copiously hirsute or pilose, the hairs often flat and twisted; cotyledons sessile at the connate-perfoliate base; peduncles about equalling their subtending petioles; leaflets of primary leaves 8–10, glabrous above; plant to 3 dm tall; (introd. in sw B.C.) . . . . *L. densiflorus*
  2 Flowers typically various shades of blue or purple, to about 1 cm long; leaflets 6–8.
    3 Seeds 2, the shaggy-villous pods less than 2 cm long; cotyledons sessile at the connate-perfoliate base; flowers scattered (not at all whorled but usually rather crowded), the corolla not ciliate-margined; peduncles shorter than their subtending petioles; leaflets glabrous above; plant to 2 dm tall; (s Alta.–Sask.) . . . . *L. pusillus*
    3 Seeds 4–8, the pods to over 2.5 cm long; cotyledons petioled; flowers distinctly whorled; peduncles commonly about equalling or surpassing their subtending leaves; plant to over 3 dm tall; (sw B.C.).
      4 Leaflets generally glabrous above (occasionally with a few scattered hairs); corolla-banner reflexed beyond the middle (toward apex) . . . . *L. polycarpus*
      4 Leaflets pubescent on both surfaces; banner reflexed near midpoint.
        5 Corolla-banner narrowly oblong, to 9 mm long and 6 mm broad; racemes to 7 cm long, with at most 5 whorls; pedicels to about 3.5 mm long . . . . *L. bicolor*
        5 Corolla-banner suborbicular, to 10 mm long and 11 mm broad; racemes to 12.5 cm long, with up to 9 whorls; pedicels to about 5.5 mm long . . . . *L. vallicola*
1 Perennials, the simple to freely branched stems mostly from a branched caudex, commonly over 5 dm tall; leaflets often over 4 cm long.
  6 Upper calyx-lip distended backward as a spur 0.5–3 mm long; flowers typically light blue to deep violet.

7 Corolla-keel ciliate only along the free (upper) margins, the wings often pubescent laterally near the tip; leaflets pubescent on both surfaces or glabrous above; (s B.C. and sw Alta.) . . . .*L. arbustus*

7 Corolla-keel ciliate below (along the dorsal suture) near the claw as well as along the free upper margins, the wings glabrous laterally near the tip (but often marginally ciliate near the claw and sometimes with stiff setaceous hairs on the surface near the claw); leaflets densely silky on both surfaces; (s B.C.; ?introd.) . . . .*L. caudatus*

6 Upper calyx-lip typically not spurred (sometimes gibbous; distended back to 0.5 mm in *L. argenteus* var. *tenellus*).

8 Corolla-banner pubescent over most of the surface of the back (if glabrous or the pubescence reduced to a patch under the upper calyx-lip, then the flowers sulphur-yellow; *L. sulphureus*).

9 Flowers pale sulphur-yellow; corolla-banner reflexed at well above the midpoint; pubescence appressed; (s B.C.) . . . .*L. sulphureus*

9 Flowers blue.

10 Corolla-banner reflexed at well above the midpoint (toward apex); pubescence of stem spreading or retrorse; (s B.C.) . . . .*L. leucophyllus*

10 Corolla-banner reflexed at about the midpoint; pubescence of stem appressed-ascending to spreading or retrorse; (s B.C. and sw Alta.) . . . .
. . . .*L. sericeus*

8 Corolla-banner glabrous on the back (or at most with a few cilia on the dorsal crest near the tip or a small patch of hairs on the groove beneath the tips of the upper calyx-lip); flowers typically blue or purple (yellow in *L. arboreus*).

11 Leaflets generally copiously silky above (occasionally glabrous above in the coastal *L. littoralis,* with decumbent to prostrate stems).

12 Plants tufted, the foliage less than 1 dm tall (the peduncles surpassing the foliage); whorls crowded, the raceme often subcapitate, at most about 6 cm long in fruit; corolla-banner to 8 mm long, obovate-oval; (mts. of s B.C.) . . . .*L. lyallii*

12 Plants tufted or matted, the folliage generally over 1 dm tall (if less than 1 dm, the orbicular corolla-banner over 1 cm long); (lower elevations).

13 Corolla-banner orbicular or broadly obovate; plants tufted, the stems bearing at most 3 leaves, the foliage commonly less than 1 dm tall; (se B.C. and sw Alta.) . . . .*L. minimus*

13 Corolla-banner suborbicular to elliptic or obovate; plants tufted or matted, the stems commonly with at least 4 leaves, the foliage extending to a height of over 1 dm.

14 Corolla-banner suborbicular; plants decumbent to prostrate, coastal; (w B.C.) . . . .*L. littoralis*

14 Corolla-banner elliptic to oblong-elliptic or obovate; plants erect.

15 Plant finely silky; corolla-banner elliptic to oblong-elliptic; (sw B.C.) . . . .*L. lepidus*

15 Plant densely hirsute, pilose, or silky; corolla-banner obovate.

16 Back (lower edge) of keel exposed below the wings; tip of corolla-banner obtusely pointed; pubescence consisting partly of ascending or spreading hispid hairs; (introd. on Vancouver Is.) . . . .*L. albicaulis*

16 Back of keel covered by the wings; tip of banner rounded.

17 Corolla-keel glabrous or with at most a few cilia toward the tip along the free (upper) margins; (Alaska– Yukon–n B.C.) . . . .*L. kuschei*

17 Corolla-keel ciliate along the greater part of the upper margins; (s B.C.–Alta.) . . . .*L. wyethii*

11 Leaflets generally glabrous above (occasionally sparsely puberulent or strigose).

18 Corolla-keel densely ciliate below (along the dorsal suture) near the

claw (as well as along most of the upper margins toward apex); petioles relatively short (generally less than twice the length of the leaflets).

19 Petioles all about the same length as the leaflets, the usually much-branched slender stem bearing axillary clusters of smaller leaves at its numerous nodes; plant subshrubby or decumbent.

20 Flowers blue; plant commonly decumbent, minutely puberulent except the glabrous upper surface of the leaflets; (sw B.C.) . . . .
. . . . L. rivularis

20 Flowers yellow; plant subshrubby, silvery-silky except the usually glabrous upper surface of the leaflets; (introd. in sw B.C.) . . . .
. . . . L. arboreus

19 Petioles to twice as long as the leaflets, these occasionally sparsely pubescent above; stem generally hollow.

21 Pubescence typically spreading, long-shaggy-lanate; bracts long and filamentose; lower calyx-lip broad and boat-shaped; (Alaska–B.C.–Alta.; introd. eastwards) . . . . L. nootkatensis

21 Pubescence appressed or hispidulous with scattered longer ascending hairs; bracts lance-subulate; lower calyx-lip narrowly lanceolate; (w Canada) . . . . L. arcticus

18 Corolla-keel glabrous or ciliate only toward tip; petiole-length various.

22 Stems slender, from underground rhizomes; (s Ont.) . . . . L. perennis

22 Stems solitary or clumped, not rhizomatous, sometimes hollow; (western species).

23 Stem hollow, often over 1.5 mm tall, bearing elongated basal petioles to 6 dm long; racemes often over 3 dm long.

24 Bracts subpersistent; flowers averaging about 1 cm long; corolla-keel ciliate; leaflets 7–11; (B.C.) . . . . L. burkei

24 Bracts early deciduous; flowers to 16 mm long; corolla-keel typically glabrous; leaflets 10–17; (Alaska–B.C.; introd. eastwards) . . . . L. polyphyllus

23 Stem slender, solid or hollow, to about 7 dm tall; leaves mostly cauline (except in L. arcticus).

25 Flowers at least 14 mm long (to 2 cm); corolla-banner reflexed at about the midpoint, glabrous; corolla-keel glabrous or ciliate; (w Canada) . . . . L. arcticus

25 Flowers at most 12 mm long; corolla-banner reflexed above the midpoint (toward apex), commonly with a small patch of fine pubescence on the surface beneath the tip of the upper calyx-lip.

26 Flowers 6 or 7 mm long; corolla-keel ciliate along the free (upper) margins; leaflets narrowly to broadly oblanceolate, glabrous above, commonly longer than the petiole; (?Alta.; s Sask.) . . . . L. parviflorus

26 Flowers at least 8 mm long (to 12 mm); leaflets generally linear to narrowly elliptic-oblanceolate, glabrous or pubescent above, about equalling the petiole.

27 Flowers 10–12 mm long; corolla-wings 4.5–6 mm broad, suborbicular as viewed laterally; (w Canada) . . . . L. argenteus

27 Flowers at most 10 mm long; corolla-wings at most 4.5 mm broad, semiovate as viewed laterally.

28 Upper calyx-lip gibbous to slightly spurred (spur to 0.5 mm long); corolla-keel ciliate along the free (upper) margins toward apex; petioles at most 4 cm long; (w Canada) . . . . L. argenteus

28 Upper calyx-lip not gibbous; corolla-keel glabrous; petioles to 12 cm long; (introd. in sw B.C.) . . . .
. . . . L. oreganus

L. albicaulis Dougl.
Native in the w U.S.A. from Wash. to Calif. and Nev.; reported by Dunn and Gillett (1966; Herb. V) as apparently introd. and established in the Victoria dist., Vancouver Is., sw B.C. [The report from P.E.I. by M.L. Fernald (Rhodora 16(185):94. 1914; Brackley Station, Queens Co., where overrunning a cemetery) is based upon *L. polyphyllus* (relevant collections in GH and CAN). (Incl. var. *bridgesii* Wats. (*L. formosus* var. *br.* (Wats.) Greene)].

L. arboreus Sims
A native of Calif.; reported by Hitchcock et al (1961) as introd., probably usually as a sand-binder, and well established along the coasts of Wash. and Oreg., and by Dunn and Gillett (1966) as introd. in sw B.C. (Vancouver Is. and adjacent islands; *see* their MAP, fig. 54, p. 62).
   A hybrid with *L. polyphyllus* is reported from sw B.C. by D.B. Dunn (Madroño 18(1):2. 1965; Vancouver Is.).

L. arbustus Dougl.
/T/W/ (Hs) Gravels and meadows to subalpine slopes (ranges of Canadian taxa outlined below), s to Calif., Nev., and Utah. MAPS and synonymy: *see* below.
1 Leaflets more or less pubescent above, linear-elliptic to oblanceolate, mostly less
   than 6 mm broad; [SE B.C.: a single station near the Mont. boundary s of Fernie; *see*
   the B.C.–Alta. MAP by Dunn and Gillett 1966: fig. 20, p. 31] . . . . . . ssp. *neolaxiflorus* Dunn
1 Leaflets glabrous or glabrate above, oblanceolate, to 1 cm broad; [*L. pseud.* Rydb.;
   L. laxiflorus var. *pseud.* (Rydb.) Sm.; s B.C. (Manning Provincial Park, SE of Hope;
   Creston; Moyie Mt., near Cranbrook) and sw Alta. (Crowsnest Pass); *see* the above-
   noted map by Dunn and Gillett; MAP: Phillips 1955: fig. 8, p. 191] . . . .
   . . . . ssp. *pseudoparviflorus* (Rydb.) Dunn

L. arcticus Wats.
/aST/WW/ (Hp (Hs)) Hummocky tundra and forest clearings to open subalpine ridges, the aggregate species from the coasts of Alaska–Yukon–Dist. Mackenzie (an isolated station also in the s Melville Pen., NE Dist. Keewatin) and N Banks Is. through B.C. and the mts. of sw Alta. to N Calif. (farther eastwards, the typical form s to s-cent. Dist. Mackenzie). MAPS and synon-ymy: *see* below.
1 Corolla-keel densely ciliate below (along the dorsal suture) near the claw and also
   along the free (upper) margins; [*L. latifolius* var. *can.* Sm., the type from Colwood,
   Vancouver Is., B.C.; sw B.C.: Vancouver Is. and adjacent islands and mainland NE to
   about 60 mi N of Kamloops; *see* the sw B.C. map by Dunn and Gillett 1966: fig. 69
   (inset), p. 77] . . . . ssp. *canadensis* (Sm.) Dunn
1 Corolla-keel totally glabrous or ciliate only along the free (upper) margins.
   2 Leaves chiefly borne along the stem, their petioles at most about 8 cm long; [*L.
      sub.* Piper & Rob.; *L. lat. (arct.)* var. *sub.* (P. & R.) Sm.; *L. cytisoides* Agardh; B.C.
      (N to ca. 56°N) and mts. of sw Alta.; MAPS: Dunn and Gillett 1966: fig. 69, p. 77;
      D.B. Dunn, Madroño 18(1): fig. 5, p. 14. 1965] . . . . ssp. *subalpinus* (Piper & Rob.) Dunn
   2 Leaves chiefly radical (at most 4 borne along the stem), their petioles to about
      1.5 dm long; [*L. borealis* Heller; *L. toklatensis* Lindl.; *L. yukonensis* Greene; *L.
      donnellyensis, L. gakonensis, L. multicaulis, L. multifolius, L. matanuskensis,* and
      L. prunifolius Sm.; *L. polyphyllus* ssp. *arct.* (Wats.) Phillips; *L. nootkatensis* var.
      kjellmanii Ostf.; N part of the range, s to Mt. Selwyn, NW-cent. B.C. at ca. 56°N;
      MAPS: Hultén 1968b:636 (also the aggregate species); Dunn and Gillett 1966: fig.
      69, p. 77; Porsild 1957: map 238, p. 190; Phillips 1955: fig. 4 (*L. poly.* ssp. *arct.*),
      p. 177; Raup 1947: pl. 29] . . . . ssp. *arcticus*

L. argenteus Pursh
/T/WW/ (Hp) Ponderosa-pine forest to subalpine ridges, the aggregate species from s B.C. (N to Kamloops; V), s Alta. (N to Lethbridge; CAN), and s Sask. (N to ca. 50°N) to Oreg. (?Calif.), Ariz., N.Mex., and S.Dak. [Forma *albiflorus* Boivin]. MAPS: Phillips 1955: fig. 7, p. 182; Dunn and Gillett 1966: fig. 47 (Canadian stations), p. 55.

The B.C. plant and some of the Alta.–Sask. material is referred by Dunn and Gillett to var. *tenellus* (Dougl.) Dunn (*L. ten.* Dougl.; *L. laxiflorus* and its var. *ten.* (Dougl.) T. & G.; corolla at most 10 mm long rather than up to 12 mm, its wings at most 4.5 mm broad and semiovate as viewed laterally rather than to 6 mm broad and suborbicular as viewed laterally). The above-noted map by Dunn and Gillett indicates the occurrence in Alta–Sask. of × *L. alpestris* Nels. (*L. macounii* and *L. pulcherrimus* Rydb.), a presumed hybrid between *L. argenteus* and *L. caudatus,* with the possible involvement of *L. arbustus.* It also indicates a station in extreme SW Man. (Melita, where introd. in a hayfield at the reclamation station and taken by H.H. Marshall in 1954, distributed as *L. argenteus*).

L. bicolor Lindl.
/t/W/ (T) Sandy or well-drained soils at or near the coast from SW B.C. (Vancouver Is. and adjacent islands; Yale, lower Fraser Valley; *see* B.C. map by Dunn and Gillett 1966: fig. 12, p. 23) to S Calif. [*L. micranthus* var. *bic.* (Lindl.) Wats.; *L. hirsutulus* Greene; incl. var. *tridentatus* Eastw.].

L. burkei Wats.
/sT/W/ (Hs) Streambanks, meadows, and moist forest from N B.C. (N to Fort Nelson, on the Liard R. at ca. 58°45′N; *see* B.C. map by Dunn and Gillett 1966: fig. 78, p. 86) to N Calif., Idaho, and Mont. [*L. polyphyllus* var. *burkei* (Wats.) Hitchc.].

L. caudatus Kellogg
Native in the W U.S.A. (N to Oreg. and Mont.) and reported from B.C. by Dunn and Gillett (1966; probably Vancouver Is.), where they consider it as possibly introduced.

L. densiflorus Benth.
Native from cent. Calif. through Baja Calif. to Chile; var. *scopulorum* Sm. (flowers pale yellowish rather than pink to reddish-purple, the type from Victoria, Vancouver Is., SW B.C.; *L. microcarpus* var. *scop.* Sm.) occurs on S Vancouver Is. (Victoria dist.) and the adjacent islands of NW Wash., where, according to Dunn and Gillett (1966), "The Canadian material is so uniform that it could represent an introduction of seed from a single source."

L. kuschei Eastw.
/Ss/W/ (Hs (Ch)) River terraces, open forest, and roadsides of Alaska (near Fairbanks), SW Yukon (type from near Carcross), and northernmost B.C. (S to ca. 59°N along the Liard R.). [*L. jacob-andersonii* and *L. porsildianus* Sm.]. MAPS: Hultén 1968*b*:637 ("Roadsides; possibly introduced and referable to some more southern species."); Dunn and Gillett 1966: fig. 75 (open circles), p. 83 (the authors suggesting a possible origin through hybridization between *L. arcticus* and *L. sericeus*).

L. lepidus Dougl.
/T/W/ (Hs) Sandy or rocky places at low to fairly high elevations from SW B.C. (S Vancouver Is.; *see* B.C. map by Dunn and Gillett 1966: fig. 37, p. 47; the report from Hyder, SE Alaska, by Hultén 1947, requires confirmation or may be based upon an introduced plant, it being referred to *L. sellulus* Kellogg by Hultén 1950, but restored to *L. lepidus* in his 1968*b* map; the report from Waterton Lakes, SW Alta., by Breitung 1957*b*, may possibly refer to *L. minimus*) to S Calif. [*L. aridus* Dougl.]. MAPS: Hultén 1968*b*:637; Phillips 1955: fig. 5, p. 177.

L. leucophyllus Dougl.
/t/W/ (Hs) Sagebrush plains to open or wooded foothills from S B.C. (Lumby dist., about 20 mi E of Vernon; V) to Calif., Utah, and Wyo. MAP: Phillips 1955: fig. 2, p. 169.

L. littoralis Dougl.   Chinook Licorice
/t/W/ (Hp (Ch)) Coastal beaches and dunes from W B.C. (Queen Charlotte Is., Vancouver Is., and the adjacent islands and mainland; *see* B.C. map by Dunn and Gillett 1966: fig. 59, p. 67) to Calif. MAP: Phillips 1955: fig. 6, p. 182.

L. lyallii Gray

/T/W/ (Hs) Open gravelly slopes and alpine meadows from sw B.C. (N to ca. 52°30′N; *see* B.C. map by Dunn and Gillett 1966: fig. 40, p. 49) to s Calif. [*L. lobbii* Gray]. MAP: Phillips 1955: fig. 5, p. 177.

L. minimus Dougl.

/T/W/ (Hs (Ch)) Mountains of E Wash., SE B.C. (Columbia Valley), sw Alta. (Crowsnest Pass and Waterton Lakes), and w Mont. [*L. ovinus* Greene].

L. nootkatensis Donn

/sT/W/ (Hp) Gravel bars and dry slopes (chiefly near the coast) from the Aleutian Is., Alaska (N to ca. 62°N), and sw Yukon to B.C. (s to Vancouver Is.; type presumably from Nootka) and the mts. of sw Alta. (Jasper dist.; introd. in Nfld. (Avalon Pen.), N.S. (Chebogue Point, Yarmouth Co., where very abundant on dry roadside banks; CAN; GH), the Azores, the British Isles, and Japan. [*L. albertensis, L. kiskensis, L. columbianus,* and *L. trifurcatus* Sm.; incl. vars. *ethel-looffiae, henry-looffiae,* and *perlanatus* Sm.]. MAPS: Hultén 1968b:636; Dunn and Gillett 1966: fig. 72, p. 80; D.B. Dunn, Madroño 18(1): fig. 6, p. 15. 1965.

The white-flowered phase has been distinguished as f. *leucanthus* Lepage (type from Kodiak Is., Alaska). Var. *fruticosus* Sims (var. *glaber* Hook.; var. *unalaskensis* Wats.; plant finely appressed-silky throughout except on the upper surface of the leaflets rather than spreading-pilose) occurs throughout the range. MAP: D.B. Dunn, Madroño 18(1): fig. 6, p. 15. 1965.

L. oreganus Heller

Native in Oreg. and known from sw B.C. (Victoria, Vancouver Is.; V), where considered probably introd. by Dunn and Gillett (1966; "However, the Vancouver Island population may represent a relict of an ancient broad-ranging one."). [Incl. var. *kincaidii* Sm. (*L. sulphureus* var. *kin.* (Sm.) Hitchc.)].

L. parviflorus Nutt.

/T/W/ (Hp) Damp woods or drier places up to fairly high elevations from s ?Alta. and s Sask. (Cypress Hills and near Weyburn, about 70 mi SE of Regina) to Utah and Colo. [*L. argenteus* var. *parv.* (Nutt.) Hitchc.]. The map of the Canadian stations by Dunn and Gillett (1966: fig. 47, p. 55) shows the two Sask. stations but none for Alta., from where they also report the species.

L. perennis L.

/t/EE/ (Hp) Sandy soils and dry open woods from Minn. and s Ont. (N to the s tip of Georgian Bay, L. Huron, in Simcoe Co.; *see* s Ont. map by Dunn and Gillett 1966: fig. 62, p. 69) to N.Y. and Maine, s to Ill., Ohio, and Fla.; introd. in Nfld. (Humber Valley; MT). MAPS: Fassett 1939:32 (indicating a single station in s Ont., presumably the Turkey Point, Norfolk Co., station on the N shore of L. Erie reported by Groh and Frankton 1948); Phillips 1955: fig. 3, p. 171.

Forma *leucanthus* Fern. (flowers white rather than blue-purple) is reported from s Ont. by Gaiser and Moore (1966; Lambton Co.; OAC), who also report f. *roseus* Britt., the roseate-flowered phase, from the same locality. Most of the Canadian material is referable to var. *occidentalis* Wats. (petioles and the upper half of the stem with long spreading hairs rather than appressed puberulent or the lower petioles with a few long hairs). Its f. *albiracemus* (Moore) Fern. is known from s Ont. (flowers white; type from Toronto). MAP: Fassett 1939:32.

L. polycarpus Greene

/t/W/ (T) Dry plains, ravines, and gravelly places from sw B.C. (s Vancouver Is. and adjacent islands; *see* B.C. map by Dunn and Gillett 1966: fig. 9, p. 21) to N Calif. [*L. micranthus* Dougl., not Guss.].

L. polyphyllus Lindl.

/sT/W/ (Hs) Shores, meadows, and roadsides and other disturbed habitats from Alaska (N to near Fairbanks; Hultén 1968b, considers all of the Alaskan material to have been introd.

but a collection in CAN from Anchorage was taken in a dry woods and the species is weedy even in its native area) through B.C. (the report from Alta. by Boivin 1966b, requires confirmation) to cent. Calif. [*L. stationis* and *L. pseudopolyphyllus* Sm.]. MAPS: Hultén 1968b:635; Dunn and Gillett 1966: fig. 75, p. 83; D.B. Dunn, Madroño 18(1): fig. 5, p. 14. 1965; Phillips 1955: fig. 4, p. 177.

This species is commonly cult. in E N. America and frequently escapes to roadsides and waste places, as in Ont. (N shore of L. Superior near Thunder Bay; Ottawa dist.), Que. (Montreal dist.; Gaspé Pen.), Nfld. (near Cornerbrook), N.B. (Fredericton; CAN), P.E.I. (see *L. albicaulis;* reports of *L. perennis* belong here according to D.S. Erskine 1960), and N.S. Some of the B.C. material is referable to var. *pallidipes* (Heller) Sm. (*L. pallidipes* Heller; stem hirsute or hispid rather than appressed-puberulent, the leaflets strigose above rather than glabrous).

L. pusillus Pursh
/T/WW/ (T) Dry sandy soils and dunes from Wash. to S Alta. (N to the South Saskatchewan R. at ca. 51°N) and S Sask. (N to Kindersley, about 100 mi NW of Swift Current; Breitung 1957a), S to Calif., Ariz., Colo., and Nebr. [*L. kingii sensu* John Macoun 1883, not Wats., relevant collections in CAN]. MAP (Canadian stations): Dunn and Gillett 1966: fig. 4, p. 16.

L. rivularis Dougl.
/t/W/ (Hp (Ch)) Gravelly prairies, streambanks, and open woods (always at low elevations) from SW B.C. (Sooke, Vancouver Is.; Herb. V; reports from elsewhere in B.C. by Henry 1915, require confirmation; reports from the Aleutian Is. are considered erroneous by Hultén 1950) to N Calif.

L. sericeus Pursh
/T/W/ (Hp) Dry plains, prairies, and slopes from S B.C. (Dry Interior N to Kamloops and Salmon Arm, E to the Alta. boundary) and SW Alta. (N to ca. 51°N; *see* the B.C.–Alta. map by Dunn and Gillett 1966: fig. 30, p. 41) to Calif., Ariz., and N.Mex. MAP and synonymy: *see* below.
1 Pubescence of stems spreading or retrorse; [S B.C.] . . . . var. *egglestonianus* Sm.
1 Pubescence of stems ascending or appressed-ascending; [S B.C.–SW Alta.].
  2 Flowers at most 11 mm long, in relatively open and lax racemes; stems rather
    freely branched . . . . var. *flexuosus* (Lindl.) Sm.
  2 Flowers to 1.5 cm long, in dense showy racemes; stems usually simple or
    sparingly branched . . . . var. *sericeus*
    3 Flowers white; [type from SW Alta.] . . . . f. *leucanthus* Boivin
    3 Flowers lavender to bluish; [*L. leucopsis* Agardh; *L. ornatus* Dougl.; MAP
    (aggregate species): Phillips 1955: fig. 1, p. 169] . . . . f. *sericeus*

L. sulphureus Dougl.
/t/W/ (Hs (Ch)) Dry sagebrush plains and clearings from S B.C. (Dry Interior N to Kamloops and in the Okanagan Valley N to near Vernon; *see* B.C. map by Dunn and Gillett 1966: fig. 23, p. 33) to Calif. [*L. bingenensis* Suksd.]. MAP: Phillips 1955: fig. 9, p. 191.

A collection in CAN from Kamloops, B.C., has been referred by Phillips to var. *subsaccatus* (Suksd.) Hitchc. (*L. bing.* var. *sub.* Suksd.; flowers blue or purplish rather than yellow).

L. vallicola Heller
/t/W/ (T) Pastures and fields from SW B.C. (S Vancouver Is.; *see* B.C. map by Dunn and Gillett 1966: fig. 15, p. 25) to S Calif. [Incl. *L. apricus* Greene].

L. wyethii Wats.
/T/W/ (Hs (Ch)) Streambanks, meadows, and moist forest to subalpine slopes from S B.C.–Alta. (N to ca. 50°N; *see* B.C.–Alta. map by Dunn and Gillett 1966: fig. 44, p. 52) to Oreg., ?Nev., Idaho, and ?Utah. [*L. humicola* Nels.; *L. prunophilus* (*L. polyphyllus* var. *prun.* (Jones) Phillips) of Canadian reports, not Jones].

MEDICAGO L.   [3688]   Medick.   Luzerne

1   Flowers blue-violet or purple, to 12 mm long; pods making 2 or 3 spirals; stems
    ascending; deep-rooted perennial; (introd.) ....*M. sativa*
1   Flowers yellow; (introd.).
    2   Flowers to 8 mm long; pods only slightly curved; stems ascending; deep-rooted
        perennial..*M. falcata*
    2   Flowers at most 5 mm long; low or diffuse, rather shallow-rooted annuals.
        3   Pods spineless.
            4   Pods reniform, 1-seeded, black when ripe....................*M. lupulina*
            4   Pods tightly coiled and forming a flattened spiral to about 1.5 cm broad,
                brown and papery when ripe ....*M. orbicularis*
        3   Pods spiny, closely coiled.
            5   Spines strongly arched; leaflets broadly obcordate, as broad as or broader
                than long, often with a dark central blotch on the upper surface; lower
                part of peduncle villous with crooked jointed hairs..............*M. arabica*
            5   Spines straightish except sometimes at the hooked tip; leaflets cuneate-
                obovate or -oblong, longer than broad.
                6   Plant densely soft-pubescent; base of stipules merely short-toothed;
                    leaflets barely emarginate ....[*M. minima*]
                6   Plant essentially glabrous; stipules laciniate at least at base; leaflets
                    distinctly emarginate.
                    7   Stipules pectinate, the blade as slender as the linear-filiform lateral
                        segments; seeds separated by cross-walls in the pod ....*M. polymorpha*
                    7   Stipules laciniate only at base, the blade broader than the lateral
                        segments; seeds not separated by cross-walls...........[*M. laciniata*]

M. arabica (L.) Huds.   Spotted Medick
Eurasian; occasionally introd. in waste places of N. America, as in s B.C. (Vancouver Is.) and
N.B. (ballast-heap at Carleton, near St. John, where taken by G.U. Hay in 1881; NBM). [*M.
polymorpha* var. *ar.* L.; *M. maculata* Sibth.].

M. falcata L.   Yellow Lucerne
Eurasian; locally introd. along roadsides and in waste places of N. America, as in Alaska (near
Fairbanks), B.C. (Kamloops; Midway), Alta. (N to Beaverlodge, 55°10′N), Sask. (N to Hudson
Bay Junction), Man. (N to near Duck Mt.), Ont. (N to Renfrew and Carleton counties), Que. (N
to the Montreal dist.), and N.S. (Hants Co.; ACAD). MAP: Hultén 1968*b*:638.

[M. laciniata L.]   Bur-Clover
[European; introd. in wool-waste and waste places of the E U.S.A. and known from Canada
through a 1904 collection in TRT by W. Scott in a ballpark at Toronto, Ont., where, however,
scarcely established. (*M. polymorpha* var. *lac.* L.).]

M. lupulina L.   Black Medick.   Lupuline
Eurasian; a common weed of dry fields, roadsides, and waste places in N. America, as in
Alaska (N to Nome and Fairbanks), B.C., Alta. (N to Fort Saskatchewan), Sask. (N to Valpa-
raiso, 52°51′N), Man. (N to The Pas), Ont. (N to Pagwa, ca. 50°N), Que. (N to L. St. John and
Anticosti Is.), Nfld., St-Pierre and Miquelon, N.B., P.E.I., and N.S.; SW Greenland. MAP: Hultén
1968*b*:639.
    Var. *glandulosa* Neilr. (peduncles and pods bearing stipitate glands rather than glabrous or
merely pilose) is the common phase throughout the above area. However, collections in CAN
from Ont. (Leamington, Essex Co.; E shore of L. Superior at Michipicoten), Que. (near Ville-
Marie, Timiskaming Co.), and N.B. (Dalhousie; Bathurst) are referable to the typical nonglandular phase.

[M. minima (L.) Bart.]   Bur-Clover
[Eurasian; locally introd. in the E U.S.A. and known in Canada through a 1904 collection in TRT by W. Scott in a ballpark at Toronto, where, however, scarcely established. (*M. poly-morpha* var. *min.* L.).]

M. orbicularis (L.) All.   Button Medick
Eurasian; apparently known in N. America only through collections from Vancouver Is., B.C., where taken by John Macoun at Nanaimo in 1887 and at Esquimault in 1914. An 1873 collection in CAN by Macoun from Belleville, Hastings Co., S Ont., is annotated "Cultivated in gardens". [*M. polymorpha* var. *orb.* L.].

M. polymorpha L.   Bur-Clover
Eurasian; introd. in waste places of N. America, as in SE Alaska (Loring; Sitka), SW B.C. (Vancouver Is. at Victoria, Nanaimo, and Esquimault; CAN), Sask. (Spalding, 52°20'N; Breitung 1957a), Ont. (N to Georgian Bay, L. Huron; CAN), Que. (Gaspé Pen. at York; GH), N.B. (Buctouche, Kent Co., where taken by Fowler in 1861; NBM; reported from St. John by John Macoun 1883), and ?N.S. ("manuals"; Groh and Frankton 1949b). [*M. hispida* Gaertn.; incl. *M. denticulata* Willd. and *M. sphaerocarpa* Bertol.]. MAP *(M. hisp.)*: Hultén 1968b:639.

M. sativa L.   Alfalfa, Lucerne.   Luzerne
Eurasian; commonly cult. in N. America and often escaping, as in Alaska (Tanana, ca. 65°N; Juneau), SW Dist. Mackenzie (N to Fort Simpson, ca. 62°N), B.C.–Alta., Sask. (Breitung 1957a), Man. (N to Gillam, about 165 mi S of Churchill), Ont. (N to Pagwa, ca. 50°N), Que. (N to the Gaspé Pen. at Tourelle), N.B., P.E.I., and N.S. MAP: Hultén 1968b:638.
   Forma *alba* Benke (flowers white rather than blue-violet to purple) is known from S Man. (Forrest; Erickson; Morden) and E Que. (Ste-Odile, Rimouski Co.). Forma *prolifera* Dore (the head of flowers replaced by a mass of minute greenish scales) is known from B.C. (Vernon) and S Man. (type from Gilbert Plains; W.G. Dore, Can. Field-Nat. 73(3):150. 1959).

MELILOTUS Mill.   [3689]   Sweet Clover, Melilot.   Mélilot

1   Corolla white, to 5 mm long, the standard somewhat longer than the wings and keel; calyx-teeth lance-subulate; pods moderately reticulate, brown when ripe, to 5 mm long, mucronate, the style usually deciduous; (introd.) . . . .*M. alba*
1   Corolla yellow; (introd.).
    2   Pods pubescent, obscurely reticulate, acute, black when ripe, to 6 mm long, the long style persistent; flowers to 6 mm long, the standard, wings, and keel all subequal; calyx-teeth lance-subulate . . . .*M. altissima*
    2   Pods glabrous; standard somewhat longer than the wings and keel.
        3   Flowers to 6 mm long, on pedicels about 2 mm long; calyx-teeth lance-subulate; pods to 5 mm long, transversely rugose, brown when ripe, the style usually deciduous . . . .*M. officinalis*
        3   Flowers about 2 mm long, on pedicels mostly less than 1 mm long; calyx-teeth obtuse; pods 2 or 3 mm long, strongly reticulate, olive-green when ripe, the style usually persistent . . . .*M. indica*

M. alba Desr.   White Melilot.   Trèfle d'odeur
Eurasian; a common weed of fields, roadsides, and waste places in N. America, as in Alaska–Yukon (N to ca. 65°N), Dist. Mackenzie (Great Slave L.), B.C.–Alta.–Sask., Man. (N to Churchill), Ont. (N to Moosonee, SW James Bay, 51°16'N), Que. (N to the Gaspé Pen.; reported from Anticosti Is. by Schmitt 1904), Labrador (N to Goose Bay, 53°20'N), Nfld., N.B., P.E.I., and N.S. MAP: Hultén 1968b:640.
   Forma *prolifera* Dore (the head of flowers replaced by a dense mass of small greenish scales) is known from the type locality, Armstrong, B.C., where found in an alfalfa experimental plot. The white-flowered Volga Sweet Clover, *M. wolgica* Poir., is reported from the forage plot area of the Research Station at Saskatoon, Sask., by G.A. Stevenson (Can. Field-Nat.

79(3):175. 1965), where it appeared to have been escaping locally to wasteland for some years. It differs from *M. alba* in its smaller flowers (about 3 mm long rather than 4 or 5 mm), longer pedicels (about equalling the flowers rather than much shorter), the calyces and pedicels commonly tinged brick-red, the calyx-teeth relatively broad.

M. altissima Thuill.
Eurasian; locally introd. along roadsides and in waste places in N. America, as in s Ont. (near Bridgeport, Waterloo Co.; OAC) and N.S. (Annapolis, Kings, Hants, and Cape Breton counties).

M. indica (L.) All.   Annual Yellow Sweet Clover
Eurasian; locally introd. along roadsides and in waste places in N. America, as in s B.C. (Vancouver Is., Lillooet, and Manning Provincial Park, SE of Hope; V), s Man. (Brandon), and N.S. (Pictou, Pictou Co., where taken by John Macoun on wharf-ballast in 1883; CAN; GH). [*Trifolium Melilotus indica* L.; *M. parviflora* Desf.].

M. officinalis (L.) Lam.   Yellow Sweet Clover.   Trèfle d'odeur jaune
Eurasian; a common weed of roadsides, fields, and waste places in N. America, as in s Alaska–Yukon–Dist. Mackenzie, B.C.–Alta.–Sask., Man. (N to Churchill), Ont. (N to Pagwa, ca. 50°N), Que. (N to Ste-Anne-de-la-Pocatière, Kamouraska Co.), Nfld., N.B., P.E.I., and N.S. [*Trifolium Melilotus off.* L.]. MAP: Hultén 1968*b*:640.

[The European *M. elegans* Salzm. is reported from s Man. by Boivin (1967*b*; waste places at Brandon, where a casual escape from experimental plantings). It differs from *M. officinalis* in its smaller flowers (to 4 mm long rather than 6 mm) and in its strongly ribbed pods that become black when ripe (rather than merely transversely wrinkled and brown when ripe).]

ONOBRYCHIS Mill.   [3780]

O. viciifolia Scop.   Sainfoin, Holy Clover
Eurasian; locally introd. or escaped from cult. in N. America and reported from Wash. and Mont. (where well established) by Hitchcock et al. (1961). It is known in Canada from B.C. (Vancouver Is., Cascade, Chilliwack, Spences Bridge, Cariboo, SE of Williams Lake, the Marble Range NW of Clinton, Manning Provincial Park, SE of Hope, and Kelowna; CAN; V), Ont. (Caledon, Peel Co.; CAN; reported from Point Abino, Welland Co., by John Macoun 1886), and s Que. (Boivin 1966*b*). [*Hedysarum (O.) onobrychis* L.; *O. sativa* Lam.].

OXYTROPIS DC.   [3767]   Stemless Locoweed

(Ref.: Barneby 1952)
1   Leaves simple or the secondary ones subpalmately 3-foliolate, glabrous beneath, sparsely pilose above or merely ciliate along the inrolled margins; scapes to 6 cm tall; flowers purple, to about 1.5 cm long; calyx to 8 mm long, densely black-villous-hirsute; pods to about 1.5 cm long, black-hairy; (Alaska) . . . . *O. mertensiana*
1   Leaves with 5 or more pinnately arranged leaflets.
    2   Leaflets mostly in whorls of 3 or 4 along the rachis; corolla roseate, violet, or purple; plants copiously silky-villous throughout.
        3   Pods minutely stipitate, only slightly surpassing the calyx-lobes, these about as long as the white-villous tube; leaflets to about 2.5 cm long; (Alaska–B.C. to W Ont.) . . . . *O. splendens*
        3   Pods sessile, much surpassing the calyx-lobes, these about 1/3 as long as the tube; calyx dark with mixed black and white hairs; leaflets less than 1 cm long; (var. *bellii*; eastern subarctic regions) . . . . *O. arctica*
    2   Leaflets not whorled (occasionally pseudo-verticillate in some of the leaves of *O. campestris* and *O. leucantha*).
        4   Flowers reflexed, at most 1 cm long; pods pendulous; stipules foliaceous, nearly free from the base of the petiole; plant loosely pilose or villous; (transcontinental) . . . . *O. deflexa*

4 Flowers (and pods) ascending to erect; corolla over 1 cm long; stipules adnate to the base of the petiole for at least half their length.
  5 Plant completely glabrous (even as to the calyces and pods), low; flowers solitary or 2 on a scape; calyx to 7 mm long; corolla dark blue, about 1.5 cm long; leaflets 3 or 4 mm long; (Alaska) . . . . [*O. glaberrima*]
  5 Plants distinctly pubescent.
    6 Racemes mostly with only 1 or 2 flowers (occasionally 3, rarely 4); corolla deep blue to violet-purple; leaflets to about 1 cm long; plants densely caespitose, rarely over 5 cm tall; (arctic and subarctic regions).
      7 Pods stipitate within the calyx (stipe to 3 mm long), ovoid-ellipsoid, papery and strongly inflated, thinly black-velvety-pubescent; calyx thinly shaggy-pilose; leaflets appressed-white-silky; (B.C. and Alta.; s Baffin Is., N Que., and N Labrador) . . . . *O. podocarpa*
      7 Pods sessile, oblong-cylindrical, their walls firm; calyx black-shaggy-villous; leaflets greyish green with scarcely silky pubescence; (western arctic and subarctic regions) . . . . . . *O. nigrescens*
    6 Racemes with usually more than 4 flowers; plants commonly taller and less densely caespitose.
      8 Corolla white to creamy or sulphur-yellow; floral bracts pilose dorsally.
        9 Marcescent stipules chestnut-brown; flowers commonly not more than 7; corolla to 1.5 cm long; leaflets thinly silky to glabrate; (transcontinental in arctic and subarctic regions) . . . . *O. maydelliana*
        9 Marcescent stipules paler; flowers generally more numerous.
          10 Corolla to over 2 cm long; leaflets densely silky-pilose, usually not more than 15 in number; (Alaska–B.C. to sw Man.) . . . . *O. sericea*
          10 Corolla usually shorter; leaflets more sparsely pilose, usually more numerous; (varieties; B.C. to Man.) . . . . *O. campestris*
      8 Corolla blue, violet, or purple.
        11 Plant more or less glandular-viscid, the calyx-teeth and pods often glandular-warty; floral bracts nearly always glabrous dorsally; (B.C. to Que.) . . . . *O. leucantha*
        11 Plant nonglandular; floral bracts pilose dorsally.
          12 Corolla at most about 18 mm long; (varieties; Ont. to Labrador, Nfld., and N.S.) . . . . *O. campestris*
          12 Corolla to 2.5 cm long.
            13 Flowers rarely more than 5, subumbellate, the short spike not elongating in fruit; calyx shaggy-villous with dark or mixed light and dark hairs, the tube to 9 mm long, the teeth to 6 mm long; mature fruit dark olive-green, pubescent, somewhat scythe-shaped, about 3 cm long including the long beak; leaflets commonly not over 1 cm long, densely white-villous beneath, glabrate above; scapes commonly not over 1 dm tall; plant very densely caespitose; (arctic and subarctic regions) . . . . *O. arctica*
            13 Flowers up to about 25; calyx-tube commonly 6 or 7 mm long; fruit (including beak) rarely over 2 cm long; leaflets commonly longer; scapes to 2 or 3 dm tall; plants less densely caespitose.
              14 Pubescence dolabriform, consisting of appressed 2-pronged hairs attached very close to one end (swivel-action may be observed under a lens by teasing longer portion of hairs with a needle); calyx-tube silky-strigose or -pilose, its teeth to 4 mm long; fruit strigose-silky or merely short-strigose; valves of the

                 sessile pod coriaceous to woody; raceme elongating in
                 fruit to over 1.5 dm; leaflets linear to elliptic or ovate,
                 to 4 cm long (when linear, usually falcate), silky-
                 canescent to sparsely hirsute or villous and greenish;
                 (s Alta. to s Man.) . . . . *O. lambertii*
          14 Pubescence not dolabriform.
              15 Calyx densely shaggy-silky, the surface of the tube
                   nearly concealed at anthesis; leaves silky-villous,
                   the scapes villous (rarely glabrate); leaflets rarely
                   more than 9, to 13 mm long; bracts linear to
                   lanceolate, rather membranous, shaggy-pilose
                   dorsally; (sw Alta.) . . . . *O. lagopus*
              15 Calyx silky-pilose with appressed hairs (these
                   sometimes mixed with a few longer hairs) or short-
                   pilose, but not densely shaggy; leaflets commonly
                   more than 9 and longer.
                16 Corolla white to pale yellow (or purple in
                   eastern varieties), the banner to 2 cm long;
                   leaflets not more than 21; (transcontinental) . . . .
                   . . . . *O. campestris*
                16 Corolla bright pink-purple (drying bluish), with a
                     white-striped blotch in the banner, this to 2.5
                   cm long; leaflets often more than 21; (s ?Alta.
                   and s Sask.) . . . . *O. besseyi*

O. arctica R. Br.

/AS/X/A/ (Hr) Gravel bars and tundra (confined in N. America to Alaska–Canada, the ranges of taxa outlined below); arctic Asia. MAPS and synonymy: *see* below.
1 Leaves to 6 cm long, with 9–13 opposite leaflets; corolla to 2.5 cm long, dark purple (drying blue); pods to 3 cm long, including the long beak; (N Alaska and the Mackenzie R. Delta to Prince Patrick Is. and Melville Is. (type locality), s to N-cent. Alaska and s-cent. Dist. Mackenzie; [*O. coronaminis* Fern.; *O. ?kobukensis* Welsh; *O. koyukukensis* Porsild; *O. roaldii* Ostenf.; MAPS: Porsild 1957: map 249, p. 192; Barneby 1952: map 12 (somewhat incomplete), p. 300; combine the maps by Hultén 1968b:659 and 665 (*O. kob.* and *O. koy.*)] . . . . var. *arctica*
1 Leaves to 1 dm long, at least some of the leaflets in whorls of 3 or 4; corolla to 2 cm long, reddish violet (drying violet); pods to 2.5 cm long, including the slender beak; ["*Spiesia Oxytropis Belli*" Britt.; *O. bellii* (Britt.) Palibine; *O. campestris* var. *bellii* (Britt.) Boivin; w-cent. Dist. Keewatin to Melville Pen. and northernmost Ungava (type from Digges Is., Hudson Strait; Wolstenholme), s to NE Man. (Churchill); MAPS: Porsild 1957: map 251, p. 192; Barneby 1952: map 12 (the Churchill and Digges Is. stations should be indicated), p. 300] . . . . var. *bellii* (Britt.) Boivin

O. besseyi (Rydb.) Blank.

/T/W/ (Hr) Shores, gravel benches, prairies, and lower foothills from Idaho and Mont. to s Sask. (Canopus, s of Moose Jaw, and Val Marie; Breitung 1957a; Boivin 1967b; concerning a collection in CAN purportedly from Alta., *see* Boivin 1967b), s to N Colo. [*Aragallus* Rydb.]. MAP: Barneby 1952: map 6 (indicating no Canadian stations), p. 231.

O. campestris (L.) DC.

/aST/(X)/EA/ (Hr) Prairies, rocky hillsides, open woods, alpine or subalpine meadows, and arctic tundra, the aggregate species from N Alaska, cent. Yukon, and the coast of Dist. Mackenzie to Banks Is., Victoria Is., Man. (N to Churchill), northernmost Ont.–Que.–Labrador, and s Baffin Is., s in the West through B.C.–Alta.–Sask.–sw Man. to N Oreg., Colo., and S.Dak., farther eastwards s to Wisc., cent. Ont. (s to Moosonee, near sw James Bay at ca. 51°10′N), E Que. (Quebec City dist. to the Côte-Nord and Gaspé Pen.), w Nfld., N.B. (St. John

R. system; not known from P.E.I.), NE N.S. (St. Paul Is.), and Maine; Eurasia. MAPS and synonymy: *see* below.

1   Corolla blue or bluish purple (at least on the keel), rarely pinkish.

    2   Leaves essentially uniform; [var. *?caerulea* of Labrador reports, not Koch; incl. var. *terrae-novae* (Fern.) Barneby (*O. ter.* Fern.); *O. johannensis* Fern. and its f. *bicensis* Vict. & Rousseau; *O. lambertii* var. *sericea* of N.B. reports, not *O. sericea* Nutt.; *O. ?uralensis* of Labrador reports, not DC.; NE Man. (Churchill) to S Baffin Is., Que. (type, as first collection cited, from l'Ile d'Orléans, near Quebec City), Labrador, W Nfld., N.B. (St. John R. system), and N.S. (St. Paul Is.; CAN); MAPS (several of them incomplete): Barneby 1952: map 8 (including inset), p. 265; Porsild 1957: map 250 *(O. ter.)*, p. 192; Fernald 1933: map 22 *(O. ter.)*, p. 275; Meusel, Jaeger, and Weinert 1965:245 *(O. johan.)*; Fassett 1939:74 *(O. johan.)*; Raymond 1950b: fig. 39 *(O. johan.)*, p. 105] . . . . var. *johannensis* Fern.

    2   Leaves strongly dimorphic, the primary ones short, with crowded ovate leaflets, the upper ones mostly about twice as long, with narrower leaflets; [incl. var *jordalii* (Porsild) Welsh (*O. jord.* Porsild); *Aragallus (O.) dispar* Nels.; N Alaska and W Dist. Mackenzie; reported from Alta. to Man. by Boivin 1966b; MAPS: Barneby 1952: map 8 (the squares not indicating any Canadian stations), p. 265; Hultén 1968b:664 (ssp. *jord.*); Olav Gjarevoll, K. Nor. Vidensk. Selsk. Skr. (1963, No. 4): fig. 18 (var. *jord.*), p. 80. 1963] . . . . var. *dispar* (Nels.) Barneby

1   Corolla white, ocholeucous, or yellow (the keel sometimes purple-spotted; var. *dispar* (the *O. jordalii* element) may be sought here).

    3   Leaves with at most 17 leaflets; scapes to about 1.5 dm tall; [*O. cus.* Greenm.; *O. paysoniana* Nels.; *Aragallus (O.) alpicola* Rydb.; Rocky Mts. of SE B.C. and SW Alta.; MAP: Barneby 1952: map 8, p. 265] . . . . var. *cusickii* (Greenm.) Barneby

    3   Leaves mostly with at least 17 (up to 33) leaflets; scapes commonly taller; [*Aragallus (O.) gracilis* Nels.; *O. alaskana* Nels.; *A. (O.) albertinus* Greene; *A. cervinus* Greene; *O. hyperborea* Porsild; *A. (O.) varians* Rydb.; *A. (O.) macounii* Greene in part; *A. villosus* Rydb., not Michx.; *O. (A.; Spiesia) monticola* Gray in larger part, not *A. mont.* Phil.; *O. lambertii sensu* Raup 1936, not Pursh, the relevant collection in CAN; *O. ?nana sensu* John Macoun 1883, not Nutt.; *O. ?argentata sensu* Richardson 1823, and Hooker 1831, not (Pall.) Pers.; Alaska–B.C. to Man.; MAPS: Barneby 1952: map 8 (combine vars. *gracilis* and *varians*), p. 265; Hultén 1968b:664 (ssp. *gr.*); Porsild 1966: map 109 (NW area; *O. varians*), p. 80] . . . . var. *gracilis* (Nels.) Barneby

O. deflexa (Pall.) DC.

/aST/X/EA/ (Hs (Ch))   Meadows, streambanks, clearings, and waste places at low elevations to alpine crests, the aggregate species from N Alaska, cent. Yukon, and the coast of Dist. Mackenzie to cent. Baffin Is., northernmost Que. (Hudson Strait), and N Labrador (an isolated station at Rowsell Harbour, ca. 59°N; M.L. Fernald, Rhodora 38(449):155. 1936), S in the West through B.C.–Alta.–Sask. and Man. (N to the Nelson R. NE of L. Winnipeg at ca. 55°N) to Calif., N.Mex., and N.Dak., farther eastwards known from cent. Ont. (S to the Actamacow R. SW of James Bay at 54°25'N), E Que. (limestone cliffs by Lac Pleureuse, N Gaspé Pen.), and W Nfld.; N Norway; Asia. MAPS and synonymy: *see* below.

1   Calyx-sinuses (except the ventral one) narrow and acute; corolla whitish, yellowish, lilac, or bluish, relatively narrow, the oblanceolate banner about 3 times longer than broad; [*O. retrorsa* Fern. and its var. *sericea* (T. & G.) Fern., not *O. sericea* Nutt.; *O. ?nana* Nutt.; *O. ?argentata sensu* Hooker 1831, and John Macoun 1883, in part, not (Pall.) Pers.; *Tium drummondii sensu* Lowe 1943, not *Astragalus drum.* Hook.; Alaska–B.C. to W Hudson Bay–James Bay; MAPS: Hultén 1968b:658; Barneby 1952: map 1 (dots; somewhat incomplete), p. 197] . . . . var. *sericea* T. & G.

1   Calyx-sinuses broad and obtuse; corolla typically bluish purple, the obcordate banner about twice longer than broad.

    2   Plant green, sparingly pilose (the hairs usually appressed), usually stemless (but 1 or 2 internodes occasionally developed); racemes usually compact, with up to

10 flowers; [incl. the small-flowered extreme, var. *parviflora* Boivin, and the reduced arctic extreme, var. *capitata* Boivin; *O. (Aragallus) foliolosa* Hook., the type locality "From Carlton-House to the Rocky Mountains, in lat. 54°"; transcontinental; MAPS: Porsild 1957: map 242 *(O. fol.),* p. 191; Barneby 1952: map 1 (somewhat incomplete northwards), p. 197; Fernald 1933: map 3 *(O. fol.;* incomplete northwards), p. 50; Hultén 1968*b*:659] . . . . . . var. *foliolosa* (Hook.) Barneby

2 Plant copiously and loosely villous-pilose, the stems with usually at least 1 well-developed internode at maturity; racemes usually elongating in fruit, with up to 20 flowers; [*Astragalus* Pall.; *Aragallus* Heller; reported from S Yukon by Barneby 1952 (*see* his MAP 1, p. 197) and from Alaska–Yukon by Hultén 1947 (*see* his MAP 826, p. 1193, this, however, including var. *sericea*)] . . . . var. *deflexa*

[*O. glaberrima* Hult.]
[An obscure species, known only from dry rocky slopes of the type locality along the upper Kurupa R. on the arctic slope of Alaska at ca. 67°30'N, 155°W. MAP: Hultén 1968*b*:662 ("Similar to *O. nigrescens* subsp. *bryophila,* and possibly a subdivision of that taxon, but totally glabrous.").]

O. lagopus Nutt.
/T/W/ (Hr (Ch)) Sagebrush plains to lower montane slopes from SW Alta. (Cardston, near the Mont. boundary; R.C. Barneby, Leaflets of Western Botany 10(2):21. 1963) to Idaho and Wyo. [*Aragallus* Greene]. MAP: Barneby 1952: map 5 (the occurrence in SW Alta. should be indicated), p. 221.

The Alta. plant is referable to var. *conjugens* Barneby (leaflets 5–9 rather than mostly at least 11, each leaflet about the same length as the leaf-rachis rather than much shorter; calyx usually persistent until after the pod dehisces rather than usually deciduous with the enclosed pod before seed dispersal).

O. lambertii Pursh
/T/WW/ (Hr) Prairies, bluffs, and badlands, on clay, limestone, or loess, from E Mont. to S Alta. (Cochrane, near Calgary; CAN), SE Sask. (N to Moose Jaw), S Man. (N to Steeprock, about 100 mi N of Portage la Prairie), and Minn., S to Ariz., N.Mex., Tex., Okla., and NW Mo. [*Aragallus* Greene; incl. f. *canadensis* Gand.]. MAP: Barneby 1952: map 10 (incomplete northwards), p. 286.

O. leucantha (Pall.) Pers.
/aST/X/eA/ (Hr (Ch)) Dryish tundra and rocky slopes at low to alpine elevations (ranges of Canadian taxa outlined below), S in the West through B.C. and SW Alta. to Calif. and Colo. (farther eastwards confined to Canada except for a station in NE Minn.); E Siberia. MAPS and synonymy: *see* below.

1 Calyx-teeth rarely as much as 2 mm long.

2 Leaflets glabrous above; calyces predominantly dark-hairy . . . . var. *hudsonica* (Greene) Boivin

3 Flowers reddish purple; [*Aragallus (O.) hudsonicus* Greene, the type from Great Whale R., Hudson Bay; *O. viscida* var. *hud.* (Greene) Barneby; Great Bear L. to Melville Pen. and E Hudson Bay–James Bay, Que.; MAPS: Porsild 1957: map 246 *(O. hud.),* p. 191; Barneby 1952: map 7 *(O. viscida* var. *hud.*), p. 240] . . . . f. *hudsonica*

3 Flowers white; [known only from the type locality on the Nauja R., Melville Pen.] . . . . f. *galactantha* Boivin

2 Leaflets pilose above; calyces predominantly white-hairy; [type from Whitehorse, the Yukon] . . . . var. *leuchippiana* Boivin

1 Calyx-teeth generally 3 or 4 mm long.

4 Pods (and ovaries) glandular-warty, otherwise glabrous or only sparingly pubescent.

5 Flowers to 17 mm long; [Alta.: N of Macleod; High River; type from Banff] . . . . var. *magnifica* Boivin

     5   Flowers at most 13 mm long; [*Aragallus (O.) viscidulus* Rydb. and its var.
        depressus Rydb.; B.C.–SW Alta.] . . . . var. *depressa* (Rydb.) Boivin
   4 Pods (and ovaries) nonglandular or the glandulosity concealed beneath a
     copious pilosity.
     6   Stipules pilose dorsally as well as more or less glandular.
         7   Pubescence of calyces predominantly dark-hairy; [*O. ixodes* Butt. & Abbe
           and its f. *ecaudata* Butt. & Abbe; endemic to the NW L. Superior region of
           Ont. and Minn.] . . . . var. *ixodes* (Butt. & Abbe) Boivin
         7   Pubescence of calyces completely white-hairy; [*O. gaspensis* Fern. &
           Kelso, the type from Mont-St-Pierre, Gaspé Pen., E Que.] . . . .
           . . . . var. *gaspensis* (Fern. & Kelso) Boivin
     6   Stipules glandular-warty but otherwise glabrous dorsally; [*Astragalus
        leucanthus* Pall.; *O. borealis* DC.; *O. uralensis (viscida)* var. *subsucculenta*
        Hook.; *O. glutinosa, O. sheldonensis,* and *O. verruculosa* Porsild; *O. viscidula*
        ssp. *sulphurea* Porsild; Alaska–Yukon–NW Dist. ?Mackenzie–N B.C. (S to
        Cassiar, ca. 58°30′N); MAPS: Hultén 1968b:667 (*O. bor.*); Barneby 1952: map 7
        (*O. viscida* var. *sub.*; not indicating the Yukon stations), p. 240]. Bernard
        Boivin (Nat. can (Que.) 94(1):77. 1967) states that *O. leuc.* var. *viscida* (Nutt.)
        Boivin is confined to the mts. of Wyo. and Colo. . . . . var. *leucantha*

O. maydelliana Trautv.
/AS/X/eA/ (Hr (Ch)) Rocky slopes, heaths, and tundra at low to moderate elevations from
the coasts of Alaska–Yukon–Dist. Mackenzie–Dist. Keewatin to N Banks Is., S Melville Is., N
Baffin Is., and northernmost Ungava–Labrador, S to S Alaska, N B.C. (near Summit Pass at
58°31′N; CAN), S Dist. Keewatin, Southampton Is., and N Que. (Hudson Bay coasts S to ca.
60°N); E Asia. [Incl. *O. campestris* var. *glabrata* Hook. (*O. glab.* (Hook.) Nels.) and the dark-
hairy extreme, *O. camp. var. melanocephala* Hook. (*O. may.* ssp. *mel.* (Hook.) Porsild)]. MAPS:
Hultén 1968b:658; Porsild 1957: map 243, p. 191, and 1966: map 105, p. 80; Raup 1947: pl. 30;
Meusel, Jaeger, and Weinert 1965:245.

O. mertensiana Turcz.
/S/W/eA/ (Hr (Ch)) Rocky and gravelly places (common in solifluction areas) at low to
moderate elevations, the range confined to Alaska (between ca. 62°30′ and 69°N) and extreme NE Siberia. [*Aragallus* Greene]. MAPS: Hultén 1968b:656, and 1947: map 832 (Alaska; incomplete), p. 1193; Barneby 1952: map 2 (inset), p. 202.

O. nigrescens (Pall.) Fisch.
/aSs/X/A/ (Hr (Ch)) Tundra and rocky slopes at low to moderate elevations, the aggregate species from the coasts of Alaska–Dist. Mackenzie–Dist. Keewatin to Banks Is., Melville
Is., and northernmost Baffin Is., S to S Alaska–Yukon, N B.C. (S to Mt. Selwyn, ca. 56°N; CAN),
Great Bear L., Southampton Is., and southernmost Baffin Is.; Asia. MAPS and synonymy (together with distinguishing keys to three other species (?"microspecies") of Alaska–Yukon,
with 1–3(4)-flowered racemes of bluish to purplish flowers, requiring further study): *see* below.
1 Old stipules dark reddish-brown; [Alaska N to ca. 68°N, the type from the Kokrines
   Mts. at ca. 65°N; MAPS: Hultén 1968b:657, and 1947: map 829, p. 1193; Barneby
   1952: map 3, p. 202] . . . . [*O. kokrinensis* Porsild]
1 Old stipules straw-colour to pale brown.
   2 Stipules glabrous on the back, their free lobes elliptic; scapes erect; [Alaska (N to
     ca. 67°30′N) and W Yukon (N to ca. 64°30′N; type from Eagle Summit); MAPS:
     Hultén 1968b:660, and 1947: map 835, p. 1193; Porsild 1966: map 107, p. 80;
     Barneby 1952: map 3, p. 202; W.J. Cody, Nat. can. (Que.) 98(2): fig. 29, p. 155.
     1971] . . . . [*O. scammaniana* Hult.]
   2 Stipules pubescent on the back when young, their free lobes relatively narrow;
     scapes weak, resting on the leaves or on the ground.
     3 Pods elliptic, glabrous or minutely strigose, their beaks abruptly hooked;
       [Alaska (N to ca. 65°30′N) and SW Yukon (type from Whitehorse); MAPS: Hultén

1968*b*:660; Porsild 1966: map 104, p. 79; W.J. Cody, Nat. can. (Que.) 98(2): fig. 20, p. 152. 1971] . . . . [*O. huddelsonii* Porsild]

3 Pods cylindric, greyish- or white-pubescent, short-beaked; [the typical phase evidently confined to Asia] . . . . [*O. nigrescens*]

    4 Entire plant white-pubescent; flowers mostly solitary; [*O. arctobia* Bunge and its var. *hyperarctica* Polunin; *O. arctica (nigr.)* var. *uniflora* Hook.; the Yukon–B.C. to Baffin Is.; MAPS: Hultén 1968*b*:662; Porsild 1957: map 244, p. 191, and 1951*b*: fig. 9, p. 143 (both as *O. arctobia*); Barneby 1952: map 3 (var. *uniflora*; his var. *nigrescens* is here interpreted as referring to the other N. American phases), p. 202; Fernald 1925: map 61 *(O. arctobia)*, p. 325] . . . . var. *arctobia* (Bunge) Gray

    4 Entire plant greyish-pubescent; flowers mostly in pairs.

        5 Plant pulvinate (cushion-like), densely lanate; [*Astragalus (O.) pygmaeus* Pall.; Alaska–Yukon–B.C.; MAPS: Hultén 1968*b*:661, and 1947: map 833a, p. 1193; Porsild 1966: map 106 *(O. pyg.)*, p. 80; Raup 1947: pl. 30 *(O. pyg.)*] . . . . var. *pygmaea* (Pall.) Cham.

        5 Plant densely caespitose (but scarcely pulvinate), hirsute . . . . var. *bryophila* (Greene) Lepage

           6 Flowers bluish or purplish; [*Aragallus bryophilus* Greene, the type from Hall Is., Alaska; Alaska–Yukon–northernmost B.C.; MAPS: Hultén 1968*b*:661, and 1947: map 833, p. 1193] . . . . f. *bryophila*

           6 Flowers white; [type from Kodiak Is., Alaska] . . . . f. *albida* Lepage

O. podocarpa Gray

/aST/D/ (Hr (Ch)) Calcareous cliffs, talus, and gravels to alpine ridges and slopes: B.C. (McCallum Mt., near South Atlin at ca. 59°30′N, and Mt. Assiniboine, near the Alta. boundary at ca. 50°N; CAN) and the mts. of sw Alta. (N to Jasper) to Mont., Wyo., and Colo.; Baffin Is. (N to ca. 65°N), N Que. (Akpatok Is. and Hope's Advance Bay, Ungava Bay), and N Labrador (between ca. 56° and 59°18′N). [*Aragallus* Greene; *O. arctica* var. *inflata* Hook. *(O. infl.* (Hook.) Steffen)]. MAPS: Porsild 1957: map 245, p. 191; *Atlas of Canada* 1957: map 18, sheet 38; Barneby 1952: map 3 (somewhat incomplete northwards), p. 202.

O. sericea Nutt.

/sT/WW/ (Hr (Ch)) Prairies to subalpine meadows and slopes from s Alaska–Yukon (N to ca. 62°N) and sw Dist. Mackenzie (at ca. 61°N; CAN) to B.C.–Alta., Sask. (Breitung 1957a), and sw Man. (sand-hills at St. Lazare, about 75 mi NW of Brandon), s to Nev., Utah, N.Mex., and Okla. [*Aragallus* Rydb.]. MAPS (aggregate species): Hultén 1968*b*:663; Barneby 1952: map 9, p. 273.

    Our plant is referable to var. *spicata* (Hook.) Barneby *(O. campestris* var. *spic.* Hook.; *O. (Aragallus) spic.* (Hook.) Standl.; *A. (O.) macounii* Greene; *A. melanodontus* Greene; flowers lemon to sulphur-yellow rather than white or cream-colour). MAP: Porsild 1966: map 108 *(O. spic.)*, p. 80.

O. splendens Dougl.

/ST/WW/ (Hr) Prairies and river gravels to subalpine meadows from Alaska–Yukon (N to ca. 67°N) to Great Slave L., Sask. (N to Cumberland House, ca. 54°N), Man. (N to Tod L., near the Sask. boundary at ca. 56°45′N), and w Ont. (NW shore of L. Superior near Thunder Bay; GH), s to N.Mex., N.Dak., and N Minn. [Var. *vestita* Hook., the type material collected in s Man. "On limestone rocks of the Red River, and south towards Pembina"; *Aragallus* Greene; *Spiesia* Ktze.; *A. (O.) caudatus* Greene; *A. galioides* Greene; incl. the less villous extreme, var. *richardsonii* Hook *(O. (A.) rich.* (Hook.) Schum.); *O. oxyphilla sensu* Richardson 1823, not DC.]. MAPS: Hultén 1968*b*:663; Barneby 1952: map 11 (the dot for N Ont. near s Hudson Bay at ca. 56°N may refer to *O. arctica* var. *bellii,* this also with at least some of its leaflets in whorls rather than pairs), p. 295.

PETALOSTEMUM Michx. [3710] Prairie-Clover

1 Flowers white; calyx-tube glabrous to finely puberulent; calyx-lobes ciliate; floral

bracts glabrous on the back or merely ciliate; leaflets 5, 7, or 9; stem and leaves
glabrous; (s Alta. to w Ont.) . . . .*P. candidum*
1   Flowers roseate to purplish; calyx-tube and floral bracts densely hairy.
   2   Leaflets at most 7, linear; spikes dense, to about 5 cm long; plant glabrous or
     sparingly hairy; (s Alta. to Ont.) . . . .*P. purpureum*
   2   Leaflets 13 or more, elliptic or oblong; spikes loosening and becoming up to over
     1 dm long; plant silky-hairy throughout; (s Sask. and sw Man.) . . . .*P. villosum*

P. candidum (Willd.) Michx.   White Prairie-Clover
/T/WW/   (Hp)   Dry plains and prairies (ranges of Canadian taxa outlined below), s to Mexico, Tex., La., and Miss. MAP and synonymy: *see* below.
1   Calyx subglabrous, its ribs low and rounded; spike scarcely loosening in fruit, its
   bracts leaving a small "heel" on falling; leaflets mostly over 2 mm broad; stems
   usually erect; [*Dalea* Willd.; *Kuhniastera* Ktze.; SE Sask. (Breitung 1957a), s Man. (N
   to Lundar, about 60 mi NW of Winnipeg), and w Ont. (Boivin 1966b); MAP: (aggregate
   species): Fassett 1939:53] . . . . .var. *candidum*
1   Calyx finely puberulent, its ribs sharp and somewhat wing-like; spike becoming
   loose, its bracts not leaving a well-marked "heel"; leaflets mostly less than 2 mm
   broad; central stems erect, the outer ones spreading or subprostrate, or all the
   stems subprostrate; [*P. occ.* (Gray) Fern.; *P. gracile* var. *oligophyllum* Torr. (*P.
   (Dalea) olig.* (Torr.) Rydb.); s Alta. (Cardston, Lethbridge, and Medicine Hat; CAN), s
   Sask. (Boulder L. and the Red Deer Lakes at ca. 52°N; CAN), and sw Man. (N to St.
   Lazare, about 75 mi NW of Brandon)] . . . . .var. *occidentale* Gray

P. purpureum (Vent.) Rydb.   Purple Prairie-Clover
/T/WW/   (Hp)   Prairies and dry hills (ranges of Canadian taxa outlined below), s to N.Mex.,
Tex., Ark., and Ala. MAP and synonymy: *see* below.
1   Flowers white; [Otterburne, SE Man.; Löve and Bernard 1959] . . . . . f. *albiflorum* Horr & McGr.
1   Flowers rose-purple.
   2   Stems densely villous; [*P. violaceus* var. *pub.* Gray; *P. molle* Rydb.; Alta. (Boivin
     1966b) and sw Sask. (Cypress Hills, Bare Hills, and Snipe L.; Breitung 1957a)] . . . .
     . . . . f. *pubescens* (Gray) Fassett
   2   Stems sparingly villous to glabrous; [*Dalea* Vent.; *Kuhniastera* MacM.; *P.
     violaceum* Michx.; Alta. (N to Edmonton), s Sask. (N to Indian Head and the Red
     Deer Lakes at ca. 52°N), s Man. (N to Garland, E of Duck Mt.), and w Ont. (near
     the s Man. boundary at Ingolf; introd. and persisting around grain elevators at
     Point Edward, Lambton Co.); MAP: Fassett 1939:58] . . . . f. *purpureum*

P. villosum Nutt.   Silky Prairie-Clover
/T/WW/   (Hp)   Prairies and dry hills from s Sask. (Mortlach, about 65 mi w of Regina; A.J.
Breitung, Am. Midl. Nat. 61(2):511. 1959) and sw Man. (N to Shilo, about 15 mi E of Brandon)
to N.Mex. and Tex. [*Dalea* Spreng.; *Kuhniastera* Ktze.]. MAP: Fassett 1939:53 (the occurrence
in Sask. should be indicated).

[PHASEOLUS L.]   [3901]

1   The pair of bracts subtending the calyx about 1/3 as long as the calyx; flowers white
   or yellowish, small; pods to about 13 cm long, the seeds white; leaflets narrowly
   ovate . . . .[*P. limensis*]
1   The pair of bracts subtending the calyx usually about equalling the calyx; leaflets
   ovate to rhombic-ovate.
   2   Flowers at least 2 cm long, normally red or scarlet; calyx-bracts linear-lanceolate
     to lanceolate; pods to 3 dm long, the nearly black seeds with red markings . . . .
     . . . .[*P. coccineus*]
   2   Flowers less than 2 cm long, white, yellowish, or violet-purple; calyx-bracts ovate,
     strongly several-nerved; pods to 2 dm long, the seeds white, brown, blue-black,
     or variously speckled . . . .[*P. vulgaris*]

[P. coccineus L.]   Scarlet Runner
[Tropical America; an occasional garden-escape in N. America but not established, as in Ont. (waste ground at Ottawa, where taken by W.H. Harrington in 1905; CAN). (*P. multiflorus* Lam.).]

[P. limensis Macfad.]   Lima Bean
[Tropical America; an occasional garden-escape in N. America but not established, as in N.S. (Kentville, Kings Co.; ACAD).]

[P. vulgaris L.]   Kidney-Bean
[Tropical America; an occasional garden-escape in N. America but not established, as in Man. (cobble beach at Grand Rapids, near the NW end of L. Winnipeg; CAN).]

[PISUM L.]   [3854]

[P. sativum L.]   Garden-Pea
[Eurasian; occasionally reseeding itself in gardens in N. America but scarcely established, as in B.C. (Boivin 1966*b*), s Man. (Otterburne, about 30 mi s of Winnipeg; Löve and Bernard 1959), s Ont. (Norfolk and Wellington counties), Nfld. (Rouleau 1956), and s Greenland.
    Var. *arvense* (L.) Poir. (*P. arvense* L., the Field-Pea; flowers coloured rather than white) has been taken along the Ottawa R. near Ottawa, Ont.]

PSORALEA L.   [3703]   Scurf-pea

1   Calyx at least 6 mm long at anthesis.
    2   Root much enlarged and tuber-like; leaflets mostly 5, oblanceolate to oblong, to 6 cm long; flowers numerous in spike-like racemes to about 1 dm long; calyx (and whole plant) long-white-hairy, the teeth somewhat longer than the tube; corolla ochroleucous to pale blue, about 1.5 cm long; (s Alta. to s Man.) . . . . *P. esculenta*
    2   Root not enlarged and tuber-like; leaflets 3, narrowly to broadly ovate, mostly not over 4 cm long; flowers up to 20 in short head-like racemes; calyx black-hairy, markedly accrescent, the teeth shorter than the tube; corolla with yellowish-green standard and purplish keel, to 12 mm long; plant sparsely short-strigose; (s B.C.) . . . . *P. physodes*
1   Calyx to about 5 mm long at anthesis, neither black-hairy nor markedly accrescent; corolla rarely over 9 mm long; leaflets oblanceolate to narrowly obovate or oblong-obovate.
    3   Leaflets 3 or 5, densely appressed-silvery-silky (the lower surface obscured by the dense pubescence), to 5 cm long; flowers to 1 cm long, deep blue, up to 4 at each node of an interrupted spike to 5 cm long; lower calyx-tooth about twice as long as the other 4; (s Alta. to s Man.) . . . . *P. argophylla*
    3   Leaflets green (the pubescence shorter and less dense, the upper surface often glabrate); flowers to 7 mm long; calyx-teeth subequal.
        4   Flowers white (or the keel blue), borne in congested racemes usually shorter than the leaves; (s Alta and s Sask.) . . . . *P. lanceolata*
        4   Flowers blue, borne in long loose interrupted racemes much surpassing the leaves; (?Alta.) . . . . [*P. tenuiflora*]

P. argophylla Pursh
/T/WW/   (Grh)   Plains and prairies from Mont. to s Alta. (N to near Calgary) and s Man. (N to Dropmore, SW of Duck Mt.), s to N.Mex. and Mo. [*Psoralidium* Rydb.]. MAP: Fassett 1939:42.

P. esculenta Nutt.   Breadroot
/T/WW/   (Grt)   Prairies and lower foothills from s Alta. (N to near Calgary) to Sask. (N to near Prince Albert) and s Man. (N to about 25 mi NW of Dauphin; J.L. Parker, Can. Field-Nat. 82(1):50. 1968), s to N.Mex., Tex., and Mo. [*Pediomelum* Rydb.; *Psor. brachiata* Dougl.]. MAP: Fassett 1939:42.

P. lanceolata Pursh
/T/WW/ (Hp) Sagebrush plains and sandy prairies from Wash. to s Alta. (N to Hilda, about 40 mi NE of Medicine Hat; CAN) and s Sask. (N to Saskatoon; CAN), s to Calif., N.Mex., and Kans. [*Psoralidium* Rydb.].

P. physodes Dougl. California-tea
/t/W/ (Hp) Open areas (commonly on logged-off land) on bushy or wooded slopes at low to high elevations from s B.C. (Vancouver Is.; CAN; reported from the upper Columbia Valley by Henry 1915) to Calif. and ?Idaho. [*Hoita* Rydb.].

[P. tenuiflora Pursh]
[The report of this species of the w U.S.A. (Mont. to Tex. and N.Dak.) from Alta. noted by Moss (1959) requires confirmation.]

ROBINIA L.   [3733]   Locust.   Robinier

1   Flowers white (rarely pink), on drooping peduncles; calyx-lobes merely acute, at most about 2 mm long; pods glabrous, to over 1 dm long, distinctly wing-margined; branchlets and leaflets glabrous or promptly glabrate; stipular spines to 2.5 cm long; (introd.) . . . . *R. pseudo-acacia*
1   Flowers pink to rose-purple; calyx-lobes acuminate, to 7 mm long; pods hispid, less than 1 dm long, their margins wingless or nearly so; (introd.).
  2   Branchlets, leaf-rachises, and peduncles clammy-viscid with conspicuous sessile or short-stalked glands; stipules 2 or 3 mm long, setaceous (rarely becoming spiny on vigorous shoots); pods glandular-hispid, with up to 9 seeds . . . . . .*R. viscosa*
  2   Branchlets, etc., scarcely viscid (glands, if present, small and long-stalked).
    3   Branchlets, leaf-rachises, and peduncles usually densely bristly-hispid with brown hairs and also somewhat pilose with softer hairs; stipular spines to 5 mm long or wanting; pods densely hispid, with rarely more than 5 seeds . . . .
. . . . *R. hispida*
    3   Branchlets puberulent; peduncles, pedicels, calyces, and pods glandular-hispid and more or less puberulent, the pods with up to 8 seeds . . . . .[*R. luxurians*]

R. hispida L.   Bristly Locust, Rose-Acacia
Native in dry woods and thickets of the E U.S.A. (N to Tenn. and Va.); cult. elsewhere and sometimes escaping, as in Ont. (Montgomery 1957), ?P.E.I. (the report by McSwain and Bain 1891, requires confirmation), and N.S. (persisting in a dump near Wolfville, Kings Co.; D.S. Erskine 1951).

[R. luxurians (Dieck) Schneid.]
[Native in the w U.S.A. (Nev. to Colo. and Tex.); a collection from N.S. has been placed here (Antigonish, Antigonish Co.; DAO; "common small roadside tree"), but with no indication as to its spreading from original plantings.]

R. pseudo-acacia L.   Black or Yellow Locust, False Acacia.   Acacia
Native in the E U.S.A. (N to Okla. and Pa.); much planted elsewhere and occasionally established as an escape, as in s B.C. (Vancouver Is.; Moodyville; Hedley, near Princeton; Yale), Ont. (N to the Ottawa dist.), Que. (N to Ste-Anne-de-la-Pocatière, Kamouraska Co.; QSA; ?escaped), N.B., P.E.I., and N.S. The native area is indicated in MAPS by Fowells (1965:642), Preston (1961:282), Hough (1947:295), Munns (1938: map 143, p. 147), and Little (1971: map 187-E).

R. viscosa Vent.   Clammy Locust
Native in the E U.S.A. (N to W.Va. and Pa.); much planted elsewhere and occasionally established as an escape, as in Ont. (N to the Ottawa dist.), Que. (N to the Montreal dist.), N.B., P.E.I., and N.S. The native area is indicated in a MAP by Hough (1947:296).

[SESBANIA Scop.]   [3747]

[S. exaltata (Raf.) Cory]   Hemp Sesbania
[Native in the E U.S.A. (Okla. and Mo. to Tex. and Ala.); introd. elsewhere, as in S Ont. (Gaiser and Moore 1966; along railway tracks at Sarnia, Lambton Co., where taken in 1960 but not found later so presumably not established). (*Darwinia* Raf.).]

SPHAEROPHYSA DC.   [3757]   Globe-Pea

S. salsula (Pall.) DC.
Asiatic; according to Hitchcock et al. (1961), now well established and rapidly spreading on alkaline soils in the W U.S.A. It is reported from SW Sask. by Boivin (1966*b*; Maple Creek, N of the Cypress Hills about 75 mi SW of Swift Current; as *Astragalus iochrous*), where perhaps brought in by oil-exploration rigs from the U.S.A. (Boivin; personal communication). [*Phaca* Pall.; *Swainsona* Taub.; *Astragalus iochrous* Barneby; *A. violaceus* St. John].

STROPHOSTYLES Ell.   [3901]

S. helvola (L.) Ell.   Wild Bean
/T/EE/   (T)   Damp thickets and shores from S.Dak. to Minn., Mich., S Ont. (N to Wellington and Wentworth counties), Que. (N to L. St. Peter according to Raymond 1950*b*; reported N to Montmagny, Montmagny Co., about 35 mi NE of Quebec City, by Marie-Victorin 1935; not known from the Atlantic Provinces), and Mass., S to Tex. and Fla. [*Phaseolus* L.; *P. diversifolius* Pers.]. MAP: Fassett 1939:127.

TEPHROSIA Pers.   [3718]

T. virginiana (L.) Pers.   Goat's-rue, Catgut
/t/EE/   (Hp)   Dry sandy woods and openings from Wisc. and Mich. to S Ont. (several localities in Norfolk Co.; CAN; TRT; the report from Man. by Rydberg 1932, requires confirmation), N.Y., N.H., and Mass., S to Tex. and Fla. [*Cracca* L.; *Galega* L.]. MAPS: Fassett 1939:65; C.E. Wood, Jr., Rhodora 51(610): map 7, p. 272. 1949.
    Var. *holosericea* (Nutt.) T. & G. (*T. hol.* Nutt.; leaflets silvery-silky on both surfaces, the plant silky-villous throughout, often very densely so, rather than more or less glabrate in age) is also indicated for Norfolk Co., S Ont., in the above-noted map by Fassett.

THERMOPSIS R. Br.   [3617]

1   Pods long-stipitate within the calyx, on spreading pedicels, the body commonly
    recurved through more than a semicircle or even forming a more or less complete
    ring; flowers about 2 cm long; leaflets oblong-lanceolate to rhombic-ovate, generally
    to about 3 cm long and 2 cm broad; stems to about 4 dm tall; (S B.C. to SW Man.) . . . .
    . . . .*T. rhombifolia*
1   Pods subsessile or short-stipitate, straight or only slightly curved; stems to over 1 m
    tall.
    2   Pods erect, appressed to the rachis (rarely somewhat spreading); corolla to 2.5
        cm long; leaflets linear-elliptic or oblanceolate to broadly ovate, to about 1 dm
        long; stems commonly rather sparingly branched, rarely over 1 m tall; (?B.C.) . . . .
        . . . .[*T. montana*]
    2   Pods spreading; corolla about 1.5 cm long; leaflets rhombic-lanceolate, to 7.5 cm
        long; stems mostly diffusely branched, to about 1.5 m tall; (introd.) . . . .[*T. mollis*]

[T. mollis (Michx.) Curtis]   Bush-pea
[Native in the E U.S.A. (Va. to Tenn., Ala., and Ga.); introd. elsewhere, as in P.E.I. (D.S. Erskine 1960; "Mount Hebert, naturalized along roadside near the Consolidated School, according to H.A. Messervy; if persistent, was in any case destroyed by road improvement."). (*Podalyria* Michx.).]

[T. montana Nutt.]
[Native in the W U.S.A. (N to Wash. and Mont.) and "To be looked for along the southern boundary of British Columbia" (John Macoun 1883). It is listed for B.C. by T.M.C. Taylor (1966b), apparently on the basis of a collection (a mere fragment of inflorescence) by Copley along the Ingenika R. at ca. 56°45′N referred by Boivin to *T. rhombifolia* but, "The habitat is wrong and the specimen is out of range by some 10 degrees of longitude. Thus we are left without convincing vouchers for either species of *Thermopsis* from British Columbia." (Incl. *T. gracilis* Howell; *T. fabacea sensu* Hooker 1831, not (Pall.) DC.).]

T. rhombifolia Nutt.   Golden Bean, Prairie-bean
/T/WW/   (Grh)   Dry prairies and ravines from ?B.C. (reported from Summerland, Erickson, and Field by Eastham 1947, but Boivin 1967b, believes that these and other B.C. reports are either based upon misidentifications or cultivated plants) to Alta. (N to near Fort Saskatchewan; CAN), Sask. (N to the Shell R. N of Prince Albert; CAN), and S Man. (N to Gilbert Plains; introd. at Churchill, where taken by Eva Beckett in 1946, "One clump only on river bank on site of old building"), S to Colo. and Nebr. [*Cytisus* Nutt.; *T. arenosa* Nels.].

TRIFOLIUM L.   [3690]   Clover, Trefoil.   Trèfle

1   Floral heads subtended by an involucre of usually united (sometimes distinct) bracts; flowers whitish or ochroleucous (but not definitely yellow) to pink, roseate, or purplish; leaflets 3; plants lightly pubescent or glabrate.
  2   Bracts of the involucre separate or the outer ones united at base; leaflets broadly oblong to obovate or obcordate; (introd.).
    3   Perennial, creeping and rooting at the nodes; floral heads to about 2 cm thick, the pink to purplish flowers to 6 mm long but the pubescent upper lip of the calyx becoming strongly inflated, reticulate, and down-curved; seeds commonly 2 (sometimes 1); stems to about 3 dm long; (introd. in S B.C.) . . . .
. . . . *T. fragiferum*
    3   Annuals, the stems not nodally rooting, to over 6 dm long; calyx glabrous or with merely ciliate teeth; seeds commonly more numerous.
      4   Floral heads to 4 cm thick, the flowers commonly at least 2 cm long, cream-colour with a dark purple keel; involucral bracts to over 1.5 cm long; calyx becoming strongly inflated; (introd. in SW B.C.) . . . .[*T. fucatum*]
      4   Floral heads to about 2 cm thick, the whitish or yellowish-white flowers less than 1 cm long; involucral bracts much smaller; (introd. in S Ont.) . . . .
. . . . [*T. alexandrinum*]
  2   Bracts of the involucre united to above the middle into a cup- or saucer-shaped, entire to deeply lobed involucre; calyx not becoming markedly inflated; (B.C.).
    5   Involucre long-villous, usually cup-shaped, with up to 12 deep lobes; calyx-teeth simple; corolla white to pale red, to 7 mm long; pods 1–2-seeded; annuals, sparingly to rather densely pubescent.
      6   Calyx usually hirsute or villous, the lower 3 of the bristle-tipped teeth at least as long as the tube and often surpassing the corolla; lobes of involucre usually nearly or quite entire; leaflets narrowly obovate, to 2.5 cm long . . . . *T. microcephalum*
      6   Calyx nearly or quite glabrous, the triangular, scarcely bristly teeth all shorter than the tube and much shorter than the corolla; lobes of involucre several-toothed; leaflets narrowly to broadly obcordate, to 1.5 cm long . . . . *T. microdon*
    5   Involucre (and calyx) nearly or quite glabrous, often flared and saucer-shaped; plants glabrous or very sparingly pubescent.
      7   Lower 3 of the setaceous calyx-teeth usually slenderly and deeply 2–3-cleft and longer than the tube; calyx with up to 20 nerves; involucre shallowly round-lobed, the lobes finely spinulose-toothed with teeth less than 2 mm long; corolla white or ochroleucous to pink, to 6 mm long, about equalling the calyx-teeth; pods usually 2-seeded; leaflets oblanceolate to obcordate,

to 3.5 cm long; stipules mostly serrate but scarcely lacerate; annual . . . .
. . . . *T. cyathiferum*
7   Lower (and upper) calyx-teeth usually entire (or merely 2-toothed just
      above the expanded basal half in *T. tridentatum* and sometimes in *T.
      oliganthum*; occasionally 2-cleft in *T. wormskjoldii*); involucre usually flared
      and saucer-shaped.
   8   Calyx-lobes usually 2-toothed above the middle (the tip and teeth
         spinulose-tipped), about equalling the tube; calyx with up to 25 nerves,
         often purplish, its upper sinus much the deepest; corolla purplish, to
         about 1.5 cm long; involucre irregularly lacerate about 1/3 to base into
         many narrow unequal teeth but not regularly lobed; leaflets linear to
         oblanceolate, elliptic, or narrowly oblong, to over 4 cm long; stipules
         bristly-lacerate; annual . . . . *T. tridentatum*
   8   Calyx-lobes usually entire (occasionally 2-cleft in *T. wormskjoldii* or
         2-toothed above the middle in *T. oliganthum*).
      9   Perennials with decumbent-based and often rhizomatous stems to 8
            dm long; calyx-lobes narrowly lanceolate-acicular, subequal,
            occasionally 2-cleft, about equalling the 10-veined tube; corolla
            reddish to purple (often white-tipped), to 18 mm long, the flowering
            heads to about 3 cm broad; involucre to 2 cm broad, from shallowly
            toothed or entire-lobed to lacerately 8–12-lobed; leaflets linear-
            elliptic to oblong-obovate . . . . *T. wormskjoldii*
      9   Annuals.
         10 Corolla-banner much inflated (sometimes nearly as broad as
            long), the corolla to 11 mm long, white to pinkish; calyx with 5 or
            6 nerves, its teeth not stiffly spinulose, the longest ones about
            equalling the tube; involucre reduced to a small ring, often entire
            but sometimes with up to 7 acutish or rounded lobes; seeds
            sometimes more than 2; leaflets linear to obcordate; stipules
            acuminate, mostly entire; (introd. in sw B.C.) . . . . . . *T. depauperatum*
         10 Corolla-banner scarcely inflated; teeth of calyx and involucre
            usually stiffly spinulose; involucres irregularly lobed and lacerate
            to about the middle or below (sometimes reduced to a mere ring
            in *T. oliganthum*); seeds 1 or 2; stipules ovate, mostly deeply
            lacerate.
            11 Calyx-tube with up to 25 nerves, the sinuses subequally cleft,
               the teeth narrowly lance-subulate, entire, considerably longer
               than the tube; corolla to 2 cm long, purplish (often white-
               tipped); leaflets elliptic-oblanceolate to obovate; stems to
               over 6 dm long . . . . *T. variegatum*
            11 Calyx usually 10-nerved, the upper sinus much the deepest,
               the triangular-acicular teeth somewhat shorter than the tube,
               sometimes with a pair of small lateral teeth above the
               broadened lower half; corolla to 8 mm long, lavender to
               purple; leaflets linear-elliptic or -oblanceolate to narrowly
               obcordate; stems commonly not over 2 dm long . . . . *T. oliganthum*
1 Floral heads not subtended by a true involucre (but the subopposite stipules of the
   upper leaves sometimes forming a false involucre).
   12 Flowers ochroleucous or creamy to yellow (or brown in age; often purplish in
      T. longipes); leaflets 3.
      13 Calyx-teeth subequal, about 1/3 the tube-length; fertile flowers cream-colour,
         subsessile, becoming reflexed; sterile flowers consisting of slender rigid
         palmately-lobed accrescent calyces; prostrate hairy annual; (introd. in B.C.) . . . . . .
         . . . . [*T. subterranean*]
      13 Calyx-teeth unequal, the 3 lower ones subulate and much longer than the 2
         relatively broader lower ones; flowers all similar and fertile.

14 Perennials with a taproot surmounted by a branched crown, the stems usually decumbent-based and rooting at the nodes; flowers over 7 mm long (heads to 3.5 cm broad), sometimes purplish, mostly spreading to erect; calyx glabrous to rather densely hairy, the lower 3 teeth up to 4 times the tube-length; leaflets mostly elliptic-lanceolate to oblanceolate (sometimes ovate or obovate), to 6 cm long, serrulate to nearly entire; leaf-petioles longer than the leaflets; plant sparsely to rather copiously pubescent; (s ?B.C.) . . . .[*T. longipes*]

14 Annuals, glabrous or sparingly pubescent, the stems procumbent to erect; flowers yellow, at most 7 mm long, pendulous or reflexed; heads to about 1.5 cm broad; calyx glabrous (or the lower 3 teeth sometimes sparsely tufted-hairy in *T. agrarium*), the lower 3 teeth at most slightly longer than the tube; leaf-petioles mostly shorter than the leaflets; (introd.).

  15 Terminal leaflet nearly or quite sessile, the leaflets oblanceolate to oblong-elliptic or -obovate; stipules linear to oblong-lanceolate, united to the petioles for up to 2/3 of their length; style about equalling the pod; mature corolla strongly striate, at least 4 mm long, the pressed heads mostly over 8 mm thick . . . .*T. agrarium*

  15 Terminal leaflet distinctly stalked, the leaflets cuneate-obovate; stipules ovate, united to the petioles for about half their length, the width of the adnate portion nearly or quite equal to the length of the free tip; style many times shorter than the pod.

    16 Corolla to 6 mm long, the standard strongly striate; heads usually with more than 30 flowers, mostly over 8 mm thick when pressed . . . .*T. procumbens*

    16 Corolla at most 3.5 mm long, the standard scarcely striate; heads usually with less than 20 flowers, mostly less than 8 mm thick when pressed . . . .*T. dubium*

12 Flowers white, pink, reddish, or purple (*T. longipes* may be sought here).

  17 Flowers mostly distinctly pedicelled, at least the lower ones pendulous or reflexed; calyx-tube glabrous (but the teeth or their bases sometimes pubescent); leaflets 3; plants glabrous or very sparingly pubescent.

    18 Stems extensively creeping, producing erect scape-like peduncles at the rooting nodes; stipules usually less than 1 cm long; corolla white or slightly pinkish-tinged, to 11 mm long; calyx glabrous, its teeth shorter than the tube; leaflets usually obcordate, retuse at summit, entire or nearly so; (introd., transcontinental) . . . .*T. repens*

    18 Stems ascending to erect (sometimes stoloniferous in *T. hybridum*); stipules to 2 cm long; at least the longer calyx-teeth longer than the tube.

      19 Calyx-teeth subulate, subequal, only slightly longer than the tube, sparingly hairy in the sinuses between their bases; flowers white to reddish, to 9 mm long, on pedicels to over 6 mm long; leaflets ovate to obovate or obcordate, essentially entire; sparingly pubescent perennial; (introd., transcontinental) . . . .*T. hybridum*

      19 Calyx-teeth at least twice the tube-length; leaflets distinctly serrulate; annuals.

        20 Calyx-teeth sparingly villous, acicular, up to 4 times as long as the tube; flowers pinkish, to 7 mm long, on pedicels to 3 mm long; leaflets oblanceolate to obcordate, retuse to rather deeply bifid at apex; plant glabrous to sparingly villous; (Vancouver Is.) . . . . .*T. bifidum*

        20 Calyx-teeth glabrous; entire plant nearly or quite glabrous.

          21 Flowers to 9 mm long, whitish to purple; rachis of inflorescence often prolonged above the flowers; calyx-teeth lanceolate-acuminate, 2 or 3 times the tube-length, the upper 2 teeth usually the longest; leaflets obovate to obcordate . . .[*T. gracilentum*]

          21 Flowers to 13 mm long, white with a roseate banner; rachis not

prolonged; calyx-teeth subulate, several times longer than the tube, subequal; leaflets oblong-obovate, rounded or slightly retuse at summit; (s Ont.) . . . . *T. reflexum*

17 Flowers sessile or subsessile.

    22 Floral heads slenderly conic or ovoid-cylindric, becoming cylindric in fruit; calyx copiously villous or pilose, its teeth aristate; leaflets 3; pubescent annuals.

        23 Free blades of stipules linear-subulate or bristle-like, to 1 cm long; heads drab or greyish, short-peduncled, to 4 cm long; flowers white or pale pink, to 6 mm long; calyx-teeth about twice the tube-length and surpassing the corolla; leaflets linear-oblanceolate or -oblong, to 2.5 cm long, subentire, mostly longer than the leaf-petioles; (introd. in s B.C. and from Ont. to N.S.) . . . . *T. arvense*

        23 Free blades of stipules ovate, with usually reddish or purplish margins; heads long-peduncled, to 7 cm long; flowers scarlet or crimson (rarely white), to 1.5 cm long; calyx-teeth only slightly longer than the tube and shorter than the corolla; leaflets broadly cuneate-obovate or obcordate, to 3 cm long, denticulate on the upper half, much shorter than the lower and middle leaf-petioles; (introd. in s B.C. and s Ont.) . . . . *T. incarnatum*

    22 Floral heads broadly ovoid to subglobose, not much longer than thick.

        24 Corollas mostly less than 1 cm long, pink to purplish (sometimes white); leaflets 3; perennials.

            25 Corolla resupinate (the banner turned outward rather than normally inward toward the centre of the head), to 6 mm long, 2 or 3 times longer than the calyx; calyx short-pubescent (to ?glabrate), becoming somewhat inflated and reticulate, its teeth much shorter than the tube; leaflets cuneate, entire or nearly so; (introd.) . . . . *[T. resupinatum]*

            25 Corolla not resupinate; calyx villous, its acicular plumose-villous teeth 2 or 3 times as long as the tube; leaflets oblanceolate to obcordate, coarsely serrulate their full length; plant villous-pubescent throughout; (introd. in sw B.C.) . . . . *[T. macraei]*

        24 Corolla over 1 cm long; leaflets serrulate; perennials or biennials.

            26 Leaflets usually 5 or more, rather thick and leathery, oblanceolate to obcordate, to 2.5 cm long; flowers pinkish to roseate, to over 2.5 cm long (heads to about 5 cm thick); calyx densely villous, the plumose-hairy teeth several times the tube-length; plant sparingly to densely pubescent; (s ?B.C.) . . . . *[T. macrocephalum]*

            26 Leaflets 3; flowers to about 2 cm long; calyx-tube to 4.5 mm long, the lowest setaceous tooth to 7 mm long, the others to 5 mm long; plants glabrous or sparingly pilose; (introd., transcontinental)

               27 Leaflets narrowly elliptic to oblong, to 6 cm long; flowers purplish; calyx-tube glabrous except for a hairy rim at the summit; stipules lance-acuminate . . . . *T. medium*

               27 Leaflets oval to obovate; flowers normally roseate; calyx-tube pubescent; stipules oval, with subulate tips . . . . *T. pratense*

T. agrarium L.   Yellow or Hop-Clover.   Trèfle jaune
Eurasian; introd. along roadsides and in dry fields and waste places of N. America, as in s Alaska and all the provinces (N to the Hamilton R. basin, Labrador) except Man. [Linnaeus' name being of doubtful application, this species should be called *T. aureum* Poll. but the name *T. agrarium* is retained here following common usage]. MAP: Hultén 1968b:644 *(T. aureum)*.

[T. alexandrinum L.]   Berseem, Egyptian Clover
[Native in Egypt and Syria; there is a collection in OAC from s Ont. (pastures and fields, Wellington Co.), where, however, evidently not established.]

T. arvense L.   Rabbit-foot-Clover, Stone-Clover
Eurasian; introd. along dry roadsides and in fields and waste places of N. America, as in s
B.C. (Vancouver Is. and adjacent islands; Yale; Arrow Lakes), Ont. (N to the Ottawa dist.),
Que. (N to Charlevoix and Temiscouata counties and Magdalen Is.), N.B., P.E.I., and N.S.

T. bifidum Gray   Pinole Clover
/t/W/   (T)   Open ground from sw B.C. (near Victoria, Vancouver Is.; CAN: Fletcher, in 1885)
to s Calif. [*T. gracilentum sensu* John Macoun 1886, not T. & G.; incl. var. *decipiens* Greene
(*T. greenei* House)].

T. cyathiferum Lindl.   Cup Clover
/T/W/   (T)   Wet meadows to dryish sandy soil from s B.C. (N to Revelstoke; CAN; reported
as probably introd. at Juneau, se Alaska, by Hitchcock et al. 1961, but not listed by Hultén
1947) to Calif. and Idaho.

T. depauperatum Desv.
Native in the w U.S.A. (cent. Oreg. to Calif.) and introd. northwards in Wash. and sw B.C.
(near Victoria and Esquimault, Vancouver Is., where first taken in 1875 by both G.M. Dawson
and John Macoun; CAN; V).

T. dubium Sibth.   Suckling Clover
European; introd. along roadsides and in fields and waste places of N. America, as in se
?Alaska (reported from Juneau), B.C. (Queen Charlotte Is.; Vancouver Is. and adjacent is-
lands and mainland), s Ont. (N to Grey and York counties), N.B., P.E.I., and N.S. [*T. minus*
Sm.]. MAP: Hultén 1968*b*:646.

T. fragiferum L.   Strawberry-Clover
Eurasian; introd. and established in waste places of N. America, as in s B.C. (Vernon; Herb. V;
reported from railway yards at Vancouver by Eastham 1947).

[T. fucatum Lindl.]   Sour Clover
[Native in Calif.; there is a collection in CAN from sw B.C. (Victoria, Vancouver Is.), where
taken in grassy places by James Fletcher in 1885 but evidently not established. (Incl. var *flavulum* (Greene) Jeps. (*T. flav.* Greene).]

[T. gracilentum T. & G.]   Pin-point Clover
[Native in the w U.S.A. (Wash. to Baja Calif.); the report from sw B.C. by John Macoun (1886;
Victoria, Vancouver Is.) is based upon *T. bifidum,* the relevant collection in CAN.]

T. hybridum L.   Alsike Clover.   Trèfle Alsike
Eurasian; introd. in fields and waste places of N. America and known from s Alaska–Yukon–
Dist. Mackenzie and all the provinces (in Man., N to Churchill; in Labrador, N to the Hamilton
R. basin); s Greenland. MAP: Hultén 1968*b*:642.
   Much of our material is referable to the small-dimensioned extreme, var. *elegans* (Savi)
Boiss. (var. *?pratense* Rabenh.; corolla at most 8 mm long rather than to 11 mm; heads at
most 2.5 cm thick rather than to 3.5 mm; leaflets less than 4 cm long rather than to 6 cm).
Forma *alloideum* Dore (inflorescence somewhat resembling a small onion-umbel, the calyx of
each floret strongly distended) is known from the type locality, Sylvania, Sask. Forma *proliferum* Dore (the flowers replaced by a dense mass of small greenish scales) is known from
the type locality, Lac-aux-Sables, Que. Both of these forms are probably mere pathological
states.

T. incarnatum L.   Crimson or Italian Clover
European; cult. for forage and occasionally spreading to roadsides and waste ground in N.
America, as in s B.C. (Vancouver Is.; Vancouver; Penticton) and s Ont. (N to Waterloo and
Wellington counties). [Incl. var. *elatius* Gibelli & Belli].

[T. longipes Nutt.]
[Native in the w U.S.A. (N to Wash. and Mont.), the report from s B.C. by John Macoun (1883) requiring confirmation. The MAPS of the area by J.M. Gillett (Can. J. Bot. 47(1): fig. 1, p. 94, and fig. 2, p. 95. 1969) indicate no Canadian stations.]

[T. macraei H. & A.]
[Native from Wash. to Baja Calif. and Chile; there is a collection in CAN from sw B.C. (Oak Bay, Victoria, Vancouver Is.), where probably introd. in an old field and taken by John Macoun in 1908, but apparently not established. (Incl. *T. albopurpureum* T. & G. and *T. dichotomum* H. & A.).]

[T. macrocephalum (Pursh) Poir.]
[Native in the w U.S.A. (Wash. and Idaho to Nev.). The Lyall report, "In the mountains on the southern boundary of British Columbia", quoted by John Macoun (1883) requires confirmation. (*Lupinaster* Pursh; *T. megacephalum* Nutt.).]
    T. lupinaster L., similar to *T. macrocephalum* in at least its upper leaves bearing more than the 3 leaflets usually characteristic of the genus (but differing as noted below), has been introd. into cent. Alaska and Greenland:
1   Calyx-teeth many times longer than the tube; flowers over 2 cm long; heads to 5 cm
    thick; leaflets oblanceolate to obcordate, broadly rounded to truncate or retuse at
    apex, to about 2.5 cm long . . . . *T. macrocephalum*
1   Calyx-teeth less than 3 times as long as the tube; flowers about 1.5 cm long; heads
    about 3 cm thick; leaflets narrowly elliptic, acute, to 4 cm. long; [cent. Alaska and
    Greenland; MAP: Hultén 1968b:641] . . . . *T. lupinaster* L.

T. medium L.   Zigzag Clover
Eurasian; introd. along roadsides and in fields and waste places of N. America, as in ?B.C. (Henry 1915), Ont. (N to North Lancaster, Glengarry Co.; Groh and Frankton 1949a), Que. (N to the Mingan Is. of the Côte-Nord), N.B. (Woodstock; GH), P.E.I. (Herbert Groh, Sci. Agric. 7: 394. 1927), and ?N.S. (John Macoun 1886; Halifax).

T. microcephalum Pursh
/T/W/   (T)   Moist meadows, sandy riverbanks, and drier hillsides from s B.C. (Vancouver Is. and adjacent islands E to the Columbia Valley and N to Revelstoke; CAN; V) and Mont. to Baja Calif. and Ariz.; introd. in cent. Alaska. MAP: Hultén 1968b:645.

T. microdon H. & A.
/t/W/   (T)   Meadows and sandy or rocky soil from sw B.C. (Vancouver Is. and adjacent islands and mainland; CAN; Henry 1915) to Calif. and S. America.

T. oliganthum Steud.
/t/W/   (T)   Moist meadows or dry rocky places from sw B.C. (Vancouver Is. and adjacent islands; CAN; V; reported E to Penticton by J.M. Macoun 1895) to Calif. [*T. pauciflorum* Nutt., not d'Urv.].

T. pratense L.   Red Clover.   Trèfle rouge
Eurasian; extensively cult. in N. America and freely escaping to roadsides, fields, and waste places (as outlined below for our area). MAP and synonymy: see below.
1   Leaflets to 7 cm long; heads 3 or 4 cm long . . . . var. *sativum* (Mill.) Schreb.
    2   Flowers whitish; [s Man. (Plumas, about 25 mi NE of Brandon) and N.S. (Wolfville,
        Kings Co.)] . . . . f. *flavicans* (Vis.) Hayek
    2   Flowers roseate; [Ont. (N to w James Bay at ca. 51°15'N), Que. (N to the Côte-
        Nord), Nfld., N.B., and N.S.] . . . . f. *sativum*
1   Leaflets usually less than 3 cm long; heads to 3 cm long . . . . var. *pratense*
    3   Flowers creamy white; [Man. and Que.; Boivin 1966b] . . . .
        . . . . f. *leucochraceum* Aschers. & Prantl

3 Flowers roseate; [incl. vars. *expansum* Haussk. and *frigidum* Gaud.; Aleutian
Is.–s Alaska–s Yukon–s Dist. Mackenzie–B.C.–Alta. to Sask., Man. (N to Gillam,
about 165 mi s of Churchill), Ont. (N to Big Trout L. at ca. 53°45′N), Que. (N to
the Côte-Nord), Labrador (N to the Hamilton R. basin), Nfld., N.B., P.E.I., and
N.S.; s Greenland; MAP (aggregate species): Hultén 1968*b*:643] . . . . f. *pratense*

T. procumbens L.   Low Hop-Clover
Eurasian; introd. along roadsides and in old fields and waste places of N. America, as in se
Alaska and most of the provinces (not yet definitely reported from Alta.). [*T. campestre*
Schreb., the name of correct usage according to recent authors]. MAP: Hultén 1968*b*:644 (*T.
camp.*).

T. reflexum L.   Buffalo-Clover
/t/EE/   (T (Hs, bien.))   Fields, roadsides, and borders of sandy woods from S.Dak. to Ind., s
Ont. (Essex and Lambton counties; John Macoun 1883; Dodge 1914; TRT; GH), and N.Y., s to
Tex. and Fla.
    The s Ont. plant is referable to var. *glabrum* Lojacono (*T. pensylvanicum sensu* Hooker
1831, perhaps not DC.; pedicels and calyces glabrous rather than pubescent or pilose, the
stem and branches nearly or quite glabrous rather than villous).

T. repens L.   White Clover.   Trèfle blanc
Eurasian; introd. along roadsides and in old fields and waste places of N. America, as in
Alaska (N to ca. 67°30′N), the Yukon, Dist. Mackenzie, and all the provinces (in Man., N to
Churchill; in Labrador, N to ca. 55°N); s Greenland. MAP: Hultén 1968*b*:642.
    Forma *alloideum* Dore (inflorescence somewhat resembling a small onion-umbel, the calyx
of each floret strongly distended) is known from the type locality, Ottawa, Ont. Forma *phyllan-
thum* (Ser.) Fiori & Beg. (calyx-lobes more or less modified to leaves; pedicels abnormally
elongated) is tentatively reported from N.B. by Boivin (1966*b*). These are perhaps mere pathological states.

[T. resupinatum L.]   Reversed Clover
[Asiatic; introd. along roadsides and in lawns and fields in N. America. The reports from Que.
by John Macoun (1883; near Quebec City) and N.B. by Fowler (1885; ballast-heaps at St.
John) require confirmation (if proven valid, the plant was evidently a casual waif and not established at either locality).]

[T. subterranean L.]
[European; collections from sw B.C. have been placed here (Saanich and Comox, Vancouver
Is.; Herb. V; "original seed introduced from New Zealand in 1936"), where, however, the spe-
cies is probably not established.]

T. tridentatum Lindl.
/t/W/   (T)   Meadows and grassy hillsides from sw B.C. (Vancouver Is. and adjacent islands
and mainland E to Chilliwack; CAN) to Calif.

T. variegatum Nutt.
/t/W/   (T)   Moist meadows to dry sandy soils from sw B.C. (Vancouver Is. and adjacent islands and mainland E to Chilliwack, Trail, and L. Okanagan; CAN; reported from St. Michael,
Alaska, where probably introd.) and Mont. to Calif. and Utah. [*T. dianthum* Greene]. MAP: Hultén 1968*b*:645.
    Var. *rostratum* (Greene) Hitchc. (*T. rost.* Greene; *T. appendiculatum* f. *rost.* (Greene)
McDerm.; corolla-keel tipped with a slender beak about 0.5 mm long rather than beakless or
the beak not over 0.3 mm long) is reported from sw B.C. by Hitchcock et al. (1961; Vancouver Is.).

T. wormskjoldii Lehm.
/T/W/   (Grh)   Coastal dunes, meadows, and streambanks from the southernmost Alaska
Panhandle (Loring, ca. 55°N) and B.C. (N to Queen Charlotte Is.) to Calif., Mexico, N.Mex.,

and Colo. [*T. fimbriatum* Lindl.; *T. heterodon* T. & G.; *T. spinulosum* Dougl.; *T. involucratum* Ortega, not Lam.]. MAP: Hultén 1968*b*:643.

TRIGONELLA L. [3687]

1 Flowers white with blue veins, numerous in dense heads; pods ovate, the slender beak longer than the body; leaves ovate to subrotund; stem ascending; (introd. from B.C. to Ont.) . . . . *T. caerulea*
1 Flowers white with pink veins, solitary or at most 5 in subumbellate heads or capitate racemes; pods somewhat curved, compressed, merely mucronate.
  2 Stem prostrate; leaves obcordate; (introd. in N.B.) . . . . [*T. ornithopodioides*]
  2 Stem erect or ascending; leaves ovate; (introd. in Ont., N.B., and N.S.) . . . . [*T. corniculata*]

T. caerulea (L.) Ser.
European; apparently recorded for N. America only from Canada, where introd. in B.C. (Boivin 1966*b*), Alta. (Groh and Frankton 1949*b*; Fenn, 52°08′N), Sask. (Swift Current and Saskatoon; Breitung 1957*a*), SW Man. (Brandon), and Ont. (Ottawa). [*Melilotus* Desr.; *Trifolium Melilotus caer.* L.].

[T. corniculata L.]
[European; apparently recorded for N. America only from Canada, where introd. (but scarcely established) in S Ont. (a ballpark at Toronto; TRT), N.B. (an early collection by Vroom from St. Stephen), and N.S. (early collections by Macoun and Burgess from ballast-heaps at Pictou, these referred by John Macoun 1890, to the closely related *T. hamosa* L.; GH).]

[T. ornithopodioides (L.) DC.]
[European; apparently recorded for N. America only from N.B. (ballast at St. John; NBM; John Macoun 1883; Fowler 1885), where not established. (*Trifolium* L.).]

ULEX L. [3681]

U. europaeus L. Gorse, Furze
European; occasionally cult. as a sand-binder in N. America and becoming established on sands, as in B.C. (Queen Charlotte Is.; Vancouver Is. and adjacent islands and mainland).

VICIA L. [3852] Vetch, Tare. Vesce

1 Tendrils none; flowers few in subsessile clusters, 2 or 3 cm long, commonly white with violet veins, the wing with a purplish-black blotch; leaflets 2 or 3 pairs, elliptic or ovate; stem square in cross-section; annual; (introd.) . . . . [*V. faba*]
1 Tendrils present.
  2 Flowers solitary or few in subsessile clusters in the upper leaf-axils; style bearded in a tuft on its lower side beneath the stigma; (introd.).
    3 Calyx irregular, the teeth all much shorter than the tube, the upper pair broadly triangular and shorter than the lower 3; flowers violet-blue, to about 1.5 cm long, up to 6 in a cluster; pods to 3 cm long; leaflets up to 9 pairs; perennials with filiform reddish stolons and moniliform tubers . . . . *V. sepium*
    3 Calyx nearly regular, the subequal linear to narrowly lanceolate teeth not much shorter than the tube; flowers usually solitary or in pairs in the upper leaf-axils; annuals.
      4 Tendrils all simple; leaflets at most 4 pairs; flowers less than 1 cm long, violet, solitary; pods to 2.5 cm long, their quadrate seeds strongly rough-wrinkled; (introd. in SW B.C.) . . . . [*V. lathyroides*]
      4 Tendrils forking; leaflets up to 8 pairs; flowers to 3 cm long, bicoloured purple and rose, mostly paired in the leaf-axils; pods to 8 cm long, their compressed-globose seeds smooth . . . . *V. sativa*

2 Flowers solitary to several or many on elongate peduncles; style pubescent at summit or bearded all around (not bearded in a tuft beneath the stigma); tendrils mostly forking.

  5 Flowers at most 8 mm long, solitary or in racemes of mostly not more than 6; leaflets linear to narrowly elliptic; annuals; (introd.).

    6 Calyx-lobes subequal; pods usually hirsute, obliquely tapering to tip, 2-seeded, to 1 cm long, becoming black; flowers whitish, 3 or 4 mm long; leaflets usually 6, 7, or 8 pairs, commonly truncate or retuse at the mucronate summit, to 1.5 cm long . . . . *V. hirsuta*

    6 Calyx-lobes unequal, the 2 linear lower ones about equalling the tube, the upper triangular ones much shorter; pods glabrous, to 1.5 cm long, symmetrically rounded to a blunt tip, 4-seeded, brown; flowers white to light purple, 7 or 8 mm long; leaflets commonly 3 or 4 pairs, acute or obtuse, 1 or 2 cm long . . . . *V. tetrasperma*

  5 Flowers either over 8 mm long or in racemes of more than 6.

    7 Mature racemes shorter than the subtending leaves, their flowers (at most 9) blue-purple, to over 2.5 cm long; calyx-lobes unequal; leaflets usually less than 9 pairs, their lateral veins prominent and rib-like beneath on drying; stipules sharply serrate; perennial; (B.C. to w Que.) . . . . . . *V. americana*

    7 Mature racemes mostly equalling or surpassing their subtending leaves, their usually more numerous flowers mostly less than 2 cm long; leaflets often more numerous, usually not prominently veiny.

      8 Flowers ochroleucous to orange, often purple-tinged; calyx about 1/2 the corolla-length, very irregular, the upper teeth scarcely 1 mm long, the lowest tooth about the length of the tube; pods to 4 cm long and 1.5 cm broad, blackening upon drying; leaflets lanceolate to oblong, to 4 cm long, up to 14 pairs; at least the basal half of the stipules sharply serrate; stems hollow, conspicuously ridged, to 2 m long and 7 mm thick; perennial; (coasts of Alaska and B.C.) . . . . *V. gigantea*

      8 Flowers purple or purplish to white (the keel then usually tipped with blue or purple); pods to 3 cm long; leaflets mostly smaller and usually not more than 12 pairs; stems usually more slender.

        9 Calyx (including the subequal broadly deltoid lobes) usually less than 3 mm long; corolla white with a blue-tipped keel, to 12 mm long; racemes lax, with up to about 20 flowers; leaflets broadly lanceolate to narrowly oblong, rounded or obscurely emarginate at the mucronate summit; perennial; (s Ont.) . . . . *V. caroliniana*

        9 Calyx (including the unequal teeth) commonly at least 4 mm long; corolla purplish or bicoloured purplish and white, to 1.5 cm long; racemes dense; leaflets linear to narrowly oblong; (introd.).

          10 Calyx nearly symmetrical at base; upper calyx-lobes broadly triangular, at most 0.7 mm long, the lower teeth lance-attenuate; corolla blue-violet or purple, the blade of the standard as long as the claw; plant more or less appressed-pubescent; perennial . . . .
. . . . *V. cracca*

          10 Calyx distinctly gibbous (inflated) on the upper (inner) side at base (the pedicel appearing ventral); upper calyx-lobes linear-triangular, to 1.5 mm long, the lower teeth linear-acicular; flowers to 1.5 cm long, bicoloured violet and white, the blade of the standard less than half as long as the claw; plants annual or biennial.

            11 Plant spreading-villous; lower calyx-teeth long-villous, to 4 mm long . . . . *V. villosa*

            11 Plant appressed-pubescent to glabrate; lower calyx-teeth short-pubescent or glabrate, 1 or 2 mm long . . . . *V. dasycarpa*

V. americana Muhl.
/ST/(X)/ (Hp) Damp or gravelly shores, thickets, and meadows from SE Alaska and W Dist. Mackenzie (N to ca. 65°N; not known from the Yukon) to B.C., Alta. (N to L. Athabasca), Sask. (N to Prince Albert), Man. (N to Churchill), Ont. (N to Fort Severn, Hudson Bay, ca. 56°N), and W Que. (N to Rupert House, SE James Bay, 51°29′N; reports E to the Gaspé Pen. and N.B. require confirmation; not known from Nfld., P.E.I., or N.S.), S to Calif., N Mexico, N.Mex., Kans., Ohio, and Va. MAPS: Hultén 1968b:670; Fassett 1939:111 (incomplete northwards).

The common plant northwards is referable to var. *minor* Hook. (type from near Carlton House, Sask.; var. *angustifolia* Nees; var. *linearis* (Nutt.) Wats. (*Lathyrus lin.* Nutt.) in large part; *V. caespitosa* Nels.; *V. sparsifolia* and *V. sylvatica* Nutt.; *V. trifida* Dietr.; leaflets linear to linear-oblong rather than elliptic to oblong or oblong-ovate). Var. *truncata* (Nutt.) Brewer (*V. oregana* and *V. truncata* Nutt.; leaflets truncate at summit rather than rounded or tapering) occurs with the typical form throughout the southern part of the range.

V. caroliniana Walt.
/t/EE/ (Hp) Rich woods and thickets from Minn. to S Ont. (N to Waterloo and Hastings counties) and N.Y., S to Okla., La., and Ga. MAP: Fassett 1939:116.

V. cracca L. Tufted Vetch, Canada-pea. Jargeau
Eurasian; widely introd. in N. America and a common weed in Alaska–Yukon (N to ca. 66°N) and all the provinces (in Man., N to York Factory; in Labrador, N to the Hamilton R. basin); S Greenland. MAP and synonymy: *see* below.
1 Peduncle and raceme together about twice the length of the subtending leaf; flowers to 15 mm long, the blade of the standard distinctly longer than the claw . . . .
. . . . var. *tenuifolia* (Roth) Beck
  2 Flowers blue-violet; [*V. tenuifolia* Roth; reported from Charlottetown, P.E.I., by D.S. Erskine 1960] . . . . f. *tenuifolia*
  2 Flowers white; [Ottawa dist., Ont.; Gillett 1958] . . . .
. . . . f. *albiflora* (Aschers. & Graebn.) Gams
1 Peduncle and raceme together usually less than twice the length of the subtending leaf; flowers to 13 mm long, the blade of the standard about equalling its claw . . . .
. . . . var. *cracca*
  3 Flowers blue-violet.
    4 Leaflets appressed-pilose to glabrate; [incl. var. *linearis* (Pet.) Gams and its f. *etiamalba* Boivin; range of the species; MAP (aggregate species): Hultén 1968b:670] . . . . f. *cracca*
    4 Leaflets silvery-silky with lustrous hairs; [E Que. (Anticosti Is.; MT) and Nfld. (Fernald 1933)] . . . . f. *sericea* (Peterm.) Beck
  3 Flowers white; [f. *albiflora* Kitt.; Ont. (Boivin 1966b), SW Que. (St. Helen's Is., Montreal; MT), and N.S. (Annapolis and Colchester counties)] . . . .
. . . . f. *albida* (Peterm.) Gams

V. dasycarpa Ten.
European; widely introd. throughout the U.S.A. but the only Canadian record appears to be a 1956 collecton by J.S. Erskine near Williamstown, Annapolis Co., N.S. (ACAD; "Abundant on sandy soil in field of rye").

[*V. faba* L.] Broad Bean
[European; an occasional garden-escape in N. America, as in ?Nfld. (Rouleau 1956; ?escaped).]

V. gigantea Hook. Giant Vetch
/sT/W/ (Hp) Thickets, clearings, and streambanks near the coast from SE Alaska (*see* Hultén 1947: map 843, p. 1194) through W B.C. to Calif. [*V. sitchensis* Bong.]. MAP: Hultén 1968b:670.

V. hirsuta (L.) S. F. Gray   Hairy Vetch
Eurasian; introd. along roadsides and in waste places of N. America, as in s B.C. (Vancouver
Is. and adjacent islands and mainland; Chilliwack), s Alta. (Olds; J.M. Macoun 1897), Ont.
(near Hamilton and Ottawa; John Macoun 1883), Que. (N to the Côte-Nord, Anticosti Is., and
Gaspé Pen.), St-Pierre and Miquelon, N.B., P.E.I., and N.S.; sw Greenland. [*Ervum* L.].

[V. lathyroides L.]
[Eurasian; reported from sw B.C. by J.M. Macoun (1913; near Langford, Vancouver Is.), where
apparently not established.]

V. sativa L.   Spring-Vetch
Eurasian; widely introd. along roadsides and in waste places of N. America (ranges of Canadian taxa outlined below). MAP and synonymy: *see* below.
1   Corolla usually less than 18 mm long and usually quite uniformly purple; pods plane,
    the seeds about 3 mm broad; leaflets commonly not more than 5 pairs, narrowly
    linear to oblong or obovate; [*V. ang.* L. and its var. *segetalis* (Thuill.) Koch; s Alaska
    (Sitka); B.C. (Vancouver Is. and adjacent islands; Hope); Man. (Fort Garry), Ont. (N
    to the Ottawa dist.), Que. (N to the Gaspé Pen.), Nfld., St-Pierre and Miquelon, N.B.,
    P.E.I., and N.S.; s Greenland; MAP (*V. ang.*): Hultén 1968*b*:669] . . . .
    . . . . var. *angustifolia* (L.) Wahl.
1   Corolla usually at least 18 mm long, the wings often reddish or violet, the remainder
    purple; pods often more or less depressed between the seeds, these about 5 mm
    broad; leaflets up to 8 pairs.
    2   Leaflets mostly linear, emarginate or short-pointed; [*V. angustifolia* var. *uncinata*
        (Desv.) Rouy; B.C. (Nanaimo, Vancouver Is.); E Que. (Douglastown, Gaspé Pen.;
        GH), Nfld., N.B., P.E.I., and N.S.] . . . . var. *linearis* Lange
    2   Leaflets elliptic to oblong-obovate, truncate or emarginate at the mucronate
        summit; [B.C. (Queen Charlotte Is.; Vancouver Is. and adjacent islands;
        Rosedale; Belrose), Alta. (Banff), Ont. (N to Prescott Co.), Que. (N to the Gaspé
        Pen.), Nfld., St-Pierre and Miquelon, N.B., P.E.I., and N.S.; Greenland] . . . . . var. *sativa*

V. sepium L.   Hedge Vetch
Eurasian; introd. along roadsides and in old fields of N. America, as in Ont. (ditches in a ravine near Hamilton, Wentworth Co., where taken by Dickson in 1895; CAN; reported from
Lambton Co. by Dodge 1915), Que. (N to the Quebec City dist.; MT), Nfld. (cemetery at St.
John's; GH), N.B., P.E.I. (Charlottetown; DAO; ACAD), and N.S.
    Var. *montana* Koch (leaves elliptic-lanceolate to narrowly ovate, tapering to summit, rather
than oval to ovate-oblong and round-tipped or emarginate, is known from Que. (Cap Rouge,
near Quebec City; MT).

V. tetrasperma (L.) Moench   Lentillon or Cicérole
Eurasian; introd. in old fields and waste places of N. America, as in s B.C. (Vancouver Is. and
adjacent islands and mainland), Ont. (N to the SE shore of L. Superior and the Ottawa dist.),
Que. (N to Chicoutimi Co., the Côte-Nord, and Gaspé Pen.; not known from Anticosti Is.),
?Nfld. (Fernald *in* Gray 1950), St-Pierre and Miquelon (Rouleau 1956; not listing the species
for Nfld.), N.B., P.E.I., and N.S. [*Ervum* L.; *V. pusilla* Muhl.].

V. villosa Roth   Hairy or Winter-Vetch
European; cult. for forage in N. America and escaping to fields and waste places, as in s
Alaska, s B.C. (Queen Charlotte Is.; Vancouver Is. and adjacent mainland; Hope; Spences
Bridge; Grand Forks), Man. (Brandon), Ont. (reported from Lambton Co. by Gaiser and Moore
1966; collections in OAC as far N as the Ottawa dist. have been referred here but the species
is not listed by Gillett 1958), Que. (Boivin 1966*b*), and N.S. (Kings, Lunenburg, and Colchester
counties; ACAD). MAP: Hultén 1968*b*:670.

LINACEAE (Flax Family)

(Ref.: J.K. Small, N. Am. Flora 25:67–84. 1907)
Herbs with simple entire sessile leaves, these commonly narrow, opposite or alternate, and ex-stipulate (but often with glands at base). Flowers regular, perfect, hypogynous, in corymbose or paniculate inflorescences. Sepals, petals, stamens, and styles each 4 or 5 and regularly alternating with one another. Ovary superior. Fruit a capsule.

1 Flowers 5-merous; sepals entire or merely ciliate, acute or acuminate; petals white, yellow, or blue, surpassing the sepals; capsule completely or partially 10-locular; leaves relatively long and narrow; stem commonly over 2 dm tall . . . . *Linum*
1 Flowers 4-merous; sepals 3-lobed across the broad summit, about equalling the white petals; capsule incompletely 8-locular; leaves ovate to oblong, usually about 4 or 5 mm long, opposite; stem filiform, to about 1 dm tall, several times dichotomously branching; (introd. in N.S.) . . . . *Millegrana*

LINUM L.   [3945]   Flax.   Lin

1 Fruiting pedicles to about 4 cm long; petals blue or white; sepals lacking marginal glands.
  2 Stems filiform, to about 3 dm tall; leaves all or mostly opposite, elliptic, to 1.5 cm long; petals white, with yellow base, at most about 5 mm long; annual; (introd.) . . . . . .
    . . . . *L. catharticum*
  2 Stems stouter and taller; leaves alternate; petals normally blue, about 1 cm long.
    3 Sepals long-acuminate, the inner ones usually with ciliate margins; petals less than 1.5 cm long; stigmas linear; leaves linear-lanceolate, 3-nerved for at least half their length; annual, mostly simple at base; (introd.) . . . . *L. usitatissimum*
    3 Sepals not acuminate, eciliate; petals over 2 cm long; stigmas capitate; leaves linear, 3-nerved only at base; perennial, usually with several stems; (B.C. to Que.) . . . . *L. perenne*
1 Fruiting pedicels mostly less than 1 cm long; petals yellow.
  4 Outer (as well as inner) sepals conspicuously glandular-serrate; styles united below; petals to 1.5 cm long; leaves mostly alternate, usually with a pair of minute dark glands at base; annuals.
    5 Capsule ovoid, about 5 mm long, its 5 carpels with a brown cartilaginous thickening at base; styles free only at tips; sepals to 8 mm long, they and the leaves finally deciduous; (s Alta. to Man.) . . . . *L. rigidum*
    5 Capsule globose-ovoid, about 3 mm long, without basal thickening, promptly splitting into 10 valves; styles free nearly to base; sepals 5 or 6 mm long, persistent; (s Man. and s Ont.) . . . . *L. sulcatum*
  4 Outer sepals entire; styles free to base; petals rarely over 1 cm long; capsules subglobose or globose-ovoid; leaves alternate above, opposite below, lacking basal glands; perennials; (s Ont.).
    6 Stems conspicuously angled with 3 narrow wings extending from the base of each leaf beyond the next leaf below; leaves more or less viscid; inflorescence paniculate; outer sepals elliptic, herbaceous, to about 2.5 mm long . . . .
      . . . . [*L. striatum*]
    6 Stem not conspicuously angled; leaves non-viscid; inflorescence corymbiform; outer sepals lance-attenuate to -ovate, to 3.5 mm long.
      7 Branches of inflorescence filiform, often flexuous, spreading-ascending, commonly themselves branching; sepals usually lacking marginal glands at least at maturity; leaves thinnish . . . . *L. virginianum*
      7 Branches of inflorescence angled, stiffly ascending, simple or only sparingly branched; leaves firm . . . . *L. medium*

L. catharticum L.   Fairy-Flax
Eurasian; locally introd. in old fields and in sandy or calcareous places of ᴇ N. America, as in

Ont. (a 1903 Ottawa collection by John Macoun in CAN; not listed by Gillett 1958), sw Que. (Farnham, Missisquoi Co.; Groh 1946), Nfld. (Corner Brook; CAN; MT), N.B. (St. Andrews, Charlotte Co.; GH), P.E.I. (Souris, Kings Co.; MT), and N.S. (Pictou, Antigonish, Richmond, and Cape Breton counties). [*Cathartolinum* Small]. MAPS: Hultén 1958: map 115, p. 134; C.M. Rogers, Brittonia 15(2): fig. 2, p. 104. 1963. *See* note under *Luzula campestris.*

L. medium (Planch.) Britt.
/T/EE/ (Hp) Dry or moist open soil (ranges of Canadian taxa outlined below), s to Tex. and Fla. MAP and synonymy: *see* below.

1 Longer sepals 2 or 3 mm long, the inner ones entire or sparingly glandular-ciliate; capsule promptly splitting into 10 valves; leaves elliptic to elliptic-obovate, at most about 40, only the upper ones with short subulate tips; [*L. (striatum) virginianum* var. *med.* Planch., the type from L. Huron, Ont.; *Cathartolinum* Small; s Ont.: Norfolk, Lincoln, Waterloo, York, Bruce, and Simcoe counties; MAP: C.M. Rogers, Brittonia 15(2): fig. 4, p. 113. 1963] . . . . var. *medium*
1 Longer sepals to 5 mm long, the inner ones copiously glandular-ciliate; capsule splitting into 5 carpels or tardily into 10 valves; leaves linear to lance-elliptic, all but the lowermost ones with prolonged subulate tips; [*L. virginianum (striatum)* var. *tex.* Planch.; s Ont.: Long Point, Norfolk Co., and near Sarnia, Lambton Co.; CAN, detd. Rogers; MAP: on the above-noted map by Rogers] . . . . var. *texanum* (Planch.) Fern.

L. perenne L. Perennial Flax
/aST/(X)/EA/ (Hp (Ch)) Dry prairies to alpine ridges (the typical form and var. *austriacum* of Eurasia found in waste places), var. *lewisii* from N Alaska–Yukon to w Victoria Is. and the coast of Dist. Mackenzie at Coronation Gulf, s through B.C.–Alta. to Baja Calif. and N Mexico; farther eastwards known from Sask. (N to Prince Albert), Man. (N to Churchill), Wisc., Ont. (N to James Bay–Hudson Bay), islands of James Bay–Hudson Bay (N to Long Is., ca. 55°N), and Que. (E James Bay coast; Nominingue, Labelle Co.); Eurasia. MAPS and synonymy: *see* below.

For a somewhat differing recent treatment, *see* Theodore Mosquin (Can. J. Bot. 49(8):1379–88. 1971, with MAP, fig. 1, p. 1381).

1 Flowers of two kinds (with styles longer than, and with styles shorter than, the stamens); mature pedicels not strongly arching; petals to 2 cm long; [*L. narbonense sensu* Montgomery 1957, not L.; introd. in s Ont.: Puslinch, Wellington Co., and Kingston, Frontenac Co., where noted by Montgomery as well established in a waste field; OAC] . . . . var. *perenne*
1 Flowers all of one kind; mature pedicels strongly arching or recurved.
2 Styles about 2 mm long, shorter than the stamens; [*L. austriacum* L.; introd. in s Ont. (Dundas, Wentworth Co.; Hespeler, Waterloo Co.)] . . . .
. . . . var. *austriacum* (L.) Schiede
2 Styles considerably longer than the stamens; [native] . . . .
. . . . var. *lewisii* (Pursh) Eat. & Wright
3 Flowers white; [Alta. (Boivin 1966b), NE Man. (Churchill), N Ont. (w James Bay–Hudson Bay N to ca. 56°30′N), and islands of James Bay–Hudson Bay (South Twin Is., Akimiski Is., and Long Is.)] . . . . f. *lepagei* (Boivin) Lepage
3 Flowers blue; [*L. lewisii* Pursh; *L. pratense* of Canadian reports, not (Norton) Small; range of the species; MAPS: Hultén 1968b:676; Porsild 1957: map 254, p. 192] . . . . f. *lewisii*

L. rigidum Pursh Yellow Flax
/T/WW/ (T) Dry prairies and foothills from s Alta. (N to Lethbridge and Medicine Hat) to Sask. (N to Saskatoon) and s Man. (N to Oak Point, about 55 mi NW of Winnipeg), s to N Mexico, N.Mex., and Tex.; introd. eastwards to Mo. [*Cathartolinum* Small; incl. *L. compactum* Nels.]. MAP: C.M. Rogers, Bull. Torrey Bot. Club 96(2): fig. 10, p. 184. 1969.

[L. striatum Walt.]
[Reports of this species of the E U.S.A. (N to Ill. and New Eng.) from s Ont. (as by John Macoun 1883 and 1886) all appear referable to *L. medium* or its var. *texanum* (relevant collection

from Toronto in CAN, revised by Rogers). The MAP by C.M. Rogers (Brittonia 15(2): fig. 5, p. 118. 1963) indicates no Canadian stations. (*Cathartolinum* Small).]

L. sulcatum Riddell   Yellow Flax
/T/EE/   (T)   Dry prairies and calcareous rocks and sands from S Man. (N to Fort Ellice, about 70 mi NW of Brandon; reports from Sask. refer largely or wholly to *L. rigidum,* relevant collections from the Qu'Appelle Valley in CAN, revised by Rogers) to S Ont. (N to Manitoulin Is., N L. Huron; reported as perhaps introd. at Salaberry-de-Valleyfield, Beauharnois Co., SW Que., by L.-R. Cayouette and C. Leduc, Nat. can. (Que.) 98(4):692. 1971), S to Tex., Ark., Ala., and Ga. [*Cathartolinum* Small]. MAPS: C.M. Rogers, Bull. Torrey Bot. Club 96(2): fig. 9, p. 184. 1969, and Brittonia 15(2): fig. 1, p. 100. 1963.

L. usitatissimum L.   Common Flax.   Lin
Eurasian; extensively cult. in N. America and escaping to old fields, roadsides, and waste places, as in ?Alaska (Boivin 1966*b*; not listed by Hultén 1947 and 1968*b*), Dist. Mackenzie (N to Fort Simpson, ca. 62°N; W.J. Cody, Can. Field-Nat. 75(2):64. 1961), SW B.C. (Vancouver Is.; Henry 1915), Alta. (Moss 1959), S Sask. (Boivin 1966*b*), Man. (N to The Pas), Ont. (N to L. Nipigon), Que. (N to Tadoussac, Saguenay Co., and the Gaspé Pen. at Matapédia), Nfld., N.B., P.E.I., and N.S.

Forma *leucanthum* Maly (flowers white rather than blue) is reported from Sask. by Boivin (1966*b*).

L. bienne Mill. of Europe (*L. angustifolium* Huds.) is reported as introd. in B.C. by Calder and Taylor (1968; New Westminster and Moresby Is., Queen Charlotte Is.). It differs from *L. usitatissimum* as follows:

1   Petals to about 15 mm long; inner sepals ciliate or not; capsules at least 10 mm long; seeds with a short obtuse beak; stem usually solitary; annual . . . . *L. usitatissimum*
1   Petals to 12 mm long; inner sepals with a scarious glandular-ciliate border; capsules about 6 mm long; seeds beakless; stems several from the base; biennial or perennial . . . . *L. bienne* Mill.

L. virginianum L.
/t/EE/   (Hp)   Open woods, thickets, and clearings from S Ont. (Essex, Lambton, Lincoln, Waterloo, Wentworth, and York counties) to Mass., S to Okla., Mich., and Pa. MAPS: C.M. Rogers, Bull. Torrey Bot. Club 96(2): fig. 8, p. 184. 1969, and Brittonia 15(2): fig. 5, p. 118. 1963.

MILLEGRANA Adans.   [3944]

M. radiola (L.) Druce   All-seed
Eurasian; known in N. America only from roadsides, old fields, and ditches near the coast of N.S. (Digby, Lunenburg, Halifax, Cape Breton, and Richmond counties). [*Linum* L.; *Radiola linoides* Roth; *R. millegrana* Sm.].

OXALIDACEAE (Wood-Sorrel Family)
(Ref.: J.K. Small, N. Am. Flora 25:25–58. 1907)

OXALIS L.   [3936]   Wood-Sorrel, Lady's-Sorrel.   Oxalide

Low herbs with sour watery juice and delicate alternate or basal 3-foliolate leaves, the leaflets obcordate, entire, sessile or nearly so. Flowers regular, perfect, hypogynous. Sepals and petals each 5. Stamens 10, alternately long and short, their filaments united at base into a short tube. Ovary superior. Fruit a thin-walled 5-locular capsule.

1   Petals white or pinkish, with lilac or reddish veins, to over 1.5 cm long; flowers solitary, the scapes with a pair of opposite minute bracts above the middle, the leaves all basal.
   2   Styles glabrous or nearly so; sepals finely and thinly pubescent; (Ont. to s Labrador, Nfld., and N.S.) . . . . *O. montana*
   2   Styles densely pubescent; sepals coarsely and densely pubescent; (s ?B.C.) . . . .
   . . . . [*O. oregana*]
1   Petals yellow; stems leafy.
   3   Petals to 2 cm long; flowers mostly 1 (sometimes 2 or 3) to a peduncle; anther-filaments hairy, connate for 2 or 3 mm; (s ?B.C.) . . . . [*O. suksdorfii*]
   3   Petals to 9 mm long; flowers often more numerous; anther-filaments glabrous.
      4   Hairs of stem, petioles, and capsules usually at least in part septate (with internal cross-walls), their blunt tips generally collapsing when dried or pressed; stipules none; plant rhizomatous, the stems commonly erect, sometimes prostrate or even matted; (transcontinental) . . . . *O. stricta*
      4   Hairs of stem, petioles, and capsules not septate, their pointed tips not collapsing when dried or pressed; stipules usually present (but often greatly reduced); plants not rhizomatous (but often more or less stoloniferous).
         5   Seeds with transverse whitish ridges; plant caespitose, the main stem erect, usually strigose with ascending hairs, the outer branches sometimes rooting at base; (s Alta. to Que.) . . . . *O. dillenii*
         5   Seeds not white-ridged; main stem creeping and rooting, the erect portion glabrous or strigose; (introd.) . . . . [*O. corniculata*]

[*O. corniculata* L.]   Creeping Lady's-Sorrel
[Eurasian; introd. in fields and waste places (particularly around greenhouses) in N. America and often reported from Canada. However, the only occurrence "in nature" in our area appears to be an 1893 collection by Macoun from ballast-heaps at Nanaimo, Vancouver Is., sw B.C., where apparently not again taken since that time. Except for collections inside greenhouses at Juneau, se Alaska, and at Acadia University, Wolfville, N.S., most or all other Canadian material and reports appear referable to *O. dillenii* or *O. stricta* (see G. Eiten, Am. Midl. Nat. 69(2):257–309. 1963). (*O. repens* Thunb.).]

O. dillenii Jacq.
/T/(X)/E/   (Hpr)   Dry places, the native range uncertain because of the weedy nature of the species and confusion with *O. stricta*. Collections in CAN from Alta. (Red Deer R., ca. 52°N), Sask. (Cypress Hills; Gander Lake, sw of Swift Current; Whitemud R.), and sw Que. (Chelsea, N of Hull) have been placed here by Eiten and it is reported as a weed of gardens and railway ballast in P.E.I. by D.S. Erskine (1960; Charlottetown and Montague). A collection in DAO from Morden, Man., has been referred to *O. stricta* var. *piletocarpa*. G. Eiten (Am. Midl. Nat. 69:301. 1963) reports ssp. *filipes* (Small) Eiten (*O. fil.* Small) from N.B.; Europe. [*O. stricta* var. *piletocarpa* Wieg.].

O. montana Raf.   Wood-Sorrel
/T/EE/   (Hrr)   Moist woods from Ont. (N to the Slate Is. in N L. Superior and Kapuskasing, 49°24′N; reports from Sask. and Man. are now generally discredited) to Que. (N to L. St. John

and the Côte-Nord), Labrador (N to the Hamilton R. basin), Nfld., N.B., P.E.I., and N.S., s to Minn., Wisc., Tenn., and N.C.; the closely related *O. acetosella* L. (petals relatively broad; capsules broadly ovoid rather than subglobose or globose; seeds with relatively strong ribbing) in Eurasia. [*O. acet.* ssp. *mont.* (Raf.) Hult.]. MAPS: Hultén 1958: map 127, p. 147; Braun 1937: fig. 7, p. 202; Meusel 1943: fig. 31b (incomplete).

Forma *rhodantha* Fern. (petals roseate or purple rather than white) is known from N.S. (Truro, Colchester Co.; NSPM).

[O. oregana Nutt.]
[The report of this species of the w U.S.A. (Wash. to Calif.) from s B.C. by John Macoun (1883; lower Fraser Valley) requires confirmation. [*O. acetosella* var. *oreg.* (Nutt.) Trel.]. MAP: Hultén 1958: map 127 (indicating no Canadian stations), p. 147.]

O. stricta L.   Pain d'oiseau or Surette
/T/X/   (Grh)   Open ground, fields, and roadsides (often weedy) from Wash. to Sask. (N to McKague, 52°37'N; CAN, distributed as *O. corniculata,* revised by Eiten), Man. (N to railway ballast at The Pas, where probably introd.), Ont. (N to the Ottawa dist.), Que. (N to the Gaspé Pen. at Matapédia), N.B., P.E.I., and N.S., s to Ariz., Okla., Tenn., and Ga.; introd. in Europe. [*Xanthoxalis* Small; *O. europaea* Jord.; *O. bushii* and *O. cymosa* Small].

[O. suksdorfii Trel.]
[The tentative report of this species of the w U.S.A. (s Wash. to N Calif.) from s B.C. by Boivin (1966b) requires confirmation.]

GERANIACEAE (Geranium Family)

(Ref.: L.T. Hanks and J.K. Small, N. Am. Flora 25(1):3–24. 1907)
Herbs with deeply lobed or compound stipulate opposite (sometimes nearly all basal) leaves. Flowers perfect, regular or somewhat irregular, hypogynous. Sepals and petals each 5, the latter alternating with 5 basal glands. Stamens usually 10 (sometimes 5 in *Geranium;* only 5 of them anther-bearing in *Erodium*). Ovary superior. Fruit consisting of 5 beaked and finally distinct 1-seeded carpels suspended from the top of the central column by their long styles.

1 Leaves pinnately compound, the leaflets themselves pinnatifid to 2-pinnate; perfect stamens 5; styles bearded within, often strongly twisted (but not upcurled) at maturity; seeds smooth; flowers relatively small, commonly in umbel-like clusters at the top of the axillary peduncles; more or less white-pilose and often glandular annuals; (introd.) . . . . *Erodium*
1 Leaves palmately lobed or divided; perfect stamens usually 10; styles not bearded, upcurving or coiling at maturity; seeds often reticulate; flowers to over 2 cm broad, usually in pedicelled pairs at the top of the axillary peduncles . . . . *Geranium*

ERODIUM L'Hér. [3927] Storksbill

1 Sepal-awns bristle-tipped; stipules and bracts acute or acuminate; anther-bearing filaments lacking teeth at base; leaves at first mostly basal on a very short stem, the sessile leaflets 2-pinnatifid, at most about 2.5 cm long . . . . *E. cicutarium*
1 Sepal-awns not bristle-tipped; stipules and bracts obtuse; anther-bearing filaments 2-toothed at base; leaflets usually short-stalked, 1-pinnatifid; plant to about 6 dm tall, densely glandular and smelling of musk . . . . *E. moschatum*

E. cicutarium (L.) L'Hér. Alfilaria, Filaria, Pin-Clover.
Eurasian; introd. in fields and waste places of N. America, as in s Alaska (Juneau), B.C. (N to Quesnel, ca. 53°N), Alta. (Moss 1959), Sask. (Regina and Kinestino; Breitung 1957a), Man. (Portage la Prairie and Winnipeg; CAN), Ont. (N to Simcoe and Hastings counties), Que. (N to the Côte-Nord and Gaspé Pen.), Labrador (Hopedale, 55°27'N; CAN), N.B. (near St. John), and N.S. (Centreville, Kings Co.); also introd. in sw Greenland (Polunin 1959). [*Geranium* L.]. MAP: Hultén 1968b:676.

E. moschatum (L.) L'Hér. Musk Storksbill
Eurasian; introd. in waste places and along roadsides in N. America, as in sw B.C. (Esquimault, Vancouver Is.; Eastham 1947), Ont. (N to Ottawa according to Montgomery 1957; not listed by Gillett 1958), and Que. (ballast around fish-houses at York, Gaspé Pen.; GH). [*Geranium* L.].

All of our material appears referable to var. *praecox* Lange (leaflets deeply 1–2-pinnately cleft rather than merely pinnatifid; sepals strongly viscid-hairy rather than glabrous or sparingly hairy).

GERANIUM L. [3924] Cranesbill, Wild Geranium

(Ref.: Jones and Jones 1943; L.T. Hanks and J.K. Small, N. Am. Flora 25(1):3–21. 1907)
1 Leaves triangular-ovate in general outline, palmately divided to near the midrib into 3–5 distinct pinnatifid leaflets, the terminal leaflet stalked; flowers small, purple; sepals bristle-tipped; carpels glabrous, at maturity detached from the upwardly recurved beak, each tipped with 2 hair-like terminal appendages; annual . . . . *G. robertianum*
1 Leaves reniform, pentagonal, or suborbicular in general outline, deeply divided, palmately parted (but not to the midrib, thus not into distinct leaflets); carpels mostly remaining attached to the beak or, if separating, lacking hair-like appendages.

  2 Flowers large, the petals usually at least 2 cm long; sepals bristle-tipped; terminal beak of mature fruit to over 1 cm long; carpels pubescent at least toward base; anthers 2 or 3 mm long; principal leaves 5–7-cleft up to 3/4 or more of the distance to base; perennials with stout rhizomes.

      3 Petals pilose on the inner surface up to half their length from base; free tips of style at least 3 mm long; pedicels reflexed and bent upward in fruit; plant glandular-pilose at least in the inflorescence; (B.C. to s Sask.).

          4 Petals pilose about 1/5 their length from base, rose-purple with darker veins (rarely white) . . . . *G. viscosissimum*

          4 Petals pilose about 1/2 their length from base, milk-white with pink or purplish veins (sometimes pink-tinged) . . . . *G. richardsonii*

      3 Petals glabrous except at the ciliate base, rose-purple or bluish purple (rarely white); free tips of style less than 3 mm long; pedicels permanently erect or ascending (not bent upward).

          5 Pedicels pubescent but not glandular.

              6 Pedicels spreading-villous; petals violet; leaves deeply parted into 5 or 7 principal segments; (introd. in SE Nfld.) . . . . [*G. ibericum*]

              6 Pedicels minutely pubescent; petals rose-purple; leaves deeply 5-parted; (Ont. and sw Que.) . . . . *G. maculatum*

          5 Pedicels densely glandular-short-villous.

              7 Anther-filaments conspicuously pilose with hairs to 3 mm long; free tips of styles at most 1/4 as long as the beak of the style-column; (Alaska–Yukon–B.C.–Alta.) . . . . *G. erianthum*

              7 Anther-filaments sparsely hairy at base with hairs less than 0.5 mm long; free tips of styles at least 1/3 as long as the beak of the style-column.

                  8 Mature style-column at most about 3 cm long, the beak to 1 cm long; (introd. from Man. to s Labrador, Nfld., and N.S.) . . . . . *G. pratense*

                  8 Mature style-column to 5 cm long, the beak at most 7 mm long; (s B.C.–Alta.) . . . . *G. oreganum*

  2 Flowers small, often shorter than or only slightly surpassing the calyx; terminal beak of mature style-column lacking or not over 6 mm long; anthers less than 1 mm long; annuals or biennials (except the perennial *G. pyrenaicum*).

      9 Sepals callous-tipped; seeds smooth or nearly so; leaves cleft usually not more than 2/3 to base; (introd.).

        10 Carpels conspicuously cross-wrinkled, glabrous; beak of mature style-column to 5 mm long; fertile stamens 10; plant usually pilose-hirsute throughout and somewhat glandular . . . . *G. molle*

        10 Carpels not cross-wrinkled, minutely pubescent; style-column beakless.

          11 Sepals less than 5 mm long, hirsute, about as long as the shallowly notched petals; pedicels minutely glandular; fertile stamens 5; carpel-bodies about 2 mm long; annual or biennial . . . . *G. pusillum*

          11 Sepals at least 5 mm long (the petals about twice as long), they and the pedicels minutely glandular, not hirsute; fertile stamens 10; carpel-bodies at least 3 mm long; leaf-lobes obovate-cuneiform in outline, irregularly 3-lobed at apex; perennial, with a thick scaly persistent stem-base . . . . *G. pyrenaicum*

      9 Sepals bristle-tipped; seeds reticulate; carpels pubescent; principal leaves cleft up to 3/4 or more to base.

        12 Fruiting pedicels much longer than the calyces; beak of fruit at least 3 mm long; carpels long-villous with ascending hairs; (transcontinental) . . . .
. . . . *G. bicknellii*

        12 Fruiting pedicels shorter than or only slightly longer than the calyces; beak of fruit 1 or 2 mm long.

          13 Carpels short-hirsute with spreading hairs; seeds strongly reticulate; lobes of middle and upper leaves acute; (introd.) . . . . *G. dissectum*

13 Carpels long-villous with ascending hairs; seeds obscurely reticulate;
leaf-lobes obtuse; (B.C. to w Ont.) . . . . *G. carolinianum*

G. bicknellii Britt.
/ST/X/ (T) Open woods, clearings, and disturbed soils (often around old campfires) from cent. Alaska–Yukon and Great Slave L. to L. Athabasca (Alta. and Sask.), Man. (N to Knife L., about 120 mi sw of Churchill), Ont. (N to the w James Bay watershed at ca. 53°N), Que. (N to the E James Bay watershed at ca. 51°30'N, L. St. John, and Bic, Rimouski Co.), Nfld., N.B., and N.S. (not known from P.E.I.), s to N Calif., Utah, Colo., Iowa, Ind., and Mass. [*G. nemorale* Suksd.]. MAP: Hultén 1968b:675.
    Much of our material is referable to the relatively northern var. *longipes* (Wats.) Fern. (*G. carolinianum* var. *long*. Wats.; *G. ?columbinum* ("*columbianum*") sensu Boivin 1967a, not L.; pubescence of inflorescence and upper part of stem rather uniformly short and gland-tipped rather than consisting of mixed long and short, often gland-tipped hairs).

G. carolinianum L.
/T/X/ (T) Dry rocky woods, fields, and waste places (tending to be weedy; ranges of Canadian taxa outlined below), s to N Calif., Mont., S.Dak., Kans., Mo., Tenn., and N.C.
1 Sepals at least 5 mm broad, 5-nerved; seeds subglobose, at least 2 mm thick; [*G. sphaerospermum* Fern., the type from Great Cloche Is., N L. Huron; B.C. (Boivin 1966b), Alta. (Moss 1959), Sask. (N to Meadow L. at ca. 54°10'N), Man. (N to Wekusko L., about 90 mi NE of The Pas), and Ont. (N to near Thunder Bay)] . . . .
. . . . var. *sphaerospermum* (Fern.) Breitung
1 Sepals less than 5 mm broad, 3-nerved; seeds oblong, less than 2 mm thick . . . .
. . . . var. *carolinianum*
    2 Flowers white; [type from near Belleville, Hastings Co., s Ont.] . . . . . f. *albiflorum* Boivin
    2 Flowers pink or roseate; [incl. var. *confertiflorum* Fern.; *G. langloisii* Greene; B.C. (Boivin 1966b) and Ont. (N to the N shore of L. Superior near Thunder Bay); reported by J.P. Anderson 1959, as introd. in several localities in Alaska; reports from Nfld. by Robinson and von Schrenk (1896), from N.B. by Fowler (1885), and from N.S. by John Macoun (1883) are based upon *G. bicknellii* (chiefly var. *longipes*), relevant collections in CAN, GH, NBM, and NSPM] . . . . f. *carolinianum*

G. dissectum L.
European; introd. along roadsides and in waste places of N. America, as in B.C. (Queen Charlotte Is.; Vancouver Is. and adjacent islands and mainland E to Chilliwack) and w Ont. (Kabitotikwia L., near Thunder Bay; TRT).

G. erianthum DC.
/ST/W/eA/ (Hs) Woods and meadows at low to fairly high elevations from the Aleutian Is., Alaska (N to ca. 64°N), and s Yukon to B.C. (s to Armstrong, about 12 mi N of Vernon; Herb. V) and Alta. (Boivin 1966b); E Asia. [*G. pratense* var. *eri*. (DC.) Boivin; *G. sylvaticum* of Alaskan reports, not L.]. MAP: Hultén 1968b:674.

[*G. ibericum* Cav.] Iberian Cranesbill
[European; an occasional garden-escape in N. America, as in SE Nfld. (a 1928 collection by Agnes Ayre at Beachy Cove, where probably not established).]

G. maculatum L. Wild or Spotted Cranesbill
/T/EE/ (Hs) Woods, thickets, and meadows from s Ont. (N to Wellington, Hastings, and Frontenac counties; reported from the mouth of the Rainy R., Lake of the Woods, by John Macoun 1883; his reports from Nfld. and N.S. require clarification) to sw Que. (Montreal dist. and Brome Co.; John Macoun 1883; Jones and Jones 1943; the report from SE Man. by Jackson et al. (1922; hence, presumably, by later authors) is based upon *G. pratense*, the relevant collection in WIN) and cent. Maine, s to Kans., Mo., Tenn., and Ga. MAP: Sister M. Celine Martin, Am. Midl. Nat. 73: fig. 1 (the s Man. station should probably be deleted), p. 112. 1965.

Forma *albiflorum* (Raf.) House (flowers white rather than rose-purple) is reported from s Ont. by Landon (1960; Norfolk Co.).

G. molle L.   Dovesfoot-Cranesbill
Eurasian; introd. in lawns and waste places of N. America, as in sw B.C. (Queen Charlotte Is.; Vancouver Is. and adjacent islands and mainland E to Chilliwack; CAN), s Ont. (near Owen Sound, Grey Co.; TRT; reported from Parkdale by John Macoun 1886), Que. (St-Luc, s of Montreal; Sillery, near Quebec City), and N.S. (Annapolis, Annapolis Co.; GH).

G. oreganum Howell
/T/W/   (Hs)   Woodlands and meadows from s B.C. (N to Spences Bridge; CAN) and sw Alta. (Crowsnest Pass and Milk River; CAN) to N Calif. [*G. incisum* Nutt., not Andrews; *G. ?fremontii sensu* John Macoun 1883, in part, not Torr.].

G. pratense L.
Eurasian; introd. along roadsides and in fields and waste places of N. America (the Canadian distribution outlined below, together with that of the closely related *G. sylvaticum* L. of Eurasia).
1   Pedicels erect after flowering; petals often more reddish than those of *G. pratense*; anther-filaments lanceolate at base; leaves less dissected than those of *G. pratense*; [introd. at Ste-Foy, near Quebec City, Que., and in w Greenland] . . . . *G. sylvaticum* L.
1   Pedicels recurved after flowering; anther-filaments broadly ovate at base; leaves copiously and deeply dissected . . . . *G. pratense*
    2   Flowers white; [St. Helen's Is., Montreal, Que.; Boivin 1966b] . . . . . . f. *albiflorum* Opiz
    2   Flowers violet-blue; [*G. maculatum sensu* Jackson et al. 1922, and later reports from Man. (relevant collection in WIN); SE Man. (Winnipeg; Shoal Lake), Ont. (N to the Ottawa dist.), Que. (N to the Gaspé Pen.), Labrador (L. Melville, Hamilton R. basin), Nfld., N.B., P.E.I., and N.S.] . . . . f. *pratense*

G. pusillum L.
Eurasian; introd. along roadsides and in fields and waste places of N. America, as in s B.C. (Vancouver Is. and adjacent islands and mainland; Agassiz; Grand Forks; Wilmer; Salmon Arm), s Man. (Brandon; CAN), s Ont. (N to Bruce and Wellington counties), and Que. (reported from near Quebec City by Raymond 1950b, and from Ste-Anne-de-la-Pocatière, Kamouraska Co., by Ernest Lepage and Lionel Cinq-Mars, Ann. ACFAS 12: 77. 1946); also introd. in sw Greenland.

G. pyrenaicum Burm. f.
European; occasionally introd. along roadsides and in waste places of N. America, as in Ont. (Ottawa dist.; Gillett 1958) and Que. (Sillery, near Quebec City; CAN; reported from l'Islet Co. by Groh and Frankton 1949b).

G. richardsonii Fisch. & Trautv.
/sT/WW/   (Hs)   Moist open woods, thickets, and meadows up to fairly high elevations from s-cent. Yukon (reports from Alaska apparently refer to a white-flowered garden form of *G. sanguineum* L.; see Hultén 1950) and sw Dist. Mackenzie (Mackenzie Mts.; CAN) to B.C.–Alta. and sw Sask. (Cypress Hills; CAN), s to s Calif., N.Mex., and S.Dak. [*G. gracilentum* Greene; *G. hookerianum* Walp.; *G. albiflorum* Hook., not Ledeb.]. MAP: Hultén 1968b:674.

G. robertianum L.   Herb-Robert.   Herbe à Robert or Herbe à l'esquinancie
/sT/X/EA/   (T)   Rocky woods, ravines, and clearings from B.C. (Vancouver Is.; Vancouver; Chilliwack; Kootenay; reported by Hultén 1947, as introd. at Juneau, SE Alaska; not known from Sask.; reports from SE Man. require confirmation) to Ont. (N to Lake of the Woods and the Ottawa dist.), Que. (N to the Côte-Nord, Anticosti Is., and Gaspé Pen.), Nfld., N.B., P.E.I., and N.S., s to Ill., Ind., Ohio, and Md.; Eurasia. [*Robertiella* Hanks]. MAP: Hultén 1968b:675.
    Forma *albiflorum* (Don) House (flowers white rather than purple) is reported from s Ont. by Boivin (1966b; Oshawa).

G. viscossimum Fisch. & Mey.

/T/WW/ (Hs) Open woods and meadows (ranges of Canadian taxa outlined below), s to Calif., Colo., and w S.Dak.

1 Lower petioles and stem glabrous to minutely strigose or appressed- to spreading-puberulent or hirsute, but not glandular; [*G. nervosum* Rydb.; *G. canum* Rydb. in large part but not as to type; *G. strigosior* St. John; *G. strigosum* of auth., not Burm. f.; B.C. (Flathead R. SE of Fernie; V) and s Alta. (Milk River Ridge; Calgary)] . . . . var. *nervosum* (Rydb.) Hitchc.

1 Lower petioles and stem hirsute and also glandular-puberulent, the plant rather uniformly glandular-puberulent above . . . . var. *viscosissimum*

  2 Flowers white; [B.C. and Alta.; Boivin 1966*b*] . . . . f. *album* (Suksd.) St. John

  2 Flowers pink-lavender to purplish; [B.C. (N to Quesnel and Mt. Robson Park), s Alta. (Waterton Lakes; Medicine Hat; Beaver R.), and s Sask. (Cypress Hills; Touchwood Hills; Killdeer; Wood Mountain)] . . . . f. *viscosissimum*

ZYGOPHYLLACEAE (Caltrop Family)

TRIBULUS L.   [3978]

Herb with hirsute stems branched from the base and forming mats to 1 m broad. Leaves opposite, pinnate, one of each pair distinctly longer than the other. Leaflets up to 8 pairs, oblong, entire, to about 1.5 cm long. Flowers pale yellow, regular, hypogynous, on slender axillary pedicels. Sepals, petals (to 5 mm long), and carpels usually 5 (sometimes 4), the carpels with usually 2 stout divergent spines to 6 mm long and a long row of tubercles, separate at maturity. Stamens usually 10 (sometimes 8). Ovary superior.

T. terrestris L.   Caltrop, Puncture-vine
Eurasian; introd. in dry fields and waste places of N. America, as in s Ont. (reported by Montgomery 1957, as taken at Kincardine, Bruce Co., by Howitt in 1927; reported from railway tracks at Sarnia, Lambton Co., by Gaiser and Moore 1966).

RUTACEAE (Rue Family)

Shrubs, semishrubs, or small trees with alternate, deeply pinnatifid or compound leaves dotted with translucent oil-glands. Flowers small, regular, hypogynous, greenish- or yellowish-white, perfect or unisexual, in umbels or cymes. Sepals and petals each 4 or 5, the stamens as many or twice as many. Ovary superior.

1 Tall shrub with thorny stems; leaves 1-pinnate, with up to 11 ovate-oblong entire or low-crenate leaflets, these pubescent beneath at least when young; flowers yellowish green, unisexual, in subsessile umbellate clusters in the axils of the previous year's branches; stamens 4 or 5; fruit consisting of up to 5 short-stalked 2-valved thick fleshy follicles, each of these with 1 or 2 seeds; (Ont. and s Que.) . . . .
. . . . *Zanthoxylum*
1 Stems unarmed.
  2 Leaves 3-foliolate, the ovate leaflets entire or serrulate; flowers greenish- or yellowish-white, both perfect and unisexual, in terminal corymbose cymes; stamens 4 or 5; fruit a thin flat orbicular broad-winged samara to 2.5 cm long; shrub or small tree; (s Ont.; introd. in Que.) . . . . *Ptelea*
  2 Leaves deeply 2(3)-pinnatifid, thickish, glaucous, the ultimate lobes narrowly obovate; flowers greenish yellow, perfect, cymose-paniculate; stamens 8 or 10; fruit a many-seeded capsule; semishrub; (introd.) . . . . *Ruta*

PTELEA L.   [4069]

P. trifoliata L.   Wafer-Ash, Stinking Ash, Hop-tree
/t/EE/   (Mc)   Moist woods, alluvial thickets, and rocky slopes and gravels from Nebr. to s Ont. (apparently native in Essex, Kent, and Welland counties; collection in TRT from London, Middlesex Co., where perhaps introd.; *see* s Ont. maps by Fox and Soper 1952: fig. 8, p. 80, and Soper and Heimburger 1961:13; introd. in sw Que. at Oka, Montreal, and Pointe-du-Lac), and N.Y., s to Tex. and Fla.; the closely related *P. angustifolia* Benth. in the w U.S.A. MAPS: Hosie 1969:258; V.L. Bailey et al., Brittonia 22(4): fig. 1, p. 347. 1970; V.L. Bailey, Brittonia 14(1): fig. 2, p. 8. 1962; Preston 1961:284, and 1947:222; Hough 1947:301; Munns 1938: map 144, p. 148.

RUTA L.   [4012]

R. graveolens L.   Common Rue, Herb-of-grace
European; a garden-escape to old pastures, roadsides, and waste places in N. America, as in Alta. (Twin Butte, sw of Lethbridge; Groh and Frankton 1949b), s Ont. (gravel bank near Hespeler, Waterloo Co.; Groh 1944a), and sw Que. (in a botanical garden at Laprairie, near Montreal, where possibly escaped).

ZANTHOXYLUM L.   [3990]

Z. americanum Mill.   Toothache-tree, Northern Prickly Ash.   Frêne épineux or Clavalier
/T/EE/   (Mc)   Rich woods and damp thickets from N.Dak. to Ont. (N to Renfrew and Carleton counties; CAN; TRT; *see* s Ont. maps by Fox and Soper 1952: fig. 7, p. 79, and Soper and Heimburger 1961:12) and sw Que. (N to s Pontiac Co. and the Montreal dist.), s to Okla., Mo., Ala., and Ga. [*Xanthoxylum* Gmel.; *Zanthoxylum ramiflorum* Michx.; *Z. fraxinifolium* Marsh.]. MAP (Canadian area): *Atlas of Canada* 1957: map 12, sheet 38.

SIMAROUBACEAE (Quassia Family)

AILANTHUS Desf.   [4124]   Tree-of-heaven

Tree with alternate pinnate leaves to about 6 dm long; leaflets numerous (up to 41), lanceolate or oblong, acuminate, to 18 cm long, mostly with 1–3 conspicuously gland-tipped teeth on each side near the base. Flowers small, green or yellowish, regular, both perfect and unisexual, hypogynous, in large terminal panicles, unpleasantly scented. Calyx-lobes and petals each 5. Stamens in staminate flowers 10, in perfect flowers 2 or 3. Ovary superior. Fruit an elongate twisted long-winged samara to 5 cm long with the seed near the centre.

A. altissima (Mill.) Swingle   Copal-tree
Asiatic; "Spread from cult. by basal suckers as well as by seed, Mass. to s Ont. and Iowa and southwards, often too aggressive." (Fernald *in* Gray 1950). Known in s Ont. from Essex, Kent, Lambton, Norfolk, Middlesex, Welland, Wentworth, Prince Edward, and Hastings counties and apparently definitely escaping in at least the first four of these (chiefly along the L. Erie shore). [*Toxicodendron* Mill.; *A. glandulosa* Desf.].

POLYGALACEAE (Milkwort Family)

POLYGALA L.   [4273]   Polygala, Milkwort

Low herbs with simple, entire or minutely serrulate, exstipulate leaves, these opposite, alternate, or whorled. Flowers perfect, hypogynous, irregular, the 2 inner of the 5 sepals (the wings) much the largest and coloured like the 3 more or less united petals. Middle petal keel-shaped and with a fringe-like crest. Stamens 6 or 8, united below and with the petals. Ovary superior. Fruit a 2-locular 2-seeded flat capsule.

(Ref.: S.F. Blake, N. Am. Flora 25(4, 5):305–70. 1924; Gillett 1968)
1   Flowers at least 1.5 cm long, long-pedicelled, up to 4 in a terminal cluster, normally rose-purple; sepals deciduous; small cleistogamous flowers scattered on subterranean branches; upper leaves ovate, petioled, crowded at the summit, the lower leaves small and scale-like, scattered; slenderly stoloniferous perennial; (Sask. to Que. and N.B.) . . . .*P. paucifolia*
1   Flowers smaller and numerous in racemes, cleistogamous ones present only in *P. polygama*; sepals persistent; leaves mostly narrower, at least the upper ones sessile.
    2   Leaves linear to narrowly lanceolate, at least the lower ones in whorls of 3 or more; flowers white, greenish, or occasionally pinkish; raceme tapering to tip, less than 5 mm thick; slender annual; (s Man. to s Que.) . . . .*P. verticillata*
    2   Leaves all alternate (atypical *P. verticillata* may be sought here).
        3   Stems solitary; racemes to about 1.5 cm thick; leaves entire; annuals.
            4   Flowers pale rose-purple or flesh-colour, to 1 cm long, in dense racemes to 4 cm long; corolla nearly 3 times as long as the wings (inner petaloid sepals), promptly deciduous; some or all of the fruits persistent below the terminal tuft of flowers; leaves linear-subulate or involute, to 12 mm long, soon deciduous; stems to 6 dm tall, simple or with a few erect branches; plant glaucous; (s Ont.) . . . .*P. incarnata*
            4   Flowers pink to rose-purple at summit, to about 6 mm long, in dense short-cylindric or head-like racemes to about 2 cm long; corolla about half as long as the wings, persistent; lower fruits promptly deciduous; leaves linear or narrowly elliptic, to 4 cm long and 5 mm broad; stems to 4 dm tall, simple or bushy-branched; (Ont. to N.S.) . . . .*P. sanguinea*
        3   Stems several from a thick woody caudex or perennial root; sepal-wings about equalling or longer than the corolla.
            5   Cleistogamous small flowers developed in 1-sided interrupted prostrate racemes at the base of the stems, the latter from a perennial root; flowers rose-purple, varying to white, to 6 mm long; principal leaves linear to oblong-oblanceolate, to 3 cm long; (Ont. to N.S.) . . . .*P. polygama*
            5   Cleistogamous flowers wanting; stems from a branching caudex.
                6   Flowers to 8 mm long, blue, pink, or white; principal leaves narrowly to broadly lanceolate, to 3.5 cm long; (introd. on Vancouver Is.) . . . .*P. vulgaris*
                6   Flowers at most about 4 mm long, white or whitish.
                    7   Leaves lanceolate to ovate, to 7 cm long and 3 cm broad, minutely and irregularly serrulate along the subcrustaceous margin, the lower leaves much reduced and often scale-like; sepal-wings suborbicular, to about 3 mm broad; capsule suborbicular, 3 or 4 mm thick; (Alta. to Que. and N.B.) . . . .*P. senega*
                    7   Leaves linear, to 2.5 cm long and 1.5 mm broad, the basal ones not markedly reduced; sepal-wings elliptic, rarely over 1.5 mm broad; (s Sask.) . . . .*P. alba*

P. alba Nutt.
/T/WW/   (Hp (Grh))   Dry prairies and rocky or gravelly hillsides from Wash. to Sask. (Bengough, Ceylon, and Roche Percee; Breitung 1957a) and Minn., s to Mexico and Tex. MAP: Gillett 1968: map d, fig. 8, p. 22.

P. incarnata L.
/t/EE/ (T) Dry soil, upland woods, and prairies from Nebr. to s Wisc., s Mich., s Ont. (Squirrel Is., Lambton Co.; CAN; OAC; an 1823 collection by Douglas from near Niagara Falls, Welland Co., noted by John Macoun 1883), Pa., and N.J., s to Mexico, Tex., and Fla. [*Galypola* Nieuwl.].

P. paucifolia Willd.   Fringed Polygala, Bird-on-the-wing
/T/EE/ (Hpr) Moist woodlands from Sask. (Shellbrook, near Prince Albert, and McKague, 52°37′N; Breitung 1957a) to Man. (N to Bear L., NW of Oxford L. at ca. 55°N), Ont. (N to Hawley L. at 54°34′N), Que. (N to L. Timiskaming at ca. 47°30′N, Anticosti Is., and the Gaspé Pen. near the mouth of the Grand R.; reported from the Côte-Nord by Saint-Cyr 1887), and N.B. (Charlotte and York counties; not known from P.E.I. or N.S.), s to Minn., Ill., Tenn., and Ga. [*Triclisperma* Nieuwl.; *P. uniflora* Michx.]. MAP: Gillett 1968: map a, fig. 8, p. 22.
    Forma *alba* Wheelock (flowers white rather than rose-purple; leaves relatively pale) is known from s Ont. (Norfolk and Bruce counties).

P. polygama Walt.
/T/EE/ (Hp) Dry sandy woods and openings from Minn. to Mich., Ont. (N to Renfrew and Carleton counties), SW Que. (along the Ottawa R. in s Pontiac Co.), and N.S. (Digby Co.; DAO; not known from N.B. or P.E.I.), s to Tex. and Fla. MAP: Gillett 1968: map b, fig. 8, p. 22.
    The report from Man. by Rydberg (1932; taken up by Lowe 1943) requires confirmation. Our material appears chiefly or wholly referable to var. *obtusata* Chodat (flowers mostly not over 4 mm apart in a close raceme, on pedicels to about 2 mm long, the sepal-wings shorter than to surpassing the capsule, rather than flowers mostly at least 4 mm apart in a loose raceme to 1.5 dm long, on pedicels to 3.5 mm long, the sepal-wings much surpassing the capsule).

P. sanguinea L.
/T/EE/ (T) Sterile fields, meadows, and open woods from Minn. to s Ont. (N to Farran Point, Stormont Co.; Dore and Gillett 1955), SW Que. (N to Nicolet and St-Maurice counties), N.B. (Gagetown, Queens Co.; DAO), P.E.I. (Cavendish, Queens Co.; ACAD), and N.S. (Hants, Cumberland, Colchester, Halifax, and Pictou counties), s to Okla., La., Tenn., and S.C. [*P. ?fastigiata* (*P. mariana* Mill.) and *P. ?nuttallii sensu* John Macoun 1883, not Nutt. nor T. & G., respectively; *P. ?cruciata sensu* Hooker 1830, not L.]. MAP: Gillett 1968: map e, fig. 8, p. 22.

P. senega L.   Seneca-Snakeroot.   Sénéca
/T/(X)/ (Hp) Dry or moist woods and prairies from s Alta. (N to near Calgary) to Sask. (N to near Prince Albert), Man. (N to near Gillam, about 165 mi s of Churchill), Ont. (N to the W James Bay watershed at ca. 53°N), Que. (N to the Harricanaw R. at ca. 49°N and Temiscouata Co.), and W N.B. (St. John R. system; not known from P.E.I. or N.S.), s to S.Dak., Ark., Tenn., and Ga. [Incl. var. *latifolia* T. & G., the broad-leaved extreme with leaves to 3.5 cm broad]. MAP: Gillett 1968: map c, fig. 8, p. 22.

P. verticillata L.
/T/EE/ (T) Moist sandy soil, grasslands, and woods (ranges of Canadian taxa outlined below), s to Utah, Colo., Tex., and Fla. MAPS and synonymy: *see* below.
1 Leaves (except the lowermost) alternate; raceme interrupted at base, the flowering
    portion to 5 cm long; corolla-wings about equalling the capsule; [*P. ambigua* Nutt.;
    SW Que.: Farnham, Missisquoi Co.; Herb. Marcel Raymond, detd. Raymond] . . . .
    . . . . var. *ambigua* (Nutt.) Wood
1 Leaves more generally whorled.
    2 Raceme dense, white or greenish, the flowering portion to 1.2 cm long, the
        peduncle to 4 cm long; pedicels to 0.3 mm long; leaves in 3's to 7's, or the
        uppermost ones and those of the branches alternate or opposite; [s Man.: N to
        Brandon and Winnipeg] . . . . var. *isocycla* Fern.
    2 Raceme lax, white or purplish, the flowering portion to 2 cm long, the peduncle
        to 7 cm long; pedicels to 1(2) mm long; lower leaves in 3's to 5's, the upper ones

(or sometimes all but those of the lower nodes) alternate; [*P. pretzii* Pennell; s Man. (N to Brandon and Winnipeg), s Ont. (Essex, Norfolk, Lambton, Welland, Lincoln, Waterloo, York, and Lanark counties), and sw Que. (N to the Montreal dist.); MAPS (aggregate species): F.W. Pennell, Bartonia 13: fig. 1, p. 10. 1931 (with which should be incorporated the map for *P. pretzii,* fig. 2, p. 14); Gillett 1968: map f, fig. 8, p. 22] . . . . var. *verticillata*

P. vulgaris L.
Eurasian; reported as introd. in sw B.C. by Eastham (1947; "apparently established near Comox, Vancouver Is."; Herb. V).

[The similar *P. serpyllifolia* Hose (*P. serpyllacea* Weihe) is reported from se Greenland by Böcher (1938; *see* his map, fig. 72, p. 139) but its occurrence there is considered very doubtful by Joergensen, Soerensen, and Westergaard (1958) and the Greenland dots on the MAP by Hultén (1958: map 79, p. 99) should probably by deleted. It differs from *P. vulgaris* in having at least the lower leaves opposite (rather than leaves all alternate) and in being generally smaller and more slender, the filiform stems scarcely woody at base.]

EUPHORBIACEAE (Spurge Family)

Herbs (*Euphorbia* with milky acrid juice) with entire or shallowly toothed leaves, these alternate, opposite, or sometimes whorled. Flowers small, regular, hypogynous, unisexual. Calyx present or wanting. Corolla usually wanting. Fruit a usually 3-locular, 3-lobed capsule with 1 or 2 seeds in each locule.

1 Perianth none, simulated by a somewhat cup-shaped outer structure (the cyathium) in which is borne a single pistillate flower (consisting of a single pistil) or (the flowers being monoecious) few to several staminate flowers (each consisting of a single stalked anther); juice milky; leaves mostly sessile . . . .*Euphorbia*
1 Perianth (usually a calyx only) present; flowers not borne in cyathia; stamens usually 8 or more; inflorescence spicate or racemose; juice not milky; leaves petioled; annuals.
  2 Plant densely soft-woolly and somewhat glandular; staminate flowers with a 5-parted calyx and 5 glands alternating with 5 densely fringed petals, the pistillate flowers apetalous, capitate-crowded at the base of the staminate spike; anthers inflexed in the bud; styles twice or thrice 2-parted; capsule usually 3-locular; leaves alternate, long-petioled, the blade elliptic to lance-oblong or oval, entire, rounded to subcordate at base; stems branching, to 2 m tall; (introd. in s Ont.) . . . . . .
  . . . . *[Croton]*
  2 Plant not woolly; anthers erect in the bud; petals none.
    3 Leaves alternate, long-petioled, coarsely crenate; bracts of pistillate flowers leaf-like, ovate to rotund, palmately cleft; staminate calyx 4-parted; stigmas cut-fringed; capsule 3-locular and 3-seeded; (Ont. to N.S.) . . . .*Acalypha*
    3 Leaves opposite, short-petioled, lanceolate to ovate-lanceolate, crenate-serrate; bracts of pistillate flowers minute; staminate calyx 3-parted; stigmas entire; capsule usually 2-locular and 2-seeded, hispid; (introd. from Ont. to N.S.) . . . .*Mercurialis*

ACALYPHA L. [4407] Three-seeded Mercury, Copperleaf. Ricinelle

1 Leaf-blades mostly rhombic-ovate, not much longer than the petioles; pistillate bracts commonly 5–7-cleft and often stipitate-glandular; (Ont. to N.S.) . . . .*A. rhomboidea*
1 Leaf-blades narrowly to broadly lanceolate, up to twice as long as the petioles; pistillate bracts 9–15-cleft, usually glandless . . . .*[A. virginica]*

A. rhomboidea Raf.
/T/EE/ (T) Dry to moist soil of fields, open woods, roadsides, and waste places (often weedy) from Minn. to Ont. (N to Carleton and Russell counties), Que. (N to Berthier, about 30 mi NE of Montreal), and N.S. (Clearland, Lunenburg Co.; CAN; not known from N.B. or P.E.I.), s to Okla., Ark., Ala., and Fla. [*A. virginica* of Canadian reports, probably not L.].

[*A. virginica* L.]
[Reports of this species of the E U.S.A. (N to Kans. and Mass.) from Canada all refer to *A. rhomboidea*. (*A. digynea* Raf.).]

[CROTON L.] [4348]

[*C. capitatus* Michx.] Hogwort, Woolly Croton
[This species of the E U.S.A. (N to Kans. and Iowa) is apparently known from Canada only through a 1901 collection by John Macoun along railway tracks at Queenston Heights, Lincoln Co., s Ont., where scarcely established.]

EUPHORBIA L.   [4498]   Spurge

(Ref.: Wheeler 1941)
1 Stems prostrate or more or less ascending but not erect, mostly much branched;
   leaves all opposite, oblique at base, mostly less than 1.5 cm long (those of *E. nutans*
   to 3.5 cm long); stipules well developed and usually persistent.
   2 Involucral glands nearly or quite unappendaged; leaves pale green, entire; plant
      glabrous; (shores of s Ont., E Que., and the Maritime Provinces) . . . . . . *E. polygonifolia*
   2 Involucral glands with white petal-like appendages.
      3 Ovaries and capsules pubescent; stems villous; leaves entire or remotely
         serrulate.
         4 Cyathium (the modified involucre) not split down the back; seeds with low
            transverse ridges; (Ont. to N.S.) . . . . *E. supina*
         4 Cyathium split down the back; seeds nearly smooth; (introd.) . . . . *E. humistrata*
      3 Ovaries and capsules glabrous.
         5 Stems more or less pubescent; leaves serrulate.
            6 Stems nearly uniformly pilose-hirsute from base to tip, procumbent;
               capsules less than 2 mm long; seeds sharply angled; leaves to 2 cm
               long; (Ont. to N.S.) . . . . *E. vermiculata*
            6 Stems merely with pilose lines or becoming glabrous, often ascending;
               capsules to 2.3 mm long; seeds obtusely angled; leaves to 3.5 cm long;
               (Ont. and sw Que.) . . . . *E. nutans*
         5 Stems glabrous.
            7 Leaves entire; seeds smooth.
               8 Leaves to 1 cm long, elliptic- or ovate-oblong; seeds about 1.5 mm
                  long; (s Man.) . . . . *E. geyeri*
               8 Leaves at most 7 mm long, roundish-ovate or -oblong, subcordate;
                  seeds about 1 mm long; (s Ont.) . . . . *E. serpens*
            7 Leaves serrulate toward apex; seeds more or less roughened.
               9 Seeds slightly pitted and with short cross-ribs; leaves mostly oblong
                  to ovate; (B.C. to Man.; introd. eastwards) . . . . *E. serpyllifolia*
               9 Seeds with 5 or 6 sharp elongate cross-ribs; leaves mostly narrowly
                  oblong; (B.C. to Que. and N.B.) . . . . *E. glyptosperma*
1 Stems erect; leaves often larger; stipules usually wanting (present but deciduous in
   E. marginata).
   10 Leafy bracts and uppermost leaves with broad white petaloid margins; glands of
      modified involucre (cyathium) with broad white petaloid appendages; leaves pale,
      entire, alternate (the involucral ones whorled), ovate, to 1 dm long; (introd.) . . . .
      . . . . *E. marginata*
   10 Bracts and leaves uniformly green.
      11 Leaves linear-filiform or narrowly linear, alternate, 1 or 2 cm long; stems
         densely tufted from extensively creeping rootstocks; (introd.) . . . . . . *E. cyparissias*
      11 Leaves broader (if rarely linear, plant annual).
         12 Involucre with a conspicuous white petal-like appendage to 1 cm broad;
            cauline leaves alternate, glabrous, entire, linear-oblong to oval, whorled or
            the uppermost opposite; stipules none or mere glands; perennial from a
            deep root; (s Ont.) . . . . *E. corollata*
         12 Involucre unappendaged; (introd.).
            13 Leaves chiefly opposite; annual or biennial.
               14 Leaves clasping by a cordate base, entire, glabrous and glaucous,
                  lanceolate to narrowly oblong, to 1.5 dm long, all opposite . . . *E. lathyrus*
               14 Leaves long-petioled, coarsely toothed, pubescent on both sides,
                  linear-lanceolate to ovate, the uppermost alternate . . . . *E. dentata*
            13 Leaves chiefly alternate (only the upper ones opposite or whorled).
               15 Leaves serrulate; annuals.
                  16 Rays of terminal umbel mostly 3; capsules covered with wart-like

projections; seeds smooth or obscurely reticulate; leaves
glabrous, the cauline ones oblong-spatulate . . . . [*E. obtusata*]
16 Rays of terminal umbel mostly 5; leaves more or less pubescent
beneath.
17 Capsules smooth; seeds conspicuously reticulate; leaves
obovate, the bracteal ones narrowed to base . . . . . *E. helioscopia*
17 Capsules covered with wart-like projections; seeds smooth
and shining; leaves narrower, the bracteal ones broad-based . . . .
. . . . *E. platyphyllos*
15 Leaves entire.
18 Rays of terminal umbel normally at least 7; seeds smooth;
cyathia to 4 mm high; perennials.
19 Stem-leaves broadly linear to linear-lanceolate or narrowly
oblanceolate; cyathia at most 3 mm high; rootstock rather
slender . . . . *E. esula*
19 Stem-leaves oblong-lanceolate to narrowly oblong; cyathia 3
or 4 mm high; rootstock to 2 cm thick . . . . *E. lucida*
18 Rays of terminal umbel 3 or 5; seeds pitted or tuberculate;
annuals.
20 Seeds finely and rather sharply tuberculate; cyathia 1 mm
high; rays of umbel 3 or 5; leaves linear-lanceolate, uniform . . . . . .
. . . . *E. exigua*
20 Seeds pitted, not tuberculate; cyathia 1 or 2 mm high; rays of
umbel usually 3; leaves broader.
21 Seeds uniformly pitted on both faces; stem-leaves
obovate, the upper ones all sessile; bracteal leaves
broadly triangular-reniform, tending to be connate . . . .
. . . . [*E. commutata*]
21 Seeds with 4 rows of 3 or 4 large pits on the outer face
and 2 longitudinal furrows on the inner face; stem-leaves
obovate to roundish, distinctly petioled; bracteal leaves
ovate . . . . *E. peplus*

[*E. commutata* Engelm.]
[This species of the E U.S.A. (N to Minn. and Pa.) is apparently known from Canada only
through collections by John Macoun in 1867 and 1871 in S Ont. (Shannonville, Hastings Co.;
CAN), where probably introd. but scarcely established.]

E. corollata L.   Flowering Spurge
/t/EE/   (Grt)   Dry open woods, fields, and roadsides from Minn. to S Ont. (N to Wellington
Co.) and N.Y., S to Tex. and Fla. [*Tithymalopsis* Small].

E. cyparissias L.   Cypress Spurge.   Rhubarbe des pauvres or Euphorbe cyprès
Eurasian; introd. along roadsides and in old fields and waste places of N. America, as in S
B.C. (Vancouver Is.; Langley; Rosedale; Penticton), Sask., S Man. (N to Winnipeg), Ont. (N to
Thunder Bay and Timmins), Que. (N to Bic, Rimouski Co.), Nfld., N.B., P.E.I., and N.S. [*Galarhoeus* Small; *Tithymalus* Hill]. MAP (Canadian stations): R.J. Moore and D.R. Lindsay, Can.
J. Bot. 31(2): fig. 1, p. 154. 1953.
A hybrid with *E. esula* (× *E. pseudo-esula* Schur) is reported from S Ont. by R.J. Moore and
Clarence Frankton (Can. Field-Nat. 83(3):243. 1969).

E. dentata Michx.
Native in the U.S.A. (Wyo. to Minn. and N.Y., S to Mexico, Tex., La., and Va.); known in Canada from roadsides and railway gravels of S Ont. (Essex, York, and Wentworth counties).
[*Poinsettia* Small; incl. *E. cuphosperma* (Engelm.) Boiss.].

E. esula L.   Wolf's-milk, Leafy Spurge
Eurasian; introd. along roadsides and sandy banks and in old fields of N. America, as in B.C.

(N to Quesnel, ca. 53°N), Alta. (N to Fort Saskatchewan), Sask. (N to Maidstone, 53°06′N), Man. (N to Gimli, about 45 mi N of Winnipeg), Ont. (N to near Thunder Bay), Que. (N to St-Nicholas, Lévis Co.), N.B. (St. Andrews, Charlotte Co.; NBM), P.E.I. (York, York Co.; D.S. Erskine 1960), and N.S. (Annapolis Co.; CAN). [*Tithymalus* Hill; incl. *E. virgata* Waldst. & Kit.]. MAP (W Canada): R.J. Moore, Can. J. Bot. 36(4): fig. 1, p. 550. 1958.

E. exigua L.
European; introd. along roadsides and in waste places of N. America, as in SW B.C. (Victoria, Vancouver Is.; CAN, detd. Mulligan), Ont. (Ottawa; Lobo Township, Middlesex Co.), and N.S. (North Sydney, Cape Breton Co.; GH). [*Tithymalus* Hill].

E. geyeri Engelm.
/T/(X)/   (T)   Dunes, sand-hills, and waste places from SW Man. (St. Lazare, about 75 mi NW of Brandon; St. Claude; Grande Clarière; CAN; DAO) and N.Dak. to Wisc., S to Colo., N.Mex., Tex., Nebr., and Ind. [*Chamaesyce* Small].

E. glyptosperma Engelm.
/T/X/   (T)   Dry open soil from B.C. (N to Williams Lake) to Alta. (N to Fort Saskatchewan), Sask. (N to Nipawin, 53°22′N), Man. (N to The Pas), Ont. (N to the N shore of L. Superior near Schreiber), Que. (N to L. Timiskaming at ca. 47°30′N), and N.B. (St. John R. system in Carleton and Victoria counties), S to Calif., Mexico, Tex., Mo., Ohio, and N.Y. MAP (incomplete northwards): Wheeler 1941: map 24, p. 173.

E. helioscopia L.   Wartweed.   Réveille-matin
Eurasian; introd. in old fields and waste places of N. America, as in S B.C. (Vancouver Is.; Windermere; Golden), Alta. (N to Fort Saskatchewan; reports from Sask. and Man. require confirmation), Ont. (N to Renfrew and Lanark counties), Que. (N to the Gaspé Pen.), St-Pierre and Miquelon, N.B., P.E.I., and N.S. [*Tithymalus* Hill].

E. humistrata Engelm.
Native in the E U.S.A. (N to E Kans. and Ohio); introd. along railways and roadsides elsewhere, as in S Ont. (Lambton, Norfolk, York, Waterloo, and Leeds counties) and SW ?Que. (Mt. Royal, Montréal; R. Campbell, Can. Rec. Sci. 6(6):342–51. 1895). [*Chamaesyce* Small].

E. lathyrus L.   Caper-Spurge, Mole-plant
European; a garden-escape to roadsides and waste places in N. America, as in SW B.C. (Victoria, Vancouver Is.; Herb. V), S Ont. (Collingwood, Simcoe Co.; OAC), and SW Que. (Laprairie, near Montreal; MT). [*Tithymalus* Hill].

E. lucida Waldst. & Kit.
European; introd. along roadsides and in old fields in N. America, as in Alta. (Edgerton and Fort Saskatchewan; CAN), Sask. (Kamsack, about 135 mi NE of Regina; Breitung 1957a), and S Ont. (York Co.; OAC; reported from Lambton Co. by Dodge 1915). [*Tithymalus* K. & G.; *E. ?agraria* Bieb.].

E. marginata Pursh   Snow-on-the-mountain
Native in the U.S.A. (Mont. to Minn., S to N.Mex., Tex., and Mo.; persisting in or escaping from gardens elsewhere, as in SW B.C. (Victoria, Vancouver Is.; Herb. V), S Man. (Winnipeg dist.: Otterburne), S Ont. (Lambton, Norfolk, York, and Glengarry counties), and SW Que. (Montreal). [*Dicrophyllum* K. & G.; *Lepadenia* Nieuwl.].

E. nutans Lag.
/T/EE/   (T)   Dry open soil, cult. fields, and waste places from Minn. to Ont. (Ottawa; CAN; not listed by Gillett 1958) and SW Que. (*E. maculata* reported from Papineau Co. and the Montreal dist. by Frère Cléonique-Joseph, Contrib. Lab. Bot. Univ. Montréal 27:28. 1936). [*E. preslii* Guss.; *E. hypericifolia* and *E. maculata* of American auth., not L.; *see* D. Burch, Rhodora 68(774):156–63. 1966].

[E. obtusata Pursh]
[This species of the E U.S.A. (N to Nebr. and Pa.) is tentatively reported from near Hamilton, Ont., and Quebec City, Que., by John Macoun (1886) and is reported from Montreal, Que., by R. Campbell (Can. Rec. Sci. 6(6):342–51. 1895). Macoun, however, believes that his own reports are probably referable to *E. platyphyllos*. (*Tithymalus* K. & G.).]

E. peplus L.   Petty Spurge
Eurasian; introd. in cult. and waste ground of N. America, as in SW B.C. (Vancouver Is. and adjacent islands and mainland; known as a greenhouse weed at Juneau, SE Alaska), Sask. (Boivin 1966b), S Man. (Winnipeg; Boissevain; Morden), Ont. (N to Ottawa), Que. (N to Quebec City), Nfld., N.B. (Richibucto, Kent Co.; Fowler 1885), P.E.I. (Charlottetown; GH), and N.S. (Windsor, Hants Co.; Pictou, Pictou Co.). [*Galarhoeus* Rydb.; *Tithymalus* Hill; *E. ?pilosa sensu* Goldie 1822, not L.].

E. platyphyllos L.
European; introd. in thickets and waste places of N. America, as in Ont. (N to Dundas and Prescott counties) and SW Que. (Oka; Montreal). [*Galarhoeus* Small].

E. polygonifolia L.   Seaside-Spurge
/T/EE/   (T)   Sandy or gravelly upper beaches and coastal dune-hollows: shores of the Great Lakes in Wisc., Mich., and S Ont. (N to the Bruce Pen., L. Huron); Atlantic coast from E Que. (Grindstone Is., Magdalen Is.; GH), N.B. (Grand Manan, Charlotte Co., and Tracadie Beach, Gloucester Co.; GH; reported from Kouchibouguac, Kent Co., by Fowler 1885), P.E.I. (Brackley Point, Queens Co.; GH), and N.S. to Ga. [*Chamaesyce* Small]. MAPS: Cain 1944: fig. 36 (incomplete northwards), p. 258; Wheeler 1941: map 42, p. 249; McLaughlin 1932: fig. 5, p. 342; Peattie 1922: fig. 2, p. 60.

E. serpens HBK.
/t/(X)/   (T)   Alluvial or rich soils from Mont. to N.Dak., Mich., and S Ont. (early collections between 1881 and 1901 in CAN from Essex, Kent, and Middlesex counties; ?extinct or ?introd.), S to Mexico, N.Mex., Tex., La., and Ala.; introd. eastwards to New Eng. and Fla. [*Chamaesyce* Small]. MAP: Wheeler 1941: map 37, p. 226.

E. serpyllifolia Pers.
/T/WW/   (T)   Sandy or alluvial soils from S B.C. (Vancouver Is.; Penticton; Columbia Valley) to Alta. (N to Lac la Biche, 54°50′N), Sask. (N to Nipawin, 53°22′N), and Man. (N to St. Lazare, about 75 mi NW of Brandon), S to Mexico, N.Mex., Tex., and W Mo.; introd. eastwards, as in Ont. (N to the N shore of L. Superior near Thunder Bay), SW Que. (Buckingham; Montreal), and N.B. (St. Leonard and Andover, Victoria Co.). [*Chamaesyce* Small]. MAP: Wheeler 1941: map 15 (incomplete northwards), p. 118.

E. supina Raf.   Milk-purslane
/T/EE/   (T)   Dry open soil and waste places from N.Dak. to Ont. (N to the Ottawa dist.), Que. (N to St-Fabien, Rimouski Co.), N.B. (Charlotte Co.; a railway weed at Charlottetown, P.E.I.), and N.S. (Kings, Hants, and Colchester counties), S to Tex. and Fla.; introd. in the W U.S.A. [*Chamaesyce* Moldenke]. MAP: Wheeler 1941: map 34 (incomplete northwards), p. 226.

E. vermiculata Raf.
/T/EE/   (T)   Dry open soil and waste places from Wisc. to Ont. (N to Ottawa), Que. (N to the Gaspé Pen. at Matapédia; Wheeler 1941), N.B., and N.S. (not known from P.E.I.), S to Wisc., Ohio, Pa., and N.J.; introd. in W N. America, as in SW B.C. (Parksville, Vancouver Is.; GH; Wheeler 1941), Ariz., and N.Mex. [*Chamaesyce* House; *E. hirsuta* (Torr.) Wieg.; *E. rafinesquii* Greene]. MAP: Wheeler 1941: map 41 (somewhat incomplete northwards), p. 249.

MERCURIALIS L.   [4371]   Mercury

M. annua L.   Boys-and-Girls
European; local in waste places and ballast-ground of N. America, as in s Ont. (wharf at Chatham, Kent Co., where taken by Cox in 1890; CAN), sw Que. (wharf at Montreal; CAN; MT), N.B. (wharf at Newcastle, Northumberland Co., where taken by Cox in 1897; CAN; reported from Buctouche, Kent Co., by Fowler 1885), and N.S. (wharf at Pictou, Pictou Co., where taken by John Macoun in 1883; CAN).

CALLITRICHACEAE (Water-Starwort Family)

CALLITRICHE L.   [4530]   Water-Starwort

Slender-stemmed aquatic herbs with entire to undulate opposite leaves, the submersed ones linear, the floating ones (when present) spatulate to obovate. Flowers unisexual, lacking a perianth, solitary or 2 or 3 in the leaf-axils. Staminate flowers consisting of a single stamen, the pistillate of a single pistil. Styles 2, filiform. Fruit nut-like, 4-locular, 4-lobed, 4-seeded.

(Ref.: Fassett 1951)

1 Pistillate flowers borne on pedicels usually several times the length of the mature fruit; styles sharply reflexed, to 2 mm long, usually persistent; carpels conspicuously wing-margined; floral bracts none or very small; leaves linear to linear-spatulate, to 12 mm long, their bases joined by a minute winged ridge; (s B.C.) . . . .*C. marginata*
1 Pistillate flowers nearly or quite sessile (the pedicel not over 1/4 the length of the fruit).
  2 Leaves metallic green, all linear, 1-nerved, their bases not joined by a ridge or wing; floral bracts none; fruit nearly orbicular, its conspicuously wing-margined carpels separated from one another by deep furrows extending nearly to the axis; (transcontinental) . . . .*C. hermaphroditica*
  2 Leaves bright green, connected at base by minute winged ridges; submersed leaves linear, 1-nerved; floating leaves often present, spatulate to obovate, 3–7-nerved; flowers 2-bracted at base; carpels of fruit separated only by shallow grooves.
    3 Carpels of fruit conspicuously wing-margined from base to summit, about as broad as long; floating leaves to 8 mm broad, 5–7-nerved; (introd. in sw B.C. and E Que.) . . . .*C. stagnalis*
    3 Carpels of fruit wingless or at most narrowly winged toward summit; floating leaves mostly smaller and 3-nerved.
      4 Fruit obovoid, longer than broad, its carpels usually narrowly wing-margined toward summit, the pit-like markings of their faces in rather regular vertical lines; styles shorter than the young fruit; floating leaves tapering to a rounded summit; (transcontinental) . . . .*C. verna*
      4 Fruit about as broad as long, its carpels with rounded scarcely winged margins (narrowly winged in *C. intermedia*), the pit-like markings of their faces irregularly distributed; styles as long as to much longer than the young fruit.
        5 Fruit obcordate and slightly heart-shaped, broadest above the middle, at least 1 mm long; submersed leaves mostly broader than the stem, their midribs scarcely excurrent; floating leaves subtruncate or broadly sloping to an obtuse summit; (transcontinental) . . . .*C. heterophylla*
        5 Fruit suborbicular, usually less than 1 mm long; submersed leaves much narrower than the strongly flattened stem, their midribs slightly excurrent as a short point; floating leaves gradually rounded to summit.
          6 Stigmas erect or ascending, often deciduous; carpels wingless or very narrowly winged; (transcontinental) . . . .*C. anceps*
          6 Stigmas sharply reflexed, usually persistent; carpels with a narrow but well-differentiated even wing; (Greenland) . . . .*C. hamulata*

C. anceps Fern.
/aST/X/G/   (HH)   Shallow pools and wet shores: Aleutian Is., Alaska (N to ca 66°N), s Yukon, and w Dist. Mackenzie (Porsild and Cody 1968); SE Hudson Bay (an island at ca. 56°15′N; CAN), Que. (N to s Ungava Bay, L. St. John, the Côte-Nord, and Shickshock Mts. of the Gaspé Pen., the type from Tabletop Mt.; not known from Anticosti Is.), Labrador (N to Okak, 57°35′N), Nfld., and N.S. (Yarmouth, Antigonish, Richmond, and Inverness counties; not listed by Roland 1947; not known from N.B. or P.E.I.) to N.Y., Vt., and Mass.; isolated in

Wash., Utah, and Ga. (and apparently in NW Man. according to Hultén's 1968*b* map); W Greenland between ca. 69° and 72°30′N; s Greenland; E Greenland at ca. 72°N. MAPS: Hultén 1968*b*:678; Fassett 1951: map 16 (somewhat incomplete), p. 189.

C. hamulata Kütz.
/aST/–/GE/   (HH)   Quiet waters in Greenland (W Greenland N to ca. 69°N, E Greenland N to ca. 64°N); Iceland; Europe. [*C. ?intermedia* Hoffm., only the foliage described; *C. int.* ssp. *ham.* (Kütz.) Clapham]. MAP *(C. int.)*: Hultén 1958: map 81, p. 101.

C. hermaphroditica L.
/aST/X/GEA/   (HH)   Quiet waters (often calcareous or brackish) from the Aleutian Is. and Alaska (N to ca. 69°N) to s-cent. Yukon, the Mackenzie R. Delta, Great Bear L., N Alta. (Wood Buffalo National Park), Sask. (N to near Saskatoon), Man. (N to Churchill), Ont. (N to NW James Bay at ca. 54°20′N; *see* James Bay watershed map by Lepage 1966: map 14, p. 232), Que. (N to NE James Bay at 54°19′N and the Côte-Nord at Blanc-Sablon), s ?Labrador (Fernald *in* Gray 1950), W Nfld., and N.B. (Restigouche and St. John counties; not known from P.E.I. or N.S.), s to cent. Calif., Colo., N Nebr., Minn., Wisc., Mich., N.Y., and Vt.; Disko Is., W Greenland, at ca. 69°30′N; Iceland; Eurasia. [*C. autumnalis* L.]. MAPS: Hultén 1968*b*:677; Fassett 1951: map 24 (incomplete northwards), p. 216.

C. heterophylla Pursh
/T/X/   (HH)   Quiet waters and muddy shores from s B.C. (N to Revelstoke; CAN; isolated stations in s Alaska at Kodiak and in the s Alaska Panhandle) and SW Alta. (Crowsnest Forest Reserve; CAN) to SE Man. (Otterburne, about 30 mi s of Winnipeg; Löve and Bernard 1959, supporting the citation from the Pembina R. by Lowe 1943; not known from Sask.), Ont. (N to the NE shore of L. Superior at Michipicoten), Que. (N to s Ungava Bay, the Côte-Nord, and Gaspé Pen.), Labrador (Nain, ca. 56°30′N; CAN), Nfld., N.B. (Madawaska Co.), and N.S. (Yarmouth and Cumberland counties; not known from P.E.I.), s to s Calif., Tex., Okla., Ohio, and Maine; S. America; (reports from Greenland probably refer to other species). MAP: Fassett 1951: map 13, p. 176.
   The plant of Alaska–B.C.–Alta. is referable largely or wholly to var. *bolanderi* (Hegelm.) Fassett (*C. bol.* Hegelm.; fruits mostly over 0.9 mm long rather than mostly less than 0.9 mm long; MAPS: Hultén 1968*b*:678; Fassett 1951: map 13, p. 176).

C. marginata Torr.
/t/W/   (HH)   Shallow pools from SW B.C. (Mittlenatch Is.; Boivin 1966*b*) to N Baja Calif. The MAP by Fassett (1951: map 4, p. 152) should be extended northwards to include the B.C. station.

C. stagnalis Scop.
European; introd. and rapidly spreading in quiet or running waters of N. America, as in SW B.C. (New Westminster) and E Que. (St. Lawrence R. estuary in Montmagny, Lévis, and l'Islet counties). MAP: Fassett 1951: map 23, p. 213.
   The B.C. material consists partly of the typical free-floating aquatic form and partly of f. *caespitosa* Glück (a terrestrial form, rooting at the nodes and forming a close turf, the tips of the stem often erect). The Que. material consists of another terrestrial form, f. *terrestris* Glück (differing from f. *caespitosa* in having very short stem-internodes (rather than about 1 cm long) and leaves at most 2.5 mm broad (rather than to 5 mm broad).

C. verna L.
/aST/X/GEA/   (HH)   Quiet waters and wet shores from N Alaska–Yukon–Dist. Mackenzie to Great Bear L., Great Slave L., L. Athabasca (Alta. and Sask.), s-cent. Dist. Keewatin, Que. (N to s Ungava Bay, L. St. John, the Côte-Nord, and Gaspé Pen.; not known from Anticosti Is.), Labrador (N to the Hamilton R. basin), Nfld., N.B., P.E.I., and N.S., s to Calif., N.Mex., Nebr., Ill., and Va.; W Greenland N to 69°45′N, E Greenland N to 72°52′N; Iceland; Eurasia. [*C. palustris* L., the name too ambiguous; *C. ?terrestris* Raf.]. MAPS: Hultén 1968*b*:677; Fassett 1951: map 10 (incomplete northwards), p. 169.

EMPETRACEAE (Crowberry Family)

Low evergreen and heath-like, trailing or bushy-branched shrubs with narrow rigid revolute alternate or subverticillate leaves. Flowers small, regular, perfect or unisexual, hypogynous. Sepals and stamens each 3 or 4. Petals 3 or none. Style 1. Ovary superior. Fruit a dry or juicy drupe with up to 9 nutlets.

1 Flowers in terminal heads, purplish, each subtended by 5 or 6 scarious bractlets in the axil of a scaly bract but with no proper calyx; drupe dry, about 1.5 mm thick; leaves mostly less than 6 mm long; plant essentially glabrous, diffusely branched; (E Que., S Nfld., P.E.I., and N.S.) . . . .*Corema*
1 Flowers subsessile in the leaf-axils.
   2 Leaves very strongly revolute (falsely tubular), to over 1 cm long; flowers red or yellowish; sepals and stamens each 2; drupe yellow or red, 2 or 3 mm thick . . . .
   . . . .*[Ceratiola]*
   2 Leaves less strongly revolute, mostly less than 8 mm long; flowers greenish, pinkish, or purplish; sepals and stamens each 3; drupe pink, red, purple, or black, usually thicker; (transcontinental) . . . .*Empetrum*

[CERATIOLA Michx.] [4541]

[C. ericoides Michx.] Rosemary
[Concerning an 1842 report of this South Carolinian species from N.S., see Fernald (1921:92).]

COREMA Don [4539] Broom-Crowberry

C. conradii Torr. Poverty-grass
/T/E/ (N (evergreen)) Sandy pine-barrens, sand-hills, and siliceous rocks from E Que. (Magdalen Is.), Nfld. (an 1890 collection by Waghorne in CAN; see Fernald 1921:92), P.E.I. (Bothwell, Murray River, and Bristol; D.S. Erskine 1960; not known from N.B.), and N.S. (many counties; see Roland 1947: map 300, p. 431), S to N.Y., Mass., and N.J. MAPS: Hultén 1958: map 271, p. 290; *Atlas of Canada* 1957: map 14, sheet 38; M.L. Fernald 1918b: map 14, pl. 13, and Rhodora 13(151): map 10, pl. 90, facing p. 140. 1911.

EMPETRUM L. [4540] Crowberry. Camarine

E. nigrum L. Black Crowberry, Curlewberry. Corbigeau
/AST/X/GEA/ (Ch (N; evergreen)) Acidic rocks, gravels, peats, and tundra, the aggregate species from the Aleutian Is. and coasts of Alaska–Yukon–Dist. Mackenzie–Dist. Keewatin to Victoria Is., Somerset Is., Ellesmere Is. (N to ca. 78°30′N), and northernmost Ungava–Labrador, S through B.C. to Calif., S Alta., Sask. (S to Crooked River, 52°51′N), Man. (S to Gilbert Plains, N of Riding Mt.), L. Superior (Minn. and Ont.; see L. Superior–Hudson Bay watershed map by J.H. Soper and E.G. Voss, Mich. Bot. 3(2): fig. 2, p. 37. 1964), Que. (S to Ste-Anne-de-la-Pocatière, Kamouraska Co.), St-Pierre and Miquelon, Nfld., N.B., P.E.I., N.S., N.Y., and Long Is.; W and E Greenland N to ca. 78°N; Iceland; Spitsbergen; Eurasia. MAPS and synonymy: see below.
1 Branchlets and margins of expanding leaves minutely stipitate-glandular, the leaves not tomentose, divergent and soon reflexed, to 7 mm long; [transcontinental] . . . .
   . . . . .var. *nigrum*
   2 Fruit black, often with a bloom; [*E. hermaphroditum* Hag.; *E. nigrum* (*eamesii*) var. *herm*. (Hag.) Soer. and its f. *ciliatum* Jordal; MAPS (aggregate species): Porsild 1957: map 255, p. 192; Hultén 1968b:716 (combine the maps for *E. nigrum* and its ssp. *hermaphroditum*); Raup 1947: pl. 30; Fernald 1925: map 1 (incomplete), p. 248] . . . . .f. *nigrum*
   2 Fruit purple; (*E. purpureum* Raf.) .f. *purpureum* (Raf.) Fern.

1   Branchlets and margins of expanding leaves white-tomentose, nonglandular, the
    leaves rarely reflexed; fruit pink to purplish-black.
    3   Fruit red to purplish-black, to 9 mm thick, the seeds at least 2 mm long; leaves
        soon loosely divergent, to about 7 mm long; [*E. atropurpureum* F. & W.; *E.
        rubrum* (*eamesii*) var. *atrop.* (F. & W.) Good; Ont. (L. Superior and s James Bay)
        to Que. (N to L. Mistassini), P.E.I., and N.S.; MAP: D. Löve, Rhodora 62(742): fig. 5
        (*E. eamesii* ssp. *atrop.*; incomplete westwards), p. 277. 1960] . . . .
        . . . . var. *atropurpureum* (Fern. & Wieg.) Boivin
    3   Fruit pink to bright red, to 5 mm thick, the seeds at most 1.5 mm long; leaves
        crowded, ascending, tardily divergent, to 4 mm long; [*E. eamesii* F. & W.; *E.
        rubrum* ssp. *eamesii* (F. & W.) Good; N.S. (Cape Breton Is.), E Que. (Côte-Nord),
        SE Labrador, and Nfld.; MAP: on the above map with var. *atrop.*] . . . .
        . . . . var. *eamesii* (Fern. & Wieg.) Boivin

LIMNANTHACEAE (Meadow-foam Family)

(Ref.: P.A. Rydberg, N. Am. Flora 25:97–100. 1910)
Low, usually glabrous, decumbent to erect, fleshy and juicy annuals of mostly moist or wet habitats. Leaves compound, 1-pinnate-pinnatifid, alternate, exstipulate. Flowers regular, perfect, hypogynous or slightly perigynous, solitary on axillary, often elongate peduncles. Sepals distinct except at base. Petals white or yellowish, withering-persistent. Stamens equal in number to the petals or twice as many. Styles equal in number to the carpels, free except at base. Ovary superior or partly inferior. Fruit consisting of up to 5 carpels, these maturing into 1-seeded, indehiscent, nutlet-like achenes free except for the common basal union of the styles.

1 Sepals and petals each usually 3 (sometimes 2 or 4), the sepals about 3 mm long, the white petals scarcely 2 mm long; stamens usually 3 or 6; nutlets usually 2 (sometimes 3), papillose-warty, about 2.5 mm long; leaflets narrowly oblanceolate or elliptic to oval, to 2 cm long; (Ont., sw Que., and N.S.) . . . . *Floerkea*
1 Sepals and petals each usually 4 or 5 (sometimes 6), the white or yellowish petals 4–15 mm long; stamens 8 or 10; nutlets usually 5 (sometimes 4); leaflets cuneate-obovate in outline, mostly pinnately 3-lobed (or the terminal leaflet 5-lobed), the linear lobes directed forward; (sw B.C.) . . . . *Limnanthes*

FLOERKEA Willd. [4542a]

F. proserpinacoides Willd.   False Mermaid
/T/D/ (T) Rich damp woods and wet calcareous rocks: Wash. to Calif., Wyo., and Colo. (the report from Victoria, Vancouver Is., B.C., by John Macoun 1883, was later (Macoun 1890) referred by him to *Limnanthes macounii*, his 1875 collection in CAN being the type of that species); Ont. (N to Carleton and Russell counties; not listed by Gillett 1958) to sw Que. (an island near Montreal and Grosse-Ile, Montmagny Co.; *see* Robert Joyal, Nat. can. (Que.) 97(5): map C and legend, fig. 2, p. 564. 1970) and N.S. (Kings and Inverness counties; ACAD; CAN; not listed by Roland 1947; not known from N.B. or P.E.I.), s to N.Dak., Tenn., Va., and Del. [Incl. the generally smaller-dimensioned western extreme, *F. occidentalis* Rydb.].

LIMNANTHES R. Br. [4542] Meadow-foam

1 Sepals and petals each usually 5; petals at least 8 (to 15) mm long; (introd. on Vancouver Is.) . . . . [*L. douglasii*]
1 Sepals and petals each usually 4; petals scarcely 5 mm long; (sw B.C.) . . . . . *L. macounii*

[L. douglasii R. Br.]
[Native in Oreg. and Calif.; a garden-escape elsewhere, as in sw ?B.C. (collection in V from a garden at Cowichan L., Vancouver Is.; "could well represent an escape, since the meadow-foams are not uncommonly cultivated."). The report from Vancouver Is. by John Macoun (1886) is based upon *L. macounii* (see below). (*Floerkea* Trel.).]

L. macounii Trel.
/t/W/ (T) Known only from sw B.C. (Vancouver Is. and adjacent islands; type from Victoria, Vancouver Is.). (*Floerkea* Trel.).
The type is an 1875 collection by John Macoun in CAN, originally reported as *Floerkea proserpinacoides* by Macoun (1883), later (Macoun 1886) referred by him to *L. douglasii* (see above), and still later (Macoun 1890; following the 1887 publication of the species by Trelease) referred by him to *L. macounii*.

ANACARDIACEAE (Cashew Family)

RHUS L.   [4594]   Sumac, Poison Ivy.   Sumac

Shrubs or small trees with alternate, 3-foliolate or pinnate leaves and resinous or milky juice. Flowers small, regular, greenish white or yellowish, both perfect and unisexual on the same plant, in panicles. Calyx-lobes, petals, and stamens each 5. Styles 3. Ovary superior. Fruit a dry or fleshy berry-like drupe.

(Ref.: Barkley 1937)
1 Fruits nearly or quite glabrous, white, grey, or yellowish, they and the flowers borne in loose axillary panicles; terminal leaflet long-stalked; plants poisonous to the touch.
2 Leaflets at least 7, entire, elliptic to oblong-obovate; peduncle to about 2 dm long; twigs glabrous and glaucous; shrub or small tree to about 7 m tall; (s Ont. and sw Que.) . . . . *R. vernix*
2 Leaflets 3, entire to irregularly few-toothed or -lobed; small shrub or climbing vine.
3 Leaflets broadly rounded to obtuse or very abruptly acutish, to 7 cm long; flowers 1 or 2 mm long, in rather loose, often reflexed panicles; fruits about 5 mm long; (sw B.C.) . . . . *R. diversiloba*
3 Leaflets acute or acuminate, to over 1.5 dm long; flowers 2 or 3 mm long, in congested ascending panicles; fruits about 4 mm long; (B.C. to N.S.) . . . . *R. radicans*
1 Fruits hairy, red; terminal leaflet sessile or nearly so.
4 Leaflets 3, coarsely dentate except toward base; flowers in several short spike-like clusters forming a panicle about 1 dm long; fruits densely soft-villous; (s Alta. and s Sask.; Ont. and sw Que.) . . . . *R. aromatica*
4 Leaflets at least 7; flowers in terminal panicles to about 4 dm long.
5 Leaf-rachis wing-margined; leaflets firm, entire or slightly toothed; fruits short-pubescent; young twigs, petioles, and leaf-rachises closely pubescent; (s Ont.) . . . . *R. copallina*
5 Leaf-rachis wingless; leaflets thin, whitened beneath, sharply serrate.
6 Plant (including fruits) densely velvety-villous; (Ont. to N.S.) . . . . *R. typhina*
6 Plant glabrous or merely short-pubescent; fruits covered with minute appressed hairs; (B.C.; Sask. to sw Que.) . . . . *R. glabra*

R. aromatica Ait.   Fragrant Sumac, Lemon-Sumac, Skunk-bush
/T/(X)/   (N)   Sand dunes, rocky soil, and dry open woods from Mont. and s Alta.–Sask. (var. *trilobata*; not known from Man.) to s Ont.–Que. (var. *aromatica*; not known from the Atlantic Provinces) and Vt., s to Baja Calif., Mexico, Tex., Miss., and N Fla. MAPS and synonymy: see below.
1 Terminal leaflet cuneate-obovate (the lateral margins nearly straight or slightly concave toward base), usually less than 4 cm long; [*R. (Schmaltzia; Toxicodendron) tri.* Nutt.; *R. canadensis* var. *tri.* (Nutt.) Gray; s Alta. (Fort Macleod; Lethbridge; Milk River; Medicine Hat) and Sask. (N to ca. 51°N); MAP *(R. tri.):* Barkley 1937: fig. 25, p. 401] . . . . var. *trilobata* (Nutt.) Gray
1 Terminal leaflet elliptic to rhombic-ovate, to about 8 m long; [*Schmaltzia* Desv.; *R. canadensis* Marsh., not Mill.; *R. crenata* (Mill.) Rydb., not Thunb.; s Ont. (N to Manitoulin Is., N L. Huron, and near Chalk River and Ottawa; see s Ont. map by Soper and Heimburger 1961) and sw Que. (N to Kingsmere, Gatineau Co., and Norway Bay, Pontiac Co.); MAP: Barkley 1937: fig. 24, p. 396] . . . . var. *aromatica*

R. copallina L.   Dwarf or Shining Sumac, Wingrib-Sumac
/t/EE/   (Mc)   Rocky or sandy ground and open woods from N Ill. to s Ont. (Norfolk, Middlesex, Lennox and Addington, and Leeds counties; see s Ont. maps by Soper and Heimburger

1961:79, and S.P. VanderKloet, Can. Field-Nat. 82(4): fig. 1, p. 292. 1968), s N.Y., and s Maine, s to E Tex. and Fla. [*Schmaltzia* Small]. MAPS: Barkley 1937: fig. 7, p. 318; Hough 1947:309.

The Canadian plant is referable largely or wholly to var. *latifolia* Engler (leaflets mostly not over 13 in number rather than up to 23, broadly oblong to narrowly ovate and strongly rounded to base along the upper margin rather than relatively narrow in outline and gradually tapering to both apex and base).

R. diversiloba T. & G.   Poison Oak or Ivy
/t/W/   (Ms)   Woods and thickets from sw B.C. (s Vancouver Is. and adjacent islands and mainland at Howe Sound; Eastham 1947; the Fort Vancouver locality cited by W.T. Gillis, Rhodora 73(794):180. 1971, is actually in NW Wash.) to Baja Calif. [*Toxicodendron* Greene]. MAP: Gillis, loc. cit., fig. 31, p. 177. The map by Barkley (1937: fig. 27, p. 421) should be extended northwards to include sw B.C.

R. glabra L.   Smooth Sumac
/T/(X)/   (N (Mc))   Dry fields and borders of woods from s B.C. (N to Lillooet and Kamloops; not known from Alta.) to Sask. (N to near the Man. boundary at ca. 54°45′N; Breitung 1957*a*), Man. (N to Lac du Bonnet, about 50 mi NE of Winnipeg), Ont. (N to Ingolf, near the Man. boundary at 49°48′N; *see* s Ont. map by Soper and Heimburger 1961:78), sw Que. (Farnham, Missisquoi Co.; Marcel Raymond, Rhodora 51(601):10. 1949), and cent. Maine, s to Nev., Mexico, Tex., and Fla. [*Schmaltzia* Small; *Toxicodendron* Ktze.; *R. canadensis* Mill.; *R. occidentalis* (Torr.) Blank.]. MAP: Barkley 1937: map 9 (incomplete northwards), p. 334.

Var. *borealis* Britt. (probably a hybrid between *R. glabra* and *R. typhina* (× *R. bor.* (Britt.) Greene; *R. pulvinata* Greene), the branches short-pilose or puberulent rather than glabrous and glaucous) is known from s Man. (Fernald *in* Gray 1950) and s Ont. (near Frankford, Middlesex Co.; CAN; reported from Strathroy, Middlesex Co., by Barkley 1937; a SE Man. station is indicated on the MAP for *R. pulvinata* by Barkley, fig. 8, p. 325, but his MAP for var. *borealis*, fig. 9, p. 334, indicates no Canadian stations).

R. radicans L.   Poison Ivy.   Herbe à la puce
/T/X/   (N (Ms))   Thickets, open woods, and sandy or rocky places (ranges of Canadian taxa outlined below), s to Ariz., Mexico, N.Mex., Tex., Kans., Ky., and Fla. MAPS and synonymy: *see* below.

1   Stem short, erect, scarcely branched, spreading by underground stolons and forming patches, the few leaves crowded near the tip; leaflets mostly irregularly dentate or undulate-lobed, the terminal one broadly ovate to subrotund, abruptly acute; [*R. rydbergii* Small; *R. toxicodendron* var. *rydb.* (Small) Garrett; s B.C. (N to Spences Bridge), Alta. (N to Edmonton), Sask. (N to Nipawin, ca. 53°20′N), Man. (N to Grand Rapids, near the NW end of L. Winnipeg), Ont. (N to the N shore of L. Superior and Timmins, 48°28′N; *see* s Ont. maps by J.H. Soper, Bull. Fed. Ont. Nat. 76:11. 1957, and Soper and Heimburger 1961:75), Que. (N to L. St. John and the Gaspé Pen.; *see* Que. maps by Laverdière, Rev. Can. Géogr. 9: fig. 1, p. 191. 1955, and 13:65. 1959, and Marie-Victorin and Rolland-Germain 1942: fig. 3, p. 10), N.B., P.E.I., and N.S.; MAP: W.T. Gillis, Rhodora 73(794): fig. 49 (*Toxicodendron rydb.*), p. 390. 1971] .... var. *rydbergii* (Small) Rehd.

1   Stem well developed, straggling or climbing by aerial rootlets, rarely trailing; leaflets entire or only obscurely toothed, the terminal one ovate, gradually acuminate; [*Toxicodendron* Ktze.; *R. toxicodendron* var. *rad.* (L.) Dippel; incl. *T. negundo* Greene; s Ont. (N to the Ottawa dist.; *see* the above-noted s Ont. maps by Soper and Soper and Heimburger), sw Que. (N to the Montreal dist.; M.L. Fernald, Rhodora 43(515):591. 1941), and N.S. (Yarmouth and Shelburne counties); MAP (aggregate species): Barkley 1937: fig. 29 (somewhat incomplete northwards), p. 428] .... var. *radicans*

R. typhina L.   Staghorn-Sumac, Velvet Sumac.   Vinaigrier
/T/EE/   (Mc)   Dry soil and rocky places from Minn. to Ont. (N to New Liskeard, 47°31′N), Que. (N to the S Gaspé Pen.), N.B., P.E.I., and N.S., S to Iowa, Ill., Ky., and N.C. [*R. hirta* (L.) Sudw.]. MAPS: Hosie 1969:260; Preston 1961:288; Hough 1947:307; Barkley 1937: fig. 8 (incomplete northwards), p. 325.

R. vernix L.   Poison Sumac
/T/EE/   (Mc)   Swampy woods from Minn. to S Ont. (N to Georgian Bay, L. Huron, and Grey Co.; *see* S Ont. map by Soper and Heimburger 1961:80), SW Que. (Papineau, Richelieu, Laprairie, Châteauguay, and Missisquoi counties), and Maine, S to E Tex. and Fla. [*Toxicodendron* Ktze.; *R. venenata* DC.]. MAPS: Hosie 1969:262; Raymond 1950b: fig. 27, p. 78; Hough 1947:311; Barkley 1937: fig. 30 (incomplete northwards), p. 439.

AQUIFOLIACEAE (Holly Family)

Shrubs with simple, alternate, entire or more or less serrate leaves, the minute stipules soon deciduous. Flowers small, regular, hypogynous, mostly polygamodioecious (mixed perfect and unisexual), solitary in the axils or in axillary cymose clusters. Calyx-lobes, whitish or yellowish petals, and stamens (alternating with the petals) each 4–9 (or the calyx-lobes minute and deciduous or obsolete). Ovary superior. Fruit a 4–9-seeded berry-like drupe; (Ont. to Nfld. and N.S.).

1   Petals whitish, obovate, slightly united at base; stamens adnate to the base of the corolla; calyx persistent in fruit; leaves more or less serrate . . . . *Ilex*
1   Petals yellowish, linear-oblong, distinct; stamens free; calyx deciduous or obsolete; drupes red; leaves essentially entire, thin, narrowly oblong to narrowly obovate; (Ont. to Nfld. and N.S.) . . . . *Nemopanthus*

ILEX L.   [4614]   Holly.   Houx

1   Leaves deciduous, dull above, glabrous or pubescent beneath, lanceolate to round-ovate, low-serrate most of their length, usually acuminate; drupes bright red; (Ont. to Nfld. and N.S.) . . . . *I. verticillata*
1   Leaves evergreen, thick and coriaceous, shining.
    2   Leaves commonly not over 5 cm long, entire or with a few low obtuse teeth above the middle; drupes finally black, mostly solitary in the leaf-axils; young twigs short-velvety; (N.S.) . . . . *I. glabra*
    2   Leaves to 1 dm long, their undulate margins sinuate-dentate with large triangular spine-pointed teeth (or on old trees largely entire); drupes scarlet, clustered in the axils . . . . [*I. aquifolium*]

[I. aquifolium L.]   English Holly
[Noted by Brayshaw (1960) as "An exotic species which may be found wild in Canada" and reported from B.C. by T.M.C. Taylor (1966b; ?escaped).]

I. glabra (L.) Gray   Inkberry, Bitter Gallberry
/T/E/ (N (evergreen))   Wet woods and swampy ground from N.S. (Digby, Yarmouth, Shelburne, Queens, Halifax, and Cape Breton counties; see N.S. map by Roland 1947: map 303, p. 435) and Maine (Isle au Haut) to Mass., Fla., and La. [*Prinos* L.; *I. ?opaca sensu* Hooker 1831, and Lindsay 1878, not Ait.]. MAP: Fernald 1921: map 3, pl. 130, facing p. 120.

I. verticillata (L.) Gray   Black Alder, Winterberry.   Apalanche
/T/EE/ (Mc)   Damp thickets and swampy ground (ranges of Canadian taxa outlined below), S to Minn., Ill., Tenn., and Ga. MAP and synonymy: see below.
1   Leaves generally broadest above the middle, less than 3 times as long as broad, glabrous beneath or sparsely pubescent along the main veins; [incl. var. *tenuifolia* (Torr.) Wats.; *Prinos* L.; *P. gronovii* Michx.; Ont. (N to Gogama, near Sudbury, 47°41'N) to Que. (N to Magdalen Is. and Rimouski and Temiscouata counties; reported from Gaspé Basin by John Macoun 1883), Nfld., St-Pierre and Miquelon, N.B., P.E.I., and N.S.; MAP: Braun 1935: fig. 3 (aggregate species; the occurrence in Nfld. should be indicated), p. 355] . . . . var. *verticillata*
1   Leaves broadest near or below the middle, generally 3 or 4 times as long as broad.
    2   Principal leaves at least 2 cm broad, thinly to densely pubescent over the lower surface; [*Prinos padifolius* Willd.; N.S.: Shelburne, Queens, and Halifax counties]. The validity of this taxon is questionable, G. Edwin (Rhodora 59(697):22. 1957) noting that individual plants may display the leaf-pubescence characteristics of the typical form on the upper leaves of branchlets . . . . . . var. *padifolia* (Willd.) T. & G.
    2   Leaves less than 2 cm broad, long-acuminate, glabrous beneath or sparingly pubescent on the veins; [*I. fast.* Bickn.; Nfld. (Humber R. system; GH) and N.S. (Yarmouth, Shelburne, and Halifax counties)] . . . . var. *fastigiata* (Bickn.) Fern.

NEMOPANTHUS Raf.   [4615]

N. mucronata (L.) Trel.   Mountain-Holly, Catberry.   Faux Houx
/T/EE/   (N)   Damp woods, thickets, and swamps from Minn. to Ont. (N to Gagoma, about 60 mi s of Timmins), Que. (N to the Marten R. SE of James Bay at 51°10′N; Dutilly and Lepage 1947), Nfld., N.B., P.E.I., and N.S., s to Ill., Ohio, and Va. [*Vaccinium* L.; *Ilex (N.) canadensis* Michx.; *N. fascicularis* Raf.].

CELASTRACEAE (Staff-tree Family)

Shrubs with simple, alternate or opposite, finely serrate leaves, the stems twining, trailing, or erect. Flowers small, regular, greenish, yellowish green, or purplish. Sepals, petals, and stamens each 4 or 5, the perigynous stamens alternating with the petals and inserted on a disc which fills the bottom of the calyx and sometimes covers the superior or partly inferior ovary. Fruit a 3-locular capsule, the seeds covered by an orange to crimson or scarlet aril.

1 Leaves alternate, elliptic to ovate-oblong, acuminate, serrulate; stems climbing by twining; branches terete; flowers greenish, perfect and unisexual mixed in small terminal racemes; fruit a 3-valved orange or bright-red capsule splitting to expose the 3–6 seeds, these enclosed in scarlet to crimson arils; (SE Sask. to N.B.) . . . . *Celastrus*
1 Leaves opposite; stems erect or trailing; branches 4-angled; flowers solitary or cymose in the leaf-axils, perfect.
  2 Leaves leathery and evergreen, glossy, lanceolate to oblong-lanceolate or oblanceolate, subsessile or short-petioled, to 3 cm long; flowers 3 or 4 mm broad, the sepals, maroon petals, and stamens each 4; capsules 3 or 4 mm long, with 1 or 2 seeds, these enclosed within thin lacerate whitish arils; stems erect, to about 1 m tall; (B.C. and SW Alta.) . . . . *Pachystima*
  2 Leaves deciduous, oblong-lanceolate to obovate; flowers 4–5-merous; capsules commonly longer and with more numerous seeds, these enclosed in orange, scarlet, or red arils . . . . *Euonymus*

CELASTRUS L.   [4625]   Staff-tree, Shrubby Bittersweet

1 Flowers 2–4 in small cymes in the leaf-axils; leaves oblong or obovate to suborbicular, acute to acuminate; (introd. in S Ont. and SW Que.) . . . . *C. orbiculatus*
1 Flowers numerous in terminal panicles to 1 dm long; leaves broadly lanceolate to ovate; (SE Sask. to N.B.) . . . . *C. scandens*

C. orbiculatus Thunb.   Oriental Bittersweet
Asiatic; an escape to roadsides, fence-rows, and thickets in N. America, as in S Ont. (near St. Williams, Norfolk Co.; CAN) and SW Que. (Mount Royal, Montreal).

C. scandens L.   Climbing Bittersweet.   Bourreau des arbres
/T/EE/   (Ms (vine))   Thickets, streambanks, and woods from SE Sask. (Estevan, about 110 mi SE of Regina; A.J. Breitung, Am. Midl. Nat. 61(2):511. 1959) to S Man. (N to Victoria Beach, about 55 mi NE of Winnipeg), Ont. (N to North Fowl L., between Lake of the Woods and Thunder Bay; F.K. Butters and E.C. Abbe, Rhodora 55(653):172. 1953), Que. (N to Ville-Marie, 47°20'N, and St-Joachim, NE of Quebec City; see Que. map by Doyon and Lavoie 1966: fig. 16, p. 818), N.B. (near Woodstock, Carleton Co., where taken by G.A. Inch in 1892 and probably now extinct; NBM; not known from P.E.I. or N.S.), S to Okla., La., Ala., and Ga. MAP: Ding Hou, Ann. Mo. Bot. Gard. 42: map 7, p. 235. 1955.

EUONYMUS L.   [4618]   Spindle-tree

1 Flowers 5-merous, greenish purple; peduncles 1–3(5)-flowered; capsules warty-tuberculate, their locules 4–10-seeded; seed-aril reddish orange to scarlet; leaves glabrous, their petioles rarely over 5 mm long.
  2 Trailing shrub or a few of the branches ascending; at least the upper leaves obtuse; (S Ont.) . . . . *E. obovatus*
  2 Erect shrub; leaves acutish . . . . [*E. americanus*]
1 Flowers 4-merous; capsules smooth, their locules 2-seeded; leaves acutish, their petioles commonly 1 or 2 cm long; erect shrubs.
  3 Leaves finely pubescent beneath; flowers brownish purple; peduncles few- to many-flowered; seed-aril reddish orange to scarlet; (S Ont.) . . . . *E. atropurpureus*

3 Leaves glabrous; peduncles 1–3(5)-flowered.
    4 Flowers brownish purple; seed-aril reddish orange to scarlet;
      (sw B.C.) . . . .*E. occidentalis*
    4 Flowers yellowish green; seed-aril orange; (introd.) . . . . *E. europaeus*

[E. americanus L.]   Strawberry-bush, Bursting-heart
[The report by Soper (1949) of this species of the E U.S.A. (N to Okla., Ind., and N.Y.) from S
Ont. is probably based upon a collection in OAC from London, Middlesex Co., which, however, may prove referable to *E. obovatus,* this reported from the same locality by John Macoun (1883; *E. amer.* var. *ob.*).]

E. atropurpureus Jacq.   Wahoo, Burning-bush
/t/EE/   (Mc)   Rich woods and thickets from N.Dak. (the reports westwards to Mont. by Rydberg 1922, and Fernald *in* Gray 1950, probably refer to *E. occidentalis* Nutt.) to Wisc., Mich., S
Ont. (N to Huron and York counties; *see* S Ont. maps by Fox and Soper 1953: fig. 23, p. 26,
and Soper and Heimburger 1961:16), and ?Maine, S to Okla., Ark., Tenn., Ala., and Va.; cult.
and natzd. elsewhere, as in sw Que. (Mount Royal, Montreal; MT). MAPS: Preston 1961:292
(the apparent extension into S N.B. should be deleted); Hough 1947:323.

E. europaeus L.   Spindle-tree
Eurasian; spread from cult. in N. America to roadsides and waste places, as in S Ont. (re-
ported from Lambton Co. by Gaiser and Moore 1966, and as very common in woods at
Guelph, Wellington Co., by Montgomery 1957) and sw Que. (Westmount, Montreal Is.).

E. obovatus Nutt.   Running Strawberry-bush
/t/EE/   (Ch (N))   Rich dry or moist woods from Ill. to Mich., S Ont. (N to Middlesex, Perth,
Peel, and York counties; *see* S Ont. map by Soper and Heimburger 1961:17), and W N.Y., S to
Mo. and Tenn. [*E. americanus* var. *ob.* (Nutt.) Voss].

E. occidentalis Nutt.   Western Wahoo
/t/W/   (N)   Woods and thickets on the W side of the Cascade Mts. from sw B.C. (collections
in V from Courtenay and vicinity, Vancouver Is., where taken by Greig in June, 1970, and by
Morton and Ahier in November, 1970) to cent. Calif. [*E. atropurpureus sensu* Hooker 1831,
not Jacq.].

PACHISTIMA Raf.   [4633]

P. myrsinites (Pursh) Raf.   Mountain-Box
/T/W/   (N)   Rocky woods, thickets, and slopes at low to medium elevations from B.C. (N to
Smithers, ca. 54°45′N) and sw Alta. (Waterton Lakes; Breitung 1957*b*) to Calif. [*Ilex* Pursh;
Myginda (Oreophila) myrtifolia Nutt. and its vars. *major* and *minor* Hook.; *Pachystima macro-
phylla* and *P. schaefferi* Farr].

STAPHYLEACEAE (Bladdernut Family)

STAPHYLEA L.   [4665]

Shrub or small tree with greenish striped branches and opposite 3-foliolate leaves, the ovate leaflets serrate, acuminate, to about 1 dm long, the terminal one long-stalked, the lateral ones short-stalked or sessile. Flowers greenish white, regular, perfect, perigynous, 5-merous, about 1 cm long, long-pedicelled in drooping terminal raceme-like panicles. Stamens 5, alternating with the petals. Fruit a large thin-walled inflated 3-locular capsule about 5 cm long.

S. trifolia L.   Bladdernut
/T/EE/   (Mc)   Rich woods and thickets from Minn. to Ont. (N to Grey and Carleton counties; *see* s Ont. maps by Fox and Soper 1952: fig. 9, p. 81, and Soper and Heimburger 1961:19, and the s Ont.–sw Que. map by W.G. Dore, Can. Field-Nat. 76(2): fig. 1, p. 101. 1962) and sw Que. (N to near L. St. Peter at Lanoraie, Berthier Co.), s to Okla., Ark., Ala., and Ga.

Forma *pyriformis* Dore (fruits pear-shaped rather than ellipsoid to subglobose) is known from Ont. (type from Ottawa) and sw Que. (St-Armand, Missisquoi Co.).

ACERACEAE (Maple Family)

ACER L.   [4720]   Maple.   Érable

Tall shrubs or trees with usually simple (compound in *A. negundo*) palmately veined and lobed opposite leaves. Flowers regular, completely or functionally unisexual. Calyx-lobes usually 5. Petals 5 or none. Stamens 3–12. Ovary superior. Fruit a pair of separable 1-seeded samaras or "keys" united at base and broadly winged on the back, the asymmetrical wing longer than the body.

1 Leaves with broad obtuse to rounded sinuses between the lobes, simple.
  2 Inflorescence racemose; flowers greenish white, petaliferous, to 1.5 cm broad; fruits golden-bristly-hairy, the wings forming an angle of less than 90°; leaves mostly deeply 5-lobed, puberulent on both faces (the lobes themselves commonly secondarily lobed but the margins otherwise entire), the larger ones to over 3 dm broad; (w B.C.) . . . . *A. macrophyllum*
  2 Inflorescence umbellate, corymbose, or subcapitate; flowers yellowish, slender-pedicelled; fruits glabrous or sparingly hairy; leaves averaging smaller.
    3 Petals conspicuous; wings of fruit nearly horizontally divergent, to about 1.5 cm broad and scarcely narrowed at base; inflorescence peduncled; pedicels glabrous, ascending; leaves 5-lobed, the lobes sharply but remotely coarse-toothed; petioles with milky juice; (introd.) . . . . *A. platanoides*
    3 Petals none; wings of fruit less divergent (commonly nearly parallel or divergent at about 45°), the inner side narrowed at base; inflorescence sessile; pedicels hairy, drooping; (native species).
      4 Leaves green or tawny beneath, with drooping margins, 3-lobed (sometimes with an obscure pair of lobes at base), the lobes entire or sinuate-lobed with rounded teeth, often overlapping above the sinuses; fresh twigs orange-brown; (Ont. and sw Que.) . . . . *A. nigrum*
      4 Leaves pale beneath, with flat margins and open sinuses, mostly 5-lobed, the lobes themselves with a few acutish lobes or coarse teeth; fresh twigs brown; (Ont. to N.S.) . . . . *A. saccharum*
1 Leaves (or leaflets of *A. negundo*) with narrow, acute or acutish sinuses between the lobes.
  5 Leaves pinnately compound, with up to 7 (sometimes 9) entire or coarsely few-toothed leaflets; wings of fruit nearly parallel; flowers lacking petals, the staminate ones slender-pedicelled in sessile clusters, the pistillate ones in drooping racemes; (essentially transcontinental, either native or introd.) . . . .
  . . . . *A. negundo*
  5 Leaves simple, palmately lobed and veined.
    6 Flowers in racemes or slender panicles, petaliferous, appearing during or after the unfolding of the leaves.
      7 Inflorescence strictly racemose, drooping; petals obovate, conspicuous; fruit ribless, the halves diverging at 90–120°; leaves 3-lobed at summit, finely and sharply doubly serrate; bark of younger parts green, striped with white; (Ont. to N.S.) . . . . *A. pensylvanicum*
      7 Inflorescence a slender panicle; petals narrower and inconspicuous; fruit commonly strongly ribbed over the seed; bark not striped.
        8 Leaves heavy, 5-lobed, coarsely crenate, glabrous and prominently ribbed beneath; panicle heavy, drooping; calyx to 5 mm long; halves of fruit diverging at about 120°; (introd.) . . . . *A. pseudoplatanus*
        8 Leaves thinner, 3-lobed (or slightly 5-lobed in *A. spicatum*), less prominently ribbed beneath; calyx smaller.
          9 Halves of fruit diverging at about 90°; flowers greenish; panicle ascending; leaves coarsely serrate, downy beneath; (Sask. to s Labrador, Nfld., and N.S.) . . . . *A. spicatum*

     9   Halves of fruit nearly parallel; flowers whitish; leaves glabrous;
         (introd.) . . . . *A. ginnala*

  6 Flowers in cormybs, umbels, or heads.
     10 Inflorescence a long-peduncled corymb; individual flowers and fruits long-
        pedicelled; petals usually present.
       11 Leaves 3–5-lobed (sometimes 3-foliolate), glabrous to sparingly
           glandular-puberulent, to nearly 1.5 dm long and nearly as broad, paler
           beneath, the lobes doubly serrate; stamens inserted at the outer edge
           of a lobed disk; sepals green; samaras divergent at usually less than
           90°; (Alaska–B.C. and sw Alta.) . . . . *A. glabrum*
       11 Leaves 7–9-lobed, more or less pilose beneath and often hairy above at
           least along the veins, to 6 cm long and usually considerably broader,
           the lobes serrate; stamens inserted between the ovary and the inner
           edge of a fleshy disk; sepals usually red; samaras nearly horizontally
           divergent; (sw B.C.) . . . . *A. circinatum*
     10 Pistillate and hermaphrodite flowers in sessile umbels; staminate flowers
        subsessile or short-pedicelled in capitate clusters; mature pairs of samaras
        with a V-shaped sinus (the long axis of the seed ascending).
       12 Petals none; flowers greenish yellow or reddish; young fruits white-
           villous, the mature halves to 8 cm long, usually hairy at base; terminal
           leaf-lobe much narrowed at base and much more than half the length
           of the blade; (Ont. to N.B.; planted elsewhere) . . . . *A. saccharinum*
       12 Petals about equalling the sepals; flowers dark red to scarlet; fruits
           glabrous, the halves at most 5 cm long; terminal leaf-lobe broadest at
           base and at most only slightly more than half the length of the blade;
           (Ont. to Nfld. and N.S.) . . . . *A. rubrum*

A. circinatum Pursh   Vine Maple
/t/W/ (Mc) Rocky woods from sw B.C. (Vancouver Is. and adjacent islands and mainland
E to Manning Provincial Park, SE of Hope; according to Hultén 1947, the report from Alaska by
M.W. Gorman, Pittonia 3:75. 1896, probably refers to *A. glabrum* var. *douglasii*) to N Calif.
[Incl. var. *fulva* Henry; *A. macounii* Greene]. MAPS: Hosie 1969:282; Canada Department of
Northern Affairs and Natural Resources 1956:248; Preston 1961:300.

A. ginnala Maxim.   Amur Maple
Asiatic; locally established in the E U.S.A. and reported by W.T. Macoun (Ont. Nat. Sci. Bull.
3:11. 1907) as reproducing naturally from seed at Ottawa, Ont. [*A. tataricum* of Canadian reports, not L.].

A. glabrum Torr.   Western Mountain-Maple
/sT/W/ (Mc (Ms)) Moist woods from the N Alaska Panhandle through B.C. and sw Alta. to
Calif., N.Mex., and Nebr. MAPS and synonymy: *see* below.
1 Branches greyish; leaves relatively deeply lobed, seldom over 6 cm broad; [w U.S.A.
   only, reports from w Canada referring to the following taxon; MAPS (aggregate
   species): Preston 1961:300, and 1947:236] . . . . [var. *glabrum*]
1 Branches reddish; leaves relatively shallowly lobed and averaging over 6 cm broad;
   [*A. douglasii* Hook.; *A. subserratum* Greene; *A. barbatum sensu* Hooker 1831, in
   part, not Michx.; Alaska Panhandle (*see* Hultén 1947: map 854, p. 1195) and w B.C.
   to s-interior B.C. and sw Alta. (Waterton Lakes; Crowsnest Forest Reserve; Banff;
   Jasper; Bow River Pass); MAPS: Hosie 1969:280; Canada Department of Northern
   Affairs and Natural Resources 1956: 246; Hultén 1968*b*:679] . . . .
   . . . . var. *douglasii* (Hook.) Dippel

A. macrophyllum Pursh   Big-leaf Maple
/t/W/ (Ms) Moist woods from B.C. (N to Queen Charlotte Is. according to the maps noted
below but only planted there according to Calder and Taylor 1968) to s Calif. MAPS: Hosie

1969:270; Fowells 1965:51; *Atlas of Canada* 1957: sheet 41; Canada Department of Northern Affairs and Natural Resources 1956:250; Preston 1961:304; Munns 1938: map 147, p. 151; Little 1971: map 95-N.

A. negundo L.   "Manitoba Maple", Box-Elder, Ash-leaf Maple.   Érable à Giguère
/T/WW/   (Ms)   Native along rivers in the U.S.A. and much planted and freely escaping else-where (the Canadian ranges of taxa outlined below scarcely reflecting the actual native north-ern limits), s to Mont., Ariz., N.Mex., Tex., and Fla.; MAPS and synonymy: *see* below.
1   Twigs finely greyish-velvety-pubescent; leaves usually with tufts of hairs in the axils
    of the larger veins . . . . var. *interius* (Britt.) Sarg.
    2   Samaras greenish or yellowish; [*A. (Negundo) interior* Britt.; apparently native
        from Alta. to w Ont.; introd. in sw Dist. Mackenzie (Fort Simpson, ca. 62°N)] . . . .
        . . . . f. *interius*
    2   Samaras blood-red when young; [Sask. and Man. (type from Delta, s end of L.
        Manitoba); introd. in P.E.I.] . . . . f. *loeveorum* Boivin
1   Twigs glabrous at least along the internodes; leaves glabrous.
    3   Twigs commonly purple beneath a heavy glaucous bloom . . . .
        . . . . var. *violaceum* (Kirsch.) Jaeg.
        4   Samaras greenish or yellowish; [*Negundo aceroides* var. *viol.* Kirsch.; *N.
            nuttallii* (Nieuwl.) Rydb.; Dist. Mackenzie–Alta. to N.B. and N.S.] . . . . . f. *violaceum*
        4   Samaras blood-red when young; [s Man., Ont. (type from Plantagenet,
            Prescott Co.), and Que.] . . . . f. *dorei* Boivin
    3   Twigs green . . . . var. *negundo*
        5   Samaras greenish or yellowish; [*A. fraxinifolium* Nutt., not *Negundium frax.*
            Raf.; *Negundo aceroides* Moench; s Man. to N.S. (but widely planted and
            possibly not native in Canada); MAPS: Little 1971: map 96-N; Hosie 1969:284;
            Canada Department of Northern Affairs and Natural Resources 1956:260;
            Preston 1961:306; Hough 1947:337; Munns 1938: map 152, p. 156] . . . . f. *negundo*
        5   Samaras blood-red when young; [s Man. and Ont. (type from near Ottawa)] . . . . . .
            . . . . f. *sanguineum* Martin

A. nigrum Michx. f.   Black Maple.   Érable noir
/T/EE/   (Ms)   Moist woods from S.Dak. to Minn., Ont. (N to the Ottawa dist.), and sw Que. (N to Pontiac, Argenteuil, and Nicolet counties; *see* the map of the N limits in Que. by Marie-Victorin 1935:397), s to La., Ala., and Ga. [*A. saccharum (saccharophorum)* var. *nigrum* (Michx. f.) Britt.]. MAPS: Fowells 1965:54; Canada Department of Northern Affairs and Natural Resources 1956:254; Preston 1961:296; Y. Desmarais, Brittonia 7(5): fig. 24, p. 368. 1952; Hough 1947:327; Munns 1938: map 149, p. 153; Little 1971: map 97-E; Hosie 1969:268.

A. pensylvanicum L.   Striped Maple, Moosewood.   Bois d'orignal or Bois barré
/T/EE/   (Ms)   Rich cool woods from Mich. to Ont. (N to the Timagami Provincial Forest at ca. 47°N; reports from Man. by Hooker 1831, and Fernald *in* Gray 1950, require confirmation), Que. (N to the Gaspé Pen. at Mont St-Pierre; reported from Anticosti Is. by Verrill 1865; the re-port from Nfld. by Reeks 1873, requires confirmation), N.B., P.E.I., and N.S., s to Ohio, Tenn., and N Ga. [*A. canadense* Marsh.; *A. striatum* Du Roi]. MAPS: Hosie 1969:278; Canada Depart-ment of Northern Affairs and Natural Resources 1956:244; Braun 1937: fig. 28, p. 202; Preston 1961:302; Hough 1947:331; Munns 1938: map 146, p. 150.

A. platanoides L.   Norway Maple.   Érable de Norvège
European; "Much planted; seedlings abundantly thriving in hedge-rows, roadside-thickets, etc." (Fernald *in* Gray 1950); known in Canada from s Ont. (Wellington and Wentworth coun-ties; F.H. Montgomery, Can. Field-Nat. 62(2):92. 1948, noting it as introd. but not indicating it as spreading; noted as planted but not spreading in Lambton Co. by Dodge 1915), sw Que., and Nfld.–N.B.–N.S. (?spreading).
Concerning its spreading by seed in Que., Dansereau (1957:43) writes, "The Norway Maple *(Acer platanoides)* in America decorates streets, parks, and lawns. It seeds abundantly, but

the seed often germinate, produce a few leaves, and then die. They rarely survive to the sapling stage. However . . . in Mt. Royal Park in Montreal several large saplings are to be seen, and on Mt. Yamaska (Quebec) a small tree was recently discovered." Forma *schwedleri* (Koch) Schwerin (leaves reddish rather than green) is reported from N.S. by Roland (1947) but without indication as to its spreading.

A. pseudo-platanus L.   Sycamore-Maple
European; "Much planted, freely establishing seedlings and sometimes estab. in fence-rows, on roadsides, etc." (Fernald *in* Gray 1950). Concerning plants of Lambton Co., s Ont., Dodge (1915) writes "Occasionally planted but not spreading." The report from Nfld. by Rouleau (1956) is probably based upon planted trees. The only record of it as actually spreading in Canada appears to be a collection in NSPM from Port Maitland, Yarmouth Co., N.S. where taken in a fence-row. There is also a collection in NBM from Halifax, N.S., probably from a planted tree.

A. rubrum L.   Red, Scarlet, Soft, or Swamp-Maple.   Plaine or Plaine rouge
/T/EE/   (Ms)   Moist uplands, alluvial soils, and swamps (ranges of Canadian taxa outlined below), s to Tex. and Fla. MAPS and synonymy: *see* below.
1   Leaves of fertile branches rounded or somewhat cuneate at base, 3-lobed, the terminal lobe to 5 cm long, the lateral lobes at most about 3 cm long; [var. *tridens* Wood; *Rufacer carolinianum* (Walt.) Small; Ont. (N to the E shore of L. Superior at Maimainse Point, ca. 47°N), Que. (N to L. Timiskaming at ca. 47°30′N), N.B. (Ingleside, Kings Co.; ACAD; GH), and N.S. (Digby, Annapolis, Shelburne, Halifax, and Inverness counties)] . . . . var. *trilobum* Koch
1   Leaves of fertile branches subcordate at base, commonly 5-lobed, the terminal lobe to 8 cm long, the upper lateral ones to 5 cm long . . . . var. *rubrum*
  2   Leaves permanently pubescent or tomentose beneath; [Que. (N to Temiscouata Co.), Nfld., and N.S.] . . . . f. *tomentosum* (Desf.) Dansereau
  2   Leaves glabrate at maturity.
    3   Branches strongly ascending; [St-Janvier, Terrebonne Co., Que.; Pierre Dansereau, Nat. can. (Que.) 72(5/6):127. 1945] . . . . f. *columnare* Rehd.
    3   Branches horizontally spreading to moderately ascending.
      4   Branches densely covered with short twigs to about 5 cm long, lacking long branchlets; [type from Havelock, Huntingdon Co., SW Que.] . . . .
        . . . . f. *breviramiusculum* Vict.
      4   Branches bearing elongate branchlets; [*Rufacer* Small; *A. coccineum* Michx. f.; Ont. (N to Rainy L., SE of Lake of the Woods, and Matheson, both ca. 48°30′N; reports from SE Man. require confirmation), Que. (N to the Gaspé Pen.), Nfld., N.B., P.E.I., and N.S.; MAPS (aggregate species): Hosie 1969:274; Fowells 1965:57; Preston 1961:298; Canada Department of Northern Affairs and Natural Resources 1956:256; Braun 1935: fig. 1, p. 352; Hough 1947:335; Munns 1938: map 151, p. 155; Little 1971: map 98-N] . . . .
        . . . . f. *rubrum*

A. saccharinum L.   Silver, White, Soft, or River-Maple.   Plaine blanche
/T/EE/   (Mg)   Apparently native in bottomlands and along streams from Minn. to Ont. (N to New Liskeard, 47°31′N), Que. (N to lakeshore woods at Ville Marie, 47°20′N; planted elsewhere, as in the s Gaspé Pen.), and N.B. (shores of the St. John R. system; occasionally planted in P.E.I. and N.S.), s to S.Dak., Okla., Tenn., and Fla.; planted westwards and occasionally escaped, as in Sask. (Moose Jaw) and Man. (Portage la Prairie). [*Argentacer* Small; *Acer dasycarpum* Ehrh.]. MAPS: Hosie 1969:272; Fowells 1965:63; Gleason and Cronquist 1964: fig. 14.7, p. 161; Canada Department of Northern Affairs and Natural Resources 1956:258; Preston 1961:298; Hough 1947:333; Munns 1938: map 150, p. 154; Little 1971: map 101-E.

A. saccharum Marsh.   Sugar- or Rock-Maple.   Érable à sucre
/T/EE/   (Mg)   Rich rocky or hilly woods (ranges of Canadian taxa outlined below), s to E Tex., Ark., and Ga. MAPS and synonymy: *see* below.

1 Lower leaf-surfaces yellowish green, the leaves to over 1.5 dm long (averaging about 13.5 cm), usually very pubescent, the hairs short and erect on the lower surface; (see *A. nigrum* in text) . . . . [var. *nigrum* (Michx. f.) Britt.]
1 Lower leaf-surfaces glaucous or whitish.
  2 Leaves at most 1 dm long, thickish, with a characteristic outline (the upper central lobe with divergent sides, its teeth rounded and blunt); [*A. gr.* Nutt.; *A. nigrum* var. *gr.* (Nutt.) Fosberg; approaching the Canadian boundary in NW Montana and to be searched for in S B.C.–Alta.; MAPS: Preston 1961:304, and 1947:234] . . . . [var. *grandidentatum* (Nutt.) Sudw.]
  2 Leaves to 1.5 dm long (averaging about 11.5 cm).
    3 Leaves densely villous on the veins beneath, rather shallowly lobed, the lobes pointed to rounded; petioles densely villous; [*A. saccharophorum* vars. *schn.* (Rehd.) Rousseau and *subvestitum* Vict. & Rolland; reported from Missisquoi Co., S Que., by Raymond 1950*b*, but the MAP by Y. Desmarais, Brittonia 7(5): fig. 24, p. 368. 1952, indicates no Canadian stations] . . . . var. *schneckii* Rehd.
    3 Leaves glabrous or sparingly appressed-short-pubescent, deeply lobed, the lobes terminated by sharp pointed teeth; petioles glabrous . . . . . . var. *saccharum*
      4 Leaves 3-lobed, coriaceous, round-reniform in outline, the lateral lobes prolonged and divergent, entire or barely shouldered; [*A. rugelii* Pax; Ont.: reported from Turkey Point, Norfolk Co., by Landon 1960 (*in* Addenda), from Pelee Is., Essex Co., by Dodge 1914, and from Batchawana Bay, L. Superior, by Hosie 1938] . . . . f. *rugelii* (Pax) Palmer & Steyerm.
      4 Leaves 5(3)-lobed, roundish in outline, the lobes often themselves shallowly lobed or toothed; [*A. saccharinum* Wang., not L.; *A. saccharophorum* Koch and its f. *angustilobatum* Vict. & Rousseau; *A. barbatum* of Canadian reports, not Michx.; W Ont. (N to L. Nipigon) to Que. (N to L. St. John and the Gaspé Pen.; reports, often on maps, from Anticosti Is., Que., and from Nfld. require confirmation), N.B., P.E.I., and N.S.; MAPS: Hosie 1969:266; Fowells 1965:66; Gleason and Cronquist 1964: fig. 14.7, p. 161; Preston 1961:296; Dansereau 1957: map 3A, p. 34; Canada Department of Northern Affairs and Natural Resources 1956:252; *Atlas of Canada* 1957: sheet 41; Y. Desmarais, Brittonia 7(5): fig. 24, p. 368. 1952; Hough 1947:325; Munns 1938: map 148, p. 152; Nichols 1935: fig. 5, p. 408; Little 1971: map 99-N] . . . . f. *saccharum*

A. spicatum Lam.   Mountain-Maple.   Plaine bâtard or Fouéreux
/sT/EE/   (Mc)   Cool rocky woods from Sask. (N to Nipawin, 53°22′N) to Man. (N to The Pas), Ont. (N to Sandy L. at ca. 53°N, 93°W), Que. (N to L. St. John, the Côte-Nord, Anticosti Is., and Gaspé Pen.), S Labrador (Hamilton R. basin; Abbe 1955), Nfld., N.B., P.E.I., and N.S., S to E Iowa, Ohio, Tenn., and N Ga. [*A. montanum* Ait.]. MAPS: Hosie 1969:276; Canada Department of Northern Affairs and Natural Resources 1956:242; Preston 1961:302; Hough 1947:329.

HIPPOCASTANACEAE (Buckeye Family)

AESCULUS L.   [4721]   Horse-Chestnut, Buckeye

Trees with large opposite palmately compound exstipulate leaves, the commonly 5 or 7 leaflets wedge-obovate, acuminate, irregularly serrate, to about 2 dm long. Flowers more or less zygomorphic, showy, perigynous, in ample terminal panicles. Calyx-lobes 5. Petals 4 or 5. Stamens 5–8. Fruit a prickly (at least when young) leathery globose capsule to 5 cm thick; (introd.).

1   Petals yellowish, the upper pair narrowly spatulate, the lateral pair oblong-ovate and
    rounded at base to a slender claw, the lowest petal wanting; panicles to about 1.5
    dm long; leaflets usually 5 . . . .[A. glabra]
1   Petals white, blotched with red or yellow at base, the upper and lateral pairs similar,
    with rotund blade cordate at base and on a slender claw, the lowest petal usually
    present, with a broad 3-nerved claw; panicles to 3 dm long; leaflets usually 7 . . . .
    . . . . .A. hippocastanum

[A. glabra Willd.]   Ohio Buckeye
[Native in the E U.S.A. (N to Nebr. and Pa.) and often planted northwards, as in s Ont. (Woodhouse Gore, Norfolk Co.; OAC; possibly established on sand dunes).]

A. hippocastanum L.   Horse-Chestnut.   Marronnier
European; often self-seeding from cult. trees in N. America, as apparently in s Ont., sw Que., ?N.B., and ?N.S. (planted in Nfld.).

BALSAMINACEAE (Touch-me-not Family)

IMPATIENS L.   [4856]   Touch-me-not, Balsam, Jewelweed.   Impatiente

Herbs with simple serrate exstipulate leaves. Flowers zygomorphic, perfect, showy, hypogynous, theoretically 5-merous. Sepals 3, the lowest one (as the flower hangs on its pedicel) much the largest, saccate, its base usually prolonged into a straight or recurved spur. Petals 3, the upper one large, the small lateral ones each consisting of a fused pair. Stamens 5. Ovary superior. Fruit a capsule bursting elastically into 5 valves.

1   Leaves mostly opposite or whorled, lanceolate to elliptic, acuminate, rounded or
       cuneate at base, sharply serrate; flowers normally purplish pink, to 4 cm long,
       commonly 5 or more together in cymes or umbel-like clusters in the axils of a few of
       the upper whorls of leaves, their short recurving spurs usually less than 6 mm long;
       (introd.) . . . . *I. glandulifera*
1   Leaves alternate, elliptic to oblong or ovate.
    2   Saccate sepal not spurred; flowers pale yellow to orange, to 2 cm long; leaves
           remotely and rather coarsely and irregularly toothed; (s B.C.) . . . . *I. ecalcarata*
    2   Saccate sepal spurred.
        3   Flowers at most about 12 mm long (excluding the short straight spur), lemon-
               yellow, not spotted, 4 or more in axillary cymes that often become raceme-like
               in fruit; leaves rather finely and sharply serrate; (introd.) . . . . *I. parviflora*
        3   Flowers at least 1.5 cm long (excluding the strongly curved spur), often
               spotted with crimson or brownish red, solitary or few in axillary racemes;
               leaves remotely and rather coarsely and irregularly toothed.
            4   Spur at most 8 mm long, bent at right angles to the sac, this normally pale
                   yellow, unspotted or sparingly spotted with brownish red, broader than
                   long, rather abruptly contracted into the spur; (s Ont. to Nfld. and N.S.) . . . . . .
                   . . . . *I. pallida*
            4   Spur about 1 cm long, strongly recurved parallel to the sac, this longer
                   than broad.
                5   Flowers normally orange and spotted, less than 2 cm long, the sac at
                       least 2/3 as broad as long, rather abruptly contracted into the spur;
                       (transcontinental) . . . . *I. capensis*
                5   Flowers pale yellow, unspotted or with numerous small dots, the sac
                       usually less than 1/2 as broad as long, gradually tapering into the spur;
                       (Alaska–B.C. to Man.) . . . . *I. noli-tangere*

I. capensis Meerb.   Spotted Touch-me-not, Snapweed.   Chou sauvage
/sT/X/   (T)   Moist woods, brooksides, and springy places (ranges of Canadian taxa outlined below), s to s B.C.–Alta., sw Mont. (Hitchcock et al. 1969), s Sask.–Man., Minn., Okla., Ark., Ala., and Fla.
1   Flowers basically whitish or cream-colour.
    2   Flowers with scattered pink to brownish-red spots; [Ont. (Timmins) and N.S.
           (Digby and Cumberland counties)] . . . . f. *albiflora* (Rand & Redf.) Fern. & Schub.
    2   Flowers with coalescing pink areas nearly masking the basic cream-colour;
           [s Ont.: Rondeau Provincial Park, Kent Co.]. . . . . . . f. *peasei* (Moore) Fern. & Schub.
1   Flowers basically lemon-yellow to orange.
    3   Flowers lemon-yellow, with crimson spots; [Ont. (w James Bay at 52°11′N), Que.
           (E James Bay N to ca. 52°15′N), N.B. (Sheffield, Sunbury Co.), and N.S.
           (Cambridge, Kings Co.)] . . . . f. *citrina* (Weath.) Fern. & Schub.
    3   Flowers basically orange.
        4   Flowers unspotted or merely slightly spotted at the throat; [Man. (Brandon;
               Flin Flon; Wekusko L., about 90 min NE of The Pas), Ont. (sw James Bay
               region at 51°38′N), and N.B. (near Fredericton)] . . . .
               . . . . f. *immaculata* (Weath.) Fern. & Schub.

4   Flowers with crimson spots; [*I. biflora* Walt.; *I. noli-tangere* ssp. *biflora* (Walt.) Hult.; *I. fulva* Nutt.; s-cent. ?Alaska (the report from Tanana Hot Springs by A.E. Porsild, Rhodora 41:(486):254. 1939, is based upon a sterile specimen in CAN that, according to Hultén 1947, does not differ in its vegetative parts from Alaskan *I. noli-tangere*; the report from Alaska by Fernald *in* Gray 1950, is probably based upon Porsild's citation); southernmost Dist. Mackenzie–B.C.–Alta. to Sask. (N to near Windrum L. at ca. 56°N), Man. (N to Flin Flon, ca. 54°50′N), Ont. (N to Sandy L. at ca. 53°N, 93°W), Que. (N to s James Bay at ca. 51°N and the Côte-Nord), Nfld., St-Pierre and Miquelon, N.B., P.E.I., and N.S.] . . . . f. *capensis*

I. ecalcarata Blank.   Western Touch-me-not
/t/W/   (T)   Moist shady places from SE B.C. (Crawford Bay, Kootenay L.; Eastham 1947; considered introd. there by Boivin 1966b) to N Oreg. and Mont. (Perhaps merely a spurless phase of *I. noli-tangere*, according to Hitchcock et al. 1961).

I. glandulifera Royle
Asiatic; introd. in roadside thickets and waste places of N. America, as in B.C. (N to Prince Rupert; Eastham 1947), Ont. (N to North Bay, near L. Nipissing, and Arnprior, Renfrew Co.), Que. (N to Sacré-Coeur, Rimouski Co.), N.B. (Charlotte and St. John counties), and N.S. (Digby, Pictou, and Cape Breton counties). [*I. roylei* Walp.].
   Forma *albida* (Hegi) Boivin (flowers white rather than red to purple) is reported from Ont. by Boivin (1966b). Forma *pallidiflora* (Hook. f.) Weath. (flowers pale pink, with reddish or brownish dots) is reported from B.C., Ont., and N.S. by Boivin (1966b) and from St. John, N.B., by C.A. Weatherby (Rhodora 48(576):414. 1946). The report of *I. noli-tangere* from a street in Ottawa, Ont., by J.M. Macoun (1906) is referable here, the relevant collection in CAN.

I. noli-tangere L.
/ST/WW/EA/   (T)   Damp thickets and springy places from cent. Alaska (*see* Hultén 1947: map 855, p. 1195) and B.C. to Alta. (N to L. Athabasca), Sask. (N to Montreal Lake, 54°03′N), and Man. (N to Wilkins Point, L. Winnipegosis, ca. 52°50′N), s to Oreg. and Idaho; Eurasia. [*I. aurella* and *I. occidentalis* Rydb.]. MAP: Hultén 1968b:679.

I. pallida Nutt.   Pale Touch-me-not
/T/EE/   (T)   Wet or springy places (chiefly calcareous) from s Ont. (N to Grey, Peel, and York counties) to Que. (N to the Gaspé Pen.), sw Nfld. (Crabbes Brook; GH), N.B. (Carleton and Victoria counties; reports from P.E.I. require confirmation), and N.S., s to Kans., Mo., Tenn., and Ga.
   The reports from B.C. by J.M. Macoun (1895) are based upon *I. noli-tangere*, the relevant collections in CAN. The reports from Sask. by Rydberg (1932) and Fernald *in* Gray (1950) require confirmation. The citation from Aweme, s Man., by Lowe (1943) is based upon *I. capensis* f. *immaculata* (relevant collection in WIN; his Riding Mountain report also probably refers to *I. capensis*).

I. parviflora DC.
Asiatic; apparently known in N. America only from shaded waste places and barnyards of sw Que. (Montreal; Pierre Dansereau, Ernest Rouleau and A. Lafond, Ann. ACFAS 8:95. 1942), P.E.I. (Charlottetown; CAN; GH), and N.S. (Wolfville, Kings Co.; E.C. Smith and J.S. Erskine, Rhodora 56(671):249. 1954).

RHAMNACEAE (Buckthorn Family)

Shrubs or small trees with simple, subentire or finely toothed, alternate (subopposite in *Rhamnus cathartica*), elliptic to ovate or obovate leaves. Flowers small, regular, perigynous, white or greenish, in umbel-like cymes, these either solitary or panicled. Petals and stamens (opposite the petals) 4 or 5, or petals none. Ovary partially inferior. Fruit a dry or fleshy, usually 3-seeded drupe.

1 Flowers white, numerous in panicled umbels; fruit dry, 3-lobed, splitting into 3
  carpels; leaves palmately 3-ribbed from the base, glandular-serrate . . . . *Ceanothus*
1 Flowers greenish or greenish white, solitary in the axils or in axillary or supra-axillary
  umbel-like cymes; fruit a finally blackish berry-like drupe; leaves pinnate-veined . . . .
  . . . . *Rhamnus*

CEANOTHUS L. [4877] Redroot. Céanothe

1 Leaves mostly narrowly elliptic or elliptic-lanceolate, obtuse to barely acute, to
  about 6 cm long and 2.5 cm broad, usually over twice as long as broad, typically
  sparsely pilose beneath; panicles several to many, terminating leafy branches of the
  season, the component umbel-like cymes very crowded; capsule 4 or 5 mm long;
  shrub to about 1 m tall; (SE Man. to Que.) . . . . *C. herbaceus*
1 Leaves ovate to ovate-elliptic, to about 1 dm long and 6 cm broad, mostly less than
  twice as long as broad; panicles usually looser, the component cymes separated by
  internodes to over 2 cm long.
  2 Leaves evergreen, typically strongly whitened beneath with a greyish
    puberulence (essentially glabrous beneath in var. *laevigatus*), glutinous-
    varnished and shining above, finely and sharply glandular-denticulate, blunt-
    tipped; capsules 4 or 5 mm long, deeply 3-lobed, crested slightly above the
    middle; (B.C. and SW Alta.) . . . . *C. velutinus*
  2 Leaves deciduous, neither strongly greyish-puberulent beneath nor shining
    above.
    3 Leaves acute or acuminate (rarely blunt); peduncles borne on leafy shoots of
      the season; shrub to about 1 m tall; (Ont. and S Que.) . . . . *C. americanus*
    3 Leaves blunt; peduncles developed from old buds, chiefly below the leafy
      shoots of the season; shrub to about 3 m tall; (B.C.) . . . . *C. sanguineus*

C. americanus L. New Jersey Tea
/T/EE/ (N) Dry open woods and gravelly or rocky barrens from Ont. (N to Renfrew and Carleton counties; *see* S Ont. map by Soper and Heimburger 1961:23; concerning reports from Man., *see* Scoggan 1957) to SW Que. (N to Pontiac, Papineau, and Argenteuil counties and the Montreal dist.) and cent. Maine, S to Ala. and Fla.

C. herbaceus Raf.
/T/EE/ (N) Sandy or rocky ground from SE Man. (N to Brokenhead, about 30 mi NE of Winnipeg) to Ont. (N to Manitoulin Is., N L. Huron, and the Ottawa dist.; *see* S Ont. map by Soper and Heimburger 1961:24), Que. (N to L. Timiskaming at ca. 47°30'N), and Maine, S to Tex., Ark., Ala., and Ga. [*C. ovatus* Desf. (*see* G.K. Brizicky, J. Arnold Arb. Harv. Univ. 45(4):471–73. 1964) and its f. *pubescens* (Wats.) Soper (*C. pub.* (Wats.) Rydb.); *C. intermedius sensu* Hooker 1831, not Pursh].

C. sanguineus Pursh Buck-brush, Tea-tree
/T/WW/ (N (Mc)) Cliffs and rocky slopes from B.C. (N to Bella Coola, ca. 52°20'N; CAN; reported N to Stuart L. at ca. 54°30'N by John Macoun 1883) to N Calif., Idaho, and Mont.; an isolated station on the Keweenaw Pen., L. Superior, Mich. [*C. oreganus* Nutt.]. MAP: Fernald 1935: map 6, p. 210.

C. velutinus Dougl.   Snow- or Tobacco-brush
/T/WW/   (N (Mc))   Cliffs and rocky slopes from B.C. (N to Stuart L. at ca. 54°30′N; CAN)
and sw Alta. (Crowsnest Pass; Waterton Lakes) to Calif., Colo., and S.Dak.

Var. *laevigatus* (Hook.) T. & G. (*C. laev.* Hook., the type from Nootka, Vancouver Is., B.C.) is
known in our area only from Vancouver Is., B.C.

RHAMNUS L.   [4875]   Buckthorn.   Nerprun

1   Shoots and branches spine-tipped; leaves subopposite, finely crenate, broadly
    elliptic to elliptic-obovate, with only 2 or 3 pairs of lateral veins; calyx-lobes, petals,
    and stamens each 4; drupes usually 4-seeded, the seeds with a deep narrow dorsal
    groove; (introd.) . . . .*R. cathartica*
1   Plant unarmed; leaves alternate or subalternate, with usually 8 or 9 pairs of lateral
    veins; flowers 5-merous; drupes with 2 or 3 seeds, the seeds scarcely grooved.
    2   Leaves essentially entire, short-oblong to obovate, slender-petioled; flowers
        perfect; petals broadly obovate; styles united to tip; (introd.) . . . .*R. frangula*
    2   Leaves closely serrulate, on relatively short and stout petioles; styles 3-cleft.
        3   Flowers 2–5 in sessile axillary umbels, functionally imperfect, the plants
            unisexual; petals usually lacking; hypanthium saucer-shaped; berries bluish
            black; leaves oblong-elliptic to -ovate, with mostly not more than 7 main
            lateral veins on each side; plants finely puberulent but the stems becoming
            glabrous; (transcontinental) . . . .*R. alnifolia*
        3   Flowers 8 or more (up to 50) in peduncled axillary umbels, perfect or
            imperfect (if the latter, plant monoecious); petals very small, shorter than the
            sepals; hypanthium cup-shaped; berries purplish black; leaves ovate-oblong
            to oblong-obovate, with usually 10–12 main lateral veins on each side; plants
            yellow- or brownish-puberulent: (s B.C.) . . . .*R. purshiana*

R. alnifolia L'Hér.   Alder-leaved Buckthorn
/sT/X/   (N)   Swamps and moist or wet meadows and woods from SE B.C. (near Flathead;
CAN) to Alta. (N to the Firebag R. at 58°43′N; CAN), Sask. (N to Windrum L. at ca. 56°N),
Man. (N to the Nelson R. at ca. 57°N), Ont. (N to the Severn R. at ca. 55°50′N), Que. (N to the
Côte-Nord, Anticosti Is., and Gaspé Pen.), Nfld., N.B., P.E.I., and N.S., s to Calif., Wyo., Nebr.,
Ohio, Pa., and N.J. [*R. alpina* Rich.; *R. franguloides* Michx.]. MAP: C.B. Wolf, Rancho Santa
Ana Bot. Gard. Monogr., Bot. Ser. 1: map 2 (somewhat incomplete northwards), p. 132. 1938.

Forma *angustifolia* Löve and Bernard (leaves relatively narrow, 3 or 4 times as long as
broad) is known from the type locality, Otterburne, Man., about 30 mi s of Winnipeg.

R. cathartica L.   Common Buckthorn.   Nerprun
Eurasian; introd. in open woods, pastures, and fence-rows of N. America, as in Sask. (near
Swift Current; Breitung 1957*a*), Man. (Brandon; DAO), Ont. (N to the Ottawa dist.), Que. (N to
the Montreal dist.), N.B., P.E.I., and N.S. (*see* Maritime Provinces map by R.P. Gorham, Acadian Naturalist 1(3):123. 1944).

[*R. davurica* Pall. of E Asia (resembling *R. cathartica* but the leaves lustrous above, acute to
acuminate at base, and with usually at least 4 pairs of lateral veins, rather than dull above,
rounded at base, and with at most 3 pairs of lateral veins) is reported by D.S. Erskine (1960)
as introd. and somewhat spreading on the Experimental Farm near Charlottetown, P.E.I.]

R. *frangula* L.   Alder-Buckthorn.   Nerprun bourdaine
Eurasian; introd. in thickets, ravines, and fence-rows of N. America, as in s Man. (Brandon),
Ont. (N to the Ottawa dist.; *see* s Ont. map by Soper and Heimburger 1961:22), Que. (N to
near Quebec City; Raymond 1950*b*), N.B., P.E.I., and N.S. (*see* Maritime Provinces map by
R.P. Gorham, Acadian Naturalist 1(3):123. 1944).

R. purshiana DC.   Cascara, Chittam-bark

/T/W/   (Mc (Ms))   Rich bottomlands and rocky slopes from B.C. (N to Shuswap L. and Revelstoke, both ca. 51°N, E to Trail; CAN) to N Calif., Idaho, and W Mont. [*Frangula* Cooper]. MAPS: Hosie 1969:286; Canada Department of Northern Affairs and Natural Resources 1956:262 (the extension northwards beyond ca. 51°N in B.C. to near Prince Rupert at ca. 54°N requires confirmation); Preston 1961:314, and 1947:242; Munns 1938: map 155, p. 159; Little 1971: map 185-N.

VITACEAE (Grape or Vine Family)

Vines (climbing by tendrils) with alternate, simple or palmately compound, toothed leaves. Flowers small, regular, more or less perigynous, greenish, perfect or unisexual, 5-merous, in peduncled panicles borne (like the tendrils) opposite the long-petioled leaves or in terminal clusters. Calyx-teeth sometimes obsolete. Stamens 5, opposite the 5 petals. Ovary partly inferior. Fruit a 2-locular, usually 4-seeded, purple-black or black berry.

1 Leaves palmately compound, with mostly 5 coarsely sharp-serrate leaflets to about 1.5 dm long, these elliptic to obovate, abruptly acuminate, cuneate at base, subsessile or on petiolules to 1.5 cm long; petals separate and spreading at anthesis; inflorescence cymosely compound . . . . *Parthenocissus*
1 Leaves simple, coarsely and sharply toothed (often lobed near apex), ovate- or rotund-cordate; petals united above, the corolla deciduous in one piece before expanding; inflorescence thyrsoid . . . . *Vitis*

PARTHENOCISSUS Planch. [4915] Virginia Creeper, Woodbine. Vigne-Vierge

1 Tendrils lacking adhesive disks, the plant resting loosely on rocks, fences, etc.; leaves green and glossy above, green beneath; cymes dichotomous (the branches regularly pairing), lacking an elongate central axis but usually with a pair of subequal divergent branches; fruit to about 1 cm thick, with 3 or 4 seeds; (Man. to N.S.) . . . . *P. inserta*
1 Tendrils with adhesive disks, the plant high-climbing on trees, walls, etc.; leaves dull pale green, somewhat paler beneath; cymes irregular, with a prolonged central axis and a solitary ascending to divergent lower branch; fruit rarely over 7 mm thick, with at most 3 seeds; (Ont. and Que.; planted elsewhere) . . . . *P. quinquefolia*

P. inserta (Kerner) Fritsch
/T/X/ (Ms (vine)) Moist woods and thickets from Mont. to Man. (N to Hecla Is., L. Winnipeg; not known from Sask.), Ont. (N to North Fowl L., W of Thunder Bay), Que. (N to Ville Marie, 47°20′N; evidently a garden-escape), P.E.I. (introd. in a railway yard at Charlottetown; GH), and N.S. (?introd.), S to Calif., N.Mex., Kans., Pa., and New Eng. [*Vitis* Kerner; *P. vitacea* (Knerr) Hitchc.].

Forma *dubia* Rehd. (leaflets pubescent rather than glabrous) is known from SW Que. (St-Armand, Missisquoi Co.; MT). Forma *macrophylla* (Lauche) Rehd. (leaflets to over 2 dm long rather than to about 12 cm long) occurs throughout the range.

P. quinquefolia (L.) Planch.
/T/EE/ (Ms (vine)) Moist woods and thickets from Ont. (N to the SE shore of L. Superior) to Que. (N to Grosse-Ile, near Quebec City; John Macoun 1883) and S Maine, S to Mexico, Tex., and Fla.; a garden-escape in Man. (N to Grand Beach, near the SE end of L. Winnipeg), Nfld., N.B., P.E.I., and N.S. [*Hedera* L.; *Ampelopsis* Michx.; *Vitis* Lam.; *Cissus hederacea* Pers.].

Forma *hirsuta* (Donn) Fern. (leaves pubescent rather than glabrous) is known from Ont. (Constance Bay, near Ottawa) and Que. (Montreal dist.).

VITIS L. [4909] Grape. Raisin or Vigne

1 A tendril or an inflorescence normally at each of 3–7 successive nodes; leaves thick, shallowly toothed and usually shallowly 3-lobed, permanently and uniformly densely rusty-tomentose beneath; berries to 2 cm thick; (introd.) . . . . *V. labrusca*
1 Tendrils and inflorescences intermittent, usually none at each third node; leaves less pubescent to glabrate or glabrous; berries at most about 12 mm thick.
  2 Leaves strongly whitened beneath, pubescent beneath at least when young with a rusty or reddish flocculent or velvety pilosity, shallowly toothed, unlobed to deeply 3–5-lobed; berries black with a thin bloom; (S Ont.) . . . . *V. aestivalis*

2 Leaves green or only slightly whitened beneath, glabrous or promptly glabrate beneath, coarsely and sharply toothed.

   3 Leaves unlobed or slightly 3-lobed (the lobes tending to point outward), coarsely serrate, persistently pubescent in the vein-axils beneath; diaphragms interrupting pith up to 5 mm thick; berries black and shining . . . . [*V. vulpina*]

   3 Leaves usually 3-lobed (the lobes tending to point forward), with coarse acuminate teeth; diaphragms at most 2 mm thick; berries black, with a heavy bloom; (Man. to N.S.) . . . . *V. riparia*

V. aestivalis Michx.   Summer- or Pigeon-Grape
/t/EE/   (Ms (vine))   Dry woods and thickets from Minn. to s Ont. (N to Simcoe and Prince Edward counties) and Mass., s to Tex. and Ga.

Some of the Ont. material is referable to var. *argentifolia* (Munson) Fern. (*V. arg.* Munson; *V. lecontiana* House; *V. ?bicolor* LeConte; plant soon glabrate rather than permanently more or less rusty-tomentose).

V. labrusca L.   Fox-Grape
Native in the E U.S.A. (Mich. to Maine, s to Tenn., Ky., and Ga.). Collections from s Ont. (N to Brockville, Leeds Co.) have been placed here but may actually consist of various "strains" of the cult. grape, *V. labruscana* Bailey, derived from *V. labrusca*.

A hybrid with the Wine Grape, × *V. vinifera* L., is reported from Hants Co., N.S., by M.L. Fernald (Rhodora 24(285):177. 1922; "A single vigorous vine of one of the commonly cultivated grapes is growing in the gravelly thicket at the foot of a railroad bank near Uniacke Lake; obviously sprung from seed thrown from the train."

V. riparia Michx.   Riverbank- or Frost-Grape.   Vigne or Raisin sauvage
/T/EE/   (Ms (vine))   Moist thickets from s Man. (N to Riding Mountain) to Ont. (N to L. Timiskaming at ca. 47°30'N and Renfrew and Carleton counties), Que. (N to Montmorency Falls, E of Quebec City), N.B. (St. John R. system; not known from P.E.I.), and N.S. (Bridgewater, Lunenburg Co.; GH; not listed by Roland 1947), s to N.Mex., Tex., Mo., Tenn., and Va.; introd. in the w U.S.A. [*V. vulpina* of most Canadian reports, not L.].

Var. *syrticola* (Fern. & Wieg.) Fern. (*V. vulpina* var. *syrt.* F. & W.; petioles and lower leaf-surfaces permanently and copiously pilose rather than glabrous or soon glabrate) is known from s Ont. (Norfolk Co.; OAC).

[*V. vulpina* L.]   Winter- or Frost-Grape
[Reports of this species of the E U.S.A. (N to Kans., Pa., and N.Y.) from Canada are wholly or chiefly based upon *V. riparia* (relevant collections in several herbaria). (*V. cordifolia* Michx.).]

TILIACEAE (Linden Family)

TILIA L.   [4964]   Linden, Basswood.   Tilleul

Trees with alternate, broadly ovate to roundish, serrate leaves distinctly oblique at the more or less cordate base. Flowers perfect, regular, hypogynous, white or cream-colour, in axillary cymes, the long peduncle attached at about the middle of a long, narrowly oblanceolate or tongue-shaped membranaceous bract (an adaptation for wind-dispersal). Sepals and petals each 5, each petal sometimes subtending a sterile stamen (staminodium; native species only). Fertile stamens numerous, distinct or (in introd. species) cohering in 5 groups. Ovary superior. Fruit globose, nut-like, dry and woody, tomentose, 1-locular, with 1 or 2 seeds.

1   An oblanceolate staminodium (sterile stamen) opposite each petal; leaves of fertile shoots to 2 dm long (those of sterile shoots often much longer), glabrous (or merely with tufts of hairs in the vein-axils beneath) to more or less pubescent over the lower surface with simple and stellate hairs; (Sask. to N.B.) . . . . *T. americana*
1   Staminodia lacking; leaves rarely over 12 cm long; (introd.).
    2   Leaves glabrous or merely with tufts of hairs in the vein-axils beneath; cymes with up to 10 flowers; fruit only slightly ribbed . . . . [*T. europaea*]
    2   Leaves pubescent all over the surface beneath with simple hairs (also with tufts of hairs in the vein-axils); cymes mostly 3-flowered; fruit strongly 3–5-ribbed . . . .
. . . . [*T. platyphyllos*]

T. americana L.   Basswood, Whitewood.   Bois blanc
/T/EE/   (Mg)   Rich woods from Sask. (Boivin 1966*b*; not listed by Breitung 1957*a*) to s Man. (Brandon to Winnipeg and southwards), Ont. (N to Lake of the Woods, Algonquin Provincial Park, and the Ottawa dist.), Que. (N to about 125 mi NW of Montreal in Labelle Co. and Ste-Anne-de-la-Pocatière, Kamouraska Co.; isolated at L. St. John), and N.B. (St. John R. system; not known from P.E.I.; planted in N.S.), s to Tex., Ark., Tenn., Ala., and Del. [*T. canadensis* Michx.; *T. glabra* Vent.; *T. neglecta* Spach; *T. pubescens* Ait.]. MAPS: Fowells 1965:693; *Atlas of Canada* 1957: sheet 41; Canada Department of Northern Affairs and Natural Resources 1956:264; Preston 1961:318; Hough 1947:351; Munns 1938: map 156, p. 160; Nichols 1935: fig. 5H; Little 1971: map 193-E; Hosie 1969:288.

[T. europaea L.]   European Linden
[European; planted as a shade tree in N. America and occasionally spreading to waste places and roadsides. It is known in Canada from Ont., Que., Nfld., N.B., P.E.I., and N.S.; however, data as to its spreading in these localities are insufficient to warrant its inclusion as an established member of our flora. [*T. ?parvifolia sensu* G. Lawson, Proc. N.S. Inst. Sci. 7:106. 1890, not Ehrh.].

According to Clapham, Tutin, and Warburg (1962), *T. europaea* is a hybrid between the European *T. cordata* Mill. (*T. parvifolia* Ehrh.) and *T. platyphyllos*.]

[T. platyphyllos Scop.]   Bigleaf Linden
[Eurasian; planted as a shade tree in N. America and occasionally spreading to roadsides and waste places. A collection in CAN from Grand Remous, Gatineau Co., Que., may belong here, as well as one from Youghal, Gloucester Co., N.B. However, it is not known to be definitely spreading in either of these localities. Its report from Ont. by Boivin (1966*b*) also requires confirmation in this regard. (*T. grandifolia* Ehrh.).]

MALVACEAE (Mallow Family)

Herbs with mucilaginous juice and alternate, palmately veined, usually shallowly toothed to deeply lobed or pinnatifid leaves (entire or obscurely toothed in *Abutilon*). Flowers commonly large and showy, regular, hypogynous. Calyx deeply 5-lobed, with or without a subtending involucre (epicalyx) of bractlets. Petals 5, distinct or barely coherent at base. Stamens numerous, their filaments united into a central column adnate to the base of the petal-claws (the anthers usually borne at the summit of the column but, in *Hibiscus,* borne along the sides). Ovary superior. Fruit usually a ring of carpels separating from the central axis at maturity (a 5-locular capsule in *Hibiscus*).

1 Carpels each containing at least 2 seeds; petals yellow or pink to purplish (rarely white); stigmas terminal and capitate at the ends of the styles.
  2 Fruit a 5-locular capsule with no central column; staminal tube bearing anthers for much of its length (but naked at the 5-toothed apex); calyx subtended at base by an involucre of usually at least 6 linear bractlets . . . . *Hibiscus*
  2 Fruit consisting of a ring of 10 or more hairy carpels separating from the central axis at maturity; leaves to about 1.5 dm long.
    3 Leaves entire or shallowly and rather remotely crenate, broadly ovate to rotund, deeply cordate at base, taper-pointed; calyx naked at base; petals bright yellow, to over 1 cm long; staminal tube bearing anthers only at summit; carpels each with 2 long radiate-divergent horn-like beaks; velvety-pubescent annual to over 1 m tall; (introd.) . . . . *Abutilon*
    3 Leaves 3–7-lobed and coarsely crenate-serrate (suggestive of those of the grape, *Vitis*), cordate-based, finely stellate-pubescent; calyx closely subtended by an involucre of 3 linear bractlets; petals rose-purplish, often over 2 cm long; stamens freed separately from the upper 3/4 of the staminal tube; carpels broadly rounded at the beakless tip; stellate-pubescent perennial to 2 m tall; (s B.C. and sw Alta.) . . . . *Iliamna*
1 Carpels 1-seeded (rarely 2-seeded in *Sphaeralcea munroana*); petals usually various shades of pink, red, blue-violet, or purple (white or pale yellow in *Sida*); staminal tube bearing anthers only toward summit or along its upper third.
  4 Stigmas terminal and capitate at the ends of the styles; calyx commonly naked at base (sometimes with 3 persistent linear bractlets in *Sphaeralcea*).
    5 Petals white or yellow; carpels usually 5 or 10, beaked at summit; (introd.) . . . . *Sida*
    5 Petals various shades of pink, red, blue-violet, or scarlet.
      6 Carpels with long awn-like beaks, hairy, their sides becoming obliterated, the firm dorsal portion embracing the seed; petals lavender to bluish, either shorter than the calyx or up to 2.5 cm long; calyx naked at base, spread out flat under the fruit; leaves ovate, merely angulate-lobed and coarsely dentate; villous-hirsute annual to about 1 m tall; (introd. in s Ont.) . . . . *[Anoda]*
      6 Carpels beakless or merely with smooth empty summits, their firm sides rugose-reticulate at least on the lower third; thick-rooted or rhizomatous perennials; (B.C. to Man.) . . . . *Sphaeralcea*
  4 Stigmas extending the full length of the inner surface of the style-branches.
    7 Carpels beaked; calyx usually naked at base; perennials.
      8 Petals red-purple (sometimes white), erose or short-fringed at the truncate summit; flowers long-peduncled; carpels 10 or more; leaves divided nearly or quite to base into 3–7 deeply 3-parted segments; plant glabrous or sparsely short-hirsute; (introd. in s Ont.) . . . . *[Callirhoë]*
      8 Petals light to deep pink, conspicuously ciliate on the claws, usually erose to deeply emarginate; flowers in spike-like to rather open racemes, strongly dimorphic (the perfect ones the largest); carpels at most 10, tardily separating; (s B.C.) . . . . *Sidalcea*

7 Carpels beakless; calyx subtended at base by usually 3 or more bractlets; (introd.).
    9 Bractlets subtending calyx relatively broad, united at base into a 6–9-cleft involucel; carpels usually at least 15 . . . . *Althaea*
    9 Bractlets usually 3 (rarely 1), linear or lanceolate.
       10 Central axis of fruit surpassing the 20 or more carpels and forming a narrow cone-like projection; petals obcordate, rose-pink or red; plant rather densely pubescent with simple and branching hairs; involucral bractlets united toward base . . . . *[Lavatera]*
       10 Central axis of fruit not as long as the 10–20 carpels; petals white to pink or purple; involucral bractlets free to base . . . . *Malva*

ABUTILON Mill. [4983] Indian Mallow

A. theophrasti Medic. Velvet-leaf
Asiatic (India); introd. into vacant lots, cult. fields, and waste places of N. America, as in sw B.C. (Lumby, lower Fraser Valley; Groh 1944*a*), Sask. (Biggar, about 55 mi w of Saskatoon), Man. (Brandon), Ont. (N to the Ottawa dist.), Que. (N to Gentilly, Nicolet Co.), P.E.I. (Charlotte-town), and N.S. (Kentville, Kings Co.; Roland 1947). [*Sida (Abutilon) abutilon* L.; *A. avicennae* Gaertn.].

ALTHAEA L. [4991] Guimauve

1 Plants hispid with swollen-based bristles, to 6 dm tall; lower leaves to 4 cm broad, reniform, more or less 5-lobed; upper leaves deeply 3–5-lobed or palmately divided; flowers to 2.5 cm broad, pale rose-purple (becoming bluish), the pedicels surpassing the leaves; annual or biennial; (introd. on Vancouver Is.) . . . . *[A. hirsuta]*
1 Plants not hispid, to over 1 m tall; flowers subsessile or on pedicels shorter than the leaves; biennial or perennial; (introd.).
    2 Flowers pale pink, to 4 or 5 cm broad, on pedicels shorter than the leaves, forming an irregular terminal racemose inflorescence; leaves velvety, folded like a fan, the lower ones roundish, to 8 cm broad, 3–5-lobed, the upper ones more ovate in outline and more deeply lobed; stems less than 1.5 m tall, branched, densely velvety with branching hairs . . . . *A. officinalis*
    2 Flowers variable in colour (often white, yellow, or red), to about 1 dm broad, more or less sessile in a long irregular spike-like inflorescence; leaves rough-hairy, to 3 dm broad, roundish-cordate, 5–7-lobed or -angled; stems to 3 m tall, mostly unbranched, rough-hairy . . . . *A. rosea*

[A. hirsuta L.]
[Eurasian; reported as introd. in sw B.C. by Eastham (1947; waste ground at Metchosin, Vancouver Is.; Herb. V), where, however, probably not established.]

A. officinalis L. Marshmallow
Eurasian; formerly cult. in N. America, the root yielding the original non-synthetic marshmallow-paste; locally introd. along the borders of saline or fresh marshes in N. America, as in Ont. (Boivin 1966*b*), sw Que. (Oka; Boucherville, near Montreal), and N.B. (Woodstock, Carleton Co.).

A. rosea Cav. Hollyhock
Eurasian; a garden-escape in N. America to waste ground or occasionally persisting in old gardens, as in B.C. (Kamloops; CAN), Man. (near Otterburne, about 30 mi s of Winnipeg; Löve and Bernard 1959), Ont. (Essex, Norfolk, Lincoln, Wellington, and Carleton counties), sw Que. (Montreal dist.), N.B. (near Woodstock, Carleton Co.), and N.S. (near Kentville, Kings Co.).

[ANODA Cav.]   [5002]

[A. cristata (L.) Schlecht.]
[A native of Mexico and the sw U.S.A.; spreading to roadsides and waste places elsewhere, as in s Ont. (St. Catherines, Lincoln Co., where taken by McCalla in 1897; CAN; reported from Pelee Is., Essex Co., by Montgomery 1957), where, however, scarcely established. (*A. lavateroides* Medic.).]

[CALLIRHOË Nutt.]   [4992]

[C. digitata Nutt.]   Poppy-Mallow
[Reported from s Ont. by Soper (1949), where, however, scarcely established.]

HIBISCUS L.   [5013]   Rose-Mallow.   Ketmie

1   Leaves ovate, coarsely serrate, finely stellate-canescent beneath; petals pink to purple (sometimes white), with dark centre, to 8 cm long; calyx finely stellate-pubescent throughout; capsule glabrous; perennial to 2.5 m tall; (s Ont.) . . . . . *H. palustris*
1   Leaves 3-parted to base into narrowly oblong to obovate, coarsely serrate to pinnatifid segments; petals pale yellow, purple at base, to 4 cm long; fruiting calyx inflated, hispid only on the purple nerves; capsule long-hirsute; rather low hairy annual; (introd.) . . . .*H. trionum*

H. palustris L.   Swamp Rose-Mallow, Sea-Hollyhock, Mallow-Rose
/t/EE/   (Hp)   Saline, brackish, or fresh marshes from Ill. to Mich., s Ont. (Essex, Kent, Lambton, Elgin, Welland, Lincoln, and Wellington counties; *see* s Ont. map by Soper 1962: fig. 18, p. 29), N.Y., and Mass., s along the coast to N.C. [*H. moscheutos* var. *purpurescens* Sweet; *H. opulifolius* Greene]. MAP: M.L. Fernald, Rhodora 44(524): fig. 1, p. 268. 1942.

H. trionum L.   Flower-of-an-hour
Eurasian; locally introd. in cult. and waste ground in N. America, as in Sask. (Regina and Vanscoy, sw of Saskatoon; Breitung 1957a), Man. (N to Grand Rapids, near the NW end of L. Winnipeg), Ont. (N to Ottawa), Que. (N to Montebello, Papineau Co., and the Montreal dist.), N.B. (St. Stephen, Charlotte Co.; Kingston, Kent Co.), P.E.I. (Hurst 1952), and N.S. (Kings and Pictou counties).

ILIAMNA Greene   [4986A (*Sphaeralcea*)]

I. rivularis (Dougl.) Greene   Wild Hollyhock
/T/W/   (Hp)   Montane slopes and cliffs E of the Cascade Mts. from s B.C. (N to Salmon Arm, about 50 mi E of Kamloops; CAN) and sw Alta. (Waterton Lakes; CAN) to Oreg. and Colo. [*Malva* Dougl.; *Phymosia* Rydb.; *Sphaeralcea* Torr.; *S. acerifolia* Nutt.].

[LAVATERA L.]   [4990]   Tree-Mallow

1   Lower and median leaves cordate-ovate, rather deeply 5-lobed, the upper ones 3-lobed or shallowly crenate to subentire; flowers rose-pink, to 7.5 cm broad; plant perennial, rather copiously hirsute with branched hairs . . . .[*L. thuringiaca*]
1   Lower and median leaves subrotund-cordate, the upper ones merely shallowly angulate or crenate to subentire; flowers rose-pink to red, to 1 dm broad; plant annual, finely pubescent to nearly glabrous . . . .[*L. trimestris*]

[L. thuringiaca L.]
[European; an occasional garden-escape in Canada but scarcely established, as in Sask. (Boivin 1966b), Man. (Minnedosa), Ont. (banks of the Rideau Canal s of Ottawa; DAO), and N.B. (Boivin 1966b).]

[L. trimestris L.]
[European; known in Canada as a garden-escape at Vaudreuil, near Montreal, Que., where, however, scarcely established.]

MALVA L.   [4992]   Mallow.   Mauve

1   Flowers solitary in the upper axils, white to pale purple, surpassing the subtending leaves; petals to over 2 cm long; stem-leaves 5–7-parted to below the middle or nearly to base; erect perennials; (introd.).
    2   Pubescence consisting of short stellate hairs; bractlets of involucre ovate to obovate, densely stellate-pubescent on the back; mature carpels glabrous or sparingly pubescent, keeled along the back; primary segments of stem-leaves merely shallowly lobed or coarsely toothed above the middle . . . . *M. alcea*
    2   Pubescence consisting of spreading simple hairs; bractlets linear to narrowly oblanceolate, ciliate but otherwise essentially glabrous; mature carpels rounded on the back, not reticulate, densely pubescent; primary segments of stem-leaves themselves deeply pinnatifid . . . . *M. moschata*
1   Flowers clustered in the axils of many leaves, surpassed by the long petioles; stem-leaves round-cordate or reniform and merely obtusely lobed; annual or biennial; (introd.).
    3   Petals rose-purple with deeper-coloured veins, to over 2 cm long; bractlets oblong-ovate; carpels rugose-reticulate on the back, glabrous or sparsely pubescent; stem erect . . . . *M. sylvestris*
    3   Petals much smaller; bractlets linear to linear-lanceolate.
        4   Petals about 1 cm long and about twice as long as the calyx; carpels with rounded margins and smooth or only slightly reticulate backs (the margins of adjacent ones meeting in a straight line).
            5   Stems usually prostrate; leaves only obscurely lobed; flowers mostly pedicelled, white or pale lilac; carpels not reticulate on their rounded densely short-hirsute backs . . . . *M. neglecta*
            5   Stems erect; leaves distinctly 5–7-lobed; flowers mostly sessile, white to purple; carpels obscurely to strongly reticulate on their flattish glabrous backs . . . . *M. verticillata*
        4   Petals barely surpassing the calyx, whitish; carpels acute-margined, their usually pubescent backs flattish and honeycomb-reticulate (the margins of adjacent ones meeting in a wavy line).
            6   Claw of petals glabrous; carpels with narrowly winged, minutely toothed angles; fruiting calyx enlarged, veiny-reticulate . . . . *M. parviflora*
            6   Claw of petals ciliate or bearded; carpels with acute wingless angles; fruiting calyx barely enlarged, scarcely reticulate . . . . *M. rotundifolia*

M. alcea L.
European; locally introd. along roadsides and in waste places of N. America, as in s Ont. (between Southampton, Bruce Co., and Owen Sound, Grey Co.; J.M. Macoun 1906), sw Que. (Gatineau, Beauce, Arthabasca, and Montmagny counties), N.B. (Woodstock, Carleton Co.; CAN), and N.S. (Boivin 1966b).

M. moschata L.   Musk-Mallow
European; persisting in old gardens or esc. to roadsides and waste places in N. America, as in s B.C. (Vancouver Is.; Abbotsford; New Westminster; Agassiz), Man. (Boivin 1966b), Ont. (N to the Ottawa dist.), Que. (N to the Gaspé Pen.), Nfld., N.B., P.E.I., and N.S.

The typical form has the basal and lower stem-leaves simple and rounded, the upper stem-leaves shallowly 5-cleft into broad, rhombic, simply-cleft lobes. Much of our material is referable to either f. *heterophylla* (Vis.) Hayek (lower leaves as in f. *moshata* but the upper leaves deeply 5-cleft, the lobes dissected into linear segments) or f. *laciniata* (Desr.) Hayek (lower, as well as upper, leaves 5-cleft, the lobes dissected into linear segments).

M. neglecta Wallr.   Fromagère
Eurasian; a common weed of barnyards, waste places, and roadsides in N. America, as in S
B.C. (N to near Kamloops), Alta., Man. (Boivin 1966*b*), Ont. (N to Timmins, 48°28'N), Que. (N
to Rimouski, Rimouski Co.), SE Nfld. (Avalon Pen.; GH), N.B., P.E.I. (Prince Co.), and N.S. [*M.
vulgaris* Fries].

M. parviflora L.
European; locally introd. in waste places of N. America, as in SW B.C. (Vancouver Is.; Elgin,
near New Westminster), Sask. (Boivin 1966*b*), and SW ?Que. (Fernald *in* Gray 1950; however,
collections in CAN from Longueuil, near Montreal, are referable to *M. rotundifolia*).

M. rotundifolia L.   Fromagère
European; introd. along roadsides and in waste places of N. America, as in S B.C. (N to
Salmon Arm and Revelstoke; V), Sask. (N to McKague, 52°37'N), Man. (N to Dauphin, N of Riding
Mt.), Ont. (N to near Thunder Bay), Que. (N to Montreal), and P.E.I. [*M. borealis* Wallm.; *M. pu-
silla* Sm.; *M neglecta* of Sask. reports, not Wallr.].

M. sylvestris L.   High Mallow
European; introd. along roadsides and in waste places of N. America, as in SW B.C. (Vancouver Is.; Vancouver), Alta. (Fort Saskatchewan; CAN; not listed by Moss 1959), Ont. (N to
Fort Francis, about 200 mi W of Thunder Bay; John Macoun 1883), and Que. (N to Ville Marie,
47°20'N; Groh and Frankton 1949*b*).
   Some of our material is referable to var. *mauritiana* (L.) Boiss. (*M. maur.* L.; plant essentially
glabrous rather than hirsute).

M. verticillata L.
Asiatic; introd. along roadsides and in waste places of N. America, as in Alta. (Boivin 1966*b*),
Sask. (N to McKague, 52°37'N), Man. (Dauphin, N of Riding Mt.), Ont. (N to Renfrew, Lanark,
and Carleton counties), Que. (N to Cap-à-l'Aigle, about 80 mi NE of Quebec City; CAN), N.B.,
P E.I., and N.S.
   Most of our material (at least from Man. westwards) is referable to var. *crispa* L. (*M. crispa*
L.; margins of the leaves crisped rather than flat).

SIDA L.   [4998]

1   Leaves broadly ovate to rotund in outline, deeply 3–7-lobed, stellate-pubescent
      when young, glabrate in age, to about 2 dm long, the long-acuminate lobes coarsely
      and irregularly serrate; petals white, to about 1 cm long; calyx terete at base, thinly
      to densely stellate-pubescent or even velvety; carpels commonly 10, each tipped
      with an erect beak about 3 mm long; perennial to about 3 m tall . . . . . . [*S. hermaphrodita*]
1   Leaves ovate-lanceolate to oblong or elliptic, merely crenate, minutely stellate-
      pubescent, to about 4 cm long, commonly with a spine-like process at the base of
      the petiole; petals pale yellow, about 5 mm long; calyx angled, thinly stellate-
      pubescent; carpels 5, pubescent at summit, each tipped with 2 erect minutely hispid
      beaks; annual to about 1 m tall . . . . *S. spinosa*

[S. hermaphrodita (L.) Rusby]   Virginia Mallow
[Native in the E U.S.A. (N to Mich. and Pa.) and a garden-escape N to Mass. (Fernald *in* Gray
1950). There is a collection in TRT from Haldimand Co., S Ont., where taken in 1951 by Bert
Miller but scarcely established. (*Napaea* L.).]

S. spinosa L.   Prickly Mallow
Native in Tropical America; introd. in open ground and waste places of N. America, as in S
Ont. (Pelee Is., Essex Co.; Point Edward, near Sarnia, Lambton Co.; near Cambridge, Water-
loo Co.; Kingston, Frontenac Co.).

SIDALCEA Gray   [4993]   Checker-Mallow

1 Stems more or less hollow, to about 1.5 m tall, from short thick ascending
   rootstocks, they and the stipules and petioles glabrous or subglabrous; calyces
   usually glabrous except for the ciliate lobes, sometimes more or less finely stellate
   all over; petals deep pink; carpels about 4 mm long, smooth (or at most slightly
   wrinkled on the margins), the beak to 1.3 mm long; (sw B.C.) . . . .*S. hendersonii*
1 Stems rarely hollow, they and the stipules, petioles, and calyces usually hirsute and
   also often stellate; carpels usually prominently reticulate on the sides and
   sometimes on the back, the beak at most 0.7 mm long.
   2 Rootstocks lacking; calyx to 9 mm long; petals light pinkish to fairly deep
      watermelon-pink; carpels about 3 mm long; stems to 1.5 m tall; (introd. in B.C.) . . . . . .
      . . . .*S. oregana*
   2 Short, thick rootstocks or trailing, rooting branches present; calyx to 12 mm
      long; carpels 3 or 4 mm long; (s ?B.C.).
      3 Petals almost white to pale pink or pink-orchid; stem to 2 m tall, the lower part
         usually hirsute with simple hairs . . . .[*S. campestris*]
      3 Petals pale to deep pinkish-rose; stem to about 1 m tall, mostly uniformly
         pubescent toward base with soft several-rayed hairs, the hairs becoming
         more finely stellate above . . . .[*S. malvaeflora*]

[S. campestris Greene]
[Reports of this species of the w U.S.A. (?Wash. and Oreg.) from B.C. (as by Rydberg 1922) require confirmation. The MAP by E.M. Roush (Ann. Mo. Bot. Gard. 18(2): fig. 1, p. 126. 1931) indicates no Canadian stations.]

S. hendersonii Wats.   Alkali-Mallow
/t/W/   (Hs)   Along the coast from sw B.C. (Vancouver Is. and adjacent islands; V; reported
E to the lower Fraser R. by Henry 1915) to Oreg. MAP: Roush, loc. cit., fig. 1, p. 126.

[S. malvaeflora (DC.) Gray]   Checker-bloom
[The reports this species of the w U.S.A. (Oreg. to Calif. and Mexico) from s B.C. by John Macoun (1883; Vancouver Is.) and J.M. Macoun (1895; Revelstoke) are based upon *S. hendersonii* and *S. oregana,* respectively, the relevant collections in CAN. The MAP by Roush (loc.
cit., fig. 1, p. 126) indicates no Canadian stations. (*Sida* DC.).]

S. oregana (Nutt.) Gray
Native in the w U.S.A. (cent. Wash. to N Calif., Utah, and Wyo.); apparently introd. in s B.C. at
Revelstoke (where taken by John Macoun in 1890 and reported by J.M. Macoun 1895, as *S.
malvaeflora*; CAN; *see* above) and Creston (Herb. V). [*Sida* Nutt.; *Sidalcea malvaeflora* var.
oregana (Nutt.) Wats., according to John Macoun 1886]. The MAP by Roush (loc. cit., fig. 1, p.
126) indicates no Canadian stations.

SPHAERALCEA St. Hil.   [4986]   False Mallow, Globe-Mallow

1 Leaves 3-parted nearly to base (commonly pedate, the lateral segments themselves
   often deeply parted), the divisions variously lobed; calyx usually not subtended by
   bractlets; petals coppery-scarlet to brick-red; carpels strongly rugose-reticulate
   except at summit; stems low and spreading, to 2 dm tall; (s B.C. to s Man.) . . .*S. coccinea*
1 Leaves merely rather coarsely crenate to shallowly 3–5-lobed; calyx closely
   subtended by an involucel of usually 3 linear bractlets; petals apricot-pink to
   reddish; carpels rugose-reticulate only on the lower third of their length; stems to 8
   dm tall; (s B.C.) . . . .*S. munroana*

S. coccinea (Nutt.) Rydb.   Scarlet Globe-Mallow
/T/WW/   (Hp)   Dry prairies and sand-hills from S B.C. (N to Kamloops) to Alta. (N to Dunvegan, 55°54′N), Sask. (N to Moose Jaw), and S Man. (N to Dropmore, about 100 mi NE of Brandon), S to Oreg., Utah, Tex., and Iowa. [*Malva* Nutt.; *Cristaria* Pursh; *Malvastrum* Gray; *Sida* DC.].

S. munroana (Dougl.) Spach
/t/W/   (Hp)   Open plains to lower montane slopes from S B.C. (Osoyoos, S of Penticton, where taken by J.M. Macoun in 1905; CAN) and W Mont. to Calif. and Utah. [*Malva* Dougl.; *Malvastrum* Gray; *Nuttallia* Nutt.].

HYPERICACEAE (St. John's-wort Family; Guttiferae)

HYPERICUM L.   [5168]   St. John's-wort.   Millepertuis

Herbs or shrubs (*H. kalmianum* and *H. spathulatum*) with opposite entire translucent-dotted exstipulate mostly sessile leaves. Flowers regular, perfect, hypogynous, usually in cymes (sometimes solitary). Sepals and petals each 5, the latter usually yellow to orange (pink to purplish in *H. virginicum*), sometimes streaked with dark lines or black-dotted near the margins. Stamens usually numerous, often grouped in definite clusters. Ovary superior. Fruit a many-seeded capsule.

1   Petals pinkish to purplish; stamens mostly 9, in 3 groups alternating with large
    orange glands; flowers in axillary or terminal clusters; leaves oblong or oblong-
    ovate, mostly cordate or subcordate at base, often purplish; herb to 6 dm tall;
    (E Sask. to S Labrador, Nfld., and N.S.) . . . .*H. virginicum*
1   Petals orange or yellow; stamens lacking intervening glands; flowers terminal or in
    terminal cymes.
    2   Styles united below and persisting as a beak on the mature capsule; stigmas
       minute, not capitate; stamens very numerous.
       3   Capsules 5 or 6 mm long, 1-locular, rounded to the beak; petals at most 1 cm
          long; leaves elliptic, rarely as much as 4 cm long; stem herbaceous, only
          obscurely 4-angled, to about 5 dm tall, from slender creeping rhizomes and
          stolons; (Ont. to Nfld. and N.S.) . . . .*H. ellipticum*
       3   Capsules to 1 cm long, usually 5-locular, tapering to the beak; petals to about
          1.5 cm long; leaves linear to narrowly oblong, commonly about 4 cm long;
          shrub to 1 m tall, with papery whitish bark, the ascending branches 4-angled,
          the branchlets 2-edged; stolons not evident; (Ont. and SW Que.) . . . .*H. kalmianum*
    2   Styles separate to base, often divergent, the capsule not beaked; stigmas
       capitate.
       4   Styles 5; capsule 5-locular; stamens very numerous, united at base into 5
          sets; flowers few, chiefly solitary at the ends of the branches, 5–7 cm broad;
          leaves lanceolate to elliptic, to 1 dm long; herb to over 1.5 m tall; (Ont. and
          S Que.) . . . .*H. pyramidatum*
       4   Styles 3; capsule 1-locular or 3-locular.
          5   Stamens mostly more than 35, united at base into 3–5 clusters; capsule
             3-locular, usually long remaining covered by the withered corolla; petals
             about twice as long as the sepals; herbs.
             6   Sepals linear-lanceolate, mostly acute or attenuate at apex, at least 3
                times as long as broad; petals orange-yellow, at most black-dotted on
                the margins only; seeds coarsely reticulate; leaves linear-oblong,
                commonly 3 or 4 cm long; stem freely branched, it and the branches
                sharply ridged below the base of each leaf; (introd.) . . . .*H. perforatum*
             6   Sepals broader in outline, less than 3 times as long as broad, acute to
                rounded at apex; petals pale to bright yellow; seeds smoothish or finely
                and very shallowly reticulate; leaves generally broader in outline; stem
                simple or sparingly branched, it and the mostly simple branches not
                ridged.
                7   Petals pale to bright yellow, merely purplish-black-dotted along the
                  margins or blackish-denticulate; stems to 8 dm tall, from elongate
                  slender rhizomes and stolons; (S B.C.–SW Alta.) . . . .*H. formosum*
                7   Petals pale yellow, conspicuously streaked with strong dark lines;
                  leaves oblong, to about 6 cm long; stem to over 1 m tall; (Ont.
                  to N.S.) . . . .*H. punctatum*
          5   Stamens not more than 35 and not in definite clusters.
             8   Shrub to 2.5 m tall, the branchlets sharply 2-edged; flowers about 2 cm
               broad, few in a terminal cyme and often additional smaller cymes from
               the upper axils; capsule 3-locular; (S Ont.) . . . .*H. spathulatum*

8 Herbs with flowers at most 1 cm broad; capsule 1-locular.
  9 Leaves subulate, scale-like and appressed, at most 3 mm long; flowers about 3 mm broad, mostly sessile and scattered along the erect branches; capsules lance-subulate; stem wiry-filiform, bushy-branched; root-annual; (s Ont. and sw Que.) . . . . *H. gentianoides*
  9 Leaves flat, linear to ovate, longer; stem simple or loosely branched, from a more or less perennial base; flowers broader.
   10 Bracts of inflorescence foliaceous; leaves elliptic or oblong to ovate or obovate.
     11 Leaves 5–7-nerved, usually less than 1.5 cm long; stem usually less than 2 dm tall, prostrate and forming dense mats from the freely rooting nodes, simple or sparingly branched above, the terminal flowers solitary or few; (sw B.C.) . . . .
        . . . . *H. anagalloides*
     11 Leaves 3–5-nerved, to over 2 cm long; stem to about 4 dm tall, merely decumbent-based, commonly freely branched above, the flowers often numerous; (Ont. to Nfld. and N.S.) . . . . . .
        . . . . *H. boreale*
   10 Bracts of inflorescence subulate.
     12 Principal leaves elliptic, 5-nerved, partly clasping; capsules ellipsoid, rounded at summit; sepals narrowly elliptic to oblong, broadest near the middle; perennial with leafy-bracted decumbent base; (Ont. to N.S.) . . . . *H. mutilum*
     12 Principal leaves linear to lanceolate or narrowly oblong; capsules ovoid, tapering to the acutish or obtuse summit; sepals lanceolate, broadest below the middle; perennial by short leafy offshoots.
       13 Leaves chiefly 5–7-nerved, lanceolate to narrowly oblong, acutish or blunt, rounded or subcordate at the sessile, more or less clasping base; (B.C. to N.S.) . . . . *H. majus*
       13 Leaves 1–3-nerved, linear to linear-oblong, rounded at tip, sessile or subsessile, not clasping.
         14 Leaves linear-oblong; capsules less than 5 mm long, many of them not developing; mature sepals less than 5 mm long; (Ont. to N.S.) . . . . *H. dissimulatum*
         14 Leaves linear to linear-oblanceolate; capsules regularly developing, to 6.5 mm long; mature sepals to 6 mm long; (s Man. to Nfld. and N.S.) . . . . *H. canadense*

H. anagalloides C. & S.   Tinker's Penny
/t/W/   (Hpr)   Moist ground at low to fairly high elevations from sw B.C. (Vancouver Is. and adjacent islands and mainland E to Chilliwack; CAN; V) and Mont. to Baja Calif. [*H. bryophytum* Elmer].

H. boreale (Britt.) Bickn.
/T/EE/   (Hpr)   Damp peat, sand, and shallow water from Ont. (N to Schreiber, N shore of L. Superior) to Que. (N to the Côte-Nord and Gaspé Pen.; not known from Anticosti Is.), Nfld., St-Pierre and Miquelon, N.B., P.E.I., and N.S., s to E Iowa, Ohio, and Va. [*H. canadense* var. *bor.* Britt.; *H. mutilum sensu* Robinson and von Schrenk 1896, not L. (relevant collection in CAN) and probably of P.E.I. reports, according to D.S. Erskine 1960].

Forma *callitrichoides* Fassett (the submersed phase with elongated, unbranched, sterile stems and roundish, thin, barely punctate leaves) is known from E Que. (Magdalen Is.; MT) and N.B. (near Newcastle, Northumberland Co.; CAN).

H. canadense L.
/T/EE/   (Hp)   Sandy or muddy shores and wet meadows from s Man. and Ont. (N to Quetico Provincial Park, about 100 mi W of Thunder Bay, and the N shore of L. Superior at Peninsula,

ca. 48°45'N) to Que. (N to Taschereau, 48°40'N), Nfld., N.B., P.E.I., and N.S., S to Iowa, Ill., Ala., and Ga.; introd. in Europe (Hultén 1958). [Incl. the reduced extreme, f. *minima* (Choisy) Rousseau].

Var. *magninsulare* Weath. (petals pale yellow, tinged with red, rather than yellow and relatively broad) is known from the type locality, Grand Manan Is., Charlotte Co., N.B.

H. dissimulatum Bickn.
/T/EE/ (Hp) Peaty or wet sandy soil and gravelly beaches from Ont. (N to the Missinaibi R. at ca. 50°N) to ?Que. (a collection in CAN from Amos, 48°34'N, has been placed here but requires confirmation) and N.S. (Yarmouth, Digby, Lunenburg, Hants, Halifax, and Pictou counties; not known from N.B. or P.E.I.), S to E N.Y.

Scarcely separable from *H. canadense* and possibly a hybrid between it and *H. boreale* or *H. mutilum*.

H. ellipticum Hook.
/T/EE/ (Hpr (Grh)) Wet ground and sandy or gravelly shores from Ont. (N to Schreiber, N shore of L. Superior; the report "Canada to Lake Winnipeg" by Hooker 1831 (the probable basis of the listing of the species for Man. by Lowe 1943, and other Man. reports) probably rests merely upon a too broad delineation of the range by Hooker) to Que. (N to the E James Bay watershed at 52°23'N, L. Mistassini, and the Gaspé Pen.), Nfld., N.B., and N.S. (not known from P.E.I.), S to N.Dak., Iowa, Ohio, and Md.

Forma *foliosum* Vict. (inflorescence surpassed by a pair of sterile branches to 9 cm long arising from the axils of the uppermost pair of leaves of the otherwise simple stem) is known from Ont. (NW shore of L. Superior near Thunder Bay) and Que. (type from the Cap Rouge R., Portneuf Co.; also known from Senneterre, Taschereau, and Duparquet). Forma *submersum* Fassett (the submersed state with simple sterile stems and thin ovate to rotund leaves) is known from Ont. (type from Pipe L., near Walford, N of L. Huron).

H. formosum HBK.
/T/W/ (Hpr) Moist places at low to fairly high elevations (ranges of Canadian taxa outlined below), S to Baja Calif. and Mexico.
1   Sepals relatively narrow and sharp-pointed, their margins often conspicuously black-striate or -glandular; [SW U.S.A. and Mexico] . . . . [var. *formosum*]
1   Sepals ovate-lanceolate or triangular, usually obtuse or rounded, more or less purplish-black-dotted.
    2   Stems mostly simple, to about 2 dm tall; leaves often relatively broad; [*H. nortoniae* Jones; reported from Glacier Park, B.C., by Eastham 1947, and from Alta. by Hitchcock et al. 1961] . . . . var. *nortoniae* (Jones) Hitchc.
    2   Stems frequently branched and often over 2 dm tall; [*H. scouleri* Hook.; S B.C. (N to Rogers Pass at Glacier) and SW Alta. (Waterton Lakes)] . . . .
    . . . . var. *scouleri* (Hook.) Coult.

H. gentianoides (L.) BSP.   Orange-grass, Pineweed
/T/EE/ (T) Sterile sandy or rocky soil from Wisc. to Ind., Ohio, S Ont. (Sandwich and Windsor, Essex Co.; CAN), SW Que. (Hull), and S Maine, S to Tex. and Fla. [*Sarothra* L.; *H. nudicaule* Walt.; *H. sarothra* Michx.].

H. kalmianum L.   Kalm's St. John's-wort
/T/EE/ (N) Rocky or sandy places (common along beaches of the Great Lakes) from Ont. (N to Manitoulin Is., N L. Huron, and Ottawa; reported NW to Sault Ste. Marie by John Macoun 1883; see S Ont. map by Soper and Heimburger 1961:83) to SW Que. (shore of the Ottawa R. in Pontiac Co.; CAN; MT) and N.Y., S to Ill., Ind., and Ohio.

H. majus (Gray) Britt.
/sT/X/ (Hp) Moist ground from S B.C. (Vancouver Is. and Kamloops; CAN) to L. Athabasca (Alta. and Sask.), Man. (N to Sasaginnigak L., about 125 mi NE of Winnipeg), Ont. (N to

Hypericum

the sw James Bay watershed at 51°27′N), Que. (N to Ste-Luce, Rimouski Co.), N.B. (Charlotte Co.; CAN; GH), P.E.I., and N.S., s to Wash., Colo., Nebr., Pa., and Del. [*H. canadense* var. *majus* Gray; *H. anagalloides sensu* John Macoun 1883, not C. & S., the relevant collection in CAN].

H. mutilum L.
/T/EE/ (Hp) Moist ground from Man. (*see* Scoggan 1957) and Ont. (N to the Ottawa dist.; TRT; reported N to the N shore of L. Superior by John Macoun and John Gibson, Can. J., n.s. 15(91). 1876, this perhaps referable to *H. boreale*) to Que. (N to the Quebec City dist. and L. St. John), N.B., and N.S. (reports from P.E.I. are based upon *H. boreale,* according to D.S. Erskine 1960), s to Tex. and Fla.

The Canadian plant appears referable to var. *parviflorum* (Willd.) Fern. (*H. parv.* Willd.; *H. ?quinquenervium* Walt; leaves elliptic, gradually rounded to apex (rather than ovate to narrowly oblong or lance-ovate), the upper ones and those of the branches tapering from base to the obtuse tip).

H. perforatum L.   Common St. John's-wort, Klamath-weed.   Pertuisane
Eurasian; a common weed of dry pastures, old fields, and roadsides in N. America, as in s B.C. (N to Enderby, N of Vernon), Ont. (N to New Liskeard, 47°31′N; the report from Man. by Lowe 1943, requires confirmation), Que. (N to Grosse-Ile, about 40 mi NE of Quebec City), Nfld., N.B., P.E.I., and N.S.

H. punctatum Lam.
/T/EE/ (Hpr (Grh)) Thickets and damp ground from Minn. to Ont. (N to the Ottawa dist.), Que. (N to Bic, Rimouski Co.; CAN), and N.S. (Baddeck, Victoria Co.; GH; not listed by Roland 1947; not known from N.B. or P.E.I.), s to Tex. and Fla. [*H. corymbosum* Muhl.; *H. maculatum* Michx.; *H. ?micranthum* Chois.].

H. pyramidatum Ait.   Great St. John's-wort
/T/EE/ (Hpr) Rich thickets and moist ground from Ont. (N to the Nation R. at Casselman, about 30 mi E of Ottawa; reports from Man. may be based upon an 1859 collection by Bourgeau in what he referred to loosely as the Lake Winnipeg Valley) to Que. (N to Argenteuil, Deux-Montagnes, and Terrebonne counties; the report N to Quebec City by John Macoun 1883, requires confirmation) and N Maine, s to Kans., Mo., Ohio, and Md. [*H. ascyroides* Willd.; *H. macrocarpum* Michx.; *H. ascyron* of American auth., not L.].

H. spathulatum (Spach) Steud.
/T/EE/ (Hpr) Wet sands and boggy or swampy ground (ranges of Canadian taxa outlined dlesex, Wellington, and Grey counties; *see* s Ont. map by Soper and Heimburger 1961:84) and s N.Y., s to Ark., Ala., and Ga. [*H. prolificum* of American auth., not L.].

H. virginicum L.   Marsh-St. John's-wort
/T/EE/ (Hpr) Wet sands and boggy or swampy ground (ranges of Canadian taxa outlined below), s to Nebr., Ark., Ala., and Ga.
1   Mature sepals to 8 mm long, acute or acuminate; styles to 3 mm long; [*Triadenum* Raf.; *Elodea (Elodes)* Nutt.; *E. campanulata* Pursh; reported from N.S. by Fernald *in* Gray 1950, reports from elsewhere in Canada referring chiefly to the following taxon] . . . .
. . . . var. *virginicum*
1   Mature sepals at most about 5 mm long; styles rarely over 1.5 mm long; [*Elodea (Triadenum) fraseri* Spach; Sask. (Amisk L., near Flin Flon at ca. 54°45′N; Breitung 1957a), Man. (N to Sasaginnigak L., about 125 mi NE of Winnipeg), Ont. (N to Kapuskasing, 49°24′N), Que. (N to the Côte-Nord, Gaspé Pen., and Magdalen Is.), s Labrador (Fernald *in* Gray 1950), Nfld., N.B., and N.S.; reported by J.M. Macoun 1913, from sw B.C. (as *Elodea campanulata;* Ucluelet, Vancouver Is., where "Introduced from the east with Cranberry plants")] . . . . var. *fraseri* (Spach) Fern.

[FRANKENIACEAE] (Frankenia Family)

[FRANKENIA L.]   [5233]

[F. pulverulenta L.]

[European; reported by Brother Louis Arsène (Rhodora 49(586):248. 1947) as taken by Le Hors in 1936 at Savoyard, Ile St-Pierre, St-Pierre and Miquelon, where introd. but perhaps not established. The family is not keyed out in the "Key to Families" but resembles the Hypericaceae in several rather technical characters, differing in its sepals being united into a tube (rather than free) and its leaves lacking the pellucid dots characteristic of species of that family.]

ELATINACEAE (Waterwort Family)

ELATINE L.   [5231]   Waterwort

Low aquatic or subaquatic mat-forming herbs with opposite, entire, linear to obovate leaves less than 1 cm long. Flowers inconspicuous, regular, hypogynous, solitary or cymose in the leaf-axils. Sepals, petals, and stamens commonly 2 or 3. Ovary superior. Fruit a many-seeded thin-walled capsule.

1   Seed-coat with elliptical pits rounded at the ends (the ends not extending between the ends of pits in adjacent rows), the pits scarcely reduced in size toward the ends of the seed; flowers usually 2-merous, the capsule usually with 2 carpels; leaves cuneate-obovate to oblong, rarely over 5 mm long and 3 mm broad; (Ont. to Nfld. and N.S.) . . . .*E. minima*
1   Seed-coat with 6-sided angular-ended pits (the ends extending between the ends of pits in adjacent rows), the pits somewhat narrower and less distinct toward the ends of the seed; flowers usually 3-merous, the capsule usually with 3 carpels; (essentially transcontinental) . . . .*E. triandra*

E. minima (Nutt.) Fisch. & Mey.
/T/EE/   (T)   Sandy or peaty shores, tidal flats, and shallow water from Minn. to Ont. (Pothole Portage in the Sudbury dist. N of L. Huron; N.C. Fassett, Rhodora 41(488):369. 1939), Que. (N to Tadoussac, Saguenay Co.), Nfld., N.B. (Welsh L., about 30 mi N of St. John; CAN), P.E.I., and N.S., s to Wisc., Mich., Va., and Md. [*Crypta* Nutt.]. MAPS: Fassett, loc. cit., map 1, p. 372; R. Gauthier and Marcel Raymond, Contrib. Inst. Bot. Univ. Montréal 64: fig. 2, p. 33. 1949.

E. triandra Schkuhr
/sT/(X)/EA/   (T)   Muddy shores and shallow water, the aggregate species from s Dist. Mackenzie (N to the N shore of Great Slave L.; CAN) and ?B.C. (reported from Alberni, Vancouver Is., by Carter and Newcombe 1921) to Alta. (near Granum, about 35 mi SE of Lethbridge), Sask. (N to Prince Albert), s Man. (near Otterburne, about 30 mi s of Winnipeg; Löve and Bernard 1959), Ont. (N to the Ottawa dist. according to Fassett's map for var. *americana*), Que. (along the Ottawa R. from Hull to Montreal, thence along fresh and tidal shores of the St. Lawrence R. estuary to St-Vallier, about 20 mi NE of Quebec City; L. St. John; Brome L., Brome Co.), and N.B. (tidal shores of the St. John, Kennebecasis, and Miramichi rivers; not known from P.E.I. or N.S.), s to s Calif., N Mexico, Tex., Okla., Mo., and Va.; Eurasia. MAPS and synonymy: *see* below.

1   Leaves obovate to broadly spatulate, to 8 mm long and 5 mm broad; seeds borne from the lower half of the central axis, ascending, with mostly at least 20 pits in each row; stems densely matted, the crowded ascending branches to about 5 cm long; [*Peplis (E.) americana* Pursh; s Man. (reported from near Otterburne by Löve and Bernard 1959) to N.B.; (reports of *E. americana* from Vancouver Is. by Eastham 1947, and from Reed L., Sask., by John Macoun 1883, probably refer to var. *triandra*); MAPS (the s Man. station should be indicated on all): N.C. Fassett, Rhodora 41(488): map 3, p. 372. 1939; M.L. Fernald, Rhodora 42(502): map 18 (E area), p. 378. 1940; R. Gauthier and Marcel Raymond, Contrib. Inst. Bot. Univ. Montréal 64: fig. 1, p. 30. 1949] . . . . .var. *americana* (Pursh) Fassett
1   Leaves linear, lanceolate, oblong, or narrowly spatulate; seeds borne along nearly the entire length of the central axis, divergent.
   2   Seeds straightish, with at most 15 pits in each row; leaves usually less than 5 mm long and 2 mm broad, commonly rounded or tapering at the apex; stems densely matted, the ascending branches rarely over 3 cm long; [*E. brachysperma* Gray; reported from Alta. by Moss 1959; the MAP by Fassett, loc. cit., map 4, p. 372, indicates no Canadian stations] . . . . .var. *brachysperma* (Gray) Fassett
   2   Seeds curved, with at least 16 pits in each row; leaves to 15 mm long and 3 mm broad, often truncate to emarginate; stems loosely matted or with submersed branches to 2 dm long; [s Dist. Mackenzie (Great Slave L.), ?B.C. (*see* var. *amer.*), Alta., and Sask.; MAP: Fassett, loc. cit., map 2 (var. *genuina*), p. 372] . . . . .var. *triandra*

CISTACEAE (Rockrose Family)

Low shrubs or herbs with simple, narrow, entire, sessile or short-petioled leaves, these alternate, opposite, or falsely verticillate (or the lower ones opposite, the upper ones alternate). Flowers perfect, hypogynous, regular except for the calyx (outer 2 bract-like sepals much smaller than the inner 3). Petals either 3, red, and minute, or 5, yellow, and much surpassing the sepals, distinct. Stamens commonly numerous. Ovary superior. Fruit a capsule.

1 Petals 3, dark red, minute, withering-persistent; style short or none; capsule imperfectly 3-locular; flowers in very numerous small cymes disposed in a large leafy panicle; base of plant often with rosettes or leafy offshoots; (E Canada) . . . . *Lechea*
1 Petals 5, yellow, much surpassing the sepals, not persistent (*Helianthemum* later producing much smaller cleistogamous flowers); capsule 1-locular.
  2 Leaves linear or scale-like, strongly overlapping; style slender, elongate; flowers solitary at the ends of short leafy lateral branches; plant low and bushy-branched, forming large mats . . . . *Hudsonia*
  2 Leaves with dilated blades, not strongly overlapping; style short or none; flowers solitary or in few-flowered cymes at the end of leafy branches, small cleistogamous ones appearing later in the season; (Man. to N.S.) . . . . . *Helianthemum*

HELIANTHEMUM Mill. [5245] Rockrose, Frostweed

1 Petaliferous (non-cleistogamous) flowers 2 or more in terminal corymbs rarely overtopped by the lateral branches, their 3 inner sepals not much longer than the outer pair; capsules distinctly 3-angled; seeds rounded at summit, finely reticulate; leaves mostly canescent above; (s Man. and s Ont.) . . . .*H. bicknellii*
1 Petaliferous flowers mostly solitary (rarely 2 on each stem) and soon overtopped by lateral branches, their 3 inner sepals up to twice as long as the outer pair; capsules subterete or obscurely 3-angled; seeds truncate at summit, strongly papillate; leaves green above; (Ont. to N.S.) . . . . *H. canadense*

H. bicknellii Fern.   Frostweed
/T/(X)/ (Ch (Hp)) Dry rocky, sandy, or clayey woods, clearings, and plains from E Wyo. to Minn., s Man. (N to Victoria Beach, about 65 mi NE of Winnipeg), s Ont. (Essex and York counties), and Md., s to Colo., Kans., Ill., Ohio, and N.C. [*H. (Crocanthemum) majus* of auth., not *Lechea major* L., basionym]. MAP: H.S. Daoud and R.L. Wilbur, Rhodora 67(771): map. 6, p. 307. 1965.

H. canadense (L.) Michx.   Frostweed
/T/EE/ (Ch (Hp)) Dry open woods, clearings, and barren places from Wisc. to Ont. (N to Constance Bay, about 30 mi W of Ottawa; possible basis of the report of *H. majus* N to Lake of the Woods by J.M. Macoun 1898), SW Que. (Ile Calumet, Pontiac Co.; Hull, Gatineau Co.), and N.S. (Kings, Queens, and Halifax counties; not known from N.B. or P.E.I.), s to Mo., Miss., Ky., and N.C. [*Cistus* L.; *Crocanthemum* Britt.]. MAP: H.S. Daoud and R.L. Wilbur, Rhodora 67(771): map 4, p. 307. 1965.

HUDSONIA L. [5247] Hudsonia. Hudsonie

1 Leaves linear-subulate, to 7 mm long, villous, appressed-ascending; flowers bright yellow, on naked pedicels to 1 cm long; capsules cylindric, pubescent at summit; (P.E.I., N.S., St-Pierre and Miquelon, and Nfld.) . . . .*H. ericoides*
1 Leaves lance-ovate, scale-like and closely appressed, at most 4 mm long, densely tomentose; flowers sulphur-yellow; (s Dist. Mackenzie and Alta. to s Labrador and P.E.I.) . . . .*H. tomentosa*

H. ericoides L.   Golden-Heather
/T/E/ (Ch) Dry sands, pinelands, and acidic rocks from Nfld. (Baccalieu Is., Barred Is.,

and the Avalon Pen.; CAN; GH), St-Pierre and Miquelon, P.E.I. (Bothwell, Kings Co.; CAN; GH), and N.S. (Shelburne, Kings, Lunenburg, and Halifax counties; not known from N.B.) to Del. and S.C. MAP: Fernald 1918a: map 5, pl. 17.

Forma *leucantha* Fern. (flowers whitish rather than bright yellow) is known from P.E.I. (type from Bothwell, Kings Co.).

H. tomentosa Nutt.   Beach-heath
/sT/EE/   (Ch)   Dunes, sandy ridges, and blow-outs (ranges of Canadian taxa outlined below), s to Minn., Ill., Ind., s Ont., s Maine, and N.C.
1   Flowers on naked pedicels to 7 mm long; capsules pubescent at summit; [N ?Alta. (L. Athabasca); Ont. (Boivin 1966b), Que. (Côte-Nord; Gaspé Pen.), P.E.I. (Bothwell, Kings Co.), and N.S. (Boivin 1966b)]. This taxon combines the characters of *H. ericoides* and *H. tomentosa* and would probably be generally accepted as of hybrid origin through this parentage but for the fact, as pointed out by Fernald *in* Gray 1950, that it extends 2,000 mi NW of the range of *H. ericoides* . . . . var. *intermedia* Peck
1   Flowers sessile or nearly so; capsules glabrous; [*H. ericoides sensu* Richardson 1823 (and probaly early reports from N.S.), not L.; Great Slave L. to L. Athabasca (Alta. and Sask.), s Man. (N to Brokenhead, about 30 mi NE of Winnipeg), Ont. (N to Lake of the Woods, the N shore of L. Superior, and Cochrane, 49°03′N), Que. (N to the St. John R. at 51°25′N and the Côte-Nord), s Labrador (Goose Bay, Hamilton R. basin), N.B., and P.E.I.] . . . . var. *tomentosa*

LECHEA L.   [5248]   Pinweed

(Ref.: Hodgdon 1938; Wilbur and Daoud 1961)
1   Outer sepals nearly equalling or distinctly surpassing the inner ones; (Ont.).
  2   Stem villous with spreading hairs; inner sepals about equalling the outer, glabrous or occasionally pilose along the keel, the fruiting calyx rounded at base; seeds lustrous; leaves of basal offshoots mostly at least 8 mm long . . . . *L. villosa*
  2   Stem pubescent with appressed or incurved hairs; inner sepals distinctly shorter than the outer, more or less villous throughout, scarcely keeled, the fruiting calyx tapering at base; seeds opaque; leaves of basal offshoots less than 8 mm long . .
     . . . . *L. minor*
1   Outer sepals at most only slightly over half as long as the inner ones (sometimes nearly equalling them in *L. maritima*).
  3   Leaves copiously appressed-canescent or strongly short-pilose, at least on the midrib and margins beneath.
    4   Leaves of basal shoots dull green, pilose over the entire surface beneath; outer sepals sometimes nearly equalling the inner; (N.B.) . . . . *L. maritima*
    4   Leaves of basal shoots bright green, pilose beneath only on the midrib and margins; outer sepals distinctly shorter than the inner; (s Ont.) . . . . *L. stricta*
  3   Leaves green, sparingly pubescent only on the midrib and margins beneath.
    5   Seeds 2–4, dark brown, flattened-ovoid, lacking an adherent coat; fruiting calyx tapering at base; (s Ont.) . . . . *L. leggettii*
    5   Seeds 4–6, light brown, shaped like a section of an orange, interruptedly coated with a gray membrane; fruiting calyx obtuse or rounded at base; (Sask. to N.S.) . . . . *L. intermedia*

L. intermedia Leggett
/T/EE/   (Hp (Ch))   Dry sterile soil from S.Dak. to Minn., SE Man. (N to Victoria Beach, about 55 mi NE of Winnipeg), Ont. (N to Quetico Provincial Park, about 100 mi W of Thunder Bay, the SE shore of L. Superior, and Renfrew and Carleton counties), SW Que. (N to L. St. Peter in Champlain and St-Maurice counties), N.B., P.E.I., and N.S., s to NW Nebr., s Ont., N.Y., and Vt.; an isolated station along the Archibald R., L. Athabasca, Sask. [Incl. vars. *depauperata* and *laurentiana* Hodgdon and *L. juniperina* Bickn.]. MAP: combine the maps by Hodgdon 1938: map 25, map 26 (var. *junip.* (Bickn.) Robins.), and map 27 (var. *laur.*), p. 120.

L. leggettii Britt.
/t/EE/ (Hp (Ch)) Dry or damp open woods, sands, and peats from N III. to Mich., s Ont. (Sandwich, Essex Co.; Toronto), N.Y., and N.J., s to La. and Fla. [Incl. *L. moniliformis* Bickn.]. MAP: combine the maps by Hodgdon 1938: map 22, map 23 (var. *mon.*), and map 24 (var. *ramosissima*), p. 120.

L. maritima Leggett
/T/E/ (Hp (Ch)) Dunes and sandy flats near the coast and slightly inland from E N.B. (Kent and Northumberland counties; CAN; GH; NSPM) and Maine to Va. [Incl. var. *subcylindrica* Hodgdon]. MAP: combine the maps by Hodgdon 1938: map 18, map 19 (var. *virginica*), and map 20 (var. *sub.*), p. 101.

L. minor L.
/T/EE/ (Hp (Ch)) Sandy woods and clearings from III. to Mich., Ont. (Essex, Norfolk, and Middlesex counties; reported N to the Ottawa dist. by Gillett 1958), Pa., and N.H., s to La. and N Fla. [*L. thymifolia* Michx.]. MAP: Hodgdon 1938: map 5, p. 55.

L. stricta Leggett
/t/EE/ (Hp (Ch)) Sandy places from Minn. to Wisc., s Ont. (near Belleville, Hastings Co., where taken by John Macoun in 1876 and 1877; Hodgdon 1938), and N.Y., s to N Nebr. and N Ind. MAP: Hodgdon 1938: map 21, p. 120.

L. villosa Ell.
/t/EE/ (Hp (Ch)) Dry sands and gravels from Kans. to Mich., s Ont. (Essex, Kent, Lambton, Norfolk, and Middlesex counties), N.Y., and N.H., s to E Tex. and Fla. [*L. minor* var. *vill.* (Ell.) Boivin]. MAP: Hodgdon 1938: map 2, p. 55.

VIOLACEAE (Violet Family)

Herbs with subentire to deeply divided, commonly cordate or reniform leaves, these alternate or all basal. Flowers zygomorphic, perfect, hypogynous, solitary and usually nodding on axillary or basal peduncles, mostly showy but often also in part cleistogamous and inconspicuous or even subterranean. Sepals, petals, and stamens each 5. Ovary superior. Fruit a 1-locular capsule, the 3 valves commonly expelling their seeds by a pinching inrolling of the margins on drying.

1   Sepals not auricled, nearly equalling the corolla; flowers greenish white, mostly less than 5 mm long, the lower petal merely gibbous or saccate at base; stamens united into a sheath around the pistil, all spurless; pedicels short, jointed above the middle, recurved, 1 or few from the median leaf-axils; leaves alternate, elliptic to ovate-oblong, tapering to base and apex, abruptly acuminate, entire or the later ones remotely toothed, more or less pubescent; (s Ont.) . . . . *Hybanthus*
1   Sepals auricled at base, shorter than the corolla; flowers white, yellow, or various shades of bluish purple, the lower petal spurred; stamens distinct, the 2 lower ones bearing spurs that extend into the corolla-spur; pedicels solitary in the leaf-axils or all basal, elongate, 2-bracted above the middle; leaves alternate or all basal, usually toothed to deeply divided, mostly cordate at base . . . . *Viola*

HYBANTHUS Jacq.   [5271]

H. concolor (Forst.) Spreng.   Green Violet
/t/EE/   (Hp)   Rich woods and ravines (chiefly calcareous) from Wisc. to Mich., s Ont. (Kent, Lambton, Huron, Middlesex, Norfolk, Oxford, Welland, and Halton counties; *see* s Ont. map by Soper 1962: fig. 18, p. 29), N.Y., and Conn., s to Kans., Miss., and Ga. [*Viola* Forst.; *Cubelium* Raf.; *Ionidium* B. & H.; *Solea* Gingins].

Forma *subglaber* (Eames) Zenkert (leaves glabrous or nearly so rather than distinctly pubescent) is known from s Ont. (near London, Middlesex Co., where taken by Burgess in 1882; John Macoun 1883).

VIOLA L.   [5274]   Violet

(Ref.: Baird 1942)
1   Plants with leafy stems, the flowers axillary; lateral petals bearded toward base (except in *V. rostrata*).
  2   Stipules broad and leaf-like, with dilated summit, deeply divided into narrow segments toward base; styles broadly clavate; fibrous-rooted annuals; (pansies; introd.).
    3   Upper leaves entire or with a single pair of low teeth near the apex, spatulate to oblanceolate, cuneate at base; lower leaves with orbicular blades; petals to about 1 cm long, bluish white to creamy, about twice as long as the sepals . . . .
        . . . . *V. kitaibeliana*
    3   Leaves all with several pairs of distinct teeth.
      4   Petals variously marked with yellow, white, or purple, to 3 times as long as the sepals; lower and median leaves rounded or cordate at base . . . . . *V. tricolor*
      4   Petals ivory or pale yellow (sometimes with purple-tinged tips), shorter to slightly longer than the sepals; lower and median leaves cuneate at base . . . . . .
          . . . . *V. arvensis*
  2   Stipules mostly narrower and bract-like, entire to merely salient-toothed or fringed; styles linear or narrowly clavate; perennials.
    5   Leaves lanceolate to narrowly ovate, nearly entire, tapering gradually into margined petioles, crowded on the short stem; stipules subentire; petals yellow, with brown-purple veins near base; spur short; (B.C. to sw Man.) . . . .
        . . . . *V. nuttallii*

    5 Leaves cordate-ovate to reniform, distinctly toothed, borne along the usually elongated stem (this sometimes very short in *V. langsdorfii*).
       6 Stipules sharply toothed or fringed (*V. langsdorfii* may sometimes key out here).
          7 Sepals ciliate; petals creamy or ivory, with prominent brown-purple veins near base; spur 3 or 4 mm long; stipules to 2.5 cm long, fringed their whole length with teeth to 5 mm long; plant essentially glabrous; (s Ont. and s ?Que.) . . . . *V. striata*
          7 Sepals eciliate; petals violet, purple, or lilac; stipules to about 1.5 cm long, toothed mostly only toward base.
             8 Spur to 1.5 cm long; petals light violet with a darker base, the lateral ones beardless; tip of style glabrous and straight; upper leaves tapering to tip; plant essentially glabrous; (Ont. and sw Que.) . . . .
. . . . *V. rostrata*
             8 Spur less than 1 cm long; lateral petals bearded; tip of style recurved and somewhat pubescent.
                9 Leaves rather thin, essentially glabrous, the upper ones with rounded tips; stipules ovate-lanceolate, their teeth to 2 mm long; flowers pale violet; (s Man. to N.S.) . . . . *V. conspersa*
                9 Leaves firm, glabrous to densely puberulent, the upper ones gradually narrowed to tip; stipules linear-lanceolate, with shorter teeth; flowers deep violet or blue-violet; (transcontinental; see *V. canina*) . . . . *V. adunca*
       6 Stipules entire or remotely short-toothed.
         10 Petals yellow to golden (the 3 lower ones purple-veined).
            11 Stems copiously soft-villous, usually leafless at base (occasionally with 1 basal leaf); leaves thickish, strongly veined, broadly ovate- to rotund-cordate, blunt-tipped, the expanding ones densely soft-pubescent; stipules ovate-oblong or semiovate, soft-pubescent; capsules white-woolly; (Man. to Que.) . . . . *V. pubescens*
            11 Stems not villous; leaves thinner; stipules usually narrower; capsules glabrous.
               12 Lateral petals beardless; style-head 2-cleft, beardless; sepals sometimes with a purple midstripe; cleistogamous flowers commonly borne in pairs in the leaf-axils; leaves cordate-rotund to reniform, ciliate, otherwise glabrous or sparingly appressed-strigose above, to about 4 cm broad; stems weak, bearing 2 or 3 leaves, from a short and usually slender but fleshy rhizome; (Alaska–Yukon–B.C.) . . . . *V. biflora*
               12 Lateral petals bearded; style-head capitate, bearded; cleistogamous flowers solitary in the leaf-axils.
                 13 Plant stoloniferous, the stolons often greatly elongate, producing new plants at their rooting nodes; flowering-stems leafy only toward base; leaves ovate-cordate to suborbicular, blunt-tipped, usually puberulent and rather conspicuously mottled with small purplish blotches that tend to form a network, persisting through the winter; (se Alaska–B.C.) . . . .
. . . . *V. sempervirens*
                 13 Plants scarcely stoloniferous.
                    14 Flowering stems leafy only near or below the middle; leaves orbicular to round-reniform, broadly rounded at summit, usually glabrous and not at all purplish-mottled; (B.C. and sw Alta.) . . . . *V. orbiculata*
                    14 Flowering stems leafy only along about the upper third of their length (long-petioled basal leaves also usually present).
                      15 Leaves mostly abruptly acute; style bearded only along

the side toward summit; (Alaska–B.C.–Alta.) . . . .
. . . . *V. glabella*

15 Leaves mostly tapering to an acuminate tip; style
bearded over the summit as well as long the side; (s
Man. to N.S.) . . . . *V. eriocarpa*

10 Petals predominantly white, violet, or blue-violet.
16 Petals predominantly white (but yellow-based and the 3 lower ones
purplish-veined); flowers about 1.5 cm long, the spur short; leaves
to about 1 dm long, acute to rather strongly acuminate, minutely
pubescent to glabrate; (B.C. to N.S.) . . . . *V. canadensis*
16 Petals blue-violet (if sometimes nearly white in *V. langsdorfii,* not
yellow-based); leaves mostly blunt to subacute.
17 Sepals conspicuously ciliate; flowers to 2 cm long, the spur
broad and saccate, never hooked, much less than half as long
as the blade of the spurred petal; head of style bearded; leaves
glabrous or puberulent; (sw B.C.) . . . . *V. howellii*
17 Sepals eciliate.
18 Flowers to 1.5 cm long, the slender spur usually over half the
length of the spurred petal and somewhat hooked; head of
style bearded; leaves glabrous to copiously puberulent;
(transcontinental; see *V. canina*) . . . . *V. adunca*
18 Flowers to 2 cm long, the spur broad and saccate, much less
than half as long as the blade of the spurred petal, never
hooked; head of style not bearded; leaves usually glabrous,
sometimes sparingly pubescent; (Alaska–Yukon–B.C.) . . . .
. . . . *V. langsdorfii*
1 Plants lacking manifest stems, the leaves and peduncles arising directly from the
caudex or from runners; perennials.
19 Leaves deeply palmately lobed or divided; flowers various shades of bluish
purple; sepals minutely ciliate; styles upwardly thickened; rhizome thick and
fleshy.
20 Flowers all petaliferous, flat and nearly rotate, the petals all beardless;
stamens exserted; style with a straight tip, persistent at the summit of one of
the mature valves; leaves deeply 3-divided, the lateral divisions 3–5-parted
into linear to narrowly spatulate segments; (s Ont.) . . . . *V. pedata*
20 Early flowers petaliferous, later flowers cleistogamous; some or all of the
petals directed forward, the 3 lower ones bearded at base; stamens not
exserted; style laterally beaked at summit.
21 Leaves minutely pubescent or glabrate, deeply 2–3-divided, the segments
again 2–3-cleft into linear or linear-lanceolate lobes; petals all bright violet;
cleistogamous flowers on slender ascending peduncles; rhizome erect;
(s Alta. to s Ont.) . . . . *V. pedatifida*
21 Leaves villous at least beneath and on the petioles, mostly less divided
and with broader segments; cleistogamous flowers on depressed short
peduncles; petals pale to deep violet; rhizome creeping or oblique.
22 Leaves all deeply divided into 5–11 fairly uniform narrow segments
(these often further dissected), the basal sinus rather broad; (s Ont.) . . . . . .
. . . . *V. palmata*
22 Earliest and latest leaves usually uncut, ovate-cordate, sparsely
pubescent; other leaves 3–5-lobed, densely villous beneath and on the
petioles, the terminal segment broad, the basal segments shaped
rather like an elephant's ear; (s ?Ont.) . . . . [*V. triloba*]
19 Leaves merely toothed or lobed, not deeply divided (early and late phases of *V.
triloba* may be sought here).
23 Leaves tapering or rounded to subtruncate at base, glabrous, very shallowly
crenate-serrate; petals white, the 3 lower ones with brown-purple veins near
the base, the lateral ones beardless or nearly so.

24 Leaf-blade lanceolate to elliptic, usually more than 3 times as long as broad, gradually tapering into the petiole; stolons often forming extensive mats by midsummer and bearing short-peduncled cleistogamous flowers at the nodes; (Ont. to St-Pierre and Miquelon and N.S.; introd. in B.C.) . . . .
. . . . *V. lanceolata*

24 Leaf-blade narrowly to broadly ovate, rarely 3 times as long as broad, rounded to subtruncate at base; cleistogamous flowers borne on prolonged peduncles chiefly from the crowns and from the first nodes of the midsummer stolons . . . . [*V. primulifolia*]

23 Leaves mostly cordate or subcordate at base.

25 Flowers yellow or white.

26 Petals bright yellow, the lower 3 with brown veins, the lateral pair bearded; cleistogamous flowers borne on prostrate or partially subterranean stolon-like branches, often forming open racemes; leaves minutely pubescent and barely unrolling at anthesis, in maturity round-elliptic to suborbicular and glabrate at least above, undulate-crenate, to 12 cm long, lying flat on the ground, the sinus narrow; (s Ont. and s Que.) . . . . *V. rotundifolia*

26 Petals white with brown-purple veins; cleistogamous flowers borne on simple aerial peduncles; leaves cordate-ovate to reniform, expanding at or before anthesis.

27 Nonstoloniferous; leaves orbicular to reniform; petals all beardless; cleistogamous flowers on prostrate or arching peduncles; seeds brown with darker brown markings; (transcontinental) . . . . . . *V. renifolia*

27 Stoloniferous.

28 Leaves glabrous, ovate to reniform; flowers at most about 1 cm long, very fragrant; lateral petals beardless or with a small tuft of hairs at base; upper petals obovate; cleistogamous flowers on ascending peduncles; seeds becoming black; stolons filiform; (transcontinental) . . . . *V. macloskeyi*

28 Leaves more or less pubescent at least when young, chiefly ovate; flowers to 1.5 cm long, only slightly fragrant; cleistogamous flowers on nearly prostrate peduncles; seeds yellowish brown; stolons cord-like.

29 Lateral petals beardless or nearly so; upper petals narrow; leaves with a few scattered hairs on the upper surface at least when young; petioles and peduncles usually reddish; (Man. to sw Que.) . . . . *V. blanda*

29 Lateral petals bearded; upper petals obovate; petioles and peduncles usually green; (Ont. to Nfld. and N.S.) . . . . . *V. incognita*

25 Flowers lilac to blue, violet, or purplish blue (except in albino forms).

30 Rhizome cord-like; sepals non-ciliate.

31 Spur to 2/3 as long as the blade of the spurred petal; petals all beardless; leaves strigose above, with a deep basal sinus, the basal lobes converging and often overlapping; nonstoloniferous; (transcontinental) . . . . *V. selkirkii*

31 Spur much shorter than the blade of the spurred petal; lateral petals usually more or less bearded at base (often beardless in *V. epipsila*); leaf-sinus open; cord-like superficial leafy stolons commonly developed as the plant matures.

32 Plants finely pubescent throughout; style ending in a slender hooked tip; seeds to 4 mm long; (garden-escape) . . . . *V. odorata*

32 Plants glabrous or sometimes slightly pubescent on the stipules and the lower leaf-surfaces, particularly along the veins; style ending in a broad disk; seeds less than 2 mm long.

33 Leaves cordate-rotund to round-reniform, commonly 3 or more present at anthesis, their tips rounded or obtuse;

bracts usually located near the middle of the peduncle; flowers lilac to almost white; stipules green, streaked with red, their margins sparingly ciliolate; (transcontinental) . . . . *V. palustris*

    33 Leaves mostly broadly ovate to round-reniform, commonly only 1 or 2 present at anthesis, their tips obtuse; bracts usually well above the middle of the peduncle; flowers commonly deeper purple; stipules purplish, apparently gland-tipped but otherwise glabrous; (Alaska–B.C. to w Ont.) . . . . . . *V. epipsila*

30 Rhizomes typically thick and fleshy, nonstoloniferous.
    34 Leaves variable as the season progresses, at one stage narrowly lanceolate to oblong-ovate, chiefly much longer than broad, often variably incised or lobed toward the rounded or subtruncate (sometimes cordate) base; petals violet or blue-violet, the 3 lower ones white at the copiously bearded base; cleistogamous flowers on erect peduncles; (Ont. to N.S.) . . . . *V. sagittata*
    34 Leaves essentially uniform throughout the season, mostly distinctly cordate, regularly toothed (not incised or lobed).
        35 Beard of lateral petals including many club-shaped hairs with knob-like tips; corolla blue-violet, usually darker toward the centre; spurred petal shorter than the lateral ones, beardless at base; sepals normally glabrous (ciliate in f. *prionosepala*); cleistogamous flowers long and slender, on erect peduncles; leaves broadly ovate; plant glabrous or nearly so; (Ont. to Nfld. and N.S.) . . . . *V. cucullata*
        35 Beard of lateral petals not strongly knobbed, the hairs mostly with slender tips; corolla deeper violet to purplish, not darkened toward the centre; spurred and lateral petals subequal.
        36 Sepals ciliate.
            37 Sepals closely long-ciliate nearly to tip, their narrow divergent auricles conspicuous; petals all more or less bearded within at base; cleistogamous flowers on ascending or erect peduncles; petioles and lower surfaces of young leaves sparsely hirsute or hispidulous; seeds with a caruncle to 0.5 mm long; (s B.C.; Ont. to Nfld. and N.S.) . . . . *V. septentrionalis*
            37 Sepals short-ciliate toward base, their broad auricles appressed; lateral petals bearded at base, the spurred petal beardless or sparingly villous; cleistogamous flowers on prostrate peduncles; petioles and lower surfaces of young leaves densely villous, the mature leaves dark green and thickish; seeds with a short caruncle; (s ?Man. to Que.) . . . . *V. sororia*
        36 Sepals not ciliate.
            38 Leaves narrowly cordate-ovate, triangular or ovate-oblong, gradually tapering to tip, their petioles and lower surfaces villous or pubescent to glabrate, their margins with at most about 12 rather coarse teeth; 3 lower petals bearded within at base; peduncles villous, those of the cleistogamous flowers ascending or erect; (?Ont. and N.B.) . . . . *V. novae-angliae*
            38 Leaves narrowly cordate-ovate to reniform, essentially glabrous except sometimes for soft pubescence in youth, more finely and abundantly toothed; peduncles glabrous.
                39 Spurred petal beardless at base, the lateral petals with a slender beard; cleistogamous flowers borne on prostrate (at first partly subterranean) to arched-

ascending peduncles; outer sepals ovate-lanceolate;
leaves broadly cordate-ovate to reniform, abruptly pointed
. . . . [*V. papilionacea*]
39 Spurred petal bearded at base (only slightly so in *V. latiuscula*); lateral petals with a conspicuous beard.
40 Spurred petal only slightly villous at base; cleistogamous flowers borne on short prostrate peduncles; sepals obtuse; leaves broadly deltoid-ovate to reniform, abruptly pointed; petioles granular-puberulent near the leaf-blade; (s ?Ont.) . . . . . .
. . . . [*V. latiuscula*]
40 Spurred petal strongly bearded at base; cleistogamous flowers borne on ascending or erect peduncles.
41 Sepals and broadly cordate-ovate to reniform leaves obtuse; seeds with prolonged caruncle; (transcontinental) . . . . *V. nephrophylla*
41 Sepals and narrowly cordate-ovate leaves acute or acutish; caruncle of seeds short; (Ont. and Que.)
. . . . *V. affinis*

V. adunca Sm.

/aST/X/G/ (Hsr) Dry to moist meadows, woods, and open ground to near timberline (ranges of Canadian taxa outlined below), s to Calif., Colo., S.Dak., Minn., Mich., s Ont., N.Y., and New Eng.; var. *minor* in w Greenland N to ca. 65°30′N, in E Greenland N to 60°32′N. MAPS and synonymy: *see* below.
1 Leaves densely puberulent, rather gradually narrowed to apex; stipules entire or short-toothed toward base . . . . var. *adunca*
  2 Flowers blue-veined but otherwise white; [type from Ile-aux-Basques, near Trois-Pistoles, Temiscouata Co., E Que.] . . . . f. *albiflora* Vict. & Rousseau
  2 Flowers violet or violet-blue; [*V. albertina, V. cardaminefolia*, and *V. subvestita* Greene; *V. montanensis* and *V. monticola* Rydb.; *V. canina* vars. *adunca* (Sm.) Gray and *longipes* (Nutt.) Wats.; *V. arenaria* of Canadian reports in part, not DC.; *V. canina* var. *rupestris sensu* John Macoun 1886, not Regel (relevant collections in CAN); s Alaska (*see* Hultén 1947: map 857, p. 1195; Hultén notes that the Yukon dot refers to the glabrous var. *minor*); Great Bear L. and L. Athabasca, Alta., through B.C. and Alta. to Sask. (N to Goldfields, near L. Athabasca), Man. (N to Flin Flon, ca. 55°N), Ont. (N to the Fawn R. at ca. 54°N, 89°W), and Que. (N to the Harricanaw R., L. St. John, the Côte-Nord, and Gaspé Pen.); MAP (aggregate species): Hultén 1968b:682] . . . . f. *adunca*
1 Leaves glabrous; stipules subentire . . . . var. *minor* (Hook.) Fern.
  3 Flowers blue-veined but otherwise white; [*V. muhlenbergiana* f. *?albiflora* Hook.; type from the banks of the Wiachouan R., Que., at ca. 56°N), ... f. *candida* Lepage
  3 Flowers violet or violet-blue; [var. *glabra* Brain.; *V. muhlenbergiana* Ging. and its var. *minor* Hook.; *V. labradorica* Schrank; *V. muhlenbergii* Torr. in part; *V. ?allionii* Pio; *V. debilis sensu* Richardson 1823, not Michx.; *V. canina* var. *sylvestris* Regel; s-cent. Yukon (*see* above) and NW Dist. Mackenzie through B.C., Alta., and Sask. to Man. (N to about 28 mi s of Churchill), northernmost Ont., Que. (N to E Hudson Bay at ca. 58°30′N and the Côte-Nord), Labrador (N to the Komaktorvik R. at 59°22′N), Nfld., N.B., P.E.I., and N.S.; w Greenland N to ca. 65°30′N, E Greenland N to 60°32′N; MAP (E N. America): Böcher 1954: fig. 14a, p. 57] . . . . f. *minor*

V. affinis Le Conte

/T/EE/ (Hr) Shores, low woods, damp thickets, and meadows from Wisc. to Ont. (N to the s James Bay watershed at ca. 51°15′N; Dutilly, Lepage, and Duman 1954) and Que. (N to Anti-costi Is. and Gaspé Pen.), s to Ark., Tenn., Ala., and Ga. [*V. venustula* Greene].
  Hybrids with *V. conspersa* and *V. sororia* are reported from s Ont. by Gaiser and Moore

(1966; Lambton Co.). Material in our area N of Ottawa and Montreal has been referred to var. *subarctica* Rousseau (*V. nephrophylla sensu* Potter 1934, not Greene; *see* Dutilly, Lepage, and Duman 1954; rhizomes slender and cord-like rather than thick and fleshy; type from Anticosti Is., E Que.).

V. arvensis Murr.   Wild Pansy.   Pensée des champs
Eurasian; a garden-escape or introd. along roadsides and in fields in N. America, as in B.C. (N to Kimsquit, NE of Ocean Falls at ca. 52°20'N; CAN), Alta. (Moss 1959), Sask. (N to Tisdale, 52°51'N), s Man. (Otterburne, about 30 mi s of Winnipeg), Ont. (N to the Ottawa dist.), Que. (N to L. St. John, the Côte-Nord, and Gaspé Pen.; *see* Que. map by Lionel Cinq-Mars, Nat. can. (Que.) 93(6): map 8, pl. 9, p. 952. 1966), Nfld., N.B., P.E.I., and N.S. [*V. tricolor* var. *arv.* (Murr.) DC.].

V. biflora L.
/ST/W/EA/   (Hs)   Rocky slopes and alpine meadows from cent. Alaska–w Yukon (N to ca. 65°45'N) to B.C. (s to Queen Charlotte Is.), with an isolated area in Colo.; Eurasia. MAP: Hultén 1968b:681.
      The plant of Queen Charlotte Is., B.C., has been separated as ssp. *carlottae* Calder & Taylor (sepals with a prominent purple midstripe, ciliate only in the upper half, rather than lacking a prominent midstripe and more extensively ciliate; type from Moresby Is., Queen Charlotte Is.; according to Eric Hultén, Sven. Bot. Tidskr. 62(4):525. 1968, a collection from Craig, Alaska, also probably belongs here).

V. blanda Willd.
/T/EE/   (Hrr)   Rich woods from Man. (N to Berens R., about 160 mi N of Winnipeg) to Ont. (N to near Lake of the Woods and the Nipigon R. N of L. Superior), sw Que. (N to the Montreal dist.), and N.H., s to Wisc., Ill., Ohio, Tenn., and Ga. [*V. amoena* Le Conte; *V. ?clandestina sensu* Hooker 1830, in part, perhaps not Pursh].

V. canadensis L.   Canada-Violet, Tall White Violet
/sT/X/   (Hs(r))   Woods, thickets, meadows, and rocky slopes (ranges of Canadian taxa outlined below), s to Ariz., N.Mex., Tex., Tenn., Ala., and S.C.
1   Stolons present; leaves often broader than long; plant pubescent; [*V. rugulosa* and
    V. rydbergii Greene; sw Dist. Mackenzie–B.C. to Alta. (N to Wood Buffalo National
    Park at 59°07'N), Sask. (N to Prince Albert), Man. (N to The Pas), and w Ont. (near
    Thunder Bay); sw ?Que. (Raymond 1950b; Missisquoi Co.)] . . . .
    . . . . var. *rugulosa* (Greene) Hitchc.
1   Stolons wanting; leaves usually longer than broad, not ciliate; plant glabrous or
    puberulent; [Ont. (N to Sandy L. at ca. 53°N), Que. (N to l'Ange-Gardien, NE of
    Quebec City; *see* Que. map by Doyon and Lavoie 1966: fig. 18, p. 819; reported N to
    Cacouna, Temiscouata Co., by Penhallow 1891), N.B. (Carleton and Victoria
    counties), and N.S. (near Newport and Wentworth, Hants Co.; not known from P.E.I.;
    reports from Nfld. require confirmation)] . . . . var. *canadensis*

V. canina L.
/aST/–/GEA/   (Hsr)   Tundra and dryish sandy or gravelly slopes of s Greenland (N to ca. 61°N; var. *montana* (L.) Lange (*V. montana* L.)); Iceland; Eurasia. MAP: Hultén 1958: map 84 (*V. mont.*), p. 103.
      This species (not keyed out above) is closely related to *V. adunca* (which *see* in the above key to *Viola* species). From *V. adunca* var. *minor,* it differs in its larger corolla with broader petals and in the absence of a basal rosette.

V. conspersa Reichenb.
/T/EE/   (Hsr)   Meadows, damp woods, and low ground from s Man. (N to Victoria Beach, about 55 mi NE of Winnipeg) to Ont. (N to Longlac, N of L. Superior at 49°47'N), Que. (N to Tadoussac, Saguenay Co., and the Gaspé Pen.), N.B., and N.S. (not known from P.E.I.), s to Tenn., Ala., and Ga. [*V. muhlenbergii* Torr.].

Reports from elsewhere in our area refer largely to *V. adunca*. Forma *masonii* (Farw.) House (flowers white rather than violet) is known from Ont. (near Fallowfield, about 11 mi SW of Ottawa; MT). A hybrid with *V. rostrata* is reported from Missisquoi Co., SW Que., by Raymond (1950*b*; × *V. malteana* House). One with *V. striata* is reported from S Ont. by Gaiser and Moore (1966; Lambton Co.).

V. cucullata Ait.
/T/EE/ (Hr) Wet meadows and swampy ground (ranges of Canadian taxa outlined below), s to Nebr., Ark., Tenn., and Ga.

1 Auricles of sepals to about 2 mm long; [E Que. (Gaspé Pen.; Magdalen Is.), Nfld. (type from near Grand Falls), N.B., and N.S.] . . . . var. *microtitis* Brain.
1 Auricles of sepals to 6 mm long . . . . var. *cucullata*
  2 Petals uniformly white; [Ont. and Que.; Boivin 1966*b*] . . . . f. *albiflora* Britt.
  2 Petals at least partly blue-violet.
    3 Petals irregularly blue-violet and white; [SW Que.; Boivin 1966*b*] . . . .
      . . . . f. *thurstonii* (Twining) House
    3 Petals uniformly blue-violet.
      4 Sepals marginally ciliate; upper surface and margins of leaves puberulent; [*V. prionosepala* Greene, the type from Chelsea, N of Hull, Que.] . . . .
        . . . . f. *prionosepala* (Greene) Brain.
      4 Sepals not ciliate; leaves essentially glabrous; [*V. ?asarifolia* Pursh; *V. ?obliqua* Hill; Ont. (N to the N shore of L. Superior at Peninsula, ca. 48°45′N), Que. (N to the Côte-Nord and Gaspé Pen.), Nfld., N.B. (provincial floral emblem), P.E.I., and N.S.; reports from Man. appear referable to *V. nephrophylla* and *V. sororia* (relevant collection in WIN)]. A collection in CAN from Hamilton, S Ont., has been referred to a purported hybrid with *V. (sagittata* var. *ovata) fimbriatula* (× *V. porteriana* Pollard). One with *V. papilionacea* is reported from S Ont. by Montgomery (1945; Waterloo Co.). One with *V. septentrionalis* (× *V. melissaefolia* Greene) is reported from Ottawa, Ont., Abbotsford, Que., P.E.I. (type locality), and N.S. Collections in CAN from St-Norbert, Arthabasca Co., SW Que., have been named a hybrid with *V. sororia,* this hybrid also being reported from S Ont. by Gaiser and Moore (1966; Lambton Co.) . . . . f. *cucullata*

V. epipsila Ledeb.
/ST/WW/EA/ (Hrr) Cool swampy places from Alaska (N to ca. 65°N) and cent. Yukon to NW Dist. Mackenzie, Great Slave L., and N Man. (s to Gillam, about 165 mi S of Churchill), s to N Calif., Utah, Colo., and S.Dak.; an isolated station in W Ont. on the N shore of L. Superior E of Nipigon, according to Hultén's map; Iceland; Eurasia. MAPS (aggregate species): Hultén 1958: map 104, p. 123; Raup 1947: pl. 30 (NW N. America; incomplete eastwards).

The plant of N. America and most of Asia is referred by Hultén (1958) to ssp. *repens* (Turcz.) Becker (*V. repens* Turcz.; *V. achyrophora* Greene; plant smaller-dimensioned and less pubescent than the typical form). The species should perhaps be merged with *V. palustris*.

V. eriocarpa Schwein.   Smooth Yellow Violet
/T/EE/ (Hsr) Damp woods and cool rocky slopes from S Man. (N to Riding Mt.; DAO) to Ont. (N to Hearst, 49°42′N), Que. (N to the Gaspé Pen.), N.B., P.E.I., and N.S., s to Okla., Ohio, Tenn., and N.C. [Incl. var. *leiocarpa* Fern. & Wieg. (*V. pensylvanica (pubescens)* var. *leio*. (F. & W.) Fern.); *V. pen*. of most Canadian reports, not Michx., which is *V. pubescens* according to G.N. Jones, Rhodora 61(728):219–20.1959]. MAP: Frère Lucien Lévesque and Pierre Dansereau, Nat. can. (Que.) 93(5): fig. 2, p. 492. 1966.

A purported hybrid with *V. pubescens* is reported from S Ont. by Soper (1949).

V. glabella Nutt.
/sT/W/ (Hsr) Moist woods and streambanks from S Alaska (N to ca. 62°N; see Hultén

1947: map 860, p. 1196) through B.C. and sw Alta. (Waterton Lakes; CAN) to N Calif. and Mont.; the report from NE Asia by Hitchcock et al. 1961, requires confirmation. [*V. canadensis (biflora)* var. *sitchensis* Ledeb.; *V. can. sensu* Bongard 1833, not L.]. MAP: Frère Lucien Lévesque and Pierre Dansereau, Nat. can. (Que.) 93(5): fig. 1, p. 492. 1966.

V. howellii Gray
/t/W/ (Hsr (Grh)) Moist woods and prairies from sw B.C. (Vancouver Is.; New Westminster; Cascade) to Calif.

V. incognita Brainerd
/T/EE/ (Hrr) Woods, thickets, and openings from Ont. (N to Schreiber, N shore of L. Superior; CAN; reported from Renison, near James Bay at ca. 51°N, by Hustich 1955) to Que. (N to SE James Bay at ca. 52°N, L. Mistassini, the Côte-Nord, Anticosti Is., and Gaspé Pen.; an isolated station near Hubbard L. at ca. 55°N; *see* Que. map by Lionel Cinq-Mars, Nat. can. (Que.) 93(6): map 12, pl. 9, p. 952. 1966), s Labrador (Forteau, 51°28′N; GH), Nfld., N.B., P.E.I., and N.S., s to N.Dak., Minn., Mich., Pa., and Del.

Much of our material is referable to var. *forbesii* Brainerd (leaves glabrous except for scattered hairs on the upper surface rather than soft-hairy beneath especially when young). A collection in CAN from Harrington Harbour, Côte-Nord, E Que., has been named a hybrid between *V. incognita* and *V. (macloskeyi* var.) *pallens*.

V. kitaibeliana Schultes   Field-Pansy
Eurasian; introd. along roadsides and in dry fields and waste places of N. America, as in s Sask. (grain-field at Tisdale; Breitung 1957a) and s Ont. (Essex, Lambton, Elgin, Norfolk, and Peel counties). [Incl. *V. rafinesquii* Greene, considered by L.H. Shinners, Rhodora 63(756):327–35. 1961, to be the native N. American representative].

V. lanceolata L.   Lance-leaved Violet
/T/EE/ (Hrr) Damp to inundated open places and woods from Nebr. to Minn., Ont. (N to Schreiber, N shore of L. Superior), Que. (N to Lac Desmarais, 117 mi N of Mount-Laurier, Labelle Co.; *see* Que. maps by Marie-Victorin and Rolland-Germain 1942: fig. 15, p. 29, and Lionel Cinq-Mars, Nat. can. (Que.) 93(6): map 9, pl. 10, p. 954. 1966), St-Pierre and Miquelon, N.B., and N.S. (not known from P.E.I.), s to E Tex. and Fla.; introd. in Wash. and sw B.C. (Eastham 1947: "Apparently well-established and spreading on blueberry farms on Lulu Is., Vancouver, presumably brought in with blueberry plants from eastern N. Am.").

V. langsdorfii (Regel) Fisch.
/ST/W/eA/ (Hsr) Moist meadows and bogs from the Aleutian Is., Alaska (N to the Seward Pen. at ca. 65°N; type from Unalaska; *see* Hultén 1947: map 861, p. 1196), and s Yukon (Porsild 1951a) through B.C. to s Oreg.; E Asia. [*V. mirabilis* var. *lang.* Regel; *V. simulata* Baker]. MAP: Hultén 1968b:681.

[V. latiuscula Greene]
[The report of this species of the E U.S.A. (N.Y. and Vt. to Va.) from s Ont. by Soper (1949; apparently based upon collections in TRT from Halton, Simcoe, and York counties) requires confirmation.]

V. macloskeyi Lloyd
/ST/X/ (Hrr) Boggy or wet ground and wet thickets, isolated stations on Great Bear L. and in cent. Dist. Keewatin (Yathkyed L. to Nueltin L.), the main area from B.C. (N to Quesnel) and s Alta. to Man. (N to Churchill; not known from Sask.), Ont. (N to the Severn R. at ca. 55°30′N), Que. (N to Leaf Bay, sw Ungava Bay at ca. 59°N, the Côte-Nord, Anticosti Is., and Gaspé Pen.), Labrador (N to Okak, 57°40′N), Nfld., N.B., P.E.I., and N.S., s to s Calif., Colo., N.Dak., Ohio, Ala., and S.C.

The typical form (leaves obscurely crenate and usually less than 2.5 cm broad) is reported from B.C. and Alta. by Hitchcock et al. (1961). Most of our more eastern material is referable to var. *pallens* (Banks) Hitchc. (*V. rotundifolia* var. *pallens* Banks; *V. pallens* (Banks) Brainerd and its var. *subreptans* Rousseau; *V. mistassinica* Greene; leaves more prominently crenate and often over 2.5 cm broad).

V. nephrophylla Greene
/ST/X/ (Hr) Moist places and gravelly shores (ranges of Canadian taxa outlined below), s to Calif., N.Mex., N.Dak., Iowa, Mich., and New Eng. MAP and synonymy: *see* below.
1 All 5 petals bearded; leaves purplish beneath, relatively thick; [*V. cognata* Greene; B.C. and Alta.; Hitchcock et al. 1961] . . . . var. *cognata* (Greene) Hitchc.
1 Upper petals not bearded; leaves usually not purplish beneath . . . . var. *nephrophylla*
  2 Petals predominantly white.
    3 Petals rather uniformly white; [Sask. (Wallwort; Breitung 1957*a*) and N.B. (Dalhousie)] . . . . f. *albinea* Farw.
    3 Petals white but spotted with blue, the veins dark blue; [type from Templeton, Gatineau Co., sw Que.; Bernard Boivin, Nat. can. (Que.) 87:49. 1960] . . . .
      . . . . f. *bicolor* Boivin
  2 Petals rich violet; [*V. macabeiana* Baker; *V. peramoena* Greene; w Dist. Mackenzie (Great Bear L.) and B.C.–Alta. to Sask. (N to McKague, ca. 52°45′N), Man. (N to the Churchill R. at ca. 57°20′N), Ont. (N to the Kapiscaw R. w of James Bay at ca. 52°30′N), Que. (N to Anticosti Is. and the Côte-Nord), Nfld., N.B., P.E.I., and N.S.; MAP (aggregate species): N.H. Russell and F.S. Crosswhite, Madroño 17(2): fig. 1 (incomplete northwards), p. 57. 1963]. A hybrid with *V. sagittata* is reported from s Ont. by Gaiser and Moore (1966; Lambton Co.) . . . .
    . . . . f. *nephrophylla*

V. novae-angliae House
/T/EE/ (Hr) Meadows, wet rocks, and gravels from Minn. to ?Ont. (collections in MT and TRT from near London, Middlesex Co., and Quetico Provincial Park, about 100 mi w of Thunder Bay, require confirmation; not known from Que., P.E.I., or N.S.), N.B. (Victoria, Charlotte, and Queens counties), and N Maine. [*V. ovata* and *V. sagittata* of early N.B. reports, not Nutt. and Ait., respectively, relevant collections in NBM].

V. nuttallii Pursh   Yellow Prairie-Violet
/T/WW/ (Hs) Dry woods, sagebrush plains, and prairies at low to moderate elevations from B.C. (N to Kamloops; CAN) to Alta. (N to Calgary; CAN), s Sask. (Cypress Hills, Wood Mountain, and Milk River; CAN), and sw Man. (Brandon; Rock Lake; 8 mi N of Minto), s to Calif., Ariz., and Mo.
1 Leaf-blades narrowly lanceolate or elliptic-lanceolate, usually at least 3 times as long as broad, narrowed to petioles nearly or quite as long; [s Alta. and s Sask.] . . . var. *nuttallii*
1 Leaf-blades usually less than 3 times as long as broad.
  2 Leaf-blades narrowly to broadly ovate, usually more or less truncate or subcordate at base, generally less than 5 cm long, glabrous or sparingly hairy; capsules glabrous; [*V. vallicola* Nels.; *V. russellii* Boivin; B.C. to Sask.] . . . .
    . . . . var. *vallicola* (Nels.) St. John
  2 Leaf-blades usually at least 5 cm long, seldom at all cordate-based; capsules often hairy.
    3 Leaves usually distinctly pubescent, the narrowly ovate blades thick and fleshy; [*V. praemorsa* Dougl.; Vancouver Is.] . . . . var. *praemorsa* (Dougl.) Wats.
    3 Leaves glabrous to moderately pubescent, the blades variable in shape but scarcely fleshy; [*V. linguaefolia* Nutt.; B.C. and Alta.] . . . . var. *major* Hook.

V. odorata L.   English or Sweet Violet
Eurasian; a garden-escape to roadsides and waste places in N. America, as in sw B.C. (Victoria, Vancouver Is.; John Macoun 1883), s Ont. (Wellington Co.; F.H. Montgomery, Can. Field-Nat. 62(3):95. 1948), Que. (Boivin 1966*b*), Nfld. (Rouleau 1956), and N.S. (John Macoun 1883).
  Forma *albiflora* Oborny (flowers white rather than rich violet) is reported from Que. by Lionel Cinq-Mars, Nat. can. (Que.) 93(6):955. 1955; Ste-Pétronille, E of Quebec City).

V. orbiculata Geyer   Round-leaved Violet
/T/W/   (Hs)   Alpine and subalpine slopes from B.C. (N to the Dean R. at ca. 52°N and Revel-stoke; reported N to Laurier Pass in the Peace River Dist. at ca. 56°N by Raup 1934) and SW Alta. (Waterton Lakes and Crowsnest Pass; CAN; DAO) to Oreg., Idaho, and Mont. [*V. sarmentosa (sempervirens)* var. *orb.* (Geyer) Gray].

V. palmata L.
/t/EE/   (Hr)   Rich deciduous woods and shaded calcareous ledges from Minn. to S Ont. (Essex, Kent, Lambton, Elgin, Waterloo, Wellington, and York counties; CAN; OAC; TRT) and S N.H., S to Miss. and Fla. [*V. cucullata* var. *pal.* (L.) Gray].

V. palustris L.   Alpine Marsh-Violet
/aST/(X)/GEA/   (Hrr)   Moist meadows and along streams from SE ?Alaska (Evans Is.; CAN; western material is referred to the doubtfully distinct *V. epipsila* ssp. *repens* by Hultén 1958 (compare his maps 103 *(V. pal.)* and 104 *(V. epip.),* p. 123)) to B.C. (N to the Beatton R. at ca. 57°N; CAN), Alta. (N to L. Athabasca; CAN), Sask. (N to Hasbala L. at 59°55'N; CAN), S Dist. Keewatin (Baralzon L. at ca. 60°N; CAN), Man., Ont. (N to near Thunder Bay), Que. (N to the George R., Ungava Bay, at 58°13'N, the Côte-Nord, Anticosti Is., and Gaspé Pen.), Labrador (N to Hopedale, 55°27'N), and Nfld. (not known from the Maritime Provinces), S in the West to Calif., Utah, and Colo. and in the East to the mts. of N.H. and Maine; W Greenland N to ca. 63°N, E Greenland N to ca. 66°N; Iceland; Europe; NW Asia. MAP: Hultén 1958: map 103 (incomplete westwards according to the present interpretation), p. 123.

The typical form has the flowers predominantly white but the 3 lowest petals more or less strongly lilac-tinged and purple-veined. Forma *albiflora* Neum. (flowers completely white except for the lilac spur) is widespread throughout our area. Var. *brevipes* (Baker) Davis (flowers white throughout) is reported from SW Alta. by Breitung (1957*b*; Waterton Lakes). M. Sorsa (Madroño 19(5):173. 1968) suggests that it may be a hybrid between *V. macloskeyi* and *V. palustris.*

[V. papilionacea Pursh]
[This species of the E U.S.A. (N to N.Dak. and Maine) is accredited to S Que. by Fernald *in* Gray (1950) and to Ont., Que., and N.S. by various other authors. However, part of these reports are referred to *V. affinis* by Lionel Cinq-Mars (Nat. can. (Que.) 93(6):937. 1966) and it is included in *V. cucullata* by Boivin (1966*b*). If warranting status as a distinct species, its occurrence in Canada requires confirmation.]

V. pedata L.   Pansy-Violet, Birdsfoot-Violet
/t/EE/   (Hr)   Dry places and open woods from Kans. to Minn., Wisc., Mich., S Ont. (Norfolk, Lambton, Waterloo, Welland, and Lincoln counties), N.Y., and N.H., S to E Tex. and Fla.

Our material is referable to var. *lineariloba* DC. (petals all lilac-purple rather than the upper ones dark violet, the lower ones lilac-purple; leaf-segments relatively narrow).

V. pedatifida Don   Larkspur-Violet or Purple Prairie-Violet
/T/(X)/   (Hr)   Prairies and dry openings from S Alta. (N to Red Deer; CAN) to S Sask. (N to Indian Head, about 40 mi E of Regina; CAN), S Man. (N to Brokenpipe L., about 15 mi NW of Dauphin; J.L. Parker, Can. Field-Nat. 76(2):125. 1962), and S Ont. (near Brantford, Brant Co., where taken by John Macoun in 1907; CAN), S to Mont., Ariz., N.Mex., Okla., Mo., and N Ohio. [*V. delphinifolia* Nutt.; *V. ?pinnata sensu* Richardson 1823, not L.].

[V. primulifolia L.]
[This species of the E U.S.A. (N to Minn. and Maine) is accredited to S Ont. and SW Que. by Fernald *in* Gray (1950; var. *acuta* (Bigel.) T. & G.), to N.B. by John Macoun (1883) and Fowler (1885), and to N.S. in the map by Braun (1937: map 13, p. 197). However, both Boivin (1966*b*) and Lionel Cinq-Mars (Nat. can. (Que.) 93(6):924. 1966) refer most or all such reports to × *V. sublanceolata* House (*V. lanceolata* × *V. (macloskeyi* var.) *pallens*).]

V. pubescens Ait.   Downy Yellow Violet
/T/EE/   (Hsr)   Rich deciduous woods from s Man. (N to Fork River, about 115 mi N of Bran-
don; WIN) to Ont. (N to L. Timiskaming at ca. 47°30′N; CAN), Que. (N to Ville-Marie, 47°20′N;
CAN; reports from the Maritime Provinces refer largely or wholly to *V. eriocarpa,* relevant col-
lections in several herbaria), and Maine, s to Nebr., Mo., Tenn., and Va. [*V. pensylvanica*
Michx. (*see* G.N. Jones, Rhodora 61(728):219–20. 1959); *V. scabriuscula* Schw.]. MAP: Frère
Lucien Lévesque and Pierre Dansereau, Nat. can. (Que.) 93(5): fig. 2, p. 492. 1966.
   Var. *peckii* House (capsules glabrous rather than white-woolly) is reported from s Ont. by
Krotkov (1940; Bruce Pen., L. Huron).

V. renifolia Gray
/ST/X/   (Hr)   Moist cool woods, swampy ground, and rocky slopes from s Alaska–Yukon
and Great Bear L. to B.C.–Alta., Sask. (N to Prince Albert), Man. (N to Churchill), Ont. (N to the
Hudson Bay watershed at ca. 56°N), James Bay (Akimiski Is.), Que. (N to Knob Lake, 54°48′N,
the Côte-Nord, Anticosti Is., and Gaspé Pen.), Labrador (N to the Hamilton R. basin), Nfld.,
N.B., P.E.I., and N.S., s to N ?Wash., Colo., S.Dak., Minn., Wisc., Mich., and Conn.
   Most of our material is referable to var. *brainerdii* (Greene) Fern. (*V. br.* Greene, the type
from near Ottawa, Ont.; petioles and leaves glabrous or soon so, rather than permanently villous). MAP: Hultén 1968b:683.

V. rostrata Pursh   Long-spurred Violet
/T/EE/   (Hsr)   Rich deciduous woods from Wisc. to Ont. (N to Carleton and Stormont coun-
ties), sw Que. (N to Contrecoeur, about 30 mi NE of Montreal; the report from Anticosti Is. by
Saint-Cyr 1887, undoubtedly refers to some other species), and Vt., s to Ala. and Ga.
   A hybrid with *V. striata* is reported from s Ont. by Boivin (1966b; Cambridge (Galt), Waterloo
Co.), in whose opinion all Canadian records of *V. rostrata* require confirmation.

V. rotundifolia Michx.   Round-leaved or Early Yellow Violet
/T/EE/   (Hrr)   Rich deciduous woods from s Ont. (N to Lincoln Co.; A. Bouchard and P.F.
Maycock, Can. J. Bot. 48(12):2290. 1970; collections in TRT from York Co. and in OAC from
Uxbridge, Ontario Co., require confirmation) to sw Que. (N to Garthby, Wolfe Co., about 70 mi
s of Quebec City; *see* s Que. map by Bouchard and Maycock, loc. cit., fig. 1, p. 2287) and
cent. Maine, s to Tenn., N Ga., and N S.C. MAPS: Bouchard and Maycock, loc. cit., fig. 3, p.
2300; Raymond 1950b: fig. 28, p. 78; Braun 1937: map 29, p. 202.

V. sagittata Ait.   Arrow-leaved Violet
/T/EE/   (Hr)   Open woods, sterile meadows, and clearings (ranges of Canadian taxa outlined below), s to E Tex. and Ga.
1   Sepals and their auricles glabrous; leaves (above the often sharply hastate-lobed
    base) narrowly lanceolate to lance-oblong, 2 or 3 times as long as broad, sparsely
    pubescent, mostly on very long slender petioles; [s Ont. (N to Waterloo, York, and
    Hastings counties) and Que. (Rouville and Bagot counties; MT; reported from
    Lorette, near Quebec City, by John Macoun 1883)] . . . . var. *sagittata*
1   Sepals and their auricles ciliate; leaves (above the unlobed or subhastately lobed
    base) oblong-ovate to broadly deltoid, mostly less than twice as long as broad,
    typically copiously pubescent, slightly shorter to longer than the petioles . . . .
    . . . . var. *ovata* (Nutt.) T. & G.
    2   Flowers in umbels of 3; [*V. fimbriatula* f. *umb.* Fern., the type from near Halifax,
        N.S.] . . . . f. *umbelliflora* (Fern.) Scoggan
    2   Flowers solitary; [*V. ovata* Nutt.; *V. fimbriatula* Sm.; Ont. (N to the Ottawa dist.),
        Que. (Rougemont, Rouville Co.; Lionel Cinq-Mars, Ann. ACFAS 22:58. 1956), N.B.
        (Grand Manan Is., Charlotte Co.), P.E.I. (near Charlottetown), and N.S.
        (Yarmouth, Digby, Annapolis, Kings, Hants, and Halifax counties)]. A hybrid with
        V. septentrionalis is reported from P.E.I. by E. Brainerd, Rhodora 6(71):217. 1904;
        a purported hybrid between this and the typical form is reported from sw Que. by
        Lionel Cinq-Mars (Nat. can. (Que.) 93(6):942. 1966; Rougemont, Rouville Co.;
        × *V. abundans* House) . . . . f. *ovata*

V. selkirkii Pursh
/aST/X/GEA/ (Hr) Woods and cool rocky slopes from the w Aleutian Is. (Attu Is.) and s Alaska–Yukon (N to ca. 62°30′N; not known from Dist. Mackenzie) to B.C.–Alta., Sask. (N to Amisk L. at ca. 55°N), Man. (N to The Pas), Ont. (N to Kapuskasing, 49°24′N), Que. (N to the Ungava Bay watershed at ca. 59°30′N, the Côte-Nord, and Gaspé Pen.; not known from Anticosti Is.; type from near Montreal), Labrador (N to Ramah, 58°54′N), Nfld., N.B., P.E.I., and N.S., s to s B.C. (Monashee Pass, about 35 mi SE of Vernon; Herb. V, detd. Baird; isolated in Colo.), Sask. (s to Mistatim, 52°52′N), Minn., Wisc., Mich., Pa., and New Eng.; w Greenland N to 63°04′N; NE Europe; Asia. MAPS: Hultén 1968b:682; Böcher 1954: fig. 17, p. 67.

V. sempervirens Greene Evergreen Violet
/T/W/ (Hsr) Moist woods from the southernmost Alaska Panhandle through B.C. (Vancouver Is. and adjacent islands and mainland N to McLeod L., ca. 54°N, E to Ymir, s of Nelson; CAN; V) to N Calif. [*V. sarmentosa* Dougl., not Bieb.]. MAP: Hultén 1968b:680.

V. septentrionalis Greene
/T/X/ (Hr) Moist open woods and clearings from s B.C. (reported from Cascade, near Vancouver, and from the Pend d'Oreille R., Kootenay Valley, by E. Brainerd, Rhodora 17:70. 1915; not known from Alta.) to ?Sask. (reported from McKague, 52°37′N, by Breitung 1957a, but a replicate in CAN is referred to *V. canadensis* var. *rugulosa* by Boivin; reports from Man. all appear to be based upon other species), Ont. (N to Kapuskasing, 49°24′N; type from near Ottawa), Que. (N to Waswanipi L. at 49°39′N, 76°30′W, and the Gaspé Pen.), Nfld., N.B., P.E.I., and N.S., s to ?Wash., Nebr., Iowa, Wisc., Tenn., and Va.
Forma *alba* Vict. & Rousseau (petals white except for the bluish veins rather than deep bluish to violet) is known from sw Que. (Kirk's Ferry, Gatineau Co.; type from Rosemere, Terrebonne Co.).

V. sororia Willd.
/T/EE/ (Hr) Moist meadows, woods, and slopes from s ?Man. (reported from Aweme, s of Brandon, by Lowe 1943; collections in CAN from near Portage la Prairie and Winnipeg have been placed here but require confirmation) to Ont. (N to Timmins, 48°28′N; CAN) and sw Que. (N to Duparquet, ca. 48°30′N), s to Okla., Mo., Ky., and N.C.
Forma *beckwithiae* House (flowers white rather than lavender or violet) is reported from sw Que. by Lionel Cinq-Mars (Nat. can. (Que.) 93(6):946. 1966; Rougemont, Rouville Co.). A hybrid with *V. triloba* (× *V. populifolia* Greene) is known from the type locality, Flamboro, Wentworth Co., s Ont.

V. striata Ait. Cream-Violet
/t/EE/ (Hs) Moist meadows and woods from Wisc., Mich., and Ohio to s Ont. (Essex, Lambton, Elgin, Middlesex, Welland, Wentworth, York, and Frontenac counties) and N.Y., s to Ark. and Ga.; a local garden-escape elsewhere, as in sw ?Que. (Montreal; John Macoun and John Gibson, Can. J., n.s. 15(91). 1876). [*V. ?ochroleuca* Schw.].

V. tricolor L. Pansy. Pensée
Eurasian; persisting in gardens or escaping to waste places in N. America, as in s B.C. (Vancouver Is.; Kootenay), Alta. (Moss 1959), Sask. (Boivin 1966b; not listed by Breitung 1957a), Man. (Brandon), Ont. (N to Nipigon, N shore of L. Superior; Montgomery 1957), Que. (N to the Côte-Nord and Gaspé Pen.), N.B., and N.S.

[V. triloba Schwein.]
[The report of this species of the E U.S.A. (N to Ill. and New Eng.) from s Ont. by Soper (1949; presumably based upon a collection in OAC from Turkey Point, Norfolk Co.) requires confirmation.]